11. Format for Bank Reconciliation:

Cash balance according to bank statement			$xxx
Add: Additions by company not on bank statement		$xx	
Bank errors		xx	xx
			$xxx
Deduct: Deductions by company not on bank statement		$xx	
Bank errors		xx	xx
Adjusted balance			$xxx
Cash balance according to company's records			$xxx
Add: Additions by bank not recorded by company ..		$xx	
Company errors		xx	xx
			$xxx
Deduct: Deductions by bank not recorded by company		$xx	
Company errors		xx	xx
Adjusted balance			$xxx

12. Inventory Costing Methods:

1. First-in, First-out (FIFO)
2. Last-in, First-out (LIFO)
3. Average Cost

13. Interest Computations:

Interest = Face Amount (or Principal) $\times$ Rate $\times$ Time

14. Methods of Determining Annual Depreciation:

STRAIGHT-LINE: $\dfrac{\text{Cost} - \text{Estimated Residual Value}}{\text{Estimated Life}}$

DOUBLE-DECLINING-BALANCE: Rate* $\times$ Book Value at Beginning of Period

*Rate is commonly twice the straight-line rate (1/Estimated Life).

15. Adjustments to Net Income (Loss) Using the Indirect Method

	Increase (Decrease)
Net income (loss)	$ XXX
Adjustments to reconcile net income to net cash flow from operating activities:	
Depreciation of fixed assets	XXX
Amortization of intangible assets	XXX
Losses on disposal of assets	XXX
Gains on disposal of assets	(XXX)
Changes in current operating assets and liabilities:	
Increases in noncash current operating assets	(XXX)
Decreases in noncash current operating assets	XXX
Increases in current operating liabilities	XXX
Decreases in current operating liabilities	(XXX)
Net cash flow from operating activities	$ XXX
	or
	$(XXX)

16. Contribution Margin Ratio = $\dfrac{\text{Sales} - \text{Variable Costs}}{\text{Sales}}$

17. Break-Even Sales (Units) = $\dfrac{\text{Fixed Costs}}{\text{Unit Contribution Margin}}$

18. Sales (Units) = $\dfrac{\text{Fixed Costs} + \text{Target Profit}}{\text{Unit Contribution Margin}}$

19. Margin of Safety = $\dfrac{\text{Sales} - \text{Sales at Break-Even Point}}{\text{Sales}}$

20. Operating Leverage = $\dfrac{\text{Contribution Margin}}{\text{Income from Operations}}$

21. Variances

$\text{Direct Materials Price Variance} = \left(\begin{array}{c} \text{Actual Price} - \\ \text{Standard Price} \end{array} \right) \times \text{Actual Quantity}$

$\text{Direct Materials Quantity Variance} = \left(\begin{array}{c} \text{Actual Quantity} - \\ \text{Standard Quantity} \end{array} \right) \times \begin{array}{c} \text{Standard} \\ \text{Price} \end{array}$

$\text{Direct Labor Rate Variance} = \left(\begin{array}{c} \text{Actual Rate per Hour} - \\ \text{Standard Rate per Hour} \end{array} \right) \times \text{Actual Hours}$

$\text{Direct Labor Time Variance} = \left(\begin{array}{c} \text{Actual Direct Labor Hours} - \\ \text{Standard Direct Labor Hours} \end{array} \right) \times \begin{array}{c} \text{Standard Rate} \\ \text{per Hour} \end{array}$

$\begin{array}{c} \text{Variable Factory} \\ \text{Overhead Controllable} \\ \text{Variance} \end{array} = \begin{array}{c} \text{Actual Variable} \\ \text{Factory} \\ \text{Overhead} \end{array} - \begin{array}{c} \text{Budgeted Variable} \\ \text{Factory Overhead} \end{array}$

$\begin{array}{c} \text{Fixed Factory} \\ \text{Overhead} \\ \text{Volume} \\ \text{Variance} \end{array} = \left(\begin{array}{c} \text{Standard Hours} \\ \text{for 100\% of} \\ \text{Normal} \\ \text{Capacity} \end{array} - \begin{array}{c} \text{Standard} \\ \text{Hours for} \\ \text{Actual Units} \\ \text{Produced} \end{array} \right) \times \begin{array}{c} \text{Fixed Factory} \\ \text{Overhead} \\ \text{Rate} \end{array}$

22. Rate of Return on Investment (ROI) = $\dfrac{\text{Income from Operations}}{\text{Invested Assets}}$

Alternative ROI Computation:

$\text{ROI} = \dfrac{\text{Income from Operations}}{\text{Sales}} \times \dfrac{\text{Sales}}{\text{Invested Assets}}$

23. Capital Investment Analysis Methods:

1. Methods That Ignore Present Values:
   A. Average Rate of Return Method
   B. Cash Payback Method
2. Methods That Use Present Values:
   A. Net Present Value Method
   B. Internal Rate of Return Method

24. Average Rate of Return = $\dfrac{\text{Estimated Average Annual Income}}{\text{Average Investment}}$

25. Present Value Index = $\dfrac{\text{Total Present Value of Net Cash Flow}}{\text{Amount to Be Invested}}$

26. Present Value Factor for an Annuity of $1 = $\dfrac{\text{Amount to Be Invested}}{\text{Equal Annual Net Cash Flows}}$

Accounting 1A: Financial Accounting

Long Beach City College

Warren/Reeve/Duchac

CENGAGE
Learning™

Australia • Brazil • Japan • Korea • Mexico • Singapore • Spain • United Kingdom • United States

CENGAGE
Learning™

Accounting 1A: Financial Accounting

Warren/Reeve/Duchac

Executive Editors:
 Maureen Staudt
 Michael Stranz

Senior Project Development Manager:
 Linda DeStefano

Marketing Specialist:
 Sara Mercurio
 Lindsay Shapiro

Senior Production / Manufacturing Manager:
 Donna M. Brown

PreMedia Supervisor:
 Joel Brennecke

Rights & Permissions Specialist:
 Kalina Hintz
 Todd Osborne

Cover Image:
 Getty Images*

* Unless otherwise noted, all cover images used by Custom Solutions, a part of Cengage Learning, have been supplied courtesy of Getty Images with the exception of the Earthview cover image, which has been supplied by the National Aeronautics and Space Administration (NASA).

ISBN-13: 978-1-111-00693-8

ISBN-10: 1-111-00693-8

Cengage Learning
5191 Natorp Boulevard
Mason, Ohio 45040
USA

Cengage Learning is a leading provider of customized learning solutions with office locations around the globe, including Singapore, the United Kingdom, Australia, Mexico, Brazil, and Japan. Locate your local office at:
international.cengage.com/region

Cengage Learning products are represented in Canada by Nelson Education, Ltd.

For your lifelong learning solutions, visit **www.cengage.com/custom**

Visit our corporate website at **www.cengage.com**

Printed in the United States of America

Brief Custom Contents

The Author Team

Carl S. Warren

Dr. Carl S. Warren is Professor Emeritus of Accounting at the University of Georgia, Athens. Dr. Warren has taught classes at the University of Georgia, University of Iowa, Michigan State University, and University of Chicago. Professor Warren focused his teaching efforts on principles of accounting and auditing. He received his Ph.D. from Michigan State University and his B.B.A. and M.A. from the University of Iowa. During his career, Dr. Warren published numerous articles in professional journals, including *The Accounting Review, Journal of Accounting Research, Journal of Accountancy, The CPA Journal,* and *Auditing: A Journal of Practice & Theory.* Dr. Warren has served on numerous committees of the American Accounting Association, the American Institute of Certified Public Accountants, and the Institute of Internal Auditors. He has also consulted with numerous companies and public accounting firms. Warren's outside interests include playing handball, golfing, skiing, backpacking, and fly-fishing.

James M. Reeve

Dr. James M. Reeve is Professor Emeritus of Accounting and Information Management at the University of Tennessee. Professor Reeve taught on the accounting faculty for 25 years, after graduating with his Ph.D. from Oklahoma State University. His teaching effort focused on undergraduate accounting principles and graduate education in the Master of Accountancy and Senior Executive MBA programs. Beyond this, Professor Reeve is also very active in the Supply Chain Certification program, which is a major executive education and research effort of the College. His research interests are varied and include work in managerial accounting, supply chain management, lean manufacturing, and information management. He has published over 40 articles in academic and professional journals, including the *Journal of Cost Management, Journal of Management Accounting Research, Accounting Review, Management Accounting Quarterly, Supply Chain Management Review,* and *Accounting Horizons.* He has consulted or provided training around the world for a wide variety of organizations, including Boeing, Procter and Gamble, Norfolk Southern, Hershey Foods, Coca-Cola, and Sony. When not writing books, Professor Reeve plays golf and is involved in faith-based activities.

Jonathan Duchac

Dr. Jonathan Duchac is the Merrill Lynch and Co. Professor of Accounting and Director of the Program in Enterprise Risk Management at Wake Forest University. He earned his Ph.D. in accounting from the University of Georgia and currently teaches introductory and advanced courses in financial accounting. Dr. Duchac has received a number of awards during his career, including the Wake Forest University Outstanding Graduate Professor Award, the T.B. Rose award for Instructional Innovation, and the University of Georgia Outstanding Teaching Assistant Award. In addition to his teaching responsibilities, Dr. Duchac has served as Accounting Advisor to Merrill Lynch Equity Research, where he worked with research analysts in reviewing and evaluating the financial reporting practices of public companies. He has testified before the U.S. House of Representatives, the Financial Accounting Standards Board, and the Securities and Exchange Commission; and has worked with a number of major public companies on financial reporting and accounting policy issues. In addition to his professional interests, Dr. Duchac is the Treasurer of The Special Children's School of Winston-Salem; a private, nonprofit developmental day school serving children with special needs. Dr. Duchac is an avid long-distance runner, mountain biker, and snow skier. His recent events include the Grandfather Mountain Marathon, the Black Mountain Marathon, the Shut-In Ridge Trail run, and NO MAAM (Nocturnal Overnight Mountain Bike Assault on Mount Mitchell).

For nearly 80 years, *Accounting* has been used effectively to teach generations of businessmen and women. The text has been used by millions of business students. For many, this book provides the only exposure to accounting principles that they will ever receive. As the most successful business textbook of all time, it continues to introduce students to accounting through a variety of time-tested ways.

The previous edition, 9e, started a new journey into learning more about the changing needs of accounting students through a variety of new and innovative research and development methods. Our Blue Sky Workshops brought accounting faculty from all over the country into our book development process in a very direct and creative way. Many of the features and themes present in this text are a result of the collaboration and countless conversations we've had with accounting instructors over the last several years. 10e continues to build on this philosophy and strives to be reflective of the suggestions and feedback we receive from instructors and students on an ongoing basis. We're very happy with the results, and think you'll be pleased with the improvements we've made to the text.

The original author of *Accounting*, James McKinsey, could not have imagined the success and influence this text has enjoyed or that his original vision would continue to lead the market into the twenty-first century. As the current authors, we appreciate the responsibility of protecting and enhancing this vision, while continuing to refine it to meet the changing needs of students and instructors. Always in touch with a tradition of excellence but never satisfied with yesterday's success, this edition enthusiastically embraces a changing environment and continues to proudly lead the way. We sincerely thank our many colleagues who have helped to make it happen.

Carl S. Warren

Jonathan Duchac

"The teaching of accounting is no longer designed to train professional accountants only. With the growing complexity of business and the constantly increasing difficulty of the problems of management, it has become essential that everyone who aspires to a position of responsibility should have a knowledge of the fundamental principles of accounting."

— James O. McKinsey, Author, first edition, 1929

Textbooks continue to play an invaluable role in the teaching and learning environment. Continuing our focus from previous editions, we reached out to accounting teachers in an effort to improve the textbook presentation. New for this edition, we have extended our discussions to reach out to students directly in order to learn what they value in a textbook. Here's a preview of some of the improvements we've made to this edition based on student input:

(NEW!) Guiding Principles System

Students can easily locate the information they need to master course concepts with the new "Guiding Principles System (GPS)." At the beginning of every chapter, this innovative system plots a course through the chapter content by displaying the chapter objectives, major topics, and related Example Exercises. The GPS reference to the chapter "At a Glance" summary completes this proven system.

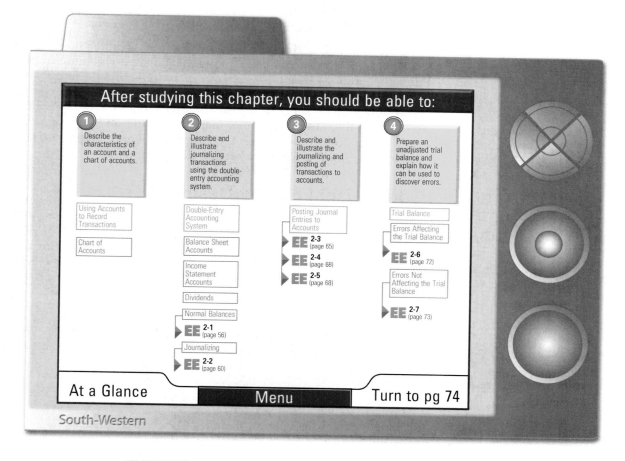

(NEW!) Written for Today's Students

Designed for today's students, the 10th edition has been extensively revised using an innovative, high-impact writing style that emphasizes topics in a concise and clearly written manner. Direct sentences, concise paragraphs, numbered lists, and step-by-step calculations provide students with an easy-to-follow structure for learning accounting. This is achieved without sacrificing content or rigor.

Leading by Example

NEW! Mornin' Joe Financial Statements

Beginning after "Accounting for Merchandising Businesses" and continuing through Chapter 13, "Investments and Fair Value Accounting," each chapter contains an excerpt from the full financial statements for Mornin' Joe, a coffee company. The addition of this new example shows students the big picture of accounting by providing a consistent reference point for users who want to see an entire set of financial statements and the way each chapter topic fits within them. The financial statements were crafted by the authors to be consistent with the presentation in each chapter.

NEW! Revised Coverage of Investments

A new chapter on investments and fair value accounting has been written to consolidate coverage of both dept and equity investments. The chapter also contains a conceptual discussion of fair value accounting and its increasing role in defining today's modern accounting methods.

NEW! IFRS Coverage

No topic is on the minds of many accounting practitioners more than the possible convergence of IFRS and GAAP. How accounting educators handle this emerging reality is perhaps even more of a question going forward. To help address this, the authors have written an appendix located in the back of the text that provides a short overview of what IFRS is and what it means for the future. In addition, an outline of many of the major differences between IFRS and GAAP that includes chapter and objective references is also included. IFRS icons now exist in the margin throughout the text to help highlight certain areas where differences exist between these standards.

NEW! Modern User-Friendly Design

Based on students' testimonials of what they find most useful, this streamlined presentation includes a wealth of helpful resources without the clutter. To update the look of the material, some exhibits use computerized spreadsheets to better reflect the changing environment of business. Visual learners will appreciate the generous number of exhibits and illustrations used to convey concepts and procedures.

Exhibit 4

Retained Earnings Statement for Merchandising Business

NetSolutions Retained Earnings Statement For the Year Ended December 31, 2011		
Retained earnings, January 1, 2011		$128,800
Net income for the year	$75,400	
Less dividends	18,000	
Increase in retained earnings		57,400
Retained earnings, December 31, 2011		$186,200

	Journal			Page 25	
Date	Description	Post. Ref.	Debit	Credit	
2011 Jan. 3	Cash		1,800		
	Sales			1,800	
	To record cash sales.				

Chapter Updates and Enhancements

The following includes some of the specific content changes that can be found in *Financial and Managerial Accounting, 10e*.

Chapter 1: Introduction to Accounting and Business

- Starbucks replaces DaimlerChrysler in opening lead-in example.
- Discussion of "types of business organizations" has been moved to later in the chapter. Proprietorships, partnerships, corporations, and limited liability companies (LLC) are now discussed with the business entity concept.
- "General-purpose financial statements" has been added as a new key term.
- New Exhibit 3 provides guidelines for ethical conduct.
- Discussion on career opportunities for accountants has been updated.
- Improved formatting of transaction discussion for NetSolutions for greater clarity.
- International Accounting Standards Board (IASB) and *International Financial Reporting Standards* are now mentioned in the discussion of generally accepted accounting principles.
- New Financial Analysis and Interpretation (FAI) box has been added that introduces the ratio for liabilities to owner's equity.

Chapter 2: Analyzing Transactions

- New chapter opener features Apple.
- New section on the double-entry accounting system (Objective 2) provides improved coverage of the rules of debit and credit for balance sheet, income statement, and owner drawing account. This discussion includes normal balances of accounts. In addition, Exhibit 3 was revised so that it better summarizes the rules of debits and credits for students to refer to when working end-of-chapter homework.
- Discussion of recording transactions in accounts has been streamlined by including the discussion of the rules of debits and credits earlier in the chapter. Also, a new more simplified format for the journal and accounts is used.
- Each illustrated transaction now includes the following sections: "Transaction, Analysis, and Journal Entry." In addition, new line art design improves the presentation of journal entries and accounts.
- Discussion of discovery and correction of errors has been revised and is now integrated into the discussion of the unadjusted trial balance.
- New FAI feature has been added that discusses horizontal analysis of financial statements.

Chapter 3: The Adjusting Process

- Discussion of the adjusting process has been revised to list the reasons for updating some accounts in the ledger under accrual accounting.
- A new Exhibit 6 on Summary of Adjustments has been developed to include the reason for each adjustment, the adjusting entry, example adjusting entries from NetSolutions, and the financial statement impact if adjusting is omitted.
- New FAI feature has been added that discusses vertical analysis of financial statements.

Chapter 4: Completing the Accounting Cycle

- New spreadsheet format provides row and column labels that are more consistent with Microsoft Excel to reflect what students will see in practice.
- Integrated all accounts necessary to complete the spreadsheet directly into the spreadsheet rather than adding them at the bottom of the spreadsheet. As reviewer feedback notes, this is consistent with using Microsoft Excel where new rows (accounts) can be directly inserted into the spreadsheet at their appropriate place.
- New exhibit for preparing the work sheet (spreadsheet) has been added that separates the individual adjustments from the adjusted trial balance totals.
- Added stepwise approach to preparing the work sheet (spreadsheet).

- Added "closing the books" as a key term. Added (permanent) descriptor to real accounts key term.
- New FAI feature covers working capital and the current ratio.

Chapter 5: Accounting for Merchandising Businesses

- New chapter opener features Dollar Tree, Inc.
- For added clarity, "transportation" terminology has been changed to "freight." For example, instead of transportation costs, we use freight costs or simply freight.
- For added clarity, this edition provides a fuller definition of debit (credit) memorandums. For efficiency, they are usually referenced as just debit memo or credit memo.
- In the appendix to this chapter (The Periodic Inventory System), "Transportation In" was switched to "Freight In" for consistency with the chapter presentation.

Chapter 6: Inventories

- Begin financial reporting illustrations using Mornin' Joe to reinforce the importance of financial statements to a business and as a framework to learn accounting.
- Significantly revised section on "Effect of Inventory Errors on the Financial Statements." Added new Exhibits 9, 10, and 11. The section begins with a list of reasons that inventory errors can occur. Further illustrations get into the effects on the income statement and balance sheet. Exhibit 9 depicts the inventory error and whether the effect is understated or overstated in terms of COMS, gross profit, and net income. Exhibit 10 shows the effects of inventory errors on two years of income statements. Exhibit 11 shows the ending error and whether it is overstated or understated as it relates to merchandise inventory, current assets, total assets, and owner's equity (capital).
- Moved the "Estimating Inventory Cost" section from the chapter to an appendix at the end of the chapter. This section describes and illustrates "retail" and the "gross profit" methods of estimating inventory. The end-of-chapter materials still include exercises and one problem (A and B) for this appendix.

Chapter 7: Sarbanes-Oxley, Internal Control, and Cash

- New illustration and journal entry for "Cash Short and Over" provides a visual presentation to reinforce this concept.
- For added clarity, "Depositor" terminology has change to "Company" in the bank reconciliations.
- Added check numbers to Exhibit 5, illustration of a bank statement. This is done based on user feedback and reflects that most banks do not return checks but simply list the cleared checks (by check number) on the bank statement.
- Added stepwise illustration of how to prepare the bank statement (see Exhibit 7).
- Used Mornin' Joe as the financial statement reporting illustration to reinforce the importance of financial statements to a business and as a framework to learn accounting.

Chapter 8: Receivables

- New chapter opener features Oakley, Inc.
- Illustrations for allowance methods revised to use the same data to facilitate comparisons of the percent of sales and aging of receivables methods.
- New Exhibit 2 comparing percent of sales and aging of receivables methods.
- New illustration of promissory note (Exhibit 4) provides a visual reference to reinforce this concept.
- Used Mornin' Joe as the financial statement reporting illustration to reinforce the importance of financial statements to a business and as a framework to learn accounting.

Chapter 9: Fixed Assets and Intangible Assets

- New Exhibit 7, Comparing Depreciation Methods, compares depreciation methods using chapter illustration.

- Exchanging of similar fixed assets moved to end of chapter appendix (Appendix 2). Related end-of-chapter materials are still included.
- Used Mornin' Joe as the financial statement reporting illustration to reinforce the importance of financial statements to a business and as a framework to learn accounting.

Chapter 10: Current Liabilities and Payroll

- Updated federal withholding table and revised chapter illustrations.
- Revised "Contingent Liabilities" section including Exhibit 10.
- Used Mornin' Joe as the financial statement reporting illustration to reinforce the importance of financial statements to a business and as a framework to learn accounting.

Chapter 11: Corporations: Organization, Stock Transactions, and Dividends

- New chapter opener features Hasbro, Inc.
- Added discussion of cumulative preferred stock with dividends in arrears.
- Used Mornin' Joe as the financial statement reporting illustration to reinforce the importance of financial statements to a business and as a framework to learn accounting.

Chapter 12: Long-Term Liabilities: Bonds and Notes

This chapter was based on Chapter 13 in 9e. Objectives for this chapter are:

- Objective 1: Compute the potential impact of long-term borrowing on earnings per share.
- Objective 2: Describe the characteristics and terminology of bonds payable.
- Objective 3: Journalize entries for bonds payable.
- Objective 4: Describe and illustrate the accounting for installment notes.
- Objective 5: Describe and illustrate the reporting of long-term liabilities including bonds and notes payable.
- A new objective has been added that includes discussion of installment notes.
- Discussion of pricing of bonds using present values moved to Appendix 1 at the end of the chapter. Related end-of-chapter is still included.
- "Effective Interest Rate Method of Amortization" is now Appendix 2 at the end of the chapter. Related end-of-chapter is still included.

NOTE: Chapter 12 from the prior edition no longer exists. The material from Chapter 12 of 9e has been redistributed as follows:

9e Chapter	Topic	10e Chapter
Chapter 12	Deferred Taxes	Appendix D (back of text)
Chapter 12	Reporting Unusual Items on the Income Statement	Chapter 15 (FSA Appendix)
Chapter 12	Earnings Per Common Share	Chapters 12, 15
Chapter 12	Comprehensive Income	Chapter 13 (Appendix 2)
Chapter 12	Accounting for Investments in Stocks	Chapter 13
Chapter 13	Characteristics of Bonds Payable	Chapter 12
Chapter 13	Payment and Redemption of Bonds Payable	Chapter 12
Chapter 13	Investments in Bonds	Chapter 13
Chapter 13	Appendix: Effective Interest Rate Method of Amortization	Chapter 12

(NEW!) Chapter 13: Investments and Fair Value Accounting

A new chapter on "Investments and Fair Value Accounting" has been written for this edition, consolidating all investments-related topics into one chapter based on market feedback. The objectives for this chapter are:

- Objective 1: Describe why companies invest in debt and equity securities.
- Objective 2: Describe and illustrate the accounting for debt investments.
- Objective 3: Describe and illustrate the accounting for equity investments.
- Objective 4: Describe and illustrate valuing and reporting investments in the financial statements.
- Objective 5: Describe fair value accounting and its implications for the future.
- Chapter opener features News Corporation.
- Appendix 1 covers accounting for held-to-maturity investments.
- Appendix 2 covers the topic of comprehensive income.

Chapter 14: Statement of Cash Flows

- Revised beginning section discussing the statement of cash flows (SCF) and illustrating the format for the SCF under the direct and indirect methods.
- Revised beginning discussion of direct method to emphasize conversion of accrual income statement to cash flows from operations (on an item-by-item basis). New graphic for conversion of interest expense to cash payments for interest provides visual reinforcement for this topic.
- Used stepwise format for preparing the statement of cash flows under indirect and direct methods.
- Used stepwise format for preparing the work sheet for the indirect method in the end-of-chapter appendix.

Chapter 15: Financial Statement Analysis

- New chapter opener features Nike, Inc.
- Real world financial statement analysis problem features data from the Nike, Inc. 2007 10K, which can be found in Appendix F in the back of the text.
- Each ratio is highlighted in a boxed screen for easier review.
- Appendix on "Unusual Items on the Income Statement" was added.

Chapter 16: Managerial Accounting Concepts and Principles

- Added a new section at the beginning of the chapter on the uses of managerial accounting, which references subsequent chapters where the uses are described and illustrated.
- Added an illustration of comparing merchandising and manufacturing income statements.
- Added format for the cost of goods manufactured statement.
- Added stepwise preparation of the cost of goods manufactured.

Chapter 17: Job Order Costing

- Added format for the entries used to dispose of overapplied or underapplied factory overhead.
- Changed order of entries so that entries for sales and cost of goods sold are shown separately from the finished goods entry for completed units.

Chapter 18: Process Cost Systems

- Revised Exhibit 2 and accompanying narrative so that Exhibit 2 ties into Exhibit 8, which illustrates entries for Frozen Delights.
- Revised illustration of cost of production report so that units are classified into groups consisting of beginning work in process units (Group 1), started and completed units (Group 2), and ending work in process units (Group 3). This aids students in computing unit costs and assigning costs to groups using first-in, first-out inventory cost flow. Accompanying exhibits and art also classify units by these groups.
- Revised and expanded the section on using the cost of production report for decision making to include an example from Frozen Delights.

Chapter 19: Cost Behavior and Cost-Volume-Profit Analysis

- Supplemented the mixed cost discussion by adding an equation for determining fixed costs.
- Added contribution margin equation to cost-volume-profit discussion.
- Added unit contribution margin equation to cost-volume-profit discussion.
- Added "change in income from operations" equation based on unit contribution margin to cost-volume-profit discussion.
- Incorporated a discussion of computing break-even in sales dollars using contribution margin ratio.
- Added a stepwise approach to discussion of preparing cost-volume-profit and profit-volume charts.
- Added equation for computing the percent change in income from operations using "operating leverage."
- Expanded discussion of margin of safety so that margin of safety may be expressed in sales dollars, units, or percent of current sales.
- Revised appendix on variable costing to include format for variable costing income statement.

Chapter 20: Variable Costing for Management Analysis

- Chapter objectives revised slightly.
- Generic absorption and variable costing income reporting formats illustrated in Objective 1, followed by numerical examples.
- Graphic on page 912 revised to include units manufactured = units sold.
- Formulas (equations) added for contribution margin analysis section, Objective 5.
- Exhibits 11, 12, and 16 revised for clarity.

Chapter 21: Budgeting

- Made minor changes to chapter objectives.
- Added stepwise approach to preparing a flexible budget.
- Modified the definition of the master budget.
- Added new classifications of budget components of the master budget as operating, investing, and financing budget components.
- Added format for determining "total units to be produced."
- Added format for determining "direct materials to be purchased."

Chapter 22: Performance Evaluation Using Variances from Standard Costs

- Added a 2nd level heading for Objective 1, "Criticisms of Standard Costs."
- Added several new headings for Objective 2, "Budget Performance Report" and "Manufacturing Cost Variances."
- Revised discussion of "Manufacturing Cost Variances" to better tie into subsequent discussion of standard cost variances.
- Utilized a new equation format for computing standard cost variances. Using these equations, a positive amount indicates an unfavorable variance while a negative amount indicates a favorable variance. Later in the chapter, positive variance amounts are recorded as debits and negative variance amounts are recorded as credits.
- Revised the factory overhead variance discussion to include equations for computing total, variable, and fixed factory overhead rates. These rates are then used to explain and illustrate the computation of the controllable factory overhead variance and the volume factory overhead variance.
- Revised the factory overhead variance discussion to use equations for computing the controllable and volume variances.
- Revised the discussion of how the total factory overhead cost variance is related to overapplied or underapplied overhead balance. Further explanation is provided to show how the overapplied or underapplied overhead balance can be separated into the controllable and volume variances.
- Added new key terms for budgeted variable factory overhead, favorable cost variance, unfavorable cost variance, and standards.

Chapter 23: Performance Evaluation for Decentralized Operations

- Modified the chapter objectives slightly.
- Added equations for computing service department charge rates.
- Presented equations for allocating service department charges to decentralized operations (divisions).
- Added example format for determining residual income.
- Added equations for computing increases and decreases in divisional income using different negotiated transfer prices.

Chapter 24: Differential Analysis and Product Pricing

- Added section on managerial decision making. Objective 1 now includes a new flowchart depicting the steps that define the decision-making process.
- Added equations (e.g., markup percentages, desired profit) to "Setting Normal Product Selling Prices" Section.
- Adopted a stepwise approach to setting normal prices for each cost-plus (total, product, variable) concept.
- Added Exhibit 11 to summarize cost-plus approaches to setting normal prices.
- Added equation to determine "contribution margin per bottleneck constraint."
- Presented equations for assessing product pricing and cost decisions related to bottlenecks.
- Added equation for determining "activity rate" in Activity-Based Costing appendix.

Chapter 25: Capital Investment Analysis

- Replaced XM Satellite Radio with Carnival Corporation as the opener vignette.
- Revised the learning objectives so that the nonpresent value (average rate of return and cash payback) methods have a separate learning objective from the present value (net present value and internal rate of return) methods.
- Added an equation for determining the "average investment" for use in the average rate of return method.
- Added an equation for determining the "cash payback period."
- Added a graphic for determining the present value of $1 along with additional explanations of present values.
- Added format for using the net present value method that is consistent with that shown in the solutions manual.
- Added an equation for determining the present value index.

Chapter 26: Cost Allocation and Activity-Based Costing

- Added discussion and illustration of conditions when a single-plantwide rate might cause product cost distortions.
- Added equations for determining activity rates.

Chapter 27: Cost Management for Just-in-Time Environments

- Chapter Objective 1 revised slightly.
- Added equation for computing "Value-Added Ratio" for lead time.
- Added equation for computing "Total Within-Batch Wait Time."
- Deleted Learning Objective 2 (Andersen Metal Fabricators" illustration) from previous edition.
- Moved discussion of JIT for nonmanufacturing setting to precede implications of JIT for cost accounting.

Financial and Managerial Accounting, 10e, is unparalleled in pedagogical innovation. Our constant dialogue with accounting faculty continues to affect how we refine and improve the text to meet the needs of today's students. Our goal is to provide a logical framework and pedagogical system that caters to how students of today study and learn.

Clear Objectives and Key Learning Outcomes

To help guide students, the authors provide clear chapter objectives and important learning outcomes. All aspects of the chapter materials relate back to these key points and outcomes, which keeps students focused on the most important topics and concepts in order to succeed in the course.

1 Describe the nature of a business, the role of accounting, and ethics in business.

EX 5-1
Determining gross profit

obj. 1

During the current year, merchandise is sold for $795,000. The cost of the merchandise sold is $477,000.

a. What is the amount of the gross profit?
b. Compute the gross profit percentage (gross profit divided by sales).
c. ⟶ Will the income statement necessarily report a net income? Explain.

Example Exercises

Example Exercises were developed to reinforce concepts and procedures in a bold, new way. Like a teacher in the classroom, students follow the authors' example to see how to complete accounting applications as they are presented in the text. This feature also provides a list of Practice Exercises that parallel the Example Exercises so students get the practice they need. In addition, the Practice Exercises also include references to the chapter Example Exercises so that students can easily cross-reference when completing homework.

See the example of the application being presented.

Follow along as the authors work through the Example Exercise.

Try these corresponding end-of-chapter exercises for practice!

Example Exercise 2-2   Journal Entry for Asset Purchase   •••••••• ➤ **2**

Prepare a journal entry for the purchase of a truck on June 3 for $42,500, paying $8,500 cash and the remainder on account.

Follow My Example 2-2

June 3	Truck	42,500	
	Cash		8,500
	Accounts Payable		34,000

➤ **For Practice: PE 2-2A, PE 2-2B**

"At a Glance" Chapter Summary

The "At a Glance" summary grid ties everything together and helps students stay on track. First, the Key Points recap the chapter content for each chapter objective. Second, the related Key Learning Outcomes list all of the expected student performance capabilities that come from completing each objective. In case students need further practice on a specific outcome, the last two columns reference related Example Exercises and their corresponding Practice Exercises. In addition, the "At a Glance" grid guides struggling students from the assignable Practice Exercises to the resources in the chapter that will help them complete their homework. Through this intuitive grid, all of the chapter pedagogy links together in one cleanly integrated summary.

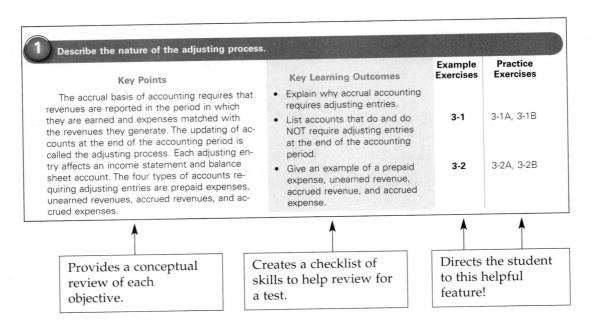

1 **Describe the nature of the adjusting process.**

Key Points	Key Learning Outcomes	Example Exercises	Practice Exercises
The accrual basis of accounting requires that revenues are reported in the period in which they are earned and expenses matched with the revenues they generate. The updating of accounts at the end of the accounting period is called the adjusting process. Each adjusting entry affects an income statement and balance sheet account. The four types of accounts requiring adjusting entries are prepaid expenses, unearned revenues, accrued revenues, and accrued expenses.	• Explain why accrual accounting requires adjusting entries. • List accounts that do and do NOT require adjusting entries at the end of the accounting period.	3-1	3-1A, 3-1B
	• Give an example of a prepaid expense, unearned revenue, accrued revenue, and accrued expense.	3-2	3-2A, 3-2B

Provides a conceptual review of each objective.

Creates a checklist of skills to help review for a test.

Directs the student to this helpful feature!

Real-World Chapter Openers

Building on the strengths of past editions, these openers continue to relate the accounting and business concepts in the chapter to students' lives. These openers employ examples of real companies and provide invaluable insight into real practice. Several of the openers created especially for this edition focus on interesting companies such as Apple; Dollar Tree; Hasbro; and News Corporation (Fox), the parent company of the hit television shows *American Idol* and *The Simpsons*.

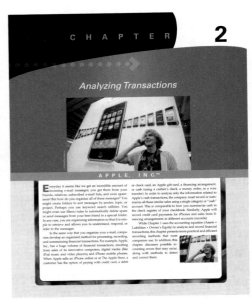

Financial Analysis and Interpretation

The "Financial Analysis and Interpretation" section at the end of each accounting chapter introduces relevant key ratios used throughout the textbook. Students connect with the business environment as they learn how stakeholders interpret financial reports. This section covers basic analysis tools that students will use again in Chapter 15, "Financial Statement Analysis." Furthermore, students get to test their proficiency with these tools through special activities and exercises at the end of each chapter. To ensure a consistent presentation, a unique icon is used for both the section and related end-of-chapter materials.

Financial Analysis and Interpretation

Comparing each item in a current statement with a total amount within that same statement is useful in analyzing relationships within a financial statement. *Vertical analysis* is the term used to describe such comparisons.

In vertical analysis of a balance sheet, each asset item is stated as a percent of the total assets. Each liability and owner's equity item is stated as a percent of the total liabilities and owner's equity. In vertical analysis of an income statement, each item is stated as a percent of revenues or fees earned.

Vertical analysis may be prepared for several periods to analyze changes in relationships over time. Vertical analysis of two years of income statements for J. Holmes, Attorney-at-Law, is shown below.

The preceding vertical analysis indicates both favorable and unfavorable trends affecting the income statement of J. Holmes, Attorney-at-Law. The increase in wages expense of 2% (32% − 30%) is an unfavorable trend, as is the increase in utilities expense of 0.7% (6.7% − 6.0%). A favorable trend is the decrease in supplies expense of 0.6% (2.0% − 1.4%). Rent expense and miscellaneous expense as a percent of fees earned were constant. The net result of these trends was that net income decreased as a percent of fees earned from 52.8% to 50.7%.

The analysis of the various percentages shown for J. Holmes, Attorney-at-Law, can be enhanced by comparisons with industry averages. Such averages are published by trade associations and financial information services. Any major differences between industry averages should be investigated.

J. Holmes, Attorney-at-Law
Income Statements
For the Years Ended December 31, 2010 and 2009

	2010 Amount	2010 Percent	2009 Amount	2009 Percent
Fees earned	$187,500	100.0%	$150,000	100.0%
Operating expenses:				
Wages expense	$ 60,000	32.0%	$ 45,000	30.0%*
Rent expense	15,000	8.0%	12,000	8.0%
Utilities expense	12,500	6.7%	9,000	6.0%
Supplies expense	2,700	1.4%	3,000	2.0%
Miscellaneous expense	2,300	1.2%	1,800	1.2%
Total operating expenses	$ 92,500	49.3%	$ 70,800	47.2%
Net income	$ 95,000	50.7%	$ 79,200	52.8%

*$45,000 ÷ $150,000

Business Connection and Comprehensive Real-World Notes

Students get a close-up look at how accounting operates in the marketplace through a variety of items in the margins and in the "Business Connection" boxed features. In addition, a variety of end-of-chapter exercises and problems employ real-world data to give students a feel for the material that accountants see daily. No matter where they are found, elements that use material from real companies are indicated with a unique icon for a consistent presentation.

Business Connection

THE ACCOUNTING EQUATION

The accounting equation serves as the basic foundation for the accounting systems of all companies. From the smallest business, such as the local convenience store, to the largest business, such as Ford Motor Company, companies use the accounting equation. Some examples taken from recent financial reports of well-known companies are shown below.

Company	Assets*	=	Liabilities	+	Owner's Equity
The Coca-Cola Company	$ 29,963	=	$13,043	+	$16,920
Circuit City Stores, Inc.	4,007	=	2,216	+	1,791
Dell Inc.	25,635	=	21,196	+	4,439
eBay Inc.	13,494	=	2,589	+	10,905
Google	18,473	=	1,433	+	17,040
McDonald's	29,024	=	13,566	+	15,458
Microsoft Corporation	63,171	=	32,074	+	31,097
Southwest Airlines Co.	13,460	=	7,011	+	6,449
Wal-Mart	151,193	=	89,620	+	61,573

*Amounts are shown in millions of dollars.

Leading by Example

Integrity, Objectivity, and Ethics in Business

In each chapter, these cases help students develop their ethical compass. Often coupled with related end-of-chapter activities, these cases can be discussed in class or students can consider the cases as they read the chapter. Both the section and related end-of-chapter materials are indicated with a unique icon for a consistent presentation.

Integrity, Objectivity, and Ethics in Business

ACCOUNTING REFORM

The financial accounting and reporting failures of Enron, WorldCom, Tyco, Xerox, and others shocked the investing public. The disclosure that some of the nation's largest and best-known corporations had overstated profits and misled investors raised the question: Where were the CPAs?

In response, Congress passed the Investor Protection, Auditor Reform, and Transparency Act of 2002, called the Sarbanes-Oxley Act. The Act establishes a Public Company Accounting Oversight Board to regulate the portion of the accounting profession that has public companies as clients. In addition, the Act prohibits auditors (CPAs) from providing certain types of nonaudit services, such as investment banking or legal services, to their clients, prohibits employment of auditors by clients for one year after they last audited the client, and increases penalties for the reporting of misleading financial statements.

Continuing Case Study

@netsolutions

Students follow a fictitious company, NetSolutions, throughout Chapters 1–5, which demonstrates a variety of transactions. The continuity of using the same company facilitates student learning especially for Chapters 1–4, which cover the accounting cycle. Also, using the same company allows students to follow the transition of the company from a service business in Chapters 1–4 to a merchandising business in Chapter 5.

Summaries

Within each chapter, these synopses draw special attention to important points and help clarify difficult concepts.

Self-Examination Questions

Five multiple-choice questions, with answers at the end of the chapter, help students review and retain chapter concepts.

Illustrative Problem and Solution

A solved problem models one or more of the chapter's assignment problems so that students can apply the modeled procedures to end-of-chapter materials.

Market Leading End-of-Chapter Material

Students need to practice accounting so that they can understand and use it. To give students the greatest possible advantage in the real world, *Financial and Managerial Accounting, 10e,* goes beyond presenting theory and procedure with comprehensive, time-tested, end-of-chapter material.

South-Western, a division of Cengage Learning, offers a vast array of online solutions to suit your course needs. Choose the product that best meets your classroom needs and course goals. Please check with your Cengage representative for more details or for ordering information.

Aplia

Founded in 2000 by economist and Stanford professor Paul Romer, Aplia is an educational technology company dedicated to improving learning by increasing student effort and engagement. Currently, our products support college-level courses and have been used by more than 650,000 students at over 750 institutions.

For students, Aplia offers a way to stay on top of coursework with regularly scheduled homework assignments. Interactive tools and content further increase engagement and understanding.

For professors, Aplia offers high-quality, auto-graded assignments, which ensure that students put forth effort on a regular basis throughout the term. These assignments have been developed for a range of textbooks and are easily customized for individual teaching schedules.

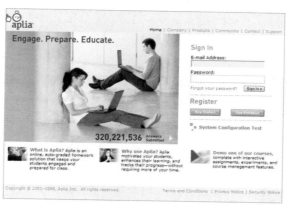

Every day, we develop our products by responding to the needs and concerns of the students and professors who use Aplia in their classrooms. As you explore the features and benefits Aplia has to offer, we hope to hear from you as well.

Welcome to Aplia.

CengageNOW *Express*

CengageNOW *Express*™ for Warren/Reeve/Duchac *Financial and Managerial Accounting*, 10e, is an online homework solution that delivers better student outcomes—NOW! CengageNOW *Express* focuses on the textbook homework that is central to success in accounting with streamlined course start-up, straightforward assignment creation, automatic grading and tracking student progress, and instant feedback for students.

- Streamlined Course Start-Up: All Brief Exercises, Exercises, Problems, and Comprehensive Problems are available immediately for students to practice.
- Straightforward Assignment Creation: Select required exercises and problems, and CengageNOW *Express* automatically applies faculty approved, Accounting Homework Options.
- Automatic grading and tracking student progress: CengageNOW *Express* grades and captures students' scores to easily monitor their progress. Export the grade book to Excel for easy data management.
- Instant feedback for students: Students stay on track with instructor-written hints and immediate feedback with every assignment. Links to the e-book, animated exercise demonstrations, and Excel spreadsheets from specific assignments are ideal for student review.

CengageNOW

CengageNOW for Warren/Reeve/Duchac *Financial and Managerial Accounting*, 10e, is a powerful and fully integrated online teaching and learning system that provides you with flexibility and control. This complete digital solution offers a comprehensive set of digital tools to power your course. CengageNOW offers the following:

- Homework, including algorithmic variations
- Integrated E-book
- Personalized Study Plans, which include a variety of multimedia assets (from exercise demonstrations to video to iPod content) for students as they master the chapter materials
- Assessment options which include the full test bank, including algorithmic variations
- Reporting capability based on AACSB, AICPA, and IMA competencies and standards
- Course Management tools, including grade book
- WebCT and Blackboard Integration

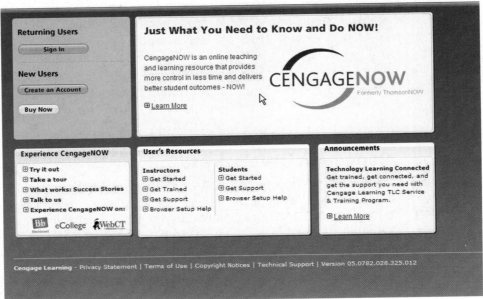

 **WebTutor™!**

Available packaged with Warren/Reeve/Duchac *Financial and Managerial Accounting*, 10e, **or for individual student purchase** Jumpstart your course with customizable, rich, text-specific content within your Course Management System.

- **Jumpstart**—Simply load a WebTutor cartridge into your Course Management System.
- **Customizable**—Easily blend, add, edit, reorganize, or delete content.
- **Content**—Rich, text-specific content, media assets, quizzing, test bank, weblinks, discussion topics, interactive games and exercises, and more.

Visit www.cengage.com for more information.

Introduction to Accounting and Business

G O O G L E™

When two teams pair up for a game of football, there is often a lot of noise. The band plays, the fans cheer, and fireworks light up the scoreboard. Obviously, the fans are committed and care about the outcome of the game. Just like fans at a football game, the owners of a business want their business to "win" against their competitors in the marketplace. While having our football team win can be a source of pride, winning in the marketplace goes beyond pride and has many tangible benefits. Companies that are winners are better able to serve customers, to provide good jobs for employees, and to make more money for the owners.

One such successful company is Google, one of the most visible companies on the Internet. Many of us cannot visit the Web without first stopping at Google to power your search. As one writer said, "Google is the closest thing the Web has

to an ultimate answer machine." And yet, Google is a free tool—no one asks for your credit card when you use any of Google's search tools. So, do you think Google has been a successful company? Does it make money? How would you know? Accounting helps to answer these questions. Google's accounting information tells us that Google is a very successful company that makes a lot of money, but not from you and me. Google makes its money from advertisers.

In this textbook, we will introduce you to accounting, the language of business. In this chapter, we begin by discussing what a business is, how it operates, and the role that accounting plays.

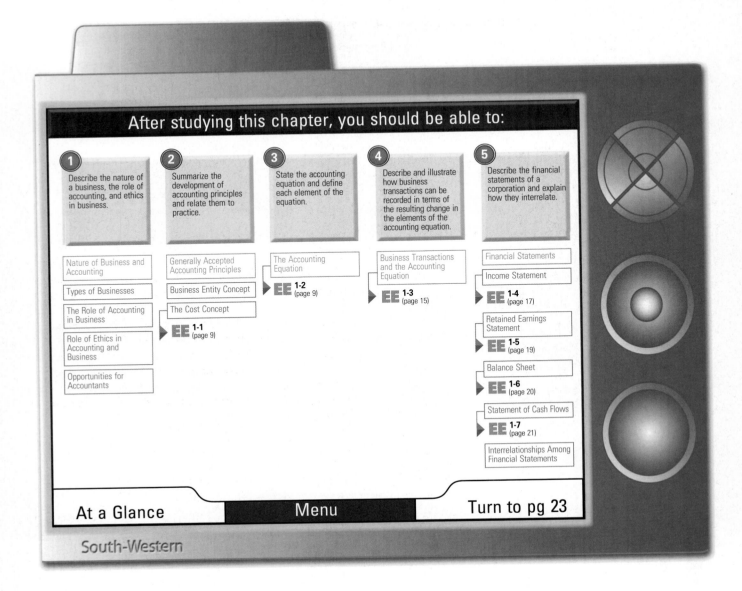

After studying this chapter, you should be able to:

1 Describe the nature of a business, the role of accounting, and ethics in business.

2 Summarize the development of accounting principles and relate them to practice.

3 State the accounting equation and define each element of the equation.

4 Describe and illustrate how business transactions can be recorded in terms of the resulting change in the elements of the accounting equation.

5 Describe the financial statements of a corporation and explain how they interrelate.

Nature of Business and Accounting

Types of Businesses

The Role of Accounting in Business

Role of Ethics in Accounting and Business

Opportunities for Accountants

Generally Accepted Accounting Principles

Business Entity Concept

The Cost Concept

EE 1-1 (page 9)

The Accounting Equation

EE 1-2 (page 9)

Business Transactions and the Accounting Equation

EE 1-3 (page 15)

Financial Statements

Income Statement

EE 1-4 (page 17)

Retained Earnings Statement

EE 1-5 (page 19)

Balance Sheet

EE 1-6 (page 20)

Statement of Cash Flows

EE 1-7 (page 21)

Interrelationships Among Financial Statements

| At a Glance | Menu | Turn to pg 23 |

South-Western

Nature of Business and Accounting

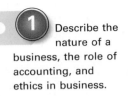

1 Describe the nature of a business, the role of accounting, and ethics in business.

A **business**[1] is an organization in which basic resources (inputs), such as materials and labor, are assembled and processed to provide goods or services (outputs) to customers. Businesses come in all sizes, from a local coffee house to Starbucks, which sells over $9 billion of coffee and related products each year.

The objective of most businesses is to earn a profit. **Profit** is the difference between the amounts received from customers for goods or services and the amounts paid for the inputs used to provide the goods or services. In this text, we focus on businesses operating to earn a profit. However many of the same concepts and principles also apply to not-for-profit organizations such as hospitals, churches, and government agencies.

Types of Businesses

Three types of businesses operated for profit include service, merchandising, and manufacturing businesses.

1 A complete glossary of terms appears at the end of the text.

Roughly eight out of every ten workers in the United States are service providers.

Each type of business and some examples are described below.

Service businesses provide services rather than products to customers.

> Delta Air Lines (transportation services)
> The Walt Disney Company (entertainment services)

Merchandising businesses sell products they purchase from other businesses to customers.

> Wal-Mart (general merchandise)
> Amazon.com (Internet books, music, videos)

Manufacturing businesses change basic inputs into products that are sold to customers.

> General Motors Corporation (cars, trucks, vans)
> Dell Inc. (personal computers)

The Role of Accounting in Business

What is the role of accounting in business? The simplest answer is that accounting provides information for managers to use in operating the business. In addition, accounting provides information to other users in assessing the economic performance and condition of the business.

> **Accounting is an information system that provides reports to users about the economic activities and condition of a business.**

Thus, **accounting** can be defined as an information system that provides reports to users about the economic activities and condition of a business. You may think of accounting as the "language of business." This is because accounting is the means by which businesses' financial information is communicated to users.

The process by which accounting provides information to users is as follows:

1. Identify users.
2. Assess users' information needs.
3. Design the accounting information system to meet users' needs.
4. Record economic data about business activities and events.
5. Prepare accounting reports for users.

As illustrated in Exhibit 1, users of accounting information can be divided into two groups: internal users and external users.

Exhibit 1

Users of Accounting Information

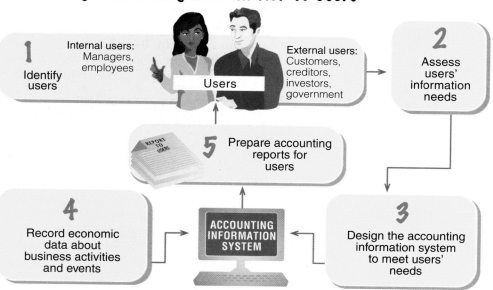

Providing Accounting Information to Users

Internal users of accounting information include managers and employees. These users are directly involved in managing and operating the business. The area of accounting that provides internal users with information is called **managerial accounting** or **management accounting**. The objective of managerial accounting is to provide relevant and timely information for managers' and employees' decision-making needs. Often times, such information is sensitive and is not distributed outside the business. Examples of sensitive information might include information about customers, prices, and plans to expand the business. Managerial accountants employed by a business are employed in **private accounting**.

External users of accounting information include customers, creditors, and the government. These users are not directly involved in managing and operating the business. The area of accounting that provides external users with information is called **financial accounting**. The objective of financial accounting is to provide relevant and timely information for the decision-making needs of users outside of the business. For example, financial reports on the operations and condition of the business are useful for banks and other creditors in deciding whether to lend money to the business. **General-purpose financial statements** are one type of financial accounting report that is distributed to external users. The term *general-purpose* refers to the wide range of decision-making needs that these reports are designed to serve. Later in this chapter, we describe and illustrate general-purpose financial statements.

Role of Ethics in Accounting and Business

The objective of accounting is to provide relevant, timely information for user decision making. Accountants must behave in an ethical manner so that the information they provide will be trustworthy and, thus, useful for decision making. Managers and employees must also behave in an ethical manner in managing and operating a business. Otherwise, no one will be willing to invest in or loan money to the business.

Ethics are moral principles that guide the conduct of individuals. Unfortunately, business managers and accountants sometimes behave in an unethical manner. A number of managers of the companies listed in Exhibit 2 engaged in accounting or business fraud. These ethical violations led to fines, firings, and lawsuits. In some cases, managers were criminally prosecuted, convicted, and sent to prison.

What went wrong for the managers and companies listed in Exhibit 2? The answer normally involved one or both of the following two factors:

Failure of Individual Character. An ethical manager and accountant is honest and fair. However, managers and accountants often face pressures from supervisors to meet company and investor expectations. In many of the cases in Exhibit 2, managers and accountants justified small ethical violations to avoid such pressures. However, these small violations became big violations as the company's financial problems became worse.

Culture of Greed and Ethical Indifference. By their behavior and attitude, senior managers set the company culture. In most of the companies listed in Exhibit 2, the senior managers created a culture of greed and indifference to the truth.

Integrity, Objectivity, and Ethics in Business

DOING THE RIGHT THING

Time Magazine named three women as "Persons of the Year 2002." Each of these not-so-ordinary women had the courage, determination, and integrity to do the right thing. Each risked their personal careers to expose shortcomings in their organizations. Sherron Watkins, an Enron vice president, wrote a letter to Enron's chairman, Kenneth Lay, warning him of improper accounting that eventually led to Enron's collapse. Cynthia Cooper, an internal accountant, informed WorldCom's Board of Directors of phony accounting that allowed WorldCom to cover up over $3 billion in losses and forced WorldCom into bankruptcy. Coleen Rowley, an FBI staff attorney, wrote a memo to FBI Director Robert Mueller, exposing how the Bureau brushed off her pleas to investigate Zacarias Moussaoui, who was indicted as a co-conspirator in the September 11 terrorist attacks.

Exhibit 2

Accounting and Business Fraud in the 2000s

Company	Nature of Accounting or Business Fraud	Result
Adelphia Communications	Rigas family treated the company assets as their own.	Bankruptcy. Rigas family members found guilty of fraud and lost their investment in the company.
American International Group, Inc. (AIG)	Used sham accounting transactions to inflate performance.	CEO resigned. Executives criminally convicted. AIG paid $126 million in fines.
America Online, Inc. and PurchasePro	Artificially inflated their financial results.	Civil charges filed against senior executives of both companies. $500 million fine.
Computer Associates International, Inc.	Fraudulently inflated its financial results.	CEO and senior executives indicted. Five executives pled guilty. $225 million fine.
Enron	Fraudulently inflated its financial results.	Bankrupcty. Senior executives criminally convicted. Over $60 billion in stock market losses.
Fannie Mae	Improperly shifted financial performance between periods.	CEO and CFO fired. Company made a $9 billion correction to previously reported earnings.
HealthSouth	Overstated performance by $4 billion in false entries.	Senior executives criminally convicted.
Qwest Communications International, Inc.	Improperly recognized $3 billion in false receipts.	CEO and six other executives criminally convicted of "massive financial fraud." $250 million SEC fine.
Tyco International, Ltd.	Failed to disclose secret loans to executives that were subsequently forgiven.	CEO forced to resign and subjected to frozen asset order and criminally convicted.
WorldCom	Misstated financial results by nearly $9 billion.	Bankruptcy. Criminal conviction of CEO and CFO. Over $100 billion in stock market losses. Directors forced to pay $18 million.
Xerox Corporation	Recognized $3 billion in revenue prior to when it should have been.	$10 million fine to SEC. Six executives forced to pay $22 million.

Exhibit 3

Guideline for Ethical Conduct

1. Identify an ethical decision by using your personal ethical standards of honesty and fairness.
2. Identify the consequences of the decision and its effect on others.
3. Consider your obligations and responsibilities to those that will be affected by your decision.
4. Make a decision that is ethical and fair to those affected by it.

As a result of the accounting and business frauds shown in Exhibit 2, Congress passed new laws to monitor the behavior of accounting and business. For example, the Sarbanes-Oxley Act of 2002 (SOX) was enacted. SOX established a new oversight body for the accounting profession called the Public Company Accounting Oversight Board (PCAOB). In addition, SOX established standards for independence, corporate responsibility, and disclosure.

How does one behave ethically when faced with financial or other types of pressure? A guideline for behaving ethically is shown in Exhibit 3.[2]

Opportunities for Accountants

Numerous career opportunities are available for students majoring in accounting. Currently, the demand for accountants exceeds the number of new graduates entering the job market. This is partly due to the increased regulation of business caused by the accounting and business frauds shown in Exhibit 2. Also, more and more businesses have come to recognize the importance and value of accounting information.

As we indicated earlier, accountants employed by a business are said to be employed in private accounting. Private accountants have a variety of possible career options within a company. Some of these career options are shown in Exhibit 4 along with their starting salaries. Accountants who provide audit services, called auditors, verify the accuracy of financial records, accounts, and systems. As shown in Exhibit 4, several private accounting careers have certification options.

Exhibit 4

Accounting Career Paths and Salaries

Accounting Career Track	Description	Career Options	Annual Starting Salaries[1]	Certification
Private Accounting	Accountants employed by companies, government, and not-for-profit entities.	Bookkeeper	$34,875	
		Payroll clerk	$33,500	Certified Payroll Professional (CPP)
		General accountant	$40,750	
		Budget analyst	$42,875	
		Cost accountant	$42,125	Certified Management Accountant (CMA)
		Internal auditor	$46,375	Certified Internal Auditor (CIA)
		Information technology auditor	$54,625	Certified Information Systems Auditor (CISA)
Public Accounting	Accountants employed individually or within a public accounting firm in tax or audit services.	Local firms	$43,625	Certified Public Accountant (CPA)
		National firms	$52,500	Certified Public Accountant (CPA)

Source: Robert Half 2008 Salary Guide (Finance and Accounting), Robert Half International, Inc.
[1]Median salaries of a reported range. Private accounting salaries are reported for large companies. Salaries may vary by region.

2 Many companies have ethical standards of conduct for managers and employees. In addition, the Institute of Management Accountants and the American Institute of Certified Public Accountants have professional codes of conduct.

Accountants and their staff who provide services on a fee basis are said to be employed in **public accounting**. In public accounting, an accountant may practice as an individual or as a member of a public accounting firm. Public accountants who have met a state's education, experience, and examination requirements may become **Certified Public Accountants (CPAs)**. CPAs generally perform general accounting, audit, or tax services. As can be seen in Exhibit 4, CPAs have slightly better starting salaries than private accountants. Career statistics indicate, however, that these salary differences tend to disappear over time.

Because all functions within a business use accounting information, experience in private or public accounting provides a solid foundation for a career. Many positions in industry and in government agencies are held by individuals with accounting backgrounds.

Integrity, Objectivity, and Ethics in Business

ACCOUNTING REFORM

The financial accounting and reporting failures of Enron, WorldCom, Tyco, Xerox, and others shocked the investing public. The disclosure that some of the nation's largest and best-known corporations had overstated profits and misled investors raised the question: Where were the CPAs?

In response, Congress passed the Investor Protection, Auditor Reform, and Transparency Act of 2002, called the Sarbanes-Oxley Act. The Act establishes a Public Company Accounting Oversight Board to regulate the portion of the accounting profession that has public companies as clients. In addition, the Act prohibits auditors (CPAs) from providing certain types of nonaudit services, such as investment banking or legal services, to their clients, prohibits employment of auditors by clients for one year after they last audited the client, and increases penalties for the reporting of misleading financial statements.

2 Summarize the development of accounting principles and relate them to practice.

Generally Accepted Accounting Principles

If a company's management could record and report financial data as it saw fit, comparisons among companies would be difficult, if not impossible. Thus, financial accountants follow **generally accepted accounting principles (GAAP)** in preparing reports. These reports allow investors and other users to compare one company to another.

Accounting principles and concepts develop from research, accepted accounting practices, and pronouncements of regulators. Within the United States, the **Financial Accounting Standards Board (FASB)** has the primary responsibility for developing accounting principles. The FASB publishes *Statements of Financial Accounting Standards* as well as *Interpretations* of these Standards. In addition, the **Securities and Exchange Commission (SEC),** an agency of the U.S. government, has authority over the accounting and financial disclosures for companies whose shares of ownership (stock) are traded and sold to the public. The SEC normally accepts the accounting principles set forth by the FASB. However, the SEC may issue *Staff Accounting Bulletins* on accounting matters that may not have been addressed by the FASB.

  Many countries outside the United States use generally accepted accounting principles adopted by the **International Accounting Standards Board (IASB).** The IASB issues *International Financial Reporting Standards (IFRSs)*. Significant differences currently exist between FASB and IASB accounting principles.[3] However, the FASB and IASB are working together to reduce and eliminate these differences into a single set of accounting principles. Such a set of worldwide accounting principles would help facilitate investment and business in an increasingly global economy.

In this chapter and text, we emphasize accounting principles and concepts. It is by this emphasis on the "why" as well as the "how" that you will gain an understanding of accounting.

3 Throughout the text we place IFRS icons like the one shown on this page to highlight items that differ between GAAP and IFRS. In addition, a brief overview of IFRS, and a summary of some key differences between GAAP and IFRS are included in Appendix G at the back of this text.

Business Entity Concept

The **business entity concept** limits the economic data in an accounting system to data related directly to the activities of the business. In other words, the business is viewed as an entity separate from its owners, creditors, or other businesses. For example, the accountant for a business with one owner would record the activities of the business only and would not record the personal activities, property, or debts of the owner.

> Under the business entity concept, the activities of a business are recorded separately from the activities of its owners, creditors, or other businesses.

A business entity may take the form of a proprietorship, partnership, corporation, or limited liability company (LLC). Each of these forms and their major characteristics are listed below.

Form of Business Entity	Characteristics
Proprietorship is owned by one individual.	• 70% of business entities in the United States. • Easy and cheap to organize. • Resources are limited to those of the owner. • Used by small businesses.
Partnership is owned by two or more individuals.	• 10% of business organizations in the United States (combined with limited liability companies). • Combines the skills and resources of more than one person.
Corporation is organized under state or federal statutes as a separate legal taxable entity.	• Generates 90% of business revenues. • 20% of the business organizations in the United States. • Ownership is divided into shares called stock. • Can obtain large amounts of resources by issuing stock. • Used by large businesses.
Limited liability company (LLC) combines the attributes of a partnership and a corporation.	• 10% of business organizations in the United States (combined with partnerships). • Often used as an alternative to a partnership. • Has tax and legal liability advantages for owners.

The three types of businesses we discussed earlier—service, merchandising, and manufacturing—may be organized as proprietorships, partnerships, corporations, or limited liability companies. Because of the large amount of resources required to operate a manufacturing business, most manufacturing businesses such as Ford Motor Company are corporations. Most large retailers such as Wal-Mart and Home Depot are also corporations.

The Cost Concept

Under the **cost concept**, amounts are initially recorded in the accounting records at their cost or purchase price. To illustrate, assume that Aaron Publishers purchased the following building on February 20, 2008:

Price listed by seller on January 1, 2008	$160,000
Aaron Publishers' initial offer to buy on January 31, 2008	140,000
Purchase price on February 20, 2008	150,000
Estimated selling price on December 31, 2010	220,000
Assessed value for property taxes, December 31, 2010	190,000

Under the cost concept, Aaron Publishers records the purchase of the building on February 20, 2008, at the purchase price of $150,000. The other amounts listed above have no effect on the accounting records.

The fact that the building has an estimated selling price on December 31, 2010, indicates that the building has increased in value. However, to use the $220,000 in the accounting records would be to record an illusory or unrealized profit. If Aaron Publishers sells the building on January 9, 2011, for $220,000, a profit of $70,000 is then realized and recorded. The new owner would record $220,000 as its cost of the building.

The cost concept also involves the objectivity and unit of measure concepts. The **objectivity concept** requires that the amounts recorded in the accounting records be based on objective evidence. In exchanges between a buyer and a seller, both try to get the best price. Only the final agreed-upon amount is objective enough to be recorded in the accounting records. If amounts in the accounting records were constantly being revised upward or downward based on offers, appraisals, and opinions, accounting reports could become unstable and unreliable.

The **unit of measure concept** requires that economic data be recorded in dollars. Money is a common unit of measurement for reporting financial data and reports.

Example Exercise 1-1   Cost Concept ········> 2

On August 25, Gallatin Repair Service extended an offer of $125,000 for land that had been priced for sale at $150,000. On September 3, Gallatin Repair Service accepted the seller's counteroffer of $137,000. On October 20, the land was assessed at a value of $98,000 for property tax purposes. On December 4, Gallatin Repair Service was offered $160,000 for the land by a national retail chain. At what value should the land be recorded in Gallatin Repair Service's records?

Follow My Example 1-1

$137,000. Under the cost concept, the land should be recorded at the cost to Gallatin Repair Service.

For Practice: PE 1-1A, PE 1-1B

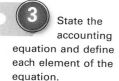

3 State the accounting equation and define each element of the equation.

The Accounting Equation

The resources owned by a business are its **assets**. Examples of assets include cash, land, buildings, and equipment. The rights or claims to the assets are divided into two types: (1) the rights of creditors and (2) the rights of owners. The rights of creditors are the debts of the business and are called **liabilities**. The rights of the owners are called **owner's equity**. The following equation shows the relationship among assets, liabilities, and owner's equity:

$$\text{Assets} = \text{Liabilities} + \text{Owner's Equity}$$

Example Exercise 1-2   Accounting Equation ········> 3

John Joos is the owner and operator of You're A Star, a motivational consulting business. At the end of its accounting period, December 31, 2009, You're A Star has assets of $800,000 and liabilities of $350,000. Using the accounting equation, determine the following amounts:

a. Owner's equity, as of December 31, 2009.
b. Owner's equity, as of December 31, 2010, assuming that assets increased by $130,000 and liabilities decreased by $25,000 during 2010.

Follow My Example 1-2

a.
$$\text{Assets} = \text{Liabilities} + \text{Owner's Equity}$$
$$\$800,000 = \$350,000 + \text{Owner's Equity}$$
$$\text{Owner's Equity} = \$450,000$$

b. First, determine the change in Owner's Equity during 2010 as follows:
$$\text{Assets} = \text{Liabilities} + \text{Owner's Equity}$$
$$\$130,000 = -\$25,000 + \text{Owner's Equity}$$
$$\text{Owner's Equity} = \$155,000$$

Next, add the change in Owner's Equity on December 31, 2009 to arrive at Owner's Equity on December 31, 2010, as shown below.

Owner's Equity on December 31, 2010 =
$$\$605,000 = \$450,000 + \$155,000$$

For Practice: PE 1-2A, PE 1-2B

This equation is called the **accounting equation**. Liabilities usually are shown before owner's equity in the accounting equation because creditors have first rights to the assets.

Given any two amounts, the accounting equation may be solved for the third unknown amount. To illustrate, if the assets owned by a business amount to $100,000 and the liabilities amount to $30,000, the owner's equity is equal to $70,000, as shown below.

Assets − Liabilities = Owner's Equity

$100,000 − $30,000 = $70,000

Business Transactions and the Accounting Equation

 4 Describe and illustrate how business transactions can be recorded in terms of the resulting change in the elements of the accounting equation.

Paying a monthly telephone bill of $168 affects a business's financial condition because it now has less cash on hand. Such an economic event or condition that directly changes an entity's financial condition or its results of operations is a **business transaction**. For example, purchasing land for $50,000 is a business transaction. In contrast, a change in a business's credit rating does not directly affect cash or any other asset, liability, or owner's equity amount.

All business transactions can be stated in terms of changes in the elements of the accounting equation. We illustrate how business transactions affect the accounting equation by using some typical transactions. As a basis for illustration, we use a business organized by Chris Clark.

Assume that on November 1, 2009, Chris Clark organizes a corporation that will be known as NetSolutions. The first phase of Chris's business plan is to operate NetSolutions as a service business assisting individuals and small businesses in developing Web pages and installing computer software. Chris expects this initial phase of the business to last one to two years. During this period, Chris plans on gathering information on the software and hardware needs of customers. During the second phase of the business plan, Chris plans to expand NetSolutions into a personalized retailer of software and hardware for individuals and small businesses.

> **All business transactions can be stated in terms of changes in the elements of the accounting equation.**

Business Connection

THE ACCOUNTING EQUATION

The accounting equation serves as the basic foundation for the accounting systems of all companies. From the smallest business, such as the local convenience store, to the largest business, such as Ford Motor Company, companies use the accounting equation. Some examples taken from recent financial reports of well-known companies are shown below.

Company	Assets*	=	Liabilities	+	Stockholders' Equity
The Coca-Cola Company	$ 29,963	=	$13,043	+	$16,920
Circuit City Stores, Inc.	4,007	=	2,216	+	1,791
Dell Inc.	25,635	=	21,196	+	4,439
eBay Inc.	13,494	=	2,589	+	10,905
Google	18,473	=	1,433	+	17,040
McDonald's	29,024	=	13,566	+	15,458
Microsoft Corporation	63,171	=	32,074	+	31,097
Southwest Airlines Co.	13,460	=	7,011	+	6,449
Wal-Mart	151,193	=	89,620	+	61,573

*Amounts are shown in millions of dollars.

Each transaction during NetSolutions' first month of operations is described in the following paragraphs. The effect of each transaction on the accounting equation is then shown.

Transaction A

> Nov. 1, 2009   Chris Clark deposits $25,000 in a bank account in the name of NetSolutions in return for shares of stock in the corporation.

Stock issued to owners (stockholders), such as Chris Clark, is referred to as **capital stock**. The owner's equity in a corporation is called **stockholders' equity**.

This transaction increases the asset (cash) on the left side of the equation by $25,000. To balance the equation, the stockholders' equity (capital stock) on the right side of the equation increases by the same amount.

The effect of this transaction on NetSolutions' accounting equation is shown below.

	Assets	=	Stockholders' Equity
	Cash	=	Capital Stock
a.	25,000		25,000

The accounting equation shown above is only for the business, NetSolutions. Under the business entity concept, Chris Clark's personal assets, such as a home or personal bank account, and personal liabilities are excluded from the equation.

Transaction B

> Nov. 5, 2009   NetSolutions paid $20,000 for the purchase of land as a future building site.

The land is located in a business park with access to transportation facilities. Chris Clark plans to rent office space and equipment during the first phase of the business plan. During the second phase, Chris plans to build an office and a warehouse on the land.

The purchase of the land changes the makeup of the assets, but it does not change the total assets. The items in the equation prior to this transaction and the effect of the transaction are shown below. The new amounts are called *balances*.

	Assets		=	Stockholders' Equity
	Cash	+ Land	=	Capital Stock
Bal.	25,000			25,000
b.	−20,000	+20,000		
Bal.	5,000	20,000		25,000

Transaction C

> Nov. 10, 2009   NetSolutions purchased supplies for $1,350 and agreed to pay the supplier in the near future.

You have probably used a credit card to buy clothing or other merchandise. In this type of transaction, you received clothing for a promise to pay your credit card bill in the future. That is, you received an asset and incurred a liability to pay a future bill. NetSolutions entered into a similar transaction by purchasing supplies for $1,350 and agreeing to pay the supplier in the near future. This type of transaction is called a purchase *on account* and is often described as follows: *Purchased supplies on account, $1,350.*

The liability created by a purchase on account is called an **account payable**. Items such as supplies that will be used in the business in the future are called **prepaid expenses**, which are assets. Thus, the effect of this transaction is to increase assets (Supplies) and liabilities (Accounts Payable) by $1,350, as follows:

	Assets			=	Liabilities + Stockholders' Equity	
					Accounts + Capital	
	Cash +	Supplies +	Land		Payable	Stock
Bal.	5,000		20,000			25,000
c.		+1,350			+1,350	
Bal.	5,000	1,350	20,000		1,350	25,000

Transaction D

> Nov. 18, 2009   NetSolutions received cash of $7,500 for providing services to customers.

You may have earned money by painting houses or mowing lawns. If so, you received money for rendering services to a customer. Likewise, a business earns money by selling goods or services to its customers. This amount is called **revenue**.

During its first month of operations, NetSolutions received cash of $7,500 for providing services to customers. The receipt of cash increases NetSolutions' assets and also increases the stockholders' equity in the business. The revenues of $7,500 are recorded in a Fees Earned column to the right of Capital Stock. The effect of this transaction is to increase Cash and Fees Earned by $7,500, as shown below.

	Assets			=	Liabilities + Stockholders' Equity		
					Accounts	Capital	Fees
	Cash +	Supplies +	Land		Payable +	Stock +	Earned
Bal.	5,000	1,350	20,000		1,350	25,000	
d.	+7,500						+7,500
Bal.	12,500	1,350	20,000		1,350	25,000	7,500

Different terms are used for the various types of revenues. As illustrated above, revenue from providing services is recorded as **fees earned**. Revenue from the sale of merchandise is recorded as **sales**. Other examples of revenue include rent, which is recorded as **rent revenue**, and interest, which is recorded as **interest revenue**.

Instead of receiving cash at the time services are provided or goods are sold, a business may accept payment at a later date. Such revenues are described as *fees earned on account* or *sales on account*. For example, if NetSolutions had provided services on account instead of for cash, transaction (d) would have been described as follows: *Fees earned on account, $7,500.*

In such cases, the firm has an **account receivable**, which is a claim against the customer. An account receivable is an asset, and the revenue is earned and recorded as if cash had been received. When customers pay their accounts, Cash increases and Accounts Receivable decreases.

Transaction E

> Nov. 30, 2009   NetSolutions paid the following expenses during the month: wages, $2,125; rent, $800; utilities, $450; and miscellaneous, $275.

During the month, NetSolutions spent cash or used up other assets in earning revenue. Assets used in this process of earning revenue are called **expenses**. Expenses include supplies used and payments for employee wages, utilities, and other services.

NetSolutions paid the following expenses during the month: wages, $2,125; rent, $800; utilities, $450; and miscellaneous, $275. Miscellaneous expenses include small amounts paid for such items as postage, coffee, and newspapers. The effect of expenses is the opposite of revenues in that expenses reduce assets and stockholders' equity. Like fees earned, the expenses are recorded in columns to the right of Capital Stock. However, since expenses reduce stockholders' equity, the expenses are entered as negative amounts. The effect of this transaction is shown below.

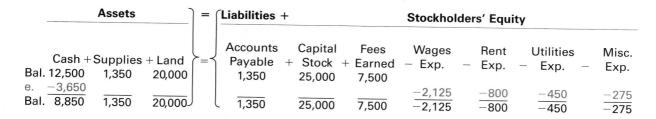

	Assets			=	Liabilities +			Stockholders' Equity			
	Cash +	Supplies +	Land	=	Accounts Payable	+ Capital Stock	+ Fees Earned	− Wages Exp.	− Rent Exp.	− Utilities Exp.	− Misc. Exp.
Bal.	12,500	1,350	20,000		1,350	25,000	7,500				
e.	−3,650							−2,125	−800	−450	−275
Bal.	8,850	1,350	20,000		1,350	25,000	7,500	−2,125	−800	−450	−275

Businesses usually record each revenue and expense transaction as it occurs. However, to simplify, we have summarized NetSolutions' revenues and expenses for the month in transactions (d) and (e).

Transaction F

Nov. 30, 2009   NetSolutions paid creditors on account, $950.

When you pay your monthly credit card bill, you decrease the cash in your checking account and decrease the amount you owe to the credit card company. Likewise, when NetSolutions pays $950 to creditors during the month, it reduces assets and liabilities, as shown below.

	Assets			=	Liabilities +			Stockholders' Equity			
	Cash +	Supplies +	Land	=	Accounts Payable	+ Capital Stock	+ Fees Earned	− Wages Exp.	− Rent Exp.	− Utilities Exp.	− Misc. Exp.
Bal.	8,850	1,350	20,000		1,350	25,000	7,500	−2,125	−800	−450	−275
f.	−950				−950						
Bal.	7,900	1,350	20,000		400	25,000	7,500	−2,125	−800	−450	−275

Paying an amount on account is different from paying an expense. The paying of an expense reduces stockholders' equity, as illustrated in transaction (e). Paying an amount on account reduces the amount owed on a liability.

Transaction G

Nov. 30, 2009   Chris Clark determined that the cost of supplies on hand at the end of the month was $550.

The cost of the supplies on hand (not yet used) at the end of the month is $550. Thus, $800 ($1,350 − $550) of supplies must have been used during the month. This decrease in supplies is recorded as an expense, as shown at the top of the next page.

	Assets		=	Liabilities +				Stockholders' Equity				
	Cash + Supplies + Land		=	Accounts Payable +	Capital Stock +	Fees Earned −	Wages Exp. −	Rent Exp. −	Supplies Exp. −	Utilities Exp. −	Misc. Exp.	
Bal.	7,900 1,350 20,000			400	25,000	7,500	−2,125	−800		−450	−275	
g.	−800								−800			
Bal.	7,900 550 20,000			400	25,000	7,500	−2,125	−800	−800	−450	−275	

Transaction H

> **Nov. 30, 2009**   NetSolutions pays $2,000 to stockholders (Chris Clark) as dividends.

Dividends are distributions of earnings to stockholders. The payment of dividends decreases cash and stockholders' equity. Like expenses, dividends are recorded in a separate column to the right of Capital Stock as a negative amount. The effect of the payment of dividends of $2,000 is shown below.

	Assets		=	Liabilities +					Stockholders' Equity			
	Cash + Supp. + Land		=	Accounts Payable +	Capital Stock	− Dividends +	Fees Earned −	Wages Exp. −	Rent Exp. −	Supplies Exp. −	Utilities Exp. −	Misc. Exp.
Bal.	7,900 550 20,000			400	25,000		7,500	−2,125	−800	−800	−450	−275
h.	−2,000					−2,000						
Bal.	5,900 550 20,000			400	25,000	−2,000	7,500	−2,125	−800	−800	−450	−275

Dividends should not be confused with expenses. Dividends do not represent assets or services used in the process of earning revenues. Instead, dividends are considered a distribution of earnings to stockholders.

Summary The transactions of NetSolutions are summarized below. Each transaction is identified by letter, and the balance of each item is shown after every transaction.

	Assets			=	Liabilities +				Stockholders' Equity				
	Cash +	Supp. +	Land	=	Accounts Payable +	Capital Stock	− Dividends	+ Earned Fees	− Wages Exp.	− Rent Exp.	Supplies Exp. −	Utilities Exp.	Misc. − Exp.
a.	+25,000					+25,000							
b.	−20,000		+20,000										
Bal.	5,000		20,000			25,000							
c.		+1,350			+1,350								
Bal.	5,000	+1,350	20,000		+1,350	25,000							
d.	+7,500							+7,500					
Bal.	12,500	1,350	20,000		1,350	25,000		7,500					
e.	−3,650								−2,125	−800		−450	−275
Bal.	8,850	1,350	20,000		1,350	25,000		7,500	−2,125	−800		−450	−275
f.	−950				−950								
Bal.	7,900	1,350	20,000		400	25,000		7,500	−2,125	−800		−450	−275
g.		−800									−800		
Bal.	7,900	550	20,000		400	25,000		7,500	−2,125	−800	−800	−450	−275
h.	−2,000						−2,000						
Bal.	5,900	550	20,000		400	25,000	−2,000	7,500	−2,125	−800	−800	−450	−275

You should note the following in the preceding summary:

1. The effect of every transaction is *an increase or a decrease in one or more of the accounting equation elements.*
2. The two sides of the accounting equation are *always equal.*
3. The stockholders' equity (owner's equity) is *increased by amounts invested by stockholders (capital stock).*
4. The stockholders' equity (owner's equity) is *increased by revenues and decreased by expenses.*
5. The stockholders' equity (owner's equity) is *decreased by dividends paid to stockholders.*

As discussed earlier, the owner's equity in a corporation is called stockholders' equity. Stockholders' equity is classified as:

1. Capital Stock
2. Retained Earnings.

Capital stock is shares of ownership distributed to investors of a corporation. It represents the portion of stockholders' equity contributed by investors. For NetSolutions, shares of capital stock of $25,000 were distributed to Chris Clark in return for investing in the business.

Retained earnings is the stockholders' equity created from business operations through revenue and expense transactions. For NetSolutions, retained earnings of $3,050 were created by its November operations (revenue and expense transactions), as shown below.

NetSolutions
Retained Earnings
November Operations
(Revenue and Expense Transactions)

	Fees Earned	–	Wages Exp.	–	Rent Exp.	–	Supplies Exp.	–	Utilities Exp.	–	Misc. Exp
Trans, d.	+7,500										
Trans, e.			−2,125		−800				−450		−275
Trans, g.							−800				
Balance,											
Nov. 30	7,500		−2,125		−800		−800		−450		−275

$3,050

Stockholders' equity created by investments by stockholders (capital stock) and by business operations (retained earnings) are reported separately. Since dividends are distributions of earnings to stockholders, dividends reduce retained earnings.

The effects of investments by stockholders, dividends, revenues, and expenses on stockholders' equity are illustrated in Exhibit 5.

Example Exercise 1-3   Transactions   4

Salvo Delivery Service is owned and operated by Joel Salvo. The following selected transactions were completed by Salvo Delivery Service during February:

1. Received cash from owner as additional investment in exchange for capital stock, $35,000.
2. Paid creditors on account, $1,800.
3. Billed customers for delivery services on account, $11,250.
4. Received cash from customers on account, $6,740.
5. Paid dividends, $1,000.

(continued)

EXHIBIT 5

Effects of Transactions on Stockholders' Equity

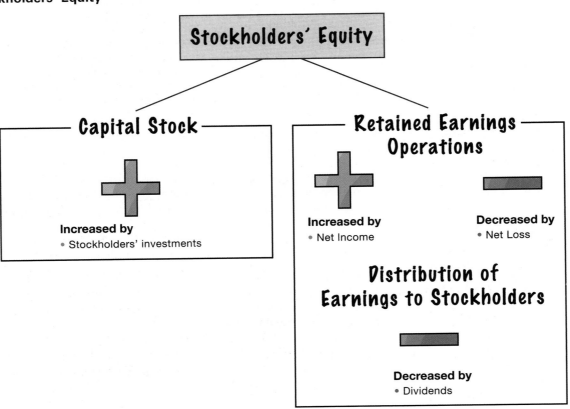

Indicate the effect of each transaction on the accounting equation elements (Assets, Liabilities, Stockholders' Equity, Dividends, Revenue, and Expense) by listing the numbers identifying the transactions, (1) through (5). Also, indicate the specific item within the accounting equation element that is affected. To illustrate, the answer to (1) is shown below.

(1) Asset (Cash) increases by $35,000; Stockholders' Equity (Capital Stock) increases by $35,000.

Follow My Example 1-3

(2) Asset (Cash) decreases by $1,800; Liability (Accounts Payable) decreases by $1,800.
(3) Asset (Accounts Receivable) increases by $11,250; Revenue (Delivery Service Fees) increases by $11,250.
(4) Asset (Cash) increases by $6,740; Asset (Accounts Receivable) decreases by $6,740.
(5) Asset (Cash) decreases by $1,000; Dividends increases by $1,000.

For Practice: PE 1-3A, PE 1-3B

Financial Statements

5 Describe the financial statements of a corporation and explain how they interrelate.

After transactions have been recorded and summarized, reports are prepared for users. The accounting reports providing this information are called **financial statements**. The primary financial statements of a corporation are the income statement, the retained earnings statement, the balance sheet, and the statement of cash flows. The order that the financial statements are prepared and the nature of each statement is described as follows.

Order Prepared	Financial Statement	Description of Statement
1.	Income statement	A summary of the revenue and expenses *for a specific period of time*, such as a month or a year.
2.	Retained earnings statement	A summary of the changes in the retained earnings for *a specific period of time*, such as a month or a year.
3.	Balance sheet	A list of the assets, liabilities, and stockholders' equity *as of a specific date*, usually at the close of the last day of a month or a year.
4.	Statement of cash flows	A summary of the cash receipts and cash payments for a *specific period of time*, such as a month or a year.

⊜netsolutions

The four financial statements and their interrelationships are illustrated in Exhibit 6, on page 18. The data for the statements are taken from the summary of transactions of NetSolutions on page 15.

All financial statements are identified by the name of the business, the title of the statement, and the *date* or *period of time*. The data presented in the income statement, the retained earnings statement, and the statement of cash flows are for a period of time. The data presented in the balance sheet are for a specific date.

Income Statement

When you buy something at a store, you may *match* the cash register total with the amount you paid the cashier and with the amount of change, if any, you received.

The income statement reports the revenues and expenses for a period of time, based on the **matching concept**. This concept is applied by *matching* the expenses with the revenue generated during a period by those expenses. The excess of the revenue over the expenses is called **net income** or **net profit**. If the expenses exceed the revenue, the excess is a **net loss**.

The revenue and expenses for NetSolutions were shown in the accounting equation as separate increases and decreases in each item. Net income for a period increases the stockholders' equity (retained earnings) for the period. A net loss decreases the stockholders' equity (retained earnings) for the period.

Example Exercise 1-4   Income Statement   •••••••▶ 5

The assets and liabilities of Chickadee Travel Service at April 30, 2010, the end of the current year, and its revenue and expenses for the year are listed below. The capital stock was $50,000 and the retained earnings was $30,000 at May 1, 2009, the beginning of the current year.

Accounts payable	$ 12,200	Miscellaneous expense	$ 12,950
Accounts receivable	31,350	Office expense	63,000
Cash	53,050	Supplies	3,350
Fees earned	263,200	Wages expense	131,700
Land	80,000		

Prepare an income statement for the current year ended April 30, 2010.

Follow My Example 1-4

Chickadee Travel Service
Income Statement
For the Year Ended April 30, 2010

Fees earned		$263,200
Expenses:		
Wages expense.	$131,700	
Office expense	63,000	
Miscellaneous expense	12,950	
Total expenses.		207,650
Net income.		$ 55,550

For Practice: PE 1-4A, PE 1-4B

Exhibit 6

Financial Statements for NetSolutions

NetSolutions
Income Statement
For the Month Ended November 30, 2009

Fees earned		$7,500
Expenses:		
Wages expense	$2,125	
Rent expense	800	
Supplies expense	800	
Utilities expense	450	
Miscellaneous expense	275	
Total expense		4,450
Net income		$3,050

NetSolutions
Retained Earnings Statement
For the Month Ended November 30, 2009

Retained earnings, November 1, 2009		$ 0
Net income for November	$3,050	
Less dividends	2,000	
Increase in retained earnings		1,050
Retained earnings, November 30, 2009		$1,050

NetSolutions
Balance Sheet
November 30, 2009

Assets		**Liabilities**	
Cash	$ 5,900	Accounts payable	$ 400
Supplies	550	**Stockholders' Equity**	
Land	20,000	Capital stock	$25,000
		Retained earnings	1,050
		Total stockholders' equity	26,050
		Total liabilities and	
Total assets	$26,450	stockholders' equity	$26,450

NetSolutions
Statement of Cash Flows
For the Month Ended November 30, 2009

Cash flows from operating activities:		
Cash received from customers	$ 7,500	
Deduct cash payments for expenses and payments		
to creditors	4,600	
Net cash flow from operating activities		$ 2,900
Cash flows from investing activities:		
Cash payments for purchase of land		(20,000)
Cash flows from financing activities:		
Cash received from issuing stock	$ 25,000	
Deduct cash dividends	2,000	
Net cash flow from financing activities		23,000
Net cash flow and November 30, 2009, cash balance		$ 5,900

The revenue, expenses, and the net income of $3,050 for NetSolutions are reported in the income statement in Exhibit 6, on page 18. The order in which the expenses are listed in the income statement varies among businesses. Most businesses list expenses in order of size, beginning with the larger items. Miscellaneous expense is usually shown as the last item, regardless of the amount.

Retained Earnings Statement

The retained earnings statement reports the changes in the retained earnings for a period of time. It is prepared *after* the income statement because the net income or net loss for the period must be reported in this statement. Similarly, it is prepared *before* the balance sheet, since the amount of retained earnings at the end of the period must be reported on the balance sheet. Because of this, the retained earnings statement is often viewed as the connecting link between the income statement and balance sheet.

The following two types of transactions affected NetSolutions' retained earnings during November:

1. Revenues and expenses, which resulted in net income of $3,050.
2. Dividends of $2,000 paid to stockholders (Chris Clark).

These transactions are summarized in the retained earnings statement for NetSolutions shown in Exhibit 6.

Since NetSolutions has been in operation for only one month, it has no retained earnings at the beginning of November. For December, however, there is a beginning balance—the balance at the end of November. This balance of $1,050 is reported on the retained earnings statement.

To illustrate, assume that NetSolutions earned net income of $4,155 and paid dividends of $2,000 during December. The retained earnings statement for NetSolutions for December is shown here.

NetSolutions
Retained Earnings Statement
For the Month Ended December 31, 2009

Retained earnings, December 1, 2009		$1,050
Net income for the month	$4,155	
Less dividends	2,000	
Increase in retained earnings		2,155
Retained earnings, December 31, 2009		$3,205

Example Exercise 1-5   Retained Earnings Statement   ▶5

Using the data for Chickadee Travel Service shown in Example Exercise 1-4, prepare a retained earnings statement for the current year ended April 30, 2010. Adam Cellini invested an additional $50,000 in the business in exchange for capital stock, and dividends of $30,000 were paid during the year.

Follow My Example 1-5

Chickadee Travel Service
Retained Earnings Statement
For the Year Ended April 30, 2010

Retained earnings, May 1, 2009		$30,000
Net income for the year	$55,550	
Less dividends	30,000	
Increase in retained earnings		25,550
Retained earnings, April 30, 2010		$55,550

For Practice: PE 1-5A, PE 1-5B

Balance Sheet

The balance sheet in Exhibit 6 reports the amounts of NetSolutions' assets, liabilities, and stockholders' equity as of November 30, 2009. The asset and liability amounts are taken from the last line of the summary of transactions on page 15. Retained earnings as of November 30, 2009, is taken from the retained earnings statement. The form of balance sheet shown in Exhibit 6 is called the **account form**. This is because it resembles the basic format of the accounting equation, with assets on the left side and the liabilities and stockholders' equity sections on the right side.[4]

The assets section of the balance sheet presents assets in the order that they will be converted into cash or used in operations. Cash is presented first, followed by receivables, supplies, prepaid insurance, and other assets. The assets of a more permanent nature are shown next, such as land, buildings, and equipment.

In the liabilities section of the balance sheet in Exhibit 6, accounts payable is the only liability. When there are two or more liabilities, each should be listed and the total amount of liabilities presented as follows:

Liabilities		
Accounts payable	$12,900	
Wages payable	2,570	
Total liabilities		$15,470

Example Exercise 1-6 Balance Sheet   5

Using the data for Chickadee Travel Service shown in Example Exercises 1-4 and 1-5, prepare the balance sheet as of April 30, 2010.

Follow My Example 1-6

Chickadee Travel Service
Balance Sheet
April 30, 2010

Assets		Liabilities	
Cash	$ 53,050	Accounts payable	$ 12,200
Accounts receivable	31,350		
Supplies	3,350	**Stockholders' Equity**	
Land	80,000	Capital stock $100,000	
		Retained earnings 55,550	
		Total stockholders' equity...	155,550
		Total liabilities and	
Total assets	$167,750	stockholders' equity.......	$167,750

For Practice: PE 1-6A, PE 1-6B

Statement of Cash Flows

The statement of cash flows consists of three sections, as shown in Exhibit 6: (1) operating activities, (2) investing activities, and (3) financing activities. Each of these sections is briefly described below.

Cash Flows from Operating Activities This section reports a summary of cash receipts and cash payments from operations. The net cash flow from operating activities normally differs from the amount of net income for the period. In Exhibit 6, NetSolutions reported net cash flows from operating activities of $2,900 and net income of $3,050. This difference occurs because revenues and expenses may not be recorded at the same time that cash is received from customers or paid to creditors.

---

4 We illustrate an alternative form of balance sheet, called the *report form*, in Chapter 5. It presents the liabilities and stockholders' equity sections below the assets section.

Cash Flows from Investing Activities This section reports the cash transactions for the acquisition and sale of relatively permanent assets. Exhibit 6 reports that NetSolutions paid $20,000 for the purchase of land during November.

Cash Flows from Financing Activities This section reports the cash transactions related to cash investments by the stockholders, borrowings, and cash dividends. Exhibit 6 shows that Chris Clark invested $25,000 in the business in exchange for capital stock and dividends of $2,000 were paid during November.

Preparing the statement of cash flows requires that each of the November cash transactions for NetSolutions be classified as operating, investing, or financing activities. Using the summary of transactions shown on page 15, the November cash transactions for NetSolutions are classified as follows:

Transaction	Amount	Cash Flow Activity
a.	$25,000	Financing (Issuance of capital stock)
b.	−20,000	Investing (Purchase of land)
d.	7,500	Operating (Fees earned)
e.	−3,650	Operating (Payment of expenses)
f.	−950	Operating (Payment of account payable)
h.	−2,000	Financing (Dividends)

Transactions (c) and (g) are not listed above since they did not involve a cash receipt or payment. In addition, the payment of accounts payable in transaction (f) is classified as an operating activity since the account payable arose from the purchase of supplies, which are used in operations. Using the preceding classifications of November cash transactions, the statement of cash flows is prepared as shown in Exhibit 6.[5]

The ending cash balance shown on the statement of cash flows is also reported on the balance sheet as of the end of the period. To illustrate, the ending cash of $5,900 reported on the November statement of cash flows in Exhibit 6 is also reported as the amount of cash on hand in the November 30, 2009, balance sheet.

Since November is NetSolutions' first period of operations, the net cash flow for November and the November 30, 2009, cash balance are the same amount, $5,900, as shown in Exhibit 6. In later periods, NetSolutions will report in its statement of cash flows a beginning cash balance, an increase or a decrease in cash for the period, and an ending cash balance. For example, assume that for December NetSolutions has a decrease in cash of $3,835. The last three lines of NetSolutions' statement of cash flows for December would be as follows:

Decrease in cash	$3,835
Cash as of December 1, 2009	5,900
Cash as of December 31, 2009	$2,065

Example Exercise 1-7   Statement of Cash Flows   •••••••• 5

A summary of cash flows for Chickadee Travel Service for the year ended April 30, 2010, is shown below.

Cash receipts:	
Cash received from customers	$251,000
Cash received from issuing capital stock	50,000
Cash payments:	
Cash paid for expenses	210,000
Cash paid for land	80,000
Cash paid for dividends	30,000

The cash balance as of May 1, 2009, was $72,050. Prepare a statement of cash flows for Chickadee Travel Service for the year ended April 30, 2010.

(*continued*)

5 This method of preparing the statement of cash flows is called the "direct method." This method and the indirect method are discussed further in Chapter 14.

Follow My Example 1-7

Chickadee Travel Service
Statement of Cash Flows
For the Year Ended April 30, 2010

Cash flows from operating activities:		
Cash received from customers....................	$251,000	
Deduct cash payments for expenses	210,000	
Net cash flows from operating activities..............		$ 41,000
Cash flows from investing activities:		
Cash payments for purchase of land		(80,000)
Cash flows from financing activities:		
Cash received from issuing capital stock	$ 50,000	
Deduct cash dividends......................	30,000	
Net cash flows from financing activities..............		20,000
Net decrease in cash during year		$ (19,000)
Cash as of May 1, 2009......................		72,050
Cash as of April 30, 2010.....................		$ 53,050

For Practice: PE 1-7A, PE 1-7B

Interrelationships Among Financial Statements

Financial statements are prepared in the order of the income statement, retained earnings statement, balance sheet, and statement of cash flows. This order is important because the financial statements are interrelated. These interrelationships for NetSolutions are shown in Exhibit 6 and are described below.[6]

Financial Statements	Interrelationship	NetSolutions Example (Exhibit 6)
Income Statement *and* Retained Earnings Statement	Net income or net loss reported on the income statement is also reported on the retained earnings statement as either an addition (net income) to or deduction (net loss) from the beginning retained earnings.	NetSolutions' net income of $3,050 for November is added to the beginning retained earnings on November 1, 2009, in the retained earnings statement.
Retained Earnings Statement *and* Balance Sheet	Retained earnings at the end of the period reported on the retained earnings statement is also reported on the balance sheet as retained earnings.	NetSolutions' retained earnings of $1,050 as of November 30, 2009, on the retained earnings statement also appears on the November 30, 2009, balance sheet as retained earnings.
Balance Sheet *and* Statement of Cash Flows	The cash reported on the balance sheet is also reported as the end-of-period cash on the statement of cash flows.	Cash of $5,900 reported on the balance sheet as of November 30, 2009, is also reported on the November statement of cash flows as the end-of-period cash.

The preceding interrelationships are important in analyzing financial statements and the impact of transactions on a business. In addition, these interrelationships serve as a check on whether the financial statements are prepared correctly. For example, if the ending cash on the statement of cash flows doesn't agree with the balance sheet cash, then an error has occurred.

---

6 Depending on the method of preparing the cash flows from operating activities section of the statement of cash flows, net income (or net loss) may also appear on the statement of cash flows. This interrelationship or method of preparing the statement of cash flows, called the "indirect method," is described and illustrated in Chapter 14.

Financial Analysis and Interpretation

Financial statements are useful to bankers, creditors, owners, and other users in analyzing and interpreting the financial performance and condition of a business. Throughout this text, we discuss various tools that are often used to analyze and interpret the financial performance and condition of a business. The first such tool we introduce is useful in analyzing the ability of a business to pay its creditors.

The relationship between liabilities and stockholders' equity, expressed as a ratio, is computed as follows:

$$\text{Ratio of Liabilities to Stockholders' Equity} = \frac{\text{Total Liabilities}}{\text{Total Stockholders' Equity}}$$

To illustrate, NetSolutions' ratio of liabilities to stockholders' equity at the end of November is 0.015, as calculated below.

$$\text{Ratio of Liabilities to Stockholders' Equity} = \frac{\$400}{\$26,050} = 0.015$$

The rights of creditors to a business's assets take precedence over the rights of stockholders. Thus, the lower the ratio of liabilities to stockholders' equity, the better able the business is to withstand poor business conditions and pay its obligations to creditors.

At a Glance 1

1 Describe the nature of a business, the role of accounting, and ethics in business.

Key Points

A business provides goods or services (outputs) to customers with the objective of earning a profit. Three types of businesses include service, merchandising, and manufacturing businesses.

Accounting, called the "language of business," is an information system that provides reports to users about the economic activities and condition of a business.

Ethics are moral principles that guide the conduct of individuals. Good ethical conduct depends on individual character and firm culture.

Accountants are engaged in private accounting or public accounting.

Key Learning Outcomes

- Distinguish among service, merchandising, and manufacturing businesses.

- Describe the role of accounting in business and explain why accounting is called the "language of business."

- Define ethics and list the two factors affecting ethical conduct.

- Describe what private and public accounting means.

	Example Exercises	Practice Exercises

2 Summarize the development of accounting principles and relate them to practice.

Key Points	Key Learning Outcomes	Example Exercises	Practice Exercises
Generally accepted accounting principles (GAAP) are used in preparing financial statements so that users can compare one company to another. Accounting principles and concepts develop from research, practice, and pronouncements of authoritative bodies such as the Financial Accounting Standards Board (FASB), Securities and Exchange Commission (SEC), and the International Accounting Standards Board (IASB). The business entity concept views the business as an entity separate from its owners, creditors, or other businesses. Businesses may be organized as proprietorships, partnerships, corporations, and limited liability companies. The cost concept requires that properties and services bought by a business be recorded in terms of actual cost. The objectivity concept requires that the accounting records and reports be based on objective evidence. The unit of measure concept requires that economic data be recorded in dollars.	• Explain what is meant by generally accepted accounting principles. • Describe how generally accepted accounting principles are developed. • Describe and give an example of what is meant by the business entity concept. • Describe the characteristics of a proprietorship, partnership, corporation, and limited liability company. • Describe and give an example of what is meant by the cost concept. • Describe and give an example of what is meant by the objectivity concept. • Describe and give an example of what is meant by the unit of measure concept.	1-1	1-1A, 1-1B

3 State the accounting equation and define each element of the equation.

Key Points	Key Learning Outcomes	Example Exercises	Practice Exercises
The resources owned by a business and the rights or claims to these resources may be stated in the form of an equation, as follows: Assets = Liabilities + Owner's Equity	• State the accounting equation. • Define assets, liabilities, and owner's equity. • Given two elements of the accounting equation, solve for the third element.	1-2	1-2A, 1-2B

4 Describe and illustrate how business transactions can be recorded in terms of the resulting change in the elements of the accounting equation.

Key Points	Key Learning Outcomes	Example Exercises	Practice Exercises
All business transactions can be stated in terms of the change in one or more of the three elements of the accounting equation.	• Define a business transaction. • Using the accounting equation as a framework, record transactions.	1-3	1-3A, 1-3B

5 Describe the financial statements of a corporation and explain how they interrelate.

Key Points

The primary financial statements of a corporation are the income statement, the retained earnings statement, the balance sheet, and the statement of cash flows. The income statement reports a period's net income or net loss, which is also reported on the retained earnings statement. The retained earnings reported on the retained earnings statement is also reported on the balance sheet. The ending cash balance is reported on the balance sheet and the statement of cash flows.

Key Learning Outcomes	Example Exercises	Practice Exercises
• List and describe the financial statements of a corporation.		
• Prepare an income statement.	1-4	1-4A, 1-4B
• Prepare a retained earnings statement.	1-5	1-5A, 1-5B
• Prepare a balance sheet.	1-6	1-6A, 1-6B
• Prepare a statement of cash flows.	1-7	1-7A, 1-7B
• Explain how the financial statements of a corporation are interrelated.		

Key Terms

account form (20)
account payable (12)
account receivable (12)
accounting (3)
accounting equation (10)
assets (9)
balance sheet (17)
business (2)
business entity concept (8)
business transaction (10)
capital stock (11)
Certified Public Accountant (CPA) (7)
corporation (8)
cost concept (8)
dividends (14)
ethics (4)
expenses (12)
fees earned (12)
financial accounting (4)

Financial Accounting Standards Board (FASB) (7)
financial statements (16)
general-purpose financial statements (4)
generally accepted accounting principles (GAAP) (7)
income statement (17)
interest revenue (12)
International Accounting Standards Board (IASB) (7)
liabilities (9)
limited liability company (LLC) (8)
management (or managerial) accounting (4)
manufacturing business (3)
matching concept (17)
merchandising business (3)
net income (or net profit) (17)
net loss (17)

objectivity concept (9)
owner's equity (9)
partnership (8)
prepaid expenses (12)
private accounting (4)
profit (2)
proprietorship (8)
public accounting (7)
rent revenue (12)
retained earnings (15)
retained earnings statement (17)
revenue (12)
sales (12)
Securities and Exchange Commission (SEC) (7)
service business (3)
statement of cash flows (17)
stockholders' equity (11)
unit of measure concept (9)

Illustrative Problem

Cecil Jameson, Attorney-at-Law, P.C. is organized as a professional corporation owned and operated by Cecil Jameson. On July 1, 2009, Cecil Jameson, Attorney-at-Law, P.C. has the following assets, liabilities, and capital stock: cash, $1,000; accounts receivable, $3,200; supplies, $850; land, $10,000; accounts payable, $1,530; capital stock, $10,000. Office space and office equipment are currently being rented, pending the construction of an office complex on land purchased last year. Business transactions during July are summarized as follows:

  a. Received cash from clients for services, $3,928.
  b. Paid creditors on account, $1,055.
  c. Received cash from Cecil Jameson as an additional investment in exchange for capital stock, $3,700.
  d. Paid office rent for the month, $1,200.
  e. Charged clients for legal services on account, $2,025.
  f. Purchased supplies on account, $245.
  g. Received cash from clients on account, $3,000.
  h. Received invoice for paralegal services from Legal Aid Inc. for July (to be paid on August 10), $1,635.
  i. Paid the following: wages expense, $850; answering service expense, $250; utilities expense, $325; and miscellaneous expense, $75.
  j. Determined that the cost of supplies on hand was $980; therefore, the cost of supplies used during the month was $115.
  k. Paid dividends of $1,000.

Instructions

1. Determine the amount of retained earnings as of July 1, 2009.
2. State the assets, liabilities, and stockholders' equity as of July 1 in equation form similar to that shown in this chapter. In tabular form below the equation, indicate the increases and decreases resulting from each transaction and the new balances after each transaction.
3. Prepare an income statement for July, a retained earnings statement for July, and a balance sheet as of July 31, 2009.
4. (Optional). Prepare a statement of cash flows for July.

Solution

1.

$$\text{Assets} - \text{Liabilities} = \text{Stockholders' Equity}$$

$$(\$1,000 + \$3,200 + \$850 + \$10,000) - \$1,530 = \text{Capital Stock} + \text{Retained Earnings}$$

$$\$15,050 - \$1,530 = \$10,000 + \text{Retained Earnings}$$

$$\$3,520 = \text{Retained Earnings}$$

2.

	Assets				=	Liabilities +		Stockholders' Equity										
	Cash +	Accts. Rec. +	Supp. +	Land	=	Accts. Pay. +	Capital Stock +	Retained Earnings −	Dividends +	Fees Earned −	Paralegal Exp. −	Wages Exp. −	Rent Exp. −	Answering Utilities Exp. −	Service Exp. −	Supp. Exp. −	Misc. Exp.		
Bal.	1,000	3,200	850	10,000		1,530	10,000	$3,520											
a.	+3,928									3,928									
Bal.	4,928	3,200	850	10,000		1,530	10,000			3,928									
b.	−1,055					−1,055													
Bal.	3,873	3,200	850	10,000		475	10,000			3,928									
c.	+3,700						+3,700												
Bal.	7,573	3,200	850	10,000		475	13,700			3,928									
d.	−1,200												−1,200						
Bal.	6,373	3,200	850	10,000		475	13,700			3,928			−1,200						
e.		+2,025								+2,025									
Bal.	6,373	5,225	850	10,000		475	13,700			5,953			−1,200						
f.			+ 245			+ 245													
Bal.	6,373	5,225	1,095	10,000		720	13,700			5,953			−1,200						
g.	+3,000	−3,000																	
Bal.	9,373	2,225	1,095	10,000		720	13,700			5,953			−1,200						
h.						+1,635					−1,635								
Bal.	9,373	2,225	1,095	10,000		2,355	13,700			5,953	−1,635		−1,200						
i.	−1,500											−850		−325	−250		−75		
Bal.	7,873	2,225	1,095	10,000		2,355	13,700			5,953	−1,635	−850	−1,200	−325	−250		−75		
j.			−115													−115			
Bal.	7,873	2,225	980	10,000		2,355	13,700			5,953	−1,635	−850	−1,200	−325	−250	−115	−75		
k.	−1,000								−1,000										
Bal.	6,873	2,225	980	10,000		2,355	13,700	$3,520	−1,000	5,953	−1,635	−850	−1,200	−325	−250	−115	−75		

3.

Cecil Jameson, Attorney-at-Law, P.C.
Income Statement
For the Month Ended July 31, 2009

Fees earned		$5,953
Expenses:		
Paralegal expense	$1,635	
Rent expense	1,200	
Wages expense	850	
Utilities expense	325	
Answering service expense	250	
Supplies expense	115	
Miscellaneous expense	75	
Total expenses		4,450
Net income		$1,503

Cecil Jameson, Attorney-at-Law, P.C.
Retained Earnings Statement
For the Month Ended July 31, 2009

Retained earnings, July 1, 2009		$3,520
Net income for the month	$1,503	
Less dividends	1,000	
Increase in retained earnings		503
Retained earnings, July 31, 2009		$4,023

(continued)

Cecil Jameson, Attorney-at-Law, P.C.
Balance Sheet
July 31, 2009

Assets		Liabilities		
Cash	$ 6,873	Accounts payable		$ 2,355
Accounts receivable	2,225	**Stockholders' Equity**		
Supplies	980	Capital stock	$13,700	
Land	10,000	Retained earnings	4,023	
		Total stockholders' equity . . .		17,723
		Total liabilities and		
Total assets	$20,078	stockholders' equity		$20,078

4. Optional.

Cecil Jameson, Attorney-at-Law, P.C.
Statement of Cash Flows
For the Month Ended July 31, 2009

Cash flows from operating activities:		
Cash received from customers.	$6,928*	
Deduct cash payments for operating expenses	3,755**	
Net cash flows from operating activities		$3,173
Cash flows from investing activities		—
Cash flows from financing activities:		
Cash received from issuing capital stock.	$3,700	
Deduct cash dividends	1,000	
Net cash flows from financing activities		2,700
Net increase in cash during year		$5,873
Cash as of July 1, 2009.		1,000
Cash as of July 31, 2009.		$6,873

*$6,928 = $3,928 + $3,000
**$3,755 = $1,055 + $1,200 + $1,500

Self-Examination Questions (Answers at End of Chapter)

1. A profit-making business operating as a separate legal entity and in which ownership is divided into shares of stock is known as a:
   A. proprietorship.   C. partnership.
   B. service business.   D. corporation.

2. The resources owned by a business are called:
   A. assets.   C. the accounting equation.
   B. liabilities.   D. stockholders' equity.

3. A listing of a business entity's assets, liabilities, and stockholders' equity as of a specific date is a(n):
   A. balance sheet.
   B. income statement.
   C. retained earnings statement.
   D. statement of cash flows.

4. If total assets increased $20,000 during a period and total liabilities increased $12,000 during the same period, the amount and direction (increase or decrease) of the change in stockholders' equity for that period is a(n):
   A. $32,000 increase.   C. $8,000 increase.
   B. $32,000 decrease.   D. $8,000 decrease.

5. If revenue was $45,000, expenses were $37,500, and dividends were $10,000, the amount of net income or net loss would be:
   A. $45,000 net income.   C. $37,500 net loss.
   B. $7,500 net income.   D. $2,500 net loss.

Eye Openers

1. What is the objective of most businesses?
2. What is the difference between a manufacturing business and a service business? Is a restaurant a manufacturing business, a service business, or both?

3. Name some users of accounting information.

4. What is the role of accounting in business?

5. Why are most large companies like Microsoft, PepsiCo, Caterpillar, and AutoZone organized as corporations?

6. Barry Bergan is the owner of Elephant Delivery Service. Recently, Barry paid interest of $3,000 on a personal loan of $40,000 that he used to begin the business. Should Elephant Delivery Service record the interest payment? Explain.

7. On April 2, Gremlin Repair Service extended an offer of $100,000 for land that had been priced for sale at $125,000. On May 10, Gremlin Repair Service accepted the seller's counteroffer of $115,000. Describe how Gremlin Repair Service should record the land.

8. a. Land with an assessed value of $300,000 for property tax purposes is acquired by a business for $475,000. Ten years later, the plot of land has an assessed value of $500,000 and the business receives an offer of $900,000 for it. Should the monetary amount assigned to the land in the business records now be increased?

   b. Assuming that the land acquired in (a) was sold for $900,000, how would the various elements of the accounting equation be affected?

9. Describe the difference between an account receivable and an account payable.

10. A business had revenues of $600,000 and operating expenses of $715,000. Did the business (a) incur a net loss or (b) realize net income?

11. A business had revenues of $687,500 and operating expenses of $492,400. Did the business (a) incur a net loss or (b) realize net income?

12. What particular item of financial or operating data appears on both the income statement and the retained earnings statement? What item appears on both the balance sheet and the retained earnings statement? What item appears on both the balance sheet and the statement of cash flows?

Practice Exercises

PE 1-1A
Cost concept
obj. 2
EE 1-1   p. 9

On February 7, Snap Repair Service extended an offer of $75,000 for land that had been priced for sale at $85,000. On February 21, Snap Repair Service accepted the seller's counteroffer of $81,000. On April 30, the land was assessed at a value of $125,000 for property tax purposes. On August 30, Snap Repair Service was offered $130,000 for the land by a national retail chain. At what value should the land be recorded in Snap Repair Service's records?

PE 1-1B
Cost concept
obj. 2
EE 1-1   p. 9

On November 23, Terrier Repair Service extended an offer of $40,000 for land that had been priced for sale at $48,500. On December 2, Terrier Repair Service accepted the seller's counteroffer of $44,000. On December 27, the land was assessed at a value of $50,000 for property tax purposes. On April 1, Terrier Repair Service was offered $75,000 for the land by a national retail chain. At what value should the land be recorded in Terrier Repair Service's records?

PE 1-2A
Accounting equation
obj. 3
EE 1-2   p. 9

Paul Eberly is the owner and operator of You're Great, a motivational consulting business. At the end of its accounting period, December 31, 2009, You're Great has assets of $475,000 and liabilities of $115,000. Using the accounting equation, determine the following amounts:

a. Owner's equity, as of December 31, 2009.

b. Owner's equity, as of December 31, 2010, assuming that assets increased by $90,000 and liabilities increased by $28,000 during 2010.

PE 1-2B
Accounting equation

obj. 3

EE 1-2   p. 9

Lynn Doyle is the owner and operator of Star LLC, a motivational consulting business. At the end of its accounting period, December 31, 2009, Star has assets of $750,000 and liabilities of $293,000. Using the accounting equation, determine the following amounts:

a. Owner's equity, as of December 31, 2009.
b. Owner's equity, as of December 31, 2010, assuming that assets increased by $75,000 and liabilities decreased by $30,000 during 2010.

PE 1-3A
Transactions

obj. 4

EE 1-3   p. 15

Zany Delivery Service is owned and operated by Joey Bryant. The following selected transactions were completed by Zany Delivery Service during February:

1. Received cash in exchange for capital stock, $15,000.
2. Paid advertising expense, $900.
3. Purchased supplies on account, $600.
4. Billed customers for delivery services on account, $9,000.
5. Received cash from customers on account, $5,500.

Indicate the effect of each transaction on the accounting equation elements (Assets, Liabilities, Stockholders' Equity, Dividends, Revenue, and Expense) by listing the numbers identifying the transactions, (1) through (5). Also, indicate the specific item within the accounting equation element that is affected. To illustrate, the answer to (1) is shown below.

(1) Asset (Cash) increases by $15,000; Stockholders' Equity (Capital Stock) increases by $15,000.

PE 1-3B
Transactions

obj. 4

EE 1-3   p. 15

Yukon Delivery Service is owned and operated by Betty Pasha. The following selected transactions were completed by Yukon Delivery Service during June:

1. Received cash in exchange for capital stock, $10,000.
2. Paid creditors on account, $1,500.
3. Billed customers for delivery services on account, $11,500.
4. Received cash from customers on account, $2,700.
5. Paid dividends, $2,000.

Indicate the effect of each transaction on the accounting equation elements (Assets, Liabilities, Stockholders' Equity, Dividends, Revenue, and Expense) by listing the numbers identifying the transactions, (1) through (5). Also, indicate the specific item within the accounting equation element that is affected. To illustrate, the answer to (1) is shown below.

(1) Asset (Cash) increases by $10,000; Stockholders' Equity (Capital Stock) increases by $10,000.

PE 1-4A
Income statement

obj. 5

EE 1-4   p. 17

The assets and liabilities of Impeccable Travel Service at November 30, 2010, the end of the current year, and its revenue and expenses for the year are listed below. The capital stock was $75,000 and the retained earnings were $305,000 at December 1, 2009, the beginning of the current year.

Accounts payable	$ 42,000	Miscellaneous expense	$ 12,700
Accounts receivable	75,500	Office expense	313,300
Cash	45,400	Supplies	5,100
Fees earned	754,000	Wages expense	450,000
Land	290,000		

Prepare an income statement for the current year ended November 30, 2010.

PE 1-4B
Income statement

obj. 5

EE 1-4   p. 17

The assets and liabilities of Express Travel Service at June 30, 2010, the end of the current year, and its revenue and expenses for the year are listed at the top of the following page. The capital stock was $35,000 and the retained earnings were $90,000 at July 1, 2009, the beginning of the current year.

Accounts payable	$ 12,000	Miscellaneous expense	$ 8,000
Accounts receivable	32,000	Office expense	111,000
Cash	78,000	Supplies	6,000
Fees earned	475,000	Wages expense	239,000
Land	150,000		

Prepare an income statement for the current year ended June 30, 2010.

PE 1-5A
Retained earnings statement
obj. 5
EE 1-5   p. 19

Using the data for Impeccable Travel Service shown in Practice Exercise 1-4A, prepare a retained earnings statement for the current year ended November 30, 2010. Charly Maves invested an additional $36,000 in the business in exchange for capital stock. Cash dividends of $20,000 were paid during the year.

PE 1-5B
Retained earnings statement
obj. 5
EE 1-5   p. 19

Using the data for Express Travel Service shown in Practice Exercise 1-4B, prepare a retained earnings statement for the current year ended June 30, 2010. Janis Paisley invested an additional $30,000 in the business in exchange for capital stock. Cash dividends of $18,000 were paid during the year.

PE 1-6A
Balance sheet
obj. 5
EE 1-6   p. 20

Using the data for Impeccable Travel Service shown in Practice Exercises 1-4A and 1-5A, prepare the balance sheet as of November 30, 2010.

PE 1-6B
Balance sheet
obj. 5
EE 1-6   p. 20

Using the data for Express Travel Service shown in Practice Exercises 1-4B and 1-5B, prepare the balance sheet as of June 30, 2010.

PE 1-7A
Statement of cash flows
obj. 5
EE 1-7   p. 21

A summary of cash flows for Impeccable Travel Service for the year ended November 30, 2010, is shown below.

Cash receipts:	
Cash received from customers	$700,000
Cash received from issuing capital stock	36,000
Cash payments:	
Cash paid for operating expenses	730,000
Cash paid for land	54,000
Cash paid for dividends	20,000

The cash balance as of December 1, 2009, was $113,400.

Prepare a statement of cash flows for Impeccable Travel Service for the year ended November 30, 2010.

PE 1-7B
Statement of cash flows
obj. 5
EE 1-7   p. 21

A summary of cash flows for Express Travel Service for the year ended June 30, 2010, is shown below.

Cash receipts:	
Cash received from customers	$460,000
Cash received from issuing capital stock	30,000
Cash payments:	
Cash paid for operating expenses	355,000
Cash paid for land	104,000
Cash paid for dividends	18,000

The cash balance as of July 1, 2009, was $65,000.

Prepare a statement of cash flows for Express Travel Service for the year ended June 30, 2010.

Exercises

EX 1-1
Types of businesses

obj. 1

Indicate whether each of the following companies is primarily a service, merchandise, or manufacturing business. If you are unfamiliar with the company, use the Internet to locate the company's home page or use the finance Web site of Yahoo.

1. H&R Block
2. eBay Inc.
3. Wal-Mart Stores, Inc.
4. Ford Motor Company
5. Citigroup
6. Boeing
7. SunTrust
8. Alcoa Inc.
9. Procter & Gamble
10. FedEx
11. Gap Inc.
12. Hilton Hospitality, Inc.
13. CVS
14. Caterpillar
15. The Dow Chemical Company

EX 1-2
Professional ethics

obj. 1

A fertilizer manufacturing company wants to relocate to Collier County. A 13-year-old report from a fired researcher at the company says the company's product is releasing toxic by-products. The company has suppressed that report. A second report commissioned by the company shows there is no problem with the fertilizer.

➤ Should the company's chief executive officer reveal the context of the unfavorable report in discussions with Collier County representatives? Discuss.

EX 1-3
Business entity concept

obj. 2

Chalet Sports sells hunting and fishing equipment and provides guided hunting and fishing trips. Chalet Sports is owned and operated by Cliff Owen, a well-known sports enthusiast and hunter. Cliff's wife, Judy, owns and operates Joliet Boutique, a women's clothing store. Cliff and Judy have established a trust fund to finance their children's college education. The trust fund is maintained by City Bank in the name of the children, John and Morgan.

For each of the following transactions, identify which of the entities listed should record the transaction in its records.

Entities	
C	Chalet Sports
B	City Bank Trust Fund
J	Joliet Boutique
X	None of the above

1. Cliff paid a local doctor for his annual physical, which was required by the workmen's compensation insurance policy carried by Chalet Sports.
2. Cliff received a cash advance from customers for a guided hunting trip.
3. Judy paid her dues to the YWCA.
4. Cliff paid a breeder's fee for an English springer spaniel to be used as a hunting guide dog.
5. Judy deposited a $5,000 personal check in the trust fund at City Bank.
6. Cliff paid for an advertisement in a hunters' magazine.
7. Judy authorized the trust fund to purchase mutual fund shares.
8. Judy donated several dresses from inventory for a local charity auction for the benefit of a women's abuse shelter.
9. Cliff paid for dinner and a movie to celebrate their fifteenth wedding anniversary.
10. Judy purchased two dozen spring dresses from a Seattle designer for a special spring sale.

EX 1-4
Accounting equation
obj. 3

✔ Coca-Cola,
$16,920

The total assets and total liabilities of Coca-Cola and PepsiCo are shown below.

	Coca-Cola (in millions)	PepsiCo (in millions)
Assets	$29,963	$29,930
Liabilities	13,043	14,483

Determine the stockholders' (owners') equity of each company.

EX 1-5
Accounting equation
obj. 3

✔ eBay, $10,905

The total assets and total liabilities of eBay and Google are shown below.

	eBay (in millions)	Google (in millions)
Assets	$ 13,494	$18,473
Liabilities	2,589	1,433

Determine the stockholders' (owners') equity of each company.

EX 1-6
Accounting equation
obj. 3

✔ a. 1,030,000

Determine the missing amount for each of the following:

	Assets	=	Liabilities	+	Stockholders' (Owners') Equity
a.	X	=	$250,000	+	$780,000
b.	$125,000	=	X	+	39,500
c.	60,000	=	7,500	+	X

EX 1-7
Accounting equation
objs. 3, 4

✔ b. $568,000

Donna Ahern is the sole stockholder and operator of Omega, a motivational consulting business. At the end of its accounting period, December 31, 2009, Omega has assets of $760,000 and liabilities of $240,000. Using the accounting equation and considering each case independently, determine the following amounts:

a. Stockholders' equity, as of December 31, 2009.

b. Stockholders' equity, as of December 31, 2010, assuming that assets increased by $120,000 and liabilities increased by $72,000 during 2010.

c. Stockholders' equity, as of December 31, 2010, assuming that assets decreased by $60,000 and liabilities increased by $21,600 during 2010.

d. Stockholders' equity, as of December 31, 2010, assuming that assets increased by $100,000 and liabilities decreased by $38,400 during 2010.

e. Net income (or net loss) during 2010, assuming that as of December 31, 2010, assets were $960,000, liabilities were $156,000, and no additional capital stock was issued or dividends distributed.

EX 1-8
Asset, liability, stock-holders' equity items
obj. 3

Indicate whether each of the following is identified with (1) an asset, (2) a liability, or (3) stockholders' equity (retained earnings):

a. accounts payable
b. cash
c. fees earned
d. land
e. supplies
f. wages expense

EX 1-9
Effect of transactions on accounting equation
obj. 4

Describe how the following business transactions affect the three elements of the accounting equation.

a. Invested cash in business in exchange for capital stock.
b. Received cash for services performed.   *(continued)*

c. Paid for utilities used in the business.

d. Purchased supplies for cash.

e. Purchased supplies on account.

EX 1-10
Effect of transactions on accounting equation

obj. **4**

✔ a. (1) increase $140,000

a. A vacant lot acquired for $150,000 is sold for $290,000 in cash. What is the effect of the sale on the total amount of the seller's (1) assets, (2) liabilities, and (3) stockholders' equity (retained earnings)?

b. Assume that the seller owes $80,000 on a loan for the land. After receiving the $290,000 cash in (a), the seller pays the $80,000 owed. What is the effect of the payment on the total amount of the seller's (1) assets, (2) liabilities, and (3) stockholders' equity (retained earnings)?

EX 1-11
Effect of transactions on stockholders' equity

obj. **4**

Indicate whether each of the following types of transactions will either (a) increase stockholders' equity or (b) decrease stockholders' equity:

1. expenses
2. revenues
3. stockholders' investments in exchange for capital stock
4. dividends

EX 1-12
Transactions

obj. **4**

The following selected transactions were completed by Lindbergh Delivery Service during October:

1. Received cash from issuing capital stock, $75,000.
2. Paid rent for October, $4,200.
3. Paid advertising expense, $4,000.
4. Received cash for providing delivery services, $39,750.
5. Purchased supplies for cash, $2,500.
6. Billed customers for delivery services on account, $81,200.
7. Paid creditors on account, $9,280.
8. Received cash from customers on account, $25,600.
9. Determined that the cost of supplies on hand was $900; therefore, $1,600 of supplies had been used during the month.
10. Paid cash dividends, $3,000.

Indicate the effect of each transaction on the accounting equation by listing the numbers identifying the transactions, (1) through (10), in a column, and inserting at the right of each number the appropriate letter from the following list:

a. Increase in an asset, decrease in another asset.

b. Increase in an asset, increase in a liability.

c. Increase in an asset, increase in stockholders' equity.

d. Decrease in an asset, decrease in a liability.

e. Decrease in an asset, decrease in stockholders' equity.

EX 1-13
Nature of transactions

obj. **4**

✔ d. $6,000

Murray Kiser operates his own catering service. Summary financial data for February are presented in equation form as follows. Each line designated by a number indicates the effect of a transaction on the equation. Each increase and decrease in stockholders' equity, except transaction (5), affects net income.

	Assets			=	Liabilities	+	Stockholders' Equity				
	Cash +	Supplies +	Land	=	Accounts Payable	+	Capital Stock +	Retained Earnings −	Dividends +	Fees Earned −	Expenses
Bal.	30,000	4,000	75,000		8,000		50,000	51,000			
1.	+35,000									35,000	
2	−15,000		+15,000								
3.	−26,000										−26,000
4.		+1,500			+1,500						
5.	−2,000								−2,000		
6.	−7,200				−7,200						
7.		−3,000									−3,000
Bal.	14,800	2,500	90,000		2,300		50,000	51,000	−2,000	35,000	−29,000

a. Describe each transaction.

b. What is the amount of net decrease in cash during the month?

c. What is the amount of net increase in stockholders' equity during the month?

d. What is the amount of the net income for the month?

e. How much of the net income for the month was retained in the business?

EX 1-14
Net income and dividends
obj. 5

The income statement of a corporation for the month of December indicates a net income of $75,000. During the same period, $100,000 in cash dividends were paid.

   Would it be correct to say that the business incurred a net loss of $25,000 during the month? Discuss.

EX 1-15
Net income and stockholders' equity for four businesses
obj. 5

✔ Saturn: Net income, $108,000

Four different corporations, Jupiter, Mercury, Saturn, and Venus, show the same balance sheet data at the beginning and end of a year. These data, exclusive of the amount of stockholders' equity, are summarized as follows:

	Total Assets	Total Liabilities
Beginning of the year	$ 810,000	$324,000
End of the year	1,296,000	540,000

On the basis of the above data and the following additional information for the year, determine the net income (or loss) of each company for the year. (*Hint:* First determine the amount of increase or decrease in stockholders' equity during the year.)

Jupiter: No additional capital stock was issued, and no dividends were paid.

Mercury: No additional capital stock was issued, but dividends of $72,000 were paid.

Saturn: Additional capital stock of $162,000 was issued, but no dividends were paid.

Venus: Additional capital stock of $162,000 was issued, and dividends of $72,000 were paid.

EX 1-16
Balance sheet items
obj. 5

From the following list of selected items taken from the records of Hoosier Appliance Service as of a specific date, identify those that would appear on the balance sheet:

1. Accounts Payable
2. Capital Stock
3. Cash
4. Fees Earned
5. Land
6. Supplies
7. Supplies Expense
8. Utilities Expense
9. Wages Expense
10. Wages Payable

EX 1-17
Income statement items
obj. **5**

Based on the data presented in Exercise 1-16, identify those items that would appear on the income statement.

EX 1-18
Retained earnings statement
obj. **5**

✔ Retained earnings, April 30, 2010: $799,100

Financial information related to Teflon Company, for the month ended April 30, 2010, is as follows:

Net income for April	$ 93,780
Dividends during April	10,000
Retained earnings, April 1, 2010	715,320

Prepare a retained earnings statement for the month ended April 30, 2010.

EX 1-19
Income statement
obj. **5**

✔ Net income: $116,600

Relax Services was organized on May 1, 2010. A summary of the revenue and expense transactions for May follows:

Fees earned	$363,200
Wages expense	187,000
Rent expense	36,000
Supplies expense	11,500
Miscellaneous expense	12,100

Prepare an income statement for the month ended May 31.

EX 1-20
Missing amounts from balance sheet and income statement data
obj. **5**

✔ (a) $46,890

One item is omitted in each of the following summaries of balance sheet and income statement data for the following four different corporations:

	Earth	Mars	Neptune	Pluto
Beginning of the year:				
Assets	$216,000	$250,000	$100,000	(d)
Liabilities	129,600	130,000	76,000	$120,000
End of the year:				
Assets	268,200	350,000	90,000	248,000
Liabilities	117,000	110,000	80,000	136,000
During the year:				
Additional issuance of capital stock	(a)	50,000	10,000	40,000
Dividends	14,400	16,000	(c)	60,000
Revenue	71,190	(b)	115,000	112,000
Expenses	38,880	64,000	122,500	128,000

Determine the missing amounts, identifying them by letter. (*Hint:* First determine the amount of increase or decrease in stockholders' equity during the year.)

EX 1-21
Balance sheets, net income
obj. **5**

✔ b. $136,275

Financial information related to Plexiglass Interiors for October and November 2010 is as follows:

	October 31, 2010	November 30, 2010
Accounts payable	$ 46,200	$ 49,800
Accounts receivable	102,000	117,375
Capital stock	50,000	50,000
Cash	?	?
Retained earnings	180,000	306,000
Supplies	9,000	7,500

a. Prepare balance sheets for Plexiglass Interiors as of October 31 and as of November 30, 2010.
b. Determine the amount of net income for November, assuming that no additional capital stock was issued and no dividends were paid during the month.
c. Determine the amount of net income for November, assuming that no additional capital stock was issued but dividends of $37,500 were paid during the month.

EX 1-22
Financial statements
obj. 5

Each of the following items is shown in the financial statements of ExxonMobil Corporation. Identify the financial statement (balance sheet or income statement) in which each item would appear.

a. Accounts payable
b. Cash equivalents
c. Crude oil inventory
d. Equipment
e. Exploration expenses
f. Income taxes payable
g. Investments
h. Long-term debt

i. Marketable securities
j. Notes and loans payable
k. Notes receivable
l. Operating expenses
m. Prepaid taxes
n. Sales
o. Selling expenses

EX 1-23
Statement of cash flows
obj. 5

Indicate whether each of the following activities would be reported on the statement of cash flows as (a) an operating activity, (b) an investing activity, or (c) a financing activity:

1. Cash received from issuing capital stock
2. Cash paid for land
3. Cash received from fees earned
4. Cash paid for expenses

EX 1-24
Statement of cash flows
obj. 5

A summary of cash flows for Pickerel Consulting Group for the year ended March 31, 2010, is shown below.

Cash receipts:	
Cash received from customers	$239,100
Cash received from issuing capital stock	50,000
Cash payments:	
Cash paid for operating expenses	162,900
Cash paid for land	75,000
Cash paid for dividends	10,000

The cash balance as of April 1, 2009, was $30,800.

Prepare a statement of cash flows for Pickerel Consulting Group for the year ended March 31, 2010.

EX 1-25
Financial statements
obj. 5

✔ Correct amount
of total assets is
$176,400

Driftwood Realty, organized July 1, 2010, is owned and operated by Steffy Owen. How many errors can you find in the following statements for Driftwood Realty, prepared after its second month of operations?

Driftwood Realty
Income Statement
August 31, 2010

Sales commissions.		$467,100
Expenses:		
Office salaries expense	$291,600	
Rent expense.	99,000	
Automobile expense	22,500	
Miscellaneous expense	7,200	
Supplies expense	2,700	
Total expenses		423,000
Net income		$134,100

Steffy Owen
Retained Earnings Statement
August 31, 2009

Retained earnings, August 17, 2010.	$ 76,100
Less dividends during August	18,000
	$ 58,100
Additional issuance of capital stock	22,500
	$ 80,600
Net income for the month.	134,100
Retained earnings, August 31, 2010.	$214,700

Balance Sheet
For the Month Ended August 31, 2010

Assets		Liabilities	
Cash.	$29,700	Accounts receivable	$128,700
Accounts payable.	34,200	Supplies	18,000
		Stockholders' Equity	
		Capital stock . . . . $ 40,000	
		Retained earnings 214,700	
		Total stockholders' equity	254,700
		Total liabilities and stockholders'	
Total assets	$63,900	equity	$401,400

EX 1-26
Ratio of liabilities to
stockholders' equity

The Home Depot, Inc., is the world's largest home improvement retailer and one of the largest retailers in the United States based on net sales volume. The Home Depot operates over 2,000 Home Depot® stores that sell a wide assortment of building materials and home improvement and lawn and garden products. The Home Depot also operates over 30 EXPO Design Center stores that offer interior design products, such as kitchen and bathroom cabinetry, tiles, flooring, and lighting fixtures, and installation services.

The Home Depot reported the following balance sheet data (in millions):

	Jan. 28, 2007	Jan. 29, 2006
Total assets	$52,263	$44,405
Total stockholders' equity	25,030	26,909

a. Determine the total liabilities as of January 28, 2007, and January 29, 2006.
b. Determine the ratio of liabilities to stockholders' equity for 2007 and 2006. Round to two decimal places.
c. What conclusions regarding the margin of protection to the creditors can you draw from (b)?

EX 1-27
Ratio of liabilities to
stockholders' equity

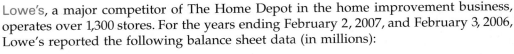

Lowe's, a major competitor of The Home Depot in the home improvement business, operates over 1,300 stores. For the years ending February 2, 2007, and February 3, 2006, Lowe's reported the following balance sheet data (in millions):

	2007	2006
Total assets	$27,767	$24,639
Total liabilities	12,042	10,343

a. Determine the total stockholders' equity as of February 2, 2007, and February 3, 2006.
b. Determine the ratio of liabilities to stockholders' equity for 2007 and 2006. Round to two decimal places.
c. What conclusions regarding the margin of protection to the creditors can you draw from (b)?
d. Using the balance sheet data for The Home Depot in Exercise 1-26, how does the ratio of liabilities to stockholders' equity of Lowe's compare to that of The Home Depot?

Problems Series A

PR 1-1A
Transactions

obj. 4

✔ Cash bal. at end
of July: $50,450

Jean Howard established an insurance agency on July 1 of the current year and completed the following transactions during July:

a. Opened a business bank account with a deposit of $50,000 in exchange for capital stock.
b. Purchased supplies on account, $1,600.
c. Paid creditors on account, $500.
d. Received cash from fees earned on insurance commissions, $9,250.
e. Paid rent on office and equipment for the month, $2,500.
f. Paid automobile expenses for month, $900, and miscellaneous expenses, $300.
g. Paid office salaries, $1,900.
h. Determined that the cost of supplies on hand was $550; therefore, the cost of supplies used was $1,050.
i. Billed insurance companies for sales commissions earned, $11,150.
j. Paid dividends, $2,700.

Instructions

1. Indicate the effect of each transaction and the balances after each transaction, using the following tabular headings:

Assets			=	Liabilities +			Stockholders' Equity					
Cash +	Accounts Receivable +	Supplies =		Accounts Payable +	Capital Stock −	Dividends +	Fees Earned −	Rent Expense −	Salaries Expense −	Supplies Expense −	Auto Expense −	Misc. Expense

2. ▬▬▶ Briefly explain why the stockholders' investments and revenues increased stockholders' equity, while dividends and expenses decreased stockholders' equity.

PR 1-2A
Financial statements

obj. 5

✔ 1. Net income:
$208,860

The amounts of the assets and liabilities of Heavenly Travel Service at April 30, 2010, the end of the current year, and its revenue and expenses for the year are listed below. The capital stock was $15,000 and retained earnings was $30,540 on May 1, 2009, the beginning of the current year. During the year, dividends of $25,000 were paid.

Accounts payable	$ 14,600	Supplies	$ 6,800
Accounts receivable	78,000	Supplies expense	13,200
Cash	159,200	Taxes expense	10,250
Fees earned	600,000	Utilities expense	49,150
Miscellaneous expense	5,000	Wages expense	232,640
Rent expense	80,900		

Instructions

1. Prepare an income statement for the current year ended April 30, 2010.
2. Prepare a retained earnings statement for the current year ended April 30, 2010.
3. Prepare a balance sheet as of April 30, 2010.

PR 1-3A
Financial statements

obj. 5

✔ 1. Net income:
$22,975

Doug Van Buren established Ohm Computer Services on July 1, 2010. The effect of each transaction and the balances after each transaction for July are shown at the top of the following page.

Instructions

1. Prepare an income statement for the month ended July 31, 2010.
2. Prepare a retained earnings statement for the month ended July 31, 2010.
3. Prepare a balance sheet as of July 31, 2010.
4. (Optional). Prepare a statement of cash flows for the month ending July 31, 2010.

	Assets			= Liabilities +		Stockholders' Equity						
	Cash	Accounts Receivable	Supplies	Accounts Payable	Capital Stock	Dividends	Fees Earned	Salaries Expense	Rent Expense	Auto Expense	Supplies Expense	Misc. Expense
a.	+30,000				+30,000							
b.			+2,600	+2,600								
Bal.	30,000		2,600	2,600	30,000							
c.	+29,500						+29,500					
Bal.	59,500		2,600	2,600	30,000		29,500					
d.	−8,000								−8,000			
Bal.	51,500		2,600	2,600	30,000		29,500		−8,000			
e.	−1,250			−1,250								
Bal.	50,250		2,600	1,350	30,000		29,500		−8,000			
f.		+20,750					+20,750					
Bal.	50,250	20,750	2,600	1,350	30,000		50,250		−8,000			
g.	−5,750									−3,875		−1,875
Bal.	44,500	20,750	2,600	1,350	30,000		50,250		−8,000	−3,875		−1,875
h.	−12,000							−12,000				
Bal.	32,500	20,750	2,600	1,350	30,000		50,250	−12,000	−8,000	−3,875		−1,875
i.			−1,525								−1,525	
Bal.	32,500	20,750	1,075	1,350	30,000		50,250	−12,000	−8,000	−3,875	−1,525	−1,875
j.	−7,500					−7,500						
Bal.	25,000	20,750	1,075	1,350	30,000	−7,500	50,250	−12,000	−8,000	−3,875	−1,525	−1,875

PR 1-4A

Transactions; financial statements

objs. 4, 5

✔ 2. Net income: $14,450

On April 1, 2010, Ryan Barnes established Coyote Realty. Ryan completed the following transactions during the month of April:

a. Opened a business bank account with a deposit of $25,000 in exchange for capital stock.
b. Paid rent on office and equipment for the month, $3,200.
c. Paid automobile expenses (including rental charge) for month, $1,200, and miscellaneous expenses, $800.
d. Purchased supplies (pens, file folders, and copy paper) on account, $900.
e. Earned sales commissions, receiving cash, $24,000.
f. Paid creditor on account, $400.
g. Paid office salaries, $3,600.
h. Paid dividends, $3,000.
i. Determined that the cost of supplies on hand was $150; therefore, the cost of supplies used was $750.

Instructions

1. Indicate the effect of each transaction and the balances after each transaction, using the following tabular headings:

	Assets		= Liabilities +		Stockholders' Equity							
Cash	+ Supplies	=	Accounts Payable	+ Capital Stock	− Dividends	+ Sales Commissions	− Office Salaries Expense	− Rent Expense	− Auto Expense	− Supplies Expense	− Misc. Expense	

2. Prepare an income statement for April, a retained earnings statement for April, and a balance sheet as of April 30.

PR 1-5A

Transactions; financial statements

objs. 4, 5

✔ 3. Net income: $13,950

Colfax Dry Cleaners is owned and operated by Maria Acosta. A building and equipment are currently being rented, pending expansion to new facilities. The actual work of dry cleaning is done by another company at wholesale rates. The assets, liabilities, and capital stock of the business on November 1, 2010, are as follows: Cash, $34,200; Accounts Receivable, $40,000; Supplies, $5,000; Land, $50,000; Accounts Payable, $16,400; Capital Stock, $10,000. Business transactions during November are summarized as follows:

a. Maria Acosta invested additional cash in the business with a deposit of $35,000 in exchange for capital stock.

b. Purchased land for use as a parking lot, paying cash of $30,000.
c. Paid rent for the month, $4,500.
d. Charged customers for dry cleaning revenue on account, $18,250.
e. Paid creditors on account, $9,000.
f. Purchased supplies on account, $2,800.
g. Received cash from cash customers for dry cleaning revenue, $31,750.
h. Received cash from customers on account, $27,800.
i. Received monthly invoice for dry cleaning expense for November (to be paid on December 10), $14,800.
j. Paid the following: wages expense, $8,200; truck expense, $1,875; utilities expense, $1,575; miscellaneous expense, $850.
k. Determined that the cost of supplies on hand was $3,550; therefore, the cost of supplies used during the month was $4,250.
l. Paid dividends, $10,000.

Instructions
1. Determine the amount of retained earnings as of November 1.
2. State the assets, liabilities, and stockholders' equity as of November 1 in equation form similar to that shown in this chapter. In tabular form below the equation, indicate increases and decreases resulting from each transaction and the new balances after each transaction.
3. Prepare an income statement for November, a retained earnings statement for November, and a balance sheet as of November 30.
4. (Optional) Prepare a statement of cash flows for November.

PR 1-6A
Missing amounts from financial statements

obj. 5

✔ g. $56,610

The financial statements at the end of Four Corners Realty's first month of operations are shown below and on the next page.

Four Corners Realty
Income Statement
For the Month Ended July 31, 2010

Fees earned		$239,700
Expenses:		
Wages expense	$ (a)	
Rent expense	24,480	
Supplies expense	20,400	
Utilities expense	13,770	
Miscellaneous expense	8,415	
Total expenses		121,890
Net income		(b)

Four Corners Realty
Retained Earnings Statement
For the Month Ended July 31, 2010

Retained earnings, July 1, 2010		$ (c)
Net income for July	$ (d)	
Less dividends	(e)	
Increase in retained earnings		(f)
Retained earnings, July 31, 2010		(g)

Four Corners Realty
Balance Sheet
July 31, 2010

Assets		Liabilities	
Cash	$150,450	Accounts payable	$12,240
Supplies	10,200	**Stockholders' Equity**	
Land	(h)	Capital stock	$ (j)
		Retained earnings	(k)
		Total stockholders' equity	(l)
		Total liabilities and	
Total assets	(i)	stockholders' equity	(m)

Four Corners Realty
Statement of Cash Flows
For the Month Ended July 31, 2010

Cash flows from operating activities:		
Cash received from customers	$ (n)	
Deduct cash payments for expenses and payments to creditors	119,850	
Net cash flow from operating activities		$ (o)
Cash flows from investing activities:		
Cash payments for acquisition of land		(367,200)
Cash flows from financing activities:		
Cash received from issuing capital stock	$459,000	
Deduct cash dividends	61,200	
Net cash flow from financing activities		(p)
Net cash flow and July 31, 2010, cash balance		(q)

Instructions
By analyzing the interrelationships among the four financial statements, determine the proper amounts for (a) through (q).

Problems Series B

PR 1-1B
Transactions

obj. 4

✔ Cash bal. at end of November: $28,100

On November 1 of the current year, Rhea Quade established a business to manage rental property. She completed the following transactions during November:

a. Opened a business bank account with a deposit of $30,000 in exchange for capital stock.
b. Purchased supplies (pens, file folders, and copy paper) on account, $1,750.
c. Received cash from fees earned for managing rental property, $3,600.
d. Paid rent on office and equipment for the month, $1,300.
e. Paid creditors on account, $500.
f. Billed customers for fees earned for managing rental property, $4,800.
g. Paid automobile expenses (including rental charges) for month, $500, and miscellaneous expenses, $200.
h. Paid office salaries, $1,000.
i. Determined that the cost of supplies on hand was $800; therefore, the cost of supplies used was $950.
j. Paid dividends, $2,000.

Instructions
1. Indicate the effect of each transaction and the balances after each transaction, using the following tabular headings:

Assets			= Liabilities +			Stockholders' Equity						
	Accounts		Accounts	Capital			Fees	Rent	Salaries	Supplies	Auto	Misc.
Cash +	Receivable +	Supplies =	Payable +	Stock	−	Dividends +	Earned −	Expense −	Expense −	Expense −	Expense −	Expense

2. ▬▬▶ Briefly explain why the stockholders' investments and revenues increased stockholders' equity, while dividends and expenses decreased stockholders' equity.

PR 1-2B
Financial statements

obj. 5

Following are the amounts of the assets and liabilities of St. Kitts Travel Agency at December 31, 2010, the end of the current year, and its revenue and expenses for the year. The capital stock was $10,000 and retained earnings was $35,000 on January 1, 2010, the beginning of the current year. During the current year, dividends of $7,500 were paid.

Accounts payable	$ 6,250	Rent expense	$12,500
Accounts receivable	21,150	Supplies	1,350
Cash	90,000	Supplies expense	1,400
Fees earned	125,000	Utilities expense	9,100
Miscellaneous expense	750	Wages expense	32,500

✔ 1. Net income:
$68,750

Instructions

1. Prepare an income statement for the current year ended December 31, 2010.
2. Prepare a retained earnings statement for the current year ended December 31, 2010.
3. Prepare a balance sheet as of December 31, 2010.

PR 1-3B
Financial statements

obj. 5

✔ 1. Net income:
$8,800

Ashley Rhymer established Fair Play Financial Services on January 1, 2010. Fair Play Financial Services offers financial planning advice to its clients. The effect of each transaction and the balances after each transaction for January are shown below.

Instructions

1. Prepare an income statement for the month ended January 31, 2010.
2. Prepare a retained earnings statement for the month ended January 31, 2010.
3. Prepare a balance sheet as of January 31, 2010.
4. (Optional). Prepare a statement of cash flows for the month ending January 31, 2010.

	Assets			=	Liabilities	+			Stockholders' Equity					
	Cash	+ Accounts Receivable	+ Supplies	=	Accounts Payable	+ Capital Stock	− Dividends	+ Fees Earned	− Salaries Expense	− Rent Expense	− Auto Expense	− Supplies Expense	− Misc. Expense
a.	+15,000					+15,000							
b.			+2,180		+2,180								
Bal.	15,000		2,180		2,180	15,000							
c.	− 600				−600								
Bal.	14,400		2,180		1,580	15,000							
d.	+28,000							+28,000					
Bal.	42,400		2,180		1,580	15,000		28,000					
e.	− 7,500									−7,500			
Bal.	34,900		2,180		1,580	15,000		28,000		−7,500			
f.	− 5,700										−4,500		−1,200
Bal.	29,200		2,180		1,580	15,000		28,000		−7,500	−4,500		−1,200
g.	−16,000								−16,000				
Bal.	13,200		2,180		1,580	15,000		28,000	−16,000	−7,500	−4,500		−1,200
h.			−1,500									−1,500	
Bal.	13,200		680		1,580	15,000		28,000	−16,000	−7,500	−4,500	−1,500	−1,200
i.		+11,500						+11,500					
Bal.	13,200	11,500	680		1,580	15,000		39,500	−16,000	−7,500	−4,500	−1,500	−1,200
j.	− 5,000						−5,000						
Bal.	8,200	11,500	680		1,580	15,000	−5,000	39,500	−16,000	−7,500	−4,500	−1,500	−1,200

PR 1-4B
Transactions;
financial statements

objs. 4, 5

✔ 2. Net income:
$9,200

On August 1, 2010, Tanja Zier established Royal Realty. Tanja completed the following transactions during the month of August:

a. Opened a business bank account with a deposit of $20,000 in exchange for capital stock.
b. Purchased supplies (pens, file folders, paper, etc.) on account, $2,650.
c. Paid creditor on account, $1,600.
d. Earned sales commissions, receiving cash, $28,750.
e. Paid rent on office and equipment for the month, $4,200.
f. Paid dividends, $5,000.
g. Paid automobile expenses (including rental charge) for month, $2,500, and miscellaneous expenses, $1,200.

(continued)

h. Paid office salaries, $10,000.
i. Determined that the cost of supplies on hand was $1,000; therefore, the cost of supplies used was $1,650.

Instructions
1. Indicate the effect of each transaction and the balances after each transaction, using the following tabular headings:

Assets		= Liabilities +			Stockholders' Equity						
							Office				
		Accounts	Capital		Sales	Salaries	Rent	Auto	Supplies	Misc.
Cash	+ Supplies =	Payable +	Stock −	Dividends +	Commissions +	Expense −	Expense −	Expense −	Expense −	Expense

2. Prepare an income statement for August, a retained earnings statement for August, and a balance sheet as of August 31.

PR 1-5B
Transactions;
financial statements

objs. 4, 5

✔ 3. Net income:
$22,050

Swan Dry Cleaners is owned and operated by Peyton Keyes. A building and equipment are currently being rented, pending expansion to new facilities. The actual work of dry cleaning is done by another company at wholesale rates. The assets, liabilities, and capital stock of the business on July 1, 2010, are as follows: Cash, $17,000; Accounts Receivable, $31,000; Supplies, $3,200; Land, $36,000; Accounts Payable, $10,400; Capital Stock, $35,000. Business transactions during July are summarized as follows:

a. Peyton Keyes invested additional cash in the business with a deposit of $25,000 in exchange for capital stock.
b. Paid $24,000 for the purchase of land as a future building site.
c. Received cash from cash customers for dry cleaning revenue, $19,500.
d. Paid rent for the month, $3,000.
e. Purchased supplies on account, $1,550.
f. Paid creditors on account, $5,100.
g. Charged customers for dry cleaning revenue on account, $24,750.
h. Received monthly invoice for dry cleaning expense for July (to be paid on August 10), $8,200.
i. Paid the following: wages expense, $5,100; truck expense, $1,200; utilities expense, $800; miscellaneous expense, $950.
j. Received cash from customers on account, $26,750.
k. Determined that the cost of supplies on hand was $1,800; therefore, the cost of supplies used during the month was $2,950.
l. Paid dividends of $18,000.

Instructions
1. Determine the amount of retained earnings as of July 1 of the current year.
2. State the assets, liabilities, and stockholders' equity as of July 1 in equation form similar to that shown in this chapter. In tabular form below the equation, indicate increases and decreases resulting from each transaction and the new balances after each transaction.
3. Prepare an income statement for July, a retained earnings statement for July, and a balance sheet as of July 31.
4. (Optional). Prepare a statement of cash flows for July.

PR 1-6B
Missing amounts
from financial
statements

obj. 5

The financial statements at the end of Palo Duro Realty's first month of operations are shown at the top of the next page.

✔ k. $180,000

Palo Duro Realty
Income Statement
For the Month Ended November 30, 2010

Fees earned		$ (a)
Expenses:		
Wages expense	$ 51,000	
Rent expense	19,200	
Supplies expense	(b)	
Utilities expense	10,800	
Miscellaneous expense	6,600	
Total expenses		105,600
Net income		$ 74,400

Palo Duro Realty
Retained Earnings Statement
For the Month Ended November 30, 2010

Retained earnings, November 1, 2010		$ (c)
Net income for November	$ (d)	
Less dividends	36,000	
Increase in retained earnings		(e)
Retained earnings, November 30, 2010		(f)

Palo Duro Realty
Balance Sheet
November 30, 2010

Assets		Liabilities	
Cash	$ 26,700	Accounts payable	$ 9,600
Supplies	21,300	**Stockholders' Equity**	
Land.	240,000	Capital stock $240,000	
		Retained earnings . . . . (h)	
		Total stockholders' equtiy	(i)
		Total liabilities and	
Total assets	(g)	stockholders' equity	(j)

Palo Duro Realty
Statement of Cash Flows
For the Month Ended November 30, 2010

Cash flows from operating activities:		
Cash received from customers.	$ (k)	
Deduct cash payments for expenses and payments to creditors	117,300	
Net cash flow from operating activities		$ (l)
Cash flows from investing activities:		
Cash payments for acquisition of land.		(m)
Cash flows from financing activities:		
Cash received from issuing capital stock	(n)	
Deduct cash dividends.	(o)	
Net cash flow from financing activities		(p)
Net cash flow and November 30, 2010, cash balance		(q)

Instructions

By analyzing the interrelationships among the four financial statements, determine the proper amounts for (a) through (q).

Continuing Problem

✔ 2.Net income: $1,480

Lee Chang enjoys listening to all types of music and owns countless CDs. Over the years, Lee has gained a local reputation for knowledge of music from classical to rap and the ability to put together sets of recordings that appeal to all ages.

During the last several months, Lee served as a guest disc jockey on a local radio station. In addition, Lee has entertained at several friends' parties as the host deejay.

On June 1, 2010, Lee established a corporation known as Music Depot. Using an extensive collection of music CDs, Lee will serve as a disc jockey on a fee basis for weddings, college parties, and other events. During June, Lee entered into the following transactions:

June 1. Deposited $8,000 in a checking account in the name of Music Depot in exchange for capital stock.
   2. Received $2,400 from a local radio station for serving as the guest disc jockey for June.
   2. Agreed to share office space with a local real estate agency, Upstairs Realty. Music Depot will pay one-fourth of the rent. In addition, Music Depot agreed to pay a portion of the salary of the receptionist and to pay one-fourth of the utilities. Paid $750 for the rent of the office.
   4. Purchased supplies (blank CDs, poster board, extension cords, etc.) from City Office Supply Co. for $350. Agreed to pay $100 within 10 days and the remainder by July 5, 2010.
   6. Paid $600 to a local radio station to advertise the services of Music Depot twice daily for two weeks.
   8. Paid $500 to a local electronics store for renting digital recording equipment.
   12. Paid $250 (music expense) to Cool Music for the use of its current music demos to make various music sets.
   13. Paid City Office Supply Co. $100 on account.
   16. Received $400 from a dentist for providing two music sets for the dentist to play for her patients.
   22. Served as disc jockey for a wedding party. The father of the bride agreed to pay $1,350 the 1st of July.
   25. Received $500 from a friend for serving as the disc jockey for a cancer charity ball hosted by the local hospital.
   29. Paid $240 (music expense) to Galaxy Music for the use of its library of music demos.
   30. Received $1,000 for serving as disc jockey for a local club's monthly dance.
   30. Paid Upstairs Realty $400 for Music Depot's share of the receptionist's salary for June.
   30. Paid Upstairs Realty $300 for Music Depot's share of the utilities for June.
   30. Determined that the cost of supplies on hand is $170. Therefore, the cost of supplies used during the month was $180.
   30. Paid for miscellaneous expenses, $150.
   30. Paid $800 royalties (music expense) to National Music Clearing for use of various artists' music during the month.
   30. Paid dividends of $200.

Instructions

1. Indicate the effect of each transaction and the balances after each transaction, using the following tabular headings:

Assets			= Liabilities +				Stockholders' Equity								
									Office	Equipment					
	Accounts		Accounts	Capital		Fees	Music	Rent	Rent	Advertising	Wages	Utilities	Supplies	Misc.
Cash +	Receivable +	Supplies =	Payable +	Stock	− Dividends +	Earned −	Expense −	Expense −	Expense −	Expense −	Expense −	Expense −	Expense −	Expense

2. Prepare an income statement for Music Depot for the month ended June 30, 2010.
3. Prepare a retained earnings statement for Music Depot for the month ended June 30, 2010.
4. Prepare a balance sheet for Music Depot as of June 30, 2010.

Special Activities

SA 1-1
Ethics and professional conduct in business

Group Project

Blake Gillis, president of Wayside Enterprises, applied for a $175,000 loan from American National Bank. The bank requested financial statements from Wayside Enterprises as a basis for granting the loan. Blake has told his accountant to provide the bank with a balance sheet. Blake has decided to omit the other financial statements because there was a net loss during the past year.

In groups of three or four, discuss the following questions:

1. Is Blake behaving in a professional manner by omitting some of the financial statements?
2. a. What types of information about their businesses would owners be willing to provide bankers? What types of information would owners not be willing to provide?
   b. What types of information about a business would bankers want before extending a loan?
   c. What common interests are shared by bankers and business owners?

SA 1-2
Net income

On August 1, 2009, Dr. Dana Hendley established Med, a medical practice organized as a professional corporation. The following conversation occurred the following February between Dr. Hendley and a former medical school classmate, Dr. Elyse Monti, at an American Medical Association convention in New York City.

Dr. Monti: Dana, good to see you again. Why didn't you call when you were in Denver? We could have had dinner together.

Dr. Hendley: Actually, I never made it to Denver this year. My husband and kids went up to our Vail condo twice, but I got stuck in Fort Lauderdale. I opened a new consulting practice this August and haven't had any time for myself since.

Dr. Monti: I heard about it . . . Med . . . something . . . right?

Dr. Hendley: Yes, Med. My husband chose the name.

Dr. Monti: I've thought about doing something like that. Are you making any money? I mean, is it worth your time?

Dr. Hendley: You wouldn't believe it. I started by opening a bank account with $30,000, and my January bank statement has a balance of $75,000. Not bad for six months—all pure profit.

Dr. Monti: Maybe I'll try it in Denver! Let's have breakfast together tomorrow and you can fill me in on the details.

➤ Comment on Dr. Hendley's statement that the difference between the opening bank balance ($30,000) and the January statement balance ($75,000) is pure profit.

SA 1-3
Transactions and financial statements

Amber Keck, a junior in college, has been seeking ways to earn extra spending money. As an active sports enthusiast, Amber plays tennis regularly at the North Fulton Tennis Club, where her family has a membership. The president of the club recently approached Amber with the proposal that she manage the club's tennis courts. Amber's primary duty would be to supervise the operation of the club's four indoor and six outdoor courts, including court reservations.

In return for her services, the club would pay Amber $200 per week, plus Amber could keep whatever she earned from lessons and the fees from the use of the ball machine. The club and Amber agreed to a one-month trial, after which both would consider an arrangement for the remaining two years of Amber's college career. On this basis, Amber organized Deuce as a proprietorship.

Small businesses such as Deuce are often organized as proprietorships. The accounting for proprietorships is similar to that for a corporation, except for owner's equity. Instead of Capital Stock and Retained Earnings, an item entitled Amber Keck,

Capital, is used to indicate owner's equity in the accounting equation. Withdrawals for personal use are handled similarly to dividends.

During June 2009, Amber managed the tennis courts and entered into the following transactions:

a. Opened a business account by depositing $1,250.
b. Paid $250 for tennis supplies (practice tennis balls, etc.).
c. Paid $150 for the rental of video equipment to be used in offering lessons during June.
d. Arranged for the rental of two ball machines during June for $200. Paid $100 in advance, with the remaining $100 due July 1.
e. Received $1,500 for lessons given during June.
f. Received $400 in fees from the use of the ball machines during June.
g. Paid $600 for salaries of part-time employees who answered the telephone and took reservations while Amber was giving lessons.
h. Paid $120 for miscellaneous expenses.
i. Received $800 from the club for managing the tennis courts during June.
j. Determined that the cost of supplies on hand at the end of the month totaled $150; therefore, the cost of supplies used was $100.
k. Withdrew $270 for personal use on June 30.

As a friend and accounting student, you have been asked by Amber to aid her in assessing the venture.

1. Indicate the effect of each transaction and the balances after each transaction, using the following tabular headings:

Assets			= Liabilities +		Owner's Equity					
Cash +	Supplies	=	Accounts Payable	+	Amber Keck, Capital −	Amber Keck, Drawing +	Service Revenue −	Salary Expense −	Rent Expense −	Supplies Expense −	Misc. Expense

2. Prepare an income statement for June.
3. Prepare a statement of owner's equity for June. The statement of owner's equity for a proprietorship is similar to the retained earnings statement for a corporation. The balance of the owner's capital as of the beginning of the period is listed first. Any investments made by the owner during the period are then listed and the net income (net loss) is added (subtracted) to determine a subtotal. From this subtotal, the owner's withdrawals are subtracted to determine the increase (decrease) in owner's equity for the period. This increase (decrease) is then added to (subtracted from) the beginning owner's equity to determine the owner's equity as of the end of the period.
4. Prepare a balance sheet as of June 30.
5. a. Assume that Amber Keck could earn $8 per hour working 30 hours a week as a waitress. Evaluate which of the two alternatives, working as a waitress or operating Deuce, would provide Amber with the most income per month.
   b. ➤ Discuss any other factors that you believe Amber should consider before discussing a long-term arrangement with the North Fulton Tennis Club.

SA 1-4
Certification requirements for accountants

By satisfying certain specific requirements, accountants may become certified as public accountants (CPAs), management accountants (CMAs), or internal auditors (CIAs). Find the certification requirements for one of these accounting groups by accessing the appropriate Internet site listed below.

Internet Project

Site	Description
http://www.ais-cpa.com	This site lists the address and/or Internet link for each state's board of accountancy. Find your state's requirements.
http://www.imanet.org	This site lists the requirements for becoming a CMA.
http://www.theiia.org	This site lists the requirements for becoming a CIA.

SA 1-5
Cash flows

Amazon.com, an Internet retailer, was incorporated and began operation in the mid-90s. On the statement of cash flows, would you expect Amazon.com's net cash flows from operating, investing, and financing activities to be positive or negative for its first three years of operations? Use the following format for your answers, and briefly explain your logic.

	First Year	Second Year	Third Year
Net cash flows from operating activities	negative		
Net cash flows from investing activities			
Net cash flows from financing activities			

SA 1-6
Financial analysis of Enron Corporation

Internet Project

The now defunct Enron Corporation, once headquartered in Houston, Texas, provided products and services for natural gas, electricity, and communications to wholesale and retail customers. Enron's operations were conducted through a variety of subsidiaries and affiliates that involved transporting gas through pipelines, transmitting electricity, and managing energy commodities. The following data were taken from Enron's financial statements:

	In millions
Total revenues	$100,789
Total costs and expenses	98,836
Operating income	1,953
Net income	979
Total assets	65,503
Total liabilities	54,033
Total stockholders' equity	11,470
Net cash flows from operating activities	4,779
Net cash flows from investing activities	(4,264)
Net cash flows from financing activities	571
Net increase in cash	1,086

The market price of Enron's stock was approximately $83 per share when the prior financial statement data were taken. However, eventually Enron's stock was selling for $0.22 per share.

➤ Review the preceding financial statement data and search the Internet for articles on Enron Corporation. Briefly explain why Enron's stock dropped so dramatically.

Answers to Self-Examination Questions

1. **D**   A corporation, organized in accordance with state or federal statutes, is a separate legal entity in which ownership is divided into shares of stock (answer D). A proprietorship (answer A) is an unincorporated business owned by one individual. A service business (answer B) provides services to its customers. It can be organized as a proprietorship, partnership, corporation, or limited liability company. A partnership (answer C) is an unincorporated business owned by two or more individuals.

2. **A**   The resources owned by a business are called assets (answer A). The debts of the business are called liabilities (answer B), and the equity of the stockholders is called stockholders' equity (answer D). The relationship between assets, liabilities, and stockholders' equity is expressed as the accounting equation (answer C).

3. **A**   The balance sheet is a listing of the assets, liabilities, and stockholders' equity of a business at a specific date (answer A). The income statement (answer B) is a summary of the revenue and expenses of a business for a specific period of time. The retained earnings statement (answer C) summarizes the changes in retained earnings for a specific period of time. The statement of cash flows (answer D) summarizes the cash receipts and cash payments for a specific period of time.

4. **C**   The accounting equation is:

   Assets = Liabilities + Stockholders' Equity

Therefore, if assets increased by $20,000 and liabilities increased by $12,000, owner's equity must have increased by $8,000 (answer C), as indicated in the following computation:

Assets	=	Liabilities +	Stockholders' Equity
+$20,000	=	+$12,000 +	Stockholders' Equity
+$20,000 − $12,000	=		Stockholders' Equity
+$8,000	=		Stockholders' Equity

5. **B** Net income is the excess of revenue over expenses, or $7,500 (answer B). If expenses exceed revenue, the difference is a net loss. Dividends are the opposite of the stockholders investing in the business and do not affect the amount of net income or net loss.

Analyzing Transactions

© AP Photo/Paul Sakuma

A P L E ,   I N C.™

Everyday it seems like we get an incredible amount of incoming e-mail messages; you get them from your friends, relatives, subscribed e-mail lists, and even spammers! But how do you organize all of these messages? You might create folders to sort messages by sender, topic, or project. Perhaps you use keyword search utilities. You might even use filters/rules to automatically delete spam or send messages from your best friend to a special folder. In any case, you are organizing information so that it is simple to retrieve and allows you to understand, respond, or refer to the messages.

In the same way that you organize your e-mail, companies develop an organized method for processing, recording, and summarizing financial transactions. For example, Apple, Inc., has a huge volume of financial transactions, resulting from sales of its innovative computers, digital media (like iPod music and video players), and iPhone mobile phones. When Apple sells an iPhone online or at The Apple Store, a customer has the option of paying with credit card, a debit

or check card, an Apple gift card, a financing arrangement, or cash (using a cashier's check, a money order, or a wire transfer). In order to analyze only the information related to Apple's cash transactions, the company must record or summarize all these similar sales using a single category or "cash" account. This is comparable to how you summarize cash in the check register of your checkbook. Similarly, Apple will record credit card payments for iPhones and sales from financing arrangements in different accounts (records).

While Chapter 1 uses the accounting equation (Assets = Liabilities + Owner's Equity) to analyze and record financial transactions, this chapter presents more practical and efficient recording methods that most companies use. In addition, this chapter discusses possible accounting errors that may occur, along with methods to detect and correct them.

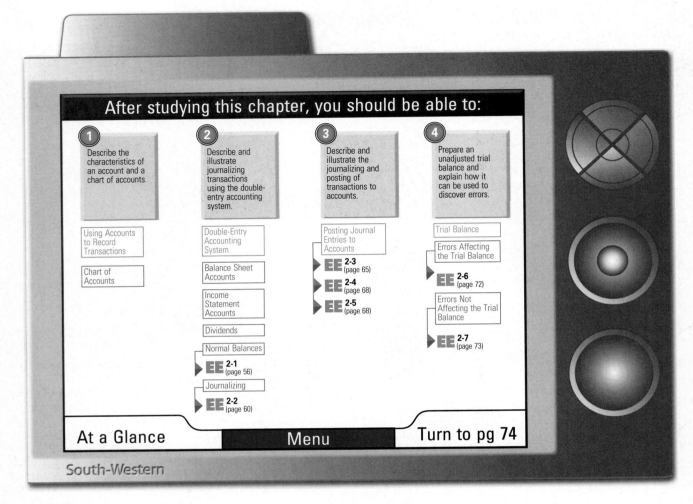

After studying this chapter, you should be able to:

1 Describe the characteristics of an account and a chart of accounts.

Using Accounts to Record Transactions

Chart of Accounts

2 Describe and illustrate journalizing transactions using the double-entry accounting system.

Double-Entry Accounting System

Balance Sheet Accounts

Income Statement Accounts

Dividends

Normal Balances

EE 2-1 (page 56)

Journalizing

EE 2-2 (page 60)

3 Describe and illustrate the journalizing and posting of transactions to accounts.

Posting Journal Entries to Accounts

EE 2-3 (page 65)

EE 2-4 (page 68)

EE 2-5 (page 68)

4 Prepare an unadjusted trial balance and explain how it can be used to discover errors.

Trial Balance

Errors Affecting the Trial Balance

EE 2-6 (page 72)

Errors Not Affecting the Trial Balance

EE 2-7 (page 73)

At a Glance   Menu   Turn to pg 74

South-Western

 Describe the characteristics of an account and a chart of accounts.

Using Accounts to Record Transactions

In Chapter 1, we recorded the November transactions for NetSolutions using the accounting equation format shown in Exhibit 1. However, this format is not efficient or practical for companies that have to record thousands or millions of transactions daily. As a result, accounting systems are designed to show the increases and decreases in each accounting equation element as a separate record. This record is called an **account**.

To illustrate, the Cash column of Exhibit 1 records the increases and decreases in cash. Likewise, the other columns in Exhibit 1 record the increases and decreases in the other accounting equation elements. Each of these columns can be organized into a separate account.

An account, in its simplest form, has three parts.

1. A title, which is the name of the accounting equation element recorded in the account.
2. A space for recording increases in the amount of the element.
3. A space for recording decreases in the amount of the element.

The account form presented below is called a **T account** because it resembles the letter T. The left side of the account is called the *debit* side, and the right side is called the *credit* side.[1]

Title	
Left side	Right side
debit	*credit*

[1] The terms *debit* and *credit* are derived from the Latin *debere* and *credere*.

Exhibit 1

NetSolutions November Transactions

	Assets			=	Liabilities	+		Stockholders' Equity						
	Cash	+ Supp. +	Land	=	Accounts Payable +	Capital Stock	− Dividends +	Fees Earned −	Wages Exp. −	Rent Exp. −	Supplies Exp. −	Utilities Exp. −	Misc. Exp.	
a.	+25,000					+25,000								
b.	−20,000		+20,000											
Bal.	5,000		20,000			25,000								
c.		+1,350			+1,350									
Bal.	5,000	1,350	20,000		1,350	25,000								
d.	+ 7,500							+7,500						
Bal.	12,500	1,350	20,000		1,350	25,000		7,500						
e.	− 3,650								−2,125	−800		−450	−275	
Bal.	8,850	1,350	20,000		1,350	25,000		7,500	−2,125	−800		−450	−275	
f.	− 950				− 950									
Bal.	7,900	1,350	20,000		400	25,000		7,500	−2,125	−800		−450	−275	
g.		− 800									−800			
Bal.	7,900	550	20,000		400	25,000		7,500	−2,125	−800	−800	−450	−275	
h.	−2,000						−2,000							
Bal.	5,900	550	20,000		400	25,000	−2,000	7,500	−2,125	−800	−800	−450	−275	

> **Amounts entered on the left side of an account are debits, and amounts entered on the right side of an account are credits.**

The amounts shown in the Cash column of Exhibit 1 would be recorded in a cash account as follows:

Cash

Debit side of account	(a) 25,000 (d) 7,500	(b) 20,000 (e) 3,650 (f) 950 (h) 2,000	Credit side of account
	Balance 5,900		

Balance of account ↑

Many times when accountants analyze complex transactions, they use T accounts to simplify the thought process. In the same way, you will find T accounts a useful device in this and later accounting courses.

Recording transactions in accounts must follow certain rules. For example, increases in assets are recorded on the **debit** (left side) of an account. Likewise, decreases in assets are recorded on the **credit** (right side) of an account. The excess of the debits of an asset account over its credits is the **balance of the account**.

To illustrate, the receipt (increase in Cash) of $25,000 in transaction (a) is entered on the debit (left) side of the cash account shown above. The letter or date of the transaction is also entered into the account. This is done so if any questions later arise related to the entry, the entry can be traced back to the underlying transaction data. In contrast, the payment (decrease in Cash) of $20,000 to purchase land in transaction (b) is entered on the credit (right) side of the account. The balance of the cash account of $5,900 is the excess of the debits over the credits as shown below.

Debits ($25,000 + $7,500)	$32,500
Less credits ($20,000 + $3,650 + $950 + $2,000)	26,600
Balance of Cash as of November 30, 2009	$ 5,900

The balance of the cash account is inserted in the account, in the Debit column. In this way, the balance is identified as a debit balance.[2] This balance represents NetSolutions' cash on hand as of November 30, 2009. This balance of $5,900 is reported on the November 30, 2009, balance sheet for NetSolutions as shown in Exhibit 6 of Chapter 1.

In an actual accounting system, a more formal account form replaces the T account. Later in this chapter, we illustrate a four-column account. The T account, however, is

---

2 The totals of the debit and credit columns may be shown separately in an account. When this is done, these amounts should be identified in some way so that they are not mistaken for entries or the ending balance of the account.

a simple way to illustrate the effects of transactions on accounts and financial statements. For this reason, T accounts are often used in business to explain transactions.

Each of the columns in Exhibit 1 can be converted into an account form in a similar manner as was done for the Cash column of Exhibit 1. However, as we mentioned earlier, recording increases and decreases in accounts must follow certain rules. We discuss these rules after we describe and illustrate the chart of accounts.

Chart of Accounts

A group of accounts for a business entity is called a **ledger**. A list of the accounts in the ledger is called a **chart of accounts**. The accounts are normally listed in the order in which they appear in the financial statements. The balance sheet accounts are listed first, in the order of assets, liabilities, and stockholders' equity. The income statement accounts are then listed in the order of revenues and expenses. Each of these major account groups is described next.

Assets are resources owned by the business entity. These resources can be physical items, such as cash and supplies, or intangibles that have value. Examples of intangible assets include patent rights, copyrights, and trademarks. Examples of other assets include accounts receivable, prepaid expenses (such as insurance), buildings, equipment, and land.

Liabilities are debts owed to outsiders (creditors). Liabilities are often identified on the balance sheet by titles that include the word *payable*. Examples of liabilities include accounts payable, notes payable, and wages payable. Cash received before services are delivered creates a liability to perform the services. These future service commitments are called *unearned revenues*. Examples of unearned revenues are magazine subscriptions received by a publisher and tuition received by a college at the beginning of a term.

Stockholders' equity is the stockholders' right to the assets of the business. Stockholders' equity is represented by the balance of the capital stock and retained earnings accounts. A **dividends** account represents distributions of earnings to stockholders.

Business Connection

THE HIJACKING RECEIVABLE

A company's chart of accounts should reflect the basic nature of its operations. Occasionally, however, transactions take place that give rise to unusual accounts. The following is a story of one such account.

During the early 1970s, before strict airport security was implemented across the United States, several airlines experienced hijacking incidents. One such incident occurred on November 10, 1972, when a Southern Airways DC-9 en route from Memphis to Miami was hijacked during a stopover in Birmingham, Alabama. The three hijackers boarded the plane in Birmingham armed with handguns and hand grenades. At gunpoint, the hijackers took the plane, the plane's crew of four, and 27 passengers to nine American cities, Toronto, and eventually to Havana, Cuba.

During the long flight, the hijackers threatened to crash the plane into the Oak Ridge, Tennessee, nuclear facilities, insisted on talking with President Nixon, and demanded a ransom of $10 million. Southern Airways, however, was only able to come up with $2 million. Eventually, the pilot talked the hijackers into settling for the $2 million when the plane landed in Chattanooga for refueling.

Upon landing in Havana, the Cuban authorities arrested the hijackers and, after a brief delay, sent the plane, passengers, and crew back to the United States. The hijackers and $2 million stayed in Cuba.

How did Southern Airways account for and report the hijacking payment in its subsequent financial statements? As you might have analyzed, the initial entry credited Cash for $2 million. The debit was to an account entitled "Hijacking Payment." This account was reported as a type of receivable under "other assets" on Southern's balance sheet. The company maintained that it would be able to collect the cash from the Cuban government and that, therefore, a receivable existed. In fact, Southern Airways was repaid $2 million by the Cuban government, which was, at that time, attempting to improve relations with the United States.

Revenues are increases in stockholders' equity (retained earnings) as a result of selling services or products to customers. Examples of revenues include fees earned, fares earned, commissions revenue, and rent revenue.

Expenses result from using up assets or consuming services in the process of generating revenues. Examples of expenses include wages expense, rent expense, utilities expense, supplies expense, and miscellaneous expense.

A chart of accounts should meet the needs of a company's managers and other users of its financial statements. The accounts within the chart of accounts are numbered for use as references. A numbering system is normally used, so that new accounts can be added without affecting other account numbers.

Exhibit 2 is NetSolutions' chart of accounts that we will use in this chapter. Additional accounts will be introduced in later chapters. In Exhibit 2, each account number has two digits. The first digit indicates the major account group of the ledger in which the account is located. Accounts beginning with 1 represent assets; 2, liabilities; 3, stockholders' equity; 4, revenue; and 5, expenses. The second digit indicates the location of the account within its group.

You should note that each of the columns in Exhibit 1 has been assigned an account number in the chart of accounts shown in Exhibit 2. In addition, we have added accounts for Accounts Receivable, Prepaid Insurance, Office Equipment, and Unearned Rent. These accounts will be used in recording NetSolutions' December transactions.

Procter & Gamble's account numbers have over 30 digits to reflect P&G's many different operations and regions.

Exhibit 2

Chart of Accounts for NetSolutions

Balance Sheet Accounts	Income Statement Accounts
1. Assets	**4. Revenue**
11 Cash	41 Fees Earned
12 Accounts Receivable	**5. Expenses**
14 Supplies	51 Wages Expense
15 Prepaid Insurance	52 Rent Expense
17 Land	54 Utilities Expense
18 Office Equipment	55 Supplies Expense
2. Liabilities	59 Miscellaneous Expense
21 Accounts Payable	
23 Unearned Rent	
3. Stockholders' Equity	
31 Capital Stock	
32 Retained Earnings	
33 Dividends	

2 Describe and illustrate journalizing transactions using the double-entry accounting system.

Double-Entry Accounting System

All businesses use what is called the **double-entry accounting system**. This system is based on the accounting equation and requires that every business transaction be recorded in at least two accounts. In addition, it requires that the total debits recorded for each transaction equal the total credits recorded. The double-entry accounting system also has specific **rules of debit and credit** for recording transactions in the accounts.

Balance Sheet Accounts

The double-entry accounting system is based on the accounting equation and specific rules for recording debits and credits. The debit and credit rules for balance sheet accounts are as follows:

Balance Sheet Accounts

ASSETS Asset Accounts		=	LIABILITIES Liability Accounts		+	STOCKHOLDERS' EQUITY Stockholders' Equity Accounts	
Debit for increases (+)	Credit for decreases (−)		Debit for decreases (−)	Credit for increases (+)		Debit for decreases (−)	Credit for increases (+)

Income Statement Accounts

The debit and credit rules for income statement accounts are based on their relationship with stockholders' equity (retained earnings). As shown above, stockholders' equity accounts are increased by credits. Since revenues increase stockholders' equity, revenue accounts are increased by credits and decreased by debits. Since stockholders' equity accounts are decreased by debits, expense accounts are increased by debits and decreased by credits. Thus, the rules of debit and credit for revenue and expense accounts are as follows:

Income Statement Accounts

Revenue Accounts		Expense Accounts	
Debit for decreases (−)	Credit for increases (+)	Debit for increases (+)	Credit for decreases (−)

Dividends

The debit and credit rules for recording dividends are based on the effect of dividends on stockholders' equity (retained earnings). Since dividends decrease stockholders' equity (retained earnings), the dividends account is increased by debits. Likewise, the dividends account is decreased by credits. Thus, the rules of debit and credit for the dividends account are as follows:

Dividends

Debit for increases (+)	Credit for decreases (−)

Normal Balances

The sum of the increases in an account is usually equal to or greater than the sum of the decreases in the account. Thus, the **normal balance of an account** is either a debit or credit depending on whether increases in the account are recorded as debits or credits. For example, since asset accounts are increased with debits, asset accounts normally have debit balances. Likewise, liability accounts normally have credit balances.

The rules of debit and credit and the normal balances of the various types of accounts are summarized in Exhibit 3. Debits and credits are sometimes abbreviated as Dr. for debit and Cr. for credit.

Example Exercise 2-1 Rules of Debit and Credit and Normal Balances ••••> ②

State for each account whether it is likely to have (a) debit entries only, (b) credit entries only, or (c) both debit and credit entries. Also, indicate its normal balance.

1. Dividends
2. Accounts Payable
3. Cash

4. Fees Earned
5. Supplies
6. Utilities Expense

Follow My Example 2-1

1. Debit entries only; normal debit balance
2. Debit and credit entries; normal credit balance
3. Debit and credit entries; normal debit balance

4. Credit entries only; normal credit balance
5. Debit and credit entries; normal debit balance
6. Debit entries only; normal debit balance

....

For Practice: PE 2-1A, PE 2-1B

Exhibit 3

Rules of Debit and Credit, Normal Balances of Accounts

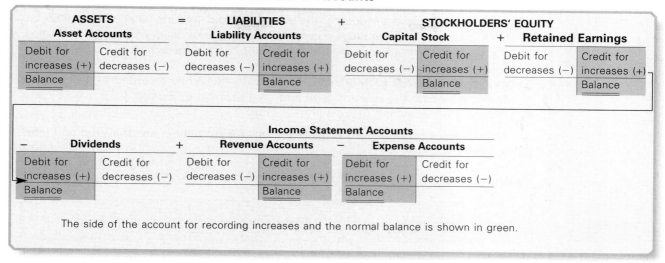

The side of the account for recording increases and the normal balance is shown in green.

When an account normally having a debit balance has a credit balance, or vice versa, an error may have occurred or an unusual situation may exist. For example, a credit balance in the office equipment account could result only from an error. This is because a business cannot have more decreases than increases of office equipment. On the other hand, a debit balance in an accounts payable account could result from an overpayment.

Journalizing

A journal can be thought of as being similar to an individual's diary of significant day-to-day life events.

Using the rules of debit and credit, transactions are initially entered in a record called a **journal**. In this way, the journal serves as a record of when transactions occurred and were recorded. To illustrate, we use the November transactions of NetSolutions from Chapter 1.

Chris Clark's first transaction (a) on November 1 was to deposit $25,000 in a bank account in the name of NetSolutions in exchange for capital stock. The effect of this transaction on the balance sheet is to increase assets (Cash) and stockholders' equity (Capital Stock) by $25,000. This transaction is recorded in the journal using the following steps:

Step 1.   The date of the transaction is entered in the Date column.

Step 2.   The title of the account to be debited is recorded at the left-hand margin under the Description column, and the amount to be debited is entered in the Debit column.

Step 3.   The title of the account to be credited is listed below and to the right of the debited account title, and the amount to be credited is entered in the Credit column.

Step 4.   A brief description may be entered below the credited account.

Step 5.   The Post. Ref. (Posting Reference) column is left blank when the journal entry is initially recorded. We will use this column later in this chapter when we transfer the journal entry amounts to the accounts in the ledger.

Using the preceding steps, transaction (a) is recorded in the journal as follows:

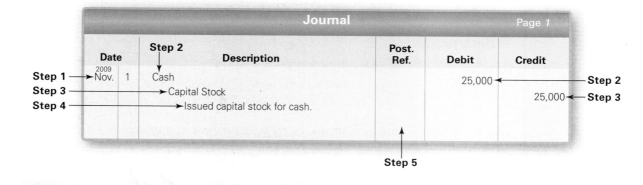

The process of recording a transaction in the journal is called **journalizing**. The entry in the journal is called a **journal entry**.

The following is a useful method for analyzing and journalizing transactions:

1. Carefully read the description of the transaction to determine whether an asset, a liability, a stockholders' equity, a revenue, an expense, or a dividend account is affected.
2. For each account affected by the transaction, determine whether the account increases or decreases.
3. Determine whether each increase or decrease should be recorded as a debit or a credit, following the rules of debit and credit shown in Exhibit 3.
4. Record the transaction using a journal entry.

The remaining transactions of NetSolutions for November are analyzed and journalized next.

Transaction B

> Nov. 5   NetSolutions paid $20,000 for the purchase of land as a future building site.

Analysis This transaction increases one asset account and decreases another. It is recorded in the journal as a $20,000 increase (debit) to Land and a $20,000 decrease (credit) to Cash.

Journal Entry

5	Land	20,000	
	Cash		20,000
	Purchased land for building site.		

Transaction C

> Nov. 10   NetSolutions purchased supplies on account for $1,350.

Analysis This transaction increases an asset account and increases a liability account. It is recorded in the journal as a $1,350 increase (debit) to Supplies and a $1,350 increase (credit) to Accounts Payable.

Journal Entry

10	Supplies	1,350	
	Accounts Payable		1,350
	Purchased supplies on account.		

Transaction D

> Nov. 18   NetSolutions received cash of $7,500 from customers for services provided.

Analysis This transaction increases an asset account and increases a revenue account. It is recorded in the journal as a $7,500 increase (debit) to Cash and a $7,500 increase (credit) to Fees Earned.

Journal Entry

18	Cash		7,500	
	Fees Earned			7,500
	Received fees from customers.			

Transaction E

> Nov. 30   NetSolutions incurred the following expenses: wages, $2,125; rent, $800; utilities, $450; and miscellaneous, $275.

Analysis This transaction increases various expense accounts and decreases an asset (Cash) account. You should note that regardless of the number of accounts, *the sum of the debits is always equal to the sum of the credits in a journal entry*. It is recorded in the journal as an increase (debit) to Wages Expense, $2,125; Rent Expense, $800; Utilities Expense, $450; Miscellaneous Expense, $275; and a decrease (credit) to Cash, $3,650.

Journal Entry

30	Wages Expense		2,125	
	Rent Expense		800	
	Utilities Expense		450	
	Miscellaneous Expense		275	
	Cash			3,650
	Paid expenses.			

Transaction F

> Nov. 30   NetSolutions paid creditors on account, $950.

Analysis This transaction decreases a liability account and decreases an asset account. It is recorded in the journal as a $950 decrease (debit) to Accounts Payable and a $950 decrease (credit) to Cash.

Journal Entry

30	Accounts Payable		950	
	Cash			950
	Paid creditors on account.			

Integrity, Objectivity, and Ethics in Business

WILL JOURNALIZING PREVENT FRAUD?

While journalizing transactions reduces the possibility of fraud, it by no means eliminates it. For example, embez- zlement can be hidden within the double-entry book- keeping system by creating fictitious suppliers to whom checks are issued.

Transaction G

Nov. 30 Chris Clark determined that the cost of supplies on hand at November 30 was $550.

Analysis NetSolutions purchased $1,350 of supplies on November 10. Thus, $800 ($1,350 − $550) of supplies must have been used during November. This transaction is recorded in the journal as an $800 increase (debit) to Supplies Expense and an $800 de- crease (credit) to Supplies.

Journal Entry

30	Supplies Expense		800	
	Supplies			800
	Supplies used during November.			

Transaction H

Nov. 30 NetSolutions paid $2,000 of dividends to stockholders.

Analysis This transaction decreases assets and stockholders' equity (retained earnings). This transaction is recorded in the journal as a $2,000 increase (debit) to Dividends and a $2,000 decrease (credit) to Cash.

Journal Entry

Journal					Page 2
Date	Description		Post. Ref.	Debit	Credit
2009 Nov.	30	Dividends		2,000	
		Cash			2,000
		Paid dividends to stockholders.			

Example Exercise 2-2 Journal Entry for Asset Purchase ·······► ②

Prepare a journal entry for the purchase of a truck on June 3 for $42,500, paying $8,500 cash and the remainder on account.

Follow My Example 2-2

June 3	Truck		42,500	
	Cash			8,500
	Accounts Payable			34,000

For Practice: PE 2-2A, PE 2-2B

Describe and illustrate the journalizing and posting of transactions to accounts.

Posting Journal Entries to Accounts

As illustrated, a transaction is first recorded in a journal. Periodically, the journal entries are transferred to the accounts in the ledger. The process of transferring the debits and credits from the journal entries to the accounts is called **posting**.

We use the December transactions of NetSolutions to illustrate posting from the journal to the ledger. By using the December transactions, we also provide an additional review of analyzing and journalizing transactions.

Transaction

> Dec. 1   NetSolutions paid a premium of $2,400 for an insurance policy for liability, theft, and fire. The policy covers a one-year period.

Analysis Advance payments of expenses such as insurance are prepaid expenses. Prepaid expenses are assets. For NetSolutions, the asset purchased is insurance protection for 12 months. This transaction is recorded as a $2,400 increase (debit) to Prepaid Insurance and a $2,400 decrease (credit) to Cash.

Journal Entry

Dec.	1	Prepaid Insurance	15	2,400	
		Cash	11		2,400
		Paid premium on one-year policy.			

The posting of the preceding December 1 transaction is shown in Exhibit 4. You will notice that the T account form is not used. In practice, the T account is usually replaced with a standard account form similar to that shown in Exhibit 4.

The debits and credits for each journal entry are posted to the accounts in the order in which they occur in the journal. To illustrate, the debit portion of the December 1 journal entry is posted to the prepaid account in Exhibit 4 using the following four steps:

Step 1.   The date (Dec. 1) of the journal entry is entered in the Date column of Prepaid Insurance.

Step 2.   The amount (2,400) is entered into the Debit column of Prepaid Insurance.

Step 3.   The journal page number (2) is entered in the Posting Reference (Post. Ref.) column of Prepaid Insurance.

Step 4.   The account number (15) is entered in the Posting Reference (Post. Ref.) column in the journal.

As shown in Exhibit 4, the credit portion of the December 1 journal entry is posted to the cash account in a similar manner.

The remaining December transactions for NetSolutions are analyzed and journalized in the following paragraphs. These transactions are posted to the ledger in Exhibit 5 on pages 69–70. To simplify, some of the December transactions are stated in summary form. For example, cash received for services is normally recorded on a daily basis. However, only summary totals are recorded at the middle and end of the month for NetSolutions.

Transaction

> Dec. 1   NetSolutions paid rent for December, $800. The company from which NetSolutions is renting its store space now requires the payment of rent on the first of each month, rather than at the end of the month.

Analysis The advance payment of rent is an asset, much like the advance payment of the insurance premium in the preceding transaction. However, unlike the insurance premium,

Exhibit 4

Diagram of the Recording and Posting of a Debit and a Credit

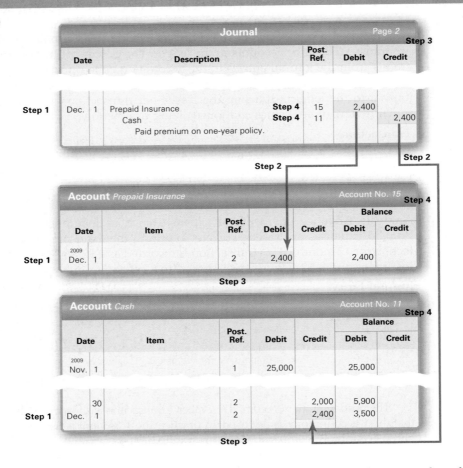

this prepaid rent will expire in one month. When an asset that is purchased will be used up in a short period of time, such as a month, it is normal to debit an expense account initially. This avoids having to transfer the balance from an asset account (Prepaid Rent) to an expense account (Rent Expense) at the end of the month. Thus, this transaction is recorded as an $800 increase (debit) to Rent Expense and an $800 decrease (credit) to Cash.

Journal Entry

	1	Rent Expense	52	800	
		Cash	11		800
		Paid rent for December.			

Transaction

> Dec. 1 NetSolutions received an offer from a local retailer to rent the land purchased on November 5. The retailer plans to use the land as a parking lot for its employees and customers. NetSolutions agreed to rent the land to the retailer for three months, with the rent payable in advance. NetSolutions received $360 for three months' rent beginning December 1.

Analysis By agreeing to rent the land and accepting the $360, NetSolutions has incurred an obligation (liability) to the retailer. This obligation is to make the land available for use for three months and not to interfere with its use. The liability created by receiving the cash in advance of providing the service is called **unearned revenue**. As time passes, the unearned rent liability will decrease and will become revenue. Thus, this transaction is recorded as a $360 increase (debit) to Cash and a $360 increase (credit) to Unearned Rent.

Journal Entry

1	Cash	11	360	
	Unearned Rent	23		360
	Received advance payment for			
	three months' rent on land.			

Transaction

| Dec. 4 | NetSolutions purchased office equipment on account from Executive Supply Co. for $1,800. |

Analysis The asset (Office Equipment) and liability accounts (Accounts Payable) increase. This transaction is recorded as a $1,800 increase (debit) to Office Equipment and a $1,800 increase (credit) to Accounts Payable.

Journal Entry

4	Office Equipment	18	1,800	
	Accounts Payable	21		1,800
	Purchased office equipment			
	on account.			

Transaction

| Dec. 6 | NetSolutions paid $180 for a newspaper advertisement. |

Analysis An expense increases and an asset (Cash) decreases. Expense items that are expected to be minor in amount are normally included as part of the miscellaneous expense. This transaction is recorded as a $180 increase (debit) to Miscellaneous Expense and a $180 decrease (credit) to Cash.

Journal Entry

6	Miscellaneous Expense	59	180	
	Cash	11		180
	Paid for newspaper ad.			

Transaction

| Dec. 11 | NetSolutions paid creditors $400. |

Analysis A liability (Accounts Payable) and an asset (Cash) decrease. This transaction is recorded as a $400 decrease (debit) to Accounts Payable and a $400 decrease (credit) to Cash.

Journal Entry

In computerized accounting systems, some transactions may be automatically authorized and recorded when certain events occur. For example, the wages of employees may be paid automatically at the end of each pay period.

11	Accounts Payable		21	400	
	Cash		11		400
	Paid creditors on account.				

Transaction

Dec. 13 NetSolutions paid a receptionist and a part-time assistant $950 for two weeks' wages.

Analysis This transaction is similar to the December 6 transaction, where an expense account is increased and Cash is decreased. This transaction is recorded as a $950 increase (debit) to Wages Expense and a $950 decrease (credit) to Cash.

Journal Entry

Journal					**Page 3**
Date		**Description**	**Post. Ref.**	**Debit**	**Credit**
2009 Dec.	13	Wages Expense	51	950	
		Cash	11		950
		Paid two weeks' wages.			

Transaction

Dec. 16 NetSolutions received $3,100 from fees earned for the first half of December.

Analysis An asset account (Cash) and a revenue account (Fees Earned) increase. This transaction is recorded as a $3,100 increase (debit) to Cash and a $3,100 increase (credit) to Fees Earned.

Journal Entry

16	Cash		11	3,100	
	Fees Earned		41		3,100
	Received fees from customers.				

Transaction

Dec. 16   Fees earned on account totaled $1,750 for the first half of December.

Analysis When a business agrees that a customer may pay for services provided at a later date, an **account receivable** is created. An account receivable is a claim against the customer. An account receivable is an asset, and the revenue is earned even though no cash has been received. Thus, this transaction is recorded as a $1,750 increase (debit) to Accounts Receivable and a $1,750 increase (credit) to Fees Earned.

Journal Entry

16	Accounts Receivable	12	1,750	
	Fees Earned	41		1,750
	Recorded fees earned on account.			

Example Exercise 2-3   Journal Entry for Fees Earned   •••••••• ❯ ③

Prepare a journal entry on August 7 for the fees earned on account, $115,000.

Follow My Example 2-3

Aug. 7	Accounts Receivable	115,000	
	Fees Earned		115,000

For Practice: PE 2-3A, PE 2-3B

Transaction

Dec. 20   NetSolutions paid $900 to Executive Supply Co. on the $1,800 debt owed from the December 4 transaction.

Analysis This is similar to the transaction of December 11. This transaction is recorded as a $900 decrease (debit) to Accounts Payable and a $900 decrease (credit) to Cash.

Journal Entry

20	Accounts Payable	21	900	
	Cash	11		900
	Paid part of amount owed to			
	Executive Supply Co.			

Transaction

Dec. 21   NetSolutions received $650 from customers in payment of their accounts.

Analysis When customers pay amounts owed for services they have previously received, one asset increases and another asset decreases. This transaction is recorded as a $650 increase (debit) to Cash and a $650 decrease (credit) to Accounts Receivable.

Journal Entry

21	Cash	11	650	
	Accounts Receivable	12		650
	Received cash from customers			
	on account.			

Transaction

Dec. 23   NetSolutions paid $1,450 for supplies.

Analysis One asset account (Supplies) increases and another asset account (Cash) decreases. This transaction is recorded as a $1,450 increase (debit) to Supplies and a $1,450 decrease (credit) to Cash.

Journal Entry

23	Supplies	14	1,450	
	Cash	11		1,450
	Purchased supplies.			

Transaction

Dec. 27   NetSolutions paid the receptionist and the part-time assistant $1,200 for two weeks' wages.

Analysis This is similar to the transaction of December 13. This transaction is recorded as a $1,200 increase (debit) to Wages Expense and a $1,200 decrease (credit) to Cash.

Journal Entry

27	Wages Expense	51	1,200	
	Cash	11		1,200
	Paid two weeks' wages.			

Transaction

Dec. 31   NetSolutions paid its $310 telephone bill for the month.

Analysis This is similar to the transaction of December 6. This transaction is recorded as a $310 increase (debit) to Utilities Expense and a $310 decrease (credit) to Cash.

Journal Entry

31	Utilities Expense	54	310	
	Cash	11		310
	Paid telephone bill.			

Transaction

Dec. 31   NetSolutions paid its $225 electric bill for the month.

Analysis This is similar to the preceding transaction. This transaction is recorded as a $225 increase (debit) to Utilities Expense and a $225 decrease (credit) to Cash.

Journal Entry

	Journal				Page 4
Date	**Description**	**Post. Ref.**	**Debit**		**Credit**
2009 Dec. 31	Utilities Expense	54	225		
	Cash	11			225
	Paid electric bill.				

Transaction

Dec. 31   NetSolutions received $2,870 from fees earned for the second half of December.

Analysis This is similar to the transaction of December 16. This transaction is recorded as a $2,870 increase (debit) to Cash and a $2,870 increase (credit) to Fees Earned.

Journal Entry

31	Cash	11	2,870	
	Fees Earned	41		2,870
	Received fees from customers.			

Transaction

Dec. 31   Fees earned on account totaled $1,120 for the second half of December.

Analysis This is similar to the transaction of December 16. This transaction is recorded as a $1,120 increase (debit) to Accounts Receivable and a $1,120 increase (credit) to Fees Earned.

Journal Entry

31	Accounts Receivable	12	1,120	
	Fees Earned	41		1,120
	Recorded fees earned on account.			

Transaction

Dec. 31   NetSolutions paid $2,000 of dividends to stockholders.

Analysis This transaction decreases stockholders' equity (retained earnings) and assets. This transaction is recorded as a $2,000 increase (debit) to Dividends and a $2,000 decrease (credit) to Cash.

Journal Entry

31	Dividends	33	2,000	
	Cash	11		2,000
	Paid dividends to stockholders.			

Example Exercise 2-4   Journal Entry for Dividends   **3**

Prepare a journal entry on December 29 for the payment of dividends of $12,000.

Follow My Example 2-4

Dec. 29   Dividends 12,000
            Cash   12,000

For Practice: PE 2-4A, PE 2-4B

Exhibit 5 shows the ledger for NetSolutions after the transactions for both November and December have been posted.

Example Exercise 2-5   Missing Amount from an Account   **3**

On March 1, the cash account balance was $22,350. During March, cash receipts totaled $241,880 and the March 31 balance was $19,125. Determine the cash payments made during March.

Follow My Example 2-5

Using the following T account, solve for the amount of cash payments (indicated by ? below).

	Cash		
Mar. 1 Bal.	22,350	?	Cash payments
Cash receipts	241,880		
Mar. 31 Bal.	19,125		

$19,125 = $22,350 + $241,880 − Cash payments
Cash payments = $22,350 + $241,880 − $19,125 = $245,105

For Practice: PE 2-5A, PE 2-5B

Exhibit 5

Ledger NetSolutions

Ledger

Account Cash — Account No. 11

Date	Item	Post. Ref.	Debit	Credit	Balance Debit	Balance Credit
2009						
Nov. 1		1	25,000		25,000	
5		1		20,000	5,000	
18		1	7,500		12,500	
30		1		3,650	8,850	
30		1		950	7,900	
30		2		2,000	5,900	
Dec. 1		2		2,400	3,500	
1		2		800	2,700	
1		2	360		3,060	
6		2		180	2,880	
11		2		400	2,480	
13		3		950	1,530	
16		3	3,100		4,630	
20		3		900	3,730	
21		3	650		4,380	
23		3		1,450	2,930	
27		3		1,200	1,730	
31		3		310	1,420	
31		4		225	1,195	
31		4	2,870		4,065	
31		4		2,000	2,065	

Account Accounts Receivable — Account No. 12

Date	Item	Post. Ref.	Debit	Credit	Balance Debit	Balance Credit
2009						
Dec. 16		3	1,750		1,750	
21		3		650	1,100	
31		4	1,120		2,220	

Account Supplies — Account No. 14

Date	Item	Post. Ref.	Debit	Credit	Balance Debit	Balance Credit
2009						
Nov. 10		1	1,350		1,350	
30		1		800	550	
Dec. 23		3	1,450		2,000	

Account Prepaid Insurance — Account No. 15

Date	Item	Post. Ref.	Debit	Credit	Balance Debit	Balance Credit
2009						
Dec. 1		2	2,400		2,400	

Account Land — Account No. 17

Date	Item	Post. Ref.	Debit	Credit	Balance Debit	Balance Credit
2009						
Nov. 5		1	20,000		20,000	

Account Office Equipment — Account No. 18

Date	Item	Post. Ref.	Debit	Credit	Balance Debit	Balance Credit
2009						
Dec. 4		2	1,800		1,800	

Account Accounts Payable — Account No. 21

Date	Item	Post. Ref.	Debit	Credit	Balance Debit	Balance Credit
2009						
Nov. 10		1		1,350		1,350
30		1	950			400
Dec. 4		2		1,800		2,200
11		2	400			1,800
20		3	900			900

Account Unearned Rent — Account No. 23

Date	Item	Post. Ref.	Debit	Credit	Balance Debit	Balance Credit
2009						
Dec. 1		2		360		360

Account Capital Stock — Account No. 31

Date	Item	Post. Ref.	Debit	Credit	Balance Debit	Balance Credit
2009						
Nov. 1		1		25,000		25,000

Account Dividends — Account No. 33

Date	Item	Post. Ref.	Debit	Credit	Balance Debit	Balance Credit
2009						
Nov. 30		2	2,000		2,000	
Dec. 31		4	2,000		4,000	

Account Fees Earned — Account No. 41

Date	Item	Post. Ref.	Debit	Credit	Balance Debit	Balance Credit
2009						
Nov. 18		1		7,500		7,500
Dec. 16		3		3,100		10,600
16		3		1,750		12,350
31		4		2,870		15,220
31		4		1,120		16,340

Account Wages Expense — Account No. 51

Date	Item	Post. Ref.	Debit	Credit	Balance Debit	Balance Credit
2009						
Nov. 30		1	2,125		2,125	
Dec. 13		3	950		3,075	
27		3	1,200		4,275	

(continued)

Exhibit 5

Ledger NetSolutions *(concluded)*

Account *Rent Expense*					Account No. 52	
		Post. Ref.	Debit	Credit	Balance Debit	Balance Credit
Date	Item	Post. Ref.	Debit	Credit	Debit	Credit
2009 Nov. 30		1	800		800	
Dec. 1		2	800		1,600	

Account *Supplies Expense*					Account No. 55	
		Post. Ref.	Debit	Credit	Balance Debit	Balance Credit
Date	Item	Post. Ref.	Debit	Credit	Debit	Credit
2009 Nov. 30		1	800		800	

Account *Utilities Expense*					Account No. 54	
		Post. Ref.	Debit	Credit	Balance Debit	Balance Credit
Date	Item	Post. Ref.	Debit	Credit	Debit	Credit
2009 Nov. 30		1	450		450	
Dec. 31		3	310		760	
31		4	225		985	

Account *Miscellaneous Expense*					Account No. 59	
		Post. Ref.	Debit	Credit	Balance Debit	Balance Credit
Date	Item	Post. Ref.	Debit	Credit	Debit	Credit
2009 Nov. 30		1	275		275	
Dec. 6		2	180		455	

4 Prepare an unadjusted trial balance and explain how it can be used to discover errors.

Trial Balance

Errors may occur in posting debits and credits from the journal to the ledger. One way to detect such errors is by preparing a **trial balance**. Double-entry accounting requires that debits must always equal credits. The trial balance verifies this equality. The steps in preparing a trial balance are as follows:

Step 1: List the name of the company, the title of the trial balance, and the date the trial balance is prepared.

Step 2: List the accounts from the ledger and enter their debit or credit balance in the Debit or Credit column of the trial balance.

Step 3: Total the Debit and Credit columns of the trial balance.

Step 4: Verify that the total of the Debit column equals the total of the Credit column.

    The trial balance for NetSolutions as of December 31, 2009, is shown in Exhibit 6. The account balances in Exhibit 6 are taken from the ledger shown in Exhibit 5. Before a trial balance is prepared, each account balance in the ledger must be determined. When the standard account form is used as in Exhibit 5, the balance of each account appears in the balance column on the same line as the last posting to the account.

    The trial balance shown in Exhibit 6 is titled an **unadjusted trial balance**. This is to distinguish it from other trial balances that we will be preparing in later chapters. These other trial balances include an adjusted trial balance and a post-closing trial balance.[3]

Errors Affecting the Trial Balance

If the trial balance totals are not equal, an error has occurred. In this case, the error must be found and corrected. A method useful in discovering errors is as follows:

1. If the difference between the Debit and Credit column totals is 10, 100, or 1,000, an error in addition may have occurred. In this case, re-add the trial balance column totals. If the error still exists, recompute the account balances.

---

3 The adjusted trial balance is discussed in Chapter 3, and the post-closing trial balance is discussed in Chapter 4.

Exhibit 6

Trial Balance

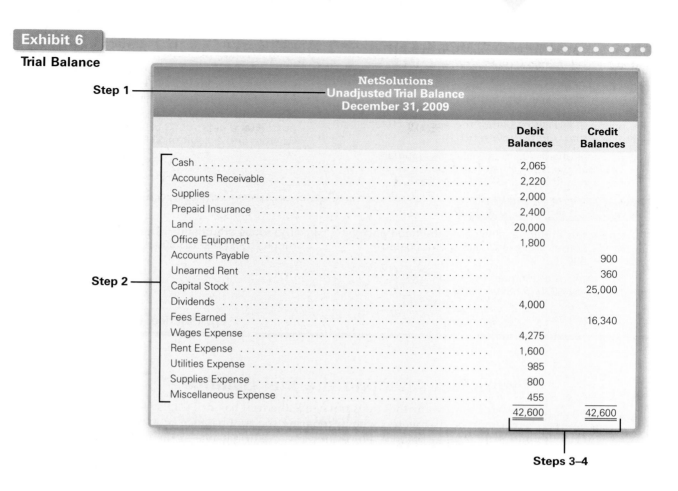

Step 1

NetSolutions
Unadjusted Trial Balance
December 31, 2009

	Debit Balances	Credit Balances
Cash	2,065	
Accounts Receivable	2,220	
Supplies	2,000	
Prepaid Insurance	2,400	
Land	20,000	
Office Equipment	1,800	
Accounts Payable		900
Unearned Rent		360
Capital Stock		25,000
Dividends	4,000	
Fees Earned		16,340
Wages Expense	4,275	
Rent Expense	1,600	
Utilities Expense	985	
Supplies Expense	800	
Miscellaneous Expense	455	
	42,600	42,600

Step 2

Steps 3–4

2. If the difference between the Debit and Credit column totals can be evenly divisible by 2, the error may be due to the entering of a debit balance as a credit balance, or vice versa. In this case, review the trial balance for account balances of one-half the difference that may have been entered in the wrong column. For example, if the Debit column total is $20,640 and the Credit column total is $20,236, the difference of $404 ($20,640 − $20,236) may be due to a credit account balance of $202 that was entered as a debit account balance.

3. If the difference between the Debit and Credit column totals is evenly divisible by 9, trace the account balances back to the ledger to see if an account balance was incorrectly copied from the ledger. Two common types of copying errors are transpositions and slides. A **transposition** occurs when the order of the digits is copied incorrectly, such as writing $542 as $452 or $524. In a **slide**, the entire number is copied incorrectly one or more spaces to the right or the left, such as writing $542.00 as $54.20 or $5,420.00. In both cases, the resulting error will be evenly divisible by 9.

4. If the difference between the Debit and Credit column totals is not evenly divisible by 2 or 9, review the ledger to see if an account balance in the amount of the error has been omitted from the trial balance. If the error is not discovered, review the journal postings to see if a posting of a debit or credit may have been omitted.

5. If an error is not discovered by the preceding steps, the accounting process must be retraced, beginning with the last journal entry.

The trial balance does not provide complete proof of the accuracy of the ledger. It indicates only that the debits and the credits are equal. This proof is of value, however, because errors often affect the equality of debits and credits.

Example Exercise 2-6   Trial Balance Errors

For each of the following errors, considered individually, indicate whether the error would cause the trial balance totals to be unequal. If the error would cause the trial balance totals to be unequal, indicate whether the debit or credit total is higher and by how much.

a. Payment of a dividend of $5,600 was journalized and posted as a debit of $6,500 to Salary Expense and a credit of $6,500 to Cash.

b. A fee of $2,850 earned from a client was debited to Accounts Receivable for $2,580 and credited to Fees Earned for $2,850.

c. A payment of $3,500 to a creditor was posted as a debit of $3,500 to Accounts Payable and a debit of $3,500 to Cash.

Follow My Example 2-6

a. The totals are equal since both the debit and credit entries were journalized and posted for $6,500.

b. The totals are unequal. The credit total is higher by $270 ($2,850 − $2,580).

c. The totals are unequal. The debit total is higher by $7,000 ($3,500 + $3,500).

For Practice: PE 2-6A, PE 2-6B

Errors Not Affecting the Trial Balance

An error may occur that does not cause the trial balance totals to be unequal. Such an error may be discovered when preparing the trial balance or may be indicated by an unusual account balance. For example, a credit balance in the supplies account indicates an error has occurred. This is because a business cannot have "negative" supplies. When such errors are discovered, they should be corrected. If the error has already been journalized and posted to the ledger, a **correcting journal entry** is normally prepared.

To illustrate, assume that on May 5 a $12,500 purchase of office equipment on account was incorrectly journalized and posted as a debit to Supplies and a credit to Accounts Payable for $12,500. This posting of the incorrect entry is shown in the following T accounts:

Incorrect:

Supplies		Accounts Payable	
12,500			12,500

Before making a correcting journal entry, it is best to determine the debit(s) and credit(s) that should have been recorded. These are shown in the following T accounts:

Correct:

Office Equipment		Accounts Payable	
12,500			12,500

Comparing the two sets of T accounts shows that the incorrect debit to Supplies may be corrected by debiting Office Equipment for $12,500 and crediting Supplies for $12,500. The following correcting journal entry is then journalized and posted:

Entry to Correct Error:

May	31	Office Equipment	18	12,500	
		Supplies	14		12,500
		To correct erroneous debit			
		to Supplies on May 5. See invoice			
		from Bell Office Equipment Co.			

Example Exercise 2-7   Correcting Entries

The following errors took place in journalizing and posting transactions:

a. Dividends of $6,000 were recorded as a debit to Office Salaries Expense and a credit to Cash.

b. Utilities Expense of $4,500 paid for the current month was recorded as a debit to Miscellaneous Expense and a credit to Accounts Payable.

Journalize the entries to correct the errors. Omit explanations.

Follow My Example 2-7

a. Dividends	6,000	
Office Salaries Expense		6,000
b. Accounts Payable	4,500	
Miscellaneous Expense		4,500
Utilities Expense	4,500	
Cash		4,500

Note: The first entry in (b) reverses the incorrect entry, and the second entry records the correct entry. These two entries could also be combined into one entry; however, preparing two entries will make it easier for someone later to understand what had happened and why the entries were necessary.

For Practice: PE 2-7A, PE 2-7B

Financial Analysis and Interpretation

A single item appearing in a financial statement is often useful in interpreting the financial results of a business. However, comparing this item in a current statement with the same item in prior statements often makes the financial information more useful. **Horizontal analysis** is the term used to describe such comparisons.

In horizontal analysis, the amount of each item on the current financial statements is compared with the same item on one or more earlier statements. The increase or decrease in the *amount* of the item is computed, together with the *percent* of increase or decrease. When two statements are being compared, the earlier statement is used as the base for computing the amount and the percent of change.

To illustrate, the horizontal analysis of two income statements for J. Holmes, Attorney-at-Law, P.C. is shown. The horizontal analysis indicates both favorable and unfavorable trends affecting the income statement of J. Holmes, Attorney-at-Law, P.C. The increase in fees earned is a favorable trend, as is the decrease in supplies expense. Unfavorable trends include the increase in wages expense, utilities expense, and miscellaneous expense. These expenses increased the same as or faster than the increase in revenues, with total operating expenses increasing by 30.6%. Overall, net income increased by $15,800, or 19.9%, a favorable trend.

The significance of the various increases and decreases in the revenue and expense items should be investigated to see if operations could be further improved. For example, the increase in utilities expense of 38.9% was the result of renting additional office space for use by a part-time law student in performing paralegal services. This explains the increase in rent expense of 25% and the increase in wages expense of 33.3%. The increase in revenues of 25% reflects the fees generated by the new paralegal.

The preceding example illustrates how horizontal analysis can be useful in interpreting and analyzing financial statements. Horizontal analyses similar to that shown can also be performed for the balance sheet, the retained earnings statement, and the statement of cash flows.

J. Holmes, Attorney-at-Law, P.C.
Income Statement
For the Years Ended December 31, 2010 and 2009

	2010	2009	Increase (Decrease) Amount	Percent
Fees earned	$187,500	$150,000	$37,500	25.0%*
Operating expenses:				
Wages expense	$ 60,000	$ 45,000	$15,000	33.3
Rent expense	15,000	12,000	3,000	25.0
Utilities expense	12,500	9,000	3,500	38.9
Supplies expense	2,700	3,000	(300)	(10.0)
Miscellaneous expense	2,300	1,800	500	27.8
Total operating expenses	$ 92,500	$ 70,800	$21,700	30.6
Net income	$ 95,000	$ 79,200	$15,800	19.9

*$37,500 ÷ $150,000

1 Describe the characteristics of an account and a chart of accounts.

Key Points	Key Learning Outcomes	Example Exercises	Practice Exercises
The record used for recording individual transactions is an account. A group of accounts is called a ledger. The simplest form of an account, a T account, has three parts: (1) a title, which is the name of the item recorded in the account; (2) a left side, called the debit side; and (3) a right side, called the credit side. Amounts entered on the left side of an account, regardless of the account title, are called debits to the account. Amounts entered on the right side of an account are called credits. Periodically, the debits in an account are added, the credits in the account are added, and the balance of the account is determined.	• Record transactions in T accounts.		
	• Determine the balance of a T account.		
The system of accounts that make up a ledger is called a chart of accounts.	• Prepare a chart of accounts for a corporation.		

2 Describe and illustrate journalizing transactions using the double-entry accounting system.

Key Points	Key Learning Outcomes	Example Exercises	Practice Exercises
The double-entry accounting system is designed so that the sum of the debits always equals the sum of the credits for each journal entry.			
Transactions are initially entered in a record called a journal. The rules of debit and credit for recording increases or decreases in asset, liability, capital stock, retained earnings, dividends, revenue, and expense accounts are shown in Exhibit 3. Each transaction is recorded so that the sum of the debits is always equal to the sum of the credits. The normal balance of an account is indicated by the side of the account (debit or credit) that receives the increases.	• Indicate the normal balance of an account.	2-1	2-1A, 2-1B
	• Journalize transactions using the rules of debit and credit.	2-2	2-2A, 2-2B

3 Describe and illustrate the journalizing and posting of transactions to accounts.

Key Points	Key Learning Outcomes	Example Exercises	Practice Exercises
Transactions are journalized and posted to the ledger using the rules of debit and credit. The debits and credits for each journal entry are posted to the accounts in the order in which they occur in the journal. In posting to the standard account, (1) the date is entered, and (2) the amount of the entry is entered. For future reference, (3) the journal page number is inserted in the Posting Reference column of the account, and (4) the account number is inserted in the Posting Reference column of the journal.	• Journalize transactions using the rules of debit and credit.	2-3 2-4	2-3A, 2-3B 2-4A, 2-4B
	• Determine whether an account has only debit entries, only credit entries, or both.		
	• Determine the normal balance of an account.		
	• Determine the missing amount from an account given its balance.	2-5	2-5A, 2-5B
	• Post journal entries to a standard account.		
	• Post journal entries to a T account.		

Prepare an unadjusted trial balance and explain how it can be used to discover errors.

Key Points

A trial balance is prepared by listing the accounts from the ledger and their balances. The totals of the Debit column and Credit column of the trial balance must be equal. If the two totals are not equal, an error has occurred. Errors may occur even though the trial balance totals are equal. Such errors may require a correcting journal entry.

Key Learning Outcomes	Example Exercises	Practice Exercises
• Prepare an unadjusted trial balance.		
• Discover errors that cause unequal totals in the trial balance.	2-6	2-6A, 2-6B
• Prepare correcting journal entries for various errors.	2-7	2-7A, 2-7B

Key Terms

account (52)
account receivable (64)
assets (54)
balance of the account (53)
chart of accounts (54)
correcting journal entry (72)
credit (53)
debit (53)
dividends (54)
double-entry accounting system (55)

expenses (55)
horizontal analysis (73)
journal (57)
journal entry (58)
journalizing (58)
ledger (54)
liabilities (54)
normal balance of an account (56)
posting (61)
revenues (55)

rules of debit and credit (55)
slide (71)
stockholders' equity (54)
T account (52)
transposition (71)
trial balance (70)
unadjusted trial balance (70)
unearned revenue (62)

Illustrative Problem

J. F. Outz, M.D., has been practicing as a cardiologist for three years in a professional corporation known as Hearts, P.C. During April 2009, Hearts completed the following transactions:

Apr. 1. Paid office rent for April, $800.
3. Purchased equipment on account, $2,100.
5. Received cash on account from patients, $3,150.
8. Purchased X-ray film and other supplies on account, $245.
9. One of the items of equipment purchased on April 3 was defective. It was returned with the permission of the supplier, who agreed to reduce the account for the amount charged for the item, $325.
12. Paid cash to creditors on account, $1,250.

Apr. 17.   Paid cash for renewal of a six-month property insurance policy, $370.

20.   Discovered that the balances of the cash account and the accounts payable account as of April 1 were overstated by $200. A payment of that amount to a creditor in March had not been recorded. Journalize the $200 payment as of April 20.

24.   Paid cash for laboratory analysis, $545.

27.   Paid dividends of $1,250.

30.   Recorded the cash received in payment of services (on a cash basis) to patients during April, $1,720.

30.   Paid salaries of receptionist and nurses, $1,725.

30.   Paid various utility expenses, $360.

30.   Recorded fees charged to patients on account for services performed in April, $5,145.

30.   Paid miscellaneous expenses, $132.

Hearts, P. C.'s account titles, numbers, and balances as of April 1 (all normal balances) are listed as follows: Cash, 11, $4,123; Accounts Receivable, 12, $6,725; Supplies, 13, $290; Prepaid Insurance, 14, $465; Equipment, 18, $19,745; Accounts Payable, 22, $765; Capital Stock, 31, $10,000; Retained Earnings, 32, $20,583; Dividends, 33; Professional Fees, 41; Salary Expense, 51; Rent Expense, 53; Laboratory Expense, 55; Utilities Expense, 56; Miscellaneous Expense, 59.

Instructions

1.   Open a ledger of standard four-column accounts for Hearts, P. C. as of April 1. Enter the balances in the appropriate balance columns and place a check mark (✔) in the Posting Reference column. (*Hint:* Verify the equality of the debit and credit balances in the ledger before proceeding with the next instruction.)

2.   Journalize each transaction in a two-column journal.

3.   Post the journal to the ledger, extending the month-end balances to the appropriate balance columns after each posting.

4.   Prepare an unadjusted trial balance as of April 30.

Solution 1., 2., and **3.**

Journal				Page 27
Date	**Description**	**Post. Ref.**	**Debit**	**Credit**
2009 Apr. 1	Rent Expense	53	800	
	Cash	11		800
	Paid office rent for April.			
3	Equipment	18	2,100	
	Accounts Payable	22		2,100
	Purchased equipment on account.			
5	Cash	11	3,150	
	Accounts Receivable	12		3,150
	Received cash on account.			
8	Supplies	13	245	
	Accounts Payable	22		245
	Purchased supplies.			
9	Accounts Payable	22	325	
	Equipment	18		325
	Returned defective equipment.			
12	Accounts Payable	22	1,250	
	Cash	11		1,250
	Paid creditors on account.			
17	Prepaid Insurance	14	370	
	Cash	11		370
	Renewed six-month property policy.			
20	Accounts Payable	22	200	
	Cash	11		200
	Recorded March payment to creditor.			

Journal				Page 28
Date	**Description**	**Post. Ref.**	**Debit**	**Credit**
2009 Apr. 24	Laboratory Expense	55	545	
	Cash	11		545
	Paid for laboratory analysis.			
27	Dividends	33	1,250	
	Cash	11		1,250
	Paid dividends.			
30	Cash	11	1,720	
	Professional Fees	41		1,720
	Received fees from patients.			
30	Salary Expense	51	1,725	
	Cash	11		1,725
	Paid salaries.			
30	Utilities Expense	56	360	
	Cash	11		360
	Paid utilities.			
30	Accounts Receivable	12	5,145	
	Professional Fees	41		5,145
	Recorded fees earned on account.			
30	Miscellaneous Expense	59	132	
	Cash	11		132
	Paid expenses.			

Ledger

Account *Cash*   Account No. 11

Date	Item	Post. Ref.	Debit	Credit	Balance Debit	Balance Credit
2009 Apr. 1	Balance	✓			4,123	
1		27		800	3,323	
5		27	3,150		6,473	
12		27		1,250	5,223	
17		27		370	4,853	
20		27		200	4,653	
24		28		545	4,108	
27		28		1,250	2,858	
30		28	1,720		4,578	
30		28		1,725	2,853	
30		28		360	2,493	
30		28		132	2,361	

Account *Accounts Receivable*   Account No. 12

Date	Item	Post. Ref.	Debit	Credit	Balance Debit	Balance Credit
2009 Apr. 1	Balance	✓			6,725	
5		27		3,150	3,575	
30		28	5,145		8,720	

Account *Supplies*   Account No. 13

Date	Item	Post. Ref.	Debit	Credit	Balance Debit	Balance Credit
2009 Apr. 1	Balance	✓			290	
8		27	245		535	

Account *Prepaid Insurance* — Account No. *14*

Date	Item	Post. Ref.	Debit	Credit	Balance Debit	Balance Credit
2009 Apr. 1	Balance	✓			465	
17		27	370		835	

Account *Equipment* — Account No. *18*

Date	Item	Post. Ref.	Debit	Credit	Balance Debit	Balance Credit
2009 Apr. 1	Balance	✓			19,745	
3		27	2,100		21,845	
9		27		325	21,520	

Account *Accounts Payable* — Account No. *22*

Date	Item	Post. Ref.	Debit	Credit	Balance Debit	Balance Credit
2009 Apr. 1	Balance	✓				7,65
3		27		2,100		2,865
8		27		245		3,110
9		27	325			2,785
12		27	1,250			1,535
20		27	200			1,335

Account *Capital Stock* — Account No. *31*

Date	Item	Post. Ref.	Debit	Credit	Balance Debit	Balance Credit
2009 Apr. 1	Balance	✓				10,000

Account *Retained Earnings* — Account No. *32*

Date	Item	Post. Ref.	Debit	Credit	Balance Debit	Balance Credit
2009 Apr. 1	Balance	✓				20,583

Account *Dividends* — Account No. *33*

Date	Item	Post. Ref.	Debit	Credit	Balance Debit	Balance Credit
2009 Apr. 27		28	1,250		1,250	

Account *Professional Fees* — Account No. *41*

Date	Item	Post. Ref.	Debit	Credit	Balance Debit	Balance Credit
2009 Apr. 30		28		1,720		1,720
30		28		5,145		6,865

Account *Salary Expense* — Account No. *51*

Date	Item	Post. Ref.	Debit	Credit	Balance Debit	Balance Credit
2009 Apr. 30		28	1,725		1,725	

Account *Rent Expense* — Account No. *53*

Date	Item	Post. Ref.	Debit	Credit	Balance Debit	Balance Credit
2009 Apr. 1		27	800		800	

Account *Laboratory Expense* — Account No. *55*

Date	Item	Post. Ref.	Debit	Credit	Balance Debit	Balance Credit
2009 Apr. 24		28	545		545	

Account *Utilities Expense* — Account No. *56*

Date	Item	Post. Ref.	Debit	Credit	Balance Debit	Balance Credit
2009 Apr. 30		28	360		360	

Account *Miscellaneous Expense* — Account No. *59*

Date	Item	Post. Ref.	Debit	Credit	Balance Debit	Balance Credit
2009 Apr. 30		28	132		132	

4.

Hearts, P.C. Unadjusted Trial Balance April 30, 2009	Debit Balances	Credit Balances
Cash	2,361	
Accounts Receivable	8,720	
Supplies	535	
Prepaid Insurance	835	
Equipment	21,520	
Accounts Payable		1,335
Capital Stock		10,000
Retained Earnings		20,583
Dividends	1,250	
Professional Fees		6,865
Salary Expense	1,725	
Rent Expense	800	
Laboratory Expense	545	
Utilities Expense	360	
Miscellaneous Expense	132	
	38,783	38,783

Self-Examination Questions (Answers at End of Chapter)

1. A debit may signify a(n):
   A. increase in an asset account.
   B. decrease in an asset account.
   C. increase in a liability account.
   D. increase in the capital stock account.

2. The type of account with a normal credit balance is:
   A. an asset.   C. a revenue.
   B. dividends.   D. an expense.

3. A debit balance in which of the following accounts would indicate a likely error?
   A. Accounts Receivable
   B. Cash
   C. Fees Earned
   D. Miscellaneous Expense

4. The receipt of cash from customers in payment of their accounts would be recorded by:
   A. a debit to Cash and a credit to Accounts Receivable.
   B. a debit to Accounts Receivable and a credit to Cash.
   C. a debit to Cash and a credit to Accounts Payable.
   D. a debit to Accounts Payable and a credit to Cash.

5. The form listing the titles and balances of the accounts in the ledger on a given date is the:
   A. income statement.
   B. balance sheet.
   C. retained earnings statement.
   D. trial balance.

Eye Openers

1. What is the difference between an account and a ledger?
2. Do the terms *debit* and *credit* signify increase or decrease or can they signify either? Explain.

3. Explain why the rules of debit and credit are the same for liability accounts and stockholders' equity accounts.

4. What is the effect (increase or decrease) of a debit to an expense account (a) in terms of stockholders' equity (retained earnings) and (b) in terms of expense?

5. What is the effect (increase or decrease) of a credit to a revenue account (a) in terms of stockholders' equity (retained earnings) and (b) in terms of revenue?

6. Carr Company adheres to a policy of depositing all cash receipts in a bank account and making all payments by check. The cash account as of March 31 has a credit balance of $1,250, and there is no undeposited cash on hand. (a) Assuming no errors occurred during journalizing or posting, what caused this unusual balance? (b) Is the $1,250 credit balance in the cash account an asset, a liability, stockholders' equity, a revenue, or an expense?

7. Longfellow Company performed services in July for a specific customer, for a fee of $8,380. Payment was received the following August. (a) Was the revenue earned in July or August? (b) What accounts should be debited and credited in (1) July and (2) August?

8. What proof is provided by a trial balance?

9. If the two totals of a trial balance are equal, does it mean that there are no errors in the accounting records? Explain.

10. Assume that a trial balance is prepared with an account balance of $18,500 listed as $1,850 and an account balance of $3,680 listed as $3,860. Identify the transposition and the slide.

11. Assume that when a purchase of supplies of $2,650 for cash was recorded, both the debit and the credit were journalized and posted as $2,560. (a) Would this error cause the trial balance to be out of balance? (b) Would the trial balance be out of balance if the $2,650 entry had been journalized correctly but the credit to Cash had been posted as $2,560?

12. Assume that JRQ Consulting erroneously recorded the payment of $10,000 of dividends as a debit to Salary Expense. (a) How would this error affect the equality of the trial balance? (b) How would this error affect the income statement, retained earnings statement, and balance sheet?

13. Assume that Beebe Realty Co. borrowed $120,000 from City Bank and Trust. In recording the transaction, Beebe erroneously recorded the receipt as a debit to Cash, $120,000, and a credit to Fees Earned, $120,000. (a) How would this error affect the equality of the trial balance? (b) How would this error affect the income statement, retained earnings statement, and balance sheet?

14. In journalizing and posting the entry to record the purchase of supplies for cash, the accounts payable account was credited in error. What is the preferred procedure to correct this error?

15. Checking accounts are the most common form of deposits for banks. Assume that Yellowstone Storage has a checking account at Livingston Savings Bank. What type of account (asset, liability, capital stock, retained earnings, revenue, expense, dividends) does the account balance of $12,100 represent from the viewpoint of (a) Yellowstone Storage and (b) Livingston Savings Bank?

Practice Exercises

PE 2-1A
Rules of debit and credit and normal balances

obj. 2

EE 2-1 p. 56

State for each account whether it is likely to have (a) debit entries only, (b) credit entries only, or (c) both debit and credit entries. Also, indicate its normal balance.

1. Accounts Payable
2. Cash
3. Dividends
4. Miscellaneous Expense
5. Prepaid Insurance
6. Rent Revenue

PE 2-1B
Rules of debit and credit and normal balances

obj. 2

EE 2-1 p. 56

State for each account whether it is likely to have (a) debit entries only, (b) credit entries only, or (c) both debit and credit entries. Also, indicate its normal balance.

1. Accounts Receivable
2. Commissions Earned
3. Notes Payable
4. Capital Stock
5. Unearned Rent
6. Wages Expense

PE 2-2A
Journal entry for asset purchase

obj. 2

EE 2-2 p. 60

Prepare a journal entry for the purchase of office supplies on October 14 for $9,000, paying $1,800 cash and the remainder on account.

PE 2-2B
Journal entry for asset purchase

obj. 2

EE 2-2 p. 60

Prepare a journal entry for the purchase of office equipment on February 3 for $18,250, paying $3,650 cash and the remainder on account.

PE 2-3A
Journal entry for fees earned

obj. 3

EE 2-3 p. 65

Prepare a journal entry on April 2 for cash received for services rendered, $3,600.

PE 2-3B
Journal entry for fees earned

obj. 3

EE 2-3 p. 65

Prepare a journal entry on November 29 for fees earned on account, $11,375.

PE 2-4A
Journal entry for dividends

obj. 3

EE 2-4 p. 68

Prepare a journal entry on January 19 for the payment of $8,500 of dividends.

PE 2-4B
Journal entry for dividends

obj. 3

EE 2-4 p. 68

Prepare a journal entry on December 23 for the payment of $6,000 of dividends.

PE 2-5A
Missing amount
from an account
obj. 3
EE 2-5   p. 68

On July 1, the supplies account balance was $1,950. During July, supplies of $6,750 were purchased, and $1,851 of supplies were on hand as of July 31. Determine supplies expense for July.

PE 2-5B
Missing amount
from an account
obj. 3
EE 2-5   p. 68

On October 1, the cash account balance was $23,600. During October, cash payments totaled $315,700, and the October 31 balance was $36,900. Determine the cash receipts during October.

PE 2-6A
Trial balance errors
obj. 4
EE 2-6   p. 72

For each of the following errors, considered individually, indicate whether the error would cause the trial balance totals to be unequal. If the error would cause the trial balance totals to be unequal, indicate whether the debit or credit total is higher and by how much.

a. The payment of cash for the purchase of office equipment of $8,000 was debited to Land for $8,000 and credited to Cash for $8,000.
b. The payment of $6,750 on account was debited to Accounts Payable for $675 and credited to Cash for $6,750.
c. The receipt of cash on account of $4,150 was recorded as a debit to Cash for $4,510 and a credit to Accounts Receivable for $4,150.

PE 2-6B
Trial balance errors
obj. 4
EE 2-6   p. 72

For each of the following errors, considered individually, indicate whether the error would cause the trial balance totals to be unequal. If the error would cause the trial balance totals to be unequal, indicate whether the debit or credit total is higher and by how much.

a. The payment of an insurance premium of $3,600 for a two-year policy was debited to Prepaid Insurance for $3,600 and credited to Cash for $6,300.
b. A payment of $725 on account was debited to Accounts Payable for $752 and credited to Cash for $752.
c. A purchase of supplies of $900 was debited to Supplies for $900 and debited to Accounts Payable for $900.

PE 2-7A
Correcting entries
obj. 4
EE 2-7   p. 73

The following errors took place in journalizing and posting transactions:
a. The receipt of $6,480 for services rendered was recorded as a debit to Accounts Receivable and a credit to Fees Earned.
b. The purchase of supplies of $1,960 on account was recorded as a debit to Office Equipment and a credit to Supplies.

Journalize the entries to correct the errors. Omit explanations.

PE 2-7B
Correcting entries
obj. 4
EE 2-7   p. 73

The following errors took place in journalizing and posting transactions:
a. Advertising expense of $950 paid for the current month was recorded as a debit to Miscellaneous Expense and a credit to Advertising Expense.
b. The payment of $1,500 from a customer on account was recorded as a debit to Cash and a credit to Accounts Payable.

Journalize the entries to correct the errors. Omit explanations.

Exercises

EX 2-1
Chart of
accounts

obj. 1

The following accounts appeared in recent financial statements of Continental Airlines:

Accounts Payable	Flight Equipment
Air Traffic Liability	Landing Fees
Aircraft Fuel Expense	Passenger Revenue
Cargo and Mail Revenue	Purchase Deposits for Flight Equipment
Commissions	Spare Parts and Supplies

Identify each account as either a balance sheet account or an income statement account. For each balance sheet account, identify it as an asset, a liability, or stockholders' equity. For each income statement account, identify it as a revenue or an expense.

EX 2-2
Chart of
accounts

obj. 1

Humvee Interiors is operated by Tony Newbaurer, an interior decorator. In the ledger of Humvee Interiors, the first digit of the account number indicates its major account classification (1—assets, 2—liabilities, 3—stockholders' equity, 4—revenues, 5—expenses). The second digit of the account number indicates the specific account within each of the preceding major account classifications.

Match each account number with its most likely account in the list below. The account numbers are 11, 12, 13, 21, 31, 32, 33, 41, 51, 52, and 53.

Accounts Payable	Land
Accounts Receivable	Miscellaneous Expense
Capital Stock	Retained Earnings
Cash	Supplies Expense
Dividends	Wages Expense
Fees Earned	

EX 2-3
Chart of
accounts

obj. 1

Monet School is a newly organized business that teaches people how to inspire and influence others. The list of accounts to be opened in the general ledger is as follows:

Accounts Payable	Prepaid Insurance
Accounts Receivable	Rent Expense
Capital Stock	Retained Earnings
Cash	Supplies
Dividends	Supplies Expense
Equipment	Unearned Rent
Fees Earned	Wages Expense
Miscellaneous Expense	

List the accounts in the order in which they should appear in the ledger of Monet School and assign account numbers. Each account number is to have two digits: the first digit is to indicate the major classification (1 for assets, etc.), and the second digit is to identify the specific account within each major classification (11 for Cash, etc.).

EX 2-4
Identifying
transactions

objs. 1, 2

Cycle Tours Co. is a travel agency. The nine transactions recorded by Cycle Tours during February 2010, its first month of operations, are indicated in the following T accounts:

Cash		Equipment		Dividends	
(1) 25,000	(2) 1,750	(3) 18,000		(9) 2,500	
(7) 10,000	(3) 3,600				
	(4) 2,700				
	(6) 7,500				
	(9) 2,500				

Accounts Receivable		Accounts Payable		Service Revenue	
(5) 13,500	(7) 10,000	(6) 7,500	(3) 14,400		(5) 13,500

Supplies		Capital Stock		Operating Expenses	
(2) 1,750	(8) 1,050		(1) 25,000	(4) 2,700	
				(8) 1,050	

Indicate for each debit and each credit: (a) whether an asset, liability, capital stock, dividends, revenue, or expense account was affected and (b) whether the account was increased (+) or decreased (−). Present your answers in the following form, with transaction (1) given as an example:

	Account Debited		Account Credited	
Transaction	Type	Effect	Type	Effect
(1)	asset	+	capital stock	+

EX 2-5
Journal entries
objs. 1,2

Based upon the T accounts in Exercise 2-4, prepare the nine journal entries from which the postings were made. Journal entry explanations may be omitted.

EX 2-6
Trial balance
obj. 4

Based upon the data presented in Exercise 2-4, prepare an unadjusted trial balance, listing the accounts in their proper order.

✔ Total Debit column:
$45,400

EX 2-7
Normal entries for accounts
obj. 2

During the month, Genesis Labs Co. has a substantial number of transactions affecting each of the following accounts. State for each account whether it is likely to have (a) debit entries only, (b) credit entries only, or (c) both debit and credit entries.

1. Accounts Payable
2. Accounts Receivable
3. Cash
4. Fees Earned
5. Insurance Expense
6. Dividends
7. Supplies Expense

EX 2-8
Normal balances of accounts
objs. 1, 2

Identify each of the following accounts of Sesame Services Co. as asset, liability, stockholders' equity, revenue, or expense, and state in each case whether the normal balance is a debit or a credit.

a. Accounts Payable
b. Accounts Receivable
c. Capital Stock
d. Cash
e. Dividends
f. Fees Earned
g. Office Equipment
h. Rent Expense
i. Supplies
j. Wages Expense

EX 2-9
Rules of debit and credit
objs. 1, 2

The following table summarizes the rules of debit and credit. For each of the items (a) through (l), indicate whether the proper answer is a debit or a credit.

	Increase	Decrease	Normal Balance
Balance sheet accounts:			
Asset	Debit	(a)	(b)
Liability	Credit	(c)	(d)
Stockholders' equity:			
Capital stock	(e)	Debit	(f)
Retained earnings	(g)	Debit	Credit
Dividends	Debit	(h)	Debit
Income statement accounts:			
Revenue	(i)	(j)	(k)
Expense	(l)	Credit	Debit

EX 2-10
Retained earnings account balance
objs. 1, 2

As of January 1, Retained Earnings had a credit balance of $37,100. During the year, dividends totaled $1,000, and the business incurred a net loss of $52,300.

a. Calculate the balance of Retained Earnings as of the end of the year.

b. Assuming that there have been no recording errors, will the balance sheet prepared at December 31 balance? Explain.

EX 2-11
Cash account balance
objs. 1, 2, 3

During the month, Racoon Co. received $319,750 in cash and paid out $269,900 in cash.
a. Do the data indicate that Racoon Co. earned $49,850 during the month? Explain.
b. If the balance of the cash account is $72,350 at the end of the month, what was the cash balance at the beginning of the month?

EX 2-12
Account balances
objs. 1, 2, 3
✔c. $284,175

a. During July, $90,300 was paid to creditors on account, and purchases on account were $115,150. Assuming the July 31 balance of Accounts Payable was $39,000, determine the account balance on July 1.
b. On May 1, the accounts receivable account balance was $36,200. During May, $315,000 was collected from customers on account. Assuming the May 31 balance was $41,600, determine the fees billed to customers on account during May.
c. On April 1, the cash account balance was $18,275. During April, cash receipts totaled $279,100 and the April 30 balance was $13,200. Determine the cash payments made during April.

EX 2-13
Transactions
obj. 2

Derby Co. has the following accounts in its ledger: Cash; Accounts Receivable; Supplies; Office Equipment; Accounts Payable; Capital Stock; Retained Earnings; Dividends; Fees Earned; Rent Expense; Advertising Expense; Utilities Expense; Miscellaneous Expense.
    Journalize the following selected transactions for March 2009 in a two-column journal. Journal entry explanations may be omitted.

Mar. 1. Paid rent for the month, $3,000.
       2. Paid advertising expense, $1,800.
       5. Paid cash for supplies, $900.
       6. Purchased office equipment on account, $12,300.
      10. Received cash from customers on account, $4,100.
      15. Paid creditor on account, $1,200.
      27. Paid cash for repairs to office equipment, $500.
      30. Paid telephone bill for the month, $180.
      31. Fees earned and billed to customers for the month, $26,800.
      31. Paid electricity bill for the month, $315.
      31. Paid dividends, $2,000.

EX 2-14
Journalizing and posting
objs. 2, 3

On August 7, 2010, Mainsail Co. purchased $2,190 of supplies on account. In Mainsail Co.'s chart of accounts, the supplies account is No. 15, and the accounts payable account is No. 21.

a. Journalize the August 7, 2010, transaction on page 19 of Mainsail Co.'s two-column journal. Include an explanation of the entry.
b. Prepare a four-column account for Supplies. Enter a debit balance of $1,050 as of August 1, 2010. Place a check mark (✔) in the Posting Reference column.
c. Prepare a four-column account for Accounts Payable. Enter a credit balance of $15,600 as of August 1, 2010. Place a check mark (✔) in the Posting Reference column.
d. Post the August 7, 2010, transaction to the accounts.

EX 2-15
Transactions and T accounts
objs. 2, 3

The following selected transactions were completed during February of the current year:

1. Billed customers for fees earned, $41,730.
2. Purchased supplies on account, $1,800.
3. Received cash from customers on account, $39,150.
4. Paid creditors on account, $1,100.

a. Journalize the above transactions in a two-column journal, using the appropriate number to identify the transactions. Journal entry explanations may be omitted.

b. Post the entries prepared in (a) to the following T accounts: Cash, Supplies, Accounts Receivable, Accounts Payable, Fees Earned. To the left of each amount posted in the accounts, place the appropriate number to identify the transactions.

EX 2-16
Trial balance
obj. 4

✔ Total of Credit
column: $696,350

The accounts in the ledger of Aznar Co. as of October 31, 2010, are listed in alphabetical order as follows. All accounts have normal balances. The balance of the cash account has been intentionally omitted.

Accounts Payable	$ 28,000	Notes Payable	$ 60,000
Accounts Receivable	56,250	Prepaid Insurance	4,500
Capital Stock	50,000	Rent Expense	90,000
Cash	?	Retained Earnings	79,850
Dividends	30,000	Supplies	3,150
Fees Earned	465,000	Supplies Expense	11,850
Insurance Expense	9,000	Unearned Rent	13,500
Land	127,500	Utilities Expense	62,250
Miscellaneous Expense	13,350	Wages Expense	262,500

Prepare an unadjusted trial balance, listing the accounts in their proper order and inserting the missing figure for cash.

EX 2-17
Effect of errors on trial balance
obj. 4

Indicate which of the following errors, each considered individually, would cause the trial balance totals to be unequal:

a. A payment of $2,150 to a creditor was posted as a debit of $2,150 to Accounts Payable and a debit of $2,150 to Cash.

b. A fee of $4,600 earned and due from a client was not debited to Accounts Receivable or credited to a revenue account, because the cash had not been received.

c. A receipt of $3,100 from an account receivable was journalized and posted as a debit of $3,100 to Cash and a credit of $3,100 to Fees Earned.

d. A payment of $10,000 for equipment purchased was posted as a debit of $1,000 to Equipment and a credit of $1,000 to Cash.

e. Payment of dividends of $15,000 was journalized and posted as a debit of $5,000 to Salary Expense and a credit of $15,000 to Cash.

EX 2-18
Errors in trial balance
obj. 4

✔ Total of Credit
column: $181,600

The following preliminary unadjusted trial balance of Nevada-For-You Co., a sports ticket agency, does not balance:

Nevada-For-You Co.
Unadjusted Trial Balance
December 31, 2010

	Debit Balances	Credit Balances
Cash	47,350	
Accounts Receivable	22,100	
Prepaid Insurance		8,000
Equipment	7,500	
Accounts Payable		12,980
Unearned Rent		2,900
Capital Stock	30,000	
Retained Earnings	52,420	
Dividends	10,000	
Service Revenue		83,750
Wages Expense		42,000
Advertising Expense	7,200	
Miscellaneous Expense		1,425
	176,570	151,055

When the ledger and other records are reviewed, you discover the following: (1) the debits and credits in the cash account total $47,350 and $33,975, respectively; (2) a billing of $2,500 to a customer on account was not posted to the accounts receivable account;

(3) a payment of $1,800 made to a creditor on account was not posted to the accounts payable account; (4) the balance of the unearned rent account is $4,250; (5) the correct balance of the equipment account is $75,000; and (6) each account has a normal balance. Prepare a corrected unadjusted trial balance.

EX 2-19
Effect of errors on trial balance
obj. 4

The following errors occurred in posting from a two-column journal:

1. A credit of $6,150 to Accounts Payable was not posted.
2. A debit of $1,500 to Cash was posted to Miscellaneous Expense.
3. A credit of $270 to Cash was posted as $720.
4. A debit of $4,520 to Wages Expense was posted as $4,250.
5. An entry debiting Accounts Receivable and crediting Fees Earned for $11,000 was not posted.
6. A debit of $900 to Accounts Payable was posted as a credit.
7. A debit of $1,150 to Supplies was posted twice.

Considering each case individually (i.e., assuming that no other errors had occurred), indicate: (a) by "yes" or "no" whether the trial balance would be out of balance; (b) if answer to (a) is "yes," the amount by which the trial balance totals would differ; and (c) whether the Debit or Credit column of the trial balance would have the larger total. Answers should be presented in the following form, with error (1) given as an example:

	(a)	(b)	(c)
Error	Out of Balance	Difference	Larger Total
1.	yes	$6,150	debit

EX 2-20
Errors in trial balance
obj. 4
✔ Total of Credit column: $1,500,000

Identify the errors in the following trial balance. All accounts have normal balances.

Burgoo Co.
Unadjusted Trial Balance
For the Month Ending March 31, 2010

	Debit Balances	Credit Balances
Cash	90,000	
Accounts Receivable		196,800
Prepaid Insurance	43,200	
Equipment	600,000	
Accounts Payable	22,200	
Salaries Payable		15,000
Capital Stock		150,000
Retained Earnings		368,400
Dividends		72,000
Service Revenue		944,400
Salary Expense	393,720	
Advertising Expense		86,400
Miscellaneous Expense	17,880	
	1,833,000	1,833,000

EX 2-21
Entries to correct errors
obj. 4

The following errors took place in journalizing and posting transactions:

a. Rent of $6,000 paid for the current month was recorded as a debit to Rent Expense and a credit to Prepaid Rent.
b. Dividends of $18,000 were recorded as a debit to Wages Expense and a credit to Cash.

Journalize the entries to correct the errors. Omit explanations.

EX 2-22
Entries to correct errors
obj. 4

The following errors took place in journalizing and posting transactions:

a. Cash of $3,750 received on account was recorded as a debit to Fees Earned and a credit to Cash.

b. A $1,500 purchase of supplies for cash was recorded as a debit to Supplies Expense and a credit to Accounts Payable.

Journalize the entries to correct the errors. Omit explanations.

EX 2-23
Horizontal analysis of income statement

The following data (in millions) is taken from the financial statements of Williams-Sonoma for years ending 2007 and 2006:

	2007	2006
Net sales (revenues)	$3,728	$3,539
Total operating expenses	3,400	3,194

a. For Williams-Sonoma, comparing 2007 with 2006, determine the amount of change in millions and the percent of change for:

   1. Net sales (revenues)

   2. Total operating expenses

b. ▬▶ What conclusions can you draw from your analysis of the net sales and the total operating expenses?

EX 2-24
Horizontal analysis of income statement

The following data were adapted from the financial statements of Kmart Corporation, prior to its filing for bankruptcy:

	In millions	
For years ending January 31	**2000**	**1999**
Sales	$ 37,028	$ 35,925
Cost of sales (expense)	(29,658)	(28,111)
Selling, general, and administrative expenses	(7,415)	(6,514)
Operating income (loss)	$ (45)	$ 1,300

a. Prepare a horizontal analysis for the income statement showing the amount and percent of change in each of the following:

   1. Sales

   2. Cost of sales

   3. Selling, general, and administative expenses

   4. Operating income (loss)

b. Comment on the results of your horizontal analysis in part (a).

Problems Series A

PR 2-1A
Entries into T accounts and trial balance

objs. 1, 2, 3, 4

✔ 3. Total of Debit column: $62,700

Travis Fortney, an architect, opened an office on April 1, 2010. During the month, he completed the following transactions connected with his professional corporation, Travis Fortney, Architect, P.C.

a. Transferred cash from a personal bank account to an account to be used for the business in exchange for capital stock, $30,000.

b. Purchased used automobile for $19,500, paying $4,500 cash and giving a note payable for the remainder.

c. Paid April rent for office and workroom, $3,000.

d. Paid cash for supplies, $1,450.

e. Purchased office and computer equipment on account, $6,000.

f. Paid cash for annual insurance policies on automobile and equipment, $2,000.

g. Received cash from a client for plans delivered, $7,500.

h. Paid cash to creditors on account, $1,750.

i. Paid cash for miscellaneous expenses, $500.

j. Received invoice for blueprint service, due in May, $1,000.

k. Recorded fee earned on plans delivered, payment to be received in May, $5,200.
l. Paid salary of assistant, $1,600.
m. Paid cash for miscellaneous expenses, $325.
n. Paid installment due on note payable, $250.
o. Paid gas, oil, and repairs on automobile for April, $400.

Instructions

1. Record the above transactions directly in the following T accounts, without journalizing: Cash; Accounts Receivable; Supplies; Prepaid Insurance; Automobiles; Equipment; Notes Payable; Accounts Payable; Capital Stock; Professional Fees; Rent Expense; Salary Expense; Blueprint Expense; Automobile Expense; Miscellaneous Expense. To the left of each amount entered in the accounts, place the appropriate letter to identify the transaction.
2. Determine account balances of the T accounts. Accounts containing a single entry only (such as Prepaid Insurance) do not need a balance.
3. Prepare an unadjusted trial balance for Travis Fortney, Architect, P.C. as of April 30, 2010.

PR 2-2A
Journal entries and
trial balance

objs. 1, 2, 3, 4

✔ 4. c. $2,725

On October 1, 2010, Cody Doerr established Banyan Realty, which completed the following transactions during the month:

a. Cody Doerr transferred cash from a personal bank account to an account to be used for the business in exchange for capital stock, $17,500.
b. Purchased supplies on account, $1,000.
c. Earned sales commissions, receiving cash, $12,250.
d. Paid rent on office and equipment for the month, $3,800.
e. Paid creditor on account, $600.
f. Paid dividends, $3,000.
g. Paid automobile expenses (including rental charge) for month, $1,500, and miscellaneous expenses, $400.
h. Paid office salaries, $3,100.
i. Determined that the cost of supplies used was $725.

Instructions

1. Journalize entries for transactions (a) through (i), using the following account titles: Cash; Supplies; Accounts Payable; Capital Stock; Dividends; Sales Commissions; Rent Expense; Office Salaries Expense; Automobile Expense; Supplies Expense; Miscellaneous Expense. Journal entry explanations may be omitted.
2. Prepare T accounts, using the account titles in (1). Post the journal entries to these accounts, placing the appropriate letter to the left of each amount to identify the transactions. Determine the account balances, after all posting is complete. Accounts containing only a single entry do not need a balance.
3. Prepare an unadjusted trial balance as of October 31, 2010.
4. Determine the following:
    a. Amount of total revenue recorded in the ledger.
    b. Amount of total expenses recorded in the ledger.
    c. Amount of net income for October.

PR 2-3A
Journal entries and
trial balance

objs. 1, 2, 3, 4

✔ 3. Total of Credit
column: $53,400

On July 1, 2010, Jessie Halverson established an interior decorating business, Photogenic Designs. During the month, Jessie Halverson completed the following transactions related to the business:

July 1. Jessie transferred cash from a personal bank account to an account to be used for the business in exchange for capital stock, $18,000.
      4. Paid rent for period of July 4 to end of month, $1,750.
     10. Purchased a truck for $15,000, paying $1,000 cash and giving a note payable for the remainder.

July 13. Purchased equipment on account, $7,000.
    14. Purchased supplies for cash, $1,200.
    15. Paid annual premiums on property and casualty insurance, $2,700.
    15. Received cash for job completed, $7,500.
    21. Paid creditor a portion of the amount owed for equipment purchased on July 13, $2,500.
    24. Recorded jobs completed on account and sent invoices to customers, $8,600.
    26. Received an invoice for truck expenses, to be paid in August, $800.
    27. Paid utilities expense, $900.
    27. Paid miscellaneous expenses, $315.
    29. Received cash from customers on account, $3,600.
    30. Paid wages of employees, $2,400.
    31. Paid dividends, $2,000.

Instructions

1. Journalize each transaction in a two-column journal, referring to the following chart of accounts in selecting the accounts to be debited and credited. (Do not insert the account numbers in the journal at this time.) Journal entry explanations may be omitted.

11	Cash	31	Capital Stock
12	Accounts Receivable	33	Dividends
13	Supplies	41	Fees Earned
14	Prepaid Insurance	51	Wages Expense
16	Equipment	53	Rent Expense
18	Truck	54	Utilities Expense
21	Notes Payable	55	Truck Expense
22	Accounts Payable	59	Miscellaneous Expense

2. Post the journal to a ledger of four-column accounts, inserting appropriate posting references as each item is posted. Extend the balances to the appropriate balance columns after each transaction is posted.
3. Prepare an unadjusted trial balance for Photogenic Designs as of July 31, 2010.

PR 2-4A
Journal entries and trial balance

objs. 1, 2, 3, 4

✔ 4. Total of Debit column: $560,750

Dodge City Realty acts as an agent in buying, selling, renting, and managing real estate. The unadjusted trial balance on July 31, 2010, is shown below.

Dodge City Realty
Unadjusted Trial Balance
July 31, 2010

		Debit Balances	Credit Balances
11	Cash	33,920	
12	Accounts Receivable	57,200	
13	Prepaid Insurance	7,200	
14	Office Supplies	1,600	
16	Land	—	
21	Accounts Payable		9,920
22	Unearned Rent		—
23	Notes Payable		—
31	Capital Stock		10,000
32	Retained Earnings		40,480
33	Dividends	25,600	
41	Fees Earned		352,000
51	Salary and Commission Expense	224,000	
52	Rent Expense	28,000	
53	Advertising Expense	22,880	
54	Automobile Expense	10,240	
59	Miscellaneous Expense	1,760	
		412,400	412,400

The following business transactions were completed by Dodge City Realty during August 2010:

Aug. 1. Purchased office supplies on account, $2,100.
      2. Paid rent on office for month, $4,000.
      3. Received cash from clients on account, $44,600.
      5. Paid annual insurance premiums, $5,700.
      9. Returned a portion of the office supplies purchased on August 1, receiving full credit for their cost, $400.
     17. Paid advertising expense, $5,500.
     23. Paid creditors on account, $4,950.
     29. Paid miscellaneous expenses, $500.
     30. Paid automobile expense (including rental charges for an automobile), $1,500.
     31. Discovered an error in computing a commission; received cash from the salesperson for the overpayment, $1,000.
     31. Paid salaries and commissions for the month, $27,800.
     31. Recorded revenue earned and billed to clients during the month, $83,000.
     31. Purchased land for a future building site for $75,000, paying $10,000 in cash and giving a note payable for the remainder.
     31. Paid dividends, $5,000.
     31. Rented land purchased on August 31 to a local university for use as a parking lot during football season (September, October, and November); received advance payment of $3,600.

Instructions

1. Record the August 1 balance of each account in the appropriate balance column of a four-column account, write *Balance* in the item section, and place a check mark (✔) in the Posting Reference column.
2. Journalize the transactions for August in a two-column journal. Journal entry explanations may be omitted.
3. Post to the ledger, extending the account balance to the appropriate balance column after each posting.
4. Prepare an unadjusted trial balance of the ledger as of August 31, 2010.

PR 2-5A
Errors in trial balance

obj. 4

✔ 7. Total of Credit
column: $43,338.10

If the working papers correlating with this textbook are not used, omit Problem 2-5A.

The following records of Hallmark Electronic Repair Inc. are presented in the working papers:

- Journal containing entries for the period May 1–31.
- Ledger to which the May entries have been posted.
- Preliminary trial balance as of May 31, which does not balance.

Locate the errors, supply the information requested, and prepare a corrected trial balance according to the following instructions. The balances recorded in the accounts as of May 1 and the entries in the journal are correctly stated. If it is necessary to correct any posted amounts in the ledger, a line should be drawn through the erroneous figure and the correct amount inserted above. Corrections or notations may be inserted on the preliminary trial balance in any manner desired. It is not necessary to complete all of the instructions if equal trial balance totals can be obtained earlier. However, the requirements of instructions (6) and (7) should be completed in any event.

Instructions

1. Verify the totals of the preliminary trial balance, inserting the correct amounts in the schedule provided in the working papers.

2. Compute the difference between the trial balance totals.
3. Compare the listings in the trial balance with the balances appearing in the ledger, and list the errors in the space provided in the working papers.
4. Verify the accuracy of the balance of each account in the ledger, and list the errors in the space provided in the working papers.
5. Trace the postings in the ledger back to the journal, using small check marks to identify items traced. Correct any amounts in the ledger that may be necessitated by errors in posting, and list the errors in the space provided in the working papers.
6. Journalize as of May 31 the payment of $120 for gas and electricity. The bill had been paid on May 31 but was inadvertently omitted from the journal. Post to the ledger. (Revise any amounts necessitated by posting this entry.)
7. Prepare a new unadjusted trial balance.

PR 2-6A
Corrected trial balance

obj. 4

✔ 1. Total of Debit column: $475,000

Yin & Yang Video has the following unadjusted trial balance as of January 31, 2010:

Yin & Yang Video
Unadjusted Trial Balance
January 31, 2010

	Debit Balances	Credit Balances
Cash	19,000	
Accounts Receivable	34,100	
Supplies	4,464	
Prepaid Insurance	4,800	
Equipment	108,000	
Notes Payable		45,000
Accounts Payable		9,650
Capital Stock		40,000
Retained Earnings		29,400
Dividends	23,500	
Fees Earned		356,000
Wages Expense	204,000	
Rent Expense	41,700	
Advertising Expense	19,800	
Gas, Electricity, and Water Expense	11,340	
	470,704	480,050

The debit and credit totals are not equal as a result of the following errors:

a. The balance of cash was overstated by $10,000.
b. A cash receipt of $6,100 was posted as a debit to Cash of $1,600.
c. A debit of $3,500 to Accounts Receivable was not posted.
d. A return of $415 of defective supplies was erroneously posted as a $451 credit to Supplies.
e. An insurance policy acquired at a cost of $800 was posted as a credit to Prepaid Insurance.
f. The balance of Notes Payable was overstated by $9,000.
g. A credit of $1,450 in Accounts Payable was overlooked when the balance of the account was determined.
h. A debit of $2,500 for dividends was posted as a debit to Capital Stock.
i. The balance of $18,900 in Advertising Expense was entered as $19,800 in the trial balance.
j. Miscellaneous Expense, with a balance of $3,060, was omitted from the trial balance.

Instructions
1. Prepare a corrected unadjusted trial balance as of January 31 of the current year.
2. ➡ Does the fact that the unadjusted trial balance in (1) is balanced mean that there are no errors in the accounts? Explain.

Problems Series B

PR 2-1B
Entries into T accounts and trial balance

objs. 1, 2, 3, 4

✔ 3. Total of Debit column: $49,625

Brandy Corbin, an architect, opened an office on July 1, 2010. During the month, she completed the following transactions connected with her professional corporation, Brandy Corbin, Architect, P.C.:

a. Transferred cash from a personal bank account to an account to be used for the business in exchange for capital stock, $20,000.
b. Paid July rent for office and workroom, $2,500.
c. Purchased used automobile for $22,300, paying $5,000 cash and giving a note payable for the remainder.
d. Purchased office and computer equipment on account, $7,000.
e. Paid cash for supplies, $1,200.
f. Paid cash for annual insurance policies, $2,400.
g. Received cash from client for plans delivered, $4,175.
h. Paid cash for miscellaneous expenses, $240.
i. Paid cash to creditors on account, $2,500.
j. Paid installment due on note payable, $300.
k. Received invoice for blueprint service, due in August, $800.
l. Recorded fee earned on plans delivered, payment to be received in August, $3,150.
m. Paid salary of assistant, $1,500.
n. Paid gas, oil, and repairs on automobile for July, $410.

Instructions

1. Record the above transactions directly in the following T accounts, without journalizing: Cash; Accounts Receivable; Supplies; Prepaid Insurance; Automobiles; Equipment; Notes Payable; Accounts Payable; Capital Stock; Professional Fees; Rent Expense; Salary Expense; Automobile Expense; Blueprint Expense; Miscellaneous Expense. To the left of the amount entered in the accounts, place the appropriate letter to identify the transaction.
2. Determine account balances of the T accounts. Accounts containing a single entry only (such as Prepaid Insurance) do not need a balance.
3. Prepare an unadjusted trial balance for Brandy Corbin, Architect, P.C. as of July 31, 2010.

PR 2-2B
Journal entries and trial balance

objs. 1, 2, 3, 4

✔ 4. c. $11,025

On August 1, 2010, Cheryl Newsome established Titus Realty, which completed the following transactions during the month:

a. Cheryl Newsome transferred cash from a personal bank account to an account to be used for the business in exchange for capital stock, $25,000.
b. Paid rent on office and equipment for the month, $2,750.
c. Purchased supplies on account, $950.
d. Paid creditor on account, $400.
e. Earned sales commissions, receiving cash, $18,100.
f. Paid automobile expenses (including rental charge) for month, $1,000, and miscellaneous expenses, $600.
g. Paid office salaries, $2,150.
h. Determined that the cost of supplies used was $575.
i. Paid dividends, $2,000.

Instructions

1. Journalize entries for transactions (a) through (i), using the following account titles: Cash; Supplies; Accounts Payable; Capital Stock; Dividends; Sales Commissions;

Office Salaries Expense; Rent Expense; Automobile Expense; Supplies Expense; Miscellaneous Expense. Explanations may be omitted.

2. Prepare T accounts, using the account titles in (1). Post the journal entries to these accounts, placing the appropriate letter to the left of each amount to identify the transactions. Determine the account balances, after all posting is complete. Accounts containing only a single entry do not need a balance.

3. Prepare an unadjusted trial balance as of August 31, 2010.

4. Determine the following:
   a. Amount of total revenue recorded in the ledger.
   b. Amount of total expenses recorded in the ledger.
   c. Amount of net income for August.

PR 2-3B
Journal entries and
trial balance

objs. 1, 2, 3, 4

✔ 3. Total of Credit
column: $57,000

On April 1, 2010, Jose Guadalupe established an interior decorating business, Lodge Designs. During the month, Jose completed the following transactions related to the business:

Apr. 1. Jose transferred cash from a personal bank account to an account to be used for the business in exchange for capital stock, $15,000.

2. Paid rent for period of April 2 to end of month, $2,350.

6. Purchased office equipment on account, $10,000.

8. Purchased a used truck for $21,000, paying $2,000 cash and giving a note payable for the remainder.

10. Purchased supplies for cash, $1,200.

12. Received cash for job completed, $8,500.

15. Paid annual premiums on property and casualty insurance, $1,800.

23. Recorded jobs completed on account and sent invoices to customers, $6,000.

24. Received an invoice for truck expenses, to be paid in April, $1,000.

29. Paid utilities expense, $1,100.

29. Paid miscellaneous expenses, $500.

30. Received cash from customers on account, $3,500.

30. Paid wages of employees, $3,000.

30. Paid creditor a portion of the amount owed for equipment purchased on April 6, $2,500.

30. Paid dividends, $1,750.

Instructions

1. Journalize each transaction in a two-column journal, referring to the following chart of accounts in selecting the accounts to be debited and credited. (Do not insert the account numbers in the journal at this time.) Explanations may be omitted.

11	Cash	31	Capital Stock
12	Accounts Receivable	33	Dividends
13	Supplies	41	Fees Earned
14	Prepaid Insurance	51	Wages Expense
16	Equipment	53	Rent Expense
18	Truck	54	Utilities Expense
21	Notes Payable	55	Truck Expense
22	Accounts Payable	59	Miscellaneous Expense

2. Post the journal to a ledger of four-column accounts, inserting appropriate posting references as each item is posted. Extend the balances to the appropriate balance columns after each transaction is posted.

3. Prepare an unadjusted trial balance for Lodge Designs as of April 30, 2010.

PR 2-4B
Journal entries and trial balance

objs. 1, 2, 3, 4

✔ 4. Total of Debit column: $264,640

Ampere Realty acts as an agent in buying, selling, renting, and managing real estate. The unadjusted trial balance on October 31, 2010, is shown below.

Ampere Realty
Unadjusted Trial Balance
October 31, 2010

		Debit Balances	Credit Balances
11	Cash	13,150	
12	Accounts Receivable	33,750	
13	Prepaid Insurance	1,500	
14	Office Supplies	900	
16	Land	—	
21	Accounts Payable		6,510
22	Unearned Rent		—
23	Notes Payable		—
31	Capital Stock		4,000
32	Retained Earnings		12,490
33	Dividends	1,000	
41	Fees Earned		130,000
51	Salary and Commission Expense	74,100	
52	Rent Expense	15,000	
53	Advertising Expense	8,900	
54	Automobile Expense	2,750	
59	Miscellaneous Expense	1,950	
		153,000	153,000

The following business transactions were completed by Ampere Realty during November 2010:

Nov. 1. Paid rent on office for month, $3,000.
      2. Purchased office supplies on account, $1,000.
      5. Paid annual insurance premiums, $2,400.
     10. Received cash from clients on account, $25,000.
     15. Purchased land for a future building site for $90,000, paying $10,000 in cash and giving a note payable for the remainder.
     17. Paid creditors on account, $2,910.
     20. Returned a portion of the office supplies purchased on November 2, receiving full credit for their cost, $200.
     23. Paid advertising expense, $1,250.
     27. Discovered an error in computing a commission; received cash from the salesperson for the overpayment, $400.
     28. Paid automobile expense (including rental charges for an automobile), $900.
     29. Paid miscellaneous expenses, $450.
     30. Recorded revenue earned and billed to clients during the month, $31,750.
     30. Paid salaries and commissions for the month, $13,500.
     30. Paid dividends, $1,000.
     30. Rented land purchased on November 15 to local merchants association for use as a parking lot in December and January, during a street rebuilding program; received advance payment of $2,000.

Instructions
1. Record the November 1, 2010, balance of each account in the appropriate balance column of a four-column account, write *Balance* in the item section, and place a check mark (✔) in the Posting Reference column.
2. Journalize the transactions for November in a two-column journal. Journal entry explanations may be omitted.
3. Post to the ledger, extending the account balance to the appropriate balance column after each posting.
4. Prepare an unadjusted trial balance of the ledger as of November 30, 2010.

PR 2-5B
Errors in trial balance

obj. 4

✔ 7. Total of Debit
column: $43,338.10

If the working papers correlating with this textbook are not used, omit Problem 2-5B.

The following records of Hallmark Electronic Repair Inc. are presented in the working papers:

- Journal containing entries for the period May 1–31.
- Ledger to which the May entries have been posted.
- Preliminary trial balance as of May 31, which does not balance.

Locate the errors, supply the information requested, and prepare a corrected trial balance according to the following instructions. The balances recorded in the accounts as of May 1 and the entries in the journal are correctly stated. If it is necessary to correct any posted amounts in the ledger, a line should be drawn through the erroneous figure and the correct amount inserted above. Corrections or notations may be inserted on the preliminary trial balance in any manner desired. It is not necessary to complete all of the instructions if equal trial balance totals can be obtained earlier. However, the requirements of instructions (6) and (7) should be completed in any event.

Instructions

1. Verify the totals of the preliminary trial balance, inserting the correct amounts in the schedule provided in the working papers.
2. Compute the difference between the trial balance totals.
3. Compare the listings in the trial balance with the balances appearing in the ledger, and list the errors in the space provided in the working papers.
4. Verify the accuracy of the balance of each account in the ledger, and list the errors in the space provided in the working papers.
5. Trace the postings in the ledger back to the journal, using small check marks to identify items traced. Correct any amounts in the ledger that may be necessitated by errors in posting, and list the errors in the space provided in the working papers.
6. Journalize as of May 31 the payment of $175 for advertising expense. The bill had been paid on May 31 but was inadvertently omitted from the journal. Post to the ledger. (Revise any amounts necessitated by posting this entry.)
7. Prepare a new unadjusted trial balance.

PR 2-6B
Corrected trial balance

obj. 4

✔ 1. Total of Debit
column: $350,000

Damascus Carpet has the following unadjusted trial balance as of August 31, 2010.

Damascus Carpet
Unadjusted Trial Balance
August 31, 2010

	Debit Balances	Credit Balances
Cash	8,650	
Accounts Receivable	21,760	
Supplies	4,195	
Prepaid Insurance	1,550	
Equipment	98,000	
Notes Payable		45,675
Accounts Payable		13,825
Capital Stock		20,000
Retained Earnings		47,200
Dividends	25,375	
Fees Earned		214,725
Wages Expense	122,500	
Rent Expense	29,050	
Advertising Expense	1,260	
Miscellaneous Expense	2,540	
	314,880	341,425

The debit and credit totals are not equal as a result of the following errors:

a. The balance of cash was understated by $5,250.
b. A cash receipt of $3,600 was posted as a debit to Cash of $6,300.
c. A debit of $2,250 to Accounts Receivable was not posted.
d. A return of $350 of defective supplies was erroneously posted as a $530 credit to Supplies.

e. An insurance policy acquired at a cost of $300 was posted as a credit to Prepaid Insurance.

f. The balance of Notes Payable was understated by $13,125.

g. A credit of $1,575 in Accounts Payable was overlooked when determining the balance of the account.

h. A debit of $6,125 for dividends was posted as a credit to Retained Earnings.

i. The balance of $12,600 in Advertising Expense was entered as $1,260 in the trial balance.

j. Gas, Electricity, and Water Expense, with a balance of $12,075 was omitted from the trial balance.

Instructions

1. Prepare a corrected unadjusted trial balance as of August 31, 2010.

2. ➤ Does the fact that the unadjusted trial balance in (1) is balanced mean that there are no errors in the accounts? Explain.

Continuing Problem

✔ 4. Total of Debit column: $38,680

The transactions completed by Music Depot during June 2010 were described at the end of Chapter 1. The following transactions were completed during July, the second month of the business's operations:

July 1. Lee Chang made an additional investment in Music Depot by depositing $2,500 in Music Depot's checking account in exchange for capital stock.

1. Instead of continuing to share office space with a local real estate agency, Lee decided to rent office space near a local music store. Paid rent for July, $2,000.

1. Paid a premium of $2,700 for a comprehensive insurance policy covering liability, theft, and fire. The policy covers a one-year period.

2. Received $1,350 on account.

3. On behalf of Music Depot, Lee signed a contract with a local radio station, WHBD, to provide guest spots for the next three months. The contract requires Music Depot to provide a guest disc jockey for 80 hours per month for a monthly fee of $3,600. Any additional hours beyond 80 will be billed to WHBD at $40 per hour. In accordance with the contract, Lee received $7,200 from WHBD as an advance payment for the first two months.

3. Paid $250 on account.

4. Paid an attorney $500 for reviewing the July 3rd contract with WHBD. (Record as Miscellaneous Expense.)

5. Purchased office equipment on account from One-Stop Office Mart, $5,000.

8. Paid for a newspaper advertisement, $200.

11. Received $800 for serving as a disc jockey for a party.

13. Paid $600 to a local audio electronics store for rental of digital recording equipment.

14. Paid wages of $1,000 to receptionist and part-time assistant.

16. Received $1,750 for serving as a disc jockey for a wedding reception.

18. Purchased supplies on account, $680.

21. Paid $420 to Upload Music for use of its current music demos in making various music sets.

22. Paid $800 to a local radio station to advertise the services of Music Depot twice daily for the remainder of July.

23. Served as disc jockey for a party for $2,500. Received $750, with the remainder due August 4, 2010.

27. Paid electric bill, $560.

July 28. Paid wages of $1,000 to receptionist and part-time assistant.
29. Paid miscellaneous expenses, $150.
30. Served as a disc jockey for a charity ball for $1,800. Received $400, with the remainder due on August 9, 2010.
31. Received $2,800 for serving as a disc jockey for a party.
31. Paid $1,100 royalties (music expense) to National Music Clearing for use of various artists' music during July.
31. Paid dividends of $1,500.

Music Depot's chart of accounts and the balance of accounts as of July 1, 2010 (all normal balances), are as follows:

11	Cash	$ 8,010	41	Fees Earned	$5,650
12	Accounts Receivable	1,350	50	Wages Expense	400
14	Supplies	170	51	Office Rent Expense	750
15	Prepaid Insurance	—	52	Equipment Rent Expense	500
17	Office Equipment	—	53	Utilities Expense	300
21	Accounts Payable	250	54	Music Expense	1,290
23	Unearned Revenue	—	55	Advertising Expense	600
31	Capital Stock	8,000	56	Supplies Expense	180
33	Dividends	200	59	Miscellaneous Expense	150

Instructions

1. Enter the July 1, 2010, account balances in the appropriate balance column of a four-column account. Write *Balance* in the Item column, and place a check mark (✔) in the Posting Reference column. (*Hint:* Verify the equality of the debit and credit balances in the ledger before proceeding with the next instruction.)
2. Analyze and journalize each transaction in a two-column journal, omitting journal entry explanations.
3. Post the journal to the ledger, extending the account balance to the appropriate balance column after each posting.
4. Prepare an unadjusted trial balance as of July 31, 2010.

Special Activities

SA 2-1
Ethics and professional conduct in business

At the end of the current month, Hannah Kinsey prepared a trial balance for Seaside Rescue Service. The credit side of the trial balance exceeds the debit side by a significant amount. Hannah has decided to add the difference to the balance of the miscellaneous expense account in order to complete the preparation of the current month's financial statements by a 5 o'clock deadline. Hannah will look for the difference next week when she has more time.

➤ Discuss whether Hannah is behaving in a professional manner.

SA 2-2
Account for revenue

Roswell College requires students to pay tuition each term before classes begin. Students who have not paid their tuition are not allowed to enroll or to attend classes.

What journal entry do you think Roswell College would use to record the receipt of the students' tuition payments? Describe the nature of each account in the entry.

SA 2-3
Record transactions

The following discussion took place between Faye Lucas, the office manager of Typhoon Data Company, and a new accountant, Steve Haack.

Steve: I've been thinking about our method of recording entries. It seems that it's inefficient.

Faye: In what way?

Steve: Well—correct me if I'm wrong—it seems like we have unnecessary steps in the process. We could easily develop a trial balance by posting our transactions directly into the ledger and bypassing the journal altogether. In this way, we could combine the recording and posting process into one step and save ourselves a lot of time. What do you think?

Faye: We need to have a talk.

━━━▶ What should Faye say to Steve?

SA 2-4
Debits and credits

Group Project

The following excerpt is from a conversation between Barb Thiel, the president and chief operating officer of Teton Construction Company, and her neighbor, Loyd Crum.

Loyd: Barb, I'm taking a course in night school, "Intro to Accounting." I was wondering—could you answer a couple of questions for me?

Barb: Well, I will if I can.

Loyd: Okay, our instructor says that it's critical we understand the basic concepts of accounting, or we'll never get beyond the first test. My problem is with those rules of debit and credit . . . you know, assets increase with debits, decrease with credits, etc.

Barb: Yes, pretty basic stuff. You just have to memorize the rules. It shouldn't be too difficult.

Loyd: Sure, I can memorize the rules, but my problem is I want to be sure I understand the basic concepts behind the rules. For example, why can't assets be increased with credits and decreased with debits like revenue? As long as everyone did it that way, why not? It would seem easier if we had the same rules for all increases and decreases in accounts. Also, why is the left side of an account called the debit side? Why couldn't it be called something simple . . . like the "LE" for Left Entry? The right side could be called just "RE" for Right Entry. Finally, why are there just two sides to an entry? Why can't there be three or four sides to an entry?

In a group of four or five, select one person to play the role of Barb and one person to play the role of Loyd.

1. ━━━▶ After listening to the conversation between Barb and Loyd, help Barb answer Loyd's questions.
2. What information (other than just debit and credit journal entries) could the accounting system gather that might be useful to Barb in managing Teton Construction Company?

SA 2-5
Transactions and income statement

Cody Packwood is planning to manage and operate Ace Caddy Service at Hattiesburg Golf and Country Club during June through August 2010. Cody will rent a small maintenance building from the country club for $600 per month and will offer caddy services, including cart rentals, to golfers. Cody has had no formal training in record keeping.

Cody keeps notes of all receipts and expenses in a shoe box. An examination of Cody's shoe box records for June revealed the following:

June   1. Withdrew $2,500 from personal bank account to be used to operate the caddy service.
       1. Paid rent to Hattiesburg Golf and Country Club, $600.
       2. Paid for golf supplies (practice balls, etc.), $750.
       3. Arranged for the rental of 25 regular (pulling) golf carts and 10 gasoline-driven carts for $2,000 per month. Paid $500 in advance, with the remaining $1,500 due June 20.
       7. Purchased supplies, including gasoline, for the golf carts on account, $500. Hattiesburg Golf and Country Club has agreed to allow Cody to store the gasoline in one of its fuel tanks at no cost.
     15. Received cash for services from June 1–15, $2,350.
     17. Paid cash to creditors on account, $500.
     20. Paid remaining rental on golf carts, $1,500.
     22. Purchased supplies, including gasoline, on account, $400.
     25. Accepted IOUs from customers on account, $1,200.
     28. Paid miscellaneous expenses, $150.
     30. Received cash for services from June 16–30, $2,650.
     30. Paid telephone and electricity (utilities) expenses, $140.
     30. Paid wages of part-time employees, $450.

June 30. Received cash in payment of IOUs on account, $800.
  30. Determined the amount of supplies on hand at the end of June, $425.

Cody has asked you several questions concerning his financial affairs to date, and he has asked you to assist with his record keeping and reporting of financial data.

a. To assist Cody with his record keeping, prepare a chart of accounts that would be appropriate for Ace Caddy Service. *Note:* Small businesses such as Ace Caddy Service are often organized as proprietorships. The accounting for proprietorships is similar to that for a corporation, except that the owner's equity accounts differ. Specifically, instead of the account for Capital Stock, a capital account entitled Cody Packwood, Capital is used to record investments in the business. In addition, instead of a dividends account, withdrawals from the business are debited to Cody Packwood, Drawing. A proprietorship has no retained earnings account.

b. Prepare an income statement for June in order to help Cody assess the profitability of Ace Caddy Service. For this purpose, the use of T accounts may be helpful in analyzing the effects of each June transaction.

c. Based on Cody's records of receipts and payments, calculate the amount of cash on hand on June 30. For this purpose, a T account for cash may be useful.

d. ━━━▶ A count of the cash on hand on June 30 totaled $3,600. Briefly discuss the possible causes of the difference between the amount of cash computed in (c) and the actual amount of cash on hand.

SA 2-6
Opportunities for accountants

<u>Internet Project</u>

The increasing complexity of the current business and regulatory environment has created an increased demand for accountants who can analyze business transactions and interpret their effects on the financial statements. In addition, a basic ability to analyze the effects of transactions is necessary to be successful in all fields of business as well as in other disciplines, such as law. To better understand the importance of accounting in today's environment, search the Internet or your local newspaper for job opportunities. One possible Internet site is **http://www.monster.com**. Then do one of the following:

1. Print a listing of at least two ads for accounting jobs. Alternatively, bring to class at least two newspaper ads for accounting jobs.
2. Print a listing of at least two ads for nonaccounting jobs for which some knowledge of accounting is preferred or necessary. Alternatively, bring to class at least two newspaper ads for such jobs.

Answers to Self-Examination Questions ● ● ● ● ●▶

1. **A** A debit may signify an increase in an asset account (answer A) or a decrease in a liability or capital stock account. A credit may signify a decrease in an asset account (answer B) or an increase in a liability or capital stock account (answers C and D).

2. **C** Liability, capital stock, retained earnings, and revenue (answer C) accounts have normal credit balances. Asset (answer A), dividends (answer B), and expense (answer D) accounts have normal debit balances.

3. **C** Accounts Receivable (answer A), Cash (answer B), and Miscellaneous Expense (answer D) would all normally have debit balances. Fees Earned should normally have a credit balance. Hence, a debit balance in Fees Earned (answer C) would indicate a likely error in the recording process.

4. **A** The receipt of cash from customers on account increases the asset Cash and decreases the asset Accounts Receivable, as indicated by answer A. Answer B has the debit and credit reversed, and answers C and D involve transactions with creditors (accounts payable) and not customers (accounts receivable).

5. **D** The trial balance (answer D) is a listing of the balances and the titles of the accounts in the ledger on a given date, so that the equality of the debits and credits in the ledger can be verified. The income statement (answer A) is a summary of revenue and expenses for a period of time. The balance sheet (answer B) is a presentation of the assets, liabilities, and stockholders' equity on a given date. The retained earnings statement (answer C) is a summary of the changes in retained earnings for a period of time.

CHAPTER 3

The Adjusting Process

MARVEL ENTERTAINMENT, INC.

Do you subscribe to any magazines? Most of us subscribe to one or more magazines such as *Cosmopolitan, Sports Illustrated, Golf Digest, Newsweek,* or *Rolling Stone.* Magazines usually require you to prepay the yearly subscription price before you receive any issues. When should the magazine company record revenue from the subscriptions?

As we discussed in Chapter 2, sometimes revenues are earned and expenses are incurred at the point cash is received or paid. For transactions such as magazine subscriptions, the revenue is earned when the magazine is delivered, not when the cash is received. Most companies are required to account for revenues and expenses when the benefit is substantially provided or consumed, which may not be when cash is received or paid.

One company that records revenue from subscriptions is Marvel Entertainment, Inc. Marvel began in 1939 as a comic book publishing company, establishing such popular comic book characters as Spider-Man®, X-Men®, Fantastic Four®, and the Avengers®. From these humble beginnings, Marvel has grown into a full-line, multi-billion-dollar entertainment company. Marvel not only publishes comic books, but it has also added feature films, such as the *Spider-Man* movies, video games, and toys to its product offerings.

Most companies, like Marvel Entertainment, are required to update their accounting records for items such as revenues earned from magazine subscriptions before preparing their financial statements. In this chapter, we describe and illustrate this updating process.

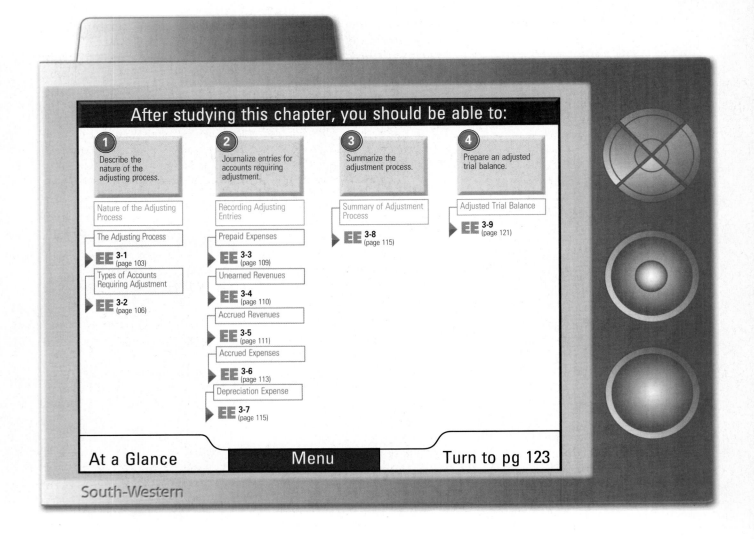

After studying this chapter, you should be able to:

1 Describe the nature of the adjusting process.

Nature of the Adjusting Process

The Adjusting Process

EE 3-1 (page 103)

Types of Accounts Requiring Adjustment

EE 3-2 (page 106)

2 Journalize entries for accounts requiring adjustment.

Recording Adjusting Entries

Prepaid Expenses

EE 3-3 (page 109)

Unearned Revenues

EE 3-4 (page 110)

Accrued Revenues

EE 3-5 (page 111)

Accrued Expenses

EE 3-6 (page 113)

Depreciation Expense

EE 3-7 (page 115)

3 Summarize the adjustment process.

Summary of Adjustment Process

EE 3-8 (page 115)

4 Prepare an adjusted trial balance.

Adjusted Trial Balance

EE 3-9 (page 121)

At a Glance   Menu   Turn to pg 123

South-Western

1 Describe the nature of the adjusting process.

Nature of the Adjusting Process

When preparing financial statements, the economic life of the business is divided into time periods. This **accounting period concept** requires that revenues and expenses be reported in the proper period. To determine the proper period, accountants use generally accepted accounting principles (GAAP). The use of the accrual basis of accounting is required by GAAP.

Under the **accrual basis of accounting**, revenues are reported in the income statement in the period in which they are earned. For example, revenue is reported when the services are provided to customers. Cash may or may not be received from customers during this period. The accounting concept supporting this reporting of revenues is called the **revenue recognition concept**.

Under the accrual basis, expenses are reported in the same period as the revenues to which they relate. For example, utility expenses incurred in December are reported as an expense and matched against December's revenues even though the utility bill may not be paid until January. The accounting concept supporting reporting revenues and related expenses in the same period is called the **matching concept**, or **matching principle**. By matching revenues and expenses, net income or loss for the period is properly reported on the income statement.

Although GAAP requires the accrual basis of accounting, some businesses use the **cash basis of accounting**. Under the cash basis of accounting, revenues and expenses are

American Airlines uses the accrual basis of accounting. Revenues are recognized when passengers take flights, not when the passenger makes the reservation or pays for the ticket.

reported in the income statement in the period in which cash is received or paid. For example, fees are recorded when cash is received from clients; likewise, wages are recorded when cash is paid to employees. The net income (or net loss) is the difference between the cash receipts (revenues) and the cash payments (expenses).

Small service businesses may use the cash basis, because they have few receivables and payables. For example, attorneys, physicians, and real estate agents often use the cash basis. For them, the cash basis provides financial statements similar to those of the accrual basis. For most large businesses, however, the cash basis will not provide accurate financial statements for user needs. For this reason, we use the accrual basis in this text.

> The matching concept supports reporting revenues and related expenses in the same period.

The Adjusting Process

At the end of the accounting period, many of the account balances in the ledger can be reported in the financial statements without change. For example, the balances of the cash and land accounts are normally the amount reported on the balance sheet.

Under the accrual basis, however, some accounts in the ledger require updating.[1] This updating is required for the following reasons:

1. Some expenses are not recorded daily. For example, the daily use of supplies would require many entries with small amounts. Also, managers usually do not need to know the amount of supplies on hand on a day-to-day basis.
2. Some revenues and expenses are incurred as time passes rather than as separate transactions. For example, rent received in advance (unearned rent) expires and becomes revenue with the passage of time. Likewise, prepaid insurance expires and becomes an expense with the passage of time.
3. Some revenues and expenses may be unrecorded. For example, a company may have provided services to customers that it has not billed or recorded at the end of the accounting period. Likewise, a company may not pay its employees until the next accounting period even though the employees have earned their wages in the current period.

> All adjusting entries affect at least one income statement account and one balance sheet account.

The analysis and updating of accounts at the end of the period before the financial statements are prepared is called the **adjusting process**. The journal entries that bring the accounts up to date at the end of the accounting period are called **adjusting entries**. All adjusting entries affect at least one income statement account and one balance sheet account. Thus, an adjusting entry will *always* involve a revenue or an expense account *and* an asset or a liability account.

Example Exercise 3-1   Accounts Requiring Adjustment   •••••••• 1

Indicate with a Yes or No whether or not each of the following accounts normally requires an adjusting entry.

a.	Cash	c.	Wages Expense	e.	Accounts Receivable
b.	Prepaid Rent	d.	Office Equipment	f.	Unearned Rent

Follow My Example 3-1

a.	No	c.	Yes	e.	Yes
b.	Yes	d.	No	f.	Yes

For Practice: PE 3-1A, PE 3-1B

---

1 Under the cash basis of accounting, accounts do not require adjusting. This is because transactions are recorded only when cash is received or paid. Thus, the matching concept is not used under the cash basis.

Types of Accounts Requiring Adjustment

Four basic types of accounts require adjusting entries as shown below.

1. Prepaid expenses
2. Unearned revenues
3. Accrued revenues
4. Accrued expenses

Prepaid expenses are the advance payment of *future* expenses and are recorded as assets when cash is paid. Prepaid expenses become expenses over time or during normal operations. To illustrate, the following transaction of NetSolutions from Chapter 2 is used.

The tuition you pay at the beginning of each term is an example of a prepaid expense to you, as a student.

| Dec. 1 | NetSolutions paid $2,400 as a premium on a one-year insurance policy. |

On December 1, the cash payment of $2,400 was recorded as a debit to Prepaid Insurance and credit to Cash for $2,400. At the end of December, only $200 ($2,400 divided by 12 months) of the insurance premium is expired and has become an expense. The remaining $2,200 of prepaid insurance will become an expense in future months. Thus, the $200 is insurance expense of December and should be recorded with an adjusting entry.

Other examples of prepaid expenses include supplies, prepaid advertising, and prepaid interest.

Unearned revenues are the advance receipt of *future* revenues and are recorded as liabilities when cash is received. Unearned revenues become earned revenues over time or during normal operations. To illustrate, we use the following December 1 transaction of NetSolutions.

| Dec. 1 | NetSolutions received $360 from a local retailer to rent land for three months. |

On December 1, the cash receipt of $360 was recorded as a debit to Cash and a credit to Unearned Rent for $360. At the end of December, $120 ($360 divided by 3 months) of the unearned rent has been earned. The remaining $240 will become rent revenue in future months. Thus, the $120 is rent revenue of December and should be recorded with an adjusting entry.

Other examples of unearned revenues include tuition received in advance by a school, an annual retainer fee received by an attorney, premiums received in advance by an insurance company, and magazine subscriptions received in advance by a publisher.

Exhibit 1 illustrates the nature of prepaid expenses and unearned revenues.

Exhibit 1

Type of Adjustments: Prepaid Expenses and Unearned Revenues

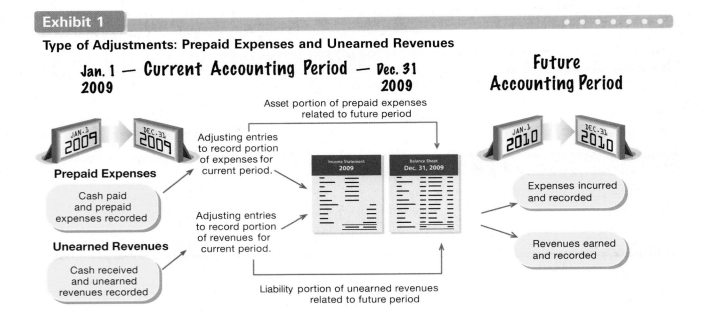

netsolutions

Accrued revenues are unrecorded revenues that have been earned and for which cash has yet to be received. Fees for services that an attorney or a doctor has provided but not yet billed are accrued revenues. To illustrate, we use the following example involving NetSolutions and one of its customers.

> **Dec. 15** NetSolutions signed an agreement with Dankner Co. on December 15 under which NetSolutions will bill Dankner Co. on the fifteenth of each month for services rendered at the rate of $20 per hour.

From December 16–31, NetSolutions provided 25 hours of service to Dankner Co. Although the revenue of $500 (25 hours × $20) has been earned, it will not be billed until January 15. Likewise, cash of $500 will not be received until Dankner pays its bill. Thus, the $500 of accrued revenue and the $500 of fees earned should be recorded with an adjusting entry on December 31.

Other examples of accrued revenues include accrued interest on notes receivable and accrued rent on property rented to others.

Accrued expenses are unrecorded expenses that have been incurred and for which cash has yet to be paid. Wages owed to employees at the end of a period but not yet paid is an accrued expense. To illustrate, the following example involving NetSolutions and its employees is used:

> **Dec. 31** NetSolutions owes its employees wages of $250 for Monday and Tuesday, December 30 and 31.

NetSolutions paid wages of $950 on December 13 and $1,200 on December 27, 2009. These payments covered the biweekly pay periods that ended on those days. As of December 31, 2009, NetSolutions owes its employees wages of $250 for Monday and Tuesday, December 30 and 31. The wages of $250 will be paid on January 10, 2010, however, they are an expense of December. Thus, $250 of accrued wages should be recorded with an adjusting entry on December 31.

Other examples of accrued expenses include accrued interest on notes payable and accrued taxes.

As illustrated above, accrued revenues are earned revenues that are unrecorded. The cash receipts for accrued revenues are normally received in the next accounting period. Accrued expenses are expenses that have been incurred, but are unrecorded. The cash payments for accrued expenses are normally paid in the next accounting period. Exhibit 2 illustrates the nature of accrued revenues and accrued expenses.

Exhibit 2

Type of Adjustments: Accrued Revenues and Expenses

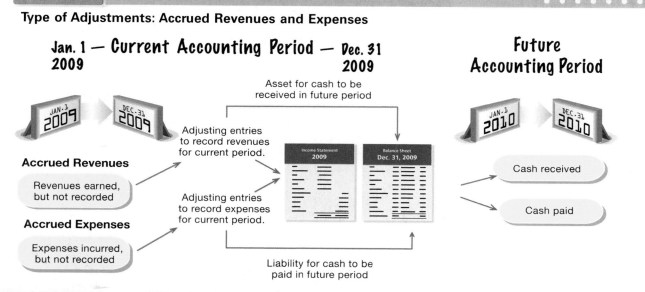

Prepaid expenses and unearned revenues are sometimes referred to as *deferrals*. This is because the recording of the related expense or revenue is deferred to a future period. Accrued revenues and accrued expenses are sometimes referred to as *accruals*. This is because the related revenue or expense should be recorded or accrued in the current period.

Example Exercise 3-2 Type of Adjustment 1

Classify the following items as (1) prepaid expense, (2) unearned revenue, (3) accrued expense, or (4) accrued revenue.

a. Wages owed but not yet paid.

b. Supplies on hand.

c. Fees received but not yet earned.

d. Fees earned but not yet received.

Follow My Example 3-2

a. Accrued expense

b. Prepaid expense

c. Unearned revenue

d. Accrued revenue

For Practice: PE 3-2A, PE 3-2B

2 Journalize entries for accounts requiring adjustment.

Recording Adjusting Entries

To illustrate adjusting entries, we use the December 31, 2009, unadjusted trial balance of NetSolutions shown in Exhibit 3. An expanded chart of accounts for NetSolutions is shown in Exhibit 4. The additional accounts used in this chapter are shown in color. The rules of debit and credit shown in Exhibit 3 of Chapter 2 are used to record the adjusting entries.

Exhibit 3

Unadjusted Trial Balance for NetSolutions

 netsolutions

NetSolutions Unadjusted Trial Balance December 31, 2009	Debit Balances	Credit Balances
Cash	2,065	
Accounts Receivable	2,220	
Supplies	2,000	
Prepaid Insurance	2,400	
Land	20,000	
Office Equipment	1,800	
Accounts Payable		900
Unearned Rent		360
Capital Stock		25,000
Dividends	4,000	
Fees Earned		16,340
Wages Expense	4,275	
Rent Expense	1,600	
Utilities Expense	985	
Supplies Expense	800	
Miscellaneous Expense	455	
	42,600	42,600

Exhibit 4

**Expanded Chart
of Accounts for
NetSolutions**

Balance Sheet Accounts		Income Statement Accounts	
1. Assets		**4. Revenue**	
11	Cash	41	Fees Earned
12	Accounts Receivable	42	Rent Revenue
14	Supplies		**5. Expenses**
15	Prepaid Insurance	51	Wages Expense
17	Land	52	Rent Expense
18	Office Equipment	53	Depreciation Expense
19	Accumulated Depreciation—Office Equipment	54	Utilities Expense
	2. Liabilities	55	Supplies Expense
21	Accounts Payable	56	Insurance Expense
22	Wages Payable	59	Miscellaneous Expense
23	Unearned Rent		
	3. Stockholders' Equity		
31	Capital Stock		
32	Retained Earnings		
33	Dividends		

Prepaid Expenses

The balance in NetSolutions' supplies account on December 31 is $2,000. Some of these supplies (CDs, paper, envelopes, etc.) were used during December, and some are still on hand (not used). If either amount is known, the other can be determined. It is normally easier to determine the cost of the supplies on hand at the end of the month than to record daily supplies used. Assuming that on December 31 the amount of supplies on hand is $760, the amount to be transferred from the asset account to the expense account is $1,240, computed as follows:

Supplies available during December (balance of account)	$2,000
Supplies on hand, December 31	760
Supplies used (amount of adjustment)	$1,240

At the end of December, the supplies expense account should be increased (debited) for $1,240, and the supplies account should be decreased (credited) for $1,240 to record the supplies used during December. The adjusting journal entry and T accounts for Supplies and Supplies Expense are as follows:

Journal					Page *5*
Date	Description	Post. Ref.	Debit	Credit	
2009 Dec. 31	Supplies Expense	55	1,240		
	Supplies	14		1,240	
	Supplies used ($2,000 − $760).				

Supplies				Supplies Expense	
Bal.	2,000	Dec. 31	1,240	Bal.	800
Adj. Bal.	760			Dec. 31	1,240
				Adj. Bal.	2,040

The adjusting entry is shown in color in the T accounts to separate it from other transactions. After the adjusting entry is recorded and posted, the supplies account has a debit balance of $760. This balance is an asset that will become an expense in a future period.

The debit balance of $2,400 in NetSolutions' prepaid insurance account represents a December 1 prepayment of insurance for 12 months. At the end of December, the insurance expense account should be increased (debited), and the prepaid insurance account should be decreased (credited) by $200, the insurance for one month. The adjusting journal entry and T accounts for Prepaid Insurance and Insurance Expense are as follows:

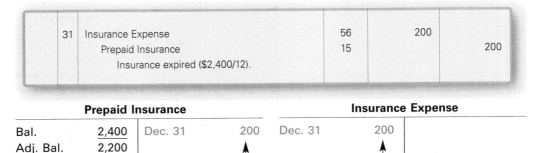

	31	Insurance Expense	56	200	
		Prepaid Insurance	15		200
		Insurance expired ($2,400/12).			

Prepaid Insurance				**Insurance Expense**	
Bal.	2,400	Dec. 31	200	Dec. 31	200
Adj. Bal.	2,200				

After the adjusting entry is recorded and posted, the prepaid insurance account has a debit balance of $2,200. This balance is an asset that will become an expense in future periods. The insurance expense account has a debit balance of $200, which is an expense of the current period.

> The adjusted balance of a prepaid expense is an asset that will become an expense in a future period.

What is the effect of omitting adjusting entries? If the preceding adjustments for supplies ($1,240) and insurance ($200) are not recorded, the financial statements prepared as of December 31 will be misstated. On the income statement, Supplies Expense and Insurance Expense will be understated by a total of $1,440 ($1,240 + $200), and net income will be overstated by $1,440. On the balance sheet, Supplies and Prepaid Insurance will be overstated by a total of $1,440. Since net income increases Retained Earnings, stockholders' equity will also be overstated by $1,440 on the balance sheet. The effects of omitting these adjusting entries on the income statement and balance sheet are as follows:

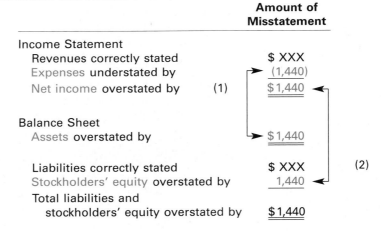

			Amount of Misstatement
Income Statement			
Revenues correctly stated			$ XXX
Expenses understated by			(1,440)
Net income overstated by	(1)		$ 1,440
Balance Sheet			
Assets overstated by			$ 1,440
Liabilities correctly stated			$ XXX
Stockholders' equity overstated by		(2)	1,440
Total liabilities and			
stockholders' equity overstated by			$ 1,440

Arrow (1) indicates the effect of the understated expenses on assets. Arrow (2) indicates the effect of the overstated net income on stockholders' equity.

Integrity, Objectivity, and Ethics in Business

FREE ISSUE

Office supplies are often available to employees on a "free issue" basis. This means that employees do not have to "sign" for the release of office supplies but merely obtain the necessary supplies from a local storage area as needed. Just because supplies are easily available, however, doesn't mean they can be taken for personal use. There are many instances where employees have been terminated for taking supplies home for personal use.

Payments for prepaid expenses are sometimes made at the beginning of the period in which they will be *entirely used or consumed*. To illustrate, we use the following December 1 transaction of NetSolutions:

> Dec. 1   NetSolutions paid rent of $800 for the month.

On December 1, the rent payment of $800 represents Prepaid Rent. However, the Prepaid Rent expires daily, and at the end of December there will be no asset left. In such cases, the payment of $800 is recorded as Rent Expense rather than as Prepaid Rent. In this way, no adjusting entry is needed at the end of the period.[2]

Example Exercise 3-3   Adjustment for Prepaid Expense   •••••••• ➤ 2

The prepaid insurance account had a beginning balance of $6,400 and was debited for $3,600 of premiums paid during the year. Journalize the adjusting entry required at the end of the year assuming the amount of unexpired insurance related to future periods is $3,250.

Follow My Example 3-3

Insurance Expense	6,750	
Prepaid Insurance		6,750
Insurance expired ($6,400 + $3,600 − $3,250).		

For Practice: PE 3-3A, PE 3-3B

Unearned Revenues

The December 31 unadjusted trial balance of NetSolutions indicates a balance in the unearned rent account of $360. This balance represents the receipt of three months rent on December 1 for December, January, and February. At the end of December, one month's rent has been earned. Thus, the unearned rent account should be decreased (debited) by $120, and the rent revenue account should be increased (credited) by $120. The $120 represents the rental revenue for one month ($360/3). The adjusting journal entry and T accounts are shown below.

31	Unearned Rent	23	120	
	Rent Revenue	42		120
	Rent earned ($360/3 months).			

Unearned Rent				**Rent Revenue**		
Dec. 31	120	Bal.	360		Dec. 31	120
		Adj. Bal.	240			

After the adjusting entry is recorded and posted, the unearned rent account has a credit balance of $240. This balance is a liability that will become revenue in a future period. Rent Revenue has a balance of $120, which is revenue of the current period.[3]

If the preceding adjustment of unearned rent and rent revenue is not recorded, the financial statements prepared on December 31 will be misstated. On the income statement, Rent Revenue and the net income will be understated by $120. On the balance sheet, Unearned Rent will be overstated by $120, and stockholders' equity (Retained Earnings) will be understated by $120. The effects of omitting this adjusting entry are shown at the top of the next page.

2 An alternative treatment of recording the cost of supplies, rent, and other prepayments of expenses is discussed in an appendix that can be downloaded from the book's companion Web site (www.cengage.com/accounting/warren)

3 An alternative treatment of recording revenues received in advance of their being earned is discussed in an appendix that can be downloaded from the book's companion Web site (www.cengage.com/accounting/warren).

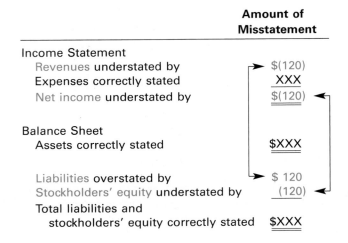

	Amount of Misstatement
Income Statement	
Revenues understated by	$(120)
Expenses correctly stated	XXX
Net income understated by	$(120)
Balance Sheet	
Assets correctly stated	$XXX
Liabilities overstated by	$ 120
Stockholders' equity understated by	(120)
Total liabilities and stockholders' equity correctly stated	$XXX

Example Exercise 3-4 Adjustment for Unearned Revenue ········» 2

The balance in the unearned fees account, before adjustment at the end of the year, is $44,900. Journalize the adjusting entry required if the amount of unearned fees at the end of the year is $22,300.

Follow My Example 3-4

Unearned Fees	22,600	
Fees Earned		22,600
Fees earned ($44,900 − $22,300).		

For Practice: PE 3-4A, PE 3-4B

Accrued Revenues

RadioShack Corporation is engaged in consumer electronics retailing. RadioShack accrues revenue for finance charges, late charges, and returned check fees related to its credit operations.

During an accounting period, some revenues are recorded only when cash is received. Thus, at the end of an accounting period, there may be revenue that has been earned *but has not been recorded*. In such cases, the revenue should be recorded by increasing (debiting) an asset account and increasing (crediting) a revenue account.

To illustrate, assume that NetSolutions signed an agreement with Dankner Co. on December 15. The agreement provides that NetSolutions will answer computer questions and render assistance to Dankner Co.'s employees. The services will be billed to Dankner Co. on the fifteenth of each month at a rate of $20 per hour. As of December 31, NetSolutions had provided 25 hours of assistance to Dankner Co. The revenue of $500 (25 hours × $20) will be billed on January 15. However, NetSolutions earned the revenue in December.

The claim against the customer for payment of the $500 is an account receivable (*an asset*). Thus, the accounts receivable account should be increased (debited) by $500 and the fees earned account should be increased (credited) by $500. The adjusting journal entry and T accounts are shown below.

31	Accounts Receivable	12	500	
	Fees Earned	41		500
	Accrued fees (25 hrs. × $20).			

Accounts Receivable			Fees Earned	
Bal.	2,220		Bal.	16,340
Dec. 31	500		Dec. 31	500
Adj. Bal.	2,720		Adj. Bal.	16,840

If the adjustment for the accrued revenue ($500) is not recorded, Fees Earned and the net income will be understated by $500 on the income statement. On the balance sheet, Accounts Receivable and stockholders' equity (Retained Earnings) will be understated by $500. The effects of omitting this adjusting entry are shown below.

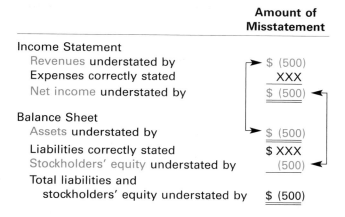

	Amount of Misstatement
Income Statement	
Revenues understated by	$ (500)
Expenses correctly stated	XXX
Net income understated by	$ (500)
Balance Sheet	
Assets understated by	$ (500)
Liabilities correctly stated	$ XXX
Stockholders' equity understated by	(500)
Total liabilities and stockholders' equity understated by	$ (500)

Example Exercise 3-5   Adjustment for Accrued Revenues   ●●●●●●●● ▶ ②

At the end of the current year, $13,680 of fees have been earned but have not been billed to clients. Journalize the adjusting entry to record the accrued fees.

Follow My Example 3-5

```
Accounts Receivable . . . . . . . . . . . . . . . . . . . . . . . . . . . . . . . . . . . . . . .  13,680
    Fees Earned   . . . . . . . . . . . . . . . . . . . . . . . . . . . . . . . . . . . . . . . . .              13,680
        Accrued fees.
```

For Practice: PE 3-5A, PE 3-5B

Accrued Expenses

Some types of services used in earning revenues are paid for *after* the service has been performed. For example, wages expense is used hour by hour, but is paid only daily, weekly, biweekly, or monthly. At the end of the accounting period, the amount of such *accrued* but unpaid items is an expense and a liability.

For example, if the last day of the employees' pay period is not the last day of the accounting period, an accrued expense (wages expense) and the related liability (wages payable) must be recorded by an adjusting entry. This adjusting entry is necessary so that expenses are properly matched to the period in which they were incurred in earning revenue.

To illustrate, NetSolutions pays its employees biweekly. During December, NetSolutions paid wages of $950 on December 13 and $1,200 on December 27. These payments covered pay periods ending on those days as shown in Exhibit 5. As of December 31, NetSolutions owes $250 of wages to employees for Monday and Tuesday, December 30 and 31. Thus, the wages expense account should be increased (debited) by $250 and the wages payable account should be increased (credited) by $250. The adjusting journal entry and T accounts are shown below.

31	Wages Expense	51	250	
	Wages Payable	22		250
	Accrued wages.			

Callaway Golf Company, a manufacturer of such innovative golf clubs as the "Big Bertha" driver, reports accrued warranty expense on its balance sheet.

Wages Expense			**Wages Payable**		
Bal.	4,275			Dec. 31	250
Dec. 31	250				
Adj. Bal.	4,525				

After the adjusting entry is recorded and posted, the debit balance of the wages expense account is $4,525. This balance of $4,525 is the wages expense for two months, November and December. The credit balance of $250 in Wages Payable is the liability for wages owed on December 31.

As shown in Exhibit 5, NetSolutions paid wages of $1,275 on January 10. This payment includes the $250 of accrued wages recorded on December 31. Thus, on January 10, the wages payable account should be decreased (debited) by $250. Also, the wages expense account should be increased (debited) by $1,025 ($1,275 − $250), which is the wages expense for January 1–10. Finally, the cash account is decreased (credited) by $1,275. The journal entry for the payment of wages on January 10 is shown below.[4]

Jan.	10	Wages Expense	51	1,025	
		Wages Payable	22	250	
		Cash	11		1,275

What would be the effect on the financial statements if the adjustment for wages ($250) is not recorded? On the income statement, Wages Expense will be understated by $250, and the net income will be overstated by $250. On the balance sheet, Wages

Exhibit 5

Accrued Wages

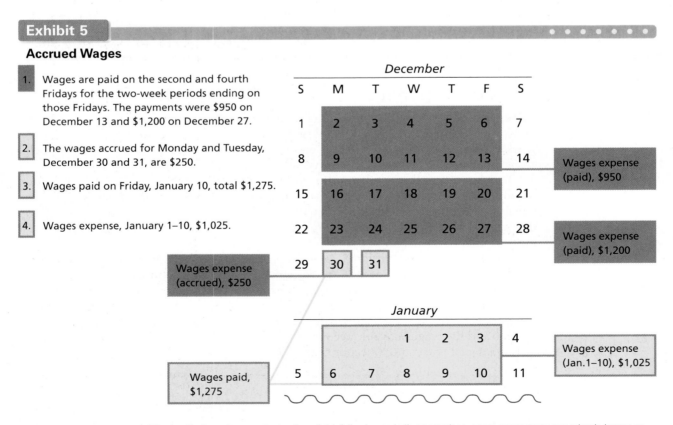

1. Wages are paid on the second and fourth Fridays for the two-week periods ending on those Fridays. The payments were $950 on December 13 and $1,200 on December 27.

2. The wages accrued for Monday and Tuesday, December 30 and 31, are $250.

3. Wages paid on Friday, January 10, total $1,275.

4. Wages expense, January 1–10, $1,025.

Wages expense (paid), $950
Wages expense (paid), $1,200
Wages expense (accrued), $250
Wages paid, $1,275
Wages expense (Jan.1–10), $1,025

4 To simplify the subsequent recording of the following period's transactions, some accountants use what is known as reversing entries for certain types of adjustments. Reversing entries are discussed and illustrated in Appendix B at the end of the textbook.

Payable will be understated by $250, and stockholders' equity (Retained Earnings) will be overstated by $250. The effects of omitting this adjusting entry are shown as follows:

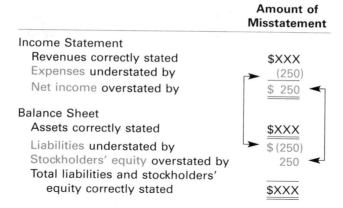

	Amount of Misstatement
Income Statement	
Revenues correctly stated	$XXX
Expenses understated by	(250)
Net income overstated by	$ 250
Balance Sheet	
Assets correctly stated	$XXX
Liabilities understated by	$ (250)
Stockholders' equity overstated by	250
Total liabilities and stockholders' equity correctly stated	$XXX

Example Exercise 3-6   Adjustment for Accrued Expense   ▸ 2

Sanregret Realty Co. pays weekly salaries of $12,500 on Friday for a five-day week ending on that day. Journalize the necessary adjusting entry at the end of the accounting period, assuming that the period ends on Thursday.

Follow My Example 3-6

Salaries Expense	10,000	
Salaries Payable		10,000
Accrued salaries [($12,500/5 days) × 4 days].		

For Practice: PE 3-6A, PE 3-6B

Depreciation Expense

Fixed assets, or **plant assets**, are physical resources that are owned and used by a business and are permanent or have a long life. Examples of fixed assets include land, buildings, and equipment. In a sense, fixed assets are a type of *long-term* prepaid expense. Because of their unique nature and long life, they are discussed separately from other prepaid expenses, such as supplies and prepaid insurance.

Fixed assets such as office equipment are used to generate revenue much like supplies are used to generate revenue. Unlike supplies, however, there is no visible reduction in the quantity of the equipment. Instead, as time passes, the equipment loses its ability to provide useful services. This decrease in usefulness is called **depreciation**.

All fixed assets, except land, lose their usefulness and, thus, are said to **depreciate**. As a fixed asset depreciates while being used to generate revenue, a portion of its cost should be recorded as an expense. This periodic expense is called **depreciation expense**.

The adjusting entry to record depreciation expense is similar to the adjusting entry for supplies used. The depreciation expense account is increased (debited) for the amount of depreciation. However, the fixed asset account is not decreased (credited). This is because both the original cost of a fixed asset and the depreciation recorded since its purchase are normally reported on the balance sheet. Instead, an account entitled **Accumulated Depreciation** is increased (credited).

Accumulated depreciation accounts are called **contra accounts**, or **contra asset accounts**. This is because accumulated depreciation accounts are deducted from their related fixed asset accounts on the balance sheet. The normal balance of a contra account is opposite to the account from which it is deducted. Since the normal balance of a fixed asset account is a debit, the normal balance of an accumulated depreciation account is a credit.

Lowe's Companies, Inc., reported land, buildings, and store equipment at a cost of over $18 billion and accumulated depreciation of over $4.1 billion.

The normal titles for fixed asset accounts and their related contra asset accounts are as follows:

Fixed Asset Account	Contra Asset Account
Land	None—Land is not depreciated.
Buildings	Accumulated Depreciation—Buildings
Store Equipment	Accumulated Depreciation—Store Equipment
Office Equipment	Accumulated Depreciation—Office Equipment

The December 31, 2009, unadjusted trial balance of NetSolutions (Exhibit 3) indicates that NetSolutions owns two fixed assets: land and office equipment. Land does not depreciate; however, an adjusting entry should be recorded for the depreciation of the office equipment for December. We assume that the office equipment has depreciated $50 during December.[5] Thus, the depreciation expense account should be increased (debited) by $50 and the accumulated depreciation—office equipment account should be increased (credited) by $50. The adjusting journal entry and T accounts are shown below.

31	Depreciation Expense	53	50	
	Accumulated Depreciation—Office Equip.	19		50
	Depreciation on office equipment.			

Office Equipment

Bal.   1,800

Accumulated Depr.—Office Equipment

Dec. 31   50

Depreciation Expense

Dec. 31   50

After the adjusting journal entry is recorded and posted, the office equipment account still has a debit balance of $1,800. This is the original cost of the office equipment that was purchased on December 4. The accumulated depreciation—office equipment account has a credit balance of $50. The difference between these two balances of $1,750 ($1,800 − $50) is the cost of the office equipment that has not yet been depreciated. This amount of $1,750 is called the **book value of the asset** (or **net book value**).

The office equipment and its related accumulated depreciation are reported on the December 31, 2009 balance sheet as follows:

Office equipment	$1,800	
Less accumulated depreciation	50	$1,750

The market value of a fixed asset usually differs from its book value. This is because depreciation is an *allocation* method, not a *valuation* method. That is, depreciation allocates the cost of a fixed asset to expense over its estimated life. Depreciation does not measure changes in market values, which vary from year to year. Thus, on December 31, 2009, the market value of NetSolutions' office equipment could be more or less than $1,750.

If the adjustment for depreciation ($50) is not recorded, Depreciation Expense on the income statement will be understated by $50, and the net income will be overstated by $50. On the balance sheet, the book value of Office Equipment and stockholders' equity (Retained Earnings) will be overstated by $50. The effects of omitting the adjustment for depreciation are shown at the top of the next page.

5 We describe and illustrate methods of computing depreciation expense in Chapter 10.

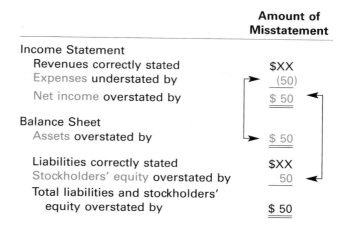

	Amount of Misstatement
Income Statement	
Revenues correctly stated	$XX
Expenses understated by	(50)
Net income overstated by	$ 50
Balance Sheet	
Assets overstated by	$ 50
Liabilities correctly stated	$XX
Stockholders' equity overstated by	50
Total liabilities and stockholders' equity overstated by	$ 50

Example Exercise 3-7   Adjustment for Depreciation ● ● ● ● ● ● ● ● ⟩ 2

The estimated amount of depreciation on equipment for the current year is $4,250. Journalize the adjusting entry to record the depreciation.

Follow My Example 3-7

```
Depreciation Expense . . . . . . . . . . . . . . . . . . . . . . . . . . . . . . . . . . . . .   4,250
    Accumulated Depreciation—Equipment . . . . . . . . . . . . . . . . . . . . . .            4,250
        Depreciation on equipment.
```

For Practice: PE 3-7A, PE 3-7B

3 Summarize the adjustment process.

@netsolutions

Summary of Adjustment Process

We have described and illustrated the basic types of adjusting entries. A summary of these basic adjustments is shown in Exhibit 6 on pages 116–117.

The adjusting entries for NetSolutions are shown in Exhibit 7 on page 118. The adjusting entries are dated as of the last day of the period. However, because collecting the adjustment data requires time, the entries are usually recorded at a later date. An explanation is included with each adjusting entry.

NetSolutions' adjusting entries have been posted to the ledger shown in Exhibit 8 on pages 119–120. The adjustments are shown in color in Exhibit 8 to distinguish them from other transactions.

Example Exercise 3-8   Effect of Omitting Adjustments ● ● ● ● ● ● ● ● ⟩ 3

For the year ending December 31, 2010, Mann Medical Co. mistakenly omitted adjusting entries for (1) $8,600 of unearned revenue that was earned, (2) earned revenue that was not billed of $12,500, and (3) accrued wages of $2,900. Indicate the combined effect of the errors on (a) revenues, (b) expenses, and (c) net income for the year ended December 31, 2010.

Follow My Example 3-8

a. Revenues were understated by $21,100 ($8,600 + $12,500).

b. Expenses were understated by $2,900.

c. Net income was understated by $18,200 ($8,600 + $12,500 − $2,900).

For Practice: PE 3-8A, PE 3-8B

Exhibit 6

Summary of Adjustments

PREPAID EXPENSES

Examples	Reason for Adjustment	Adjusting Entry		Examples from NetSolutions		Financial Statement Impact if Adjusting Entry Is Omitted	
			Dr.	Cr.			

Supplies, Prepaid Insurance	Prepaid expenses (assets) have been used or consumed in the business operations.	Expense
		Asset
				Supplies Expense
				  Supplies
					1,240
					1,240
						Income Statement:
						  Revenues
						  Expenses
						  Net income
						Balance Sheet:
						  Assets
						  Liabilities
						  Stockholders' equity
						  (Retained Earnings)
							No effect
							Understated
							Overstated
							
							Overstated
							No effect
							Overstated

					Insurance Expense 200 Prepaid Insurance 200		

UNEARNED REVENUES

Examples	Reason for Adjustment	Adjusting Entry		Examples from NetSolutions		Financial Statement Impact if Adjusting Entry Is Omitted	
			Dr.	Cr.			

Unearned rent, magazine subscriptions received in advance, fees received in advance of services	Cash received before the services have been provided is recorded as a liability. Some services have been provided to customer before the end of the accounting period.	Liability
		Revenue
				Unearned Rent
				  Rent Revenue
					120
					120
						Income Statement:
						  Revenues
						  Expenses
						  Net income
						Balance Sheet:
						  Assets
						  Liabilities
						  Stockholders' equity
						  (Retained Earnings)
							Understated
							No effect
							Understated
							
							No effect
							Overstated
							Understated

ACCRUED REVENUES

Examples	Reason for Adjustment	Adjusting Entry		Examples from NetSolutions		Financial Statement Impact if Adjusting Entry Is Omitted	
			Dr.	Cr.			

Services performed but not billed, interest to be received	Services have been provided to the customer but have not been billed or recorded. Interest has been earned, but has not been received or recorded.	Asset
		Revenue
				Accounts Receivable 500
				  Fees Earned
					500	Income Statement:
						  Revenues
						  Expenses
						  Net income
						Balance Sheet:
						  Assets
						  Liabilities
						  Stockholders' equity
						  (Retained Earnings)
							Understated
							No effect
							Understated
							
							Understated
							No effect
							Understated

ACCRUED EXPENSES

Examples	Reason for Adjustment	Adjusting Entry	Examples from NetSolutions	Financial Statement Impact if Adjusting Entry Is Omitted
Wages or salaries incurred but not paid, interest incurred but not paid	Expenses have been incurred but have not been paid or recorded.	Expense Dr. Liability Cr.	Wages Expense 250 Wages Payable 250	Income Statement: Revenues No effect Expenses Understated Net income Overstated Balance Sheet: Assets No effect Liabilities Understated Stockholders' equity Overstated (Retained Earnings)

DEPRECIATION

Examples	Reason for Adjustment	Adjusting Entry	Examples from NetSolutions	Financial Statement Impact if Adjusting Entry Is Omitted
Depreciation of equipment and buildings	Fixed assets depreciate as they are used or consumed in the business operations.	Expense Dr. Contra Asset Cr.	Depreciation Expense— Office Equipment 50 Accumulated Depr.— Office Equipment 50	Income Statement: Revenues No effect Expenses Understated Net income Overstated Balance Sheet: Assets Overstated Liabilities No effect Stockholders' equity Overstated (Retained Earnings)

Exhibit 7

Adjusting Entries— NetSolutions

		Journal			Page *5*
Date		Description	Post. Ref.	Debit	Credit
2009 Dec.	31	Adjusting Entries			
		Supplies Expense	55	1,240	
		Supplies	14		1,240
		Supplies used ($2,000 – $760).			
	31	Insurance Expense	56	200	
		Prepaid Insurance	15		200
		Insurance expired ($2,400/12 months).			
	31	Unearned Rent	23	120	
		Rent Revenue	42		120
		Rent earned ($360/3 months).			
	31	Accounts Receivable	12	500	
		Fees Earned	41		500
		Accrued fees (25 hrs. × $20).			
	31	Wages Expense	51	250	
		Wages Payable	22		250
		Accrued wages.			
	31	Depreciation Expense	53	50	
		Accum. Depreciation—Office Equipment	19		50
		Depreciation on office equipment.			

One way for an accountant to check whether all adjustments have been made is to compare the current period's adjustments with those of the prior period.

Business Connection

MICROSOFT CORPORATION

Microsoft Corporation develops, manufactures, licenses, and supports a wide range of computer software products, including Windows Vista, Windows XP, Word, Excel, and the Xbox® gaming system. When Microsoft sells its products, it incurs an obligation to support its software with technical support and periodic updates. As a result, not all the revenue is earned on the date of sale; some of the revenue on the date of sale is unearned. The portion of revenue related to support services, such as updates and technical support, is earned as time passes and support is provided to customers. Thus, each year Microsoft makes adjusting entries transferring some of its unearned revenue to revenue. The following excerpts were taken from Microsoft's 2007 financial statements:

> The percentage of revenue recorded as unearned … ranges from approximately 15% to 25% of the sales price for Windows XP Home, approximately 5% to 15% of the sales price for Windows XP Professional, …

Unearned Revenue:

	June 30, 2007	June 30, 2006
Unearned revenue (in millions)	$12,646	$10,902

During the year ending June 30, 2008, Microsoft expects to record over $10,779 million of unearned revenue as revenue. At the same time, Microsoft will record additional unearned revenue from current period sales.

Source: Taken from Microsoft's June 30, 2007, annual report.

Exhibit 8

Ledger with Adjusting Entries—NetSolutions

Account Cash — Account No. 11

Date	Item	Post. Ref.	Debit	Credit	Balance Debit	Balance Credit
2009 Nov. 1		1	25,000		25,000	
5		1		20,000	5,000	
18		1	7,500		12,500	
30		1		3,650	8,850	
30		1		950	7,900	
30		2		2,000	5,900	
Dec. 1		2		2,400	3,500	
1		2		800	2,700	
1		2	360		3,060	
6		2		180	2,880	
11		2		400	2,480	
13		3		950	1,530	
16		3	3,100		4,630	
20		3		900	3,730	
21		3	650		4,380	
23		3		1,450	2,930	
27		3		1,200	1,730	
31		3		310	1,420	
31		4		225	1,195	
31		4	2,870		4,065	
31		4		2,000	2,065	

Account Accounts Receivable — Account No. 12

Date	Item	Post. Ref.	Debit	Credit	Balance Debit	Balance Credit
2009 Dec. 16		3	1,750		1,750	
21		3		650	1,100	
31		4	1,120		2,220	
31	Adjusting	5	500		2,720	

Account Supplies — Account No. 14

Date	Item	Post. Ref.	Debit	Credit	Balance Debit	Balance Credit
2009 Nov. 10		1	1,350		1,350	
30		1		800	550	
Dec. 23		3	1,450		2,000	
31	Adjusting	5		1,240	760	

Account Prepaid Insurance — Account No. 15

Date	Item	Post. Ref.	Debit	Credit	Balance Debit	Balance Credit
2009 Dec. 1		2	2,400		2,400	
31	Adjusting	5		200	2,200	

Account Land — Account No. 17

Date	Item	Post. Ref.	Debit	Credit	Balance Debit	Balance Credit
2009 Nov. 5		1	20,000		20,000	

Account Office Equipment — Account No. 18

Date	Item	Post. Ref.	Debit	Credit	Balance Debit	Balance Credit
2009 Dec. 4		2	1,800		1,800	

Account Acc. Depr.—Office Equip. — Account No. 19

Date	Item	Post. Ref.	Debit	Credit	Balance Debit	Balance Credit
2009 Dec. 31	Adjusting	5		50		50

Account Accounts Payable — Account No. 21

Date	Item	Post. Ref.	Debit	Credit	Balance Debit	Balance Credit
2009 Nov. 10		1		1,350		1,350
30		1	950			400
Dec. 4		2		1,800		2,200
11		2	400			1,800
20		3	900			900

Account Wages Payable — Account No. 22

Date	Item	Post. Ref.	Debit	Credit	Balance Debit	Balance Credit
2009 Dec. 31	Adjusting	5		250		250

Account Unearned Rent — Account No. 23

Date	Item	Post. Ref.	Debit	Credit	Balance Debit	Balance Credit
2009 Dec. 1		2		360		360
31	Adjusting	5	120			240

Account Capital Stock — Account No. 31

Date	Item	Post. Ref.	Debit	Credit	Balance Debit	Balance Credit
2009 Nov. 1		1		25,000		25,000

(continued)

Exhibit 8

Ledger with Adjusting Entries—NetSolutions *(concluded)*

Account *Dividends*   Account No. *33*

Date	Item	Post. Ref.	Debit	Credit	Balance Debit	Balance Credit
2009						
Nov. 30		2	2,000		2,000	
Dec. 31		4	2,000		4,000	

Account *Fees Earned*   Account No. *41*

Date	Item	Post. Ref.	Debit	Credit	Balance Debit	Balance Credit
2009						
Nov. 18		1		7,500		7,500
Dec. 16		3		3,100		10,600
16		3		1,750		12,350
31		4		2,870		15,220
31		4		1,120		16,340
31	Adjusting	5		500		16,840

Account *Rent Revenue*   Account No. *42*

Date	Item	Post. Ref.	Debit	Credit	Balance Debit	Balance Credit
2009						
Dec. 31	Adjusting	5		120		120

Account *Wages Expense*   Account No. *51*

Date	Item	Post. Ref.	Debit	Credit	Balance Debit	Balance Credit
2009						
Nov. 30		1	2,125		2,125	
Dec. 13		3	950		3,075	
27		3	1,200		4,275	
31	Adjusting	5	250		4,525	

Account *Rent Expense*   Account No. *52*

Date	Item	Post. Ref.	Debit	Credit	Balance Debit	Balance Credit
2009						
Nov. 30		1	800		800	
Dec. 1		2	800		1,600	

Account *Depreciation Expense*   Account No. *53*

Date	Item	Post. Ref.	Debit	Credit	Balance Debit	Balance Credit
2009						
Dec. 31	Adjusting	5	50		50	

Account *Utilities Expense*   Account No. *54*

Date	Item	Post. Ref.	Debit	Credit	Balance Debit	Balance Credit
2009						
Nov. 30		1	450		450	
Dec. 31		3	310		760	
31		4	225		985	

Account *Supplies Expense*   Account No. *55*

Date	Item	Post. Ref.	Debit	Credit	Balance Debit	Balance Credit
2009						
Nov. 30		1	800		800	
Dec. 31	Adjusting	5	1,240		2,040	

Account *Insurance Expense*   Account No. *56*

Date	Item	Post. Ref.	Debit	Credit	Balance Debit	Balance Credit
2009						
Dec. 31	Adjusting	5	200		200	

Account *Miscellaneous Expense*   Account No. *59*

Date	Item	Post. Ref.	Debit	Credit	Balance Debit	Balance Credit
2009						
Nov. 30		1	275		275	
Dec. 6		2	180		455	

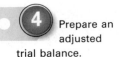

4 Prepare an adjusted trial balance.

Adjusted Trial Balance

After the adjusting entries have been posted, an **adjusted trial balance** is prepared. The adjusted trial balance verifies the equality of the total debit and credit balances before the financial statements are prepared. If the adjusted trial balance does not balance, an error has occurred. However, as we discussed in Chapter 2, errors may occur even though the adjusted trial balance totals agree. For example, if an adjusting entry were omitted, the adjusted trial balance totals would still agree.

@netsolutions   Exhibit 9 shows the adjusted trial balance for NetSolutions as of December 31, 2009. In Chapter 4, we discuss how financial statements, including a classified balance sheet, can be prepared from an adjusted trial balance.

Exhibit 9

Adjusted Trial Balance

NetSolutions
Adjusted Trial Balance
December 31, 2009

	Debit Balances	Credit Balances
Cash	2,065	
Accounts Receivable	2,720	
Supplies	760	
Prepaid Insurance	2,200	
Land	20,000	
Office Equipment	1,800	
Accumulated Depreciation—Office Equipment		50
Accounts Payable		900
Wages Payable		250
Unearned Rent		240
Capital Stock		25,000
Dividends	4,000	
Fees Earned		16,840
Rent Revenue		120
Wages Expense	4,525	
Rent Expense	1,600	
Depreciation Expense	50	
Utilities Expense	985	
Supplies Expense	2,040	
Insurance Expense	200	
Miscellaneous Expense	455	
	43,400	43,400

Example Exercise 3-9 Effect of Errors on Adjusted Trial Balance 4

For each of the following errors, considered individually, indicate whether the error would cause the adjusted trial balance totals to be unequal. If the error would cause the adjusted trial balance totals to be unequal, indicate whether the debit or credit total is higher and by how much.

a. The adjustment for accrued fees of $5,340 was journalized as a debit to Accounts Payable for $5,340 and a credit to Fees Earned of $5,340.

b. The adjustment for depreciation of $3,260 was journalized as a debit to Depreciation Expense for $3,620 and a credit to Accumulated Depreciation for $3,260.

Follow My Example 3-9

a. The totals are equal even though the debit should have been to Accounts Receivable instead of Accounts Payable.

b. The totals are unequal. The debit total is higher by $360 ($3,620 − $3,260).

For Practice: PE 3-9A, PE 3-9B

Financial Analysis and Interpretation

Comparing each item in a current statement with a total amount within that same statement is useful in analyzing relationships within a financial statement. *Vertical analysis* is the term used to describe such comparisons.

In vertical analysis of a balance sheet, each asset item is stated as a percent of the total assets. Each liability and stockholders' equity item is stated as a percent of the total liabilities and stockholders' equity. In vertical analysis of an income statement, each item is stated as a percent of revenues or fees earned.

Vertical analysis may be prepared for several periods to analyze changes in relationships over time. Vertical analysis of two years of income statements for J. Holmes, Attorney at Law, P.C. is shown below.

The preceding vertical analysis indicates both favorable and unfavorable trends affecting the income statement of J. Holmes, Attorney at Law, P.C. The increase in wages expense of 2% (32% − 30%) is an unfavorable trend, as is the increase in utilities expense of 0.7% (6.7% − 6.0%). A favorable trend is the decrease in supplies expense of 0.6% (2.0% − 1.4%). Rent expense and miscellaneous expense as a percent of fees earned were constant. The net result of these trends was that net income decreased as a percent of fees earned from 52.8% to 50.7%.

The analysis of the various percentages shown for J. Holmes, Attorney at Law, P.C. can be enhanced by comparisons with industry averages. Such averages are published by trade associations and financial information services. Any major differences between industry averages should be investigated.

J. Holmes, Attorney at Law, P.C.
Income Statements
For the Years Ended December 31, 2010 and 2009

	2010		2009	
	Amount	Percent	Amount	Percent
Fees earned	$187,500	100.0%	$150,000	100.0%
Operating expenses:				
Wages expense	$ 60,000	32.0%	$ 45,000	30.0%*
Rent expense	15,000	8.0%	12,000	8.0%
Utilities expense	12,500	6.7%	9,000	6.0%
Supplies expense	2,700	1.4%	3,000	2.0%
Miscellaneous expense	2,300	1.2%	1,800	1.2%
Total operating expenses	$ 92,500	49.3%	$ 70,800	47.2%
Net income	$ 95,000	50.7%	$ 79,200	52.8%

*$45,000 ÷ $150,000

f·a·i

1 Describe the nature of the adjusting process.

Key Points

The accrual basis of accounting requires that revenues are reported in the period in which they are earned and expenses matched with the revenues they generate. The updating of accounts at the end of the accounting period is called the adjusting process. Each adjusting entry affects an income statement and balance sheet account. The four types of accounts requiring adjusting entries are prepaid expenses, unearned revenues, accrued revenues, and accrued expenses.

Key Learning Outcomes	Example Exercises	Practice Exercises
• Explain why accrual accounting requires adjusting entries.		
• List accounts that do and do NOT require adjusting entries at the end of the accounting period.	3-1	3-1A, 3-1B
• Give an example of a prepaid expense, unearned revenue, accrued revenue, and accrued expense.	3-2	3-2A, 3-2B

2 Journalize entries for accounts requiring adjustment.

Key Points

Adjusting entries illustrated in this chapter include prepaid expenses, unearned revenues, accrued revenues, and accrued expenses. In addition, the adjusting entry necessary to record depreciation on fixed assets was illustrated.

Key Learning Outcomes	Example Exercises	Practice Exercises
• Prepare an adjusting entry for a prepaid expense.	3-3	3-3A, 3-3B
• Prepare an adjusting entry for an unearned revenue.	3-4	3-4A, 3-4B
• Prepare an adjusting entry for an accrued revenue.	3-5	3-5A, 3-5B
• Prepare an adjusting entry for an accrued expense.	3-6	3-6A, 3-6B
• Prepare an adjusting entry for depreciation expense.	3-7	3-7A, 3-7B

3 Summarize the adjustment process.

Key Points

A summary of adjustments, including the type of adjustment, reason for the adjustment, the adjusting entry, and the effect of omitting an adjustment on the financial statements, is shown in Exhibit 6.

Key Learning Outcomes	Example Exercises	Practice Exercises
• Determine the effect on the income statement and balance sheet of omitting an adjusting entry for prepaid expense, unearned revenue, accrued revenue, accrued expense, and depreciation.	3-8	3-8A, 3-8B

4 Prepare an adjusted trial balance.

Key Points

After all the adjusting entries have been posted, the equality of the total debit balances and total credit balances is verified by an adjusted trial balance.

Key Learning Outcomes	Example Exercises	Practice Exercises
• Prepare an adjusted trial balance.		
• Determine the effect of errors on the equality of the adjusted trial balance.	3-9	3-9A, 3-9B

Key Terms

accounting period concept (102)
accrual basis of accounting (102)
accrued expenses (105)
accrued revenues (105)
accumulated depreciation (113)
adjusted trial balance (120)
adjusting entries (103)

adjusting process (103)
book value of the asset (or net book value) (114)
cash basis of accounting (102)
contra account (or contra asset account) (113)
depreciate (113)
depreciation (113)

depreciation expense (113)
fixed assets (or plant assets) (113)
matching concept (or matching principle) (102)
prepaid expenses (104)
revenue recognition concept (102)
unearned revenues (104)

Illustrative Problem

Three years ago, T. Roderick organized Harbor Realty Inc. At July 31, 2010, the end of the current year, the unadjusted trial balance of Harbor Realty Inc. appears as shown below.

Harbor Realty Inc.
Unadjusted Trial Balance
July 31, 2010

	Debit Balances	Credit Balances
Cash	3,425	
Accounts Receivable	7,000	
Supplies	1,270	
Prepaid Insurance	620	
Office Equipment	51,650	
Accumulated Depreciation—Office Equipment		9,700
Accounts Payable		925
Wages Payable		0
Unearned Fees		1,250
Capital Stock		5,000
Retained Earnings		24,000
Dividends	5,200	
Fees Earned		59,125
Wages Expense	22,415	
Depreciation Expense	0	
Rent Expense	4,200	
Utilities Expense	2,715	
Supplies Expense	0	
Insurance Expense	0	
Miscellaneous Expense	1,505	
	100,000	100,000

The data needed to determine year-end adjustments are as follows:
a. Supplies on hand at July 31, 2010, $380.
b. Insurance premiums expired during the year, $315.
c. Depreciation of equipment during the year, $4,950.
d. Wages accrued but not paid at July 31, 2010, $440.
e. Accrued fees earned but not recorded at July 31, 2010, $1,000.
f. Unearned fees on July 31, 2010, $750.

Instructions

1. Prepare the necessary adjusting journal entries. Include journal entry explanations.
2. Determine the balance of the accounts affected by the adjusting entries, and prepare an adjusted trial balance.

Solution

1.

	Journal			
Date	**Description**	**Post. Ref.**	**Debit**	**Credit**
2010 July 31	Supplies Expense		890	
	Supplies			890
	Supplies used ($1,270 – $380).			
31	Insurance Expense		315	
	Prepaid Insurance			315
	Insurance expired.			
31	Depreciation Expense		4,950	
	Accumulated Depreciation—Office Equipment			4,950
	Depreciation expense.			
31	Wages Expense		440	
	Wages Payable			440
	Accrued wages.			
31	Accounts Receivable		1,000	
	Fees Earned			1,000
	Accrued fees.			
31	Unearned Fees		500	
	Fees Earned			500
	Fees earned ($1,250 – $750).			

2.

Harbor Realty Inc.
Adjusted Trial Balance
July 31, 2010

	Debit Balances	Credit Balances
Cash	3,425	
Accounts Receivable	8,000	
Supplies	380	
Prepaid Insurance	305	
Office Equipment	51,650	
Accumulated Depreciation—Office Equipment		14,650
Accounts Payable		925
Wages Payable		440
Unearned Fees		750
Capital Stock		5,000
Retained Earnings		24,000
Dividends	5,200	
Fees Earned		60,625
Wages Expense	22,855	
Depreciation Expense	4,950	
Rent Expense	4,200	
Utilities Expense	2,715	
Supplies Expense	890	
Insurance Expense	315	
Miscellaneous Expense	1,505	
	106,390	106,390

Self-Examination Questions (Answers at End of Chapter)

1. Which of the following items represents a deferral?
   A. Prepaid insurance
   B. Wages payable
   C. Fees earned
   D. Accumulated depreciation

2. If the supplies account, before adjustment on May 31, indicated a balance of $2,250, and supplies on hand at May 31 totaled $950, the adjusting entry would be:
   A. debit Supplies, $950; credit Supplies Expense, $950.
   B. debit Supplies, $1,300; credit Supplies Expense, $1,300.
   C. debit Supplies Expense, $950; credit Supplies, $950.
   D. debit Supplies Expense, $1,300; credit Supplies, $1,300.

3. The balance in the unearned rent account for Jones Co. as of December 31 is $1,200. If Jones Co. failed to record the adjusting entry for $600 of rent earned during December, the effect on the balance sheet and income statement for December would be:
   A. assets understated $600; net income overstated $600.

   B. liabilities understated $600; net income understated $600.
   C. liabilities overstated $600; net income understated $600.
   D. liabilities overstated $600; net income overstated $600.

4. If the estimated amount of depreciation on equipment for a period is $2,000, the adjusting entry to record depreciation would be:
   A. debit Depreciation Expense, $2,000; credit Equipment, $2,000.
   B. debit Equipment, $2,000; credit Depreciation Expense, $2,000.
   C. debit Depreciation Expense, $2,000; credit Accumulated Depreciation, $2,000.
   D. debit Accumulated Depreciation, $2,000; credit Depreciation Expense, $2,000.

5. If the equipment account has a balance of $22,500 and its accumulated depreciation account has a balance of $14,000, the book value of the equipment would be:
   A. $36,500.
   B. $22,500.
   C. $14,000.
   D. $8,500.

Eye Openers

1. How are revenues and expenses reported on the income statement under (a) the cash basis of accounting and (b) the accrual basis of accounting?
2. Fees for services provided are billed to a customer during 2009. The customer remits the amount owed in 2010. During which year would the revenues be reported on the income statement under (a) the cash basis? (b) the accrual basis?
3. Employees performed services in 2009, but the wages were not paid until 2010. During which year would the wages expense be reported on the income statement under (a) the cash basis? (b) the accrual basis?
4. Is the matching concept related to (a) the cash basis of accounting or (b) the accrual basis of accounting?
5. Is the cash balance on the unadjusted trial balance the amount that should normally be reported on the balance sheet? Explain.
6. Is the supplies balance on the unadjusted trial balance the amount that should normally be reported on the balance sheet? Explain.
7. Why are adjusting entries needed at the end of an accounting period?
8. What is the difference between *adjusting entries* and *correcting entries*?
9. Identify the four different categories of adjusting entries frequently required at the end of an accounting period.
10. If the effect of the debit portion of an adjusting entry is to increase the balance of an asset account, which of the following statements describes the effect of the credit portion of the entry?
    a. Increases the balance of a liability account.
    b. Increases the balance of a revenue account.
    c. Increases the balance of an expense account.
11. If the effect of the credit portion of an adjusting entry is to increase the balance of a liability account, which of the following statements describes the effect of the debit portion of the entry?
    a. Increases the balance of an expense account.
    b. Increases the balance of a revenue account.
    c. Increases the balance of an asset account.
12. Does every adjusting entry have an effect on determining the amount of net income for a period? Explain.
13. What is the nature of the balance in the prepaid insurance account at the end of the accounting period (a) before adjustment? (b) after adjustment?
14. On July 1 of the current year, a business paid the July rent on the building that it occupies. (a) Do the rights acquired at July 1 represent an asset or an expense? (b) What is the justification for debiting Rent Expense at the time of payment?
15. (a) Explain the purpose of the two accounts: Depreciation Expense and Accumulated Depreciation. (b) What is the normal balance of each account? (c) Is it customary for the balances of the two accounts to be equal in amount? (d) In what financial statements, if any, will each account appear?

Practice Exercises

● ● ● ● ◯ ❯❯

PE 3-1A
Accounts requiring adjustment
obj. 1
EE 3-1   p. 103

Indicate with a Yes or No whether or not each of the following accounts normally requires an adjusting entry.

a. Building
b. Cash
c. Interest Payable
d. Miscellaneous Expense
e. Capital Stock
f. Prepaid Insurance

PE 3-1B
Accounts requiring adjustment
obj. 1
EE 3-1   p. 103

Indicate with a Yes or No whether or not each of the following accounts normally requires an adjusting entry.

a. Accumulated Depreciation
b. Dividends
c. Land
d. Salaries Payable
e. Supplies
f. Unearned Rent

PE 3-2A
Type of adjustment
obj. 1
EE 3-2   p. 106

Classify the following items as (1) prepaid expense, (2) unearned revenue, (3) accrued revenue, or (4) accrued expense.

a. Cash received for use of land next month
b. Fees earned but not received
c. Rent expense owed but not yet paid
d. Supplies on hand

PE 3-2B
Type of adjustment
obj. 1
EE 3-2   p. 106

Classify the following items as (1) prepaid expense, (2) unearned revenue, (3) accrued revenue, or (4) accrued expense.

a. Cash received for services not yet rendered
b. Insurance paid
c. Rent revenue earned but not received
d. Salaries owed but not yet paid

PE 3-3A
Adjustment for prepaid expense
obj. 2
EE 3-3   p. 109

The prepaid insurance account had a beginning balance of $6,000 and was debited for $7,200 of premiums paid during the year. Journalize the adjusting entry required at the end of the year assuming the amount of unexpired insurance related to future periods is $4,200.

PE 3-3B
Adjustment for prepaid expense
obj. 2
EE 3-3   p. 109

The supplies account had a beginning balance of $1,815 and was debited for $3,790 for supplies purchased during the year. Journalize the adjusting entry required at the end of the year assuming the amount of supplies on hand is $1,675.

PE 3-4A
Adjustment for unearned revenue
obj. 2
EE 3-4   p. 110

On October 1, 2009, Nautilus Co. received $15,300 for the rent of land for 12 months. Journalize the adjusting entry required for unearned rent on December 31, 2009.

PE 3-4B
Adjustment for unearned revenue
obj. 2
EE 3-4   p. 110

The balance in the unearned fees account, before adjustment at the end of the year, is $31,850. Journalize the adjusting entry required assuming the amount of unearned fees at the end of the year is $6,195.

PE 3-5A
Adjustment for accrued revenues
obj. 2
EE 3-5   p. 111

At the end of the current year, $12,400 of fees have been earned but have not been billed to clients. Journalize the adjusting entry to record the accrued fees.

PE 3-5B
Adjustment for accrued revenues
obj. 2
EE 3-5   p. 111

At the end of the current year, $9,134 of fees have been earned but have not been billed to clients. Journalize the adjusting entry to record the accrued fees.

PE 3-6A
Adjustment for
accrued expense

obj. 2

EE 3-6   p. 113

Haifa Realty Co. pays weekly salaries of $29,100 on Monday for a six-day workweek ending the preceding Saturday. Journalize the necessary adjusting entry at the end of the accounting period assuming that the period ends on Thursday.

PE 3-6B
Adjustment for
accrued expense

obj. 2

EE 3-6   p. 113

Colossal Realty Co. pays weekly salaries of $19,375 on Friday for a five-day workweek ending on that day. Journalize the necessary adjusting entry at the end of the accounting period assuming that the period ends on Tuesday.

PE 3-7A
Adjustment for
depreciation

obj. 2

EE 3-7   p. 115

The estimated amount of depreciation on equipment for the current year is $5,500. Journalize the adjusting entry to record the depreciation.

PE 3-7B
Adjustment for
depreciation

obj. 2

EE 3-7   p. 115

The estimated amount of depreciation on equipment for the current year is $3,200. Journalize the adjusting entry to record the depreciation.

PE 3-8A
Effect of omitting
adjustments

obj. 3

EE 3-8   p. 115

For the year ending November 30, 2010, Towson Medical Services Co. mistakenly omitted adjusting entries for (1) $1,430 of supplies that were used, (2) unearned revenue of $11,150 that was earned, and (3) insurance of $6,000 that expired. Indicate the combined effect of the errors on (a) revenues, (b) expenses, and (c) net income for the year ended November 30, 2010.

PE 3-8B
Effect of omitting
adjustments

obj. 3

EE 3-8   p. 115

For the year ending February 28, 2009, Samaritan Medical Co. mistakenly omitted adjusting entries for (1) depreciation of $4,100, (2) fees earned that were not billed of $15,300, and (3) accrued wages of $3,750. Indicate the combined effect of the errors on (a) revenues, (b) expenses, and (c) net income for the year ended February 28, 2009.

PE 3-9A
Effect of errors on
adjusted trial balance

obj. 4

EE 3-9   p. 121

For each of the following errors, considered individually, indicate whether the error would cause the adjusted trial balance totals to be unequal. If the error would cause the adjusted trial balance totals to be unequal, indicate whether the debit or credit total is higher and by how much.

a. The adjustment for accrued wages of $4,150 was journalized as a debit to Wages Expense for $4,150 and a credit to Accounts Payable for $4,150.

b. The entry for $1,290 of supplies used during the period was journalized as a debit to Supplies Expense of $1,290 and a credit to Supplies of $1,920.

PE 3-9B
Effect of errors on
adjusted trial balance

obj. 4

EE 3-9   p. 121

For each of the following errors, considered individually, indicate whether the error would cause the adjusted trial balance totals to be unequal. If the error would cause the adjusted trial balance totals to be unequal, indicate whether the debit or credit total is higher and by how much.

a. The adjustment of $8,175 for accrued fees earned was journalized as a debit to Accounts Receivable for $8,175 and a credit to Fees Earned for $8,157.

b. The adjustment of depreciation of $2,700 was omitted from the end-of-period adjusting entries.

Exercises

EX 3-1
Classifying types of adjustments
obj. 1

Classify the following items as (a) prepaid expense, (b) unearned revenue, (c) accrued revenue, or (d) accrued expense.

1. A two-year premium paid on a fire insurance policy.
2. Fees earned but not yet received.
3. Fees received but not yet earned.
4. Salary owed but not yet paid.
5. Subscriptions received in advance by a magazine publisher.
6. Supplies on hand.
7. Taxes owed but payable in the following period.
8. Utilities owed but not yet paid.

EX 3-2
Classifying adjusting entries
obj. 1

The following accounts were taken from the unadjusted trial balance of Washington Co., a congressional lobbying firm. Indicate whether or not each account would normally require an adjusting entry. If the account normally requires an adjusting entry, use the following notation to indicate the type of adjustment:

AE—Accrued Expense
AR—Accrued Revenue
PE—Prepaid Expense
UR—Unearned Revenue

To illustrate, the answer for the first account is shown below.

Account	Answer
Accounts Receivable	Normally requires adjustment (AR).
Capital Stock	
Cash	
Dividends	
Interest Payable	
Interest Receivable	
Land	
Office Equipment	
Prepaid Rent	
Retained Earnings	
Supplies	
Unearned Fees	
Wages Expense	

EX 3-3
Adjusting entry for supplies
obj. 2

The balance in the supplies account, before adjustment at the end of the year, is $1,736. Journalize the adjusting entry required if the amount of supplies on hand at the end of the year is $813.

EX 3-4
Determining supplies purchased
obj. 2

The supplies and supplies expense accounts at December 31, after adjusting entries have been posted at the end of the first year of operations, are shown in the following T accounts:

Supplies				Supplies Expense	
Bal.	675			Bal.	2,718

Determine the amount of supplies purchased during the year.

EX 3-5
Effect of omitting adjusting entry
objs. 2, 3

At March 31, the end of the first month of operations, the usual adjusting entry transferring prepaid insurance expired to an expense account is omitted. Which items will be incorrectly stated, because of the error, on (a) the income statement for March and (b) the balance sheet as of March 31? Also indicate whether the items in error will be overstated or understated.

EX 3-6
Adjusting entries for prepaid insurance
obj. **2**

The balance in the prepaid insurance account, before adjustment at the end of the year, is $11,500. Journalize the adjusting entry required under each of the following *alternatives* for determining the amount of the adjustment: (a) the amount of insurance expired during the year is $8,750; (b) the amount of unexpired insurance applicable to future periods is $2,750.

EX 3-7
Adjusting entries for prepaid insurance
obj. **2**

The prepaid insurance account had a balance of $5,400 at the beginning of the year. The account was debited for $6,000 for premiums on policies purchased during the year. Journalize the adjusting entry required at the end of the year for each of the following situations: (a) the amount of unexpired insurance applicable to future periods is $1,000; (b) the amount of insurance expired during the year is $10,400.

EX 3-8
Adjusting entries for unearned fees
obj. **2**

✔ Amount of entry: $21,175

The balance in the unearned fees account, before adjustment at the end of the year, is $38,375. Journalize the adjusting entry required if the amount of unearned fees at the end of the year is $17,200.

EX 3-9
Effect of omitting adjusting entry
objs. **2, 3**

At the end of February, the first month of the business year, the usual adjusting entry transferring rent earned to a revenue account from the unearned rent account was omitted. Indicate which items will be incorrectly stated, because of the error, on (a) the income statement for February and (b) the balance sheet as of February 28. Also indicate whether the items in error will be overstated or understated.

EX 3-10
Adjusting entry for accrued fees
obj. **2**

At the end of the current year, $8,140 of fees have been earned but have not been billed to clients.

a. Journalize the adjusting entry to record the accrued fees.
b. If the cash basis rather than the accrual basis had been used, would an adjusting entry have been necessary? Explain.

EX 3-11
Adjusting entries for unearned and accrued fees
obj. **2**

The balance in the unearned fees account, before adjustment at the end of the year, is $112,790. Of these fees, $69,735 have been earned. In addition, $13,200 of fees have been earned but have not been billed. Journalize the adjusting entries (a) to adjust the unearned fees account and (b) to record the accrued fees.

EX 3-12
Effect of omitting adjusting entry
objs. **2, 3**

The adjusting entry for accrued fees was omitted at March 31, the end of the current year. Indicate which items will be in error, because of the omission, on (a) the income statement for the current year and (b) the balance sheet as of March 31. Also indicate whether the items in error will be overstated or understated.

EX 3-13
Adjusting entries for accrued salaries

obj. 2

✔ a. Amount of entry: $2,220

Canyon Realty Co. pays weekly salaries of $3,700 on Friday for a five-day workweek ending on that day. Journalize the necessary adjusting entry at the end of the accounting period assuming that the period ends (a) on Wednesday and (b) on Thursday.

EX 3-14
Determining wages paid

obj. 2

The wages payable and wages expense accounts at October 31, after adjusting entries have been posted at the end of the first month of operations, are shown in the following T accounts:

Wages Payable				Wages Expense	
	Bal.	3,175	Bal.	93,800	

Determine the amount of wages paid during the month.

EX 3-15
Effect of omitting adjusting entry

objs. 2, 3

Accrued salaries of $4,950 owed to employees for December 30 and 31 are not considered in preparing the financial statements for the year ended December 31. Indicate which items will be erroneously stated, because of the error, on (a) the income statement for the year and (b) the balance sheet as of December 31. Also indicate whether the items in error will be overstated or understated.

EX 3-16
Effect of omitting adjusting entry

objs. 2, 3

Assume that the error in Exercise 3-15 was not corrected and that the $4,950 of accrued salaries was included in the first salary payment in January. Indicate which items will be erroneously stated, because of failure to correct the initial error, on (a) the income statement for the month of January and (b) the balance sheet as of January 31.

EX 3-17
Adjusting entries for prepaid and accrued taxes

obj. 2

✔ b. $24,750

Northwest Financial Services was organized on April 1 of the current year. On April 2, Northwest prepaid $4,500 to the city for taxes (license fees) for the *next* 12 months and debited the prepaid taxes account. Northwest is also required to pay in January an annual tax (on property) for the *previous* calendar year. The estimated amount of the property tax for the current year (April 1 to December 31) is $21,375.

a. Journalize the two adjusting entries required to bring the accounts affected by the two taxes up to date as of December 31, the end of the current year.
b. What is the amount of tax expense for the current year?

EX 3-18
Adjustment for depreciation

obj. 2

The estimated amount of depreciation on equipment for the current year is $1,840. Journalize the adjusting entry to record the depreciation.

EX 3-19
Determining fixed asset's book value

obj. 2

The balance in the equipment account is $925,700, and the balance in the accumulated depreciation—equipment account is $311,100.

a. What is the book value of the equipment?
b. Does the balance in the accumulated depreciation account mean that the equipment's loss of value is $311,100? Explain.

EX 3-20
Book value of fixed assets

obj. 2

In a recent balance sheet, Microsoft Corporation reported *Property, Plant, and Equipment* of $7,223 million and *Accumulated Depreciation* of $4,179 million.

a. What was the book value of the fixed assets?
b. Would the book value of Microsoft Corporation's fixed assets normally approximate their fair market values?

EX 3-21
Effects of errors on
financial statements

objs. 2, 3

For a recent period, the balance sheet for Circuit City Stores, Inc., reported accrued expenses of $464,511,000. For the same period, Circuit City reported income before income taxes of $151,112,000. Assume that the accrued expenses apply to the current period and were not recorded at the end of the current period. What would have been the income (loss) before income taxes?

EX 3-22
Effects of errors on
financial statements

objs. 2, 3

For a recent year, the balance sheet for The Campbell Soup Company includes accrued expenses of $1,022,000,000. The income before taxes for The Campbell Soup Company for the year was $1,001,000,000.

a. Assume the accruals apply to the current year and were not recorded at the end of the year. By how much would income before taxes have been misstated?
b. What is the percentage of the misstatement in (a) to the reported income of $1,001,000,000? Round to one decimal place.

EX 3-23
Effects of errors on
financial statements

objs. 2, 3

✔ 1. a. Revenue
understated,
$21,950

The accountant for Mystic Medical Co., a medical services consulting firm, mistakenly omitted adjusting entries for (a) unearned revenue earned during the year ($21,950) and (b) accrued wages ($6,100). Indicate the effect of each error, considered individually, on the income statement for the current year ended July 31. Also indicate the effect of each error on the July 31 balance sheet. Set up a table similar to the following, and record your answers by inserting the dollar amount in the appropriate spaces. Insert a zero if the error does not affect the item.

	Error (a)		Error (b)	
	Over-stated	Under-stated	Over-stated	Under-stated
1. Revenue for the year would be	$ ____	$ ____	$ ____	$ ____
2. Expenses for the year would be	$ ____	$ ____	$ ____	$ ____
3. Net income for the year would be	$ ____	$ ____	$ ____	$ ____
4. Assets at July 31 would be	$ ____	$ ____	$ ____	$ ____
5. Liabilities at July 31 would be	$ ____	$ ____	$ ____	$ ____
6. Stockholders' equity at July 31 would be	$ ____	$ ____	$ ____	$ ____

EX 3-24
Effects of errors on
financial statements

objs. 2, 3

If the net income for the current year had been $424,300 in Exercise 3-23, what would have been the correct net income if the proper adjusting entries had been made?

EX 3-25
Adjusting entries for
depreciation; effect of
error

objs. 2, 3

On December 31, a business estimates depreciation on equipment used during the first year of operations to be $12,200.

a. Journalize the adjusting entry required as of December 31.
b. If the adjusting entry in (a) were omitted, which items would be erroneously stated on (1) the income statement for the year and (2) the balance sheet as of December 31?

EX 3-26
**Adjusting entries
from trial balances**

obj. 4

The unadjusted and adjusted trial balances for Glockenspiel Services Co. on March 31, 2010, are shown below.

Glockenspiel Services Co.
Trial Balance
March 31, 2010

	Unadjusted		Adjusted	
	Debit Balances	Credit Balances	Debit Balances	Credit Balances
Cash	16		16	
Accounts Receivable	38		42	
Supplies	12		9	
Prepaid Insurance	20		12	
Land	26		26	
Equipment	40		40	
Accumulated Depreciation—Equipment		8		13
Accounts Payable		26		26
Wages Payable		0		1
Capital Stock		40		40
Retained Earnings		52		52
Dividends	8		8	
Fees Earned		74		78
Wages Expense	24		25	
Rent Expense	8		8	
Insurance Expense	0		8	
Utilities Expense	4		4	
Depreciation Expense	0		5	
Supplies Expense	0		3	
Miscellaneous Expense	4		4	
	200	200	210	210

Journalize the five entries that adjusted the accounts at March 31, 2010. None of the accounts were affected by more than one adjusting entry.

EX 3-27
**Adjusting entries
from trial balances**

obj. 4

✔ Corrected trial
balance totals,
$621,900

The accountant for Rooster Laundry prepared the following unadjusted and adjusted trial balances. Assume that all balances in the unadjusted trial balance and the amounts of the adjustments are correct. Identify the errors in the accountant's adjusting entries.

Rooster Laundry
Trial Balance
January 31, 2010

	Unadjusted		Adjusted	
	Debit Balances	Credit Balances	Debit Balances	Credit Balances
Cash	15,000		15,000	
Accounts Receivable	36,500		44,000	
Laundry Supplies	7,500		11,000	
Prepaid Insurance*	10,400		2,800	
Laundry Equipment	280,000		268,000	
Accumulated Depreciation		96,000		96,000
Accounts Payable		19,200		19,200
Wages Payable				2,400
Capital Stock		30,000		30,000
Retained Earnings		90,600		90,600
Dividends	57,550		57,550	
Laundry Revenue		364,200		364,200
Wages Expense	98,400		98,400	
Rent Expense	51,150		51,150	
Utilities Expense	37,000		37,000	
Depreciation Expense			12,000	
Laundry Supplies Expense			3,500	
Insurance Expense			1,600	
Miscellaneous Expense	6,500		6,500	
	600,000	600,000	608,500	602,400

*$7,600 of insurance expired during the year.

EX 3-28

Vertical analysis of income statement

The following data (in millions) is taken from the financial statements of Williams-Sonoma for the years ending 2007 and 2006:

	2007	2006
Net sales (revenues)	$3,728	$3,539
Net income	209	215

a. Determine the amount of change (in millions) and percent of change in net income for 2007.
b. Determine the percentage relationship between net income and net sales (net income divided by net sales) for 2007 and 2008.
c. What conclusions can you draw from your analysis?

EX 3-29

Vertical analysis of income statement

The following income statement data (in thousands) for Dell Inc. and Gateway, Inc., were taken from their recent annual reports:

	Dell	Gateway
Net sales	$35,404,000	$ 4,171,325
Cost of goods sold (expense)	(29,055,000)	(3,605,120)
Operating expenses	(3,505,000)	(1,077,447)
Operating income (loss)	$ 2,844,000	$ (511,242)

a. Prepare a vertical analysis of the income statement for Dell.
b. Prepare a vertical analysis of the income statement for Gateway.
c. Based on (a) and (b), how does Dell compare to Gateway?

Problems Series A

PR 3-1A

Adjusting entries

obj. 2

On August 31, 2010, the following data were accumulated to assist the accountant in preparing the adjusting entries for Cobalt Realty:

a. Fees accrued but unbilled at August 31 are $9,560.
b. The supplies account balance on August 31 is $3,150. The supplies on hand at August 31 are $900.
c. Wages accrued but not paid at August 31 are $1,200.
d. The unearned rent account balance at August 31 is $9,375, representing the receipt of an advance payment on August 1 of three months' rent from tenants.
e. Depreciation of office equipment is $1,600.

Instructions

1. Journalize the adjusting entries required at August 31, 2010.
2. Briefly explain the difference between adjusting entries and entries that would be made to correct errors.

PR 3-2A

Adjusting entries

obj. 2

Selected account balances before adjustment for Oval Realty at April 30, 2010, the end of the current year, are shown at the top of the next page.

	Debits	Credits
Accounts Receivable	$ 65,000	
Accumulated Depreciation		$ 10,000
Depreciation Expense	—	
Equipment	100,000	
Fees Earned		379,500
Prepaid Rent	8,200	
Rent Expense	—	
Supplies	1,950	
Supplies Expense	—	
Unearned Fees		9,000
Wages Expense	128,000	
Wages Payable		—

Data needed for year-end adjustments are as follows:

a. Supplies on hand at April 30, $600.
b. Depreciation of equipment during year, $1,000.
c. Rent expired during year, $6,000.
d. Wages accrued but not paid at April 30, $1,900.
e. Unearned fees at April 30, $3,750.
f. Unbilled fees at April 30, $4,500.

Instructions

Journalize the six adjusting entries required at April 30, based on the data presented.

PR 3-3A
Adjusting entries

obj. 2

Wind River Outfitters Co., an outfitter store for fishing treks, prepared the following unadjusted trial balance at the end of its first year of operations:

Wind River Outfitters Co.
Unadjusted Trial Balance
February 28, 2010

	Debit Balances	Credit Balances
Cash	13,200	
Accounts Receivable	43,800	
Supplies	3,600	
Equipment	81,000	
Accounts Payable		6,100
Unearned Fees		9,600
Capital Stock		20,000
Retained Earnings		91,400
Dividends	5,000	
Fees Earned		147,900
Wages Expense	76,400	
Rent Expense	27,500	
Utilities Expense	21,000	
Miscellaneous Expense	3,500	
	275,000	275,000

For preparing the adjusting entries, the following data were assembled:

a. Supplies on hand on February 28 were $750.
b. Fees earned but unbilled on February 28 were $2,900.
c. Depreciation of equipment was estimated to be $5,400 for the year.
d. Unpaid wages accrued on February 28 were $800.
e. The balance in unearned fees represented the February 1 receipt in advance for services to be provided. Only $1,600 of the services was provided between February 1 and February 28.

Instructions

Journalize the adjusting entries necessary on February 28.

PR 3-4A
Adjusting entries
objs. 2, 3, 4

Billy Board Company specializes in the maintenance and repair of signs, such as billboards. On March 31, 2010, the accountant for Billy Board Company prepared the following trial balances:

Billy Board Company
Trial Balance
March 31, 2010

	Unadjusted		Adjusted	
	Debit Balances	Credit Balances	Debit Balances	Credit Balances
Cash	4,750		4,750	
Accounts Receivable	17,400		17,400	
Supplies	6,200		1,850	
Prepaid Insurance	9,000		3,600	
Land	50,000		50,000	
Buildings	120,000		120,000	
Accumulated Depreciation—Buildings		51,500		58,100
Trucks	75,000		75,000	
Accumulated Depreciation—Trucks		12,000		14,300
Accounts Payable		6,920		7,520
Salaries Payable		—		1,180
Unearned Service Fees		10,500		5,100
Capital Stock		50,000		50,000
Retained Earnings		106,400		106,400
Dividends	7,500		7,500	
Service Fees Earned		162,680		168,080
Salary Expense	80,000		81,180	
Depreciation Expense—Trucks	—		2,300	
Rent Expense	11,900		11,900	
Supplies Expense	—		4,350	
Utilities Expense	6,200		6,800	
Depreciation Expense—Buildings	—		6,600	
Taxes Expense	2,900		2,900	
Insurance Expense	—		5,400	
Miscellaneous Expense	9,150		9,150	
	400,000	400,000	410,680	410,680

Instructions

Journalize the seven entries that adjusted the accounts at March 31. None of the accounts were affected by more than one adjusting entry.

PR 3-5A
Adjusting entries and
adjusted trial balances
objs. 2, 3, 4

✔ 2. Total of Debit
column: $333,050

Jacksonville Financial Services Co., which specializes in appliance repair services, is owned and operated by Cindy Latty. Jacksonville Financial Services Co.'s accounting clerk prepared the unadjusted trial balance at December 31, 2010, shown below.

Jacksonville Financial Services Co.
Unadjusted Trial Balance
December 31, 2010

	Debit Balances	Credit Balances
Cash	10,200	
Accounts Receivable	34,750	
Prepaid Insurance	6,000	
Supplies	1,725	
Land	50,000	
Building	80,750	
Accumulated Depreciation—Building		37,850
Equipment	45,000	
Accumulated Depreciation—Equipment		17,650
Accounts Payable		3,750
Unearned Rent		3,600
Capital Stock		25,000
Retained Earnings		78,550
Dividends	8,000	
Fees Earned		158,600
Salaries and Wages Expense	56,850	
Utilities Expense	14,100	
Advertising Expense	7,500	
Repairs Expense	6,100	
Miscellaneous Expense	4,025	
	325,000	325,000

The data needed to determine year-end adjustments are as follows:

a. Depreciation of building for the year, $2,100.
b. Depreciation of equipment for the year, $3,000.
c. Accrued salaries and wages at December 31, $800.
d. Unexpired insurance at December 31, $1,500.
e. Fees earned but unbilled on December 31, $2,150.
f. Supplies on hand at December 31, $600.
g. Rent unearned at December 31, $1,500.

Instructions

1. Journalize the adjusting entries. Add additional accounts as needed.
2. Determine the balances of the accounts affected by the adjusting entries and prepare an adjusted trial balance.

PR 3-6A
Adjusting entries and errors

obj. 3

✔ 2. Corrected Net Income: $135,375

At the end of July, the first month of operations, the following selected data were taken from the financial statements of Monita Forche, Attorney at Law, P.C.:

Net income for July	$135,800
Total assets at July 31	750,000
Total liabilities at July 31	250,000
Total stockholders' equity at July 31	500,000

In preparing the financial statements, adjustments for the following data were overlooked:

a. Unbilled fees earned at July 31, $6,700.
b. Depreciation of equipment for July, $3,000.
c. Accrued wages at July 31, $2,150.
d. Supplies used during July, $1,975.

Instructions

1. Journalize the entries to record the omitted adjustments.
2. Determine the correct amount of net income for July and the total assets, liabilities, and stockholders' equity at July 31. In addition to indicating the corrected amounts, indicate the effect of each omitted adjustment by setting up and completing a columnar table similar to the following. Adjustment (a) is presented as an example.

	Net Income	Total Assets	= Total Liabilities	+ Total Stockholders' Equity
Reported amounts	$135,800	$750,000	$250,000	$500,000
Corrections:				
Adjustment (a)	+6,700	+6,700	0	+6,700
Adjustment (b)				
Adjustment (c)				
Adjustment (d)				
Corrected amounts				

Problems Series B

PR 3-1B
Adjusting entries

obj. 2

On March 31, 2010, the following data were accumulated to assist the accountant in preparing the adjusting entries for Hackney Realty:

a. The supplies account balance on March 31 is $2,315. The supplies on hand on March 31 are $990.
b. The unearned rent account balance on March 31 is $7,950, representing the receipt of an advance payment on March 1 of three months' rent from tenants.
c. Wages accrued but not paid at March 31 are $800.

d. Fees accrued but unbilled at March 31 are $7,100.
e. Depreciation of office equipment is $700.

Instructions

1. Journalize the adjusting entries required at March 31, 2010.
2. Briefly explain the difference between adjusting entries and entries that would be made to correct errors.

PR 3-2B
Adjusting entries
obj. 2

Selected account balances before adjustment for Perfect Realty at October 31, 2010, the end of the current year, are as follows:

	Debits	Credits
Accounts Receivable	$ 40,000	
Equipment	100,000	
Accumulated Depreciation		$ 12,000
Prepaid Rent	9,000	
Supplies	1,800	
Wages Payable		—
Unearned Fees		6,000
Fees Earned		215,000
Wages Expense	75,000	
Rent Expense	—	
Depreciation Expense	—	
Supplies Expense	—	

Data needed for year-end adjustments are as follows:

a. Unbilled fees at October 31, $2,900.
b. Supplies on hand at October 31, $400.
c. Rent expired, $6,000.
d. Depreciation of equipment during year, $3,000.
e. Unearned fees at October 31, $800.
f. Wages accrued but not paid at October 31, $1,400.

Instructions

Journalize the six adjusting entries required at October 31, based on the data presented.

PR 3-3B
Adjusting entries
obj. 2

Chinook Company, an electronics repair store, prepared the unadjusted trial balance shown below at the end of its first year of operations.

Chinook Company
Unadjusted Trial Balance
November 30, 2010

	Debit Balances	Credit Balances
Cash	6,900	
Accounts Receivable	45,000	
Supplies	10,800	
Equipment	227,400	
Accounts Payable		10,500
Unearned Fees		12,000
Capital Stock		20,000
Retained Earnings		136,000
Dividends	9,000	
Fees Earned		271,500
Wages Expense	63,000	
Rent Expense	48,000	
Utilities Expense	34,500	
Miscellaneous Expense	5,400	
	450,000	450,000

For preparing the adjusting entries, the following data were assembled:

a. Fees earned but unbilled on November 30 were $1,300.
b. Supplies on hand on November 30 were $3,100.
c. Depreciation of equipment was estimated to be $3,500 for the year.
d. The balance in unearned fees represented the November 1 receipt in advance for services to be provided. Only $4,000 of the services was provided between November 1 and November 30.
e. Unpaid wages accrued on November 30 were $900.

Instructions

Journalize the adjusting entries necessary on November 30, 2010.

PR 3-4B
Adjusting entries
objs. **2, 3, 4**

Luxor Company specializes in the repair of music equipment and is owned and operated by Amy Busby. On November 30, 2010, the end of the current year, the accountant for Luxor Company prepared the following trial balances:

Luxor Company
Trial Balance
November 30, 2010

	Unadjusted		Adjusted	
	Debit Balances	Credit Balances	Debit Balances	Credit Balances
Cash	38,250		38,250	
Accounts Receivable	109,500		109,500	
Supplies	11,250		2,700	
Prepaid Insurance	14,250		4,500	
Equipment	360,450		360,450	
Accumulated Depreciation—Equipment		94,500		102,000
Automobiles	109,500		109,500	
Accumulated Depreciation—Automobiles		54,750		61,200
Accounts Payable		24,930		26,400
Salaries Payable		—		6,000
Unearned Service Fees		18,000		8,700
Capital Stock		150,000		150,000
Retained Earnings		244,020		244,020
Dividends	75,000		75,000	
Service Fees Earned		733,800		743,100
Salary Expense	516,900		522,900	
Rent Expense	54,000		54,000	
Supplies Expense	—		8,550	
Depreciation Expense—Equipment	—		7,500	
Depreciation Expense—Automobiles	—		6,450	
Utilities Expense	12,900		14,370	
Taxes Expense	8,175		8,175	
Insurance Expense	—		9,750	
Miscellaneous Expense	9,825		9,825	
	1,320,000	1,320,000	1,341,420	1,341,420

Instructions

Journalize the seven entries that adjusted the accounts at November 30. None of the accounts were affected by more than one adjusting entry.

PR 3-5B
Adjusting entries and adjusted trial balances
objs. **2, 3, 4**

✔ 2. Total of Debit column: $822,180

Misfire Company is a small editorial services company owned and operated by Pedro Borman. On August 31, 2010, the end of the current year, Misfire Company's accounting clerk prepared the unadjusted trial balance shown on the next page.
　The data needed to determine year-end adjustments are as follows:

a. Unexpired insurance at August 31, $1,800.
b. Supplies on hand at August 31, $750.
c. Depreciation of building for the year, $2,000.
d. Depreciation of equipment for the year, $5,000.
e. Rent unearned at August 31, $2,850.

f. Accrued salaries and wages at August 31, $2,800.
g. Fees earned but unbilled on August 31, $12,380.

Misfire Company
Unadjusted Trial Balance
August 31, 2010

	Debit Balances	Credit Balances
Cash	7,500	
Accounts Receivable	38,400	
Prepaid Insurance	7,200	
Supplies	1,980	
Land	112,500	
Building	200,250	
Accumulated Depreciation—Building		137,550
Equipment	135,300	
Accumulated Depreciation—Equipment		97,950
Accounts Payable		12,150
Unearned Rent		6,750
Capital Stock		100,000
Retained Earnings		121,000
Dividends	15,000	
Fees Earned		324,600
Salaries and Wages Expense	193,370	
Utilities Expense	42,375	
Advertising Expense	22,800	
Repairs Expense	17,250	
Miscellaneous Expense	6,075	
	800,000	800,000

Instructions

1. Journalize the adjusting entries. Add additional accounts as needed.
2. Determine the balances of the accounts affected by the adjusting entries, and prepare an adjusted trial balance.

PR 3-6B
Adjusting entries and errors

obj. 3

✔ 2 Corrected Net Income: $136,850

At the end of April, the first month of operations, the following selected data were taken from the financial statements of Beth Cato, Attorney at Law, P.C.:

Net income for April	$125,750
Total assets at April 30	500,000
Total liabilities at April 30	180,000
Total stockholders' equity at April 30	320,000

In preparing the financial statements, adjustments for the following data were overlooked:

a. Supplies used during April, $3,100.
b. Unbilled fees earned at April 30, $18,750.
c. Depreciation of equipment for April, $2,700.
d. Accrued wages at April 30, $1,850.

Instructions

1. Journalize the entries to record the omitted adjustments.
2. Determine the correct amount of net income for April and the total assets, liabilities, and stockholders' equity at April 30. In addition to indicating the corrected amounts, indicate the effect of each omitted adjustment by setting up and completing a columnar table similar to the following. Adjustment (a) is presented as an example.

	Net Income	Total Assets =	Total Liabilities +	Total Stockholders' Equity
Reported amounts	$125,750	$500,000	$180,000	$320,000
Corrections:				
Adjustment (a)	−3,100	−3,100	0	−3,100
Adjustment (b)				
Adjustment (c)				
Adjustment (d)				
Corrected amounts				

Continuing Problem

✔ 3. Total of Debit
column: $40,460

The unadjusted trial balance that you prepared for Music Depot at the end of Chapter 2 should appear as follows:

Music Depot
Unadjusted Trial Balance
July 31, 2010

	Debit Balances	Credit Balances
Cash	12,780	
Accounts Receivable	3,150	
Supplies	850	
Prepaid Insurance	2,700	
Office Equipment	5,000	
Accounts Payable		5,680
Unearned Revenue		7,200
Capital Stock		10,500
Dividends	1,700	
Fees Earned		15,300
Wages Expense	2,400	
Office Rent Expense	2,750	
Equipment Rent Expense	1,100	
Utilities Expense	860	
Music Expense	2,810	
Advertising Expense	1,600	
Supplies Expense	180	
Miscellaneous Expense	800	
	38,680	38,680

The data needed to determine adjustments for the two-month period ending July 31, 2010, are as follows:

a. During July, Music Depot provided guest disc jockeys for WHBD for a total of 120 hours. For information on the amount of the accrued revenue to be billed to WHBD, see the contract described in the July 3, 2010, transaction at the end of Chapter 2.

b. Supplies on hand at July 31, $175.

c. The balance of the prepaid insurance account relates to the July 1, 2010, transaction at the end of Chapter 2.

d. Depreciation of the office equipment is $60.

e. The balance of the unearned revenue account relates to the contract between Music Depot and WHBD, described in the July 3, 2010, transaction at the end of Chapter 2.

f. Accrued wages as of July 31, 2010, were $120.

Instructions

1. Prepare adjusting journal entries. You will need the following additional accounts:

    18 Accumulated Depreciation—Office Equipment
    22 Wages Payable
    57 Insurance Expense
    58 Depreciation Expense

2. Post the adjusting entries, inserting balances in the accounts affected.

3. Prepare an adjusted trial balance.

Special Activities

SA 3-1
Ethics and professional conduct in business

Cliff Hall opened Meridian Co. on January 1, 2009. At the end of the first year, the business needed additional capital. On behalf of Meridian, Cliff applied to Federal National Bank for a loan of $300,000. Based on Meridian financial statements, which had been prepared on a cash basis, the Federal National Bank loan officer rejected the loan as too risky.

After receiving the rejection notice, Cliff instructed his accountant to prepare the financial statements on an accrual basis. These statements included $48,500 in accounts receivable and $15,650 in accounts payable. Cliff then instructed his accountant to record an additional $20,000 of accounts receivable for commissions on property for which a contract had been signed on December 28, 2009, but which would not be formally "closed" and the title transferred until January 5, 2010.

Cliff then applied for a $300,000 loan from First City Bank, using the revised financial statements. On this application, Cliff indicated that he had not previously been rejected for credit.

Discuss the ethical and professional conduct of Cliff Hall in applying for the loan from First City Bank.

SA 3-2
Accrued expense

On December 30, 2010, you buy a Ford Expedition. It comes with a three-year, 36,000-mile warranty. On March 5, 2011, you return the Expedition to the dealership for some basic repairs covered under the warranty. The cost of the repairs to the dealership is $1,645. In what year, 2010 or 2011, should Ford Motor Company recognize the cost of the warranty repairs as an expense?

SA 3-3
Accrued revenue

The following is an excerpt from a conversation between Joel Loomis and Krista Truitt just before they boarded a flight to Paris on Delta Air Lines. They are going to Paris to attend their company's annual sales conference.

Joel: Krista, aren't you taking an introductory accounting course at college?

Krista: Yes, I decided it's about time I learned something about accounting. You know, our annual bonuses are based on the sales figures that come from the accounting department.

Joel: I guess I never really thought about it.

Krista: You should think about it! Last year, I placed a $750,000 order on December 28. But when I got my bonus, the $750,000 sale wasn't included. They said it hadn't been shipped until January 3, so it would have to count in next year's bonus.

Joel: A real bummer!

Krista: Right! I was counting on that bonus including the $750,000 sale.

Joel: Did you complain?

Krista: Yes, but it didn't do any good. Ashley, the head accountant, said something about matching revenues and expenses. Also, something about not recording revenues until the sale is final. I figure I'd take the accounting course and find out whether she's just jerking me around.

Joel: I never really thought about it. When do you think Delta Air Lines will record its revenues from this flight?

Krista: Hmmm . . . I guess it could record the revenue when it sells the ticket . . . or . . . when the boarding passes are taken at the door . . . or . . . when we get off the plane . . . or when our company pays for the tickets . . . or . . . I don't know. I'll ask my accounting instructor.

Discuss when Delta Air Lines should recognize the revenue from ticket sales to properly match revenues and expenses.

SA 3-4
Adjustments and
financial statements

Several years ago, your brother opened Niagara Appliance Repairs. He made a small initial investment and added money from his personal bank account as needed. He withdrew money for living expenses at irregular intervals. As the business grew, he hired an assistant. He is now considering adding more employees, purchasing additional service trucks, and purchasing the building he now rents. To secure funds for the expansion, your brother submitted a loan application to the bank and included the most recent financial statements (shown below) prepared from accounts maintained by a part-time bookkeeper.

Niagara Appliance Repairs
Income Statement
For the Year Ended October 31, 2010

Service revenue		$112,500
Less: Rent paid	$31,200	
Wages paid	24,750	
Supplies paid	7,000	
Utilities paid	6,500	
Insurance paid	3,600	
Miscellaneous payments	9,100	82,150
Net income		$ 30,350

(continued)

Niagara Appliance Repairs
Balance Sheet
October 31, 2010

Assets

Cash	$15,900
Amounts due from customers	18,750
Truck	55,350
Total assets	$90,000

Equities

Owner's equity	$90,000

After reviewing the financial statements, the loan officer at the bank asked your brother if he used the accrual basis of accounting for revenues and expenses. Your brother responded that he did and that is why he included an account for "Amounts Due from Customers." The loan officer then asked whether or not the accounts were adjusted prior to the preparation of the statements. Your brother answered that they had not been adjusted.

a. Why do you think the loan officer suspected that the accounts had not been ad-justed prior to the preparation of the statements?
b. Indicate possible accounts that might need to be adjusted before an accurate set of financial statements could be prepared.

SA 3-5
Codes of ethics

Group Project

Obtain a copy of your college or university's student code of conduct. In groups of three or four, answer the following question:

1. Compare this code of conduct with the accountant's Codes of Professional Conduct, which is linked to the text Web site at **academic.cengage.com/accounting/warren**.
2. One of your classmates asks you for permission to copy your homework, which your instructor will be collecting and grading for part of your overall term grade. Although your instructor has not stated whether one student may or may not copy another student's homework, is it ethical for you to allow your classmate to copy your homework? Is it ethical for your classmate to copy your homework?

Answers to Self-Examination Questions

1. **A**   A deferral is the delay in recording an ex-pense already paid, such as prepaid insurance (answer A). Wages payable (answer B) is con-sidered an accrued expense or accrued liability. Fees earned (answer C) is a revenue item. Accumulated depreciation (answer D) is a con-tra account to a fixed asset.

2. **D**   The balance in the supplies account, before adjustment, represents the amount of supplies available. From this amount ($2,250) is subtracted the amount of supplies on hand ($950) to deter-mine the supplies used ($1,300). Since increases in expense accounts are recorded by debits and decreases in asset accounts are recorded by cred-its, answer D is the correct entry.

3. **C**   The failure to record the adjusting entry deb-iting Unearned Rent, $600, and crediting Rent Revenue, $600, would have the effect of over-stating liabilities by $600 and understating net income by $600 (answer C).

4. **C**   Since increases in expense accounts (such as depreciation expense) are recorded by debits and it is customary to record the decreases in useful-ness of fixed assets as credits to accumulated de-preciation accounts, answer C is the correct entry.

5. **D**   The book value of a fixed asset is the differ-ence between the balance in the asset account and the balance in the related accumulated de-preciation account, or $22,500 − $14,000, as in-dicated by answer D ($8,500).

CHAPTER 4

Completing the Accounting Cycle

ELECTRONIC ARTS INC.

Most of us have had to file a personal tax return. At the beginning of the year, you estimate your upcoming income and decide whether you need to increase your payroll tax withholdings or perhaps pay estimated taxes. During the year, you earn income and enter into tax-related transactions, such as making charitable contributions. At the end of the year, your employer sends you a tax withholding information form (W-2) form, and you collect the tax records needed for completing your yearly tax forms. As the next year begins, you start the cycle all over again.

Businesses also go through a cycle of activities. For example, Electronic Arts Inc., the world's largest developer and marketer of electronic game software, begins its cycle by developing new or revised game titles, such as Madden NFL Football®, Need for Speed®, Tiger Woods PGA Tour®, The Sims®, and The Lord of the Rings®. These games are marketed and sold throughout the year. During the year, operating transactions of the business are recorded. For Electronic Arts, such transactions include the salaries for game developers, advertising expenditures, costs for producing and packaging games, and game revenues. At the end of the year, financial statements are prepared that summarize the operating activities for the year. Electronic Arts publishes these statements on its Web site at **http://investor.ea.com**. Finally, before the start of the next year, the accounts are readied for recording the operations of the next year.

As we saw in Chapter 1, the initial cycle for NetSolutions began with Chris Clark's investment in the business on November 1, 2009. The cycle continued with recording NetSolutions' transactions for November and December, as we discussed and illustrated in Chapters 1 and 2. In Chapter 3, the cycle continued when the adjusting entries for the two months ending December 31, 2009, were recorded. In this chapter, we complete the cycle for NetSolutions by preparing financial statements and getting the accounts ready for recording transactions of the next period.

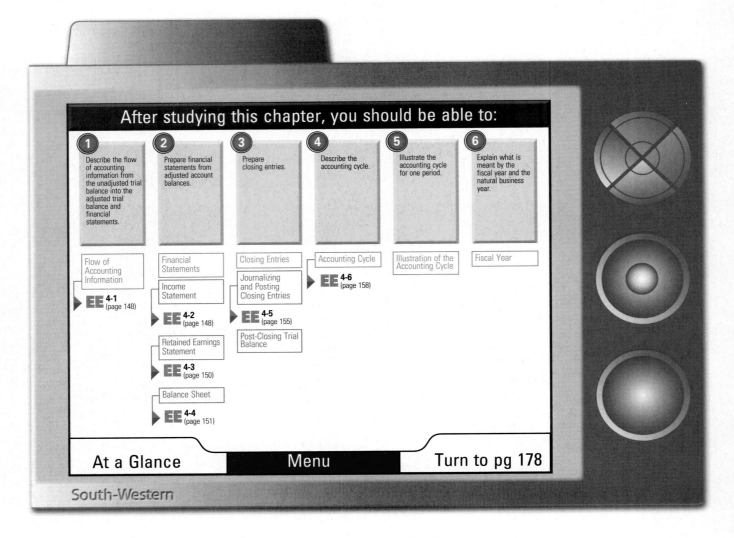

After studying this chapter, you should be able to:

1 Describe the flow of accounting information from the unadjusted trial balance into the adjusted trial balance and financial statements.

2 Prepare financial statements from adjusted account balances.

3 Prepare closing entries.

4 Describe the accounting cycle.

5 Illustrate the accounting cycle for one period.

6 Explain what is meant by the fiscal year and the natural business year.

Flow of Accounting Information

EE 4-1 (page 148)

Financial Statements

Income Statement

EE 4-2 (page 148)

Retained Earnings Statement

EE 4-3 (page 150)

Balance Sheet

EE 4-4 (page 151)

Closing Entries

Journalizing and Posting Closing Entries

EE 4-5 (page 155)

Post-Closing Trial Balance

Accounting Cycle

EE 4-6 (page 158)

Illustration of the Accounting Cycle

Fiscal Year

At a Glance   Menu   Turn to pg 178

South-Western

---

1 Describe the flow of accounting information from the unadjusted trial balance into the adjusted trial balance and financial statements.

@netsolutions

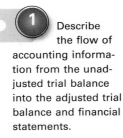

Many companies use Microsoft's Excel® software to prepare end-of-period spreadsheets (work sheets).

Flow of Accounting Information

The end-of-period process by which accounts are adjusted and the financial statements are prepared is one of the most important in accounting. Using our illustration of NetSolutions from Chapters 1–3, this process is summarized in spreadsheet form in Exhibit 1.

Exhibit 1 begins with the unadjusted trial balance as of the end of the period. The unadjusted trial balance verifies that the total of the debit balances equals the total of the credit balances. If the trial balance totals are unequal, an error has occurred. Any error must be found and corrected before the end-of-period process can continue.

The adjustments for NetSolutions from Chapter 3 are shown in the Adjustments columns of Exhibit 1. Cross-referencing (by letters) the debit and credit of each adjustment is useful in reviewing the impact of the adjustments on the unadjusted account balances. The adjustments are normally entered in the order in which the data are assembled. If the titles of the accounts to be adjusted do not appear in the unadjusted trial balance, the accounts are inserted in their proper order in the Account Title column. The total of the Adjustments columns verifies that the debits equals the credits for the adjustment data and adjusting entries. The total of the Debit column must equal the total of the Credit column.

The adjustment data are added to or subtracted from the amounts in the Unadjusted Trial Balance columns to arrive at the Adjusted Trial Balance columns. In this way, the Adjusted Trial Balance columns of Exhibit 1 illustrate the impact of the adjusting entries on the unadjusted accounts. The totals of the Adjusted Trial Balance columns verify the equality of the totals of the debit and credit balances after adjustment.

Exhibit 1 also illustrates the flow of accounts from the adjusted trial balance into the financial statements as follows:

1. The revenue and expense accounts are extended to (flow into) the Income Statement columns.

2. At the bottom of the Income Statement columns, the net income or net loss for the period is the difference between the total Credit Column (revenues) and the total Debit column (expenses). If the Income Statement Credit column total (revenues) is greater than the Income Statement Debit column total (expenses), the difference is the net income. If the Income Statement Debit column total is greater than the Income Statement Credit column total, the difference is a net loss. Exhibit 1 shows that NetSolutions had net income of $7,105 for the period.

3. The assets, liabilities, capital stock, and dividends accounts are extended (flow into) to the Balance Sheet columns.

4. At the bottom of the Balance Sheet column, the net income or net loss for the period is the difference between the total Debit column and the total Credit column. Since net income increases stockholders' equity (retained earnings), NetSolutions' net income of $7,105 is shown in the Balance Sheet Credit column.

To summarize, Exhibit 1 illustrates the end-of-period process by which accounts are adjusted. In addition, Exhibit 1 illustrates how the adjusted accounts flow into the financial statements. The financial statements for NetSolutions can be prepared directly from Exhibit 1.

The spreadsheet in Exhibit 1 is not a required part of the accounting process. However, many accountants prepare such a spreadsheet, often called a work sheet, in manual or electronic form, as part of their normal end-of-period process. The primary advantage in doing so is that it allows managers and accountants to see the impact of the adjustments on the financial statements. This is especially useful for adjustments

Exhibit 1

End-of-Period Spreadsheet (Work Sheet)

	A	B	C	D	E	F	G	H	I	J	K
1					NetSolutions						
2					End-of-Period Spreadsheet (Work Sheet)						
3					For the Two Months Ended December 31, 2009						
4		Unadjusted				Adjusted					
5		Trial Balance		Adjustments		Trial Balance		Income Statement		Balance Sheet	
6	Account Title	Dr.	Cr.	Dr.	Cr.	Dr.	Cr.	Dr.	Cr.	Dr.	Cr.
7											
8	Cash	2,065				2,065				2,065	
9	Accounts Receivable	2,220		(d) 500		2,720				2,720	
10	Supplies	2,000			(a) 1,240	760				760	
11	Prepaid Insurance	2,400			(b) 200	2,200				2,200	
12	Land	20,000				20,000				20,000	
13	Office Equipment	1,800				1,800				1,800	
14	Accumulated Depreciation				(f) 50		50				50
15	Accounts Payable		900				900				900
16	Wages Payable				(e) 250		250				250
17	Unearned Rent		360	(c) 120			240				240
18	Capital Stock		25,000				25,000				25,000
19	Dividends	4,000				4,000				4,000	
20	Fees Earned		16,340		(d) 500		16,840		16,840		
21	Rent Revenue				(c) 120		120		120		
22	Wages Expense	4,275		(e) 250		4,525		4,525			
23	Rent Expense	1,600				1,600		1,600			
24	Depreciation Expense			(f) 50		50		50			
25	Utilities Expense	985				985		985			
26	Supplies Expense	800		(a) 1,240		2,040		2,040			
27	Insurance Expense			(b) 200		200		200			
28	Miscellaneous Expense	455				455		455			
29		42,600	42,600	2,360	2,360	43,400	43,400	9,855	16,960	33,545	26,440
30	Net income							7,105			7,105
31								16,960	16,960	33,545	33,545
32											

that depend upon estimates. We discuss such estimates and their impact on the financial statements in later chapters.[1]

Example Exercise 4-1   Flow of Accounts into Financial Statements

The balances for the accounts listed below appear in the Adjusted Trial Balance columns of the end-of-period spreadsheet (work sheet). Indicate whether each balance should be extended to (a) an Income Statement column or (b) a Balance Sheet column.

1. Dividends
2. Utilities Expense
3. Accumulated Depreciation—Equipment
4. Unearned Rent

5. Fees Earned
6. Accounts Payable
7. Rent Revenue
8. Supplies

Follow My Example 4-1

1. Balance Sheet column
2. Income Statement column
3. Balance Sheet column
4. Balance Sheet column

5. Income Statement column
6. Balance Sheet column
7. Income Statement column
8. Balance Sheet column

For Practice: PE 4-1A, PE 4-1B

Prepare financial statements from adjusted account balances.

Financial Statements

Using Exhibit 1, the financial statements for NetSolutions can be prepared. The income statement, the retained earnings statement, and the balance sheet are shown in Exhibit 2.

Income Statement

@netsolutions

The income statement is prepared directly from the Income Statement or Adjusted Trial Balance columns of Exhibit 1 beginning with fees earned of $16,840. The expenses in the income statement in Exhibit 2 are listed in order of size, beginning with the larger items. Miscellaneous expense is the last item, regardless of its amount.

Example Exercise 4-2   Determining Net Income from End-of-Period Spreadsheet

In the Balance Sheet columns of the end-of-period spreadsheet (work sheet) for Dimple Consulting Co. for the current year, the Debit column total is $678,450, and the Credit column total is $599,750 before the amount for net income or net loss has been included. In preparing the income statement from the end-of-period spreadsheet (work sheet), what is the amount of net income or net loss?

Follow My Example 4-2

A net income of $78,700 ($678,450 − $599,750) would be reported. When the Debit column of the Balance Sheet columns is more than the Credit column, net income is reported. If the Credit column exceeds the Debit column, a net loss is reported.

For Practice: PE 4-2A, PE 4-2B

Integrity, Objectivity, and Ethics in Business

THE ROUND TRIP

A common type of fraud involves artificially inflating revenue. One fraudulent method of inflating revenue is called "round tripping." Under this scheme, a selling company (S) "lends" money to a customer company (C). The money is then used by C to purchase a product from S. Thus, S sells product to C and is paid with the money just loaned to C! This looks like a sale in the accounting records, but in reality, S is shipping free product. The fraud is exposed when it is determined that there was no intent to repay the original loan.

---

1 The appendix to this chapter describes and illustrates how to prepare the end-of-period spreadsheet (work sheet).

Exhibit 2

Financial Statements Prepared from Work Sheet

NetSolutions
Income Statement
For the Two Months Ended December 31, 2009

Fees earned	$16,840	
Rent revenue	120	
Total revenues		$16,960
Expenses:		
Wages expense	$4,525	
Supplies expense	2,040	
Rent expense	1,600	
Utilities expense	985	
Insurance expense	200	
Depreciation expense	50	
Miscellaneous expense	455	
Total expenses		9,855
Net income		$ 7,105

NetSolutions
Retained Earnings Statement
For the Two Months Ended December 31, 2009

Retained earnings, November 1, 2009		$ 0
Net income for November and December	$7,105	
Less dividends	4,000	
Increase in retained earnings		3,105
Retained earnings, December 31, 2009		$3,105

NetSolutions
Balance Sheet
December 31, 2009

Assets			Liabilities		
Current assets:			Current liabilities:		
Cash	$ 2,065		Accounts payable	$900	
Accounts receivable	2,720		Wages payable	250	
Supplies	760		Unearned rent	240	
Prepaid insurance	2,200		Total liabilities		$ 1,390
Total current assets		$ 7,745			
Property, plant, and equipment:					
Land	$20,000				
Office equipment	$1,800		**Stockholders' Equity**		
Less accum. depreciation 50	1,750		Capital stock	$25,000	
Total property, plant,			Retained earnings	3,105	
and equipment		21,750	Total stockholders' equity		28,105
Total assets		$29,495	Total liabilities and stockholders' equity		$29,495

Retained Earnings Statement

The first item normally presented on the retained earnings statement is the balance of the retained earnings account at the beginning of the period. Since NetSolutions began operations on November 1, this balance is zero in Exhibit 2. Then, the retained earnings statement shows the net income for the two months ended December 31, 2009. The amount of dividends is deducted from the net income to arrive at the retained earnings as of December 31, 2009.

For the following period, the beginning balance of retained earnings for NetSolutions is the ending balance that was reported for the previous period. For example, assume that during 2010, NetSolutions earned net income of $149,695 and paid dividends of $24,000. The retained earnings statement for the year ending December 31, 2010, for NetSolutions is as follows:

NetSolutions
Retained Earnings Statement
For the Month Ended December 31, 2010

Retained earnings, January 1, 2010		$ 3,105
Net income for the year	$149,695	
Less dividends	24,000	
Increase in retained earnings		125,695
Retained earnings, December 31, 2010		$128,800

For NetSolutions, the amount of dividends was less than the net income. If the dividends had exceeded the net income, the order of the net income and the dividends would have been reversed. The difference between the two items would then be deducted from the beginning Retained Earnings balance. Other factors, such as a net loss, may also require some change in the form of the retained earnings statement, as shown in the following example:

Retained earnings, January 1, 20—		$45,000
Net loss for the year	$5,600	
Dividends	9,500	
Decrease in retained earnings		15,100
Retained earnings, December 31, 20—		$29,900

Example Exercise 4-3 Retained Earnings Statement ●●●●●●●● 2

Zack Gaddis owns and operates Gaddis Employment Services. On January 1, 2009, Retained Earnings had a balance of $186,000. During the year, an additional $40,000 of capital stock was issued for cash and dividends of $25,000 were paid. For the year ended December 31, 2009, Gaddis Employment Services reported a net income of $18,750. Prepare a retained earnings statement for the year ended December 31, 2009.

Follow My Example 4-3

GADDIS EMPLOYMENT SERVICES
RETAINED EARNINGS STATEMENT
For the Year Ended December 31, 2009

Retained earnings, January 1, 2009		$186,000
Dividends	$ 25,000	
Less net income	18,750	
Decrease in retained earnings		6,250
Retained earnings, December 31, 2009		$179,750

For Practice: PE 4-3A, PE 4-3B

Balance Sheet

The balance sheet is prepared directly from the Balance Sheet or Adjusted Trial Balance columns of Exhibit 1 beginning with Cash of $2,065.

The balance sheet in Exhibit 2 shows subsections for assets and liabilities. Such a balance sheet is a *classified balance sheet*. These subsections are described next.

> **Two common classes of assets are current assets and property, plant, and equipment.**

Assets Assets are commonly divided into two sections on the balance sheet: (1) current assets and (2) property, plant, and equipment.

Current Assets Cash and other assets that are expected to be converted to cash or sold or used up usually within one year or less, through the normal operations of the business, are called **current assets.** In addition to cash, the current assets may include notes receivable, accounts receivable, supplies, and other prepaid expenses.

Notes receivable are amounts that customers owe. They are written promises to pay the amount of the note and interest. Accounts receivable are also amounts customers owe, but they are less formal than notes. Accounts receivable normally result from providing services or selling merchandise on account. Notes receivable and accounts receivable are current assets because they are usually converted to cash within one year or less.

Property, Plant, and Equipment The property, plant, and equipment section may also be described as **fixed assets** or **plant assets.** These assets include equipment, machinery, buildings, and land. With the exception of land, as we discussed in Chapter 3, fixed assets depreciate over a period of time. The cost, accumulated depreciation, and book value of each major type of fixed asset are normally reported on the balance sheet or in the notes to the financial statements.

> **Two common classes of liabilities are current liabilities and long-term liabilities.**

Liabilities Liabilities are the amounts the business owes to creditors. Liabilities are commonly divided into two sections on the balance sheet: (1) current liabilities and (2) long-term liabilities.

Current Liabilities Liabilities that will be due within a short time (usually one year or less) and that are to be paid out of current assets are called **current liabilities.** The most common liabilities in this group are notes payable and accounts payable. Other current liabilities may include Wages Payable, Interest Payable, Taxes Payable, and Unearned Fees.

Long-Term Liabilities Liabilities that will not be due for a long time (usually more than one year) are called **long-term liabilities.** If NetSolutions had long-term liabilities, they would be reported below the current liabilities. As long-term liabilities come due and are to be paid within one year, they are reported as current liabilities. If they are to be renewed rather than paid, they would continue to be reported as long term. When an asset is pledged as security for a liability, the obligation may be called a *mortgage note payable* or a *mortgage payable.*

Stockholders' Equity The stockholders' right to the assets of the business is presented on the balance sheet below the liabilities section. The stockholders' equity consists of capital stock and retained earnings. The stockholders' equity is added to the total liabilities, and this total must be equal to the total assets.

Example Exercise 4-4 Classified Balance Sheet •••••••••▷ 2

The following accounts appear in an adjusted trial balance of Hindsight Consulting. Indicate whether each account would be reported in the (a) current asset; (b) property, plant, and equipment; (c) current liability; (d) long-term liability; or (e) stockholders' equity section of the December 31, 2009, balance sheet of Hindsight Consulting.

1. Capital Stock
2. Notes Receivable (due in 6 months)
3. Notes Payable (due in 2011)
4. Land
5. Cash
6. Unearned Rent (3 months)
7. Accumulated Depreciation—Equipment
8. Accounts Payable

(continued)

Follow My Example 4-4

1. Stockholders' equity
2. Current asset
3. Long-term liability
4. Property, plant, and equipment

5. Current asset
6. Current liability
7. Property, plant, and equipment
8. Current liability

For Practice: PE 4-4A, PE 4-4B

Business Connection

INTERNATIONAL DIFFERENCES

Financial statements prepared under accounting practices in other countries often differ from those prepared under generally accepted accounting principles in the United States. This is to be expected, since cultures and market structures differ from country to country.

To illustrate, BMW Group prepares its financial statements under International Financial Reporting Standards as adopted by the European Union. In doing so, BMW's balance sheet reports fixed assets first, followed by current assets. It also reports stockholders' equity before the liabilities. In contrast, balance sheets prepared under U.S. accounting principles report current assets followed by fixed assets and current liabilities followed by long-term liabilities and stockholders' equity. The U.S. form of balance sheet is organized to emphasize creditor interpretation and analysis. For example, current assets and current liabilities are presented first to facilitate their interpretation and analysis by creditors. Likewise, to emphasize their importance, liabilities are reported before stockholders' equity.

Regardless of these differences, the basic principles underlying the accounting equation and the double-entry accounting system are the same in Germany and the United States. Even though differences in recording and reporting exist, the accounting equation holds true: the total assets still equal the total liabilities and stockholders' equity.

---

3 Prepare closing entries.

⊜netsolutions

Closing Entries

As discussed in Chapter 3, the adjusting entries are recorded in the journal at the end of the accounting period. For NetSolutions, the adjusting entries are shown in Exhibit 7 of Chapter 3.

After the adjusting entries are posted to NetSolutions' ledger, shown in Exhibit 6 (on pages 156–157), the ledger agrees with the data reported on the financial statements.

The balances of the accounts reported on the balance sheet are carried forward from year to year. Because they are relatively permanent, these accounts are called **permanent accounts** or **real accounts**. For example, Cash, Accounts Receivable, Equipment, Accumulated Depreciation, Accounts Payable, Capital Stock, and Retained Earnings are all permanent accounts.

The balances of the accounts reported on the income statement are not carried forward from year to year. Also, the balance of the dividends account, which is reported on the retained earnings statement, is not carried forward. Because these accounts report amounts for only one period, they are called **temporary accounts** or **nominal accounts**. Temporary accounts are not carried forward because they relate only to one period. For example, the Fees Earned of $16,840 and Wages Expense of $4,525 for NetSolutions shown in Exhibit 2 are for the two months ending December 31, 2009, and should not be carried forward to 2010.

At the beginning of the next period, temporary accounts should have zero balances. To achieve this, temporary account balances are transferred to permanent accounts at the end of the accounting period. The entries that transfer these balances are called **closing entries**. The transfer process is called the **closing process** and is sometimes referred to as **closing the books**.

> **Closing entries transfer the balances of temporary accounts to the retained earnings account.**

The closing process involves the following four steps:

1. Revenue account balances are transferred to an account called Income Summary.
2. Expense account balances are transferred to an account called Income Summary.
3. The balance of Income Summary (net income or net loss) is transferred to the retained earnings account.
4. The balance of the dividends account is transferred to the retained earnings account.

Exhibit 3 diagrams the closing process.

Exhibit 3

The Closing Process

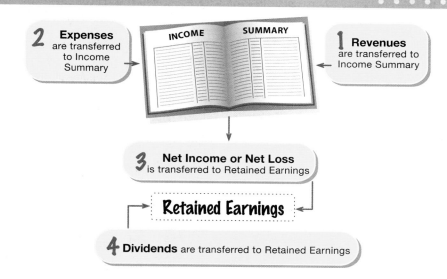

Income Summary is a temporary account that is only used during the closing process. At the beginning of the closing process, Income Summary has no balance. During the closing process, Income Summary will be debited and credited for various amounts. At the end of the closing process, Income Summary will again have no balance. Because Income Summary has the effect of clearing the revenue and expense accounts of their balances, it is sometimes called a **clearing account**. Other titles used for this account include Revenue and Expense Summary, Profit and Loss Summary, and Income and Expense Summary.

> The income summary account does not appear on the financial statements.

The four closing entries required in the closing process are as follows:

1. Debit each revenue account for its balance and credit Income Summary for the total revenue.
2. Credit each expense account for its balance and debit Income Summary for the total expenses.
3. Debit Income Summary for its balance and credit the retained earnings account.
4. Debit the retained earnings account for the balance of the dividends account and credit the dividends account.

In the case of a net loss, Income Summary will have a debit balance after the first two closing entries. In this case, credit Income Summary for the amount of its balance and debit the retained earnings account for the amount of the net loss.

Closing entries are recorded in the journal and are dated as of the last day of the accounting period. In the journal, closing entries are recorded immediately following the adjusting entries. The caption, *Closing Entries*, is often inserted above the closing entries to separate them from the adjusting entries.

It is possible to close the temporary revenue and expense accounts without using a clearing account such as Income Summary. In this case, the balances of the revenue and expense accounts are closed directly to the retained earnings account. This process may be used in a computerized accounting system. In a manual system, the use of an income summary account aids in detecting and correcting errors.

Journalizing and Posting Closing Entries

A flowchart of the four closing entries for NetSolutions is shown in Exhibit 4. The balances in the accounts are those shown in the Adjusted Trial Balance columns of the end-of-period spreadsheet shown in Exhibit 1.

Exhibit 4

Flowchart of Closing Entries for NetSolutions

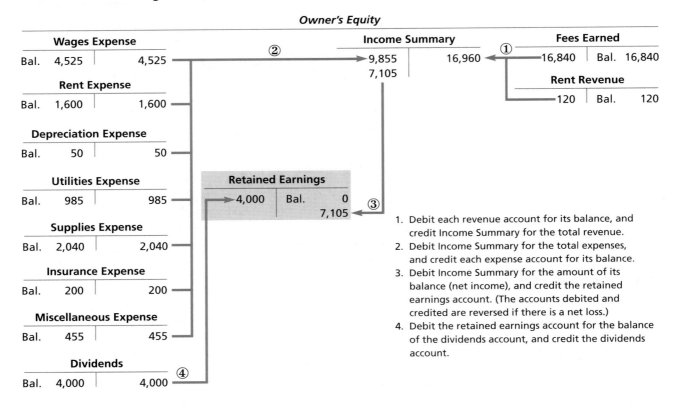

The closing entries for NetSolutions are shown in Exhibit 5. The account titles and balances for the these entries may be obtained from the end-of-period spreadsheet, the adjusted trial balance, the income statement, the retained earnings statement, or the ledger.

The closing entries are posted to NetSolutions ledger as shown in Exhibit 6 (pages 156–157). Income Summary has been added to NetSolutions' ledger in Exhibit 6 as account number 34. After the closing entries are posted, NetSolutions' ledger has the following characteristics:

1. The balance of Retained Earnings of $3,105 agrees with the amount reported on the retained earnings statement and the balance sheet.
2. The revenue, expense, and dividends accounts will have zero balances.

As shown in Exhibit 6, the closing entries are normally identified in the ledger as "Closing." In addition, a line is often inserted in both balance columns after a closing entry is posted. This separates next period's revenue, expense, and dividend transactions from those of the current period. Next period's transactions will be posted directly below the closing entry.

Exhibit 5

Closing Entries for NetSolutions

Journal   Page *6*

Date		Description	Post. Ref.	Debit	Credit
		Closing Entries			
2009 Dec.	31	Fees Earned	41	16,840	
		Rent Revenue	42	120	
		Income Summary	34		16,960
	31	Income Summary	34	9,855	
		Wages Expense	51		4,525
		Rent Expense	52		1,600
		Depreciation Expense	53		50
		Utilities Expense	54		985
		Supplies Expense	55		2,040
		Insurance Expense	56		200
		Miscellaneous Expense	59		455
	31	Income Summary	34	7,105	
		Retained Earnings	32		7,105
	31	Retained Earnings	32	4,000	
		Dividends	33		4,000

Example Exercise 4-5   Closing Entries   **3**

After the accounts have been adjusted at July 31, the end of the fiscal year, the following balances are taken from the ledger of Cabriolet Services Co.:

Retained Earnings	$615,850
Dividends	25,000
Fees Earned	380,450
Wages Expense	250,000
Rent Expense	65,000
Supplies Expense	18,250
Miscellaneous Expense	6,200

Journalize the four entries required to close the accounts.

Follow My Example 4-5

July	31	Fees Earned	380,450	
		Income Summary		380,450
	31	Income Summary	339,450	
		Wages Expense		250,000
		Rent Expense		65,000
		Supplies Expense		18,250
		Miscellaneous Expense		6,200
	31	Income Summary	41,000	
		Retained Earnings		41,000
	31	Retained Earnings	25,000	
		Dividends		25,000

For Practice: PE 4-5A, PE 4-5B

Exhibit 6

Ledger for NetSolutions

Ledger

Account Cash — Account No. 11

Date	Item	Post. Ref.	Debit	Credit	Balance Debit	Balance Credit
2009 Nov. 1		1	25,000		25,000	
5		1		20,000	5,000	
18		1	7,500		12,500	
30		1		3,650	8,850	
30		1		950	7,900	
30		2		2,000	5,900	
Dec. 1		2		2,400	3,500	
1		2		800	2,700	
1		2	360		3,060	
6		2		180	2,880	
11		2		400	2,480	
13		3		950	1,530	
16		3	3,100		4,630	
20		3		900	3,730	
21		3	650		4,380	
23		3		1,450	2,930	
27		3		1,200	1,730	
31		3		310	1,420	
31		4		225	1,195	
31		4	2,870		4,065	
31		4		2,000	2,065	

Account Accounts Receivable — Account No. 12

Date	Item	Post. Ref.	Debit	Credit	Balance Debit	Balance Credit
2009 Dec. 16		3	1,750		1,750	
21		3		650	1,100	
31		4	1,120		2,220	
31	Adjusting	5	500		2,720	

Account Supplies — Account No. 14

Date	Item	Post. Ref.	Debit	Credit	Balance Debit	Balance Credit
2009 Nov. 10		1	1,350		1,350	
30		1		800	550	
23		3	1,450		2,000	
Dec. 31	Adjusting	5		1,240	760	

Account Prepaid Insurance — Account No. 15

Date	Item	Post. Ref.	Debit	Credit	Balance Debit	Balance Credit
2009 Dec. 1		2	2,400		2,400	
31	Adjusting	5		200	2,200	

Account Land — Account No. 17

Date	Item	Post. Ref.	Debit	Credit	Balance Debit	Balance Credit
2009 Nov. 5		1	20,000		20,000	

Account Office Equipment — Account No. 18

Date	Item	Post. Ref.	Debit	Credit	Balance Debit	Balance Credit
2009 Dec. 4		2	1,800		1,800	

Account Accumulated Depreciation — Account No. 19

Date	Item	Post. Ref.	Debit	Credit	Balance Debit	Balance Credit
2009 Dec. 31	Adjusting	5		50		50

Account Accounts Payable — Account No. 21

Date	Item	Post. Ref.	Debit	Credit	Balance Debit	Balance Credit
2009 Nov. 10		1		1,350		1,350
30		1	950			400
Dec. 4		2		1,800		2,200
11		2	400			1,800
20		3	900			900

Account Wages Payable — Account No. 22

Date	Item	Post. Ref.	Debit	Credit	Balance Debit	Balance Credit
2009 Dec. 31	Adjusting	5		250		250

Account Unearned Rent — Account No. 23

Date	Item	Post. Ref.	Debit	Credit	Balance Debit	Balance Credit
2009 Dec. 1		2		360		360
31	Adjusting	5	120			240

Account Capital Stock — Account No. 31

Date	Item	Post. Ref.	Debit	Credit	Balance Debit	Balance Credit
2009 Nov. 1		1		25,000		25,000

Account Retained Earnings — Account No. 32

Date	Item	Post. Ref.	Debit	Credit	Balance Debit	Balance Credit
2009 Dec. 31	Closing	6		7,105		7,105
31	Closing	6	4,000			3,105

Account Dividends — Account No. 33

Date	Item	Post. Ref.	Debit	Credit	Balance Debit	Balance Credit
2009 Nov. 30		2	2,000		2,000	
Dec. 31		4	2,000		4,000	
31	Closing	6		4,000	—	—

Exhibit 6
(continued)

Account *Income Summary* — Account No. 34

Date	Item	Post. Ref.	Debit	Credit	Balance Debit	Balance Credit
2009						
Dec. 31	Closing	6		16,960		16,960
31	Closing	6	9,855			7,105
31	Closing	6	7,105		—	—

Account *Fees Earned* — Account No. 41

Date	Item	Post. Ref.	Debit	Credit	Balance Debit	Balance Credit
2009						
Nov. 18		1		7,500		7,500
Dec. 16		3		3,100		10,600
16		3		1,750		12,350
31		4		2,870		15,220
31		4		1,120		16,340
31	Adjusting	5		500		16,840
31	Closing	6	16,840		—	—

Account *Rent Revenue* — Account No. 42

Date	Item	Post. Ref.	Debit	Credit	Balance Debit	Balance Credit
2009						
Dec. 31	Adjusting	5		120		120
31	Closing	6	120		—	—

Account *Wages Expense* — Account No. 51

Date	Item	Post. Ref.	Debit	Credit	Balance Debit	Balance Credit
2009						
Nov. 30		1	2,125		2,125	
Dec. 13		3	950		3,075	
27		3	1,200		4,275	
31	Adjusting	5	250		4,525	
31	Closing	6		4,525	—	—

Account *Rent Expense* — Account No. 52

Date	Item	Post. Ref.	Debit	Credit	Balance Debit	Balance Credit
2009						
Nov. 30		1	800		800	
Dec. 1		2	800		1,600	
31	Closing	6		1,600	—	—

Account *Depreciation Expense* — Account No. 53

Date	Item	Post. Ref.	Debit	Credit	Balance Debit	Balance Credit
2009						
Dec. 31	Adjusting	5	50		50	
31	Closing	6		50	—	—

Account *Utilities Expense* — Account No. 54

Date	Item	Post. Ref.	Debit	Credit	Balance Debit	Balance Credit
2009						
Nov. 30		1	450		450	
Dec. 31		3	310		760	
31		4	225		985	
31	Closing	6		985	—	—

Account *Supplies Expense* — Account No. 55

Date	Item	Post. Ref.	Debit	Credit	Balance Debit	Balance Credit
2009						
Nov. 30		1	800		800	
Dec. 31	Adjusting	5	1,240		2,040	
31	Closing	6		2,040	—	—

Account *Insurance Expense* — Account No. 56

Date	Item	Post. Ref.	Debit	Credit	Balance Debit	Balance Credit
2009						
Dec. 31	Adjusting	5	200		200	
31	Closing	6		200	—	—

Account *Miscellaneous Expense* — Account No. 59

Date	Item	Post. Ref.	Debit	Credit	Balance Debit	Balance Credit
2009						
Nov. 30		1	275		275	
Dec. 6		2	180		455	
31	Closing	6		455	—	—

Post-Closing Trial Balance

A post-closing trial balance is prepared after the closing entries have been posted. The purpose of the post-closing (after closing) trial balance is to verify that the ledger is in balance at the beginning of the next period. The accounts and amounts should agree exactly with the accounts and amounts listed on the balance sheet at the end of the period. The post-closing trial balance for NetSolutions is shown in Exhibit 7.

Exhibit 7

Post-Closing Trial Balance

NetSolutions Post-Closing Trial Balance December 31, 2009	Debit Balances	Credit Balances
Cash	2,065	
Accounts Receivable	2,720	
Supplies	760	
Prepaid Insurance	2,200	
Land	20,000	
Office Equipment	1,800	
Accumulated Depreciation		50
Accounts Payable		900
Wages Payable		250
Unearned Rent		240
Capital Stock		25,000
Retained Earnings		3,105
	29,545	29,545

Describe the accounting cycle.

Accounting Cycle

The accounting process that begins with analyzing and journalizing transactions and ends with the post-closing trial balance is called the **accounting cycle**. The steps in the accounting cycle are as follows:

1. Transactions are analyzed and recorded in the journal.
2. Transactions are posted to the ledger.
3. An unadjusted trial balance is prepared.
4. Adjustment data are assembled and analyzed.
5. An optional end-of-period spreadsheet (work sheet) is prepared.
6. Adjusting entries are journalized and posted to the ledger.
7. An adjusted trial balance is prepared.
8. Financial statements are prepared.
9. Closing entries are journalized and posted to the ledger.
10. A post-closing trial balance is prepared.[2]

Exhibit 8 illustrates the accounting cycle in graphic form. It also illustrates how the accounting cycle begins with the source documents for a transaction and flows through the accounting system and into the financial statements.

Example Exercise 4-6   Accounting Cycle   4

From the following list of steps in the accounting cycle, identify what two steps are missing.

a. Transactions are analyzed and recorded in the journal.
b. Transactions are posted to the ledger.
c. Adjustment data are assembled and analyzed.
d. An optional end-of-period spreadsheet (work sheet) is prepared.
e. Adjusting entries are journalized and posted to the ledger.
f. Financial statements are prepared.
g. Closing entries are journalized and posted to the ledger.
h. A post-closing trial balance is prepared.

(continued)

2 Some accountants include the journalizing and posting of "reversing entries" as the last step in the accounting cycle. Because reversing entries are not required, we describe and illustrate them in Appendix B at the end of the book.

Follow My Example 4-6

The following two steps are missing: (1) the preparation of an unadjusted trial balance and (2) the preparation of the adjusted trial balance. The unadjusted trial balance should be prepared after step (b). The adjusted trial balance should be prepared after step (e).

For Practice: PE 4-6A, PE 4-6B

Exhibit 8

Accounting Cycle

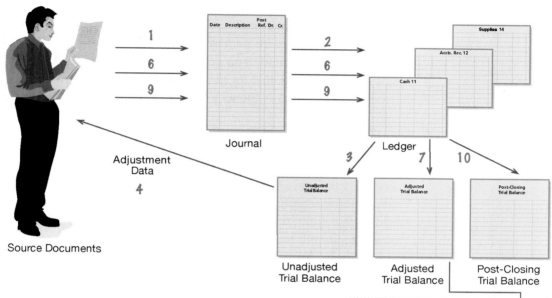

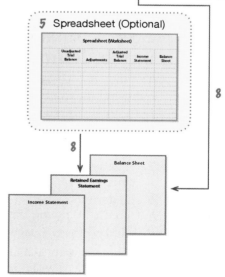

Financial Statements

Accounting Cycle Steps

1 Transactions are analyzed and recorded in the journal.

2 Transactions are posted to the ledger.

3 An unadjusted trial balance is prepared.

4 Adjustment data are assembled and analyzed.

5 An optional end-of-period spreadsheet (work sheet) is prepared.

6 Adjusting entries are journalized and posted to the ledger.

7 An adjusted trial balance is prepared.

8 Financial statements are prepared.

9 Closing entries are journalized and posted to the ledger.

10 A post-closing trial balance is prepared.

5 Illustrate the accounting cycle for one period.

Illustration of the Accounting Cycle

In this section, we will illustate the complete accounting cycle for one period. We assume that for several years Kelly Pitney has operated a part-time consulting business from her home. As of April 1, 2010, Kelly decided to move to rented quarters and to operate the business on a full-time basis as a professional corporation. The business will be known as Kelly Consulting, P.C. During April, Kelly Consulting entered into the following transactions:

Apr. 1. The following assets were received from Kelly Pitney in exchange for capital stock: cash, $13,100; accounts receivable, $3,000; supplies, $1,400; and office equipment, $12,500. There were no liabilities received.

   1. Paid three months' rent on a lease rental contract, $4,800.
   2. Paid the premiums on property and casualty insurance policies, $1,800.
   4. Received cash from clients as an advance payment for services to be provided and recorded it as unearned fees, $5,000.
   5. Purchased additional office equipment on account from Office Station Co., $2,000.
   6. Received cash from clients on account, $1,800.
   10. Paid cash for a newspaper advertisement, $120.
   12. Paid Office Station Co. for part of the debt incurred on April 5, $1,200.
   12. Recorded services provided on account for the period April 1–12, $4,200.
   14. Paid part-time receptionist for two weeks' salary, $750.
   17. Recorded cash from cash clients for fees earned during the period April 1–16, $6,250.
   18. Paid cash for supplies, $800.
   20. Recorded services provided on account for the period April 13–20, $2,100.
   24. Recorded cash from cash clients for fees earned for the period April 17–24, $3,850.
   26. Received cash from clients on account, $5,600.
   27. Paid part-time receptionist for two weeks' salary, $750.
   29. Paid telephone bill for April, $130.
   30. Paid electricity bill for April, $200.
   30. Recorded cash from cash clients for fees earned for the period April 25–30, $3,050.
   30. Recorded services provided on account for the remainder of April, $1,500.
   30. Paid dividends of $6,000.

Step 1. Analyzing and Recording Transactions in the Journal

The first step in the accounting cycle is to analyze and record transactions in the journal using the double-entry accounting system. As we illustrated in Chapter 2, transactions are analyzed and journalized using the following steps:

1. Carefully read the description of the transaction to determine whether an asset, liability, capital stock, retained earnings, revenue, expense, or dividends account is affected.
2. For each account affected by the transaction, determine whether the account increases or decreases.
3. Determine whether each increase or decrease should be recorded as a debit or a credit, following the rules of debit and credit shown in Exhibit 3 of Chapter 2.
4. Record the transaction using a journal entry.

The company's chart of accounts is useful in determining which accounts are affected by the transaction. The chart of accounts for Kelly Consulting is as follows:

11 Cash	32 Retained Earnings
12 Accounts Receivable	33 Dividends
14 Supplies	34 Income Summary
15 Prepaid Rent	41 Fees Earned
16 Prepaid Insurance	51 Salary Expense
18 Office Equipment	52 Rent Expense
19 Accumulated Depreciation	53 Supplies Expense
21 Accounts Payable	54 Depreciation Expense
22 Salaries Payable	55 Insurance Expense
23 Unearned Fees	59 Miscellaneous Expense
31 Capital Stock	

After analyzing each of Kelly Consulting's transactions for April, the journal entries are recorded as shown in Exhibit 9.

Step 2. Posting Transactions to the Ledger

Periodically, the transactions recorded in the journal are posted to the accounts in the ledger. The debits and credits for each journal entry are posted to the accounts in the order in which they occur in the journal. As we illustrated in Chapters 2 and 3, journal entries are posted to the accounts using the following four steps.

1. The date is entered in the Date column of the account.
2. The amount is entered into the Debit or Credit column of the account.
3. The journal page number is entered in the Posting Reference column.
4. The account number is entered in the Posting Reference (Post. Ref.) column in the journal.

The journal entries for Kelly Consulting have been posted to the ledger shown in Exhibit 17 on pages 168–170.

Exhibit 9

Journal Entries for April, Kelly Consulting, P.C.

Journal — Page 1

Date		Description	Post. Ref.	Debit	Credit
2010 Apr.	1	Cash	11	13,100	
		Accounts Receivable	12	3,000	
		Supplies	14	1,400	
		Office Equipment	18	12,500	
		Capital Stock	31		30,000
	1	Prepaid Rent	15	4,800	
		Cash	11		4,800
	2	Prepaid Insurance	16	1,800	
		Cash	11		1,800
	4	Cash	11	5,000	
		Unearned Fees	23		5,000
	5	Office Equipment	18	2,000	
		Accounts Payable	21		2,000
	6	Cash	11	1,800	
		Accounts Receivable	12		1,800
	10	Miscellaneous Expense	59	120	
		Cash	11		120
	12	Accounts Payable	21	1,200	
		Cash	11		1,200
	12	Accounts Receivable	12	4,200	
		Fees Earned	41		4,200
	14	Salary Expense	51	750	
		Cash	11		750

(continued)

Exhibit 9

Journal Entries for April, Kelly Consulting, P.C. (continued)

Date		Description	Post. Ref.	Debit	Credit
2010					
Apr.	17	Cash	11	6,250	
		Fees Earned	41		6,250
	18	Supplies	14	800	
		Cash	11		800
	20	Accounts Receivable	12	2,100	
		Fees Earned	41		2,100
	24	Cash	11	3,850	
		Fees Earned	41		3,850
	26	Cash	11	5,600	
		Accounts Receivable	12		5,600
	27	Salary Expense	51	750	
		Cash	11		750
	29	Miscellaneous Expense	59	130	
		Cash	11		130
	30	Miscellaneous Expense	59	200	
		Cash	11		200
	30	Cash	11	3,050	
		Fees Earned	41		3,050
	30	Accounts Receivable	12	1,500	
		Fees Earned	41		1,500
	30	Dividends	33	6,000	
		Cash	11		6,000

Journal — Page 2

Step 3. Preparing an Unadjusted Trial Balance

An unadjusted trial balance is prepared to determine whether any errors have been made in posting the debits and credits to the ledger. The unadjusted trial balance does not provide complete proof of the accuracy of the ledger. It indicates only that the debits and the credits are equal. This proof is of value, however, because errors often affect the equality of debits and credits. If the two totals of a trial balance are not equal, an error has occurred that must be discovered and corrected.

The unadjusted trial balance for Kelly Consulting is shown in Exhibit 10. The unadjusted account balances shown in Exhibit 10 were taken from Kelly Consulting's ledger shown in Exhibit 17, on pages 168–170, before any adjusting entries were recorded.

Step 4. Assembling and Analyzing Adjustment Data

Before the financial statements can be prepared, the accounts must be updated. The four types of accounts that normally require adjustment include prepaid expenses, unearned revenue, accrued revenue, and accrued expenses. In addition, depreciation

Exhibit 10

Unadjusted Trial Balance, Kelly Consulting, P.C.

Kelly Consulting, P.C.
Unadjusted Trial Balance
April 30, 2010

	Debit Balances	Credit Balances
Cash	22,100	
Accounts Receivable	3,400	
Supplies	2,200	
Prepaid Rent	4,800	
Prepaid Insurance	1,800	
Office Equipment	14,500	
Accumulated Depreciation		0
Accounts Payable		800
Salaries Payable		0
Unearned Fees		5,000
Capital Stock		30,000
Dividends	6,000	
Fees Earned		20,950
Salary Expense	1,500	
Rent Expense	0	
Supplies Expense	0	
Depreciation Expense	0	
Insurance Expense	0	
Miscellaneous Expense	450	
	56,750	56,750

expense must be recorded for fixed assets other than land. The following data have been assembled on April 30, 2010, for analysis of possible adjustments for Kelly Consulting:

a.   Insurance expired during April is $300.
b.   Supplies on hand on April 30 are $1,350.
c.   Depreciation of office equipment for April is $330.
d.   Accrued receptionist salary on April 30 is $120.
e.   Rent expired during April is $1,600.
f.   Unearned fees on April 30 are $2,500.

Step 5. Preparing an Optional End-of-Period Spreadsheet (Work Sheet)

Although an end-of-period spreadsheet (work sheet) is not required, it is useful in showing the flow of accounting information from the unadjusted trial balance to the adjusted trial balance and financial statements. In addition, an end-of-period spreadsheet is useful in analyzing the impact of proposed adjustments on the financial statements. The end-of-period spreadsheet for Kelly Consulting is shown in Exhibit 11.

Step 6. Journalizing and Posting Adjusting Entries

Based on the adjustment data shown in step 4, adjusting entries for Kelly Consulting are prepared as shown in Exhibit 12. Each adjusting entry affects at least one income statement account and one balance sheet account. Explanations for each adjustment including any computations are normally included with each adjusting entry.

Exhibit 11

End-of-Period Spreadsheet (Work Sheet)

	A	B	C	D	E	F	G	H	I	J	K
1		Kelly Consulting, P. C.									
2		End-of-Period Spreadsheet (Work Sheet)									
3		For the Month Ended April 30, 2010									
4		Unadjusted				Adjusted					
5		Trial Balance		Adjustments		Trial Balance		Income Statement		Balance Sheet	
6	Account Title	Dr.	Cr.	Dr.	Cr.	Dr.	Cr.	Dr.	Cr.	Dr.	Cr.
7											
8	Cash	22,100				22,100				22,100	
9	Accounts Receivable	3,400				3,400				3,400	
10	Supplies	2,200			(b) 850	1,350				1,350	
11	Prepaid Rent	4,800			(e) 1,600	3,200				3,200	
12	Prepaid Insurance	1,800			(a) 300	1,500				1,500	
13	Office Equipment	14,500				14,500				14,500	
14	Accum. Depreciation				(c) 330		330				330
15	Accounts Payable		800				800				800
16	Salaries Payable				(d) 120		120				120
17	Unearned Fees		5,000	(f) 2,500			2,500				2,500
18	Capital Stock		30,000				30,000				30,000
19	Dividends	6,000				6,000				6,000	
20	Fees Earned		20,950		(f) 2,500		23,450		23,450		
21	Salary Expense	1,500		(d) 120		1,620		1,620			
22	Rent Expense			(e) 1,600		1,600		1,600			
23	Supplies Expense			(b) 850		850		850			
24	Depreciation Expense			(c) 330		330		330			
25	Insurance Expense			(a) 300		300		300			
26	Miscellaneous Expense	450				450		450			
27		56,750	56,750	5,700	5,700	57,200	57,200	5,150	23,450	52,050	33,750
28	Net income							18,300			18,300
29								23,450	23,450	52,050	52,050

Exhibit 12

Adjusting Entries, Kelly Consulting, P.C.

Date			Post. Ref.	Debit	Credit
		Adjusting Entries			
2010 Apr.	30	Insurance Expense	55	300	
		Prepaid Insurance	16		300
		Expired Insurance.			
	30	Supplies Expense	53	850	
		Supplies	14		850
		Supplies used ($2,200 – $1,350).			
	30	Depreciation Expense	54	330	
		Accumulated Depreciation	19		330
		Depreciation of office equipment.			
	30	Salary Expense	51	120	
		Salaries Payable	22		120
		Accrued salary.			
	30	Rent Expense	52	1,600	
		Prepaid Rent	15		1,600
		Rent expired during April.			
	30	Unearned Fees	23	2,500	
		Fees Earned	41		2,500
		Fees earned ($5,000 – $2,500).			

Journal — Page 3

Each of the adjusting entries shown in Exhibit 12 is posted to Kelly Consulting's ledger shown in Exhibit 17 on pages 168–170. The adjusting entries are identified in the ledger as "Adjusting."

Step 7. Preparing an Adjusted Trial Balance

After the adjustments have been journalized and posted, an adjusted trial balance is prepared to verify the equality of the total of the debit and credit balances. This is the last step before preparing the financial statements. If the adjusted trial balance does not balance, an error has occurred and must be found and corrected. The adjusted trial balance for Kelly Consulting as of April 30, 2010, is shown in Exhibit 13.

Step 8. Preparing the Financial Statements

The most important outcome of the accounting cycle is the financial statements. The income statement is prepared first, followed by the retained earnings statement and then the balance sheet. The statements can be prepared directly from the adjusted trial balance, the end-of-period spreadsheet, or the ledger. The net income or net loss shown on the income statement is reported on the retained earnings statement along with any dividends. The ending retained earnings is reported on the balance sheet. The total stockholders' equity (capital stock plus retained earnings) is added with total liabilities to equal total assets.

The financial statements for Kelly Consulting are shown in Exhibit 14. Kelly Consulting earned net income of $18,300 for April. As of April 30, 2010, Kelly Consulting has total assets of $45,720, total liabilities of $3,420, and total stockholders' equity of $42,300.

Exhibit 13

Adjusted Trial Balance, Kelly Consulting, P.C.

Kelly Consulting, P.C.
Adjusted Trial Balance
April 30, 2010

	Debit Balances	Credit Balances
Cash	22,100	
Accounts Receivable	3,400	
Supplies	1,350	
Prepaid Rent	3,200	
Prepaid Insurance	1,500	
Office Equipment	14,500	
Accumulated Depreciation		330
Accounts Payable		800
Salaries Payable		120
Unearned Fees		2,500
Capital Stock		30,000
Dividends	6,000	
Fees Earned		23,450
Salary Expense	1,620	
Rent Expense	1,600	
Supplies Expense	850	
Depreciation Expense	330	
Insurance Expense	300	
Miscellaneous Expense	450	
	57,200	57,200

Exhibit 14

Financial
Statements,
Kelly
Consulting, P.C.

Kelly Consulting, P.C.
Income Statement
For the Month Ended April 30, 2010

Fees earned		$23,450
Expenses:		
Salary expense	$1,620	
Rent expense	1,600	
Supplies expense	850	
Depreciation expense	330	
Insurance expense	300	
Miscellaneous expense	450	
Total expenses		5,150
Net income		$18,300

Kelly Consulting, P.C.
Retained Earnings Statement
For the Month Ended April 30, 2010

Retained earnings, April 1, 2010		$ 0
Net income for the month	$18,300	
Less dividends	6,000	
Increase in retained earnings		12,300
Retained earnings, April 30, 2010		$12,300

Kelly Consulting, P.C.
Balance Sheet
April 30, 2010

Assets

Current assets:		
Cash	$22,100	
Accounts receivable	3,400	
Supplies	1,350	
Prepaid rent	3,200	
Prepaid insurance	1,500	
Total current assets		$31,550
Property, plant, and equipment:		
Office equipment	$14,500	
Less accumulated depreciation	330	
Total property, plant, and equipment		14,170
Total assets		$45,720

Liabilities

Current liabilities:		
Accounts payable	$ 800	
Salaries payable	120	
Unearned fees	2,500	
Total liabilities		$ 3,420
Stockholders' Equity		
Capital stock	$30,000	
Retained earnings	12,300	
Total stockholders' equity		42,300
Total liabilities and stockholders' equity		$45,720

Step 9. Journalizing and Posting Closing Entries

As described earlier in this chapter, four closing entries are required at the end of an accounting period. These four closing entries are as follows:

1. Debit each revenue account for its balance and credit Income Summary for the total revenue.
2. Credit each expense account for its balance and debit Income Summary for the total expenses.
3. Debit Income Summary for its balance and credit the retained earnings account.
4. Debit the retained earnings account for the balance of the dividends account and credit the dividends account.

The four closing entries for Kelly Consulting are shown in Exhibit 15. The closing entries are posted to Kelly Consulting's ledger as shown in Exhibit 17 (pages 168–170). After the closing entries are posted, Kelly Consulting's ledger has the following characteristics:

1. The balance of Retained Earnings of $12,300 agrees with the amount reported on the retained earnings statement and the balance sheet.
2. The revenue, expense, and dividends accounts will have zero balances.

The closing entries are normally identified in the ledger as "Closing." In addition, a line is often inserted in both balance columns after a closing entry is posted. This separates next period's revenue, expense, and withdrawal transactions from those of the current period.

Step 10. Preparing a Post-Closing Trial Balance

A post-closing trial balance is prepared after the closing entries have been posted. The purpose of the post-closing trial balance is to verify that the ledger is in balance at the beginning of the next period. The accounts and amounts in the post-closing trial balance

Exhibit 15

Closing Entries, Kelly Consulting, P.C.

Date		Description	Post. Ref.	Debit	Credit
		Journal			Page 4
		Closing Entries			
2010 Apr.	30	Fees Earned	41	23,450	
		Income Summary	34		23,450
	30	Income Summary	34	5,150	
		Salary Expense	51		1,620
		Rent Expense	52		1,600
		Supplies Expense	53		850
		Depreciation Expense	54		330
		Insurance Expense	55		300
		Miscellaneous Expense	59		450
	30	Income Summary	34	18,300	
		Retained Earnings	32		18,300
	30	Retained Earnings	32	6,000	
		Dividends	33		6,000

Exhibit 16

Post-Closing Trial Balance, Kelly Consulting, P.C.

Kelly Consulting, P.C. Post-Closing Trial Balance April 30, 2010	Debit Balances	Credit Balances
Cash	22,100	
Accounts Receivable	3,400	
Supplies	1,350	
Prepaid Rent	3,200	
Prepaid Insurance	1,500	
Office Equipment	14,500	
Accumulated Depreciation		330
Accounts Payable		800
Salaries Payable		120
Unearned Fees		2,500
Capital Stock		30,000
Retained Earnings		12,300
	46,050	46,050

should agree exactly with the accounts and amounts listed on the balance sheet at the end of the period.

The post-closing trial balance for Kelly Consulting is shown in Exhibit 16. The balances shown in the post-closing trial balance are taken from the ending balances in the ledger shown in Exhibit 17. These balances agree with the amounts shown on Kelly Consulting's balance sheet in Exhibit 14.

Exhibit 17

Ledger, Kelly Consulting, P.C.

Ledger

Account Cash   Account No. 11

Date	Item	Post. Ref.	Debit	Credit	Balance Debit	Balance Credit
2010						
Apr. 1		1	13,100		13,100	
1		1		4,800	8,300	
2		1		1,800	6,500	
4		1	5,000		11,500	
6		1	1,800		13,300	
10		1		120	13,180	
12		1		1,200	11,980	
14		1		750	11,230	
17		2	6,250		17,480	
18		2		800	16,680	
24		2	3,850		20,530	
26		2	5,600		26,130	
27		2		750	25,380	
29		2		130	25,250	
30		2		200	25,050	
30		2	3,050		28,100	
30		2		6,000	22,100	

Account Accounts Receivable   Account No. 12

Date	Item	Post. Ref.	Debit	Credit	Balance Debit	Balance Credit
2010						
Apr. 1		1	3,000		3,000	
6		1		1,800	1,200	
12		1	4,200		5,400	
20		2	2,100		7,500	
26		2		5,600	1,900	
30		2	1,500		3,400	

Account Supplies   Account No. 14

Date	Item	Post. Ref.	Debit	Credit	Balance Debit	Balance Credit
2010						
Apr. 1		1	1,400		1,400	
18		2	800		2,200	
30	Adjusting	3		850	1,350	

Exhibit 17

Ledger, Kelly Consulting, P.C. *(continued)*

Account *Prepaid Rent* — Account No. *15*

Date	Item	Post. Ref.	Debit	Credit	Balance Debit	Balance Credit
2010						
Apr. 1		1	4,800		4,800	
30	Adjusting	3		1,600	3,200	

Account *Prepaid Insurance* — Account No. *16*

Date	Item	Post. Ref.	Debit	Credit	Balance Debit	Balance Credit
2010						
Apr. 2		1	1,800		1,800	
30	Adjusting	3		300	1,500	

Account *Office Equipment* — Account No. *18*

Date	Item	Post. Ref.	Debit	Credit	Balance Debit	Balance Credit
2010						
Apr. 1		1	12,500		12,500	
5		1	2,000		14,500	

Account *Accumulated Depreciation* — Account No. *19*

Date	Item	Post. Ref.	Debit	Credit	Balance Debit	Balance Credit
2010						
Apr. 30	Adjusting	3		330		330

Account *Accounts Payable* — Account No. *21*

Date	Item	Post. Ref.	Debit	Credit	Balance Debit	Balance Credit
2010						
Apr. 5		1		2,000		2,000
12		1	1,200			800

Account *Salaries Payable* — Account No. *22*

Date	Item	Post. Ref.	Debit	Credit	Balance Debit	Balance Credit
2010						
Apr. 30	Adjusting	3		120		120

Account *Unearned Fees* — Account No. *23*

Date	Item	Post. Ref.	Debit	Credit	Balance Debit	Balance Credit
2010						
Apr. 4		1		5,000		5,000
30	Adjusting	3	2,500			2,500

Account *Capital Stock* — Account No. *31*

Date	Item	Post. Ref.	Debit	Credit	Balance Debit	Balance Credit
2010						
Apr. 1		1		30,000		30,000

Account *Retained Earnings* — Account No. *32*

Date	Item	Post. Ref.	Debit	Credit	Balance Debit	Balance Credit
2010						
Apr. 1		1				0
30	Closing	4		18,300		18,300
30	Closing	4	6,000			12,300

Account *Dividends* — Account No. *33*

Date	Item	Post. Ref.	Debit	Credit	Balance Debit	Balance Credit
2010						
Apr. 30		2	6,000		6,000	
30	Closing	4		6,000	—	—

Account *Income Summary* — Account No. *34*

Date	Item	Post. Ref.	Debit	Credit	Balance Debit	Balance Credit
2010						
Apr. 30	Closing	4		23,450		23,450
30	Closing	4	5,150			18,300
30	Closing	4	18,300		—	—

Account *Fees Earned* — Account No. *41*

Date	Item	Post. Ref.	Debit	Credit	Balance Debit	Balance Credit
2010						
Apr. 12		1		4,200		4,200
17		2		6,250		10,450
20		2		2,100		12,550
24		2		3,850		16,400
30		2		3,050		19,450
30		2		1,500		20,950
30	Adjusting	3		2,500		23,450
30	Closing	4	23,450		—	—

Account *Salary Expense* — Account No. *51*

Date	Item	Post. Ref.	Debit	Credit	Balance Debit	Balance Credit
2010						
Apr. 14		1	750		750	
27		2	750		1,500	
30	Adjusting	3	120		1,620	
30	Closing	4		1,620	—	—

Account *Rent Expense* — Account No. *52*

Date	Item	Post. Ref.	Debit	Credit	Balance Debit	Balance Credit
2010						
Apr. 30	Adjusting	3	1,600		1,600	
30	Closing	4		1,600	—	—

(continued)

Exhibit 17

Ledger, Kelly Consulting, P.C. (concluded)

Account *Supplies Expense*   Account No. *53*

Date	Item	Post. Ref.	Debit	Credit	Balance Debit	Balance Credit
2010						
Apr. 30	Adjusting	3	850		850	
30	Closing	4		850	—	—

Account *Insurance Expense*   Account No. *55*

Date	Item	Post. Ref.	Debit	Credit	Balance Debit	Balance Credit
2010						
Apr. 30	Adjusting	3	300		300	
30	Closing	4		300	—	—

Account *Depreciation Expense*   Account No. *54*

Date	Item	Post. Ref.	Debit	Credit	Balance Debit	Balance Credit
2010						
Apr. 30	Adjusting	3	330		330	
30	Closing	4		330	—	—

Account *Miscellaneous Expense*   Account No. *59*

Date	Item	Post. Ref.	Debit	Credit	Balance Debit	Balance Credit
2010						
Apr. 10		1	120		120	
29		2	130		250	
30		2	200		450	
30	Closing	4		450	—	—

6 Explain what is meant by the fiscal year and the natural business year.

Fiscal Year

The annual accounting period adopted by a business is known as its **fiscal year**. Fiscal years begin with the first day of the month selected and end on the last day of the following twelfth month. The period most commonly used is the calendar year. Other periods are not unusual, especially for businesses organized as corporations. For example, a corporation may adopt a fiscal year that ends when business activities have reached the lowest point in its annual operating cycle. Such a fiscal year is called the **natural business year**. At the low point in its operating cycle, a business has more time to analyze the results of operations and to prepare financial statements.

Because companies with fiscal years often have highly seasonal operations, investors and others should be careful in interpreting partial-year reports for such companies. That is, you should expect the results of operations for these companies to vary significantly throughout the fiscal year.

The financial history of a business may be shown by a series of balance sheets and income statements for several fiscal years. If the life of a business is expressed by a line moving from left to right, the series of balance sheets and income statements may be graphed as follows:

Percentage of Companies with Fiscal Years Ending in:

January	5%	July	2%
February	1	August	2
March	3	September	7
April	2	October	3
May	3	November	2
June	7	December	63

Source: *Accounting Trends & Techniques*, 61st edition, 2007 (New York: American Institute of Certified Public Accountants).

Financial History of a Business

Income Statement for the year ended Dec. 31, 2008

Dec. 31 2008

Balance Sheet Dec. 31, 2008

Income Statement for the year ended Dec. 31, 2009

Dec. 31 2009

Balance Sheet Dec. 31, 2009

Income Statement for the year ended Dec. 31, 2010

Dec. 31 2010

Balance Sheet Dec. 31, 2010

Financial Analysis and Interpretation

The ability of a business to pay its debts is called *solvency*. Two financial measures for evaluating a business's short-term solvency are working capital and the current ratio. *Working capital* is the excess of the current assets of a business over its current liabilities, as shown below.

Working Capital = Current Assets − Current Liabilities

An excess of the current assets over the current liabilities implies that the business is able to pay its current liabilities. If the current liabilities are greater than the current assets, the business may not be able to pay its debts and continue in business.

To illustrate, NetSolutions' working capital at the end of 2009 is $675 as computed below. This amount of working capital implies that NetSolutions can pay its current liabilities.

Working Capital = Current Assets − Current Liabilities
Working Capital = $7,745 − $1,390
Working Capital = $6,355

The *current ratio* is another means of expressing the relationship between current assets and current liabilities.

The current ratio is computed by dividing current assets by current liabilities, as shown below.

Current Ratio = Current Assets/Current Liabilities

To illustrate, the current ratio for NetSolutions at the end of 2009 is 5.8, computed as follows:

Current Ratio = Current Assets/Current Liabilities
Current Ratio = $7,745/$1,390 = 5.8

The current ratio is useful in making comparisons across companies and with industry averages. To illustrate, assume that as of December 31, 2009, the working capital of a company that competes with NetSolutions is much greater than $675 but its current ratio is only 0.7. Considering these facts alone, NetSolutions is in a more favorable position to obtain short-term credit, even though the competing company has a greater amount of working capital.

f·a·i

A P P E N D I X   1

End-of-Period Spreadsheet (Work Sheet)

Accountants often use working papers for analyzing and summarizing data. Such working papers are not a formal part of the accounting records. This is in contrast to the chart of accounts, the journal, and the ledger, which are essential parts of an accounting system. Working papers are usually prepared by using a computer spreadsheet program such as Microsoft's Excel.®

@netsolutions

The end-of-period spreadsheet (work sheet) shown in Exhibit 1 is a working paper used to summarize adjusting entries and the account balances for the financial statements. In companies with few accounts and adjustments, an end-of-period spreadsheet may not be necessary. For example, the financial statements for NetSolutions can be prepared directly from the Adjusted Trial Balance columns in Exhibit 1. However, many companies use an end-of-period spreadsheet as an aid to analyzing adjustment data and preparing the financial statements.

Exhibits 18 through 22 on pages 172–177 illustrate the step-by-step process of how to prepare an end-of-period spreadsheet. As a basis for this illustration, we use NetSolutions.

Step 1. Enter the Title

The spreadsheet is started by entering the following data:

1. Name of the business: *NetSolutions*
2. Type of working paper: *End-of-Period Spreadsheet*
3. The period of time: *For the Two Months Ended December 31, 2009*

Exhibit 18 shows the preceding data entered for NetSolutions.

Exhibit 18

Spreadsheet (Work Sheet) with Unadjusted Trial Balance Entered

	A	B	C	D	E	F	G	H	I	J	K
1					NetSolutions						
2					End-of-Period Spreadsheet (Work Sheet)						
3					For the Two Months Ended December 31, 2009						
4		Unadjusted				Adjusted					
5		Trial Balance		Adjustments		Trial Balance		Income Statement		Balance Sheet	
6	Account Title	Dr.	Cr.	Dr.	Cr.	Dr.	Cr.	Dr.	Cr.	Dr.	Cr.
7											
8	Cash	2,065									
9	Accounts Receivable	2,220									
10	Supplies	2,000									
11	Prepaid Insurance	2,400									
12	Land	20,000									
13	Office Equipment	1,800									
14	Accumulated Depreciation										
15	Accounts Payable		900								
16	Wages Payable										
17	Unearned Rent		360								
18	Capital Stock		25,000								
19	Dividends	4,000									
20	Fees Earned		16,340								
21	Rent Revenue										
22	Wages Expense	4,275									
23	Rent Expense	1,600									
24	Depreciation Expense										
25	Utilities Expense	985									
26	Supplies Expense	800									
27	Insurance Expense										
28	Miscellaneous Expense	455									
29		42,600	42,600								
30											
31											
32											

> The spreadsheet (work sheet) is used for summarizing the effects of adjusting entries. It also aids in preparing financial statements.

Step 2. Enter the Unadjusted Trial Balance

Enter the unadjusted trial balance on the spreadsheet. The spreadsheet in Exhibit 18 shows the unadjusted trial balance for NetSolutions at December 31, 2009.

Step 3. Enter the Adjustments

The adjustments for NetSolutions from Chapter 3 are entered in the Adjustments columns, as shown in Exhibit 19. Cross-referencing (by letters) the debit and credit of each adjustment is useful in reviewing the spreadsheet. It is also helpful for identifying the adjusting entries that need to be recorded in the journal. This cross-referencing process is sometimes referred to as *keying* the adjustments.

The adjustments are normally entered in the order in which the data are assembled. If the titles of the accounts to be adjusted do not appear in the unadjusted trial balance, the accounts are inserted in their proper order in the Account Title column.

The adjusting entries for NetSolutions that are entered in the Adjustments columns are as follows:

(a) **Supplies**. The supplies account has a debit balance of $2,000. The cost of the supplies on hand at the end of the period is $760. The supplies expense for December is the difference between the two amounts, or $1,240 ($2,000 − $760). The adjustment is entered as (1) $1,240 in the Adjustments Debit column on the same line as Supplies Expense and (2) $1,240 in the Adjustments Credit column on the same line as Supplies.

Exhibit 19

Spreadsheet (Work Sheet) with Unadjusted Trial Balance and Adjustments

	A	B	C	D	E	F	G	H	I	J	K
1				NetSolutions							
2				End-of-Period Spreadsheet (Work Sheet)							
3				For the Two Months Ended December 31, 2009							
4		Unadjusted				Adjusted					
5		Trial Balance		Adjustments		Trial Balance		Income Statement		Balance Sheet	
6	Account Title	Dr.	Cr.	Dr.	Cr.	Dr.	Cr.	Dr.	Cr.	Dr.	Cr.
7											
8	Cash	2,065									
9	Accounts Receivable	2,220		(d) 500							
10	Supplies	2,000			(a) 1,240						
11	Prepaid Insurance	2,400			(b) 200						
12	Land	20,000									
13	Office Equipment	1,800									
14	Accumulated Depreciation				(f) 50						
15	Accounts Payable		900								
16	Wages Payable				(e) 250						
17	Unearned Rent		360	(c) 120							
18	Capital Stock		25,000								
19	Dividends	4,000									
20	Fees Earned		16,340		(d) 500						
21	Rent Revenue				(c) 120						
22	Wages Expense	4,275		(e) 250							
23	Rent Expense	1,600									
24	Depreciation Expense			(f) 50							
25	Utilities Expense	985									
26	Supplies Expense	800		(a) 1,240							
27	Insurance Expense			(b) 200							
28	Miscellaneous Expense	455									
29		42,600	42,600	2,360	2,360						
30											
31											
32											

The adjustments on the spreadsheet (work sheet) are used in preparing the adjusting journal entries.

(b) **Prepaid Insurance.** The prepaid insurance account has a debit balance of $2,400. This balance represents the prepayment of insurance for 12 months beginning December 1. Thus, the insurance expense for December is $200 ($2,400 ÷ 12). The adjustment is entered as (1) $200 in the Adjustments Debit column on the same line as Insurance Expense and (2) $200 in the Adjustments Credit column on the same line as Prepaid Insurance.

(c) **Unearned Rent.** The unearned rent account had a credit balance of $360. This balance represents the receipt of three months' rent, beginning with December. Thus, the rent revenue for December is $120 ($360 ÷ 3). The adjustment is entered as (1) $120 in the Adjustments Debit column on the same line as Unearned Rent and (2) $120 in the Adjustments Credit column on the same line as Rent Revenue.

(d) **Accrued Fees.** Fees accrued at the end of December but not recorded total $500. This amount is an increase in an asset and an increase in revenue. The adjustment is entered as (1) $500 in the Adjustments Debit Column on the same line as Accounts Receivable and (2) $500 in the Adjustments Credit column on the same line as Fees Earned.

(e) **Wages.** Wages accrued but not paid at the end of December total $250. This amount is an increase in expenses and an increase in liabilities. The adjustment is entered as (1) $250 in the Adjustments Debit column on the same line as Wages Expense and (2) $250 in the Adjustments Credit column on the same line as Wages Payable.

(f) **Depreciation.** Depreciation of the office equipment is $50 for December. The adjustment is entered as (1) $50 in the Adjustments Debit column on the same line as Depreciation Expense and (2) $50 in the Adjustments Credit column on the same line as Accumulated Depreciation.

After the adjustments have been entered, the Adjustments columns are totaled to verify the equality of the debits and credits. The total of the Debit column must equal the total of the Credit column.

Step 4. Enter the Adjusted Trial Balance

The adjusted trial balance is entered by combining the adjustments with the unadjusted balances for each account. The adjusted amounts are then extended to the Adjusted Trial Balance columns, as shown in Exhibit 20.

Exhibit 20

Spreadsheet (Work Sheet) with Unadjusted Trial Balance, Adjustments, and Adjusted Trial Balance Entered

	A	B	C	D	E	F	G	H	I	J	K
1					NetSolutions						
2				End-of-Period Spreadsheet (Work Sheet)							
3				For the Two Months Ended December 31, 2009							
4		Unadjusted				Adjusted					
5		Trial Balance		Adjustments		Trial Balance		Income Statement		Balance Sheet	
6	Account Title	Dr.	Cr.	Dr.	Cr.	Dr.	Cr.	Dr.	Cr.	Dr.	Cr.
7											
8	Cash	2,065				2,065					
9	Accounts Receivable	2,220		(d) 500		2,720					
10	Supplies	2,000			(a) 1,240	760					
11	Prepaid Insurance	2,400			(b) 200	2,200					
12	Land	20,000				20,000					
13	Office Equipment	1,800				1,800					
14	Accumulated Depreciation				(f) 50		50				
15	Accounts Payable		900				900				
16	Wages Payable				(e) 250		250				
17	Unearned Rent		360	(c) 120			240				
18	Capital Stock		25,000				25,000				
19	Dividends	4,000				4,000					
20	Fees Earned		16,340		(d) 500		16,840				
21	Rent Revenue				(c) 120		120				
22	Wages Expense	4,275		(e) 250		4,525					
23	Rent Expense	1,600				1,600					
24	Depreciation Expense			(f) 50		50					
25	Utilities Expense	985				985					
26	Supplies Expense	800		(a) 1,240		2,040					
27	Insurance Expense			(b) 200		200					
28	Miscellaneous Expense	455				455					
29		42,600	42,600	2,360	2,360	43,400	43,400				
30											
31											
32											

The adjusted trial balance amounts are determined by adding the adjustments to or subtracting the adjustments from the trial balance amounts. For example, the Wages Expense debit of $4,525 is the trial balance amount of $4,275 plus the $250 adjustment debit.

To illustrate, the cash amount of $2,065 is extended to the Adjusted Trial Balance Debit column since no adjustments affected Cash. Accounts Receivable has an initial balance of $2,220 and a debit adjustment of $500. Thus, $2,720 ($2,220 + $500) is entered in the Adjusted Trial Balance Debit column for Accounts Receivable. The same process continues until all account balances are extended to the Adjusted Trial Balance columns.

After the accounts and adjustments have been extended, the Adjusted Trial Balance columns are totaled to verify the equality of debits and credits. The total of the Debit column must equal the total of the Credit column.

Step 5. Extend the Accounts to the Income Statement and Balance Sheet Columns

The adjusted trial balance amounts are extended to the Income Statement and Balance Sheet columns. The amounts for revenues and expenses are extended to the Income Statement column. The amounts for assets, liabilities, capital stock, retained earnings and dividends are extended to the Balance Sheet columns.[3]

The first account listed in the Adjusted Trial Balance columns is Cash with a debit balance of $2,065. Cash is an asset, is listed on the balance sheet, and has a debit balance. Therefore, $2,065 is extended to the Balance Sheet Debit column. The Fees Earned balance of $16,840 is extended to the Income Statement Credit column. The same process continues until all account balances have been extended to the proper columns, as shown in Exhibit 21.

Step 6. Total the Income Statement and Balance Sheet Columns, Compute the Net Income or Net Loss, and Complete the Spreadsheet

After the account balances are extended to the Income Statement and Balance Sheet columns, each of the columns is totaled. The difference between the two Income Statement column totals is the amount of the net income or the net loss for the period. This difference (net income or net loss) will also be the difference between the two Balance Sheet column totals.

If the Income Statement Credit column total (total revenue) is greater than the Income Statement Debit column total (total expenses), the difference is the net income. If the Income Statement Debit column total is greater than the Income Statement Credit column total, the difference is a net loss.

As shown in Exhibit 22, the total of the Income Statement Credit column is $16,960, and the total of the Income Statement Debit column is $9,855. Thus, the net income for NetSolutions is $7,105 as shown below.

Total of Income Statement Credit column (revenues)	$16,960
Total of Income Statement Debit column (expenses)	9,855
Net income (excess of revenues over expenses)	$ 7,105

The amount of the net income, $7,105, is entered in the Income Statement Debit column and the Balance Sheet Credit column. *Net income* is also entered in the Account Title column. Entering the net income of $7,105 in the Balance Sheet Credit column has the effect of transferring the net balance of the revenue and expense accounts to the retained earnings account.

If there was a net loss instead of net income, the amount of the net loss would be entered in the Income Statement Credit column and the Balance Sheet Debit column. *Net loss* would also be entered in the Account Title column.

After the net income or net loss is entered on the spreadsheet, the Income Statement and Balance Sheet columns are totaled. The totals of the two Income Statement columns must now be equal. The totals of the two Balance Sheet columns must also be equal.

---

3 The balances of the retained earnings and dividends accounts are extended to the Balance Sheet columns because the spreadsheet does not have separate Retained Earnings Statement columns.

Exhibit 21

Spreadsheet (Work Sheet) with Amounts Extended to Income Statement and Balance Sheet Columns

	A	B	C	D	E	F	G	H	I	J	K
1				NetSolutions							
2				End-of-Period Spreadsheet (Work Sheet)							
3				For the Two Months Ended December 31, 2009							
4		Unadjusted				Adjusted					
5		Trial Balance		Adjustments		Trial Balance		Income Statement		Balance Sheet	
6	Account Title	Dr.	Cr.	Dr.	Cr.	Dr.	Cr.	Dr.	Cr.	Dr.	Cr.
7											
8	Cash	2,065				2,065				2,065	
9	Accounts Receivable	2,220		(d) 500		2,720				2,720	
10	Supplies	2,000			(a) 1,240	760				760	
11	Prepaid Insurance	2,400			(b) 200	2,200				2,200	
12	Land	20,000				20,000				20,000	
13	Office Equipment	1,800				1,800				1,800	
14	Accumulated Depreciation				(f) 50		50				50
15	Accounts Payable		900				900				900
16	Wages Payable				(e) 250		250				250
17	Unearned Rent		360	(c) 120			240				240
18	Capital Stock		25,000				25,000				25,000
19	Dividends	4,000				4,000				4,000	
20	Fees Earned		16,340		(d) 500		16,840		16,840		
21	Rent Revenue				(c) 120		120		120		
22	Wages Expense	4,275		(e) 250		4,525		4,525			
23	Rent Expense	1,600				1,600		1,600			
24	Depreciation Expense			(f) 50		50		50			
25	Utilities Expense	985				985		985			
26	Supplies Expense	800		(a) 1,240		2,040		2,040			
27	Insurance Expense			(b) 200		200		200			
28	Miscellaneous Expense	455				455		455			
29		42,600	42,600	2,360	2,360	43,400	43,400				
30											
31											
32											

The revenue and expense amounts are extended to (entered in) the Income Statement columns.

The asset, liability, capital stock, and dividends amounts are extended to (entered in) the Balance Sheet columns.

Preparing the Financial Statements from the Spreadsheet

The spreadsheet can be used to prepare the income statement, the retained earnings statement, and the balance sheet shown in Exhibit 2. The income statement is normally prepared directly from the spreadsheet. The expenses are listed in the income statement in Exhibit 2 in order of size, beginning with the larger items. Miscellaneous expense is the last item, regardless of its amount.

The first item normally presented on the retained earnings statement is the balance of the retained earnings account at the beginning of the period. This amount along with the net income (or net loss) and the dividends shown in the spreadsheet, are used to determine the ending retained earnings account balance.

Exhibit 22

Completed Spreadsheet (Work Sheet) with Net Income Shown

	A	B	C	D	E	F	G	H	I	J	K
1				NetSolutions							
2				End-of-Period Spreadsheet (Work Sheet)							
3				For the Two Months Ended December 31, 2009							
4		Unadjusted				Adjusted					
5		Trial Balance		Adjustments		Trial Balance		Income Statement		Balance Sheet	
6	Account Title	Dr.	Cr.	Dr.	Cr.	Dr.	Cr.	Dr.	Cr.	Dr.	Cr.
7											
8	Cash	2,065				2,065				2,065	
9	Accounts Receivable	2,220		(d) 500		2,720				2,720	
10	Supplies	2,000			(a) 1,240	760				760	
11	Prepaid Insurance	2,400			(b) 200	2,200				2,200	
12	Land	20,000				20,000				20,000	
13	Office Equipment	1,800				1,800				1,800	
14	Accumulated Depreciation				(f) 50		50				50
15	Accounts Payable		900				900				900
16	Wages Payable				(e) 250		250				250
17	Unearned Rent		360	(c) 120			240				240
18	Capital Stock		25,000				25,000				25,000
19	Dividends	4,000				4,000				4,000	
20	Fees Earned		16,340		(d) 500		16,840		16,840		
21	Rent Revenue				(c) 120		120		120		
22	Wages Expense	4,275		(e) 250		4,525		4,525			
23	Rent Expense	1,600				1,600		1,600			
24	Depreciation Expense			(f) 50		50		50			
25	Utilities Expense	985				985		985			
26	Supplies Expense	800		(a) 1,240		2,040		2,040			
27	Insurance Expense			(b) 200		200		200			
28	Miscellaneous Expense	455				455		455			
29		42,600	42,600	2,360	2,360	43,400	43,400	9,855	16,960	33,545	26,440
30	Net income							7,105			7,105
31								16,960	16,960	33,545	33,545
32											

> The difference between the Income Statement column totals is the net income (or net loss) for the period. The difference between the Balance Sheet column totals is also the net income (or net loss) for the period.

The balance sheet can be prepared directly from the spreadsheet columns except for the ending balance of retained earnings. The ending balance of retained earnings is taken from the retained earnings statement.

When a spreadsheet is used, the adjusting and closing entries are normally not journalized or posted until after the spreadsheet and financial statements have been prepared. The data for the adjusting entries are taken from the adjustments columns of the spreadsheet. The data for the first two closing entries are taken from the Income Statement columns of the spreadsheet. The amount for the third closing entry is the net income or net loss appearing at the bottom of the spreadsheet. The amount for the fourth closing entry is the dividends account balance that appears in the Balance Sheet Debit column of the spreadsheet.

1 Describe the flow of accounting information from the unadjusted trial balance into the adjusted trial balance and financial statements.

Key Points	Key Learning Outcomes	Example Exercises	Practice Exercises
Exhibit 1 illustrates the end-of-period process by which accounts are adjusted and how the adjusted accounts flow into the financial statements.	• Using an end-of-period spreadsheet (work sheet), describe how the unadjusted trial balance accounts are affected by adjustments and how the adjusted trial balance accounts flow into the income statement and balance sheet.	4-1	4-1A, 4-1B

2 Prepare financial statements from adjusted account balances.

Key Points	Key Learning Outcomes	Example Exercises	Practice Exercises
Using the end-of-period spreadsheet (work sheet) shown in Exhibit 1, the income statement and balance sheet for NetSolutions can be prepared. The retained earnings statement is prepared by listing the beginning balance of retained earnings, adding net income (subtracting a net loss), and deducting dividends. A classified balance sheet has sections for current assets; property, plant, and equipment; current liabilities; long-term liabilities; and stockholders' equity.	• Describe how the net income or net loss from the period can be determined from an end-of-period spreadsheet (work sheet).		
	• Prepare an income statement, retained earnings statement, and a balance sheet.	4-2 4-3	4-2A, 4-2B 4-3A, 4-3B
	• Indicate how accounts would be reported in a classified balance sheet.	4-4	4-4A, 4-4B

3 Prepare closing entries.

Key Points	Key Learning Outcomes	Example Exercises	Practice Exercises
Four entries are required in closing the temporary accounts. The first entry closes the revenue accounts to Income Summary. The second entry closes the expense accounts to Income Summary. The third entry closes the balance of Income Summary (net income or net loss) to the retained earnings account. The fourth entry closes the dividends account to the retained earnings account.	• Prepare the closing entry for revenues.	4-5	4-5A, 4-5B
	• Prepare the closing entry for expenses.	4-5	4-5A, 4-5B
	• Prepare the closing entry for transferring the balance of Income Summary to the retained earnings account.	4-5	4-5A, 4-5B
After the closing entries have been posted to the ledger, the balance in the retained earnings account agrees with the amount reported on the retained earnings statement and balance sheet. In addition, the revenue, expense, and dividends accounts will have zero balances.	• Prepare the closing entry for the dividends account.	4-5	4-5A, 4-5B

(continued)

4 Describe the accounting cycle.

		Example Exercises	Practice Exercises
Key Points	**Key Learning Outcomes**		

The 10 basic steps of the accounting cycle are as follows:

1. Transactions are analyzed and recorded in the journal.
2. Transactions are posted to the ledger.
3. An unadjusted trial balance is prepared.
4. Adjustment data are assembled and analyzed.
5. An optional end-of-period spreadsheet (work sheet) is prepared.
6. Adjusting entries are journalized and posted to the ledger.
7. An adjusted trial balance is prepared.
8. Financial statements are prepared.
9. Closing entries are journalized and posted to the ledger.
10. A post-closing trial balance is prepared.

- List the 10 steps of the accounting cycle.
- Determine whether any steps are out of order in a listing of accounting cycle steps.
- Determine whether there are any missing steps in a listing of accounting cycle steps.

4-6 4-6A, 4-6B

5 Illustrate the accounting cycle for one period.

		Example Exercises	Practice Exercises
Key Points	**Key Learning Outcomes**		

The complete accounting cycle for Kelly Consulting, P.C. for the month of April is described and illustrated on pages 159–170.

- Complete the accounting cycle for a period from beginning to end.

6 Explain what is meant by the fiscal year and the natural business year.

		Example Exercises	Practice Exercises
Key Points	**Key Learning Outcomes**		

The annual accounting period adopted by a business is its fiscal year. A company's fiscal year that ends when business activities have reached the lowest point in its annual operating cycle is called the natural business year.

- Explain why companies use a fiscal year that is different from the calendar year.

Key Terms

accounting cycle (158)
clearing account (153)
closing entries (152)
closing process (152)
closing the books (152)
current assets (151)

current liabilities (151)
fiscal year (170)
fixed (plant) assets (151)
Income Summary (153)
long-term liabilities (151)
natural business year (170)

notes receivable (151)
real (permanent) accounts (152)
temporary (nominal) accounts (152)

Illustrative Problem

Three years ago, T. Roderick organized Harbor Realty Inc. At July 31, 2010, the end of the current fiscal year, the following end-of-period spreadsheet (work sheet) was prepared:

	A	B	C	D	E	F	G	H	I	J	K
1					Harbor Realty Inc.						
2					End-of-Period Spreadsheet (Work Sheet)						
3					For the Year Ended July 31, 2010						
4		Unadjusted				Adjusted					
5		Trial Balance		Adjustments		Trial Balance		Income Statement		Balance Sheet	
6	**Account Title**	Dr.	Cr.	Dr.	Cr.	Dr.	Cr.	Dr.	Cr.	Dr.	Cr.
7	Cash	3,425				3,425				3,425	
8	Accounts Receivable	7,000		(e) 1,000		8,000				8,000	
9	Supplies	1,270			(a) 890	380				380	
10	Prepaid Insurance	620			(b) 315	305				305	
11	Office Equipment	51,650				51,650				51,650	
12	Accum. Depreciation		9,700		(c) 4,950		14,650				14,650
13	Accounts Payable		925				925				925
14	Unearned Fees		1,250	(f) 500			750				750
15	Wages Payable				(d) 440		440				440
16	Capital Stock		5,000				5,000				5,000
17	Retained Earnings		24,000				24,000				24,000
18	Dividends	5,200				5,200				5,200	
19	Fees Earned		59,125		(e) 1,000		60,625		60,625		
20					(f) 500						
21	Wages Expense	22,415		(d) 440		22,855		22,855			
22	Depreciation Expense			(c) 4,950		4,950		4,950			
23	Rent Expense	4,200				4,200		4,200			
24	Utilities Expense	2,715				2,715		2,715			
25	Supplies Expense			(a) 890		890		890			
26	Insurance Expense			(b) 315		315		315			
27	Miscellaneous Expense	1,505				1,505		1,505			
28		100,000	100,000	8,095	8,095	106,390	106,390	37,430	60,625	68,960	45,765
29	Net income							23,195			23,195
30								60,625	60,625	68,960	68,960
31											

Instructions

1. Prepare an income statement, a retained earnings statement, and a balance sheet.
2. On the basis of the data in the end-of-period spreadsheet (work sheet), journalize the closing entries.

Solution

1.

Harbor Realty Inc.
Income Statement
For the Year Ended July 31, 2010

Fees earned		$60,625
Expenses:		
Wages expense	$22,855	
Depreciation expense	4,950	
Rent expense	4,200	
Utilities expense	2,715	
Supplies expense	890	
Insurance expense	315	
Miscellaneous expense	1,505	
Total expenses		37,430
Net income		$23,195

Harbor Realty Inc.
Retained Earnings Statement
For the Year Ended July 31, 2010

Retained earnings, August 1, 2009		$24,000
Net income for the year	$23,195	
Less dividends	5,200	
Increase in retained earnings		17,995
Retained earnings, July 31, 2010		$41,995

Harbor Realty Inc.
Balance Sheet
July 31, 2010

Assets			Liabilities		
Current assets:			Current liabilities:		
Cash	$ 3,425		Accounts payable	$ 925	
Accounts receivable	8,000		Unearned fees	750	
Supplies	380		Wages payable	440	
Prepaid insurance	305		Total liabilities		$ 2,115
Total current assets		$12,110			
Property, plant, and equipment:			**Stockholders' Equity**		
Office equipment	$51,650		Capital stock	$ 5,000	
Less accumulated depreciation	14,650		Retained earnings	41,995	
Total property, plant,			Total stockholders' equity		46,995
and equipment		37,000	Total liabilities and		
Total assets		$49,110	stockholders' equity		$49,110

2.

			Journal			Page
Date			Description	Post. Ref.	Debit	Credit
			Closing Entries			
2010 July	31		Fees Earned		60,625	
			Income Summary			60,625
	31		Income Summary		37,430	
			Wages Expense			22,855
			Depreciation Expense			4,950
			Rent Expense			4,200
			Utilities Expense			2,715
			Supplies Expense			890
			Insurance Expense			315
			Miscellaneous Expense			1,505
	31		Income Summary		23,195	
			Retained Earnings			23,195
	31		Retained Earnings		5,200	
			Dividends			5,200

Self-Examination Questions

1. Which of the following accounts in the Adjusted Trial Balance columns of the end-of-period spreadsheet (work sheet) would be extended to the Balance Sheet columns?
   A. Utilities Expense   C. Dividends
   B. Rent Revenue   D. Miscellaneous Expense

2. Which of the following accounts would be classified as a current asset on the balance sheet?
   A. Office Equipment
   B. Land
   C. Accumulated Depreciation
   D. Accounts Receivable

3. Which of the following entries closes the dividends account at the end of the period?
   A. Debit the dividends account, credit the income summary account.
   B. Debit the retained earnings account, credit the dividends account.

   C. Debit the income summary account, credit the dividends account.
   D. Debit the dividends account, credit the retained earnings account.

4. Which of the following accounts would *not* be closed to the income summary account at the end of a period?
   A. Fees Earned
   B. Wages Expense
   C. Rent Expense
   D. Accumulated Depreciation

5. Which of the following accounts would *not* be included in a post-closing trial balance?
   A. Cash
   B. Fees Earned
   C. Accumulated Depreciation
   D. Capital Stock

Eye Openers

1. Why do some accountants prepare an end-of-period spreadsheet (work sheet)?
2. Is the end-of-period spreadsheet (work sheet) a substitute for the financial statements? Discuss.
3. In the Income Statement columns of the end-of-period spreadsheet (work sheet) for Steward Consulting Co. for the current year, the Debit column total is $675,450 and the Credit column total is $915,800 before the amount for net income or net loss has been included. In preparing the income statement from the end-of-period spreadsheet (work sheet), what is the amount of net income or net loss?
4. Describe the nature of the assets that compose the following sections of a balance sheet: (a) current assets, (b) property, plant, and equipment.
5. What is the difference between a current liability and a long-term liability?
6. What types of accounts are referred to as temporary accounts?
7. Why are closing entries required at the end of an accounting period?
8. What is the difference between adjusting entries and closing entries?
9. Describe the four entries that close the temporary accounts.
10. What is the purpose of the post-closing trial balance?
11. (a) What is the most important output of the accounting cycle? (b) Do all companies have an accounting cycle? Explain.
12. What is the natural business year?
13. Why might a department store select a fiscal year ending January 31, rather than a fiscal year ending December 31?
14. The fiscal years for several well-known companies are as follows:

Company	Fiscal Year Ending	Company	Fiscal Year Ending
Kmart	January 30	Toys "R" Us, Inc.	February 3
JCPenney	January 26	Federated Department Stores, Inc.	February 3
Target Corp.	January 28	The Limited, Inc.	February 2

What general characteristic shared by these companies explains why they do not have fiscal years ending December 31?

Practice Exercises

PE 4-1A
Flow of accounts into financial statements
obj. 1
EE 4-1   p. 148

The balances for the accounts listed below appear in the Adjusted Trial Balance columns of the end-of-period spreadsheet (work sheet). Indicate whether each balance should be extended to (a) an Income Statement column or (b) a Balance Sheet column.

1. Accumulated Depreciation—Equipment
2. Cash
3. Commissions Earned
4. Insurance Expense
5. Prepaid Rent
6. Supplies
7. Dividends
8. Wages Expense

PE 4-1B
Flow of accounts into financial statements
obj. 1
EE 4-1   p. 148

The balances for the accounts listed below appear in the Adjusted Trial Balance columns of the end-of-period spreadsheet (work sheet). Indicate whether each balance should be extended to (a) an Income Statement column or (b) a Balance Sheet column.

1. Accounts Payable
2. Depreciation Expense—Equipment
3. Capital Stock
4. Office Equipment
5. Rent Revenue
6. Supplies Expense
7. Unearned Service Revenue
8. Wages Payable

PE 4-2A
Determining net
income from the
end-of-period spread-
sheet (work sheet)

obj. 2

EE 4-2 p. 148

In the Income Statement columns of the end-of-period spreadsheet (work sheet) for El Dorado Consulting Co. for the current year, the Debit column total is $186,200 and the Credit column total is $233,400 before the amount for net income or net loss has been included. In preparing the income statement from the end-of-period spreadsheet (work sheet), what is the amount of net income or net loss?

PE 4-2B
Determining net
income from the
end-of-period spread-
sheet (work sheet)

obj. 2

EE 4-2 p. 148

In the Balance Sheet columns of the end-of-period spreadsheet (work sheet) for Lancaster Consulting Co. for the current year, the Debit column total is $375,000 and the Credit column total is $505,200 before the amount for net income or net loss has been included. In preparing the income statement from the end-of-period spreadsheet (work sheet), what is the amount of net income or net loss?

PE 4-3A
Retained earnings
statement

obj. 2

EE 4-3 p. 150

Meg Ostermiller owns and operates 4U Delivery Services. On January 1, 2009, Retained Earnings had a balance of $900,500. During the year, no additional capital stock was issued and dividends of $60,000 were paid. For the year ended December 31, 2009, 4U Delivery Services reported a net loss of $24,900. Prepare a retained earnings statement for the year ended December 31, 2009.

PE 4-3B
Retained earnings
statement

obj. 2

EE 4-3 p. 150

Rod Zoot owns and operates Steuben Advertising Services. On January 1, 2009, Retained Earnings had a balance of $475,000. During the year, an additional $75,000 of capital stock was issued and dividends of $30,000 were paid. For the year ended December 31, 2009, Steuben Advertising Services reported a net income of $110,000. Prepare a retained earnings statement for the year ended December 31, 2009.

PE 4-4A
Classified balance
sheet

obj. 2

EE 4-4 p. 151

The following accounts appear in an adjusted trial balance of Gondola Consulting. Indicate whether each account would be reported in the (a) current asset; (b) property, plant, and equipment; (c) current liability; (d) long-term liability; or (e) stockholders' equity section of the December 31, 2009, balance sheet of Gondola Consulting.

1. Accounts Payable
2. Accounts Receivable
3. Accumulated Depreciation—Equipment
4. Cash

5. Capital Stock
6. Note Payable (due in 2016)
7. Supplies
8. Wages Payable

PE 4-4B
Classified balance
sheet

obj. 2

EE 4-4 p. 151

The following accounts appear in an adjusted trial balance of Resolve Consulting. Indicate whether each account would be reported in the (a) current asset; (b) property, plant, and equipment; (c) current liability; (d) long-term liability; or (e) stockholders' equity section of the December 31, 2009, balance sheet of Resolve Consulting.

1. Building
2. Capital Stock
3. Mortgage Payable (due in 2015)
4. Prepaid Rent

5. Salaries Payable
6. Supplies
7. Taxes Payable
8. Unearned Service Fees

PE 4-5A
Closing entries
obj. 3
EE 4-5   p. 155

After the account have been adjusted at November 30, the end of the fiscal year, the following balances were taken from the ledger of Pond Landscaping Co.:

Capital Stock	$100,000
Retained Earnings	878,500
Dividends	50,000
Fees Earned	779,000
Wages Expense	389,000
Rent Expense	60,000
Supplies Expense	7,200
Miscellaneous Expense	11,400

Journalize the four entries required to close the accounts.

PE 4-5B
Closing entries
obj. 3
EE 4-5   p. 155

After the accounts have been adjusted at July 31, the end of the fiscal year, the following balances were taken from the ledger of Rabbit Delivery Services Co.:

Capital Stock	$250,000
Retained Earnings	480,000
Dividends	20,000
Fees Earned	515,000
Wages Expense	480,000
Rent Expense	75,000
Supplies Expense	12,100
Miscellaneous Expense	4,000

Journalize the four entries required to close the accounts.

PE 4-6A
Accounting cycle
obj. 4
EE 4-6   p. 158

From the following list of steps in the accounting cycle, identify what two steps are missing.

a. Transactions are analyzed and recorded in the journal.
b. Transactions are posted to the ledger.
c. An unadjusted trial balance is prepared.
d. An optional end-of-period spreadsheet (work sheet) is prepared.
e. Adjusting entries are journalized and posted to the ledger.
f. An adjusted trial balance is prepared.
g. Financial statements are prepared.
h. A post-closing trial balance is prepared.

PE 4-6B
Accounting cycle
obj. 4
EE 4-6   p. 158

From the following list of steps in the accounting cycle, identify what two steps are missing.

a. Transactions are analyzed and recorded in the journal.
b. An unadjusted trial balance is prepared.
c. Adjustment data are assembled and analyzed.
d. An optional end-of-period spreadsheet (work sheet) is prepared.
e. Adjusting entries are journalized and posted to the ledger.
f. An adjusted trial balance is prepared.
g. Closing entries are journalized and posted to the ledger.
h. A post-closing trial balance is prepared.

Exercises

EX 4-1
Extending account balances in an end-of-period spreadsheet (work sheet)

objs. 1, 2

The balances for the accounts listed below appear in the Adjusted Trial Balance columns of the end-of-period spreadsheet (work sheet). Indicate whether each balance should be extended to (a) an Income Statement column or (b) a Balance Sheet column.

1. Accounts Payable
2. Accounts Receivable
3. Cash
4. Dividends
5. Fees Earned

6. Supplies
7. Unearned Rent
8. Utilities Expense
9. Wages Expense
10. Wages Payable

EX 4-2
Classifying accounts

objs. 1, 2

Balances for each of the following accounts appear in an adjusted trial balance. Identify each as (a) asset, (b) liability, (c) revenue, or (d) expense.

1. Accounts Payable
2. Equipment
3. Fees Earned
4. Insurance Expense
5. Prepaid Advertising
6. Prepaid Insurance

7. Rent Revenue
8. Salary Expense
9. Salary Payable
10. Supplies
11. Supplies Expense
12. Unearned Rent

EX 4-3
Financial statements from the end-of-period spreadsheet (work sheet)

objs. 1, 2

Alpine Consulting is a consulting firm owned and operated by Scott Young. The end-of-period spreadsheet (work sheet) shown below was prepared for the year ended March 31, 2010.

	A	B	C	D	E	F	G	H	I	J	K
1					Alpine Consulting						
2					End-of-Period Spreadsheet (Work Sheet)						
3					For the Year Ended March 31, 2010						
4		Unadjusted				Adjusted					
5		Trial Balance		Adjustments		Trial Balance		Income Statement		Balance Sheet	
6	Account Title	Dr.	Cr.	Dr.	Cr.	Dr.	Cr.	Dr.	Cr.	Dr.	Cr.
7											
8	Cash	9,500				9,500				9,500	
9	Accounts Receivable	22,500				22,500				22,500	
10	Supplies	2,400			(a) 1,850	550				550	
11	Office Equipment	18,500				18,500				18,500	
12	Accumulated Depreciation		2,500		(b) 1,200		3,700				3,700
13	Accounts Payable		6,100				6,100				6,100
14	Salaries Payable				(c) 200		200				200
15	Capital Stock		10,000				10,000				10,000
16	Retained Earnings		12,600				12,600				12,600
17	Dividends	3,000				3,000				3,000	
18	Fees Earned		43,800				43,800		43,800		
19	Salary Expense	17,250		(c) 200		17,450		17,450			
20	Supplies Expense			(a) 1,850		1,850		1,850			
21	Depreciation Expense			(b) 1,200		1,200		1,200			
22	Miscellaneous Expense	1,850				1,850		1,850			
23		75,000	75,000	3,250	3,250	76,400	76,400	22,350	43,800	54,050	32,600
24	Net income							21,450			21,450
25								43,800	43,800	54,050	54,050
26											

Based on the preceding spreadsheet, prepare an income statement, retained earnings statement, and balance sheet for Alpine Consulting.

EX 4-4
Financial statements from the end-of-period spreadsheet (work sheet)

objs. 1, 2

Aardvark Consulting is a consulting firm owned and operated by Jan Sullivan. The following end-of-period spreadsheet (work sheet) was prepared for the year ended November 30, 2010.

	A	B	C	D	E	F	G	H	I	J	K
1		Aardvark Consulting									
2		End-of-Period Spreadsheet (Work Sheet)									
3		For the Year Ended November 30, 2010									
4		Unadjusted				Adjusted					
5		Trial Balance		Adjustments		Trial Balance		Income Statement		Balance Sheet	
6	Account Title	Dr.	Cr.	Dr.	Cr.	Dr.	Cr.	Dr.	Cr.	Dr.	Cr.
7											
8	Cash	7,500				7,500				7,500	
9	Accounts Receivable	18,500				18,500				18,500	
10	Supplies	3,000			(a) 2,250	750				750	
11	Office Equipment	30,500				30,500				30,500	
12	Accumulated Depreciation		4,500		(b) 900		5,400				5,400
13	Accounts Payable		3,300				3,300				3,300
14	Salaries Payable				(c) 400		400				400
15	Capital Stock		8,000				8,000				8,000
16	Retained Earnings		19,200				19,200				19,200
17	Dividends	2,000				2,000				2,000	
18	Fees Earned		60,000				60,000		60,000		
19	Salary Expense	32,000		(c) 400		32,400		32,400			
20	Supplies Expense			(a) 2,250		2,250		2,250			
21	Depreciation Expense			(b) 900		900		900			
22	Miscellaneous Expense	1,500				1,500		1,500			
23		95,000	95,000	3,550	3,550	96,300	96,300	37,050	60,000	59,250	36,300
24	Net income							22,950			22,950
25								60,000	60,000	59,250	59,250
26											

Based upon the preceding spreadsheet, prepare an income statement, retained earnings statement, and balance sheet for Aardvark Consulting.

EX 4-5
Income statement

obj. 2

✔ Net income, $112,000

The following account balances were taken from the adjusted trial balance for 3 Rivers Messenger Service, a delivery service firm, for the current fiscal year ended September 30, 2010:

Depreciation Expense	$ 8,000	Rent Expense	$ 60,500
Fees Earned	425,000	Salaries Expense	213,800
Insurance Expense	1,500	Supplies Expense	2,750
Miscellaneous Expense	3,250	Utilities Expense	23,200

Prepare an income statement.

EX 4-6
Income statement; net loss

obj. 2

✔ Net loss, $44,275

The following revenue and expense account balances were taken from the ledger of Infinet Services Co. after the accounts had been adjusted on January 31, 2010, the end of the current fiscal year:

Depreciation Expense	$12,200	Service Revenue	$233,900
Insurance Expense	6,000	Supplies Expense	2,875
Miscellaneous Expense	4,750	Utilities Expense	18,750
Rent Expense	49,300	Wages Expense	184,300

Prepare an income statement.

EX 4-7
Income statement

obj. 2

FedEx Corporation had the following revenue and expense account balances (in millions) at its fiscal year-end of May 31, 2007:

Depreciation	$ 845	Purchased Transportation	$ 1,097
Fuel	2,946	Rentals and Landing Fees	1,598
Maintenance and Repairs	1,440	Revenues	22,527
Other Expense (Income) Net	4,566	Salaries and Employee Benefits	8,051
Provision for Income Taxes	733		

Internet Project

✔ a. Net income:
$1,251

a. Prepare an income statement.

b. ➤ Compare your income statement with the related income statement that is available at the FedEx Corporation Web site, which is linked to the text's Web site at **www.cengage.com/accounting/warren**. What similarities and differences do you see?

EX 4-8
Retained earnings statement
obj. 2

✔ Retained earnings, Mar. 31, 2010:
$899,900

Jackrabbit Systems Co. offers its services to residents in the Santa Cruz area. Selected accounts from the ledger of Jackrabbit Systems Co. for the current fiscal year ended March 31, 2010, are as follows:

Retained Earnings					Dividends			
Mar. 31	32,000	Apr. 1 (2009)	611,900	June 30	8,000	Mar. 31	32,000	
		Mar. 31	320,000	Sept. 30	8,000			
				Dec. 31	8,000			
				Mar. 31	8,000			

Income Summary			
Mar. 31	600,000	Mar. 31	920,000
31	320,000		

Prepare a retained earnings statement for the year.

EX 4-9
Retained earnings statement; net loss
obj. 2

✔ Retained earnings, June 30, 2010:
$201,300

Selected accounts from the ledger of Picasso Sports for the current fiscal year ended June 30, 2010, are as follows:

Retained Earnings					Dividends			
June 30	32,300	July 1 (2009)	237,600	Sept. 30	1,000	June 30	4,000	
30	4,000			Dec. 31	1,000			
				May 31	1,000			
				June 30	1,000			

Income Summary			
June 30	511,900	June 30	479,600
		30	32,300

Prepare a retained earnings statement for the year.

EX 4-10
Classifying assets
obj. 2

Identify each of the following as (a) a current asset or (b) property, plant, and equipment:

1. Accounts receivable
2. Building
3. Cash
4. Equipment
5. Prepaid rent
6. Supplies

EX 4-11
Balance sheet classification
obj. 2

At the balance sheet date, a business owes a mortgage note payable of $360,000, the terms of which provide for monthly payments of $2,000.

➤ Explain how the liability should be classified on the balance sheet.

EX 4-12
Balance sheet
obj. 2

✔ Total assets:
$187,500

Optimum Weight Co. offers personal weight reduction consulting services to individuals. After all the accounts have been closed on June 30, 2010, the end of the current fiscal year, the balances of selected accounts from the ledger of Optimum Weight Co. are as follows:

Accounts Payable	$ 8,625	Prepaid Insurance	$ 4,800
Accounts Receivable	20,780	Prepaid Rent	3,000
Accumulated Depreciation—Equipment	25,975	Retained Earnings	133,000
Capital Stock	40,000	Salaries Payable	3,375
Cash	?	Supplies	520
Equipment	75,000	Unearned Fees	2,500
Land	100,000		

Prepare a classified balance sheet that includes the correct balance for Cash.

EX 4-13
Balance sheet
obj. 2

✔ Corrected balance sheet, total assets: $540,000

List the errors you find in the following balance sheet. Prepare a corrected balance sheet.

Cabana Services Co.
Balance Sheet
For the Year Ended August 31, 2010

Assets			Liabilities		
Current assets:			Current liabilities:		
Cash	$ 15,840		Accounts receivable	$ 41,250	
Accounts payable	20,370		Accum. depr.—building	260,100	
Supplies	4,950		Accum. depr.—equipment	55,440	
Prepaid insurance	14,400		Net income	75,000	
Land	180,000		Total liabilities		$431,790
Total current assets		$235,560			
Property, plant,			**Stockholders' Equity**		
and equipment:			Wages payable	$ 4,020	
Building	$470,100		Capital stock	75,000	
Equipment	129,000		Retained earnings	440,610	
Total property, plant,			Total stockholders' equity		519,630
and equipment		715,860	Total liabilities and		
Total assets		$951,420	stockholders' equity		$951,420

EX 4-14
Identifying accounts to be closed
obj. 3

From the following list, identify the accounts that should be closed to Income Summary at the end of the fiscal year:

a. Accounts Receivable
b. Accumulated Depreciation—Equipment
c. Depreciation Expense—Equipment
d. Equipment
e. Capital Stock
f. Dividends
g. Fees Earned
h. Land
i. Supplies
j. Supplies Expense
k. Wages Expense
l. Wages Payable

EX 4-15
Closing entries
obj. 3

Prior to its closing, Income Summary had total debits of $432,200 and total credits of $572,600.

Briefly explain the purpose served by the income summary account and the nature of the entries that resulted in the $432,200 and the $572,600.

EX 4-16
Closing entries with net income
obj. 3

After all revenue and expense accounts have been closed at the end of the fiscal year, Income Summary has a debit of $193,400 and a credit of $258,600. At the same date, Retained Earnings has a credit balance of $300,000, and Dividends has a balance of $25,000. (a) Journalize the entries required to complete the closing of the accounts. (b) Determine the amount of Retained Earnings at the end of the period.

EX 4-17
Closing entries with net loss
obj. 3

Marina Services Co. offers its services to individuals desiring to improve their personal images. After the accounts have been adjusted at July 31, the end of the fiscal year, the following balances were taken from the ledger of Marina Services Co.

Capital Stock	$100,000	Wages Expense	$190,000
Retained Earnings	380,000	Rent Expense	45,000
Dividends	30,000	Supplies Expense	11,200
Fees Earned	215,000	Miscellaneous Expense	5,100

Journalize the four entries required to close the accounts.

EX 4-18
Identifying
permanent accounts

obj. 3

Which of the following accounts will usually appear in the post-closing trial balance?

a. Accounts Payable
b. Accumulated Depreciation
c. Capital Stock
d. Dividends
e. Cash
f. Depreciation Expense

g. Fees Earned
h. Office Equipment
i. Salaries Expense
j. Salaries Payable
k. Supplies

EX 4-19
Post-closing trial
balance

obj. 3

✔ Correct column
totals, $175,000

An accountant prepared the following post-closing trial balance:

La Jolla Billiards Co.
Post-Closing Trial Balance
October 31, 2010

	Debit Balances	Credit Balances
Cash	13,200	
Accounts Receivable	29,350	
Supplies		1,850
Equipment		130,600
Accumulated Depreciation—Equipment	43,500	
Accounts Payable	15,800	
Salaries Payable		1,500
Unearned Rent	6,000	
Capital Stock	35,000	
Retained Earnings		73,200
	142,850	207,150

Prepare a corrected post-closing trial balance. Assume that all accounts have normal balances and that the amounts shown are correct.

EX 4-20
Steps in the
accounting cycle

obj. 4

Rearrange the following steps in the accounting cycle in proper sequence:

a. An unadjusted trial balance is prepared.
b. Transactions are posted to the ledger.
c. Transactions are analyzed and recorded in the journal.
d. An optional end-of-period spreadsheet (work sheet) is prepared.
e. An adjusted trial balance is prepared.
f. Financial statements are prepared.
g. A post-closing trial balance is prepared.
h. Adjustment data are asssembled and analyzed.
i. Closing entries are journalized and posted to the ledger.
j. Adjusting entries are journalized and posted to the ledger.

EX 4-21
Appendix: Steps in
completing an end-
of-period spreadsheet
(work sheet)

The steps performed in completing an end-of-period spreadsheet (work sheet) are listed below in random order.

a. Add the Debit and Credit columns of the Unadjusted Trial Balance columns of the spreadsheet (work sheet) to verify that the totals are equal.
b. Add the Debit and Credit columns of the Balance Sheet and Income Statement columns of the spreadsheet (work sheet) to verify that the totals are equal.
c. Add or deduct adjusting entry data to trial balance amounts, and extend amounts to the Adjusted Trial Balance columns.
d. Add the Debit and Credit columns of the Adjustments columns of the spreadsheet (work sheet) to verify that the totals are equal.

e. Add the Debit and Credit columns of the Balance Sheet and Income Statement columns of the spreadsheet (work sheet) to determine the amount of net income or net loss for the period.

f. Add the Debit and Credit columns of the Adjusted Trial Balance columns of the spreadsheet (work sheet) to verify that the totals are equal.

g. Enter the adjusting entries into the spreadsheet (work sheet), based on the adjustment data.

h. Enter the amount of net income or net loss for the period in the proper Income Statement column and Balance Sheet column.

i. Enter the unadjusted account balances from the general ledger into the Unadjusted Trial Balance columns of the spreadsheet (work sheet).

j. Extend the adjusted trial balance amounts to the Income Statement columns and the Balance Sheet columns.

Indicate the order in which the preceding steps would be performed in preparing and completing a spreadsheet (work sheet).

EX 4-22
Appendix:
Adjustment data on an end-of-period spreadsheet (work sheet)

✔ Total debits of Adjustments column: $16

Homeland Security Services Co. offers security services to business clients. The trial balance for Homeland Security Services Co. has been prepared on the end-of-period spreadsheet (work sheet) for the year ended October 31, 2010, shown below.

Homeland Security Services Co.
End-of-Period Spreadsheet (Work Sheet)
For the Year Ended October 31, 2010

Account Title	Unadjusted Trial Balance		Adjustments		Adjusted Trial Balance	
	Dr.	Cr.	Dr.	Cr.	Dr.	Cr.
Cash	6					
Accounts Receivable	40					
Supplies	4					
Prepaid Insurance	6					
Land	50					
Equipment	20					
Accum. Depr.—Equipment		2				
Accounts Payable		18				
Wages Payable		0				
Capital Stock		15				
Retained Earnings		70				
Dividends	4					
Fees Earned		45				
Wages Expense	10					
Rent Expense	6					
Insurance Expense	0					
Utilities Expense	3					
Supplies Expense	0					
Depreciation Expense	0					
Miscellaneous Expense	1					
	150	150				

The data for year-end adjustments are as follows:

a. Fees earned, but not yet billed, $4.
b. Supplies on hand, $1.
c. Insurance premiums expired, $5.
d. Depreciation expense, $2.
e. Wages accrued, but not paid, $2.

Enter the adjustment data, and place the balances in the Adjusted Trial Balance columns.

EX 4-23
Appendix: Completing an end-of-period spreadsheet (work sheet)

✔ Net income: $17

Homeland Security Services Co. offers security services to business clients. Complete the following end-of-period spreadsheet (work sheet) for Homeland Security Services Co.

Homeland Security Services Co.
End-of-Period Spreadsheet (Work Sheet)
For the Year Ended October 31, 2010

Account Title	Adjusted Trial Balance Dr.	Adjusted Trial Balance Cr.	Income Statement Dr.	Income Statement Cr.	Balance Sheet Dr.	Balance Sheet Cr.
Cash	6					
Accounts Receivable	44					
Supplies	1					
Prepaid Insurance	1					
Land	50					
Equipment	20					
Accum. Depr.—Equipment		4				
Accounts Payable		18				
Wages Payable		2				
Capital Stock		15				
Retained Earnings		70				
Dividends	4					
Fees Earned		49				
Wages Expense	12					
Rent Expense	6					
Insurance Expense	5					
Utilities Expense	3					
Supplies Expense	3					
Depreciation Expense	2					
Miscellaneous Expense	1					
	158	158				
Net income (loss)						

EX 4-24
Appendix: Financial statements from an end-of-period spreadsheet (work sheet)

✔ Retained Earnings, October 31, 2010: $83

Based on the data in Exercise 4-23, prepare an income statement, retained earnings statement, and balance sheet for Homeland Security Services Co.

EX 4-25
Appendix: Adjusting entries from an end-of-period spreadsheet (work sheet)

Based on the data in Exercise 4-22, prepare the adjusting entries for Homeland Security Services Co.

EX 4-26
Appendix: Closing entries from an end-of-period spreadsheet (work sheet)

Based on the data in Exercise 4-23, prepare the closing entries for Homeland Security Services Co.

EX 4-27
Working capital and current ratio

The following data (in thousands) were taken from recent financial statements of Under Armour, Inc.:

| | December 31 | |
	2007	2006
Current assets	$322,245	$244,952
Current liabilities	95,699	71,563

a. Compute the working capital and the current ratio as of December 31, 2007 and 2006. Round to two decimal places.
b. What conclusions concerning the company's ability to meet its financial obligations can you draw from part (a)?

EX 4-28
Working capital and current ratio

The following data (in thousands) were taken from recent financial statements of Starbucks Corporation:

	Sept. 30, 2007	Oct. 1, 2006
Current assets	$1,696,487	$1,529,788
Current liabilities	2,155,566	1,935,620

a. Compute the working capital and the current ratio as of September 30, 2007 and October 1, 2006. Round to two decimal places.
b. What conclusions concerning the company's ability to meet its financial obligations can you draw from part (a)?

Problems Series A

PR 4-1A
Financial statements and closing entries

objs. 1, 2, 3

✔ 1. Net loss: $14,150

Prison Watch Company offers legal consulting advice to prison inmates. Prison Watch Company prepared the end-of-period spreadsheet (work sheet) at the top of the following page at June 30, 2010, the end of the current fiscal year.

Instructions

1. Prepare an income statement for the year ended June 30.
2. Prepare a retained earnings statement for the year ended June 30.
3. Prepare a balance sheet as of June 30.
4. On the basis of the end-of-period spreadsheet (work sheet), journalize the closing entries.
5. Prepare a post-closing trial balance.

	A	B	C	D	E	F	G	H	I	J	K
1				Prison Watch Company							
2				End-of-Period Spreadsheet (Work Sheet)							
3				For the Year Ended June 30, 2010							
4		Unadjusted Trial Balance		Adjustments		Adjusted Trial Balance		Income Statement		Balance Sheet	
5											
6	Account Title	Dr.	Cr.	Dr.	Cr.	Dr.	Cr.	Dr.	Cr.	Dr.	Cr.
7											
8	Cash	5,100				5,100				5,100	
9	Accounts Receivable	12,750		(a) 1,200		13,950				13,950	
10	Prepaid Insurance	3,600			(b) 900	2,700				2,700	
11	Supplies	2,025			(c) 1,525	500				500	
12	Land	80,000				80,000				80,000	
13	Building	200,000				200,000				200,000	
14	Acc. Depr.—Building		90,000		(d) 2,500		92,500				92,500
15	Equipment	140,000				140,000				140,000	
16	Acc. Depr.—Equipment		54,450		(e) 6,000		60,450				60,450
17	Accounts Payable		9,750				9,750				9,750
18	Sal. & Wages Payable				(f) 1,900		1,900				1,900
19	Unearned Rent		4,500	(g) 4,000			500				500
20	Capital Stock		125,000				125,000				125,000
21	Retained Earnings		186,300				186,300				186,300
22	Dividends	20,000				20,000				20,000	
23	Fees Revenue		280,000		(a) 1,200		281,200		281,200		
24	Rent Revenue				(g) 4,000		4,000		4,000		
25	Salaries & Wages Expense	145,100		(f) 1,900		147,000		147,000			
26	Advertising Expense	86,800				86,800		86,800			
27	Utilities Expense	30,000				30,000		30,000			
28	Travel Expense	18,750				18,750		18,750			
29	Depr. Exp.—Equipment			(e) 6,000		6,000		6,000			
30	Depr. Exp.—Building			(d) 2,500		2,500		2,500			
31	Supplies Expense			(c) 1,525		1,525		1,525			
32	Insurance Expense			(b) 900		900		900			
33	Misc. Expense	5,875				5,875		5,875			
34		750,000	750,000	18,025	18,025	761,600	761,600	299,350	285,200	462,250	476,400
35	Net loss								14,150	14,150	
36								299,350	299,350	476,400	476,400
37											

PR 4-2A
Financial statements and closing entries
objs. 2, 3

✔ 1. Retained Earnings, March 31: $317,000

The Hometown Services Company is a financial planning services firm owned and operated by Jane Maines. As of March 31, 2010, the end of the current fiscal year, the accountant for The Hometown Services Company prepared an end-of-period spreadsheet (work sheet), part of which is shown at the top of the next page.

Instructions
1. Prepare an income statement, a retained earnings statement, and a balance sheet.
2. Journalize the entries that were required to close the accounts at March 31.
3. If the balance of Retained Earnings increased $35,000 after the closing entries were posted, and the dividends remained the same, what was the amount of net income or net loss?

	A	H	I	J	K
		\multicolumn{5}{c}{The Hometown Services Company}				
1		The Hometown Services Company				
2		End-of-Period Spreadsheet (Work Sheet)				
3		For the Year Ended March 31, 2010				
4			Income Statement		Balance Sheet	
5			Dr.	Cr.	Dr.	Cr.
6	Cash				12,950	
7	Accounts Receivable				28,150	
8	Supplies				4,400	
9	Prepaid Insurance				9,500	
10	Land				100,000	
11	Buildings				360,000	
12	Accumulated Depreciation—Buildings					117,200
13	Equipment				260,000	
14	Accumulated Depreciation—Equipment					152,700
15	Accounts Payable					33,300
16	Salaries Payable					3,300
17	Unearned Rent					1,500
18	Capital Stock					150,000
19	Retained Earnings					277,600
20	Dividends				25,000	
21	Service Fees			475,000		
22	Rent Revenue			5,000		
23	Salary Expense		340,600			
24	Depreciation Expense—Equipment		18,500			
25	Rent Expense		15,500			
26	Supplies Expense		10,950			
27	Utilities Expense		9,900			
28	Depreciation Expense—Buildings		6,600			
29	Repairs Expense		5,450			
30	Insurance Expense		3,000			
31	Miscellaneous Expense		5,100			
32			415,600	480,000	800,000	735,600
33	Net income		64,400			64,400
34			480,000	480,000	800,000	800,000
35						

PR 4-3A
T accounts, adjusting entries, financial statements, and closing entries; optional end-of-period spreadsheet (work sheet)

objs. 2, 3

✔ 2. Net income: $36,700

The unadjusted trial balance of Surf Suds Laundry at October 31, 2010, the end of the current fiscal year, is shown below.

Surf Suds Laundry
Unadjusted Trial Balance
October 31, 2010

	Debit Balances	Credit Balances
Cash	4,350	
Laundry Supplies	11,250	
Prepaid Insurance	7,200	
Laundry Equipment	163,500	
Accumulated Depreciation		61,500
Accounts Payable		9,300
Capital Stock		8,000
Retained Earnings		48,700
Dividends	3,000	
Laundry Revenue		247,500
Wages Expense	107,250	
Rent Expense	54,000	
Utilities Expense	20,400	
Miscellaneous Expense	4,050	
	375,000	375,000

The data needed to determine year-end adjustments are as follows:

a. Wages accrued but not paid at October 31 are $1,250.
b. Depreciation of equipment during the year is $9,500.
c. Laundry supplies on hand at October 31 are $2,900.
d. Insurance premiums expired during the year are $6,000.

Instructions

1. For each account listed in the unadjusted trial balance, enter the balance in a T account. Identify the balance as "Oct. 31 Bal." In addition, add T accounts for Wages Payable, Depreciation Expense, Laundry Supplies Expense, Insurance Expense, and Income Summary.
2. **Optional:** Enter the unadjusted trial balance on an end-of-period spreadsheet (work sheet) and complete the spreadsheet. Add the accounts listed in Part (1) as needed.
3. Journalize and post the adjusting entries. Identify the adjustments by "Adj." and the new balances as "Adj. Bal."
4. Prepare an adjusted trial balance.
5. Prepare an income statement, a retained earnings statement, and a balance sheet.
6. Journalize and post the closing entries. Identify the closing entries by "Clos."
7. Prepare a post-closing trial balance.

PR 4-4A

Ledger accounts, adjusting entries, financial statements, and closing entries; optional end-of-period spreadsheet (work sheet)

objs. 2, 3

✔ 4. Net income: $22,645

If the working papers correlating with this textbook are not used, omit Problem 4-4A.

The ledger and trial balance of Mechanical Services Co. as of July 31, 2010, the end of the first month of its current fiscal year, are presented in the working papers.
    Data needed to determine the necessary adjusting entries are as follows:

a. Service revenue accrued at July 31 is $3,000.
b. Supplies on hand at July 31 are $1,475.
c. Insurance premiums expired during July are $1,200.
d. Depreciation of the building during July is $1,300.
e. Depreciation of equipment during July is $1,250.
f. Unearned rent at July 31 is $1,700.
g. Wages accrued but not paid at July 31 are $500.

Instructions

1. **Optional:** Complete the end-of-period spreadsheet (work sheet) using the adjustment data shown above.
2. Journalize and post the adjusting entries, inserting balances in the accounts affected.
3. Prepare an adjusted trial balance.
4. Prepare an income statement, a retained earnings statement, and a balance sheet.
5. Journalize and post the closing entries. Indicate closed accounts by inserting a line in both Balance columns opposite the closing entry. Insert the new balance of the capital account.
6. Prepare a post-closing trial balance.

PR 4-5A

Ledger accounts, adjusting entries, financial statements, and closing entries; optional end-of-period spreadsheet (work sheet)

objs. 2, 3

The unadjusted trial balance of Loose Leaf Co. at December 31, 2010, the end of the current year, is shown at the top of the next page. The data needed to determine year-end adjustments are as follows:

a. Supplies on hand at December 31 are $1,500.
b. Insurance premiums expired during the year are $2,500.
c. Depreciation of equipment during the year is $4,700.
d. Depreciation of trucks during the year is $3,100.
e. Wages accrued but not paid at December 31 are $750.

Loose Leaf Co.
Unadjusted Trial Balance
December 31, 2010

	Debit Balances	Credit Balances
11 Cash	1,825	
13 Supplies	4,820	
14 Prepaid Insurance	7,500	
16 Equipment	70,200	
17 Accumulated Depreciation—Equipment		12,050
18 Trucks	50,000	
19 Accumulated Depreciation—Trucks		27,100
21 Accounts Payable		12,015
31 Capital Stock		3,000
32 Retained Earnings		24,885
33 Dividends	2,500	
41 Service Revenue		120,950
51 Wages Expense	48,010	
53 Rent Expense	7,600	
55 Truck Expense	5,350	
59 Miscellaneous Expense	2,195	
	200,000	200,000

Instructions

1. For each account listed in the unadjusted trial balance, enter the balance in the appropriate Balance column of a four-column account and place a check mark (✔) in the Posting Reference column.
2. **Optional:** Enter the unadjusted trial balance on an end-of-period spreadsheet (work sheet) and complete the spreadsheet. Add the accounts listed in part (3) as needed.
3. Journalize and post the adjusting entries, inserting balances in the accounts affected. The following additional accounts from Loose Leaf's chart of accounts should be used: Wages Payable, 22; Supplies Expense, 52; Depreciation Expense—Equipment, 54; Depreciation Expense—Trucks, 56; Insurance Expense, 57.
4. Prepare an adjusted trial balance.
5. Prepare an income statement, a retained earnings statement, and a balance sheet.
6. Journalize and post the closing entries. (Income Summary is account #34 in the chart of accounts.) Indicate closed accounts by inserting a line in both Balance columns opposite the closing entry.
7. Prepare a post-closing trial balance.

PR 4-6A
Complete accounting cycle

objs. 4, 5, 6

For the past several years, Emily Page has operated a part-time consulting business from her home. As of June 1, 2010, Emily decided to move to rented quarters and to operate the business as a professional corporation, which was to be known as Bottom Line Consulting, P.C., on a full-time basis. Bottom Line Consulting entered into the following transactions during June:

June 1. The following assets were received from Emily Page in exchange for capital stock: cash, $20,000; accounts receivable, $4,500; supplies, $2,000; and office equipment, $11,500. There were no liabilities received.

1. Paid three months' rent on a lease rental contract, $6,000.
2. Paid the premiums on property and casualty insurance policies, $2,400.
4. Received cash from clients as an advance payment for services to be provided and recorded it as unearned fees, $2,700.
5. Purchased additional office equipment on account from Office Depot Co., $3,500.
6. Received cash from clients on account, $3,000.
10. Paid cash for a newspaper advertisement, $200.
12. Paid Office Depot Co. for part of the debt incurred on June 5, $750.

June 12. Recorded services provided on account for the period June 1–12, $5,100.
    14. Paid part-time receptionist for two weeks' salary, $1,100.
    17. Recorded cash from cash clients for fees earned during the period June 1–16, $6,500.
    18. Paid cash for supplies, $750.
    20. Recorded services provided on account for the period June 13–20, $3,100.
    24. Recorded cash from cash clients for fees earned for the period June 17–24, $5,150.
    26. Received cash from clients on account, $6,900.
    27. Paid part-time receptionist for two weeks' salary, $1,100.
    29. Paid telephone bill for June, $150.
    30. Paid electricity bill for June, $400.
    30. Recorded cash from cash clients for fees earned for the period June 25–30, $2,500.
    30. Recorded services provided on account for the remainder of June, $1,000.
    30. Paid dividends of $5,000.

Instructions

1. Journalize each transaction in a two-column journal, referring to the following chart of accounts in selecting the accounts to be debited and credited. (Do not insert the account numbers in the journal at this time.)

11	Cash	31	Capital Stock
12	Accounts Receivable	32	Retained Earnings
14	Supplies	33	Dividends
15	Prepaid Rent	41	Fees Earned
16	Prepaid Insurance	51	Salary Expense
18	Office Equipment	52	Rent Expense
19	Accumulated Depreciation	53	Supplies Expense
21	Accounts Payable	54	Depreciation Expense
22	Salaries Payable	55	Insurance Expense
23	Unearned Fees	59	Miscellaneous Expense

2. Post the journal to a ledger of four-column accounts.
3. Prepare an unadjusted trial balance.
4. At the end of June, the following adjustment data were assembled. Analyze and use these data to complete parts (5) and (6).
   a. Insurance expired during June is $200.
   b. Supplies on hand on June 30 are $650.
   c. Depreciation of office equipment for June is $250.
   d. Accrued receptionist salary on June 30 is $220.
   e. Rent expired during June is $2,000.
   f. Unearned fees on June 30 are $1,875.
5. **Optional:** Enter the unadjusted trial balance on an end-of-period spreadsheet (work sheet) and complete the spreadsheet.
6. Journalize and post the adjusting entries.
7. Prepare an adjusted trial balance.
8. Prepare an income statement, a retained earnings statement, and a balance sheet.
9. Prepare and post the closing entries. (Income Summary is account #34 in the chart of accounts.) Indicate closed accounts by inserting a line in both the Balance columns opposite the closing entry.
10. Prepare a post-closing trial balance.

Problems Series B

PR 4-1B
Financial statements and closing entries

objs. 1, 2, 3

Lightworks Company maintains and repairs warning lights, such as those found on radio towers and lighthouses. Lightworks Company prepared the end-of-period spreadsheet (work sheet) shown below at July 31, 2010, the end of the current fiscal year:

	A	B	C	D	E	F	G	H	I	J	K
1				\multicolumn{4}{c} Lightworks Company					
2				End-of-Period Spreadsheet (Work Sheet)							
3				For the Year Ended July 31, 2010							
4		Unadjusted				Adjusted					
5		Trial Balance		Adjustments		Trial Balance		Income Statement		Balance Sheet	
6	Account Title	Dr.	Cr.	Dr.	Cr.	Dr.	Cr.	Dr.	Cr.	Dr.	Cr.
7											
8	Cash	5,800				5,800				5,800	
9	Accounts Receivable	18,900		(a) 3,300		22,200				22,200	
10	Prepaid Insurance	4,200			(b) 3,000	1,200				1,200	
11	Supplies	2,730			(c) 1,900	830				830	
12	Land	98,000				98,000				98,000	
13	Building	200,000				200,000				200,000	
14	Acc. Depr.—Building		100,300		(d) 1,400		101,700				101,700
15	Equipment	101,000				101,000				101,000	
16	Acc. Depr.—Equipment		85,100		(e) 3,200		88,300				88,300
17	Accounts Payable		5,700				5,700				5,700
18	Salaries & Wages Payable				(f) 1,800		1,800				1,800
19	Unearned Rent		2,100	(g) 1,000			1,100				1,100
20	Capital Stock		40,000				40,000				40,000
21	Retained Earnings		63,100				63,100				63,100
22	Dividends	10,000				10,000				10,000	
23	Fees Revenue		303,700		(a) 3,300		307,000		307,000		
24	Rent Revenue				(g) 1,000		1,000		1,000		
25	Salaries & Wages Expense	113,100		(f) 1,800		114,900		114,900			
26	Advertising Expense	21,700				21,700		21,700			
27	Utilities Expense	11,400				11,400		11,400			
28	Repairs Expense	8,850				8,850		8,850			
29	Depr. Exp.—Equipment			(e) 3,200		3,200		3,200			
30	Insurance Expense			(b) 3,000		3,000		3,000			
31	Supplies Expense			(c) 1,900		1,900		1,900			
32	Depr. Exp.—Building			(d) 1,400		1,400		1,400			
33	Misc. Expense	4,320				4,320		4,320			
34		600,000	600,000	15,600	15,600	609,700	609,700	170,670	308,000	439,030	301,700
35	Net income							137,330			137,330
36								308,000	308,000	439,030	439,030
37											

✔ 1. Net income: $137,330

Instructions

1. Prepare an income statement for the year ended July 31.
2. Prepare a retained earnings statement for the year ended July 31.
3. Prepare a balance sheet as of July 31.
4. Based upon the end-of-period spreadsheet (work sheet), journalize the closing entries.
5. Prepare a post-closing trial balance.

PR 4-2B
Financial statements and closing entries

objs. 2, 3

✔ 1. Curtis Graves, capital, November 30: $176,300

Suspicions Company is an investigative services firm that is owned and operated by Curtis Graves. On November 30, 2010, the end of the current fiscal year, the accountant for Suspicions Company prepared an end-of-period spreadsheet (work sheet), a part of which is shown below.

	A	H	I	J	K
1	Suspicions Company				
2	End-of-Period Spreadsheet (Work Sheet)				
3	For the Year Ended November 30, 2010				
		Income Statement		Balance Sheet	
4		Dr.	Cr.	Dr.	Cr.
5	Cash			11,500	
6	Accounts Receivable			47,200	
7	Supplies			3,500	
8	Prepaid Insurance			4,800	
9	Equipment			175,000	
10	Accumulated Depreciation—Equipment				55,200
11	Accounts Payable				6,000
12	Salaries Payable				1,500
13	Unearned Rent				3,000
14	Capital Stock				30,000
15	Retained Earnings				142,800
16	Dividends			30,000	
17	Service Fees		480,000		
18	Rent Revenue		20,000		
19	Salary Expense	375,000			
20	Rent Expense	62,500			
21	Supplies Expense	9,000			
22	Depreciation Expense—Equipment	5,000			
23	Utilities Expense	4,400			
24	Repairs Expense	3,200			
25	Insurance Expense	2,800			
26	Miscellaneous Expense	4,600			
27		466,500	500,000	272,000	238,500
28	Net income	33,500			33,500
29		500,000	500,000	272,000	272,000
30					

Instructions
1. Prepare an income statement, retained earnings statement, and a balance sheet.
2. Journalize the entries that were required to close the accounts at November 30.
3. If Retained Earnings decreased $40,000 after the closing entries were posted, and the dividends remained the same, what was the amount of net income or net loss?

PR 4-3B
T accounts, adjusting entries, financial statements, and closing entries; optional end-of-period spreadsheet (work sheet)

objs. 2, 3

✔ 2. Net income: $35,900

The unadjusted trial balance of Ocean Breeze Laundromat at April 30, 2010, the end of the current fiscal year, is shown below.

Ocean Breeze Laundromat
Unadjusted Trial Balance
April 30, 2010

	Debit Balances	Credit Balances
Cash	11,000	
Laundry Supplies	18,900	
Prepaid Insurance	8,600	
Laundry Equipment	284,000	
Accumulated Depreciation		150,400
Accounts Payable		9,800
Capital Stock		25,000
Retained Earnings		82,600
Dividends	8,400	
Laundry Revenue		232,200
Wages Expense	104,000	
Rent Expense	39,300	
Utilities Expense	20,400	
Miscellaneous Expense	5,400	
	500,000	500,000

The data needed to determine year-end adjustments are as follows:

a. Laundry supplies on hand at April 30 are $4,000.
b. Insurance premiums expired during the year are $5,200.
c. Depreciation of equipment during the year is $6,000.
d. Wages accrued but not paid at April 30 are $1,100.

Instructions

1. For each account listed in the unadjusted trial balance, enter the balance in a T account. Identify the balance as "April 30 Bal." In addition, add T accounts for Wages Payable, Depreciation Expense, Laundry Supplies Expense, Insurance Expense, and Income Summary.
2. **Optional:** Enter the unadjusted trial balance on an end-of-period spreadsheet (work sheet) and complete the spreadsheet. Add the accounts listed in part (1) as needed.
3. Journalize and post the adjusting entries. Identify the adjustments by "Adj." and the new balances as "Adj. Bal."
4. Prepare an adjusted trial balance.
5. Prepare an income statement, a retained earnings statement, and a balance sheet.
6. Journalize and post the closing entries. Identify the closing entries by "Clos."
7. Prepare a post-closing trial balance.

PR 4-4B
Ledger accounts, adjusting entries, financial statements, and closing entries; optional end-of-period spreadsheet (work sheet)

obj. **2, 3**

✔ 4. Net income: $22,820

If the working papers correlating with this textbook are not used, omit Problem 4-4B.

The ledger and trial balance of Handy Man Services Co. as of July 31, 2010, the end of the first month of its current fiscal year, are presented in the working papers.

Data needed to determine the necessary adjusting entries are as follows:

a. Service revenue accrued at July 31 is $2,200.
b. Supplies on hand at July 31 are $1,450.
c. Insurance premiums expired during July are $800.
d. Depreciation of the building during July is $1,000.
e. Depreciation of equipment during July is $750.
f. Unearned rent at July 31 is $1,800.
g. Wages accrued at July 31 are $600.

Instructions

1. **Optional:** Complete the end-of-period spreadsheet (work sheet) using the adjustment data shown above.
2. Journalize and post the adjusting entries, inserting balances in the accounts affected.
3. Prepare an adjusted trial balance.
4. Prepare an income statement, a retained earnings statement, and a balance sheet.
5. Journalize and post the closing entries. Indicate closed accounts by inserting a line in both Balance columns opposite the closing entry. Insert the new balance of the capital account.
6. Prepare a post-closing trial balance.

PR 4-5B
Ledger accounts, adjusting entries, financial statements, and closing entries; optional spreadsheet (work sheet)

objs. 2, 3

✔ 5. Net income: $35,635

The unadjusted trial balance of Fix-It Co. at February 28, 2010, the end of the current year, is shown below.

Fix-It Co.
Unadjusted Trial Balance
February 28, 2010

		Debit Balances	Credit Balances
11	Cash	3,950	
13	Supplies	15,295	
14	Prepaid Insurance	2,735	
16	Equipment	100,650	
17	Accumulated Depreciation—Equipment		21,209
18	Trucks	36,300	
19	Accumulated Depreciation—Trucks		7,400
21	Accounts Payable		4,015
31	Capital Stock		10,000
32	Retained Earnings		62,426
33	Dividends	5,000	
41	Service Revenue		119,950
51	Wages Expense	39,925	
53	Rent Expense	10,600	
55	Truck Expense	7,350	
59	Miscellaneous Expense	3,195	
		225,000	225,000

The data needed to determine year-end adjustments are as follows:

a. Supplies on hand at February 28 are $4,000.
b. Insurance premiums expired during year are $2,000.
c. Depreciation of equipment during year is $6,000.
d. Depreciation of trucks during year is $3,500.
e. Wages accrued but not paid at February 28 are $450.

Instructions

1. For each account listed in the trial balance, enter the balance in the appropriate Balance column of a four-column account and place a check mark (✔) in the Posting Reference column.
2. **Optional:** Enter the unadjusted trial balance on an end-of-period spreadsheet (work sheet) and complete the spreadsheet. Add the accounts listed in part (3) as needed.
3. Journalize and post the adjusting entries, inserting balances in the accounts affected. The following additional accounts from Fix-It's chart of accounts should be used: Wages Payable, 22; Supplies Expense, 52; Depreciation Expense—Equipment, 54; Depreciation Expense—Trucks, 56; Insurance Expense, 57.
4. Prepare an adjusted trial balance.
5. Prepare an income statement, a retained earnings statement, and a balance sheet.
6. Journalize and post the closing entries. (Income Summary is account #34 in the chart of accounts.) Indicate closed accounts by inserting a line in both Balance columns opposite the closing entry.
7. Prepare a post-closing trial balance.

PR 4-6B
Complete accounting cycle

objs. 4, 5, 6

For the past several years, Kareem Ismail has operated a part-time consulting business from his home as a professional corporation. As of October 1, 2010, Kareem decided to move to rented quarters and to operate the business, which was to be known as Iron Mountain Consulting, P.C., on a full-time basis. Iron Mountain Consulting entered into the following transactions during October:

Oct.   1.   The following assets were received from Kareem Ismail in exchange for capital stock: cash, $18,000 accounts receivable, $5,000 supplies, $1,500; and office equipment, $10,750. There were no liabilities received.

✔ 8. Net income: $26,100

Oct. 1. Paid three months' rent on a lease rental contract, $4,800.
2. Paid the premiums on property and casualty insurance policies, $2,700.
4. Received cash from clients as an advance payment for services to be provided and recorded it as unearned fees, $3,150.
5. Purchased additional office equipment on account from Office Station Co., $1,250.
6. Received cash from clients on account, $2,000.
10. Paid cash for a newspaper advertisement, $325.
12. Paid Office Station Co. for part of the debt incurred on October 5, $750.
12. Recorded services provided on account for the period October 1–12, $5,750.
14. Paid part-time receptionist for two weeks' salary, $900.
17. Recorded cash from cash clients for fees earned during the period October 1–17, $9,250.
18. Paid cash for supplies, $600.
20. Recorded services provided on account for the period October 13–20, $4,100.
24. Recorded cash from cash clients for fees earned for the period October 17–24, $4,850.
26. Received cash from clients on account, $3,450.
27. Paid part-time receptionist for two weeks' salary, $900.
29. Paid telephone bill for October, $250.
31. Paid electricity bill for October, $300.
31. Recorded cash from cash clients for fees earned for the period October 25–31, $3,975.
31. Recorded services provided on account for the remainder of October, $2,500.
31. Paid dividends of $7,500.

Instructions

1. Journalize each transaction in a two-column journal, referring to the following chart of accounts in selecting the accounts to be debited and credited. (Do not insert the account numbers in the journal at this time.)

11	Cash	31	Capital Stock
12	Accounts Receivable	32	Retained Earnings
14	Supplies	33	Dividends
15	Prepaid Rent	41	Fees Earned
16	Prepaid Insurance	51	Salary Expense
18	Office Equipment	52	Rent Expense
19	Accumulated Depreciation	53	Supplies Expense
21	Accounts Payable	54	Depreciation Expense
22	Salaries Payable	55	Insurance Expense
23	Unearned Fees	59	Miscellaneous Expense

2. Post the journal to a ledger of four-column accounts.
3. Prepare an unadjusted trial balance.
4. At the end of October, the following adjustment data were assembled. Analyze and use these data to complete parts (5) and (6).
   a. Insurance expired during October is $225.
   b. Supplies on hand on October 31 are $875.
   c. Depreciation of office equipment for October is $400.
   d. Accrued receptionist salary on October 31 is $200.
   e. Rent expired during October is $1,600.
   f. Unearned fees on October 31 are $1,150.
5. **Optional:** Enter the unadjusted trial balance on an end-of-period spreadsheet (work sheet) and complete the spreadsheet.
6. Journalize and post the adjusting entries.
7. Prepare an adjusted trial balance.
8. Prepare an income statement, a retained earnings statement, and a balance sheet.
9. Prepare and post the closing entries. (Income Summary is account #34 in the chart of accounts.) Indicate closed accounts by inserting a line in both the Balance columns opposite the closing entry.
10. Prepare a post-closing trial balance.

Continuing Problem

✔ 2. Net income:
$6,920

The unadjusted trial balance of Music Depot as of July 31, 2010, along with the adjustment data for the two months ended July 31, 2010, are shown in Chapter 3.

Based upon the adjustment data, the adjusted trial balance shown below was prepared.

Music Depot
Adjusted Trial Balance
July 31, 2010

	Debit Balances	Credit Balances
Cash	12,780	
Accounts Receivable	4,750	
Supplies	175	
Prepaid Insurance	2,475	
Office Equipment	5,000	
Accumulated Depreciation—Office Equipment		60
Accounts Payable		5,680
Wages Payable		120
Unearned Revenue		3,600
Capital Stock		10,500
Dividends	1,700	
Fees Earned		20,500
Wages Expense	2,520	
Office Rent Expense	2,750	
Equipment Rent Expense	1,100	
Utilities Expense	860	
Music Expense	2,810	
Advertising Expense	1,600	
Supplies Expense	855	
Insurance Expense	225	
Depreciation Expense	60	
Miscellaneous Expense	800	
	40,460	40,460

Instructions

1. **Optional.** Using the data from Chapter 3, prepare an end-of-period spreadsheet (work sheet).
2. Prepare an income statement, a retained earning statement, and a balance sheet.
3. Journalize and post the closing entries. The income summary account is #34 in the ledger of Music Depot. Indicate closed accounts by inserting a line in both Balance columns opposite the closing entry.
4. Prepare a post-closing trial balance.

Comprehensive Problem 1

✔ 8. Net income,
$27,665

Kelly Pitney began her consulting business, Kelly Consulting, P.C., on April 1, 2010. The accounting cycle for Kelly Consulting for April, including financial statements, was illustrated on pages 159–170. During May, Kelly Consulting entered into the following transactions:

May 3. Received cash from clients as an advance payment for services to be provided and recorded it as unearned fees, $2,500.
     5. Received cash from clients on account, $1,750.
     9. Paid cash for a newspaper advertisement, $300.
   13. Paid Office Station Co. for part of the debt incurred on April 5, $400.
   15. Recorded services provided on account for the period May 1–15, $6,100.
   16. Paid part-time receptionist for two weeks' salary including the amount owed on April 30, $750.

May 17. Recorded cash from cash clients for fees earned during the period May 1–16, $8,200.
   20. Purchased supplies on account, $400.
   21. Recorded services provided on account for the period May 16–20, $3,900.
   25. Recorded cash from cash clients for fees earned for the period May 17–23, $5,100.
   27. Received cash from clients on account, $9,500.
   28. Paid part-time receptionist for two weeks' salary, $750.
   30. Paid telephone bill for May, $120.
   31. Paid electricity bill for May, $290.
   31. Recorded cash from cash clients for fees earned for the period May 26–31, $3,875.
   31. Recorded services provided on account for the remainder of May, $3,200.
   31. Paid dividends of $8,000.

Instructions

1. The chart of accounts for Kelly Consulting is shown on page 160, and the post-closing trial balance as of April 30, 2010, is shown on page 168. For each account in the post-closing trial balance, enter the balance in the appropriate Balance column of a four-column account. Date the balances May 1, 2010, and place a check mark (✔) in the Posting Reference column. Journalize each of the May transactions in a two-column journal using Kelly Consulting's chart of accounts. (Do not insert the account numbers in the journal at this time.)
2. Post the journal to a ledger of four-column accounts.
3. Prepare an unadjusted trial balance.
4. At the end of May, the following adjustment data were assembled. Analyze and use these data to complete parts (5) and (6).
   a. Insurance expired during May is $300.
   b. Supplies on hand on May 31 are $600.
   c. Depreciation of office equipment for May is $330.
   d. Accrued receptionist salary on May 31 is $240.
   e. Rent expired during May is $1,600.
   f. Unearned fees on May 31 are $2,000.
5. **Optional:** Enter the unadjusted trial balance on an end-of-period spreadsheet (work sheet) and complete the spreadsheet.
6. Journalize and post the adjusting entries.
7. Prepare an adjusted trial balance.
8. Prepare an income statement, a retained earnings statement, and a balance sheet.
9. Prepare and post the closing entries. (Income Summary is account #34 in the chart of accounts.) Indicate closed accounts by inserting a line in both the Balance columns opposite the closing entry.
10. Prepare a post-closing trial balance.

Special Activities

SA 4-1
Ethics and professional conduct in business

Pixel Graphics is a graphics arts design consulting firm. Marcie Biel, its treasurer and vice president of finance, has prepared a classified balance sheet as of August 31, 2010, the end of its fiscal year. This balance sheet will be submitted with Pixel Graphics' loan application to Planet Trust & Savings Bank.

In the Current Assets section of the balance sheet, Marcie reported a $75,000 receivable from Chas Gaddis, the president of Pixel Graphics, as a trade account receivable. Chas borrowed the money from Pixel Graphics in November 2008 for a down payment on a new home. He has orally assured Marcie that he will pay off the account receivable within the next year. Marcie reported the $75,000 in the same manner on the preceding year's balance sheet.

➤ Evaluate whether it is acceptable for Marcie Biel to prepare the August 31, 2010, balance sheet in the manner indicated above.

SA 4-2
Financial statements

The following is an excerpt from a telephone conversation between Alice Lutz, president of DeSoto Supplies Co., and Victor Hood, owner of Hood Employment Co.

Alice: Victor, you're going to have to do a better job of finding me a new computer programmer. That last guy was great at programming, but he didn't have any common sense.

Victor: What do you mean? The guy had a master's degree with straight A's.

Alice: Yes, well, last month he developed a new financial reporting system. He said we could do away with manually preparing an end-of-period spreadsheet (work sheet) and financial statements. The computer would automatically generate our financial statements with "a push of a button."

Victor: So what's the big deal? Sounds to me like it would save you time and effort.

Alice: Right! The balance sheet showed a minus for supplies!

Victor: Minus supplies? How can that be?

Alice: That's what I asked.

Victor: So, what did he say?

Alice: Well, after he checked the program, he said that it must be right. The minuses were greater than the pluses. . . .

Victor: Didn't he know that Supplies can't have a credit balance—it must have a debit balance?

Alice: He asked me what a debit and credit were.

Victor: I see your point.

1. ➤ Comment on (a) the desirability of computerizing DeSoto Supplies Co.'s financial reporting system, (b) the elimination of the end-of-period spreadsheet (work sheet) in a computerized accounting system, and (c) the computer programmer's lack of accounting knowledge.
2. ➤ Explain to the programmer why Supplies could not have a credit balance.

SA 4-3
Financial statements

Assume that you recently accepted a position with Stockman National Bank as an assistant loan officer. As one of your first duties, you have been assigned the responsibility of evaluating a loan request for $90,000 from Goldworks.com, a small corporation. In support of the loan application, Yolanda Tovar, owner and sole stockholder, submitted a "Statement of Accounts" (trial balance) for the first year of operations ended March 31, 2010.

Goldworks.com
Statement of Accounts
March 31, 2010

Cash	4,100	
Billings Due from Others	30,140	
Supplies (chemicals, etc.)	14,940	
Trucks	52,740	
Equipment	16,180	
Amounts Owed to Others		5,700
Investment in Business		47,000
Service Revenue		147,300
Wages Expense	60,100	
Utilities Expense	14,660	
Rent Expense	4,800	
Insurance Expense	1,400	
Other Expenses	940	
	200,000	200,000

1. ➤ Explain to Yolanda Tovar why a set of financial statements (income statement, retained earnings statement, and balance sheet) would be useful to you in evaluating the loan request.
2. In discussing the "Statement of Accounts" with Yolanda Tovar, you discovered that the accounts had not been adjusted at March 31. Analyze the "Statement of Accounts" and indicate possible adjusting entries that might be necessary before an accurate set of financial statements could be prepared.
3. ➤ Assuming that an accurate set of financial statements will be submitted by Yolanda Tovar in a few days, what other considerations or information would you require before making a decision on the loan request?

SA 4-4
Compare balance sheets

Group Project

Internet Project

In groups of three or four, compare the balance sheets of two different companies, and present to the class a summary of the similarities and differences of the two companies. You may obtain the balance sheets you need from one of the following sources:

1. Your school or local library.
2. The investor relations department of each company.
3. The company's Web site on the Internet.
4. EDGAR (Electronic Data Gathering, Analysis, and Retrieval), the electronic archives of financial statements filed with the Securities and Exchange Commission.

SEC documents can be retrieved using the EdgarScan™ service at **http://sec.gov.** To obtain annual report information, click on "Search for Company Filing," click on "Companies & Other Filers," type in the company name, and then click on "Find Companies." Click on the CIK related to the company name, search for Form 10-K, and click on "Retrieve Selected Findings." Finally, click on the "html" for the latest period and the related document.

Answers to Self-Examination Questions

1. **C** The dividends account, (answer C), would be extended to the Balance Sheet columns of the work sheet. Utilities Expense (answer A), Rent Revenue (answer B), and Miscellaneous Expense (answer D) would all be extended to the Income Statement columns of the work sheet.

2. **D** Cash or other assets that are expected to be converted to cash or sold or used up within one year or less, through the normal operations of the business, are classified as current assets on the balance sheet. Accounts Receivable (answer D) is a current asset, since it will normally be converted to cash within one year. Office Equipment (answer A), Land (answer B), and Accumulated Depreciation (answer C) are all reported in the property, plant, and equipment section of the balance sheet.

3. **B** The entry to close the dividends account is to debit the retained earnings account and credit the dividends account (answer B).

4. **D** Since all revenue and expense accounts are closed at the end of the period, Fees Earned (answer A), Wages Expense (answer B), and Rent Expense (answer C) would all be closed to Income Summary. Accumulated Depreciation (answer D) is a contra asset account that is not closed.

5. **B** Since the post-closing trial balance includes only balance sheet accounts (all of the revenue, expense, and dividends accounts are closed), Cash (answer A), Accumulated Depreciation (answer C), and Capital Stock (answer D) would appear on the post-closing trial balance. Fees Earned (answer B) is a temporary account that is closed prior to preparing the post-closing trial balance.

CHAPTER 5

Accounting for Merchandising Businesses

DOLLAR TREE STORES, INC.

When you are low on cash but need to pick up party supplies, housewares, or other consumer items, where do you go? Many shoppers are turning to Dollar Tree Stores, Inc., the nation's largest single price point dollar retailer with over 3,400 stores in 48 states. For the fixed price of $1 on all merchandise in its stores, this retailer has worked hard on its concept to provide "new treasures" every week for the entire family.

Despite the fact that every item costs only $1, the accounting for a merchandiser, like Dollar Tree, is more complex than for a service company. This is because a service company sells only services and has no inventory. With Dollar Tree's locations and merchandise, the company must design its accounting system to not only record the receipt of goods for resale, but also to keep track of

what merchandise is available for sale as well as where the merchandise is located. In addition, Dollar Tree must record the sales and costs of the goods sold for each of its stores. Finally, Dollar Tree must record such data as delivery costs, merchandise discounts, and merchandise returns.

In this chapter, we focus on the accounting principles and concepts for a merchandising business. In doing so, we highlight the basic differences between merchandiser and service company activities. We then describe and illustrate the financial statements of a merchandising business and accounting for merchandise transactions.

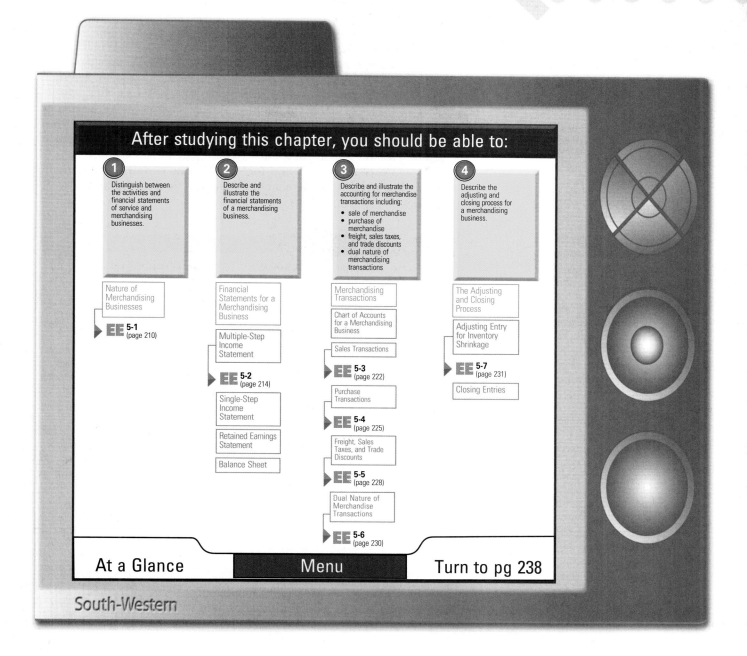

After studying this chapter, you should be able to:

1 Distinguish between the activities and financial statements of service and merchandising businesses.

Nature of Merchandising Businesses

EE 5-1 (page 210)

2 Describe and illustrate the financial statements of a merchandising business.

Financial Statements for a Merchandising Business

Multiple-Step Income Statement

EE 5-2 (page 214)

Single-Step Income Statement

Retained Earnings Statement

Balance Sheet

3 Describe and illustrate the accounting for merchandise transactions including:
- sale of merchandise
- purchase of merchandise
- freight, sales taxes, and trade discounts
- dual nature of merchandising transactions

Merchandising Transactions

Chart of Accounts for a Merchandising Business

Sales Transactions

EE 5-3 (page 222)

Purchase Transactions

EE 5-4 (page 225)

Freight, Sales Taxes, and Trade Discounts

EE 5-5 (page 228)

Dual Nature of Merchandise Transactions

EE 5-6 (page 230)

4 Describe the adjusting and closing process for a merchandising business.

The Adjusting and Closing Process

Adjusting Entry for Inventory Shrinkage

EE 5-7 (page 231)

Closing Entries

At a Glance   Menu   Turn to pg 238

South-Western

1 Distinguish between the activities and financial statements of service and merchandising businesses.

Nature of Merchandising Businesses

The activities of a service business differ from those of a merchandising business. These differences are illustrated in the following condensed income statements:

Service Business		Merchandising Business	
Fees earned	$XXX	Sales	$XXX
Operating expenses	−XXX	Cost of merchandise sold	−XXX
Net income	$XXX	Gross profit	$XXX
		Operating expenses	−XXX
		Net income	$XXX

The revenue activities of a service business involve providing services to customers. On the income statement for a service business, the revenues from services are reported as *fees earned*. The operating expenses incurred in providing the services are subtracted from the fees earned to arrive at *net income*.

Sales −	**Cost of Merchandise Sold**	= **Gross Profit**
Gross Profit −	**Operating Expenses**	= **Net Income**

In contrast, the revenue activities of a merchandising business involve the buying and selling of merchandise. A merchandising business first purchases merchandise to sell to its customers. When this merchandise is sold, the revenue is reported as sales, and its cost is recognized as an expense. This expense is called the **cost of merchandise sold**. The cost of merchandise sold is subtracted from sales to arrive at gross profit. This amount is called **gross profit** because it is the profit *before* deducting operating expenses.

Merchandise on hand (not sold) at the end of an accounting period is called **merchandise inventory**. Merchandise inventory is reported as a current asset on the balance sheet.

Example Exercise 5-1   Gross Profit   ●●●●●●●●❯ 1

During the current year, merchandise is sold for $250,000 cash and for $975,000 on account. The cost of the merchandise sold is $735,000. What is the amount of the gross profit?

Follow My Example 5-1

The gross profit is $490,000 ($250,000 + $975,000 − $735,000).

....

For Practice: PE 5-1A, PE 5-1B

The Operating Cycle

The operations of a merchandising business involve the purchase of merchandise for sale (purchasing), the sale of the products to customers (sales), and the receipt of cash from customers (collection). This overall process is referred to as the *operating cycle*. Thus, the operating cycle begins with spending cash, and it ends with receiving cash from customers. The operating cycle for a merchandising business is shown to the right.

Operating cycles for retailers are usually shorter than for manufacturers because retailers purchase goods in a form ready for sale to the customer. Of course, some retailers will have shorter operating cycles than others

because of the nature of their products. For example, a jewelry store or an automobile dealer normally has a longer operating cycle than a consumer electronics store or a grocery store.

Businesses with longer operating cycles normally have higher profit margins on their products than businesses with shorter operating cycles. For example, it is not unusual for jewelry stores to price their jewelry at 30%–50% above cost. In contrast, grocery stores operate on very small profit margins, often below 5%. Grocery stores make up the difference by selling their products more quickly.

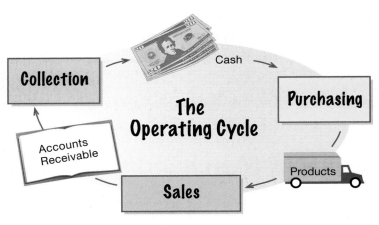

---

2   Describe and illustrate the financial statements of a merchandising business.

@netsolutions

Financial Statements for a Merchandising Business

In this section, we illustrate the financial statements for NetSolutions after it becomes a retailer of computer hardware and software. During 2009, Chris Clark implemented the second phase of NetSolutions' business plan. In doing so, Chris notified clients that beginning July 1, 2010, NetSolutions would no longer offer consulting services. Instead, it would become a retailer.

NetSolutions' business strategy is to offer personalized service to individuals and small businesses who are upgrading or purchasing new computer systems. NetSolutions' personal service includes a no-obligation, on-site assessment of the customer's computer needs. By providing personalized service and follow-up, Chris feels that NetSolutions can compete effectively against such retailers as Best Buy and Office Depot, Inc.

Multiple-Step Income Statement

The 2011 income statement for NetSolutions is shown in Exhibit 1.[1] This form of income statement, called a **multiple-step income statement**, contains several sections, subsections, and subtotals.

Revenue from Sales This section of the multiple-step income statement consists of sales, sales returns and allowances, sales discounts, and net sales. This section, as shown in Exhibit 1, is as follows:

Revenue from sales:			
Sales			$720,185
Less: Sales returns and allowances	$6,140		
Sales discounts	5,790	11,930	
Net sales			$708,255

Exhibit 1

Multiple-Step Income Statement

NetSolutions
Income Statement
For the Year Ended December 31, 2011

Revenue from sales:			
Sales		$720,185	
Less: Sales returns and allowances	$ 6,140		
Sales discounts	5,790	11,930	
Net sales			$708,255
Cost of merchandise sold			525,305
Gross profit			$182,950
Operating expenses:			
Selling expenses:			
Sales salaries expense	$53,430		
Advertising expense	10,860		
Depreciation expense—store equipment	3,100		
Delivery expense	2,800		
Miscellaneous selling expense	630		
Total selling expenses		$ 70,820	
Administrative expenses:			
Office salaries expense	$21,020		
Rent expense	8,100		
Depreciation expense—office equipment	2,490		
Insurance expense	1,910		
Office supplies expense	610		
Misc. administrative expense	760		
Total administrative expenses		34,890	
Total operating expenses			105,710
Income from operations			$ 77,240
Other income and expense:			
Rent revenue		$ 600	
Interest expense		(2,440)	(1,840)
Net income			$ 75,400

---

1 We use the NetSolutions income statement for 2011 as a basis for illustration because, as will be shown, it allows us to better illustrate the computation of the cost of merchandise sold.

Sales is the total amount charged customers for merchandise sold, including cash sales and sales on account. During 2011, NetSolutions sold merchandise of $720,185 for cash or on account.

Sales returns and allowances are granted by the seller to customers for damaged or defective merchandise. In such cases, the customer may either return the merchandise or accept an allowance from the seller. NetSolutions reported $6,140 of sales returns and allowances during 2011.

Sales discounts are granted by the seller to customers for early payment of amounts owed. For example, a seller may offer a customer a 2% discount on a sale of $10,000 if the customer pays within 10 days. If the customer pays within the 10-day period, the seller receives cash of $9,800, and the buyer receives a discount of $200 ($10,000 × 2%). NetSolutions reported $5,790 of sales discounts during 2011.

Net sales is determined by subtracting sales returns and allowances and sales discounts from sales. As shown above, NetSolutions reported $708,255 of net sales during 2011. Some companies report only net sales and report sales, sales returns and allowances, and sales discounts in notes to the financial statements.

Cost of Merchandise Sold

The cost of merchandise sold is the cost of the merchandise sold to customers. NetSolutions reported cost of merchandise sold of $525,305 during 2011. To illustrate how cost of merchandise sold is determined, we use data from when NetSolutions began its merchandising operations on July 1, 2010.

Purchases July 1–December 31, 2010	$340,000
Merchandise inventory on December 31, 2010	59,700

Since NetSolutions had only $59,700 of merchandise left on December 31, 2010, it must have sold merchandise that cost $280,300 during 2010 as shown below.

Purchases	$340,000
Less merchandise inventory, December 31, 2010	59,700
Cost of merchandise sold	$280,300

To continue, assume the following 2011 data for NetSolutions:

Purchases of merchandise	$521,980
Purchases returns and allowances	9,100
Purchases discounts	2,525
Freight in on merchandise purchased	17,400

Sellers may grant a buyer sales returns and allowances for returned or damaged merchandise. From a buyer's perspective, such allowances are called **purchases returns and allowances**. Likewise, sellers may grant a buyer a sales discount for early payment of the amount owed. From a buyer's perspective, such discounts are called **purchases discounts**. Purchases returns and allowances and purchases discounts are subtracted from purchases to arrive at **net purchases** as shown below for NetSolutions.

Periodic

Purchases		$521,980
Less: Purchases returns and allowances	$9,100	
Purchases discounts	2,525	11,625
Net purchases		$510,355

Freight costs incurred in obtaining the merchandise increase the cost of the merchandise purchased. These costs are called **freight in**. Adding freight in to net purchases yields the **cost of merchandise purchased** as shown below for NetSolutions.

Net purchases	$510,355
Add freight in	17,400
Cost of merchandise purchased	$527,755

The beginning inventory is added to the cost of merchandise purchased to determine the **merchandise available for sale** for the period. The ending inventory of

NetSolutions on December 31, 2010, $59,700, becomes the beginning (January 1, 2011) inventory for 2011. Thus, the merchandise available for sale for NetSolutions during 2011 is $587,455 as shown below.

Merchandise inventory, January 1, 2011	$ 59,700
Cost of merchandise purchased	527,755
Cost of merchandise available for sale	$587,455

The ending inventory is then subtracted from the merchandise available for sale to yield the cost of merchandise sold. Assuming the ending inventory on December 31, 2011, is $62,150, the cost of merchandise sold for NetSolutions is $525,305 as shown in Exhibit 1 and below.

Cost of merchandise available for sale	$587,455
Less merchandise inventory, December 31, 2011	62,150
Cost of merchandise sold	$525,305

In the preceding computation, merchandise inventory at the end of the period is subtracted from the merchandise available for sale to determine the cost of merchandise sold. The merchandise inventory at the end of the period is determined by taking a physical count of inventory on hand. This method of determining the cost of merchandise sold and the amount of merchandise on hand is called the **periodic inventory system**. Under the periodic inventory system, the inventory records do not show the amount available for sale or the amount sold during the period. Instead, the cost of merchandise sold is computed and reported as shown in Exhibit 2.

Under the **perpetual inventory system** of accounting, each purchase and sale of merchandise is recorded in the inventory and the cost of merchandise sold accounts. As a result, the amounts of merchandise available for sale and sold are continuously (perpetually) updated in the inventory records. Because many retailers use computerized systems, the perpetual inventory system is widely used. For example, such systems may use bar codes, such as the one on the back of this textbook. An optical scanner reads the bar code to record merchandise purchased and sold.

Businesses using a perpetual inventory system report the cost of merchandise sold as a single line on the income statement. An example of such reporting is illustrated in Exhibit 1 for NetSolutions.

Because of its wide use, we use the perpetual inventory system in the remainder of this chapter. The periodic inventory system is described and illustrated in the appendix to this chapter.

Retailers, such as Best Buy, Sears Holding Corporation, and Wal-Mart, and grocery store chains, such as Winn-Dixie Stores, Inc. and Kroger, use bar codes and optical scanners as part of their computerized inventory systems.

Exhibit 2

Cost of Merchandise Sold

periodic

Merchandise inventory, January 1, 2011			$ 59,700
Purchases		$521,980	
Less: Purchases returns and allowances	$9,100		
Purchases discounts	2,525	11,625	
Net purchases		$510,355	
Add freight in		17,400	
Cost of merchandise purchased			527,755
Merchandise available for sale			$587,455
Less merchandise inventory, December 31, 2011 . .			62,150
Cost of merchandise sold			$525,305

Gross Profit Gross profit is computed by subtracting the cost of merchandise sold from net sales, as shown below.

Net sales	$708,255
Cost of merchandise sold	525,305
Gross profit	$182,950

As shown above and in Exhibit 1, NetSolutions has gross profit of $182,950 in 2011.

Income from Operations **Income from operations**, sometimes called **operating income**, is determined by subtracting operating expenses from gross profit. Operating expenses are normally classified as either selling expenses or administrative expenses.

Selling expenses are incurred directly in the selling of merchandise. Examples of selling expenses include sales salaries, store supplies used, depreciation of store equipment, delivery expense, and advertising.

Administrative expenses, sometimes called **general expenses**, are incurred in the administration or general operations of the business. Examples of administrative expenses include office salaries, depreciation of office equipment, and office supplies used.

Each selling and administrative expense may be reported separately as shown in Exhibit 1. However, many companies report selling, administrative, and operating expenses as single line items as shown below for NetSolutions.

Gross profit		$182,950
Operating expenses:		
Selling expenses	$70,820	
Administrative expenses	34,890	
Total operating expenses		105,710
Income from operations		$ 77,240

Other Income and Expense Other income and expense items are not related to the primary operations of the business. **Other income** is revenue from sources other than the primary operating activity of a business. Examples of other income include income from interest, rent, and gains resulting from the sale of fixed assets. **Other expense** is an expense that cannot be traced directly to the normal operations of the business. Examples of other expenses include interest expense and losses from disposing of fixed assets.

Other income and other expense are offset against each other on the income statement. If the total of other income exceeds the total of other expense, the difference is added to income from operations to determine net income. If the reverse is true, the difference is subtracted from income from operations. The other income and expense items of NetSolutions are reported as shown below and in Exhibit 1.

Income from operations		$77,240
Other income and expense:		
Rent revenue	$ 600	
Interest expense	(2,440)	(1,840)
Net income		$75,400

Example Exercise 5-2 Cost of Merchandise Sold ● ● ● ● ● ● ● ● ▶ ②

Based on the following data, determine the cost of merchandise sold for May. Follow the format used in Exhibit 2.

Merchandise inventory, May 1	$121,200
Merchandise inventory, May 31	142,000
Purchases	985,000
Purchases returns and allowances	23,500
Purchases discounts.	21,000
Freight in.	11,300

(continued)

Follow My Example 5-2

Cost of merchandise sold:			
Merchandise inventory, May 1			$ 121,200
Purchases		$985,000	
Less: Purchases returns and allowances	$23,500		
Purchases discounts	21,000	44,500	
Net purchases		$940,500	
Add freight in		11,300	
Cost of merchandise purchased			951,800
Merchandise available for sale			$1,073,000
Less merchandise inventory, May 31			142,000
Cost of merchandise sold			$ 931,000

For Practice: PE 5-2A, PE 5-2B

Single-Step Income Statement

An alternate form of income statement is the **single-step income statement**. As shown in Exhibit 3, the income statement for NetSolutions deducts the total of all expenses *in one step* from the total of all revenues.

The single-step form emphasizes total revenues and total expenses in determining net income. A criticism of the single-step form is that gross profit and income from operations are not reported.

Retained Earnings Statement

The retained earnings statement for NetSolutions is shown in Exhibit 4. This statement is prepared in the same manner as for a service business.

Balance Sheet

The balance sheet may be presented with assets on the left-hand side and the liabilities and stockholders' equity on the right-hand side. This form of the balance sheet is called the **account form**. The balance sheet may also be presented in a downward sequence in three sections. This form of balance sheet is called the **report form**. The report form

Exhibit 3

Single-Step Income Statement

NetSolutions
Income Statement
For the Year Ended December 31, 2011

Revenues:		
Net sales		$708,255
Rent revenue		600
Total revenues		$708,855
Expenses:		
Cost of merchandise sold	$525,305	
Selling expenses	70,820	
Administrative expenses	34,890	
Interest expense	2,440	
Total expenses		633,455
Net income		$ 75,400

Exhibit 4

Retained Earnings Statement for Merchandising Business

NetSolutions
Retained Earnings Statement
For the Year Ended December 31, 2011

Retained earnings, January 1, 2011		$128,800
Net income for the year	$75,400	
Less dividends	18,000	
Increase in retained earnings		57,400
Retained earnings, December 31, 2011		$186,200

of balance sheet for NetSolutions is shown in Exhibit 5. In Exhibit 5, merchandise inventory is reported as a current asset and the current portion of the note payable of $5,000 is reported as a current liability.

Exhibit 5

Report Form of Balance Sheet

NetSolutions
Balance Sheet
December 31, 2011

Assets

Current assets:			
Cash		$ 52,950	
Accounts receivable		91,080	
Merchandise inventory		62,150	
Office supplies		480	
Prepaid insurance		2,650	
Total current assets			$209,310
Property, plant, and equipment:			
Land		$ 20,000	
Store equipment	$27,100		
Less accumulated depreciation	5,700	21,400	
Office equipment	$15,570		
Less accumulated depreciation	4,720	10,850	
Total property, plant, and equipment			52,250
Total assets			$261,560

Liabilities

Current liabilities:		
Accounts payable	$ 22,420	
Note payable (current portion)	5,000	
Salaries payable	1,140	
Unearned rent	1,800	
Total current liabilities		$ 30,360
Long-term liabilities:		
Note payable (final payment due 2021)		20,000
Total liabilities		$ 50,360

Stockholders' Equity

Capital stock	$ 25,000	
Retained earnings	186,200	
Total stockholders' equity		211,200
Total liabilities and stockholders' equity		$261,560

Business Connection

H&R BLOCK VERSUS THE HOME DEPOT

H&R Block is a service business that primarily offers tax planning and preparation to its customers. The Home Depot is a large home improvement retailer. The differences in the operations of a service and merchandise business are illustrated in their income statements, as shown below.

H&R Block
Condensed Income Statement
For the Year Ending April 30, 2007
(in millions)

Revenue.	$4,021
Operating expenses	3,361
Operating income	$ 660
Other income (expense)	(24)
Income before taxes	$ 636
Income taxes	262
Net income	$ 374

As discussed in a later chapter, corporations are subject to income taxes. Thus, the income statements of H&R Block and The Home Depot report "income taxes" as a deduction from "income before income taxes" in arriving at net income. This is in contrast to a proprietorship, which is not subject to income taxes.

The Home Depot
Condensed Income Statement
For the Year Ending January 28, 2007
(in millions)

Net sales	$90,837
Cost of merchandise sold	61,054
Gross profit	$29,783
Operating expenses	20,110
Operating income	$ 9,673
Other income (expense)	(365)
Income before taxes	$ 9,308
Income taxes	3,547
Net income	$ 5,761

3 Describe and illustrate the accounting for merchandise transactions including:
• sale of merchandise
• purchase of merchandise
• freight, sales taxes, and trade discounts
• dual nature of merchandising transactions

@netsolutions

Merchandising Transactions

In the prior section, we described and illustrated the financial statements of a merchandising business, NetSolutions. In this section, we describe and illustrate the recording of merchandise transactions. We begin by describing the chart of accounts for a merchandising business.

Chart of Accounts for a Merchandising Business

The chart of accounts for a merchandising business should reflect the elements of the financial statements. The chart of accounts for NetSolutions is shown in Exhibit 6. The accounts related to merchandising transactions are shown in color.

As shown in Exhibit 6, NetSolutions' chart of accounts consists of three-digit account numbers. The first digit indicates the major financial statement classification (1 for assets, 2 for liabilities, and so on). The second digit indicates the subclassification (e.g., 11 for current assets, 12 for noncurrent assets). The third digit identifies the specific account (e.g., 110 for Cash, 123 for Store Equipment). Using a three-digit numbering system makes it easier to add new accounts as they are needed.

Sales Transactions

Merchandise transactions are recorded using the rules of debit and credit that we described and illustrated in Chapter 2. Exhibit 3, shown on page 57 of Chapter 2, summarizes these rules.

The accounting system used in the preceding chapters is often modified to more efficiently record transactions. For example, an accounting system should be designed to provide information on the amounts due from various customers (accounts receivable) and amounts owed to various creditors (accounts payable). A separate account for each customer and creditor could be added to the ledger. However, as the number of customers and creditors increased, the ledger would become large and awkward to use.

A large number of individual accounts with a common characteristic can be grouped together in a separate ledger, called a **subsidiary ledger**. The primary ledger, which contains all of the balance sheet and income statement accounts, is then called the **general ledger**. Each subsidiary ledger is represented in the general ledger by a summarizing

Chart of Accounts for NetSolutions, a Merchandising Business

Balance Sheet Accounts	Income Statement Accounts
100 Assets	**400 Revenues**
110 Cash	410 Sales
112 Accounts Receivable	411 Sales Returns and Allowances
115 Merchandise Inventory	412 Sales Discounts
116 Office Supplies	**500 Costs and Expenses**
117 Prepaid Insurance	510 Cost of Merchandise Sold
120 Land	520 Sales Salaries Expense
123 Store Equipment	521 Advertising Expense
124 Accumulated Depreciation—Store Equipment	522 Depreciation Expense—Store Equipment
125 Office Equipment	523 Delivery Expense
126 Accumulated Depreciation—Office Equipment	529 Miscellaneous Selling Expense
	530 Office Salaries Expense
200 Liabilities	531 Rent Expense
210 Accounts Payable	532 Depreciation Expense—Office Equipment
211 Salaries Payable	533 Insurance Expense
212 Unearned Rent	534 Office Supplies Expense
215 Notes Payable	539 Misc. Administrative Expense
300 Stockholders' Equity	**600 Other Income**
310 Capital Stock	610 Rent Revenue
311 Retained Earnings	**700 Other Expense**
312 Dividends	710 Interest Expense
313 Income Summary	

account, called a **controlling account**. The sum of the balances of the accounts in the subsidiary ledger must equal the balance of the related controlling account. Thus, a subsidiary ledger is a secondary ledger that supports a controlling account in the general ledger.

Common subsidiary ledgers are:[2]

1. The **accounts receivable subsidiary ledger**, or *customers ledger*, lists the individual customer accounts in alphabetical order. The controlling account in the general ledger is Accounts Receivable.

2. The **accounts payable subsidiary ledger**, or *creditors ledger*, lists individual creditor accounts in alphabetical order. The controlling account in the general ledger is Accounts Payable.

3. The **inventory subsidiary ledger**, or *inventory ledger*, lists individual inventory by item (bar code) number. The controlling account in the general ledger is Inventory. An inventory subsidiary ledger is used in a perpetual inventory system.

In this section, sales transactions involving cash sales and sales on account are illustrated. In addition, sales discounts and sales returns transactions are illustrated.

Cash Sales A business may sell merchandise for cash. Cash sales are normally entered (rung up) on a cash register and recorded in the accounts. To illustrate, assume that on January 3, NetSolutions sells merchandise for $1,800. These cash sales are recorded as follows:

	Journal			Page 25
Date	Description	Post. Ref.	Debit	Credit
2011 Jan. 3	Cash		1,800	
	Sales			1,800
	To record cash sales.			

Using the perpetual inventory system, the cost of merchandise sold and the decrease in merchandise inventory are also recorded. In this way, the merchandise inventory account indicates the amount of merchandise on hand (not sold).

To illustrate, assume that the cost of merchandise sold on January 3 is $1,200. The entry to record the cost of merchandise sold and the decrease in the merchandise inventory is as follows:

Jan.	3	Cost of Merchandise Sold	1,200	
		Merchandise Inventory		1,200
		To record the cost of merchandise sold.		

Sales may be made to customers using credit cards such as MasterCard or VISA. Such sales are recorded as cash sales. This is because these sales are normally processed by a clearing-house that contacts the bank that issued the card. The issuing bank then electronically transfers cash directly to the retailer's bank account.[3] Thus, the retailer normally receives cash within a few days of making the credit card sale.

If the customers in the preceding sales had used MasterCards to pay for their purchases, the sales would be recorded exactly as shown in the preceding entry. Any processing fees charged by the clearing-house or issuing bank are periodically recorded as an expense. This expense is normally reported on the income statement as an administrative expense. To illustrate, assume that NetSolutions paid credit card processing fees of $48 on January 31. These fees would be recorded as follows:

Jan.	31	Credit Card Expense	48	
		Cash		48
		To record service charges on credit card sales for the month.		

Instead of using MasterCard or VISA, a customer may use a credit card that is not issued by a bank. For example, a customer might use an American Express card. If the seller uses a clearing-house, the clearing-house will collect the receivable and transfer the cash to the retailer's bank account similar to the way it would have if the customer had used MasterCard or VISA. Large businesses, however, may not use a clearing-house. In such cases, nonbank credit card sales must first be reported to the card company before cash is received. Thus, a receivable is created with the nonbank credit card company. However, since most retailers use clearing-houses to process both bank and nonbank credit cards, we will record all credit card sales as cash sales.

Sales on Account A business may sell merchandise on account. The seller records such sales as a debit to Accounts Receivable and a credit to Sales. An example of an entry for a NetSolutions sale on account of $510 follows. The cost of merchandise sold was $280.

A retailer may accept MasterCard or VISA but not American Express. Why? The service fees that credit card companies charge retailers are the primary reason that some businesses do not accept all credit cards. For example, American Express Co.'s service fees are normally higher than MasterCard's or VISA's. As a result, some retailers choose not to accept American Express cards. The disadvantage of this practice is that the retailer may lose customers to competitors who do accept American Express cards.

Jan.	12	Accounts Receivable—Sims Co.	510	
		Sales		510
		Invoice No. 7172.		
	12	Cost of Merchandise Sold	280	
		Merchandise Inventory		280
		Cost of merch. sold on Invoice No. 7172.		

3 CyberSource is one of the major credit card clearing-houses. For a more detailed description of how credit card sales are processed, see the following CyberSource Web page: **http://www.cybersource.com/products_and_services/global_payment_services/credit_card_processing/howitworks.xml**.

Sales Discounts The terms of a sale are normally indicated on the **invoice** or bill that the seller sends to the buyer. An example of a sales invoice for NetSolutions is shown in Exhibit 7.

Exhibit 7

Invoice

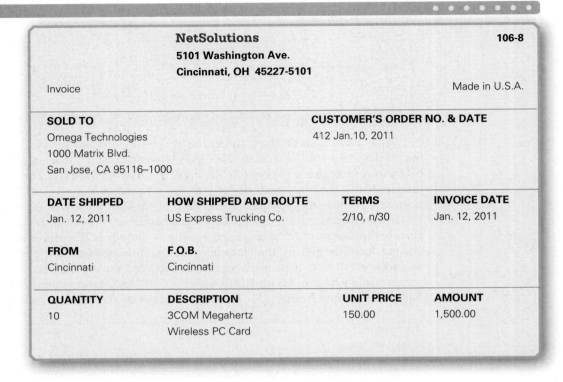

NetSolutions		106-8
5101 Washington Ave.		
Cincinnati, OH 45227-5101		
Invoice		Made in U.S.A.

SOLD TO	**CUSTOMER'S ORDER NO. & DATE**
Omega Technologies	412 Jan.10, 2011
1000 Matrix Blvd.	
San Jose, CA 95116–1000	

DATE SHIPPED	**HOW SHIPPED AND ROUTE**	**TERMS**	**INVOICE DATE**
Jan. 12, 2011	US Express Trucking Co.	2/10, n/30	Jan. 12, 2011

FROM	**F.O.B.**
Cincinnati	Cincinnati

QUANTITY	**DESCRIPTION**	**UNIT PRICE**	**AMOUNT**
10	3COM Megahertz Wireless PC Card	150.00	1,500.00

The terms for when payments for merchandise are to be made are called the **credit terms.** If payment is required on delivery, the terms are *cash* or *net cash.* Otherwise, the buyer is allowed an amount of time, known as the **credit period,** in which to pay.

The credit period usually begins with the date of the sale as shown on the invoice. If payment is due within a stated number of days after the invoice date, such as 30 days, the terms are *net 30 days.* These terms may be written as *n/30.*[4] If payment is due by the end of the month in which the sale was made, the terms are written as *n/eom.*

To encourage the buyer to pay before the end of the credit period, the seller may offer a discount. For example, a seller may offer a 2% discount if the buyer pays within 10 days of the invoice date. If the buyer does not take the discount, the total amount is due within 30 days. These terms are expressed as *2/10, n/30* and are read as *2% discount if paid within 10 days, net amount due within 30 days.* The credit terms of 2/10, n/30 are summarized in Exhibit 8, using the invoice in Exhibit 7.

Exhibit 8

Credit Terms

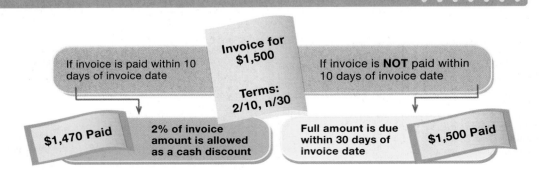

4 The word *net* as used here does not have the usual meaning of a number after deductions have been subtracted, as in *net income.*

Discounts taken by the buyer for early payment are recorded as sales discounts by the seller. Managers usually want to know the amount of the sales discounts for a period. For this reason, sales discounts are recorded in a separate sales discounts account, which is a *contra* (or *offsetting*) account to Sales.

To illustrate, assume that NetSolutions receives $1,470 on January 22 for the invoice shown in Exhibit 7. Since the invoice was paid within the discount period (10 days), the buyer deducted $30 ($1,500 × 2%) from the invoice amount. NetSolutions would record the receipt of the cash as follows:

Jan.	22	Cash	1,470	
		Sales Discounts	30	
		Accounts Receivable—Omega Technologies		1,500
		Collection on Invoice No. 106-8, less		
		2% discount.		

Book publishers often experience large returns if a book is not immediately successful. For example, 35% of adult hardcover books shipped to retailers are returned to publishers, according to the Association of American Publishers.

Sales Returns and Allowances Merchandise sold may be returned to the seller (sales return). In other cases, the seller may reduce the initial selling price (sales allowance). This might occur if the merchandise is defective, damaged during shipment, or does not meet the buyer's expectations.

If the return or allowance is for a sale on account, the seller usually issues the buyer a **credit memorandum**, often called a **credit memo**. A credit memo authorizes a credit to (decreases) the buyer's account receivable. A credit memo indicates the amount and reason for the credit. An example of a credit memo issued by NetSolutions is shown in Exhibit 9.

Like sales discounts, sales returns and allowances reduce sales revenue. Also, returns often result in additional shipping and handling expenses. Thus, managers usually want to know the amount of returns and allowances for a period. For this reason, sales returns and allowances are recorded in a separate sales returns and allowances account, which is is a *contra* (or *offsetting*) account to Sales.

The seller debits Sales Returns and Allowances for the amount of the return or allowance. If the sale was on account, the seller credits Accounts Receivable. Using a perpetual inventory system, the seller must also debit (increase) Merchandise Inventory and decrease (credit) Cost of Merchandise Sold for the cost of the returned merchandise.

To illustrate, we use the credit memo shown in Exhibit 9. The selling price of the merchandise returned in Exhibit 9 is $225. Assuming that the cost of the

Exhibit 9

Credit Memo

NetSolutions   No. 32
5101 Washington Ave.
Cincinnati, OH 45227-5101

CREDIT MEMO

TO	DATE
Krier Company	January 13, 2011
7608 Melton Avenue	
Los Angeles, CA 90025-3942	

WE CREDIT YOUR ACCOUNT AS FOLLOWS

| 1 | Graphic Video Card | 225.00 |

merchandise returned is $140, the sales return and allowance would be recorded as follows:

Jan.	13	Sales Returns and Allowances	225	
		Accounts Receivable—Krier Company		225
		Credit Memo No. 32.		

Jan.	13	Merchandise Inventory	140	
		Cost of Merchandise Sold		140
		Cost of merchandise returned, Credit		
		Memo No. 32.		

A buyer may pay for merchandise and then later return it. In this case, the seller may do one of the following:

1. Issue a credit that is applied against the buyer's other receivables.
2. Issue a cash refund.

If the credit is applied against the buyer's other receivables, the seller records the credit with entries similar to those shown above. If cash is refunded, the seller debits Sales Returns and Allowances and credits Cash.

Example Exercise 5-3 Sales Transactions 3

Journalize the following merchandise transactions:
a. Sold merchandise on account, $7,500 with terms 2/10, n/30. The cost of the merchandise sold was $5,625.
b. Received payment less the discount.

Follow My Example 5-3

a.	Accounts Receivable	7,500	
	Sales		7,500
	Cost of Merchandise Sold	5,625	
	Merchandise Inventory		5,625
b.	Cash	7,350	
	Sales Discounts	150	
	Accounts Receivable		7,500

For Practice: PE 5-3A, PE 5-3B

Integrity, Objectivity, and Ethics in Business

THE CASE OF THE FRAUDULENT PRICE TAGS

One of the challenges for a retailer is policing its sales return policy. There are many ways in which customers can unethically or illegally abuse such policies. In one case, a couple was accused of attaching Marshalls' store price tags to cheaper merchandise bought or obtained elsewhere. The couple then returned the cheaper goods and received the substantially higher refund amount. Company security officials discovered the fraud and had the couple arrested after they had allegedly bilked the company for over $1 million.

Purchase Transactions

Under the perpetual inventory system, cash purchases of merchandise are recorded as follows:

		Journal			Page 24
Date		**Description**	**Post. Ref.**	**Debit**	**Credit**
2011 Jan.	3	Merchandise Inventory		2,510	
		Cash			2,510
		Purchased inventory from Bowen Co.			

Purchases of merchandise on account are recorded as follows:

Jan.	4	Merchandise Inventory		9,250	
		Accounts Payable—Thomas Corporation			9,250
		Purchased inventory on account.			

Purchases Discounts Purchases discounts taken by a buyer reduce the cost of the merchandise purchased. Even if the buyer has to borrow to pay within a discount period, it is normally to the buyer's advantage to do so. For this reason, accounting systems are normally designed so that all available discounts are taken.

To illustrate, assume that NetSolutions purchased merchandise from Alpha Technologies as follows:

Invoice Date	Invoice Amount	Terms
March 12	$3,000	2/10, n/30

The last day of the discount period is March 22 (March 12 + 10 days). Assume that in order to pay the invoice on March 22, NetSolutions borrows $2,940, which is $3,000 less the discount of $60 ($3,000 × 2%). If we also assume an annual interest rate of 6% and a 360-day year, the interest on the loan of $2,940 for the remaining 20 days of the credit period is $9.80 ($2,940 × 6% × 20/360).

The net savings to NetSolutions of taking the discount is $50.20, computed as follows:

Discount of 2% on $3,000	$60.00
Interest for 20 days at a rate of 6% on $2,940	9.80
Savings from taking the discount	$50.20

The savings can also be seen by comparing the interest rate on the money *saved* by taking the discount and the interest rate on the money *borrowed* to take the discount. The interest rate on the money saved in the prior example is estimated by converting 2% for 20 days to a yearly rate, as follows:

$$2\% \times \frac{360 \text{ days}}{20 \text{ days}} = 2\% \times 18 = 36\%$$

NetSolutions borrowed $2,940 at 6% to take the discount. If NetSolutions does not take the discount, it *pays* an estimated interest rate of 36% for using the $2,940 for the remaining 20 days of the credit period. Thus, buyers should normally take all available purchase discounts.

Should you pay your bills, such as utility bills and credit card bills, as soon as they are received? Probably not. Most bills that you receive do not offer discounts for early payment. Rather, the bills normally indicate only a due date and perhaps a penalty for late payment. Many times you receive bills weeks before their due date. In such cases, it is to your advantage to file the bill by its due date in a folder or other organizer, such as a desk calendar, and mail the payment a few days before it is due. This way, you can use your money to earn interest on your checking or savings account.

Under the perpetual inventory system, the buyer initially debits Merchandise Inventory for the amount of the invoice. When paying the invoice within the discount period, the buyer credits Merchandise Inventory for the amount of the discount. In this way, Merchandise Inventory shows the *net* cost to the buyer.

To illustrate, NetSolutions would record the Alpha Technologies invoice and its payment at the end of the discount period as follows:

Mar.	12	Merchandise Inventory	3,000	
		Accounts Payable—Alpha Technologies		3,000
	22	Accounts Payable—Alpha Technologies	3,000	
		Cash		2,940
		Merchandise Inventory		60

Assume that NetSolutions does not take the discount, but instead pays the invoice on April 11. In this case, NetSolutions would record the payment on April 11 as follows:

Apr.	11	Accounts Payable—Alpha Technologies	3,000	
		Cash		3,000

Purchases Returns and Allowances A buyer may return merchandise (purchases return) or request a price allowance (purchases allowance) from the seller. In both cases, the buyer normally sends the seller a debit memorandum. A **debit memorandum**, often called a **debit memo**, is shown in Exhibit 10. A debit memo informs the seller of the amount the buyer proposes to *debit* to the account payable due the seller. It also states the reasons for the return or the request for the price allowance.

The buyer may use the debit memo as the basis for recording the return or allowance or wait for approval from the seller (creditor). In either case, the buyer debits Accounts Payable and credits Merchandise Inventory.

Exhibit 10

Debit Memo

NetSolutions   No. 18
5101 Washington Ave.
Cincinnati, OH 45227-5101

DEBIT MEMO

TO	DATE
Maxim Systems	March 7, 2011
7519 East Willson Ave.	
Seattle, WA 98101–7519	

WE DEBIT YOUR ACCOUNT AS FOLLOWS

10 Server Network Interface Cards, your Invoice No. 7291,	@ 90.00	900.00
are being returned via parcel post. Our order specified No. 825X.		

To illustrate, NetSolutions records the return of the merchandise indicated in the debit memo in Exhibit 10 as follows:

Mar.	7	Accounts Payable—Maxim Systems	900	
		Merchandise Inventory		900
		Debit Memo No. 18.		

A buyer may return merchandise or be granted a price allowance before paying an invoice. In this case, the amount of the debit memo is deducted from the invoice. The amount is deducted before the purchase discount is computed.

To illustrate, assume the following data concerning a purchase of merchandise by NetSolutions on May 2:

May   2. Purchased $5,000 of merchandise on account from Delta Data Link, terms 2/10, n/30.
       4. Returned $3,000 of the merchandise purchased on March 2.
       12. Paid for the purchase of May 2 less the return and discount.

NetSolutions would record these transactions as follows:

May	2	Merchandise Inventory	5,000	
		Accounts Payable—Delta Data Link		5,000
		Purchased merchandise.		
	4	Accounts Payable—Delta Data Link	3,000	
		Merchandise Inventory		3,000
		Returned portion of merch. purchased.		
	12	Accounts Payable—Delta Data Link	2,000	
		Cash		1,960
		Merchandise Inventory		40
		Paid invoice [($5,000 − $3,000) × 2%		
		= $40; $2,000 − $40 = $1,960].		

Example Exercise 5-4   Purchase Transactions   3

Rofles Company purchased merchandise on account from a supplier for $11,500, terms 2/10, n/30. Rofles Company returned $3,000 of the merchandise and received full credit.

a. If Rofles Company pays the invoice within the discount period, what is the amount of cash required for the payment?
b. Under a perpetual inventory system, what account is credited by Rofles Company to record the return?

Follow My Example 5-4

a. $8,330. Purchase of $11,500 less the return of $3,000 less the discount of $170 [($11,500 − $3,000) × 2%].
b. Merchandise Inventory

For Practice: PE 5-4A, PE 5-4B

Freight, Sales Taxes, and Trade Discounts

Purchases and sales of merchandise often involve freight and sales taxes. Also, the seller may offer buyers trade discounts.

Freight The terms of a sale indicate when ownership (title) of the merchandise passes from the seller to the buyer. This point determines whether the buyer or the seller pays the freight costs.[5]

> **The buyer bears the freight costs if the shipping terms are FOB shipping point.**

The ownership of the merchandise may pass to the buyer when the seller delivers the merchandise to the freight carrier. In this case, the terms are said to be **FOB (free on board) shipping point**. This term means that the buyer pays the freight costs from the shipping point to the final destination. Such costs are part of the buyer's total cost of purchasing inventory and are added to the cost of the inventory by debiting Merchandise Inventory.

To illustrate, assume that on June 10, NetSolutions purchased merchandise as follows:

June 10. Purchased merchandise from Magna Data, $900, terms FOB shipping point.
10. Paid freight of $50 on June 10 purchase from Magna Data.

NetSolutions would record these two transactions as follows:

Sometimes FOB shipping point and FOB destination are expressed in terms of the location at which the title to the merchandise passes to the buyer. For example, if Toyota Motor Corporation's assembly plant in Osaka, Japan, sells automobiles to a dealer in Chicago, FOB shipping point could be expressed as FOB Osaka. Likewise, FOB destination could be expressed as FOB Chicago.

June	10	Merchandise Inventory		900	
		Accounts Payable—Magna Data			900
		Purchased merchandise, terms FOB shipping point.			
	10	Merchandise Inventory		50	
		Cash			50
		Paid shipping cost on merchandise purchased.			

> **The seller bears the freight costs if the shipping terms are FOB destination.**

The ownership of the merchandise may pass to the buyer when the buyer receives the merchandise. In this case, the terms are said to be **FOB (free on board) destination**. This term means that the seller pays the freight costs from the shipping point to the buyer's final destination. When the seller pays the delivery charges, the seller debits Delivery Expense or Freight Out. Delivery Expense is reported on the seller's income statement as a selling expense.

To illustrate, assume that NetSolutions sells merchandise as follows:

June 15. Sold merchandise to Kranz Company on account, $700, terms FOB destination. The cost of the merchandise sold is $480.
15. NetSolutions pays freight of $40 on the sale of June 15.

NetSolutions records the sale, the cost of the sale, and the freight cost as follows:

---

5 The passage of title also determines whether the buyer or seller must pay other costs, such as the cost of insurance, while the merchandise is in transit.

June	15	Accounts Receivable—Kranz Company	700	
		Sales		700
		Sold merchandise, terms FOB destination.		
	15	Cost of Merchandise Sold	480	
		Merchandise Inventory		480
		Recorded cost of merchandise sold to Kranz Company.		
	15	Delivery Expense	40	
		Cash		40
		Paid shipping cost on merch. sold.		

The seller may prepay the freight, even though the terms are FOB shipping point. The seller will then add the freight to the invoice. The buyer debits Merchandise Inventory for the total amount of the invoice, including the freight. Any discount terms would not apply to the prepaid freight.

To illustrate, assume that NetSolutions sells merchandise as follows:

June 20.   Sold merchandise to Planter Company on account, $800, terms FOB shipping point. NetSolutions paid freight of $45, which was added to the invoice. The cost of the merchandise sold is $360.

NetSolutions records the sale, the cost of the sale, and the freight as follows:

June	20	Accounts Receivable—Planter Company	800	
		Sales		800
		Sold merch., terms FOB shipping point.		
	20	Cost of Merchandise Sold	360	
		Merchandise Inventory		360
		Recorded cost of merchandise sold to Planter Company.		
	20	Accounts Receivable—Planter Company	45	
		Cash		45
		Prepaid shipping cost on merch. sold.		

Shipping terms, the passage of title, and whether the buyer or seller is to pay the freight costs are summarized in Exhibit 11.

Exhibit 11

Freight Terms

Example Exercise 5-5   Freight Terms

••••••••> 3

Determine the amount to be paid in full settlement of each of invoices (a) and (b), assuming that credit for returns and allowances was received prior to payment and that all invoices were paid within the discount period.

	Merchandise	Freight Paid by Seller	Freight Terms	Returns and Allowances
a.	$4,500	$200	FOB shipping point, 1/10, n/30	$ 800
b.	5,000	60	FOB destination, 2/10, n/30	2,500

Follow My Example 5-5

a. $3,863. Purchase of $4,500 less return of $800 less the discount of $37 [($4,500 − $800) × 1%] plus $200 of shipping.

b. $2,450. Purchase of $5,000 less return of $2,500 less the discount of $50 [($5,000 − $2,500) × 2%].

For Practice: PE 5-5A, PE 5-5B

Sales Taxes Almost all states levy a tax on sales of merchandise.[6] The liability for the sales tax is incurred when the sale is made.

At the time of a cash sale, the seller collects the sales tax. When a sale is made on account, the seller charges the tax to the buyer by debiting Accounts Receivable. The seller credits the sales account for the amount of the sale and credits the tax to Sales Tax Payable. For example, the seller would record a sale of $100 on account, subject to a tax of 6%, as follows:

The six states with the highest state sales tax (including the local option) are Tennessee, Louisiana, Washington, New York, Arkansas, and Alabama. Some states have no sales tax, including Alaska, Delaware, Montana, New Hampshire, and Oregon.

Aug.	12	Accounts Receivable—Lemon Co.		106	
		Sales			100
		Sales Tax Payable			6
		Invoice No. 339.			

On a regular basis, the seller pays to the taxing authority (state) the amount of the sales tax collected. The seller records such a payment as follows:

Business collects sales tax from customers

Customer

Sept.	15	Sales Tax Payable		2,900	
		Cash			2,900
		Payment for sales taxes collected during August.			

State

Business remits sales tax to state

Trade Discounts *Wholesalers* are companies that sell merchandise to other businesses rather than to the public. Many wholesalers publish sales catalogs. Rather than updating their catalogs, wholesalers may publish price updates. These updates may include large discounts from the catalog list prices. In addition, wholesalers often offer special discounts to government agencies or businesses that order large quantities. Such discounts are called **trade discounts**.

Sellers and buyers do not normally record the list prices of merchandise and trade discounts in their accounts. For example, assume that an item has a list price of $1,000 and a 40% trade discount. The seller records the sale of the item at $600 [$1,000 less the trade discount of $400 ($1,000 × 40%)]. Likewise, the buyer records the purchase at $600.

6 Businesses that purchase merchandise for resale to others are normally exempt from paying sales taxes on their purchases. Only final buyers of merchandise normally pay sales taxes.

Dual Nature of Merchandise Transactions

Each merchandising transaction affects a buyer and a seller. In the illustration below, we show how the same transactions would be recorded by the seller and the buyer. In this example, the seller is Scully Company and the buyer is Burton Co.

Transaction	Scully Company (Seller)	Burton Co. (Buyer)

July 1. Scully Company sold merchandise on account to Burton Co., $7,500, terms FOB shipping point, n/45. The cost of the merchandise sold was $4,500.	Accounts Receivable—Burton Co. . 7,500
	    Sales 7,500
	
	Cost of Merchandise Sold 4,500
	    Merchandise Inventory 4,500
		Merchandise Inventory 7,500
		    Accounts Payable—Scully Co. 7,500

July 2. Burton Co. paid freight of $150 on July 1 purchase from Scully Company.	No entry.	Merchandise Inventory . . . . 150 Cash 150

July 5. Scully Company sold merchandise on account to Burton Co., $5,000, terms FOB destination, n/30. The cost of the merchandise sold was $3,500.	Accounts Receivable—Burton Co. . 5,000
	    Sales 5,000
	
	Cost of Merchandise Sold 3,500
	    Merchandise Inventory 3,500
		Merchandise Inventory 5,000
		    Accounts Payable—Scully Co. 5,000

July 7. Scully Company paid freight of $250 for delivery of merchandise sold to Burton Co. on July 5.	Delivery Expense . . . . 250 Cash 250	No entry.

July 13. Scully Company issued Burton Co. a credit memo for merchandise returned, $1,000. The merchandise had been purchased by Burton Co. on account on July 5. The cost of the merchandise returned was $700.	Sales Returns and Allowances . . . 1,000
	    Accounts Receivable—Burton Co. 1,000
	
	Merchandise Inventory 700
	    Cost of Merchandise Sold. 700
		Accounts Payable—Scully Co. . . 1,000
		    Merchandise Inventory 1,000

July 15. Scully Company received payment from Burton Co. for purchase of July 5.	Cash 4,000
	    Accounts Receivable—Burton Co. 4,000
		Accounts Payable—Scully Co. . . 4,000
		    Cash 4,000

July 18. Scully Company sold merchandise on account to Burton Co., $12,000, terms FOB shipping point, 2/10, n/eom. Scully Company prepaid freight of $500, which was added to the invoice. The cost of the merchandise sold was $7,200.	Accounts Receivable—Burton Co. 12,000
	    Sales 12,000
	
	Accounts Receivable—Burton Co. . . 500
	    Cash 500
	
	Cost of Merchandise Sold 7,200
	    Merchandise Inventory 7,200
		Merchandise Inventory 12,500
		    Accounts Payable—Scully Co. 12,500

July 28. Scully Company received payment from Burton Co. for purchase of July 18, less discount (2% × $12,000).	Cash 12,260
	Sales Discounts 240
	    Accounts Receivable—Burton Co. 12,500
		Accounts Payable—Scully Co. . 12,500
		    Merchandise Inventory 240
		    Cash 12,260

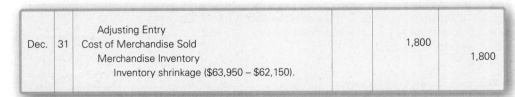

Example Exercise 5-6 Transactions for Buyer and Seller 3

Sievert Co. sold merchandise to Bray Co. on account, $11,500, terms 2/15, n/30. The cost of the merchandise sold is $6,900. Sievert Co. issued a credit memo for $900 for merchandise returned and later received the amount due within the discount period. The cost of the merchandise returned was $540. Journalize Sievert Co.'s and Bray Co.'s entries for the payment of the amount due.

Follow My Example 5-6

Sievert Co. journal entries:

Cash ($11,500 − $900 − $212)	10,388	
Sales Discounts [($11,500 − $900) × 2%]	212	
Accounts Receivable—Bray Co. ($11,500 − $900)		10,600

Bray Co. journal entries:

Accounts Payable—Sievert Co. ($11,500 − $900)	10,600	
Merchandise Inventory [($11,500 − $900) × 2%]		212
Cash ($11,500 − $900 − $212)		10,388

For Practice: PE 5-6A, PE 5-6B

4 Describe the adjusting and closing process for a merchandising business.

@netsolutions

The Adjusting and Closing Process

We have described and illustrated the chart of accounts and the recording of transactions for a merchandising business, NetSolutions. We have also illustrated the preparation of financial statements. In the remainder of this chapter, we describe the adjusting and closing process for a merchandising business. In this discussion, we will focus on the elements of the accounting cycle that differ from those of a service business.

Adjusting Entry for Inventory Shrinkage

$62,150
Actual Inventory per Physical Count

$1,800
Shrinkage

$63,950
Available for Sale per Records

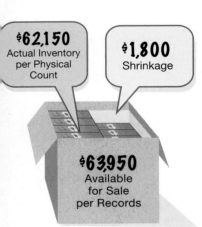

Under the perpetual inventory system, the merchandise inventory account is continually updated for purchase and sales transactions. As a result, the balance of the merchandise inventory account is the amount of merchandise available for sale at that point in time. However, retailers normally experience some loss of inventory due to shoplifting, employee theft, or errors. Thus, the physical inventory on hand at the end of the accounting period is usually less than the balance of Merchandise Inventory. This difference is called **inventory shrinkage** or **inventory shortage**.

To illustrate, NetSolutions' inventory records indicate the following on December 31, 2011:

	Dec. 31, 2011
Account balance of Merchandise Inventory	$63,950
Physical merchandise inventory on hand	62,150
Inventory shrinkage	$ 1,800

At the end of the accounting period, inventory shrinkage is recorded by the following adjusting entry:

Dec.	31	Adjusting Entry		
		Cost of Merchandise Sold	1,800	
		Merchandise Inventory		1,800
		Inventory shrinkage ($63,950 − $62,150).		

Retailers lose an estimated $30 billion to inventory shrinkage. The primary causes of the shrinkage are employee theft and shoplifting.

After the preceding entry is recorded, the balance of Merchandise Inventory agrees with the physical inventory on hand at the end of the period. Since inventory shrinkage cannot be totally eliminated, it is considered a normal cost of operations. If, however, the amount of the shrinkage is unusually large, it may be disclosed separately on the income statement. In such cases, the shrinkage may be recorded in a separate account, such as Loss from Merchandise Inventory Shrinkage.[7]

Example Exercise 5-7   Inventory Shrinkage    4

Pulmonary Company's perpetual inventory records indicate that $382,800 of merchandise should be on hand on March 31, 2010. The physical inventory indicates that $371,250 of merchandise is actually on hand. Journalize the adjusting entry for the inventory shrinkage for Pulmonary Company for the year ended March 31, 2010. Assume that the inventory shrinkage is a normal amount.

Follow My Example 5-7

Mar. 31	Cost of Merchandise Sold	11,550	
	Merchandise Inventory		11,550
	Inventory shrinkage ($382,800 − $371,250).		

For Practice: PE 5-7A, PE 5-7B

Closing Entries

The closing entries for a merchandising business are similar to those for a service business. The four closing entries for a merchandising business are as follows:

1. Debit each temporary account with a credit balance, such as Sales, for its balance and credit Income Summary.
2. Credit each temporary account with a debit balance, such as the various expenses, and credit Income Summary. Since Sales Returns and Allowances, Sales Discounts, and Cost of Merchandise Sold are temporary accounts with debit balances, they are credited for their balances.
3. Debit Income Summary for the amount of its balance (net income) and credit the retained earnings account. The accounts debited and credited are reversed if there is a net loss.
4. Debit the retained earnings account for the balance of the dividends account and credit the dividends account.

The four closing entries for NetSolutions are shown at the top of the following page.

NetSolutions' income summary account after the closing entries have been posted is as follows:

Account Income Summary					Account No. *313*	
					Balance	
Date	Item	Post. Ref.	Debit	Credit	Debit	Credit
2011						
Dec. 31	Revenues	29		720,785		720,785
31	Expenses	29	645,385			75,400
31	Net income	29	75,400		—	—

After the closing entries are posted to the accounts, a post-closing trial balance is prepared. The only accounts that should appear on the post-closing trial balance are the asset, contra asset, liability, and stockholders' equity accounts with balances. These are the same accounts that appear on the end-of-period balance sheet. If the two totals of the trial balance columns are not equal, an error has occurred that must be found and corrected.

7 The adjusting process for a merchandising business may be aided by preparing an end-of-period spreadsheet (work sheet). An end-of-period spreadsheet (work sheet) for a merchandising business is described and illustrated in Appendix D.

Journal					**Page 29**
Date		**Item**	**Post. Ref.**	**Debit**	**Credit**
		Closing Entries			
2011 Dec.	31	Sales	410	720,185	
		Rent Revenue	610	600	
		Income Summary	313		720,785
	31	Income Summary	313	645,385	
		Sales Returns and Allowances	411		6,140
		Sales Discounts	412		5,790
		Cost of Merchandise Sold	510		525,305
		Sales Salaries Expense	520		53,430
		Advertising Expense	521		10,860
		Depr. Expense—Store Equipment	522		3,100
		Delivery Expense	523		2,800
		Miscellaneous Selling Expense	529		630
		Office Salaries Expense	530		21,020
		Rent Expense	531		8,100
		Depr. Expense—Office Equipment	532		2,490
		Insurance Expense	533		1,910
		Office Supplies Expense	534		610
		Misc. Administrative Expense	539		760
		Interest Expense	710		2,440
	31	Income Summary	313	75,400	
		Retained Earnings	311		75,400
	31	Retained Earnings	311	18,000	
		Dividends	312		18,000

Financial Analysis and Interpretation

The ratio of net sales to assets measures how effectively a business is using its assets to generate sales. A high ratio indicates an effective use of assets. The assets used in computing the ratio may be the total assets at the end of the year, the average of the total assets at the beginning and end of the year, or the average of the monthly assets. For our purposes, we will use the average of the total assets at the beginning and end of the year. The ratio is computed as follows:

$$\text{Ratio of Net Sales to Assets} = \frac{\text{Net Sales}}{\text{Average Total Assets}}$$

To illustrate the use of this ratio, the following data (in millions) are taken from annual reports of Sears Holding Corporation and JCPenney:

	Sears	JCPenney
Total revenues (net sales)	$50,703	$19,903
Total assets:		
Beginning of year	27,397	12,673
End of year	30,066	12,461

The ratio of net sales to assets for each company is as follows:

	Sears	JCPenney
Ratio of net sales to assets	1.76*	1.58**

*$50,703/[($27,397 + $30,066)/2]
**$19,903/[($12,673 + $12,461)/2]

Based on these ratios, Sears appears better than JCPenney in utilizing its assets to generate sales. Comparing this ratio over time for both Sears and JCPenney, as well as comparing it with industry averages, would provide a better basis for interpreting the financial performance of each company.

Integrity, Objectivity, and Ethics in Business

THE COST OF EMPLOYEE THEFT

One survey reported that the 23 largest U.S. retail store chains have lost over $6 billion to shoplifting and employee theft. Of this amount, only 1.93% of the losses resulted in any recovery. The stores apprehended over 530,000 shoplifters and dishonest employees.

Approximately 1 out of every 28 employees was apprehended for theft from his or her employer. Each dishonest employee stole approximately 6.6 times the amount stolen by shoplifters ($851 vs. $129).

Source: Jack L. Hayes International, 19th Annual Retail Theft Survey, 2007.

A P P E N D I X

The Periodic Inventory System

Throughout this chapter, the perpetual inventory system was used to record purchases and sales of merchandise. Not all merchandise businesses, however, use the perpetual inventory system. For example, small merchandise businesses, such as a local hardware store, may use a manual accounting system. A manual perpetual inventory system is time consuming and costly to maintain. In this case, the periodic inventory system may be used.

Cost of Merchandise Sold Using the Periodic Inventory System

@netsolutions

In the periodic inventory system, sales are recorded in the same manner as in the perpetual inventory system. However, cost of merchandise sold is not recorded on the date of sale. Instead, cost of merchandise sold is determined as shown in Exhibit 12 for NetSolutions.

Exhibit 12

Determining Cost of Merchandise Sold Using the Periodic System

Merchandise inventory, January 1, 2011			$ 59,700
Purchases		$521,980	
Less: Purchases returns and allowances	$9,100		
Purchases discounts	2,525	11,625	
Net purchases		$510,355	
Add freight in		17,400	
Cost of merchandise purchased			527,755
Merchandise available for sale			$587,455
Less merchandise inventory, December 31, 2011			62,150
Cost of merchandise sold			$525,305

Chart of Accounts Under the Periodic Inventory System

The chart of accounts under a periodic inventory system is shown in Exhibit 13. The accounts used to record transactions under the periodic inventory system are highlighted in Exhibit 13.

Exhibit 13

Chart of Accounts Under the Periodic Inventory System

Balance Sheet Accounts	Income Statement Accounts
100 Assets	**400 Revenues**
110 Cash	410 Sales
111 Notes Receivable	411 Sales Returns and Allowances
112 Accounts Receivable	412 Sales Discounts
115 Merchandise Inventory	**500 Costs and Expenses**
116 Office Supplies	510 Purchases
117 Prepaid Insurance	511 Purchases Returns and Allowances
120 Land	512 Purchases Discounts
123 Store Equipment	513 Freight In
124 Accumulated Depreciation—Store Equipment	520 Sales Salaries Expense
125 Office Equipment	521 Advertising Expense
126 Accumulated Depreciation—Office Equipment	522 Depreciation Expense—Store Equipment
200 Liabilities	523 Delivery Expense
210 Accounts Payable	529 Miscellaneous Selling Expense
211 Salaries Payable	530 Office Salaries Expense
212 Unearned Rent	531 Rent Expense
215 Notes Payable	532 Depreciation Expense—Office Equipment
300 Stockholders' Equity	533 Insurance Expense
310 Capital Stock	534 Office Supplies Expense
311 Retained Earnings	539 Misc. Administrative Expense
312 Dividends	**600 Other Income**
313 Income Summary	610 Rent Revenue
	700 Other Expense
	710 Interest Expense

Recording Merchandise Transactions Under the Periodic Inventory System

Using the periodic inventory system, purchases of inventory are not recorded in the merchandise inventory account. Instead, purchases, purchases discounts, and purchases returns and allowances accounts are used. In addition, the sales of merchandise are not recorded in the inventory account. Thus, there is no detailed record of the amount of inventory on hand at any given time. At the end of the period, a physical count of merchandise inventory on hand is taken. This physical count is used to determine the cost of merchandise sold as shown in Exhibit 12.

The use of purchases, purchases discounts, purchases returns and allowances, and freight in accounts are described below.

Purchases Purchases of inventory are recorded in a purchases account rather than in the merchandise inventory account. Purchases is debited for the invoice amount of a purchase.

Purchases Discounts Purchases discounts are normally recorded in a separate purchases discounts account. The balance of the purchases discounts account is reported as a deduction from Purchases for the period. Thus, Purchases Discounts is a contra (or offsetting) account to Purchases.

Purchases Returns and Allowances Purchases returns and allowances are recorded in a similar manner as purchases discounts. A separate purchases returns and allowances account is used to record returns and allowances. Purchases returns and allowances are reported as a deduction from Purchases for the period. Thus, Purchases Returns and Allowances is a contra (or offsetting) account to Purchases.

Freight In When merchandise is purchased FOB shipping point, the buyer pays for the freight. Under the periodic inventory system, freight paid when purchasing merchandise FOB shipping point is debited to Freight In, Transportation In, or a similar account.

The preceding periodic inventory accounts and their effect on the cost of merchandise purchased are summarized below.

Account	Entry to Increase (Decrease)	Normal Balance	Effect on Cost of Merchandise Purchased
Purchases	Debit	Debit	Increases
Purchases Discounts	Credit	Credit	Decreases
Purchases Returns and Allowances	Credit	Credit	Decreases
Freight In	Debit	Debit	Increases

Exhibit 14 illustrates the recording of merchandise transactions using the periodic system. As a review, Exhibit 14 also illustrates how each transaction would have been recorded using the perpetual system.

Adjusting Process Under the Periodic Inventory System

The adjusting process is the same under the periodic and perpetual inventory systems except for the inventory shrinkage adjustment. The ending merchandise inventory is determined by a physical count under both systems.

Under the perpetual inventory system, the ending inventory physical count is compared to the balance of Merchandise Inventory. The difference is the amount of inventory shrinkage. The inventory shrinkage is then recorded as a debit to Cost of Merchandise Sold and a credit to Merchandise Inventory.

Under the periodic inventory system, the merchandise inventory account is not kept up to date for purchases and sales. As a result, the inventory shrinkage cannot be directly determined. Instead, any inventory shrinkage is included indirectly in the computation of cost of merchandise sold as shown in Exhibit 12. This is a major disadvantage of the periodic inventory system. That is, under the periodic inventory system, inventory shrinkage is not separately determined.

Financial Statements Under the Periodic Inventory System

The financial statements are similar under the perpetual and periodic inventory systems. When a multiple-step income statement is prepared, cost of merchandise sold may be reported as shown in Exhibit 12.

Exhibit 14

Transactions Using the Periodic and Perpetual Inventory Systems

Transaction	Periodic Inventory System		Perpetual Inventory System	

June 5. Purchased $30,000 of merchandise on account, terms 2/10, n/30.	Purchases 30,000
	   Accounts Payable . . . .
		
		30,000
			Merchandise Inventory 30,000
			   Accounts Payable . . . .
				
				30,000

June 8. Returned merchandise purchased on account on June 5, $500.	Accounts Payable 500
	   Purchases Returns and Allowances
		
		500
			Accounts Payable 500
			   Merchandise Inventory . . . .
				
				500

June 15. Paid for purchase of June 5, less return of $500 and discount of $590 [($30,000 − $500) × 2%].	Accounts Payable 29,500
	   Cash . . . .
	   Purchases Discounts . . . .
		
		28,910
		590
			Accounts Payable 29,500
			   Cash . . . .
			   Merchandise Inventory . . . .
				
				28,910
				590

June 18. Sold merchandise on account, $12,500, 1/10, n/30. The cost of the merchandise sold was $9,000.	Accounts Receivable 12,500
	   Sales . . . .
		
		12,500
			Accounts Receivable 12,500
			   Sales . . . .
			Cost of Merchandise Sold 9,000
			   Merchandise Inventory . . . .
				
				12,500
				
				9,000

June 21. Received merchandise returned on account, $4,000. The cost of the merchandise returned was $2,800.	Sales Returns and Allowances . . 4,000
	   Accounts Receivable . . . .
		
		4,000
			Sales Returns and Allowances . . 4,000
			   Accounts Receivable . . . .
			Merchandise Inventory 2,800
			   Cost of Merchandise Sold . .
				
				4,000
				
				2,800

June 22. Purchased merchandise, $15,000, terms FOB shipping point, 2/15, n/30, with prepaid freight of $750 added to the invoice.	Purchases 15,000
	Freight In 750
	   Accounts Payable . . . .
		
		15,750
			Merchandise Inventory 15,750
			   Accounts Payable . . . .
				
				15,750

June 28. Received $8,415 as payment on account from June 18 sale less return of June 21 and less discount of $85 [($12,500 − $4,000) × 1%].	Cash 8,415
	Sales Discounts 85
	   Accounts Receivable . . . .
		
		8,500
			Cash 8,415
			Sales Discounts 85
			   Accounts Receivable . . . .
				
				8,500

June 29. Received $19,600 from cash sales. The cost of the merchandise sold was $13,800.	Cash 19,600
	   Sales . . . .
		
		19,600
			Cash 19,600
			   Sales . . . .
			Cost of Merchandise Sold 13,800
			   Merchandise Inventory . . . .
				
				19,600
				
				13,800

Closing Entries Under the Periodic Inventory System

The closing entries differ in the periodic inventory system in that there is no cost of merchandise sold account to close to Income Summary. Instead, the purchases, purchases discounts, purchases returns and allowances, and freight in accounts are closed to Income Summary. In addition, the merchandise inventory account is adjusted to the end-of-period physical inventory count during the closing process.

The four closing entries under the periodic inventory system are as follows:

1. Debit each temporary account with a credit balance, such as Sales, for its balance and credit Income Summary. Since Purchases Discounts and Purchases Returns

and Allowances are temporary accounts with credit balances, they are debited for their balances. In addition, Merchandise Inventory is debited for its end-of-period balance based on the end-of-period physical inventory.

2. Credit each temporary account with a debit balance, such as the various expenses, and debit Income Summary. Since Sales Returns and Allowances, Sales Discounts, Purchases, and Freight In are temporary accounts with debit balances, they are credited for their balances. In addition, Merchandise Inventory is credited for its balance as of the beginning of the period.

3. Debit Income Summary for the amount of its balance (net income) and credit the retained earnings account. The accounts debited and credited are reversed if there is a net loss.

4. Debit the retained earnings account for the balance of the dividends account and credit the dividends account.

The four closing entries for NetSolutions under the periodic inventory system are:

Journal

Date		Item	Post. Ref.	Debit	Credit
2011		Closing Entries			
Dec.	31	Merchandise Inventory	115	62,150	
		Sales	410	720,185	
		Purchases Returns and Allowances	511	9,100	
		Purchases Discounts	512	2,525	
		Rent Revenue	610	600	
		Income Summary	313		794,560
	31	Income Summary	313	719,160	
		Merchandise Inventory	115		59,700
		Sales Returns and Allowances	411		6,140
		Sales Discounts	412		5,790
		Purchases	510		521,980
		Freight In	513		17,400
		Sales Salaries Expense	520		53,430
		Advertising Expense	521		10,860
		Depreciation Expense—Store Equipment	522		3,100
		Delivery Expense	523		2,800
		Miscellaneous Selling Expense	529		630
		Office Salaries Expense	530		21,020
		Rent Expense	531		8,100
		Depreciation Expense—Office Equipment	532		2,490
		Insurance Expense	533		1,910
		Office Supplies Expense	534		610
		Miscellaneous Administrative Expense	539		760
		Interest Expense	710		2,440
	31	Income Summary	313	75,400	
		Retained Earnings	311		75,400
	31	Retained Earnings	311	18,000	
		Dividends	312		18,000

In the first closing entry, Merchandise Inventory is debited for $62,150. This is the ending physical inventory count on December 31, 2011. In the second closing entry, Merchandise Inventory is credited for its January 1, 2011, balance of $59,700. In this way, the closing entries highlight the importance of the beginning and ending balances of Merchandise Inventory in determining cost of merchandise sold, as shown in Exhibit 12. After the closing entries are posted, Merchandise Inventory will have a balance of $62,150. This is the amount reported on the December 31, 2011, balance sheet.

In the preceding closing entries, the periodic accounts are highlighted in color. Under the perpetual inventory system, the highlighted periodic inventory accounts are replaced by the cost of merchandise sold account.

At a Glance 5 ● ● ●

1   Distinguish between the activities and financial statements of service and merchandising businesses.

Key Points	Key Learning Outcomes	Example Exercises	Practice Exercises
The primary differences between a service business and a merchandising business relate to revenue activities. Merchandising businesses purchase merchandise for selling to customers. On a merchandising business's income statement, revenue from selling merchandise is reported as sales. The cost of the merchandise sold is subtracted from sales to arrive at gross profit. The operating expenses are subtracted from gross profit to arrive at net income. Merchandise inventory, which is merchandise not sold, is reported as a current asset on the balance sheet.	• Describe how the activities of a service and a merchandising business differ. • Describe the differences between the income statements of a service and a merchandising business. • Compute gross profit. • Describe how merchandise inventory is reported on the balance sheet.	5-1	5-1A, 5-1B

2   Describe and illustrate the financial statements of a merchandising business.

Key Points	Key Learning Outcomes	Example Exercises	Practice Exercises
The multiple-step income statement of a merchandiser reports sales, sales returns and allowances, sales discounts, and net sales. The cost of the merchandise sold is subtracted from net sales to determine the gross profit. The cost of merchandise sold is determined by using either the periodic or perpetual inventory system. Operating income is determined by subtracting operating expenses from gross profit. Operating expenses are normally classified as selling or administrative expenses. Net income is determined by adding or subtracting the net of other income and expense. The income statement may also be reported in a single-step form. The retained earnings statement is similar to that for a service business. The balance sheet reports merchandise inventory at the end of the period as a current asset.	• Prepare a multiple-step income statement for a merchandising business. • Describe how cost of merchandise sold is determined under a periodic inventory system. • Compute cost of merchandise sold under a periodic inventory system as shown in Exhibit 2. • Prepare a single-step income statement. • Prepare a retained earnings statement for a merchandising business. • Prepare a balance sheet for a merchandising business.	5-2	5-2A, 5-2B

Describe and illustrate the accounting for merchandise transactions including:
- sale of merchandise
- purchase of merchandise
- freight, sales taxes, and trade discounts
- dual nature of merchandising transactions

Key Points	Key Learning Outcomes	Example Exercises	Practice Exercises
Sales of merchandise for cash or on account are recorded by crediting Sales. Under the perpetual inventory system, the cost of merchandise sold and the reduction in merchandise inventory are also recorded for the sale. For sales of merchandise on account, the credit terms may allow discounts for early payment. Such discounts are recorded by the seller as a debit to Sales Discounts. Sales discounts are reported as a deduction from the amount initially recorded in Sales. Likewise, when merchandise is returned or a price adjustment is granted, the seller debits Sales Returns and Allowances.	• Prepare journal entries to record sales of merchandise for cash or using a credit card.		
	• Prepare journal entries to record sales of merchandise on account.	5-3	5-3A, 5-3B
	• Prepare journal entries to record sales discounts and sales returns and allowances.	5-3	5-3A, 5-3B
Purchases of merchandise for cash or on account are recorded by debiting Merchandise Inventory. For purchases of merchandise on account, the credit terms may allow cash discounts for early payment. Such purchases discounts are viewed as a reduction in the cost of the merchandise purchased. When merchandise is returned or a price adjustment is granted, the buyer credits Merchandise Inventory.	• Prepare journal entries to record the purchase of merchandise for cash.		
	• Prepare journal entries to record the purchase of merchandise on account.	5-4	5-4A, 5-4B
	• Prepare journal entries to record purchases discounts and purchases returns and allowances.	5-4	5-4A, 5-4B
When merchandise is shipped FOB shipping point, the buyer pays the freight and debits Merchandise Inventory. When merchandise is shipped FOB destination, the seller pays the freight and debits Delivery Expense or Freight Out. If the seller prepays freight as a convenience to the buyer, the seller debits Accounts Receivable for the costs.	• Prepare journal entries for freight from the point of view of the buyer and seller.		
	• Determine the total cost of the purchase of merchandise under differing freight terms.	5-5	5-5A, 5-5B
The liability for sales tax is incurred when the sale is made and is recorded by the seller as a credit to the sales tax payable account. When the amount of the sales tax is paid to the taxing unit, Sales Tax Payable is debited and Cash is credited.	• Prepare journal entries for the collection and payment of sales taxes by the seller.		
Many wholesalers offer trade discounts, which are discounts off the list prices of merchandise. Normally, neither the seller nor the buyer records the list price and the related trade discount in the accounts.	• Determine the cost of merchandise purchased when a trade discount is offered by the seller.		
Each merchandising transaction affects a buyer and a seller. The illustration in this chapter shows how the same transactions would be recorded by both.	• Record the same merchandise transactions for the buyer and seller.	5-6	5-6A, 5-6B

4 Describe the adjusting and closing process for a merchandising business.

		Example Exercises	Practice Exercises

Key Points

The accounting cycle for a merchandising business is similar to that of a service business. However, a merchandiser is likely to experience inventory shrinkage, which must be recorded. The normal adjusting entry is to debit Cost of Merchandise Sold and credit Merchandise Inventory for the amount of the shrinkage.

The closing entries for a merchandising business are similar to those for a service business. The first entry closes sales and other revenue to Income Summary. The second entry closes cost of merchandise sold, sales discounts, sales returns and allowances, and other expenses to Income Summary. The third entry closes the balance of Income Summary (the net income or net loss) to the retained earnings account. The fourth entry closes the dividends account to the retained earnings account.

Key Learning Outcomes

- Prepare the adjusting journal entry for inventory shrinkage.

  Example Exercises: **5-7**   Practice Exercises: 5-7A, 5-7B

- Prepare the closing entries for a merchandising business.

Key Terms

account form (215)
accounts payable subsidiary ledger (218)
accounts receivable subsidiary ledger (218)
administrative expenses (general expenses) (214)
controlling account (218)
cost of merchandise purchased (212)
cost of merchandise sold (210)
credit memorandum (credit memo) (221)
credit period (220)
credit terms (220)
debit memorandum (debit memo) (224)
FOB (free on board) destination (226)

FOB (free on board) shipping point (226)
freight in (212)
general ledger (217)
gross profit (210)
income from operations (operating income) (214)
inventory shrinkage (inventory shortage) (230)
inventory subsidiary ledger (218)
invoice (220)
merchandise available for sale (212)
merchandise inventory (210)
multiple-step income statement (211)
net purchases (212)
net sales (212)

other expense (214)
other income (214)
periodic inventory system (213)
perpetual inventory system (213)
purchases discounts (212)
purchases returns and allowances (212)
report form (215)
sales (212)
sales discounts (212)
sales returns and allowances (212)
selling expenses (214)
single-step income statement (215)
subsidiary ledger (217)
trade discounts (228)

Illustrative Problem ● ● ● ● ➤

The following transactions were completed by Montrose Company during May of the current year. Montrose Company uses a perpetual inventory system.

May 3. Purchased merchandise on account from Floyd Co., $4,000, terms FOB shipping point, 2/10, n/30, with prepaid freight of $120 added to the invoice.

  5. Purchased merchandise on account from Kramer Co., $8,500, terms FOB destination, 1/10, n/30.

  6. Sold merchandise on account to C. F. Howell Co., list price $4,000, trade discount 30%, terms 2/10, n/30. The cost of the merchandise sold was $1,125.

  8. Purchased office supplies for cash, $150.

  10. Returned merchandise purchased on May 5 from Kramer Co., $1,300.

  13. Paid Floyd Co. on account for purchase of May 3, less discount.

  14. Purchased merchandise for cash, $10,500.

  15. Paid Kramer Co. on account for purchase of May 5, less return of May 10 and discount.

  16. Received cash on account from sale of May 6 to C. F. Howell Co., less discount.

  19. Sold merchandise on MasterCard credit cards, $2,450. The cost of the merchandise sold was $980.

  22. Sold merchandise on account to Comer Co., $3,480, terms 2/10, n/30. The cost of the merchandise sold was $1,400.

  24. Sold merchandise for cash, $4,350. The cost of the merchandise sold was $1,750.

  25. Received merchandise returned by Comer Co. from sale on May 22, $1,480. The cost of the returned merchandise was $600.

  31. Paid a service processing fee of $140 for MasterCard sales.

Instructions

1. Journalize the preceding transactions.
2. Journalize the adjusting entry for merchandise inventory shrinkage, $3,750.

Solution

1.

May	3	Merchandise Inventory	4,120	
		Accounts Payable—Floyd Co.		4,120
	5	Merchandise Inventory	8,500	
		Accounts Payable—Kramer Co.		8,500
	6	Accounts Receivable—C. F. Howell Co.	2,800	
		Sales		2,800
		[$4,000 − (30% × $4,000)].		
	6	Cost of Merchandise Sold	1,125	
		Merchandise Inventory		1,125
	8	Office Supplies	150	
		Cash		150
	10	Accounts Payable—Kramer Co.	1,300	
		Merchandise Inventory		1,300
	13	Accounts Payable—Floyd Co.	4,120	
		Merchandise Inventory		80
		Cash		4,040
		[$4,000 − (2% × $4,000) + $120].		
	14	Merchandise Inventory	10,500	
		Cash		10,500
	15	Accounts Payable—Kramer Co.	7,200	
		Merchandise Inventory		72
		Cash		7,128
		[($8,500 − $1,300) × 1% = $72;		
		$8,500 − $1,300 − $72 = $7,128].		

May 16	Cash		2,744	
	Sales Discounts		56	
	Accounts Receivable—C. F. Howell Co.			2,800
19	Cash		2,450	
	Sales			2,450
19	Cost of Merchandise Sold		980	
	Merchandise Inventory			980
22	Accounts Receivable—Comer Co.		3,480	
	Sales			3,480
22	Cost of Merchandise Sold		1,400	
	Merchandise Inventory			1,400
24	Cash		4,350	
	Sales			4,350
24	Cost of Merchandise Sold		1,750	
	Merchandise Inventory			1,750
25	Sales Returns and Allowances		1,480	
	Accounts Receivable—Comer Co.			1,480
25	Merchandise Inventory		600	
	Cost of Merchandise Sold			600
31	Credit Card Expense		140	
	Cash			140
2. May 31	Cost of Merchandise Sold		3,750	
	Merchandise Inventory			3,750
	Inventory shrinkage.			

Self-Examination Questions (Answers at End of Chapter)

1. If merchandise purchased on account is returned, the buyer may inform the seller of the details by issuing a(n):
   A. debit memo.   C. invoice.
   B. credit memo.   D. bill.

2. If merchandise is sold on account to a customer for $1,000, terms FOB shipping point, 1/10, n/30, and the seller prepays $50 in freight, the amount of the discount for early payment would be:
   A. $0.   C. $10.00.
   B. $5.00.   D. $10.50.

3. The income statement in which the total of all expenses is deducted from the total of all revenues is termed the:
   A. multiple-step form.   C. account form.
   B. single-step form.   D. report form.

4. On a multiple-step income statement, the excess of net sales over the cost of merchandise sold is called:
   A. operating income.
   B. income from operations.
   C. gross profit.
   D. net income.

5. Which of the following expenses would normally be classified as other expense on a multiple-step income statement?
   A. Depreciation expense—office equipment
   B. Sales salaries expense
   C. Insurance expense
   D. Interest expense

Eye Openers

1. What distinguishes a merchandising business from a service business?
2. Can a business earn a gross profit but incur a net loss? Explain.
3. In computing the cost of merchandise sold, does each of the following items increase or decrease that cost? (a) freight, (b) beginning merchandise inventory, (c) purchase discounts, (d) ending merchandise inventory
4. Describe how the periodic system differs from the perpetual system of accounting for merchandise inventory.

5. Differentiate between the multiple-step and the single-step forms of the income statement.
6. What are the major advantages and disadvantages of the single-step form of income statement compared to the multiple-step statement?
7. What type of revenue is reported in the Other income section of the multiple-step income statement?
8. Name at least three accounts that would normally appear in the chart of accounts of a merchandising business but would not appear in the chart of accounts of a service business.
9. How are sales to customers using MasterCard and VISA recorded?
10. The credit period during which the buyer of merchandise is allowed to pay usually begins with what date?
11. What is the meaning of (a) 1/15, n/60; (b) n/30; (c) n/eom?
12. What is the nature of (a) a credit memo issued by the seller of merchandise, (b) a debit memo issued by the buyer of merchandise?
13. Who bears the freight when the terms of sale are (a) FOB shipping point, (b) FOB destination?
14. Business Outfitters Inc., which uses a perpetual inventory system, experienced a normal inventory shrinkage of $9,175. What accounts would be debited and credited to record the adjustment for the inventory shrinkage at the end of the accounting period?
15. Assume that Business Outfitters Inc. in Eye Opener 14 experienced an abnormal inventory shrinkage of $80,750. Business Outfitters Inc. has decided to record the abnormal inventory shrinkage so that it would be separately disclosed on the income statement. What account would be debited for the abnormal inventory shrinkage?

Practice Exercises

PE 5-1A
Gross profit

obj. 1

EE 5-1   p. 210

During the current year, merchandise is sold for $32,800 cash and $379,500 on account. The cost of the merchandise sold is $250,000. What is the amount of the gross profit?

PE 5-1B
Gross profit

obj. 1

EE 5-1   p. 210

During the current year, merchandise is sold for $375,000 cash and $815,000 on account. The cost of the merchandise sold is $700,000. What is the amount of the gross profit?

PE 5-2A
Cost of merchandise sold

obj. 2

EE 5-2   p. 214

Based on the following data, determine the cost of merchandise sold for June:

Merchandise inventory, June 1	$ 35,500
Merchandise inventory, June 30	40,500
Purchases	384,000
Purchases returns and allowances	11,000
Purchases discounts	3,000
Freight in	6,000

PE 5-2B
Cost of merchandise sold

obj. 2

EE 5-2   p. 214

Based on the following data, determine the cost of merchandise sold for August:

Merchandise inventory, August 1	$120,000
Merchandise inventory, August 31	150,000
Purchases	780,000
Purchases returns and allowances	20,000
Purchases discounts	10,000
Freight in	5,000

PE 5-3A
Sales transactions
obj. 3

EE 5-3 p. 222

Journalize the following merchandise transactions:
a. Sold merchandise on account, $41,000 with terms 1/10, n/30. The cost of the merchandise sold was $22,500.
b. Received payment less the discount.

PE 5-3B
Sales transactions
obj. 3

EE 5-3 p. 222

Journalize the following merchandise transactions:
a. Sold merchandise on account, $16,000 with terms 2/10, n/30. The cost of the merchandise sold was $9,600.
b. Received payment less the discount.

PE 5-4A
Purchase transactions
obj. 3

EE 5-4 p. 225

Kosmos Company purchased merchandise on account from a supplier for $21,500, terms 1/10, n/30. Kosmos Company returned $1,500 of the merchandise and received full credit.
a. If Kosmos Company pays the invoice within the discount period, what is the amount of cash required for the payment?
b. Under a perpetual inventory system, what account is debited by Kosmos Company to record the return?

PE 5-4B
Purchase transactions
obj. 3

EE 5-4 p. 225

Enduro Tile Company purchased merchandise on account from a supplier for $8,000, terms 2/10, n/30. Enduro Tile Company returned $3,500 of the merchandise and received full credit.
a. If Enduro Tile Company pays the invoice within the discount period, what is the amount of cash required for the payment?
b. Under a perpetual inventory system, what account is credited by Enduro Tile Company to record the return?

PE 5-5A
Freight terms
obj. 3

EE 5-5 p. 228

Determine the amount to be paid in full settlement of each of invoices (a) and (b), assuming that credit for returns and allowances was received prior to payment and that all invoices were paid within the discount period.

	Merchandise	Freight Paid by Seller	Freight Terms	Returns and Allowances
a.	$13,150	$450	FOB destination, 1/10, n/30	$4,150
b.	32,100	900	FOB shipping point, 2/10, n/30	5,000

PE 5-5B
Freight terms
obj. 3

EE 5-5 p. 228

Determine the amount to be paid in full settlement of each of invoices (a) and (b), assuming that credit for returns and allowances was received prior to payment and that all invoices were paid within the discount period.

	Merchandise	Freight Paid by Seller	Freight Terms	Returns and Allowances
a.	$9,000	$300	FOB shipping point, 1/10, n/30	$2,500
b.	7,500	200	FOB destination, 2/10, n/30	400

PE 5-6A
Transactions for buyer and seller
obj. 3

EE 5-6 p. 230

Saddlebag Co. sold merchandise to Bioscan Co. on account, $17,500, terms FOB shipping point, 2/10, n/30. The cost of the merchandise sold is $10,000. Saddlebag Co. paid freight of $600 and later received the amount due within the discount period. Journalize Saddlebag Co.'s and Bioscan Co.'s entries for the payment of the amount due.

PE 5-6B
Transactions for buyer and seller
obj. 3

EE 5-6 p. 230

Santana Co. sold merchandise to Birch Co. on account, $6,000, terms 2/15, n/30. The cost of the merchandise sold is $4,000. Santana Co. issued a credit memo for $800 for merchandise returned and later received the amount due within the discount period. The cost of the merchandise returned was $550. Journalize Santana Co.'s and Birch Co.'s entries for the payment of the amount due.

PE 5-7A
Inventory shrinkage
obj. 4

EE 5-7 p. 231

Retro Company's perpetual inventory records indicate that $975,000 of merchandise should be on hand on October 31, 2010. The physical inventory indicates that $894,750 of merchandise is actually on hand. Journalize the adjusting entry for the inventory shrinkage for Retro Company for the year ended October 31, 2010. Assume that the inventory shrinkage is a normal amount.

PE 5-7B
Inventory shrinkage
obj. 4

EE 5-7 p. 231

Hairology Company's perpetual inventory records indicate that $120,500 of merchandise should be on hand on April 30, 2010. The physical inventory indicates that $115,850 of merchandise is actually on hand. Journalize the adjusting entry for the inventory shrinkage for Hairology Company for the year ended April 30, 2010. Assume that the inventory shrinkage is a normal amount.

Exercises

EX 5-1
Determining gross profit
obj. 1

During the current year, merchandise is sold for $795,000. The cost of the merchandise sold is $477,000.

a. What is the amount of the gross profit?
b. Compute the gross profit percentage (gross profit divided by sales).
c. ➤ Will the income statement necessarily report a net income? Explain.

EX 5-2
Determining cost of merchandise sold
obj. 1

In 2007, Best Buy reported revenue of $35,934 million. Its gross profit was $8,769 million. What was the amount of Best Buy's cost of merchandise sold?

EX 5-3
Identify items missing in determining cost of merchandise sold
obj. 2

For (a) through (d), identify the items designated by "X" and "Y."

a. Purchases − (X + Y) = Net purchases.
b. Net purchases + X = Cost of merchandise purchased.
c. Merchandise inventory (beginning) + Cost of merchandise purchased = X.
d. Merchandise available for sale − X = Cost of merchandise sold.

EX 5-4
Cost of merchandise sold and related items
obj. 2

✔ a. Cost of merchandise sold, $1,400,600

The following data were extracted from the accounting records of Wedgeforth Company for the year ended November 30, 2010:

Merchandise inventory, December 1, 2009	$ 210,000
Merchandise inventory, November 30, 2010	185,000
Purchases	1,400,000
Purchases returns and allowances	20,000
Purchases discounts	18,500
Sales	2,250,000
Freight in	14,100

a. Prepare the cost of merchandise sold section of the income statement for the year ended November 30, 2010, using the periodic inventory system.
b. Determine the gross profit to be reported on the income statement for the year ended November 30, 2010.

EX 5-5
Cost of merchandise sold

obj. 2

✔ Correct cost of merchandise sold, $953,500

Identify the errors in the following schedule of cost of merchandise sold for the current year ended July 31, 2010:

Cost of merchandise sold:			
Merchandise inventory, July 31, 2010			$ 140,000
Purchases		$975,000	
Plus: Purchases returns and allowances	$12,000		
Purchases discounts	8,000	20,000	
Gross purchases		$995,000	
Less freight in		13,500	
Cost of merchandise purchased			981,500
Merchandise available for sale			$1,121,500
Less merchandise inventory, August 1, 2009			125,000
Cost of merchandise sold			$ 996,500

EX 5-6
Income statement for merchandiser

obj. 2

For the fiscal year, sales were $5,280,000, sales discounts were $100,000, sales returns and allowances were $75,000, and the cost of merchandise sold was $3,000,000.

a. What was the amount of net sales?
b. What was the amount of gross profit?

EX 5-7
Income statement for merchandiser

obj. 2

The following expenses were incurred by a merchandising business during the year. In which expense section of the income statement should each be reported: (a) selling, (b) administrative, or (c) other?

1. Advertising expense
2. Depreciation expense on store equipment
3. Insurance expense on office equipment
4. Interest expense on notes payable
5. Rent expense on office building
6. Salaries of office personnel
7. Salary of sales manager
8. Sales supplies used

EX 5-8
Single-step income statement

obj. 2

✔ Net income: $1,320,000

Summary operating data for Paper Plus Company during the current year ended June 30, 2010, are as follows: cost of merchandise sold, $4,000,000; administrative expenses, $500,000; interest expense, $30,000; rent revenue, $100,000; net sales, $6,500,000; and selling expenses, $750,000. Prepare a single-step income statement.

EX 5-9
Multiple-step income statement

obj. 2

Identify the errors in the following income statement:

Armortec Company
Income Statement
For the Year Ended February 28, 2010

Revenue from sales:			
Sales		$5,345,800	
Add: Sales returns and allowances	$120,000		
Sales discounts	60,000	180,000	
Gross sales			$5,525,800
Cost of merchandise sold			3,100,800
Income from operations			$2,425,000
Expenses:			
Selling expenses		$ 800,000	
Administrative expenses		600,000	
Delivery expense		50,000	
Total expenses			1,450,000
			$ 975,000
Other expense:			
Interest revenue			40,000
Gross profit			$ 935,000

EX 5-10
Determining amounts for items omitted from income statement

obj. 2

✔ a. $15,000
✔ h. $520,000

Two items are omitted in each of the following four lists of income statement data. Determine the amounts of the missing items, identifying them by letter.

Sales	$250,000	$600,000	$1,000,000	$ (g)
Sales returns and allowances	(a)	30,000	(e)	7,500
Sales discounts	10,000	18,000	40,000	11,500
Net sales	225,000	(c)	910,000	(h)
Cost of merchandise sold	(b)	330,000	(f)	400,000
Gross profit	90,000	(d)	286,500	120,000

EX 5-11
Multiple-step income statement

obj. 2

✔ a. Net income: $275,000

On March 31, 2010, the balances of the accounts appearing in the ledger of El Dorado Furnishings Company, a furniture wholesaler, are as follows:

Administrative Expenses	$ 250,000	Office Supplies	$ 21,200
Building	1,025,000	Retained Earnigs	937,600
Capital Stock	200,000	Salaries Payable	6,000
Cash	97,000	Sales	2,550,000
Cost of Merchandise Sold	1,400,000	Sales Discounts	40,000
Dividends	50,000	Sales Returns and Allowances	160,000
Interest Expense	15,000	Selling Expenses	410,000
Merchandise Inventory	260,000	Store Supplies	15,400
Notes Payable	59,000		

a. Prepare a multiple-step income statement for the year ended March 31, 2010.
b. Compare the major advantages and disadvantages of the multiple-step and single-step forms of income statements.

EX 5-12
Chart of accounts

obj. 3

Frazee Paints Co. is a newly organized business with a list of accounts arranged in alphabetical order below.

Accounts Payable
Accounts Receivable
Accumulated Depreciation—Office Equipment
Accumulated Depreciation—Store Equipment
Advertising Expense
Capital Stock
Cash
Cost of Merchandise Sold
Delivery Expense
Depreciation Expense—Office Equipment
Depreciation Expense—Store Equipment
Dividends
Income Summary
Insurance Expense
Interest Expense
Land
Merchandise Inventory
Miscellaneous Administrative Expense

Miscellaneous Selling Expense
Notes Payable
Office Equipment
Office Salaries Expense
Office Supplies
Office Supplies Expense
Prepaid Insurance
Rent Expense
Retained Earnings
Salaries Payable
Sales
Sales Discounts
Sales Returns and Allowances
Sales Salaries Expense
Store Equipment
Store Supplies
Store Supplies Expense

Construct a chart of accounts, assigning account numbers and arranging the accounts in balance sheet and income statement order, as illustrated in Exhibit 6. Each account number is three digits: the first digit is to indicate the major classification ("1" for assets, and so on); the second digit is to indicate the subclassification ("11" for current assets, and so on); and the third digit is to identify the specific account ("110" for Cash, and so on).

EX 5-13
Sales-related transactions, including the use of credit cards

obj. 3

Journalize the entries for the following transactions:

a. Sold merchandise for cash, $18,500. The cost of the merchandise sold was $11,000.
b. Sold merchandise on account, $12,000. The cost of the merchandise sold was $7,200.
c. Sold merchandise to customers who used MasterCard and VISA, $115,200. The cost of the merchandise sold was $70,000.
d. Sold merchandise to customers who used American Express, $45,000. The cost of the merchandise sold was $27,000.
e. Received an invoice from National Credit Co. for $5,600, representing a service fee paid for processing MasterCard, VISA, and American Express sales.

EX 5-14
Sales returns and allowances

obj. 3

During the year, sales returns and allowances totaled $65,900. The cost of the merchandise returned was $40,000. The accountant recorded all the returns and allowances by debiting the sales account and crediting Cost of Merchandise Sold for $65,900.
━━▶ Was the accountant's method of recording returns acceptable? Explain. In your explanation, include the advantages of using a sales returns and allowances account.

EX 5-15
Sales-related transactions

obj. 3

After the amount due on a sale of $25,000, terms 1/10, n/eom, is received from a customer within the discount period, the seller consents to the return of the entire shipment. The cost of the merchandise returned was $15,000. (a) What is the amount of the refund owed to the customer? (b) Journalize the entries made by the seller to record the return and the refund.

EX 5-16
Sales-related transactions

obj. 3

The debits and credits for three related transactions are presented in the following T accounts. Describe each transaction.

Cash					Sales		
(5)	17,640					(1)	20,000

Accounts Receivable					Sales Discounts		
(1)	20,000	(3)	2,000	(5)	360		
		(5)	18,000				

Merchandise Inventory					Sales Returns and Allowances		
(4)	1,000	(2)	12,000	(3)	2,000		

				Cost of Merchandise Sold			
				(2)	12,000	(4)	1,000

EX 5-17
Sales-related transactions

obj. 3

✔ d. $12,775

Merchandise is sold on account to a customer for $12,500, terms FOB shipping point, 1/10, n/30. The seller paid the freight of $400. Determine the following: (a) amount of the sale, (b) amount debited to Accounts Receivable, (c) amount of the discount for early payment, and (d) amount due within the discount period.

EX 5-18
Purchase-related transaction

obj. 3

Newgen Company purchased merchandise on account from a supplier for $9,000, terms 2/10, n/30. Newgen Company returned $1,200 of the merchandise and received full credit.

a. If Newgen Company pays the invoice within the discount period, what is the amount of cash required for the payment?
b. Under a perpetual inventory system, what account is credited by Newgen Company to record the return?

EX 5-19
Purchase-related transactions

obj. 3

A retailer is considering the purchase of 100 units of a specific item from either of two suppliers. Their offers are as follows:

A: $200 a unit, total of $20,000, 2/10, n/30, no charge for freight.
B: $195 a unit, total of $19,500, 1/10, n/30, plus freight of $400.

Which of the two offers, A or B, yields the lower price?

EX 5-20
Purchase-related transactions

obj. 3

The debits and credits from four related transactions are presented in the following T accounts. Describe each transaction.

Cash					Accounts Payable		
		(2)	250	(3)	500	(1)	8,000
		(4)	7,350	(4)	7,500		

Merchandise Inventory			
(1)	8,000	(3)	500
(2)	250	(4)	150

EX 5-21
Purchase-related
transactions

obj. 3

✔ (c) Cash, cr.
$14,700

Versailles Co., a women's clothing store, purchased $18,000 of merchandise from a supplier on account, terms FOB destination, 2/10, n/30. Versailles Co. returned $3,000 of the merchandise, receiving a credit memo, and then paid the amount due within the discount period. Journalize Versailles Co.'s entries to record (a) the purchase, (b) the merchandise return, and (c) the payment.

EX 5-22
Purchase-related
transactions

obj. 3

✔ (e) Cash, dr. $900

Journalize entries for the following related transactions of Westcoast Diagnostic Company:
a. Purchased $25,000 of merchandise from Presidio Co. on account, terms 2/10, n/30.
b. Paid the amount owed on the invoice within the discount period.
c. Discovered that $5,000 of the merchandise was defective and returned items, receiving credit.
d. Purchased $4,000 of merchandise from Presidio Co. on account, terms n/30.
e. Received a check for the balance owed from the return in (c), after deducting for the purchase in (d).

EX 5-23
Determining
amounts to be paid
on invoices

obj. 3

✔ a. $14,200

Determine the amount to be paid in full settlement of each of the following invoices, assuming that credit for returns and allowances was received prior to payment and that all invoices were paid within the discount period.

	Merchandise	Freight Paid by Seller		Returns and Allowances
a.	$15,000	—	FOB destination, n/30	$ 800
b.	10,000	$400	FOB shipping point, 2/10, n/30	1,200
c.	8,250	—	FOB shipping point, 1/10, n/30	750
d.	2,900	125	FOB shipping point, 2/10, n/30	400
e.	3,850	—	FOB destination, 2/10, n/30	—

EX 5-24
Sales tax

obj. 3

✔ c. $14,850

A sale of merchandise on account for $13,750 is subject to an 8% sales tax. (a) Should the sales tax be recorded at the time of sale or when payment is received? (b) What is the amount of the sale? (c) What is the amount debited to Accounts Receivable? (d) What is the title of the account to which the $1,100 ($13,750 × 8%) is credited?

EX 5-25
Sales tax
transactions

obj. 3

Journalize the entries to record the following selected transactions:
a. Sold $3,400 of merchandise on account, subject to a sales tax of 5%. The cost of the merchandise sold was $2,000.
b. Paid $41,950 to the state sales tax department for taxes collected.

EX 5-26
Sales-related
transactions

obj. 3

Summit Co., a furniture wholesaler, sells merchandise to Bitone Co. on account, $23,400, terms 2/10, n/30. The cost of the merchandise sold is $14,000. Summit Co. issues a credit memo for $4,400 for merchandise returned and subsequently receives the amount due within the discount period. The cost of the merchandise returned is $2,600. Journalize Summit Co.'s entries for (a) the sale, including the cost of the merchandise sold, (b) the credit memo, including the cost of the returned merchandise, and (c) the receipt of the check for the amount due from Bitone Co.

EX 5-27
Purchase-related
transactions

obj. 3

Based on the data presented in Exercise 5-26, journalize Bitone Co.'s entries for (a) the purchase, (b) the return of the merchandise for credit, and (c) the payment of the invoice within the discount period.

EX 5-28
Normal balances
of merchandise
accounts

obj. 3

What is the normal balance of the following accounts: (a) Cost of Merchandise Sold, (b) Delivery Expense, (c) Merchandise Inventory, (d) Sales, (e) Sales Discounts, (f) Sales Returns and Allowances, (g) Sales Tax Payable?

EX 5-29
Adjusting entry for merchandise inventory shrinkage
obj. 4

Iverson Tile Co.'s perpetual inventory records indicate that $675,150 of merchandise should be on hand on December 31, 2010. The physical inventory indicates that $649,780 of merchandise is actually on hand. Journalize the adjusting entry for the inventory shrinkage for Iverson Tile Co. for the year ended December 31, 2010.

EX 5-30
Closing the accounts of a merchandiser
obj. 4

From the following list, identify the accounts that should be closed to Income Summary at the end of the fiscal year under a perpetual inventory system: (a) Accounts Payable, (b) Advertising Expense, (c) Cost of Merchandise Sold, (d) Dividends, (e) Merchandise Inventory, (f) Sales, (g) Sales Discounts, (h) Sales Returns and Allowances, (i) Supplies, (j) Supplies Expense, (k) Wages Payable.

EX 5-31
Closing entries; net income
obj. 4

Based on the data presented in Exercise 5-11, journalize the closing entries.

EX 5-32
Closing entries
obj. 4

On May 31, 2010, the balances of the accounts appearing in the ledger of Champion Interiors Company, a furniture wholesaler, are as follows:

Accumulated Depr.—Building	$ 30,460	Retained Earnings	$116,155
Administrative Expenses	65,300	Salaries Payable	680
Building	55,680	Sales	313,540
Capital Stock	25,000	Sales Discounts	18,000
Cash	8,840	Sales Returns and Allow.	12,000
Cost of Merchandise Sold	188,000	Sales Tax Payable	4,900
Dividends	7,950	Selling Expenses	124,000
Interest Expense	1,920	Store Supplies	4,580
Merchandise Inventory	26,000	Store Supplies Expenses	2,465
Notes Payable	24,000		

Prepare the May 31, 2010, closing entries for Champion Interiors Company.

Appendix
EX 5-33
Accounts for periodic and perpetual inventory systems

Indicate which of the following accounts would be included in the chart of accounts of a merchandising company using either the (a) periodic inventory system or (b) perpetual inventory system. If the account would be included in the chart of accounts of a company using the periodic and perpetual systems, indicate (c) for both.

(1)	Cost of Merchandise Sold	(6)	Purchases Returns and Allowances
(2)	Delivery Expense	(7)	Sales
(3)	Merchandise Inventory	(8)	Sales Discounts
(4)	Purchases	(9)	Sales Returns and Allowances
(5)	Purchases Discounts	(10)	Freight In

Appendix
EX 5-34
Rules of debit and credit for periodic inventory accounts

Complete the following table by indicating for (a) through (g) whether the proper answer is debit or credit.

Account	Increase	Decrease	Normal Balance
Purchases	debit	(a)	(b)
Purchases Discounts	(c)	debit	credit
Purchases Returns and Allowances	credit	(d)	(e)
Freight In	(f)	credit	(g)

Appendix
EX 5-35
Journal entries using the periodic inventory system

The following selected transactions were completed by Artic Company during February of the current year. Artic Company uses the periodic inventory system.

Feb. 2.   Purchased $17,500 of merchandise on account, FOB shipping point, terms 2/15, n/30.

Feb. 5. Paid freight of $300 on the February 2 purchase.
6. Returned $2,000 of the merchandise purchased on February 2.
13. Sold merchandise on account, $9,000, FOB destination, 2/10, n/30. The cost of merchandise sold was $6,600.
15. Paid freight of $100 for the merchandise sold on February 13.
17. Paid for the purchase of February 2 less the return and discount.
23. Received payment on account for the sale of February 13 less the discount.

Journalize the entries to record the transactions of Artic Company.

**Appendix
EX 5-36**
Journal entries using perpetual inventory system

Using the data shown in Exercise 5-35, journalize the entries for the transactions assuming that Artic Company uses the perpetual inventory system.

**Appendix
EX 5-37**
Closing entries using periodic inventory system

Aladdin Company is a small rug retailer owned and operated by Lin Endsley. After the accounts have been adjusted on October 31, the following account balances were taken from the ledger:

Advertising Expense	$ 16,500
Depreciation Expense	4,000
Dividends	30,000
Freight In	8,000
Merchandise Inventory, October 1	43,800
Merchandise Inventory, October 31	35,750
Miscellaneous Expense	1,750
Purchases	560,000
Purchases Discounts	12,000
Purchases Returns and Allowances	6,000
Salaries Expense	80,000
Sales	890,000
Sales Discounts	5,000
Sales Returns and Allowances	10,000

Journalize the closing entries on October 31.

EX 5-38
Ratio of net sales to total assets

The Home Depot reported the following data (in millions) in its financial statements:

	2007	2006
Net sales	$90,837	$81,511
Total assets at the end of the year	52,263	44,482
Total assets at the beginning of the year	44,482	38,907

a. Determine the ratio of net sales to average total assets for The Home Depot for 2007 and 2006. Round to two decimal places.
b. What conclusions can be drawn from these ratios concerning the trend in the ability of The Home Depot to effectively use its assets to generate sales?

EX 5-39
Ratio of net sales to total assets

Kroger, a national supermarket chain, reported the following data (in millions) in its financial statements for 2007:

Total revenue	$66,111
Total assets at end of year	21,215
Total assets at beginning of year	20,482

a. Compute the ratio of net sales to assets for 2007. Round to two decimal places.
b. Would you expect the ratio of net sales to assets for Kroger to be similar to or different from that of Tiffany & Co.? Tiffany is the large North American retailer of jewelry, with a ratio of net sales to average total assets of 0.94.

Problems Series A

PR 5-1A

Multiple-step income statement and report form of balance sheet

obj. 2

✔ 1. Net income: $120,000

The following selected accounts and their current balances appear in the ledger of Case-It Co. for the fiscal year ended November 30, 2010:

Cash	$ 37,700	Sales	$2,703,600
Accounts Receivable	111,600	Sales Returns and Allowances	37,800
Merchandise Inventory	180,000	Sales Discounts	19,800
Office Supplies	5,000	Cost of Merchandise Sold	1,926,000
Prepaid Insurance	12,000	Sales Salaries Expense	378,000
Office Equipment	115,200	Advertising Expense	50,900
Accumulated Depreciation—		Depreciation Expense—	
Office Equipment	49,500	Store Equipment	8,300
Store Equipment	311,500	Miscellaneous Selling Expense	2,000
Accumulated Depreciation—		Office Salaries Expense	73,800
Store Equipment	87,500	Rent Expense	39,900
Accounts Payable	48,600	Insurance Expense	22,950
Salaries Payable	3,600	Depreciation Expense—	
Note Payable		Office Equipment	16,200
(final payment due 2025)	54,000	Office Supplies Expense	1,650
Capital Stock	50,000	Miscellaneous Administrative	
Retained Earnings	404,800	Expense	1,900
Dividends	45,000	Interest Expense	4,400

Instructions

1. Prepare a multiple-step income statement.
2. Prepare a retained earnings statement.
3. Prepare a report form of balance sheet, assuming that the current portion of the note payable is $8,000.
4. Briefly explain (a) how multiple-step and single-step income statements differ and (b) how report-form and account-form balance sheets differ.

PR 5-2A

Single-step income statement and account form of balance sheet

objs. 2, 4

✔ 3. Total assets: $636,000

Selected accounts and related amounts for Case-It Co. for the fiscal year ended November 30, 2010, are presented in Problem 5-1A.

Instructions

1. Prepare a single-step income statement in the format shown in Exhibit 3.
2. Prepare a retained earnings statement.
3. Prepare an account form of balance sheet, assuming that the current portion of the note payable is $8,000.
4. Prepare closing entries as of November 30, 2010.

PR 5-3A

Sales-related transactions

obj. 3

The following selected transactions were completed by Rayne Supplies Co., which sells irrigation supplies primarily to wholesalers and occasionally to retail customers:

Aug. 1. Sold merchandise on account to Tomahawk Co., $12,500, terms FOB shipping point, n/eom. The cost of merchandise sold was $7,500.

2. Sold merchandise for $20,000 plus 7% sales tax to retail cash customers. The cost of merchandise sold was $13,100.

5. Sold merchandise on account to Epworth Company, $30,000, terms FOB destination, 1/10, n/30. The cost of merchandise sold was $19,500.

8. Sold merchandise for $11,500 plus 7% sales tax to retail customers who used VISA cards. The cost of merchandise sold was $7,000.

13. Sold merchandise to customers who used MasterCard cards, $8,000. The cost of merchandise sold was $5,000.

Aug. 14. Sold merchandise on account to Osgood Co., $11,800, terms FOB shipping point, 1/10, n/30. The cost of merchandise sold was $7,000.

15. Received check for amount due from Epworth Company for sale on August 5.

16. Issued credit memo for $1,800 to Osgood Co. for merchandise returned from sale on August 14. The cost of the merchandise returned was $1,000.

18. Sold merchandise on account to Horton Company, $6,850, terms FOB shipping point, 2/10, n/30. Paid $210 for freight and added it to the invoice. The cost of merchandise sold was $4,100.

24. Received check for amount due from Osgood Co. for sale on August 14 less credit memo of August 16 and discount.

28. Received check for amount due from Horton Company for sale of August 18.

31. Paid Piper Delivery Service $2,100 for merchandise delivered during August to customers under shipping terms of FOB destination.

31. Received check for amount due from Tomahawk Co. for sale of August 1.

Sept. 3. Paid First Federal Bank $980 for service fees for handling MasterCard and VISA sales during August.

10. Paid $1,750 to state sales tax division for taxes owed on sales.

Instructions
Journalize the entries to record the transactions of Rayne Supplies Co.

PR 5-4A
Purchase-related transactions

obj. 3

The following selected transactions were completed by Padre Co. during October of the current year:

Oct. 1. Purchased merchandise from Wood Co., $15,500, terms FOB shipping point, 2/10, n/eom. Prepaid freight of $400 was added to the invoice.

5. Purchased merchandise from Davis Co., $14,150, terms FOB destination, n/30.

10. Paid Wood Co. for invoice of October 1, less discount.

13. Purchased merchandise from Folts Co., $8,000, terms FOB destination, 1/10, n/30.

14. Issued debit memo to Folts Co. for $1,500 of merchandise returned from purchase on October 13.

18. Purchased merchandise from Lakey Company, $12,250, terms FOB shipping point, n/eom.

18. Paid freight of $180 on October 18 purchase from Lakey Company.

19. Purchased merchandise from Noman Co., $11,150, terms FOB destination, 2/10, n/30.

23. Paid Folts Co. for invoice of October 13, less debit memo of October 14 and discount.

29. Paid Noman Co. for invoice of October 19, less discount.

31. Paid Lakey Company for invoice of October 18.

31. Paid Davis Co. for invoice of October 5.

Instructions
Journalize the entries to record the transactions of Padre Co. for October.

PR 5-5A
Sales-related and purchase-related transactions

obj. 3

The following were selected from among the transactions completed by Sandusky Company during December of the current year:

Dec. 3. Purchased merchandise on account from Hillsboro Co., list price $38,000, trade discount 25%, terms FOB shipping point, 2/10, n/30, with prepaid freight of $900 added to the invoice.

5. Purchased merchandise on account from Deepwater Co., $18,750, terms FOB destination, 2/10, n/30.

Dec. 6. Sold merchandise on account to Zion Co., list price $27,000, trade discount 35%, terms 2/10, n/30. The cost of the merchandise sold was $14,000.

7. Returned $3,000 of merchandise purchased on December 5 from Deepwater Co.

13. Paid Hillsboro Co. on account for purchase of December 3, less discount.

15. Paid Deepwater Co. on account for purchase of December 5, less return of December 7 and discount.

16. Received cash on account from sale of December 6 to Zion Co., less discount.

19. Sold merchandise on MasterCard, $58,000. The cost of the merchandise sold was $34,800.

22. Sold merchandise on account to Smith River Co., $15,400, terms 2/10, n/30. The cost of the merchandise sold was $9,000.

23. Sold merchandise for cash, $33,600. The cost of the merchandise sold was $20,000.

28. Received merchandise returned by Smith River Co. from sale on December 22, $2,400. The cost of the returned merchandise was $1,400.

31. Paid MasterCard service fee of $1,750.

Instructions

Journalize the transactions.

PR 5-6A
Sales-related and purchase-related transactions for seller and buyer

obj. 3

The following selected transactions were completed during November between Sycamore Company and Bonita Company:

Nov. 2. Sycamore Company sold merchandise on account to Bonita Company, $16,000, terms FOB shipping point, 2/10, n/30. Sycamore Company paid freight of $375, which was added to the invoice. The cost of the merchandise sold was $10,000.

8. Sycamore Company sold merchandise on account to Bonita Company, $24,750, terms FOB destination, 1/15, n/eom. The cost of the merchandise sold was $14,850.

8. Sycamore Company paid freight of $640 for delivery of merchandise sold to Bonita Company on November 8.

12. Bonita Company returned $5,750 of merchandise purchased on account on November 8 from Sycamore Company. The cost of the merchandise returned was $3,000.

12. Bonita Company paid Sycamore Company for purchase of November 2, less discount.

23. Bonita Company paid Sycamore Company for purchase of November 8, less discount and less return of November 12.

24. Sycamore Company sold merchandise on account to Bonita Company, $13,200, terms FOB shipping point, n/eom. The cost of the merchandise sold was $8,000.

26. Bonita Company paid freight of $290 on November 24 purchase from Sycamore Company.

30. Bonita Company paid Sycamore Company on account for purchase of November 24.

Instructions

Journalize the November transactions for (1) Sycamore Company and (2) Bonita Company.

Appendix
PR 5-7A
Purchase-related transactions using periodic inventory system

Selected transactions for Padre Co. during October of the current year are listed in Problem 5-4A.

Instructions

Journalize the entries to record the transactions of Padre Co. for October using the periodic inventory system.

Appendix
PR 5-8A
Sales-related and purchase-related transactions using periodic inventory system

Selected transactions for Sandusky Company during December of the current year are listed in Problem 5-5A.

Instructions

Journalize the entries to record the transactions of Sandusky Company for December using the periodic inventory system.

Appendix
PR 5-9A
Sales-related and purchase-related transactions for buyer and seller using periodic inventory system

Selected transactions during November between Sycamore Company and Bonita Company are listed in Problem 5-6A.

Instructions

Journalize the entries to record the transactions for (1) Sycamore Company and (2) Bonita Company assuming that both companies use the periodic inventory system.

Appendix
PR 5-10A
Periodic inventory accounts, multiple-step income statement, closing entries

obj. 2

✔ 2 Net income, $362,600

On June 30, 2010, the balances of the accounts appearing in the ledger of Andover Company are as follows:

Cash	$ 36,600	Sales Discounts	$ 18,750
Accounts Receivable	144,250	Purchases	1,073,000
Merchandise Inventory, July 1, 2009	175,450	Purchases Returns and Allowances	12,000
Office Supplies	6,050	Purchases Discounts	9,000
Prepaid Insurance	9,000	Freight In	21,800
Land	70,000	Sales Salaries Expense	312,500
Store Equipment	341,550	Advertising Expense	110,000
Accumulated Depreciation—		Delivery Expense	18,000
Store Equipment	11,800	Depreciation Expense—	
Office Equipment	157,000	Store Equipment	11,800
Accumulated Depreciation—		Miscellaneous Selling Expense	21,400
Office Equipment	32,500	Office Salaries Expense	200,000
Accounts Payable	55,650	Rent Expense	62,500
Salaries Payable	5,900	Insurance Expense	6,000
Unearned Rent	16,600	Office Supplies Expense	4,600
Notes Payable	25,000	Depreciation Expense—	
Capital Stock	90,000	Office Equipment	3,000
Retained Earnings	290,100	Miscellaneous Administrative Expense	11,700
Dividends	37,500	Rent Revenue	12,500
Sales	2,212,900	Interest Expense	1,500
Sales Returns and Allowances	20,000		

Instructions

1. Does Andover Company use a periodic or perpetual inventory system? Explain.
2. Prepare a multiple-step income statement for Andover Company for the year ended June 30, 2010. The merchandise inventory as of June 30, 2010, was $188,200.
3. Prepare the closing entries for Andover Company as of June 30, 2010.

Problems Series B

PR 5-1B
Multiple-step income statement and report form of balance sheet
obj. 2

✔ 1. Net income: $300,000

The following selected accounts and their current balances appear in the ledger of Drapery Land Co. for the fiscal year ended July 31, 2010:

Cash	$161,250	Sales	$3,855,000
Accounts Receivable	363,000	Sales Returns and Allowances	69,300
Merchandise Inventory	525,000	Sales Discounts	65,700
Office Supplies	16,800	Cost of Merchandise Sold	2,325,000
Prepaid Insurance	10,200	Sales Salaries Expense	519,600
Office Equipment	255,000	Advertising Expense	131,400
Accumulated Depreciation—		Depreciation Expense—	
Office Equipment	138,400	Store Equipment	19,200
Store Equipment	759,000	Miscellaneous Selling Expense	4,800
Accumulated Depreciation—		Office Salaries Expense	252,450
Store Equipment	102,600	Rent Expense	94,050
Accounts Payable	166,800	Depreciation Expense—	
Salaries Payable	7,200	Office Equipment	38,100
Note Payable		Insurance Expense	11,700
(final payment due 2020)	168,000	Office Supplies Expense	3,200
Capital Stock	500,000	Miscellaneous Administrative	
Retained Earnings	812,250	Expense	5,500
Dividends	105,000	Interest Expense	15,000

Instructions
1. Prepare a multiple-step income statement.
2. Prepare a retained earnings statement.
3. Prepare a report form of balance sheet, assuming that the current portion of the note payable is $16,800.
4. Briefly explain (a) how multiple-step and single-step income statements differ and (b) how report-form and account-form balance sheets differ.

PR 5-2B
Single-step income statement and account form of balance sheet
objs. 2, 4

✔ 3. Total assets: $1,849,250

Selected accounts and related amounts for Drapery Land Co. for the fiscal year ended July 31, 2010, are presented in Problem 5-1B.

Instructions
1. Prepare a single-step income statement in the format shown in Exhibit 3.
2. Prepare a retained earnings statement.
3. Prepare an account form of balance sheet, assuming that the current portion of the note payable is $16,800.
4. Prepare closing entries as of July 31, 2010.

PR 5-3B
Sales-related transactions
obj. 3

The following selected transactions were completed by Yukon Supply Co., which sells office supplies primarily to wholesalers and occasionally to retail customers:

Jan. 2. Sold merchandise on account to Oakley Co., $8,000, terms FOB destination, 1/10, n/30. The cost of the merchandise sold was $4,500.
3. Sold merchandise for $21,800 plus 8% sales tax to retail cash customers. The cost of merchandise sold was $13,000.
4. Sold merchandise on account to Rawlins Co., $7,500, terms FOB shipping point, n/eom. The cost of merchandise sold was $4,200.
5. Sold merchandise for $10,000 plus 8% sales tax to retail customers who used MasterCard. The cost of merchandise sold was $6,000.
12. Received check for amount due from Oakley Co. for sale on January 2.
14. Sold merchandise to customers who used American Express cards, $6,000. The cost of merchandise sold was $3,200.

Jan. 16. Sold merchandise on account to Keystone Co., $16,500, terms FOB shipping point, 1/10, n/30. The cost of merchandise sold was $10,000.

18. Issued credit memo for $2,000 to Keystone Co. for merchandise returned from sale on January 16. The cost of the merchandise returned was $1,200.

19. Sold merchandise on account to Cooney Co., $15,750, terms FOB shipping point, 2/10, n/30. Added $400 to the invoice for prepaid freight. The cost of merchandise sold was $9,500.

26. Received check for amount due from Keystone Co. for sale on January 16 less credit memo of January 18 and discount.

28. Received check for amount due from Cooney Co. for sale of January 19.

31. Received check for amount due from Rawlins Co. for sale of January 4.

31. Paid Black Hawk Delivery Service $3,875 for merchandise delivered during January to customers under shipping terms of FOB destination.

Feb. 3. Paid City Bank $1,150 for service fees for handling MasterCard and American Express sales during January.

15. Paid $3,600 to state sales tax division for taxes owed on sales.

Instructions

Journalize the entries to record the transactions of Yukon Supply Co.

PR 5-4B
Purchase-related transactions

obj. 3

The following selected transactions were completed by Silvertree Company during January of the current year:

Jan. 1. Purchased merchandise from Guinn Co., $13,600, terms FOB destination, n/30.

3. Purchased merchandise from Cybernet Co., $18,000, terms FOB shipping point, 2/10, n/eom. Prepaid freight of $300 was added to the invoice.

4. Purchased merchandise from Berry Co., $22,000, terms FOB destination, 2/10, n/30.

6. Issued debit memo to Berry Co. for $3,500 of merchandise returned from purchase on January 4.

13. Paid Cybernet Co. for invoice of January 3, less discount.

14. Paid Berry Co. for invoice of January 4, less debit memo of January 6 and discount.

19. Purchased merchandise from Cleghorne Co., $18,000, terms FOB shipping point, n/eom.

19. Paid freight of $500 on January 19 purchase from Cleghorne Co.

20. Purchased merchandise from Lenn Co., $10,000, terms FOB destination, 1/10, n/30.

30. Paid Lenn Co. for invoice of January 20, less discount.

31. Paid Guinn Co. for invoice of January 1.

31. Paid Cleghorne Co. for invoice of January 19.

Instructions

Journalize the entries to record the transactions of Silvertree Company for January.

PR 5-5B
Sales-related and purchase-related transactions

obj. 3

The following were selected from among the transactions completed by Calworks Company during April of the current year:

Apr. 3. Purchased merchandise on account from Prescott Co., list price $42,000, trade discount 40%, terms FOB destination, 2/10, n/30.

4. Sold merchandise for cash, $18,200. The cost of the merchandise sold was $11,000.

5. Purchased merchandise on account from Stafford Co., $21,300, terms FOB shipping point, 2/10, n/30, with prepaid freight of $600 added to the invoice.

6. Returned $6,000 of merchandise purchased on April 3 from Prescott Co.

11. Sold merchandise on account to Logan Co., list price $8,500, trade discount 20%, terms 1/10, n/30. The cost of the merchandise sold was $4,500.

13. Paid Prescott Co. on account for purchase of April 3, less return of April 6 and discount.

14. Sold merchandise on VISA, $60,000. The cost of the merchandise sold was $36,000.

Apr. 15. Paid Stafford Co. on account for purchase of April 5, less discount.

21. Received cash on account from sale of April 11 to Logan Co., less discount.

24. Sold merchandise on account to Alma Co., $9,200, terms 1/10, n/30. The cost of the merchandise sold was $5,500.

28. Paid VISA service fee of $1,800.

30. Received merchandise returned by Alma Co. from sale on April 24, $1,200. The cost of the returned merchandise was $720.

Instructions
Journalize the transactions.

PR 5-6B
Sales-related and purchase-related transactions for seller and buyer

obj. 3

The following selected transactions were completed during August between Salem Company and Boulder Co.:

Aug. 1. Salem Company sold merchandise on account to Boulder Co., $28,600, terms FOB destination, 2/15, n/eom. The cost of the merchandise sold was $17,000.

2. Salem Company paid freight of $500 for delivery of merchandise sold to Boulder Co. on August 1.

5. Salem Company sold merchandise on account to Boulder Co., $18,000, terms FOB shipping point, n/eom. The cost of the merchandise sold was $10,800.

6. Boulder Co. returned $1,600 of merchandise purchased on account on August 1 from Salem Company. The cost of the merchandise returned was $960.

9. Boulder Co. paid freight of $350 on August 5 purchase from Salem Company.

15. Salem Company sold merchandise on account to Boulder Co., $36,200, terms FOB shipping point, 1/10, n/30. Salem Company paid freight of $900, which was added to the invoice. The cost of the merchandise sold was $19,600.

16. Boulder Co. paid Salem Company for purchase of August 1, less discount and less return of August 6.

25. Boulder Co. paid Salem Company on account for purchase of August 15, less discount.

31. Boulder Co. paid Salem Company on account for purchase of August 5.

Instructions
Journalize the August transactions for (1) Salem Company and (2) Boulder Co.

Appendix PR 5-7B
Purchase-related transactions using periodic inventory system

Selected transactions for Silvertree Company during January of the current year are listed in Problem 5-4B.

Instructions
Journalize the entries to record the transactions of Silvertree Company for January using the periodic inventory system.

Appendix PR 5-8B
Sales-related and purchase-related transactions using periodic inventory system

Selected transactions for Calworks Company during April of the current year are listed in Problem 5-5B.

Instructions
Journalize the entries to record the transactions of Calworks Company for April using the periodic inventory system.

Appendix PR 5-9B
Sales-related and purchase-related transactions for buyer and seller using periodic inventory system

Selected transactions during August between Salem Company and Boulder Co. are listed in Problem 5-6B.

Instructions
Journalize the entries to record the transactions for (1) Salem Company and (2) Boulder Co. assuming that both companies use the periodic inventory system.

**Appendix
PR 5-10B**
Periodic inventory ac-
counts, multiple-step
income statement,
closing entries

✔ 2 Net income,
$181,350

On October 31, 2010, the balances of the accounts appearing in the ledger of Triple Creek Company are as follows:

Cash	$ 18,300	Sales Returns and Allowances	$ 10,000
Accounts Receivable	72,000	Sales Discounts	9,300
Merchandise Inventory,		Purchases	536,500
November 1, 2009	87,700	Purchases Returns and Allowances	6,000
Office Supplies	3,000	Purchases Discounts	4,500
Prepaid Insurance	4,500	Freight In	10,900
Land	35,000	Sales Salaries Expense	156,250
Store Equipment	170,000	Advertising Expense	55,000
Accum. Depr.—Store Equip.	55,900	Delivery Expense	9,000
Office Equipment	78,500	Depr. Expense—Store Equip.	5,900
Accum. Depr.—Office Equip.	16,250	Miscellaneous Selling Expense	10,700
Accounts Payable	27,800	Office Salaries Expense	100,000
Salaries Payable	3,000	Rent Expense	31,250
Unearned Rent	8,300	Insurance Expense	3,000
Notes Payable	12,500	Office Supplies Expense	2,300
Capital Stock	75,000	Depr. Expense—Office Equip.	1,500
Retained Earnings	114,050	Miscellaneous Administrative Expense	5,850
Dividends	18,750	Rent Revenue	6,250
Sales	1,106,400	Interest Expense	750

Instructions
1. Does Triple Creek Company use a periodic or perpetual inventory system? Explain.
2. Prepare a multiple-step income statement for Triple Creek Company for the year ended October 31, 2010. The merchandise inventory as of October 31, 2010, was $94,100.
3. Prepare the closing entries for Triple Creek Company as of October 31, 2010.

Comprehensive Problem 2

✔ 8. Net income:
$693,800

South Coast Boards Co. is a merchandising business. The account balances for South Coast Boards Co. as of July 1, 2010 (unless otherwise indicated), are as follows:

110	Cash	$ 63,600	410	Sales	$3,221,100
112	Accounts Receivable	153,900	411	Sales Returns & Allowances	92,700
115	Merchandise Inventory	602,400	412	Sales Discounts	59,400
116	Prepaid Insurance	16,800	510	Cost of Merchandise Sold	1,623,000
117	Store Supplies	11,400	520	Sales Salaries Expense	334,800
123	Store Equipment	469,500	521	Advertising Expense	81,000
124	Accum. Depr.—Store Equip.	56,700	522	Depreciation Expense	—
210	Accounts Payable	96,600	523	Store Supplies Expense	—
211	Salaries Payable	—	529	Misc. Selling Expense	12,600
310	Capital Stock	100,000	530	Office Salaries Expense	182,100
311	Retained Earnings, Aug. 1, 2009	455,300	531	Rent Expense	83,700
312	Dividends	135,000	532	Insurance Expense	—
313	Income Summary	—	539	Misc. Administrative Expense	7,800

During July, the last month of the fiscal year, the following transactions were completed:

July 1. Paid rent for July, $5,000.
   3. Purchased merchandise on account from Belmont Co., terms 2/10, n/30, FOB shipping point, $40,000.
   4. Paid freight on purchase of July 3, $600.
   6. Sold merchandise on account to Modesto Co., terms 2/10, n/30, FOB shipping point, $25,000. The cost of the merchandise sold was $15,000.
   7. Received $26,500 cash from Yuba Co. on account, no discount.
   10. Sold merchandise for cash, $80,000. The cost of the merchandise sold was $50,000.
   13. Paid for merchandise purchased on July 3, less discount.
   14. Received merchandise returned on sale of July 6, $6,000. The cost of the merchandise returned was $4,500.
   15. Paid advertising expense for last half of July, $7,500.
   16. Received cash from sale of July 6, less return of July 14 and discount.

July 19. Purchased merchandise for cash, $36,000.

19. Paid $18,000 to Bakke Co. on account, no discount.

20. Sold merchandise on account to Reedley Co., terms 1/10, n/30, FOB shipping point, $40,000. The cost of the merchandise sold was $25,000.

21. For the convenience of the customer, paid freight on sale of July 20, $1,100.

21. Received $17,600 cash from Owen Co. on account, no discount.

21. Purchased merchandise on account from Nye Co., terms 1/10, n/30, FOB destination, $20,000.

24. Returned $2,000 of damaged merchandise purchased on July 21, receiving credit from the seller.

26. Refunded cash on sales made for cash, $3,000. The cost of the merchandise returned was $1,800.

28. Paid sales salaries of $22,800 and office salaries of $15,200.

29. Purchased store supplies for cash, $2,400.

30. Sold merchandise on account to Whitetail Co., terms 2/10, n/30, FOB shipping point, $18,750. The cost of the merchandise sold was $11,250.

30. Received cash from sale of July 20, less discount, plus freight paid on July 21.

31. Paid for purchase of July 21, less return of July 24 and discount.

Instructions

1. Enter the balances of each of the accounts in the appropriate balance column of a four-column account. Write *Balance* in the item section, and place a check mark (✓) in the Posting Reference column. Journalize the transactions for July.

2. Post the journal to the general ledger, extending the month-end balances to the appropriate balance columns after all posting is completed. In this problem, you are not required to update or post to the accounts receivable and accounts payable subsidiary ledgers.

3. Prepare an unadjusted trial balance.

4. At the end of July, the following adjustment data were assembled. Analyze and use these data to complete (5) and (6).

a. Merchandise inventory on July 31		$589,850
b. Insurance expired during the year		12,500
c. Store supplies on hand on July 31		4,700
d. Depreciation for the current year		18,800
e. Accrued salaries on July 31:		
Sales salaries	$4,400	
Office salaries	2,700	7,100

5. **Optional:** Enter the unadjusted trial balance on a 10-column end-of-period spreadsheet (work sheet), and complete the spreadsheet. See Appendix D for how to prepare an end-of-period spreadsheet (work sheet) for a merchandising business.

6. Journalize and post the adjusting entries.

7. Prepare an adjusted trial balance.

8. Prepare an income statement, a retained earnings statement, and a balance sheet.

9. Prepare and post the closing entries. Indicate closed accounts by inserting a line in both the Balance columns opposite the closing entry. Insert the new balance in the retained earnings account.

10. Prepare a post-closing trial balance.

Special Activities

SA 5-1

Ethics and professional conduct in business

On February 15, 2010, Tropical Connection Company, a garden retailer, purchased $25,000 of seed, terms 2/10, n/30, from Midwest Seed Co. Even though the discount period had expired, Lydia DeLay subtracted the discount of $500 when she processed the documents for payment on March 16, 2010.

━━━━► Discuss whether Lydia DeLay behaved in a professional manner by subtracting the discount, even though the discount period had expired.

SA 5-2
Purchases discounts and accounts payable

The Encore Video Store Co. is owned and operated by Sergio Alonzo. The following is an excerpt from a conversation between Sergio Alonzo and Suzie Engel, the chief accountant for The Encore Video Store.

Sergio: Suzie, I've got a question about this recent balance sheet.

Suzie: Sure, what's your question?

Sergio: Well, as you know, I'm applying for a bank loan to finance our new store in Cherokee, and I noticed that the accounts payable are listed as $120,000.

Suzie: That's right. Approximately $100,000 of that represents amounts due our suppliers, and the remainder is miscellaneous payables to creditors for utilities, office equipment, supplies, etc.

Sergio: That's what I thought. But as you know, we normally receive a 2% discount from our suppliers for earlier payment, and we always try to take the discount.

Suzie: That's right. I can't remember the last time we missed a discount.

Sergio: Well, in that case, it seems to me the accounts payable should be listed minus the 2% discount. Let's list the accounts payable due suppliers as $98,000, rather than $100,000. Every little bit helps. You never know. It might make the difference between getting the loan and not.

➤ How would you respond to Sergio Alonzo's request?

SA 5-3
Determining cost of purchase

The following is an excerpt from a conversation between Ted Mackie and Laurie Van Dorn. Ted is debating whether to buy a stereo system from Classic Audio, a locally owned electronics store, or Sound Unlimited, an online electronics company.

Ted: Laurie, I don't know what to do about buying my new stereo.

Laurie: What's the problem?

Ted: Well, I can buy it locally at Classic Audio for $490.00. However, Sound Unlimited has the same system listed for $499.99.

Laurie: So what's the big deal? Buy it from Classic Audio.

Ted: It's not quite that simple. Sound Unlimited said something about not having to pay sales tax, since I was out of state.

Laurie: Yes, that's a good point. If you buy it at Classic Audio, they'll charge you 6% sales tax.

Ted: But Sound Unlimited charges $13.99 for shipping and handling. If I have them send it next-day air, it'll cost $24.99 for shipping and handling.

Laurie: I guess it is a little confusing.

Ted: That's not all. Classic Audio will give an additional 1% discount if I pay cash. Otherwise, they will let me use my VISA, or I can pay it off in three monthly installments.

Laurie: Anything else???

Ted: Well . . . Sound Unlimited says I have to charge it on my VISA. They don't accept checks.

Laurie: I am not surprised. Many online stores don't accept checks.

Ted: I give up. What would you do?

1. Assuming that Sound Unlimited doesn't charge sales tax on the sale to Ted, which company is offering the best buy?
2. ➤ What might be some considerations other than price that might influence Ted's decision on where to buy the stereo system?

SA 5-4
Sales discounts

Your sister operates Ennis Parts Company, an online boat parts distributorship that is in its third year of operation. The income statement is shown at the top of the following page and was recently prepared for the year ended March 31, 2010.

　　Your sister is considering a proposal to increase net income by offering sales discounts of 2/15, n/30, and by shipping all merchandise FOB shipping point. Currently, no sales discounts are allowed and merchandise is shipped FOB destination. It is estimated that these credit terms will increase net sales by 15%. The ratio of the cost of merchandise sold to net sales is expected to be 65%. All selling and administrative expenses are expected to remain unchanged, except for store supplies, miscellaneous selling, office supplies, and miscellaneous administrative expenses, which are expected to increase proportionately with increased net sales. The amounts of these preceding items for the year ended March 31, 2010, were as follows:

Ennis Parts Company
Income Statement
For the Year Ended March 31, 2010

Revenues:		
Net sales		$400,000
Interest revenue		5,000
Total revenues		$405,000
Expenses:		
Cost of merchandise sold	$260,000	
Selling expenses	45,000	
Administrative expenses	24,275	
Interest expense	7,500	
Total expenses		336,775
Net income		$ 68,225

Store supplies expense	$6,000	Office supplies expense	$1,000
Miscellaneous selling expense	1,500	Miscellaneous administrative expense	500

The other income and other expense items will remain unchanged. The shipment of all merchandise FOB shipping point will eliminate all delivery expenses, which for the year ended March 31, 2010, were $9,375.

1. Prepare a projected single-step income statement for the year ending March 31, 2011, based on the proposal. Assume all sales are collected within the discount period.
2. a. ━━━━▶ Based on the projected income statement in (1), would you recommend the implementation of the proposed changes?
   b. Describe any possible concerns you may have related to the proposed changes described in (1).

SA 5-5
Shopping for a television

Group Project

Assume that you are planning to purchase a 50-inch plasma television. In groups of three or four, determine the lowest cost for the television, considering the available alternatives and the advantages and disadvantages of each alternative. For example, you could purchase locally, through mail order, or through an Internet shopping service. Consider such factors as delivery charges, interest-free financing, discounts, coupons, and availability of warranty services. Prepare a report for presentation to the class.

Answers to Self-Examination Questions ● ● ● ●❯

1. **A** A debit memo (answer A), issued by the buyer, indicates the amount the buyer proposes to debit to the accounts payable account. A credit memo (answer B), issued by the seller, indicates the amount the seller proposes to credit to the accounts receivable account. An invoice (answer C) or a bill (answer D), issued by the seller, indicates the amount and terms of the sale.

2. **C** The amount of discount for early payment is $10 (answer C), or 1% of $1,000. Although the $50 of freight paid by the seller is debited to the customer's account, the customer is not entitled to a discount on that amount.

3. **B** The single-step form of income statement (answer B) is so named because the total of all expenses is deducted in one step from the total of all revenues. The multiple-step form (answer A) includes numerous sections and subsections with several subtotals. The account form (answer C)

and the report form (answer D) are two common forms of the balance sheet.

4. **C** Gross profit (answer C) is the excess of net sales over the cost of merchandise sold. Operating income (answer A) or income from operations (answer B) is the excess of gross profit over operating expenses. Net income (answer D) is the final figure on the income statement after all revenues and expenses have been reported.

5. **D** Expenses such as interest expense (answer D) that cannot be associated directly with operations are identified as *other expense* or *nonoperating expense.* Depreciation expense—office equipment (answer A) is an administrative expense. Sales salaries expense (answer B) is a selling expense. Insurance expense (answer C) is a mixed expense with elements of both selling expense and administrative expense. For small businesses, insurance expense is usually reported as an administrative expense.

CHAPTER 6

Inventories

BEST BUY

Assume that in September you purchased a Philips HDTV plasma television from Best Buy. At the same time, you purchased a Sony surround sound system for $299.99. You liked your surround sound so well that in November you purchased an identical Sony system on sale for $249.99 for your bedroom TV. Over the holidays, you moved to a new apartment and in the process of unpacking discovered that one of the Sony surround sound systems was missing. Luckily, your renters/homeowners insurance policy will cover the theft, but the insurance company needs to know the cost of the system that was stolen.

The Sony systems were identical. However, to respond to the insurance company, you will need to identify which system was stolen. Was it the first system, which cost $299.99, or was it the second system, which cost $249.99? Whichever assumption you make may determine the amount that you receive from the insurance company.

Merchandising businesses such as Best Buy make similar assumptions when identical merchandise is purchased at different costs. For example, Best Buy may have purchased thousands of Sony surround sound systems over the past year at different costs. At the end of a period, some of the Sony systems will still be in inventory, and some will have been sold. But which costs relate to the sold systems, and which costs relate to the Sony systems still in inventory? Best Buy's assumption about inventory costs can involve large dollar amounts and, thus, can have a significant impact on the financial statements. For example, Best Buy reported $4,028 million of inventory on March 3, 2007, and net income of $1,377 million for the year.

In this chapter, we will discuss such issues as how to determine the cost of merchandise in inventory and the cost of merchandise sold. However, we begin this chapter by discussing the importance of control over inventory.

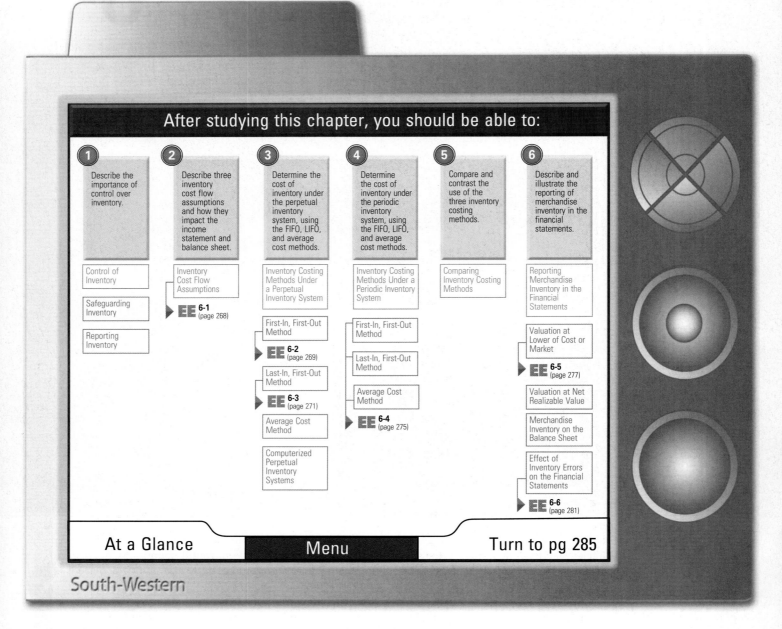

After studying this chapter, you should be able to:

1 Describe the importance of control over inventory.

2 Describe three inventory cost flow assumptions and how they impact the income statement and balance sheet.

3 Determine the cost of inventory under the perpetual inventory system, using the FIFO, LIFO, and average cost methods.

4 Determine the cost of inventory under the periodic inventory system, using the FIFO, LIFO, and average cost methods.

5 Compare and contrast the use of the three inventory costing methods.

6 Describe and illustrate the reporting of merchandise inventory in the financial statements.

Control of Inventory

Safeguarding Inventory

Reporting Inventory

Inventory Cost Flow Assumptions

EE 6-1 (page 268)

Inventory Costing Methods Under a Perpetual Inventory System

First-In, First-Out Method

EE 6-2 (page 269)

Last-In, First-Out Method

EE 6-3 (page 271)

Average Cost Method

Computerized Perpetual Inventory Systems

Inventory Costing Methods Under a Periodic Inventory System

First-In, First-Out Method

Last-In, First-Out Method

Average Cost Method

EE 6-4 (page 275)

Comparing Inventory Costing Methods

Reporting Merchandise Inventory in the Financial Statements

Valuation at Lower of Cost or Market

EE 6-5 (page 277)

Valuation at Net Realizable Value

Merchandise Inventory on the Balance Sheet

Effect of Inventory Errors on the Financial Statements

EE 6-6 (page 281)

At a Glance | Menu | Turn to pg 285

South-Western

 **1** Describe the importance of control over inventory.

Control of Inventory

Two primary objectives of control over inventory are as follows:[1]

1. Safeguarding the inventory from damage or theft.
2. Reporting inventory in the financial statements.

Safeguarding Inventory

Controls for safeguarding inventory begin as soon as the inventory is ordered. The following documents are often used for inventory control:

> Purchase order
> Receiving report
> Vendor's invoice

1 Additional controls used by businesses are described and illustrated in Chapter 7, "Sarbanes-Oxley, Internal Control, and Cash."

The **purchase order** authorizes the purchase of the inventory from an approved vendor. As soon as the inventory is received, a receiving report is completed. The **receiving report** establishes an initial record of the receipt of the inventory. To make sure the inventory received is what was ordered, the receiving report is compared with the company's purchase order. The price, quantity, and description of the item on the purchase order and receiving report are then compared to the vendor's invoice. If the receiving report, purchase order, and vendor's invoice agree, the inventory is recorded in the accounting records. If any differences exist, they should be investigated and reconciled.

Recording inventory using a perpetual inventory system is also an effective means of control. The amount of inventory is always available in the **inventory subsidiary ledger**. This helps keep inventory quantities at proper levels. For example, comparing inventory quantities with maximum and minimum levels allows for the timely reordering of inventory and prevents ordering excess inventory.

Finally, controls for safeguarding inventory should include security measures to prevent damage and customer or employee theft. Some examples of security measures include the following:

1. Storing inventory in areas that are restricted to only authorized employees.
2. Locking high-priced inventory in cabinets.
3. Using two-way mirrors, cameras, security tags, and guards.

Reporting Inventory

A **physical inventory** or count of inventory should be taken near year-end to make sure that the quantity of inventory reported in the financial statements is accurate. After the quantity of inventory on hand is determined, the cost of the inventory is assigned for reporting in the financial statements. Most companies assign costs to inventory using one of three inventory cost flow assumptions.

 2 Describe three inventory cost flow assumptions and how they impact the income statement and balance sheet.

Inventory Cost Flow Assumptions

An accounting issue arises when identical units of merchandise are acquired at different unit costs during a period. In such cases, when an item is sold, it is necessary to determine its cost using a cost flow assumption and related inventory cost flow method. Three common cost flow assumptions and related inventory cost flow methods are shown below.

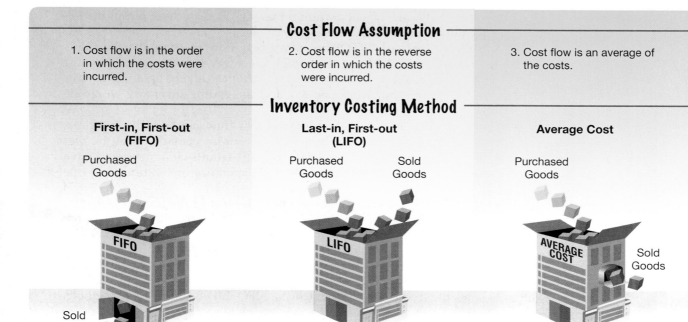

To illustrate, assume that three identical units of merchandise are purchased during May, as follows:

			Units	Cost
May	10	Purchase	1	$ 9
	18	Purchase	1	13
	24	Purchase	1	14
Total			3	$36

Average cost per unit: $12 ($36 ÷ 3 units)

Assume that one unit is sold on May 30 for $20. Depending upon which unit was sold, the gross profit varies from $11 to $6 as shown below.

	May 10 Unit Sold	May 18 Unit Sold	May 24 Unit Sold
Sales	$20	$20	$20
Cost of merchandise sold	9	13	14
Gross profit	$11	$ 7	$ 6
Ending inventory	$27	$23	$22
	($13 + $14)	($9 + $14)	($9 + $13)

The specific identification method is normally used by automobile dealerships, jewelry stores, and art galleries.

Under the **specific identification inventory cost flow method**, the unit sold is identified with a specific purchase. The ending inventory is made up of the remaining units on hand. Thus, the gross profit, cost of merchandise sold, and ending inventory can vary as shown above. For example, if the May 18 unit was sold, the cost of merchandise sold is $13, the gross profit is $7, and the ending inventory is $23.

The specific identification method is not practical unless each inventory unit can be separately identified. For example, an automobile dealer may use the specific identification method since each automobile has a unique serial number. However, most businesses cannot identify each inventory unit separately. In such cases, one of the following three inventory cost flow methods is used.

Under the **first-in, first-out (FIFO) inventory cost flow method**, the first units purchased are assumed to be sold and the ending inventory is made up of the most recent purchases. In the preceding example, the May 10 unit would be assumed to have been sold. Thus, the gross profit would be $11, and the ending inventory would be $27 ($13 + $14).

Under the **last-in, first-out (LIFO) inventory cost flow method**, the last units purchased are assumed to be sold and the ending inventory is made up of the first purchases. In the preceding example, the May 24 unit would be assumed to have been sold. Thus, the gross profit would be $6, and the ending inventory would be $22 ($9 + $13).

Under the **average inventory cost flow method**, the cost of the units sold and in ending inventory is an average of the purchase costs. In the preceding example, the cost of the unit sold would be $12 ($36 ÷ 3 units), the gross profit would be $8 ($20 − $12), and the ending inventory would be $24 ($12 × 2 units).

The three inventory cost flow methods, FIFO, LIFO, and average, are shown in Exhibit 1.

Exhibit 2 shows the frequency with which the FIFO, LIFO, and average methods are used.

Exhibit 1

Inventory Costing Methods

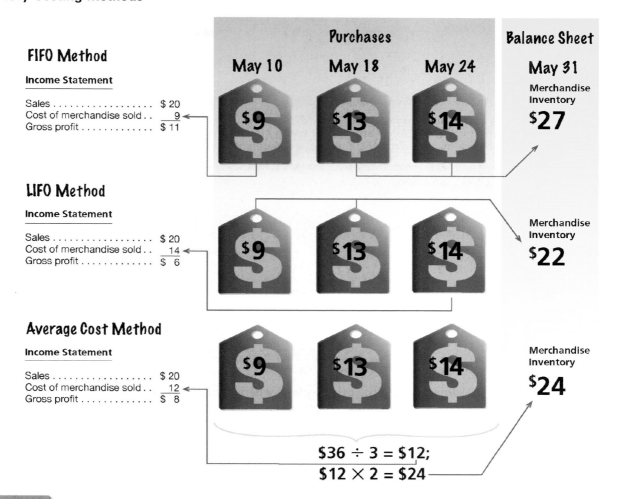

FIFO Method

Income Statement

Sales . . . . $ 20
Cost of merchandise sold . . ___9__
Gross profit . . . . $ 11

LIFO Method

Income Statement

Sales . . . . $ 20
Cost of merchandise sold . . __14__
Gross profit . . . . $ 6

Average Cost Method

Income Statement

Sales . . . . $ 20
Cost of merchandise sold . . __12__
Gross profit . . . . $ 8

Purchases

May 10   May 18   May 24

$9 $13 $14

Balance Sheet

May 31

Merchandise Inventory
$27

Merchandise Inventory
$22

Merchandise Inventory
$24

$36 ÷ 3 = $12;
$12 × 2 = $24

Exhibit 2

Use of Inventory Costing Methods*

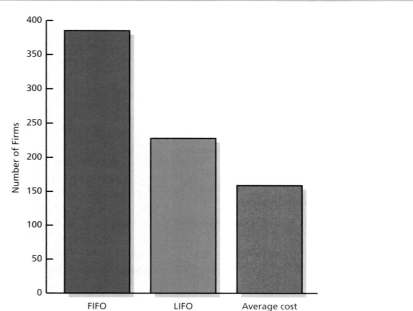

Source: *Accounting Trends and Techniques*, 61st edition, 2007 (New York: American Institute of Certified Public Accountants).

*Firms may be counted more than once for using multiple methods.

Example Exercise 6-1   Cost Flow Methods   ●●●●●●●● ➤ ②

Three identical units of Item QBM are purchased during February, as shown below.

Item QBM		Units	Cost
Feb. 8	Purchase	1	$ 45
15	Purchase	1	48
26	Purchase	1	51
	Total	3	$144
	Average cost per unit		$ 48 ($144 ÷ 3 units)

Assume that one unit is sold on February 27 for $70.

Determine the gross profit for February and ending inventory on February 28 using the (a) first-in, first-out (FIFO); (b) last-in, first-out (LIFO); and (c) average cost methods.

Follow My Example 6-1

		Gross Profit	Ending Inventory
a.	First-in, first-out (FIFO)	$25 ($70 − $45)	$99 ($48 + $51)
b.	Last-in, first-out (LIFO)	$19 ($70 − $51)	$93 ($45 + $48)
c.	Average cost	$22 ($70 − $48)	$96 ($48 × 2)

For Practice: PE 6-1A, PE 6-1B

---

③ Determine the cost of inventory under the perpetual inventory system, using the FIFO, LIFO, and average cost methods.

Although e-tailers, such as eToys Direct, Inc., Amazon.com, and Furniture.com, Inc., don't have retail stores, they still take possession of inventory in warehouses. Thus, they must account for inventory as illustrated in this chapter.

Inventory Costing Methods Under a Perpetual Inventory System

As illustrated in the prior section, when identical units of an item are purchased at different unit costs, an inventory cost flow method must be used. This is true regardless of whether the perpetual or periodic inventory system is used.

In this section, the FIFO, LIFO, and average cost methods are illustrated under a perpetual inventory system. For purposes of illustration, the data for Item 127B are used, as shown below.

Item 127B		Units	Cost
Jan. 1	Inventory	100	$20
4	Sale	70	
10	Purchase	80	21
22	Sale	40	
28	Sale	20	
30	Purchase	100	22

First-In, First-Out Method

When the FIFO method is used, costs are included in cost of merchandise sold in the order in which they were purchased. This is often the same as the physical flow of the merchandise. Thus, the FIFO method often provides results that are about the same as those that would have been obtained using the specific identification method. For example, grocery stores shelve milk and other perishable products by expiration dates. Products with early expiration dates are stocked in front. In this way, the oldest products (earliest purchases) are sold first.

> Using FIFO, costs are included in the merchandise sold in the order in which they were incurred.

To illustrate, Exhibit 3 shows use of FIFO under a perpetual inventory system for Item 127B. The journal entries and the inventory subsidiary ledger for Item 127B are shown in Exhibit 3 as follows:

1. The beginning balance on January 1 is $2,000 (100 units at a unit cost of $20).
2. On January 4, 70 units were sold at a price of $30 each for sales of $2,100 (70 units × $30). The cost of merchandise sold is $1,400 (70 units at a unit cost of $20). After the sale, there remains $600 of inventory (30 units at a unit cost of $20).

Exhibit 3

Entries and Perpetual Inventory Account (FIFO)

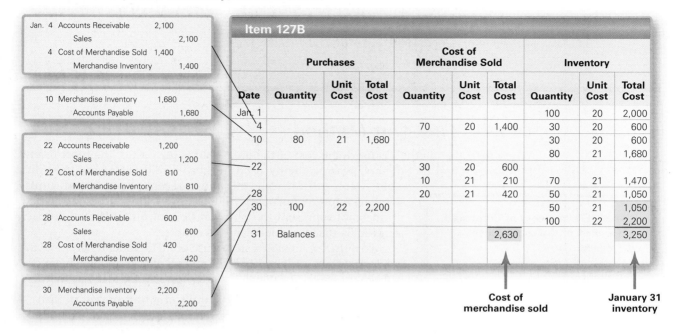

Jan. 4	Accounts Receivable	2,100	
	Sales		2,100
4	Cost of Merchandise Sold	1,400	
	Merchandise Inventory		1,400
10	Merchandise Inventory	1,680	
	Accounts Payable		1,680
22	Accounts Receivable	1,200	
	Sales		1,200
22	Cost of Merchandise Sold	810	
	Merchandise Inventory		810
28	Accounts Receivable	600	
	Sales		600
28	Cost of Merchandise Sold	420	
	Merchandise Inventory		420
30	Merchandise Inventory	2,200	
	Accounts Payable		2,200

Item 127B

		Purchases			Cost of Merchandise Sold			Inventory		
Date	Quantity	Unit Cost	Total Cost	Quantity	Unit Cost	Total Cost	Quantity	Unit Cost	Total Cost
Jan. 1							100	20	2,000
4				70	20	1,400	30	20	600
10	80	21	1,680				30	20	600
							80	21	1,680
22				30	20	600			
				10	21	210	70	21	1,470
28				20	21	420	50	21	1,050
30	100	22	2,200				50	21	1,050
							100	22	2,200
31	Balances					2,630			3,250

Cost of merchandise sold

January 31 inventory

3. On January 10, $1,680 is purchased (80 units at a unit cost of $21). After the purchase, the inventory is reported on two lines, $600 (30 units at a unit cost of $20) from the beginning inventory and $1,680 (80 units at a unit cost of $21) from the January 10 purchase.

4. On January 22, 40 units are sold at a price of $30 each for sales of $1,200 (40 units × $30). Using FIFO, the cost of merchandise sold of $810 consists of $600 (30 units at a unit cost of $20) from the beginning inventory plus $210 (10 units at a unit cost of $21) from the January 10 purchase. After the sale, there remains $1,470 of inventory (70 units at a unit cost of $21) from the January 10 purchase.

5. The January 28 sale and January 30 purchase are recorded in a similar manner.

6. The ending balance on January 31 is $3,250. This balance is made up of two layers of inventory as follows:

	Date of Purchase	Quantity	Unit Cost	Total Cost
Layer 1:	Jan. 10	50	$21	$1,050
Layer 2:	Jan. 30	100	22	2,200
Total		150		$3,250

Example Exercise 6-2   Perpetual Inventory Using FIFO   >> 3

Beginning inventory, purchases, and sales for Item ER27 are as follows:

Nov.	1	Inventory	40 units at $5
	5	Sale	32 units
	11	Purchase	60 units at $7
	21	Sale	45 units

Assuming a perpetual inventory system and using the first-in, first-out (FIFO) method, determine (a) the cost of merchandise sold on November 21 and (b) the inventory on November 30.

(continued)

Follow My Example 6-2

a. Cost of merchandise sold (November 21):

8 units at $5	$ 40
37 units at $7	259
45 units	$299

b. Inventory, November 30:

$161 = (23 units × $7)

For Practice: PE 6-2A, PE 6-2B

Last-In, First-Out Method

When the LIFO method is used, the cost of the units sold is the cost of the most recent purchases. The LIFO method was originally used in those rare cases where the units sold were taken from the most recently purchased units. However, for tax purposes, LIFO is now widely used even when it does not represent the physical flow of units. The tax impact of LIFO is discussed later in this chapter.

> **Using LIFO, the cost of units sold is the cost of the most recent purchases.**

To illustrate, Exhibit 4 shows use of LIFO under a perpetual inventory system for Item 127B. The journal entries and the inventory subsidiary ledger for Item 127B are shown in Exhibit 4 as follows:

1. The beginning balance on January 1 is $2,000 (100 units at a unit of cost of $20).
2. On January 4, 70 units were sold at a price of $30 each for sales of $2,100 (70 units × $30). The cost of merchandise sold is $1,400 (70 units at a unit cost of $20). After the sale, there remains $600 of inventory (30 units at a unit cost of $20).
3. On January 10, $1,680 is purchased (80 units at a unit cost of $21). After the purchase, the inventory is reported on two lines, $600 (30 units at a unit cost of $20) from the beginning inventory and $1,680 (80 units at $21 per unit) from the January 10 purchase.
4. On January 22, 40 units are sold at a price of $30 each for sales of $1,200 (40 units × $30). Using LIFO, the cost of merchandise sold is $840 (40 units at unit cost of $21) from the January 10 purchase. After the sale, there remains $1,440 of inventory

Exhibit 4

Entries and Perpetual Inventory Account (LIFO)

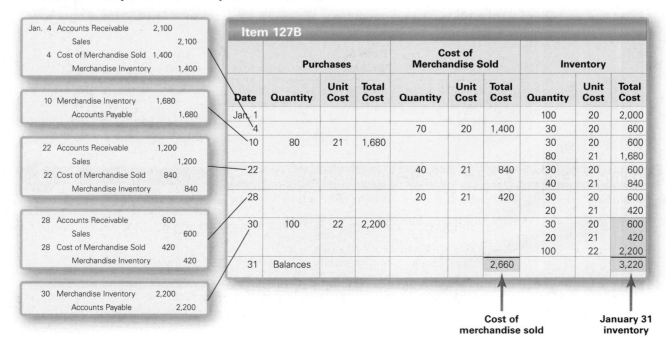

Jan. 4	Accounts Receivable	2,100	
	Sales		2,100
4	Cost of Merchandise Sold	1,400	
	Merchandise Inventory		1,400
10	Merchandise Inventory	1,680	
	Accounts Payable		1,680
22	Accounts Receivable	1,200	
	Sales		1,200
22	Cost of Merchandise Sold	840	
	Merchandise Inventory		840
28	Accounts Receivable	600	
	Sales		600
28	Cost of Merchandise Sold	420	
	Merchandise Inventory		420
30	Merchandise Inventory	2,200	
	Accounts Payable		2,200

Item 127B

Date	Purchases Quantity	Unit Cost	Total Cost	Cost of Merchandise Sold Quantity	Unit Cost	Total Cost	Inventory Quantity	Unit Cost	Total Cost
Jan. 1							100	20	2,000
4				70	20	1,400	30	20	600
10	80	21	1,680				30	20	600
							80	21	1,680
22				40	21	840	30	20	600
							40	21	840
28				20	21	420	30	20	600
							20	21	420
30	100	22	2,200				30	20	600
							20	21	420
							100	22	2,200
31	Balances					2,660			3,220

Cost of merchandise sold

January 31 inventory

consisting of $600 (30 units at a unit cost of $20) from the beginning inventory and $840 (40 units at a unit cost of $21) from the January 10 purchase.

5. The January 28 sale and January 30 purchase are recorded in a similar manner.
6. The ending balance on January 31 is $3,220. This balance is made up of three layers of inventory as follows:

	Date of Purchase	Quantity	Unit Cost	Total Cost
Layer 1:	Beg. inv. (Jan. 1)	30	$20	$ 600
Layer 2:	Jan. 10	20	21	420
Layer 3:	Jan. 30	100	22	2,200
Total		150		$3,220

When the LIFO method is used, the inventory subsidiary ledger is sometimes maintained in units only. The units are converted to dollars when the financial statements are prepared at the end of the period.

Example Exercise 6-3   Perpetual Inventory Using LIFO  3

Beginning inventory, purchases, and sales for Item ER27 are as follows:

Nov.	1	Inventory	40 units at $5
	5	Sale	32 units
	11	Purchase	60 units at $7
	21	Sale	45 units

Assuming a perpetual inventory system and using the last-in, first-out (LIFO) method, determine (a) the cost of the merchandise sold on November 21 and (b) the inventory on November 30.

Follow My Example 6-3

a. Cost of merchandise sold (November 21):

$315 = (45 units × $7)

b. Inventory, November 30:

8 units at $5	$ 40
15 units at $7	105
23 units	$145

For Practice: PE 6-3A, PE 6-3B

Average Cost Method

When the average cost method is used in a perpetual inventory system, an average unit cost for each item is computed each time a purchase is made. This unit cost is then used to determine the cost of each sale until another purchase is made and a new average is computed. This averaging technique is called a *moving average*. Since the average cost method is rarely used in a perpetual inventory system, it is not illustrated.

Computerized Perpetual Inventory Systems

A perpetual inventory system may be used in a manual accounting system. However, if there are many inventory transactions, such a system is costly and time consuming. In most cases, perpetual inventory systems are computerized.

A computerized perpetual inventory system for a retail store could be used as follows:

1. Each inventory item, including description, quantity, and unit size, is stored electronically in an inventory file. The total of the file equals the balance of Merchandise Inventory in the general ledger.

Wal-Mart, Target, and other retailers use bar code scanners as part of their perpetual inventory systems.

2. Each time an item is purchased or returned by a customer, the inventory file is updated by scanning the item's bar code.

3. Each time an item is sold, the item's bar code is scanned at the cash register and the inventory files are updated.

4. After a physical inventory is taken, the inventory count data are used to update the inventory file. A listing of inventory overages and shortages is printed, and any unusual amounts are investigated.

Computerized perpetual inventory systems are useful to managers in controlling and managing inventory. For example, fast selling items can be reordered before the stock runs out. Sales patterns can also be analyzed to determine when to mark down merchandise or when to restock seasonal merchandise. Finally, inventory data can be used in evaluating advertising campaigns and sales promotions.

4 Determine the cost of inventory under the periodic inventory system, using the FIFO, LIFO, and average cost methods.

Inventory Costing Methods Under a Periodic Inventory System

When the periodic inventory system is used, only revenue is recorded each time a sale is made. No entry is made at the time of the sale to record the cost of the merchandise sold. At the end of the accounting period, a physical inventory is taken to determine the cost of the inventory and the cost of the merchandise sold.[2]

Like the perpetual inventory system, a cost flow assumption must be made when identical units are acquired at different unit costs during a period. In such cases, the FIFO, LIFO, or average cost method is used.

First-In, First-Out Method

To illustrate the use of the FIFO method in a periodic inventory system, we use the same data for Item 127B as in the perpetual inventory example. The beginning inventory entry and purchases of Item 127B in January are as follows:

Jan.	1	Inventory	100 units at	$20	$2,000
	10	Purchase	80 units at	21	1,680
	30	Purchase	100 units at	22	2,200
Available for sale during month			280		$5,880

The physical count on January 31 shows that 150 units are on hand. Using the FIFO method, the cost of the merchandise on hand at the end of the period is made up of the most recent costs. The cost of the 150 units in ending inventory on January 31 is determined as follows:

Most recent costs, January 30 purchase	100 units at	$22	$2,200
Next most recent costs, January 10 purchase	50 units at	$21	1,050
Inventory, January 31	150 units		$3,250

Deducting the cost of the January 31 inventory of $3,250 from the cost of merchandise available for sale of $5,880 yields the cost of merchandise sold of $2,630, as shown below.

Beginning inventory, January 1	$2,000
Purchases ($1,680 + $2,200)	3,880
Cost of merchandise available for sale in January	$5,880
Less ending inventory, January 31	3,250
Cost of merchandise sold	$2,630

2 Determining the cost of merchandise sold using the periodic system was illustrated in Chapter 5.

The $3,250 cost of the ending merchandise inventory on January 31 is made up of the most recent costs. The $2,630 cost of merchandise sold is made up of the beginning inventory and the earliest costs. Exhibit 5 shows the relationship of the cost of merchandise sold for January and the ending inventory on January 31.

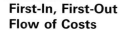
Exhibit 5

First-In, First-Out Flow of Costs

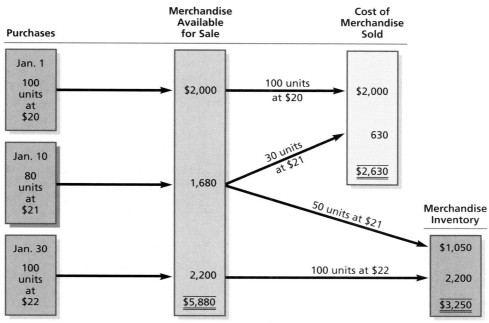

Last-In, First-Out Method

IFRS   IFRS

When the LIFO method is used, the cost of merchandise on hand at the end of the period is made up of the earliest costs. Based on the same data as in the FIFO example, the cost of the 150 units in ending inventory on January 31 is determined as follows:

Beginning inventory, January 1	100 units at	$20	$2,000
Next earliest costs, January 10	50 units at	$21	1,050
Inventory, January 31	150 units		$3,050

Deducting the cost of the January 31 inventory of $3,050 from the cost of merchandise available for sale of $5,880 yields the cost of merchandise sold of $2,830, as shown below.

Beginning inventory, January 1	$2,000
Purchases ($1,680 + $2,200)	3,880
Cost of merchandise available for sale in January	$5,880
Less ending inventory, January 31	3,050
Cost of merchandise sold	$2,830

The $3,050 cost of the ending merchandise inventory on January 31 is made up of the earliest costs. The $2,830 cost of merchandise sold is made up of the most recent costs. Exhibit 6 shows the relationship of the cost of merchandise sold for January and the ending inventory on January 31.

Exhibit 6

Last-In, First-Out Flow of Costs

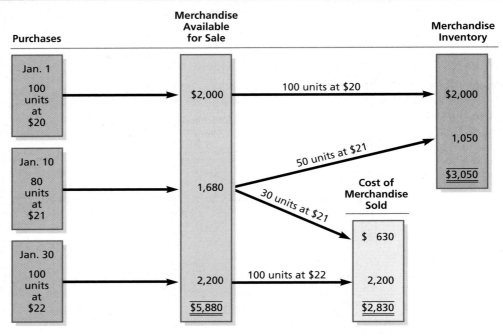

Average Cost Method

The average cost method is sometimes called the *weighted average method*. The average cost method uses the average unit cost for determining cost of merchandise sold and the ending merchandise inventory. If purchases are relatively uniform during a period, the average cost method provides results that are similar to the physical flow of goods.

The weighted average unit cost is determined as follows:

$$\text{Average Unit Cost} = \frac{\text{Total Cost of Units Available for Sale}}{\text{Units Available for Sale}}$$

To illustrate, we use the data for Item 127B as follows:

$$\text{Average Unit Cost} = \frac{\text{Total Cost of Units Available for Sale}}{\text{Units Available for Sale}} = \frac{\$5,880}{280 \text{ units}}$$

$$\text{Average Unit Cost} = \$21 \text{ per unit}$$

The cost of the January 31 ending inventory is as follows:

Inventory, January 31: $3,150 (150 units × $21)

Deducting the cost of the January 31 inventory of $3,150 from the cost of merchandise available for sale of $5,880 yields the cost of merchandise sold of $2,730, as shown below.

Beginning inventory, January 1	$2,000
Purchases ($1,680 + $2,200)	3,880
Cost of merchandise available for sale in January	$5,880
Less ending inventory, January 31	3,150
Cost of merchandise sold	$2,730

The cost of merchandise sold could also be computed by multiplying the number of units sold by the average cost as follows:

Cost of merchandise sold: $2,730 (130 units × $21)

Example Exercise 6-4 Periodic Inventory Using FIFO, LIFO, Average Cost Methods

The units of an item available for sale during the year were as follows:

Jan. 1	Inventory	6 units at $50	$ 300
Mar. 20	Purchase	14 units at $55	770
Oct. 30	Purchase	20 units at $62	1,240
	Available for sale	40 units	$2,310

There are 16 units of the item in the physical inventory at December 31. The periodic inventory system is used. Determine the inventory cost using (a) the first-in, first-out (FIFO) method, (b) the last-in, first-out (LIFO) method, and (c) the average cost method.

Follow My Example 6-4

a. First-in, first-out (FIFO) method: $992 = (16 units × $62)

b. Last-in, first-out (LIFO) method: $850 = (6 units × $50) + (10 units × $55)

c. Average cost method: $924 (16 units × $57.75), where average cost = $57.75 = $2,310/40 units

For Practice: PE 6-4A, PE 6-4B

---

5 Compare and contrast the use of the three inventory costing methods.

Comparing Inventory Costing Methods

A different cost flow is assumed for the FIFO, LIFO, and average inventory cost flow methods. As a result, the three methods normally yield different amounts for the following:

1. Cost of merchandise sold
2. Gross profit
3. Net income
4. Ending merchandise inventory

Using the periodic inventory system illustration with sales of $3,900 (130 units × $30), these differences are illustrated below.[3]

Partial Income Statements

	First-In, First-Out		Average Cost		Last-In, First-Out	
Net sales		$3,900		$3,900		$3,900
Cost of merchandise sold:						
Beginning inventory	$2,000		$2,000		$2,000	
Purchases	3,880		3,880		3,880	
Merchandise available for sale	$5,880		$5,880		$5,880	
Less ending inventory	3,250		3,150		3,050	
Cost of merchandise sold		2,630		2,730		2,830
Gross profit		$1,270		$1,170		$1,070

The preceding differences show the effect of increasing costs (prices). If costs (prices) remain the same, all three methods would yield the same results. However, costs (prices) normally do change. The effects of changing costs (prices) on the FIFO and LIFO methods are summarized in Exhibit 7. The average cost method will always yield results between those of FIFO and LIFO.

3 Similar results would also occur when comparing inventory costing methods under a perpetual inventory system.

Exhibit 7		Increasing Costs (Prices)		Decreasing Costs (Prices)	
Effects of Changing Costs (Prices): FIFO and LIFO Cost Methods		Highest Amount	Lowest Amount	Highest Amount	Lowest Amount
	Cost of merchandise sold	LIFO	FIFO	FIFO	LIFO
	Gross profit	FIFO	LIFO	LIFO	FIFO
	Net income	FIFO	LIFO	LIFO	FIFO
	Ending merchandise inventory	FIFO	LIFO	LIFO	FIFO

FIFO reports higher gross profit and net income than the LIFO method when costs (prices) are increasing, as shown in Exhibit 7. However, in periods of rapidly rising costs, the inventory that is sold must be replaced at increasingly higher costs. In such cases, the larger FIFO gross profit and net income are sometimes called *inventory profits* or *illusory profits*.

During a period of increasing costs, LIFO matches more recent costs against sales on the income statement. Thus, it can be argued that the LIFO method more nearly matches current costs with current revenues. LIFO also offers an income tax savings during periods of increasing costs. This is because LIFO reports the lowest amount of gross profit and, thus, taxable net income. However, under LIFO, the ending inventory on the balance sheet may be quite different from its current replacement cost. In such cases, the financial statements normally include a note that estimates what the inventory would have been if FIFO had been used.

The average cost method is, in a sense, a compromise between FIFO and LIFO. The effect of cost (price) trends is averaged in determining the cost of merchandise sold and the ending inventory. For a series of purchases, the average cost will be the same, regardless of whether costs are increasing or decreasing. For example, reversing the sequence of unit costs presented in the prior illustration does not affect the average unit cost nor the amounts reported for cost of merchandise sold, gross profit, or ending inventory.

Integrity, Objectivity, and Ethics in Business

WHERE'S THE BONUS?

Managers are often given bonuses based on reported earnings numbers. This can create a conflict. LIFO can improve the value of the company through lower taxes. However, in periods of rising costs (prices), LIFO also produces a lower earnings number and, therefore, lower management bonuses. Ethically, managers should select accounting procedures that will maximize the value of the firm, rather than their own compensation. Compensation specialists can help avoid this ethical dilemma by adjusting the bonus plan for the accounting procedure differences.

6 Describe and illustrate the reporting of merchandise inventory in the financial statements.

Reporting Merchandise Inventory in the Financial Statements

Cost is the primary basis for valuing and reporting inventories in the financial statements. However, inventory may be valued at other than cost in the following cases:

1. The cost of replacing items in inventory is below the recorded cost.
2. The inventory cannot be sold at normal prices due to imperfections, style changes, or other causes.

Valuation at Lower of Cost or Market

Dell Inc. recorded over $39.3 million of charges (expenses) in writing down its inventory of notebook computers. The remaining inventories of computers were then sold at significantly reduced prices.

If the cost of replacing inventory is lower than its recorded purchase cost, the **lower-of-cost-or-market (LCM) method** is used to value the inventory. *Market*, as used in *lower of cost or market*, is the cost to replace the inventory. The market value is based on normal quantities that would be purchased from suppliers.

The lower-of-cost-or-market method can be applied in one of three ways. The cost, market price, and any declines could be determined for the following:

1. Each item in the inventory.
2. Each major class or category of inventory.
3. Total inventory as a whole.

The amount of any price decline is included in the cost of merchandise sold. This, in turn, reduces gross profit and net income in the period in which the price declines occur. This matching of price declines to the period in which they occur is the primary advantage of using the lower-of-cost-or-market method.

To illustrate, assume the following data for 400 identical units of Item A in inventory on December 31, 2010:

Unit purchased cost	$10.25
Replacement cost on December 31, 2010	9.50

Since Item A could be replaced at $9.50 a unit, $9.50 is used under the lower-of-cost-or-market method.

Exhibit 8 illustrates applying the lower-of-cost-or-market method to each inventory item (A, B, C, and D). As applied on an item-by-item basis, the total lower-of-cost-or-market is $15,070, which is a market decline of $450 ($15,520 − $15,070). This market decline of $450 is included in the cost of merchandise sold.

In Exhibit 8, Items A, B, C, and D could be viewed as a class of inventory items. If the lower-of-cost-or-market method is applied to the class, the inventory would be valued at $15,472, which is a market decline of $48 ($15,520 − $15,472). Likewise, if Items A, B, C, and D make up the total inventory, the lower-of-cost-or-market method as applied to the total inventory would be the same amount, $15,472.

Exhibit 8

Determining Inventory at Lower of Cost or Market

	A	B	C	D	E	F	G
1			Unit	Unit		Total	
2		Inventory	Cost	Market			Lower
3	Item	Quantity	Price	Price	Cost	Market	of C or M
4	A	400	$10.25	$ 9.50	$ 4,100	$ 3,800	$ 3,800
5	B	120	22.50	24.10	2,700	2,892	2,700
6	C	600	8.00	7.75	4,800	4,650	4,650
7	D	280	14.00	14.75	3,920	4,130	3,920
8	Total				$15,520	$15,472	$15,070
9							

Example Exercise 6-5 Lower-of-Cost-or-Market Method •••••••• 6

On the basis of the following data, determine the value of the inventory at the lower of cost or market. Apply lower of cost or market to each inventory item as shown in Exhibit 8.

Item	Inventory Quantity	Unit Cost Price	Unit Market Price
C17Y	10	$ 39	$40
B563	7	110	98

(continued)

Follow My Example 6-5

	A	B	C	D	E	F	G
1			Unit	Unit	Total		
2		Inventory	Cost	Market			Lower
3	Item	Quantity	Price	Price	Cost	Market	of C or M
4	C17Y	10	$ 39	$ 40	$ 390	$ 400	$ 390
5	B563	7	110	98	770	686	686
6	Total				$1,160	$1,086	$1,076
7							
8							
9							

For Practice: PE 6-5A, PE 6-5B

Valuation at Net Realizable Value

Merchandise that is out of date, spoiled, or damaged can often be sold only at a price below its original cost. Such merchandise should be valued at its **net realizable value**. Net realizable value is determined as follows:

Net Realizable Value = Estimated Selling Price − Direct Costs of Disposal

Direct costs of disposal include selling expenses such as special advertising or sales commissions on sale. To illustrate, assume the following data about an item of damaged merchandise:

Original cost	$1,000
Estimated selling price	800
Selling expenses	150

The merchandise should be valued at its net realizable value of $650 as shown below.

Net Realizable Value = $800 − $150 = $650

Merchandise Inventory on the Balance Sheet

Merchandise inventory is usually reported in the Current Assets section of the balance sheet. In addition to this amount, the following are reported:

1. The method of determining the cost of the inventory (FIFO, LIFO, or average)
2. The method of valuing the inventory (cost or the lower of cost or market)

The financial statement reporting for the topics covered in Chapters 6–13 are illustrated using excerpts from the financial statements of Mornin' Joe. Mornin' Joe is a fictitious company that offers drip and espresso coffee in a coffeehouse setting. The complete financial statements of Mornin' Joe are illustrated at the end of Chapter 13 (pages 614–616)

The balance sheet presentation for merchandise inventory for Mornin' Joe is as follows:

Mornin' Joe
Balance Sheet
December 31, 2010

Current assets:		
Cash and cash equivalents		$235,000
Trading investments (at cost)	$420,000	
Plus valuation allowance on trading investments	45,000	465,000
Accounts receivable	$305,000	
Less allowance for doubtful accounts	12,300	292,700
Merchandise inventory—at lower of cost		
(first-in, first-out method) or market		120,000

It is not unusual for a large business to use different costing methods for segments of its inventories. Also, a business may change its inventory costing method. In such cases, the effect of the change and the reason for the change are disclosed in the financial statements.

Effect of Inventory Errors on the Financial Statements

Any errors in merchandise inventory will affect the balance sheet and income statement. Some reasons that inventory errors may occur include the following:

1. Physical inventory on hand was miscounted.
2. Costs were incorrectly assigned to inventory. For example, the FIFO, LIFO, or average cost method was incorrectly applied.
3. Inventory in transit was incorrectly included or excluded from inventory.
4. Consigned inventory was incorrectly included or excluded from inventory.

Inventory errors often arise from merchandise that is in transit at year-end. As discussed in Chapter 5, shipping terms determine when the title to merchandise passes. When goods are purchased or sold *FOB shipping point,* title passes to the buyer when the goods are shipped. When the terms are *FOB destination,* title passes to the buyer when the goods are received.

To illustrate, assume that SysExpress ordered the following merchandise from American Products:

Date ordered:	December 27, 2009
Amount:	$10,000
Terms:	FOB shipping point, 2/10, n/30
Date shipped by seller:	December 30
Date delivered:	January 3, 2010

When SysExpress counts its physical inventory on December 31, 2009, the merchandise is still in transit. In such cases, it would be easy for SysExpress to not include the $10,000 of merchandise in its December 31 physical inventory. However, since the merchandise was purchased *FOB shipping point,* SysExpress owns the merchandise. Thus, it should be included in the ending December 31 inventory even though it is not on hand. Likewise, any merchandise *sold* by SysExpress *FOB destination* is still SysExpress's inventory even if it is in transit to the buyer on December 31.

Inventory errors often arise from **consigned inventory**. Manufacturers sometimes ship merchandise to retailers who act as the manufacturer's selling agent. The manufacturer, called the **consignor**, retains title until the goods are sold. Such merchandise is said to be shipped *on consignment* to the retailer, called the **consignee**. Any unsold merchandise at year-end is a part of the manufacturer's (consignor's) inventory, even though the merchandise is in the hands of the retailer (consignee). At year-end, it would be easy for the retailer (consignee) to incorrectly include the consigned merchandise in its physical inventory. Likewise, the manufacturer (consignor) should include consigned inventory in its physical inventory even though the inventory is not on hand.

Income Statement Effects Inventory errors will misstate the income statement amounts for cost of merchandise sold, gross profit, and net income. The effects of inventory errors on the current period's income statement are summarized in Exhibit 9.

Exhibit 9

Effect of Inventory Errors on Current Period's Income Statement

	Income Statement Effect		
Inventory Error	Cost of Merchandise Sold	Gross Profit	Net Income
Beginning inventory is:			
Understated	*Understated*	*Overstated*	*Overstated*
Overstated	*Overstated*	*Understated*	*Understated*
Ending inventory is:			
Understated	*Overstated*	*Understated*	*Understated*
Overstated	*Understated*	*Overstated*	*Overstated*

To illustrate, we use the income statements of SysExpress shown in Exhibit 10.[4]

On December 31, 2009, assume that SysExpress incorrectly records its physical inventory as $50,000 instead of the correct amount of $60,000. Thus, the December 31, 2009, inventory is understated by $10,000 ($60,000 − $50,000). As a result, the cost of merchandise sold is overstated by $10,000. The gross profit and the net income for the year will also be understated by $10,000.

Exhibit 10

Effects of Inventory Errors on Two Years' Income Statements

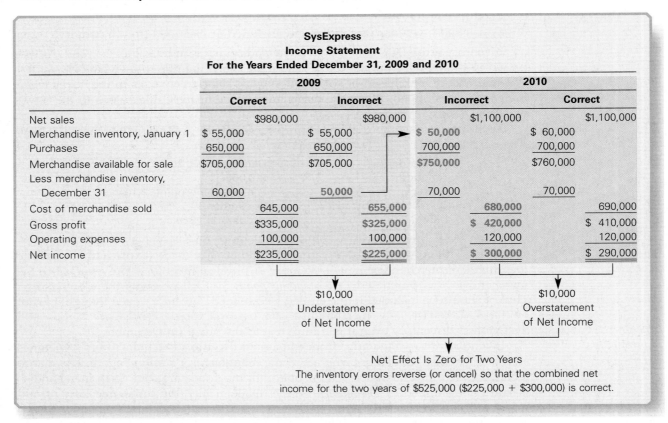

SysExpress
Income Statement
For the Years Ended December 31, 2009 and 2010

	2009		2010	
	Correct	Incorrect	Incorrect	Correct
Net sales	$980,000	$980,000	$1,100,000	$1,100,000
Merchandise inventory, January 1	$ 55,000	$ 55,000	$ 50,000	$ 60,000
Purchases	650,000	650,000	700,000	700,000
Merchandise available for sale	$705,000	$705,000	$750,000	$760,000
Less merchandise inventory, December 31	60,000	50,000	70,000	70,000
Cost of merchandise sold	645,000	655,000	680,000	690,000
Gross profit	$335,000	$325,000	$ 420,000	$ 410,000
Operating expenses	100,000	100,000	120,000	120,000
Net income	$235,000	$225,000	$ 300,000	$ 290,000

$10,000
Understatement
of Net Income

$10,000
Overstatement
of Net Income

Net Effect Is Zero for Two Years
The inventory errors reverse (or cancel) so that the combined net income for the two years of $525,000 ($225,000 + $300,000) is correct.

The December 31, 2009, merchandise inventory becomes the January 1, 2010, inventory. Thus, the beginning inventory for 2010 is understated by $10,000. As a result, the cost of merchandise sold is understated by $10,000 for 2010. The gross profit and net income for 2010 will be overstated by $10,000.

As shown in Exhibit 10, since the ending inventory of one period is the beginning inventory of the next period, the effects of inventory errors carry forward to the next period. Specifically, if uncorrected, the effects of inventory errors reverse themselves in the next period. In Exhibit 10, the combined net income for the two years of $525,000 is correct even though the 2009 and 2010 income statements were incorrect.

Balance Sheet Effects Inventory errors misstate the merchandise inventory, current assets, total assets, and stockholders' equity (retained earnings) on the balance sheet. The effects of inventory errors on the current period's balance sheet are summarized in Exhibit 11.

---

4 We will illustrate the effect of inventory errors using the periodic system. This is because it is easier to see the impact of inventory errors on the income statement using the periodic system. The effect of inventory errors would be the same under the perpetual inventory system.

Exhibit 11

Effect of Inventory Errors on Current Period's Balance Sheet

Ending Inventory Error	Balance Sheet Effect			
	Merchandise Inventory	Current Assets	Total Assets	Stockholders' Equity (Retained Earnings)
Understated	Understated	Understated	Understated	Understated
Overstated	Overstated	Overstated	Overstated	Overstated

For the SysExpress illustration shown in Exhibit 10, the December 31, 2009, ending inventory was understated by $10,000. As a result, the merchandise inventory, current assets, and total assets would be understated by $10,000 on the December 31, 2009, balance sheet. Because the ending physical inventory is understated, the cost of merchandise sold for 2009 will be overstated by $10,000. Thus, the gross profit and the net income for 2009 are understated by $10,000. Since the net income is closed to Retained Earnings at the end of the period, the stockholders' equity (retained earnings) on the December 31, 2009, balance sheet is also understated by $10,000.

As discussed above, inventory errors reverse themselves within two years. As a result, the balance sheet will be correct as of December 31, 2010. Using the SysExpress illustration from Exhibit 10, these effects are summarized below.

	Amount of Misstatement	
Balance Sheet:	December 31, 2009	December 31, 2010
Merchandise inventory overstated (understated)	$(10,000)	Correct
Current assets overstated (understated)	(10,000)	Correct
Total assets overstated (understated)	(10,000)	Correct
Stockholders' equity (retained earnings) overstated (understated)	(10,000)	Correct
Income Statement:	2009	2010
Cost of merchandise sold overstated (understated)	$ 10,000	$(10,000)
Gross profit overstated (understated)	(10,000)	10,000
Net income overstated (understated)	(10,000)	10,000

Example Exercise 6-6   Effect of Inventory Errors   6

Zula Repair Shop incorrectly counted its December 31, 2010, inventory as $250,000 instead of the correct amount of $220,000. Indicate the effect of the misstatement on Zula's December 31, 2010, balance sheet and income statement for the year ended December 31, 2010.

Follow My Example 6-6

	Amount of Misstatement Overstatement (Understatement)
Balance Sheet:	
Merchandise inventory overstated	$ 30,000
Current assets overstated	30,000
Total assets overstated	30,000
Stockholders' equity (retained earnings) overstated	30,000
Income Statement:	
Cost of merchandise sold understated	$(30,000)
Gross profit overstated	30,000
Net income overstated	30,000

For Practice: PE 6-6A, PE 6-6B

Business Connection

RAPID INVENTORY AT COSTCO

Costco Wholesale Corporation operates over 300 membership warehouses that offer members low prices on a limited selection of nationally branded and selected private label products. Costco emphasizes high sales volumes and rapid inventory turnover. This enables Costco to operate profitably at significantly lower gross margins than traditional wholesalers, discount retailers, and supermarkets. In addition, Costco's rapid turnover provides it the opportunity to conserve on its cash, as described below.

Because of its high sales volume and rapid inventory turnover, Costco generally has the opportunity to receive cash from the sale of a substantial portion of its inventory at mature warehouse operations before it is required to pay all its merchandise vendors, even though Costco takes advantage of early payment terms to obtain payment discounts. As sales in a given warehouse increase and

inventory turnover becomes more rapid, a greater percentage of the inventory is financed through payment terms provided by vendors rather than by working capital (cash).

© DON RYAN/ASSOCIATED PRESS

Financial Analysis and Interpretation

A merchandising business should keep enough inventory on hand to meet the needs of its customers. A failure to do so may result in lost sales. At the same time, too much inventory ties up funds that could be used to improve operations. In addition, excess inventory increases expenses such as storage, insurance, and property taxes. Finally, excess inventory increases the risk of losses due to price declines, damage, or changes in customers' tastes.

Two measures to analyze the efficiency and effectiveness of inventory are the inventory turnover and the number of days' sales in inventory.

Inventory turnover measures the relationship between cost of merchandise sold and the amount of inventory carried during the period. It is computed as follows:

$$\text{Inventory Turnover} = \frac{\text{Cost of Merchandise Sold}}{\text{Average Inventory}}$$

To illustrate, the following data (in thousands) have been taken from annual reports for SUPERVALU Inc. and Zale Corporation:

	SUPERVALU	Zale
Cost of merchandise sold . .	$29,267,000	$1,194,399
Inventories:		
Beginning of year	$ 954,200	$ 903,294
End of year	$ 2,749,000	$1,021,164
Average	$ 1,851,600	$ 962,229
Inventory turnover.	15.8	1.2

The inventory turnover is 15.8 for SUPERVALU and 1.2 for Zale. Generally, the larger the inventory turnover, the more efficient and effective the management of inventory. However, differences in companies and industries may be

too great to allow specific statements as to what is a good inventory turnover. For example, SUPERVALU is a leading food distributor in the United States. Because SUPERVALU's inventory is perishable, we would expect it to have a high inventory turnover. In contrast, Zale Corporation is a large retailer of fine jewelry in the United States. Thus, we would expect Zale to have a lower inventory turnover than SUPERVALU.

The **number of days' sales in inventory** is a rough measure of the length of time it takes to acquire, sell, and replace the inventory. It is computed as follows:

Number of Days' Sales in Inventory

$$= \frac{\text{Average Inventory}}{\text{Average Daily Cost of Merchandise Sold}}$$

The average daily cost of merchandise sold is determined by dividing the cost of merchandise sold by 365. The number of days' sales in inventory for SUPERVALU and Zale is computed as shown below.

	SUPERVALU	Zale
Average daily cost of merchandise sold:		
$29,267,000/365	$ 80,184	
$1,194,399/365		$ 3,272
Average inventory.	$1,851,600	$962,229
Number of days' sales		
in inventory	23.1 days	294.1 days

Generally, the lower the number of days' sales in inventory, the better. As with inventory turnover, we should expect differences among industries, such as those for SUPERVALU and Zale.

f·a·i

A P P E N D I X

Estimating Inventory Cost

A business may need to estimate the amount of inventory for the following reasons:

1. Perpetual inventory records are not maintained.
2. A disaster such as a fire or flood has destroyed the inventory records and the inventory.
3. Monthly or quarterly financial statements are needed, but a physical inventory is taken only once a year.

This appendix describes and illustrates two widely used methods of estimating inventory cost.

Retail Method of Inventory Costing

The **retail inventory method** of estimating inventory cost requires costs and retail prices to be maintained for the merchandise available for sale. A ratio of cost to retail price is then used to convert ending inventory at retail to estimate the ending inventory cost.

The retail inventory method is applied as follows:

Step 1. Determine the total merchandise available for sale at cost and retail.
Step 2. Determine the ratio of the cost to retail of the merchandise available for sale.
Step 3. Determine the ending inventory at retail by deducting the net sales from the merchandise available for sale at retail.
Step 4. Estimate the ending inventory cost by multiplying the ending inventory at retail by the cost to retail ratio.

Exhibit 12 illustrates the retail inventory method.

Exhibit 12

Determining Inventory by the Retail Method

	A	B	C
1		Cost	Retail
2	Merchandise inventory, January 1	$19,400	$ 36,000
3	Purchases in January (net)	42,600	64,000
Step 1 → 4	Merchandise available for sale	$62,000	$100,000
Step 2 → 5	Ratio of cost to retail price: $\frac{\$62,000}{\$100,000} = 62\%$		
6	Sales for January (net)		70,000
Step 3 → 7	Merchandise inventory, January 31, at retail		$ 30,000
Step 4 → 8	Merchandise inventory, January 31, at estimated cost		
9	($30,000 × 62%)		$ 18,600
10			

When estimating the cost to retail ratio, the mix of items in the ending inventory is assumed to be the same as the merchandise available for sale. If the ending inventory is made up of different classes of merchandise, cost to retail ratios may be developed for each class of inventory.

An advantage of the retail method is that it provides inventory figures for preparing monthly statements. Department stores and similar retailers often determine gross profit and operating income each month, but may take a physical inventory only once or twice a year. Thus, the retail method allows management to monitor operations more closely.

The retail method may also be used as an aid in taking a physical inventory. In this case, the items are counted and recorded at their retail (selling) prices instead of their costs. The physical inventory at retail is then converted to cost by using the cost to retail ratio.

Gross Profit Method of Inventory Costing

The **gross profit method** uses the estimated gross profit for the period to estimate the inventory at the end of the period. The gross profit is estimated from the preceding year, adjusted for any current-period changes in the cost and sales prices.

The gross profit method is applied as follows:

Step 1. Determine the merchandise available for sale at cost.

Step 2. Determine the estimated gross profit by multiplying the net sales by the gross profit percentage.

Step 3. Determine the estimated cost of merchandise sold by deducting the estimated gross profit from the net sales.

Step 4. Estimate the ending inventory cost by deducting the estimated cost of merchandise sold from the merchandise available for sale.

Exhibit 13 illustrates the gross profit method.

Exhibit 13

Estimating Inventory by Gross Profit Method

	A	B	C
1			Cost
2	Merchandise inventory, January 1		$ 57,000
3	Purchases in January (net)		180,000
Step 1 → 4	Merchandise available for sale		$237,000
5	Sales for January (net)	$250,000	
Step 2 → 6	Less estimated gross profit ($250,000 × 30%)	75,000	
Step 3 → 7	Estimated cost of merchandise sold		175,000
Step 4 → 8	Estimated merchandise inventory, January 31		$ 62,000
9			

The gross profit method is useful for estimating inventories for monthly or quarterly financial statements. It is also useful in estimating the cost of merchandise destroyed by fire or other disasters.

1 Describe the importance of control over inventory.

Key Points	Key Learning Outcomes	Example Exercises	Practice Exercises
Two primary objectives of control over inventory are safeguarding the inventory and properly reporting it in the financial statements. The perpetual inventory system enhances control over inventory. In addition, a physical inventory count should be taken periodically to detect shortages as well as to deter employee thefts.	• Describe controls for safeguarding inventory. • Describe how a perpetual inventory system enhances control over inventory. • Describe why taking a physical inventory enhances control over inventory.		

2 Describe three inventory cost flow assumptions and how they impact the income statement and balance sheet.

Key Points	Key Learning Outcomes	Example Exercises	Practice Exercises
The three common inventory cost flow assumptions used in business are the (1) first-in, first-out method (FIFO); (2) last-in, first-out method (LIFO); and (3) average cost method. The choice of a cost flow assumption directly affects the income statement and balance sheet.	• Describe the FIFO, LIFO, and average cost flow methods. • Describe how choice of a cost flow method affects the income statement and balance sheet.	6-1	6-1A, 6-1B

3 Determine the cost of inventory under the perpetual inventory system, using the FIFO, LIFO, and average cost methods.

Key Points	Key Learning Outcomes	Example Exercises	Practice Exercises
In a perpetual inventory system, the number of units and the cost of each type of merchandise are recorded in an inventory subsidiary ledger, with a separate account for each type of merchandise.	• Determine the cost of inventory and cost of merchandise sold using a perpetual inventory system under the FIFO method.	6-2	6-2A, 6-2B
	• Determine the cost of inventory and cost of merchandise sold using a perpetual inventory system under the LIFO method.	6-3	6-3A, 6-3B

4 Determine the cost of inventory under the periodic inventory system, using the FIFO, LIFO, and average cost methods.

Key Points	Key Learning Outcomes	Example Exercises	Practice Exercises
In a periodic inventory system, a physical inventory is taken to determine the cost of the inventory and the cost of merchandise sold.	• Determine the cost of inventory and cost of merchandise sold using a periodic inventory system under the FIFO method.	**6-4**	6-4A, 6-4B
	• Determine the cost of inventory and cost of merchandise sold using a periodic inventory system under the LIFO method.	**6-4**	6-4A, 6-4B
	• Determine the cost of inventory and cost of merchandise sold using a periodic inventory system under the average cost method.	**6-4**	6-4A, 6-4B

5 Compare and contrast the use of the three inventory costing methods.

Key Points	Key Learning Outcomes	Example Exercises	Practice Exercises
The three inventory costing methods will normally yield different amounts for (1) the ending inventory, (2) the cost of merchandise sold for the period, and (3) the gross profit (and net income) for the period.	• Indicate which inventory cost flow method will yield the highest and lowest ending inventory and net income during periods of increasing prices. • Indicate which inventory cost flow method will yield the highest and lowest ending inventory and net income during periods of decreasing prices.		

6 Describe and illustrate the reporting of merchandise inventory in the financial statements.

Key Points	Key Learning Outcomes	Example Exercises	Practice Exercises
The lower of cost or market is used to value inventory. Inventory that is out of date, spoiled, or damaged is valued at its net realizable value. Merchandise inventory is usually presented in the Current Assets section of the balance sheet, following receivables. The method of determining the cost and valuing the inventory is reported. Errors in reporting inventory based on the physical inventory will affect the balance sheet and income statement.	• Determine inventory using lower of cost or market. • Illustrate the use of net realizable value for spoiled or damaged inventory. • Prepare the Current Assets section of the balance sheet that includes inventory. • Determine the effect of inventory errors on the balance sheet and income statement.	**6-5** **6-6**	6-5A, 6-5B 6-6A, 6-6B

Key Terms

average inventory cost flow
method (266)

consigned inventory (279)

consignee (279)

consignor (279)

first-in, first-out (FIFO)
inventory cost flow
method (266)

gross profit method (284)

inventory subsidiary
ledger (265)

inventory turnover (282)

last-in, first-out (LIFO)
inventory cost flow
method (266)

lower-of-cost-or-market (LCM)
method (277)

net realizable value (278)

number of days' sales in
inventory (282)

physical inventory (265)

purchase order (265)

receiving report (265)

retail inventory
method (283)

specific identification inventory
cost flow method (264)

Illustrative Problem

Stewart Co.'s beginning inventory and purchases during the year ended December 31, 2010, were as follows:

		Units	Unit Cost	Total Cost
January 1	Inventory	1,000	$50.00	$ 50,000
March 10	Purchase	1,200	52.50	63,000
June 25	Sold 800 units			
August 30	Purchase	800	55.00	44,000
October 5	Sold 1,500 units			
November 26	Purchase	2,000	56.00	112,000
December 31	Sold 1,000 units			
Total		5,000		$269,000

Instructions

1. Determine the cost of inventory on December 31, 2010, using the perpetual inventory system and each of the following inventory costing methods:
   a. first-in, first-out
   b. last-in, first-out
2. Determine the cost of inventory on December 31, 2010, using the periodic inventory system and each of the following inventory costing methods:
   a. first-in, first-out
   b. last-in, first-out
   c. average cost
3. Appendix: Assume that during the fiscal year ended December 31, 2010, sales were $290,000 and the estimated gross profit rate was 40%. Estimate the ending inventory at December 31, 2010, using the gross profit method.

Solution

1. a. First-in, first-out method: $95,200 (shown on page 288)
   b. Last-in, first-out method: $91,000 ($35,000 + $56,000) (shown on page 288)
2. a. First-in, first-out method:
      1,700 units at $56 = $95,200
   b. Last-in, first-out method:

1,000 units at $50.00	$50,000
700 units at $52.50	36,750
1,700 units	$86,750

1. a. First-in, first-out method: $95,200

Date	Purchases Quantity	Purchases Unit Cost	Purchases Total Cost	Cost of Merchandise Sold Quantity	Cost of Merchandise Sold Unit Cost	Cost of Merchandise Sold Total Cost	Inventory Quantity	Inventory Unit Cost	Inventory Total Cost
2010 Jan. 1							1,000	50.00	50,000
Mar. 10	1,200	52.50	63,000				1,000	50.00	50,000
							1,200	52.50	63,000
June 25				800	50.00	40,000	200	50.00	10,000
							1,200	52.50	63,000
Aug. 30	800	55.00	44,000				200	50.00	10,000
							1,200	52.50	63,000
							800	55.00	44,000
Oct. 5				200	50.00	10,000	700	55.00	38,500
				1,200	52.50	63,000			
				100	55.00	5,500			
Nov. 26	2,000	56.00	112,000				700	55.00	38,500
							2,000	56.00	112,000
Dec. 31				700	55.00	38,500	1,700	56.00	95,200
				300	56.00	16,800			
31 Balances						173,800			95,200

b. Last-in, first-out method: $91,000 ($35,000 + $56,000)

Date	Purchases Quantity	Purchases Unit Cost	Purchases Total Cost	Cost of Merchandise Sold Quantity	Cost of Merchandise Sold Unit Cost	Cost of Merchandise Sold Total Cost	Inventory Quantity	Inventory Unit Cost	Inventory Total Cost
2010 Jan. 1							1,000	50.00	50,000
Mar. 10	1,200	52.50	63,000				1,000	50.00	50,000
							1,200	52.50	63,000
June 25				800	52.50	42,000	1,000	50.00	50,000
							400	52.50	21,000
Aug. 30	800	55.00	44,000				1,000	50.00	50,000
							400	52.50	21,000
							800	55.00	44,000
Oct. 5				800	55.00	44,000	700	50.00	35,000
				400	52.50	21,000			
				300	50.00	15,000			
Nov. 26	2,000	56.00	112,000				700	50.00	35,000
							2,000	56.00	112,000
Dec. 31				1,000	56.00	56,000	700	50.00	35,000
							1,000	56.00	56,000
31 Balances						178,000			91,000

c. Average cost method:

Average cost per unit: $269,000/5,000 units = $53.80

Inventory, December 31, 2010:   1,700 units at $53.80 = $91,460

3. Appendix:

Merchandise inventory, January 1, 2010	$ 50,000
Purchases (net)	219,000
Merchandise available for sale	$269,000
Sales (net) $290,000	
Less estimated gross profit ($290,000 × 40%) 116,000	
Estimated cost of merchandise sold	174,000
Estimated merchandise inventory, December 31, 2010	$ 95,000

Self-Examination Questions (Answers at End of Chapter)

1. The inventory costing method that is based on the assumption that costs should be charged against revenue in the order in which they were incurred is:
   A. FIFO.
   B. LIFO.
   C. average cost.
   D. perpetual inventory.

2. The following units of a particular item were purchased and sold during the period:

Beginning inventory	40 units at $20
First purchase	50 units at $21
Second purchase	50 units at $22
First sale	110 units
Third purchase	50 units at $23
Second sale	45 units

   What is the cost of the 35 units on hand at the end of the period as determined under the perpetual inventory system by the LIFO costing method?
   A. $715
   B. $705
   C. $700
   D. $805

3. The following units of a particular item were available for sale during the period:

Beginning inventory	40 units at $20
First purchase	50 units at $21
Second purchase	50 units at $22
Third purchase	50 units at $23

   What is the unit cost of the 35 units on hand at the end of the period as determined under the periodic inventory system by the FIFO costing method?
   A. $20
   B. $21
   C. $22
   D. $23

4. If merchandise inventory is being valued at cost and the price level is steadily rising, the method of costing that will yield the highest net income is:
   A. LIFO.
   B. FIFO.
   C. average.
   D. periodic.

5. If the inventory at the end of the year is understated by $7,500, the error will cause an:
   A. understatement of cost of merchandise sold for the year by $7,500.
   B. overstatement of gross profit for the year by $7,500.
   C. overstatement of merchandise inventory for the year by $7,500.
   D. understatement of net income for the year by $7,500.

Eye Openers

1. Before inventory purchases are recorded, the receiving report should be reconciled to what documents?
2. What security measures may be used by retailers to protect merchandise inventory from customer theft?
3. Which inventory system provides the more effective means of controlling inventories (perpetual or periodic)? Why?
4. Why is it important to periodically take a physical inventory if the perpetual system is used?
5. Do the terms *FIFO* and *LIFO* refer to techniques used in determining quantities of the various classes of merchandise on hand? Explain.
6. Does the term *last-in* in the LIFO method mean that the items in the inventory are assumed to be the most recent (last) acquisitions? Explain.
7. If merchandise inventory is being valued at cost and the price level is decreasing, which of the three methods of costing—FIFO, LIFO, or average cost—will yield (a) the highest inventory cost, (b) the lowest inventory cost, (c) the highest gross profit, and (d) the lowest gross profit?
8. Which of the three methods of inventory costing—FIFO, LIFO, or average cost—will in general yield an inventory cost most nearly approximating current replacement cost?
9. If inventory is being valued at cost and the price level is steadily rising, which of the three methods of costing—FIFO, LIFO, or average cost—will yield the lowest annual income tax expense? Explain.
10. Can a company change its method of costing inventory? Explain.
11. Because of imperfections, an item of merchandise cannot be sold at its normal selling price. How should this item be valued for financial statement purposes?

12. How is the method of determining the cost of the inventory and the method of valuing it disclosed in the financial statements?
13. The inventory at the end of the year was understated by $12,750. (a) Did the error cause an overstatement or an understatement of the gross profit for the year? (b) Which items on the balance sheet at the end of the year were overstated or understated as a result of the error?
14. Funtime Co. sold merchandise to Jaffe Company on December 31, FOB shipping point. If the merchandise is in transit on December 31, the end of the fiscal year, which company would report it in its financial statements? Explain.
15. A manufacturer shipped merchandise to a retailer on a consignment basis. If the merchandise is unsold at the end of the period, in whose inventory should the merchandise be included?

Practice Exercises

PE 6-1A
Cost flow methods

obj. 2

EE 6-1   p. 268

Three identical units of Item WH4 are purchased during June, as shown below.

Item WH4		Units	Cost
June 3	Purchase	1	$ 30
10	Purchase	1	36
19	Purchase	1	42
Total		3	$108
Average cost per unit			$ 36 ($108 ÷ 3 units)

Assume that one unit is sold on June 23 for $53.
  Determine the gross profit for June and ending inventory on June 30 using the (a) first-in, first-out (FIFO); (b) last-in, first-out (LIFO); and (c) average cost methods.

PE 6-1B
Cost flow methods

obj. 2

EE 6-1   p. 268

Three identical units of Item JC07 are purchased during August, as shown below.

Item JC07		Units	Cost
Aug. 7	Purchase	1	$ 80
13	Purchase	1	84
25	Purchase	1	88
Total		3	$252
Average cost per unit			$ 84 ($252 ÷ 3 units)

Assume that one unit is sold on August 30 for $125.
  Determine the gross profit for August and ending inventory on August 31 using the (a) first-in, first-out (FIFO); (b) last-in, first-out (LIFO); and (c) average cost methods.

PE 6-2A
Perpetual inventory using FIFO

obj. 3

EE 6-2   p. 269

Beginning inventory, purchases, and sales for Item VX48 are as follows:

July 1	Inventory	100 units at $8
8	Sale	90 units
15	Purchase	125 units at $12
25	Sale	60 units

Assuming a perpetual inventory system and using the first-in, first-out (FIFO) method, determine (a) the cost of merchandise sold on July 25 and (b) the inventory on July 31.

PE 6-2B
Perpetual inventory using FIFO

obj. 3

EE 6-2   p. 269

Beginning inventory, purchases, and sales for Item CJ10 are as follows:

Apr. 1	Inventory	30 units at $70
8	Sale	18 units
15	Purchase	25 units at $72
24	Sale	15 units

Assuming a perpetual inventory system and using the first-in, first-out (FIFO) method, determine (a) the cost of merchandise sold on April 24 and (b) the inventory on April 30.

PE 6-3A
Perpetual inventory
using LIFO

obj. 3

EE 6-3   p. 271

Beginning inventory, purchases, and sales for Item VX48 are as follows:

July 1	Inventory	100 units at $8
8	Sale	90 units
15	Purchase	125 units at $12
25	Sale	60 units

Assuming a perpetual inventory system and using the last-in, first-out (LIFO) method, determine (a) the cost of merchandise sold on July 25 and (b) the inventory on July 31.

PE 6-3B
Perpetual inventory
using LIFO

obj. 3

EE 6-3   p. 271

Beginning inventory, purchases, and sales for Item CJ10 are as follows:

Apr. 1	Inventory	30 units at $70
8	Sale	18 units
15	Purchase	25 units at $72
24	Sale	15 units

Assuming a perpetual inventory system and using the last-in, first-out (LIFO) method, determine (a) the cost of merchandise sold on April 24 and (b) the inventory on April 30.

PE 6-4A
Periodic inventory
using FIFO, LIFO,
average cost
methods

obj. 4

EE 6-4   p. 275

The units of an item available for sale during the year were as follows:

Jan. 1	Inventory	5 units at $120	$ 600
Feb. 13	Purchase	65 units at $114	7,410
Oct. 30	Purchase	10 units at $119	1,190
	Available for sale	80 units	$9,200

There are 24 units of the item in the physical inventory at December 31. The periodic inventory system is used. Determine the inventory cost using (a) the first-in, first-out (FIFO) method; (b) the last-in, first-out (LIFO) method; and (c) the average cost method.

PE 6-4B
Periodic inventory
using FIFO, LIFO,
average cost
methods

obj. 4

EE 6-4   p. 275

The units of an item available for sale during the year were as follows:

Jan. 1	Inventory	60 units at $45	$ 2,700
Apr. 20	Purchase	90 units at $50	4,500
Nov. 30	Purchase	75 units at $54	4,050
	Available for sale	225 units	$11,250

There are 48 units of the item in the physical inventory at December 31. The periodic inventory system is used. Determine the inventory cost using (a) the first-in, first-out (FIFO) method; (b) the last-in, first-out (LIFO) method; and (c) the average cost method.

PE 6-5A
Lower-of-cost-or-
market method

obj. 6

EE 6-5   p. 277

On the basis of the following data, determine the value of the inventory at the lower of cost or market. Apply lower of cost or market to each inventory item as shown in Exhibit 8.

Item	Inventory Quantity	Unit Cost Price	Unit Market Price
Alpha	400	$ 6	$ 5
Beta	350	12	14

PE 6-5B
Lower-of-cost-or-
market method

obj. 6

EE 6-5   p. 277

On the basis of the following data, determine the value of the inventory at the lower of cost or market. Apply lower of cost or market to each inventory item as shown in Exhibit 8.

Item	Inventory Quantity	Unit Cost Price	Unit Market Price
Widget	100	$30	$27
Gidget	75	24	25

PE 6-6A
Effect of inventory
errors

obj. 6

EE 6-6   p. 281

During the taking of its physical inventory on December 31, 2010, Euro Bath Company incorrectly counted its inventory as $496,000 instead of the correct amount of $480,000. Indicate the effect of the misstatement on Euro Bath's December 31, 2010, balance sheet and income statement for the year ended December 31, 2010.

PE 6-6B
Effect of inventory errors

obj. 6

EE 6-6   p. 281

During the taking of its physical inventory on December 31, 2010, Best Interiors Company incorrectly counted its inventory as $145,000 instead of the correct amount of $175,000. Indicate the effect of the misstatement on Best Interiors' December 31, 2010, balance sheet and income statement for the year ended December 31, 2010.

Exercises

EX 6-1
Control of inventories

obj. 1

Hammer & Nails Hardware Store currently uses a periodic inventory system. Alice Asaki, the owner, is considering the purchase of a computer system that would make it feasible to switch to a perpetual inventory system.

Alice is unhappy with the periodic inventory system because it does not provide timely information on inventory levels. Alice has noticed on several occasions that the store runs out of good-selling items, while too many poor-selling items are on hand.

Alice is also concerned about lost sales while a physical inventory is being taken. Hammer & Nails Hardware currently takes a physical inventory twice a year. To minimize distractions, the store is closed on the day inventory is taken. Alice believes that closing the store is the only way to get an accurate inventory count.

➤ Will switching to a perpetual inventory system strengthen Hammer & Nails Hardware's control over inventory items? Will switching to a perpetual inventory system eliminate the need for a physical inventory count? Explain.

EX 6-2
Control of inventories

obj. 1

Fly Away Luggage Shop is a small retail establishment located in a large shopping mall. This shop has implemented the following procedures regarding inventory items:

a. Whenever Fly Away receives a shipment of new inventory, the items are taken directly to the stockroom. Fly Away's accountant uses the vendor's invoice to record the amount of inventory received.

b. Since the shop carries mostly high-quality, designer luggage, all inventory items are tagged with a control device that activates an alarm if a tagged item is removed from the store.

c. Since the display area of the store is limited, only a sample of each piece of luggage is kept on the selling floor. Whenever a customer selects a piece of luggage, the salesclerk gets the appropriate piece from the store's stockroom. Since all salesclerks need access to the stockroom, it is not locked. The stockroom is adjacent to the break room used by all mall employees.

➤ State whether each of these procedures is appropriate or inappropriate. If it is inappropriate, state why.

EX 6-3
Perpetual inventory using FIFO

objs. 2, 3

✔ Inventory balance, April 30, $3,750

Beginning inventory, purchases, and sales data for portable video CD players are as follows:

Apr. 1	Inventory	50 units at $35
5	Sale	40 units
14	Purchase	60 units at $36
21	Sale	35 units
23	Sale	10 units
30	Purchase	75 units at $38

The business maintains a perpetual inventory system, costing by the first-in, first-out method. Determine the cost of the merchandise sold for each sale and the inventory balance after each sale, presenting the data in the form illustrated in Exhibit 3.

EX 6-4
Perpetual inventory using LIFO
objs. **2, 3**

✔ Inventory balance, April 30, $3,740

Assume that the business in Exercise 6-3 maintains a perpetual inventory system, costing by the last-in, first-out method. Determine the cost of merchandise sold for each sale and the inventory balance after each sale, presenting the data in the form illustrated in Exhibit 4.

EX 6-5
Perpetual inventory using LIFO
objs. **2, 3**

✔ Inventory balance, March 31, $14,600

Beginning inventory, purchases, and sales data for cell phones for March are as follows:

Inventory		Purchases		Sales	
March 1	1,000 units at $40	March 5	500 units at $42	March 8	700 units
		20	450 units at $44	14	600 units
				31	300 units

Assuming that the perpetual inventory system is used, costing by the LIFO method, determine the cost of merchandise sold for each sale and the inventory balance after each sale, presenting the data in the form illustrated in Exhibit 4.

EX 6-6
Perpetual inventory using FIFO
objs. **2, 3**

✔ Inventory balance, March 31, $15,400

Assume that the business in Exercise 6-5 maintains a perpetual inventory system, costing by the first-in, first-out method. Determine the cost of merchandise sold for each sale and the inventory balance after each sale, presenting the data in the form illustrated in Exhibit 3.

EX 6-7
FIFO, LIFO costs under perpetual inventory system
objs. **2, 3**
✔ a. $19,200

The following units of a particular item were available for sale during the year:

Beginning inventory	150 units at $75
Sale	120 units at $125
First purchase	400 units at $78
Sale	200 units at $125
Second purchase	300 units at $80
Sale	290 units at $125

The firm uses the perpetual inventory system, and there are 240 units of the item on hand at the end of the year. What is the total cost of the ending inventory according to (a) FIFO, (b) LIFO?

EX 6-8
Periodic inventory by three methods
objs. **2, 4**
✔ b. $6,414

The units of an item available for sale during the year were as follows:

Jan. 1	Inventory	27 units at $120
Feb. 17	Purchase	54 units at $138
July 21	Purchase	63 units at $156
Nov. 23	Purchase	36 units at $165

There are 50 units of the item in the physical inventory at December 31. The periodic inventory system is used. Determine the inventory cost by (a) the first-in, first-out method, (b) the last-in, first-out method, and (c) the average cost method.

EX 6-9
Periodic inventory by three methods; cost of merchandise sold

objs. 2, 4

✔ a. Inventory, $2,508

The units of an item available for sale during the year were as follows:

Jan. 1	Inventory	42 units at $60
Mar. 10	Purchase	58 units at $65
Aug. 30	Purchase	20 units at $68
Dec. 12	Purchase	30 units at $70

There are 36 units of the item in the physical inventory at December 31. The periodic inventory system is used. Determine the inventory cost and the cost of merchandise sold by three methods, presenting your answers in the following form:

	Cost	
Inventory Method	**Merchandise Inventory**	**Merchandise Sold**
a. First-in, first-out	$	$
b. Last-in, first-out		
c. Average cost		

EX 6-10
Comparing inventory methods

obj. 5

Assume that a firm separately determined inventory under FIFO and LIFO and then compared the results.

1. In each space below, place the correct sign [less than (<), greater than (>), or equal (=)] for each comparison, assuming periods of rising prices.

a. FIFO inventory	_____	LIFO inventory
b. FIFO cost of goods sold	_____	LIFO cost of goods sold
c. FIFO net income	_____	LIFO net income
d. FIFO income tax	_____	LIFO income tax

2. Why would management prefer to use LIFO over FIFO in periods of rising prices?

EX 6-11
Lower-of-cost-or-market inventory

obj. 6

✔ LCM: $16,990

On the basis of the following data, determine the value of the inventory at the lower of cost or market. Assemble the data in the form illustrated in Exhibit 8.

Commodity	Inventory Quantity	Unit Cost Price	Unit Market Price
Aquarius	20	$ 80	$ 92
Capricorn	50	70	65
Leo	8	300	280
Scorpio	30	40	30
Taurus	100	90	94

EX 6-12
Merchandise inventory on the balance sheet

obj. 6

Based on the data in Exercise 6-11 and assuming that cost was determined by the FIFO method, show how the merchandise inventory would appear on the balance sheet.

EX 6-13
Effect of errors in physical inventory

obj. 6

Montana White Water Co. sells canoes, kayaks, whitewater rafts, and other boating supplies. During the taking of its physical inventory on December 31, 2010, Montana White Water incorrectly counted its inventory as $315,600 instead of the correct amount of $325,000.

a. State the effect of the error on the December 31, 2010, balance sheet of Montana White Water.
b. State the effect of the error on the income statement of Montana White Water for the year ended December 31, 2010.

EX 6-14
Effect of errors in physical inventory

obj. 6

Boss Motorcycle Shop sells motorcycles, ATVs, and other related supplies and accessories. During the taking of its physical inventory on December 31, 2010, Boss Motorcycle Shop incorrectly counted its inventory as $195,750 instead of the correct amount of $188,200.

a. State the effect of the error on the December 31, 2010, balance sheet of Boss Motorcycle Shop.
b. State the effect of the error on the income statement of Boss Motorcycle Shop for the year ended December 31, 2010.

EX 6-15
Error in inventory
obj. 6

During 2010, the accountant discovered that the physical inventory at the end of 2009 had been understated by $11,900. Instead of correcting the error, however, the accountant assumed that an $11,900 overstatement of the physical inventory in 2010 would balance out the error.

➤ Are there any flaws in the accountant's assumption? Explain.

Appendix
EX 6-16
Retail inventory
method

A business using the retail method of inventory costing determines that merchandise inventory at retail is $950,000. If the ratio of cost to retail price is 66%, what is the amount of inventory to be reported on the financial statements?

Appendix
EX 6-17
Retail inventory
method

A business using the retail method of inventory costing determines that merchandise inventory at retail is $880,000. If the ratio of cost to retail price is 65%, what is the amount of inventory to be reported on the financial statements?

Appendix
EX 6-18
Retail inventory
method

A business using the retail method of inventory costing determines that merchandise inventory at retail is $375,000. If the ratio of cost to retail price is 60%, what is the amount of inventory to be reported on the financial statements?

Appendix
EX 6-19
Retail inventory
method

✔ Inventory, April
30: $165,000

On the basis of the following data, estimate the cost of the merchandise inventory at April 30 by the retail method:

		Cost	Retail
April 1	Merchandise inventory	$ 180,000	$ 300,000
April 1–30	Purchases (net)	1,200,000	2,000,000
April 1–30	Sales (net)		2,025,000

Appendix
EX 6-20
Gross profit
inventory method

The merchandise inventory was destroyed by fire on October 11. The following data were obtained from the accounting records:

Jan. 1	Merchandise inventory	$ 260,000
Jan. 1–Oct. 11	Purchases (net)	1,900,000
	Sales (net)	3,200,000
	Estimated gross profit rate	40% .4

a. Estimate the cost of the merchandise destroyed.
b. Briefly describe the situations in which the gross profit method is useful.

Appendix
EX 6-21
Gross profit
method

Based on the following data, estimate the cost of ending merchandise inventory:

Sales (net)	$4,800,000
Estimated gross profit rate	40%
Beginning merchandise inventory	$ 250,000
Purchases (net)	2,900,000
Merchandise available for sale	$3,150,000

Appendix
EX 6-22
Gross profit
method

Based on the following data, estimate the cost of ending merchandise inventory:

Sales (net)	$1,500,000
Estimated gross profit rate	38%
Beginning merchandise inventory	$ 80,000
Purchases (net)	948,000
Merchandise available for sale	$1,028,000

EX 6-23
Inventory turnover

The following data were taken from recent annual reports of Apple Computer, Inc., a manufacturer of personal computers and related products, and American Greetings Corporation, a manufacturer and distributor of greeting cards and related products:

	Apple	American Greetings
Cost of goods sold	$13,717,000,000	$826,791,000
Inventory, end of year	270,000,000	187,817,000
Inventory, beginning of the year	165,000,000	230,308,000

a. Determine the inventory turnover for Apple and American Greetings. Round to one decimal place.
b. Would you expect American Greetings' inventory turnover to be higher or lower than Apple's? Why?

EX 6-24
Inventory turnover and number of days' sales in inventory

✔ a. Kroger, 33 days' sales in inventory

Kroger, Safeway Inc., and Winn-Dixie Stores Inc. are three grocery chains in the United States. Inventory management is an important aspect of the grocery retail business. Recent balance sheets for these three companies indicated the following merchandise inventory information:

	Merchandise Inventory	
	End of Year (in millions)	Beginning of Year (in millions)
Kroger	$4,609	$4,486
Safeway	2,643	2,766
Winn-Dixie	523	798

The cost of goods sold for each company were:

	Cost of Goods Sold (in millions)
Kroger	$50,115
Safeway	28,604
Winn-Dixie	5,327

a. Determine the number of days' sales in inventory and inventory turnover for the three companies. Round to the nearest day and one decimal place.
b. Interpret your results in (a).
c. If Safeway had Kroger's number of days' sales in inventory, how much additional cash flow (round to nearest million) would have been generated from the smaller inventory relative to its actual average inventory position?

Problems Series A

PR 6-1A
FIFO perpetual inventory

objs. 2, 3

✔ 3. $1,413,500

The beginning inventory of merchandise at Waldo Co. and data on purchases and sales for a three-month period are as follows:

Date	Transaction	Number of Units	Per Unit	Total
March 3	Inventory	60	$1,500	$ 90,000
8	Purchase	120	1,800	216,000
11	Sale	80	5,000	400,000
30	Sale	50	5,000	250,000
April 8	Purchase	100	2,000	200,000
10	Sale	60	5,000	300,000
19	Sale	30	5,000	150,000
28	Purchase	100	2,200	220,000
May 5	Sale	60	5,250	315,000
16	Sale	80	5,250	420,000
21	Purchase	180	2,400	432,000
28	Sale	90	5,250	472,500

Instructions

1. Record the inventory, purchases, and cost of merchandise sold data in a perpetual inventory record similar to the one illustrated in Exhibit 3, using the first-in, first-out method.
2. Determine the total sales and the total cost of merchandise sold for the period. Journalize the entries in the sales and cost of merchandise sold accounts. Assume that all sales were on account.
3. Determine the gross profit from sales for the period.
4. Determine the ending inventory cost.

PR 6-2A
LIFO perpetual inventory

objs. 2, 3

✔ 2. Gross profit, $1,395,500

The beginning inventory for Waldo Co. and data on purchases and sales for a three-month period are shown in Problem 6-1A.

Instructions

1. Record the inventory, purchases, and cost of merchandise sold data in a perpetual inventory record similar to the one illustrated in Exhibit 4, using the last-in, first-out method.
2. Determine the total sales, the total cost of merchandise sold, and the gross profit from sales for the period.
3. Determine the ending inventory cost.

PR 6-3A
Periodic inventory by three methods

objs. 2, 4

✔ 1. $15,583

Artic Appliances uses the periodic inventory system. Details regarding the inventory of appliances at January 1, 2010, purchases invoices during the year, and the inventory count at December 31, 2010, are summarized as follows:

| Model | Inventory, January 1 | Purchases Invoices | | | Inventory Count, December 31 |
		1st	2nd	3rd	
BB900	27 at $213	21 at $215	18 at $222	18 at $225	30
C911	10 at 60	6 at 65	2 at 65	2 at 70	4
L100	6 at 305	3 at 310	3 at 316	4 at 317	4
N201	2 at 520	2 at 527	2 at 530	2 at 535	4
Q73	6 at 520	8 at 531	4 at 549	6 at 542	7
Z120	—	4 at 222	4 at 232	—	2
ZZRF	8 at 70	12 at 72	16 at 74	14 at 78	12

Instructions

1. Determine the cost of the inventory on December 31, 2010, by the first-in, first-out method. Present data in columnar form, using the following headings:

Model	Quantity	Unit Cost	Total Cost

If the inventory of a particular model comprises one entire purchase plus a portion of another purchase acquired at a different unit cost, use a separate line for each purchase.
2. Determine the cost of the inventory on December 31, 2010, by the last-in, first-out method, following the procedures indicated in (1).
3. Determine the cost of the inventory on December 31, 2010, by the average cost method, using the columnar headings indicated in (1).
4. ━━━━➤ Discuss which method (FIFO or LIFO) would be preferred for income tax purposes in periods of (a) rising prices and (b) declining prices.

PR 6-4A
Lower-of-cost-or-market inventory

obj. 6

✔ Total LCM, $43,096

If the working papers correlating with this textbook are not used, omit Problem 6-4A.
Data on the physical inventory of Winesap Co. as of December 31, 2010, are presented in the working papers. The quantity of each commodity on hand has been determined and recorded on the inventory sheet. Unit market prices have also been determined as of December 31 and recorded on the sheet. The inventory is to be determined at cost and also at the lower of cost or market, using the first-in, first-out method. Quantity and cost data from the last purchases invoice of the year and the next-to-the-last purchases invoice are summarized as follows:

Description	Last Purchases Invoice		Next-to-the-Last Purchases Invoice	
	Quantity Purchased	Unit Cost	Quantity Purchased	Unit Cost
Alpha 10	30	$ 60	40	$ 59
Beta 30	25	170	15	180
Charlie 4	20	132	15	131
Echo 9	150	25	100	27
Frank 6	6	550	15	540
George 15	90	16	100	15
Killo 6	8	400	4	398
Quebec 12	500	6	500	7
Romeo 7	75	25	80	26
Sierra 3	5	250	4	260
Washburn 2	100	15	115	14
X-Ray 4	10	750	8	740

Instructions

Record the appropriate unit costs on the inventory sheet, and complete the pricing of the inventory. When there are two different unit costs applicable to an item:

1. Draw a line through the quantity, and insert the quantity and unit cost of the last purchase.
2. On the following line, insert the quantity and unit cost of the next-to-the-last purchase.
3. Total the cost and market columns and insert the lower of the two totals in the Lower of C or M column. The first item on the inventory sheet has been completed as an example.

Appendix PR 6-5A

Retail method; gross profit method

✔ 1. $351,500

Selected data on merchandise inventory, purchases, and sales for Clairemont Co. and Malibu Co. are as follows:

	Cost	Retail
Clairemont Co.		
Merchandise inventory, July 1	$ 300,000	$ 400,000
Transactions during July:		
Purchases (net)	3,400,000	4,600,000
Sales		4,715,000
Sales returns and allowances		190,000
Malibu Co.		
Merchandise inventory, February 1	$ 225,000	
Transactions during February and March:		
Purchases (net)	3,200,000	
Sales	5,200,000	
Sales returns and allowances	95,000	
Estimated gross profit rate	38%	

Instructions

1. Determine the estimated cost of the merchandise inventory of Clairemont Co. on July 31 by the retail method, presenting details of the computations.
2. a. Estimate the cost of the merchandise inventory of Malibu Co. on March 31 by the gross profit method, presenting details of the computations.
   b. Assume that Malibu Co. took a physical inventory on March 31 and discovered that $243,250 of merchandise was on hand. What was the estimated loss of inventory due to theft or damage during February and March?

Problems Series B

PR 6-1B

FIFO perpetual inventory

The beginning inventory at Thoreau Office Supplies and data on purchases and sales for a three-month period are as follows:

objs. 2, 3

✔ 3. $13,270

Date	Transaction	Number of Units	Per Unit	Total
Jan. 1	Inventory	75	$20	$1,500
10	Purchase	200	21	4,200
28	Sale	100	40	4,000
30	Sale	110	40	4,400
Feb. 5	Sale	20	44	880
10	Purchase	120	22	2,640
16	Sale	90	42	3,780
28	Sale	50	45	2,250
Mar. 5	Purchase	175	24	4,200
14	Sale	120	50	6,000
25	Purchase	150	25	3,750
30	Sale	100	50	5,000

Instructions
1. Record the inventory, purchases, and cost of merchandise sold data in a perpetual inventory record similar to the one illustrated in Exhibit 3, using the first-in, first-out method.
2. Determine the total sales and the total cost of merchandise sold for the period. Journalize the entries in the sales and cost of merchandise sold accounts. Assume that all sales were on account.
3. Determine the gross profit from sales for the period.
4. Determine the ending inventory cost.

PR 6-2B
LIFO perpetual inventory

objs. 2, 3

✔ 2. Gross profit, $13,090

The beginning inventory at Thoreau Office Supplies and data on purchases and sales for a three-month period are shown in Problem 6-1B.

Instructions
1. Record the inventory, purchases, and cost of merchandise sold data in a perpetual inventory record similar to the one illustrated in Exhibit 4, using the last-in, first-out method.
2. Determine the total sales, the total cost of merchandise sold, and the gross profit from sales for the period.
3. Determine the ending inventory cost.

PR 6-3B
Periodic inventory by three methods

objs. 2, 4

✔ 1. $7,581

Bulldog Appliances uses the periodic inventory system. Details regarding the inventory of appliances at August 1, 2009, purchases invoices during the year, and the inventory count at July 31, 2010, are summarized as follows:

Model	Inventory, August 1	Purchases Invoices 1st	Purchases Invoices 2nd	Purchases Invoices 3rd	Inventory Count, July 31
ALN3	16 at $ 88	8 at $ 79	6 at $ 85	12 at $ 92	16
UGA1	1 at 75	1 at 65	5 at 68	3 at 70	4
SL89	7 at 242	6 at 250	5 at 260	10 at 259	9
F69	6 at 80	5 at 82	8 at 89	8 at 90	6
H60W	2 at 108	2 at 110	3 at 128	3 at 130	5
J600T	5 at 160	4 at 170	4 at 175	7 at 180	8
ZZH0	—	7 at 75	7 at 100	7 at 101	9

Instructions
1. Determine the cost of the inventory on July 31, 2010, by the first-in, first-out method. Present data in columnar form, using the following headings:

Model	Quantity	Unit Cost	Total Cost

If the inventory of a particular model comprises one entire purchase plus a portion of another purchase acquired at a different unit cost, use a separate line for each purchase.

2. Determine the cost of the inventory on July 31, 2010, by the last-in, first-out method, following the procedures indicated in (1).
3. Determine the cost of the inventory on July 31, 2010, by the average cost method, using the columnar headings indicated in (1).
4. ━━━▶ Discuss which method (FIFO or LIFO) would be preferred for income tax purposes in periods of (a) rising prices and (b) declining prices.

PR 6-4B
Lower-of-cost-or-market inventory

obj. 6

✔ Total LCM, $44,146

If the working papers correlating with this textbook are not used, omit Problem 6-4B.

Data on the physical inventory of Zircon Company as of December 31, 2010, are presented in the working papers. The quantity of each commodity on hand has been determined and recorded on the inventory sheet. Unit market prices have also been determined as of December 31 and recorded on the sheet. The inventory is to be determined at cost and also at the lower of cost or market, using the first-in, first-out method. Quantity and cost data from the last purchases invoice of the year and the next-to-the-last purchases invoice are summarized as follows:

Description	Last Purchases Invoice		Next-to-the-Last Purchases Invoice	
	Quantity Purchased	Unit Cost	Quantity Purchased	Unit Cost
Alpha 10	30	$ 60	30	$ 59
Beta 30	35	175	20	180
Charlie 4	20	130	25	129
Echo 9	150	26	100	27
Frank 6	10	565	10	560
George 15	100	15	100	14
Killo 6	10	385	5	384
Quebec 12	400	7	500	6
Romeo 7	80	22	50	21
Sierra 3	5	250	4	260
Washburn 2	90	24	80	22
X-Ray 4	10	750	9	745

Instructions

Record the appropriate unit costs on the inventory sheet, and complete the pricing of the inventory. When there are two different unit costs applicable to an item, proceed as follows:

1. Draw a line through the quantity, and insert the quantity and unit cost of the last purchase.
2. On the following line, insert the quantity and unit cost of the next-to-the-last purchase.
3. Total the cost and market columns and insert the lower of the two totals in the Lower of C or M column. The first item on the inventory sheet has been completed as an example.

Appendix PR 6-5B
Retail method; gross profit method

✔ 1. $340,000

Selected data on merchandise inventory, purchases, and sales for Gainesville Co. and Tallahassee Co. are as follows:

	Cost	Retail
Gainesville Co.		
Merchandise inventory, April 1	$ 200,000	$ 300,000
Transactions during April:		
Purchases (net)	2,520,000	3,700,000
Sales		3,550,000
Sales returns and allowances		50,000
Tallahassee Co.		
Merchandise inventory, October 1	$ 300,000	
Transactions during October through December:		
Purchases (net)	1,800,000	
Sales	2,796,000	
Sales returns and allowances	96,000	
Estimated gross profit rate	36%	

Instructions

1. Determine the estimated cost of the merchandise inventory of Gainesville Co. on April 30 by the retail method, presenting details of the computations.
2. a. Estimate the cost of the merchandise inventory of Tallahassee Co. on December 31 by the gross profit method, presenting details of the computations.
   b. Assume that Tallahassee Co. took a physical inventory on December 31 and discovered that $358,500 of merchandise was on hand. What was the estimated loss of inventory due to theft or damage during October through December?

Special Activities

SA 6-1
Ethics and profes-
sional conduct in
business

Ebba Co. is experiencing a decrease in sales and operating income for the fiscal year ending December 31, 2010. Cody Bryant, controller of Ebba Co., has suggested that all orders received before the end of the fiscal year be shipped by midnight, December 31, 2010, even if the shipping department must work overtime. Since Ebba Co. ships all merchandise FOB shipping point, it would record all such shipments as sales for the year ending December 31, 2010, thereby offsetting some of the decreases in sales and operating income.

Discuss whether Cody Bryant is behaving in a professional manner.

SA 6-2
LIFO and inventory
flow

The following is an excerpt from a conversation between Chad Lindy, the warehouse manager for House of Foods Wholesale Co., and its accountant, Summer Roseberry. Wholesale operates a large regional warehouse that supplies produce and other grocery products to grocery stores in smaller communities.

Chad: Summer, can you explain what's going on here with these monthly statements?

Summer: Sure, Chad. How can I help you?

Chad: I don't understand this last-in, first-out inventory procedure. It just doesn't make sense.

Summer: Well, what it means is that we assume that the last goods we receive are the first ones sold. So the inventory is made up of the items we purchased first.

Chad: Yes, but that's my problem. It doesn't work that way! We always distribute the oldest produce first. Some of that produce is perishable! We can't keep any of it very long or it'll spoil.

Summer: Chad, you don't understand. We only *assume* that the products we distribute are the last ones received. We don't actually have to distribute the goods in this way.

Chad: I always thought that accounting was supposed to show what really happened. It all sounds like "make believe" to me! Why not report what really happens?

Respond to Chad's concerns.

SA 6-3
Costing inventory

Mimotopes Company began operations in 2009 by selling a single product. Data on purchases and sales for the year were as follows:

Purchases:

Date	Units Purchased	Unit Cost	Total Cost
April 6	15,500	$12.20	$ 189,100
May 18	16,500	13.00	214,500
June 6	20,000	13.20	264,000
July 10	20,000	14.00	280,000
August 10	13,600	14.25	193,800
October 25	6,400	14.50	92,800
November 4	4,000	14.95	59,800
December 10	4,000	16.00	64,000
	100,000		$1,358,000

(continued)

Sales:

April	8,000 units
May	8,000
June	10,000
July	12,000
August	14,000
September	14,000
October	9,000
November	5,000
December	4,000
Total units	84,000
Total sales	$1,300,000

On January 6, 2010, the president of the company, Mohammad Zanelli, asked for your advice on costing the 16,000-unit physical inventory that was taken on December 31, 2009. Moreover, since the firm plans to expand its product line, he asked for your advice on the use of a perpetual inventory system in the future.

1. Determine the cost of the December 31, 2009, inventory under the periodic system, using the (a) first-in, first-out method, (b) last-in, first-out method, and (c) average cost method.
2. Determine the gross profit for the year under each of the three methods in (1).
3. a. ➤ Explain varying viewpoints why each of the three inventory costing methods may best reflect the results of operations for 2009.
   b. ➤ Which of the three inventory costing methods may best reflect the replacement cost of the inventory on the balance sheet as of December 31, 2009?
   c. ➤ Which inventory costing method would you choose to use for income tax purposes? Why?
   d. ➤ Discuss the advantages and disadvantages of using a perpetual inventory system. From the data presented in this case, is there any indication of the adequacy of inventory levels during the year?

SA 6-4
Inventory ratios for Dell and HP

Dell Inc. and Hewlett-Packard Development Company, L.P. (HP) are both manufacturers of computer equipment and peripherals. However, the two companies follow two different strategies. Dell follows primarily a build-to-order strategy, where the consumer orders the computer from a Web page. The order is then manufactured and shipped to the customer within days of the order. In contrast, HP follows a build-to-stock strategy, where the computer is first built for inventory, then sold from inventory to retailers, such as Best Buy. The two strategies can be seen in the difference between the inventory turnover and number of days' sales in inventory ratios for the two companies. The following financial statement information is provided for Dell and HP for a recent fiscal year (in millions):

	Dell	HP
Inventory, beginning of period	$ 459	$ 6,877
Inventory, end of period	576	7,750
Cost of goods sold	45,958	69,178

a. Determine the inventory turnover ratio and number of days' sales in inventory ratio for each company. Round to one decimal place.
b. ➤ Interpret the difference between the ratios for the two companies.

SA 6-5
Comparing inventory ratios for two companies

Tiffany Co. is a high-end jewelry retailer, while Amazon.com uses its e-commerce services, features, and technologies to sell its products through the Internet. Recent balance sheet inventory disclosures for Tiffany and Amazon.com (in thousands) are as follows:

	End-of-Period Inventory	Beginning-of-Period Inventory
Tiffany Co.	$1,214,622	$1,060,164
Amazon.com	877,000	566,000

The cost of merchandise sold reported by each company was as follows:

	Tiffany Co.	Amazon.com
Cost of merchandise sold	$1,172,646	$8,255,000

a. Determine the inventory turnover and number of days' sales in inventory for Tiffany and Amazon.com. Round to two decimal places.

b. 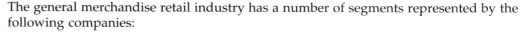 Interpret your results.

SA 6-6
**Comparing inventory
ratios for three
companies**

The general merchandise retail industry has a number of segments represented by the following companies:

Company Name	Merchandise Concept
Costco Wholesale Corporation	Membership warehouse
Wal-Mart	Discount general merchandise
JCPenney	Department store

For a recent year, the following cost of merchandise sold and beginning and ending inventories have been provided from corporate annual reports (in millions) for these three companies:

	Costco	Wal-Mart	JCPenney
Cost of merchandise sold	$52,746	$264,152	$12,078
Merchandise inventory, beginning	4,015	32,191	3,210
Merchandise inventory, ending	4,569	33,685	3,400

a. Determine the inventory turnover ratio for all three companies. Round to one decimal place.

b. Determine the number of days' sales in inventory for all three companies. Round to one decimal place.

c. ━━━━▶ Interpret these results based on each company's merchandise concept.

Answers to Self-Examination Questions

1. **A** The FIFO method (answer A) is based on the assumption that costs are charged against revenue in the order in which they were incurred. The LIFO method (answer B) charges the most recent costs incurred against revenue, and the average cost method (answer C) charges a weighted average of unit costs of items sold against revenue. The perpetual inventory system (answer D) is a system and not a method of costing.

2. **A** The LIFO method of costing is based on the assumption that costs should be charged against revenue in the reverse order in which costs were incurred. Thus, the oldest costs are assigned to inventory. Thirty of the 35 units would be assigned a unit cost of $20 (since 10 of the beginning inventory units were sold on the first sale), and the remaining 5 units would be assigned a cost of $23, for a total of $715 (answer A).

3. **D** The FIFO method of costing is based on the assumption that costs should be charged against revenue in the order in which they were incurred (first-in, first-out). Thus, the most recent costs are assigned to inventory. The 35 units would be assigned a unit cost of $23 (answer D).

4. **B** When the price level is steadily rising, the earlier unit costs are lower than recent unit costs. Under the FIFO method (answer B), these earlier costs are matched against revenue to yield the highest possible net income. The periodic inventory system (answer D) is a system and not a method of costing.

5. **D** The understatement of inventory by $7,500 at the end of the year will cause the cost of merchandise sold for the year to be overstated by $7,500, the gross profit for the year to be understated by $7,500, the merchandise inventory to be understated by $7,500, and the net income for the year to be understated by $7,500 (answer D).

CHAPTER 7

Sarbanes-Oxley, Internal Control, and Cash

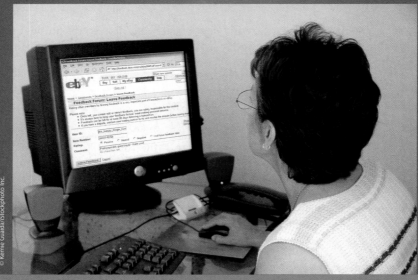

© Kemie Guaida/iStockphoto Inc.

e B A Y   I N C.

Controls are a part of your everyday life. At one extreme, laws are used to limit your behavior. For example, the speed limit is a control on your driving, designed for traffic safety. In addition, you are also affected by many nonlegal controls. For example, you can keep credit card receipts in order to compare your transactions to the monthly credit card statement. Comparing receipts to the monthly statement is a control designed to catch mistakes made by the credit card company. Likewise, recording checks in your checkbook is a control that you can use at the end of the month to verify the accuracy of your bank statement. In addition, banks give you a personal identification number (PIN) as a control against unauthorized access to your cash if you lose your automated teller machine (ATM) card. Dairies use freshness dating on their milk containers as a control to prevent the purchase or sale of soured milk. As you can see, you use and encounter controls every day.

Just as there are many examples of controls throughout society, businesses must also implement controls to help guide the behavior of their managers, employees, and customers. For example, eBay Inc. maintains an Internet-based marketplace for the sale of goods and services. Using eBay's online platform, buyers and sellers can browse, buy, and sell a wide variety of items including antiques and used cars. However, in order to maintain the integrity and trust of its buyers and sellers, eBay must have controls to ensure that buyers pay for their items and sellers don't misrepresent their items or fail to deliver sales. One such control eBay uses is a feedback forum that estabilishes buyer and seller reputations. A prospective buyer or seller can view the member's reputation and feedback comments before completing a transaction. Dishonest or unfair trading can lead to a negative reputation and even suspension or cancellation of the member's ability to trade on eBay.

In this chapter, we will discuss controls that can be included in accounting systems to provide reasonable assurance that the financial statements are reliable. We also discuss controls over cash that you can use to determine whether your bank has made any errors in your account. We begin this chapter by discussing the Sarbanes-Oxley Act of 2002 and its impact on controls and financial reporting.

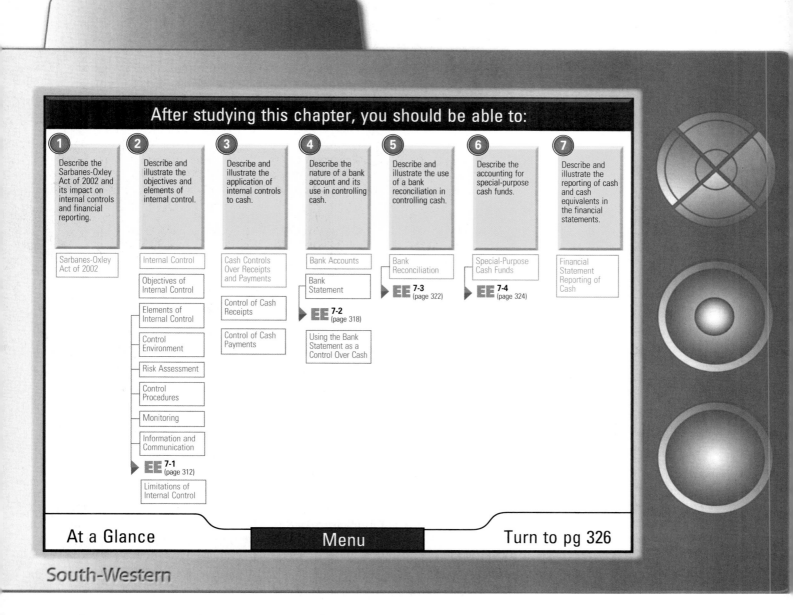

After studying this chapter, you should be able to:

1 Describe the Sarbanes-Oxley Act of 2002 and its impact on internal controls and financial reporting.

Sarbanes-Oxley Act of 2002

2 Describe and illustrate the objectives and elements of internal control.

Internal Control

Objectives of Internal Control

Elements of Internal Control

Control Environment

Risk Assessment

Control Procedures

Monitoring

Information and Communication

▶ **EE** 7-1 (page 312)

Limitations of Internal Control

3 Describe and illustrate the application of internal controls to cash.

Cash Controls Over Receipts and Payments

Control of Cash Receipts

Control of Cash Payments

4 Describe the nature of a bank account and its use in controlling cash.

Bank Accounts

Bank Statement

▶ **EE** 7-2 (page 318)

Using the Bank Statement as a Control Over Cash

5 Describe and illustrate the use of a bank reconciliation in controlling cash.

Bank Reconciliation

▶ **EE** 7-3 (page 322)

6 Describe the accounting for special-purpose cash funds.

Special-Purpose Cash Funds

▶ **EE** 7-4 (page 324)

7 Describe and illustrate the reporting of cash and cash equivalents in the financial statements.

Financial Statement Reporting of Cash

At a Glance   Menu   Turn to pg 326

South-Western

---

1 Describe the Sarbanes-Oxley Act of 2002 and its impact on internal controls and financial reporting.

The ex-CEO of WorldCom, Bernard Ebbers, was sentenced to 25 years in prison.

Sarbanes-Oxley Act of 2002

During the financial scandals of the early 2000s, stockholders, creditors, and other investors lost billions of dollars.[1] As a result, the United States Congress passed the **Sarbanes-Oxley Act of 2002**. This act, often referred to as *Sarbanes-Oxley*, is one of the most important laws affecting U.S. companies in recent history. The purpose of Sarbanes-Oxley is to restore public confidence and trust in the financial reporting of companies.

Sarbanes-Oxley applies only to companies whose stock is traded on public exchanges, referred to as *publicly held companies*. However, Sarbanes-Oxley highlighted the importance of assessing the financial controls and reporting of all companies. As a result, companies of all sizes have been influenced by Sarbanes-Oxley.

Sarbanes-Oxley emphasizes the importance of effective internal control.[2] **Internal control** is defined as the procedures and processes used by a company to:

1 Exhibit 2 in Chapter 1 briefly summarizes these scandals.

2 Sarbanes-Oxley also has important implications for corporate governance and the regulation of the public accounting profession. This chapter, however, focuses on the internal control implications of Sarbanes-Oxley.

1. Safeguard its assets.
2. Process information accurately.
3. Ensure compliance with laws and regulations.

Sarbanes-Oxley requires companies to maintain effective internal controls over the recording of transactions and the preparing of financial statements. Such controls are important because they deter fraud and prevent misleading financial statements as shown below.

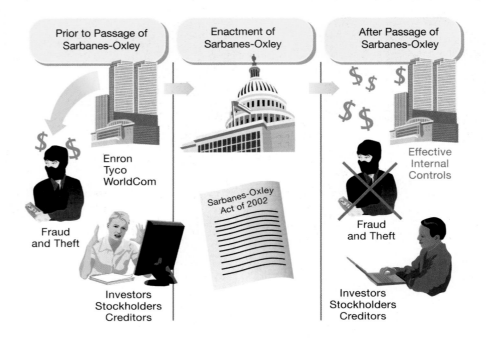

It is estimated that companies spend millions each year to comply with the requirements of Sarbanes-Oxley.

Sarbanes-Oxley also requires companies and their independent accountants to report on the effectiveness of the company's internal controls.[3] These reports are required to be filed with the company's annual 10-K report with the Securities and Exchange Commission. Companies are also encouraged to include these reports in their annual reports to stockholders. An example of such a report by the management of Nike is shown in Exhibit 1.

Exhibit 1

Sarbanes-Oxley Report of Nike

Management's Annual Report on Internal Control Over Financial Reporting

Management is responsible for establishing and maintaining adequate internal control over financial reporting . . . , Under the supervision and with the participation of our Chief Executive Officer and Chief Financial Officer, our management conducted an evaluation of the effectiveness of our internal control over financial reporting based upon the framework in *Internal Control—Integrated Framework* issued by the Committee of Sponsoring Organizations of the Treadway Commission. Based on that evaluation, our management concluded that our internal control over financial reporting is effective as of May 31, 2007. . . .

PricewaterhouseCoopers LLP, an independent registered public accounting firm, has audited . . . management's assessment of the effectiveness of our internal control over financial reporting . . . and . . . the effectiveness of our internal control over financial reporting . . . as stated in their report . . . .

MARK G. PARKER
Chief Executive Officer and President

DONALD W. BLAIR
Chief Financial Officer

3 These reporting requirements are required under Section 404 of the act. As a result, these requirements and reports are often referred to as 404 requirements and 404 reports.

Exhibit 1 indicates that Nike based its evaluation of internal controls on *Internal Control—Integrated Framework*, which was issued by the Committee of Sponsoring Organizations (COSO) of the Treadway Commission. This framework is the standard by which companies design, analyze, and evaluate internal controls. For this reason, this framework is used as the basis for discussing internal controls.

Internal Control

2 Describe and illustrate the objectives and elements of internal control.

Internal Control—Integrated Framework is the standard by which companies design, analyze, and evaluate internal control.[4] In this section, the objectives of internal control are described followed by a discussion of how these objectives can be achieved through the *Integrated Framework*'s five elements of internal control.

Objectives of Internal Control

Information on *Internal Control—Integrated Framework* can be found on COSO's Web site at http://www.coso.org/.

The objectives of internal control are to provide reasonable assurance that:

1. Assets are safeguarded and used for business purposes.
2. Business information is accurate.
3. Employees and managers comply with laws and regulations.

These objectives are illustrated below.

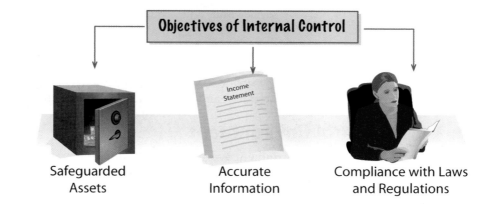

Safeguarded Assets   Accurate Information   Compliance with Laws and Regulations

The Association of Certified Fraud Examiners has estimated that businesses will lose over $650 billion, or around 5% of revenue, to employee fraud.

Source: *2006 Report to the Nation: Occupational Fraud and Abuse,* Association of Certified Fraud Examiners.

Internal control can safeguard assets by preventing theft, fraud, misuse, or misplacement. A serious concern of internal control is preventing employee fraud. **Employee fraud** is the intentional act of deceiving an employer for personal gain. Such fraud may range from minor overstating of a travel expense report to stealing millions of dollars. Employees stealing from a business often adjust the accounting records in order to hide their fraud. Thus, employee fraud usually affects the accuracy of business information.

Accurate information is necessary to successfully operate a business. Businesses must also comply with laws, regulations, and financial reporting standards. Examples of such standards include environmental regulations, safety regulations, and generally accepted accounting principles (GAAP).

Elements of Internal Control

The three internal control objectives can be achieved by applying the five **elements of internal control** set forth by the *Integrated Framework*.[5] These elements are as follows:

1. Control environment
2. Risk assessment

---

4 *Internal Control—Integrated Framework* by the Committee of Sponsoring Organizations of the Treadway Commission, 1992.
5 Ibid., 12–14.

3. Control procedures
4. Monitoring
5. Information and communication

The elements of internal control are illustrated in Exhibit 2.

Exhibit 2

Elements of Internal Control

In Exhibit 2, the elements of internal control form an umbrella over the business to protect it from control threats. The control environment is the size of the umbrella. Risk assessment, control procedures, and monitoring are the fabric of the umbrella, which keep it from leaking. Information and communication connect the umbrella to management.

Control Environment

The **control environment** is the overall attitude of management and employees about the importance of controls. Three factors influencing a company's control environment are as follows:

1. Management's philosophy and operating style
2. The company's organizational structure
3. The company's personnel policies

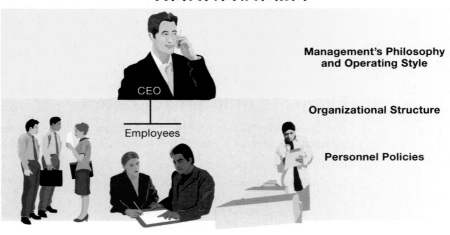

Management's philosophy and operating style relates to whether management emphasizes the importance of internal controls. An emphasis on controls and adherence to control policies creates an effective control environment. In contrast, over-emphasizing operating goals and tolerating deviations from control policies creates an ineffective control environment.

The business's organizational structure is the framework for planning and controlling operations. For example, a retail store chain might organize each of its stores as separate business units. Each store manager has full authority over pricing and other operating activities. In such a structure, each store manager has the responsibility for establishing an effective control environment.

The business's personnel policies involve the hiring, training, evaluation, compensation, and promotion of employees. In addition, job descriptions, employee codes of ethics, and conflict-of-interest policies are part of the personnel policies. Such policies can enhance the internal control environment if they provide reasonable assurance that only competent, honest employees are hired and retained.

Risk Assessment

All businesses face risks such as changes in customer requirements, competitive threats, regulatory changes, and changes in economic factors. Management should identify such risks, analyze their significance, assess their likelihood of occurring, and take any necessary actions to minimize them.

Control Procedures

A bank officer who was not required to take vacations stole almost $5 million by printing fake certificates of deposit. The theft was discovered when the bank began requiring all employees to take vacations.

Control procedures provide reasonable assurance that business goals will be achieved, including the prevention of fraud. Control procedures, which constitute one of the most important elements of internal control, include the following as shown in Exhibit 3.

1. Competent personnel, rotating duties, and mandatory vacations
2. Separating responsibilities for related operations
3. Separating operations, custody of assets, and accounting
4. Proofs and security measures

Exhibit 3

Internal Control Procedures

Control Threats

Control Procedures
Competent personnel, rotating duties, and mandatory vacations
Separating responsibilities for related operations
Separating operations, custody of assets, and accounting
Proofs and security measures

Management   Business

Competent Personnel, Rotating Duties, and Mandatory Vacations A successful company needs competent employees who are able to perform the duties that they are assigned. Procedures should be established for properly training and supervising employees. It is also advisable to rotate duties of accounting personnel and mandate vacations for all employees. In this way, employees are encouraged to adhere to procedures. Cases of employee fraud are often discovered when a long-term employee, who never took vacations, missed work because of an illness or another unavoidable reason.

An accounting clerk for the Grant County (Washington) Alcoholism Program was in charge of collecting money, making deposits, and keeping the records. While the clerk was away on maternity leave, the replacement clerk discovered a fraud: $17,800 in fees had been collected but had been hidden for personal gain.

Separating Responsibilities for Related Operations The responsibility for related operations should be divided among two or more persons. This decreases the possibility of errors and fraud. For example, if the same person orders supplies, verifies the receipt of the supplies, and pays the supplier, the following abuses may occur:

1. Orders may be placed on the basis of friendship with a supplier, rather than on price, quality, and other objective factors.
2. The quantity and quality of supplies received may not be verified; thus, the company may pay for supplies not received or that are of poor quality.
3. Supplies may be stolen by the employee.
4. The validity and accuracy of invoices may not be verified; hence, the company may pay false or inaccurate invoices.

For the preceding reasons, the responsibilities for purchasing, receiving, and paying for supplies should be divided among three persons or departments.

An accounts payable clerk created false invoices and submitted them for payment. The clerk obtained the checks, cashed them, and stole thousands of dollars.

Separating Operations, Custody of Assets, and Accounting The responsibilities for operations, custody of assets, and accounting should be separated. In this way, the accounting records serve as an independent check on the operating managers and the employees who have custody of assets.

To illustrate, employees who handle cash receipts should not record cash receipts in the accounting records. To do so would allow employees to borrow or steal cash and hide the theft in the accounting records. Likewise, operating managers should not also record the results of operations. To do so would allow the managers to distort the accounting reports to show favorable results, which might allow them to receive larger bonuses.

Proofs and Security Measures Proofs and security measures are used to safeguard assets and ensure reliable accounting data. Proofs involve procedures such as authorization, approval, and reconciliation. For example, an employee planning to travel on company business may be required to complete a "travel request" form for a manager's authorization and approval.

Integrity, Objectivity, and Ethics in Business

TIPS ON PREVENTING EMPLOYEE FRAUD IN SMALL COMPANIES

- Do not have the same employee write company checks and keep the books. Look for payments to vendors you don't know or payments to vendors whose names appear to be misspelled.
- If your business has a computer system, restrict access to accounting files as much as possible. Also, keep a backup copy of your accounting files and store it at an off-site location.
- Be wary of anybody working in finance that declines to take vacations. They may be afraid that a replacement will uncover fraud.

- Require and monitor supporting documentation (such as vendor invoices) before signing checks.
- Track the number of credit card bills you sign monthly.
- Limit and monitor access to important documents and supplies, such as blank checks and signature stamps.
- Check W-2 forms against your payroll annually to make sure you're not carrying any fictitious employees.
- Rely on yourself, not on your accountant, to spot fraud.

Source: Steve Kaufman, "Embezzlement Common at Small Companies," Knight-Ridder Newspapers, reported in *Athens Daily News/Athens Banner-Herald*, March 10, 1996, p. 4D.

Documents used for authorization and approval should be prenumbered, accounted for, and safeguarded. Prenumbering of documents helps prevent transactions from being recorded more than once or not at all. In addition, accounting for and safeguarding prenumbered documents helps prevent fraudulent transactions from being recorded. For example, blank checks are prenumbered and safeguarded. Once a payment has been properly authorized and approved, the checks are filled out and issued.

Reconciliations are also an important control. Later in this chapter, the use of bank reconciliations as an aid in controlling cash is described and illustrated.

Security measures involve measures to safeguard assets. For example, cash on hand should be kept in a cash register or safe. Inventory not on display should be stored in a locked storeroom or warehouse. Accounting records such as the accounts receivable subsidiary ledger should also be safeguarded to prevent their loss. For example, electronically maintained accounting records should be safeguarded with access codes and backed up so that any lost or damaged files could be recovered if necessary.

A 24-hour convenience store could use a security guard, video cameras, and an alarm system to deter robberies.

Monitoring

Monitoring the internal control system is used to locate weaknesses and improve controls. Monitoring often includes observing employee behavior and the accounting system for indicators of control problems. Some such indicators are shown in Exhibit 4.[6]

Evaluations of controls are often performed when there are major changes in strategy, senior management, business structure, or operations. Internal auditors, who are independent of operations, usually perform such evaluations. Internal auditors are also responsible for day-to-day monitoring of controls. External auditors also evaluate and report on internal control as part of their annual financial statement audit.

Exhibit 4

Warning Signs of Internal Control Problems

Warning signs with regard to people

1. Abrupt change in lifestyle (without winning the lottery).
2. Close social relationships with suppliers.
3. Refusing to take a vacation.
4. Frequent borrowing from other employees.
5. Excessive use of alcohol or drugs.

Warning signs from the accounting system

1. Missing documents or gaps in transaction numbers (could mean documents are being used for fraudulent transactions).
2. An unusual increase in customer refunds (refunds may be phony).
3. Differences between daily cash receipts and bank deposits (could mean receipts are being pocketed before being deposited).
4. Sudden increase in slow payments (employee may be pocketing the payments).
5. Backlog in recording transactions (possibly an attempt to delay detection of fraud).

6 Edwin C. Bliss, "Employee Theft," *Boardroom Reports*, July 15, 1994, pp. 5–6.

Information and Communication

Information and communication is an essential element of internal control. Information about the control environment, risk assessment, control procedures, and monitoring is used by management for guiding operations and ensuring compliance with reporting, legal, and regulatory requirements. Management also uses external information to assess events and conditions that impact decision making and external reporting. For example, management uses pronouncements of the Financial Accounting Standards Board (FASB) to assess the impact of changes in reporting standards on the financial statements.

Example Exercise 7-1   Internal Control Elements   ·········▶ 2

Identify each of the following as relating to (a) the control environment, (b) risk assessment, or (c) control procedures.

1. Mandatory vacations
2. Personnel policies
3. Report of outside consultants on future market changes

Follow My Example 7-1

1. (c) control procedures
2. (a) the control environment
3. (b) risk assessment

For Practice: PE 7-1A, PE 7-1B

Limitations of Internal Control

Internal control systems can provide only reasonable assurance for safeguarding assets, processing accurate information, and compliance with laws and regulations. In other words, internal controls are not a guarantee. This is due to the following factors:

1. The human element of controls
2. Cost-benefit considerations

The *human element* recognizes that controls are applied and used by humans. As a result, human errors can occur because of fatigue, carelessness, confusion, or misjudgment. For example, an employee may unintentionally shortchange a customer or miscount the amount of inventory received from a supplier. In addition, two or more employees may collude together to defeat or circumvent internal controls. This latter case often involves fraud and the theft of assets. For example, the cashier and the accounts receivable clerk might collude to steal customer payments on account.

Cost-benefit considerations recognize that cost of internal controls should not exceed their benefits. For example, retail stores could eliminate shoplifting by searching all customers before they leave the store. However, such a control procedure would upset customers and result in lost sales. Instead, retailers use cameras or signs saying *We prosecute all shoplifters*.

3 Describe and illustrate the application of internal controls to cash.

Cash Controls Over Receipts and Payments

Cash includes coins, currency (paper money), checks, and money orders. Money on deposit with a bank or other financial institution that is available for withdrawal is also considered cash. Normally, you can think of cash as anything that a bank would accept for deposit in your account. For example, a check made payable to you could normally be deposited in a bank and, thus, is considered cash.

Businesses usually have several bank accounts. For example, a business might have one bank account for general cash payments and another for payroll. A separate ledger account is normally used for each bank account. For example, a bank account at City Bank could be identified in the ledger as *Cash in Bank—City Bank*. To simplify, we will assume in this chapter that a company has only *one* bank account, which is identified in the ledger as *Cash*.

Cash is the asset most likely to be stolen or used improperly in a business. For this reason, businesses must carefully control cash and cash transactions.

Control of Cash Receipts

To protect cash from theft and misuse, a business must control cash from the time it is received until it is deposited in a bank. Businesses normally receive cash from two main sources.

1. Customers purchasing products or services
2. Customers making payments on account

Cash Received from Cash Sales   An important control to protect cash received in over-the-counter sales is a cash register. The use of a cash register to control cash is shown below.

The Internet has given rise to a form of cash called "cybercash," which is used for Internet transactions, such as being used in conjunction with PayPal.

Fast-food restaurants, such as McDonald's, receive cash primarily from over-the-counter sales. Internet retailers, such Amazon.com, receive cash primarily through electronic funds transfers from credit card companies.

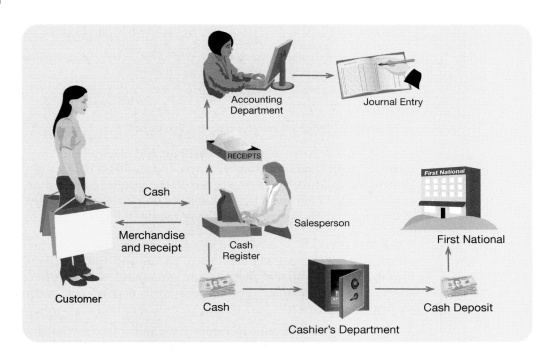

A cash register controls cash as follows:

1. At the beginning of every work shift, each cash register clerk is given a cash drawer containing a predetermined amount of cash. This amount is used for making change for customers and is sometimes called a *change fund*.
2. When a salesperson enters the amount of a sale, the cash register displays the amount to the customer. This allows the customer to verify that the clerk has charged the correct amount. The customer also receives a cash receipt.

3. At the end of the shift, the clerk and the supervisor count the cash in the clerk's cash drawer. The amount of cash in each drawer should equal the beginning amount of cash plus the cash sales for the day.

4. The supervisor takes the cash to the Cashier's Department where it is placed in a safe.

5. The supervisor forwards the clerk's cash register receipts to the Accounting Department.

6. The cashier prepares a bank deposit ticket.

7. The cashier deposits the cash in the bank, or the cash is picked up by an armored car service, such as Wells Fargo.

8. The Accounting Department summarizes the cash receipts and records the day's cash sales.

9. When cash is deposited in the bank, the bank normally stamps a duplicate copy of the deposit ticket with the amount received. This bank receipt is returned to the Accounting Department, where it is compared to the total amount that should have been deposited. This control helps ensure that all the cash is deposited and that no cash is lost or stolen on the way to the bank. Any shortages are thus promptly detected.

Salespersons may make errors in making change for customers or in ringing up cash sales. As a result, the amount of cash on hand may differ from the amount of cash sales. Such differences are recorded in a **cash short and over account**.

To illustrate, assume the following cash register data for May 3:

| Cash register total for cash sales | $35,690 |
| Cash receipts from cash sales | 35,668 |

The cash sales, receipts, and shortage of $22 ($35,690 − $35,668) would be recorded as follows:

May	3	Cash	35,668	
		Cash Short and Over	22	
		Sales		35,690

If there had been cash over, Cash Short and Over would have been credited for the overage. At the end of the accounting period, a debit balance in Cash Short and Over is included in Miscellaneous expense on the income statement. A credit balance is included in the Other income section. If a salesperson consistently has large cash short and over amounts, the supervisor may require the clerk to take additional training.

Cash Received in the Mail Cash is received in the mail when customers pay their bills. This cash is usually in the form of checks and money orders. Most companies design their invoices so that customers return a portion of the invoice, called a *remittance advice*, with their payment. Remittance advices may be used to control cash received in the mail as follows:

1. An employee opens the incoming mail and compares the amount of cash received with the amount shown on the remittance advice. If a customer does not return a remittance advice, the employee prepares one. The remittance advice serves as a record of the cash initially received. It also helps ensure that the posting to the customer's account is for the amount of cash received.

2. The employee opening the mail stamps checks and money orders "For Deposit Only" in the bank account of the business.

3. The remittance advices and their summary totals are delivered to the Accounting Department.

4. All cash and money orders are delivered to the Cashier's Department.

5. The cashier prepares a bank deposit ticket.

6. The cashier deposits the cash in the bank, or the cash is picked up by an armored car service, such as Wells Fargo.

7. An accounting clerk records the cash received and posts the amounts to the customer accounts.

8. When cash is deposited in the bank, the bank normally stamps a duplicate copy of the deposit ticket with the amount received. This bank receipt is returned to the Accounting Department, where it is compared to the total amount that should have been deposited. This control helps ensure that all cash is deposited and that no cash is lost or stolen on the way to the bank. Any shortages are thus promptly detected.

Separating the duties of the Cashier's Department, which handles cash, and the Accounting Department, which records cash, is a control. If Accounting Department employees both handle and record cash, an employee could steal cash and change the accounting records to hide the theft.

Cash Received by EFT Cash may also be received from customers through **electronic funds transfer (EFT)**. For example, customers may authorize automatic electronic transfers from their checking accounts to pay monthly bills for such items as cell phone, Internet, and electric services. In such cases, the company sends the customer's bank a signed form from the customer authorizing the monthly electronic transfers. Each month, the company notifies the customer's bank of the amount of the transfer and the date the transfer should take place. On the due date, the company records the electronic transfer as a receipt of cash to its bank account and posts the amount paid to the customer's account.

Companies encourage customers to use EFT for the following reasons:

1. EFTs cost less than receiving cash payments through the mail.

2. EFTs enhance internal controls over cash since the cash is received directly by the bank without any employees handling cash.

3. EFTs reduce late payments from customers and speed up the processing of cash receipts.

Howard Schultz & Associates (HS&A) specializes in reviewing cash payments for its clients. HS&A searches for errors, such as duplicate payments, failures to take discounts, and inaccurate computations. Amounts recovered for clients range from thousands to millions of dollars.

Control of Cash Payments

The control of cash payments should provide reasonable assurance that:

1. Payments are made for only authorized transactions.

2. Cash is used effectively and efficiently. For example, controls should ensure that all available purchase discounts are taken.

In a small business, an owner/manager may authorize payments based on personal knowledge. In a large business, however, purchasing goods, inspecting the goods received, and verifying the invoices are usually performed by different employees. These duties must be coordinated to ensure that proper payments are made to creditors. One system used for this purpose is the voucher system.

Voucher System A **voucher system** is a set of procedures for authorizing and recording liabilities and cash payments. A **voucher** is any document that serves as proof of authority to pay cash or issue an electronic funds transfer. An invoice that has been approved for payment could be considered a voucher. In many businesses, however, a voucher is a special form used to record data about a liability and the details of its payment.

In a manual system, a voucher is normally prepared after all necessary supporting documents have been received. For the purchase of goods, a voucher is supported by the supplier's invoice, a purchase order, and a receiving report. After a voucher is prepared, it is submitted for approval. Once approved, the voucher is recorded in the accounts and filed by due date. Upon payment, the voucher is recorded in the same manner as the payment of an account payable.

Many businesses and individuals are now using Internet banking services, which provide for the payment of funds electronically.

In a computerized system, data from the supporting documents (such as purchase orders, receiving reports, and suppliers' invoices) are entered directly into computer files. At the due date, the checks are automatically generated and mailed to creditors. At that time, the voucher is electronically transferred to a paid voucher file.

Cash Paid by EFT Cash can also be paid by electronic funds transfer systems. For example, many companies pay their employees by EFT. Under such a system, employees authorize the deposit of their payroll checks directly into their checking accounts. Each pay period, the company transfers the employees' net pay to their checking accounts through the use of EFT. Many companies also use EFT systems to pay their suppliers and other vendors.

Bank Accounts

④ Describe the nature of a bank account and its use in controlling cash.

A major reason that companies use bank accounts is for internal control. Some of the control advantages of using bank accounts are as follows:

1. Bank accounts reduce the amount of cash on hand.
2. Bank accounts provide an independent recording of cash transactions. Reconciling the balance of the cash account in the company's records with the cash balance according to the bank is an important control.
3. Use of bank accounts facilitates the transfer of funds using EFT systems.

Bank Statement

Banks usually maintain a record of all checking account transactions. A summary of all transactions, called a **bank statement**, is mailed to the company (depositor) or made available online, usually each month. The bank statement shows the beginning balance, additions, deductions, and the ending balance. A typical bank statement is shown in Exhibit 5.

Checks or copies of the checks listed in the order that they were paid by the bank may accompany the bank statement. If paid checks are returned, they are stamped "Paid," together with the date of payment. Many banks no longer return checks or check copies. Instead, the check payment information is available online.

The company's checking account balance *in the bank records* is a liability. Thus, in the bank's records, the company's account has a credit balance. Since the bank statement is prepared from the bank's point of view, a credit memo entry on the bank statement indicates an increase (a credit) to the company's account. Likewise, a debit memo entry on the bank statement indicates a decrease (a debit) in the company's account. This relationship is shown below.

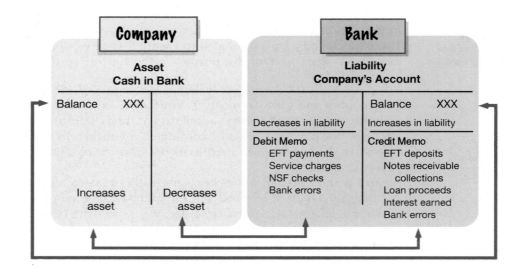

Exhibit 5

Bank Statement

				MEMBER FDIC				PAGE 1

VALLEY NATIONAL BANK OF LOS ANGELES

LOS ANGELES, CA 90020-4253   (310)555-5151

POWER NETWORKING
1000 Belkin Street
Los Angeles, CA 90014 -1000

ACCOUNT NUMBER	1627042
FROM 6/30/09 TO 7/31/09	
BALANCE	4,218.60
22 DEPOSITS	13,749.75
52 WITHDRAWALS	14,698.57
3 OTHER DEBITS AND CREDITS	90.00CR
NEW BALANCE	3,359.78

CHECKS AND OTHER DEBITS						DEPOSITS	DATE	BALANCE
No. 850	819.40	No. 852	122.54			585.75	07/01	3,862.41
No. 854	369.50	No. 853	20.15			421.53	07/02	3,894.29
No. 851	600.00	No. 856	190.70	No. 857	52.50	781.30	07/03	3,832.39
No. 855	25.93	No. 858	160.00			662.50	07/05	4,308.96
No. 860	921.20	NSF	300.00			503.18	07/07	3,590.94

No. 880	32.26	No. 877	535.09			ACH 932.00	07/29	4,136.66
No. 881	21.10	No. 879	732.26	No. 882	126.20	705.21	07/30	3,962.31
		SC	18.00			MS 408.00	07/30	4,352.31
No. 874	26.12	ACH	1,615.13			648.72	07/31	3,359.78

EC	ERROR CORRECTION	ACH	AUTOMATED CLEARING HOUSE
MS	MISCELLANEOUS		
NSF	NOT SUFFICIENT FUNDS	SC	SERVICE CHARGE

THE RECONCILEMENT OF THIS STATEMENT WITH YOUR RECORDS IS ESSENTIAL. ANY ERROR OR EXCEPTION SHOULD BE REPORTED IMMEDIATELY.

A bank makes credit entries (issues credit memos) for the following:

1. Deposits made by electronic funds transfer (EFT)
2. Collections of note receivable for the company
3. Proceeds for a loan made to the company by the bank
4. Interest earned on the company's account
5. Correction (if any) of bank errors

A bank makes debit entries (issues debit memos) for the following:

1. Payments made by electronic funds transfer (EFT)
2. Service charges
3. Customer checks returned for not sufficient funds
4. Correction (if any) of bank errors

Customers' checks returned for not sufficient funds, called *NSF checks*, are customer checks that were initially deposited, but were not paid by the customer's bank. Since the company's bank credited the customer's check to the company's account when it was deposited, the bank debits the company's account (issues a debit memo) when the check is returned without payment.

The reason for a credit or debit memo entry is indicated on the bank statement. Exhibit 5 identifies the following types of credit and debit memo entries:

EC: Error correction to correct bank error
NSF: Not sufficient funds check
SC: Service charge
ACH: Automated clearing house entry for electronic funds transfer
MS: Miscellaneous item such as collection of a note receivable on behalf of the company or receipt of a loan by the company from the bank

The above list includes the notation "ACH" for electronic funds transfers. ACH is a network for clearing electronic funds transfers among individuals, companies, and banks.[7] Because electronic funds transfers may be either deposits or payments, ACH entries may indicate either a debit or credit entry to the company's account. Likewise, entries to correct bank errors and miscellaneous items may indicate a debit or credit entry to the company's account.

Example Exercise 7-2   Items on Company's Bank Statement

The following items may appear on a bank statement:

1. NSF check
2. EFT deposit
3. Service charge
4. Bank correction of an error from recording a $400 check as $40

Using the format shown below, indicate whether the item would appear as a debit or credit memo on the bank statement and whether the item would increase or decrease the balance of the company's account.

Item No.	Appears on the Bank Statement as a Debit or Credit Memo	Increases or Decreases the Balance of the Company's Bank Account

Follow My Example 7-2

Item No.	Appears on the Bank Statement as a Debit or Credit Memo	Increases or Decreases the Balance of the Company's Bank Account
1	debit memo	decreases
2	credit memo	increases
3	debit memo	decreases
4	debit memo	decreases

For Practice: PE 7-2A, PE 7-2B

Using the Bank Statement as a Control Over Cash

The bank statement is a primary control that a company uses over cash. A company uses the bank's statement as a control by comparing the company's recording of cash transactions to those recorded by the bank.

The cash balance shown by a bank statement is usually different from the company's cash balance, as shown in Exhibit 6.

Exhibit 6

**Power
Networking's
Records and
Bank Statement**

Bank Statement		
Beginning balance		$ 4,218.60
Additions:		
Deposits	$13,749.75	
Miscellaneous	408.00	14,157.75
Deductions:		
Checks	$14,698.57	
NSF check	300.00	
Service charge	18.00	(15,016.57)
Ending balance		$ 3,359.78

Power Networking Records	
Beginning balance	$ 4,227.60
Deposits	14,565.95
Checks	(16,243.56)
Ending balance	$ 2,549.99

Power Networking
should determine
the reason for the
difference in these
two amounts.

Differences between the company and bank balance may arise because of a delay by either the company or bank in recording transactions. For example, there is normally a time lag of one or more days between the date a check is written and the date that it is paid by the bank. Likewise, there is normally a time lag between when the company mails a deposit to the bank (or uses the night depository) and when the bank receives and records the deposit.

Differences may also arise because the bank has debited or credited the company's account for transactions that the company will not know about until the bank statement is received. Finally, differences may arise from errors made by either the company or the bank. For example, the company may incorrectly post to Cash a check written for $4,500 as $450. Likewise, a bank may incorrectly record the amount of a check.

Integrity, Objectivity, and Ethics in Business

CHECK FRAUD

Check fraud involves counterfeiting, altering, or otherwise manipulating the information on checks in order to fraudulently cash a check. According to the National Check Fraud Center, check fraud and counterfeiting are among the fastest growing problems affecting the financial system, generating over $10 billion in losses annually. Criminals perpetrate the fraud by taking blank checks from your checkbook, finding a canceled check in the garbage, or removing a check you have mailed to pay bills. Consumers can prevent check fraud by carefully storing blank checks, placing outgoing mail in postal mailboxes, and shredding canceled checks.

Bank Reconciliation

5 Describe and
illustrate the
use of a bank reconciliation in controlling
cash.

A **bank reconciliation** is an analysis of the items and amounts that result in the cash balance reported in the bank statement to differ from the balance of the cash account in the ledger. The adjusted cash balance determined in the bank reconciliation is reported on the balance sheet.

A bank reconciliation is usually divided into two sections as follows:

1. The *bank section* begins with the cash balance according to the bank statement and ends with the *adjusted balance*.

2. The *company section* begins with the cash balance according to the company's records and ends with the *adjusted balance*.

The *adjusted balance* from bank and company sections must be equal. The format of the bank reconciliation is shown below.

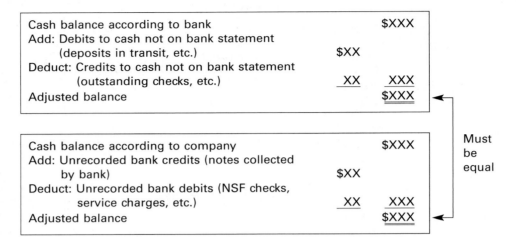

Cash balance according to bank		$XXX
Add: Debits to cash not on bank statement		
(deposits in transit, etc.)	$XX	
Deduct: Credits to cash not on bank statement		
(outstanding checks, etc.)	XX	XXX
Adjusted balance		$XXX

Cash balance according to company		$XXX
Add: Unrecorded bank credits (notes collected		
by bank)	$XX	
Deduct: Unrecorded bank debits (NSF checks,		
service charges, etc.)	XX	XXX
Adjusted balance		$XXX

Must
be
equal

A bank reconciliation is prepared using the following steps:

Bank Section of Reconciliation

Step 1.   Enter the *Cash balance according to bank* from the ending cash balance according to the bank statement.

Step 2.   *Add deposits not recorded by the bank.*
Identify deposits not recorded by the bank by comparing each deposit listed on the bank statement with unrecorded deposits appearing in the preceding period's reconciliation and with the current period's deposits.

Examples: Deposits in transit at the end of the period.

Step 3.   *Deduct outstanding checks that have not been paid by the bank.*
Identify outstanding checks by comparing paid checks with outstanding checks appearing on the preceding period's reconciliation and with recorded checks.

Examples: Outstanding checks at the end of the period.

Step 4.   Determine the *Adjusted balance* by adding Step 2 and deducting Step 3.

Company Section of Reconciliation

Step 5.   Enter the *Cash balance according to company* from the ending cash balance in the ledger.

Step 6.   *Add credit memos that have not been recorded.*
Identify the bank credit memos that have not been recorded by comparing the bank statement credit memos to entries in the journal.

Examples: A note receivable and interest that the bank has collected for the company.

Step 7.   *Deduct debit memos that have not been recorded.*
Identify the bank debit memos that have not been recorded by comparing the bank statement debit memos to entries in the journal.

Examples: Customers' not sufficient funds (NSF) checks; bank service charges.

Step 8.   Determine the *Adjusted balance* by adding Step 6 and deducting Step 7.

Step 9.   Verify that the Adjusted balances determined in Steps 4 and 8 are equal.

The adjusted balances in the bank and company sections of the reconciliation must be equal. If the balances are not equal, an item has been overlooked and must be found.

Sometimes, the adjusted balances are not equal because either the company or the bank has made an error. In such cases, the error is often discovered by comparing the amount of each item (deposit and check) on the bank statement with that in the company's records.

Any bank or company errors discovered should be added or deducted from the bank or company section of the reconciliation depending on the nature of the error. For example, assume that the bank incorrectly recorded a company check for $50 as $500. This bank error of $450 ($500 − $50) would be added to the bank balance in the bank section of the reconciliation. In addition, the bank would be notified of the error so that it could be corrected. On the other hand, assume that the company recorded a deposit of $1,200 as $2,100. This company error of $900 ($2,100 − $1,200) would be deducted from the cash balance in the company section of the bank reconciliation. The company would later correct the error using a journal entry.

To illustrate, we will use the bank statement for Power Networking in Exhibit 5. This bank statement shows a balance of $3,359.78 as of July 31. The cash balance in Power Networking's ledger on the same date is $2,549.99. Using the preceding steps, the following reconciling items were identified:

Step 2. Deposit of July 31, not recorded on bank statement: $816.20
Step 3. Outstanding checks:

Check No. 812	$1,061.00
Check No. 878	435.39
Check No. 883	48.60
Total	$1,544.99

Step 6. Note receivable of $400 plus interest of $8 collected by bank not recorded in the journal as indicated by a credit memo of $408.
Step 7. Check from customer (Thomas Ivey) for $300 returned by bank because of insufficient funds (NSF) as indicated by a debit memo of $300.00.
Bank service charges of $18, not recorded in the journal as indicated by a debit memo of $18.00.

In addition, an error of $9 was discovered. This error occurred when Check No. 879 for $732.26 to Taylor Co., on account, was recorded in the company's journal as $723.26.

The bank reconciliation, based on the Exhibit 5 bank statement and the preceding reconciling items, is shown in Exhibit 7.

The company's records do not need to be updated for any items in the *bank section* of the reconciliation. This section begins with the cash balance according to the bank statement. However, the bank should be notified of any errors that need to be corrected.

The company's records do need to be updated for any items in the *company section* of the bank reconciliation. The company's records are updated using journal entries. For example, journal entries should be made for any unrecorded bank memos and any company errors.

The journal entries for Power Networking, based on the bank reconciliation shown in Exhibit 7, are as follows:

July	31	Cash		408	
		Notes Receivable			400
		Interest Revenue			8
	31	Accounts Receivable—Thomas Ivey		300	
		Miscellaneous Expense		18	
		Accounts Payable—Taylor Co.		9	
		Cash			327

Exhibit 7

Bank Reconciliation for Power Networking

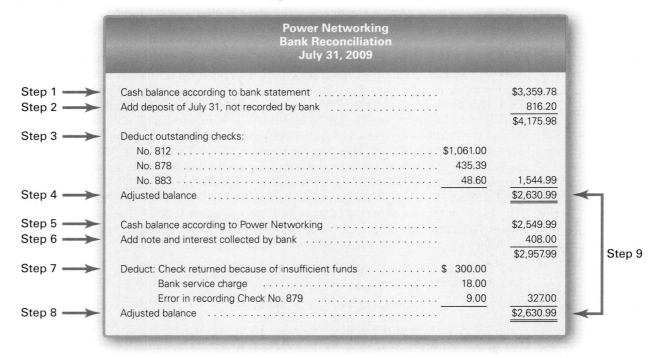

Power Networking
Bank Reconciliation
July 31, 2009

Step 1 →	Cash balance according to bank statement		$3,359.78
Step 2 →	Add deposit of July 31, not recorded by bank		816.20
			$4,175.98
Step 3 →	Deduct outstanding checks:		
	No. 812	$1,061.00	
	No. 878	435.39	
	No. 883	48.60	1,544.99
Step 4 →	Adjusted balance		$2,630.99
Step 5 →	Cash balance according to Power Networking		$2,549.99
Step 6 →	Add note and interest collected by bank		408.00
			$2,957.99
Step 7 →	Deduct: Check returned because of insufficient funds	$ 300.00	
	Bank service charge	18.00	
	Error in recording Check No. 879	9.00	327.00
Step 8 →	Adjusted balance		$2,630.99

Step 9

After the preceding journal entries are recorded and posted, the cash account will have a debit balance of $2,630.99. This cash balance agrees with the adjusted balance shown on the bank reconciliation. This is the amount of cash on July 31 and is the amount that is reported on Power Networking's July 31 balance sheet.

Businesses may reconcile their bank accounts in a slightly different format from that shown in Exhibit 7. Regardless, the objective is to control cash by reconciling the company's records with the bank statement. In doing so, any errors or misuse of cash may be detected.

To enhance internal control, the bank reconciliation should be prepared by an employee who does not take part in or record cash transactions. Otherwise, mistakes may occur, and it is more likely that cash will be stolen or misapplied. For example, an employee who handles cash and also reconciles the bank statement could steal a cash deposit, omit the deposit from the accounts, and omit it from the reconciliation.

Bank reconciliations are also important computerized systems where deposits and checks are stored in electronic files and records. Some systems use computer software to determine the difference between the bank statement and company cash balances. The software then adjusts for deposits in transit and outstanding checks. Any remaining differences are reported for further analysis.

Example Exercise 7-3 Bank Reconciliation •••••••▶ **5**

The following data were gathered to use in reconciling the bank account of Photo Op:

Balance per bank	$14,500
Balance per company records	13,875
Bank service charges	75
Deposit in transit	3,750
NSF check	800
Outstanding checks	5,250

a. What is the adjusted balance on the bank reconciliation?

b. Journalize any necessary entries for Photo Op based on the bank reconciliation.

(continued)

Follow My Example 7-3

a. $13,000, as shown below.

Bank section of reconciliation: $14,500 + $3,750 − $5,250 = $13,000
Company section of reconciliation: $13,875 − $75 − $800 = $13,000

b. Accounts Receivable   800
Miscellaneous Expense   75
   Cash.   875

For Practice: PE 7-3A, PE 7-3B

Integrity, Objectivity, and Ethics in Business

BANK ERROR IN YOUR FAVOR

You may sometime have a bank error in your favor, such as a misposted deposit. Such errors are not a case of "found money," as in the Monopoly® game. Bank control

systems quickly discover most errors and make automatic adjustments. Even so, you have a legal responsibility to report the error and return the money to the bank.

6 Describe the accounting for special-purpose cash funds.

Special-Purpose Cash Funds

A company often has to pay small amounts for such items as postage, office supplies, or minor repairs. Although small, such payments may occur often enough to total a significant amount. Thus, it is desirable to control such payments. However, writing a check for each small payment is not practical. Instead, a special cash fund, called a **petty cash fund**, is used.

A petty cash fund is established by estimating the amount of payments needed from the fund during a period, such as a week or a month. A check is then written and cashed for this amount. The money obtained from cashing the check is then given to an employee, called the *petty cash custodian*. The petty cash custodian disburses monies from the fund as needed. For control purposes, the company may place restrictions on the maximum amount and the types of payments that can be made from the fund. Each time money is paid from petty cash, the custodian records the details on a petty cash receipts form.

The petty cash fund is normally replenished at periodic intervals, when it is depleted, or reaches a minimum amount. When a petty cash fund is replenished, the accounts debited are determined by summarizing the petty cash receipts. A check is then written for this amount, payable to Petty Cash.

To illustrate, assume that a petty cash fund of $500 is established on August 1. The entry to record this transaction is as follows:

| Aug. | 1 | Petty Cash | 500 | |
| | | Cash | | 500 |

The only time Petty Cash is debited is when the fund is initially established, as shown in the preceding entry, or when the fund is being increased. The only time Petty Cash is credited is when the fund is being decreased.

At the end of August, the petty cash receipts indicate expenditures for the following items:

Office supplies	$380
Postage (debit Office Supplies)	22
Store supplies	35
Miscellaneous administrative expense	30
Total	$467

The entry to replenish the petty cash fund on August 31 is as follows:

Aug.	31	Office Supplies	402	
		Store Supplies	35	
		Miscellaneous Administrative Expense	30	
		Cash		467

Petty Cash is not debited when the fund is replenished. Instead, the accounts affected by the petty cash disbursements are debited, as shown in the preceding entry. Replenishing the petty cash fund restores the fund to its original amount of $500.

Companies often use other cash funds for special needs, such as payroll or travel expenses. Such funds are called **special-purpose funds**. For example, each salesperson might be given $1,000 for travel-related expenses. Periodically, each salesperson submits an expense report, and the fund is replenished. Special-purpose funds are established and controlled in a manner similar to that of the petty cash fund.

Example Exercise 7-4 Petty Cash Fund   •••••••➤ 6

Prepare journal entries for each of the following:
a. Issued a check to establish a petty cash fund of $500.
b. The amount of cash in the petty cash fund is $120. Issued a check to replenish the fund, based on the following summary of petty cash receipts: office supplies, $300 and miscellaneous administrative expense, $75. Record any missing funds in the cash short and over account.

Follow My Example 7-4

a.	Petty Cash	500	
	Cash		500
b.	Office Supplies.	300	
	Miscellaneous Administrative Expense	75	
	Cash Short and Over	5	
	Cash		380

For Practice: PE 7-4A, PE 7-4B

 Describe and illustrate the reporting of cash and cash equivalents in the financial statements.

Financial Statement Reporting of Cash

Cash is normally listed as the first asset in the Current Assets section of the balance sheet. Most companies present only a single cash amount on the balance sheet by combining all their bank and cash fund accounts.

A company may temporarily have excess cash. In such cases, the company normally invests in highly liquid investments in order to earn interest. These investments are called **cash equivalents**.[8] Examples of cash equivalents include U.S. Treasury bills, notes issued by major corporations (referred to as commercial paper), and money market funds. In such cases, companies usually report *Cash and cash equivalents* as one amount on the balance sheet.

The balance sheet presentation for cash for Mornin' Joe is shown below.

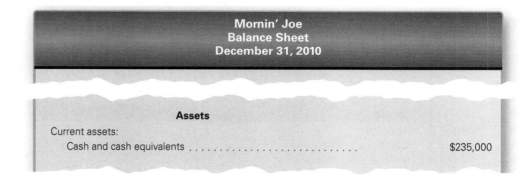

**Mornin' Joe
Balance Sheet
December 31, 2010**

Assets

Current assets:

Cash and cash equivalents $235,000

Banks may require that companies maintain minimum cash balances in their bank accounts. Such a balance is called a **compensating balance**. This is often required by the bank as part of a loan agreement or line of credit. A *line of credit* is a preapproved amount the bank is willing to lend to a customer upon request. Compensating balance requirements are normally disclosed in notes to the financial statements.

Financial Analysis and Interpretation

For companies that are either starting up or in financial distress, cash is critical for their survival. In their first few years of operations, startup companies often report losses and negative net cash flows. In these cases, the ratio of cash to monthly cash expenses (negative cash flow for operating activities) is useful for assessing how long a company can continue to operate without additional financing or without generating positive cash flows from operations. Likewise, this ratio can be used to assess how long a business may continue to operate when experiencing financial distress. In computing cash to monthly cash expenses, the amount of cash on hand can be taken from the balance sheet, while the monthly cash expenses can be estimated from the operating activities section of the statement of cash flows.

The ratio of cash to monthly cash expenses is computed by first determining the monthly cash expenses. The monthly cash expenses are determined as follows:

$$\text{Monthly Cash Expenses} = \frac{\text{Negative Cash Flows from Operations}}{12}$$

The ratio of cash to monthly cash expenses can then be computed as follows:

$$\text{Ratio of Cash to Monthly Cash Expenses} = \frac{\text{Cash and Cash Equivalents as of Year-End}}{\text{Monthly Cash Expenses}}$$

To illustrate these ratios, we use Northwest Airlines Corporation, a major carrier of passengers and cargo with service to approximately 900 cities in 160 countries. For the year ending December 31, 2005, Northwest Airlines reported the following data (in millions):

Negative cash flows from operations	$ (436)
Cash and cash equivalents as of December 31, 2005	1,284

Based on the preceding data, the monthly cash expenses, sometimes referred to as cash burn, were $36.3 million per month ($436/12). Thus, as of December 31, 2005, the cash to monthly cash expenses ratio was 35.4 ($1,284/$36.3). That is, as of December 31, 2005, Northwest would run out of cash in less than three years unless it changes its operations, sells investments, or raises additional financing. Northwest Airlines was able to reorganize and for the year ending December 31, 2006, generated $1,245 million in positive cash flows from operations.

f·a·i

---

8 To be classified a cash equivalent, according to FASB Statement No. 95, the investment is expected to be converted to cash within 90 days.

Business Connection

MICROSOFT CORPORATION

Microsoft Corporation develops, manufactures, licenses, and supports software products for computing devices. Microsoft software products include computer operating systems, such as Windows, and application software, such as Microsoft Word™ and Excel.™ Microsoft is actively involved in the video game market through its Xbox and is also involved in online products and services.

Microsoft is known for its strong cash position. Microsoft's June 30, 2007, balance sheet reported over $23 billion of cash and short-term investments, as shown below.

Balance Sheet June 30, 2007 (In millions) Assets	
Current assets:	
Cash and cash equivalents..	$ 6,111
Short-term investments...	17,300
Total cash and short-term investments............................	$23,411

The cash and cash equivalents of $6,111 million are further described in the notes to the financial statements, as shown below.

Cash and equivalents:	
Cash	$3,040
Mutual funds	132
Commercial paper	179
U.S. government and agency securities	1
Corporate notes and bonds	2,425
Municipal securities	334
Total cash and equivalents	$6,111

 • • • *At a Glance* **7**

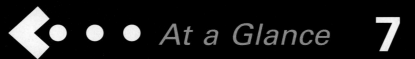

1 Describe the Sarbanes-Oxley Act of 2002 and its impact on internal controls and financial reporting.

Key Points	Key Learning Outcomes	Example Exercises	Practice Exercises
The purpose of the Sarbanes-Oxley Act of 2002 is to restore public confidence and trust in the financial statements of companies. Sarbanes-Oxley requires companies to maintain strong and effective internal controls and to report on the effectiveness of the internal controls.	• Describe why Congress passed Sarbanes-Oxley. • Describe the purpose of Sarbanes-Oxley. • Define *internal control*.		

2. Describe and illustrate the objectives and elements of internal control.

Key Points	Key Learning Outcomes	Example Exercises	Practice Exercises
The objectives of internal control are to provide reasonable assurance that (1) assets are safeguarded and used for business purposes, (2) business information is accurate, and (3) laws and regulations are complied with. The elements of internal control are the control environment, risk assessment, control procedures, monitoring, and information and communication.	• List the objectives of internal control. • List the elements of internal control. • Describe each element of internal control and factors influencing each element.	7-1	7-1A, 7-1B

3. Describe and illustrate the application of internal controls to cash.

Key Points	Key Learning Outcomes	Example Exercises	Practice Exercises
A cash register is one of the most important controls to protect cash received in over-the-counter sales. A remittance advice is a control for cash received through the mail. Separating the duties of handling cash and recording cash is also a control. A voucher system is a control system for cash payments that uses a set of procedures for authorizing and recording liabilities and cash payments. Many companies use electronic funds transfers to enhance their control over cash receipts and cash payments.	• Describe and give examples of controls for cash received from cash sales, cash received in the mail, and cash received by EFT. • Describe and give examples of controls for cash payments made using a voucher system and cash payments made by EFT.		

4. Describe the nature of a bank account and its use in controlling cash.

Key Points	Key Learning Outcomes	Example Exercises	Practice Exercises
Bank accounts help control cash by reducing the amount of cash on hand and facilitating the transfer of cash between businesses and locations. In addition, the bank statement allows a business to reconcile the cash transactions recorded in the accounting records to those recorded by the bank.	• Describe how the use of bank accounts helps control cash. • Describe a bank statement and provide examples of items that appear on a bank statement as debit and credit memos.	7-2	7-2A, 7-2B

5. Describe and illustrate the use of a bank reconciliation in controlling cash.

Key Points	Key Learning Outcomes	Example Exercises	Practice Exercises
The bank reconciliation begins with the cash balance according to the bank statement. This balance is adjusted for the company's changes in cash that do not appear on the bank statement and for any bank errors. The second section begins with the cash balance according to the company's records. This balance is adjusted for the bank's changes in cash that do not appear on the company's records and for any company errors. The adjusted balances for the two sections must be equal. The items in the company section must be journalized on the company's records.	• Describe a bank reconciliation. • Prepare a bank reconciliation. • Journalize any necessary entries on the company's records based on the bank reconciliation.	7-3 7-3	7-3A, 7-3B 7-3A, 7-3B

Key Points	Key Learning Outcomes	Example Exercises	Practice Exercises
Special-purpose cash funds, such as a petty cash fund or travel funds, are used by businesses to meet specific needs. Each fund is established by cashing a check for the amount of cash needed. At periodic intervals, the fund is replenished and the disbursements recorded.	• Describe the use of special-purpose cash funds.		
	• Journalize the entry to establish a petty cash fund.	**7-4**	7-4A, 7-4B
	• Journalize the entry to replenish a petty cash fund.	**7-4**	7-4A, 7-4B

7 Describe and illustrate the reporting of cash and cash equivalents in the financial statements.

Key Points	Key Learning Outcomes	Example Exercises	Practice Exercises
Cash is listed as the first asset in the Current Assets section of the balance sheet. Companies that have invested excess cash in highly liquid investments usually report *Cash and cash equivalents* on the balance sheet.	• Describe the reporting of cash and cash equivalents in the financial statements.		
	• Illustrate the reporting of cash and cash equivalents in the financial statements.		

Key Terms

bank reconciliation (319)
bank statement (316)
cash (312)
cash equivalents (325)
cash short and over
   account (314)

compensating balance (325)
control environment (308)
electronic funds transfer
   (EFT) (315)
elements of internal control (307)
employee fraud (307)

internal control (305)
petty cash fund (323)
Sarbanes-Oxley Act of 2002 (305)
special-purpose funds (324)
voucher (315)
voucher system (315)

Illustrative Problem

The bank statement for Urethane Company for June 30, 2009, indicates a balance of $9,143.11. All cash receipts are deposited each evening in a night depository, after banking hours. The accounting records indicate the following summary data for cash receipts and payments for June:

Cash balance as of June 1	$ 3,943.50
Total cash receipts for June	28,971.60
Total amount of checks issued in June	28,388.85

Comparing the bank statement and the accompanying canceled checks and memos with the records reveals the following reconciling items:

a. The bank had collected for Urethane Company $1,030 on a note left for collection. The face amount of the note was $1,000.
b. A deposit of $1,852.21, representing receipts of June 30, had been made too late to appear on the bank statement.
c. Checks outstanding totaled $5,265.27.
d. A check drawn for $139 had been incorrectly charged by the bank as $157.
e. A check for $30 returned with the statement had been recorded in the company's records as $240. The check was for the payment of an obligation to Avery Equipment Company for the purchase of office supplies on account.
f. Bank service charges for June amounted to $18.20.

Instructions

1. Prepare a bank reconciliation for June.
2. Journalize the entries that should be made by Urethane Company.

Solution

1.

Urethane Company
Bank Reconciliation
June 30, 2009

Cash balance according to bank statement		$ 9,143.11
Add: Deposit of June 30 not recorded by bank	$1,852.21	
Bank error in charging check as $157		
instead of $139	18.00	1,870.21
		$11,013.32
Deduct: Outstanding checks		5,265.27
Adjusted balance		$ 5,748.05
Cash balance according to company's records		$ 4,526.25*
Add: Proceeds of note collected by bank,		
including $30 interest	$1,030.00	
Error in recording check	210.00	1,240.00
		$ 5,766.25
Deduct: Bank service charges		18.20
Adjusted balance		$ 5,748.05
*$3,943.50 + $28,971.60 − $28,388.85		

2.

June	30	Cash	1,240.00	
		Notes Receivable		1,000.00
		Interest Revenue		30.00
		Accounts Payable—Avery Equipment Company		210.00
	30	Miscellaneous Administrative Expense	18.20	
		Cash		18.20

Self-Examination Questions (Answers at End of Chapter)

1. Which of the following is *not* an element of internal control?
   A. Control environment
   B. Monitoring
   C. Compliance with laws and regulations
   D. Control procedures

2. The bank erroneously charged Tropical Services' account for $450.50 for a check that was correctly written and recorded by Tropical Services as $540.50. To reconcile the bank account of Tropical Services at the end of the month, you would:
   A. add $90 to the cash balance according to the bank statement.
   B. add $90 to the cash balance according to Tropical Services' records.
   C. deduct $90 from the cash balance according to the bank statement.
   D. deduct $90 from the cash balance according to Tropical Services' records.

3. In preparing a bank reconciliation, the amount of checks outstanding would be:
   A. added to the cash balance according to the bank statement.
   B. deducted from the cash balance according to the bank statement.
   C. added to the cash balance according to the company's records.
   D. deducted from the cash balance according to the company's records.

4. Journal entries based on the bank reconciliation are required for:
   A. additions to the cash balance according to the company's records.
   B. deductions from the cash balance according to the company's records.
   C. both A and B.
   D. neither A nor B.

5. A petty cash fund is:
   A. used to pay relatively small amounts.
   B. established by estimating the amount of cash needed for disbursements of relatively small amounts during a specified period.
   C. reimbursed when the amount of money in the fund is reduced to a predetermined minimum amount.
   D. all of the above.

Eye Openers

1. (a) Why did Congress pass the Sarbanes-Oxley Act of 2002? (b) What is the purpose of the Sarbanes-Oxley Act of 2002?
2. Define *internal control*.
3. (a) Name and describe the five elements of internal control. (b) Is any one element of internal control more important than another?
4. How does a policy of rotating clerical employees from job to job aid in strengthening the control procedures within the control environment? Explain.
5. Why should the responsibility for a sequence of related operations be divided among different persons? Explain.
6. Why should the employee who handles cash receipts not have the responsibility for maintaining the accounts receivable records? Explain.
7. In an attempt to improve operating efficiency, one employee was made responsible for all purchasing, receiving, and storing of supplies. Is this organizational change wise from an internal control standpoint? Explain.
8. The ticket seller at a movie theater doubles as a ticket taker for a few minutes each day while the ticket taker is on a break. Which control procedure of a business's system of internal control is violated in this situation?
9. Why should the responsibility for maintaining the accounting records be separated from the responsibility for operations? Explain.
10. Assume that Yvonne Dauphin, accounts payable clerk for Bedell Inc., stole $73,250 by paying fictitious invoices for goods that were never received. The clerk set up accounts in the names of the fictitious companies and cashed the checks at a local bank. Describe a control procedure that would have prevented or detected the fraud.
11. Before a voucher for the purchase of merchandise is approved for payment, supporting documents should be compared to verify the accuracy of the liability. Give an example of supporting documents for the purchase of merchandise.

12. The accounting clerk pays all obligations by prenumbered checks. What are the strengths and weaknesses in the internal control over cash payments in this situation?

13. The balance of Cash is likely to differ from the bank statement balance. What two factors are likely to be responsible for the difference?

14. What is the purpose of preparing a bank reconciliation?

15. Do items reported as credits on the bank statement represent (a) additions made by the bank to the company's balance or (b) deductions made by the bank from the company's balance? Explain.

16. Oak Grove Inc. has a petty cash fund of $1,500. (a) Since the petty cash fund is only $1,500, should Oak Grove Inc. implement controls over petty cash? (b) What controls, if any, could be used for the petty cash fund?

17. (a) How are cash equivalents reported in the financial statements? (b) What are some examples of cash equivalents?

Practice Exercises

PE 7-1A
Internal control elements

obj. 2

EE 7-1   p. 312

Identify each of the following as relating to (a) the control environment, (b) control procedures, or (c) monitoring.

1. Hiring of external auditors to review the adequacy of controls
2. Personnel policies
3. Safeguarding inventory in a locked warehouse

PE 7-1B
Internal control elements

obj. 2

EE 7-1   p. 312

Identify each of the following as relating to (a) the control environment, (b) control procedures, or (c) information and communication.

1. Management's philosophy and operating style
2. Report of internal auditors
3. Separating related operations

PE 7-2A
Items on company's bank statement

obj. 4

EE 7-2   p. 318

The following items may appear on a bank statement:

1. Bank correction of an error from posting another customer's check to the company's account
2. EFT deposit
3. Loan proceeds
4. NSF check

Using the format shown below, indicate whether each item would appear as a debit or credit memo on the bank statement and whether the item would increase or decrease the balance of the company's account.

Item No.	Appears on the Bank Statement as a Debit or Credit Memo	Increases or Decreases the Balance of the Company's Bank Account

---

PE 7-2B
Items on company's bank statement

obj. 4

EE 7-2   p. 318

The following items may appear on a bank statement:

1. Bank correction of an error from recording a $3,200 deposit as $2,300
2. EFT payment
3. Note collected for company
4. Service charge

Using the format shown below, indicate whether each item would appear as a debit or credit memo on the bank statement and whether the item would increase or decrease the balance of the company's account.

Item No.	Appears on the Bank Statement as a Debit or Credit Memo	Increases or Decreases the Balance of the Company's Bank Account

PE 7-3A
Bank reconciliation

obj. 5

EE 7-3 p. 322

The following data were gathered to use in reconciling the bank account of East Meets West Company:

Balance per bank	$19,340
Balance per company records	6,480
Bank service charges	50
Deposit in transit	2,500
Note collected by bank with $250 interest	8,250
Outstanding checks	7,160

a. What is the adjusted balance on the bank reconciliation?
b. Journalize any necessary entries for East Meets West Company based on the bank reconciliation.

PE 7-3B
Bank reconciliation

obj. 5

EE 7-3 p. 322

The following data were gathered to use in reconciling the bank account of Crescent Moon Company:

Balance per bank	$11,200
Balance per company records	9,295
Bank service charges	25
Deposit in transit	1,650
NSF check	600
Outstanding checks	4,180

a. What is the adjusted balance on the bank reconciliation?
b. Journalize any necessary entries for Crescent Moon Company based on the bank reconciliation.

PE 7-4A
Petty cash fund

obj. 6

EE 7-4 p. 324

Prepare journal entries for each of the following:
a. Issued a check to establish a petty cash fund of $300.
b. The amount of cash in the petty cash fund is $95. Issued a check to replenish the fund, based on the following summary of petty cash receipts: store supplies, $120 and miscellaneous selling expense, $75. Record any missing funds in the cash short and over account.

PE 7-4B
Petty cash fund

obj. 6

EE 7-4 p. 324

Prepare journal entries for each of the following:
a. Issued a check to establish a petty cash fund of $500.
b. The amount of cash in the petty cash fund is $140. Issued a check to replenish the fund, based on the following summary of petty cash receipts: repair expense, $260 and miscellaneous selling expense, $84. Record any missing funds in the cash short and over account.

Exertises

EX 7-1
Sarbanes-Oxley internal control report

obj. 1

Using Wikpedia (www.wikpedia.com), look up the entry for Sarbanes-Oxley Act. Look over the table of contents and find the section that describes Section 404.
 What does Section 404 require of management's internal control report?

EX 7-2
Internal controls

objs. 2, 3

Blake Gable has recently been hired as the manager of Jittery Jim's Canyon Coffee. Jittery Jim's Canyon Coffee is a national chain of franchised coffee shops. During his first month as store manager, Blake encountered the following internal control situations:

a. Blake caught an employee putting a case of 100 single-serving tea bags in her car. Not wanting to create a scene, Blake smiled and said, "I don't think you're putting those tea bags on the right shelf. Don't they belong inside the coffee shop?" The employee returned the tea bags to the stockroom.
b. Jittery Jim's Canyon Coffee has one cash register. Prior to Blake's joining the coffee shop, each employee working on a shift would take a customer order, accept payment, and then prepare the order. Blake made one employee on each shift responsible for taking orders and accepting the customer's payment. Other employees prepare the orders.
c. Since only one employee uses the cash register, that employee is responsible for counting the cash at the end of the shift and verifying that the cash in the drawer matches the amount of cash sales recorded by the cash register. Blake expects each cashier to balance the drawer to the penny *every* time—no exceptions.

➤ State whether you agree or disagree with Blake's method of handling each situation and explain your answer.

EX 7-3
Internal controls

objs. 2, 3

Anasazi Earth Clothing is a retail store specializing in women's clothing. The store has established a liberal return policy for the holiday season in order to encourage gift purchases. Any item purchased during November and December may be returned through January 31, with a receipt, for cash or exchange. If the customer does not have a receipt, cash will still be refunded for any item under $100. If the item is more than $100, a check is mailed to the customer.

Whenever an item is returned, a store clerk completes a return slip, which the customer signs. The return slip is placed in a special box. The store manager visits the return counter approximately once every two hours to authorize the return slips. Clerks are instructed to place the returned merchandise on the proper rack on the selling floor as soon as possible.

This year, returns at Anasazi Earth Clothing have reached an all-time high. There are a large number of returns under $100 without receipts.

a. ➤ How can sales clerks employed at Anasazi Earth Clothing use the store's return policy to steal money from the cash register?
b. ➤ What internal control weaknesses do you see in the return policy that make cash thefts easier?
c. ➤ Would issuing a store credit in place of a cash refund for all merchandise returned without a receipt reduce the possibility of theft? List some advantages and disadvantages of issuing a store credit in place of a cash refund.
d. ➤ Assume that Anasazi Earth Clothing is committed to the current policy of issuing cash refunds without a receipt. What changes could be made in the store's procedures regarding customer refunds in order to improve internal control?

EX 7-4
Internal controls for bank lending

objs. 2, 3

First Kenmore Bank provides loans to businesses in the community through its Commercial Lending Department. Small loans (less than $100,000) may be approved by an individual loan officer, while larger loans (greater than $100,000) must be approved by a board of loan officers. Once a loan is approved, the funds are made available to the loan applicant under agreed-upon terms. The president of First Kenmore Bank has instituted a policy whereby he has the individual authority to approve loans up to $5,000,000. The president believes that this policy will allow flexibility to approve loans to valued clients much quicker than under the previous policy.

➤ As an internal auditor of First Kenmore Bank, how would you respond to this change in policy?

EX 7-5
Internal controls
objs. 2, 3

One of the largest losses in history from unauthorized securities trading involved a securities trader for the French bank, Societe Generale. The trader was able to circumvent internal controls and create over $7 billion in trading losses in six months. The trader apparently escaped detection by using knowledge of the bank's internal control systems learned from a previous back-office monitoring job. Much of this monitoring involved the use of software to monitor trades. In addition, traders are usually kept to tight spending limits. Apparently, these controls failed in this case.

What general weaknesses in Societe Generale's internal controls contributed to the occurrence and size of the losses?

EX 7-6
Internal controls
objs. 2, 3

An employee of JHT Holdings, Inc., a trucking company, was responsible for resolving roadway accident claims under $25,000. The employee created fake accident claims and wrote settlement checks of between $5,000 and $25,000 to friends or acquaintances acting as phony "victims." One friend recruited subordinates at his place of work to cash some of the checks. Beyond this, the JHT employee also recruited lawyers, who he paid to represent both the trucking company and the fake victims in the bogus accident settlements. When the lawyers cashed the checks, they allegedly split the money with the corrupt JHT employee. This fraud went undetected for two years.

Why would it take so long to discover such a fraud?

EX 7-7
Internal controls
objs. 2, 3

Bizarro Sound Co. discovered a fraud whereby one of its front office administrative employees used company funds to purchase goods, such as computers, digital cameras, compact disk players, and other electronic items for her own use. The fraud was discovered when employees noticed an increase in delivery frequency from vendors and the use of unusual vendors. After some investigation, it was discovered that the employee would alter the description or change the quantity on an invoice in order to explain the cost on the bill.

What general internal control weaknesses contributed to this fraud?

EX 7-8
Financial statement fraud
objs. 2, 3

A former chairman, CFO, and controller of Donnkenny, Inc., an apparel company that makes sportswear for Pierre Cardin and Victoria Jones, pleaded guilty to financial statement fraud. These managers used false journal entries to record fictitious sales, hid inventory in public warehouses so that it could be recorded as "sold," and required sales orders to be backdated so that the sale could be moved back to an earlier period. The combined effect of these actions caused $25 million out of $40 million in quarterly sales to be phony.

a. Why might control procedures listed in this chapter be insufficient in stopping this type of fraud?
b. How could this type of fraud be stopped?

EX 7-9
Internal control of cash receipts
objs. 2, 3

The procedures used for over-the-counter receipts are as follows. At the close of each day's business, the sales clerks count the cash in their respective cash drawers, after which they determine the amount recorded by the cash register and prepare the memo cash form, noting any discrepancies. An employee from the cashier's office counts the cash, compares the total with the memo, and takes the cash to the cashier's office.

a. Indicate the weak link in internal control.
b. How can the weakness be corrected?

EX 7-10
Internal control of cash receipts
objs. 2, 3

Victor Blackmon works at the drive-through window of Buffalo Bob's Burgers. Occasionally, when a drive-through customer orders, Victor fills the order and pockets the customer's money. He does not ring up the order on the cash register.

Identify the internal control weaknesses that exist at Buffalo Bob's Burgers, and discuss what can be done to prevent this theft.

EX 7-11
Internal control of
cash receipts

objs. 2, 3

The mailroom employees send all remittances and remittance advices to the cashier. The cashier deposits the cash in the bank and forwards the remittance advices and duplicate deposit slips to the Accounting Department.

a. ➤ Indicate the weak link in internal control in the handling of cash receipts.
b. ➤ How can the weakness be corrected?

EX 7-12
Entry for cash sales;
cash short

objs. 2, 3

The actual cash received from cash sales was $36,183, and the amount indicated by the cash register total was $36,197. Journalize the entry to record the cash receipts and cash sales.

EX 7-13
Entry for cash sales;
cash over

objs. 2, 3

The actual cash received from cash sales was $11,279, and the amount indicated by the cash register total was $11,256. Journalize the entry to record the cash receipts and cash sales.

EX 7-14
Internal control of
cash payments

objs. 2, 3

El Cordova Co. is a small merchandising company with a manual accounting system. An investigation revealed that in spite of a sufficient bank balance, a significant amount of available cash discounts had been lost because of failure to make timely payments. In addition, it was discovered that the invoices for several purchases had been paid twice. ➤ Outline procedures for the payment of vendors' invoices, so that the possibilities of losing available cash discounts and of paying an invoice a second time will be minimized.

EX 7-15
Internal control of
cash payments

objs. 2, 3

Digital Com Company, a communications equipment manufacturer, recently fell victim to a fraud scheme developed by one of its employees. To understand the scheme, it is necessary to review Digital Com's procedures for the purchase of services.

The purchasing agent is responsible for ordering services (such as repairs to a photocopy machine or office cleaning) after receiving a service requisition from an authorized manager. However, since no tangible goods are delivered, a receiving report is not prepared. When the Accounting Department receives an invoice billing Digital Com for a service call, the accounts payable clerk calls the manager who requested the service in order to verify that it was performed.

The fraud scheme involves Matt DuBois, the manager of plant and facilities. Matt arranged for his uncle's company, Urban Industrial Supply and Service, to be placed on Digital Com's approved vendor list. Matt did not disclose the family relationship.

On several occasions, Matt would submit a requisition for services to be provided by Urban Industrial Supply and Service. However, the service requested was really not needed, and it was never performed. Urban would bill Digital Com for the service and then split the cash payment with Matt.

➤ Explain what changes should be made to Digital Com's procedures for ordering and paying for services in order to prevent such occurrences in the future.

EX 7-16
Bank reconciliation

obj. 5

Identify each of the following reconciling items as: (a) an addition to the cash balance according to the bank statement, (b) a deduction from the cash balance according to the bank statement, (c) an addition to the cash balance according to the company's records, or (d) a deduction from the cash balance according to the company's records. (None of the transactions reported by bank debit and credit memos have been recorded by the company.)

1. Bank service charges, $15.
2. Check drawn by company for $160 but incorrectly recorded as $610.

3. Check for $500 incorrectly charged by bank as $5,000.
4. Check of a customer returned by bank to company because of insufficient funds, $3,000.
5. Deposit in transit, $15,500.
6. Outstanding checks, $9,600.
7. Note collected by bank, $10,000.

EX 7-17
Entries based on
bank reconciliation

obj. 5

Which of the reconciling items listed in Exercise 7-16 require an entry in the company's accounts?

EX 7-18
Bank reconciliation

obj. 5

✔ Adjusted balance:
$13,680

The following data were accumulated for use in reconciling the bank account of Commander Co. for March:

a. Cash balance according to the company's records at March 31, $13,065.
b. Cash balance according to the bank statement at March 31, $12,750.
c. Checks outstanding, $4,170.
d. Deposit in transit, not recorded by bank, $5,100.
e. A check for $180 in payment of an account was erroneously recorded in the check register as $810.
f. Bank debit memo for service charges, $15.

Prepare a bank reconciliation, using the format shown in Exhibit 7.

EX 7-19
Entries for bank
reconciliation

obj. 5

Using the data presented in Exercise 7-18, journalize the entry or entries that should be made by the company.

EX 7-20
Entries for note
collected by bank

obj. 5

Accompanying a bank statement for Euthenics Company is a credit memo for $18,270, representing the principal ($18,000) and interest ($270) on a note that had been collected by the bank. The company had been notified by the bank at the time of the collection, but had made no entries. Journalize the entry that should be made by the company to bring the accounting records up to date.

EX 7-21
Bank reconciliation

obj. 5

✔ Adjusted balance:
$11,740

An accounting clerk for Grebe Co. prepared the following bank reconciliation:

Grebe Co.
Bank Reconciliation
August 31, 2010

Cash balance according to company's records		$ 4,690
Add: Outstanding checks	$3,110	
Error by Grebe Co. in recording Check		
No. 1115 as $940 instead of $490	450	
Note for $6,500 collected by bank, including interest.	6,630	10,190
Deduct: Deposit in transit on August 31	$4,725	$14,880
Bank service charges	30	4,755
Cash balance according to bank statement		$10,125

a. From the data in the above bank reconciliation, prepare a new bank reconciliation for Grebe Co., using the format shown in the illustrative problem.
b. If a balance sheet were prepared for Grebe Co. on August 31, 2010, what amount should be reported for cash?

EX 7-22
Bank reconciliation

obj. 5

✔ Corrected
adjusted balance:
$11,960

Identify the errors in the following bank reconciliation:

Rakestraw Co.
Bank Reconciliation
For the Month Ended April 30, 2010

Cash balance according to bank statement.		$11,320
Add outstanding checks:		
No. 315	$ 450	
360	615	
364	850	
365	775	2,690
		$14,010
Deduct deposit of April 30, not recorded by bank.		3,330
Adjusted balance		$10,680
Cash balance according to company's records.		$ 7,003
Add: Proceeds of note collected by bank:		
Principal $4,000		
Interest 120	$4,120	
Service charges	18	4,138
		$11,141
Deduct: Check returned because of insufficient funds	$ 945	
Error in recording April 20 deposit of $5,300 as $3,500 .	1,800	2,745
Adjusted balance		$ 8,396

EX 7-23
Using bank reconciliation to determine cash receipts stolen

objs. 2, 3, 5

First Impressions Co. records all cash receipts on the basis of its cash register tapes. First Impressions Co. discovered during June 2010 that one of its sales clerks had stolen an undetermined amount of cash receipts when she took the daily deposits to the bank. The following data have been gathered for June:

Cash in bank according to the general ledger	$ 7,865
Cash according to the June 30, 2010, bank statement	18,175
Outstanding checks as of June 30, 2010	5,190
Bank service charge for June	25
Note receivable, including interest collected by bank in June	8,400

No deposits were in transit on June 30.

a. Determine the amount of cash receipts stolen by the sales clerk.
b. ➤ What accounting controls would have prevented or detected this theft?

EX 7-24
Petty cash fund entries

obj. 6

Journalize the entries to record the following:

a. Check No. 8193 is issued to establish a petty cash fund of $800.
b. The amount of cash in the petty cash fund is now $294. Check No. 8336 is issued to replenish the fund, based on the following summary of petty cash receipts: office supplies, $295; miscellaneous selling expense, $120; miscellaneous administrative expense, $75. (Since the amount of the check to replenish the fund plus the balance in the fund do not equal $800, record the discrepancy in the cash short and over account.)

EX 7-25
Variation in cash flows

obj. 7

Mattel, Inc., designs, manufactures, and markets toy products worldwide. Mattel's toys include Barbie™ fashion dolls and accessories, Hot Wheels™, and Fisher-Price brands. For a recent year, Mattel reported the following net cash flows from operating activities (in thousands):

First quarter ending March 31	$ (326,536)
Second quarter ending June 30	(165,047)
Third quarter ending September 30	(9,738)
Fourth quarter December 31	1,243,603

➤ Explain why Mattel reports negative net cash flows from operating activities during the first three quarters yet reports positive cash flows for the fourth quarter and net positive cash flows for the year.

EX 7-26
Cash to monthly
cash expenses ratio

During 2010, Bezel Inc. has monthly cash expenses of $250,000. On December 31, 2010, the cash balance is $1,750,000.

a. Compute the ratio of cash to monthly cash expenses.
b. ➤ Based on (a), what are the implications for Bezel Inc.?

EX 7-27
Cash to monthly
cash expenses ratio

Delta Air Lines is one of the major airlines in the United States and the world. It provides passenger and cargo services for over 200 domestic U.S. cities as well as 70 international cities. It operates a fleet of over 800 aircraft and is headquartered in Atlanta, Georgia. Delta reported the following financial data (in millions) for the year ended December 31, 2004:

Net cash flows from operating activities	$(1,123)
Cash, December 31, 2004	1,811

a. Determine the monthly cash expenses. Round to one decimal place.
b. Determine the ratio of cash to monthly expenses. Round to one decimal place.
c. ➤ Based on your analysis, do you believe that Delta will remain in business?

EX 7-28
Cash to monthly
cash expenses ratio

Acusphere, Inc., is a specialty pharmaceutical company that develops new drugs and improved formulations of existing drugs using its proprietary microparticle technology. Currently, the company has three products in development in the areas of cardiology, oncology, and asthma. Acusphere reported the following data (in thousands) for the years ending December 31, 2006, 2005, 2004, and 2003:

	2006	2005	2004	2003
Cash as of December 31*	$ 59,750	$ 51,112	$ 45,180	$ 54,562
Net cash flows from operating activities	(48,089)	(30,683)	(19,319)	(15,507)

*Includes cash equivalents and short-term investments.

1. Determine the monthly cash expenses for 2006, 2005, 2004, and 2003. Round to one decimal place.
2. Determine the ratio of cash to monthly expenses as of December 31, 2006, 2005, 2004, and 2003. Round to one decimal place.
3. ➤ Based on (1) and (2), comment on Acusphere's ratio of cash to monthly operating expenses for 2006, 2005, 2004, and 2003.

Problems Series A

PR 7-1A
Evaluate internal
control of cash
objs. 2, 3

The following procedures were recently installed by The Louver Shop:

a. Each cashier is assigned a separate cash register drawer to which no other cashier has access.
b. At the end of a shift, each cashier counts the cash in his or her cash register, unlocks the cash register record, and compares the amount of cash with the amount on the record to determine cash shortages and overages.
c. Vouchers and all supporting documents are perforated with a PAID designation after being paid by the treasurer.
d. Disbursements are made from the petty cash fund only after a petty cash receipt has been completed and signed by the payee.
e. All sales are rung up on the cash register, and a receipt is given to the customer. All sales are recorded on a record locked inside the cash register.
f. Checks received through the mail are given daily to the accounts receivable clerk for recording collections on account and for depositing in the bank.
g. The bank reconciliation is prepared by the accountant.

Instructions

→ Indicate whether each of the procedures of internal control over cash represents (1) a strength or (2) a weakness. For each weakness, indicate why it exists.

PR 7-2A
Transactions for petty cash, cash short and over

objs. 3, 6

Hallihan Company completed the following selected transactions during June 2010:

June 1. Established a petty cash fund of $500.

12. The cash sales for the day, according to the cash register records, totaled $13,115. The actual cash received from cash sales was $13,129.

30. Petty cash on hand was $38. Replenished the petty cash fund for the following disbursements, each evidenced by a petty cash receipt:

June 2. Store supplies, $55.

10. Express charges on merchandise purchased, $80 (Merchandise Inventory).

14. Office supplies, $35.

15. Office supplies, $40.

18. Postage stamps, $42 (Office Supplies).

20. Repair to fax, $100 (Miscellaneous Administrative Expense).

21. Repair to office door lock, $35 (Miscellaneous Administrative Expense).

22. Postage due on special delivery letter, $27 (Miscellaneous Administrative Expense).

28. Express charges on merchandise purchased, $40 (Merchandise Inventory).

30. The cash sales for the day, according to the cash register records, totaled $16,850. The actual cash received from cash sales was $16,833.

30. Increased the petty cash fund by $125.

Instructions
Journalize the transactions.

PR 7-3A
Bank reconciliation and entries

obj. 5

✔ 1. Adjusted balance: $13,445

The cash account for Interactive Systems at February 28, 2010, indicated a balance of $7,635. The bank statement indicated a balance of $13,333 on February 28, 2010. Comparing the bank statement and the accompanying canceled checks and memos with the records reveals the following reconciling items:

a. Checks outstanding totaled $4,118.
b. A deposit of $4,500, representing receipts of February 28, had been made too late to appear on the bank statement.
c. The bank had collected $5,200 on a note left for collection. The face of the note was $5,000.
d. A check for $290 returned with the statement had been incorrectly recorded by Interactive Systems as $920. The check was for the payment of an obligation to Busser Co. for the purchase of office supplies on account.
e. A check drawn for $415 had been incorrectly charged by the bank as $145.
f. Bank service charges for February amounted to $20.

Instructions
1. Prepare a bank reconciliation.
2. Journalize the necessary entries. The accounts have not been closed.

PR 7-4A
Bank reconciliation and entries

obj. 5

✔ 1. Adjusted balance: $15,430

The cash account for Fred's Sports Co. on June 1, 2010, indicated a balance of $16,515. During June, the total cash deposited was $40,150, and checks written totaled $43,600. The bank statement indicated a balance of $18,175 on June 30, 2010. Comparing the bank statement, the canceled checks, and the accompanying memos with the records revealed the following reconciling items:

a. Checks outstanding totaled $6,840.
b. A deposit of $4,275, representing receipts of June 30, had been made too late to appear on the bank statement.

c. A check for $640 had been incorrectly charged by the bank as $460.

d. A check for $80 returned with the statement had been recorded by Fred's Sports Co. as $800. The check was for the payment of an obligation to Miliski Co. on account.

e. The bank had collected for Fred's Sports Co. $3,240 on a note left for collection. The face of the note was $3,000.

f. Bank service charges for June amounted to $35.

g. A check for $1,560 from ChimTech Co. was returned by the bank because of insufficient funds.

Instructions

1. Prepare a bank reconciliation as of June 30.

2. Journalize the necessary entries. The accounts have not been closed.

PR 7-5A
Bank reconciliation and entries

obj. 5

✔ 1. Adjusted balance: $11,178.59

Rocky Mountain Interiors deposits all cash receipts each Wednesday and Friday in a night depository, after banking hours. The data required to reconcile the bank statement as of July 31 have been taken from various documents and records and are reproduced as follows. The sources of the data are printed in capital letters. All checks were written for payments on account.

BANK RECONCILIATION FOR PRECEDING MONTH (DATED JUNE 30):

Cash balance according to bank statement..........................		$ 9,422.80
Add deposit of June 30, not recorded by bank		780.80
		$10,203.60
Deduct outstanding checks:		
No. 580	$310.10	
No. 602	85.50	
No. 612	92.50	
No. 613	137.50	625.60
Adjusted balance		$ 9,578.00
Cash balance according to company's records		$ 9,605.70
Deduct service charges		27.70
Adjusted balance		$ 9,578.00

CASH ACCOUNT:
   Balance as of July 1 $9,578.00

CHECKS WRITTEN:
   Number and amount of each check issued in July:

Check No.	Amount	Check No.	Amount	Check No.	Amount
614	$243.50	621	$309.50	628	$ 837.70
615	350.10	622	Void	629	329.90
616	279.90	623	Void	630	882.80
617	395.50	624	707.01	631	1,081.56
618	435.40	625	158.63	632	62.40
619	320.10	626	550.03	633	310.08
620	328.87	627	318.73	634	503.30

Total amount of checks issued in July $8,405.01

```
                                          MEMBER FDIC                          PAGE    1

A B  AMERICAN NATIONAL BANK               ACCOUNT NUMBER
     OF DETROIT                           FROM   7/01/20–  TO  7/31/20–
DETROIT, MI 48201-2500    (313)933-8547   BALANCE              9,422.80

                                       9  DEPOSITS             6,086.35

                                      20  WITHDRAWALS          8,237.41

          ROCKY MOUNTAIN INTERIORS     4  OTHER DEBITS
                                          AND CREDITS          3,685.00CR

                                          NEW BALANCE         10,956.74

*– – – – – CHECKS AND OTHER DEBITS – – – – – * – DEPOSITS – * – DATE – * – BALANCE– *

No.580  310.10   No.612    92.50              780.80      07/01    9,801.00
No.602   85.50   No.614   243.50              569.50      07/03   10,041.50
No.615  350.10   No.616   279.90              701.80      07/06   10,113.30
No.617  395.50   No.618   435.40              819.24      07/11   10,101.64
No.619  320.10   No.620   238.87              580.70      07/13   10,123.37
No.621  309.50   No.624   707.01    MS  4,000.00          07/14   13,106.86
No.625  158.63   No.626   550.03    MS    160.00          07/14   12,558.20
No.627  318.73   No.629   329.90              600.10      07/17   12,509.67
No.630  882.80   No.631 1,081.56  NSF 450.00              07/20   10,095.31
No.628  837.70   No.633   310.08              701.26      07/21    9,648.79
                                              731.45      07/24   10,380.24
                                              601.50      07/28   10,981.74
                      SC     25.00                        07/31   10,956.74

         EC — ERROR CORRECTION              OD — OVERDRAFT
         MS — MISCELLANEOUS                 PS — PAYMENT STOPPED
         NSF — NOT SUFFICIENT FUNDS         SC — SERVICE CHARGE

   * * *                     * * *                        * * *
        THE RECONCILEMENT OF THIS STATEMENT WITH YOUR RECORDS IS ESSENTIAL.
           ANY ERROR OR EXCEPTION SHOULD BE REPORTED IMMEDIATELY.
```

CASH RECEIPTS FOR MONTH OF JULY   6,158.60

DUPLICATE DEPOSIT TICKETS:
Date and amount of each deposit in July:

Date	Amount	Date	Amount	Date	Amount
July 2	$569.50	July 12	$508.70	July 23	$731.45
5	701.80	16	600.10	26	601.50
9	819.24	19	701.26	31	925.05

Instructions

1. Prepare a bank reconciliation as of July 31. If errors in recording deposits or checks are discovered, assume that the errors were made by the company. Assume that all deposits are from cash sales. All checks are written to satisfy accounts payable.
2. Journalize the necessary entries. The accounts have not been closed.
3. What is the amount of Cash that should appear on the balance sheet as of July 31?
4. ◢◤ Assume that a canceled check for $125 has been incorrectly recorded by the bank as $1,250. Briefly explain how the error would be included in a bank reconciliation and how it should be corrected.

Problems Series B

PR 7-1B
Evaluating internal
control of cash

objs. 2, 3

The following procedures were recently installed by C&G Hydraulics Company:

a. The bank reconciliation is prepared by the cashier, who works under the supervision of the treasurer.
b. All mail is opened by the mail clerk, who forwards all cash remittances to the cashier. The cashier prepares a listing of the cash receipts and forwards a copy of the list to the accounts receivable clerk for recording in the accounts.
c. At the end of the day, cash register clerks are required to use their own funds to make up any cash shortages in their registers.
d. At the end of each day, all cash receipts are placed in the bank's night depository.
e. At the end of each day, an accounting clerk compares the duplicate copy of the daily cash deposit slip with the deposit receipt obtained from the bank.
f. The accounts payable clerk prepares a voucher for each disbursement. The voucher along with the supporting documentation is forwarded to the treasurer's office for approval.
g. After necessary approvals have been obtained for the payment of a voucher, the treasurer signs and mails the check. The treasurer then stamps the voucher and supporting documentation as paid and returns the voucher and supporting documentation to the accounts payable clerk for filing.
h. Along with petty cash expense receipts for postage, office supplies, etc., several post-dated employee checks are in the petty cash fund.

Instructions
➡ Indicate whether each of the procedures of internal control over cash represents (1) a strength or (2) a weakness. For each weakness, indicate why it exists.

PR 7-2B
Transactions for
petty cash, cash
short and over

objs. 3, 6

Padilla's Restoration Company completed the following selected transactions during March 2010:

Mar. 1. Established a petty cash fund of $800.
    10. The cash sales for the day, according to the cash register records, totaled $11,368. The actual cash received from cash sales was $11,375.
    31. Petty cash on hand was $193. Replenished the petty cash fund for the following disbursements, each evidenced by a petty cash receipt:
    Mar. 3. Store supplies, $275.
        7. Express charges on merchandise sold, $120 (Delivery Expense).
        9. Office supplies, $18.
      13. Office supplies, $13.
      19. Postage stamps, $9 (Office Supplies).
      21. Repair to office file cabinet lock, $40 (Miscellaneous Administrative Expense).
      22. Postage due on special delivery letter, $18 (Miscellaneous Administrative Expense).
      24. Express charges on merchandise sold, $90 (Delivery Expense).
      30. Office supplies, $16.
    31. The cash sales for the day, according to the cash register records, totaled $14,690. The actual cash received from cash sales was $14,675.
    31. Decreased the petty cash fund by $50.

Instructions
Journalize the transactions.

PR 7-3B
Bank reconciliation
and entries

obj. **5**

✔ 1. Adjusted
balance: $8,613

The cash account for Discount Medical Co. at April 30, 2010, indicated a balance of $4,604. The bank statement indicated a balance of $9,158 on April 30, 2010. Comparing the bank statement and the accompanying canceled checks and memos with the records revealed the following reconciling items:

a. Checks outstanding totaled $5,225.
b. A deposit of $3,150, representing receipts of April 30, had been made too late to appear on the bank statement.
c. The bank had collected $4,120 on a note left for collection. The face of the note was $4,000.
d. A check for $2,490 returned with the statement had been incorrectly recorded by Discount Medical Co. as $2,409. The check was for the payment of an obligation to Goldstein Co. for the purchase of office equipment on account.
e. A check drawn for $170 had been erroneously charged by the bank as $1,700.
f. Bank service charges for April amounted to $30.

Instructions
1. Prepare a bank reconciliation.
2. Journalize the necessary entries. The accounts have not been closed.

PR 7-4B
Bank reconciliation
and entries

obj. **5**

✔ 1. Adjusted
balance: $9,360

The cash account for Inky's Bike Co. at July 1, 2010, indicated a balance of $12,470. During July, the total cash deposited was $26,680, and checks written totaled $31,500. The bank statement indicated a balance of $16,750 on July 31. Comparing the bank statement, the canceled checks, and the accompanying memos with the records revealed the following reconciling items:

a. Checks outstanding totaled $12,850.
b. A deposit of $5,100, representing receipts of July 31, had been made too late to appear on the bank statement.
c. The bank had collected for Inky's Bike Co. $2,675 on a note left for collection. The face of the note was $2,500.
d. A check for $370 returned with the statement had been incorrectly charged by the bank as $730.
e. A check for $320 returned with the statement had been recorded by Inky's Bike Co. as $230. The check was for the payment of an obligation to Ranchwood Co. on account.
f. Bank service charges for July amounted to $25.
g. A check for $850 from Hallock Co. was returned by the bank because of insufficient funds.

Instructions
1. Prepare a bank reconciliation as of July 31.
2. Journalize the necessary entries. The accounts have not been closed.

PR 7-5B
Bank reconciliation
and entries

obj. **5**

✔ 1. Adjusted
balance: $13,893.32

Reydell Furniture Company deposits all cash receipts each Wednesday and Friday in a night depository, after banking hours. The data required to reconcile the bank statement as of June 30 have been taken from various documents and records and are reproduced as follows. The sources of the data are printed in capital letters. All checks were written for payments on account.

JUNE BANK STATEMENT:

```
                                    MEMBER FDIC              PAGE    1
          AMERICAN NATIONAL BANK         ACCOUNT NUMBER
          OF DETROIT                     FROM 6/01/20–    TO 6/30/20–
  DETROIT, MI 48201-2500   (313)933-8547   BALANCE           9,447.20
                                         9 DEPOSITS          8,691.77
                                        20 WITHDRAWALS       8,014.37
  REYDELL FURNITURE COMPANY              4 OTHER DEBITS
                                           AND CREDITS       3,370.00CR
                                           NEW BALANCE      13,494.60
```

* – – – CHECKS AND OTHER DEBITS – – – * – – DEPOSITS – – * – DATE – * – – BALANCE – – *						
No.731	162.15	No.736	345.95	690.25	6/01	9,629.35
No.739	60.55	No.740	237.50	1,080.50	6/02	10,411.80
No.741	495.15	No.742	501.90	854.17	6/04	10,268.92
No.743	671.30	No.744	506.88	840.50	6/09	9,931.24
No.745	117.25	No.746	298.66	MS 3,500.00	6/09	13,015.33
No.748	450.90	No.749	640.13	MS 210.00	6/09	12,134.30
No.750	276.77	No.751	299.37	896.61	6/11	12,454.77
No.752	537.01	No.753	380.95	882.95	6/16	12,419.76
No.754	449.75	No.755	272.75	1,606.74	6/18	13,304.00
No.757	407.95	No.759	901.50	897.34	6/23	12,891.89
				942.71	6/25	13,834.60
			NSF 300.00		6/28	13,534.60
			SC 40.00		6/30	13,494.60

```
   EC — ERROR CORRECTION          OD — OVERDRAFT
   MS — MISCELLANEOUS             PS — PAYMENT STOPPED
   NSF — NOT SUFFICIENT FUNDS     SC — SERVICE CHARGE
   ***                    ***                    ***
```

THE RECONCILEMENT OF THIS STATEMENT WITH YOUR RECORDS IS ESSENTIAL.
ANY ERROR OR EXCEPTION SHOULD BE REPORTED IMMEDIATELY.

CASH ACCOUNT:
Balance as of June 1 .... $9,317.40

CASH RECEIPTS FOR MONTH OF JUNE $9,601.58

DUPLICATE DEPOSIT TICKETS:
Date and amount of each deposit in June:

Date	Amount	Date	Amount	Date	Amount
June 1	$1,080.50	June 10	$ 896.61	June 22	$ 987.34
3	854.17	15	882.95	24	942.71
8	840.50	17	1,606.74	30	1,510.06

CHECKS WRITTEN:
Number and amount of each check issued in June:

Check No.	Amount	Check No.	Amount	Check No.	Amount
740	$237.50	747	Void	754	$ 449.75
741	495.15	748	$ 450.90	755	272.75
742	501.90	749	640.13	756	113.95
743	671.30	750	276.77	757	407.95
744	506.88	751	299.37	758	259.60
745	117.25	752	537.01	759	901.50
746	298.66	753	830.95	760	486.39

Total amount of checks issued in June $8,755.66

BANK RECONCILIATION FOR PRECEDING MONTH:

Reydell Furniture Company
Bank Reconciliation
May 31, 20—

Cash balance according to bank statement		$ 9,447.20
Add deposit for May 31, not recorded by bank		690.25
		$10,137.45
Deduct outstanding checks:		
No. 731	$162.15	
736	345.95	
738	251.40	
739	60.55	820.05
Adjusted balance		$ 9,317.40
Cash balance according to company's records		$ 9,352.50
Deduct service charges		35.10
Adjusted balance		$ 9,317.40

Instructions
1. Prepare a bank reconciliation as of June 30. If errors in recording deposits or checks are discovered, assume that the errors were made by the company. Assume that all deposits are from cash sales. All checks are written to satisfy accounts payable.
2. Journalize the necessary entries. The accounts have not been closed.
3. What is the amount of Cash that should appear on the balance sheet as of June 30?
4. ▬▬▶ Assume that a canceled check for $260 has been incorrectly recorded by the bank as $620. Briefly explain how the error would be included in a bank reconciliation and how it should be corrected.

Special Activities ● ● ● ● ● ▶

SA 7-1
Ethics and professional conduct in business

During the preparation of the bank reconciliation for New Concepts Co., Peter Fikes, the assistant controller, discovered that City National Bank incorrectly recorded a $710 check written by New Concepts Co. as $170. Peter has decided not to notify the bank but wait for the bank to detect the error. Peter plans to record the $540 error as Other Income if the bank fails to detect the error within the next three months.
▬▬▶ Discuss whether Peter is behaving in a professional manner.

SA 7-2
Internal controls

The following is an excerpt from a conversation between two sales clerks, Ross Maas and Shu Lyons. Both Ross and Shu are employed by Hawkins Electronics, a locally owned and operated electronics retail store.

Ross: Did you hear the news?

Shu: What news?

Ross: Jane and Rachel were both arrested this morning.

Shu: What? Arrested? You're putting me on!

Ross: No, really! The police arrested them first thing this morning. Put them in handcuffs, read them their rights—the whole works. It was unreal!

Shu: What did they do?

Ross: Well, apparently they were filling out merchandise refund forms for fictitious customers and then taking the cash.

Shu: I guess I never thought of that. How did they catch them?

Ross: The store manager noticed that returns were twice that of last year and seemed to be increasing. When he confronted Jane, she became flustered and admitted to taking the cash, apparently over $7,000 in just three months. They're going over the last six months' transactions to try to determine how much Rachel stole. She apparently started stealing first.

▬▬▶ Suggest appropriate control procedures that would have prevented or detected the theft of cash.

SA 7-3
Internal controls

The following is an excerpt from a conversation between the store manager of Yoder Brothers Grocery Stores, Lori Colburn, and Terry Whipple, president of Yoder Brothers Grocery Stores.

Terry: Lori, I'm concerned about this new scanning system.

Lori: What's the problem?

Terry: Well, how do we know the clerks are ringing up all the merchandise?

Lori: That's one of the strong points about the system. The scanner automatically rings up each item, based on its bar code. We update the prices daily, so we're sure that the sale is rung up for the right price.

Terry: That's not my concern. What keeps a clerk from pretending to scan items and then simply not charging his friends? If his friends were buying 10-15 items, it would be easy for the clerk to pass through several items with his finger over the bar code or just pass the merchandise through the scanner with the wrong side showing. It would look normal for anyone observing. In the old days, we at least could hear the cash register ringing up each sale.

Lori: I see your point.

➤ Suggest ways that Yoder Brothers Grocery Stores could prevent or detect the theft of merchandise as described.

SA 7-4
Ethics and professional conduct in business

Ryan Egan and Jack Moody are both cash register clerks for Organic Markets. Lee Sorrell is the store manager for Organic Markets. The following is an excerpt of a conversation between Ryan and Jack:

Ryan: Jack, how long have you been working for Organic Markets?

Jack: Almost five years this November. You just started two weeks ago . . . right?

Ryan: Yes. Do you mind if I ask you a question?

Jack: No, go ahead.

Ryan: What I want to know is, have they always had this rule that if your cash register is short at the end of the day, you have to make up the shortage out of your own pocket?

Jack: Yes, as long as I've been working here.

Ryan: Well, it's the pits. Last week I had to pay in almost $40.

Jack: It's not that big a deal. I just make sure that I'm not short at the end of the day.

Ryan: How do you do that?

Jack: I just shortchange a few customers early in the day. There are a few jerks that deserve it anyway. Most of the time, their attention is elsewhere and they don't think to check their change.

Ryan: What happens if you're over at the end of the day?

Jack: Lee lets me keep it as long as it doesn't get to be too large. I've not been short in over a year. I usually clear about $20 to $30 extra per day.

➤ Discuss this case from the viewpoint of proper controls and professional behavior.

SA 7-5
Bank reconciliation and internal control

The records of Anacker Company indicate a July 31 cash balance of $9,400, which includes undeposited receipts for July 30 and 31. The cash balance on the bank statement as of July 31 is $6,575. This balance includes a note of $4,000 plus $160 interest collected by the bank but not recorded in the journal. Checks outstanding on July 31 were as follows: No. 370, $580; No. 379, $615; No. 390, $900; No. 1148, $225; No. 1149, $300; and No. 1151, $750.

On July 3, the cashier resigned, effective at the end of the month. Before leaving on July 31, the cashier prepared the following bank reconciliation:

Cash balance per books, July 31		$ 9,400
Add outstanding checks:		
No. 1148	$225	
1149	300	
1151	750	1,175
		$10,575
Less undeposited receipts		4,000
Cash balance per bank, July 31		$ 6,575
Deduct unrecorded note with interest		4,160
True cash, July 31		$ 2,415

```
        Calculator Tape of Outstanding Checks:
                      0 *
                    225 +
                    300 +
                    750 +
                  1,175 *
```

Subsequently, the owner of Anacker Company discovered that the cashier had stolen an unknown amount of undeposited receipts, leaving only $1,000 to be deposited on July 31. The owner, a close family friend, has asked your help in determining the amount that the former cashier has stolen.

1. Determine the amount the cashier stole from Anacker Company. Show your computations in good form.
2. How did the cashier attempt to conceal the theft?
3. a. Identify two major weaknesses in internal controls, which allowed the cashier to steal the undeposited cash receipts.
   b. ━━━━━► Recommend improvements in internal controls, so that similar types of thefts of undeposited cash receipts can be prevented.

SA 7-6
Observe internal controls over cash

Group Project

Select a business in your community and observe its internal controls over cash receipts and cash payments. The business could be a bank or a bookstore, restaurant, department store, or other retailer. In groups of three or four, identify and discuss the similarities and differences in each business's cash internal controls.

SA 7-7
Cash to monthly cash expenses ratio

OccuLogix, Inc., provides treatments for eye diseases, including age-related macular degeneration (AMD). The company's treatment system, called the RHEO system, consists of an Octonova pump and disposable treatment sets that improve microcirculation in the eye by filtering high molecular weight proteins and other macromolecules from the patient's plasma. OccuLogix reported the following data (in thousands) for the years ending December 31, 2006, 2005, 2004, and 2003:

	2006	2005	2004	2003
Cash as of December 31*	$15,536	$41,268	$60,040	$1,239
Net cash flows from operating activities	(14,548)	(18,710)	(5,382)	(2,375)

*Includes cash equivalents and short-term investments.

1. Determine the monthly cash expenses for 2006, 2005, 2004, and 2003. Round to one decimal place.
2. Determine the ratio of cash to monthly expenses as of December 31, 2006, 2005, 2004, and 2003. Round to one decimal place.
3. ━━━━━► Based on (1) and (2), comment on OccuLogix's ratio of cash to monthly operating expenses for 2006, 2005, 2004, and 2003.

Answers to Self-Examination Questions

1. **C** Compliance with laws and regulations (answer C) is an objective, not an element, of internal control. The control environment (answer A), monitoring (answer B), control procedures (answer D), risk assessment, and information and communication are the five elements of internal control.

2. **C** The error was made by the bank, so the cash balance according to the bank statement needs to be adjusted. Since the bank deducted $90 ($540.50 −$450.50) too little, the error of $90 should be deducted from the cash balance according to the bank statement (answer C).

3. **B** On any specific date, the cash account in a company's ledger may not agree with the account in the bank's ledger because of delays and/or errors by either party in recording transactions. The purpose of a bank reconciliation, therefore, is to determine the reasons for any differences between the two account balances. All errors should then be corrected by the company or the bank, as appropriate. In arriving at the adjusted cash balance according to the bank statement, outstanding checks must be deducted (answer B) to adjust for checks that have been written by the company but that have not yet been presented to the bank for payment.

4. **C** All reconciling items that are added to and deducted from the cash balance according to the company's records on the bank reconciliation (answer C) require that journal entries be made by the company to correct errors made in recording transactions or to bring the cash account up to date for delays in recording transactions.

5. **D** To avoid the delay, annoyance, and expense that is associated with paying all obligations by check, relatively small amounts (answer A) are paid from a petty cash fund. The fund is established by estimating the amount of cash needed to pay these small amounts during a specified period (answer B), and it is then reimbursed when the amount of money in the fund is reduced to a predetermined minimum amount (answer C).

CHAPTER 8

Receivables

OAKLEY, INC.

The sale and purchase of merchandise involves the exchange of goods for cash. However, the point at which cash actually changes hands varies with the transaction. Consider transactions by Oakley, Inc., a worldwide leader in the design, development, manufacture, and distribution of premium sunglasses, goggles, prescription eyewear, apparel, footwear, and accessories. Not only does the company sell its products through three different company-owned retail chains, but it also has approximately 10,000 independent distributors.

If you were to buy a pair of sunglasses at an Oakley Vault, which is one of the company's retail outlet stores, you would have to pay cash or use a credit card to pay for the glasses before you left the store. However, Oakley allows its distributors to purchase sunglasses "on account." These sales on account are recorded as receivables due from the distributors.

As an individual, you also might build up a trusted financial history with a local company or department store that would allow you to purchase merchandise on account. Like Oakley's distributors, your purchase on account would be recorded as an account receivable. Such credit transactions facilitate sales and are a significant current asset for many businesses. In this chapter, we will describe common classifications of receivables, illustrate how to account for uncollectible receivables, and demonstrate the reporting of receivables on the balance sheet.

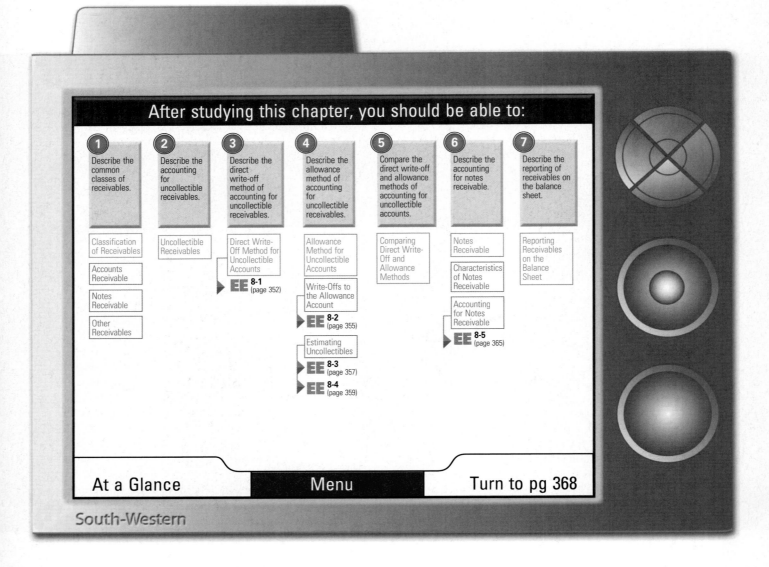

After studying this chapter, you should be able to:

1 Describe the common classes of receivables.

2 Describe the accounting for uncollectible receivables.

3 Describe the direct write-off method of accounting for uncollectible receivables.

4 Describe the allowance method of accounting for uncollectible receivables.

5 Compare the direct write-off and allowance methods of accounting for uncollectible accounts.

6 Describe the accounting for notes receivable.

7 Describe the reporting of receivables on the balance sheet.

Classification of Receivables

Accounts Receivable

Notes Receivable

Other Receivables

Uncollectible Receivables

Direct Write-Off Method for Uncollectible Accounts

EE 8-1 (page 352)

Allowance Method for Uncollectible Accounts

Write-Offs to the Allowance Account

EE 8-2 (page 355)

Estimating Uncollectibles

EE 8-3 (page 357)

EE 8-4 (page 359)

Comparing Direct Write-Off and Allowance Methods

Notes Receivable

Characteristics of Notes Receivable

Accounting for Notes Receivable

EE 8-5 (page 365)

Reporting Receivables on the Balance Sheet

At a Glance   Menu   Turn to pg 368

South-Western

1 Describe the common classes of receivables.

Classification of Receivables

The receivables that result from sales on account are normally accounts receivable or notes receivable. The term **receivables** includes all money claims against other entities, including people, companies, and other organizations. Receivables are usually a significant portion of the total current assets.

Accounts Receivable

The most common transaction creating a receivable is selling merchandise or services on account (on credit). The receivable is recorded as a debit to Accounts Receivable. Such **accounts receivable** are normally collected within a short period, such as 30 or 60 days. They are classified on the balance sheet as a current asset.

Notes Receivable

Notes receivable are amounts that customers owe for which a formal, written instrument of credit has been issued. If notes receivable are expected to be collected within a year, they are classified on the balance sheet as a current asset.

Notes are often used for credit periods of more than 60 days. For example, an automobile dealer may require a down payment at the time of sale and accept a note or a series of notes for the remainder. Such notes usually provide for monthly payments.

An annual report of La-Z-Boy Incorporated reported that receivables made up over 48% of La-Z-Boy's current assets.

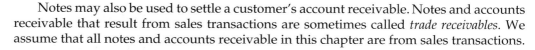

If you have purchased an automobile on credit, you probably signed a note. From your viewpoint, the note is a note payable. From the creditor's viewpoint, the note is a note receivable.

Notes may also be used to settle a customer's account receivable. Notes and accounts receivable that result from sales transactions are sometimes called *trade receivables*. We assume that all notes and accounts receivable in this chapter are from sales transactions.

Other Receivables

Other receivables include interest receivable, taxes receivable, and receivables from officers or employees. Other receivables are normally reported separately on the balance sheet. If they are expected to be collected within one year, they are classified as current assets. If collection is expected beyond one year, they are classified as noncurrent assets and reported under the caption *Investments*.

Uncollectible Receivables

2 Describe the accounting for uncollectible receivables.

In prior chapters, the accounting for sales of merchandise or services on account (on credit) was described and illustrated. A major issue that has not yet been discussed is that some customers will not pay their accounts. That is, some accounts receivable will be uncollectible.

Companies may shift the risk of uncollectible receivables to other companies. For example, some retailers do not accept sales on account, but will only accept cash or credit cards. Such policies shift the risk to the credit card companies.

Companies may also sell their receivables. This is often the case when a company issues its own credit card. For example, Macy's and JCPenney issue their own credit cards. Selling receivables is called *factoring* the receivables. The buyer of the receivables is called a *factor*. An advantage of factoring is that the company selling its receivables immediately receives cash for operating and other needs. Also, depending on the factoring agreement, some of the risk of uncollectible accounts is shifted to the factor.

Regardless of how careful a company is in granting credit, some credit sales will be uncollectible. The operating expense recorded from uncollectible receivables is called **bad debt expense**, *uncollectible accounts expense*, or *doubtful accounts expense*.

There is no general rule for when an account becomes uncollectible. Some indications that an account may be uncollectible include the following:

1. The receivable is past due.
2. The customer does not respond to the company's attempts to collect.
3. The customer files for bankruptcy.
4. The customer closes its business.
5. The company cannot locate the customer.

Adams, Stevens & Bradley, Ltd. is a collection agency that operates on a contingency basis. That is, its fees are based on what it collects.

If a customer doesn't pay, a company may turn the account over to a collection agency. After the collection agency attempts to collect payment, any remaining balance in the account is considered worthless.

The two methods of accounting for uncollectible receivables are as follows:

1. The **direct write-off method** records bad debt expense only when an account is determined to be worthless.
2. The **allowance method** records bad debt expense by estimating uncollectible accounts at the end of the accounting period.

The direct write-off method is often used by small companies and companies with few receivables.[1] Generally accepted accounting principles (GAAP), however, require companies with a large amount of receivables to use the allowance method. As a result, most well-known companies such as General Electric, Pepsi, Intel, and FedEx use the allowance method.

---

1 The direct write-off method is also required for federal income tax purposes.

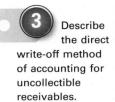

3 Describe the direct write-off method of accounting for uncollectible receivables.

Direct Write-Off Method for Uncollectible Accounts

Under the direct write-off method, Bad Debt Expense is not recorded until the customer's account is determined to be worthless. At that time, the customer's account receivable is written off.

To illustrate, assume that a $4,200 account receivable from D. L. Ross has been determined to be uncollectible. The entry to write off the account is as follows:

| May | 10 | Bad Debt Expense | 4,200 | |
| | | Accounts Receivable—D. L. Ross | | 4,200 |

An account receivable that has been written off may be collected later. In such cases, the account is reinstated by an entry that reverses the write-off entry. The cash received in payment is then recorded as a receipt on account.

To illustrate, assume that the D. L. Ross account of $4,200 written off on May 10 is later collected on November 21. The reinstatement and receipt of cash is recorded as follows:

Nov.	21	Accounts Receivable—D. L. Ross	4,200	
		Bad Debt Expense		4,200
	21	Cash	4,200	
		Accounts Receivable—D. L. Ross		4,200

The direct write-off method is used by businesses that sell most of their goods or services for cash or accept only MasterCard or VISA, which are recorded as cash sales. In such cases, receivables are a small part of the current assets and any bad debt expense is small. Examples of such businesses are a restaurant, a convenience store, and a small retail store.

Example Exercise 8-1   Direct Write-Off Method ••••••••> 3

Journalize the following transactions using the direct write-off method of accounting for uncollectible receivables:

July 9. Received $1,200 from Jay Burke and wrote off the remainder owed of $3,900 as uncollectible.
Oct. 11. Reinstated the account of Jay Burke and received $3,900 cash in full payment.

Follow My Example 8-1

July	9	Cash	1,200	
		Bad Debt Expense	3,900	
		Accounts Receivable—Jay Burke		5,100
Oct.	11	Accounts Receivable—Jay Burke	3,900	
		Bad Debt Expense		3,900
	11	Cash	3,900	
		Accounts Receivable—Jay Burke		3,900

For Practice: PE 8-1A, PE 8-1B

Describe the allowance method of accounting for uncollectible receivables.

Allowance Method for Uncollectible Accounts

The allowance method estimates the uncollectible accounts receivable at the end of the accounting period. Based on this estimate, Bad Debt Expense is recorded by an adjusting entry.

To illustrate, assume that ExTone Company began operations August 1. As of the end of its accounting period on December 31, 2009, ExTone has an accounts receivable balance of $200,000. This balance includes some past due accounts. Based on industry averages, ExTone estimates that $30,000 of the December 31 accounts receivable will be uncollectible. However, on December 31, ExTone doesn't know which customer accounts will be uncollectible. Thus, specific customer accounts cannot be decreased or credited. Instead, a contra asset account, **Allowance for Doubtful Accounts**, is credited for the estimated bad debts.

Using the $30,000 estimate, the following adjusting entry is made on December 31:

2009				
Dec.	31	Bad Debt Expense	30,000	
		Allowance for Doubtful Accounts		30,000
		Uncollectible accounts estimate.		

> **The adjusting entry reduces receivables to their net realizable value and matches the uncollectible expense with revenues.**

The preceding adjusting entry affects the income statement and balance sheet. On the income statement, the $30,000 of Bad Debt Expense will be matched against the related revenues of the period. On the balance sheet, the value of the receivables is reduced to the amount that is expected to be collected or realized. This amount, $170,000 ($200,000 − $30,000), is called the **net realizable value** of the receivables.

After the preceding adjusting entry is recorded, Accounts Receivable still has a debit balance of $200,000. This balance is the total amount owed by customers on account on December 31 as supported by the accounts receivable subsidiary ledger. The accounts receivable contra account, Allowance for Doubtful Accounts, has a credit balance of $30,000.

Integrity, Objectivity, and Ethics in Business

SELLER BEWARE

A company in financial distress will still try to purchase goods and services on account. In these cases, rather than "buyer beware," it is more like "seller beware." Sellers must be careful in advancing credit to such companies, because trade creditors have low priority for cash payments in the event of bankruptcy. To help suppliers, third-party services specialize in evaluating financially distressed customers. These services analyze credit risk for these firms by evaluating recent management payment decisions (who is getting paid and when), court actions (if in bankruptcy), and other supplier credit tightening or suspension actions. Such information helps monitor and adjust trade credit amounts and terms with the financially distressed customer.

Write-Offs to the Allowance Account

When a customer's account is identified as uncollectible, it is written off against the allowance account. This requires the company to remove the specific accounts receivable and an equal amount from the allowance account.

To illustrate, on January 21, 2010, John Parker's account of $6,000 with ExTone Company is written off as follows:

2010 Jan.	21	Allowance for Doubtful Accounts	6,000	
		Accounts Receivable—John Parker		6,000

At the end of a period, Allowance for Doubtful Accounts will normally have a balance. This is because Allowance for Doubtful Accounts is based on an estimate. As a result, the total write-offs to the allowance account during the period will rarely equal the balance of the account at the beginning of the period. The allowance account will have a credit balance at the end of the period if the write-offs during the period are less than the beginning balance. It will have a debit balance if the write-offs exceed the beginning balance.

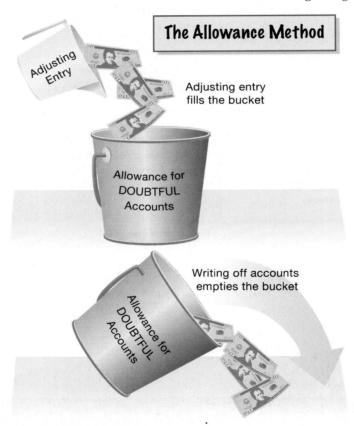

The Allowance Method

Adjusting Entry

Adjusting entry fills the bucket

Allowance for DOUBTFUL Accounts

Writing off accounts empties the bucket

Allowance for DOUBTFUL Accounts

To illustrate, assume that during 2010 ExTone Company writes off $26,750 of uncollectible accounts, including the $6,000 account of John Parker recorded on January 21. Allowance for Doubtful Accounts will have a credit balance of $3,250 ($30,000 − $26,750), as shown below.

ALLOWANCE FOR DOUBTFUL ACCOUNTS

		Jan. 1, 2010 Balance	30,000
Total accounts written off $26,750	Jan. 21 6,000		
	Feb. 2 3,900		
	⋮ ⋮		
		Dec. 31, 2010 Unadjusted balance	3,250

If ExTone Company had written off $32,100 in accounts receivable during 2010, Allowance for Doubtful Accounts would have a debit balance of $2,100, as shown below.

ALLOWANCE FOR DOUBTFUL ACCOUNTS

			Jan. 1, 2010	Balance	30,000
Total accounts written off $32,100	Jan. 21	6,000			
	Feb. 2	3,900			
	⋮	⋮			
Dec. 31, 2010 Unadjusted balance 2,100					

The allowance account balances (credit balance of $3,250 and debit balance of $2,100) in the preceding illustrations are *before* the end-of-period adjusting entry. After the end-of-period adjusting entry is recorded, Allowance for Doubtful Accounts should always have a credit balance.

An account receivable that has been written off against the allowance account may be collected later. Like the direct write-off method, the account is reinstated by an entry that reverses the write-off entry. The cash received in payment is then recorded as a receipt on account.

To illustrate, assume that Nancy Smith's account of $5,000 which was written off on April 2 is collected later on June 10. ExTone Company records the reinstatement and the collection as follows:

June	10	Accounts Receivable—Nancy Smith	5,000	
		Allowance for Doubtful Accounts		5,000
	10	Cash	5,000	
		Accounts Receivable—Nancy Smith		5,000

Example Exercise 8-2   Allowance Method  4

Journalize the following transactions using the allowance method of accounting for uncollectible receivables.

July 9.   Received $1,200 from Jay Burke and wrote off the remainder owed of $3,900 as uncollectible.
Oct. 11.   Reinstated the account of Jay Burke and received $3,900 cash in full payment.

Follow My Example 8-2

July 9	Cash	1,200	
	Allowance for Doubtful Accounts	3,900	
	Accounts Receivable—Jay Burke		5,100
Oct. 11	Accounts Receivable—Jay Burke	3,900	
	Allowance for Doubtful Accounts		3,900
11	Cash	3,900	
	Accounts Receivable—Jay Burke		3,900

For Practice: PE 8-2A, PE 8-2B

Estimating Uncollectibles

The allowance method requires an estimate of uncollectible accounts at the end of the period. This estimate is normally based on past experience, industry averages, and forecasts of the future.

The two methods used to estimate uncollectible accounts are as follows:

1. Percent of sales method.
2. Analysis of receivables method.

Percent of Sales Method
Since accounts receivable are created by credit sales, uncollectible accounts can be estimated as a percent of credit sales. If the portion of credit sales to sales is relatively constant, the percent may be applied to total sales or net sales.

To illustrate, assume the following data for ExTone Company on December 31, 2010, before any adjustments:

Balance of Accounts Receivable	$240,000
Balance of Allowance for Doubtful Accounts	3,250 (Cr.)
Total credit sales	3,000,000
Bad debt as a percent of credit sales	$\frac{3}{4}\%$

Bad Debt Expense of $22,500 is estimated as follows:

Bad Debt Expense = Credit Sales × Bad Debt as a Percent of Credit Sales
Bad Debt Expense = $3,000,000 × $\frac{3}{4}\%$ = $22,500

The adjusting entry for uncollectible accounts on December 31, 2010, is as follows:

Dec.	31	Bad Debt Expense	22,500	
		Allowance for Doubtful Accounts		22,500
		Uncollectible accounts estimate.		
		($3,000,000 × 0.0075 = $22,500)		

After the adjusting entry is posted to the ledger, Bad Debt Expense will have an adjusted balance of $22,500. Allowance for Doubtful Accounts will have an adjusted balance of $25,750 ($3,250 + $22,500). Both T accounts are shown below.

BAD DEBT EXPENSE

Dec. 31, 2010	Adjusting entry	22,500
Dec. 31	Adjusted balance	22,500

ALLOWANCE FOR DOUBTFUL ACCOUNTS

			Jan. 1, 2010	Balance	30,000
Total accounts	Jan. 21	6,000			
written off $26,750	Feb. 2	3,900			
	⋮	⋮			
			Dec. 31	Unadjusted balance	3,250
			Dec. 31	Adjusting entry	22,500
			Dec. 31	Adjusted balance	25,750

Under the percent of sales method, the amount of the adjusting entry is the amount estimated for Bad Debt Expense. This estimate is credited to whatever the unadjusted balance is for Allowance for Doubtful Accounts.

To illustrate, assume that in the preceding example the unadjusted balance of Allowance for Doubtful Accounts on December 31, 2010, had been a $2,100 debit balance instead of a $3,250 credit balance. The adjustment would still have been

> The estimate based on sales is added to any balance in Allowance for Doubtful Accounts.

$22,500. However, the December 31, 2010, ending adjusted balance of Allowance for Doubtful Accounts would have been $20,400 ($22,500 − $2,100).

Example Exercise 8-3   Percent of Sales Method   ● ● ● ● ● ● ● ● ⟩ 4

At the end of the current year, Accounts Receivable has a balance of $800,000; Allowance for Doubtful Accounts has a credit balance of $7,500; and net sales for the year total $3,500,000. Bad debt expense is estimated at ½ of 1% of net sales.

Determine (a) the amount of the adjusting entry for uncollectible accounts; (b) the adjusted balances of Accounts Receivable, Allowance for Doubtful Accounts, and Bad Debt Expense; and (c) the net realizable value of accounts receivable.

Follow My Example 8-3

a. $17,500 ($3,500,000 × 0.005)

		Adjusted Balance
b.	Accounts Receivable	$800,000
	Allowance for Doubtful Accounts ($7,500 + $17,500)	25,000
	Bad Debt Expense	17,500

c. $775,000 ($800,000 − $25,000)

For Practice: PE 8-3A, PE 8-3B

Analysis of Receivables Method   The analysis of receivables method is based on the assumption that the longer an account receivable is outstanding, the less likely that it will be collected. The analysis of receivables method is applied as follows:

The percentage of uncollectible accounts will vary across companies and industries. For example, in their recent annual reports, JCPenney reported 1.7% of its receivables as uncollectible, Deere & Company (manufacturer of John Deere tractors, etc.) reported only 1.0% of its dealer receivables as uncollectible, and HCA Inc., a hospital management company, reported 42% of its receivables as uncollectible.

Step 1.   The due date of each account receivable is determined.

Step 2.   The number of days each account is past due is determined. This is the number of days between the due date of the account and the date of the analysis.

Step 3.   Each account is placed in an aged class according to its days past due. Typical aged classes include the following:

  Not past due
  1–30 days past due
  31–60 days past due
  61–90 days past due
  91–180 days past due
  181–365 days past due
  Over 365 days past due

Step 4.   The totals for each aged class are determined.

Step 5.   The total for each aged class is multiplied by an estimated percentage of uncollectible accounts for that class.

Step 6.   The estimated total of uncollectible accounts is determined as the sum of the uncollectible accounts for each aged class.

The preceding steps are summarized in an aging schedule, and this overall process is called **aging the receivables**.

To illustrate, assume that ExTone Company uses the analysis of receivables method instead of the percent of sales method. ExTone prepared an aging schedule for its accounts receivable of $240,000 as of December 31, 2010, as shown in Exhibit 1.

Exhibit 1

Aging of Receivables Schedule
December 31, 2010

		A	B	C	D	E	F	G	H	I
	1			**Not**			**Days Past Due**			
	2			**Past**						**Over**
	3	**Customer**	**Balance**	**Due**	**1–30**	**31–60**	**61–90**	**91–180**	**181–365**	**365**
	4	Ashby & Co.	1,500			1,500				
	5	B. T. Barr	6,100					3,500	2,600	
	6	Brock Co.	4,700	4,700						
Steps 1–3	21									
	22	Saxon Woods Co.	600					600		
Step 4	23	Total	240,000	125,000	64,000	13,100	8,900	5,000	10,000	14,000
Step 5	24	Percent uncollectible		2%	5%	10%	20%	30%	50%	80%
Step 6	25	Estimate of uncollectible accounts	26,490	2,500	3,200	1,310	1,780	1,500	5,000	11,200

Assume that ExTone Company sold merchandise to Saxon Woods Co. on August 29 with terms 2/10, n/30. Thus, the due date (Step 1) of Saxon Woods' account is September 28, as shown below.

Credit terms, net	30 days
Less: Aug. 29 to Aug. 30	2 days
Days in September	28 days

As of December 31, Saxon Woods' account is 94 days past due (Step 2), as shown below.

<table>
<tr><td>Number of days past due in September</td><td>2 days (30 – 28)</td></tr>
<tr><td>Number of days past due in October</td><td>31 days</td></tr>
<tr><td>Number of days past due in November</td><td>30 days</td></tr>
<tr><td>Number of days past due in December</td><td>31 days</td></tr>
<tr><td>Total number of days past due</td><td>94 days</td></tr>
</table>

> The estimate based on receivables is compared to the balance in the allowance account to determine the amount of the adjusting entry.

Exhibit 1 shows that the $600 account receivable for Saxon Woods Co. was placed in the 91–180 days past due class (Step 3).

The total for each of the aged classes is determined (Step 4). Exhibit 1 shows that $125,000 of the accounts receivable are not past due, while $64,000 are 1–30 days past due. ExTone Company applies a different estimated percentage of uncollectible accounts to the totals of each of the aged classes (Step 5). As shown in Exhibit 1, the percent is 2% for accounts not past due, while the percent is 80% for accounts over 365 days past due.

The sum of the estimated uncollectible accounts for each aged class (Step 6) is the estimated uncollectible accounts on December 31, 2010. This is the desired adjusted balance for Allowance for Doubtful Accounts. For ExTone Company, this amount is $26,490, as shown in Exhibit 1.

Comparing the estimate of $26,490 with the unadjusted balance of the allowance account determines the amount of the adjustment for Bad Debt Expense. For ExTone, the unadjusted balance of the allowance account is a credit balance of $3,250. The amount to be added to this balance is therefore $23,240 ($26,490 − $3,250). The adjusting entry is as follows:

Dec.	31	Bad Debt Expense	23,240	
		Allowance for Doubtful Accounts		23,240
		Uncollectible accounts estimate.		
		($26,490 − $3,250)		

The Commercial Collection Agency Section of the Commercial Law League of America reported the following collection rates by number of months past due:

After the preceding adjusting entry is posted to the ledger, Bad Debt Expense will have an adjusted balance of $23,240. Allowance for Doubtful Accounts will have an adjusted balance of $26,490, and the net realizable value of the receivables is $213,510 ($240,000 − $26,490). Both T accounts are shown below.

BAD DEBT EXPENSE

| Dec. 31, 2010 | Adjusting entry | 23,240 |
| Dec. 31 | Adjusting balance | 23,240 |

ALLOWANCE FOR DOUBTFUL ACCOUNTS

	Dec. 31, 2010	Unadjusted balance	3,250
	Dec. 31	Adjusting entry	23,240
	Dec. 31	Adjusted balance	26,490

Bar chart: Number of Months Past Due (1, 2, 3, 6, 9, 12, 24) with collection rates 93.4%, 84.6%, 72.9%, 57.0%, 41.9%, 25.4%, 12.5%.

Under the analysis of receivables method, the amount of the adjusting entry is the amount that will yield an adjusted balance for Allowance for Doubtful Accounts equal to that estimated by the aging schedule.

To illustrate, if the unadjusted balance of the allowance account had been a debit balance of $2,100, the amount of the adjustment would have been $28,590 ($26,490 + $2,100). In this case, Bad Debt Expense would have an adjusted balance of $28,590. However, the adjusted balance of Allowance for Doubtful Accounts would still have been $26,490. After the adjusting entry is posted, both T accounts are shown below.

BAD DEBT EXPENSE

| Dec. 31, 2010 | Adjusting entry | 28,590 |
| Dec. 31 | Adjusting balance | 28,590 |

ALLOWANCE FOR DOUBTFUL ACCOUNTS

Dec. 31, 2010	Unadjusted balance	2,100			
			Aug. 31	Adjusted entry	28,590
			Aug. 31	Adjusted balance	26,490

Example Exercise 8-4   Analysis of Receivables Method   ●●●●●●●> ④

At the end of the current year, Accounts Receivable has a balance of $800,000; Allowance for Doubtful Accounts has a credit balance of $7,500; and net sales for the year total $3,500,000. Using the aging method, the balance of Allowance for Doubtful Accounts is estimated as $30,000.

Determine (a) the amount of the adjusting entry for uncollectible accounts; (b) the adjusted balances of Accounts Receivable, Allowance for Doubtful Accounts, and Bad Debt Expense; and (c) the net realizable value of accounts receivable.

Follow My Example 8-4

a. $22,500 ($30,000 − $7,500)

	Adjusted Balance
b. Accounts Receivable	$800,000
Allowance for Doubtful Accounts	30,000
Bad Debt Expense	22,500

c. $770,000 ($800,000 − $30,000)

For Practice: PE 8-4A, PE 8-4B

Comparing Estimation Methods Both the percent of sales and analysis of receivables methods estimate uncollectible accounts. However, each method has a slightly different focus and financial statement emphasis.

Under the percent of sales method, Bad Debt Expense is the focus of the estimation process. The percent of sales method places more emphasis on matching revenues and expenses and, thus, emphasizes the income statement. That is, the amount of the adjusting entry is based on the estimate of Bad Debt Expense for the period. Allowance for Doubtful Accounts is then credited for this amount.

Under the analysis of receivables method, Allowance for Doubtful Accounts is the focus of the estimation process. The analysis of receivables method places more emphasis on the net realizable value of the receivables and, thus, emphasizes the balance sheet. That is, the amount of the adjusting entry is the amount that will yield an adjusted balance for Allowance for Doubtful Accounts equal to that estimated by the aging schedule. Bad Debt Expense is then debited for this amount.

Exhibit 2 summarizes these differences between the percent of sales and the analysis of receivables methods. Exhibit 2 also shows the results of the ExTone Company illustration for the percent of sales and analysis of receivables methods. The amounts shown in Exhibit 2 assume that an unadjusted credit balance of $3,250 for Allowance for Doubtful Accounts. While the methods normally yield different amounts for any one period, over several periods the amounts should be similar.

Exhibit 2

Differences Between Estimation Methods

	Focus of Method	Financial Statement Emphasis	ExTone Company Example	
			Bad Debt Expense Estimate **	Allowance for Doubtful Accounts Estimate
Percent of Sales Method	Bad Debt Expense Estimate	Income Statement	$22,500	$25,750* ($22,500 + $3,250)
Analysis of Receivables Method	Allowance for Doubtful Accounts Estimate	Balance Sheet	$23,240* ($26,490 − $3,250)	$26,490

*Indicates that the estimate was derived (sometimes called plugged) from the estimate on which this method focuses.
** Amount of adjusting entry.

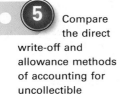

5 Compare the direct write-off and allowance methods of accounting for uncollectible accounts.

Comparing Direct Write-Off and Allowance Methods

The journal entries for the direct write-off and allowance methods are illustrated and compared in this section. As a basis for our illustration, the following selected transactions, taken from the records of Hobbs Company for the year ending December 31, 2009, are used:

Mar. 1. Wrote off account of C. York, $3,650.
Apr. 12. Received $2,250 as partial payment on the $5,500 account of Cary Bradshaw. Wrote off the remaining balance as uncollectible.
June 22. Received the $3,650 from C. York, which had been written off on March 1. Reinstated the account and recorded the cash receipt.
Sept. 7. Wrote off the following accounts as uncollectible (record as one journal entry):

Jason Bigg	$1,100	Stanford Noonan	$1,360
Steve Bradey	2,220	Aiden Wyman	990
Samantha Neeley	775		

Dec. 31. Hobbs Company uses the percent of credit sales method of estimating uncollectible expenses. Based on past history and industry averages, 1.25% of credit sales are expected to be uncollectible. Hobbs recorded $3,400,000 of credit sales during 2009.

Exhibit 3 illustrates the journal entries for Hobbs Company using the direct write-off and allowance methods. Using the direct write-off method, there is no adjusting entry on December 31 for uncollectible accounts. In contrast, the allowance method records an adjusting entry for estimated uncollectible accounts of $42,500.

Exhibit 3

Comparing Direct Write-Off and Allowance Methods

		Direct Write-Off Method			Allowance Method		
2009 Mar.	1	Bad Debt Expense	3,650		Allowance for Doubtful Accounts	3,650	
		Accounts Receivable—C. York		3,650	Accounts Receivable—C. York		3,650
Apr.	12	Cash	2,250		Cash	2,250	
		Bad Debt Expense	3,250		Allowance for Doubtful Accounts	3,250	
		Accounts Receivable—Cary Bradshaw		5,500	Accounts Receivable—Cary Bradshaw		5,500
June	22	Accounts Receivable—C. York	3,650		Accounts Receivable—C. York	3,650	
		Bad Debt Expense		3,650	Allowance for Doubtful Accounts		3,650
	22	Cash	3,650		Cash	3,650	
		Accounts Receivable—C. York		3,650	Accounts Receivable—C. York		3,650
Sept.	7	Bad Debt Expense	6,445		Allowance for Doubtful Accounts	6,445	
		Accounts Receivable—Jason Bigg		1,100	Accounts Receivable—Jason Bigg		1,100
		Accounts Receivable—Steve Bradey		2,220	Accounts Receivable—Steve Bradey		2,220
		Accounts Receivable—Samantha Neeley		775	Accounts Receivable—Samantha Neeley		775
		Accounts Receivable—Stanford Noonan		1,360	Accounts Receivable—Stanford Noonan		1,360
		Accounts Receivable—Aiden Wyman		990	Accounts Receivable—Aiden Wyman		990
Dec.	31	No Entry			Bad Debt Expense	42,500	
					Allowance for Doubtful Accounts		42,500
					Uncollectible accounts estimate. ($3,400,000 × 0.0125 = $42,500)		

The primary differences between the direct write-off and allowance methods are summarized below.

COMPARING THE DIRECT WRITE-OFF AND ALLOWANCE METHODS

	Direct Write-Off Method	Allowance Method
Bad debt expense is recorded	When the specific customer accounts are determined to be uncollectible.	Using estimate based on (1) a percent of sales or (2) an analysis of receivables.
Allowance account	No allowance account is used.	The allowance account is used.
Primary users	Small companies and companies with few receivables.	Large companies and those with a large amount of receivables.

Integrity, Objectivity, and Ethics in Business

RECEIVABLES FRAUD

Financial reporting frauds are often tied to accounts receivable, because receivables allow companies to record revenue before cash is received. Take, for example, the case of entrepreneur Michael Weinstein, who acquired Coated Sales, Inc. with the dream of growing the small specialty company into a major corporation. To acquire funding that would facilitate this growth, Weinstein had to artificially boost the company's sales. He accomplished this by adding millions in false accounts receivable to existing customer accounts.

The company's auditors began to sense a problem when they called one of the company's customers to confirm a large order. When the customer denied placing the order, the auditors began to investigate the company's receivables more closely. Their analysis revealed a fraud which overstated profits by $55 million and forced the company into bankruptcy, costing investors and creditors over $160 million.

Source: Joseph T. Wells, "Follow Fraud to the Likely Perpetrator," *The Journal of Accountancy*, March 2001.

6 Describe the accounting for notes receivable.

Notes Receivable

A note has some advantages over an account receivable. By signing a note, the debtor recognizes the debt and agrees to pay it according to its terms. Thus, a note is a stronger legal claim.

Characteristics of Notes Receivable

A promissory note is a written promise to pay the face amount, usually with interest, on demand or at a date in the future.[2] Characteristics of a promissory note are as follows:

1. The *maker* is the party making the promise to pay.
2. The *payee* is the party to whom the note is payable.
3. The *face amount* is the amount the note is written for on its face.
4. The *issuance date* is the date a note is issued.
5. The *due date* or *maturity date* is the date the note is to be paid.
6. The *term* of a note is the amount of time between the issuance and due dates.
7. The *interest rate* is that rate of interest that must be paid on the face amount for the term of the note.

Exhibit 4 illustrates a promissory note. The maker of the note is Selig Company, and the payee is Pearland Company. The face value of the note is $2,000, and the issuance date is March 16, 2009. The term of the note is 90 days, which results in a due date of June 14, 2009, as shown below and at the top of page 410.

Days in March	31 days
Minus issuance date of note	16
Days remaining in March	15 days
Add days in April	30
Add days in May	31
Add days in June (due date of June 14)	14
Term of note	90 days

2 You may see references to non-interest-bearing notes. Such notes are not widely used and carry an assumed or implicit interest rate.

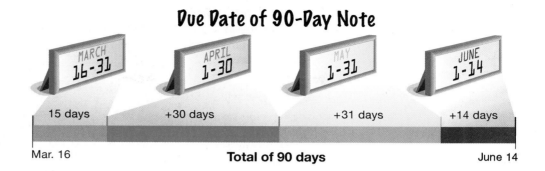

Due Date of 90-Day Note

| 15 days | +30 days | +31 days | +14 days |

Mar. 16   **Total of 90 days**   June 14

In Exhibit 4, the term of the note is 90 days and has an interest rate of 10%.

Exhibit 4

Promissory Note

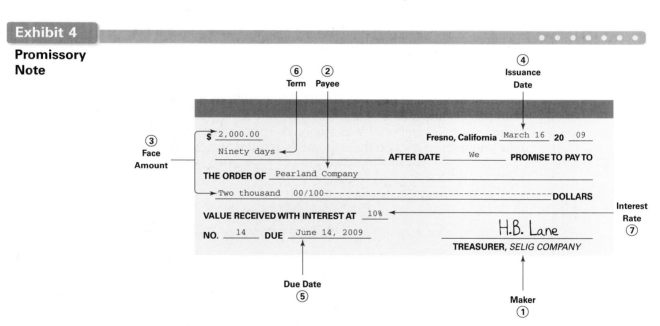

The interest on a note is computed as follows:

$$\text{Interest} = \text{Face Amount} \times \text{Interest Rate} \times (\text{Term}/360 \text{ days})$$

The interest rate is stated on an annual (yearly) basis, while the term is expressed as days. Thus, the interest on the note in Exhibit 4 is computed as follows:

$$\text{Interest} = \$2,000 \times 10\% \times (90/360) = \$50$$

To simplify, we will use 360 days per year. In practice, companies such as banks and mortgage companies use the exact number of days in a year, 365.

The **maturity value** is the amount that must be paid at the due date of the note, which is the sum of the face amount and the interest. The maturity value of the note in Exhibit 4 is $2,050 ($2,000 + $50).

Accounting for Notes Receivable

A promissory note may be received by a company from a customer to replace an account receivable. In such cases, the promissory note is recorded as a note receivable.[3]

Your credit card balances that are not paid at the end of the month incur an interest charge expressed as a percent per month. Interest charges of 1½% per month are common. Such charges approximate an annual interest rate of 18% per year (1½% × 12). Thus, if you can borrow money at less than 18%, you are better off borrowing the money to pay off the credit card balance.

3 The accounting for notes payable is described and illustrated in Chapter 12.

To illustrate, assume that a company accepts a 30-day, 12% note dated November 21, 2010, in settlement of the account of W. A. Bunn Co., which is past due and has a balance of $6,000. The company records the receipt of the note as follows:

Nov.	21	Notes Receivable—W. A. Bunn Co.	6,000	
		Accounts Receivable—W. A. Bunn Co.		6,000

At the due date, the company records the receipt of $6,060 ($6,000 face amount plus $60 interest) as follows:

Dec.	21	Cash	6,060	
		Notes Receivable—W. A. Bunn Co.		6,000
		Interest Revenue		60
		$6,060 = [$6,000 + ($6,000 × 12% × 30/360)].		

If the maker of a note fails to pay the note on the due date, the note is a **dishonored note receivable**. A company that holds a dishonored note transfers the face amount of the note plus any interest due back to an accounts receivable account. For example, assume that the $6,000, 30-day, 12% note received from W. A. Bunn Co. and recorded on November 21 is dishonored. The company holding the note transfers the note and interest back to the customer's account as follows:

Dec.	21	Accounts Receivable—W. A. Bunn Co.	6,060	
		Notes Receivable—W. A. Bunn Co.		6,000
		Interest Revenue		60

The company has earned the interest of $60, even though the note is dishonored. If the account receivable is uncollectible, the company will write off $6,060 against Allowance for Doubtful Accounts.

A company receiving a note should record an adjusting entry for any accrued interest at the end of the period. For example, assume that Crawford Company issues a $4,000, 90-day, 12% note dated December 1, 2010, to settle its account receivable. If the accounting period ends on December 31, the company receiving the note would record the following entries:

2010				
Dec.	1	Notes Receivable—Crawford Company	4,000	
		Accounts Receivable—Crawford Company		4,000
	31	Interest Receivable	40	
		Interest Revenue		40
		Accrued interest.		
		($4,000 × 12% × 30/360)		
2011				
Mar.	1	Cash	4,120	
		Notes Receivable—Crawford Company		4,000
		Interest Receivable		40
		Interest Revenue		80
		Total interest of $120.		
		($4,000 × 12% × 90/360)		

The interest revenue account is closed at the end of each accounting period. The amount of interest revenue is normally reported in the Other income section of the income statement.

Example Exercise 8-5   Note Receivable   • • • • • • • • > 6

Same Day Surgery Center received a 120-day, 6% note for $40,000, dated March 14 from a patient on account.

a. Determine the due date of the note.
b. Determine the maturity value of the note.
c. Journalize the entry to record the receipt of the payment of the note at maturity.

Follow My Example 8-5

a. The due date of the note is July 12, determined as follows:

March	17 days (31 − 14)
April	30 days
May	31 days
June	30 days
July	12 days
Total	120 days

b. $40,800 [$40,000 + ($40,000 × 6% × 120/360)]

c. July 12   Cash   40,800
                 Notes Receivable   40,000
                 Interest Revenue   800

For Practice: PE 8-5A, PE 8-5B

7   Describe the reporting of receivables on the balance sheet.

Reporting Receivables on the Balance Sheet

All receivables that are expected to be realized in cash within a year are reported in the Current Assets section of the balance sheet. Current assets are normally reported in the order of their liquidity, beginning with cash and cash equivalents.

The balance sheet presentation for receivables for Mornin' Joe is shown below.

Mornin' Joe Balance Sheet December 31, 2010		

Assets		
Current assets:		
Cash and cash equivalents		$235,000
Trading investments (at cost)	$420,000	
Plus valuation allowance for trading investments	45,000	465,000
Accounts receivable	$305,000	
Less allowance for doubtful accounts	12,300	292,700

In Mornin Joe's financial statements, the allowance for doubtful accounts is subtracted from accounts receivable. Some companies report receivables at their net realizable value with a note showing the amount of the allowance.

Other disclosures related to receivables are reported either on the face of the financial statements or in the financial statement notes. Such disclosures include the market (fair) value of the receivables. In addition, if unusual credit risks exist within the receivables, the nature of the risks are disclosed. For example, if the majority of the receivables are due from one customer or are due from customers located in one area of the country or one industry, these facts are disclosed.[4]

Financial Analysis and Interpretation

Two financial measures that are especially useful in evaluating efficiency in collecting receivables are (1) the accounts receivable turnover and (2) the number of days' sales in receivables.

The **accounts receivable turnover** measures how frequently during the year the accounts receivable are being converted to cash. For example, with credit terms of 2/10, n/30, the accounts receivable should turn over more than 12 times per year. The accounts receivable turnover is computed as follows:[5]

$$\text{Accounts Receivable Turnover} = \frac{\text{Net Sales}}{\text{Average Accounts Receivable}}$$

The average accounts receivable can be determined by using monthly data or by simply adding the beginning and ending accounts receivable balances and dividing by two. For example, using the following financial data (in millions) for FedEx, the 2007 and 2006 accounts receivable turnover is computed as 10.5 and 7.7, respectively.

	2007		2006		2005
Net sales	$22,527		$21,296		—
Accounts receivable	1,429		2,860		$2,703
Average accounts receivable	2,145	[($1,429 + $2,860)/2]	2,782	[($2,860 + $2,703)/2]	
Accounts receivable turnover	10.5	($22,527/$2,145)	7.7	($21,296/$2,782)	

Comparing 2007 and 2006 indicates that the accounts receivable turnover has increased from 7.7 to 10.5. Thus, FedEx's management of accounts receivable has improved in 2007.

The **number of days' sales in receivables** is an estimate of the length of time the accounts receivable have been outstanding. With credit terms of 2/10, n/30, the number of days' sales in receivables should be less than 20 days. It is computed as follows:

$$\text{Number of Days' Sales in Receivables} = \frac{\text{Average Accounts Receivable}}{\text{Average Daily Sales}}$$

Average daily sales are determined by dividing net sales by 365 days. For example, using the preceding data for FedEx, the number of days' sales in receivables is 34.8 and 47.7 for 2007 and 2006, respectively, as shown below.

	2007		2006	
Net sales	$22,527		$21,296	
Average accounts receivable	2,145	[($1,429 + $2,860)/2]	2,782	[($2,860 + $2,703)/2]
Average daily sales	61.7	($22,527/365)	58.3	($21,296/365)
Days' sales in receivables	34.8	($2,145/61.7)	47.7	($2,782/58.3)

The number of days' sales in receivables confirms an improvement in managing accounts receivable during 2007. That is, the efficiency in collecting accounts receivable has improved when the number of days' sales in receivables decreases. During 2007, FedEx's days in receivables decreased from 47.7 in 2006 to 34.8. However, these measures should also be compared with similar companies within the industry.

---

4 *Statement of Financial Accounting Standards No. 105,* "Disclosures of Information about Financial Instruments with Off-Balance Sheet Risk and Financial Instruments with Concentrations of Credit Risk," and *No. 107,* "Disclosures about Fair Value of Financial Instruments" (Norwalk, CT: Financial Accounting Standards Board).

5 If known, credit sales can be used in the numerator. However, because credit sales are not normally disclosed to external users, most analysts use net sales in the numerator.

Business Connection

DELTA AIR LINES

Delta Air Lines is a major air carrier that services cities throughout the United States and the world. In its operations, Delta generates accounts receivable as reported in the following note to its financial statements:

Our accounts receivable are generated largely from the sale of passenger airline tickets and cargo transportation services. The majority of these sales are processed through major credit card companies, resulting in accounts receivable which are generally short-term in duration. We also have receivables from the sale of mileage

credits to partners, such as credit card companies, hotels and car rental agencies, that participate in our SkyMiles program. We believe that the credit risk associated with these receivables is minimal and that the allowance for uncollectible accounts that we have provided is appropriate.

In its December 31, 2007, balance sheet, Delta reported the following accounts receivable (in millions):

	Dec. 31, 2007	Dec. 31, 2006
Current Assets:		
...		
Accounts receivable, net of an allowance for uncollectible accounts of $26 at December 31, 2007 and $21 at December 31, 2006	$1,066	$915

A P P E N D I X

Discounting Notes Receivable

A company may endorse a note receivable and transfer it to a bank in return for cash. This is called *discounting notes receivable*. The bank pays cash (the *proceeds*) to the company after deducting a *discount* (interest). The discount is computed using a *discount rate* on the maturity value of the note for the discount period. The *discount period* is the time that the bank must hold the note before it becomes due.

To illustrate, assume that on May 3 a note receivable from Pryor & Co is discounted by Deacon Company at its bank. The related data are as follows:

Face amount of note	$1,800
Issuance date of note	April 8
Interest rate on note	12%
Term of note	90 days
Due date of note	July 7
Maturity value of note	$1,854 [$1,800 + ($1,800 × 12% × 90/360)]
Discount date	May 3
Discount period	65 days (May 3 to July 7)
Discount rate	14%
Discount	$46.87 ($1,854 × 14% × 65/360)
Discount proceeds	$1,807.13 ($1,854.00 − $46.87)

Deacon Company records the receipt of the proceeds as follows:

May	3	Cash	1,807.13	
		Notes Receivable		1,800.00
		Interest Revenue		7.13
		Discounted $1,800, 90-day, 12% note at 14%.		

If the proceeds had been less than the face amount, Deacon Company would have recorded the excess of the face amount over the proceeds as interest expense. For example, if the proceeds had been $1,785, Deacon Company would have recorded interest expense of $15 ($1,800 − $1,785). The length of the discount period, interest rate, and discount rate determine whether interest expense or interest revenue is recorded.

Without a statement limiting responsibility, Deacon Company must pay the maturity value of the note if the maker defaults. This potential liability is called a *contingent liability*. If the maker pays the maturity value, the contingent liability ceases to exist. If, on the other hand, the maker dishonors the note, the contingent liability becomes a liability that must be paid.

If a discounted note receivable is dishonored, the bank notifies the company and asks for payment. In some cases, the bank may charge a *protest fee* on dishonored notes. The entire amount paid to the bank, including the maturity value and protest fee, is debited to the account receivable of the maker.

To illustrate, assume that Pryor & Co. dishonors the $1,800, 90-day, 12% note that was discounted on May 3. The bank charges a protest fee of $12. Deacon Company's entry to record the payment to the bank is as follows:

July	7	Accounts Receivable—Pryor & Co.	1,866	
		Cash		1,866
		Paid dishonored, discounted note (maturity value of $1,854 plus protest fee of $12).		

At a Glance 8

1 Describe the common classes of receivables.

Key Points	Key Learning Outcomes	Example Exercises	Practice Exercises
The term *receivables* includes all money claims against other entities, including people, business firms, and other organizations. Receivables are normally classified as accounts receivable, notes receivable, or other receivables.	• Define the term *receivables*. • List some common classifications of receivables.		

2 Describe the accounting for uncollectible receivables.

Key Points	Key Learning Outcomes	Example Exercises	Practice Exercises
Regardless of the care used in granting credit and the collection procedures used, a part of the credit sales will not be collectible. The operating expense recorded from uncollectible receivables is called *bad debt expense.* The two methods of accounting for uncollectible receivables are the direct write-off method and the allowance method.	• Describe how a company may shift the risk of uncollectible receivables to other companies. • List factors that indicate an account receivable is uncollectible. • Describe two methods of accounting for uncollectible accounts receivable.		

3 Describe the direct write-off method of accounting for uncollectible receivables.

Key Points	Key Learning Outcomes	Example Exercises	Practice Exercises
Under the direct write-off method, the entry to write off an account debits Bad Debt Expense and credits Accounts Receivable. Neither an allowance account nor an adjusting entry is needed at the end of the period.	• Prepare journal entries to write off an account using the direct method.	8-1	8-1A, 8-1B
	• Prepare journal entries for the reinstatement and collection of an account previously written off.	8-1	8-1A, 8-1B

4 Describe the allowance method of accounting for uncollectible receivables.

Key Points	Key Learning Outcomes	Example Exercises	Practice Exercises
Under the allowance method, an adjusting entry is made for uncollectible accounts. When an account is determined to be uncollectible, it is written off against the allowance account. The allowance account normally has a credit balance after the adjusting entry has been posted and is a contra asset account. The estimate of uncollectibles may be based on a percent of sales or an analysis of receivables. Using the percent of sales, the adjusting entry is made without regard to the balance of the allowance account. Using the analysis of receivables, the adjusting entry is made so that the balance of the allowance account will equal the estimated uncollectibles at the end of the period.	• Prepare journal entries to write off an account using the allowance method.	8-2	8-2A, 8-2B
	• Prepare journal entries for the reinstatement and collection of an account previously written off.	8-2	8-2A, 8-2B
	• Determine the adjustment, bad debt expense, and net realizable value of accounts receivable using the percent of sales method.	8-3	8-3A, 8-3B
	• Determine the adjustment, bad debt expense, and net realizable value of accounts receivable using the analysis of receivables method.	8-4	8-4A, 8-4B

Compare the direct write-off and allowance methods of accounting for uncollectible accounts.

		Example Exercises	Practice Exercises
Key Points	**Key Learning Outcomes**		
The direct write-off and allowance methods of accounting for uncollectible accounts are recorded differently in the accounts and presented differently in the financial statements. Exhibit 3 illustrates both methods of accounting for uncollectible accounts.	• Describe the differences in accounting for uncollectible accounts under the direct write-off and allowance methods.		
	• Record journal entries using the direct write-off and allowance methods.		

6

Describe the accounting for notes receivable.

		Example Exercises	Practice Exercises
Key Points	**Key Learning Outcomes**		
A note received in settlement of an account receivable is recorded as a debit to Notes Receivable and a credit to Accounts Receivable. When a note matures, Cash is debited, Notes Receivable is credited, and Interest Revenue is credited. If the maker of a note fails to pay the debt on the due date, the dishonored note is recorded by debiting an accounts receivable account for the amount of the claim against the maker of the note.	• Describe the characteristics of a note receivable.		
	• Determine the due date and maturity value of a note receivable.	**8-5**	8-5A, 8-5B
	• Prepare journal entries for the receipt of the payment of a note receivable.	**8-5**	8-5A, 8-5B
	• Prepare a journal entry for the dishonored note receivable.		

7

Describe the reporting of receivables on the balance sheet.

		Example Exercises	Practice Exercises
Key Points	**Key Learning Outcomes**		
All receivables that are expected to be realized in cash within a year are reported in the Current Assets section of the balance sheet in the order in which they can be converted to cash in normal operations. In addition to the allowance for doubtful accounts, additional receivable disclosures include the market (fair) value and unusual credit risks.	• Describe how receivables are reported in the Current Assets section of the balance sheet.		
	• Describe disclosures related to receivables that should be reported in the financial statements.		

Key Terms

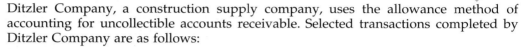

accounts receivable (350)
accounts receivable
   turnover (366)
aging the receivables (357)
Allowance for Doubtful
   Accounts (353)

allowance method (351)
bad debt expense (351)
direct write-off method (351)
dishonored note
   receivable (364)
maturity value (363)

net realizable value (353)
notes receivable (350)
number of days' sales
   in receivables (366)
receivables (350)

Illustrative Problem

Ditzler Company, a construction supply company, uses the allowance method of accounting for uncollectible accounts receivable. Selected transactions completed by Ditzler Company are as follows:

Feb. 1. Sold merchandise on account to Ames Co., $8,000. The cost of the merchandise sold was $4,500.

Mar. 15. Accepted a 60-day, 12% note for $8,000 from Ames Co. on account.

Apr. 9. Wrote off a $2,500 account from Dorset Co. as uncollectible.

    21. Loaned $7,500 cash to Jill Klein, receiving a 90-day, 14% note.

May 14. Received the interest due from Ames Co. and a new 90-day, 14% note as a renewal of the loan. (Record both the debit and the credit to the notes receivable account.)

June 13. Reinstated the account of Dorset Co., written off on April 9, and received $2,500 in full payment.

July 20. Jill Klein dishonored her note.

Aug. 12. Received from Ames Co. the amount due on its note of May 14.

    19. Received from Jill Klein the amount owed on the dishonored note, plus interest for 30 days at 15%, computed on the maturity value of the note.

Dec. 16. Accepted a 60-day, 12% note for $12,000 from Global Company on account.

    31. It is estimated that 3% of the credit sales of $1,375,000 for the year ended December 31 will be uncollectible.

Instructions

1. Journalize the transactions.
2. Journalize the adjusting entry to record the accrued interest on December 31 on the Global Company note.

Solution

1.

Feb.	1	Accounts Receivable—Ames Co.	8,000.00	
		Sales		8,000.00
	1	Cost of Merchandise Sold	4,500.00	
		Merchandise Inventory		4,500.00
Mar.	15	Notes Receivable—Ames Co.	8,000.00	
		Accounts Receivable—Ames Co.		8,000.00
Apr.	9	Allowance for Doubtful Accounts	2,500.00	
		Accounts Receivable—Dorset Co.		2,500.00
	21	Notes Receivable—Jill Klein	7,500.00	
		Cash		7,500.00
May	14	Notes Receivable—Ames Co.	8,000.00	
		Cash	160.00	
		Notes Receivable—Ames Co.		8,000.00
		Interest Revenue		160.00
June	13	Accounts Receivable—Dorset Co.	2,500.00	
		Allowance for Doubtful Accounts		2,500.00
	13	Cash	2,500.00	
		Accounts Receivable—Dorset Co.		2,500.00
July	20	Accounts Receivable—Jill Klein	7,762.50	
		Notes Receivable—Jill Klein		7,500.00
		Interest Revenue		262.50
Aug.	12	Cash	8,280.00	
		Notes Receivable—Ames Co.		8,000.00
		Interest Revenue		280.00
	19	Cash	7,859.53	
		Accounts Receivable—Jill Klein		7,762.50
		Interest Revenue		97.03
		($7,762.50 × 15% × 30/360).		
Dec.	16	Notes Receivable—Global Company	12,000.00	
		Accounts Receivable—Global Company		12,000.00
	31	Bad Debt Expense	41,250.00	
		Allowance for Doubtful Accounts		41,250.00
		Uncollectible accounts estimate.		
		($1,375,000 × 3%)		

2.

Dec.	31	Interest Receivable	60.00	
		Interest Revenue		60.00
		Accrued interest.		
		($12,000 × 12% × 15/360)		

Self-Examination Questions (Answers at End of Chapter)

1. At the end of the fiscal year, before the accounts are adjusted, Accounts Receivable has a balance of $200,000 and Allowance for Doubtful Accounts has a credit balance of $2,500. If the estimate of uncollectible accounts determined by aging the receivables is $8,500, the amount of bad debt expense is:
   A. $2,500.
   B. $6,000.
   C. $8,500.
   D. $11,000.

2. At the end of the fiscal year, Accounts Receivable has a balance of $100,000 and Allowance for Doubtful Accounts has a balance of $7,000. The expected net realizable value of the accounts receivable is:
   A. $7,000.
   B. $93,000.
   C. $100,000.
   D. $107,000.

3. What is the maturity value of a 90-day, 12% note for $10,000?
   A. $8,800
   B. $10,000
   C. $10,300
   D. $11,200

4. What is the due date of a $12,000, 90-day, 8% note receivable dated August 5?
   A. October 31
   B. November 2
   C. November 3
   D. November 4

5. When a note receivable is dishonored, Accounts Receivable is debited for what amount?
   A. The face value of the note
   B. The maturity value of the note
   C. The maturity value of the note less accrued interest
   D. The maturity value of the note plus accrued interest

Eye Openers

1. What are the three classifications of receivables?
2. What types of transactions give rise to accounts receivable?
3. In what section of the balance sheet should a note receivable be listed if its term is (a) 90 days, (b) six years?
4. Give two examples of other receivables.
5. Gallatin Hardware is a small hardware store in the rural township of Willow Creek that rarely extends credit to its customers in the form of an account receivable. The few customers that are allowed to carry accounts receivable are long-time residents of Willow Creek and have a history of doing business at Gallatin Hardware. What method of accounting for uncollectible receivables should Gallatin Hardware use? Why?
6. Which of the two methods of accounting for uncollectible accounts provides for the recognition of the expense at the earlier date?
7. What kind of an account (asset, liability, etc.) is Allowance for Doubtful Accounts, and is its normal balance a debit or a credit?
8. After the accounts are adjusted and closed at the end of the fiscal year, Accounts Receivable has a balance of $298,150 and Allowance for Doubtful Accounts has a balance of $31,200. Describe how the accounts receivable and the allowance for doubtful accounts are reported on the balance sheet.
9. A firm has consistently adjusted its allowance account at the end of the fiscal year by adding a fixed percent of the period's net sales on account. After seven years, the balance in Allowance for Doubtful Accounts has become very large in relationship to the balance in Accounts Receivable. Give two possible explanations.
10. Which of the two methods of estimating uncollectibles provides for the most accurate estimate of the current net realizable value of the receivables?
11. For a business, what are the advantages of a note receivable in comparison to an account receivable?
12. Blanchard Company issued a note receivable to Tucker Company. (a) Who is the payee? (b) What is the title of the account used by Tucker Company in recording the note?
13. If a note provides for payment of principal of $90,000 and interest at the rate of 7%, will the interest amount to $6,300? Explain.

14. The maker of a $10,000, 8%, 90-day note receivable failed to pay the note on the due date of June 30. What accounts should be debited and credited by the payee to record the dishonored note receivable?
15. The note receivable dishonored in Eye Opener 14 is paid on July 30 by the maker, plus interest for 30 days, 10%. What entry should be made to record the receipt of the payment?
16. Under what section should accounts receivable be reported on the balance sheet?

Practice Exercises

PE 8-1A
Direct write-off method
obj. 3
EE 8-1   p. 352

Journalize the following transactions using the direct write-off method of accounting for uncollectible receivables:

Sept. 19.   Received $100 from Pat Roark and wrote off the remainder owed of $500 as uncollectible.
Dec. 20.   Reinstated the account of Pat Roark and received $500 cash in full payment.

PE 8-1B
Direct write-off method
obj. 3
EE 8-1   p. 352

Journalize the following transactions using the direct write-off method of accounting for uncollectible receivables:

Feb. 25.   Received $500 from Jason Wilcox and wrote off the remainder owed of $4,000 as uncollectible.
May 9.   Reinstated the account of Jason Wilcox and received $4,000 cash in full payment.

PE 8-2A
Allowance method
obj. 4
EE 8-2   p. 355

Journalize the following transactions using the allowance method of accounting for uncollectible receivables:

Sept. 19.   Received $100 from Pat Roark and wrote off the remainder owed of $500 as uncollectible.
Dec. 20.   Reinstated the account of Pat Roark and received $500 cash in full payment.

PE 8-2B
Allowance method
obj. 4
EE 8-2   p. 355

Journalize the following transactions using the allowance method of accounting for uncollectible receivables:

Feb. 25.   Received $500 from Jason Wilcox and wrote off the remainder owed of $4,000 as uncollectible.
May 9.   Reinstated the account of Jason Wilcox and received $4,000 cash in full payment.

PE 8-3A
Percent of sales method
obj. 4
EE 8-3   p. 357

At the end of the current year, Accounts Receivable has a balance of $1,400,000; Allowance for Doubtful Accounts has a debit balance of $2,250; and net sales for the year total $9,500,000. Bad debt expense is estimated at $\frac{1}{4}$ of 1% of net sales.
Determine (1) the amount of the adjusting entry for uncollectible accounts; (2) the adjusted balances of Accounts Receivable, Allowance for Doubtful Accounts, and Bad Debt Expense; and (3) the net realizable value of accounts receivable.

PE 8-3B
Percent of sales method
obj. 4

At the end of the current year, Accounts Receivable has a balance of $750,000; Allowance for Doubtful Accounts has a credit balance of $11,250; and net sales for the year total $4,100,000. Bad debt expense is estimated at $\frac{1}{2}$ of 1% of net sales.

EE 8-3   p. 357 — Determine (1) the amount of the adjusting entry for uncollectible accounts; (2) the adjusted balances of Accounts Receivable, Allowance for Doubtful Accounts, and Bad Debt Expense; and (3) the net realizable value of accounts receivable.

PE 8-4A
Analysis of
receivables method

obj. 4

EE 8-4   p. 359

At the end of the current year, Accounts Receivable has a balance of $1,400,000; Allowance for Doubtful Accounts has a debit balance of $2,250; and net sales for the year total $9,500,000. Using the aging method, the balance of Allowance for Doubtful Accounts is estimated as $24,000.

Determine (1) the amount of the adjusting entry for uncollectible accounts; (2) the adjusted balances of Accounts Receivable, Allowance for Doubtful Accounts, and Bad Debt Expense; and (3) the net realizable value of accounts receivable.

PE 8-4B
Analysis of
receivables method

obj. 4

EE 8-4   p. 359

At the end of the current year, Accounts Receivable has a balance of $750,000; Allowance for Doubtful Accounts has a credit balance of $11,250; and net sales for the year total $4,150,000. Using the aging method, the balance of Allowance for Doubtful Accounts is estimated as $30,000.

Determine (1) the amount of the adjusting entry for uncollectible accounts; (2) the adjusted balances of Accounts Receivable, Allowance for Doubtful Accounts, and Bad Debt Expense; and (3) the net realizable value of accounts receivable.

PE 8-5A
Note receivable

obj. 6

EE 8-5   p. 365

Cannondale Supply Company received a 120-day, 9% note for $200,000, dated March 13 from a customer on account.

a. Determine the due date of the note.
b. Determine the maturity value of the note.
c. Journalize the entry to record the receipt of the payment of the note at maturity.

PE 8-5B
Note receivable

obj. 6

EE 8-5   p. 365

Northrop Supply Company received a 30-day, 6% note for $40,000, dated September 23 from a customer on account.

a. Determine the due date of the note.
b. Determine the maturity value of the note.
c. Journalize the entry to record the receipt of the payment of the note at maturity.

Exercises

EX 8-1
Classifications of
receivables

obj. 1

Boeing is one of the world's major aerospace firms, with operations involving commercial aircraft, military aircraft, missiles, satellite systems, and information and battle management systems. As of December 31, 2007, Boeing had $2,838 million of receivables involving U.S. government contracts and $1,232 million of receivables involving commercial aircraft customers, such as Delta Air Lines and United Airlines.

Should Boeing report these receivables separately in the financial statements, or combine them into one overall accounts receivable amount? Explain.

EX 8-2
Nature of
uncollectible
accounts

The MGM Mirage owns and operates casinos including the MGM Grand and the Bellagio in Las Vegas, Nevada. As of December 31, 2007, the MGM Mirage reported accounts and notes receivable of $452,945,000 and allowance for doubtful accounts of $90,024,000.

obj. 2

✔ a. 19.9%

Johnson & Johnson manufactures and sells a wide range of health care products including Band-Aids and Tylenol. As of December 31, 2007, Johnson & Johnson reported accounts receivable of $9,444,000,000 and allowance for doubtful accounts of $193,000,000.

a. Compute the percentage of the allowance for doubtful accounts to the accounts and notes receivable as of December 31, 2007, for The MGM Mirage.

b. Compute the percentage of the allowance for doubtful accounts to the accounts receivable as of December 31, 2007, for Johnson & Johnson.

c. ➤ Discuss possible reasons for the difference in the two ratios computed in (a) and (b).

EX 8-3
Entries for uncollectible accounts, using direct write-off method

obj. 3

Journalize the following transactions in the accounts of Laser Tech Co., a medical equipment company that uses the direct write-off method of accounting for uncollectible receivables:

Feb. 23. Sold merchandise on account to Dr. Judith Salazar, $41,500. The cost of the merchandise sold was $22,300.

May 10. Received $10,000 from Dr. Judith Salazar and wrote off the remainder owed on the sale of February 23 as uncollectible.

Dec. 2. Reinstated the account of Dr. Judith Salazar that had been written off on May 10 and received $31,500 cash in full payment.

EX 8-4
Entries for uncollectible receivables, using allowance method

obj. 4

Journalize the following transactions in the accounts of Food Unlimited Company, a restaurant supply company that uses the allowance method of accounting for uncollectible receivables:

Jan. 18. Sold merchandise on account to Wings Co., $13,200. The cost of the merchandise sold was $9,500.

Mar. 31. Received $5,000 from Wings Co. and wrote off the remainder owed on the sale of January 18 as uncollectible.

Sept. 3. Reinstated the account of Wings Co. that had been written off on March 31 and received $8,200 cash in full payment.

EX 8-5
Entries to write off accounts receivable

objs. 3, 4

Tech Savvy, a computer consulting firm, has decided to write off the $8,375 balance of an account owed by a customer, Nick Wadle. Journalize the entry to record the write-off, assuming that (a) the direct write-off method is used and (b) the allowance method is used.

EX 8-6
Providing for doubtful accounts

obj. 4

✔ a. $23,500
✔ b. $24,800

At the end of the current year, the accounts receivable account has a debit balance of $825,000 and net sales for the year total $9,400,000. Determine the amount of the adjusting entry to provide for doubtful accounts under each of the following assumptions:

a. The allowance account before adjustment has a credit balance of $11,200. Bad debt expense is estimated at 1/4 of 1% of net sales.

b. The allowance account before adjustment has a credit balance of $11,200. An aging of the accounts in the customer ledger indicates estimated doubtful accounts of $36,000.

c. The allowance account before adjustment has a debit balance of $6,000. Bad debt expense is estimated at 1/2 of 1% of net sales.

d. The allowance account before adjustment has a debit balance of $6,000. An aging of the accounts in the customer ledger indicates estimated doubtful accounts of $49,500.

EX 8-7
Number of days past due

Bubba's Auto Supply distributes new and used automobile parts to local dealers throughout the Southeast. Bubba's credit terms are n/30. As of the end of business on July 31, the following accounts receivable were past due:

obj. 4

✔ AAA Pickup
Shop, 62 days

Account	Due Date	Amount
AAA Pickup Shop	May 30	$6,000
Best Auto	July 14	3,000
Downtown Repair	March 18	2,000
Luke's Auto Repair	June 1	5,000
New or Used Auto	June 18	750
Sally's	April 12	2,800
Trident Auto	May 31	1,500
Washburn Repair & Tow	March 13	7,500

Determine the number of days each account is past due.

EX 8-8
Aging-of-receivables schedule

obj. 4

The accounts receivable clerk for Summit Industries prepared the following partially completed aging-of-receivables schedule as of the end of business on November 30:

	A	B	C	D	E	F	G
1			Not		Days Past Due		
2			Past				Over
3	Customer	Balance	Due	1–30	31–60	61–90	90
4	Abbott Brothers Inc.	2,000	2,000				
5	Alonso Company	1,500		1,500			
21	Ziel Company	5,000				5,000	
22	Subtotals	807,500	475,000	180,000	78,500	42,300	31,700

The following accounts were unintentionally omitted from the aging schedule and not included in the subtotals above:

Customer	Balance	Due Date
Cottonwood Industries	$14,300	July 6
Fargo Company	17,700	September 17
Garfield Inc.	8,500	October 17
Sadler Company	10,000	November 2
Twitty Company	25,000	December 23

a. Determine the number of days past due for each of the preceding accounts.
b. Complete the aging-of-receivables schedule by including the omitted accounts.

EX 8-9
Estimating allowance for doubtful accounts

obj. 4

✔ $77,800

Summit Industries has a past history of uncollectible accounts, as shown below. Estimate the allowance for doubtful accounts, based on the aging-of-receivables schedule you completed in Exercise 8-8.

Age Class	Percent Uncollectible
Not past due	1%
1–30 days past due	6
31–60 days past due	20
61–90 days past due	35
Over 90 days past due	50

EX 8-10
Adjustment for uncollectible accounts

obj. 4

Using data in Exercise 8-8, assume that the allowance for doubtful accounts for Summit Industries has a credit balance of $16,175 before adjustment on November 30. Journalize the adjusting entry for uncollectible accounts as of November 30.

EX 8-11
Estimating doubtful accounts
obj. 4

Fonda Bikes Co. is a wholesaler of motorcycle supplies. An aging of the company's accounts receivable on December 31, 2010, and a historical analysis of the percentage of uncollectible accounts in each age category are as follows:

Age Interval	Balance	Percent Uncollectible
Not past due	$567,000	$\frac{1}{2}\%$
1–30 days past due	58,000	3
31–60 days past due	29,000	7
61–90 days past due	20,500	15
91–180 days past due	15,000	40
Over 180 days past due	10,500	75
	$700,000	

Estimate what the proper balance of the allowance for doubtful accounts should be as of December 31, 2010.

EX 8-12
Entry for uncollectible accounts
obj. 4

Using the data in Exercise 8-11, assume that the allowance for doubtful accounts for Fonda Bikes Co. had a debit balance of $4,145 as of December 31, 2010.
Journalize the adjusting entry for uncollectible accounts as of December 31, 2010.

EX 8-13
Entries for bad debt expense under the direct write-off and allowance methods
obj. 5

✔ c. $6,025 higher

The following selected transactions were taken from the records of Lights of the West Company for the first year of its operations ending December 31, 2010:

Jan. 24. Wrote off account of J. Huntley, $3,000.
Feb. 17. Received $1,500 as partial payment on the $4,000 account of Karlene Solomon. Wrote off the remaining balance as uncollectible.
May 29. Received $3,000 from J. Huntley, which had been written off on January 24. Reinstated the account and recorded the cash receipt.
Nov. 30. Wrote off the following accounts as uncollectible (record as one journal entry):

Don O'Leary	$2,000
Kim Snider	1,500
Jennifer Kerlin	900
Tracy Lane	1,250
Lynn Fuqua	450

Dec. 31. Lights of the West Company uses the percent of credit sales method of estimating uncollectible accounts expense. Based on past history and industry averages, 1½% of credit sales are expected to be uncollectible. Lights of the West Company recorded $975,000 of credit sales during 2010.

a. Journalize the transactions for 2010 under the direct write-off method.
b. Journalize the transactions for 2010 under the allowance method.
c. ⬤━━━▶ How much higher (lower) would Lights of the West Company's net income have been under the direct write-off method than under the allowance method?

EX 8-14
Entries for bad debt expense under the direct write-off and allowance methods
obj. 5

✔ c. $17,200 higher

The following selected transactions were taken from the records of Burrito Company for the year ending December 31, 2010:

Mar. 13. Wrote off account of B. Hall, $4,200.
Apr. 19. Received $3,000 as partial payment on the $7,500 account of M. Rainey. Wrote off the remaining balance as uncollectible.
July 9. Received the $4,200 from B. Hall, which had been written off on March 13. Reinstated the account and recorded the cash receipt.
Nov. 23. Wrote off the following accounts as uncollectible (record as one journal entry):

Rai Quinn	$1,200
P. Newman	750
Ned Berry	2,900
Mary Adams	1,675
Nichole Chapin	480

Dec. 31.   The company prepared the following aging schedule for its accounts receivable:

Aging Class (Number of Days Past Due)	Receivables Balance on December 31	Estimated Percent of Uncollectible Accounts
0–30 days	$200,000	2%
31–60 days	75,000	8
61–90 days	24,000	25
91–120 days	9,000	40
More than 120 days	12,000	80
Total receivables	$320,000	

a. Journalize the transactions for 2010 under the direct write-off method.
b. Journalize the transactions for 2010 under the allowance method, assuming that the allowance account had a beginning balance of $12,000 on January 1, 2010, and the company uses the analysis of receivables method.
c. ▬▬▶ How much higher (lower) would Burrito's 2010 net income have been under the direct write-off method than under the allowance method?

EX 8-15
Effect of doubtful accounts on net income
obj. 5

During its first year of operations, Master Plumbing Supply Co. had net sales of $3,500,000, wrote off $50,000 of accounts as uncollectible using the direct write-off method, and reported net income of $390,500. Determine what the net income would have been if the allowance method had been used, and the company estimated that 1¾% of net sales would be uncollectible.

EX 8-16
Effect of doubtful accounts on net income
obj. 5
✔ b. $24,750 credit balance

Using the data in Exercise 8-15, assume that during the second year of operations Master Plumbing Supply Co. had net sales of $4,200,000, wrote off $60,000 of accounts as uncollectible using the direct write-off method, and reported net income of $425,000.

a. Determine what net income would have been in the second year if the allowance method (using 1¾% of net sales) had been used in both the first and second years.
b. Determine what the balance of the allowance for doubtful accounts would have been at the end of the second year if the allowance method had been used in both the first and second years.

EX 8-17
Entries for bad debt expense under the direct write-off and allowance methods
obj. 5
✔ c. $7,000 higher

Isner Company wrote off the following accounts receivable as uncollectible for the first year of its operations ending December 31, 2010:

Customer	Amount
L. Hearn	$10,000
Carrie Murray	9,500
Kelly Salkin	13,100
Shana Wagnon	2,400
Total	$35,000

a. Journalize the write-offs for 2010 under the direct write-off method.
b. Journalize the write-offs for 2010 under the allowance method. Also, journalize the adjusting entry for uncollectible accounts. The company recorded $2,400,000 of credit sales during 2010. Based on past history and industry averages, 1¾% of credit sales are expected to be uncollectible.
c. How much higher (lower) would Isner Company's 2010 net income have been under the direct write-off method than under the allowance method?

EX 8-18
Entries for bad debt expense under the direct write-off and allowance methods

obj. 5

OK International wrote off the following accounts receivable as uncollectible for the year ending December 31, 2010:

Customer	Amount
Eva Fry	$ 6,500
Lance Landau	11,200
Marcie Moffet	3,800
Jose Reis	3,500
Total	$25,000

The company prepared the following aging schedule for its accounts receivable on December 31, 2010:

Aging Class (Number of Days Past Due)	Receivables Balance on December 31	Estimated Percent of Uncollectible Accounts
0–30 days	$480,000	1%
31–60 days	100,000	3
61–90 days	40,000	20
91–120 days	25,000	30
More than 120 days	5,000	40
Total receivables	$650,000	

a. Journalize the write-offs for 2010 under the direct write-off method.
b. Journalize the write-offs and the year-end adjusting entry for 2010 under the allowance method, assuming that the allowance account had a beginning balance of $22,500 on January 1, 2010, and the company uses the analysis of receivables method.

EX 8-19
Determine due date and interest on notes

obj. 6

✔ d. May 5, $225

Determine the due date and the amount of interest due at maturity on the following notes:

	Date of Note	Face Amount	Interest Rate	Term of Note
a.	October 1	$10,500	8%	60 days
b.	August 30	18,000	10	120 days
c.	May 30	12,000	12	90 days
d.	March 6	15,000	9	60 days
e.	May 23	9,000	10	60 days

EX 8-20
Entries for notes receivable

obj. 6

✔ b. $40,600

South Bay Interior Decorators issued a 90-day, 6% note for $40,000, dated April 15, to Miami Furniture Company on account.

a. Determine the due date of the note.
b. Determine the maturity value of the note.
c. Journalize the entries to record the following: (1) receipt of the note by Miami Furniture and (2) receipt of payment of the note at maturity.

EX 8-21
Entries for notes receivable

obj. 6

The series of seven transactions recorded in the following T accounts were related to a sale to a customer on account and the receipt of the amount owed. Briefly describe each transaction.

CASH				NOTES RECEIVABLE			
(7)	30,955			(5)	30,000	(6)	30,000

ACCOUNTS RECEIVABLE				SALES RETURNS AND ALLOWANCES			
(1)	35,000	(3)	5,000	(3)	5,000		
(6)	30,750	(5)	30,000				
		(7)	30,750				

MERCHANDISE INVENTORY				COST OF MERCHANDISE SOLD			
(4)	3,000	(2)	21,000	(2)	21,000	(4)	3,000

SALES				INTEREST REVENUE			
		(1)	35,000			(6)	750
						(7)	205

EX 8-22
Entries for notes receivable, including year-end entries

obj. 6

The following selected transactions were completed by Alcor Co., a supplier of Velcro™ for clothing:

2009
Dec. 13.   Received from Penick Clothing & Bags Co., on account, an $84,000, 90-day, 9% note dated December 13.
      31.   Recorded an adjusting entry for accrued interest on the note of December 13.
      31.   Recorded the closing entry for interest revenue.

2010
Mar. 12.   Received payment of note and interest from Penick Clothing & Bags Co.

Journalize the transactions.

EX 8-23
Entries for receipt and dishonor of note receivable

obj. 6

Journalize the following transactions of Funhouse Productions:

July   8.   Received a $120,000, 90-day, 8% note dated July 8 from Mystic Mermaid Company on account.
Oct.   6.   The note is dishonored by Mystic Mermaid Company.
Nov. 5.   Received the amount due on the dishonored note plus interest for 30 days at 10% on the total amount charged to Mystic Mermaid Company on October 6.

EX 8-24
Entries for receipt and dishonor of notes receivable

objs. 4, 6

Journalize the following transactions in the accounts of Lemon Grove Co., which operates a riverboat casino:

Mar.   1.   Received a $30,000, 60-day, 6% note dated March 1 from Bradshaw Co. on account.
      18.   Received a $25,000, 60-day, 9% note dated March 18 from Soto Co. on account.
Apr. 30.   The note dated March 1 from Bradshaw Co. is dishonored, and the customer's account is charged for the note, including interest.
May 17.   The note dated March 18 from Soto Co. is dishonored, and the customer's account is charged for the note, including interest.
July 29.   Cash is received for the amount due on the dishonored note dated March 1 plus interest for 90 days at 8% on the total amount debited to Bradshaw Co. on April 30.
Aug. 23.   Wrote off against the allowance account the amount charged to Soto Co. on May 17 for the dishonored note dated March 18.

EX 8-25
Receivables on the balance sheet

obj. 7

List any errors you can find in the following partial balance sheet:

Jennett Company
Balance Sheet
December 31, 2010

Assets		
Current assets:		
Cash		$ 95,000
Notes receivable	$250,000	
Less interest receivable	15,000	235,000
Accounts receivable	$398,000	
Plus allowance for doubtful accounts	36,000	434,000

Appendix
EX 8-26
Discounting notes receivable

✔ a. $61,800

D. Stoner Co., a building construction company, holds a 120-day, 9% note for $60,000, dated August 7, which was received from a customer on account. On October 6, the note is discounted at the bank at the rate of 12%.

a. Determine the maturity value of the note.
b. Determine the number of days in the discount period.
c. Determine the amount of the discount.
d. Determine the amount of the proceeds.
e. Journalize the entry to record the discounting of the note on October 6.

**Appendix
EX 8-27**

**Entries for receipt
and discounting of
note receivable and
dishonored notes**

Journalize the following transactions in the accounts of Zion Theater Productions:

Mar. 1. Received a $40,000, 90-day, 8% note dated March 1 from Gymboree Company on account.

31. Discounted the note at Security Credit Bank at 10%.

May 30. The note is dishonored by Gymboree Company; paid the bank the amount due on the note, plus a protest fee of $200.

June 29. Received the amount due on the dishonored note plus interest for 30 days at 12% on the total amount charged to Gymboree Company on May 30.

EX 8-28

**Accounts receivable
turnover and days'
sales in receivables**

✔ a. 2007: 8.4

Polo Ralph Lauren Corporation designs, markets, and distributes a variety of apparel, home decor, accessory, and fragrance products. The company's products include such brands as Polo by Ralph Lauren, Ralph Lauren Purple Label, Ralph Lauren, Polo Jeans Co., and Chaps. Polo Ralph Lauren reported the following (in thousands):

	For the Period Ending	
	March 31, 2007	April 1, 2006
Net sales	$4,295,400	$3,746,300
Accounts receivable	511,900	516,600

Assume that accounts receivable (in millions) were $530,503 at the beginning of the 2006 fiscal year.

a. Compute the accounts receivable turnover for 2007 and 2006. Round to one decimal place.

b. Compute the days' sales in receivables for 2007 and 2006. Round to one decimal place.

c. ➤ What conclusions can be drawn from these analyses regarding Ralph Lauren's efficiency in collecting receivables?

EX 8-29

**Accounts receivable
turnover and days'
sales in receivables**

✔ a. 2007: 9.0

H.J. Heinz Company was founded in 1869 at Sharpsburg, Pennsylvania, by Henry J. Heinz. The company manufactures and markets food products throughout the world, including ketchup, condiments and sauces, frozen food, pet food, soups, and tuna. For the fiscal years 2007 and 2006, H.J. Heinz reported the following (in thousands):

	Year Ending	
	May 2, 2007	May 3, 2006
Net sales	$9,001,630	$8,643,438
Accounts receivable	996,852	1,002,125

Assume that the accounts receivable (in thousands) were $1,092,394 at the beginning of 2006.

a. Compute the accounts receivable turnover for 2007 and 2006. Round to one decimal place.

b. Compute the days' sales in receivables at the end of 2007 and 2006. Round to one decimal place.

c. ➤ What conclusions can be drawn from these analyses regarding Heinz's efficiency in collecting receivables?

EX 8-30

**Accounts receivable
turnover and days'
sales in receivables**

The Limited, Inc., sells women's and men's clothing through specialty retail stores. The Limited sells women's intimate apparel and personal care products through Victoria's Secret and Bath & Body Works stores. The Limited reported the following (in millions):

	For the Period Ending	
	Feb. 3, 2007	Jan. 28, 2006
Net sales	$10,671	$9,699
Accounts receivable	176	182

Assume that accounts receivable (in millions) were $128 on January 29, 2005.

a. Compute the accounts receivable turnover for 2007 and 2006. Round to one decimal place.

b. Compute the day's sales in receivables for 2007 and 2006. Round to one decimal place.

c. ———➤ What conclusions can be drawn from these analyses regarding The Limited's efficiency in collecting receivables?

EX 8-31
Accounts receivable turnover

Use the data in Exercises 8-29 and 8-30 to analyze the accounts receivable turnover ratios of H.J. Heinz Company and The Limited, Inc.

a. Compute the average accounts receivable turnover ratio for The Limited, Inc., and H.J. Heinz Company for the years shown in Exercises 8-29 and 8-30.

b. ———➤ Does The Limited or H.J. Heinz Company have the higher average accounts receivable turnover ratio?

c. ———➤ Explain the logic underlying your answer in (b).

Problems Series A ● ● ● ● ●➤

PR 8-1A
Entries related to uncollectible accounts

obj. 4

KLOOSTER & ALLEN

✔ 3. $918,750

The following transactions were completed by The Bronze Gallery during the current fiscal year ended December 31:

June 6. Reinstated the account of Ian Netti, which had been written off in the preceding year as uncollectible. Journalized the receipt of $1,945 cash in full payment of Ian's account.

July 19. Wrote off the $11,150 balance owed by Rancho Rigging Co., which is bankrupt.

Aug. 13. Received 35% of the $20,000 balance owed by Santori Co., a bankrupt business, and wrote off the remainder as uncollectible.

Sept. 2. Reinstated the account of Sheryl Capers, which had been written off two years earlier as uncollectible. Recorded the receipt of $3,170 cash in full payment.

Dec. 31. Wrote off the following accounts as uncollectible (compound entry): Jacoba Co., $8,390; Garcia Co., $2,500; Summit Furniture, $6,400; Jill DePuy, $1,800.

   31. Based on an analysis of the $960,750 of accounts receivable, it was estimated that $42,000 will be uncollectible. Journalized the adjusting entry.

Instructions

1. Record the January 1 credit balance of $40,000 in a T account for Allowance for Doubtful Accounts.

2. Journalize the transactions. Post each entry that affects the following T accounts and determine the new balances:

Allowance for Doubtful Accounts
Bad Debt Expense

3. Determine the expected net realizable value of the accounts receivable as of December 31.

4. Assuming that instead of basing the provision for uncollectible accounts on an analysis of receivables, the adjusting entry on December 31 had been based on an estimated expense of ¾ of 1% of the net sales of $6,000,000 for the year, determine the following:

a. Bad debt expense for the year.

b. Balance in the allowance account after the adjustment of December 31.

c. Expected net realizable value of the accounts receivable as of December 31.

PR 8-2A
Aging of receivables; estimating allowance for doubtful accounts

obj. 4

✔ 3. $67,210

Wigs Plus Company supplies wigs and hair care products to beauty salons through-out California and the Pacific Northwest. The accounts receivable clerk for Wigs Plus prepared the following partially completed aging-of-receivables schedule as of the end of business on December 31, 2009:

	A	B	C	D	E	F	G	H
1			Not		Days Past Due			
2			Past					
3	Customer	Balance	Due	1–30	31–60	61–90	91–120	Over 120
4	Alpha Beauty	20,000	20,000					
5	Blonde Wigs	11,000			11,000			
30	Zahn's Beauty	2,900		2,900				
31	Subtotals	900,000	498,600	217,250	98,750	33,300	29,950	22,150

The following accounts were unintentionally omitted from the aging schedule:

Customer	Due Date	Balance
Sun Coast Beauty	May 30, 2009	$2,850
Paradise Beauty Store	Sept. 15, 2009	6,050
Helix Hair Products	Oct. 17, 2009	800
Hairy's Hair Care	Oct. 20, 2009	2,000
Surf Images	Nov. 18, 2009	700
Oh The Hair	Nov. 29, 2009	3,500
Mountain Coatings	Dec. 1, 2009	2,250
Lasting Images	Jan. 9, 2010	7,400

Wigs Plus has a past history of uncollectible accounts by age category, as follows:

Age Class	Percent Uncollectible
Not past due	2%
1–30 days past due	4
31–60 days past due	10
61–90 days past due	15
91–120 days past due	35
Over 120 days past due	80

Instructions
1. Determine the number of days past due for each of the preceding accounts.
2. Complete the aging-of-receivables schedule.
3. Estimate the allowance for doubtful accounts, based on the aging-of-receivables schedule.
4. Assume that the allowance for doubtful accounts for Wigs Plus has a credit balance of $1,710 before adjustment on December 31, 2009. Journalize the adjustment for uncollectible accounts.

PR 8-3A
Compare two methods of accounting for uncollectible receivables

objs. 3, 4, 5

✔ 1. Year 4: Balance of allowance account, end of year, $13,350

J. J. Technology Company, which operates a chain of 30 electronics supply stores, has just completed its fourth year of operations. The direct write-off method of recording bad debt expense has been used during the entire period. Because of substantial increases in sales volume and the amount of uncollectible accounts, the firm is considering changing to the allowance method. Information is requested as to the effect that an annual provision of $\frac{1}{2}$% of sales would have had on the amount of bad debt expense reported for each of the past four years. It is also considered desirable to know what the balance of Allowance for Doubtful Accounts would have been at the end of each year. The following data have been obtained from the accounts:

Year	Sales	Uncollectible Accounts Written Off	Year of Origin of Accounts Receivable Written Off as Uncollectible 1st	2nd	3rd	4th
1st	$1,300,000	$ 1,200	$1,200			
2nd	1,750,000	3,000	1,400	$1,600		
3rd	3,000,000	13,000	3,800	3,000	$6,200	
4th	3,600,000	17,700		4,000	6,100	$7,600

Instructions

1. Assemble the desired data, using the following column headings:

	Bad Debt Expense			
Year	Expense Actually Reported	Expense Based on Estimate	Increase (Decrease) in Amount of Expense	Balance of Allowance Account, End of Year

2. ▬▬▶ Experience during the first four years of operations indicated that the receivables were either collected within two years or had to be written off as uncollectible. Does the estimate of $\frac{1}{2}$% of sales appear to be reasonably close to the actual experience with uncollectible accounts originating during the first two years? Explain.

PR 8-4A
Details of notes receivable and related entries

obj. 6

✔1. Note 2: Due date, Sept. 13; Interest due at maturity, $150

Boutique Ads Co. produces advertising videos. During the last six months of the current fiscal year, Boutique Ads Co. received the following notes:

	Date	Face Amount	Term	Interest Rate
1.	May 9	$19,200	45 days	9%
2.	July 15	11,250	60 days	8
3.	Aug. 1	43,200	90 days	7
4.	Sept. 4	20,000	90 days	6
5.	Nov. 26	13,500	60 days	8
6.	Dec. 16	21,600	60 days	13

Instructions

1. Determine for each note (a) the due date and (b) the amount of interest due at maturity, identifying each note by number.
2. Journalize the entry to record the dishonor of Note (3) on its due date.
3. Journalize the adjusting entry to record the accrued interest on Notes (5) and (6) on December 31.
4. Journalize the entries to record the receipt of the amounts due on Notes (5) and (6) in January and February.

PR 8-5A
Notes receivable entries

obj. 6

The following data relate to notes receivable and interest for Vidovich Co., a financial services company. (All notes are dated as of the day they are received.)

Mar. 3. Received a $72,000, 9%, 60-day note on account.
      25. Received a $10,000, 8%, 90-day note on account.
May   2. Received $73,080 on note of March 3.
      16. Received a $40,000, 7%, 90-day note on account.
      31. Received a $25,000, 6%, 30-day note on account.
June 23. Received $10,200 on note of March 25.
      30. Received $25,125 on note of May 31.
July 1. Received a $7,500, 12%, 30-day note on account.
      31. Received $7,575 on note of July 1.
Aug. 14. Received $40,700 on note of May 16.

Instructions
Journalize the entries to record the transactions.

PR 8-6A
Sales and notes receivable transactions

obj. 6

The following were selected from among the transactions completed during the current year by Bonita Co., an appliance wholesale company:

Jan. 20. Sold merchandise on account to Wilding Co., $30,750. The cost of merchandise sold was $18,600.
Mar. 3. Accepted a 60-day, 8% note for $30,750 from Wilding Co. on account.
May   2. Received from Wilding Co. the amount due on the note of March 3.
June 10. Sold merchandise on account to Foyers for $13,600. The cost of merchandise sold was $8,200.

June 15. Loaned $18,000 cash to Michele Hobson, receiving a 30-day, 6% note.

20. Received from Foyers the amount due on the invoice of June 10, less 2% discount.

July 15. Received the interest due from Michele Hobson and a new 60-day, 9% note as a renewal of the loan of June 15. (Record both the debit and the credit to the notes receivable account.)

Sept. 13. Received from Michele Hobson the amount due on her note of July 15.

13. Sold merchandise on account to Rainbow Co., $20,000. The cost of merchandise sold was $11,500.

Oct. 12. Accepted a 60-day, 6% note for $20,000 from Rainbow Co. on account.

Dec. 11. Rainbow Co. dishonored the note dated October 12.

26. Received from Rainbow Co. the amount owed on the dishonored note, plus interest for 15 days at 12% computed on the maturity value of the note.

Instructions
Journalize the transactions.

Problems Series B

PR 8-1B
Entries related to uncollectible accounts

obj. 4

✔ 3. $750,375

The following transactions were completed by Interia Management Company during the current fiscal year ended December 31:

Feb. 24. Received 40% of the $18,000 balance owed by Broudy Co., a bankrupt business, and wrote off the remainder as uncollectible.

May 3. Reinstated the account of Irma Alonso, which had been written off in the preceding year as uncollectible. Journalized the receipt of $1,725 cash in full payment of Alonso's account.

Aug. 9. Wrote off the $3,600 balance owed by Tux Time Co., which has no assets.

Nov. 20. Reinstated the account of Pexis Co., which had been written off in the preceding year as uncollectible. Journalized the receipt of $6,140 cash in full payment of the account.

Dec. 31. Wrote off the following accounts as uncollectible (compound entry): Siena Co., $2,400; Kommers Co., $1,800; Butte Distributors, $6,000; Ed Ballantyne, $1,750.

31. Based on an analysis of the $768,375 of accounts receivable, it was estimated that $18,000 will be uncollectible. Journalized the adjusting entry.

Instructions
1. Record the January 1 credit balance of $15,500 in a T account for Allowance for Doubtful Accounts.
2. Journalize the transactions. Post each entry that affects the following selected T accounts and determine the new balances:

Allowance for Doubtful Accounts
Bad Debt Expense

3. Determine the expected net realizable value of the accounts receivable as of December 31.
4. Assuming that instead of basing the provision for uncollectible accounts on an analysis of receivables, the adjusting entry on December 31 had been based on an estimated expense of $\frac{1}{2}$ of 1% of the net sales of $4,100,000 for the year, determine the following:
   a. Bad debt expense for the year.
   b. Balance in the allowance account after the adjustment of December 31.
   c. Expected net realizable value of the accounts receivable as of December 31.

PR 8-2B

Aging of receivables; estimating allowance for doubtful accounts

obj. **4**

✔ 3. $72,270

Cutthroat Company supplies flies and fishing gear to sporting goods stores and outfitters throughout the western United States. The accounts receivable clerk for Cutthroat prepared the following partially completed aging-of-receivables schedule as of the end of business on December 31, 2009:

	A	B	C	D	E	F	G	H
1			Not		Days Past Due			
2			Past					
3	Customer	Balance	Due	1–30	31–60	61–90	91–120	Over 120
4	Alder Fishery	15,000	15,000					
5	Brown Trout	5,500			5,500			
30	Zug Bug Sports	2,900		2,900				
31	Subtotals	850,000	422,450	247,250	103,850	33,300	25,000	18,150

The following accounts were unintentionally omitted from the aging schedule:

Customer	Due Date	Balance
AAA Sports & Flies	June 14, 2009	$2,850
Blackmon Flies	Aug. 30, 2009	1,200
Charlie's Fish Co.	Sept. 30, 2009	1,800
Firehole Sports	Oct. 17, 2009	600
Green River Sports	Nov. 7, 2009	950
Smith River Co.	Nov. 28, 2009	2,200
Wintson Company	Dec. 1, 2009	2,250
Wolfe Bug Sports	Jan. 6, 2010	6,550

Cutthroat Company has a past history of uncollectible accounts by age category, as follows:

Age Class	Percent Uncollectible
Not past due	2%
1–30 days past due	5
31–60 days past due	10
61–90 days past due	25
91–120 days past due	45
Over 120 days past due	90

Instructions

1. Determine the number of days past due for each of the preceding accounts.
2. Complete the aging-of-receivables schedule.
3. Estimate the allowance for doubtful accounts, based on the aging-of-receivables schedule.
4. Assume that the allowance for doubtful accounts for Cutthroat Company has a debit balance of $1,370 before adjustment on December 31, 2009. Journalize the adjusting entry for uncollectible accounts.

PR 8-3B

Compare two methods of accounting for uncollectible receivables

objs. **3, 4, 5**

✔ 1. Year 4: Balance of allowance account, end of year, $13,700

Maywood Company, a telephone service and supply company, has just completed its fourth year of operations. The direct write-off method of recording bad debt expense has been used during the entire period. Because of substantial increases in sales volume and the amount of uncollectible accounts, the firm is considering changing to the allowance method. Information is requested as to the effect that an annual provision of $3/4$% of sales would have had on the amount of bad debt expense reported for each of the past four years. It is also considered desirable to know what the balance of Allowance for Doubtful Accounts would have been at the end of each year. The following data have been obtained from the accounts:

Year	Sales	Uncollectible Accounts Written Off	Year of Origin of Accounts Receivable Written Off as Uncollectible			
			1st	2nd	3rd	4th
1st	$ 680,000	$2,600	$2,600			
2nd	800,000	3,100	2,000	$1,100		
3rd	1,000,000	6,000	750	4,200	$1,050	
4th	2,000,000	8,200		1,260	2,700	$4,240

Instructions

1. Assemble the desired data, using the following column headings:

	Bad Debt Expense			
Year	Expense Actually Reported	Expense Based on Estimate	Increase (Decrease) in Amount of Expense	Balance of Allowance Account, End of Year

2. ━━━▶ Experience during the first four years of operations indicated that the receivables were either collected within two years or had to be written off as uncollectible. Does the estimate of ¾% of sales appear to be reasonably close to the actual experience with uncollectible accounts originating during the first two years? Explain.

PR 8-4B
Details of notes receivable and related entries

obj. 6

✔ 1. Note 2: Due date, July 26; Interest due at maturity, $185

Hauser Co. wholesales bathroom fixtures. During the current fiscal year, Hauser Co. received the following notes:

	Date	Face Amount	Term	Interest Rate
1.	Apr. 4	$30,000	60 days	8%
2.	June 26	18,500	30 days	12
3.	July 5	16,200	120 days	6
4.	Oct. 31	36,000	60 days	9
5.	Nov. 23	21,000	60 days	6
6.	Dec. 27	40,500	30 days	12

Instructions

1. Determine for each note (a) the due date and (b) the amount of interest due at maturity, identifying each note by number.
2. Journalize the entry to record the dishonor of Note (3) on its due date.
3. Journalize the adjusting entry to record the accrued interest on Notes (5) and (6) on December 31.
4. Journalize the entries to record the receipt of the amounts due on Notes (5) and (6) in January.

PR 8-5B
Notes receivable entries

obj. 6

The following data relate to notes receivable and interest for Optic Co., a cable manufacturer and supplier. (All notes are dated as of the day they are received.)

June 10. Received a $15,000, 9%, 60-day note on account.
July 13. Received a $54,000, 10%, 120-day note on account.
Aug. 9. Received $15,225 on note of June 10.
Sept. 4. Received a $24,000, 9%, 60-day note on account.
Nov. 3. Received $24,360 on note of September 4.
　　5. Received a $24,000, 7%, 30-day note on account.
　　10. Received $55,800 on note of July 13.
　　30. Received a $15,000, 10%, 30-day note on account.
Dec. 5. Received $24,140 on note of November 5.
　　30. Received $15,125 on note of November 30.

Instructions

Journalize entries to record the transactions.

PR 8-6B
Sales and notes
receivable
transactions

obj. 6

KLOOSTER
& ALLEN

The following were selected from among the transactions completed by Mair Co. during the current year. Mair Co. sells and installs home and business security systems.

Jan. 10.   Loaned $12,000 cash to Jas Caudel, receiving a 90-day, 8% note.
Feb. 4.   Sold merchandise on account to Periman & Co., $28,000. The cost of the merchandise sold was $16,500.
      13.   Sold merchandise on account to Centennial Co., $30,000. The cost of merchandise sold was $17,600.
Mar. 6.   Accepted a 60-day, 6% note for $28,000 from Periman & Co. on account.
      14.   Accepted a 60-day, 12% note for $30,000 from Centennial Co. on account.
Apr. 10.   Received the interest due from Jas Caudel and a new 90-day, 10% note as a renewal of the loan of January 10. (Record both the debit and the credit to the notes receivable account.)
May   5.   Received from Periman & Co. the amount due on the note of March 6.
      13.   Centennial Co. dishonored its note dated March 14.
June 12.   Received from Centennial Co. the amount owed on the dishonored note, plus interest for 30 days at 12% computed on the maturity value of the note.
July 9.   Received from Jas Caudel the amount due on his note of April 10.
Aug. 10.   Sold merchandise on account to Lindenfield Co., $13,600. The cost of the merchandise sold was $8,000.
      20.   Received from Lindenfield Co. the amount of the invoice of August 10, less 1% discount.

Instructions
Journalize the transactions.

Special Activities

SA 8-1
Ethics and
professional conduct
in business

Mirna Gaymer, vice president of operations for Rocky Mountain County Bank, has instructed the bank's computer programmer to use a 365-day year to compute interest on depository accounts (payables). Mirna also instructed the programmer to use a 360-day year to compute interest on loans (receivables).
➤ Discuss whether Mirna is behaving in a professional manner.

SA 8-2
Estimate
uncollectible
accounts

For several years, Halsey Co.'s sales have been on a "cash only" basis. On January 1, 2007, however, Halsey Co. began offering credit on terms of n/30. The amount of the adjusting entry to record the estimated uncollectible receivables at the end of each year has been ¼ of 1% of credit sales, which is the rate reported as the average for the industry. Credit sales and the year-end credit balances in Allowance for Doubtful Accounts for the past four years are as follows:

Year	Credit Sales	Allowance for Doubtful Accounts
2007	$6,120,000	$ 6,390
2008	6,300,000	11,880
2009	6,390,000	17,000
2010	6,540,000	24,600

Javier Cernao, president of Halsey Co., is concerned that the method used to account for and write off uncollectible receivables is unsatisfactory. He has asked for your advice in the analysis of past operations in this area and for recommendations for change.

1. Determine the amount of (a) the addition to Allowance for Doubtful Accounts and (b) the accounts written off for each of the four years.
2. a. ➤ Advise Javier Cernao as to whether the estimate of ¼ of 1% of credit sales appears reasonable.

(continued)

b. ➤ Assume that after discussing (a) with Javier Cernao, he asked you what action might be taken to determine what the balance of Allowance for Doubtful Accounts should be at December 31, 2010, and what possible changes, if any, you might recommend in accounting for uncollectible receivables. How would you respond?

SA 8-3
Accounts receivable turnover and days' sales in receivables

Best Buy is a specialty retailer of consumer electronics, including personal computers, entertainment software, and appliances. Best Buy operates retail stores in addition to the Best Buy, Media Play, On Cue, and Magnolia Hi-Fi Web sites. For two recent years, Best Buy reported the following (in millions):

	Year Ending	
	Mar. 3, 2007	**Feb. 25, 2006**
Net sales	$35,934	$30,848
Accounts receivable at end of year	548	506

Assume that the accounts receivable (in millions) were $375 at the beginning of the year ending February 25, 2006.

1. Compute the accounts receivable turnover for 2007 and 2006. Round to one decimal place.
2. Compute the days' sales in receivables at the end of 2007 and 2006.
3. ➤ What conclusions can be drawn from (1) and (2) regarding Best Buy's efficiency in collecting receivables?
4. ➤ For its years ending in 2007 and 2006, Circuit City Stores, Inc., has an accounts receivable turnover of 30.7 and 50.6, respectively. Compare Best Buy's efficiency in collecting receivables with that of Circuit City.
5. ➤ What assumption did we make about sales for the Circuit City and Best Buy ratio computations that might distort the two company ratios and therefore cause the ratios not to be comparable?

SA 8-4
Accounts receivable turnover and days' sales in receivables

Apple Computer, Inc., designs, manufactures, and markets personal computers and related personal computing and communicating solutions for sale primarily to education, creative, consumer, and business customers. Substantially all of the company's net sales over the last five years are from sales of its Macs, Ipods, and related software and peripherals. For two recent fiscal years, Apple reported the following (in millions):

	Year Ending	
	Sept. 30, 2006	**Sept. 24, 2005**
Net sales	$19,315	$13,931
Accounts receivable at end of year	1,252	895

Assume that the accounts receivable (in millions) were $774 at the beginning of 2005.

1. Compute the accounts receivable turnover for 2006 and 2005. Round to one decimal place.
2. Compute the days' sales in receivables at the end of 2006 and 2005.
3. ➤ What conclusions can be drawn from (1) and (2) regarding Apple's efficiency in collecting receivables?

SA 8-5
Accounts receivable turnover and days' sales in receivables

EarthLink, Inc., is a nationwide Internet Service Provider (ISP). EarthLink provides a variety of services to its customers, including narrowband access, broadband or high-speed access, and Web hosting services. For two recent years, EarthLink reported the following (in thousands):

	Year Ending	
	Dec. 31, 2006	**Dec. 31, 2005**
Net sales	$1,301,267	$1,290,072
Accounts receivable at end of year	51,054	36,033

Assume that the accounts receivable (in thousands) were $30,733 at January 1, 2005.

1. Compute the accounts receivable turnover for 2006 and 2005. Round to one decimal place.
2. Compute the days' sales in receivables at the end of 2006 and 2005.
3. ⬛➤ What conclusions can be drawn from (1) and (2) regarding EarthLink's efficiency in collecting receivables?
4. ⬛➤ Given the nature of EarthLink's operations, do you believe EarthLink's accounts receivable turnover ratio would be higher or lower than a typical manufacturing company, such as Boeing or Kellogg Company? Explain.

SA 8-6
Accounts receivable turnover

The accounts receivable turnover ratio will vary across companies, depending on the nature of the company's operations. For example, an accounts receivable turnover of 6 for an Internet Service Provider is unacceptable but might be excellent for a manufacturer of specialty milling equipment. A list of well-known companies follows.

Alcoa Inc.	The Coca-Cola Company	Kroger
AutoZone, Inc.	Delta Air Lines	Procter & Gamble
Barnes & Noble, Inc.	The Home Depot	Wal-Mart
Caterpillar	IBM	Whirlpool Corporation

1. Categorize each of the preceding companies as to whether its turnover ratio is likely to be above or below 15.
2. ⬛➤ Based on (1), identify a characteristic of companies with accounts receivable turnover ratios above 15.

Answers to Self-Examination Questions

1. **B** The estimate of uncollectible accounts, $8,500 (answer C), is the amount of the desired balance of Allowance for Doubtful Accounts after adjustment. The amount of the current provision to be made for uncollectible accounts expense is thus $6,000 (answer B), which is the amount that must be added to the Allowance for Doubtful Accounts credit balance of $2,500 (answer A) so that the account will have the desired balance of $8,500.

2. **B** The amount expected to be realized from accounts receivable is the balance of Accounts Receivable, $100,000, less the balance of Allowance for Doubtful Accounts, $7,000, or $93,000 (answer B).

3. **C** Maturity value is the amount that is due at the maturity or due date. The maturity value of $10,300 (answer C) is determined as follows:

Face amount of note	$10,000
Plus interest ($10,000 × 0.12 × 90/360)	300
Maturity value of note	$10,300

4. **C** November 3 is the due date of a $12,000, 90-day, 8% note receivable dated August 5 [26 days in August (31 days − 5 days) + 30 days in September + 31 days in October + 3 days in November].

5. **B** If a note is dishonored, Accounts Receivable is debited for the maturity value of the note (answer B). The maturity value of the note is its face value (answer A) plus the accrued interest. The maturity value of the note less accrued interest (answer C) is equal to the face value of the note. The maturity value of the note plus accrued interest (answer D) is incorrect, since the interest would be added twice.

CHAPTER 9

Fixed Assets and Intangible Assets

© AP Photo/W. A. Harewood

FATBURGER INC.

Do you remember purchasing your first car? You probably didn't buy your first car like you would buy a CD. Purchasing a new or used car is expensive. In addition, you would drive (use) the car for the next 3–5 years or longer. As a result, you might spend hours or weeks considering different makes and models, safety ratings, warranties, and operating costs before deciding on the final purchase.

Like buying her first car, Lovie Yancey spent a lot of time before deciding to open her first restaurant. In 1952, she created the biggest, juiciest hamburger that anyone had ever seen. She called it a Fatburger. The restaurant initially started as a 24-hour operation to cater to the schedules of professional musicians. As a fan of popular music and its performers, Yancey played rhythm and blues, jazz, and blues recordings for her customers. Fatburger's popularity with entertainers was illustrated when its name was used in a 1992 rap by Ice Cube. "Two in the mornin' got the Fatburger," Cube said, in "It Was a Good Day," a track on his *Predator* album.

The demand for this incredible burger was such that, in 1980, Ms. Yancey decided to offer Fatburger franchise opportunities. In 1990, with the goal of expanding Fatburger throughout the world, Fatburger Inc. purchased the business from Ms. Yancey. Today, Fatburger has grown to a multi-restaurant chain with owners and investors such as talk show host Montel Williams, Cincinnati Bengals' tackle Willie Anderson, comedian David Spade, and musicians Cher, Janet Jackson, and Pharrell.

So, how much would it cost you to open a Fatburger restaurant? The total investment begins at over $750,000 per restaurant. Thus, in starting a Fatburger restaurant, you would be making a significant investment that would affect your life for years to come. In this chapter, we discuss the accounting for investments in fixed assets such as those used to open a Fatburger restaurant. We also explain how to determine the portion of the fixed asset that becomes an expense over time. Finally, we discuss the accounting for the disposal of fixed assets and accounting for intangible assets such as patents and copyrights. **http://www.fatburger.com**

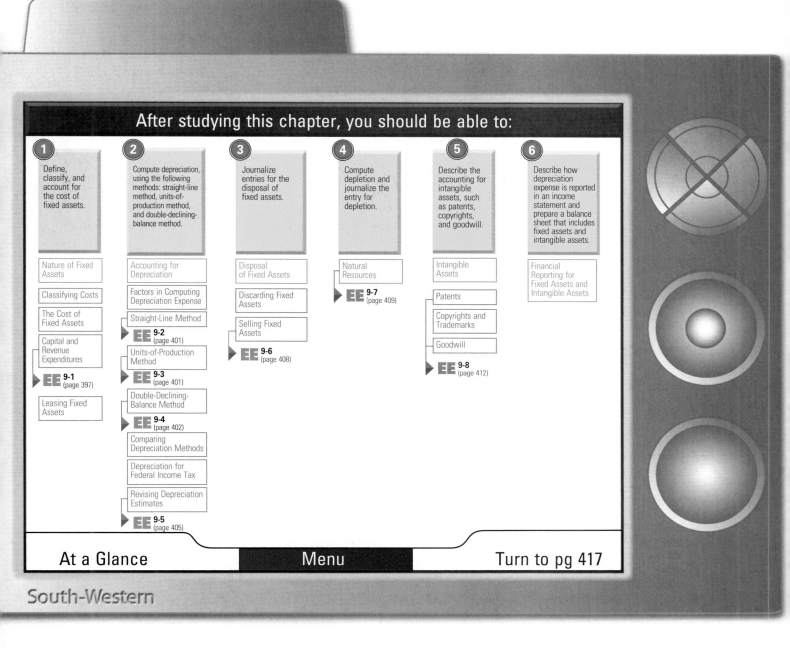

After studying this chapter, you should be able to:

1 Define, classify, and account for the cost of fixed assets.

- Nature of Fixed Assets
- Classifying Costs
- The Cost of Fixed Assets
- Capital and Revenue Expenditures
  ▶ **EE** 9-1 (page 397)
- Leasing Fixed Assets

2 Compute depreciation, using the following methods: straight-line method, units-of-production method, and double-declining-balance method.

- Accounting for Depreciation
- Factors in Computing Depreciation Expense
- Straight-Line Method
  ▶ **EE** 9-2 (page 401)
- Units-of-Production Method
  ▶ **EE** 9-3 (page 401)
- Double-Declining-Balance Method
  ▶ **EE** 9-4 (page 402)
- Comparing Depreciation Methods
- Depreciation for Federal Income Tax
- Revising Depreciation Estimates
  ▶ **EE** 9-5 (page 405)

3 Journalize entries for the disposal of fixed assets.

- Disposal of Fixed Assets
- Discarding Fixed Assets
- Selling Fixed Assets
  ▶ **EE** 9-6 (page 408)

4 Compute depletion and journalize the entry for depletion.

- Natural Resources
  ▶ **EE** 9-7 (page 409)

5 Describe the accounting for intangible assets, such as patents, copyrights, and goodwill.

- Intangible Assets
- Patents
- Copyrights and Trademarks
- Goodwill
  ▶ **EE** 9-8 (page 412)

6 Describe how depreciation expense is reported in an income statement and prepare a balance sheet that includes fixed assets and intangible assets.

- Financial Reporting for Fixed Assets and Intangible Assets

| At a Glance | Menu | Turn to pg 417 |

South-Western

1 Define, classify, and account for the cost of fixed assets.

Nature of Fixed Assets

Fixed assets are long-term or relatively permanent assets such as equipment, machinery, buildings, and land. Other descriptive titles for fixed assets are *plant assets* or *property, plant, and equipment*. Fixed assets have the following characteristics:

1. They exist physically and, thus, are *tangible* assets.
2. They are owned and used by the company in its normal operations.
3. They are not offered for sale as part of normal operations.

Exhibit 1 shows the percent of fixed assets to total assets for some select companies. As shown in Exhibit 1, fixed assets are often a significant portion of the total assets of a company.

Exhibit 1

Fixed Assets as a Percent of Total Assets— Selected Companies

	Fixed Assets as a Percent of Total Assets
Alcoa Inc.	40%
ExxonMobil Corporation	60
Ford Motor Company	35
Kroger	55
Marriott International, Inc.	31
United Parcel Service, Inc.	53
Verizon Communications	45
Walgreen Co.	46
Wal-Mart	53

Classifying Costs

A cost that has been incurred may be classified as a fixed asset, an investment, or an expense. Exhibit 2 shows how to determine the proper classification of a cost and, thus, how it should be recorded. As shown in Exhibit 2, classifying a cost involves the following steps:

IFRS IFRS

Step 1. Is the purchased item (cost) long-lived?

If *yes*, the item is capitalized as an asset on the balance sheet as either a fixed asset or an investment. Proceed to Step 2.

If *no*, the item is classified and recorded as an *expense*.

Step 2. Is the asset used in normal operations?

If *yes*, the asset is classified and recorded as a *fixed asset*.

If *no*, the asset is classified and recorded as an *investment*.

Costs that are classified and recorded as fixed assets include the purchase of land, buildings, or equipment. Such assets normally last more than a year and are used in

Exhibit 2

Classifying Costs

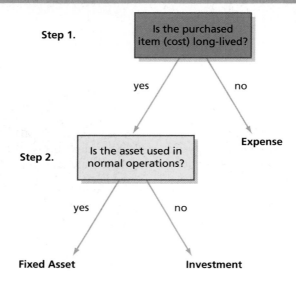

the normal operations. However, standby equipment for use during peak periods or when other equipment breaks down is still classified as a fixed asset even though it is not used very often. In contrast, fixed assets that have been abandoned or are no longer used in operations are not fixed assets.

Although fixed assets may be sold, they should not be offered for sale as part of normal operations. For example, cars and trucks offered for sale by an automotive dealership are not fixed assets of the dealership. On the other hand, a tow truck used in the normal operations of the dealership is a fixed asset of the dealership.

Investments are long-lived assets that are not used in the normal operations and are held for future resale. Such assets are reported on the balance sheet in a section entitled *Investments*. For example, undeveloped land acquired for future resale would be classified and reported as an investment, not land.

The Cost of Fixed Assets

The costs of acquiring fixed assets include all amounts spent to get the asset in place and ready for use. For example, freight costs and the costs of installing equipment are part of the asset's total cost.

Exhibit 3 summarizes some of the common costs of acquiring fixed assets. These costs are recorded by debiting the related fixed asset account, such as Land,[1] Building, Land Improvements, or Machinery and Equipment.

Only costs necessary for preparing the fixed asset for use are included as a cost of the asset. Unnecessary costs that do not increase the asset's usefulness are

Exhibit 3

Costs of Acquiring Fixed Assets

Building	Machinery & Equipment	Land
• Architects' fees	• Sales taxes	• Purchase price
• Engineers' fees	• Freight	• Sales taxes
• Insurance costs incurred during construction	• Installation	• Permits from government agencies
• Interest on money borrowed to finance construction	• Repairs (purchase of used equipment)	• Broker's commissions
• Walkways to and around the building	• Reconditioning (purchase of used equipment)	• Title fees
• Sales taxes	• Insurance while in transit	• Surveying fees
• Repairs (purchase of existing building)	• Assembly	• Delinquent real estate taxes
• Reconditioning (purchase of existing building)	• Modifying for use	• Removing unwanted building less any salvage
• Modifying for use	• Testing for use	• Grading and leveling
• Permits from government agencies	• Permits from government agencies	• Paving a public street bordering the land

Land Improvements

• Trees and shrubs
• Fences
• Outdoor lighting
• Paved parking areas

---

1 As discussed here, land is assumed to be used only as a location or site and not for its mineral deposits or other natural resources.

recorded as an expense. For example, the following costs are included as an expense:

1. Vandalism
2. Mistakes in installation
3. Uninsured theft
4. Damage during unpacking and installing
5. Fines for not obtaining proper permits from governmental agencies

Intel Corporation recently reported almost $3 billion of construction in progress, which was 7% of its total fixed assets.

A company may incur costs associated with constructing a fixed asset such as a new building. The direct costs incurred in the construction, such as labor and materials, should be capitalized as a debit to an account entitled Construction in Progress. When the construction is complete, the costs are reclassified by crediting Construction in Progress and debiting the proper fixed asset account such as Building. For some companies, construction in progress can be significant.

Capital and Revenue Expenditures

Once a fixed asset has been acquired and placed in service, costs may be incurred for ordinary maintenance and repairs. In addition, costs may be incurred for improving an asset or for extraordinary repairs that extend the asset's useful life. Costs that benefit only the current period are called **revenue expenditures**. Costs that improve the asset or extend its useful life are **capital expenditures**.[2]

Ordinary Maintenance and Repairs Costs related to the ordinary maintenance and repairs of a fixed asset are recorded as an expense of the current period. Such expenditures are *revenue expenditures* and are recorded as increases to Repairs and Maintenance Expense. For example, $300 paid for a tune-up of a delivery truck is recorded as follows:

Repairs and Maintenance Expense	300	
Cash		300

Asset Improvements After a fixed asset has been placed in service, costs may be incurred to improve the asset. For example, the service value of a delivery truck might be improved by adding a $5,500 hydraulic lift to allow for easier and quicker loading of cargo. Such costs are *capital expenditures* and are recorded as increases to the fixed asset account. In the case of the hydraulic lift, the expenditure is recorded as follows:

Delivery Truck	5,500	
Cash		5,500

Because the cost of the delivery truck has increased, depreciation for the truck would also change over its remaining useful life.

Extraordinary Repairs After a fixed asset has been placed in service, costs may be incurred to extend the asset's useful life. For example, the engine of a forklift that is near the end of its useful life may be overhauled at a cost of $4,500, extending its useful life by eight years. Such costs are *capital expenditures* and are recorded as a decrease in an accumulated depreciation account. In the case of the forklift, the expenditure is recorded as follows:

Accumulated Depreciation—Forklift	4,500	
Cash		4,500

2 Differences between GAAP and IFRS regarding the accounting for fixed assets (including the treatment of capital and revenue expenditures) are shown in Exhibit 1 of Appendix G at the back of this text.

Integrity, Objectivity, and Ethics in Business

CAPITAL CRIME

One of the largest alleged accounting frauds in history involved the improper accounting for capital expenditures. WorldCom, the second largest telecommunications company in the United States at the time, improperly treated maintenance expenditures on its telecommunications network as capital expenditures. As a result, the company had to restate its prior years' earnings downward by nearly $4 billion to correct this error. The company declared bankruptcy within months of disclosing the error, and the CEO was sentenced to 25 years in prison.

Because the forklift's remaining useful life has changed, depreciation for the forklift would also change based on the new book value of the forklift.

The accounting for revenue and capital expenditures is summarized below.

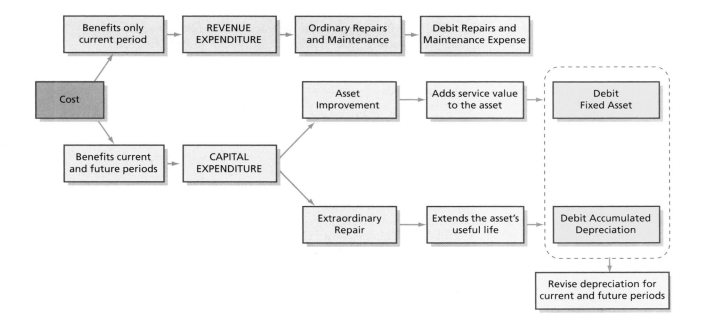

Example Exercise 9-1   Capital and Revenue Expenditures   1

On June 18, GTS Co. paid $1,200 to upgrade a hydraulic lift and $45 for an oil change for one of its delivery trucks. Journalize the entries for the hydraulic lift upgrade and oil change expenditures.

Follow My Example 9-1

June 18	Delivery Truck	1,200	
	Cash		1,200
18	Repairs and Maintenance Expense	45	
	Cash		45

For Practice: PE 9-1A, PE 9-1B

Leasing Fixed Assets

A *lease* is a contract for the use of an asset for a period of time. Leases are often used in business. For example, automobiles, computers, medical equipment, buildings, and airplanes are often leased.

The two parties to a lease contract are as follows:

1. The *lessor* is the party who owns the asset.
2. The *lessee* is the party to whom the rights to use the asset are granted by the lessor.

On December 31, 2007, Delta Air Lines operated 137 aircraft under operating leases and 48 aircraft under capital leases with future lease commitments of over $8 billion.

Under a lease contract, the lessee pays rent on a periodic basis for the lease term. The lessee accounts for a lease contract in one of two ways depending on how the lease contract is classified. A lease contract can be classified as either a:

1. *Capital lease* or
2. *Operating lease*

A **capital lease** is accounted for as if the lessee has purchased the asset. The lessee debits an asset account for the fair market value of the asset and credits a long-term lease liability account. The asset is then written off as an expense (amortized) over the life of the capital lease. The accounting for capital leases is discussed in more advanced accounting texts.

An **operating lease** is accounted for as if the lessee is renting the asset for the lease term. The lessee records operating lease payments by debiting *Rent Expense* and crediting *Cash*. The lessee's future lease obligations are not recorded in the accounts. However, such obligations are disclosed in notes to the financial statements.

The asset rentals described in earlier chapters of this text were accounted for as operating leases. To simplify, all leases are assumed to be operating leases throughout this text.

Accounting for Depreciation

2 Compute depreciation, using the following methods: straight-line method, units-of-production method, and double-declining-balance method.

Fixed assets, with the exception of land, lose their ability, over time, to provide services. Thus, the costs of fixed assets such as equipment and buildings should be recorded as an expense over their useful lives. This periodic recording of the cost of fixed assets as an expense is called **depreciation**. Because land has an unlimited life, it is not depreciated.

The adjusting entry to record depreciation debits *Depreciation Expense* and credits a *contra asset* account entitled *Accumulated Depreciation* or *Allowance for Depreciation*. The use of a contra asset account allows the original cost to remain unchanged in the fixed asset account.

Depreciation can be caused by physical or functional factors.

> **The adjusting entry to record depreciation debits Depreciation Expense and credits Accumulated Depreciation.**

1. *Physical depreciation* factors include wear and tear during use or from exposure to weather.
2. *Functional depreciation* factors include obsolescence and changes in customer needs that cause the asset to no longer provide services for which it was intended. For example, equipment may become obsolete due to changing technology.

Would you have more cash if you depreciated your car? The answer is no. Depreciation does not affect your cash flows. Likewise, depreciation does not affect the cash flows of a business. However, depreciation is subtracted in determining net income.

Two common misunderstandings that exist about *depreciation* as used in accounting include:

1. Depreciation does not measure a decline in the market value of a fixed asset. Instead, depreciation is an allocation of a fixed asset's cost to expense over the asset's useful life. Thus, the book value of a fixed asset (cost less accumulated depreciation) usually does not agree with the asset's market value. This is justified in accounting because a fixed asset is for use in a company's operations rather than for resale.
2. Depreciation does not provide cash to replace fixed assets as they wear out. This misunderstanding may occur because depreciation, unlike most expenses, does not require an outlay of cash when it is recorded.

Factors in Computing Depreciation Expense

Three factors determine the depreciation expense for a fixed asset. These three factors are as follows:

1. The asset's initial cost
2. The asset's expected useful life
3. The asset's estimated residual value

The initial *cost* of a fixed asset is determined using the concepts discussed and illustrated earlier in this chapter.

The *expected useful life* of a fixed asset is estimated at the time the asset is placed into service. Estimates of expected useful lives are available from industry trade associations. The Internal Revenue Service also publishes guidelines for useful lives, which may be helpful for financial reporting purposes. However, it is not uncommon for different companies to use a different useful life for similar assets.

JCPenney depreciates buildings over 50 years, while Tandy Corporation depreciates buildings over 10–40 years.

The **residual value** of a fixed asset at the end of its useful life is estimated at the time the asset is placed into service. Residual value is sometimes referred to as *scrap value*, *salvage value*, or *trade-in value*. The difference between a fixed asset's initial cost and its residual value is called the asset's *depreciable cost*. The depreciable cost is the amount of the asset's cost that is allocated over its useful life as depreciation expense. If a fixed asset has no residual value, then its entire cost should be allocated to depreciation.

Exhibit 4 shows the relationship between depreciation expense and a fixed asset's initial cost, expected useful life, and estimated residual value.

Exhibit 4

Depreciation Expense Factors

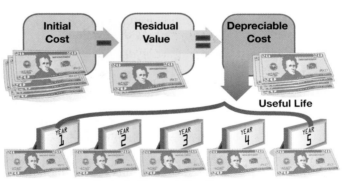

Periodic Depreciation Expense

For an asset placed into or taken out of service during the first half of a month, many companies compute depreciation on the asset for the entire month. That is, the asset is treated as having been purchased or sold on the first day of *that* month. Likewise, purchases and sales during the second half of a month are treated as having occurred on the first day of the *next* month. To simplify, this practice is used in this chapter.

The three depreciation methods used most often are as follows:[3]

1. Straight-line depreciation
2. Units-of-production depreciation
3. Double-declining-balance depreciation

Exhibit 5 shows how often these methods are used in financial statements.

It is not necessary that a company use one method of computing depreciation for all of its fixed assets. For example, a company may use one method for depreciating

---

3 Another method not often used today, called the *sum-of-the-years-digits method*, is described and illustrated in Appendix 1 at the end of this chapter.

Use of Depreciation Methods

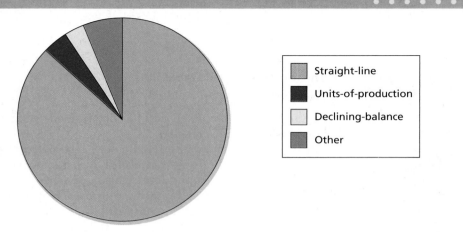

	Straight-line
	Units-of-production
	Declining-balance
	Other

Source: *Accounting Trends & Techniques,* 61st ed., American Institute of Certified Public Accountants, New York, 2007.

equipment and another method for depreciating buildings. A company may also use different methods for determining income and property taxes.

Straight-Line Method

The **straight-line method** provides for the same amount of depreciation expense for each year of the asset's useful life. As shown in Exhibit 5, the straight-line method is the most widely used depreciation method.

To illustrate, assume that equipment was purchased on January 1 as follows:

Initial cost	$24,000
Expected useful life	5 years
Estimated residual value	$2,000

The annual straight-line depreciation of $4,400 is computed below.

$$\text{Annual Depreciation} = \frac{\text{Cost} - \text{Residual Value}}{\text{Useful Life}} = \frac{\$24,000 - \$2,000}{5 \text{ Years}} = \$4,400$$

If an asset is used for only part of a year, the annual depreciation is prorated. For example, assume that the preceding equipment was purchased and placed into service on October 1. The depreciation for the year ending December 31 would be **$1,100**, computed as follows:

$$\text{First-Year Partial Depreciation} = \$4,400 \times 3/12 = \$1,100$$

The computation of straight-line depreciation may be simplified by converting the annual depreciation to a percentage of depreciable cost.[4] The straight-line percentage is determined by dividing 100% by the number of years of expected useful life, as shown below.

Expected Years of Useful Life	Straight-Line Percentage
5 years	20% (100%/5)
8 years	12.5% (100%/8)
10 years	10% (100%/10)
20 years	5% (100%/20)
25 years	4% (100%/25)

For the preceding equipment, the annual depreciation of $4,400 can be computed by multiplying the depreciable cost of $22,000 by 20% (100%/5).

As shown above, the straight-line method is simple to use. When an asset's revenues are about the same from period to period, straight-line depreciation provides a good matching of depreciation expense with the asset's revenues.

4 The depreciation rate may also be expressed as a fraction. For example, the annual straight-line rate for an asset with a three-year useful life is 1/3.

Example Exercise 9-2   Straight-Line Depreciation

Equipment acquired at the beginning of the year at a cost of $125,000 has an estimated residual value of $5,000 and an estimated useful life of 10 years. Determine (a) the depreciable cost, (b) the straight-line rate, and (c) the annual straight-line depreciation.

Follow My Example 9-2

a. $120,000 ($125,000 − $5,000)

b. 10% = 1/10

c. $12,000 ($120,000 × 10%), or ($120,000/10 years)

For Practice: PE 9-2A, PE 9-2B

Norfolk Southern Corporation depreciates its train engines based on hours of operation.

Units-of-Production Method

The **units-of-production method** provides the same amount of depreciation expense for each unit of production. Depending on the asset, the units of production can be expressed in terms of hours, miles driven, or quantity produced.

The units-of-production method is applied in two steps.

Step 1. Determine the depreciation per unit as:

$$\text{Depreciation per Unit} = \frac{\text{Cost} - \text{Residual Value}}{\text{Total Units of Production}}$$

Step 2. Compute the depreciation expense as:

Depreciation Expense = Depreciation per Unit × Total Units of Production Used

To illustrate, assume that the equipment in the preceding example is expected to have a useful life of 10,000 operating hours. During the year, the equipment was operated 2,100 hours. The units-of-production depreciation for the year is **$4,620**, as shown below.

Step 1. Determine the depreciation per hour as:

$$\text{Depreciation per Hour} = \frac{\text{Cost} - \text{Residual Value}}{\text{Total Units of Production}} = \frac{\$24,000 - \$2,000}{10,000 \text{ Hours}} = \$2.20 \text{ per Hour}$$

Step 2. Compute the depreciation expense as:

Depreciation Expense = Depreciation per Unit × Total Units of Production Used

Depreciation Expense = $2.20 per Hour × 2,100 Hours = $4,620

The units-of-production method is often used when a fixed asset's in-service time (or use) varies from year to year. In such cases, the units-of-production method matches depreciation expense with the asset's revenues.

Example Exercise 9-3   Units-of-Production Depreciation

Equipment acquired at a cost of $180,000 has an estimated residual value of $10,000, has an estimated useful life of 40,000 hours, and was operated 3,600 hours during the year. Determine (a) the depreciable cost, (b) the depreciation rate, and (c) the units-of-production depreciation for the year.

Follow My Example 9-3

a. $170,000 ($180,000 − $10,000)

b. $4.25 per hour ($170,000/40,000 hours)

c. $15,300 (3,600 hours × $4.25)

For Practice: PE 9-3A, PE 9-3B

Double-Declining-Balance Method

The **double-declining-balance method** provides for a declining periodic expense over the expected useful life of the asset. The double-declining-balance method is applied in three steps.

Step 1. Determine the straight-line percentage using the expected useful life.

Step 2. Determine the double-declining-balance rate by multiplying the straight-line rate from Step 1 by two.

Step 3. Compute the depreciation expense by multiplying the double-declining-balance rate from Step 2 times the book value of the asset.

To illustrate, the equipment purchased in the preceding example is used to compute double-declining-balance depreciation. For the first year, the depreciation is **$9,600**, as shown below.

Step 1. Straight-line percentage = 20% (100%/5)

Step 2. Double-declining-balance rate = 40% (20% × 2)

Step 3. Depreciation expense = $9,600 ($24,000 × 40%)

For the first year, the book value of the equipment is its initial cost of $24,000. After the first year, the **book value** (cost minus accumulated depreciation) declines and, thus, the depreciation also declines. The double-declining-balance depreciation for the full five-year life of the equipment is shown below.

Year	Cost	Acc. Dep. at Beginning of Year	Book Value at Beginning of Year	Double-Declining-Balance Rate	Depreciation for Year	Book Value at End of Year
1	$24,000		$24,000.00 ×	40%	$9,600.00	$14,400.00
2	24,000	$ 9,600.00	14,400.00 ×	40%	5,760.00	8,640.00
3	24,000	15,360.00	8,640.00 ×	40%	3,456.00	5,184.00
4	24,000	18,816.00	5,184.00 ×	40%	2,073.60	3,110.40
5	24,000	20,889.60	3,110.40	—	1,110.40	2,000.00

When the double-declining-balance method is used, the estimated residual value is *not* considered. However, the asset should not be depreciated below its estimated residual value. In the above example, the estimated residual value was $2,000. Therefore, the depreciation for the fifth year is $1,110.40 ($3,110.40 − $2,000.00) instead of $1,244.16 (40% × $3,110.40).

Like straight-line depreciation, if an asset is used for only part of a year, the annual depreciation is prorated. For example, assume that the preceding equipment was purchased and placed into service on October 1. The depreciation for the year ending December 31 would be $2,400, computed as follows:

First-Year Partial Depreciation = $9,600 × 3/12 = $2,400

The depreciation for the second year would then be $8,640, computed as follows:

Second-Year Depreciation = $8,640 = [40% × ($24,000 − $2,400)]

The double-declining-balance method provides a higher depreciation in the first year of the asset's use, followed by declining depreciation amounts. For this reason, the double-declining-balance method is called an **accelerated depreciation method**.

An asset's revenues are often greater in the early years of its use than in later years. In such cases, the double-declining-balance method provides a good matching of depreciation expense with the asset's revenues.

Example Exercise 9-4 Double-Declining-Balance Depreciation   2

Equipment acquired at the beginning of the year at a cost of $125,000 has an estimated residual value of $5,000 and an estimated useful life of 10 years. Determine (a) the double-declining-balance rate and (b) the double-declining-balance depreciation for the first year.

Follow My Example 9-4

a. 20% [(1/10) × 2]
b. $25,000 ($125,000 × 20%)

For Practice: PE 9-4A, PE 9-4B

Comparing Depreciation Methods

The three depreciation methods are summarized in Exhibit 6. All three methods allocate a portion of the total cost of an asset to an accounting period, while never depreciating an asset below its residual value.

Exhibit 6

Summary of Depreciation Methods

Method	Useful Life	Depreciable Cost	Depreciation Rate	Depreciation Expense
Straight-line	Years	Cost less residual value	Straight-line rate*	Constant
Units-of-production	Total units of production	Cost less residual value	(Cost − Residual value)/Total units of production	Variable
Double-declining-balance	Years	Declining book value, but not below residual value	Straight-line rate* × 2	Declining

*Straight-line rate = (1/Useful life)

The straight-line method provides for the same periodic amounts of depreciation expense over the life of the asset. The units-of-production method provides for periodic amounts of depreciation expense that vary, depending on the amount the asset is used. The double-declining-balance method provides for a higher depreciation amount in the first year of the asset's use, followed by declining amounts.

The depreciation for the straight-line, units-of-production, and double-declining-balance methods is shown in Exhibit 7. The depreciation in Exhibit 7 is based on the

Exhibit 7

Comparing Depreciation Methods

	Depreciation Expense		
Year	Straight-Line Method	Units-of-Production Method	Double-Declining-Balance Method
1	$ 4,400*	$ 4,620 ($2.20 × 2,100 hrs.)	$ 9,600.00 ($24,000 × 40%)
2	4,400	3,300 ($2.20 × 1,500 hrs.)	5,760.00 ($14,400 × 40%)
3	4,400	5,720 ($2.20 × 2,600 hrs.)	3,456.00 ($8,640 × 40%)
4	4,400	3,960 ($2.20 × 1,800 hrs.)	2,073.60 ($5,184 × 40%)
5	4,400	4,400 ($2.20 × 2,000 hrs.)	1,110.40**
Total	$22,000	$22,000	$22,000.00

*$4,400 = ($24,000 − $2,000)/5 years
**$3,110.40 − $2,000.00 because the equipment cannot be depreciated below its residual value of $2,000.

equipment purchased in our prior illustrations. For the units-of-production method, we assume that the equipment was used as follows:

Year 1	2,100 hours
Year 2	1,500
Year 3	2,600
Year 4	1,800
Year 5	2,000
Total	10,000 hours

Depreciation for Federal Income Tax

Tax Code Section 179 allows a business to deduct a portion of the cost of qualified property in the year it is placed into service.

The Internal Revenue Code uses the *Modified Accelerated Cost Recovery System (MACRS)* to compute depreciation for tax purposes. MACRS has eight classes of useful life and depreciation rates for each class. Two of the most common classes are the five-year class and the seven-year class.[5] The five-year class includes automobiles and light-duty trucks. The seven-year class includes most machinery and equipment. Depreciation for these two classes is similar to that computed using the double-declining-balance method.

In using the MACRS rates, residual value is ignored. Also, all fixed assets are assumed to be put in and taken out of service in the middle of the year. For the five-year-class assets, depreciation is spread over six years, as shown below.

Year	MACRS 5-Year-Class Depreciation Rates
1	20.0%
2	32.0
3	19.2
4	11.5
5	11.5
6	5.8
	100.0%

To simplify, a company will sometimes use MACRS for both financial statement and tax purposes. This is acceptable if MACRS does not result in significantly different amounts than would have been reported using one of the three depreciation methods discussed in this chapter.

Revising Depreciation Estimates

St. Paul Companies recently shortened the useful life of its application software at its data center.

Estimates of residual values and useful lives of fixed assets may change due to abnormal wear and tear or obsolescence. When new estimates are determined, they are used to determine the depreciation expense in future periods. The depreciation expense recorded in earlier years is not affected.[6]

To illustrate, assume the following data for a machine that was purchased on January 1, 2009:

Initial machine cost	$140,000
Expected useful life	5 years
Estimated residual value	$10,000
Annual depreciation using the straight-line method	
[($140,000 − $10,000)/5 years]	$26,000

---

5 Real estate is in either a 27½-year or a 31½-year class and is depreciated by the straight-line method.

6 *Statement of Financial Accounting Standards No. 154*, "Accounting Changes and Error Corrections" (Financial Accounting Standards Board, Norwalk, CT: 2005).

At the end of 2010, the machine's book value (undepreciated cost) is $88,000, as shown below.

Initial machine cost	$140,000
Less accumulated depreciation ($26,000 per year × 2 years)	52,000
Book value (undepreciated cost), end of second year	$ 88,000

During 2011, the company estimates that the machine's remaining useful life is eight years (instead of three) and that its residual value is $8,000 (instead of $10,000). The depreciation expense for each of the remaining eight years is $10,000, computed as follows:

Book value (undepreciated cost), end of second year	$88,000
Less revised estimated residual value	8,000
Revised remaining depreciable cost	$80,000
Revised annual depreciation expense [($88,000 − $8,000)/8 years]	$10,000

Exhibit 8 shows the book value of the asset over its original and revised lives. After the depreciation is revised at the end of 2010, book value declines at a slower rate. At the end of year 2018, the book value reaches the revised residual value of $8,000.

Exhibit 8

Book Value of Asset with Change in Estimate

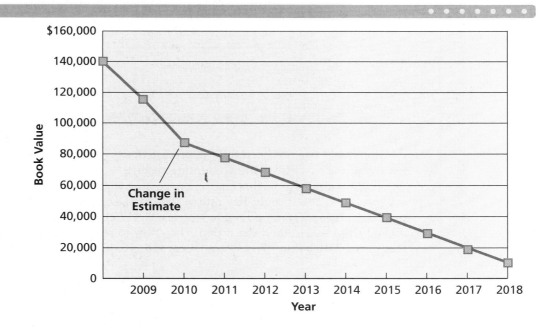

Example Exercise 9-5   Revision of Depreciation   2

A warehouse with a cost of $500,000 has an estimated residual value of $120,000, has an estimated useful life of 40 years, and is depreciated by the straight-line method. (a) Determine the amount of the annual depreciation. (b) Determine the book value at the end of the twentieth year of use. (c) Assuming that at the start of the twenty-first year the remaining life is estimated to be 25 years and the residual value is estimated to be $150,000, determine the depreciation expense for each of the remaining 25 years.

Follow My Example 9-5

a. $9,500 [($500,000 − $120,000)/40]
b. $310,000 [$500,000 − ($9,500 × 20)]
c. $6,400 [($310,000 − $150,000)/25]

For Practice: PE 9-5A, PE 9-5B

Disposal of Fixed Assets

Journalize entries for the disposal of fixed assets.

Fixed assets that are no longer useful may be discarded or sold.[7] In such cases, the fixed asset is removed from the accounts. Just because a fixed asset is fully depreciated, however, does not mean that it should be removed from the accounts.

> **The entry to record the disposal of a fixed asset removes the cost of the asset and its accumulated depreciation from the accounts.**

If a fixed asset is still being used, its cost and accumulated depreciation should remain in the ledger even if the asset is fully depreciated. This maintains accountability for the asset in the ledger. If the asset was removed from the ledger, the accounts would contain no evidence of the continued existence of the asset. In addition, cost and accumulated depreciation data on such assets are often needed for property tax and income tax reports.

Discarding Fixed Assets

If a fixed asset is no longer used and has no residual value, it is discarded. For example, assume that a fixed asset that is fully depreciated and has no residual value is discarded. The entry to record the discarding removes the asset and its related accumulated depreciation from the ledger.

To illustrate, assume that equipment acquired at a cost of $25,000 is fully depreciated at December 31, 2009. On February 14, 2010, the equipment is discarded. The entry to record the discard is as follows:

Feb.	14	Accumulated Depreciation—Equipment	25,000	
		Equipment		25,000
		To write off equipment discarded.		

If an asset has not been fully depreciated, depreciation should be recorded before removing the asset from the accounting records.

To illustrate, assume that equipment costing $6,000 with no estimated residual value is depreciated at a straight-line rate of 10%. On December 31, 2009, the accumulated depreciation balance, after adjusting entries, is $4,750. On March 24, 2010, the asset is removed from service and discarded. The entry to record the depreciation for the three months of 2010 before the asset is discarded is as follows:

Mar.	24	Depreciation Expense—Equipment	150	
		Accumulated Depreciation—Equipment		150
		To record current depreciation on equipment discarded ($600 × 3/12).		

The discarding of the equipment is then recorded as follows:

Mar.	24	Accumulated Depreciation—Equipment	4,900	
		Loss on Disposal of Equipment	1,100	
		Equipment		6,000
		To write off equipment discarded.		

7 The accounting for the exchange of fixed assets is described and illustrated in Appendix 2 at the end of this chapter.

The loss of $1,100 is recorded because the balance of the accumulated depreciation account ($4,900) is less than the balance in the equipment account ($6,000). Losses on the discarding of fixed assets are nonoperating items and are normally reported in the Other expense section of the income statement.

Selling Fixed Assets

The entry to record the sale of a fixed asset is similar to the entries for discarding an asset. The only difference is that the receipt of cash is also recorded. If the selling price is more than the book value of the asset, a gain is recorded. If the selling price is less than the book value, a loss is recorded.

To illustrate, assume that equipment is purchased at a cost of $10,000 with no estimated residual value and is depreciated at a straight-line rate of 10%. The equipment is sold for cash on October 12 of the eighth year of its use. The balance of the accumulated depreciation account as of the preceding December 31 is $7,000. The entry to update the depreciation for the nine months of the current year is as follows:

Oct.	12	Depreciation Expense—Equipment	750	
		Accumulated Depreciation—Equipment		750
		To record current depreciation on		
		equipment sold ($10,000 × $^9/_{12}$ × 10%).		

After the current depreciation is recorded, the book value of the asset is $2,250 ($10,000 − $7,750). The entries to record the sale, assuming three different selling prices, are as follows:

Sold at book value, for $2,250. No gain or loss.

Oct.	12	Cash	2,250	
		Accumulated Depreciation—Equipment	7,750	
		Equipment		10,000

Sold below book value, for $1,000. Loss of $1,250.

Oct.	12	Cash	1,000	
		Accumulated Depreciation—Equipment	7,750	
		Loss on Sale of Equipment	1,250	
		Equipment		10,000

Sold above book value, for $2,800. Gain of $550.

Oct.	12	Cash	2,800	
		Accumulated Depreciation—Equipment	7,750	
		Equipment		10,000
		Gain on Sale of Equipment		550

Example Exercise 9-6   Sale of Equipment

Equipment was acquired at the beginning of the year at a cost of $91,000. The equipment was depreciated using the straight-line method based on an estimated useful life of nine years and an estimated residual value of $10,000.

a.   What was the depreciation for the first year?

b.   Assuming the equipment was sold at the end of the second year for $78,000, determine the gain or loss on sale of the equipment.

c.   Journalize the entry to record the sale.

Follow My Example 9-6

a. $9,000 [($91,000 − $10,000)/9]

b. $5,000 gain {$78,000 − [$91,000 − ($9,000 × 2)]}

c.   Cash   78,000
    Accumulated Depreciation—Equipment   18,000
        Equipment   91,000
        Gain on Sale of Equipment   5,000

For Practice: PE 9-6A, PE 9-6B

4 Compute depletion and journalize the entry for depletion.

Natural Resources

The fixed assets of some companies include timber, metal ores, minerals, or other natural resources. As these resources are harvested or mined and then sold, a portion of their cost is debited to an expense account. This process of transferring the cost of natural resources to an expense account is called **depletion**.

Depletion is determined as follows:[8]

Step 1.   Determine the depletion rate as:

$$\text{Depletion Rate} = \frac{\text{Cost of Resource}}{\text{Estimated Total Units of Resource}}$$

Step 2.   Multiply the depletion rate by the quantity extracted from the resource during the period.

$$\text{Depletion Expense} = \text{Depletion Rate} \times \text{Quantity Extracted}$$

To illustrate, assume that Karst Company purchased mining rights as follows:

Cost of mineral deposit	$400,000
Estimated total units of resource	1,000,000 tons
Tons mined during year	90,000 tons

The depletion expense of $36,000 for the year is computed, as shown below.

Step 1.

$$\text{Depletion Rate} = \frac{\text{Cost of Resource}}{\text{Estimated Total Units of Resource}} = \frac{\$400,000}{1,000,000 \text{ Tons}} = \$0.40 \text{ per Ton}$$

Step 2.

$$\text{Depletion Expense} = \$0.40 \text{ per Ton} \times 90,000 \text{ Tons} = \$36,000$$

8 We assume that there is no significant residual value left after all the natural resource is extracted.

The adjusting entry to record the depletion is shown below.

Dec.	31	Depletion Expense	36,000	
		Accumulated Depletion		36,000
		Depletion of mineral deposit.		

Like the accumulated depreciation account, Accumulated Depletion is a *contra asset* account. It is reported on the balance sheet as a deduction from the cost of the mineral deposit.

Example Exercise 9-7   Depletion **4**

Earth's Treasures Mining Co. acquired mineral rights for $45,000,000. The mineral deposit is estimated at 50,000,000 tons. During the current year, 12,600,000 tons were mined and sold.

a. Determine the depletion rate.

b. Determine the amount of depletion expense for the current year.

c. Journalize the adjusting entry on December 31 to recognize the depletion expense.

Follow My Example 9-7

a. $0.90 per ton ($45,000,000/50,000,000 tons)

b. $11,340,000 (12,600,000 tons × $0.90 per ton)

c. Dec. 31   Depletion Expense.   11,340,000

        Accumulated Depletion.   11,340,000

        Depletion of mineral deposit.

For Practice: PE 9-7A, PE 9-7B

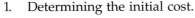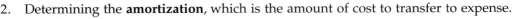

5 Describe the accounting for intangible assets, such as patents, copyrights, and goodwill.

Intangible Assets

Patents, copyrights, trademarks, and goodwill are long-lived assets that are used in the operations of a business and are not held for sale. These assets are called **intangible assets** because they do not exist physically.

The accounting for intangible assets is similar to that for fixed assets. The major issues are:

 IFRS ◀ **IFRS**

1. Determining the initial cost.

2. Determining the **amortization**, which is the amount of cost to transfer to expense.

Amortization results from the passage of time or a decline in the usefulness of the intangible asset.

Patents

Manufacturers may acquire exclusive rights to produce and sell goods with one or more unique features. Such rights are granted by **patents,** which the federal government issues to inventors. These rights continue in effect for 20 years. A business may purchase patent rights from others, or it may obtain patents developed by its own research and development.

Apple Computer, Inc., amortizes intangible assets over 3–10 years.

The initial cost of a purchased patent, including any legal fees, is debited to an asset account. This cost is written off, or amortized, over the years of the patent's expected useful life. The expected useful life of a patent may be less than its legal life. For example, a patent may become worthless due to changing technology or consumer tastes.

Patent amortization is normally computed using the straight-line method. The amortization is recorded by debiting an amortization expense account and crediting the patents account. A separate contra asset account is usually *not* used for intangible assets.

To illustrate, assume that at the beginning of its fiscal year, a company acquires patent rights for $100,000. Although the patent will not expire for 14 years, its remaining useful life is estimated as five years. The adjusting entry to amortize the patent at the end of the year is as follows:

Dec.	31	Amortization Expense—Patents		20,000	
		Patents			20,000
		Patent amortization ($100,000/5).			

Some companies develop their own patents through research and development. In such cases, any *research and development costs* are usually recorded as current operating expenses in the period in which they are incurred. This accounting for research and development costs is justified on the basis that any future benefits from research and development are highly uncertain.

Copyrights and Trademarks

Sony Corporation of America amortizes its artist contracts and music catalogs over 16 years and 21 years.

Coke® is one of the world's most recognizable trademarks. As stated in *LIFE,* "Two-thirds of the earth is covered by water; the rest is covered by Coke. If the French are known for wine and the Germans for beer, America achieved global beverage dominance with fizzy water and caramel color."

The exclusive right to publish and sell a literary, artistic, or musical composition is granted by a **copyright**. Copyrights are issued by the federal government and extend for 70 years beyond the author's death. The costs of a copyright include all costs of creating the work plus any other costs of obtaining the copyright. A copyright that is purchased is recorded at the price paid for it. Copyrights are amortized over their estimated useful lives.

A **trademark** is a name, term, or symbol used to identify a business and its products. Most businesses identify their trademarks with ® in their advertisements and on their products.

Under federal law, businesses can protect their trademarks by registering them for 10 years and renewing the registration for 10-year periods. Like a copyright, the legal costs of registering a trademark are recorded as an asset.

If a trademark is purchased from another business, its cost is recorded as an asset. In such cases, the cost of the trademark is considered to have an indefinite useful life. Thus, trademarks are not amortized. Instead, trademarks are reviewed periodically for impaired value. When a trademark is impaired, the trademark should be written down and a loss recognized.

Integrity, Objectivity, and Ethics in Business

21ST CENTURY PIRATES

Pirated software is a major concern of software companies. For example, during a recent global sweep, Microsoft Corporation seized nearly 5 million units of counterfeit Microsoft software with an estimated retail value of $1.7 billion. U.S. copyright laws and practices are sometimes ignored or disputed in other parts of the world.

Businesses must honor the copyrights held by software companies by eliminating pirated software from corporate computers. The Business Software Alliance (BSA) represents the largest software companies in campaigns to investigate illegal use of unlicensed software by businesses. The BSA estimates software industry losses of nearly $12 billion annually from software piracy. Employees using pirated software on business assets risk bringing legal penalties to themselves and their employers.

eBay recorded an impairment of $1.39 billion in the goodwill created from its purchase of Skype.

Goodwill

Goodwill refers to an intangible asset of a business that is created from such favorable factors as location, product quality, reputation, and managerial skill. Goodwill allows a business to earn a greater rate of return than normal.

Generally accepted accounting principles (GAAP) allow goodwill to be recorded only if it is objectively determined by a transaction. An example of such a transaction is the purchase of a business at a price in excess of the fair value of its net assets (assets − liabilities). The excess is recorded as goodwill and reported as an intangible asset.

Unlike patents and copyrights, goodwill is not amortized. However, a loss should be recorded if the future prospects of the purchased firm become impaired. This loss would normally be disclosed in the Other expense section of the income statement.

To illustrate, assume that on December 31 FaceCard Company has determined that $250,000 of the goodwill created from the purchase of electronic systems is impaired. The entry to record the impairment is as follows:

Dec.	31	Loss from Impaired Goodwill	250,000	
		Goodwill		250,000
		Impaired goodwill.		

Exhibit 9 shows intangible asset disclosures for 600 large firms. Goodwill is the most often reported intangible asset. This is because goodwill arises from merger transactions, which are common.

Exhibit 9

Frequency of Intangible Asset Disclosures for 600 Firms

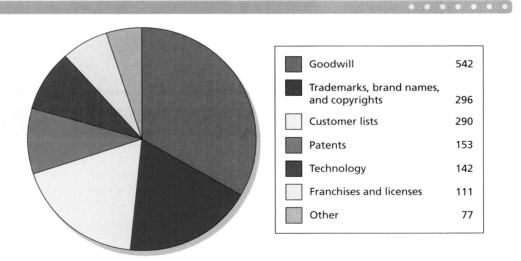

Goodwill	542
Trademarks, brand names, and copyrights	296
Customer lists	290
Patents	153
Technology	142
Franchises and licenses	111
Other	77

Source: Accounting Trends & Techniques, 61st ed., American Institute of Certified Public Accountants, New York, 2007.
Note: Some firms have multiple disclosures.

Exhibit 10 summarizes the characteristics of intangible assets.

Exhibit 10

Comparison of Intangible Assets

Intangible Asset	Description	Amortization Period	Periodic Expense
Patent	Exclusive right to benefit from an innovation.	Estimated useful life not to exceed legal life.	Amortization expense.
Copyright	Exclusive right to benefit from a literary, artistic, or musical composition.	Estimated useful life not to exceed legal life.	Amortization expense.
Trademark	Exclusive use of a name, term, or symbol.	None	Impairment loss if fair value less than carrying value (impaired).
Goodwill	Excess of purchase price of a business over the fair value of its net assets (assets − liabilities).	None	Impairment loss if fair value less than carrying value (impaired).

Example Exercise 9-8 Impaired Goodwill and Amortization of Patent

On December 31, it was estimated that goodwill of $40,000 was impaired. In addition, a patent with an estimated useful economic life of 12 years was acquired for $84,000 on July 1.

a. Journalize the adjusting entry on December 31 for the impaired goodwill.

b. Journalize the adjusting entry on December 31 for the amortization of the patent rights.

Follow My Example 9-8

a. Dec. 31	Loss from Impaired Goodwill		40,000	
	Goodwill			40,000
	Impaired goodwill.			
b. Dec. 31	Amortization Expense—Patents		3,500	
	Patents			3,500
	Amortized patent rights [($84,000/12) × (6/12)].			

For Practice: PE 9-8A, PE 9-8B

Integrity, Objectivity, and Ethics in Business

WHEN DOES GOODWILL BECOME WORTHLESS?

The timing and amount of goodwill write-offs can be very subjective. Managers and their accountants should fairly estimate the value of goodwill and record goodwill impairment when it occurs. It would be unethical to delay a write-down of goodwill when it is determined that the asset is impaired.

6 Describe how depreciation expense is reported in an income statement and prepare a balance sheet that includes fixed assets and intangible assets.

Financial Reporting for Fixed Assets and Intangible Assets

In the income statement, depreciation and amortization expense should be reported separately or disclosed in a note. A description of the methods used in computing depreciation should also be reported.

In the balance sheet, each class of fixed assets should be disclosed on the face of the statement or in the notes. The related accumulated depreciation should also be disclosed, either by class or in total. The fixed assets may be shown at their *book value* (cost less accumulated depreciation), which can also be described as their *net* amount.

If there are many classes of fixed assets, a single amount may be presented in the balance sheet, supported by a note with a separate listing. Fixed assets may be reported under the more descriptive caption of property, plant, and equipment.

Intangible assets are usually reported in the balance sheet in a separate section following fixed assets. The balance of each class of intangible assets should be disclosed net of any amortization.

The balance sheet presentation for Mornin' Joe's fixed and intangible assets is shown below.

Mornin' Joe
Balance Sheet
December 31, 2010

Property, plant, and equipment:			
Land			$1,850,000
Buildings	$2,650,000		
Less accumulated depreciation	420,000	2,230,000	
Office equipment	$ 350,000		
Less accumulated depreciation	102,000	248,000	
Total property, plant, and equipment			$4,328,000
Intangible assets:			
Patents			140,000

The cost and related accumulated depletion of mineral rights are normally shown as part of the Fixed Assets section of the balance sheet. The mineral rights may be shown net of depletion on the face of the balance sheet. In such cases, a supporting note discloses the accumulated depletion.

Business Connection

HUB-AND-SPOKE OR POINT-TO-POINT?

Southwest Airlines Co. uses a simple fare structure, featuring low, unrestricted, unlimited, everyday coach fares. These fares are made possible by Southwest's use of a point-to-point, rather than a hub-and-spoke, business approach. United Airlines, Inc., Delta Air Lines, and American Airlines employ a hub-and-spoke approach in which an airline establishes major hubs that serve as connecting links to other cities. For example, Delta has established major connecting hubs in Atlanta, Cincinnati, and Salt Lake City. In contrast, Southwest focuses on point-to-point service between selected cities with over 400 one-way, nonstop city pairs with an average length of just over 600 miles and average flying time of 1.8 hours. As a result, Southwest minimizes connections, delays, and total trip time. Southwest also focuses on serving conveniently located satellite or downtown airports, such as Dallas Love Field, Houston Hobby, and Chicago Midway. Because these airports are normally less congested than hub airports, Southwest is better able to maintain high employee productivity and reliable on-time performance. This operating approach permits the company to achieve high utilization of its fixed assets, such as its 737 aircraft. For example, aircraft are scheduled to minimize time spent at the gate, thereby reducing the number of aircraft and gate facilities that would otherwise be required.

© AP Photo/Matt Slocum

Financial Analysis and Interpretation

Fixed assets can be evaluated by their ability to generate revenue. One measure of the revenue-generating ability of fixed assets is the fixed asset turnover ratio. The **fixed asset turnover ratio** measures the number of dollars of revenue earned per dollar of fixed assets and is computed as follows:

Fixed Asset Turnover Ratio

$$= \frac{\text{Revenue}}{\text{Average Book Value of Fixed Assets}}$$

To illustrate, the following fixed asset balance sheet information is used for Marriott International, Inc.:

	December 29, 2006 (in millions)	December 30, 2005 (in millions)
Property and equipment (net)	$1,238	$2,341

Marriott reported revenue of $12,160 million for 2006. Thus, the fixed asset turnover ratio is calculated as follows:

$$\text{Fixed Asset Turnover Ratio} = \frac{\$12,160}{(\$1,238 + \$2,341)/2} = 6.80$$

For every dollar of fixed assets, Marriott earns $6.80 of revenue. The larger this ratio, the more efficiently a business is using its fixed assets. This ratio can be compared across time within a single firm or to other companies in the industry to evaluate overall fixed asset turnover performance.

The fixed asset turnover ratio for a number of different companies is shown below. The smaller ratios are associated with companies that require large fixed asset investments. The larger fixed asset turnover ratios are associated with firms that are more labor-intensive and require smaller fixed asset investments.

Company (industry)	Fixed Asset Turnover Ratio
Comcast Corporation (cable)	1.25
Google (Internet)	6.32
Manpower Inc. (temporary employment)	88.14
Norfolk Southern Corporation (railroad)	0.45
Ruby Tuesday, Inc. (restaurant)	1.40
Southwest Airlines Co. (airline)	0.93

APPENDIX 1

A recent edition of *Accounting Trends & Techniques* reported that only 1%–2% of the surveyed companies now use this method for financial reporting purposes.

Sum-of-the-Years-Digits Depreciation

Under the *sum-of-the-years-digits method*, depreciation expense is determined by multiplying the original cost of the asset less its estimated residual value by a smaller fraction each year. Thus, the sum-of-the-years-digits method is similar to the double-declining-balance method in that the depreciation expense declines each year.

The denominator of the fraction used in determining the depreciation expense is the sum of the digits of the years of the asset's useful life. For example, an asset with a useful life of five years would have a denominator of 15 (5 + 4 + 3 + 2 + 1). The denominator can also be determined using the following formula where N is the useful life of the assest:

$$\text{Sum of Years of Useful Life} = \frac{N(N + 1)}{2} = \frac{5(5 + 1)}{2} = 15$$

The numerator of the fraction is the number of years of useful life remaining at the beginning of each year for which depreciation is being computed. Thus, the numerator decreases each year by 1. For a useful life of five years, the numerator is 5 the first year, 4 the second year, 3 the third year, and so on.

To illustrate, the equipment example from the illustrations for the straight-line, units-of-production, and double-declining-balance methods is used. This equipment was purchased on January 1 as follows:

Initial cost	$24,000
Expected useful life	5 years
Estimated residual value	$2,000

Using the sum-of-the-years-digits method, the depreciation is computed as shown below.

Year	Cost Less Residual Value	Rate	Depreciation for Year	Acc. Dep. at End of Year	Book Value at End of Year
1	$22,000	$5/15$	$7,333.33	$ 7,333.33	$16,666.67
2	22,000	$4/15$	5,866.67	13,200.00	10,800.00
3	22,000	$3/15$	4,400.00	17,600.00	6,400.00
4	22,000	$2/15$	2,933.33	20,533.33	3,466.67
5	22,000	$1/15$	1,466.67	22,000.00	2,000.00

If an asset is used for only part of a year, the annual depreciation is prorated. For example, assume that the preceding equipment was purchased and placed into service on October 1. The depreciation for the year ending December 31 would be **$1,833.33**, computed as follows:

$$\text{First-Year Partial Depreciation} = \$7,333.33 \times 3/12 = \$1,833.33$$

The depreciation for the second year would then be **$6,966.67**, computed as follows:

$$\text{Second-Year Depreciation} = (9/12 \times 5/15 \times \$22,000) + (3/12 \times 4/15 \times \$22,000)$$

$$\text{Second-Year Depreciation} = \$5,500.00 + \$1,466.67 = \$6,966.67$$

At one time, the sum-of-the-years-digits method of depreciation was widely used. However, MACRS and current tax law changes have limited its use.

A P P E N D I X   2

Exchanging Similar Fixed Assets

Old equipment is often traded in for new equipment having a similar use. In such cases, the seller allows the buyer an amount for the old equipment traded in. This amount, called the **trade-in allowance**, may be either greater or less than the book value of the old equipment. The remaining balance—the amount owed—is either paid in cash or recorded as a liability. It is normally called **boot**, which is its tax name.

Accounting for the exchange of similar assets depends on whether the transaction has *commercial substance*.[9] An exchange has commercial substance if future cash flows change as a result of the exchange. If an exchange of similar assets has commercial substance, a gain or loss is recognized based on the difference between the book value of the asset given up (exchanged) and the fair market value of the asset received. In such cases, the exchange is accounted for similar to that of a sale of a fixed asset.

9 *Statement of Financial Accounting Standards No. 153*, "Exchanges of Nonmonetary Assets" (Financial Accounting Standards Board, Norwalk, CT: 2004).

Gain on Exchange

To illustrate a gain on an exchange of similar assets, assume the following:

Similar equipment acquired (new):

Price (fair market value) of new equipment	$5,000
Trade-in allowance on old equipment	1,100
Cash paid at June 19, date of exchange	$3,900

Equipment traded in (old):

Cost of old equipment	$4,000
Accumulated depreciation at date of exchange	3,200
Book value at June 19, date of exchange	$ 800

The entry to record this exchange and payment of cash is as follows:

June 19	Accumulated Depreciation—Equipment	3,200	
	Equipment (new equipment)	5,000	
	Equipment (old equipment)		4,000
	Cash		3,900
	Gain on Exchange of Equipment		300

The gain on the exchange, $300, is the difference between the fair market value of the new asset of $5,000 and the book value of the old asset traded in of $800 plus the cash paid of $3,900 as shown below.

Price (fair market value) of new equipment		$5,000
Less assets given up in exchange:		
Book value of old equipment ($4,000 − $3,200)	$ 800	
Cash paid on the exchange	3,900	4,700
Gain on exchange of assets		$ 300

Loss on Exchange

To illustrate a loss on an exchange of similar assets, assume that instead of a trade-in allowance of $1,100, a trade-in allowance of only $675 was allowed in the preceding example. In this case, the cash paid on the exchange is $4,325 as shown below.

Price (fair market value) of new equipment	$5,000
Trade-in allowance of old equipment	675
Cash paid at June 19, date of exchange	$4,325

The entry to record this exchange and payment of cash is as follows:

June 19	Accumulated Depreciation—Equipment	3,200	
	Equipment (new equipment)	5,000	
	Loss on Exchange of Equipment	125	
	Equipment (old equipment)		4,000
	Cash		4,325

The loss on the exchange, $125, is the difference between the fair market value of the new asset of $5,000 and the book value of the old asset traded in of $800 plus the cash paid of $4,325 as shown below.

Price (fair market value) of new equipment		$5,000
Less assets given up in exchange:		
Book value of old equipment ($4,000 − $3,200)	$ 800	
Cash paid on the exchange	4,325	5,125
Loss on exchange of assets		$ (125)

In those cases where an asset exchange *lacks commercial substance*, no gain is recognized on the exchange. Instead, the cost of the new asset is adjusted for any gain. For example, in the first illustration, the gain of $300 would be subtracted from the purchase price of $5,000 and the new asset would be recorded at $4,700. Accounting for the exchange of assets that lack commercial substance is discussed in more advanced accounting texts.[10]

---

10 The exchange of similar assets also involves complex tax issues that are discussed in advanced accounting courses.

1 Define, classify, and account for the cost of fixed assets.

Key Points	Key Learning Outcomes	Example Exercises	Practice Exercises
Fixed assets are long-term tangible assets that are owned by the business and are used in the normal operations of the business such as equipment, buildings, and land. The initial cost of a fixed asset includes all amounts spent to get the asset in place and ready for use. Once an asset is placed into service, revenue and capital expenditures may be incurred. Revenue expenditures include ordinary repairs and maintenance. Capital expenditures include asset improvements and extraordinary repairs. Fixed assets may also be leased and accounted for as capital or operating leases.	• Define *fixed assets*. • List types of costs that should and should not be included in the cost of a fixed asset. • Provide examples of ordinary repairs, asset improvements, and extraordinary repairs. • Prepare journal entries for ordinary repairs, asset improvements, and extraordinary repairs.	9-1	9-1A, 9-1B

2 Compute depreciation, using the following methods: straight-line method, units-of-production method, and double-declining-balance method.

Key Points	Key Learning Outcomes	Example Exercises	Practice Exercises
All fixed assets except land lose their ability to provide services and should be depreciated over time. Three factors are considered in determining depreciation: (1) the fixed asset's initial cost, (2) the useful life of the asset, and (3) the residual value of the asset. The straight-line method spreads the initial cost less the residual value equally over the useful life. The units-of-production method spreads the initial cost less the residual value equally over the units expected to be produced by the asset during its useful life. The double-declining-balance method is applied by multiplying the declining book value of the asset by twice the straight-line rate. Depreciation may be revised for changes in an asset's useful life or residual value. Such changes affect future depreciation.	• Define and describe *depreciation*. • List the factors used in determining depreciation. • Compute straight-line depreciation. • Compute units-of-production depreciation. • Compute double-declining-balance depreciation. • Compute revised depreciation for a change in an asset's useful life and residual value.	 9-2 9-3 9-4 9-5	 9-2A, 9-2B 9-3A, 9-3B 9-4A, 9-4B 9-5A, 9-5B

3 Journalize entries for the disposal of fixed assets.

Key Points	Key Learning Outcomes	Example Exercises	Practice Exercises
To record disposals of fixed assets, any depreciation for the current period should be recorded, and the book value of the asset is then removed from the accounts. For assets discarded from service, a loss may be recorded for any remaining book value of the asset. When a fixed asset is sold, the book value is removed, and the cash or other asset received is recorded. If the selling price is more than the book value of the asset, the transaction results in a gain. If the selling price is less than the book value, there is a loss.	• Prepare the journal entry for discarding a fixed asset. • Prepare journal entries for the sale of a fixed asset.	 9-6	 9-6A, 9-6B

4 Compute depletion and journalize the entry for depletion.

Key Points	Key Learning Outcomes	Example Exercises	Practice Exercises
The amount of periodic depletion is computed by multiplying the quantity of minerals extracted during the period by a depletion rate. The depletion rate is computed by dividing the cost of the mineral deposit by its estimated total units of resources. The entry to record depletion debits a depletion expense account and credits an accumulated depletion account.	• Define and describe *depletion*. • Compute a depletion rate. • Prepare the journal entry to record depletion.	 9-7 9-7	 9-7A, 9-7B 9-7A, 9-7B

5 Describe the accounting for intangible assets, such as patents, copyrights, and goodwill.

Key Points	Key Learning Outcomes	Example Exercises	Practice Exercises
Long-term assets such as patents, copyrights, trademarks, and goodwill that are without physical attributes but are used in the business are intangible assets. The initial cost of an intangible asset should be debited to an asset account. The cost of patents and copyrights should be amortized over the years of the asset's expected usefulness by debiting an expense account and crediting the intangible asset account. Trademarks and goodwill are not amortized, but are written down only upon impairment.	• Define, describe, and provide examples of intangible assets. • Prepare a journal entry for the purchase of an intangible asset. • Prepare a journal entry to amortize the costs of patents and copyrights. • Prepare the journal entry to record the impairment of goodwill.	 9-8 9-8	 9-8A, 9-8B 9-8A, 9-8B

Describe how depreciation expense is reported in an income statement and prepare a balance sheet that includes fixed assets and intangible assets.

Key Points	Key Learning Outcomes	Example Exercises	Practice Exercises
The amount of depreciation expense and the method or methods used in computing depreciation should be disclosed in the financial statements. In addition, each major class of fixed assets should be disclosed, along with the related accumulated depreciation. Intangible assets are usually presented in the balance sheet in a separate section immediately following fixed assets. Each major class of intangible assets should be disclosed at an amount net of the amortization recorded to date.	• Describe and illustrate how fixed assets are reported in the income statement and balance sheet. • Describe and illustrate how intangible assets are reported in the income statement and balance sheet.		

Key Terms

accelerated depreciation method (402)
amortization (409)
book value (402)
boot (415)
capital expenditures (396)
capital lease (398)
copyright (410)

depletion (408)
depreciation (398)
double-declining-balance method (402)
fixed asset turnover ratio (414)
fixed assets (393)
goodwill (411)
intangible assets (409)

operating lease (398)
patents (409)
residual value (399)
revenue expenditures (396)
straight-line method (400)
trade-in allowance (415)
trademark (410)
units-of-production method (401)

Illustrative Problem

McCollum Company, a furniture wholesaler, acquired new equipment at a cost of $150,000 at the beginning of the fiscal year. The equipment has an estimated life of five years and an estimated residual value of $12,000. Ellen McCollum, the president, has requested information regarding alternative depreciation methods.

Instructions

1. Determine the annual depreciation for each of the five years of estimated useful life of the equipment, the accumulated depreciation at the end of each year, and the book value of the equipment at the end of each year by (a) the straight-line method and (b) the double-declining-balance method.
2. Assume that the equipment was depreciated under the double-declining-balance method. In the first week of the fifth year, the equipment was sold for $10,000. Journalize the entry to record the sale.

Solution

1.

	Year	Depreciation Expense	Accumulated Depreciation, End of Year	Book Value, End of Year
a.	1	$27,600*	$ 27,600	$122,400
	2	27,600	55,200	94,800
	3	27,600	82,800	67,200
	4	27,600	110,400	39,600
	5	27,600	138,000	12,000

*$27,600 = ($150,000 − $12,000) ÷ 5

	Year	Depreciation Expense	Accumulated Depreciation, End of Year	Book Value, End of Year
b.	1	$60,000**	$ 60,000	$ 90,000
	2	36,000	96,000	54,000
	3	21,600	117,600	32,400
	4	12,960	130,560	19,440
	5	7,440***	138,000	12,000

**$60,000 = $150,000 × 40%
***The asset is not depreciated below the estimated residual value of $12,000.
  $7,440 = $150,000 − $130,560 − $12,000

2.

Cash	10,000	
Accumulated Depreciation—Equipment	130,560	
Loss on Sale of Equipment	9,440	
Equipment		150,000

Self-Examination Questions (Answers at End of Chapter)

1. Which of the following expenditures incurred in connection with acquiring machinery is a proper charge to the asset account?
   A. Freight
   B. Installation costs
   C. Both A and B
   D. Neither A nor B

2. What is the amount of depreciation, using the double-declining-balance method for the second year of use for equipment costing $9,000, with an estimated residual value of $600 and an estimated life of three years?
   A. $6,000
   B. $3,000
   C. $2,000
   D. $400

3. An example of an accelerated depreciation method is:
   A. straight-line.
   B. double-declining-balance.
   C. units-of-production.
   D. depletion.

4. Equipment purchased on January 3, 2008, for $80,000 was depreciated using the straight-line method based upon a 5-year life and $7,500 residual value. The equipment was sold on December 31, 2010, for $40,000. What is the gain on the sale of the equipment?
   A. $3,500
   B. $14,500
   C. $36,500
   D. $43,500

5. Which of the following is an example of an intangible asset?
   A. Patents
   B. Goodwill
   C. Copyrights
   D. All of the above

Eye Openers

1. Which of the following qualities are characteristic of fixed assets? (a) tangible, (b) capable of repeated use in the operations of the business, (c) held for sale in the normal course of business, (d) used rarely in the operations of the business, (e) long-lived.

2. Mancini Office Supplies has a fleet of automobiles and trucks for use by salespersons and for delivery of office supplies and equipment. East Village Auto Sales Co. has automobiles and trucks for sale. Under what caption would the automobiles and trucks be reported in the balance sheet of (a) Mancini Office Supplies, (b) East Village Auto Sales Co.?

3. Just Animals Co. acquired an adjacent vacant lot with the hope of selling it in the future at a gain. The lot is not intended to be used in Just Animals' business operations. Where should such real estate be listed in the balance sheet?

4. My Mother's Closet Company solicited bids from several contractors to construct an addition to its office building. The lowest bid received was for $375,000. My Mother's Closet Company decided to construct the addition itself at a cost of $298,500. What amount should be recorded in the building account?

5. Distinguish between the accounting for capital expenditures and revenue expenditures.

6. Immediately after a used truck is acquired, a new motor is installed at a total cost of $3,175. Is this a capital expenditure or a revenue expenditure?

7. How does the accounting for a capital lease differ from the accounting for an operating lease?

8. Are the amounts at which fixed assets are reported in the balance sheet their approximate market values as of the balance sheet date? Discuss.

9. a. Does the recognition of depreciation in the accounts provide a special cash fund for the replacement of fixed assets? Explain.
   b. Describe the nature of depreciation as the term is used in accounting.

10. Pac Vac Company purchased a machine that has a manufacturer's suggested life of 15 years. The company plans to use the machine on a special project that will last 12 years. At the completion of the project, the machine will be sold. Over how many years should the machine be depreciated?

11. Is it necessary for a business to use the same method of computing depreciation (a) for all classes of its depreciable assets, (b) for financial statement purposes and in determining income taxes?

12. a. Under what conditions is the use of an accelerated depreciation method most appropriate?
    b. Why is an accelerated depreciation method often used for income tax purposes?
    c. What is the Modified Accelerated Cost Recovery System (MACRS), and under what conditions is it used?

13. A company revised the estimated useful lives of its fixed assets, which resulted in an increase in the remaining lives of several assets. Can the company include, as income of the current period, the cumulative effect of the changes, which reduces the depreciation expense of past periods? Discuss.

14. For some of the fixed assets of a business, the balance in Accumulated Depreciation is exactly equal to the cost of the asset. (a) Is it permissible to record additional depreciation on the assets if they are still useful to the business? Explain. (b) When should an entry be made to remove the cost and the accumulated depreciation from the accounts?

15. a. Over what period of time should the cost of a patent acquired by purchase be amortized?
    b. In general, what is the required accounting treatment for research and development costs?
    c. How should goodwill be amortized?

Practice Exercises

PE 9-1A
Capital and revenue
expenditures

obj. 1

EE 9-1 p. 397

On May 27, Linoleum Associates Co. paid $950 to repair the transmission on one of its delivery vans. In addition, Linoleum Associates paid $450 to install a GPS system in its van. Journalize the entries for the transmission and GPS system expenditures.

PE 9-1B
Capital and revenue
expenditures

obj. 1

EE 9-1 p. 397

On October 9, Wonder Inflatables Co. paid $1,150 to install a hydraulic lift and $40 for an air filter for one of its delivery trucks. Journalize the entries for the new lift and air filter expenditures.

PE 9-2A
Straight-line
depreciation

obj. 2

EE 9-2 p. 401

A building acquired at the beginning of the year at a cost of $485,000 has an estimated residual value of $75,000 and an estimated useful life of 25 years. Determine (a) the depreciable cost, (b) the straight-line rate, and (c) the annual straight-line depreciation.

PE 9-2B
Straight-line
depreciation

obj. 2

EE 9-2 p. 401

Equipment acquired at the beginning of the year at a cost of $125,000 has an estimated residual value of $5,000 and an estimated useful life of eight years. Determine (a) the depreciable cost, (b) the straight-line rate, and (c) the annual straight-line depreciation.

PE 9-3A
Units-of-production
depreciation

obj. 2

EE 9-3 p. 401

A truck acquired at a cost of $134,000 has an estimated residual value of $35,000, has an estimated useful life of 300,000 miles, and was driven 52,000 miles during the year. Determine (a) the depreciable cost, (b) the depreciation rate, and (c) the units-of-production depreciation for the year.

PE 9-3B
Units-of-production
depreciation

obj. 2

EE 9-3 p. 401

A tractor acquired at a cost of $95,000 has an estimated residual value of $15,000, has an estimated useful life of 40,000 hours, and was operated 5,100 hours during the year. Determine (a) the depreciable cost, (b) the depreciation rate, and (c) the units-of-production depreciation for the year.

PE 9-4A
Double-declining-
balance depreciation

obj. 2

EE 9-4 p. 402

A building acquired at the beginning of the year at a cost of $650,000 has an estimated residual value of $125,000 and an estimated useful life of 40 years. Determine (a) the double-declining-balance rate and (b) the double-declining-balance depreciation for the first year.

PE 9-4B
Double-declining-
balance depreciation

obj. 2

EE 9-4 p. 402

Equipment acquired at the beginning of the year at a cost of $145,000 has an estimated residual value of $18,000 and an estimated useful life of five years. Determine (a) the double-declining-balance rate and (b) the double-declining-balance depreciation for the first year.

PE 9-5A
Revision of
depreciation

obj. 2

EE 9-5   p. 405

Equipment with a cost of $250,000 has an estimated residual value of $34,000, has an estimated useful life of 18 years, and is depreciated by the straight-line method. (a) Determine the amount of the annual depreciation. (b) Determine the book value at the end of the tenth year of use. (c) Assuming that at the start of the eleventh year the remaining life is estimated to be eight years and the residual value is estimated to be $6,000, determine the depreciation expense for each of the remaining eight years.

PE 9-5B
Revision of
depreciation

obj. 2

EE 9-5   p. 405

A truck with a cost of $80,000 has an estimated residual value of $15,000, has an estimated useful life of eight years, and is depreciated by the straight-line method. (a) Determine the amount of the annual depreciation. (b) Determine the book value at the end of the fourth year of use. (c) Assuming that at the start of the fifth year the remaining life is estimated to be five years and the residual value is estimated to be $10,000, determine the depreciation expense for each of the remaining five years.

PE 9-6A
Sale of equipment

obj. 3

EE 9-6   p. 408

Equipment was acquired at the beginning of the year at a cost of $324,000. The equipment was depreciated using the double-declining-balance method based on an estimated useful life of eight years and an estimated residual value of $43,000.

a. What was the depreciation for the first year?
b. Assuming the equipment was sold at the end of the second year for $200,000, determine the gain or loss on the sale of the equipment.
c. Journalize the entry to record the sale.

PE 9-6B
Sale of equipment

obj. 3

EE 9-6   p. 408

Equipment was acquired at the beginning of the year at a cost of $160,000. The equipment was depreciated using the straight-line method based on an estimated useful life of 15 years and an estimated residual value of $17,500.

a. What was the depreciation for the first year?
b. Assuming the equipment was sold at the end of the sixth year for $90,000, determine the gain or loss on the sale of the equipment.
c. Journalize the entry to record the sale.

PE 9-7A
Depletion

obj. 4

EE 9-7   p. 409

Montana Mining Co. acquired mineral rights for $120,000,000. The mineral deposit is estimated at 200,000,000 tons. During the current year, 31,155,000 tons were mined and sold.

a. Determine the depletion rate.
b. Determine the amount of depletion expense for the current year.
c. Journalize the adjusting entry on December 31 to recognize the depletion expense.

PE 9-7B
Depletion

obj. 4

EE 9-7   p. 409

Cooke City Mining Co. acquired mineral rights for $50,000,000. The mineral deposit is estimated at 125,000,000 tons. During the current year, 42,385,000 tons were mined and sold.

a. Determine the depletion rate.
b. Determine the amount of depletion expense for the current year.
c. Journalize the adjusting entry on December 31 to recognize the depletion expense.

PE 9-8A
Impaired goodwill
and amortization of
patent

obj. 5

EE 9-8   p. 412

On December 31, it was estimated that goodwill of $500,000 was impaired. In addition, a patent with an estimated useful economic life of eight years was acquired for $388,000 on July 1.

a. Journalize the adjusting entry on December 31 for the impaired goodwill.
b. Journalize the adjusting entry on December 31 for the amortization of the patent rights.

PE 9-8B
Impaired goodwill and amortization of patent

obj. 5

EE 9-8 p. 412

On December 31, it was estimated that goodwill of $875,000 was impaired. In addition, a patent with an estimated useful economic life of 17 years was acquired for $425,000 on April 1.

a. Journalize the adjusting entry on December 31 for the impaired goodwill.
b. Journalize the adjusting entry on December 31 for the amortization of the patent rights.

Exercises

EX 9-1
Costs of acquiring fixed assets

obj. 1

Catherine Simpkins owns and operates Speedy Print Co. During February, Speedy Print Co. incurred the following costs in acquiring two printing presses. One printing press was new, and the other was used by a business that recently filed for bankruptcy.

Costs related to new printing press:

1. Sales tax on purchase price
2. Freight
3. Special foundation
4. Insurance while in transit
5. New parts to replace those damaged in unloading
6. Fee paid to factory representative for installation

Costs related to used printing press:

7. Fees paid to attorney to review purchase agreement
8. Freight
9. Installation
10. Repair of vandalism during installation
11. Replacement of worn-out parts
12. Repair of damage incurred in reconditioning the press

a. Indicate which costs incurred in acquiring the new printing press should be debited to the asset account.
b. Indicate which costs incurred in acquiring the used printing press should be debited to the asset account.

EX 9-2
Determine cost of land

obj. 1

Bridger Ski Co. has developed a tract of land into a ski resort. The company has cut the trees, cleared and graded the land and hills, and constructed ski lifts. (a) Should the tree cutting, land clearing, and grading costs of constructing the ski slopes be debited to the land account? (b) If such costs are debited to Land, should they be depreciated?

EX 9-3
Determine cost of land

obj. 1

✔ $327,425

Fastball Delivery Company acquired an adjacent lot to construct a new warehouse, paying $30,000 and giving a short-term note for $270,000. Legal fees paid were $1,425, delinquent taxes assumed were $12,000, and fees paid to remove an old building from the land were $18,500. Materials salvaged from the demolition of the building were sold for $4,500. A contractor was paid $910,000 to construct a new warehouse. Determine the cost of the land to be reported on the balance sheet.

EX 9-4
Capital and revenue expenditures

obj. 1

Connect Lines Co. incurred the following costs related to trucks and vans used in operating its delivery service:

1. Replaced a truck's suspension system with a new suspension system that allows for the delivery of heavier loads.
2. Installed a hydraulic lift to a van.

3. Repaired a flat tire on one of the vans.
4. Overhauled the engine on one of the trucks purchased three years ago.
5. Removed a two-way radio from one of the trucks and installed a new radio with a greater range of communication.
6. Rebuilt the transmission on one of the vans that had been driven 40,000 miles. The van was no longer under warranty.
7. Changed the radiator fluid on a truck that had been in service for the past four years.
8. Tinted the back and side windows of one of the vans to discourage theft of contents.
9. Changed the oil and greased the joints of all the trucks and vans.
10. Installed security systems on four of the newer trucks.

Classify each of the costs as a capital expenditure or a revenue expenditure.

EX 9-5
Capital and revenue expenditures

obj. 1

Jaime Baldwin owns and operates Love Transport Co. During the past year, Jaime incurred the following costs related to an 18-wheel truck:

1. Changed engine oil.
2. Installed a wind deflector on top of the cab to increase fuel mileage.
3. Replaced fog and cab light bulbs.
4. Modified the factory-installed turbo charger with a special-order kit designed to add 50 more horsepower to the engine performance.
5. Replaced a headlight that had burned out.
6. Removed the old CB radio and replaced it with a newer model with a greater range.
7. Replaced the old radar detector with a newer model that detects the KA frequencies now used by many of the state patrol radar guns. The detector is wired directly into the cab, so that it is partially hidden. In addition, Jaime fastened the detector to the truck with a locking device that prevents its removal.
8. Replaced the hydraulic brake system that had begun to fail during his latest trip through the Rocky Mountains.
9. Installed a television in the sleeping compartment of the truck.
10. Replaced a shock absorber that had worn out.

Classify each of the costs as a capital expenditure or a revenue expenditure.

EX 9-6
Capital and revenue expenditures

obj. 1

Easy Move Company made the following expenditures on one of its delivery trucks:

Feb. 16.   Replaced transmission at a cost of $3,150.
July 15.   Paid $1,100 for installation of a hydraulic lift.
Oct.   3.   Paid $72 to change the oil and air filter.

Prepare journal entries for each expenditure.

EX 9-7
Nature of depreciation

obj. 2

Legacy Ironworks Co. reported $3,175,000 for equipment and $2,683,000 for accumulated depreciation—equipment on its balance sheet.
━━━━▶ Does this mean (a) that the replacement cost of the equipment is $3,175,000 and (b) that $2,683,000 is set aside in a special fund for the replacement of the equipment? Explain.

EX 9-8
Straight-line depreciation rates

obj. 2

✔ c. 10%

Convert each of the following estimates of useful life to a straight-line depreciation rate, stated as a percentage, assuming that the residual value of the fixed asset is to be ignored: (a) 2 years, (b) 8 years, (c) 10 years, (d) 20 years, (e) 25 years, (f) 40 years, (g) 50 years.

EX 9-9
Straight-line depreciation

obj. 2

✔ $3,350

A refrigerator used by a meat processor has a cost of $93,750, an estimated residual value of $10,000, and an estimated useful life of 25 years. What is the amount of the annual depreciation computed by the straight-line method?

EX 9-10
Depreciation by units-of-production method

obj. 2

✔ $276

A diesel-powered generator with a cost of $145,000 and estimated residual value of $7,000 is expected to have a useful operating life of 75,000 hours. During July, the generator was operated 150 hours. Determine the depreciation for the month.

EX 9-11
Depreciation by units-of-production method

obj. 2

✔ a. Truck #1, credit Accumulated Depreciation, $6,670

Prior to adjustment at the end of the year, the balance in Trucks is $250,900 and the balance in Accumulated Depreciation—Trucks is $88,200. Details of the subsidiary ledger are as follows:

Truck No.	Cost	Estimated Residual Value	Estimated Useful Life	Accumulated Depreciation at Beginning of Year	Miles Operated During Year
1	$50,000	$ 6,500	150,000 miles	—	23,000 miles
2	72,900	9,900	300,000	$60,000	25,000
3	38,000	3,000	200,000	8,050	36,000
4	90,000	13,000	200,000	20,150	40,000

a. Determine the depreciation rates per mile and the amount to be credited to the accumulated depreciation section of each of the subsidiary accounts for the miles operated during the current year.
b. Journalize the entry to record depreciation for the year.

EX 9-12
Depreciation by two methods

obj. 2

✔ a. $3,750

A Kubota tractor acquired on January 9 at a cost of $75,000 has an estimated useful life of 20 years. Assuming that it will have no residual value, determine the depreciation for each of the first two years (a) by the straight-line method and (b) by the double-declining-balance method.

EX 9-13
Depreciation by two methods

obj. 2

✔ a. $19,000

A storage tank acquired at the beginning of the fiscal year at a cost of $172,000 has an estimated residual value of $20,000 and an estimated useful life of eight years. Determine the following: (a) the amount of annual depreciation by the straight-line method and (b) the amount of depreciation for the first and second years computed by the double-declining-balance method.

EX 9-14
Partial-year depreciation

obj. 2

✔ a. First year, $2,000

Sandblasting equipment acquired at a cost of $85,000 has an estimated residual value of $5,000 and an estimated useful life of 10 years. It was placed in service on October 1 of the current fiscal year, which ends on December 31. Determine the depreciation for the current fiscal year and for the following fiscal year by (a) the straight-line method and (b) the double-declining-balance method.

EX 9-15
Revision of depreciation

obj. 2

✔ a. $17,500

A building with a cost of $1,050,000 has an estimated residual value of $420,000, has an estimated useful life of 36 years, and is depreciated by the straight-line method. (a) What is the amount of the annual depreciation? (b) What is the book value at the end of the twentieth year of use? (c) If at the start of the twenty-first year it is estimated that the remaining life is 20 years and that the residual value is $300,000, what is the depreciation expense for each of the remaining 20 years?

EX 9-16
Capital expenditure and depreciation

objs. 1, 2

✔ b. Depreciation Expense, $600

Crane Company purchased and installed carpet in its new general offices on March 30 for a total cost of $12,000. The carpet is estimated to have a 15-year useful life and no residual value.

a. Prepare the journal entries necessary for recording the purchase of the new carpet.
b. Record the December 31 adjusting entry for the partial-year depreciation expense for the carpet, assuming that Crane Company uses the straight-line method.

EX 9-17
Entries for sale of fixed asset
obj. **3**

Equipment acquired on January 3, 2007, at a cost of $504,000, has an estimated useful life of 12 years, has an estimated residual value of $42,000, and is depreciated by the straight-line method.

a. What was the book value of the equipment at December 31, 2010, the end of the year?
b. Assuming that the equipment was sold on April 1, 2011, for $315,000, journalize the entries to record (1) depreciation for the three months until the sale date, and (2) the sale of the equipment.

EX 9-18
Disposal of fixed asset
obj. **3**
✔ b. $177,750

Equipment acquired on January 3, 2007, at a cost of $265,500, has an estimated useful life of eight years and an estimated residual value of $31,500.

a. What was the annual amount of depreciation for the years 2007, 2008, and 2009, using the straight-line method of depreciation?
b. What was the book value of the equipment on January 1, 2010?
c. Assuming that the equipment was sold on January 4, 2010, for $168,500, journalize the entry to record the sale.
d. Assuming that the equipment had been sold on January 4, 2010, for $180,000 instead of $168,500, journalize the entry to record the sale.

EX 9-19
Depletion entries
obj. **4**
✔ a. $2,475,000

Cikan Mining Co. acquired mineral rights for $16,200,000. The mineral deposit is estimated at 90,000,000 tons. During the current year, 13,750,000 tons were mined and sold.

a. Determine the amount of depletion expense for the current year.
b. Journalize the adjusting entry to recognize the depletion expense.

EX 9-20
Amortization entries
obj. **5**
✔ a. $57,500

Isolution Company acquired patent rights on January 4, 2007, for $750,000. The patent has a useful life equal to its legal life of 15 years. On January 7, 2010, Isolution successfully defended the patent in a lawsuit at a cost of $90,000.

a. Determine the patent amortization expense for the current year ended December 31, 2010.
b. Journalize the adjusting entry to recognize the amortization.

EX 9-21
Book value of fixed assets
obj. **6**

Apple Computer, Inc., designs, manufactures, and markets personal computers and related software. Apple also manufactures and distributes music players (Ipod) along with related accessories and services including the online distribution of third-party music. The following information was taken from a recent annual report of Apple:

Property, Plant, and Equipment (in millions):

	Current Year	Preceding Year
Land and buildings	$626	$361
Machinery, equipment, and internal-use software	595	470
Office furniture and equipment	94	81
Other fixed assets related to leases	760	569
Accumulated depreciation and amortization	794	664

a. Compute the book value of the fixed assets for the current year and the preceding year and explain the differences, if any.
b. ⬛⬛⬛➤ Would you normally expect the book value of fixed assets to increase or decrease during the year?

EX 9-22
Balance sheet
presentation

obj. 6

List the errors you find in the following partial balance sheet:

Hobart Company
Balance Sheet
December 31, 2010

Assets

Total current assets $350,000

Property, plant, and equipment:	Replacement Cost	Accumulated Depreciation	Book Value
Land	$ 60,000	$ 12,000	$ 48,000
Buildings	156,000	45,600	110,400
Factory equipment	330,000	175,200	154,800
Office equipment	72,000	48,000	24,000
Patents	48,000	—	48,000
Goodwill	27,000	3,000	24,000
Total property, plant, and equipment	$693,000	$283,800	409,200

Appendix 1
EX 9-23
Sum-of-the-years-
digits depreciation

✔ First year: $7,143

Based on the data in Exercise 9-12, determine the depreciation for the Kubota tractor for each of the first two years, using the sum-of-the-years-digits depreciation method. Round to the nearest dollar.

Appendix 1
EX 9-24
Sum-of-the-years-
digits depreciation

✔ First year:
$33,778

Based on the data in Exercise 9-13, determine the depreciation for the storage tank for each of the first two years, using the sum-of-the-years-digits depreciation method. Round to the nearest dollar.

Appendix 1
EX 9-25
Partial-year depreciation

✔ First year: $3,636

Based on the data in Exercise 9-14, determine the depreciation for the sandblasting equipment for each of the first two years, using the sum-of-the-years-digits depreciation method. Round to the nearest dollar.

Appendix 2
EX 9-26
Asset traded for
similar asset

✔ a. $180,000

A printing press priced at a fair market value of $300,000 is acquired in a transaction that has commercial substance by trading in a similar press and paying cash for the difference between the trade-in allowance and the price of the new press.

a. Assuming that the trade-in allowance is $120,000, what is the amount of cash given?
b. Assuming that the book value of the press traded in is $115,500, what is the gain or loss on the exchange?

Appendix 2
EX 9-27
Asset traded for
similar asset

✔ a. $180,000

Assume the same facts as in Exercise 9-26, except that the book value of the press traded in is $127,750. (a) What is the amount of cash given? (b) What is the gain or loss on the exchange?

Appendix 2
EX 9-28
Entries for trade of
fixed asset

On October 1, Hot Springs Co., a water distiller, acquired new bottling equipment with a list price (fair market value) of $462,000. Hot Springs received a trade-in allowance of $96,000 on the old equipment of a similar type and paid cash of $366,000. The following information about the old equipment is obtained from the account in the equipment ledger: cost, $336,000; accumulated depreciation on December 31, the end of the preceding fiscal year, $220,000; annual depreciation, $20,000. Assuming the exchange has commercial substance, journalize the entries to record (a) the current depreciation of the old equipment to the date of trade-in and (b) the exchange transaction on October 1.

Appendix 2
EX 9-29
Entries for trade of
fixed asset

On April 1, Gyminny Delivery Services acquired a new truck with a list price (fair market value) of $150,000. Gyminny received a trade-in allowance of $30,000 on an old truck of similar type and paid cash of $120,000. The following information about the old truck is obtained from the account in the equipment ledger: cost, $96,000; accumulated depreciation on December 31, the end of the preceding fiscal year, $64,000; annual depreciation, $16,000. Assuming the exchange has commercial substance, journalize the entries to record (a) the current depreciation of the old truck to the date of trade-in and (b) the transaction on April 1.

EX 9-30
Fixed asset turnover
ratio

Verizon Communications is a major telecommunications company in the United States. Verizon's balance sheet disclosed the following information regarding fixed assets:

	Dec. 31, 2007 (in millions)	Dec. 31, 2006 (in millions)
Plant, property, and equipment	$213,994	$204,109
Less accumulated depreciation	128,700	121,753
	$ 85,294	$ 82,356

Verizon's revenue for 2007 was $93,469 million. The fixed asset turnover for the telecommunications industry averages 1.10.

a. Determine Verizon's fixed asset turnover ratio. Round to two decimal places.
b. ▬▬▶ Interpret Verizon's fixed asset turnover ratio.

EX 9-31
Fixed asset turnover
ratio

The following table shows the revenue and average net fixed assets (in millions) for a recent fiscal year for Best Buy and Circuit City Stores, Inc.:

	Revenue	Average Net Fixed Assets
Best Buy	$35,934	$2,825
Circuit City Stores, Inc.	12,430	880

a. Compute the fixed asset turnover for each company. Round to two decimal places.
b. ▬▬▶ Which company uses its fixed assets more efficiently? Explain.

Problems Series A ● ● ● ●▶

PR 9-1A
Allocate payments
and receipts to fixed
asset accounts

obj. 1

✔ Land, $469,450

The following payments and receipts are related to land, land improvements, and buildings acquired for use in a wholesale apparel business. The receipts are identified by an asterisk.

a. Finder's fee paid to real estate agency .... $ 4,000
b. Cost of real estate acquired as a plant site: Land 375,000
                                                     Building 25,000
c. Fee paid to attorney for title search 2,500
d. Delinquent real estate taxes on property, assumed by purchaser ... 31,750
e. Architect's and engineer's fees for plans and supervision 36,000
f. Cost of removing building purchased with land in (b) 10,000
g. Proceeds from sale of salvage materials from old building 3,000*

h. Cost of filling and grading land	$ 15,200
i. Premium on one-year insurance policy during construction	5,400
j. Money borrowed to pay building contractor	600,000*
k. Special assessment paid to city for extension of water main to the property	9,000
l. Cost of repairing windstorm damage during construction	3,000
m. Cost of repairing vandalism damage during construction	1,800
n. Cost of trees and shrubbery planted	12,000
o. Cost of paving parking lot to be used by customers	14,500
p. Interest incurred on building loan during construction	33,000
q. Proceeds from insurance company for windstorm and vandalism damage	4,500*
r. Payment to building contractor for new building	700,000
s. Refund of premium on insurance policy (j) canceled after 10 months	450*

Instructions

1. Assign each payment and receipt to Land (unlimited life), Land Improvements (limited life), Building, or Other Accounts. Indicate receipts by an asterisk. Identify each item by letter and list the amounts in columnar form, as follows:

Item	Land	Land Improvements	Building	Other Accounts

2. Determine the amount debited to Land, Land Improvements, and Building.
3. ━━━▶ The costs assigned to the land, which is used as a plant site, will not be depreciated, while the costs assigned to land improvements will be depreciated. Explain this seemingly contradictory application of the concept of depreciation.

PR 9-2A
Compare three depreciation methods
obj. 2

✔ a. 2009: straight-line depreciation, $86,000

Newbirth Coatings Company purchased waterproofing equipment on January 2, 2009, for $380,000. The equipment was expected to have a useful life of four years, or 8,000 operating hours, and a residual value of $36,000. The equipment was used for 3,000 hours during 2009, 2,500 hours in 2010, 1,400 hours in 2011, and 1,100 hours in 2012.

Instructions

Determine the amount of depreciation expense for the years ended December 31, 2009, 2010, 2011, and 2012, by (a) the straight-line method, (b) the units-of-production method, and (c) the double-declining-balance method. Also determine the total depreciation expense for the four years by each method. The following columnar headings are suggested for recording the depreciation expense amounts:

	Depreciation Expense		
Year	Straight-Line Method	Units-of-Production Method	Double-Declining-Balance Method

---

PR 9-3A
Depreciation by three methods; partial years
obj. 2

✔ a. 2008, $7,600

Razar Sharp Company purchased tool sharpening equipment on July 1, 2008, for $48,600. The equipment was expected to have a useful life of three years, or 7,500 operating hours, and a residual value of $3,000. The equipment was used for 1,800 hours during 2008, 2,600 hours in 2009, 2,000 hours in 2010, and 1,100 hours in 2011.

Instructions

Determine the amount of depreciation expense for the years ended December 31, 2008, 2009, 2010, and 2011, by (a) the straight-line method, (b) the units-of-production method, and (c) the double-declining-balance method.

PR 9-4A
Depreciation by two methods; sale of fixed asset
objs. 2, 3

New tire retreading equipment, acquired at a cost of $144,000 at the beginning of a fiscal year, has an estimated useful life of four years and an estimated residual value of $10,800. The manager requested information regarding the effect of alternative methods on the amount of depreciation expense each year. On the basis of the data presented to the manager, the double-declining-balance method was selected.

✔ 1. b. Year 1,
$72,000 depreciation
expense

In the first week of the fourth year, the equipment was sold for $19,750.

Instructions

1. Determine the annual depreciation expense for each of the estimated four years of use, the accumulated depreciation at the end of each year, and the book value of the equipment at the end of each year by (a) the straight-line method and (b) the double-declining-balance method. The following columnar headings are suggested for each schedule:

Year	Depreciation Expense	Accumulated Depreciation, End of Year	Book Value, End of Year

2. Journalize the entry to record the sale.
3. Journalize the entry to record the sale, assuming that the equipment sold for $14,900 instead of $19,750.

PR 9-5A
Transactions for fixed assets, including sale
objs. **1, 2, 3**

The following transactions, adjusting entries, and closing entries were completed by King Furniture Co. during a three-year period. All are related to the use of delivery equipment. The double-declining-balance method of depreciation is used.

2008

Jan. 7.   Purchased a used delivery truck for $45,600, paying cash.

Feb. 27.   Paid garage $130 for changing the oil, replacing the oil filter, and tuning the engine on the delivery truck.

Dec. 31.   Recorded depreciation on the truck for the fiscal year. The estimated useful life of the truck is eight years, with a residual value of $10,000 for the truck.

2009

Jan. 8.   Purchased a new truck for $75,000, paying cash.

Mar. 13.   Paid garage $200 to tune the engine and make other minor repairs on the used truck.

Apr. 30.   Sold the used truck for $30,000. (Record depreciation to date in 2009 for the truck.)

Dec. 31.   Record depreciation for the new truck. It has an estimated trade-in value of $13,500 and an estimated life of 10 years.

2010

July 1.   Purchased a new truck for $82,000, paying cash.

Oct. 4.   Sold the truck purchased January 8, 2009, for $53,000. (Record depreciation for the year.)

Dec. 31.   Recorded depreciation on the remaining truck. It has an estimated residual value of $15,000 and an estimated useful life of 10 years.

Instructions
Journalize the transactions and the adjusting entries.

PR 9-6A
Amortization and depletion entries
objs. **4, 5**

✔ 1. b. $33,750

Data related to the acquisition of timber rights and intangible assets during the current year ended December 31 are as follows:

a. On December 31, the company determined that $20,000,000 of goodwill was impaired.

b. Governmental and legal costs of $675,000 were incurred on June 30 in obtaining a patent with an estimated economic life of 10 years. Amortization is to be for one-half year.

c. Timber rights on a tract of land were purchased for $1,665,000 on February 16. The stand of timber is estimated at 9,000,000 board feet. During the current year, 2,400,000 board feet of timber were cut and sold.

Instructions

1. Determine the amount of the amortization, depletion, or impairment for the current year for each of the foregoing items.

2. Journalize the adjusting entries to record the amortization, depletion, or impairment for each item.

Problems Series B

PR 9-1B
Allocate payments and receipts to fixed asset accounts

obj. 1

✔ Land, $356,200

The following payments and receipts are related to land, land improvements, and buildings acquired for use in a wholesale ceramic business. The receipts are identified by an asterisk.

a.	Fee paid to attorney for title search	$ 1,500
b.	Cost of real estate acquired as a plant site: Land	270,000
	Building	30,000
c.	Special assessment paid to city for extension of water main to the property	20,000
d.	Cost of razing and removing building	5,000
e.	Proceeds from sale of salvage materials from old building	3,600*
f.	Delinquent real estate taxes on property, assumed by purchaser ...	15,800
g.	Premium on one-year insurance policy during construction	4,200
h.	Cost of filling and grading land	17,500
i.	Architect's and engineer's fees for plans and supervision	18,000
j.	Money borrowed to pay building contractor	750,000*
k.	Cost of repairing windstorm damage during construction	4,500
l.	Cost of paving parking lot to be used by customers	15,000
m.	Cost of trees and shrubbery planted	9,000
n.	Cost of floodlights installed on parking lot	1,100
o.	Cost of repairing vandalism damage during construction	1,500
p.	Proceeds from insurance company for windstorm and vandalism damage	6,000*
q.	Payment to building contractor for new building	800,000
r.	Interest incurred on building loan during construction	45,000
s.	Refund of premium on insurance policy (g) canceled after 11 months	350*

Instructions

1. Assign each payment and receipt to Land (unlimited life), Land Improvements (limited life), Building, or Other Accounts. Indicate receipts by an asterisk. Identify each item by letter and list the amounts in columnar form, as follows:

Item	Land	Land Improvements	Building	Other Accounts

2. Determine the amount debited to Land, Land Improvements, and Building.
3. ➤ The costs assigned to the land, which is used as a plant site, will not be depreciated, while the costs assigned to land improvements will be depreciated. Explain this seemingly contradictory application of the concept of depreciation.

PR 9-2B
Compare three depreciation methods

obj. 2

✔ a. 2008: straight-line depreciation, $21,000

Mammoth Company purchased packaging equipment on January 3, 2008, for $67,500. The equipment was expected to have a useful life of three years, or 25,000 operating hours, and a residual value of $4,500. The equipment was used for 12,000 hours during 2008, 9,000 hours in 2009, and 4,000 hours in 2010.

Instructions

Determine the amount of depreciation expense for the years ended December 31, 2008, 2009, and 2010, by (a) the straight-line method, (b) the units-of-production method, and (c) the double-declining-balance method. Also determine the total depreciation expense for the three years by each method. The following columnar headings are suggested for recording the depreciation expense amounts:

	Depreciation Expense		
Year	Straight-Line Method	Units-of-Production Method	Double-Declining-Balance Method

PR 9-3B

Depreciation by three methods; partial years

obj. 2

✔ a. 2008: $2,510

Quality IDs Company purchased plastic laminating equipment on July 1, 2008, for $15,660. The equipment was expected to have a useful life of three years, or 18,825 operating hours, and a residual value of $600. The equipment was used for 3,750 hours during 2008, 7,500 hours in 2009, 5,000 hours in 2010, and 2,575 hours in 2011.

Instructions

Determine the amount of depreciation expense for the years ended December 31, 2008, 2009, 2010, and 2011, by (a) the straight-line method, (b) the units-of-production method, and (c) the double-declining-balance method. Round to the nearest dollar.

PR 9-4B

Depreciation by two methods; sale of fixed asset

objs. 2, 3

✔ 1. b. Year 1: $52,500 depreciation expense

New lithographic equipment, acquired at a cost of $131,250 at the beginning of a fiscal year, has an estimated useful life of five years and an estimated residual value of $11,250. The manager requested information regarding the effect of alternative methods on the amount of depreciation expense each year. On the basis of the data presented to the manager, the double-declining-balance method was selected.

In the first week of the fifth year, the equipment was sold for $21,500.

Instructions

1. Determine the annual depreciation expense for each of the estimated five years of use, the accumulated depreciation at the end of each year, and the book value of the equipment at the end of each year by (a) the straight-line method and (b) the double-declining-balance method. The following columnar headings are suggested for each schedule:

Year	Depreciation Expense	Accumulated Depreciation, End of Year	Book Value, End of Year

2. Journalize the entry to record the sale.
3. Journalize the entry to record the sale, assuming that the equipment was sold for $12,500 instead of $21,500.

PR 9-5B

Transactions for fixed assets, including sale

objs. 1, 2, 3

The following transactions, adjusting entries, and closing entries were completed by Trail Creek Furniture Co. during a three-year period. All are related to the use of delivery equipment. The double-declining-balance method of depreciation is used.

2008

Jan. 6.   Purchased a used delivery truck for $24,000, paying cash.
July 19. Paid garage $500 for miscellaneous repairs to the truck.
Dec. 31. Recorded depreciation on the truck for the year. The estimated useful life of the truck is four years, with a residual value of $4,000 for the truck.

2009

Jan. 2.   Purchased a new truck for $69,000, paying cash.
Aug. 1.   Sold the used truck for $10,250. (Record depreciation to date in 2009 for the truck.)
Oct. 24. Paid garage $415 for miscellaneous repairs to the truck.
Dec. 31. Record depreciation for the new truck. It has an estimated residual value of $15,000 and an estimated life of five years.

2010

July 1.   Purchased a new truck for $70,000, paying cash.
Oct. 1.   Sold the truck purchased January 2, 2009, for $25,000. (Record depreciation for the year.)
Dec. 31. Recorded depreciation on the remaining truck. It has an estimated residual value of $18,000 and an estimated useful life of eight years.

Instructions

Journalize the transactions and the adjusting entries.

PR 9-6B
Amortization and
depletion entries

objs. **4, 5**

✔ 1. a. $356,200

Data related to the acquisition of timber rights and intangible assets during the current year ended December 31 are as follows:

a. Timber rights on a tract of land were purchased for $1,170,000 on July 5. The stand of timber is estimated at 4,500,000 board feet. During the current year, 1,370,000 board feet of timber were cut and sold.

b. On December 31, the company determined that $5,000,000 of goodwill was impaired.

c. Governmental and legal costs of $234,000 were incurred on April 4 in obtaining a patent with an estimated economic life of 12 years. Amortization is to be for three-fourths of a year.

Instructions

1. Determine the amount of the amortization, depletion, or impairment for the current year for each of the foregoing items.

2. Journalize the adjusting entries required to record the amortization, depletion, or impairment for each item.

Special Activities

SA 9-1
Ethics and profes-
sional conduct in
business

Esteban Appleby, CPA, is an assistant to the controller of Summerfield Consulting Co. In his spare time, Esteban also prepares tax returns and performs general accounting services for clients. Frequently, Esteban performs these services after his normal working hours, using Summerfield Consulting Co.'s computers and laser printers. Occasionally, Esteban's clients will call him at the office during regular working hours. ➤ Discuss whether Esteban is performing in a professional manner.

SA 9-2
Financial vs. tax
depreciation

The following is an excerpt from a conversation between two employees of Quantum Technologies, Pat Gapp and Faye Dalby. Pat is the accounts payable clerk, and Faye is the cashier.

Pat: Faye, could I get your opinion on something?

Faye: Sure, Pat.

Pat: Do you know Julie, the fixed assets clerk?

Faye: I know who she is, but I don't know her real well. Why?

Pat: Well, I was talking to her at lunch last Monday about how she liked her job, etc. You know, the usual . . . and she mentioned something about having to keep two sets of books . . . one for taxes and one for the financial statements. That can't be good accounting, can it? What do you think?

Faye: Two sets of books? It doesn't sound right.

Pat: It doesn't seem right to me either. I was always taught that you had to use generally accepted accounting principles. How can there be two sets of books? What can be the difference between the two?

➤ How would you respond to Faye and Pat if you were Julie?

SA 9-3
Effect of depreciation
on net income

Lonesome Dove Construction Co. specializes in building replicas of historic houses. Mike Jahn, president of Lonesome Dove Construction, is considering the purchase of various items of equipment on July 1, 2008, for $200,000. The equipment would have a useful life of five years and no residual value. In the past, all equipment has been leased. For tax purposes, Mike is considering depreciating the equipment by the straight-line method. He discussed the matter with his CPA and learned that, although the straight-line method could be elected, it was to his advantage to use the Modified Accelerated Cost Recovery System (MACRS) for tax purposes. He asked for your advice as to which method to use for tax purposes.

1. Compute depreciation for each of the years (2008, 2009, 2010, 2011, 2012, and 2013) of useful life by (a) the straight-line method and (b) MACRS. In using the straight-line method, one-half year's depreciation should be computed for 2008 and 2013. Use the MACRS rates presented on page 404.

2. Assuming that income before depreciation and income tax is estimated to be $500,000 uniformly per year and that the income tax rate is 40%, compute the net

income for each of the years 2008, 2009, 2010, 2011, 2012, and 2013, if (a) the straight-line method is used and (b) MACRS is used.

3. ━━━▶ What factors would you present for Mike's consideration in the selection of a depreciation method?

SA 9-4
Shopping for a delivery truck

Group Project

You are planning to acquire a delivery truck for use in your business for five years. In groups of three or four, explore a local dealer's purchase and leasing options for the truck. Summarize the costs of purchasing versus leasing, and list other factors that might help you decide whether to buy or lease the truck.

SA 9-5
Applying for patents, copyrights, and trademarks

Internet Project

Go to the Internet and review the procedures for applying for a patent, a copyright, and a trademark. One Internet site that is useful for this purpose is **idresearch.com,** which is linked to the text's Web site at **academic.cengage.com/accounting/warren.** Prepare a written summary of these procedures.

SA 9-6
Fixed asset turnover: three industries

The following table shows the revenues and average net fixed assets for a recent fiscal year for three different companies from three different industries: retailing, manufacturing, and communications.

	Revenues (in millions)	Average Net Fixed Assets (in millions)
Wal-Mart	$348,650	$83,865
Alcoa Inc.	30,379	14,495
Comcast Corporation	24,966	20,009

a. For each company, determine the fixed asset turnover ratio. Round to two decimal places.
b. Explain Wal-Mart's ratio relative to the other two companies.

Answers to Self-Examination Questions

1. **C** All amounts spent to get a fixed asset (such as machinery) in place and ready for use are proper charges to the asset account. In the case of machinery acquired, the freight (answer A) and the installation costs (answer B) are both (answer C) proper charges to the machinery account.

2. **C** The periodic charge for depreciation under the double-declining-balance method for the second year is determined by first computing the depreciation charge for the first year. The depreciation for the first year of $6,000 (answer A) is computed by multiplying the cost of the equipment, $9,000, by 2/3 (the straight-line rate of 1/3 multiplied by 2). The depreciation for the second year of $2,000 (answer C) is then determined by multiplying the book value at the end of the

first year, $3,000 (the cost of $9,000 minus the first-year depreciation of $6,000), by 2/3. The third year's depreciation is $400 (answer D). It is determined by multiplying the book value at the end of the second year, $1,000, by 2/3, thus yielding $667. However, the equipment cannot be depreciated below its residual value of $600; thus, the third-year depreciation is $400 ($1,000 − $600).

3. **B** A depreciation method that provides for a higher depreciation amount in the first year of the use of an asset and a gradually declining periodic amount thereafter is called an accelerated depreciation method. The double-declining-balance method (answer B) is an example of such a method.

4. **A** A gain of $3,500 was recognized on the sale of the equipment as shown below.

Annual depreciation ($80,000 − $7,500)/5 years	$14,500 (Answer B)
Cost of equipment	$80,000
Accumulated depreciation on December 31, 2010 ($14,500 × 3)	43,500 (Answer D)
Book value of equipment on December 31, 2010	$36,500 (Answer C)
Selling price	$40,000
Book value of equipment on December 31, 2010	36,500
Gain on sale of equipment	$ 3,500

5. **D** Long-lived assets that are useful in operations, not held for sale, and without physical qualities are called intangible assets. Patents, goodwill, and copyrights are examples of intangible assets (answer D).

CHAPTER 10

Current Liabilities and Payroll

PANERA BREAD

anks and other financial institutions provide loans or credit to buyers for purchases of various items. Using credit to purchase items is probably as old as commerce itself. In fact, the Babylonians were lending money to support trade as early as 1300 B.C. The use of credit provides *individuals* convenience and buying power. Credit cards provide individuals convenience over writing checks and make purchasing over the Internet easier. Credit cards also provide individuals control over cash by providing documentation of their purchases through receipt of monthly credit card statements and by allowing them to avoid carrying large amounts of cash and to purchase items before they are paid.

Short-term credit is also used by *businesses* to provide convenience in purchasing items for manufacture or resale. More importantly, short-term credit gives a business control over the payment for goods and services. For example, Panera Bread, a chain of bakery-cafés located

throughout the United States, uses short-term trade credit, or accounts payable, to purchase ingredients for making bread products in its bakeries. Short-term trade credit gives Panera control over cash payments by separating the purchase function from the payment function. Thus, the employee responsible for purchasing the bakery ingredients is separated from the employee responsible for paying for the purchase. This separation of duties can help prevent unauthorized purchases or payments.

In addition to accounts payable, a business like Panera Bread can also have current liabilities related to payroll, payroll taxes, employee benefits, short-term notes, unearned revenue, and contingencies. We will discuss each of these types of current liabilities in this chapter.

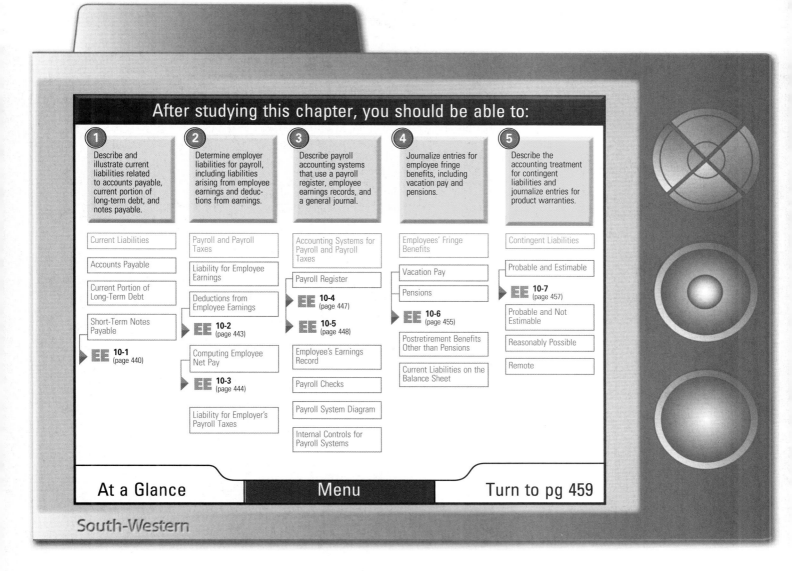

After studying this chapter, you should be able to:

1 Describe and illustrate current liabilities related to accounts payable, current portion of long-term debt, and notes payable.

2 Determine employer liabilities for payroll, including liabilities arising from employee earnings and deductions from earnings.

3 Describe payroll accounting systems that use a payroll register, employee earnings records, and a general journal.

4 Journalize entries for employee fringe benefits, including vacation pay and pensions.

5 Describe the accounting treatment for contingent liabilities and journalize entries for product warranties.

Current Liabilities

Accounts Payable

Current Portion of Long-Term Debt

Short-Term Notes Payable

EE 10-1 (page 440)

Payroll and Payroll Taxes

Liability for Employee Earnings

Deductions from Employee Earnings

EE 10-2 (page 443)

Computing Employee Net Pay

EE 10-3 (page 444)

Liability for Employer's Payroll Taxes

Accounting Systems for Payroll and Payroll Taxes

Payroll Register

EE 10-4 (page 447)

EE 10-5 (page 448)

Employee's Earnings Record

Payroll Checks

Payroll System Diagram

Internal Controls for Payroll Systems

Employees' Fringe Benefits

Vacation Pay

Pensions

EE 10-6 (page 455)

Postretirement Benefits Other than Pensions

Current Liabilities on the Balance Sheet

Contingent Liabilities

Probable and Estimable

EE 10-7 (page 457)

Probable and Not Estimable

Reasonably Possible

Remote

At a Glance   **Menu**   **Turn to pg 459**

South-Western

1 Describe and illustrate current liabilities related to accounts payable, current portion of long-term debt, and notes payable.

Current Liabilities

When a company or a bank advances *credit,* it is making a loan. The company or bank is called a *creditor* (or *lender*). The individuals or companies receiving the loan are called *debtors* (or *borrowers*).

Debt is recorded as a liability by the debtor. *Long-term liabilities* are debt due beyond one year. Thus, a 30-year mortgage used to purchase property is a long-term liability. *Current liabilities* are debt that will be paid out of current assets and are due within one year.

Three types of current liabilities are discussed in this section—accounts payable, current portion of long-term debt, and notes payable.

Accounts Payable

Accounts payable transactions have been described and illustrated in earlier chapters. These transactions involved a variety of purchases on account, including the purchase of merchandise and supplies. For most companies, accounts payable is the largest current liability. Exhibit 1 shows the accounts payable balance as a percent of total current liabilities for a number of companies.

Exhibit 1

Accounts Payable as a Percent of Total Current Liabilities

Company	Accounts Payable as a Percent of Total Current Liabilities
Alcoa Inc.	39%
AT&T	16
Gap Inc.	47
IBM	22
Nissan Motor Co. Ltd.	25
Rite Aid Corp.	51
ChevronTexaco	54

Current Portion of Long-Term Debt

Long-term liabilities are often paid back in periodic payments, called *installments*. Such installments that are due *within* the coming year are classified as a current liability. The installments due *after* the coming year are classified as a long-term liability.

To illustrate, Starbucks Corporation reported the following debt payments schedule in its September 30, 2007, annual report to shareholders:

Fiscal year ending	
2008	$ 775,000
2009	789,000
2010	337,000
2011	56,000
2012	0
Thereafter	550,000,000
Total principal payments	$551,957,000

The debt of $775,000 due in 2008 would be reported as a current liability on the September 30, 2007, balance sheet. The remaining debt of $551,182,000 ($551,957,000 − $775,000) would be reported as a long-term liability on the balance sheet.

Short-Term Notes Payable

Notes may be issued to purchase merchandise or other assets. Notes may also be issued to creditors to satisfy an account payable created earlier.[1]

To illustrate, assume that Nature's Sunshine Company issued a 90-day, 12% note for $1,000, dated August 1, 2009, to Murray Co. for a $1,000 overdue account. The entry to record the issuance of the note is as follows:

Aug.	1	Accounts Payable—Murray Co.	1,000	
		Notes Payable		1,000
		Issued a 90-day, 12% note on account.		

---

1 The accounting for notes received to satisfy an account receivable was described and illustrated in Chapter 8, Receivables.

When the note matures, the entry to record the payment of $1,000 plus $30 interest ($1,000 × 12% × 90/360) is as follows:

Oct.	30	Notes Payable	1,000	
		Interest Expense	30	
		Cash		1,030
		Paid principal and interest due on note.		

The interest expense is reported in the Other expense section of the income statement for the year ended December 31, 2009. The interest expense account is closed at December 31.

Each note transaction affects a debtor (borrower) and creditor (lender). The following illustration shows how the same transactions are recorded by the debtor and creditor. In this illustration, the debtor (borrower) is Bowden Co., and the creditor (lender) is Coker Co.

	Bowden Co. (Borrower)			**Coker Co. (Creditor)**		
May 1. Bowden Co. purchased merchandise on account from Coker Co., $10,000, 2/10, n/30. The merchandise cost Coker Co. $7,500.	Merchandise Inventory Accounts Payable	10,000	10,000	Accounts Receivable Sales	10,000	10,000
				Cost of Merchandise Sold Merchandise Inventory	7,500	7,500
May 31. Bowden Co. issued a 60-day, 12% note for $10,000 to Coker Co. on account.	Accounts Payable Notes Payable	10,000	10,000	Notes Receivable Accounts Receivable	10,000	10,000
July 30. Bowden Co. paid Coker Co. the amount due on the note of May 31. Interest: $10,000 × 12% × 60/360.	Notes Payable Interest Expense Cash	10,000 200	10,200	Cash Interest Revenue Notes Receivable	10,200	200 10,000

A company may borrow from a bank by issuing a note. To illustrate, assume that on September 19 Iceburg Company issues a $4,000, 90-day, 15% note to First National Bank. The entry to record the issuance of the note is as follows:

Sept.	19	Cash	4,000	
		Notes Payable		4,000
		Issued a 90-day, 15% note to First National Bank.		

On the due date of the note (December 18), Iceburg Company owes $4,000 plus interest of $150 ($4,000 × 15% × 90/360). The entry to record the payment of the note is as follows:

Dec.	18	Notes Payable	4,000	
		Interest Expense	150	
		Cash		4,150
		Paid principal and interest due on note.		

The U.S. Treasury issues short-term treasury bills to investors at a discount.

In some cases, a *discounted note* may be issued rather than an interest-bearing note. A discounted note has the following characteristics:

1. The creditor (lender) requires an interest rate, called the *discount rate*.
2. Interest, called the *discount*, is computed on the face amount of the note.
3. The debtor (borrower) receives the face amount of the note less the discount, called the *proceeds*.
4. The debtor pays the face amount of the note on the due date.

To illustrate, assume that on August 10, Cary Company issues a $20,000, 90-day discounted note to Western National Bank. The discount rate is 15%, and the amount of the discount is $750 ($20,000 × 15% × 90/360). Thus, the proceeds received by Cary Company are $19,250. The entry by Cary Company is as follows:

Aug.	10	Cash	19,250	
		Interest Expense	750	
		Notes Payable		20,000
		Issued a 90-day discounted note to Western National Bank at a 15% discount rate.		

The entry when Cary Company pays the discounted note on November 8 is as follows:[2]

Nov.	8	Notes Payable	20,000	
		Cash		20,000
		Paid note due.		

Other current liabilities that have been discussed in earlier chapters include accrued expenses, unearned revenue, and interest payable. The accounting for wages and salaries, termed *payroll accounting*, is discussed next.

Example Exercise 10-1 Proceeds from Notes Payable

On July 1, Bella Salon Company issued a 60-day note with a face amount of $60,000 to Delilah Hair Products Company for merchandise inventory.

a. Determine the proceeds of the note, assuming the note carries an interest rate of 6%.
b. Determine the proceeds of the note, assuming the note is discounted at 6%.

Follow My Example 10-1

a. $60,000.
b. $59,400 [$60,000 − ($60,000 × 6% × 60/360)].

....

For Practice: PE 10-1A, PE 10-1B

---

2 If the accounting period ends before a discounted note is paid, an adjusting entry should record the prepaid (deferred) interest that is not yet an expense. This deferred interest would be deducted from Notes Payable in the Current Liabilities section of the balance sheet.

Determine employer liabilities for payroll, including liabilities arising from employee earnings and deductions from earnings.

Payroll and Payroll Taxes

In accounting, **payroll** refers to the amount paid employees for services they provided during the period. A company's payroll is important for the following reasons:

1. Employees are sensitive to payroll errors and irregularities.
2. Good employee morale requires payroll to be paid timely and accurately.
3. Payroll is subject to federal and state regulations.
4. Payroll and related payroll taxes significantly affect the net income of most companies.

Liability for Employee Earnings

Salary usually refers to payment for managerial and administrative services. Salary is normally expressed in terms of a month or a year. *Wages* usually refers to payment for employee manual labor. The rate of wages is normally stated on an hourly or a weekly

> **Employee salaries and wages are expenses to an employer.**

basis. The salary or wage of an employee may be increased by bonuses, commissions, profit sharing, or cost-of-living adjustments.

Companies engaged in interstate commerce must follow the Fair Labor Standards Act. This act, sometimes called the Federal Wage and Hour Law, requires employers to pay a minimum rate of $1\frac{1}{2}$ times the regular rate for all hours worked in excess of 40 hours per week. Exemptions are provided for executive, administrative, and some supervisory positions. Increased rates for working overtime, nights, or holidays are common, even when not required by law. These rates may be as much as twice the regular rate.

Information on average salaries for a variety of professions can be found on Internet job sites such as **monster.com**.

To illustrate computing an employee's earnings, assume that John T. McGrath is a salesperson employed by McDermott Supply Co. McGrath's regular rate is $34 per hour, and any hours worked in excess of 40 hours per week are paid at $1\frac{1}{2}$ times the regular rate. McGrath worked 42 hours for the week ended December 27. His earnings of **$1,462** for the week are computed as follows:

Earnings at regular rate (40 hrs. × $34)	$1,360
Earnings at overtime rate [2 hrs. × ($34 × $1\frac{1}{2}$)]	102
Total earnings	**$1,462**

Deductions from Employee Earnings

The total earnings of an employee for a payroll period, including any overtime pay, are called **gross pay**. From this amount is subtracted one or more *deductions* to arrive at the **net pay**. Net pay is the amount paid the employee. The deductions normally include federal, state, and local income taxes, medical insurance, and pension contributions.

Income Taxes Employers normally withhold a portion of employee earnings for payment of the employees' federal income tax. Each employee authorizes the amount to be withheld by completing an "Employee's Withholding Allowance Certificate," called a W-4. Exhibit 2 is the W-4 form submitted by John T. McGrath.

On the W-4, an employee indicates marital status and the number of withholding allowances. A single employee may claim one withholding allowance. A married employee may claim an additional allowance for a spouse. An employee may also claim an allowance for each dependent other than a spouse. Each allowance reduces the federal income tax withheld from the employee's check. Exhibit 2 indicates that John T. McGrath is single and, thus, claimed one withholding allowance.

The federal income tax withheld depends on each employee's gross pay and W-4 allowance. Withholding tables issued by the Internal Revenue Service (IRS) are used to determine amounts to withhold. Exhibit 3 is an example of an IRS wage withholding table for a single person who is paid weekly.[3]

---

3 IRS withholding tables are also available for married employees and for pay periods other than weekly.

Exhibit 2

Employee's Withholding Allowance Certificate (W-4 Form)

Cut here and give Form W-4 to your employer. Keep the top part for your records.

Form **W-4**	**Employee's Withholding Allowance Certificate**	OMB No. 1545-0074
Department of the Treasury Internal Revenue Service	▶ Whether you are entitled to claim a certain number of allowances or exemption from withholding is subject to review by the IRS. Your employer may be required to send a copy of this form to the IRS.	**2008**

1 Type or print your first name and middle initial. **John T.**	Last name **McGrath**	2 Your social security number **381 ¦ 48¦ 9120**

Home address (number and street or rural route)
1830 4th Street

3 ☒ Single ☐ Married ☐ Married, but withhold at higher Single rate.
Note. If married, but legally separated, or spouse is a nonresident alien, check the "Single" box.

City or town, state, and ZIP code
Clinton, Iowa 52732-6142

4 If your last name differs from that shown on your social security card, check here. You must call 1-800-772-1213 for a new card. ▶ ☐

5	Total number of allowances you are claiming (from line **H** above **or** from the applicable worksheet on page 2)	5	1
6	Additional amount, if any, you want withheld from each paycheck	6	$
7	I claim exemption from withholding for 2008, and I certify that I meet **both** of the following conditions for exemption.		

• Last year I had a right to a refund of **all** federal income tax withheld because I had **no** tax liability and
• This year I expect a refund of **all** federal income tax withheld because I expect to have **no** tax liability.
If you meet both conditions, write "Exempt" here . . . . ▶ | 7 |

Under penalties of perjury, I declare that I have examined this certificate and to the best of my knowledge and belief, it is true, correct, and complete.

Employee's signature
(Form is not valid unless you sign it.) ▶ *John T. McGrath*   Date ▶ June 2, 2008

8 Employer's name and address (Employer: Complete lines 8 and 10 only if sending to the IRS.)	9 Office code (optional)	10 Employer identification number (EIN)

Cat. No. 10220Q   Form **W-4** (2008)

In Exhibit 3, each row is the employee's wages after deducting the employee's withholding allowances. Each year, the amount of the standard withholding allowance is determined by the IRS. For a single person paid weekly, we assume the standard withholding allowance to be deducted in Exhibit 3 is $67.[4] Thus, if two withholding allowances are claimed, $134 ($67 × 2) is deducted.

To illustrate, John T. McGrath made $1,462 for the week ended December 27. McGrath's W-4 claims one withholding allowance of $67. Thus, the wages used in determining McGrath's withholding bracket in Exhibit 3 are $1,395 ($1,462 − $67).

After the person's withholding wage bracket has been computed, the federal income tax to be withheld is determined as follows:

Step 1. Locate the proper withholding wage bracket in Exhibit 3.

McGrath's wages after deducting one standard IRS withholding allowance are $1,395 ($1,462 − $67). Therefore, the wage bracket for McGrath is $653–$1,533.

Step 2. Compute the withholding for the proper wage bracket using the directions in the two right-hand columns in Exhibit 3.

For McGrath's wage bracket, the withholding is computed as "$82.95 plus 25% of the excess over $653." Hence, McGrath's withholding is $268.45, as shown below.

Initial withholding from wage bracket	$ 82.95
Plus [25% × ($1,395 − $653)]	185.50
Total withholding	$268.45

Exhibit 3

Wage Bracket Withholding Table

Table for Percentage Method of Withholding WEEKLY Payroll Period

(a) SINGLE person (including head of household) —

If the amount of wages (after subtracting withholding allowances) is:		The amount of income tax to withhold is:	
Not over $51		$0	

Over—	But not over—		of excess over—
$51	—$198 . .	10%	—$51
$198	—$653 . .	$14.70 plus 15%	—$198
$653	—$1,533 . .	$82.95 plus 25%	—$653	◀— McGrath wage bracket
$1,533	—$3,202 . .	$302.95 plus 28%	—$1,533
$3,202	—$6,916 . .	$770.27 plus 33%	—$3,202
$6,916	. . . .	$1,995.89 plus 35%	—$6,916

Source: Publication 15, *Employer's Tax Guide*, Internal Revenue Service, 2008.

4 The actual IRS standard withholding allowance changes every year and was $67.31 for 2008.

Residents of New York City must pay federal, state, and city income taxes.

Employers may also be required to withhold state or city income taxes. The amounts to be withheld are determined on state-by-state and city-by-city bases.

Example Exercise 10-2   Federal Income Tax Withholding ········⟩ 2

Karen Dunn's weekly gross earnings for the present week were $2,250. Dunn has two exemptions. Using the wage bracket withholding table in Exhibit 3 with a $67 standard withholding allowance for each exemption, what is Dunn's federal income tax withholding?

Follow My Example 10-2

Total wage payment		$ 2,250
One allowance (provided by IRS)	$67	
Multiplied by allowances claimed on Form W-4	× 2	134
Amount subject to withholding		$ 2,116
Initial withholding from wage bracket in Exhibit 3		$302.95
Plus additional withholding: 28% of excess over $1,533		163.24*
Federal income tax withholding		$466.19

*28% × ($2,116 − $1,533)

For Practice: PE 10-2A, PE 10-2B

FICA Tax Employers are required by the Federal Insurance Contributions Act (FICA) to withhold a portion of the earnings of each employee. The **FICA tax** withheld contributes to the following two federal programs:

1. *Social security*, which provides payments for retirees, survivors, and disability insurance (OASDI).
2. *Medicare*, which provides health insurance for senior citizens.

The amount withheld from each employee is based on the employee's earnings *paid* in the *calendar* year. The withholding tax rates and maximum earnings subject to tax are often revised by Congress. To simplify, this chapter assumes the following rates and earnings subject to tax:

1. Social security: 6% on the first $100,000 of annual earnings
2. Medicare: 1.5% on all earnings

To illustrate, assume that John T. McGrath's annual earnings prior to the payroll period ending on December 27 total $99,038. Since McGrath's earnings for the week are $1,462, the total FICA tax to be withheld is **$79.65**, as shown below.

Earnings subject to 6% social security tax		
($100,000 − $99,038)	$ 962	
Social security tax rate	× 6%	
Social security tax		$57.72
Earnings subject to 1.5% Medicare tax	$1,462	
Medicare tax rate	× 1.5%	
Medicare tax		21.93
Total FICA tax		$79.65

Other Deductions Employees may choose to have additional amounts deducted from their gross pay. For example, an employee may authorize deductions for retirement savings, charitable contributions, or life insurance. A union contract may also require the deduction of union dues.

Computing Employee Net Pay

Gross earnings less payroll deductions equals *net pay*, sometimes called *take-home pay*. Assuming that John T. McGrath authorized deductions for retirement savings and for a United Fund contribution, McGrath's net pay for the week ended December 27 is $1,088.90, as shown below.

Gross earnings for the week		$1,462.00
Deductions:		
Social security tax	$ 57.72	
Medicare tax	21.93	
Federal income tax	268.45	
Retirement savings	20.00	
United Fund	5.00	
Total deductions		373.10
Net pay		$1,088.90

Example Exercise 10-3 Employee Net Pay ••••••••> 2

Karen Dunn's weekly gross earnings for the week ending December 3 were $2,250, and her federal income tax withholding was $466.19. Prior to this week, Dunn had earned $98,000 for the year. Assuming the social security rate is 6% on the first $100,000 of annual earnings and Medicare is 1.5% of all earnings, what is Dunn's net pay?

Follow My Example 10-3

Total wage payment			$2,250.00
Less: Federal income tax withholding		$466.19	
Earnings subject to social security tax ($100,000 − $98,000)	$2,000		
Social security tax rate	× 6%		
Social security tax		120.00	
Medicare tax ($2,250 × 1.5%)		33.75	619.94
Net pay			$1,630.06

For Practice: PE 10-3A, PE 10-3B

Liability for Employer's Payroll Taxes

Employers are subject to the following payroll taxes for amounts paid their employees:

1. *FICA Tax*: Employers must match the employee's FICA tax contribution.

2. *Federal Unemployment Compensation Tax (FUTA)*: This employer tax provides for temporary payments to those who become unemployed. The tax collected by the federal government is allocated among the states for use in state programs rather than paid directly to employees. Congress often revises the FUTA tax rate and maximum earnings subject to tax. In this chapter, the FUTA rate and earnings subject to tax are assumed to be 6.2% on the first $7,000 of annual earnings paid each employee during the calendar year.

3. *State Unemployment Compensation Tax (SUTA)*: This employer tax also provides temporary payments to those who become unemployed. The FUTA and SUTA programs are closely coordinated, with the states distributing the unemployment checks.[5] SUTA tax rates and earnings subject to tax vary by state.[6]

5 This rate may be reduced to 0.8% for credits for state unemployment compensation tax.

6 As of January 1, 2008, the maximum state rate credited against the federal unemployment rate was 5.4% of the first $7,000 of each employee's earnings during a calendar year.

The preceding employer taxes are an operating expense of the company. Exhibit 4 summarizes the responsibility for employee and employer payroll taxes.

Exhibit 4

Responsibility for Tax Payments

Employee		**Business**
Social security tax		Social security tax
Medicare tax	**Government**	Medicare tax
Federal withholding tax		Federal unemployment compensation tax
		State unemployment compensation tax

Business Connection

THE MOST YOU WILL EVER PAY

In 1936, the Social Security Board described how the tax was expected to affect a worker's pay, as follows:

The taxes called for in this law will be paid both by your employer and by you. For the next 3 years you will pay maybe 15 cents a week, maybe 25 cents a week, maybe 30 cents or more, according to what you earn. That is to say, during the next 3 years, beginning January 1, 1937, you will pay 1 cent for every dollar you earn, and at the same time your employer will pay 1 cent for every dollar you earn, up to $3,000 a year. . . .

    . . . Beginning in 1940 you will pay, and your employer will pay, 1½ cents for each dollar you earn, up to $3,000

a year . . . and then beginning in 1943, you will pay 2 cents, and so will your employer, for every dollar you earn for the next three years. After that, you and your employer will each pay half a cent more for 3 years, and finally, beginning in 1949, . . . you and your employer will each pay 3 cents on each dollar you earn, up to $3,000 a year. That is the most you will ever pay.

The rate on January 1, 2008, was 7.65 cents per dollar earned (7.65%). The social security portion was 6.20% on the first $102,000 of earnings. The Medicare portion was 1.45% on all earnings.

Source: Arthur Lodge, "That Is the Most You Will Ever Pay," *Journal of Accountancy*, October 1985, p. 44.

Integrity, Objectivity, and Ethics in Business

RESUMÉ PADDING

Misrepresenting your accomplishments on your resumé could come back to haunt you. In one case, the chief financial officer (CFO) of Veritas Software was forced to resign his position when it was discovered that he had

lied about earning an MBA from Stanford University, when in actuality he had earned only an undergraduate degree from Idaho State University.

Source: Reuters News Service, October 4, 2002.

---

3 Describe payroll accounting systems that use a payroll register, employee earnings records, and a general journal.

Accounting Systems for Payroll and Payroll Taxes

Payroll systems should be designed to:

1. Pay employees accurately and timely.
2. Meet regulatory requirements of federal, state, and local agencies.
3. Provide useful data for management decision-making needs.

Although payroll systems differ among companies, the major elements of most payroll systems are:

1. Payroll register
2. Employee's earnings record
3. Payroll checks

Payroll Register

The **payroll register** is a multicolumn report used for summarizing the data for each payroll period. Although payroll registers vary by company, a payroll register normally includes the following columns:

1. Employee name	8. Federal income tax withheld
2. Total hours worked	9. Retirement savings withheld
3. Regular earnings	10. Miscellaneous items withheld
4. Overtime earnings	11. Total withholdings
5. Total gross earnings	12. Net pay
6. Social security tax withheld	13. Check number of payroll check issued
7. Medicare tax withheld	14. Accounts debited for payroll expense

Exhibit 5 illustrates a payroll register. The right-hand columns of the payroll register indicate the accounts debited for the payroll expense. These columns are often referred to as the *payroll distribution*.

Recording Employees' Earnings The column totals of the payroll register provide the basis for recording the journal entry for payroll. The entry based on the payroll register in Exhibit 5 is shown on the next page.

Payroll taxes become a liability to the employer when the payroll is paid.

Recording and Paying Payroll Taxes Payroll taxes are recorded as liabilities when the payroll is *paid* to employees. In addition, employers compute and report payroll taxes on a *calendar-year* basis, which may differ from the company's fiscal year.

Exhibit 5

Payroll Register

	Employee Name	Total Hours	Earnings		
			Regular	Overtime	Total
1	Abrams, Julie S.	40	500.00		500.00
2	Elrod, Fred G.	44	392.00	58.80	450.80
3	Gomez, Jose C.	40	840.00		840.00
4	McGrath, John T.	42	1,360.00	102.00	1,462.00
25	Wilkes, Glenn K.	40	480.00		480.00
26	Zumpano, Michael W.	40	600.00		600.00
27	Total		13,328.00	574.00	13,902.00
28					

Dec.	27	Sales Salaries Expense	11,122.00	
		Office Salaries Expense	2,780.00	
		Social Security Tax Payable		643.07
		Medicare Tax Payable		208.53
		Employees Federal Income Tax Payable		3,332.00
		Retirement Savings Deductions Payable		680.00
		United Fund Deductions Payable		470.00
		Accounts Receivable—Fred G. Elrod (emp.)		50.00
		Salaries Payable		8,518.40
		Payroll for week ended December 27.		

Example Exercise 10-4   Journalize Period Payroll   ·········▶ ③

The payroll register of Chen Engineering Services indicates $900 of social security withheld and $225 of Medicare tax withheld on total salaries of $15,000 for the period. Federal withholding for the period totaled $2,925.

Provide the journal entry for the period's payroll.

Follow My Example 10-4

Salaries Expense	15,000	
Social Security Tax Payable		900
Medicare Tax Payable		225
Employees Federal Withholding Tax Payable		2,925
Salaries Payable		10,950

For Practice: PE 10-4A, PE 10-4B

To illustrate, assume that Everson Company's fiscal year ends on April 30. Also, assume the following payroll data on December 31, 2009:

Wages owed employees on December 31	$26,000
Wages subject to payroll taxes:	
Social security tax (6.0%)	$18,000
Medicare tax (1.5%)	26,000
State (5.4%) and federal (0.8%)	
unemployment compensation tax	1,000

Exhibit 5   · · · · · · · ·

(Concluded)

	Deductions						Paid		Accounts Debited		
	Social Security Tax	Medicare Tax	Federal Income Tax	Retirement Savings	Misc.	Total	Net Pay	Check No.	Sales Salaries Expense	Office Salaries Expense	
1	30.00	7.50	74.00	20.00	UF 10.00	141.50	358.50	6857	500.00		1
2	27.05	6.76	62.00		AR 50.00	145.81	304.99	6858		450.80	2
3	50.40	12.60	131.00	25.00	UF 10.00	229.00	611.00	6859	840.00		3
4	57.72	21.93	268.45	20.00	UF 5.00	373.10	1,088.90	6860	1,462.00		4
25	28.80	7.20	69.00	10.00		115.00	365.00	6880	480.00		25
26	36.00	9.00	79.00	5.00	UF 2.00	131.00	469.00	6881		600.00	26
27	643.07	208.53	3,332.00	680.00	UF 470.00	5,383.60	8,518.40		11,122.00	2,780.00	27
28					AR 50.00						28

Miscellaneous Deductions: UF—United Fund; AR—Accounts Receivable

If the payroll is paid on December 31, the payroll taxes are computed as follows:

Social security	$1,080 ($18,000 × 6.0%)
Medicare tax	390 ($26,000 × 1.5%)
State unemployment compensation tax (SUTA)	54 ($1,000 × 5.4%)
Federal unemployment compensation tax (FUTA)	8 ($1,000 × 0.8%)
Total payroll taxes	$1,532

If the payroll is paid on January 2, however, the *entire* $26,000 is subject to *all* payroll taxes. This is because the maximum earnings limit for social security and unemployment taxes starts on January 1 of each year. Thus, if the payroll is paid on January 2, the payroll taxes are computed as follows:

Social security	$1,560 ($26,000 × 6.0%)
Medicare tax	390 ($26,000 × 1.5%)
State unemployment compensation tax (SUTA)	1,404 ($26,000 × 5.4%)
Federal unemployment compensation tax (FUTA)	208 ($26,000 × 0.8%)
Total payroll taxes	$3,562

The payroll register in Exhibit 5 indicates that social security tax of $643.07 and Medicare tax of $208.53 were withheld. Employers must match the employees' FICA contributions. Thus, the employer's social security and Medicare payroll tax will also be $643.07 and $208.53, respectively.

Assume that in Exhibit 5 the earnings subject to state and federal unemployment compensation taxes are $2,710. In addition, assume a SUTA rate of 5.4% and a FUTA rate of 0.8%. The payroll taxes based on Exhibit 5 are $1,019.62, as shown below.

Social security	$ 643.07 (from Social Security Tax column of Exhibit 5)
Medicare tax	208.53 (from Medicare Tax column of Exhibit 5)
SUTA	146.34 ($2,710 × 5.4%)
FUTA	21.68 ($2,710 × 0.8%)
Total payroll taxes	$1,019.62

The entry to journalize the payroll tax expense for Exhibit 5 is shown below.

Dec.	27	Payroll Tax Expense	1,019.62	
		Social Security Tax Payable		643.07
		Medicare Tax Payable		208.53
		State Unemployment Tax Payable		146.34
		Federal Unemployment Tax Payable		21.68
		Payroll taxes for week ended		
		December 27.		

The preceding entry records a liability for each payroll tax. When the payroll taxes are paid, an entry is recorded debiting the payroll tax liability accounts and crediting Cash.

Example Exercise 10-5 Journalize Payroll Tax

The payroll register of Chen Engineering Services indicates $900 of social security withheld and $225 of Medicare tax withheld on total salaries of $15,000 for the period. Assume earnings subject to state and federal unemployment compensation taxes are $5,250, at the federal rate of 0.8% and the state rate of 5.4%. Provide the journal entry to record the payroll tax expense for the period.

Follow My Example 10-5

Payroll Tax Expense	1,450.50	
Social Security Tax Payable		900.00
Medicare Tax Payable		225.00
State Unemployment Tax Payable		283.50*
Federal Unemployment Tax Payable		42.00**

*$5,250 × 5.4%

**$5,250 × 0.8%

For Practice: PE 10-5A, PE 10-5B

Employee's Earnings Record

Each employee's earnings to date must be determined at the end of each payroll period. This total is necessary for computing the employee's social security tax withholding and the employer's payroll taxes. Thus, detailed payroll records must be kept for each employee. This record is called an **employee's earnings record**.

Exhibit 6, on pages 450–451, shows a portion of John T. McGrath's employee's earnings record. An employee's earnings record and the payroll register are interrelated. For example, McGrath's earnings record for December 27 can be traced to the fourth line of the payroll register in Exhibit 5.

As shown in Exhibit 6, an employee's earnings record has quarterly and yearly totals. These totals are used for tax, insurance, and other reports. For example, one such report is the Wage and Tax Statement, commonly called a *W-2*. This form is provided annually to each employee as well as to the Social Security Administration. The W-2 shown below is based on John T. McGrath's employee's earnings record shown in Exhibit 6.

22222 Void ☐	a Employee's social security number 381-48-9120	For Office Use Only ▶ OMB No. 1545–0008	
b Employer identification number (EIN) 61-8436524		1 Wages, tips, other compensation 100,500.00	2 Federal income tax withheld 21,387.65
c Employer's name, address, and ZIP code McDermott Supply Co. 415 5th Ave. So. Dubuque, IA 52736-0142		3 Social security wages 100,000.00	4 Social security tax withheld 6,000.00
		5 Medical wages and tips 100,500.00	6 Medicare tax withheld 1,507.50
		7 Social security tips	8 Allocated tips
d Control number		9 Advance EIC payment	10 Dependent care benefits
e Employee's first name and initial Last name Suff. John T. McGrath		11 Nonqualified plans	12a See instructions for box 12
1830 4th St. Clinton, IA 52732-6142		13 Statutory employee ☐ Retirement plan ☐ Third party sick pay ☐	12b
		14 Other	12c
			12d
f Employee's address, and ZIP code			
15 State Employer's state ID number IA	16 State wages, tips, etc. 17 State income tax	18 Local wages, tips, etc. 19 Local income tax	20 Locality name Dubuque

Form **W-2** **Wage and Tax Statement**   **2009**

Copy A For Social Security Administration — Send this entire page with Form W-3 to the Social Security Administration; photocopies are **not** acceptable.

Department of the Treasury—Internal Revenue Service

For Privacy Act and Paperwork Reduction Act Notice, see back of Copy D.

Cat. No. 10134D

Do Not Cut, Fold, or Staple Forms on This Page — Do Not Cut, Fold, or Staple Forms on This Page

Payroll Checks

Companies may pay employees, especially part-time employees, by issuing *payroll checks*. Each check includes a detachable statement showing how the net pay was computed. Exhibit 7, on page 452, illustrates a payroll check for John T. McGrath.

Exhibit 6

Employee's Earnings Record

John T. McGrath
1830 4th St.
Clinton, IA 52732-6142   PHONE: 555-3148

| SINGLE | NUMBER OF WITHHOLDING ALLOWANCES: 1 | PAY RATE: | $1,360.00 Per Week |

OCCUPATION: Salesperson   EQUIVALENT HOURLY RATE: $34

	Period Ending	Total Hours	Regular Earnings	Overtime Earnings	Total Earnings	Total	
42	SEPT. 27	53	1,360.00	663.00	2,023.00	75,565.00	42
43	THIRD QUARTER		17,680.00	7,605.00	25,285.00		43
44	OCT. 4	51	1,360.00	561.00	1,921.00	77,486.00	44
50	NOV. 15	50	1,360.00	510.00	1,870.00	89,382.00	50
51	NOV. 22	53	1,360.00	663.00	2,023.00	91,405.00	51
52	NOV. 29	47	1,360.00	357.00	1,717.00	93,122.00	52
53	DEC. 6	53	1,360.00	663.00	2,023.00	95,145.00	53
54	DEC.13	52	1,360.00	612.00	1,972.00	97,117.00	54
55	DEC. 20	51	1,360.00	561.00	1,921.00	99,038.00	55
56	DEC. 27	42	1,360.00	102.00	1,462.00	100,500.00	56
57	FOURTH QUARTER		17,680.00	7,255.00	24,935.00		57
58	YEARLY TOTAL		70,720.00	29,780.00	100,500.00		58

Most companies issuing payroll checks use a special payroll bank account. In such cases, payroll is processed as follows:

1. The total net pay for the period is determined from the payroll register.
2. The company authorizes an electronic funds transfer (EFT) from its regular bank account to the special payroll bank account for the total net pay.
3. Individual payroll checks are written from the payroll account.
4. The numbers of the payroll checks are inserted in the payroll register.

An advantage of using a separate payroll bank account is that reconciling the bank statements is simplified. In addition, a payroll bank account establishes control over payroll checks and, thus, prevents their theft or misuse.

Many companies use electronic funds transfer to pay their employees. In such cases, each pay period an employee's net pay is deposited directly into the employee checking account. Later, employees receive a payroll statement summarizing how the net pay was computed.

Payroll System Diagram

Exhibit 8, on page 452, shows the flow of data and the interactions among the elements of a payroll system. As shown in Exhibit 8, the inputs into a payroll system may be classified as:

1. Constants, which are data that remain unchanged from payroll to payroll.

    Examples: Employee names, social security numbers, marital status, number of income tax withholding allowances, rates of pay, tax rates, and withholding tables.

Exhibit 6

(Concluded)

SOC. SEC. NO.: 381-48-9120		**EMPLOYEE NO.: 814**

DATE OF BIRTH: February 15, 1982

DATE EMPLOYMENT TERMINATED:

	Deductions						Paid		
	Social Security Tax	**Medicare Tax**	**Federal Income Tax**	**Retirement Savings**	**Other**		**Total**	**Net Amount**	**Check No.**	
42	121.38	30.35	429.83	20.00			601.56	1,421.44	6175	42
43	1,517.10	379.28	5,391.71	260.00	UF	40.00	7,588.09	17,696.91		43
44	115.26	28.82	401.27	20.00			565.35	1,355.65	6225	44
50	112.20	28.05	386.99	20.00			547.24	1,322.76	6530	50
51	121.38	30.35	429.83	20.00			601.56	1,421.44	6582	51
52	103.02	25.76	344.15	20.00			492.93	1,224.07	6640	52
53	121.38	30.35	429.83	20.00	UF	5.00	606.56	1,416.44	6688	53
54	118.32	29.58	415.55	20.00			583.45	1,388.55	6743	54
55	115.26	28.82	401.27	20.00			565.35	1,355.65	6801	55
56	57.72	21.93	268.45	20.00	UF	5.00	373.10	1,088.90	6860	56
57	1,466.10	374.03	5,293.71	260.00	UF	15.00	7,408.84	17,526.16		57
58	6,000.00	1,507.50	21,387.65	1,040.00	UF	100.00	30,035.15	70,464.85		58

Many computerized payroll systems are offered on the Internet for a monthly fee. Internet-based payroll systems have the advantage of maintaining current federal and state tax rates.

2. Variables, which are data that change from payroll to payroll.

   Examples: Number of hours or days worked for each employee, accrued days of sick leave, vacation credits, total earnings to date, and total taxes withheld.

In a computerized accounting system, constants are stored within a payroll file. The variables are input each pay period by a payroll clerk. In some systems, employees swipe their identification (ID) cards when they report for and leave work. In such cases, the hours worked by each employee are automatically updated.

A computerized payroll system also maintains electronic versions of the payroll register and employee earnings records. Payroll system outputs, such as payroll checks, EFTs, and tax records, are automatically produced each pay period.

Internal Controls for Payroll Systems

Payroll frauds often involve a supervisor who cashes the payroll checks of fictitious employees or fired employees who are kept on the payroll.

The cash payment controls described in Chapter 7, *Sarbanes-Oxley, Internal Control, and Cash,* also apply to payrolls. Some examples of payroll controls include the following:

1. If a check-signing machine is used, blank payroll checks and access to the machine should be restricted to prevent their theft or misuse.

2. The hiring and firing of employees should be properly authorized and approved in writing.

3. All changes in pay rates should be properly authorized and approved in writing.

Exhibit 7

Payroll Check

MS McDermott Supply Co.
415 5th Ave. So.
Dubuque, IA 52736-0142

John T. McGrath
1830 4th St.
Clinton, IA 52732-6142

Check Number: 6860
Pay Period Ending: 12/27/09

HOURS & EARNINGS		TAXES & DEDUCTIONS		
DESCRIPTION	AMOUNT	DESCRIPTION	CURRENT AMOUNT	Y-T-D AMOUNT
Rate of Pay Reg.	34	Social Security Tax	57.72	6,000.00
Rate of Pay O.T.	51	Medicare Tax	21.93	1,507.50
Hours Worked Reg.	40	Fed. Income Tax	268.45	21,387.65
Hours Worked O.T.	2	U.S. Savings Bonds	20.00	1,040.00
		United Fund	5.00	100.00
Net Pay	1,088.90			
Total Gross Pay	1,462.00	Total	373.10	30,035.15
Total Gross Y-T-D	100,500.00			

STATEMENT OF EARNINGS. DETACH AND KEEP FOR YOUR RECORDS

MS McDermott Supply Co.
415 5th Ave. So.
Dubuque, IA 52736-0142

Pay Period Ending: 12/27/09

LaGesse Savings & Loan
33 Katie Avenue, Suite 33
Clinton, IA 52736-3581

24-2/531

6860

PAY ONE THOUSAND EIGHTY-EIGHT AND 90/100 . . . . **DOLLARS**

To the Order of   JOHN T. MCGRATH
1830 4TH ST.
CLINTON, IA 52732-6142

$1,088.90

Franklin D. McDermott

⑈6860⑈ ⑆153111123⑆ ⑈938540 2⑈

---

4. Employees should be observed when arriving for work to verify that employees are "checking in" for work only once and only for themselves. Employees may "check in" for work by using a time card or by swiping their employee ID card.

5. Payroll checks should be distributed by someone other than employee supervisors.

6. A special payroll bank account should be used.

Exhibit 8

Flow of Data in a Payroll System

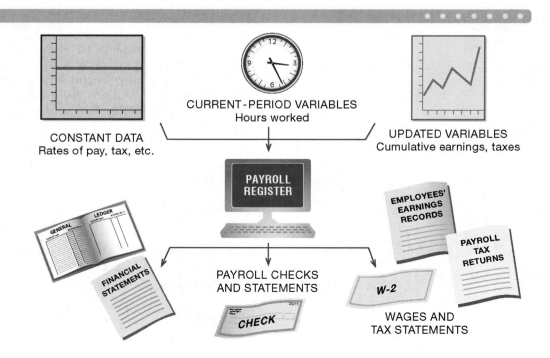

CONSTANT DATA
Rates of pay, tax, etc.

CURRENT-PERIOD VARIABLES
Hours worked

UPDATED VARIABLES
Cumulative earnings, taxes

PAYROLL REGISTER

FINANCIAL STATEMENTS

PAYROLL CHECKS AND STATEMENTS

EMPLOYEES' EARNINGS RECORDS

W-2

PAYROLL TAX RETURNS

WAGES AND TAX STATEMENTS

Integrity, Objectivity, and Ethics in Business

$8 MILLION FOR 18 MINUTES OF WORK

Computer system controls can be very important in issuing payroll checks. In one case, a Detroit school-teacher was paid $4,015,625 after deducting $3,884,375 in payroll deductions for 18 minutes of overtime work. The error was caused by a computer glitch when the teacher's employee identification number was substituted incorrectly in the "hourly wage" field and wasn't

caught by the payroll software. After six days, the error was discovered and the money was returned. "One of the things that came with (the software) is a fail-safe that prevents that. It doesn't work," a financial officer said. The district has since installed a program to flag any paycheck exceeding $10,000.

Source: Associated Press, September 27, 2002.

4 Journalize entries for employee fringe benefits, including vacation pay and pensions.

Employees' Fringe Benefits

Many companies provide their employees benefits in addition to salary and wages earned. Such **fringe benefits** may include vacation, medical, and retirement benefits. Exhibit 9 shows these three fringe benefits as a percent of total payroll costs.[7]

Exhibit 9

Benefit Dollars as a Percent of Payroll Costs

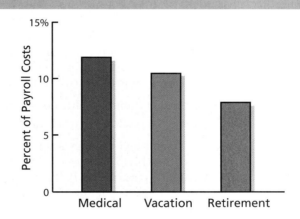

The U.S. Chamber of Commerce estimates that fringe benefits, excluding FICA, average about 33% of gross pay.

The cost of employee fringe benefits is recorded as an expense by the employer. To match revenues and expenses, the estimated cost of fringe benefits is recorded as an expense during the period in which the employees earn the benefits.

Vacation Pay

Most employers provide employees vacations, sometimes called *compensated absences*. The liability to pay for employee vacations could be accrued as a liability at the end of each pay period. However, many companies wait and record an adjusting entry for accrued vacation at the end of the year.

To illustrate, assume that employees earn one day of vacation for each month worked. The estimated vacation pay for the year ending December 31 is $325,000. The adjusting entry for the accrued vacation is shown below.

Vacation pay becomes the employer's liability as the employee earns vacation rights.

Dec.	31	Vacation Pay Expense		325,000	
		Vacation Pay Payable			325,000
		Accrued vacation pay for the year.			

Employees may be required to take all their vacation time within one year. In such cases, any accrued vacation pay will be paid within one year. Thus, the vacation pay payable is reported as a current liability on the balance sheet. If employees are allowed to accumulate their vacation pay, the estimated vacation pay payable that will *not* be taken within a year is reported as a long-term liability.

When employees take vacations, the liability for vacation pay is decreased by debiting Vacation Pay Payable. Salaries or Wages Payable and the other related payroll accounts for taxes and withholdings are credited.

Pensions

A **pension** is a cash payment to retired employees. Pension rights are accrued by employees as they work, based on the employer's pension plan. Two basic types of pension plans are:

1. Defined contribution plan
2. Defined benefit plan

In 90% of 401k plans, the employer matches some portion of the employee's contribution. As a result, nearly 70% of eligible employees elect to enroll in a 401k.

Source: "Employees Sluggish in Interacting with 401k Plans," Hewitt Associates, December 26, 2005.

In a **defined contribution plan**, the company invests contributions on behalf of the employee during the employee's working years. Normally, the employee and employer contribute to the plan. The employee's pension depends on the total contributions and the investment returns earned on those contributions.

One of the more popular defined contribution plans is the 401k plan. Under this plan, employees contribute a portion of their gross pay to investments, such as mutual funds. A 401k plan offers employees two advantages.

1. The employee contribution is deducted before taxes.
2. The contributions and related earnings are not taxed until withdrawn at retirement.

In most cases, the employer matches some portion of the employee's contribution. The employer's cost is debited to *Pension Expense*. To illustrate, assume that Heaven Scent Perfumes Company contributes 10% of employee monthly salaries to an employee 401k plan. Assuming $500,000 of monthly salaries, the journal entry to record the monthly contribution is shown below.

Dec.	31	Pension Expense		50,000	
		Cash			50,000
		Contributed 10% of monthly salaries to pension plan.			

Twenty percent of private industry uses defined benefit plans, while 43% uses defined contribution plans.

Source: Bureau of Labor Statistics, "Employee Benefits in Private Industry," 2007.

In a **defined benefit plan**, the company pays the employee a fixed annual pension based on a formula. The formula is normally based on such factors as the employee's years of service, age, and past salary.

Annual Pension = 1.5% × Years of Service × Highest 3-Year Average Salary

In a defined benefit plan, the employer is obligated to pay for (fund) the employee's future pension benefits. As a result, many companies are replacing their defined benefit plans with defined contribution plans.

The pension cost of a defined benefit plan is debited to *Pension Expense*. Cash is credited for the amount contributed (funded) by the employer. Any unfunded amount is credited to *Unfunded Pension Liability*.

To illustrate, assume that the defined benefit plan of Hinkle Co. requires an annual pension cost of $80,000. This annual contribution is based on estimates of Hinkle's future pension liabilities. On December 31, Hinkle Co. pays $60,000 to the pension fund. The entry to record the payment and unfunded liability is shown below.

Dec.	31	Pension Expense	80,000	
		Cash		60,000
		Unfunded Pension Liability		20,000
		Annual pension cost and contribution.		

If the unfunded pension liability is to be paid within one year, it is reported as a current liability on the balance sheet. Any portion of the unfunded pension liability that will be paid beyond one year is a long-term liability.

The accounting for pensions is complex due to the uncertainties of estimating future pension liabilities. These estimates depend on such factors as employee life expectancies, employee turnover, expected employee compensation levels, and investment income on pension contributions. Additional accounting and disclosures related to pensions are covered in advanced accounting courses.

Example Exercise 10-6   Vacation Pay and Pension Benefits   •••••••> 4

Manfield Services Company provides its employees vacation benefits and a defined contribution pension plan. Employees earned vacation pay of $44,000 for the period. The pension plan requires a contribution to the plan administrator equal to 8% of employee salaries. Salaries were $450,000 during the period.
   Provide the journal entry for the (a) vacation pay and (b) pension benefit.

Follow My Example 10-6

a.	Vacation Pay Expense	44,000	
	Vacation Pay Payable		44,000
	Vacation pay accrued for the period.		

b.	Pension Expense	36,000	
	Cash		36,000
	Pension contribution, 8% of $450,000 salary.		

For Practice: PE 10-6A, PE 10-6B

Postretirement Benefits Other than Pensions

Employees may earn rights to other postretirement benefits from their employer. Such benefits may include dental care, eye care, medical care, life insurance, tuition assistance, tax services, and legal services.

The accounting for other postretirement benefits is similar to that of defined benefit pension plans. The estimate of the annual benefits expense is recorded by debiting *Postretirement Benefits Expense*. If the benefits are fully funded, Cash is credited for the same amount. If the benefits are not fully funded, a postretirement benefits plan liability account is also credited.

The financial statements should disclose the nature of the postretirement benefit liabilities. These disclosures are usually included as notes to the financial statements. Additional accounting and disclosures for postretirement benefits are covered in advanced accounting courses.

Current Liabilities on the Balance Sheet

Accounts payable, the current portion of long-term debt, notes payable, and any other debts that are due within one year are reported as current liabilities on the balance sheet. The balance sheet presentation of current liabilities for Mornin' Joe is as follows:

Mornin' Joe
Balance Sheet
December 31, 2010

Liabilities

Current liabilities:

Accounts payable	$133,000
Notes payable (current portion)	200,000
Salaries and wages payable	42,000
Payroll taxes payable	16,400
Interest payable	40,000
Total current liabilities	$431,400

5 Describe the accounting treatment for contingent liabilities and journalize entries for product warranties.

Contingent Liabilities

Some liabilities may arise from past transactions if certain events occur in the future. These *potential* liabilities are called **contingent liabilities**.

The accounting for contingent liabilities depends on the following two factors:

1. Likelihood of occurring: Probable, reasonably possible, or remote
2. Measurement: Estimable or not estimable

The likelihood that the event creating the liability occurring is classified as *probable, reasonably possible,* or *remote.* The ability to estimate the potential liability is classified as *estimable* or *not estimable.*

Probable and Estimable

If a contingent liability is *probable* and the amount of the liability can be *reasonably estimated,* it is recorded and disclosed. The liability is recorded by debiting an expense and crediting a liability.

To illustrate, assume that during June a company sold a product for $60,000 that includes a 36-month warranty for repairs. The average cost of repairs over the warranty period is 5% of the sales price. The entry to record the estimated product warranty expense for June is as shown below.

The estimated costs of warranty work on new car sales are a contingent liability for Ford Motor Company.

June	30	Product Warranty Expense	3,000	
		Product Warranty Payable		3,000
		Warranty expense for June, 5% × $60,000.		

The preceding entry records warranty expense in the same period in which the sale is recorded. In this way, warranty expense is matched with the related revenue (sales).

If the product is repaired under warranty, the repair costs are recorded by debiting *Product Warranty Payable* and crediting *Cash, Supplies, Wages Payable,* or other appropriate accounts. Thus, if a $200 part is replaced under warranty on August 16, the entry is as follows:

Aug.	16	Product Warranty Payable		200	
		Supplies			200
		Replaced defective part under warranty.			

Example Exercise 10-7   Estimated Warranty Liability   •••••••• ❯ 5

Cook-Rite Co. sold $140,000 of kitchen appliances during August under a six-month warranty. The cost to repair defects under the warranty is estimated at 6% of the sales price. On September 11, a customer required a $200 part replacement, plus $90 of labor under the warranty.

Provide the journal entry for (a) the estimated warranty expense on August 31 and (b) the September 11 warranty work.

Follow My Example 10-7

a. Product Warranty Expense 8,400
     Product Warranty Payable 8,400
        To record warranty expense for August, 6% × $140,000.

b. Product Warranty Payable 290
     Supplies 200
     Wages Payable 90
        Replaced defective part under warranty.

For Practice: PE 10-7A, PE 10-7B

Probable and Not Estimable

A contingent liability may be probable, but cannot be estimated. In this case, the contingent liability is disclosed in the notes to the financial statements. For example, a company may have accidentally polluted a local river by dumping waste products. At the end of the period, the cost of the cleanup and any fines may not be able to be estimated.

Reasonably Possible

A contingent liability may be only possible. For example, a company may have lost a lawsuit for infringing on another company's patent rights. However, the verdict is under appeal and the company's lawyers feel that the verdict will be reversed or significantly reduced. In this case, the contingent liability is disclosed in the notes to the financial statements.

Remote

A contingent liability may be remote. For example, a ski resort may be sued for injuries incurred by skiers. In most cases, the courts have found that a skier accepts the risk of injury when participating in the activity. Thus, unless the ski resort is grossly negligent, the resort will not incur a liability for ski injuries. In such cases, no disclosure needs to be made in the notes to the financial statements.

The accounting treatment of contingent liabilities is summarized in Exhibit 10.

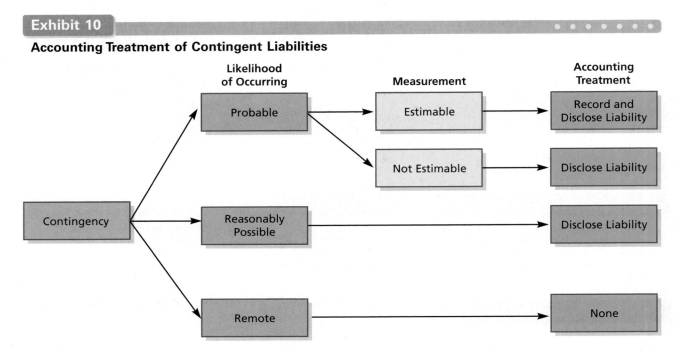

Exhibit 10

Accounting Treatment of Contingent Liabilities

Common examples of contingent liabilities disclosed in notes to the financial statements are litigation, environmental matters, guarantees, and contingencies from the sale of receivables.

An example of a contingent liability disclosure from a recent annual report of Google Inc. is shown below.

> —*Certain entities have also filed copyright claims against us, alleging that certain of our products, including Google Web Search, Google News, Google Image Search, and Google Book Search, infringe their rights. Adverse results in these lawsuits may include awards of damages and may also result in, or even compel, a change in our business practices, which could result in a loss of revenue for us or otherwise harm our business.*
>
> —*Although the results of litigation and claims cannot be predicted with certainty, we believe that the final outcome of the matters discussed above will not have a material adverse effect on our business. . . .*

Professional judgment is necessary in distinguishing between classes of contingent liabilities. This is especially the case when distinguishing between probable and reasonably possible contingent liabilities.

Integrity, Objectivity, and Ethics in Business

TODAY'S MISTAKES CAN BE TOMORROW'S LIABILITY

Environmental and public health claims are quickly growing into some of the largest contingent liabilities facing companies. For example, tobacco, asbestos, and environmental cleanup claims have reached billions of dollars and have led to a number of corporate bankruptcies. Managers must be careful that today's decisions do not become tomorrow's nightmare.

Financial Analysis and Interpretation

The Current Assets and Current Liabilities sections of the balance sheet for Noble Co. and Hart Co. are illustrated as follows:

	Noble Co.	Hart Co.
Current assets:		
Cash	$147,000	$120,000
Accounts receivable (net)	84,000	472,000
Inventory	150,000	200,000
Total current assets	$381,000	$792,000
Current liabilities:		
Accounts payable	$ 75,000	$227,000
Wages payable	30,000	193,000
Notes payable	115,000	320,000
Total current liabilities	$220,000	$740,000

We can use this information to evaluate Noble's and Hart's ability to pay their current liabilities within a short period of time, using the **quick ratio** or *acid-test ratio*. The quick ratio is computed as follows:

$$\text{Quick Ratio} = \frac{\text{Quick Assets}}{\text{Current Liabilities}}$$

The quick ratio measures the "instant" debt-paying ability of a company, using quick assets. **Quick assets** are cash, receivables, and other current assets that can quickly be converted into cash. It is often considered desirable to have a quick ratio exceeding 1.0. A ratio less than 1.0 would indicate that current liabilities cannot be covered by cash and "near cash" assets.

To illustrate, the quick ratios for both companies would be as follows:

$$\text{Noble Co.:} \frac{\$147,000 + \$84,000}{\$220,000} = 1.05$$

$$\text{Hart Co.:} \frac{\$120,000 + \$472,000}{\$740,000} = 0.80$$

As you can see, Noble Co. has quick assets in excess of current liabilities, or a quick ratio of 1.05. The ratio exceeds 1.0, indicating that the quick assets should be sufficient to meet current liabilities. Hart Co., however, has a quick ratio of 0.8. Its quick assets will not be sufficient to cover the current liabilities. Hart could solve this problem by working with a bank to convert its short-term debt of $320,000 into a long-term obligation. This would remove the notes payable from current liabilities. If Hart did this, then its quick ratio would improve to 1.4 ($592,000/ $420,000), which would be sufficient for quick assets to cover current liabilities.

At a Glance 10 ● ● ●➤

1 Describe and illustrate current liabilities related to accounts payable, current portion of long-term debt, and notes payable.

Key Points	Key Learning Outcomes	Example Exercises	Practice Exercises
Current liabilities are obligations that are to be paid out of current assets and are due within a short time, usually within one year. The three primary types of current liabilities are accounts payable, notes payable, and current portion of long-term debt.	• Identify and define the most frequently reported current liabilities on the balance sheet.		
	• Determine the interest from interest-bearing and discounted notes payable.	10-1	10-1A, 10-1B

2 Determine employer liabilities for payroll, including liabilities arising from employee earnings and deductions from earnings.

Key Points	Key Learning Outcomes	Example Exercises	Practice Exercises
An employer's liability for payroll is determined from employee total earnings, including overtime pay. From this amount, employee deductions are subtracted to arrive at the net pay to be paid to each employee. Most employers also incur liabilities for payroll taxes, such as social security tax, Medicare tax, federal unemployment compensation tax, and state unemployment compensation tax.	• Compute the federal withholding tax from a wage bracket withholding table.	**10-2**	10-2A, 10-2B
	• Compute employee net pay, including deductions for social security and Medicare tax.	**10-3**	10-3A, 10-3B

3 Describe payroll accounting systems that use a payroll register, employee earnings records, and a general journal.

Key Points	Key Learning Outcomes	Example Exercises	Practice Exercises
The payroll register is used in assembling and summarizing the data needed for each payroll period. The payroll register is supported by a detailed payroll record for each employee, called an *employee's earnings record*.	• Journalize the employee's earnings, net pay, and payroll liabilities from the payroll register.	**10-4**	10-4A, 10-4B
	• Journalize the payroll tax expense.	**10-5**	10-5A, 10-5B
	• Describe elements of a payroll system, including the employee's earnings record, payroll checks, and internal controls.		

4 Journalize entries for employee fringe benefits, including vacation pay and pensions.

Key Points	Key Learning Outcomes	Example Exercises	Practice Exercises
Fringe benefits are expenses of the period in which the employees earn the benefits. Fringe benefits are recorded by debiting an expense account and crediting a liability account.	• Journalize vacation pay.	**10-6**	10-6A, 10-6B
	• Distinguish and journalize defined contribution and defined benefit pension plans.	**10-6**	10-6A, 10-6B

5 Describe the accounting treatment for contingent liabilities and journalize entries for product warranties.

Key Points	Key Learning Outcomes	Example Exercises	Practice Exercises
A contingent liability is a potential obligation that results from a past transaction but depends on a future event. The accounting for contingent liabilities is summarized in Exhibit 10.	• Describe the accounting for contingent liabilities.		
	• Journalize estimated warranty obligations and services granted under warranty.	**10-7**	10-7A, 10-7B

Key Terms

contingent liabilities (456)
defined benefit plan (454)
defined contribution plan (454)
employee's earnings record (449)
FICA tax (443)

fringe benefits (453)
gross pay (441)
net pay (441)
payroll (441)
payroll register (446)

pension (454)
quick assets (459)
quick ratio (459)

Illustrative Problem

Selected transactions of Taylor Company, completed during the fiscal year ended December 31, are as follows:

Mar. 1. Purchased merchandise on account from Kelvin Co., $20,000.

Apr. 10. Issued a 60-day, 12% note for $20,000 to Kelvin Co. on account.

June 9. Paid Kelvin Co. the amount owed on the note of April 10.

Aug. 1. Issued a $50,000, 90-day note to Harold Co. in exchange for a building. Harold Co. discounted the note at 15%.

Oct. 30. Paid Harold Co. the amount due on the note of August 1.

Dec. 27. Journalized the entry to record the biweekly payroll. A summary of the payroll record follows:

Salary distribution:		
Sales	$63,400	
Officers	36,600	
Office	10,000	$110,000
Deductions:		
Social security tax	$ 5,050	
Medicare tax	1,650	
Federal income tax withheld	17,600	
State income tax withheld	4,950	
Savings bond deductions	850	
Medical insurance deductions	1,120	31,220
Net amount		$ 78,780

27. Journalized the entry to record payroll taxes for social security and Medicare from the biweekly payroll.

30. Issued a check in payment of liabilities for employees' federal income tax of $17,600, social security tax of $10,100, and Medicare tax of $3,300.

31. Issued a check for $9,500 to the pension fund trustee to fully fund the pension cost for December.

31. Journalized an entry to record the employees' accrued vacation pay, $36,100.

31. Journalized an entry to record the estimated accrued product warranty liability, $37,240.

Instructions

Journalize the preceding transactions.

Solution

			Debit	Credit
Mar.	1	Merchandise Inventory	20,000	
		Accounts Payable—Kelvin Co.		20,000
Apr.	10	Accounts Payable—Kelvin Co.	20,000	
		Notes Payable		20,000
June	9	Notes Payable	20,000	
		Interest Expense	400	
		Cash		20,400
Aug.	1	Building	48,125	
		Interest Expense	1,875	
		Notes Payable		50,000
Oct.	30	Notes Payable	50,000	
		Cash		50,000
Dec.	27	Sales Salaries Expense	63,400	
		Officers Salaries Expense	36,600	
		Office Salaries Expense	10,000	
		Social Security Tax Payable		5,050
		Medicare Tax Payable		1,650
		Employees Federal Income Tax Payable		17,600
		Employees State Income Tax Payable		4,950
		Bond Deductions Payable		850
		Medical Insurance Payable		1,120
		Salaries Payable		78,780
	27	Payroll Tax Expense	6,700	
		Social Security Tax Payable		5,050
		Medicare Tax Payable		1,650
	30	Employees Federal Income Tax Payable	17,600	
		Social Security Tax Payable	10,100	
		Medicare Tax Payable	3,300	
		Cash		31,000
	31	Pension Expense	9,500	
		Cash		9,500
		Fund pension cost.		
	31	Vacation Pay Expense	36,100	
		Vacation Pay Payable		36,100
		Accrue vacation pay.		
	31	Product Warranty Expense	37,240	
		Product Warranty Payable		37,240
		Accrue warranty expense.		

Self-Examination Questions (Answers at End of Chapter)

1. A business issued a $5,000, 60-day, 12% note to the bank. The amount due at maturity is:
   - A. $4,900.
   - B. $5,000.
   - C. $5,100.
   - D. $5,600.

2. A business issued a $5,000, 60-day note to a supplier, which discounted the note at 12%. The proceeds are:
   - A. $4,400.
   - B. $4,900.
   - C. $5,000.
   - D. $5,100.

3. Which of the following taxes are employers usually not required to withhold from employees?
   - A. Federal income tax
   - B. Federal unemployment compensation tax
   - C. Medicare tax
   - D. State and local income tax

4. An employee's rate of pay is $40 per hour, with time and a half for all hours worked in excess of 40 during a week. The social security rate is 6.0% on the first $100,000 of annual earnings, and the Medicare rate is 1.5% on all earnings. The following additional data are available:

Hours worked during current week	45
Year's cumulative earnings prior to current week	$99,400
Federal income tax withheld	$450

   Based on these data, the amount of the employee's net pay for the current week is:
   - A. $1,307.50.
   - B. $1,405.00.
   - C. $1,450.00.
   - D. $1,385.50.

5. Within limitations on the maximum earnings subject to the tax, employers do not incur an expense for which of the following payroll taxes?
   - A. Social security tax
   - B. Federal unemployment compensation tax
   - C. State unemployment compensation tax
   - D. Employees' federal income tax

Eye Openers

1. Does a discounted note payable provide credit without interest? Discuss.
2. Employees are subject to taxes withheld from their paychecks.
   a. List the federal taxes withheld from most employee paychecks.
   b. Give the title of the accounts credited by amounts withheld.
3. For each of the following payroll-related taxes, indicate whether there is a ceiling on the annual earnings subject to the tax: (a) federal income tax, (b) Medicare tax, (c) social security tax, (d) federal unemployment compensation tax.
4. Why are deductions from employees' earnings classified as liabilities for the employer?
5. Taylor Company, with 20 employees, is expanding operations. It is trying to decide whether to hire one full-time employee for $25,000 or two part-time employees for a total of $25,000. Would any of the employer's payroll taxes discussed in this chapter have a bearing on this decision? Explain.
6. For each of the following payroll-related taxes, indicate whether they generally apply to (a) employees only, (b) employers only, or (c) both employees and employers:
   1. Federal income tax
   2. Medicare tax
   3. Social security tax
   4. Federal unemployment compensation tax
   5. State unemployment compensation tax
7. What are the principal reasons for using a special payroll checking account?
8. In a payroll system, what types of input data are referred to as (a) constants and (b) variables?
9. Explain how a payroll system that is properly designed and operated tends to ensure that (a) wages paid are based on hours actually worked and (b) payroll checks are not issued to fictitious employees.
10. To match revenues and expenses properly, should the expense for employee vacation pay be recorded in the period during which the vacation privilege is earned or during the period in which the vacation is taken? Discuss.

11. Identify several factors that influence the future pension obligation of an employer under a defined benefit pension plan.

12. When should the liability associated with a product warranty be recorded? Discuss.

13. General Motors Corporation reported $10.1 billion of product warranties in the Current Liabilities section of a recent balance sheet. How would costs of repairing a defective product be recorded?

14. The "Questions and Answers Technical Hotline" in the *Journal of Accountancy* included the following question:

Several years ago, Company B instituted legal action against Company A. Under a memorandum of settlement and agreement, Company A agreed to pay Company B a total of $17,500 in three installments—$5,000 on March 1, $7,500 on July 1, and the remaining $5,000 on December 31. Company A paid the first two installments during its fiscal year ended September 30. Should the unpaid amount of $5,000 be presented as a current liability at September 30?

How would you answer this question?

Practice Exercises

PE 10-1A
Proceeds from notes payable
obj. 1
EE 10-1 p. 440

On September 1, Klondike Co. issued a 60-day note with a face amount of $100,000 to Arctic Apparel Co. for merchandise inventory.

a. Determine the proceeds of the note, assuming the note carries an interest rate of 6%.
b. Determine the proceeds of the note, assuming the note is discounted at 6%.

PE 10-1B
Proceeds from notes payable
obj. 1
EE 10-1 p. 440

On February 1, Electronic Warehouse Co. issued a 45-day note with a face amount of $80,000 to Yamura Products Co. for cash.

a. Determine the proceeds of the note, assuming the note carries an interest rate of 10%.
b. Determine the proceeds of the note, assuming the note is discounted at 10%.

PE 10-2A
Federal income tax withholding
obj. 2
EE 10-2 p. 443

Todd Hackworth's weekly gross earnings for the present week were $2,000. Hackworth has two exemptions. Using the wage bracket withholding table in Exhibit 3 with a $67 standard withholding allowance for each exemption, what is Hackworth's federal income tax withholding?

PE 10-2B
Federal income tax withholding
obj. 2
EE 10-2 p. 443

Robert Clowney's weekly gross earnings for the present week were $800. Clowney has one exemption. Using the wage bracket withholding table in Exhibit 3 with a $67 standard withholding allowance for each exemption, what is Clowney's federal income tax withholding?

PE 10-3A
Employee net pay
obj. 2
EE 10-3 p. 444

Todd Hackworth's weekly gross earnings for the week ending December 18 were $2,000, and his federal income tax withholding was $396.19. Prior to this week, Hackworth had earned $98,500 for the year. Assuming the social security rate is 6% on the first $100,000 of annual earnings and Medicare is 1.5% of all earnings, what is Hackworth's net pay?

PE 10-3B
Employee net pay

obj. 2

EE 10-3   p. 444

Robert Clowney's weekly gross earnings for the week ending September 5 were $800, and his federal income tax withholding was $102.95. Prior to this week, Clowney had earned $24,000 for the year. Assuming the social security rate is 6% on the first $100,000 of annual earnings and Medicare is 1.5% of all earnings, what is Clowney's net pay?

PE 10-4A
Journalize period
payroll

obj. 3

EE 10-4   p. 447

The payroll register of Woodard Construction Co. indicates $2,552 of social security withheld and $660 of Medicare tax withheld on total salaries of $44,000 for the period. Federal withholding for the period totaled $8,712.

Provide the journal entry for the period's payroll.

PE 10-4B
Journalize period
payroll

obj. 3

EE 10-4   p. 447

The payroll register of Salem Communications Co. indicates $29,580 of social security withheld and $7,650 of Medicare tax withheld on total salaries of $510,000 for the period. Retirement savings withheld from employee paychecks were $30,600 for the period. Federal withholding for the period totaled $100,980.

Provide the journal entry for the period's payroll.

PE 10-5A
Journalize payroll tax

obj. 3

EE 10-5   p. 448

The payroll register of Woodard Construction Co. indicates $2,552 of social security withheld and $660 of Medicare tax withheld on total salaries of $44,000 for the period. Assume earnings subject to state and federal unemployment compensation taxes are $10,500, at the federal rate of 0.8% and the state rate of 5.4%.

Provide the journal entry to record the payroll tax expense for the period.

PE 10-5B
Journalize payroll tax

obj. 3

EE 10-5   p. 448

The payroll register of Salem Communications Co. indicates $29,580 of social security withheld and $7,650 of Medicare tax withheld on total salaries of $510,000 for the period. Assume earnings subject to state and federal unemployment compensation taxes are $16,000, at the federal rate of 0.8% and the state rate of 5.4%.

Provide the journal entry to record the payroll tax expense for the period.

PE 10-6A
Vacation pay and
pension benefits

obj. 4

EE 10-6   p. 455

Blount Company provides its employees with vacation benefits and a defined contribution pension plan. Employees earned vacation pay of $30,000 for the period. The pension plan requires a contribution to the plan administrator equal to 10% of employee salaries. Salaries were $400,000 during the period.

Provide the journal entry for the (a) vacation pay and (b) pension benefit.

PE 10-6B
Vacation pay and
pension benefits

obj. 4

EE 10-6   p. 455

Hobson Equipment Company provides its employees vacation benefits and a defined benefit pension plan. Employees earned vacation pay of $20,000 for the period. The pension formula calculated a pension cost of $140,000. Only $106,000 was contributed to the pension plan administrator.

Provide the journal entry for the (a) vacation pay and (b) pension benefit.

PE 10-7A
Estimated warranty
liability

obj. 5

EE 10-7   p. 457

Akine Co. sold $600,000 of equipment during April under a one-year warranty. The cost to repair defects under the warranty is estimated at 6% of the sales price. On August 4, a customer required a $140 part replacement, plus $80 of labor under the warranty.

Provide the journal entry for (a) the estimated warranty expense on April 30 and (b) the August 4 warranty work.

PE 10-7B
Estimated warranty
liability

obj. 5

EE 10-7   p. 457

Robin Industries sold $350,000 of consumer electronics during May under a nine-month warranty. The cost to repair defects under the warranty is estimated at 3% of the sales price. On July 16, a customer was given $140 cash under terms of the warranty.

Provide the journal entry for (a) the estimated warranty expense on May 31 and (b) the July 16 cash payment.

Exercises

EX 10-1
Current liabilities

obj. 1

✔ Total current
liabilities, $790,000

I-Generation Co. sold 14,000 annual subscriptions of *Climber's World* for $60 during December 2010. These new subscribers will receive monthly issues, beginning in January 2011. In addition, the business had taxable income of $400,000 during the first calendar quarter of 2011. The federal tax rate is 40%. A quarterly tax payment will be made on April 7, 2011.

Prepare the Current Liabilities section of the balance sheet for I-Generation Co. on March 31, 2011.

EX 10-2
Entries for
discounting notes
payable

obj. 1

U-Build It Warehouse issues a 45-day note for $800,000 to Thomson Home Furnishings Co. for merchandise inventory. Thomson Home Furnishings Co. discounts the note at 7%.

a. Journalize U-Build It Warehouse's entries to record:
   1. the issuance of the note.
   2. the payment of the note at maturity.
b. Journalize Thomson Home Furnishings Co.'s entries to record:
   1. the receipt of the note.
   2. the receipt of the payment of the note at maturity.

EX 10-3
Evaluate alternative
notes

obj. 1

A borrower has two alternatives for a loan: (1) issue a $240,000, 60-day, 8% note or (2) issue a $240,000, 60-day note that the creditor discounts at 8%.

a. Calculate the amount of the interest expense for each option.
b. Determine the proceeds received by the borrower in each situation.
c. ➤ Which alternative is more favorable to the borrower? Explain.

EX 10-4
Entries for notes
payable

obj. 1

A business issued a 30-day, 4% note for $60,000 to a creditor on account. Journalize the entries to record (a) the issuance of the note and (b) the payment of the note at maturity, including interest.

EX 10-5
Entries for
discounted note
payable

obj. 1

A business issued a 60-day note for $45,000 to a creditor on account. The note was discounted at 6%. Journalize the entries to record (a) the issuance of the note and (b) the payment of the note at maturity.

EX 10-6
Fixed asset
purchases with note

obj. 1

On June 30, Rioux Management Company purchased land for $400,000 and a building for $600,000, paying $500,000 cash and issuing a 6% note for the balance, secured by a mortgage on the property. The terms of the note provide for 20 semiannual payments of $25,000 on the principal plus the interest accrued from the date of the preceding payment. Journalize the entry to record (a) the transaction on June 30, (b) the payment of the first installment on December 31, and (c) the payment of the second installment the following June 30.

EX 10-7
Current portion of
long-term debt

obj. 1

P.F. Chang's China Bistro, Inc., the operator of P.F. Chang restaurants, reported the following information about its long-term debt in the notes to a recent financial statement:

Long-term debt is comprised of the following:

	December 31,	
	2006	**2005**
Notes payable	$19,210,000	$10,470,000
Less current portion	(5,487,000)	(5,110,000)
Long-term debt	$13,723,000	$ 5,360,000

a. How much of the notes payable was disclosed as a current liability on the December 31, 2006, balance sheet?
b. How much did the total current liabilities change between 2005 and 2006 as a result of the current portion of long-term debt?
c. If P.F. Chang's did not issue additional notes payable during 2007, what would be the total notes payable on December 31, 2007?

EX 10-8
Calculate payroll

obj. 2

✔ b. Net pay,
$2,061.00

An employee earns $40 per hour and 1.75 times that rate for all hours in excess of 40 hours per week. Assume that the employee worked 60 hours during the week, and that the gross pay prior to the current week totaled $58,000. Assume further that the social security tax rate was 6.0% (on earnings up to $100,000), the Medicare tax rate was 1.5%, and federal income tax to be withheld was $714.

a. Determine the gross pay for the week.
b. Determine the net pay for the week.

EX 10-9
Calculate payroll

obj. 2

✔ Administrator net
pay, $1,423.57

Reaves Professional Services has three employees—a consultant, a computer programmer, and an administrator. The following payroll information is available for each employee:

	Consultant	Computer Programmer	Administrator
Regular earnings rate	$3,000 per week	$24 per hour	$36 per hour
Overtime earnings rate	Not applicable	2 times hourly rate	2 times hourly rate
Gross pay prior to current pay period	$118,000	$45,000	$99,000
Number of withholding allowances	2	1	2

For the current pay period, the computer programmer worked 50 hours and the administrator worked 46 hours. The federal income tax withheld for all three employees, who are single, can be determined from the wage bracket withholding table in Exhibit 3 in the chapter. Assume further that the social security tax rate was 6.0% on the first $100,000 of annual earnings, the Medicare tax rate was 1.5%, and one withholding allowance is $67.

Determine the gross pay and the net pay for each of the three employees for the current pay period.

EX 10-10
Summary payroll data

objs. 2, 3

✔ a. (3) Total earnings, $400,000

In the following summary of data for a payroll period, some amounts have been intentionally omitted:

Earnings:	
1. At regular rate	?
2. At overtime rate	$ 60,000
3. Total earnings	?
Deductions:	
4. Social security tax	23,200
5. Medicare tax	6,000
6. Income tax withheld	99,600
7. Medical insurance	14,000
8. Union dues	?
9. Total deductions	147,800
10. Net amount paid	252,200
Accounts debited:	
11. Factory Wages	210,000
12. Sales Salaries	?
13. Office Salaries	80,000

a. Calculate the amounts omitted in lines (1), (3), (8), and (12).
b. Journalize the entry to record the payroll accrual.
c. Journalize the entry to record the payment of the payroll.
d. ━━━▶ From the data given in this exercise and your answer to (a), would you conclude that this payroll was paid sometime during the first few weeks of the calendar year? Explain.

EX 10-11
Payroll tax entries

obj. 3

According to a summary of the payroll of Scofield Industries Co., $600,000 was subject to the 6.0% social security tax and $740,000 was subject to the 1.5% Medicare tax. Also, $20,000 was subject to state and federal unemployment taxes.

a. Calculate the employer's payroll taxes, using the following rates: state unemployment, 4.2%; federal unemployment, 0.8%.
b. Journalize the entry to record the accrual of payroll taxes.

EX 10-12
Payroll entries

obj. 3

The payroll register for Gentry Company for the week ended December 17 indicated the following:

Salaries	$540,000
Social security tax withheld	25,380
Medicare tax withheld	8,100
Federal income tax withheld	108,000

In addition, state and federal unemployment taxes were calculated at the rate of 5.2% and 0.8%, respectively, on $10,000 of salaries.

a. Journalize the entry to record the payroll for the week of December 17.
b. Journalize the entry to record the payroll tax expense incurred for the week of December 17.

EX 10-13
Payroll entries

obj. 3

Thorup Company had gross wages of $200,000 during the week ended December 10. The amount of wages subject to social security tax was $180,000, while the amount of wages subject to federal and state unemployment taxes was $25,000. Tax rates are as follows:

Social security	6.0%
Medicare	1.5%
State unemployment	5.3%
Federal unemployment	0.8%

The total amount withheld from employee wages for federal taxes was $40,000.

a. Journalize the entry to record the payroll for the week of December 10.
b. Journalize the entry to record the payroll tax expense incurred for the week of December 10.

EX 10-14
Payroll internal control procedures
obj. 3

Hillman Pizza is a pizza restaurant specializing in the sale of pizza by the slice. The store employs 7 full-time and 13 part-time workers. The store's weekly payroll averages $3,800 for all 20 workers.

Hillman Pizza uses a personal computer to assist in preparing paychecks. Each week, the store's accountant collects employee time cards and enters the hours worked into the payroll program. The payroll program calculates each employee's pay and prints a paycheck. The accountant uses a check-signing machine to sign the paychecks. Next, the restaurant's owner authorizes the transfer of funds from the restaurant's regular bank account to the payroll account.

For the week of July 11, the accountant accidentally recorded 250 hours worked instead of 40 hours for one of the full-time employees.

➤ Does Hillman Pizza have internal controls in place to catch this error? If so, how will this error be detected?

EX 10-15
Internal control procedures
obj. 3

Kailua Motors is a small manufacturer of specialty electric motors. The company employs 26 production workers and 7 administrative persons. The following procedures are used to process the company's weekly payroll:

a. All employees are required to record their hours worked by clocking in and out on a time clock. Employees must clock out for lunch break. Due to congestion around the time clock area at lunch time, management has not objected to having one employee clock in and out for an entire department.
b. Whenever a salaried employee is terminated, Personnel authorizes Payroll to remove the employee from the payroll system. However, this procedure is not required when an hourly worker is terminated. Hourly employees only receive a paycheck if their time cards show hours worked. The computer automatically drops an employee from the payroll system when that employee has six consecutive weeks with no hours worked.
c. Whenever an employee receives a pay raise, the supervisor must fill out a wage adjustment form, which is signed by the company president. This form is used to change the employee's wage rate in the payroll system.
d. Kailua Motors maintains a separate checking account for payroll checks. Each week, the total net pay for all employees is transferred from the company's regular bank account to the payroll account.
e. Paychecks are signed by using a check-signing machine. This machine is located in the main office so that it can be easily accessed by anyone needing a check signed.

➤ State whether each of the procedures is appropriate or inappropriate after considering the principles of internal control. If a procedure is inappropriate, describe the appropriate procedure.

EX 10-16
Payroll procedures
obj. 3

The fiscal year for Grain-Crop Stores Inc. ends on June 30. In addition, the company computes and reports payroll taxes on a fiscal-year basis. Thus, it applies social security and FUTA maximum earnings limitations to the fiscal-year payroll.

➤ What is wrong with these procedures for accounting for payroll taxes?

EX 10-17
Accrued vacation pay
obj. 4

A business provides its employees with varying amounts of vacation per year, depending on the length of employment. The estimated amount of the current year's vacation pay is $80,400. Journalize the adjusting entry required on January 31, the end of the first month of the current year, to record the accrued vacation pay.

EX 10-18
Pension plan entries
obj. 4

Washington Co. operates a chain of bookstores. The company maintains a defined contribution pension plan for its employees. The plan requires quarterly installments to be paid to the funding agent, Hamilton Funds, by the fifteenth of the month following the end of each quarter. Assuming that the pension cost is $124,600 for the quarter ended December 31, journalize entries to record (a) the accrued pension liability on December 31 and (b) the payment to the funding agent on January 15.

EX 10-19
Defined benefit pension plan terms
obj. **4**

In a recent year's financial statements, Procter & Gamble showed an unfunded pension liability of $2,637 million and a periodic pension cost of $183 million.

   Explain the meaning of the $2,637 million unfunded pension liability and the $183 million periodic pension cost.

EX 10-20
Accrued product warranty
obj. **5**

Lachgar Industries warrants its products for one year. The estimated product warranty is 4% of sales. Assume that sales were $210,000 for June. In July, a customer received warranty repairs requiring $140 of parts and $95 of labor.

a. Journalize the adjusting entry required at June 30, the end of the first month of the current fiscal year, to record the accrued product warranty.
b. Journalize the entry to record the warranty work provided in July.

EX 10-21
Accrued product warranty
obj. **5**

Ford Motor Company disclosed estimated product warranty payable for comparative years as follows:

	(in millions)	
	12/31/06	12/31/05
Current estimated product warranty payable	$13,644	$13,074
Noncurrent estimated product warranty payable	8,289	7,359
Total	$21,933	$20,433

Ford's sales were $160,123 million in 2005 and increased to $176,896 million in 2006. Assume that the total paid on warranty claims during 2006 was $14,000 million.

a. ⟶ Why are short- and long-term estimated warranty liabilities separately disclosed?
b. Provide the journal entry for the 2006 product warranty expense.

EX 10-22
Contingent liabilities
obj. **5**

Several months ago, Welker Chemical Company experienced a hazardous materials spill at one of its plants. As a result, the Environmental Protection Agency (EPA) fined the company $410,000. The company is contesting the fine. In addition, an employee is seeking $400,000 damages related to the spill. Lastly, a homeowner has sued the company for $260,000. The homeowner lives 30 miles from the plant, but believes that the incident has reduced the home's resale value by $260,000.

   Welker's legal counsel believes that it is probable that the EPA fine will stand. In addition, counsel indicates that an out-of-court settlement of $170,000 has recently been reached with the employee. The final papers will be signed next week. Counsel believes that the homeowner's case is much weaker and will be decided in favor of Welker. Other litigation related to the spill is possible, but the damage amounts are uncertain.

a. Journalize the contingent liabilities associated with the hazardous materials spill. Use the account "Damage Awards and Fines" to recognize the expense for the period.
b. ⟶ Prepare a note disclosure relating to this incident.

EX 10-23
Quick ratio

✔ a. 2010: 1.10

Austin Technology Co. had the following current assets and liabilities for two comparative years:

	Dec. 31, 2010	Dec. 31, 2009
Current assets:		
Cash	$370,000	$ 448,000
Accounts receivable	400,000	410,000
Inventory	220,000	180,000
Total current assets	$990,000	$1,038,000

	Dec. 31, 2010	Dec. 31, 2009
Current liabilities:		
Current portion of long-term debt	$110,000	$ 100,000
Accounts payable	220,000	200,000
Accrued and other current liabilities	370,000	360,000
Total current liabilities	$700,000	$ 660,000

a. Determine the quick ratio for December 31, 2010 and 2009.
b. ━━━▶ Interpret the change in the quick ratio between the two balance sheet dates.

EX 10-24
Quick ratio

The current assets and current liabilities for Apple Computer, Inc., and Dell Inc. are shown as follows at the end of a recent fiscal period:

	Apple Computer, Inc. (in millions) Sept. 29, 2007	Dell Inc. (in millions) Feb. 2, 2007
Current assets:		
Cash and cash equivalents	$ 9,352	$ 9,546
Short-term investments	6,034	752
Accounts receivable	4,029	6,152
Inventories	346	660
Other current assets*	2,195	2,829
Total current assets	$21,956	$19,939
Current liabilities:		
Accounts payable	$ 4,970	$10,430
Accrued and other current liabilities	4,329	7,361
Total current liabilities	$ 9,299	$17,791

*These represent prepaid expense and other nonquick current assets.

a. Determine the quick ratio for both companies.
b. ━━━▶ Interpret the quick ratio difference between the two companies.

Problems Series A ● ● ● ● ▶

PR 10-1A
Liability transactions

objs. **1**, **5**

The following items were selected from among the transactions completed by Emerald Bay Stores Co. during the current year:

Jan. 15.   Purchased merchandise on account from Hood Co., $220,000, terms n/30.
Feb. 14.   Issued a 60-day, 6% note for $220,000 to Hood Co., on account.
Apr. 15.   Paid Hood Co. the amount owed on the note of February 14.
June 2.   Borrowed $187,500 from Acme Bank, issuing a 60-day, 8% note.
July 10.   Purchased tools by issuing a $190,000, 90-day note to Columbia Supply Co., which discounted the note at the rate of 6%.
Aug. 1.   Paid Acme Bank the interest due on the note of June 2 and renewed the loan by issuing a new 60-day, 10% note for $187,500. (Journalize both the debit and credit to the notes payable account.)
Sept. 30.   Paid Acme Bank the amount due on the note of August 1.
Oct. 8.   Paid Columbia Supply Co. the amount due on the note of July 10.
Dec. 1.   Purchased office equipment from Mountain Equipment Co. for $120,000, paying $20,000 and issuing a series of ten 6% notes for $10,000 each, coming due at 30-day intervals.
5.   Settled a product liability lawsuit with a customer for $76,000, payable in January. Emerald Bay accrued the loss in a litigation claims payable account.
31.   Paid the amount due Mountain Equipment Co. on the first note in the series issued on December 1.

Instructions
1. Journalize the transactions.
2. Journalize the adjusting entry for each of the following accrued expenses at the end of the current year: (a) product warranty cost, $16,400; (b) interest on the nine remaining notes owed to Mountain Equipment Co.

PR 10-2A
Entries for payroll and payroll taxes

objs. 2, 3

✔ 1. (b) Dr. Payroll Tax Expense, $36,026

The following information about the payroll for the week ended December 30 was obtained from the records of Arnsparger Equipment Co.:

Salaries:		Deductions:	
Sales salaries	$244,000	Income tax withheld	$ 88,704
Warehouse salaries	135,000	Social security tax withheld	27,216
Office salaries	125,000	Medicare tax withheld	7,560
	$504,000	U.S. savings bonds	11,088
		Group insurance	9,072
			$143,640

Tax rates assumed:
Social security, 6% on first $100,000 of employee annual earnings
Medicare, 1.5%
State unemployment (employer only), 4.2%
Federal unemployment (employer only), 0.8%

Instructions
1. Assuming that the payroll for the last week of the year is to be paid on December 31, journalize the following entries:
   a. December 30, to record the payroll.
   b. December 30, to record the employer's payroll taxes on the payroll to be paid on December 31. Of the total payroll for the last week of the year, $25,000 is subject to unemployment compensation taxes.
2. Assuming that the payroll for the last week of the year is to be paid on January 5 of the following fiscal year, journalize the following entries:
   a. December 30, to record the payroll.
   b. January 5, to record the employer's payroll taxes on the payroll to be paid on January 5.

PR 10-3A
Wage and tax statement data on employer FICA tax

objs. 2, 3

✔ 2. (e) $28,503.00

Gridiron Concepts Co. began business on January 2, 2009. Salaries were paid to employees on the last day of each month, and social security tax, Medicare tax, and federal income tax were withheld in the required amounts. An employee who is hired in the middle of the month receives half the monthly salary for that month. All required payroll tax reports were filed, and the correct amount of payroll taxes was remitted by the company for the calendar year. Early in 2010, before the Wage and Tax Statements (Form W-2) could be prepared for distribution to employees and for filing with the Social Security Administration, the employees' earnings records were inadvertently destroyed.

None of the employees resigned or were discharged during the year, and there were no changes in salary rates. The social security tax was withheld at the rate of 6.0% on the first $100,000 of salary and Medicare tax at the rate of 1.5% on salary. Data on dates of employment, salary rates, and employees' income taxes withheld, which are summarized as follows, were obtained from personnel records and payroll records:

Employee	Date First Employed	Monthly Salary	Monthly Income Tax Withheld
Brooks	Jan. 2	$ 3,400	$ 502
Croom	June 16	5,600	1,052
Fulmer	Apr. 1	2,500	310
Johnson	Oct. 1	2,500	310
Nutt	Jan. 2	10,000	2,253
Richt	Jan. 16	3,600	552
Spurrier	Mar. 1	8,600	1,861

Instructions

1. Calculate the amounts to be reported on each employee's Wage and Tax Statement (Form W-2) for 2009, arranging the data in the following form:

Employee	Gross Earnings	Federal Income Tax Withheld	Social Security Tax Withheld	Medicare Tax Withheld

2. Calculate the following employer payroll taxes for the year: (a) social security; (b) Medicare; (c) state unemployment compensation at 4.8% on the first $8,000 of each employee's earnings; (d) federal unemployment compensation at 0.8% on the first $8,000 of each employee's earnings; (e) total.

PR 10-4A
Payroll register
objs. 2, 3

✔ 3. Dr. Payroll Tax
Expense, $773.71

If the working papers correlating with this textbook are not used, omit Problem 10-4A.

The payroll register for Namesake Co. for the week ended September 12, 2010, is presented in the working papers.

Instructions

1. Journalize the entry to record the payroll for the week.
2. Journalize the entry to record the issuance of the checks to employees.
3. Journalize the entry to record the employer's payroll taxes for the week. Assume the following tax rates: state unemployment, 3.2%; federal unemployment, 0.8%. Of the earnings, $1,500 is subject to unemployment taxes.
4. Journalize the entry to record a check issued on September 15 to Fourth National Bank in payment of employees' income taxes, $1,944.78, social security taxes, $1,084.32, and Medicare taxes, $343.10.

PR 10-5A
Payroll register
objs. 2, 3

✔ 1. Total net
amount payable,
$9,260.56

The following data for Enrichment Industries, Inc. relate to the payroll for the week ended December 10, 2010:

Employee	Hours Worked	Hourly Rate	Weekly Salary	Federal Income Tax	U.S. Savings Bonds	Accumulated Earnings, Dec. 3
Beilein	32	$16.00		$102.40	10	$ 24,576
Calhoun	50	32.00		369.60	10	84,480
Calipari	40	28.00		240.80	20	53,760
Knight	42	32.00		316.48		66,048
Odom			$3,400	748.00	90	163,200
Olson			1,600	384.00		76,800
Pitino	34	18.00		91.80		29,376
Ryan	44	34.00		297.16	20	75,072
Thompson	40	26.00		218.40	35	49,920

Employees Olson and Odom are office staff, and all of the other employees are sales personnel. All sales personnel are paid $1\frac{1}{2}$ times the regular rate for all hours in excess of 40 hours per week. The social security tax rate is 6.0% on the first $100,000 of each employee's annual earnings, and Medicare tax is 1.5% of each employee's annual earnings. The next payroll check to be used is No. 345.

Instructions

1. Prepare a payroll register for Enrichment Industries, Inc. for the week ended December 10, 2010. Use the following columns for the payroll register: Name, Total Hours, Regular Earnings, Overtime Earnings, Total Earnings, Social Security Tax, Medicare Tax, Federal Income Tax, U.S. Savings Bonds, Total Deductions, Net Pay, Ck. No., Sales Salaries Expense, and Office Salaries Expense.
2. Journalize the entry to record the payroll for the week.

PR 10-6A
Payroll accounts and
year-end entries
objs. 2, 3, 4

The following accounts, with the balances indicated, appear in the ledger of Wadsley Gifts Co. on December 1 of the current year:

211	Salaries Payable	—	218	Bond Deductions Payable	$	2,800
212	Social Security Tax Payable	$ 7,234	219	Medical Insurance Payable		22,000
213	Medicare Tax Payable	1,904	611	Operations Salaries Expense		766,000
214	Employees Federal Income Tax Payable	11,739	711	Officers Salaries Expense		504,000
215	Employees State Income Tax Payable	11,422	712	Office Salaries Expense		126,000
216	State Unemployment Tax Payable	1,200	719	Payroll Tax Expense		109,318
217	Federal Unemployment Tax Payable	400				

The following transactions relating to payroll, payroll deductions, and payroll taxes occurred during December:

Dec. 2. Issued Check No. 321 for $2,800 to Johnson Bank to purchase U.S. savings bonds for employees.

3. Issued Check No. 322 to Johnson Bank for $20,877, in payment of $7,234 of social security tax, $1,904 of Medicare tax, and $11,739 of employees' federal income tax due.

14. Journalized the entry to record the biweekly payroll. A summary of the payroll record follows:

Salary distribution:		
Operations	$34,800	
Officers	22,900	
Office	5,700	$63,400
Deductions:		
Social security tax	$ 3,550	
Medicare tax	951	
Federal income tax withheld	11,285	
State income tax withheld	2,853	
Savings bond deductions	1,400	
Medical insurance deductions	3,667	23,706
Net amount		$39,694

14. Issued Check No. 331 in payment of the net amount of the biweekly payroll.

14. Journalized the entry to record payroll taxes on employees' earnings of December 14: social security tax, $3,550; Medicare tax, $951; state unemployment tax, $300; federal unemployment tax, $100.

17. Issued Check No. 335 to Johnson Bank for $20,287, in payment of $7,100 of social security tax, $1,902 of Medicare tax, and $11,285 of employees' federal income tax due.

18. Issued Check No. 340 to Tidy Insurance Company for $22,000, in payment of the semiannual premium on the group medical insurance policy.

28. Journalized the entry to record the biweekly payroll. A summary of the payroll record follows:

Salary distribution:		
Operations	$34,200	
Officers	22,400	
Office	5,400	$62,000
Deductions:		
Social security tax	$ 3,348	
Medicare tax	930	
Federal income tax withheld	11,036	
State income tax withheld	2,790	
Savings bond deductions	1,400	19,504
Net amount		$42,496

28. Issued Check No. 352 in payment of the net amount of the biweekly payroll.

28. Journalized the entry to record payroll taxes on employees' earnings of December 28: social security tax, $3,348; Medicare tax, $930; state unemployment tax, $150; federal unemployment tax, $50.

30. Issued Check No. 354 to Johnson Bank for $2,800 to purchase U.S. savings bonds for employees.

30. Issued Check No. 356 for $17,065 to Johnson Bank in payment of employees' state income tax due on December 31.

Dec. 31.   Paid $34,000 to the employee pension plan. The annual pension cost is $40,000. (Record both the payment and unfunded pension liability.)

Instructions
1. Journalize the transactions.
2. Journalize the following adjusting entries on December 31:
    a. Salaries accrued: operations salaries, $3,420; officers salaries, $2,240; office salaries, $540. The payroll taxes are immaterial and are not accrued.
    b. Vacation pay, $11,500.

Problems Series B

PR 10-1B
Liability transactions

objs. **1, 5**

The following items were selected from among the transactions completed by Paulson, Inc. during the current year:

Apr.   1.   Borrowed $60,000 from McCaw Company, issuing a 45-day, 6% note for that amount.
    26.   Purchased equipment by issuing a $160,000, 180-day note to Houston Manufacturing Co., which discounted the note at the rate of 8%.
May 16.   Paid McCaw Company the interest due on the note of April 1 and renewed the loan by issuing a new 30-day, 10% note for $60,000. (Record both the debit and credit to the notes payable account.)
June 15.   Paid McCaw Company the amount due on the note of May 16.
Sept. 3.   Purchased merchandise on account from Oatley Co., $42,000, terms, n/30.
Oct.   3.   Issued a 30-day, 9% note for $42,000 to Oatley Co., on account.
    23.   Paid Houston Manufacturing Co. the amount due on the note of April 26.
Nov. 2.   Paid Oatley Co. the amount owed on the note of October 3.
    10.   Purchased store equipment from Biden Technology Co. for $200,000, paying $60,000 and issuing a series of seven 9% notes for $20,000 each, coming due at 30-day intervals.
Dec. 10.   Paid the amount due Biden Technology Co. on the first note in the series issued on November 10.
    16.   Settled a personal injury lawsuit with a customer for $42,500, to be paid in January. Paulson, Inc. accrued the loss in a litigation claims payable account.

Instructions
1. Journalize the transactions.
2. Journalize the adjusting entry for each of the following accrued expenses at the end of the current year:
    a. Product warranty cost, $10,400.
    b. Interest on the six remaining notes owed to Biden Technology Co.

PR 10-2B
Entries for payroll and payroll taxes

objs. **2, 3**

✔ 1. (b) Dr. Payroll Tax Expense, $68,304

The following information about the payroll for the week ended December 30 was obtained from the records of Vienna Co.:

Salaries:		Deductions:	
Sales salaries	$ 670,000	Income tax withheld	$198,744
Warehouse salaries	110,000	Social security tax withheld	51,714
Office salaries	234,000	Medicare tax withheld	15,210
	$1,014,000	U.S. savings bonds	30,420
		Group insurance	45,630
			$341,718

Tax rates assumed:
Social security, 6% on first $100,000 of employee annual earnings
Medicare, 1.5%
State unemployment (employer only), 3.8%
Federal unemployment (employer only), 0.8%

Instructions

1. Assuming that the payroll for the last week of the year is to be paid on December 31, journalize the following entries:
   a. December 30, to record the payroll.
   b. December 30, to record the employer's payroll taxes on the payroll to be paid on December 31. Of the total payroll for the last week of the year, $30,000 is subject to unemployment compensation taxes.
2. Assuming that the payroll for the last week of the year is to be paid on January 4 of the following fiscal year, journalize the following entries:
   a. December 30, to record the payroll.
   b. January 4, to record the employer's payroll taxes on the payroll to be paid on January 4.

PR 10-3B
Wage and tax statement data and employer FICA tax

objs. 2, 3

✔ 2. (e) $26,019.00

CTU Industries, Inc., began business on January 2, 2009. Salaries were paid to employees on the last day of each month, and social security tax, Medicare tax, and federal income tax were withheld in the required amounts. An employee who is hired in the middle of the month receives half the monthly salary for that month. All required payroll tax reports were filed, and the correct amount of payroll taxes was remitted by the company for the calendar year. Early in 2010, before the Wage and Tax Statements (Form W-2) could be prepared for distribution to employees and for filing with the Social Security Administration, the employees' earnings records were inadvertently destroyed.

None of the employees resigned or were discharged during the year, and there were no changes in salary rates. The social security tax was withheld at the rate of 6.0% on the first $100,000 of salary and Medicare tax at the rate of 1.5% on salary. Data on dates of employment, salary rates, and employees' income taxes withheld, which are summarized as follows, were obtained from personnel records and payroll records:

Employee	Date First Employed	Monthly Salary	Monthly Income Tax Withheld
Brown	Aug. 1	$3,600	$ 552
Carroll	Jan. 2	9,500	2,113
Grobe	May 1	6,500	1,277
Meyer	July 1	4,200	702
Saban	Jan. 2	5,100	927
Tressel	Apr. 16	3,200	452
Weis	Oct. 1	3,000	402

Instructions

1. Calculate the amounts to be reported on each employee's Wage and Tax Statement (Form W-2) for 2009, arranging the data in the following form:

Employee	Gross Earnings	Federal Income Tax Withheld	Social Security Tax Withheld	Medicare Tax Withheld

2. Calculate the following employer payroll taxes for the year: (a) social security; (b) Medicare; (c) state unemployment compensation at 4.8% on the first $10,000 of each employee's earnings; (d) federal unemployment compensation at 0.8% on the first $10,000 of each employee's earnings; (e) total.

PR 10-4B
Payroll register

objs. 2, 3

✔ 3. Dr. Payroll Tax Expense, $788.40

If the working papers correlating with this textbook are not used, omit Problem 10-4B.

The payroll register for Gogol Manufacturing Co. for the week ended September 12, 2010, is presented in the working papers.

Instructions

1. Journalize the entry to record the payroll for the week.
2. Journalize the entry to record the issuance of the checks to employees.
3. Journalize the entry to record the employer's payroll taxes for the week. Assume the following tax rates: state unemployment, 3.2%; federal unemployment, 0.8%. Of the earnings, $1,800 is subject to unemployment taxes.
4. Journalize the entry to record a check issued on September 15 to Third National Bank in payment of employees' income taxes, $2,337.88, social security taxes, $1,021.44, and Medicare taxes, $411.36.

PR 10-5B
Payroll register

objs. 2, 3

✔ 1. Total net amount payable, $8,610.31

The following data for Burtard Industries, Inc., relate to the payroll for the week ended December 10, 2010:

Employee	Hours Worked	Hourly Rate	Weekly Salary	Federal Income Tax	U.S. Savings Bonds	Accumulated Earnings, Dec. 3
Barnes			$3,000	$645.00		$144,000
Calhoun	50	$32.00		369.60	20	84,480
Crean			1,800	432.00	50	86,400
Donovan	34	20.00		136.00		32,640
Izzo	45	25.00		178.13		57,000
Matta	46	24.00		223.44	25	56,448
Self	40	23.00		193.20	40	44,160
Smith	40	22.00		202.40	30	42,240
Williams	36	18.00		142.56	30	31,104

Employees Barnes and Crean are office staff, and all of the other employees are sales personnel. All sales personnel are paid 1½ times the regular rate for all hours in excess of 40 hours per week. The social security tax rate is 6.0% on the first $100,000 of each employee's annual earnings, and Medicare tax is 1.5% of each employee's annual earnings. The next payroll check to be used is No. 652.

Instructions
1. Prepare a payroll register for Burtard Industries, Inc. for the week ended December 10, 2010. Use the following columns for the payroll register: Name, Total Hours, Regular Earnings, Overtime Earnings, Total Earnings, Social Security Tax, Medicare Tax, Federal Income Tax, U.S. Savings Bonds, Total Deductions, Net Pay, Ck. No., Sales Salaries Expense, and Office Salaries Expense.
2. Journalize the entry to record the payroll for the week.

PR 10-6B
Payroll accounts and year-end entries

objs. 2, 3, 4

The following accounts, with the balances indicated, appear in the ledger of Yukon Kayak Co. on December 1 of the current year:

211	Salaries Payable	—	218	Bond Deductions Payable	$	1,800
212	Social Security Tax Payable	$4,880	219	Medical Insurance Payable		2,000
213	Medicare Tax Payable	1,236	611	Sales Salaries Expense		556,000
214	Employees Federal Income Tax Payable	7,540	711	Officers Salaries Expense		266,400
215	Employees State Income Tax Payable	7,038	712	Office Salaries Expense		99,200
216	State Unemployment Tax Payable	1,000	719	Payroll Tax Expense		74,316
217	Federal Unemployment Tax Payable	280				

The following transactions relating to payroll, payroll deductions, and payroll taxes occurred during December:

Dec. 1.   Issued Check No. 510 to Tidy Insurance Company for $2,000, in payment of the semiannual premium on the group medical insurance policy.

2.   Issued Check No. 511 to Johnson Bank for $13,656, in payment for $4,880 of social security tax, $1,236 of Medicare tax, and $7,540 of employees' federal income tax due.

3.   Issued Check No. 512 for $1,800 to Johnson Bank to purchase U.S. savings bonds for employees.

14.   Journalized the entry to record the biweekly payroll. A summary of the payroll record follows:

Salary distribution:		
Sales	$25,000	
Officers	12,100	
Office	4,500	$41,600

Deductions:		
Social security tax	$ 2,288	
Medicare tax	624	
Federal income tax withheld	7,405	
State income tax withheld	1,872	
Savings bond deductions	900	
Medical insurance deductions	333	13,422
Net amount		$28,178

Dec. 14.   Issued Check No. 520 in payment of the net amount of the biweekly payroll.

14.   Journalized the entry to record payroll taxes on employees' earnings of December 14: social security tax, $2,288; Medicare tax, $624; state unemployment tax, $250; federal unemployment tax, $60.

17.   Issued Check No. 528 to Johnson Bank for $13,229, in payment for $4,576 of social security tax, $1,248 of Medicare tax, and $7,405 of employees' federal income tax due.

28.   Journalized the entry to record the biweekly payroll. A summary of the payroll record follows:

Salary distribution:

Sales	$25,400	
Officers	12,400	
Office	4,800	$42,600

Deductions:

Social security tax	$ 2,300	
Medicare tax	639	
Federal income tax withheld	7,583	
State income tax withheld	1,917	
Savings bond deductions	900	13,339
Net amount		$29,261

28.   Issued Check No. 540 for the net amount of the biweekly payroll.

28.   Journalized the entry to record payroll taxes on employees' earnings of December 28: social security tax, $2,300; Medicare tax, $639; state unemployment tax, $120; federal unemployment tax, $30.

30.   Issued Check No. 551 for $10,827 to Johnson Bank, in payment of employees' state income tax due on December 31.

30.   Issued Check No. 552 to Johnson Bank for $1,800 to purchase U.S. savings bonds for employees.

31.   Paid $44,000 to the employee pension plan. The annual pension cost is $52,000. (Record both the payment and the unfunded pension liability.)

Instructions
1. Journalize the transactions.
2. Journalize the following adjusting entries on December 31:
   a. Salaries accrued: sales salaries, $2,540; officers salaries, $1,240; office salaries, $480. The payroll taxes are immaterial and are not accrued.
   b. Vacation pay, $10,600.

Comprehensive Problem 3

✔ 5. Total assets, $1,567,300

Selected transactions completed by Blackwell Company during its first fiscal year ending December 31 were as follows:

Jan.   2.   Issued a check to establish a petty cash fund of $2,000.

Mar. 4.   Replenished the petty cash fund, based on the following summary of petty cash receipts: office supplies, $789; miscellaneous selling expense, $256; miscellaneous administrative expense, $378.

Apr. 5.   Purchased $14,000 of merchandise on account, terms 1/10, n/30. The perpetual inventory system is used to account for inventory.

May 7.   Paid the invoice of April 5 after the discount period had passed.

10.   Received cash from daily cash sales for $9,455. The amount indicated by the cash register was $9,545.

June 2.   Received a 60-day, 9% note for $80,000 on the Stevens account.

Aug. 1.   Received amount owed on June 2 note, plus interest at the maturity date.

8.   Received $3,400 on the Jacobs account and wrote off the remainder owed on a $4,000 accounts receivable balance. (The allowance method is used in accounting for uncollectible receivables.)

Aug. 25. Reinstated the Jacobs account written off on August 8 and received $600 cash in full payment.

Sept. 2. Purchased land by issuing a $300,000, 90-day note to Ace Development Co., which discounted it at 10%.

Oct. 2. Sold office equipment in exchange for $60,000 cash plus receipt of a $40,000, 120-day, 6% note. The equipment had cost $140,000 and had accumulated depreciation of $25,000 as of October 1.

Nov. 30. Journalized the monthly payroll for November, based on the following data:

Salaries		Deductions	
Sales salaries	$60,400	Income tax withheld	$17,082
Office salaries	34,500	Social security tax withheld	5,450
	$94,900	Medicare tax withheld	1,424

Unemployment tax rates:	
State unemployment	4.0%
Federal unemployment	0.8%
Amount subject to unemployment taxes:	
State unemployment	$4,000
Federal unemployment	4,000

30. Journalized the employer's payroll taxes on the payroll.

Dec. 1. Journalized the payment of the September 2 note at maturity.

30. The pension cost for the year was $85,000, of which $62,400 was paid to the pension plan trustee.

Instructions

1. Journalize the selected transactions.
2. Based on the following data, prepare a bank reconciliation for December of the current year:
   a. Balance according to the bank statement at December 31, $126,400.
   b. Balance according to the ledger at December 31, $109,650.
   c. Checks outstanding at December 31, $30,600.
   d. Deposit in transit, not recorded by bank, $13,200.
   e. Bank debit memo for service charges, $350.
   f. A check for $530 in payment of an invoice was incorrectly recorded in the accounts as $230.
3. Based on the bank reconciliation prepared in (2), journalize the entry or entries to be made by Blackwell Company.
4. Based on the following selected data, journalize the adjusting entries as of December 31 of the current year:
   a. Estimated uncollectible accounts at December 31, $7,200, based on an aging of accounts receivable. The balance of Allowance for Doubtful Accounts at December 31 was $750 (debit).
   b. The physical inventory on December 31 indicated an inventory shrinkage of $1,480.
   c. Prepaid insurance expired during the year, $10,200.
   d. Office supplies used during the year, $1,760.
   e. Depreciation is computed as follows:

Asset	Cost	Residual Value	Acquisition Date	Useful Life in Years	Depreciation Method Used
Buildings	$400,000	$ 0	January 2	40	Straight-line
Office Equip.	110,000	10,000	July 1	4	Straight-line
Store Equip.	50,000	5,000	January 3	8	Double-declining-balance (at twice the straight-line rate)

   f. A patent costing $22,500 when acquired on January 2 has a remaining legal life of 10 years and is expected to have value for five years.
   g. The cost of mineral rights was $220,000. Of the estimated deposit of 400,000 tons of ore, 24,000 tons were mined and sold during the year.
   h. Vacation pay expense for December, $4,800.

    i. A product warranty was granted beginning December 1 and covering a one-year period. The estimated cost is 2.5% of sales, which totaled $840,000 in December.

    j. Interest was accrued on the note receivable received on October 2.

5. Based on the following information and the post-closing trial balance shown below, prepare a balance sheet in report form at December 31 of the current year.

The merchandise inventory is stated at cost by the LIFO method.

The product warranty payable is a current liability.

Vacation pay payable:
Current liability	$3,200
Long-term liability	1,600

The unfunded pension liability is a long-term liability.

Notes payable:
Current liability	$25,000
Long-term liability	75,000

Blackwell Company
Post-Closing Trial Balance
December 31, 2010

	Debit Balances	Credit Balances
Petty Cash	2,000	
Cash	109,000	
Notes Receivable	40,000	
Accounts Receivable	210,000	
Allowance for Doubtful Accounts		7,200
Merchandise Inventory	144,200	
Interest Receivable	600	
Prepaid Insurance	20,400	
Office Supplies	6,000	
Land	292,500	
Buildings	400,000	
Accumulated Depreciation—Buildings		10,000
Office Equipment	110,000	
Accumulated Depreciation—Office Equipment		12,500
Store Equipment	50,000	
Accumulated Depreciation—Store Equipment		12,500
Mineral Rights	220,000	
Accumulated Depletion		13,200
Patents	18,000	
Social Security Tax Payable		10,420
Medicare Tax Payable		2,550
Employees Federal Income Tax Payable		17,260
State Unemployment Tax Payable		100
Federal Unemployment Tax Payable		20
Salaries Payable		85,000
Accounts Payable		140,000
Interest Payable		3,200
Product Warranty Payable		21,000
Vacation Pay Payable		4,800
Unfunded Pension Liability		22,600
Notes Payable		100,000
Capital Stock		400,000
Retained Earnings		760,350
	1,622,700	1,622,700

6. On February 7 of the following year, the merchandise inventory was destroyed by fire. Based on the following data obtained from the accounting records, estimate the cost of the merchandise destroyed:

Jan. 1 Merchandise inventory	$144,200
Jan. 1–Feb. 7 Purchases (net)	40,000
Jan. 1–Feb. 7 Sales (net)	70,000
Estimated gross profit rate	40%

Special Activities

SA 10-1
Ethics and professional conduct in business

Suzanne Thompson is a certified public accountant (CPA) and staff accountant for Deuel and Soldner, a local CPA firm. It had been the policy of the firm to provide a holiday bonus equal to two weeks' salary to all employees. The firm's new management team announced on November 15 that a bonus equal to only one week's salary would be made available to employees this year. Suzanne thought that this policy was unfair because she and her coworkers planned on the full two-week bonus. The two-week bonus had been given for 10 straight years, so it seemed as though the firm had breached an implied commitment. Thus, Suzanne decided that she would make up the lost bonus week by working an extra six hours of overtime per week over the next five weeks until the end of the year. Deuel and Soldner's policy is to pay overtime at 150% of straight time.

Suzanne's supervisor was surprised to see overtime being reported, since there is generally very little additional or unusual client service demands at the end of the calendar year. However, the overtime was not questioned, since firm employees are on the "honor system" in reporting their overtime.

➡ Discuss whether the firm is acting in an ethical manner by changing the bonus. Is Suzanne behaving in an ethical manner?

SA 10-2
Recognizing pension expense

The annual examination of Tidal Company's financial statements by its external public accounting firm (auditors) is nearing completion. The following conversation took place between the controller of Tidal Company (Jose) and the audit manager from the public accounting firm (Cara).

Cara: You know, Jose, we are about to wrap up our audit for this fiscal year. Yet, there is one item still to be resolved.

Jose: What's that?

Cara: Well, as you know, at the beginning of the year, Tidal began a defined benefit pension plan. This plan promises your employees an annual payment when they retire, using a formula based on their salaries at retirement and their years of service. I believe that a pension expense should be recognized this year, equal to the amount of pension earned by your employees.

Jose: Wait a minute. I think you have it all wrong. The company doesn't have a pension expense until it actually pays the pension in cash when the employee retires. After all, some of these employees may not reach retirement, and if they don't, the company doesn't owe them anything.

Cara: You're not really seeing this the right way. The pension is earned by your employees during their working years. You actually make the payment much later—when they retire. It's like one long accrual—much like incurring wages in one period and paying them in the next. Thus, I think that you should recognize the expense in the period the pension is earned by the employees.

Jose: Let me see if I've got this straight. I should recognize an expense this period for something that may or may not be paid to the employees in 20 or 30 years, when they finally retire. How am I supposed to determine what the expense is for the current year? The amount of the final retirement depends on many uncertainties: salary levels, employee longevity, mortality rates, and interest earned on investments to fund the pension. I don't think that an amount can be determined, even if I accepted your arguments.

➡ Evaluate Cara's position. Is she right or is Jose correct?

SA 10-3
Executive bonuses and accounting methods

Paul Sheile, the owner of Sheile Trucking Company, initiated an executive bonus plan for his chief executive officer (CEO). The new plan provides a bonus to the CEO equal to 3% of the income before taxes. Upon learning of the new bonus arrangement, the CEO issued instructions to change the company's accounting for trucks. The CEO has asked the controller to make the following two changes:

a. Change from the double-declining-balance method to the straight-line method of depreciation.

b. Add 50% to the useful lives of all trucks.

➡ Why did the CEO ask for these changes? How would you respond to the CEO's request?

SA 10-4
Ethics and professional conduct in business

Fio Barellis was discussing summer employment with Sara Rida, president of Xanadu Construction Service:

Sara: I'm glad that you're thinking about joining us for the summer. We could certainly use the help.

Fio: Sounds good. I enjoy outdoor work, and I could use the money to help with next year's school expenses.

Sara: I've got a plan that can help you out on that. As you know, I'll pay you $12 per hour, but in addition, I'd like to pay you with cash. Since you're only working for the summer, it really doesn't make sense for me to go to the trouble of formally putting you on our payroll system. In fact, I do some jobs for my clients on a strictly cash basis, so it would be easy to just pay you that way.

Fio: Well, that's a bit unusual, but I guess money is money.

Sara: Yeah, not only that, it's tax-free!

Fio: What do you mean?

Sara: Didn't you know? Any money that you receive in cash is not reported to the IRS on a W-2 form; therefore, the IRS doesn't know about the income—hence, it's the same as tax-free earnings.

a. ➤ Why does Sara Rida want to conduct business transactions using cash (not check or credit card)?

b. ➤ How should Fio respond to Sara's suggestion?

SA 10-5
Payroll forms

Group Project

Internet Project

Payroll accounting involves the use of government-supplied forms to account for payroll taxes. Three common forms are the W-2, Form 940, and Form 941. Form a team with three of your classmates and retrieve copies of each of these forms. They may be obtained from a local IRS office, found at a library, or downloaded from the Internet at **http://www.irs.gov** (go to Forms and Publications).

➤ Briefly describe the purpose of each of the three forms.

SA 10-6
Contingent liabilities

Internet Project

Altria Group, Inc., has over 24 pages dedicated to describing contingent liabilities in the notes to recent financial statements. These pages include extensive descriptions of multiple contingent liabilities. Use the Internet to research Altria Group, Inc., at **http://www.altria.com**.

a. What are the major business units of Altria Group?

b. Based on your understanding of this company, why would Altria Group require 11 pages of contingency disclosure?

Answers to Self-Examination Questions

1. **C** The maturity value is $5,100, determined as follows:

Face amount of note	$5,000
Plus interest ($5,000 × 12% × 60/360)	100
Maturity value	$5,100

2. **B** The net amount available to a borrower from discounting a note payable is called the proceeds. The proceeds of $4,900 (answer B) is determined as follows:

Face amount of note	$5,000
Less discount ($5,000 × 12% × 60/360)	100
Proceeds	$4,900

3. **B** Employers are usually required to withhold a portion of their employees' earnings for payment of federal income taxes (answer A), Medicare tax (answer C), and state and local income taxes (answer D). Generally, federal unemployment compensation taxes (answer B) are levied against the employer only and thus are not deducted from employee earnings.

4. **D** The amount of net pay of $1,385.50 (answer D) is determined as follows:

Gross pay:			
40 hours at $40		$1,600.00	
5 hours at $60		300.00	$1,900.00
Deductions:			
Federal income tax withheld		$ 450.00	
FICA:			
Social security tax ($600 × 0.06)	$36.00		
Medicare tax ($1,900 × 0.015)	28.50	64.50	514.50
			$1,385.50

5. **D** The employer incurs an expense for social security tax (answer A), federal unemployment compensation tax (answer B), and state unemployment compensation tax (answer C). The employees' federal income tax (answer D) is not an expense of the employer. It is withheld from the employees' earnings.

Corporations: Organization, Stock Transactions, and Dividends

© Susan Van Etten

H A S B R O

If you purchase a share of stock from Hasbro, you own a small interest in the company. You may request a Hasbro stock certificate as an indication of your ownership.

As you may know, Hasbro is one of the world's largest toy manufacturers and produces popular children's toys such as G.I. Joe, Play-Doh, Tonka toys, Mr. Potato Head, and Nerf balls. In addition, Hasbro manufactures family entertainment products such as Monopoly, Scrabble, and Trivial Pursuit under the Milton Bradley and Parker Brothers labels. In fact, the stock certificate of Hasbro has a picture of Uncle Pennybags, the Monopoly game icon, printed on it.

Purchasing a share of stock from Hasbro may be a great gift idea for the "hard-to-shop-for person." However, a stock certificate represents more than just a picture that you can frame. In fact, the stock certificate is a document that reflects legal ownership of the future financial prospects of Hasbro. In addition, as a shareholder, it represents your claim against the assets and earnings of the corporation.

If you are purchasing Hasbro stock as an investment, you should analyze Hasbro's financial statements and management's plans for the future. For example, Hasbro has a unique relationship with Disney that allows it to produce and sell licensed Disney products. Should this Disney relationship affect how much you are willing to pay for the stock? Also, you might want to know if Hasbro plans to pay cash dividends or whether management is considering issuing additional shares of stock.

In this chapter, we describe and illustrate the nature of corporations including the accounting for stock and dividends. This discussion will aid you in making decisions such as whether or not to buy Hasbro stock.

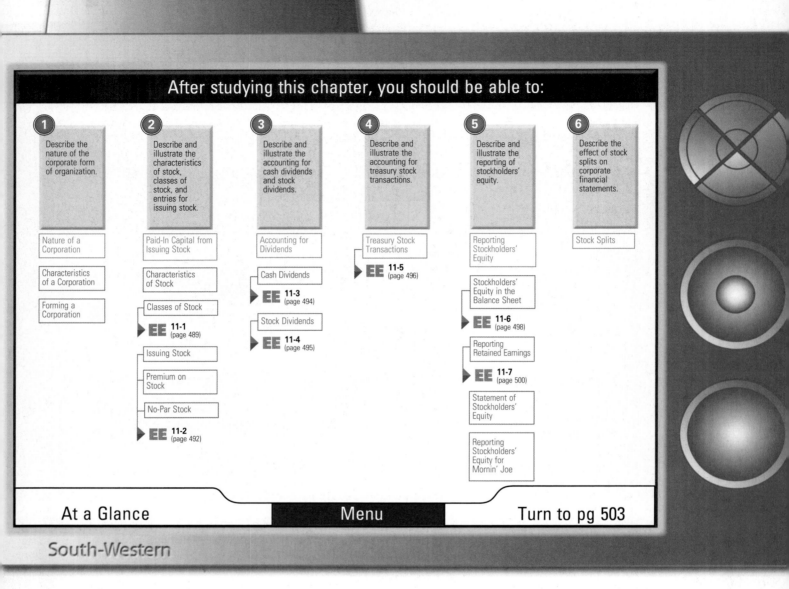

After studying this chapter, you should be able to:

1 Describe the nature of the corporate form of organization.

Nature of a Corporation

Characteristics of a Corporation

Forming a Corporation

2 Describe and illustrate the characteristics of stock, classes of stock, and entries for issuing stock.

Paid-In Capital from Issuing Stock

Characteristics of Stock

Classes of Stock

EE 11-1 (page 489)

Issuing Stock

Premium on Stock

No-Par Stock

EE 11-2 (page 492)

3 Describe and illustrate the accounting for cash dividends and stock dividends.

Accounting for Dividends

Cash Dividends

EE 11-3 (page 494)

Stock Dividends

EE 11-4 (page 495)

4 Describe and illustrate the accounting for treasury stock transactions.

Treasury Stock Transactions

EE 11-5 (page 496)

5 Describe and illustrate the reporting of stockholders' equity.

Reporting Stockholders' Equity

Stockholders' Equity in the Balance Sheet

EE 11-6 (page 498)

Reporting Retained Earnings

EE 11-7 (page 500)

Statement of Stockholders' Equity

Reporting Stockholders' Equity for Mornin' Joe

6 Describe the effect of stock splits on corporate financial statements.

Stock Splits

At a Glance   Menu   Turn to pg 503

South-Western

---

1 Describe the nature of the corporate form of organization.

A corporation was defined in the Dartmouth College case of 1819, in which Chief Justice Marshall of the United States Supreme Court stated: "A corporation is an artificial being, invisible, intangible, and existing only in contemplation of the law."

Nature of a Corporation

Most large businesses are organized as corporations. As a result, corporations generate more than 90% of the total business dollars in the United States. In contrast, most small businesses are organized as proprietorships, partnerships, or limited liability companies.

Characteristics of a Corporation

A *corporation* is a legal entity, distinct and separate from the individuals who create and operate it. As a legal entity, a corporation may acquire, own, and dispose of property in its own name. It may also incur liabilities and enter into contracts. Most importantly, it can sell shares of ownership, called **stock**. This characteristic gives corporations the ability to raise large amounts of capital.

The **stockholders** or *shareholders* who own the stock own the corporation. They can buy and sell stock without affecting the corporation's operations or continued

The Coca-Cola Company is a well-known public corporation. Mars, Incorporated, which is owned by family members, is a well-known private corporation.

existence. Corporations whose shares of stock are traded in public markets are called *public corporations.* Corporations whose shares are not traded publicly are usually owned by a small group of investors and are called *nonpublic* or *private corporations.*

The stockholders of a corporation have *limited liability.* This means that creditors usually may not go beyond the assets of the corporation to satisfy their claims. Thus, the financial loss that a stockholder may suffer is limited to the amount invested.

The stockholders control a corporation by electing a *board of directors.* This board meets periodically to establish corporate policies. It also selects the chief executive officer (CEO) and other major officers to manage the corporation's day-to-day affairs. Exhibit 1 shows the organizational structure of a corporation.

| Exhibit 1 |

Organizational Structure of a Corporation

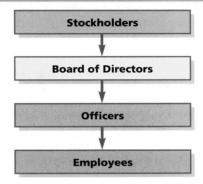

As a separate entity, a corporation is subject to taxes. For example, corporations must pay federal income taxes on their income.[1] Thus, corporate income that is distributed to stockholders in the form of *dividends* has already been taxed. In turn, stockholders must pay income taxes on the dividends they receive. This *double taxation* of corporate earnings is a major disadvantage of the corporate form.[2] The advantages and disadvantages of the corporate form are listed in Exhibit 2.

> **Corporations have a separate legal existence, transferable units of ownership, and limited stockholder liability.**

Integrity, Objectivity, and Ethics in Business

THE RESPONSIBLE BOARD

Recent accounting scandals, such as those involving Enron, WorldCom, and Fannie Mae, have highlighted the roles of boards of directors in executing their responsibilities. For example, eighteen of Enron's former directors and their insurance providers have settled shareholder litigation for $168 million, of which $13 million is to come from the directors' personal assets. Board members are now on notice that their directorship responsibilities are being taken seriously by stockholders.

Forming a Corporation

The first step in forming a corporation is to file an *application of incorporation* with the state. State incorporation laws differ, and corporations often organize in those states with the more favorable laws. For this reason, more than half of the largest companies are incorporated in Delaware. Exhibit 3 lists some corporations, their states of incorporation, and the location of their headquarters.

After the application of incorporation has been approved, the state grants a *charter* or *articles of incorporation.* The articles of incorporation formally create the corporation.[3]

---

1 A majority of states also require corporations to pay income taxes.
2 Dividends presently receive a preferential individual tax rate of 15% to reduce the impact of double taxation.
3 The articles of incorporation may also restrict a corporation's activities in certain areas, such as owning certain types of real estate, conducting certain types of business activities, or purchasing its own stock.

Exhibit 2

Advantages and Disadvantages of the Corporate Form

Advantages	Explanation
Separate legal existence	A corporation exists separately from its owners.
Continuous life	A corporation's life is separate from its owners; therefore, it exists indefinitely.
Raising large amounts of capital	The corporate form is suited for raising large amounts of money from shareholders.
Ownership rights are easily transferable	A corporation sells shares of ownership, called *stock*. The stockholders of a public company can transfer their shares of stock to other stockholders through stock markets, such as the New York Stock Exchange.
Limited liability	A corporation's creditors usually may not go beyond the assets of the corporation to satisfy their claims. Thus, the financial loss that a stockholder may suffer is limited to the amount invested.
Disadvantages	
Owner is separate from management	Stockholders control management through a board of directors. The board of directors should represent shareholder interests; however, the board is often more closely tied to management than to shareholders. As a result, the board of directors and management may not always behave in the best interests of stockholders.
Double taxation of dividends	As a separate legal entity, a corporation is subject to taxation. Thus, net income distributed as dividends will be taxed once at the corporation level, and then again at the individual level.
Regulatory costs	Corporations must satisfy many requirements such as those required by the Sarbanes-Oxley Act of 2002.

A Financial Executives International survey estimated that Sarbanes-Oxley costs the average public company over $3 million per year.

The corporate management and board of directors then prepare a set of *bylaws*, which are the rules and procedures for conducting the corporation's affairs.

Costs may be incurred in organizing a corporation. These costs include legal fees, taxes, state incorporation fees, license fees, and promotional costs. Such costs are debited to an expense account entitled *Organizational Expenses*.

To illustrate, a corporation's organizing costs of $8,500 on January 5 are recorded as shown below.

Jan.	5	Organizational Expenses	8,500	
		Cash		8,500
		Paid costs of organizing the corporation.		

Exhibit 3

Examples of Corporations and Their States of Incorporation

Corporation	State of Incorporation	Headquarters
Caterpillar	Delaware	Peoria, Ill.
Delta Air Lines	Delaware	Atlanta, Ga.
The Dow Chemical Company	Delaware	Midland, Mich.
General Electric Company	New York	Fairfield, Conn.
The Home Depot	Delaware	Atlanta, Ga.
Kellogg Company	Delaware	Battle Creek, Mich.
3M	Delaware	St. Paul, Minn.
R.J. Reynolds Tobacco Company	Delaware	Winston-Salem, N.C.
Starbucks Corporation	Washington	Seattle, Wash.
Sun Microsystems, Inc.	Delaware	Palo Alto, Calif.
The Washington Post Company	Delaware	Washington, D.C.
Whirlpool Corporation	Delaware	Benton Harbor, Mich.

Integrity, Objectivity, and Ethics in Business

NOT-FOR-PROFIT, OR NOT?

Corporations can be formed for not-for-profit purposes by making a request to the Internal Revenue Service under *Internal Revenue Code* section 501(c)3. Such corporations, such as the Sierra Club and the National Audubon Society, are exempt from federal taxes. Forming businesses inside a 501(c)3 exempt organization that competes with profit-making (and hence, tax-paying) businesses is very controversial. For example, should the local YMCA receive a tax exemption for providing similar services as the local health club business? The IRS is now challenging such businesses and is withholding 501(c)3 status to many organizations due to this issue.

Paid-In Capital from Issuing Stock

2 Describe and illustrate the characteristics of stock, classes of stock, and entries for issuing stock.

As described and illustrated in earlier chapters, the two main sources of stockholders' equity are paid-in capital (or contributed capital) and retained earnings. The main source of paid-in capital is from issuing stock.

Characteristics of Stock

Authorized

Issued

Outstanding

Number of shares authorized, issued, and outstanding

Some corporations have stopped issuing stock certificates except on special request. In these cases, the corporation maintains records of ownership.

The number of shares of stock that a corporation is *authorized* to issue is stated in its charter. The term *issued* refers to the shares issued to the stockholders. A corporation may reacquire some of the stock that it has issued. The stock remaining in the hands of stockholders is then called **outstanding stock**. The relationship between authorized, issued, and outstanding stock is shown in the graphic at the left.

Upon request, corporations may issue stock certificates to stockholders to document their ownership. Printed on a stock certificate is the name of the company, the name of the stockholder, and the number of shares owned. The stock certificate may also indicate a dollar amount assigned to each share of stock, called **par** value. Stock may be issued without par, in which case it is called *no-par stock*. In some states, the board of directors of a corporation is required to assign a *stated value* to no-par stock.

Corporations have limited liability and, thus, creditors have no claim against stockholders' personal assets. To protect creditors, however, some states require corporations to maintain a minimum amount of paid-in capital. This minimum amount, called *legal capital*, usually includes the par or stated value of the shares issued.

The major rights that accompany ownership of a share of stock are as follows:

1. The right to vote in matters concerning the corporation.
2. The right to share in distributions of earnings.
3. The right to share in assets on liquidation.

These stock rights normally vary with the class of stock.

Classes of Stock

The two primary classes of paid-in capital are common stock and preferred stock.

When only one class of stock is issued, it is called **common stock**. Each share of common stock has equal rights.

A corporation may also issue one or more classes of stock with various preference rights such as a preference to dividends. Such a stock is called a **preferred stock**. The dividend rights of preferred stock are stated either as dollars per share or as a percent of par. For

example, a $50 par value preferred stock with a $4 per share dividend may be described as either: [4]

$4 preferred stock, $50 par

or

8% preferred stock, $50 par

Because they have first rights (preference) to any dividends, preferred stockholders have a greater chance of receiving dividends than common stockholders. However, since dividends are normally based on earnings, a corporation cannot guarantee dividends even to preferred stockholders.

The payment of dividends is authorized by the corporation's board of directors. When authorized, the directors are said to have *declared* a dividend.

Cumulative preferred stock has a right to receive regular dividends that were not declared (paid) in prior years. Noncumulative preferred stock does not have this right.

Cumulative preferred stock dividends that have not been paid in prior years are said to be **in arrears**. Any preferred dividends in arrears must be paid before any common stock dividends are paid. In addition, any dividends in arrears are normally disclosed in notes to the financial statements.

To illustrate, assume that a corporation has issued the following preferred and common stock:

1,000 shares of $4 cumulative preferred stock, $50 par
4,000 shares of common stock, $15 par

The corporation was organized on January 1, 2008, and paid no dividends in 2008 and 2009. In 2010, the corporation paid dividends of $22,000. Exhibit 4 shows how the $22,000 of dividends paid in 2010 is distributed between the preferred and common stockholders.

In addition to dividend preference, preferred stock may be given preferences to assets if the corporation goes out of business and is liquidated. However, claims of

---

Exhibit 4

Dividends to Cumulative Preferred Stock

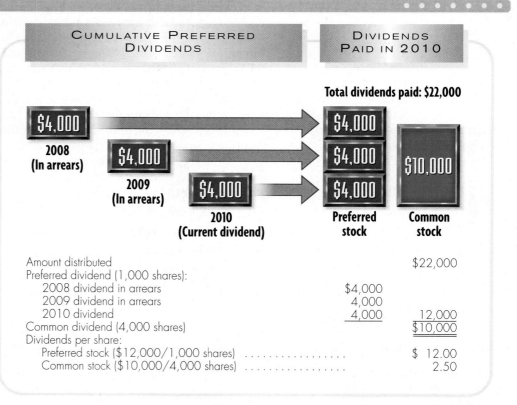

Amount distributed		$22,000
Preferred dividend (1,000 shares):		
2008 dividend in arrears	$4,000	
2009 dividend in arrears	4,000	
2010 dividend	4,000	12,000
Common dividend (4,000 shares)		$10,000
Dividends per share:		
Preferred stock ($12,000/1,000 shares)		$ 12.00
Common stock ($10,000/4,000 shares)		2.50

---

4 In some cases, preferred stock may receive additional dividends if certain conditions are met. Such stock, called *participating preferred stock*, is not often used.

Example Exercise 11-1 Dividends per Share

Sandpiper Company has 20,000 shares of 1% cumulative preferred stock of $100 par and 100,000 shares of $50 par common stock. The following amounts were distributed as dividends:

Year 1 $10,000
Year 2   45,000
Year 3   80,000

Determine the dividends per share for preferred and common stock for each year.

Follow My Example 11-1

	Year 1	Year 2	Year 3
Amount distributed	$10,000	$45,000	$80,000
Preferred dividend (20,000 shares)	10,000	30,000*	20,000
Common dividend (100,000 shares)	$ 0	$15,000	$60,000

*($10,000 + $20,000)

Dividends per share:			
Preferred stock	$0.50	$1.50	$1.00
Common stock	None	$0.15	$0.60

For Practice: PE 11-1A, PE 11-1B

creditors must be satisfied first. Preferred stockholders are next in line to receive any remaining assets, followed by the common stockholders.

Issuing Stock

A separate account is used for recording the amount of each class of stock issued to investors in a corporation. For example, assume that a corporation is authorized to issue 10,000 shares of $100 par preferred stock and 100,000 shares of $20 par common stock. The corporation issued 5,000 shares of preferred stock and 50,000 shares of common stock at par for cash. The corporation's entry to record the stock issue is as follows:[5]

Cash		1,500,000	
Preferred Stock			500,000
Common Stock			1,000,000
Issued preferred stock and common			
stock at par for cash.			

Stock is often issued by a corporation at a price other than its par. The price at which stock is sold depends on a variety of factors, such as the following:

1. The financial condition, earnings record, and dividend record of the corporation.
2. Investor expectations of the corporation's potential earning power.
3. General business and economic conditions and expectations.

If stock is issued (sold) for a price that is more than its par, the stock has been sold at a **premium**. For example, if common stock with a par of $50 is sold for $60 per share, the stock has sold at a premium of $10.

If stock is issued (sold) for a price that is less than its par, the stock has been sold at a **discount**. For example, if common stock with a par of $50 is sold for $45 per share, the stock has sold at a discount of $5. Many states do not permit stock to be sold at a discount. In other states, stock may be sold at a discount in only unusual cases. Since stock is rarely sold at a discount, it is not illustrated.

5 The accounting for investments in stocks from the point of view of the investor is discussed in Chapter 13.

In order to distribute dividends, financial statements, and other reports, a corporation must keep track of its stockholders. Large public corporations normally use a financial institution, such as a bank, for this purpose.[6] In such cases, the financial institution is referred to as a *transfer agent* or *registrar*.

Premium on Stock

When stock is issued at a premium, Cash is debited for the amount received. Common Stock or Preferred Stock is credited for the par amount. The excess of the amount paid over par is part of the paid-in capital. An account entitled *Paid-In Capital in Excess of Par* is credited for this amount.

To illustrate, assume that Caldwell Company issues 2,000 shares of $50 par preferred stock for cash at $55. The entry to record this transaction is as follows:

Cash	110,000	
Preferred Stock		100,000
Paid-In Capital in Excess of Par— Preferred Stock		10,000
Issued $50 par preferred stock at $55.		

When stock is issued in exchange for assets other than cash, such as land, buildings, and equipment, the assets acquired are recorded at their fair market value. If this value cannot be determined, the fair market price of the stock issued is used.

To illustrate, assume that a corporation acquired land with a fair market value that cannot be determined. In exchange, the corporation issued 10,000 shares of its $10 par common. If the stock has a market price of $12 per share, the transaction is recorded as follows:

Land	120,000	
Common Stock		100,000
Paid-In Capital in Excess of Par		20,000
Issued $10 par common stock, valued		
at $12 per share, for land.		

No-Par Stock

In most states, no-par preferred and common stock may be issued. When no-par stock is issued, Cash is debited and Common Stock is credited for the proceeds. As no-par stock is issued over time, this entry is the same even if the issuing price varies.

To illustrate, assume that on January 9 a corporation issues 10,000 shares of no-par common stock at $40 a share. On June 27, the corporation issues an additional 1,000 shares at $36. The entries to record these issuances of the no-par stock are as follows:

---

6 Small corporations may use a subsidiary ledger, called a *stockholders ledger*. In this case, the stock accounts (Preferred Stock and Common Stock) are controlling accounts for the subsidiary ledger.

Jan.	9	Cash	400,000	
		Common Stock		400,000
		Issued 10,000 shares of no-par		
		common at $40.		
June	27	Cash	36,000	
		Common Stock		36,000
		Issued 1,000 shares of no-par		
		common at $36.		

Business Connection

CISCO SYSTEMS, INC.

Cisco Systems, Inc., manufactures and sells networking and communications products worldwide. Some excerpts of its bylaws are shown below.

ARTICLE 2
SHAREHOLDERS' MEETINGS
Section 2.01 Annual Meetings. The annual meeting of the shareholders of the Corporation . . . shall be held each year on the second Thursday in November at 10:00 A.M. . . .

ARTICLE 3
BOARD OF DIRECTORS
Section 3.02 Number and Qualification of Directors. The number of authorized directors of this Corporation shall be not less than eight (8) nor more than fifteen (15), . . . to be (determined) by . . . the Board of Directors or shareholders.

Section 3.04 Special Meetings. Special meetings of the Board of Directors may be called at any time by the Chairman of the Board, the President of the Corporation or any two (2) directors.

ARTICLE 4
OFFICERS
Section 4.01 Number and Term. The officers of the Corporation shall include a President, a Secretary and a Chief Financial Officer, all of which shall be chosen by the Board of Directors. . . .

Section 4.05 Chairman of the Board. The Chairman of the Board shall preside at all meetings of the Board of Directors.

© AP PHOTO/PAUL SAKUMA

Section 4.06 President. The President shall be the general manager and chief executive officer of the Corporation, . . . shall preside at all meetings of shareholders, shall have general supervision of the affairs of the Corporation. . . .

Section 4.08 Secretary. The Secretary shall keep . . . minutes of all meetings, shall have charge of the seal and the corporate books. . . .

Section 4.10 Treasurer. The Treasurer shall have custody of all moneys and securities of the Corporation and shall keep regular books of account. . . .

Section 5.04 Fiscal Year. The fiscal year of the Corporation shall end on the last Saturday of July.

In some states, no-par stock may be assigned a *stated value per share*. The stated value is recorded like a par value. Any excess of the proceeds over the stated value is credited to *Paid-In Capital in Excess of Stated Value.*

To illustrate, assume that in the preceding example the no-par common stock is assigned a stated value of $25. The issuance of the stock on January 9 and June 27 is recorded as follows:

Jan.	9	Cash	400,000	
		Common Stock		250,000
		Paid-In Capital in Excess of Stated Value		150,000
		Issued 10,000 shares of no-par common at $40; stated value, $25.		
June	27	Cash	36,000	
		Common Stock		25,000
		Paid-In Capital in Excess of Stated Value		11,000
		Issued 1,000 shares of no-par common at $36; stated value, $25.		

Example Exercise 11-2   Entries for Issuing Stock   ●●●●●●●> 2

On March 6, Limerick Corporation issued for cash 15,000 shares of no-par common stock at $30. On April 13, Limerick issued at par 1,000 shares of 4%, $40 par preferred stock for cash. On May 19, Limerick issued for cash 15,000 shares of 4%, $40 par preferred stock at $42.

Journalize the entries to record the March 6, April 13, and May 19 transactions.

Follow My Example 11-2

Mar.	6	Cash	450,000	
		Common Stock		450,000
		(15,000 shares × $30).		
Apr.	13	Cash	40,000	
		Preferred Stock		40,000
		(1,000 shares × $40).		
May	19	Cash	630,000	
		Preferred Stock		600,000
		Paid-In Capital in Excess of Par		30,000
		(15,000 shares × $42).		

For Practice: PE 11-2A, PE 11-2B

---

3 Describe and illustrate the accounting for cash dividends and stock dividends.

Accounting for Dividends

When a board of directors declares a cash dividend, it authorizes the distribution of cash to stockholders. When a board of directors declares a stock dividend, it authorizes the distribution of its stock. In both cases, declaring a dividend reduces the retained earnings of the corporation.[7]

Cash Dividends

A cash distribution of earnings by a corporation to its shareholders is a **cash dividend**. Although dividends may be paid in other assets, cash dividends are the most common.

Three conditions for a cash dividend are as follows:

1. Sufficient retained earnings
2. Sufficient cash
3. Formal action by the board of directors

There must be a sufficient (large enough) balance in Retained Earnings to declare a cash dividend. That is, the balance of Retained Earnings must be large enough so that the dividend does not create a debit balance in the retained earnings account. However,

[7] In rare cases, when a corporation is reducing its operations or going out of business, a dividend may be a distribution of paid-in capital. Such a dividend is called a *liquidating dividend*.

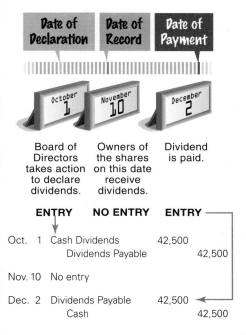

Date of Declaration	Date of Record	Date of Payment
October 1	November 10	December 2
Board of Directors takes action to declare dividends.	Owners of the shares on this date receive dividends.	Dividend is paid.
ENTRY	**NO ENTRY**	**ENTRY**

Oct. 1 Cash Dividends   42,500
       Dividends Payable   42,500

Nov. 10 No entry

Dec. 2 Dividends Payable   42,500
       Cash   42,500

The Campbell Soup Company declared on March 27 a quarterly cash dividend of $0.22 to common stockholders of record as of the close of business on April 17, payable on April 28.

a large Retained Earnings balance does not mean that there is cash available to pay dividends. This is because the balances of Cash and Retained Earnings are often unrelated.

Even if there are sufficient retained earnings and cash, a corporation's board of directors is not required to pay dividends. Nevertheless, many corporations pay quarterly cash dividends to make their stock more attractive to investors. *Special* or *extra* dividends may also be paid when a corporation experiences higher than normal profits.

Three dates included in a dividend announcement are as follows:

1. Date of declaration
2. Date of record
3. Date of payment

The *date of declaration* is the date the board of directors formally authorizes the payment of the dividend. On this date, the corporation incurs the liability to pay the amount of the dividend.

The *date of record* is the date the corporation uses to determine which stockholders will receive the dividend. During the period of time between the date of declaration and the date of record, the stock price is quoted as selling *with-dividends*. This means that any investors purchasing the stock before the date of record will receive the dividend.

The *date of payment* is the date the corporation will pay the dividend to the stockholders who owned the stock on the date of record. During the period of time between the record date and the payment date, the stock price is quoted as selling *ex-dividends*. This means that since the date of record has passed, any new investors will not receive the dividend.

To illustrate, assume that on October 1 Hiber Corporation declares the cash dividends shown below with a date of record of November 10 and a date of payment of December 2.

	Dividend per Share	Total Dividends
Preferred stock, $100 par, 5,000 shares outstanding	$2.50	$12,500
Common stock, $10 par, 100,000 shares outstanding	$0.30	30,000
Total		$42,500

On October 1, the declaration date, Hiber Corporation records the following entry:

Oct.	1	Cash Dividends	42,500	
		Cash Dividends Payable		42,500
		Declared cash dividends.		

On November 10, the date of record, no entry is necessary. This date merely determines which stockholders will receive the dividends.

On December 2, the date of payment, Hiber Corporation records the payment of the dividends as follows:

Dec.	2	Cash Dividends Payable	42,500	
		Cash		42,500
		Paid cash dividends.		

At the end of the accounting period, the balance in Cash Dividends will be transferred to Retained Earnings as part of the closing process. This closing entry debits Retained Earnings and credits Cash Dividends for the balance of the cash dividends account. If the cash dividends have not been paid by the end of the period, Cash Dividends Payable will be reported on the balance sheet as a current liability.

Example Exercise 11-3 Entries for Cash Dividends

The important dates in connection with a cash dividend of $75,000 on a corporation's common stock are February 26, March 30, and April 2. Journalize the entries required on each date.

Follow My Example 11-3

Feb. 26	Cash Dividends	75,000	
	Cash Dividends Payable		75,000
Mar. 30	No entry required.		
Apr. 2	Cash Dividends Payable	75,000	
	Cash		75,000

For Practice: PE 11-3A, PE 11-3B

Integrity, Objectivity, and Ethics in Business

THE PROFESSOR WHO KNEW TOO MUCH

A major Midwestern university released a quarterly "American Customer Satisfaction Index" based on its research of customers of popular U.S. products and services. Before the release of the index to the public, the professor in charge of the research bought and sold stocks of some of the companies in the report. The professor was quoted as saying that he thought it was important to test his theories of customer satisfaction with "real" [his own] money.

Is this proper or ethical? Apparently, the dean of the Business School didn't think so. In a statement to the press, the dean stated: "I have instructed anyone affiliated with the (index) not to make personal use of information gathered in the course of producing the quarterly index, prior to the index's release to the general public, and they [the researchers] have agreed."

Sources: Jon E. Hilsenrath and Dan Morse, "Researcher Uses Index to Buy, Short Stocks," *The Wall Street Journal*, February 18, 2003; and Jon E. Hilsenrath, "Satisfaction Theory: Mixed Results," *The Wall Street Journal*, February 19, 2003.

Stock Dividends

A **stock dividend** is a distribution of shares of stock to stockholders. Stock dividends are normally declared only on common stock and issued to common stockholders.

The recording of a stock dividend affects only stockholders' equity. Specifically, the amount of the stock dividend is transferred from Retained Earnings to Paid-In Capital. The amount transferred is normally the fair value (market price) of the shares issued in the stock dividend.[8]

To illustrate, assume that the stockholders' equity accounts of Hendrix Corporation as of December 15 are as follows:

Common Stock, $20 par (2,000,000 shares issued)	$40,000,000
Paid-In Capital in Excess of Par—Common Stock	9,000,000
Retained Earnings	26,600,000

On December 15, Hendrix Corporation declares a stock dividend of 5% or 100,000 shares (2,000,000 shares × 5%) to be issued on January 10 to stockholders of record on December 31. The market price of the stock on December 15 (the date of declaration) is $31 per share.

The entry to record the stock dividend is as follows:

Dec.	15	Stock Dividends	3,100,000	
		Stock Dividends Distributable		2,000,000
		Paid-In Capital in Excess of Par—Common Stock		1,100,000
		Declared 5% (100,000 share) stock dividend on $20 par common stock with a market price of $31 per share.		

---

8 The use of fair market value is justified as long as the number of shares issued for the stock dividend is small (less than 25% of the shares outstanding).

After the preceding entry is recorded, Stock Dividends will have a debit balance of $3,100,000. Like cash dividends, the stock dividends account is closed to Retained Earnings at the end of the accounting period. This closing entry debits Retained Earnings and credits Stock Dividends.

At the end of the period, the *stock dividends distributable* and *paid-in capital in excess of par—common stock* accounts are reported in the Paid-In Capital section of the balance sheet. Thus, the effect of the preceding stock dividend is to transfer $3,100,000 of retained earnings to paid-in capital.

On January 10, the stock dividend is distributed to stockholders by issuing 100,000 shares of common stock. The issuance of the stock is recorded by the following entry:

Jan.	10	Stock Dividends Distributable	2,000,000	
		Common Stock		2,000,000
		Issued stock as stock dividend.		

A stock dividend does not change the assets, liabilities, or total stockholders' equity of a corporation. Likewise, a stock dividend does not change an individual stockholder's proportionate interest (equity) in the corporation.

To illustrate, assume a stockholder owns 1,000 of a corporation's 10,000 shares outstanding. If the corporation declares a 6% stock dividend, the stockholder's proportionate interest will not change as shown below.

	Before **Stock Dividend**	*After* **Stock Dividend**
Total shares issued	10,000	10,600 [10,000 + (10,000 × 6%)]
Number of shares owned	1,000	1,060 [1,000 + (1,000 × 6%)]
Proportionate ownership	10% (1,000/10,000)	10% (1,060/10,600)

Example Exercise 11-4   Entries for Stock Dividends   •••••••• ▶ ③

Vienna Highlights Corporation has 150,000 shares of $100 par common stock outstanding. On June 14, Vienna Highlights declared a 4% stock dividend to be issued August 15 to stockholders of record on July 1. The market price of the stock was $110 per share on June 14.

Journalize the entries required on June 14, July 1, and August 15.

Follow My Example 11-4

June 14	Stock Dividends (150,000 × 4% × $110)	660,000	
	Stock Dividends Distributable (6,000 × $100)		600,000
	Paid-In Capital in Excess of Par—Common Stock		
	($660,000 − $600,000)		60,000
July 1	No entry required.		
Aug. 15	Stock Dividends Distributable	600,000	
	Common Stock		600,000

For Practice: PE 11-4A, PE 11-4B

④ Describe and illustrate the accounting for treasury stock transactions.

Treasury Stock Transactions

Treasury stock is stock that a corporation has issued and then reacquired. A corporation may reacquire (purchase) its own stock for a variety of reasons including the following:

1. To provide shares for resale to employees,
2. To reissue as bonuses to employees, or
3. To support the market price of the stock

The *cost method* is normally used for recording the purchase and resale of treasury stock.[9] Using the cost method, *Treasury Stock* is debited for the cost (purchase price) of the stock. When the stock is resold, Treasury Stock is credited for its cost. Any difference between the cost and the selling price is debited or credited to *Paid-In Capital from Sale of Treasury Stock*.

To illustrate, assume that a corporation has the following paid-in capital on January 1:

Common stock, $25 par (20,000 shares authorized and issued)	$500,000
Excess of issue price over par	150,000
	$650,000

On February 13, the corporation purchases 1,000 shares of its common stock at $45 per share. The entry to record the purchase of the treasury stock is as follows:

Feb.	13	Treasury Stock	45,000	
		Cash		45,000
		Purchased 1,000 shares of treasury stock at $45.		

On April 29, the corporation sells 600 shares of the treasury stock for $60. The entry to record the sale is as follows:

Apr.	29	Cash	36,000	
		Treasury Stock		27,000
		Paid-In Capital from Sale of Treasury Stock		9,000
		Sold 600 shares of treasury stock at $60.		

A sale of treasury stock may result in a decrease in paid-in capital. To the extent that Paid-In Capital from Sale of Treasury Stock has a credit balance, it is debited for any such decrease. Any remaining decrease is then debited to the retained earnings account.

To illustrate, assume that on October 4, the corporation sells the remaining 400 shares of treasury stock for $40 per share. The entry to record the sale is as follows:

Oct.	4	Cash	16,000	
		Paid-In Capital from Sale of Treasury Stock	2,000	
		Treasury Stock		18,000
		Sold 400 shares of treasury stock at $40.		

The October 4 entry shown above decreases paid-in capital by $2,000. Since Paid-In Capital from Sale of Treasury Stock has a credit balance of $9,000, the entire $2,000 was debited to Paid-In Capital from Sale of Treasury Stock.

No dividends (cash or stock) are paid on the shares of treasury stock. To do so would result in the corporation earning dividend revenue from itself.

Example Exercise 11-5   Entries for Treasury Stock   •••••••> 4

On May 3, Buzz Off Corporation reacquired 3,200 shares of its common stock at $42 per share. On July 22, Buzz Off sold 2,000 of the reacquired shares at $47 per share. On August 30, Buzz Off sold the remaining shares at $40 per share.

Journalize the transactions of May 3, July 22, and August 30.

(continued)

Follow My Example 11-5

May 3	Treasury Stock (3,200 × $42)	134,400	
	Cash		134,400
July 22	Cash (2,000 × $47)	94,000	
	Treasury Stock (2,000 × $42)		84,000
	Paid-In Capital from Sale of Treasury Stock		
	[2,000 × ($47 − $42)]		10,000
Aug. 30	Cash (1,200 × $40)	48,000	
	Paid-In Capital from Sale of Treasury Stock [1,200 × ($42 − $40)]	2,400	
	Treasury Stock (1,200 × $42)		50,400

For Practice: PE 11-5A, PE 11-5B

5 Describe and illustrate the reporting of stockholders' equity.

Reporting Stockholders' Equity

As with other sections of the balance sheet, alternative terms and formats may be used in reporting stockholders' equity. Also, changes in retained earnings and paid-in capital may be reported in separate statements or notes to the financial statements.

Stockholders' Equity in the Balance Sheet

Exhibit 5 shows two methods for reporting stockholders' equity for the December 31, 2010, balance sheet for Telex Inc.

Method 1. Each class of stock is reported, followed by its related paid-in capital accounts. Retained earnings is then reported followed by a deduction for treasury stock.

Method 2. The stock accounts are reported, followed by the paid-in capital reported as a single item, Additional paid-in capital. Retained earnings is then reported followed by a deduction for treasury stock.

Exhibit 5

Stockholders' Equity Section of a Balance Sheet

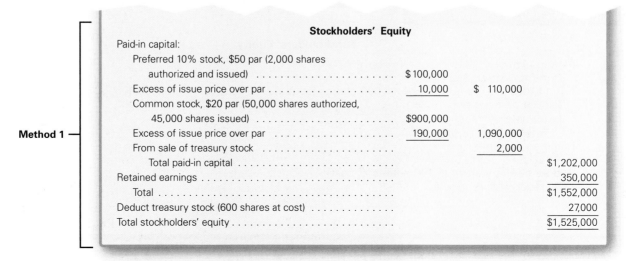

Telex Inc.
Balance Sheet
December 31, 2010

Stockholders' Equity

Paid-in capital:		
Preferred 10% stock, $50 par (2,000 shares authorized and issued) $100,000		
Excess of issue price over par 10,000	$ 110,000	
Common stock, $20 par (50,000 shares authorized, 45,000 shares issued) $900,000		
Excess of issue price over par 190,000	1,090,000	
From sale of treasury stock	2,000	
Total paid-in capital		$1,202,000
Retained earnings		350,000
Total		$1,552,000
Deduct treasury stock (600 shares at cost)		27,000
Total stockholders' equity.......................		$1,525,000

Method 1

(continued)

Exhibit 5 (continued)

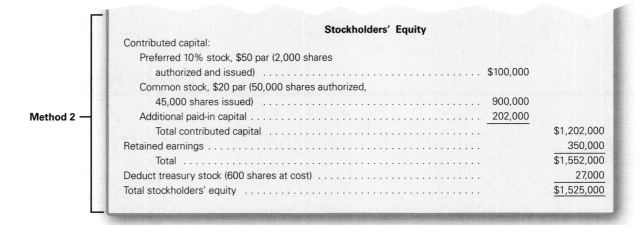

Method 2

Telex Inc.
Balance Sheet
December 31, 2010

Stockholders' Equity

Contributed capital:
Preferred 10% stock, $50 par (2,000 shares
authorized and issued) $100,000
Common stock, $20 par (50,000 shares authorized,
45,000 shares issued) 900,000
Additional paid-in capital 202,000
Total contributed capital $1,202,000
Retained earnings 350,000
Total $1,552,000
Deduct treasury stock (600 shares at cost) 27,000
Total stockholders' equity $1,525,000

Significant changes in stockholders' equity during a period may also be presented in a statement of stockholders' equity or in the notes to the financial statements. The statement of stockholders' equity is illustrated later in this section.

Relevant rights and privileges of the various classes of stock outstanding should also be reported.[10] Examples include dividend and liquidation preferences, conversion rights, and redemption rights. Such information may be disclosed on the face of the balance sheet or in the notes to the financial statements.

Example Exercise 11-6   Reporting Stockholders' Equity   5

Using the following accounts and balances, prepare the Stockholders' Equity section of the balance sheet. Forty thousand shares of common stock are authorized, and 5,000 shares have been reacquired.

Common Stock, $50 par	$1,500,000
Paid-In Capital in Excess of Par	160,000
Paid-In Capital from Sale of Treasury Stock	44,000
Retained Earnings	4,395,000
Treasury Stock	120,000

Follow My Example 11-6

Stockholders' Equity

Paid-in capital:
Common stock, $50 par
(40,000 shares authorized, 30,000 shares issued) $1,500,000
Excess of issue price over par 160,000 $1,660,000
From sale of treasury stock 44,000
Total paid-in capital $1,704,000
Retained earnings 4,395,000
Total. $6,099,000
Deduct treasury stock (5,000 shares at cost). 120,000
Total stockholders' equity $5,979,000

For Practice: PE 11-6A, PE 11-6B

10 *Statement of Financial Accounting Standards No. 129,* "Disclosure Information about Capital Structure" (Financial Accounting Standards Board, Norwalk, CT: 1997).

Reporting Retained Earnings

Changes in retained earnings may be reported using one of the following:

1. Separate retained earnings statement
2. Combined income and retained earnings statement
3. Statement of stockholders' equity

Changes in retained earnings may be reported in a separate retained earnings statement. When a separate retained earnings statement is prepared, the beginning balance of retained earnings is reported. The net income is then added (or net loss is subtracted) and any dividends are subtracted to arrive at the ending retained earnings for the period.

To illustrate, a retained earnings statement for Telex Inc. is shown in Exhibit 6.

Exhibit 6

Retained Earnings Statement

Telex Inc. Retained Earnings Statement For the Year Ended December 31, 2010			
Retained earnings, January 1, 2010			$245,000
Net income		$180,000	
Less dividends:			
Preferred stock	$10,000		
Common stock	65,000	75,000	
Increase in retained earnings			105,000
Retained earnings, December 31, 2010			$350,000

Changes in retained earnings may also be reported in combination with the income statement. This format emphasizes net income as the connecting link between the income statement and ending retained earnings. Since this format is not often used, we do not illustrate it.

Changes in retained earnings may also be reported in a statement of stockholders' equity. An example of reporting changes in retained earnings in a statement of stockholders' equity for Telex Inc. is shown in Exhibit 7.

Restrictions The use of retained earnings for payment of dividends may be restricted by action of a corporation's board of directors. Such **restrictions,** sometimes called *appropriations,* remain part of the retained earnings.

Restrictions of retained earnings are classified as:

The 2007 edition of *Accounting Trends & Techniques* indicated that 0.5% of the companies surveyed presented a separate statement of retained earnings, 0.5% presented a combined income and retained earnings statement, and 1% presented changes in retained earnings in the notes to the financial statements. The other 98% of the companies presented changes in retained earnings in a statement of stockholders' equity.

1. *Legal.* State laws may require a restriction of retained earnings.

> Example: States may restrict retained earnings by the amount of treasury stock purchased. In this way, legal capital cannot be used for dividends.

2. *Contractual.* A corporation may enter into contracts that require restrictions of retained earnings.

> Example: A bank loan may restrict retained earnings so that money for repaying the loan cannot be used for dividends.

3. *Discretionary.* A corporation's board of directors may restrict retained earnings voluntarily.

> Example: The board may restrict retained earnings and, thus, limit dividend distributions so that more money is available for expanding the business.

Restrictions of retained earnings must be disclosed in the financial statements. Such disclosures are usually included in the notes to the financial statements.

Example Exercise 11-7   Retained Earnings Statement

Dry Creek Cameras Inc. reported the following results for the year ending March 31, 2010:

Retained earnings, April 1, 2009	$3,338,500
Net income	461,500
Cash dividends declared	80,000
Stock dividends declared	120,000

Prepare a retained earnings statement for the fiscal year ended March 31, 2010.

Follow My Example 11-7

Dry Creek Cameras Inc.
Retained Earnings Statement
For the Year Ended March 31, 2010

Retained earnings, April 1, 2009		$3,338,500
Net income	$461,500	
Less dividends declared	200,000	
Increase in retained earnings		261,500
Retained earnings, March 31, 2010		$3,600,000

For Practice: PE 11-7A, PE 11-7B

Prior Period Adjustments An error may arise from a mathematical mistake or from a mistake in applying accounting principles. Such errors may not be discovered within the same period in which they occur. In such cases, the effect of the error should not affect the current period's net income. Instead, the correction of the error, called a **prior period adjustment**, is reported in the retained earnings statement. Such corrections are reported as an adjustment to the beginning balance of retained earnings.[11]

Statement of Stockholders' Equity

When the only change in stockholders' equity is due to net income or net loss and dividends, a retained earnings statement is sufficient. However, when a corporation also has changes in stock and paid-in capital accounts, a **statement of stockholders' equity** is normally prepared.

A statement of stockholders' equity is normally prepared in a columnar format. Each column is a major stockholders' equity classification. Changes in each classification are then described in the left-hand column. Exhibit 7 illustrates a statement of stockholders' equity for Telex Inc.

Exhibit 7

Statement of Stockholders' Equity

Telex Inc.
Statement of Stockholders' Equity
For the Year Ended December 31, 2010

	Preferred Stock	Common Stock	Additional Paid-In Capital	Retained Earnings	Treasury Stock	Total
Balance, January 1, 2010	$100,000	$850,000	$177,000	$245,000	$ (17,000)	$1,355,000
Net income				180,000		180,000
Dividends on preferred stock				(10,000)		(10,000)
Dividends on common stock				(65,000)		(65,000)
Issuance of additional common stock . .		50,000	25,000			75,000
Purchase of treasury stock					(10,000)	(10,000)
Balance, December 31, 2010	$100,000	$900,000	$202,000	$350,000	$ (27,000)	$1,525,000

Reporting Stockholders' Equity for Mornin' Joe

Mornin' Joe reports stockholders' equity in its balance sheet. Mornin' Joe also includes a retained earnings statement and statement of stockholders' equity in its financial statements.

The Stockholders' Equity section of Mornin' Joe's balance sheet as of December 31, 2010, is shown below.

Mornin' Joe
Balance Sheet
December 31, 2010

Stockholders' Equity

Paid-in capital:		
Preferred 10% stock, $50 par (6,000 shares		
authorized and issued)	$ 300,000	
Excess of issue price over par	50,000	$ 350,000
Common stock, $20 par (50,000 shares authorized,		
45,000 shares issued)	$ 900,000	
Excess of issue price over par	1,450,000	2,350,000
Total paid-in capital		$2,700,000
Retained earnings		1,200,300
Total		$3,900,300
Deduct treasury stock (1,000 shares at cost)		46,000
Total stockholders' equity		$3,854,300
Total liabilities and stockholders' equity		$6,169,700

Mornin' Joe's retained earnings statement for the year ended December 31, 2010, is as follows:

Mornin' Joe
Retained Earnings Statement
For the Year Ended December 31, 2010

Retained earnings, January 1, 2010			$ 852,700
Net income		$421,600	
Less dividends:			
Preferred stock	$30,000		
Common stock	44,000	74,000	
Increase in retained earnings			347,600
Retained earnings, December 31, 2010			$1,200,300

The statement of stockholders' equity for Mornin' Joe is shown below.

Mornin' Joe
Statement of Stockholders' Equity
For the Year Ended December 31, 2010

	Preferred Stock	Common Stock	Additional Paid-In Capital	Retained Earnings	Treasury Stock	Total
Balance, January 1, 2010	$300,000	$800,000	$1,325,000	$ 852,700	$ (36,000)	$3,241,700
Net income				421,600		421,600
Dividends on preferred stock				(30,000)		(30,000)
Dividends on common stock				(44,000)		(44,000)
Issuance of additional common stock		100,000	175,000			275,000
Purchase of treasury stock					(10,000)	(10,000)
Balance, December 31, 2010	$300,000	$900,000	$1,500,000	$1,200,300	$ (46,000)	$3,854,300

6 Describe the effect of stock splits on corporate financial statements.

When Nature's Sunshine Products, Inc., declared a 2-for-1 stock split, the company president said:

We believe the split will place our stock price in a range attractive to both individual and institutional investors, broadening the market for the stock.

Stock Splits

A **stock split** is a process by which a corporation reduces the par or stated value of its common stock and issues a proportionate number of additional shares. A stock split applies to all common shares including the unissued, issued, and treasury shares.

A major objective of a stock split is to reduce the market price per share of the stock. This, in turn, attracts more investors to the stock and broadens the types and numbers of stockholders.

To illustrate, assume that Rojek Corporation has 10,000 shares of $100 par common stock outstanding with a current market price of $150 per share. The board of directors declares the following stock split:

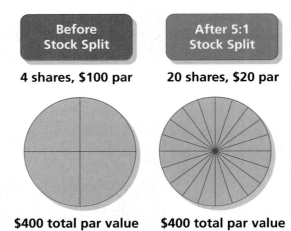

1. Each common shareholder will receive 5 shares for each share held. This is called a 5-for-1 stock split. As a result, 50,000 shares (10,000 shares × 5) will be outstanding.
2. The par of each share of common stock will be reduced to $20 ($100/5).

The par value of the common stock outstanding is $1,000,000 both before and after the stock split as shown below.

	Before Split	After Split
Number of shares	10,000	50,000
Par value per share	× $100	× $20
Total	$1,000,000	$1,000,000

In addition, each Rojek Corporation shareholder owns the same total par amount of stock before and after the stock split. For example, a stockholder who owned 4 shares of $100 par stock before the split (total par of $400) would own 20 shares of $20 par stock after the split (total par of $400). Only the number of shares and the par value per share have changed.

> **A stock split does not require a journal entry.**

Since there are more shares outstanding after the stock split, the market price of the stock should decrease. For example, in the preceding example, there would be 5 times as many shares outstanding after the split. Thus, the market price of the stock would be expected to fall from $150 to about $30 ($150/5).

Stock splits do not require a journal entry since only the par (or stated) value and number of shares outstanding have changed. However, the details of stock splits are normally disclosed in the notes to the financial statements.

Financial Analysis and Interpretation

The amount of net income is often used by investors and creditors in evaluating a company's profitability. However, net income by itself is difficult to use in comparing companies of different sizes. Also, trends in net income may be difficult to evaluate if there have been significant changes in a company's stockholders' equity. Thus, the profitability of companies is often expressed as earnings per share. **Earnings per common share (EPS)**, sometimes called *basic earnings per share,* is the net income per share of common stock outstanding during a period. Corporations whose stock is traded in a public market must report earnings per common share on their income statements.

The earnings per share is calculated as follows:

Earnings per Share

$$= \frac{\text{Net Income} - \text{Preferred Dividends}}{\text{Number of Common Shares Outstanding}}$$

If a company has preferred stock outstanding, the net income must be reduced by the amount of any preferred dividends since the numerator represents only those earnings available to the common shareholders. When the number of common shares outstanding has changed during the period, a weighted average number of shares outstanding is used in the denominator.

Earnings per share can be used to compare two companies with different net incomes. For example, the following data are available for a recent year for Blockbuster Inc. and Netflix, Inc., which are two companies in the video rental business:

	Blockbuster Inc. (in millions)	Netflix, Inc. (in millions)
Net income	$54.7	$49.1
Preferred dividends	$11.3	$0.0
Number of common shares outstanding	187.1	62.6

The earnings per share for both companies can be calculated as follows:

$$\text{Blockbuster Inc:} \quad \frac{\$54.7 - \$11.3}{187.1 \text{ common shares outstanding}}$$

$$= \$0.23 \text{ per common share}$$

$$\text{Netflix, Inc.:} \quad \frac{\$49.1}{62.6 \text{ common shares outstanding}}$$

$$= \$0.78 \text{ per common share}$$

Thus, while the net income of Blockbuster exceeds that of Netflix, the earnings per share of Netflix is more than three times as great as Blockbuster. This results from Blockbuster's preferred dividends and Netflix's much fewer shares outstanding. Not surprisingly, the stock price of Netflix ($21.60) is greater than Blockbuster's ($3.25), reflecting the superior earnings per share performance.

At a Glance 11 ● ● ●>

1 Describe the nature of the corporate form of organization.

Key Points	Key Learning Outcomes	Example Exercises	Practice Exercises
Corporations have a separate legal existence, transferable units of stock, unlimited life, and limited stockholders' liability. The advantages and disadvantages of the corporate form are summarized in Exhibit 2. Costs incurred in organizing a corporation are debited to Organizational Expenses.	• Describe the characteristics of corporations. • List the advantages and disadvantages of the corporate form. • Prepare a journal entry for the costs of organizing a corporation.		

2 Describe and illustrate the characteristics of stock, classes of stock, and entries for issuing stock.

Key Points	Key Learning Outcomes	Example Exercises	Practice Exercises
The main source of paid-in capital is from issuing common and preferred stock. Stock issued at par is recorded by debiting Cash and crediting the class of stock issued for its par amount. Stock issued for more than par is recorded by debiting Cash, crediting the class of stock for its par, and crediting Paid-In Capital in Excess of Par for the difference. When stock is issued in exchange for assets other than cash, the assets acquired are recorded at their fair market value. When no-par stock is issued, the entire proceeds are credited to the stock account. No-par stock may be assigned a stated value per share, and the excess of the proceeds over the stated value may be credited to Paid-In Capital in Excess of Stated Value.	• Describe the characteristics of common and preferred stock including rights to dividends.	**11-1**	11-1A, 11-1B
	• Journalize the entry for common and preferred stock issued at par.	**11-2**	11-2A, 11-2B
	• Journalize the entry for common and preferred stock issued at more than par.	**11-2**	11-2A, 11-2B
	• Journalize the entry for issuing no-par stock.	**11-2**	11-2A, 11-2B

3 Describe and illustrate the accounting for cash dividends and stock dividends.

Key Points	Key Learning Outcomes	Example Exercises	Practice Exercises
The entry to record a declaration of cash dividends debits Dividends and credits Dividends Payable. When a stock dividend is declared, Stock Dividends is debited for the fair value of the stock to be issued. Stock Dividends Distributable is credited for the par or stated value of the common stock to be issued. The difference between the fair value of the stock and its par or stated value is credited to Paid-In Capital in Excess of Par—Common Stock. When the stock is issued on the date of payment, Stock Dividends Distributable is debited and Common Stock is credited for the par or stated value of the stock issued.	• Journalize the entries for the declaration and payment of cash dividends.	**11-3**	11-3A, 11-3B
	• Journalize the entries for the declaration and payment of stock dividends.	**11-4**	11-4A, 11-4B

4 Describe and illustrate the accounting for treasury stock transactions.

Key Points	Key Learning Outcomes	Example Exercises	Practice Exercises
When a corporation buys its own stock, the cost method of accounting is normally used. Treasury Stock is debited for its cost, and Cash is credited. If the stock is resold, Treasury Stock is credited for its cost and any difference between the cost and the selling price is normally debited or credited to Paid-In Capital from Sale of Treasury Stock.	• Define *treasury stock*.		
	• Describe the accounting for treasury stock.		
	• Journalize entries for the purchase and sale of treasury stock.	**11-5**	11-5A, 11-5B

Describe and illustrate the reporting of stockholders' equity.

Key Points	Key Learning Outcomes	Example Exercises	Practice Exercises
Two alternatives for reporting stockholders' equity are shown in Exhibit 5. Changes in retained earnings are reported in a retained earnings statement, as shown in Exhibit 6. Restrictions to retained earnings should be disclosed. Any prior period adjustments are reported in the retained earnings statement. Changes in stockholders' equity may be reported on a statement of stockholders' equity, as shown in Exhibit 7.	• Prepare the Stockholders' Equity section of the balance sheet.	**11-6**	11-6A, 11-6B
	• Prepare a retained earnings statement.	**11-7**	11-7A, 11-7B
	• Describe retained earnings restrictions and prior period adjustments.		
	• Prepare a statement of stockholders' equity.		

6 Describe the effect of stock splits on corporate financial statements.

Key Points	Key Learning Outcomes	Example Exercises	Practice Exercises
When a corporation reduces the par or stated value of its common stock and issues a proportionate number of additional shares, a stock split has occurred. There are no changes in the balances of any accounts, and no entry is required for a stock split.	• Define and give an example of a stock split.		
	• Describe the accounting for and effects of a stock split on the financial statements.		

Key Terms

cash dividend (492)
common stock (487)
cumulative preferred stock (488)
discount (489)
earnings per common share (EPS) (503)
in arrears (488)
outstanding stock (487)

par (487)
preferred stock (487)
premium (489)
prior period adjustments (500)
restrictions (499)
statement of stockholders' equity (500)
stock (484)

stock dividend (494)
stock split (502)
stockholders (484)
treasury stock (495)

Illustrative Problem

Altenburg Inc. is a lighting fixture wholesaler located in Arizona. During its current fiscal year, ended December 31, 2010, Altenburg Inc. completed the following selected transactions:

Feb. 3. Purchased 2,500 shares of its own common stock at $26, recording the stock at cost. (Prior to the purchase, there were 40,000 shares of $20 par common stock outstanding.)

May 1. Declared a semiannual dividend of $1 on the 10,000 shares of preferred stock and a 30¢ dividend on the common stock to stockholders of record on May 31, payable on June 15.

June 15. Paid the cash dividends.

Sept. 23. Sold 1,000 shares of treasury stock at $28, receiving cash.

Nov. 1. Declared semiannual dividends of $1 on the preferred stock and 30¢ on the common stock. In addition, a 5% common stock dividend was declared on the common stock outstanding, to be capitalized at the fair market value of the common stock, which is estimated at $30.

Dec. 1. Paid the cash dividends and issued the certificates for the common stock dividend.

Instructions

Journalize the entries to record the transactions for Altenburg Inc.

Solution

2010				
Feb.	3	Treasury Stock	65,000	
		Cash		65,000
May	1	Cash Dividends	21,250	
		Cash Dividends Payable		21,250
		(10,000 × $1) + [(40,000 − 2,500) × $0.30].		
June	15	Cash Dividends Payable	21,250	
		Cash		21,250
Sept.	23	Cash	28,000	
		Treasury Stock		26,000
		Paid-In Capital from Sale of Treasury Stock		2,000
Nov.	1	Cash Dividends	21,550	
		Cash Dividends Payable		21,550
		(10,000 × $1) + [(40,000 − 1,500) × $0.30].		
	1	Stock Dividends	57,750*	
		Stock Dividends Distributable		38,500
		Paid-In Capital in Excess of Par—Common Stock		19,250
		*(40,000 − 1,500) × 5% × $30.		
Dec.	1	Cash Dividends Payable	21,550	
		Stock Dividends Distributable	38,500	
		Cash		21,550
		Common Stock		38,500

Self-Examination Questions (Answers at End of Chapter)

1. Which of the following is a disadvantage of the corporate form of organization?
   A. Limited liability
   B. Continuous life
   C. Owner is separate from management
   D. Ability to raise capital
2. Paid-in capital for a corporation may arise from which of the following sources?
   A. Issuing preferred stock
   B. Issuing common stock
   C. Selling the corporation's treasury stock
   D. All of the above
3. The Stockholders' Equity section of the balance sheet may include:
   A. Common Stock.
   B. Stock Dividends Distributable.
   C. Preferred Stock.
   D. All of the above.
4. If a corporation reacquires its own stock, the stock is listed on the balance sheet in the:
   A. Current Assets section.
   B. Long-Term Liabilities section.
   C. Stockholders' Equity section.
   D. Investments section.
5. A corporation has issued 25,000 shares of $100 par common stock and holds 3,000 of these shares as treasury stock. If the corporation declares a $2 per share cash dividend, what amount will be recorded as cash dividends?
   A. $22,000   C. $44,000
   B. $25,000   D. $50,000

Eye Openers

1. Describe the stockholders' liability to creditors of a corporation.
2. Why are most large businesses organized as corporations?
3. Of two corporations organized at approximately the same time and engaged in competing businesses, one issued $100 par common stock, and the other issued $0.01 par common stock. Do the par designations provide any indication as to which stock is preferable as an investment? Explain.
4. A stockbroker advises a client to "buy preferred stock. . . . With that type of stock, . . . [you] will never have to worry about losing the dividends." Is the broker right?
5. What are some of the factors that influence the market price of a corporation's stock?
6. When a corporation issues stock at a premium, is the premium income? Explain.
7. (a) What are the three conditions for the declaration and payment of a cash dividend? (b) The dates in connection with the declaration of a cash dividend are February 16, March 18, and April 17. Identify each date.
8. A corporation with both preferred stock and common stock outstanding has a substantial credit balance in its retained earnings account at the beginning of the current fiscal year. Although net income for the current year is sufficient to pay the preferred dividend of $125,000 each quarter and a common dividend of $300,000 each quarter, the board of directors declares dividends only on the preferred stock. Suggest possible reasons for passing the dividends on the common stock.
9. An owner of 500 shares of Microshop Company common stock receives a stock dividend of 5 shares. (a) What is the effect of the stock dividend on the stockholder's proportionate interest (equity) in the corporation? (b) How does the total equity of 505 shares compare with the total equity of 500 shares before the stock dividend?
10. a. Where should a declared but unpaid cash dividend be reported on the balance sheet?
    b. Where should a declared but unissued stock dividend be reported on the balance sheet?
11. a. In what respect does treasury stock differ from unissued stock?
    b. How should treasury stock be presented on the balance sheet?
12. A corporation reacquires 10,000 shares of its own $25 par common stock for $450,000, recording it at cost. (a) What effect does this transaction have on revenue or expense of the period? (b) What effect does it have on stockholders' equity?

13. The treasury stock in Eye Opener 12 is resold for $615,000. (a) What is the effect on the corporation's revenue of the period? (b) What is the effect on stockholders' equity?
14. What is the primary advantage of combining the retained earnings statement with the income statement?
15. What are the three classifications of restrictions of retained earnings, and how are such restrictions normally reported in the financial statements?
16. Indicate how prior period adjustments would be reported on the financial statements presented only for the current period.
17. When is a statement of stockholders' equity normally prepared?
18. What is the primary purpose of a stock split?

Practice Exercises

PE 11-1A
Dividends per share
obj. 2
EE 11-1   p. 489

Taiwanese Company has 5,000 shares of 4% cumulative preferred stock of $40 par and 10,000 shares of $90 par common stock. The following amounts were distributed as dividends:

Year 1	$15,000
Year 2	5,000
Year 3	62,000

Determine the dividends per share for preferred and common stock for each year.

PE 11-1B
Dividends per share
obj. 2
EE 11-1   p. 489

Master Craftmen Company has 10,000 shares of 2% cumulative preferred stock of $50 par and 25,000 shares of $75 par common stock. The following amounts were distributed as dividends:

Year 1	$30,000
Year 2	6,000
Year 3	80,000

Determine the dividends per share for preferred and common stock for each year.

PE 11-2A
Entries for issuing stock
obj. 2
EE 11-2   p. 492

On July 3, Hanoi Artifacts Corporation issued for cash 450,000 shares of no-par common stock at $2.50. On September 1, Hanoi Artifacts issued 10,000 shares of 2%, $25 preferred stock at par for cash. On October 30, Hanoi Artifacts issued for cash 7,500 shares of 2%, $25 par preferred stock at $30.

Journalize the entries to record the July 3, September 1, and October 30 transactions.

PE 11-2B
Entries for issuing stock
obj. 2
EE 11-2   p. 492

On February 13, Elman Corporation issued for cash 75,000 shares of no-par common stock (with a stated value of $125) at $140. On September 9, Elman issued 15,000 shares of 1%, $60 preferred stock at par for cash. On November 23, Elman issued for cash 8,000 shares of 1%, $60 par preferred stock at $70.

Journalize the entries to record the February 13, September 9, and November 23 transactions.

PE 11-3A
Entries for cash dividends
obj. 3
EE 11-3   p. 494

The important dates in connection with a cash dividend of $112,750 on a corporation's common stock are October 6, November 5, and December 5. Journalize the entries required on each date.

PE 11-3B
Entries for cash dividends
obj. 3
EE 11-3   p. 494

The important dates in connection with a cash dividend of $61,500 on a corporation's common stock are July 1, August 1, and September 30. Journalize the entries required on each date.

PE 11-4A
Entries for stock dividends
obj. 3
EE 11-4 p. 495

Self Storage Corporation has 100,000 shares of $40 par common stock outstanding. On May 10, Self Storage Corporation declared a 2% stock dividend to be issued August 1 to stockholders of record on June 9. The market price of the stock was $48 per share on May 10.

Journalize the entries required on May 10, June 9, and August 1.

PE 11-4B
Entries for stock dividends
obj. 3
EE 11-4 p. 495

Spectrum Corporation has 600,000 shares of $75 par common stock outstanding. On February 13, Spectrum Corporation declared a 4% stock dividend to be issued April 30 to stockholders of record on March 14. The market price of the stock was $90 per share on February 13.

Journalize the entries required on February 13, March 14, and April 30.

PE 11-5A
Entries for treasury stock
obj. 4
EE 11-5 p. 496

On October 3, Valley Clothing Inc. reacquired 10,000 shares of its common stock at $9 per share. On November 15, Valley Clothing sold 6,800 of the reacquired shares at $12 per share. On December 22, Valley Clothing sold the remaining shares at $7 per share.

Journalize the transactions of October 3, November 15, and December 22.

PE 11-5B
Entries for treasury stock
obj. 4
EE 11-5 p. 496

On February 1, Motorsports Inc. reacquired 7,500 shares of its common stock at $30 per share. On March 15, Motorsports sold 4,500 of the reacquired shares at $34 per share. On June 2, Motorsports sold the remaining shares at $28 per share.

Journalize the transactions of February 1, March 15, and June 2.

PE 11-6A
Reporting stockholders' equity
obj. 5
EE 11-6 p. 498

Using the following accounts and balances, prepare the Stockholders' Equity section of the balance sheet. Seventy thousand shares of common stock are authorized, and 7,500 shares have been reacquired.

Common Stock, $75 par	$4,725,000
Paid-In Capital in Excess of Par	679,000
Paid-In Capital from Sale of Treasury Stock	25,200
Retained Earnings	2,032,800
Treasury Stock	588,000

PE 11-6B
Reporting stockholders' equity
obj. 5
EE 11-6 p. 498

Using the following accounts and balances, prepare the Stockholders' Equity section of the balance sheet. Sixty thousand shares of common stock are authorized, and 4,000 shares have been reacquired.

Common Stock, $80 par	$4,000,000
Paid-In Capital in Excess of Par	630,000
Paid-In Capital from Sale of Treasury Stock	66,000
Retained Earnings	2,220,000
Treasury Stock	360,000

PE 11-7A
Retained earnings statement
obj. 5
EE 11-7 p. 500

Hornblower Cruises Inc. reported the following results for the year ending October 31, 2010:

Retained earnings, November 1, 2009	$1,500,000
Net income	475,000
Cash dividends declared	50,000
Stock dividends declared	300,000

Prepare a retained earnings statement for the fiscal year ended October 31, 2010.

PE 11-7B
Retained earnings statement
obj. 5
EE 11-7 p. 500

Frontier Leaders Inc. reported the following results for the year ending July 31, 2010:

Retained earnings, August 1, 2009	$875,000
Net income	260,000
Cash dividends declared	20,000
Stock dividends declared	100,000

Prepare a retained earnings statement for the fiscal year ended July 31, 2010.

Exercises

EX 11-1
Dividends per share
obj. 2

✔ Preferred stock,
1st year: $2.00

Fairmount Inc., a developer of radiology equipment, has stock outstanding as follows: 15,000 shares of cumulative 2%, preferred stock of $150 par, and 50,000 shares of $5 par common. During its first four years of operations, the following amounts were distributed as dividends: first year, $30,000; second year, $42,000; third year, $90,000; fourth year, $120,000. Calculate the dividends per share on each class of stock for each of the four years.

EX 11-2
Dividends per share
obj. 2

✔ Preferred stock,
1st year: $0.15

Michelangelo Inc., a software development firm, has stock outstanding as follows: 20,000 shares of cumulative 1%, preferred stock of $25 par, and 25,000 shares of $100 par common. During its first four years of operations, the following amounts were distributed as dividends: first year, $3,000; second year, $4,000; third year, $30,000; fourth year, $80,000. Calculate the dividends per share on each class of stock for each of the four years.

EX 11-3
Entries for issuing par stock
obj. 2

On February 10, Peerless Rocks Inc., a marble contractor, issued for cash 40,000 shares of $10 par common stock at $34, and on May 9, it issued for cash 100,000 shares of $5 par preferred stock at $7.

a. Journalize the entries for February 10 and May 9.
b. What is the total amount invested (total paid-in capital) by all stockholders as of May 9?

EX 11-4
Entries for issuing no-par stock
obj. 2

On June 4, Magic Carpet Inc., a carpet wholesaler, issued for cash 250,000 shares of no-par common stock (with a stated value of $3) at $12, and on October 9, it issued for cash 25,000 shares of $75 par preferred stock at $80.

a. Journalize the entries for June 4 and October 9, assuming that the common stock is to be credited with the stated value.
b. What is the total amount invested (total paid-in capital) by all stockholders as of October 9?

EX 11-5
Issuing stock for assets other than cash
obj. 2

On January 30, Lift Time Corporation, a wholesaler of hydraulic lifts, acquired land in exchange for 18,000 shares of $10 par common stock with a current market price of $15. Journalize the entry to record the transaction.

EX 11-6
Selected stock transactions
obj. 2

Rocky Mountain Sounds Corp., an electric guitar retailer, was organized by Cathy Dewitt, Melody Leimbach, and Mario Torres. The charter authorized 250,000 shares of common stock with a par of $40. The following transactions affecting stockholders' equity were completed during the first year of operations:

a. Issued 10,000 shares of stock at par to Cathy Dewitt for cash.
b. Issued 750 shares of stock at par to Mario Torres for promotional services provided in connection with the organization of the corporation, and issued 20,000 shares of stock at par to Mario Torres for cash.
c. Purchased land and a building from Melody Leimbach. The building is mortgaged for $400,000 for 20 years at 7%, and there is accrued interest of $7,000 on the mortgage note at the time of the purchase. It is agreed that the land is to be priced at $125,000 and the building at $600,000, and that Melody Leimbach's equity will be exchanged for stock at par. The corporation agreed to assume responsibility for paying the mortgage note and the accrued interest.

Journalize the entries to record the transactions.

EX 11-7
Issuing stock
obj. 2

Cashman Nursery, with an authorization of 25,000 shares of preferred stock and 300,000 shares of common stock, completed several transactions involving its stock on July 30, the first day of operations. The trial balance at the close of the day follows:

Cash	475,000	
Land	125,000	
Buildings	200,000	
Preferred 2% Stock, $100 par		250,000
Paid-In Capital in Excess of Par—Preferred Stock		75,000
Common Stock, $40 par		300,000
Paid-In Capital in Excess of Par—Common Stock		175,000
	800,000	800,000

All shares within each class of stock were sold at the same price. The preferred stock was issued in exchange for the land and buildings.

Journalize the two entries to record the transactions summarized in the trial balance.

EX 11-8
Issuing stock
obj. 2

Newgen Products Inc., a wholesaler of office products, was organized on February 20 of the current year, with an authorization of 75,000 shares of 2% preferred stock, $50 par and 400,000 shares of $15 par common stock. The following selected transactions were completed during the first year of operations:

Feb.   20. Issued 150,000 shares of common stock at par for cash.
        26. Issued 500 shares of common stock at par to an attorney in payment of legal fees for organizing the corporation.
Mar.   6. Issued 18,000 shares of common stock in exchange for land, buildings, and equipment with fair market prices of $50,000, $275,000, and $60,000, respectively.
Apr.   30. Issued 20,000 shares of preferred stock at $60 for cash.

Journalize the transactions.

EX 11-9
Entries for cash dividends
obj. 3

The important dates in connection with a cash dividend of $69,500 on a corporation's common stock are May 3, June 17, and August 1. Journalize the entries required on each date.

EX 11-10
Entries for stock dividends
obj. 3

✔ b. (1) $12,000,000
   (3) $57,000,000

Organic Health Co. is an HMO for businesses in the Chicago area. The following account balances appear on the balance sheet of Organic Health Co.: Common stock (300,000 shares authorized), $100 par, $10,000,000; Paid-in capital in excess of par—common stock, $2,000,000; and Retained earnings, $45,000,000. The board of directors declared a 2% stock dividend when the market price of the stock was $125 a share. Organic Health Co. reported no income or loss for the current year.

a. Journalize the entries to record (1) the declaration of the dividend, capitalizing an amount equal to market value, and (2) the issuance of the stock certificates.
b. Determine the following amounts before the stock dividend was declared: (1) total paid-in capital, (2) total retained earnings, and (3) total stockholders' equity.
c. Determine the following amounts after the stock dividend was declared and closing entries were recorded at the end of the year: (1) total paid-in capital, (2) total retained earnings, and (3) total stockholders' equity.

EX 11-11
Treasury stock transactions
obj. 4

✔ b. $32,000 credit

Beaverhead Creek Inc. bottles and distributes spring water. On March 4 of the current year, Beaverhead Creek reacquired 5,000 shares of its common stock at $90 per share. On August 7, Beaverhead Creek sold 3,500 of the reacquired shares at $100 per share. The remaining 1,500 shares were sold at $88 per share on November 29.

a. Journalize the transactions of March 4, August 7, and November 29.
b. What is the balance in Paid-In Capital from Sale of Treasury Stock on December 31 of the current year?
c. ▬▬▶ For what reasons might Beaverhead Creek have purchased the treasury stock?

EX 11-12
Treasury stock transactions
objs. 4, 5

✔ b. $54,000 credit

Augusta Gardens Inc. develops and produces spraying equipment for lawn maintenance and industrial uses. On August 30 of the current year, Augusta Gardens Inc. reacquired 17,500 shares of its common stock at $42 per share. On October 31, 14,000 of the reacquired shares were sold at $45 per share, and on November 10, 2,000 of the reacquired shares were sold at $48.

a. Journalize the transactions of August 30, October 31, and November 10.
b. What is the balance in Paid-In Capital from Sale of Treasury Stock on December 31 of the current year?
c. What is the balance in Treasury Stock on December 31 of the current year?
d. How will the balance in Treasury Stock be reported on the balance sheet?

EX 11-13
Treasury stock transactions
objs. 4, 5

✔ b. $37,000 credit

Sweet Water Inc. bottles and distributes spring water. On July 15 of the current year, Sweet Water Inc. reacquired 24,000 shares of its common stock at $60 per share. On August 10, Sweet Water Inc. sold 19,000 of the reacquired shares at $63 per share. The remaining 5,000 shares were sold at $56 per share on December 18.

a. Journalize the transactions of July 15, August 10, and December 18.
b. What is the balance in Paid-In Capital from Sale of Treasury Stock on December 31 of the current year?
c. Where will the balance in Paid-In Capital from Sale of Treasury Stock be reported on the balance sheet?
d. ➤ For what reasons might Sweet Water Inc. have purchased the treasury stock?

EX 11-14
Reporting paid-in capital
obj. 5

✔ Total paid-in capital, $2,225,000

The following accounts and their balances were selected from the unadjusted trial balance of REO Inc., a freight forwarder, at October 31, the end of the current fiscal year:

Preferred 2% Stock, $100 par	$ 750,000
Paid-In Capital in Excess of Par—Preferred Stock	90,000
Common Stock, no par, $5 stated value	400,000
Paid-In Capital in Excess of Stated Value—Common Stock	960,000
Paid-In Capital from Sale of Treasury Stock	25,000
Retained Earnings	3,150,000

Prepare the Paid-In Capital portion of the Stockholders' Equity section of the balance sheet. There are 250,000 shares of common stock authorized and 20,000 shares of preferred stock authorized.

EX 11-15
Stockholders' Equity section of balance sheet
obj. 5

✔ Total stockholders' equity, $4,350,000

The following accounts and their balances appear in the ledger of Newberry Properties Inc. on June 30 of the current year:

Common Stock, $75 par	$1,350,000
Paid-In Capital in Excess of Par	108,000
Paid-In Capital from Sale of Treasury Stock	12,000
Retained Earnings	2,950,000
Treasury Stock	70,000

Prepare the Stockholders' Equity section of the balance sheet as of June 30. Forty thousand shares of common stock are authorized, and 875 shares have been reacquired.

EX 11-16
Stockholders' Equity section of balance sheet
obj. 5

✔ Total stockholders' equity, $5,985,000

Race Car Inc. retails racing products for BMWs, Porsches, and Ferraris. The following accounts and their balances appear in the ledger of Race Car Inc. on April 30, the end of the current year:

Common Stock, $10 par	$ 400,000
Paid-In Capital in Excess of Par—Common Stock	120,000
Paid-In Capital in Excess of Par—Preferred Stock	90,000
Paid-In Capital from Sale of Treasury Stock—Common	30,000
Preferred 4% Stock, $50 par	1,500,000
Retained Earnings	3,900,000
Treasury Stock—Common	55,000

Fifty thousand shares of preferred and 200,000 shares of common stock are authorized. There are 5,000 shares of common stock held as treasury stock.

Prepare the Stockholders' Equity section of the balance sheet as of April 30, the end of the current year.

EX 11-17
Retained earnings statement
obj. 5

✔ Retained earnings, January 31, $3,375,000

Bancroft Corporation, a manufacturer of industrial pumps, reports the following results for the year ending January 31, 2010:

Retained earnings, February 1, 2009	$3,175,500
Net income	415,000
Cash dividends declared	75,500
Stock dividends declared	140,000

Prepare a retained earnings statement for the fiscal year ended January 31, 2010.

EX 11-18
Stockholders' Equity section of balance sheet
obj. 5

✔ Corrected total stockholders' equity, $16,758,000

List the errors in the following Stockholders' Equity section of the balance sheet prepared as of the end of the current year.

Stockholders' Equity

Paid-in capital:			
Preferred 2% stock, $150 par			
(10,000 shares authorized and issued)		$1,500,000	
Excess of issue price over par		250,000	$ 1,750,000
Retained earnings			1,450,000
Treasury stock (6,000 shares at cost)			432,000
Dividends payable			135,000
Total paid-in capital			$ 3,767,000
Common stock, $75 par (250,000 shares			
authorized, 180,000 shares issued)			14,040,000
Organizing costs			50,000
Total stockholders' equity			$17,857,000

EX 11-19
Statement of stockholders' equity
obj. 5

✔ Total stockholders' equity, Dec. 31, $7,182,000

The stockholders' equity T accounts of For All Occasions Greeting Cards Inc. for the current fiscal year ended December 31, 2010, are as follows. Prepare a statement of stockholders' equity for the fiscal year ended December 31, 2010.

COMMON STOCK

	Jan.	1	Balance	2,000,000
	Feb.	20	Issued	
			18,000 shares	900,000
	Dec.	31	Balance	2,900,000

PAID-IN CAPITAL IN EXCESS OF PAR

	Jan.	1	Balance	320,000
	Feb.	20	Issued	
			18,000 shares	216,000
	Dec.	31	Balance	536,000

TREASURY STOCK

July 19	Purchased	
	3,000 shares	144,000

RETAINED EARNINGS

June 30	Dividend	50,000	Jan.	1	Balance	3,480,000
Dec. 30	Dividend	50,000	Dec.	31	Closing	
					(net income)	510,000
			Dec.	31	Balance	3,890,000

EX 11-20
Effect of stock split
obj. 6

Mia Restaurant Corporation wholesales ovens and ranges to restaurants throughout the Southwest. Mia Restaurant Corporation, which had 40,000 shares of common stock outstanding, declared a 4-for-1 stock split (3 additional shares for each share issued).

a. What will be the number of shares outstanding after the split?
b. If the common stock had a market price of $300 per share before the stock split, what would be an approximate market price per share after the split?

EX 11-21
Effect of cash dividend and stock split
objs. 3, 6

Indicate whether the following actions would (+) increase, (−) decrease, or (0) not affect Indigo Inc.'s total assets, liabilities, and stockholders' equity:

	Assets	Liabilities	Stockholders' Equity
(1) Declaring a cash dividend	_____	_____	_____
(2) Paying the cash dividend declared in (1)	_____	_____	_____
(3) Authorizing and issuing stock certificates in a stock split	_____	_____	_____
(4) Declaring a stock dividend	_____	_____	_____
(5) Issuing stock certificates for the stock dividend declared in (4)	_____	_____	_____

EX 11-22
Selected dividend transactions, stock split
objs. 3, 6

Selected transactions completed by Hartwell Boating Supply Corporation during the current fiscal year are as follows:

Feb. 3. Split the common stock 2 for 1 and reduced the par from $40 to $20 per share. After the split, there were 250,000 common shares outstanding.
Apr. 10. Declared semiannual dividends of $1.50 on 18,000 shares of preferred stock and $0.08 on the common stock to stockholders of record on May 10, payable on June 9.
June 9. Paid the cash dividends.
Oct. 10. Declared semiannual dividends of $1.50 on the preferred stock and $0.04 on the common stock (before the stock dividend). In addition, a 2% common stock dividend was declared on the common stock outstanding. The fair market value of the common stock is estimated at $36.
Dec. 9. Paid the cash dividends and issued the certificates for the common stock dividend.

Journalize the transactions.

EX 11-23
EPS

Crystal Arts, Inc., had earnings of $160,000 for 2010. The company had 20,000 shares of common stock outstanding during the year. In addition, the company issued 2,000 shares of $100 par value preferred stock on January 3, 2010. The preferred stock has a dividend of $7 per share. There were no transactions in either common or preferred stock during 2010.
Determine the basic earnings per share for Crystal Arts.

EX 11-24
EPS

Procter & Gamble (P&G) is one of the largest consumer products companies in the world, famous for such brands as Crest® and Tide®. Financial information for the company for three recent years is as follows:

	Fiscal Years Ended (in millions)		
	2007	2006	2005
Net income	$10,340	$8,684	$6,923
Preferred dividends	$161	$148	$136
Common shares outstanding	3,159	3,055	2,515

a. Determine the earnings per share for fiscal years 2007, 2006, and 2005.
b. Evaluate the growth in earnings per share for the three years in comparison to the growth in net income for the three years.

EX 11-25
EPS

Staples and OfficeMax are two companies competing in the retail office supply business. OfficeMax had a net income of $91,721,000 for a recent year, while Staples had a net income of $973,577,000. OfficeMax had preferred stock of $54,735,000 with a preferred dividend of 7.375% on that amount. Staples had no preferred stock. The outstanding common shares for each company were as follows:

	Common Shares
OfficeMax	73,142,000
Staples	720,528,000

a. Determine the earnings per share for each company.
b. Evaluate the relative profitability of the two companies.

Problems Series A

PR 11-1A
Dividends on
preferred and
common stock

obj. 2

✔ 1. Common
dividends in 2007:
$8,000

Bridger Bike Corp. manufactures mountain bikes and distributes them through retail outlets in Montana, Idaho, Oregon, and Washington. Bridger Bike Corp. has declared the following annual dividends over a six-year period ending December 31 of each year: 2005, $5,000; 2006, $18,000; 2007, $45,000; 2008, $45,000; 2009, $60,000; and 2010, $67,000. During the entire period, the outstanding stock of the company was composed of 10,000 shares of 2% cumulative preferred stock, $100 par, and 25,000 shares of common stock, $1 par.

Instructions

1. Determine the total dividends and the per-share dividends declared on each class of stock for each of the six years. There were no dividends in arrears on January 1, 2005. Summarize the data in tabular form, using the following column headings:

Year	Total Dividends	Preferred Dividends		Common Dividends	
		Total	Per Share	Total	Per Share
2005	$ 5,000				
2006	18,000				
2007	45,000				
2008	45,000				
2009	60,000				
2010	67,000				

2. Determine the average annual dividend per share for each class of stock for the six-year period.
3. Assuming a market price of $125 for the preferred stock and $8 for the common stock, calculate the average annual percentage return on initial shareholders' investment, based on the average annual dividend per share (a) for preferred stock and (b) for common stock.

PR 11-2A
Stock transaction for
corporate expansion

obj. 2

KLOOSTER
& ALLEN

Sheldon Optics produces medical lasers for use in hospitals. The accounts and their balances appear in the ledger of Sheldon Optics on October 31 of the current year as follows:

Preferred 2% Stock, $80 par (50,000 shares authorized, 25,000 shares issued)	$ 2,000,000
Paid-In Capital in Excess of Par—Preferred Stock	75,000
Common Stock, $100 par (500,000 shares authorized, 50,000 shares issued)	5,000,000
Paid-In Capital in Excess of Par—Common Stock	600,000
Retained Earnings	16,750,000

At the annual stockholders' meeting on December 7, the board of directors presented a plan for modernizing and expanding plant operations at a cost of approximately $5,300,000. The plan provided (a) that the corporation borrow $2,000,000, (b) that 15,000 shares of the unissued preferred stock be issued through an underwriter, and (c) that a building, valued at $1,850,000, and the land on which it is located, valued at $162,500, be acquired in accordance with preliminary negotiations by the issuance of 17,500 shares of common stock. The plan was approved by the stockholders and accomplished by the following transactions:

Jan. 10. Borrowed $2,000,000 from Whitefish National Bank, giving a 7% mortgage note.

21. Issued 15,000 shares of preferred stock, receiving $84.50 per share in cash.

31. Issued 17,500 shares of common stock in exchange for land and a building, according to the plan.

No other transactions occurred during January.

Instructions
Journalize the entries to record the foregoing transactions.

PR 11-3A
Selected stock transactions

objs. **2, 3, 4**

✔ f. Cash dividends, $387,050

Coil Welding Corporation sells and services pipe welding equipment in California. The following selected accounts appear in the ledger of Coil Welding Corporation on February 1, 2010, the beginning of the current fiscal year:

Preferred 2% Stock, $25 par (50,000 shares authorized, 40,000 shares issued)	$ 1,000,000
Paid-In Capital in Excess of Par—Preferred Stock	240,000
Common Stock, $5 par (1,000,000 shares authorized, 750,000 shares issued)	3,750,000
Paid-In Capital in Excess of Par—Common Stock	6,000,000
Retained Earnings	36,785,000

During the year, the corporation completed a number of transactions affecting the stockholders' equity. They are summarized as follows:

a. Purchased 60,000 shares of treasury common for $540,000.
b. Sold 42,000 shares of treasury common for $462,000.
c. Issued 7,500 shares of preferred 2% stock at $38.
d. Issued 120,000 shares of common stock at $15, receiving cash.
e. Sold 13,000 shares of treasury common for $110,500.
f. Declared cash dividends of $0.50 per share on preferred stock and $0.42 per share on common stock.
g. Paid the cash dividends.

Instructions
Journalize the entries to record the transactions. Identify each entry by letter.

PR 11-4A
Entries for selected corporate transactions

objs. **2, 3, 4, 5**

✔ 4. Total stockholders' equity, $11,407,975

Krisch Enterprises Inc. produces aeronautical navigation equipment. The stockholders' equity accounts of Krisch Enterprises Inc., with balances on January 1, 2010, are as follows:

Common Stock, $20 stated value (250,000 shares authorized, 175,000 shares issued)	$3,500,000
Paid-In Capital in Excess of Stated Value	1,750,000
Retained Earnings	4,600,000
Treasury Stock (40,000 shares, at cost)	1,000,000

The following selected transactions occurred during the year:

Jan. 6. Paid cash dividends of $0.40 per share on the common stock. The dividend had been properly recorded when declared on November 29 of the preceding fiscal year for $54,000.

Mar. 9. Sold all of the treasury stock for $1,350,000.

Apr. 3. Issued 50,000 shares of common stock for $1,700,000.

July 30. Declared a 2% stock dividend on common stock, to be capitalized at the market price of the stock, which is $36 per share.

Aug. 30. Issued the certificates for the dividend declared on July 30.

Nov. 7. Purchased 25,000 shares of treasury stock for $800,000.

Dec. 30. Declared a $0.45-per-share dividend on common stock.

31. Closed the credit balance of the income summary account, $400,000.

31. Closed the two dividends accounts to Retained Earnings.

Instructions

1. Enter the January 1 balances in T accounts for the stockholders' equity accounts listed. Also prepare T accounts for the following: Paid-In Capital from Sale of Treasury Stock; Stock Dividends Distributable; Stock Dividends; Cash Dividends.

2. Journalize the entries to record the transactions, and post to the eight selected accounts.

3. Prepare a retained earnings statement for the year ended December 31, 2010.

4. Prepare the Stockholders' Equity section of the December 31, 2010, balance sheet.

PR 11-5A
Entries for selected corporate transactions

objs. 2, 3, 4, 6

✔ Sept. 1, Cash dividends, $165,750

Porto Bay Corporation manufactures and distributes leisure clothing. Selected transactions completed by Porto Bay during the current fiscal year are as follows:

Jan. 10. Split the common stock 4 for 1 and reduced the par from $100 to $25 per share. After the split, there were 500,000 common shares outstanding.

Mar. 1. Declared semiannual dividends of $1.20 on 80,000 shares of preferred stock and $0.24 on the 500,000 shares of $25 par common stock to stockholders of record on March 31, payable on April 30.

Apr. 30. Paid the cash dividends.

July 9. Purchased 75,000 shares of the corporation's own common stock at $26, recording the stock at cost.

Aug. 29. Sold 40,000 shares of treasury stock at $32, receiving cash.

Sept. 1. Declared semiannual dividends of $1.20 on the preferred stock and $0.15 on the common stock (before the stock dividend). In addition, a 1% common stock dividend was declared on the common stock outstanding, to be capitalized at the fair market value of the common stock, which is estimated at $30.

Oct. 31. Paid the cash dividends and issued the certificates for the common stock dividend.

Instructions
Journalize the transactions.

Problems Series B

PR 11-1B
Dividends on preferred and common stock

obj. 2

✔ 1. Common dividends in 2007: $16,500

Lone Star Theatre Inc. owns and operates movie theaters throughout Arizona and Texas. Lone Star Theatre has declared the following annual dividends over a six-year period: 2005, $7,500; 2006, $9,000; 2007, $30,000; 2008, $30,000; 2009, $40,000; and 2010, $48,500. During the entire period ending December 31 of each year, the outstanding stock of the company was composed of 10,000 shares of cumulative, 2% preferred stock, $50 par, and 50,000 shares of common stock, $1 par.

Instructions

1. Calculate the total dividends and the per-share dividends declared on each class of stock for each of the six years. There were no dividends in arrears on January 1, 2005. Summarize the data in tabular form, using the following column headings:

Year	Total Dividends	Preferred Dividends		Common Dividends	
		Total	Per Share	Total	Per Share
2005	$ 7,500				
2006	9,000				
2007	30,000				
2008	30,000				
2009	40,000				
2010	48,500				

2. Calculate the average annual dividend per share for each class of stock for the six-year period.
3. Assuming a market price per share of $40 for the preferred stock and $5 for the common stock, calculate the average annual percentage return on initial shareholders' investment, based on the average annual dividend per share (a) for preferred stock and (b) for common stock.

PR 11-2B
Stock transactions
for corporate
expansion

obj. 2

On February 28 of the current year, the following accounts and their balances appear in the ledger of Wild Things Corp., a meat processor:

Preferred 2% Stock, $25 par (75,000 shares authorized, 30,000 shares issued)	$ 750,000
Paid-In Capital in Excess of Par—Preferred Stock.	120,000
Common Stock, $30 par (400,000 shares authorized, 250,000 shares issued)	7,500,000
Paid-In Capital in Excess of Par—Common Stock	500,000
Retained Earnings	12,180,000

At the annual stockholders' meeting on April 2, the board of directors presented a plan for modernizing and expanding plant operations at a cost of approximately $3,650,000. The plan provided (a) that a building, valued at $1,680,000, and the land on which it is located, valued at $420,000, be acquired in accordance with preliminary negotiations by the issuance of 65,000 shares of common stock, (b) that 21,000 shares of the unissued preferred stock be issued through an underwriter, and (c) that the corporation borrow $700,000. The plan was approved by the stockholders and accomplished by the following transactions:

June 9. Issued 65,000 shares of common stock in exchange for land and a building, according to the plan.
    13. Issued 21,000 shares of preferred stock, receiving $40 per share in cash.
    25. Borrowed $700,000 from Wasburn City Bank, giving an 8% mortgage note.

No other transactions occurred during June.

Instructions
Journalize the entries to record the foregoing transactions.

PR 11-3B
Selected stock
transactions

objs. 2, 3, 4

f. Cash dividends,
$73,200

The following selected accounts appear in the ledger of Okie Environmental Corporation on August 1, 2010, the beginning of the current fiscal year:

Preferred 2% Stock, $50 par (40,000 shares authorized, 20,000 shares issued)	$1,000,000
Paid-In Capital in Excess of Par—Preferred Stock	100,000
Common Stock, $75 par (100,000 shares authorized, 40,000 shares issued)	3,000,000
Paid-In Capital in Excess of Par—Common Stock	150,000
Retained Earnings	8,170,000

During the year, the corporation completed a number of transactions affecting the stockholders' equity. They are summarized as follows:

a. Issued 17,500 shares of common stock at $81, receiving cash.
b. Issued 8,000 shares of preferred 2% stock at $63.
c. Purchased 5,000 shares of treasury common for $390,000.

d. Sold 3,000 shares of treasury common for $240,000.

e. Sold 1,000 shares of treasury common for $75,000.

f. Declared cash dividends of $1 per share on preferred stock and $0.80 per share on common stock.

g. Paid the cash dividends.

Instructions

Journalize the entries to record the transactions. Identify each entry by letter.

PR 11-4B
Entries for selected corporate transactions

objs. 2, 3, 4, 5

✔ 4. Total stockholders' equity, $11,853,400

Ivy Enterprises Inc. manufactures bathroom fixtures. The stockholders' equity accounts of Ivy Enterprises Inc., with balances on January 1, 2010, are as follows:

Common Stock, $8 stated value (600,000 shares authorized, 400,000 shares issued)	$3,200,000
Paid-In Capital in Excess of Stated Value	600,000
Retained Earnings	7,100,000
Treasury Stock (30,000 shares, at cost).	240,000

The following selected transactions occurred during the year:

Jan.   7. Paid cash dividends of $0.18 per share on the common stock. The dividend had been properly recorded when declared on November 30 of the preceding fiscal year for $66,600.

Feb.   9. Issued 50,000 shares of common stock for $600,000.

May 21. Sold all of the treasury stock for $300,000.

July   1. Declared a 4% stock dividend on common stock, to be capitalized at the market price of the stock, which is $13 per share.

Aug. 15. Issued the certificates for the dividend declared on July 1.

Sept. 30. Purchased 10,000 shares of treasury stock for $100,000.

Dec. 27. Declared a $0.20-per-share dividend on common stock.

    31. Closed the credit balance of the income summary account, $485,000.

    31. Closed the two dividends accounts to Retained Earnings.

Instructions

1. Enter the January 1 balances in T accounts for the stockholders' equity accounts listed. Also prepare T accounts for the following: Paid-In Capital from Sale of Treasury Stock; Stock Dividends Distributable; Stock Dividends; Cash Dividends.

2. Journalize the entries to record the transactions, and post to the eight selected accounts.

3. Prepare a retained earnings statement for the year ended December 31, 2010.

4. Prepare the Stockholders' Equity section of the December 31, 2010, balance sheet.

PR 11-5B
Entries for selected corporate transactions

objs. 2, 3, 4, 6

✔ Nov. 15, cash dividends, $138,400

Selected transactions completed by Kearny Boating Corporation during the current fiscal year are as follows:

Jan.   8. Split the common stock 3 for 1 and reduced the par from $75 to $25 per share. After the split, there were 600,000 common shares outstanding.

Feb. 13. Purchased 30,000 shares of the corporation's own common stock at $27, recording the stock at cost.

May   1. Declared semiannual dividends of $0.80 on 25,000 shares of preferred stock and $0.18 on the common stock to stockholders of record on May 15, payable on June 1.

June   1. Paid the cash dividends.

Aug.   5. Sold 22,000 shares of treasury stock at $34, receiving cash.

Nov. 15. Declared semiannual dividends of $0.80 on the preferred stock and $0.20 on the common stock (before the stock dividend). In addition, a 2% common stock dividend was declared on the common stock outstanding. The fair market value of the common stock is estimated at $40.

Dec. 31. Paid the cash dividends and issued the certificates for the common stock dividend.

Instructions

Journalize the transactions.

Special Activities

SA 11-1
**Board of directors'
actions**

Bernie Ebbers, the CEO of WorldCom, a major telecommunications company, was having personal financial troubles. Ebbers pledged a large stake of his WorldCom stock as security for some personal loans. As the price of WorldCom stock sank, Ebbers' bankers threatened to sell his stock in order to protect their loans. To avoid having his stock sold, Ebbers asked the board of directors of WorldCom to loan him nearly $400 million of corporate assets at 2.5% interest to pay off his bankers. The board agreed to lend him the money.

➤ Comment on the decision of the board of directors in this situation.

SA 11-2
**Ethics and profes-
sional conduct in
business**

Jas Bosley and Nadine Jaffe are organizing Precious Metals Unlimited Inc. to undertake a high-risk gold-mining venture in Canada. Jas and Nadine tentatively plan to request authorization for 90,000,000 shares of common stock to be sold to the general public. Jas and Nadine have decided to establish par of $0.10 per share in order to appeal to a wide variety of potential investors. Jas and Nadine feel that investors would be more willing to invest in the company if they received a large quantity of shares for what might appear to be a "bargain" price.

➤ Discuss whether Jas and Nadine are behaving in a professional manner.

SA 11-3
Issuing stock

Biosciences Unlimited Inc. began operations on January 2, 2010, with the issuance of 100,000 shares of $50 par common stock. The sole stockholders of Biosciences Unlimited Inc. are Rafel Baltis and Dr. Oscar Hansel, who organized Biosciences Unlimited Inc. with the objective of developing a new flu vaccine. Dr. Hansel claims that the flu vaccine, which is nearing the final development stage, will protect individuals against 90% of the flu types that have been medically identified. To complete the project, Biosciences Unlimited Inc. needs $10,000,000 of additional funds. The local banks have been unwilling to loan the funds because of the lack of sufficient collateral and the riskiness of the business.

The following is a conversation between Rafel Baltis, the chief executive officer of Biosciences Unlimited Inc., and Dr. Oscar Hansel, the leading researcher:

Rafel: What are we going to do? The banks won't loan us any more money, and we've got to have $10 million to complete the project. We are so close! It would be a disaster to quit now. The only thing I can think of is to issue additional stock. Do you have any suggestions?

Oscar: I guess you're right. But if the banks won't loan us any more money, how do you think we can find any investors to buy stock?

Rafel: I've been thinking about that. What if we promise the investors that we will pay them 2% of net sales until they have received an amount equal to what they paid for the stock?

Oscar: What happens when we pay back the $10 million? Do the investors get to keep the stock? If they do, it'll dilute our ownership.

Rafel: How about, if after we pay back the $10 million, we make them turn in their stock for $100 per share? That's twice what they paid for it, plus they would have already gotten all their money back. That's a $100 profit per share for the investors.

Oscar: It could work. We get our money, but don't have to pay any interest, dividends, or the $50 until we start generating net sales. At the same time, the investors could get their money back plus $50 per share.

Rafel: We'll need current financial statements for the new investors. I'll get our accountant working on them and contact our attorney to draw up a legally binding contract for the new investors. Yes, this could work.

In late 2010, the attorney and the various regulatory authorities approved the new stock offering, and 200,000 shares of common stock were privately sold to new investors at the stock's par of $50.

In preparing financial statements for 2010, Rafel Baltis and Emma Cavins, the controller for Biosciences Unlimited Inc., have the following conversation:

Emma: Rafel, I've got a problem.

Rafel: What's that, Emma?

Emma: Issuing common stock to raise that additional $10 million was a great idea. But . . .

Rafel: But what?

Emma: I've got to prepare the 2010 annual financial statements, and I am not sure how to classify the common stock.

Rafel: What do you mean? It's common stock.

Emma: I'm not so sure. I called the auditor and explained how we are contractually obligated to pay the new stockholders 2% of net sales until $50 per share is paid. Then, we may be obligated to pay them $100 per share.

Rafel: So . . .

Emma: So the auditor thinks that we should classify the additional issuance of $10 million as debt, not stock! And, if we put the $10 million on the balance sheet as debt, we will violate our other loan agreements with the banks. And, if these agreements are violated, the banks may call in all our debt immediately. If they do that, we are in deep trouble. We'll probably have to file for bankruptcy. We just don't have the cash to pay off the banks.

1. ━━━▶ Discuss the arguments for and against classifying the issuance of the $10 million of stock as debt.
2. ━━━▶ What do you think might be a practical solution to this classification problem?

SA 11-4
Interpret stock exchange listing

The following stock exchange data for General Electric was taken from the Yahoo! Finance Web site on April 18, 2008:

Gen Electric Co (NYSE: GE)

Last Trade:	32.5815
Trade Time:	11:03 AM ET
Change:	▲0.5615
	(1.75%)
Prev. Clos:	32.02
1y Target Est:	36.92
Day's Range:	32.27–32.57
52wk Range:	31.55–42.15
Volume:	25,922,495

a. If you owned 500 shares of GE, what amount would you receive as a quarterly dividend?
b. Compute the percentage increase in price from the Previous Close to the Last Trade. Round to two decimal places.
c. What is GE's percentage change in market price from the 52 week low to the Previous Close on April 17, 2008? Round to one decimal place.
d. If you bought 500 shares of GE at the Last Trade price on April 18, 2008, how much would it cost, and who gets the money?

SA 11-5
Dividends

Rainbow Designs Inc. has paid quarterly cash dividends since 1997. These dividends have steadily increased from $0.05 per share to the latest dividend declaration of $0.40 per share. The board of directors would like to continue this trend and is hesitant to suspend or decrease the amount of quarterly dividends. Unfortunately, sales dropped sharply in the fourth quarter of 2010 because of worsening economic conditions and increased competition. As a result, the board is uncertain as to whether it should declare a dividend for the last quarter of 2010.

On November 1, 2010, Rainbow Designs Inc. borrowed $1,200,000 from Washington National Bank to use in modernizing its retail stores and to expand its product line in reaction to its competition. The terms of the 10-year, 6% loan require Rainbow Designs Inc. to:

a. Pay monthly interest on the last day of the month.
b. Pay $120,000 of the principal each November 1, beginning in 2011.

c. Maintain a current ratio (current assets/current liabilities) of 2.

d. Maintain a minimum balance (a compensating balance) of $60,000 in its Washington National Bank account.

On December 31, 2010, $300,000 of the $1,200,000 loan had been disbursed in modernization of the retail stores and in expansion of the product line. Rainbow Designs Inc.'s balance sheet as of December 31, 2010, is shown below.

Rainbow Designs Inc.
Balance Sheet
December 31, 2010

Assets

Current assets:			
Cash.			$ 96,000
Marketable securities			900,000
Accounts receivable		$ 219,600	
Less allowance for doubtful accounts		15,600	204,000
Merchandise inventory			300,000
Prepaid expenses			10,800
Total current assets			$1,510,800
Property, plant, and equipment:			
Land.			$ 360,000
Buildings	$2,280,000		
Less accumulated depreciation	516,000	1,764,000	
Equipment	$1,104,000		
Less accumulated depreciation	264,000	840,000	
Total property, plant, and equipment.			2,964,000
Total assets			$4,474,800

Liabilities

Current liabilities:			
Accounts payable.		$ 172,320	
Notes payable (Washington National Bank)		120,000	
Salaries payable.		7,680	
Total current liabilities.			$ 300,000
Long-term liabilities:			
Notes payable (Washington National Bank)			1,080,000
Total liabilities			$1,380,000

Stockholders' Equity

Paid-in capital:			
Common stock, $20 par (100,000 shares authorized, 60,000 shares issued)		$1,200,000	
Excess of issue price over par		96,000	
Total paid-in capital.		$1,296,000	
Retained earnings		1,798,800	
Total stockholders' equity.			3,094,800
Total liabilities and stockholders' equity			$4,474,800

The board of directors is scheduled to meet January 5, 2011, to discuss the results of operations for 2010 and to consider the declaration of dividends for the fourth quarter of 2010. The chairman of the board has asked for your advice on the declaration of dividends.

1. ➤ What factors should the board consider in deciding whether to declare a cash dividend?

2. ➤ The board is considering the declaration of a stock dividend instead of a cash dividend. Discuss the issuance of a stock dividend from the point of view of (a) a stockholder and (b) the board of directors.

SA 11-6
Profiling a corporation

Select a public corporation you are familiar with or which interests you. Using the Internet, your school library, and other sources, develop a short (1 to 2 pages) profile of the corporation. Include in your profile the following information:

1. Name of the corporation.
2. State of incorporation.
3. Nature of its operations.
4. Total assets for the most recent balance sheet.
5. Total revenues for the most recent income statement.
6. Net income for the most recent income statement.
7. Classes of stock outstanding.
8. Market price of the stock outstanding.
9. High and low price of the stock for the past year.
10. Dividends paid for each share of stock during the past year.

In groups of three or four, discuss each corporate profile. Select one of the corporations, assuming that your group has $100,000 to invest in its stock. Summarize why your group selected the corporation it did and how financial accounting information may have affected your decision. Keep track of the performance of your corporation's stock for the remainder of the term.

Note: Most major corporations maintain "home pages" on the Internet. This home page provides a variety of information on the corporation and often includes the corporation's financial statements. In addition, the New York Stock Exchange Web site (**http://www.nyse.com**) includes links to the home pages of many listed companies. Financial statements can also be accessed using EDGAR, the electronic archives of financial statements filed with the Securities and Exchange Commission (SEC).

SEC documents can also be retrieved using the EdgarScan™ service at **http://www.sec.gov/edgar/searchedgar/webusers.htm**. To obtain annual report information, key in a company name in the appropriate space. Edgar will list the reports available to you for the company you've selected. Select the most recent annual report filing, identified as a 10-K or 10-K405.

Answers to Self-Examination Questions

1. **C** The separation of the owner from management (answer C) is a disadvantage of the corporate form of organization. This is because management may not always behave in the best interests of the owners. Limited liability (answer A), continuous life (answer B), and the ability to raise capital (answer D) are all advantages of the corporate form of organization.

2. **D** Paid-in capital is one of the two major subdivisions of the stockholders' equity of a corporation. It may result from many sources, including the issuance of preferred stock (answer A), issuing common stock (answer B), or the sale of a corporation's treasury stock (answer C).

3. **D** The Stockholders' Equity section of corporate balance sheets is divided into two principal subsections: (1) investments contributed by the stockholders and others and (2) net income

retained in the business. Included as part of the investments by stockholders and others is the par of common stock (answer A), stock dividends distributable (answer B), and the par of preferred stock (answer C).

4. **C** Reacquired stock, known as *treasury stock*, should be listed in the Stockholders' Equity section (answer C) of the balance sheet. The price paid for the treasury stock is deducted from the total of all the stockholders' equity accounts.

5. **C** If a corporation that holds treasury stock declares a cash dividend, the dividends are not paid on the treasury shares. To do so would place the corporation in the position of earning income through dealing with itself. Thus, the corporation will record $44,000 (answer C) as cash dividends [(25,000 shares issued less 3,000 shares held as treasury stock) × $2 per share dividend].

Investments and Fair Value Accounting

N E W S   C O R P O R A T I O N

You invest cash to earn more cash. For example, you could deposit cash in a bank account to earn interest. You could also invest cash in preferred or common stocks and in corporate or U.S. government notes and bonds.

Preferred and common stock can be purchased through a stock exchange, such as the New York Stock Exchange (NYSE). Preferred stock is purchased primarily with the expectation of earning dividends. Common stock is purchased with the expectation of earning dividends or realizing gains from a price increase in the stock.

Corporate and U.S. government bonds can also be purchased through a bond exchange. Bonds are purchased with the primary expectation of earning interest revenue.

Companies make investments for many of the same reasons that you would as an individual. For example, News Corporation, a diversified media company, which

produces such popular television shows as *The Simpsons* and *American Idol*, has invested $636 million of available cash in stocks and bonds. These investments are held by News Corporation for interest, dividends, and expected price increases.

Companies, however, unlike most individuals, also purchase significant amounts of the outstanding common stock of other companies for strategic reasons. For example, to expand its online presence, News Corporation recently acquired all of the stock of MySpace, the popular social networking Web site.

Investments in debt and equity securities give rise to a number of accounting issues. These issues are described and illustrated in this chapter.

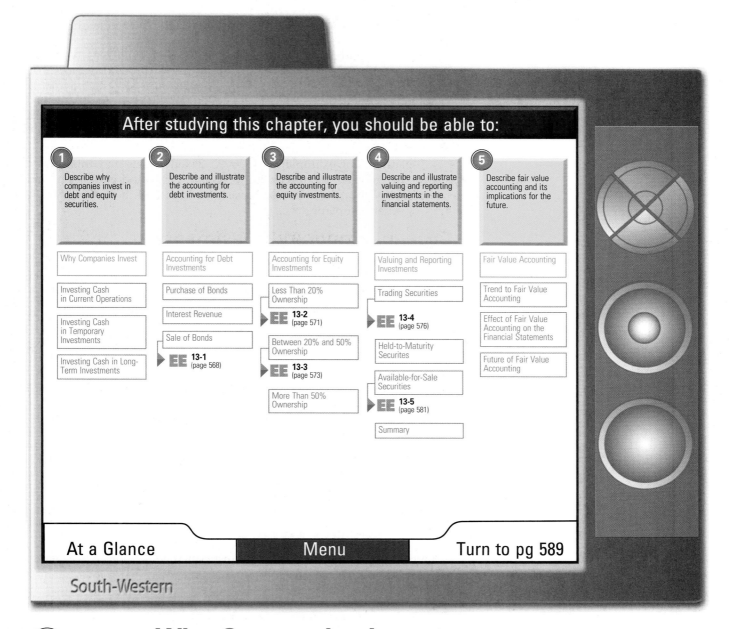

After studying this chapter, you should be able to:

1 Describe why companies invest in debt and equity securities.

- Why Companies Invest
- Investing Cash in Current Operations
- Investing Cash in Temporary Investments
- Investing Cash in Long-Term Investments

2 Describe and illustrate the accounting for debt investments.

- Accounting for Debt Investments
- Purchase of Bonds
- Interest Revenue
- Sale of Bonds
- **EE 13-1** (page 568)

3 Describe and illustrate the accounting for equity investments.

- Accounting for Equity Investments
- Less Than 20% Ownership
- **EE 13-2** (page 571)
- Between 20% and 50% Ownership
- **EE 13-3** (page 573)
- More Than 50% Ownership

4 Describe and illustrate valuing and reporting investments in the financial statements.

- Valuing and Reporting Investments
- Trading Securities
- **EE 13-4** (page 576)
- Held-to-Maturity Securites
- Available-for-Sale Securities
- **EE 13-5** (page 581)
- Summary

5 Describe fair value accounting and its implications for the future.

- Fair Value Accounting
- Trend to Fair Value Accounting
- Effect of Fair Value Accounting on the Financial Statements
- Future of Fair Value Accounting

At a Glance   Menu   Turn to pg 589

South-Western

1 Describe why companies invest in debt and equity securities.

Why Companies Invest

Most companies generate cash from their operations. This cash can be used for the following purposes:

1. Investing in current operations
2. Investing in temporary investments to earn additional revenue
3. Investing in long-term investments in stock of other companies for strategic reasons

Investing Cash in Current Operations

Cash is often used to support the current operating activities of a company. For example, cash may be used to replace worn-out equipment or to purchase new, more efficient, and productive equipment. In addition, cash may be reinvested in the company to expand its current operations. For example, a retailer based in the northwest United States might decide to expand by opening stores in the midwest.

To support its current level of operations, a company also uses cash to pay suppliers or other creditors. For example, suppliers must be paid to ensure that the company will be able to continue to purchase merchandise on account. The company may also have issued notes or bonds payable to finance its current operations. The interest on the notes or bonds must be paid.

Cash is also used to pay dividends to preferred or common stockholders. In order to maintain its ability to raise cash (capital), a company must reward (pay) investors for the use of their funds. For preferred stockholders, this reward is primarily the payment of dividends on a regular basis. For common stockholders, this reward may be in the form of an increasing stock price from improving prospects of the company. The reward for common stockholders may also take the form of cash dividends.

The accounting for the use of cash in current operations has been described and illustrated in earlier chapters. For example, Chapter 9, "Fixed Assets and Intangible Assets," illustrated the use of cash for purchasing property, plant, and equipment. In this chapter, we describe and illustrate the use of cash for investing in temporary investments and stock of other companies.

Investing Cash in Temporary Investments

A company may temporarily have excess cash that is not needed for use in its current operations. This is often the case when a company has a seasonal operating cycle. For example, a significant portion of the annual merchandise sales of a retailer occurs during the fall holiday season. As a result, retailers often experience a large increase in cash during this period, which is not needed until the spring buying season.

Instead of letting excess cash remain idle in a checking account, most companies invest their excess cash in temporary investments. In doing so, companies invest in securities such as:

1. **Debt securities**, which are notes and bonds that pay interest and have a fixed maturity date.
2. **Equity securities**, which are preferred and common stock that represent ownership in a company and do not have a fixed maturity date.

Investments in debt and equity securities, termed **Investments** or *Temporary Investments*, are reported in the Current Assets section of the balance sheet.

The primary objective of investing in temporary investments is to:

1. earn interest revenue
2. receive dividends
3. realize gains from increases in the market price of the securities.

Investments in certificates of deposit and other securities that do not normally change in value are disclosed on the balance sheet as *cash and cash equivalents*. Such investments are held primarily for their interest revenue.

Investing Cash in Long-Term Investments

SuperValu, a retail grocer, purchased Albertson's, another retail grocer, to form the third largest grocery retailing company in the United States.

The Walt Disney Company purchased Pixar Animation Studios to increase Disney's ability to produce and market animation movies.

A company may invest cash in the debt or equity of another company as a long-term investment. Long-term investments may be held for the same investment objectives as temporary investments. However, long-term investments often involve the purchase of a significant portion of the stock of another company. Such investments usually have a strategic purpose, such as:

1. *Reduction of costs*: When one company buys another company, the combined company may be able to reduce administrative expenses. For example, a combined company does not need two chief executive officers (CEOs) or chief financial officers (CFOs).
2. *Replacement of management*: If the purchased company has been mismanaged, the acquiring company may replace the company's management and, thus, improve operations and profits.
3. *Expansion*: The acquiring company may purchase a company because it has a complementary product line, territory, or customer base. The new combined company may be able to serve customers better than the two companies could separately.
4. *Integration*: A company may integrate operations by acquiring a supplier or customer. Acquiring a supplier may provide a more stable or uninterrupted supply of resources. Acquiring a customer may also provide a market for the company's products or services.

Describe and illustrate the accounting for debt investments.

Accounting for Debt Investments

Debt securities include notes and bonds, issued by corporations and governmental organizations. Most companies invest excess cash in bonds as investments to earn interest revenue.

The accounting for bond investments[1] includes recording the following:

1. Purchase of bonds
2. Interest revenue
3. Sale of bonds

Purchase of Bonds

The purchase of bonds is recorded by debiting an investments account for the purchase price of the bonds, including any brokerage commissions. If the bonds are purchased between interest dates, the purchase price includes accrued interest since the last interest payment. This is because the seller has earned the accrued interest, but the buyer will receive the accrued interest when it is paid.

To illustrate, assume that Homer Company purchases $18,000 of U.S. Treasury bonds at their face value on March 17, 2010, plus accrued interest for 45 days. The bonds have an interest rate of 6%, payable on July 31 and January 31.

The entry to record the purchase of Treasury bonds is as follows:

2010					
Mar.	17	Investments—U.S. Treasury Bonds		18,000	
		Interest Receivable		135	
		Cash			18,135
		Purchased $18,000, 6% Treasury bonds.			

Since Homer Company purchased the bonds on March 17, it is also purchasing the accrued interest for 45 days (January 31 to March 17). The accrued interest of $135 is computed as follows:[2]

$$\text{Accrued Interest} = \$18,000 \times 6\% \times (45/360) = \$135$$

The accrued interest is recorded by debiting Interest Receivable for $135. Bond Investments is debited for the purchase price of the bonds of $18,000.

Interest Revenue

On July 31, Homer Company receives a semiannual interest payment of $540 ($18,000 × 6% × ½). The $540 interest includes the $135 accrued interest that Homer Company purchased with the bonds on March 17. Thus, Homer Company has earned $405 ($540 − $135) of interest revenue since purchasing the bonds.

The receipt of the interest on July 31 is recorded as follows:

2010					
July	31	Cash		540	
		Interest Receivable			135
		Interest Revenue			405
		Received semiannual interest.			

---

1 Debt investments may also include installment notes and short-term notes. The basic accounting for notes is similar to bonds and, thus, is not illustrated.
2 To simplify, a 360-day year is used to compute interest.

Homer Company's accounting period ends on December 31. Thus, an adjusting entry must be made to accrue interest for five months (August 1 to December 31) of $450 ($18,000 × 6% × 5/12). The adjusting entry to record the accrued interest is as follows:

2010 Dec.	31	Interest Receivable	450	
		Interest Revenue		450
		Accrued interest.		

For the year ended December 31, 2010, Homer Company would report *Interest revenue* of $855 ($405 + $450) as part of *Other income* on its income statement.

The receipt of the semiannual interest of $540 on January 31, 2011, is recorded as follows:

2011 Jan.	31	Cash	540	
		Interest Revenue		90
		Interest Receivable		450
		Received interest on Treasury bonds.		

Sale of Bonds

The sale of a bond investment normally results in a gain or loss. If the proceeds from the sale exceed the book value (cost) of the bonds, then a gain is recorded. If the proceeds are less than the book value (cost) of the bonds, a loss is recorded.

To illustrate, on January 31, 2011, Homer Company sells the Treasury bonds at 98, which is a price equal to 98% of par value. The sale results in a loss of $360, as shown below.

Proceeds from sale	$17,640*
Less book value (cost) of the bonds	18,000
Loss on sale of bonds	$ (360)

*($18,000 × 98%)

The entry to record the sale is as follows:

2011 Jan.	31	Cash	17,640	
		Loss on Sale of Investment	360	
		Investments—U.S. Treasury Bonds		18,000
		Sale of U.S. Treasury bonds.		

There is no accrued interest upon the sale since the interest payment date is also January 31. If the sale were between interest dates, interest accrued since the last interest payment date would be added to the sale proceeds and credited to Interest Revenue. The loss on the sale of bond investments is reported as part of *Other income (loss)* on Homer Company's income statement.

Example Exercise 13-1 Bond Transactions ·······> 2

Journalize the entries to record the following selected bond investment transactions for Tyler Company:

1. Purchased for cash $40,000 of Tyler Company 10% bonds at 100 plus accrued interest of $320.
2. Received the first semiannual interest.
3. Sold $30,000 of the bonds at 102 plus accrued interest of $110.

(continued)

Follow My Example 13-1

1. Investments—Tyler Company Bonds	40,000	
Interest Receivable	320	
Cash		40,320
2. Cash	2,000*	
Interest Receivable		320
Interest Revenue		1,680
*$40,000 × 10% × ½		
3. Cash	30,710*	
Interest Revenue		110
Gain on Sale of Investments		600
Investments—Tyler Company Bonds		30,000

*Sale proceeds ($30,000 × 102%)	$30,600
Accrued interest	110
Total proceeds from sale	$30,710

For Practice: PE 13-1A, PE 13-1B

Accounting for Equity Investments

3 Describe and illustrate the accounting for equity investments.

A company may invest in the preferred or common stock of another company. The company investing in another company's stock is the **investor**. The company whose stock is purchased is the **investee**.

The percent of the investee's outstanding stock purchased by the investor determines the degree of control that the investor has over the investee. This, in turn, determines the accounting method used to record the stock investment as shown in Exhibit 1.

Exhibit 1

Stock Investments

Percent of Outstanding Stock Owned by Investor	Degree of Control of Investor over Investee	Accounting Method
Less than 20%	No control	Cost method
Between 20% and 50%	Significant influence	Equity method
Greater than 50%	Control	Consolidation

Less Than 20% Ownership

If the investor purchases less than 20% of the outstanding stock of the investee, the investor is considered to have no control over the investee. In this case, it is assumed that the investor purchased the stock primarily to earn dividends or realize gains on price increases of the stock.

Investments of less than 20% of the investee's outstanding stock are accounted for using the **cost method**. Under the cost method, entries are recorded for the following transactions:

1. Purchase of stock
2. Receipt of dividends
3. Sale of stock

Purchase of Stock The purchase of stock is recorded at its cost. Any brokerage commissions are included as part of the cost.

To illustrate, assume that on May 1, Bart Company purchases 2,000 shares of Lisa Company common stock at $49.90 per share plus a brokerage fee of $200. The entry to record the purchase of the stock is as follows:

May	1	Investments—Lisa Company Stock	100,000	
		Cash		100,000
		Purchased 2,000 shares of Lisa Company common stock [($49.90 × 2,000 shares) + $200].		

Receipt of Dividends On July 31, Bart Company receives a dividend of $0.40 per share from Lisa Company. The entry to record the receipt of the dividend is as follows:

July	31	Cash	800	
		Dividend Revenue		800
		Received dividend on Lisa Company common stock (2,000 shares × $0.40).		

Dividend revenue is reported as part of *Other income* on Bart Company's income statement.

Sale of Stock The sale of a stock investment normally results in a gain or loss. A gain is recorded if the proceeds from the sale exceed the book value (cost) of the stock. A loss is recorded if the proceeds from the sale are less than the book value (cost).

To illustrate, on September 1, Bart Company sells 1,500 shares of Lisa Company stock for $54.50 per share, less a $160 commission. The sale results in a gain of $6,590, as shown below.

Proceeds from sale	$81,590*
Book value (cost) of the stock	75,000**
Gain on sale	$ 6,590

*[($54.50 × 1,500 shares) − $160
**($100,000/2,000 shares) × 1,500 shares

The entry to record the sale is as follows:

Sept.	1	Cash	81,590	
		Gain on Sale of Investments		6,590
		Investments—Lisa Company Stock		75,000
		Sale of 1,500 shares of Lisa Company common stock.		

The gain on the sale of investments is reported as part of *Other income* on Bart Company's income statement.

Example Exercise 13-2   Stock Transactions   •••••••> ③

On September 1, 1,500 shares of Monroe Company are acquired at a price of $24 per share plus a $40 brokerage fee. On October 14, a $0.60 per share dividend was received on the Monroe Company stock. On November 11, 750 shares (half) of Monroe Company stock were sold for $20 per share, less a $45 brokerage fee. Prepare the journal entries for the original purchase, dividend, and sale.

Follow My Example 13-2

Sept. 1	Investments—Monroe Company Stock	36,040*	
	Cash		36,040
	*(1,500 shares × $24 per share) + $40		
Oct. 14	Cash	900*	
	Dividend Revenue		900
	*$0.60 per share × 1,500 shares		
Nov. 11	Cash	14,955*	
	Loss on Sale of Investments	3,065	
	Investments—Monroe Company Stock		18,020**
	*(750 shares × $20) − $45		
	**$36,040 × ½		

For Practice: PE 13-2A, PE 13-2B

Starbucks Corporation has a 40% ownership interest in Starbucks Coffee Japan, Ltd. Thus, Starbucks Corporation has significant influence over the operations of Starbucks Coffee Japan, Ltd.

Between 20% and 50% Ownership

If the investor purchases between 20% and 50% of the outstanding stock of the investee, the investor is considered to have a significant influence over the investee. In this case, it is assumed that the investor purchased the stock primarily for strategic reasons such as developing a supplier relationship.

Investments of between 20% and 50% of the investee's outstanding stock are accounted for using the **equity method**. Under the equity method, the stock is recorded initially at its cost, including any brokerage commissions. This is the same as under the cost method.

Under the equity method, the investment account is adjusted for the investor's share of the *net income* and *dividends* of the investee. These adjustments are as follows:

1. *Net Income:* The investor records its share of the net income of the investee as an increase in the investment account. Its share of any net loss is recorded as a decrease in the investment account.

2. *Dividends:* The investor's share of cash dividends received from the investee decreases the investment account.

Purchase of Stock   To illustrate, assume that Simpson Inc. purchased its 40% interest in Flanders Corporation's common stock on January 2, 2010, for $350,000. The entry to record the purchase is as follows:

2010				
Jan.	2	Investment in Flanders Corporation Stock	350,000	
		Cash		350,000
		Purchased 40% of Flanders		
		Corporation stock.		

Recording Investee Net Income

For the year ended December 31, 2010, Flanders Corporation reported net income of $105,000. Under the equity method, Simpson Inc. (the investor) records its share of Flanders net income as follows:

2010				
Dec.	31	Investment in Flanders Corporation Stock	42,000	
		Income of Flanders Corporation		42,000
		Record 40% share of Flanders		
		Corporation net income.		

Income of Flanders Corporation is reported on Simpson Inc.'s income statement. Depending on its significance, it may be reported separately or as part of *Other income*.

Recording Investee Dividends

During the year, Flanders declared and paid cash dividends of $45,000. Under the equity method, Simpson Inc. (the investor) records its share of Flanders' dividends as follows:

2010				
Dec.	31	Cash	18,000	
		Investment in Flanders Corporation Stock		18,000
		Record 40% share of Flanders		
		Corporation dividends.		

The effect of recording 40% of Flanders Corporation's net income and dividends is to increase the investment account by $24,000 ($42,000 − $18,000). Thus, Investment in Flanders Corporation Stock increases from $350,000 to $374,000, as shown below.

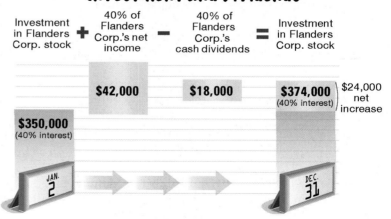

Investment and Dividends

Under the equity method, the investment account reflects the investor's proportional changes in the net book value of the investee. For example, Flanders Corporation's net book value increased by $60,000 (net income of $105,000 less dividends of $45,000) during the year. As a result, Simpson's share of Flanders' net book value increased by $24,000 ($60,000 × 40%).

Sale of Stock

Under the equity method, a gain or loss is normally recorded from the sale of an investment. A gain is recorded if the proceeds exceed the *book value* of the investment. A loss is recorded if the proceeds are less than the *book value* of the investment.

To illustrate, if Simpson Inc. sold Flanders Corporation's stock on January 1, 2011, for $400,000, a gain of $26,000 would be reported, as shown below.

Proceeds from sale	$400,000
Book value of stock investment	374,000
Gain on sale	$ 26,000

The entry to record the sale is as follows:

2011 Jan.	1	Cash	400,000	
		Investment in Flanders Corporation Stock		374,000
		Gain on Sale of Flanders Corporation Stock		26,000
		Sale of Flanders Corporation stock.		

Example Exercise 13-3 Equity Method ••••••• ⟩ 3

On January 2, Olson Company acquired 35% of the outstanding stock of Bryant Company for $140,000. For the year ending December 31, Bryant Company earned income of $44,000 and paid dividends of $20,000. Prepare the entries for Olson Company for the purchase of the stock, share of Bryant income, and dividends received from Bryant Company.

Follow My Example 13-3

Jan. 2	Investment in Bryant Company Stock	140,000	
	Cash		140,000
Dec. 31	Investment in Bryant Company Stock	15,400*	
	Income of Bryant Company		15,400
	*Record 35% of Bryant income, 35% × $44,000		
Dec. 31	Cash	7,000*	
	Investment in Bryant Company Stock		7,000
	*35% × $20,000		

For Practice: PE 13-3A, PE 13-3B

To expand its Internet presence, Google purchased 100% of YouTube's outstanding stock.

More Than 50% Ownership

If the investor purchases more than 50% of the outstanding stock of the investee, the investor is considered to have control over the investee. In this case, it is assumed that the investor purchased the stock of the investee primarily for strategic reasons.

The purchase of more than 50% ownership of the investee's stock is termed a **business combination**. Companies may combine in order to produce more efficiently, diversify product lines, expand geographically, or acquire know-how.

A corporation owning all or a majority of the voting stock of another corporation is called a **parent company**. The corporation that is controlled is called the **subsidiary company**.

Parent and subsidiary corporations often continue to maintain separate accounting records and prepare their own financial statements. In such cases, at the end of the year, the financial statements of the parent and subsidiary are combined and reported as a single company. These combined financial statements are called **consolidated financial statements**. Such statements are normally identified by adding *and Subsidiary(ies)* to the name of the parent corporation or by adding *Consolidated* to the statement title.

To the external stakeholders of the parent company, consolidated financial statements are more meaningful than separate statements for each corporation. This is because the parent company, in substance, controls the subsidiaries. The accounting for business combinations, including preparing consolidated financial statements, is described and illustrated in advanced accounting courses and textbooks.

Valuing and Reporting Investments

4 Describe and illustrate valuing and reporting investments in the financial statements.

Debt and equity securities are *financial assets* that are often traded on public exchanges such as the New York Stock Exchange. As a result, their market value can be observed and, thus, objectively determined.

For this reason, generally accepted accounting principles (GAAP) allow some debt and equity securities to be valued in the accounting records and financial statements at their fair market values. In contrast, GAAP requires tangible assets such as property, plant, and equipment to be valued and reported at their net book values (cost less accumulated depreciation).

For purposes of valuing and reporting, debt and equity securities are classified as follows:

1. Trading securities
2. Held-to-maturity securities
3. Available-for-sale securities

Trading Securities

Trading securities are debt and equity securities that are purchased and sold to earn short-term profits from changes in their market prices. Trading securities are often held by banks, mutual funds, insurance companies, and other financial institutions.

SunTrust Banks Inc. holds $2 billion in trading securities as current assets.

Because trading securities are held as a short-term investment, they are reported as a current asset on the balance sheet. Trading securities are valued as a portfolio (group) of securities using the securities' fair values. **Fair value** is the market price that the company would receive for a security if it were sold. Changes in fair value of the portfolio (group) of trading securities are recognized as an **unrealized gain or loss** for the period.

To illustrate, assume Maggie Company purchased a portfolio of trading securities during 2009. On December 31, 2009, the cost and fair values of the securities were as follows:

Name	Number of Shares	Total Cost	Total Fair Value
Armour Company	400	$ 5,000	$ 7,200
Maven, Inc.	500	11,000	7,500
Polaris Co.	200	8,000	10,600
Total		$24,000	$25,300

The portfolio of trading securities is reported at its fair value of $25,300. An adjusting entry is made to record the increase in fair value of $1,300 ($25,300 – $24,000). In order to maintain a record of the original cost of the securities, a valuation account, called *Valuation Allowance for Trading Investments*, is debited for $1,300 and *Unrealized Gain on Trading Investments* is credited for $1,300. The adjusting entry on December 31, 2009, to record the fair value of the portfolio of trading securities is shown below.

2009				
Dec.	31	Valuation Allowance for Trading Investments	1,300	
		Unrealized Gain on Trading Investments		1,300
		To record increase in fair value of		
		trading securities.		

The *Unrealized Gain on Trading Investments* is reported on the income statement. Depending on its significance, it may be reported separately or as *Other income* on the income statement. The valuation allowance is reported on the December 31, 2009, balance sheet as follows:

Maggie Company
Balance Sheet (selected items)
December 31, 2009

Current assets:		
Cash...		$120,000
Trading investments (at cost)	$24,000	
Plus valuation allowance for trading investments..............	1,300	
Trading investments (at fair value)		25,300

On September 10, 2010, Maggie Company purchases 300 shares of Zane Inc. as a trading security for $12 per share, including a brokerage commission. The entry to record this transaction is as follows:

Sept.	10	Trading Investments—Zane Inc.	3,600	
		Cash		3,600

Assume that on December 31, 2010, the cost and fair valuation of the portfolio of trading securities are as follows:

Name	Number of Shares	Total Cost	Total Fair Value
Armour Company	400	$ 5,000	$ 5,500
Maven, Inc.	500	11,000	9,000
Polaris Co.	200	8,000	7,000
Zane Inc.	300	3,600	3,000
Total		$27,600	$24,500

The Valuation Allowance for Trading Investments account should have a credit balance on December 31, 2010, of $3,100 ($27,600 − $24,500). *Before* adjustment, Valuation Allowance for Trading Investments has a debit balance of $1,300, which is its ending balance for the prior year (2009). On December 31, 2010, this prior year balance must be adjusted to a credit balance of $3,100. In order to do this, a credit adjustment of $4,400 is required, as shown below.

Valuation allowance for trading investments, January 1, 2010	$1,300	Dr.
Trading investments at cost, December 31, 2010	$27,600	
Trading investments at fair value, December 31, 2010	24,500	
Valuation allowance for trading investments, December 31, 2010	3,100	Cr.
Adjustment	$4,400	Cr.

The adjusting entry on December 31, 2010, is as follows:

2010				
Dec.	31	Unrealized Loss on Trading Investments	4,400	
		Valuation Allowance for Trading Investments		4,400
		To record decrease in fair value of		
		trading investments.		

The Valuation Allowance for Trading Investments account after the December 31, 2010, adjusting entry is as follows:

Valuation Allowance for Trading Investments

2009			2010		
Dec. 31 Adj.	1,300				
Dec. 31 Bal.	1,300				
2010			2010		
Jan. 1 Bal.	1,300		Dec. 31 Adj.	4,400	
			Dec. 31 Bal.	3,100	

A debit balance in Valuation Allowance for Trading Investments is added to the investment account, while a credit balance is subtracted from the investment account.

The *Unrealized Loss on Trading Investments* is reported on the income statement separately, or as part of *Other income (loss)*, depending on its significance. The valuation allowance is reported on the December 31, 2010, balance sheet as follows:

Maggie Company
Balance Sheet
December 31, 2010

Current assets:		
Cash		$146,000
Trading investments (at cost)	$27,600	
Less valuation allowance for trading investments	3,100	
Trading investments (at fair value)		24,500

Example Exercise 13-4   Valuing Trading Securities at Fair Value

On January 1, 2010, Valuation Allowance for Trading Investments has a debit balance of $23,500. On December 31, 2010, the cost of the trading securities portfolio was $79,200, and the fair value was $95,000. Prepare the December 31, 2010, adjusting journal entry to record the unrealized gain or loss on trading investments.

Continued

Follow My Example 13-4

2010
Dec. 31   Unrealized Loss on Trading Investments   7,700
                  Valuation Allowance for Trading Investments 7,700*
                  To record decrease in fair value of trading investments.

Valuation allowance for trading investments, January 1, 2010		$23,500 Dr.
Trading investments at cost, December 31, 2010	$79,200	
Trading investments at fair value, December 31, 2010	95,000	
Valuation allowance for trading investments, December 31, 2010 . .		15,800 Dr.
*Adjustment.		$ 7,700 Cr.

For Practice: PE 13-4A, PE 13-4B

Integrity, Objectivity, and Ethics in Business

SUB-PRIME WOES

Many of the largest U.S. banks provided mortgages to marginally qualified borrowers. Such loans were termed "sub-prime" loans. These loans were then packaged into securities that were sold to investors. Often, the banks earned attractive fees for creating these financial products. Unfortunately, many weak borrowers were unable to make their mortgage payments, which resulted in defaults on the mortgages. These defaults caused the packaged securities that held these loans to fall in value. As a result, many investors, including the banks themselves, were required to recognize large losses from declines in

fair value of these securities. Some of these losses were as follows:

UBS	$37 billion
Merrill Lynch & Co.	34 billion
Citigroup	30 billion

These losses were some of the largest in the history of these companies. Since the losses were immediately disclosed and recognized, they were never hidden from company stakeholders. This is because the accounting rules require such losses to be recognized even if the securities are not sold.

Held-to-Maturity Securities

Held-to-maturity securities are debt investments, such as notes or bonds, that a company intends to hold until their maturity date. Held-to-maturity securities are primarily purchased to earn interest revenue.

If a held-to-maturity security will mature within a year, it is reported as a current asset on the balance sheet. Held-to-maturity securities maturing beyond a year are reported as noncurrent assets.

Only securities with maturity dates such as corporate notes and bonds are classified as held-to-maturity securities. Equity securities are not held-to-maturity securities because they have no maturity date.

Held-to-maturity bond investments are recorded at their cost, including any brokerage commissions, as illustrated earlier in this chapter. If the interest rate on the bonds differs from the market rate of interest, the bonds may be purchased at a premium or discount. In such cases, the premium or discount is amortized over the life of the bonds.

Held-to-maturity bond investments are reported on the balance sheet at their amortized cost. The accounting for held-to-maturity bond investments, including premium and discount amortization, is described and illustrated in Appendix 1 at the end of this chapter.

Merrill Lynch & Co. reported $254 million in municipal bonds as held-to-maturity securities in its current assets.

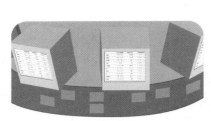

Available-for-Sale Securities

Available-for-sale securities are debt and equity securities that are not classified as trading or held-to-maturity securities. For example, bonds that management does not intend to hold to maturity are classified as available-for-sale securities.

The accounting for available-for-sale securities is similar to the accounting for trading securities except for the reporting of changes in fair values. Specifically, changes in the fair values of trading securities are reported as an unrealized gain or loss on the income statement. In contrast, changes in the fair values of available-for-sale securities are reported as part of stockholders' equity and, thus, excluded from the income statement.

To illustrate, assume that Maggie Company purchased securities during 2009 as available-for-sale securities instead of trading securities. On December 31, 2009, the cost and fair values of the securities were as follows:

Microsoft Corporation holds over $17 billion in available-for-sale securities as current assets.

Name	Number of Shares	Total Cost	Total Fair Value
Armour Company	400	$ 5,000	$ 7,200
Maven, Inc.	500	11,000	7,500
Polaris Co.	200	8,000	10,600
Total		$24,000	$25,300

The portfolio of available-for-sale securities is reported at its fair value of $25,300. An adjusting entry is made to record the increase in fair value of $1,300 ($25,300 − $24,000). In order to maintain a record of the original cost of the securities, a valuation account, called *Valuation Allowance for Available-for-Sale Investments*, is debited for $1,300. This account is similar to the valuation account used for trading securities.

Unlike trading securities, the December 31, 2009, adjusting entry credits a stockholders' equity account instead of an income statement account.[3] The $1,300 gain is credited to *Unrealized Gain (Loss) on Available-for-Sale Investments*.

The adjusting entry on December 31, 2009, to record the fair value of the portfolio of available-for-sale securities is as follows:

2009				
Dec.	31	Valuation Allowance for Available-for-Sale Investments	1,300	
		Unrealized Gain (Loss) on Available-for-Sale Investments		1,300
		To record increase in fair value of available-for-sale investments.		

A credit balance in Unrealized Gain (Loss) on Available-for-Sale Investments is added to stockholders' equity, while a debit balance is subtracted from stockholders' equity.

---

3 This is a rare exception to the rule that every adjusting entry must affect an income statement and a balance sheet account.

The valuation allowance and the unrealized gain are reported on the December 31, 2009, balance sheet as follows:

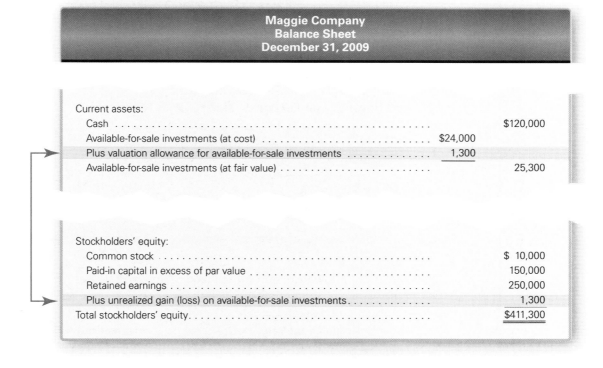

Maggie Company
Balance Sheet
December 31, 2009

Current assets:		
Cash		$120,000
Available-for-sale investments (at cost)	$24,000	
Plus valuation allowance for available-for-sale investments	1,300	
Available-for-sale investments (at fair value)		25,300
Stockholders' equity:		
Common stock		$ 10,000
Paid-in capital in excess of par value		150,000
Retained earnings		250,000
Plus unrealized gain (loss) on available-for-sale investments		1,300
Total stockholders' equity		$411,300

As shown above, Unrealized Gain (Loss) on Available-for-Sale Investments is reported as an addition to stockholders' equity. In future years, the cumulative effects of unrealized gains and losses are reported in this account. Because 2009 was the first year that Maggie Company purchased available-for-sale securities, the unrealized gain is reported as the balance of *Unrealized Gain (Loss) on Available-for-Sale Investments.*

On September 10, 2010, Maggie Company purchases 300 shares of Zane Inc. as an available-for-sale security for $12 per share, including brokerage commission. The entry to record this transaction would be as follows:

2010				
Sept.	10	Available-for-Sale Investments—Zane Inc.	3,600	
		Cash		3,600

On December 31, 2010, the cost and fair valuation of the portfolio of available-for-sale securities are as follows:

Name	Number of Shares	Total Cost	Total Fair Value
Armour Company	400	$ 5,000	$ 5,500
Maven, Inc.	500	11,000	9,000
Polaris Co.	200	8,000	7,000
Zane Inc.	300	3,600	3,000
Total		$27,600	$24,500

Valuation Allowance for Available-for-Sale Investments should have a credit balance on December 31, 2010, of $3,100 ($27,600 − $24,500). *Before* adjustment, Valuation Allowance for Available-for-Sale Investments has a debit balance of $1,300. Thus, Valuation Allowance for Available-for-Sale Investments must be adjusted on December 31, 2010, by a credit for $4,400 as shown at the top of the next page.

Valuation allowance for available-for-sale investments, January 1, 2010		$1,300 Dr.
Available-for-sale investments at cost, December 31, 2010	$27,600	
Available-for-sale investments at fair value, December 31, 2010	24,500	
Valuation allowance for available-for-sale investments, December 31, 2010		3,100 Cr.
Adjustment		$4,400 Cr.

The adjusting entry on December 31, 2010, is as follows:

2010				
Dec.	31	Unrealized Gain (Loss) on Available-for-Sale Investments	4,400	
		Valuation Allowance for Available-for-Sale Investments		4,400
		To record decrease in fair value of available-for-sale investments.		

The valuation allowance and unrealized gains and losses accounts after the December 31, 2010, adjusting entry are as follows:

Valuation Allowance for Available-for-Sale Investments		**Unrealized Gain (Loss) on Available-for-Sale Investments**	
2009 Dec. 31 Adj. 1,300 Dec. 31 Bal. 1,300			2009 Dec. 31 Adj. 1,300 Dec. 31 Bal. 1,300
2010 Jan. 1 Bal. 1,300	2010 Dec. 31 Adj. 4,400 Dec. 31 Bal. 3,100	2010 Dec. 31 Adj. 4,400 Dec. 31 Bal. 3,100	2010 Jan. 1 Bal. 1,300

The valuation allowance and unrealized gain (loss) are reported on the December 31, 2010, balance sheet as follows:

Maggie Company
Balance Sheet
December 31, 2010

Current assets:		
Cash...		$146,000
Available-for-sale investments (at cost)............................	$27,600	
Less valuation allowance for available-for-sale investments	3,100	
Available-for-sale investments (at fair value)		24,500
Stockholders' equity:		
Common stock......................................		$ 10,000
Paid-in capital in excess of par value		150,000
Retained earnings		320,000
Less unrealized gain (loss) on available-for-sale investments.............		(3,100)
Total stockholders' equity		$476,900

Example Exercise 13-5   Valuing Available-for-Sale Securities at Fair Value

On January 1, 2010, Valuation Allowance for Available-for-Sale Investments has a credit balance of $9,000. On December 31, 2010, the cost of the available-for-sale securities was $45,700, and the fair value was $37,200.
    Prepare the adjusting entry to record the unrealized gain or loss for available-for-sale investments on December 31, 2010.

Follow My Example 13-5

```
2010
Dec. 31    Valuation Allowance for Available-for-Sale Investments   .....        500*
                Unrealized Gain (Loss) on Available-for-Sale
                Investments  . . . . . . . . . . . . . . . . . . . . . . . . . . . . .              500
                    To record increase in fair value of available-for-sale
                    securities.
```

Valuation allowance for available-for-sale investments, January 1, 2010	$9,000	Cr.
Available-for-sale investments at cost, December 31, 2010	$45,700	
Available-for-sale investments at fair value, December 31, 2010	37,200	
Valuation allowance for available-for-sale investments, December 31, 2010	8,500	Cr.
*Adjustment	$ 500	Dr.

For Practice: PE 13-5A, PE 13-5B

Summary

Exhibit 2 summarizes the valuation and balance sheet reporting of trading, held-to-maturity, and available-for-sale securities.

Exhibit 2

Summary of Valuing and Reporting of Investments

	Trading Securities	Held-to-Maturity Securities	Available-for-Sale Securities
Valued at:	**Fair Value**	**Amortized Cost**	**Fair Value**
Changes in valuation are reported as:	Unrealized gain or loss is reported on income statement as Other income (loss).	Premium or discount amortization is reported as part of interest revenue on the income statement.	Accumulated unrealized gain or loss is reported in stockholders' equity on the balance sheet.
Reported on the balance sheet as:	Cost of investments plus or minus valuation allowance.	Amortized cost of investment.	Cost of investments plus or minus valuation allowance.
Classified on balance sheet as:	A current asset.	Either as a current or noncurrent asset, depending on management's intent.	Either as a current or noncurrent asset, depending on management's intent.

Common stock investments in trading and available-for-sale securities are normally less than 20% of the outstanding common stock of the investee. The portfolios are reported at fair value using the valuation allowance account, while the individual securities are accounted for using the cost method. Investments between 20 and 50% of the outstanding common stock of the investee are accounted for using the equity method illustrated earlier in this chapter. Such investments, however, are permitted to be valued using fair values. To simplify, it is assumed that the investor does not elect this option.

Common stock investments of more than 50% of the outstanding stock of the investee are reported as part of the consolidated financial statements of the parent company. Thus, using fair values for such investments is not an option.

The balance sheet reporting the investments of Mornin' Joe is shown below.

Mornin' Joe
Balance Sheet
December 31, 2010

Assets

Current assets:		
Cash and cash equivalents		$235,000
Trading investments (at cost)	$420,000	
Plus valuation allowance for trading investments	45,000	465,000
Accounts receivable	$305,000	
Less allowance for doubtful accounts	12,300	292,700
Merchandise inventory—at lower of cost		
(first-in, first-out method) or market		120,000
Prepaid insurance		24,000
Total current assets		$1,136,700
Investments:		
Investment in AM Coffee (equity method)		565,000
Property, plant, and equipment:		

Mornin' Joe invests in trading securities and does not have investments in held-to-maturity or available-for-sale securities. Mornin' Joe also owns 40% of AM Coffee Corporation, which is accounted for using the equity method. Mornin' Joe intends to keep its investment in AM Coffee indefinitely for strategic reasons; thus, its investment in AM Coffee is classified as a noncurrent asset. Such investments are normally reported before property, plant, and equipment.

Mornin' Joe reported an Unrealized Gain on Trading Investments of $5,000 and Equity Income in AM Coffee of $57,000 in the Other income and expense section of its income statement, as shown below.

Mornin' Joe
Income Statement
For the Year Ended December 31, 2010

Revenue from sales:			
Sales		$5,450,000	
Less: Sales returns and allowances	$26,500		
Sales discounts	21,400	47,900	
Net sales			$5,402,100
Cost of merchandise sold			2,160,000
Gross profit			$3,242,100
Total operating expenses			2,608,700
Income from operations			$ 633,400
Other income and expense:			
Interest revenue		$ 18,000	
Interest expense		(136,000)	
Loss on disposal of fixed asset		(23,000)	
Unrealized gain on trading investments		5,000	
Equity income in AM Coffee		57,000	(79,000)
Income before income taxes			$ 554,400
Income tax expense			132,800
Net income			$ 421,600

Business Connection

WARREN BUFFETT: THE SAGE OF OMAHA

Beginning in 1962, Warren Buffett, one of the world's wealthiest and most successful investors, began buying shares of Berkshire Hathaway. He eventually took control of the company and transformed it from a textile manufacturing company into an investment holding company. Today, Berkshire Hathaway holds over $133 billion in cash and cash equivalents, equity securities, and debt securities. Berkshire's largest holdings include The Coca-Cola Company, American Express, Wells Fargo, and Procter & Gamble. Berkshire Class A common stock trades near $130,000 per share, the highest priced share on the New York Stock Exchange. These shares would have given an investor a nearly 1,600% return since 1990.

Buffett compares his investment style to hitting a baseball: "Ted Williams, one of the greatest hitters in the game, stated, 'my argument is, to be a good hitter, you've got to get a good ball to hit. It's the first rule of the book. If I have to bite at stuff that is out of my happy zone, I'm not a .344 hitter. I might only be a .250 hitter.'" Buffett states, "Charlie (Buffett's partner) and I agree and will try to wait for (investment) opportunities that are well within our 'happy zone.'"[4]

Warren Buffett as the CEO of Berkshire Hathaway earns a salary of only $100,000 per year, which is the lowest CEO salary for a company of its size in the United States. However, he personally owns approximately 38% of the company, making him worth over $40 billion. What will Buffett do with this wealth? He has decided to give nearly all of it to philanthropic causes through the Bill and Melinda Gates Foundation.

Fair Value Accounting

5 Describe fair value accounting and its implications for the future.

Fair value is the price that would be received for selling an asset or paying off a liability. Fair value assumes that the asset is sold or the liability paid off under *normal* rather than under distressed conditions.

As illustrated earlier, generally accepted accounting principles require the use of fair values for valuing and reporting debt and equity securities held as trading or available-for-sale investments. In addition, accounts receivable is recorded and reported at an amount that approximates its fair value. This is because accounts receivable is reported at its net realizable value. In addition, accounts receivable is a current asset that will be collected (converted to cash) within a relatively short period. Likewise, accounts payable are recorded and reported at approximately their fair value.

In contrast, many assets and liabilities are recorded and reported at amounts that differ significantly from their fair values. For example, when equipment or other property, plant, and equipment assets are purchased, they are initially recorded at their fair values. That is, they are recorded at their purchase price (initial cost). However, their initial cost, called *historical cost*, is not adjusted for changes in fair values. Instead, equipment is depreciated over its useful life. As a result, the book value of property, plant, and equipment normally differs significantly from its fair value. Likewise, held-to-maturity securities are valued at their amortized cost rather than at their fair values.

Trend to Fair Value Accounting

A current trend is for the Financial Accounting Standards Board (FASB) and other accounting regulators to adopt accounting principles using fair values for valuing and reporting assets and liabilities. Factors contributing to this trend include the following:

1. Current generally accepted accounting principles are a hybrid of varying measurement methods that often conflict with each other. For example, property, plant, and equipment are normally reported at their depreciated book values. However,

GAAP require that if a fixed asset value is *impaired*, that it be written down to its fair value. Such conflicting accounting principles could confuse users of financial statements.

2. A greater percentage of the total assets of many companies consists of financial assets such as receivables and securities. Fair values for such assets can often be readily obtained from stock market quotations or computed using current interest rates and present values. Likewise, many liabilities can be readily valued using market quotations or current interest rates and present values.

3. The world economy has created pressure on accounting regulators to adopt a worldwide set of accounting principles and standards. *International Financial Reporting Standards (IFRSs)* are issued by the International Accounting Standards Board *(IASB)* and are used by the European Economic Union (EU). As a result, the FASB is under increasing pressure to conform U.S. standards with International Financial Reporting Standards. One area where differences exist is in the use of fair values, which are more often used by International Financial Reporting Standards.

While there is an increasing trend to fair value accounting, using fair values has several potential disadvantages. Some of these disadvantages include the following:

1. Fair values may not be readily obtainable for some assets or liabilities. As a result, accounting reports may become more subjective and less reliable. For example, fair values (market quotations) are normally available for trading and available-for-sale securities. However, fair values may not be as available for assets such as property, plant, and equipment or intangible assets such as goodwill.

2. Fair values make it more difficult to compare companies if companies use different methods of determining (measuring) fair values. This would be especially true for assets and liabilities for which fair values are not readily available.

3. Using fair values could result in more fluctuations in accounting reports because fair values normally change from year to year. Such volatility may confuse users of the financial statements. It may also make it more difficult for users to determine current operating trends and to predict future trends.

Effect of Fair Value Accounting on the Financial Statements

The use of fair values for valuing assets and liabilities affects the financial statements. Specifically, the balance sheet and income statement could be affected.

Balance Sheet When an asset or a liability is reported at its fair value, any difference between the asset's original cost or prior period's fair value must be recorded. As we illustrated for trading and available-for-sale securities, one method for doing this is to use a valuation allowance. The account, *Valuation Allowance for Trading Investments*, was used earlier in this chapter to adjust trading securities to their fair values. Similar accounts could be used for the other assets and liabilities.

In addition, the unrealized gain or loss on changes in fair values must be recorded. One method reports these unrealized gains and losses as part of stockholders' equity. This method was illustrated earlier in this chapter for *available-for-sale* securities.

Income Statement Instead of recording the unrealized gain or loss on changes in fair values as part of stockholders' equity, the unrealized gains or losses may be reported on the income statement. This method was illustrated earlier in this chapter for *trading* securities.

As shown above, differences exist as to how to best report changes in fair values—that is, whether to report gains or losses on fair values on the income statement or the balance sheet.

In an attempt to bridge these differences, the FASB introduced the concepts of *comprehensive income* and *accumulated other comprehensive income*. These concepts are described in Appendix 2 to this chapter.

Future of Fair Value Accounting

The use of fair value accounting was described and illustrated in this chapter for trading and available-for-sale securities. The FASB and other accounting regulators are continuing to explore the use of fair value accounting for other assets and liabilities. For example, the FASB recently issued *Statement of Financial Accounting Standards No. 159*, "The Fair Value Option for Financial Assets and Financial Liabilities," which expands the use of fair value reporting for financial assets and liabilities.[5]

─── Financial Analysis and Interpretation ───

The dividend yield indicates the rate of return to stockholders in terms of cash dividend distributions. Although the dividend yield can be computed for both preferred and common stock, it is most often computed for common stock. This is because most preferred stock has a stated dividend rate or amount. In contrast, the amount of common stock dividends normally varies with the profitability of the corporation.

The dividend yield is computed by dividing the annual dividends paid per share of common stock by the market price per share at a specific date, as shown below.

$$\text{Dividend Yield} = \frac{\text{Dividends per Share of Common Stock}}{\text{Market Price per Share of Common Stock}}$$

To illustrate, the market price of Mattel, Inc., common stock was $19.09 on April 29, 2008. During the preceding year, Mattel had paid dividends of $0.75 per share. Thus, the dividend yield of Mattel's common stock is 3.93% ($0.75/$19.09). Because the market price of a corporation's stock will vary from day to day, its dividend yield will also vary from day to day. Fortunately, the dividend yield is provided with newspaper listings of market prices and most Internet quotation services, such as from Yahoo's Finance Web site.

The recent dividend yields for some selected companies are as follows:

Company	Dividend Yield (%)
Apple	None
Bank of America	6.76
Coca-Cola Company	2.59
General Motors	4.72
Hewlett-Packard	0.67
The Home Depot	3.07
Microsoft	1.54

As can be seen, the dividend yield varies widely across firms. Growth companies often do not pay dividends, but instead, reinvest their earnings in research and development, such as with Apple.

A P P E N D I X   1

Accounting for Held-to-Maturity Investments

Held-to-maturity securities are debt investments such as notes or bonds that a company intends to hold until their maturity date. This appendix describes and illustrates the accounting for bonds purchased as a held-to-maturity investment when the price of the bond differs from par value.

Purchase of Bonds

Bonds may be purchased directly from the issuing corporation or through a bond exchange such as the New York Bond Exchange. Daily bond quotations are available from bond exchanges that include the following:

1.   Interest rate
2.   Maturity date

---

5 *Statement of Financial Accounting Standards No. 159*, "The Fair Value Option for Financial Assets and Financial Liabilities" (Norwalk, CT: Financial Accounting Standards Board, 2007).

3. Volume of sales
4. High, low, and closing prices for the day

Prices for bonds are quoted as a percentage of the face amount. Thus, the price of a $1,000 bond quoted at 99.5 would be $995, while the price of a $1,000 bond quoted at 104.25 would be $1,042.50.

The cost of a bond investment includes all costs related to the purchase including any brokerage commissions. When bonds are purchased between interest dates, the buyer normally pays the seller the interest accrued from the last interest payment date to the date of purchase. The accounting for the purchase of a bond, which included accrued interest, was illustrated in this chapter.

Bonds may be purchased at a price other than their face amount. Bonds are purchased at a premium or discount as follows:

1. If the coupon bond rate of interest is *more than* the market rate of interest for equivalent investments, bonds are purchased at a *premium*. That is, the bonds are purchased for more than their face amount.

2. If the coupon bond rate of interest is *less than* the market rate of interest for equivalent investments, bonds are purchased at a *discount*. That is, the bonds are purchased for less than their face amount.

The cost of a bond investment is recorded in an investment account, *Investment—Bonds*. The face amount of the bond and related premium or discount are normally not recorded in separate accounts. This is different from the accounting for bonds payable for which separate premium and discount accounts are used. However, like bonds payable, any premium or discount on a bond investment is amortized over the remaining life of the bonds.

Amortization of Premium or Discount

Any premium or discount on a bond investment should be amortized over the remaining life of the bond. The amortization affects the investment and interest revenue accounts as follows:

1. Bond *Premium* Amortization: Decreases Investment—Bonds and decreases Interest Revenue as shown in the following journal entry:

Interest Revenue	XXX	
Investment—Bonds		XXX
To amortize premium		
on bond investment.		

2. Bond *Discount* Amortization: Increases Investment—Bonds and increases Interest Revenue as shown in the following journal entry:

Investment—Bonds	XXX	
Interest Revenue		XXX
To amortize discount		
on bond investment.		

The amortization on bond investments is usually recorded at the end of the period as an adjusting entry. The amortization can be computed using the straight-line or interest methods.

To illustrate, assume that on April 1, 2010, Crenshaw Inc. purchases 10-year, 8% bonds on their issuance date directly from XPS Corporation as a held-to-maturity investment. The bonds pay semiannual interest and were purchased at a discount as follows:

Face amount of bonds	$50,000
Less discount on bonds	(6,000)
Purchase price of bonds	$44,000

The entries related to the bond investment during 2010 are as follows:

Purchase of bonds on April 1, 2010.

2010 Apr.	1	Investment—XPS Corporation Bonds	44,000	
		Cash		44,000
		Purchase of bonds as held-to-maturity investment.		

Receipt of semiannual interest on October 1.

Oct.	1	Cash	2,000	
		Interest Revenue		2,000
		Receipt of semiannual interest ($50,000 × 8% × ½).		

Adjusting entry for 3 months of accrued interest on December 31.

Dec.	31	Interest Receivable	1,000	
		Interest Revenue		1,000
		Accrued interest ($50,000 × 8% × ¼).		

Adjusting entry for amortization of discount on December 31 using the straight-line method.

Dec.	31	Investment—XPS Corporation Bonds	450	
		Interest Revenue		450
		Amortization of discount on bond investment ($6,000/120 months) = $50 per month $50 × 9 months = $450.		

Receipt of Maturity Value of Bond

At the maturity date of the bonds, any premium or discount will be fully amortized, and the book value (carrying value) of the bond investment account will equal the face amount of the bonds. At the maturity date, the investor will receive the face amount of the bonds.

To illustrate, the XPS Corporation bonds mature on April 1, 2020. At that date, the $6,000 discount will have been totally amortized, and Investment—XPS Corporation

Bonds will have a balance of $50,000. The receipt of the face amount of the bonds on April 1, 2020, is recorded as follows:

2020					
Apr.	1	Cash		50,000	
		Investment—XPS Corporation Bonds			50,000
		Receipt of maturity value of			
		bond investment.			

A P P E N D I X   2

Comprehensive Income

Comprehensive income is defined as all changes in stockholders' equity during a period, except those resulting from dividends and stockholders' investments. Comprehensive income is computed by adding or subtracting *other comprehensive income* from net income as follows:

Net income	$XXX
Other comprehensive income	XXX
Comprehensive income	$XXX

Other comprehensive income items include unrealized gains and losses on available-for-sale securities as well as other items such as foreign currency and pension liability adjustments. The *cumulative* effect of other comprehensive income is reported on the balance sheet, as **accumulated other comprehensive income**.

Companies may report comprehensive income in the financial statements as follows:

1. On the income statement
2. In a separate statement of comprehensive income
3. In the statement of stockholders' equity

Companies may use terms other than comprehensive income, such as *total nonowner changes in equity.*

In the earlier illustration, Maggie Company had reported an unrealized gain on available-for-sale investments of $1,300. This unrealized gain would be reported in the Stockholders' Equity section of its 2009 balance sheet as follows:

Maggie Company
Balance Sheet
December 31, 2009

Stockholders' equity:	
Common stock	$ 10,000
Paid-in capital in excess of par value	150,000
Retained earnings	250,000
Plus unrealized gain (loss) on available-for-sale investments	1,300
Total stockholders' equity	$411,300

Alternatively, Maggie Company could have reported the unrealized gain as part of accumulated other comprehensive income as follows:

Maggie Company
Balance Sheet
December 31, 2009

Stockholders' equity:	
Common stock	$ 10,000
Paid-in capital in excess of par value	150,000
Retained earnings	250,000
Accumulated other comprehensive income:	
Unrealized gain on available-for-sale investments	1,300
Total stockholders' equity	$411,300

At a Glance   13 • • •➤

1   Describe why companies invest in debt and equity securities.

Key Points	Key Learning Outcomes	Example Exercises	Practice Exercises
Cash can be used to (1) invest in current operations such as plant and equipment, (2) invest to earn additional revenue in marketable securities, or (3) invest in marketable securities for strategic reasons. Strategic investments are made to reduce costs, replace management, expand, or integrate operations.	• Describe the ways excess cash is used by a business.		
	• Describe the purpose of temporary investments.		
	• Describe the strategic purpose of long-term investments.		

2   Describe and illustrate the accounting for debt investments.

Key Points	Key Learning Outcomes	Example Exercises	Practice Exercises
The accounting for debt investments includes recording the purchase, interest revenue, and sale of the debt. Both the purchase and sale date may include accrued interest.	• Prepare journal entries to record the purchase of a debt investment, including accrued interest.	13-1	13-1A, 13-1B
	• Prepare journal entries for interest revenue from debt investments.	13-1	13-1A, 13-1B
	• Prepare journal entries to record the sale of a debt investment at a gain or loss.	13-1	13-1A, 13-1B

Describe and illustrate the accounting for equity investments.

		Example Exercises	Practice Exercises
Key Points	**Key Learning Outcomes**		

Key Points

The accounting for equity investments differs depending on the degree of control. Accounting for investments of less than 20% of the outstanding stock (no control) of the investee includes recording the purchase of stock, receipt of dividends, and sale of stock at a gain or loss. Influential investments of 20%–50% of the outstanding stock of an investee are accounted for under the *equity method*. Under the equity method, the investment is debited for the proportional share of earnings of the investee and credited for dividends received. An investment for more than 50% of the outstanding stock of an investee is treated as a *business combination* and accounted for using *consolidated financial statements*.

Key Learning Outcomes

Key Learning Outcomes	Example Exercises	Practice Exercises
• Describe the accounting for less than 20%, 20%–50%, and greater than 50% investments.		
• Prepare journal entries to record the purchase of a stock investment.	**13-2**	13-2A, 13-2B
• Prepare journal entries for receipt of dividends.	**13-2**	13-2A, 13-2B
• Prepare journal entries for the sale of a stock investment at a gain or loss.	**13-2**	13-2A, 13-2B
• Prepare journal entries for the equity earnings of an equity method investee.	**13-3**	13-3A, 13-3B
• Prepare journal entries for the dividends received from an equity method investee.	**13-3**	13-3A, 13-3B
• Describe a business combination, parent company, and subsidiary company.		
• Describe consolidated financial statements.		

Describe and illustrate valuing and reporting investments in the financial statements.

Key Points

Debt and equity securities are classified as (1) trading securities, (2) held-to-maturity securities, and (3) available-for-sale securities for reporting and valuation purposes. *Trading securities* are debt and equity securities purchased and sold to earn short-term profits. They are valued at *fair value*, which is the market price that a company would receive if the security were sold. Unrealized gains or losses from the change in fair value are reported on the income statement. *Held-to-maturity* investments are debt securities that are intended to be held until their maturity date. Held-to-maturity debt investments are valued at amortized cost. *Available-for-sale securities* are debt and equity securities that are not classified as trading or held-to-maturity. Available-for-sale securities are reported at fair value with unrealized gains or losses from changes in fair value being recognized in the Stockholders' Equity section of the balance sheet.

Key Learning Outcomes

Key Learning Outcomes	Example Exercises	Practice Exercises
• Describe trading securities, held-to-maturity securities, and available-for-sale securities.		
• Prepare journal entries to record the change in the fair value of a trading security portfolio.	**13-4**	13-4A, 13-4B
• Describe and illustrate the reporting of trading securities on the balance sheet.		
• Describe the accounting for held-to-maturity debt securities.		
• Prepare journal entries to record the change in fair value of an available-for-sale security portfolio.	**13-5**	13-5A, 13-5B
• Describe and illustrate the reporting of available-for-sale securities on the balance sheet.		

Describe fair value accounting and its implications for the future.

Key Points	Key Learning Outcomes	Example Exercises	Practice Exercises
There is a trend toward fair value accounting in generally accepted accounting principles (GAAP). One advantage of this trend is a convergence of U.S. GAAP with International Accounting Standards. Some disadvantages of using fair value accounting are that fair values may not be obtainable for some items and fair values are difficult to compare across companies. Since fair value reporting affects the financial statements, using fair value accounting could create more fluctuations in valuations and earnings.	• Describe the reasons why there is a trend toward fair value accounting. • Describe the disadvantages of fair value accounting. • Describe how fair value accounting impacts the balance sheet and income statement. • Describe the future of fair value accounting.		

Key Terms

available-for-sale securities (578)
business combination (573)
consolidated financial statements (573)
cost method (569)
debt securities (566)

equity method (571)
equity securities (566)
fair value (574)
held-to-maturity securities (577)
investee (569)
investments (566)

investor (569)
parent company (573)
subsidiary company (573)
trading securities (574)
unrealized gain or loss (574)

Illustrative Problem

The following selected investment transactions were completed by Rosewell Company during 2010, its first year of operations:

2010

Jan. 11. Purchased 800 shares of Bryan Company stock as an available-for-sale security at $23 per share plus an $80 brokerage commission.

Feb. 6. Purchased $40,000 of 8% U.S. Treasury bonds at par value plus accrued interest for 36 days. The bonds pay interest on January 1 and July 1. The bonds were classified as held-to-maturity securities.

Mar. 3. Purchased 1,900 shares of Cohen Company stock as a trading security at $48 per share plus a $152 brokerage commission.

Apr. 5. Purchased 2,400 shares of Lyons Inc. stock as an available-for-sale security at $68 per share plus a $120 brokerage commission.

May 12. Purchased 200,000 shares of Myers Company at $37 per share plus an $8,000 brokerage commission. Myers Company has 800,000 common shares issued and outstanding. The equity method was used for this investment.

July 1. Received semiannual interest on bonds purchased on February 6.

Aug. 29. Sold 1,200 shares of Cohen Company stock at $61 per share less a $90 brokerage commission.

Oct. 5. Received an $0.80-per-share dividend on Bryan Company stock.

Nov. 11. Received a $1.10-per-share dividend on Myers Company stock.

16. Purchased 3,000 shares of Morningside Company stock as a trading security for $52 per share plus a $150 brokerage commission.

Dec. 31. Accrued interest on February 6 bonds.

31. Recorded Rosewell's share of Myers Company earnings of $146,000 for the year.

31. Prepared adjusting entries for the portfolios of trading and available-for-sale securities based upon the following fair values (stock prices):

Bryan Company	$21
Cohen Company	43
Lyons Inc.	88
Myers Company	40
Morningside Company	45

Instructions

1. Journalize the preceding transactions.
2. Prepare the balance sheet disclosure for Rosewell Company's investments on December 31, 2010.

Solution

1.

2010					
Jan.	11	Available-for-Sale Investments—Bryan Company		18,480*	
		Cash			18,480
		*(800 shares × $23 per share) + $80			

Feb.	6	Investments—U.S. Treasury Bonds		40,000	
		Interest Receivable		320*	
		Cash			40,320
		*$40,000 × 8% × (36 days/360 days)			

Mar.	3	Trading Investments—Cohen Company		91,352*	
		Cash			91,352
		*(1,900 shares × $48 per share) + $152			

Apr.	5	Available-for-Sale Investments—Lyons Inc.		163,320*	
		Cash			163,320
		*(2,400 shares × $68 per share) + $120			

2010 May	12	Investment in Myers Company	7,408,000*	
		Cash		7,408,000
		*(200,000 shares × $37 per share) + $8,000		

July	1	Cash	1,600*	
		Interest Receivable		320
		Interest Revenue		1,280
		*$40,000 × 8% × ½		

Aug.	29	Cash	73,110*	
		Trading Investments—Cohen Company		57,696**
		Gain on Sale of Investments		15,414
		*(1,200 shares × $61 per share) − $90		
		**1,200 shares × ($91,352/1,900 shares)		

Oct.	5	Cash	640	
		Dividend Revenue		640
		*800 shares × $0.80 per share		

Nov.	11	Cash	220,000	
		Investment in Myers Company Stock		220,000
		*200,000 shares × $1.10 per share		

Nov.	16	Trading Investments—Morningside Company	156,150*	
		Cash		156,150
		*(3,000 shares × $52 per share) + $150		

Dec.	31	Interest Receivable	1,600	
		Interest Revenue		1,600
		Accrued interest, $40,000 × 8% × ½.		

Dec.	31	Investment in Myers Company Stock	36,500	
		Income of Myers Company		36,500
		Record equity income,		
		$146,000 × (200,000 shares/800,000 shares).		

2010 Dec.	31	Unrealized Loss on Trading Investments	24,706	
		Valuation Allowance for Trading Investments		24,706
		Record decease in fair value of trading investments, $165,100 − $189,806.		

Name	Number of Shares	Total Cost	Total Fair Value
Cohen Company	700	$ 33,656	$ 30,100*
Morningside Company	3,000	156,150	135,000**
Total		$189,806	$165,100

*700 shares × $43 per share
**3,000 shares × $45 per share

Note: Myers Company is valued using the equity method; thus, the fair value is not used.

Dec.	31	Valuation Allowance for Available-for-Sale Investments	46,200	
		Unrealized Gain (Loss) on Available-for-Sale Investments		46,200
		Record increase in fair value of available-for-sale investments, $228,000 − $181,800.		

Name	Number of Shares	Total Cost	Total Fair Value
Bryan Company	800	$ 18,480	$ 16,800*
Lyons Inc.	2,400	163,320	211,200**
Total		$181,800	$228,000

*800 shares × $21 per share
**2,400 shares × $88 per share

2.

Rosewell Company
Balance Sheet (Selected)
December 31, 2010

Current assets:		
Cash.		$XXX,XXX
Trading investments (at cost)	$189,806	
Less valuation allowance for trading investments	24,706	
Trading investments at fair value		165,100
Available-for-sale investments (at cost)	$181,800	
Plus valuation allowance for available-for-sale investments . .	46,200	
Available-for-sale investments at fair value		228,000
Stockholders' equity:		
Common stock		$ XX,XXX
Paid-in capital in excess of par value		XXX,XXX
Retained earnings		XXX,XXX
Plus unrealized gain (loss) on available-for-sale investments .		46,200
Total stockholders' equity		$XXX,XXX

Self-Examination Questions (Answers at End of Chapter)

1. An investment is made on May 24 for $50,000, 5% bonds at par value. Interest is payable on March 31 and September 30. What is the accrued interest on the purchase date?
   A. $167
   B. $375
   C. $625
   D. $875

2. On January 15 of the current year, Thomas Company purchased 1,400 shares of Dillon Company at a price of $23 per share plus a $70 brokerage commission. On April 10, Thomas Company subsequently sold 800 shares of Dillon Company for $20 per share less a $50 brokerage commission. Determine the loss on sale of investment.
   A. $2,400
   B. $2,420
   C. $2,490
   D. $2,520

3. Cole Company owns 40% of Barnwell Inc. During the current year, Barnwell reported net income of $200,000 and declared dividends of $60,000. How much would Cole Company increase Investment in Barnwell Inc. Stock for the current year?
   A. $24,000
   B. $56,000
   C. $80,000
   D. $104,000

4. On December 31, 2010, Southern Life Insurance Co. had investments in trading securities of $450,000 and a debit balance in Valuation Allowance for Trading Investments of $32,000. On December 31, 2011, the portfolio of trading securities had a cost of $500,000 and a fair value of $520,000. What was the unrealized gain or loss on the trading investments reported on the income statement for 2011?
   A. $12,000 unrealized loss
   B. $12,000 unrealized gain
   C. $20,000 unrealized gain
   D. $52,000 unrealized gain

5. On December 31, 2010, Naples Company had investments in available-for-sale securities of $200,000 and a credit balance in Valuation Allowance for Available-for-Sale Investments of $20,000. On December 31, 2011, the portfolio of available-for-sale securities had a cost of $215,000 and a fair value of $250,000. What was the unrealized gain or loss from available-for-sale securities reported on the income statement for 2011?
   A. $0
   B. $15,000 unrealized gain
   C. $20,000 unrealized gain
   D. $55,000 unrealized gain

Eye Openers

1. Why might a business invest in another company's stock?
2. If a bond is purchased between interest payment periods, how is the accrued interest treated?
3. Why would there be a gain or loss on the sale of a bond investment?
4. When is using the cost method the appropriate accounting for equity investments?
5. How does the accounting for a dividend received differ between the cost method and the equity method?
6. How are brokerage commissions treated under the cost method of accounting for equity investments?
7. How is the income of the investor impacted by equity method investments?
8. If an investor owns more than 50% of an investee, how is this treated on the investor's financial statements?

9. Google Inc. recently purchased all of the outstanding common stock of YouTube. Which is the parent company, and which is the subsidiary company in this transaction?
10. What is the major difference in the accounting for a portfolio of trading securities and a portfolio of available-for-sale securities?
11. If Valuation Allowance for Trading Investments has a credit balance, how is it treated on the balance sheet?
12. Are held-to-maturity securities (a) equity investments, (b) debt investments, or (c) both?
13. How would a debit balance in Unrealized Gain (Loss) on Available-for-Sale Investments be disclosed in the financial statements?
14. What would cause Unrealized Gain (Loss) on Available-for-Sale Investments to go from a $12,000 debit balance at the beginning of the year to a $1,000 credit balance at the end of the year?
15. What is the evidence of the trend toward fair value accounting?
16. What are some potential disadvantages of fair value accounting?

Practice Exercises

● ● ● ● ➤➤

PE 13-1A
Bond transactions
obj. 2
EE 13-1   p. 568

Journalize the entries to record the following selected bond investment transactions for Olson Technologies:

a. Purchased for cash $90,000 of Hart Industries 7% bonds at 100 plus accrued interest of $1,050.
b. Received first semiannual interest.
c. Sold $60,000 of the bonds at 102 plus accrued interest of $750.

PE 13-1B
Bond transactions
obj. 2
EE 13-1   p. 568

Journalize the entries to record the following selected bond investment transactions for First Union:

a. Purchased for cash $400,000 of Medford City 5% bonds at 100 plus accrued interest of $4,500.
b. Received first semiannual interest.
c. Sold $250,000 of the bonds at 97 plus accrued interest of $1,800.

PE 13-2A
Stock transactions
obj. 3
EE 13-2   p. 571

On August 15, 2,500 shares of Collins Company are acquired at a price of $51 per share plus a $125 brokerage fee. On September 10, a $1.10-per-share dividend was received on the Collins Company stock. On October 5, 1,000 shares of the Collins Company stock were sold for $45 per share less a $50 brokerage fee. Prepare the journal entries for the original purchase, dividend, and sale.

PE 13-2B
Stock transactions
obj. 3
EE 13-2   p. 571

On February 12, 6,000 shares of Gilbert Company are acquired at a price of $22 per share plus a $240 brokerage fee. On April 22, a $0.42-per-share dividend was received on the Gilbert Company stock. On May 10, 4,000 shares of the Gilbert Company stock were sold for $28 per share less a $160 brokerage fee. Prepare the journal entries for the original purchase, dividend, and sale.

PE 13-3A
Equity method
obj. 3
EE 13-3   p. 573

On January 2, Leonard Company acquired 30% of the outstanding stock of Bristol Company for $350,000. For the year ending December 31, Bristol Company earned income of $90,000 and paid dividends of $28,000. Prepare the entries for Leonard Company for the purchase of the stock, share of Bristol income, and dividends received from Bristol Company.

PE 13-3B
Equity method
obj. 3
EE 13-3   p. 573

On January 2, Trey Company acquired 40% of the outstanding stock of Manning Company for $205,000. For the year ending December 31, Manning Company earned income of $48,000 and paid dividends of $14,000. Prepare the entries for Trey Company for the purchase of the stock, share of Manning income, and dividends received from Manning Company.

PE 13-4A
Valuing trading securities at fair value
obj. 4
EE 13-4   p. 576

On January 1, 2010, Valuation Allowance for Trading Investments has a credit balance of $8,700. On December 31, 2010, the cost of the trading securities portfolio was $52,400, and the fair value was $53,000. Prepare the December 31, 2010, adjusting journal entry to record the unrealized gain or loss on trading investments.

PE 13-4B
Valuing trading securities at fair value
obj. 4
EE 13-4   p. 576

On January 1, 2010, Valuation Allowance for Trading Investments has a credit balance of $1,200. On December 31, 2010, the cost of the trading securities portfolio was $99,600, and the fair value was $91,200. Prepare the December 31, 2010 adjusting journal entry to record the unrealized gain or loss on trading investments.

PE 13-5A
Valuing available-for-sale securities at fair value

obj. 4

EE 13-5   p. 581

On January 1, 2010, Valuation Allowance for Available-for-Sale Securities has a debit balance of $1,500. On December 31, 2010, the cost of the available-for-sale securities was $67,500, and the fair value was $69,200. Prepare the adjusting entry to record the unrealized gain or loss for available-for-sale securities on December 31, 2010.

PE 13-5B
Valuing available-for-sale securities at fair value

obj. 4

EE 13-5   p. 581

On January 1, 2010, Valuation Allowance for Available-for-Sale Securities has a credit balance of $3,400. On December 31, 2010, the cost of the available-for-sale securities was $35,700, and the fair value was $30,100. Prepare the adjusting entry to record the unrealized gain or loss for available-for-sale securities on December 31, 2010.

Exercises

EX 13-1
Entries for investments in bonds, interest, and sale of bonds

obj. 2

Mercer Investments acquired $120,000 Jericho Corp., 6% bonds at par value on September 1, 2010. The bonds pay interest on September 1 and March 1. On March 1, 2011, Mercer sold $40,000 par value Jericho Corp. bonds at 102.

Journalize the entries to record the following:

a. The initial acquisition of the Jericho Corp. bonds on September 1, 2010.
b. The adjusting entry for 4 months of accrued interest earned on the Jericho Corp. bonds on December 31, 2010.
c. The receipt of semiannual interest on March 1, 2011.
d. The sale of $40,000 Jericho Corp. bonds on March 1, 2011, at 102.

EX 13-2
Entries for investment in bonds, interest, and sale of bonds

obj. 2

✔ c. Dec. 1, Loss on sale of investments, $20

Lance Co. purchased $36,000 of 6%, 10-year Bergen County bonds on July 12, 2010, directly from the county at par value. The bonds pay semiannual interest on May 1 and November 1. On December 1, 2010, Lance Co. sold $14,000 of the Bergen County bonds at 102 plus $70 accrued interest, less a $300 brokerage commission.

Provide the journal entries for:

a. the purchase of the bonds on July 12, plus 72 days of accrued interest.
b. semiannual interest on November 1.
c. sale of the bonds on December 1.
d. the adjusting entry for accrued interest of $220 on December 31.

EX 13-3
Entries for investment in bonds, interest, and sale of bonds

obj. 2

The following bond investment transactions were completed during 2010 by Torrence Company:

Jan. 21. Purchased 30, $1,000 par value government bonds at 100 plus 20 days' accrued interest. The bonds pay 6% annual interest on June 30 and January 1.
June 30. Received semiannual interest on bond investment.
Sept. 5. Sold 12, $1,000 par value bonds at 98 plus $134 accrued interest.

a. Journalize the entries for these transactions.
b. Provide the December 31, 2010, adjusting journal entry for semiannual interest earned from the bond coupon.

EX 13-4
Interest on bond investments

obj. 2

On May 1, 2010, Carly Company purchased $84,000 of 5%, 12-year Baltimore Company bonds at par plus 2 months' accrued interest. The bonds pay interest on March 1 and September 1. On October 1, 2010, Carly Company sold $30,000 of the Baltimore Company bonds acquired on May 1, plus one month accrued interest. On December 31, 2010, four months' interest was accrued for the remaining bonds.

Determine the interest earned by Carly Company on Baltimore Company bonds for 2010.

EX 13-5
Entries for investment in stock, receipt of dividends, and sale of shares

obj. 3

✔ c. Gain on sale of investments, $6,875

On February 17, Asher Corporation acquired 3,000 shares of the 100,000 outstanding shares of Dan Co. common stock at $28.90 plus commission charges of $300. On July 11, a cash dividend of $0.95 per share was received. On December 4, 1,000 shares were sold at $36, less commission charges of $125.

Record the entries for (a) the purchase of stock, (b) the receipt of dividends, and (c) the sale of 1,000 shares.

EX 13-6
Entries for investment in stock, receipt of dividends, and sale of shares

obj. 3

✔ June 3, Loss on sale of investments, $12,725

The following equity investment-related transactions were completed by Lance Company in 2010:

Jan. 12. Purchased 1,800 shares of Baxter Company for a price of $56.50 per share plus a brokerage commission of $90.

Apr. 10. Received a quarterly dividend of $0.25 per share on the Baxter Company investment.

June 3. Sold 1,200 shares for a price of $46 per share less a brokerage commission of $65.

Journalize the entries for these transactions.

EX 13-7
Entries for stock investments, dividends, and sale of stock

obj. 3

✔ Nov. 14, Dividend revenue, $150

Plumbline Tech Corp. manufactures surveying equipment. Journalize the entries to record the following selected equity investment transactions completed by Plumbline during 2010:

Feb.   2. Purchased for cash 900 shares of Devon Inc. stock for $54 per share plus a $450 brokerage commission.

Apr. 16. Received dividends of $0.25 per share on Devon Inc. stock.

June 17. Purchased 600 shares of Devon Inc. stock for $65 per share plus a $300 brokerage commission.

Aug. 19. Sold 1,000 shares of Devon Inc. stock for $70 per share less a $500 brokerage commission. Plumbline assumes that the first investments purchased are the first investments sold.

Nov. 14. Received dividends of $0.30 per share on Devon Inc. stock.

EX 13-8
Entries for available-for-sale stock investments and dividends

obj. 3

During 2010, its first year of operations, LandStar Corporation purchased the following securities classified as available-for-sale securities:

Security	Shares Purchased	Cost	Cash Dividends Received
Tekniks Inc.	2,800	$78,400	$560
Lakeshore Corp.	1,200	16,800	240

a. Record the purchase of the investments for cash.
b. Record the receipt of the dividends.

EX 13-9
Equity method for stock investment

obj. 3

At a total cost of $710,000, Abbott Corporation acquired 50,000 shares of Costello Corp. common stock as a long-term investment. Abbott Corporation uses the equity method of accounting for this investment. Costello Corp. has 200,000 shares of common stock outstanding, including the shares acquired by Abbott Corporation.

Journalize the entries by Abbott Corporation to record the following information:

a. Costello Corp. reports net income of $1,280,000 for the current period.
b. A cash dividend of $1.40 per common share is paid by Costello Corp. during the current period.

EX 13-10
Equity method for stock investment

obj. 3

✔ b. $4,565,760

On January 15, 2010, National Star Inc. purchased 80,000 shares of Krypton Labs Inc. directly from one of the founders for a price of $55 per share. Krypton has 250,000 shares outstanding, including the National Star shares. On July 2, 2010, Krypton paid $217,000 in total dividends to its shareholders. On December 31, 2010, Krypton reported a net income of $735,000 for the year. National Star uses the equity method in accounting for its investment in Krypton Labs.

a. Provide the National Star Inc. journal entries for the transactions involving its investment in Krypton Labs Inc. during 2010.
b. Determine the December 31, 2010, balance of Investment in Krypton Labs Inc. Stock.

EX 13-11
Equity method for stock investment

obj. 3

Corvis Company's balance sheet disclosed its long-term investment in Mid-American Company under the equity method for comparative years as follows:

	Dec. 31, 2011	Dec. 31, 2010
Investment in Mid-American Company stock (in millions)	$98	$90

In addition, the 2011 Corvis Company income statement disclosed equity earnings in the Mid-American Company investment as $10 million. Corvis Company neither purchased nor sold Mid-American Company stock during 2011. The fair value of Mid-American Company stock investment on December 31, 2011, was $107.

Explain the change in the Investment in Mid-American Company Stock balance sheet account from December 31, 2010, to December 31, 2011.

EX 13-12
Missing statement items, trading investments

obj. 4

✔ g. $7,000

Lydell Capital, Inc., makes investments in trading securities. Selected income statement items for the years ended December 31, 2010 and 2011, plus selected items from comparative balance sheets, are as follows:

Lydell Capital, Inc.
Selected Income Statement Items
For the Years Ended December 31, 2010 and 2011

	2010	2011
Operating income	a.	e.
Unrealized gain (loss)	b.	$(2,000)
Net income	c.	14,000

Lydell Capital, Inc.
Selected Balance Sheet Items
December 31, 2009, 2010, and 2011

	Dec. 31, 2009	Dec. 31, 2010	Dec. 31, 2011
Trading investments, at cost	$123,000	$146,000	$172,000
Valuation allowance for trading investments	(6,000)	9,000	g.
Trading investments, at fair value	d.	f.	h.
Retained earnings	$145,000	$192,000	i.

There were no dividends.
Determine the missing lettered items.

EX 13-13
Fair value journal entries, trading investments

obj. 4

The investments of Commerce Bank Inc. include 12,000 shares of RadTek Inc. common stock purchased on February 21, 2010, for $16 per share. These shares were classified as trading securities. As of the December 31, 2010, balance sheet date, assume that the share price increased to $21 per share. As of the December 31, 2011, balance sheet date, assume that the share price declined to $20 per share. The investment was held through December 31, 2011.

a. Journalize the entries to record the adjustment of the RadTek Inc. investment to fair value on December 31, 2010, and December 31, 2011.
b. Where is the unrealized gain or unrealized loss for trading investments disclosed on the financial statements?

EX 13-14
Fair value journal
entries, trading
investments

objs. 3, 4

Horizon Bancorp Inc. purchased a portfolio of trading securities during 2009. The cost and fair value of this portfolio on December 31, 2009, was as follows:

Name	Number of Shares	Total Cost	Total Fair Value
Apex, Inc.	1,200	$16,000	$15,000
Evans Company	700	23,000	21,500
Poole Company	300	9,000	9,200
Total		$48,000	$45,700

On April 3, 2010, Horizon Bancorp Inc. purchased 500 shares of Cable, Inc., at $30 per share plus a $100 brokerage fee. On December 31, 2010, the trading security portfolio had the following cost and fair value:

Name	Number of Shares	Total Cost	Total Fair Value
Apex, Inc.	1,200	$16,000	$16,400
Cable, Inc.	500	15,100	17,500
Evans Company	700	23,000	22,000
Poole Company	300	9,000	12,400
Total		$63,100	$68,300

Provide the journal entries to record the following:
a. The adjustment of the trading security portfolio to fair value on December 31, 2009.
b. The April 3, 2010, purchase of Cable, Inc., stock.
c. The adjustment of the trading securities portfolio to fair value on December 31, 2010.

EX 13-15
Fair value journal
entries, trading
investments

obj. 4

✔ a. 2. Dec. 31,
2010, Unrealized
loss on trading
investments, $4,900

Union Financial Services, Inc., purchased the following trading securities during 2009, its first year of operations:

Name	Number of Shares	Cost
B&T Transportation, Inc.	3,400	$ 67,100
Citrus Foods, Inc.	1,800	29,700
Stuart Housewares, Inc.	800	19,700
Total		$116,500

The market price per share for the trading security portfolio on December 31, 2009, and December 31, 2010, was as follows:

	Market Price per Share	
	Dec. 31, 2009	Dec. 31, 2010
B&T Transportation, Inc.	$25.00	$24.00
Citrus Foods, Inc.	17.50	18.00
Stuart Housewares, Inc.	23.00	20.00

a. Provide the journal entry to adjust the trading security portfolio to fair value on:
   1. December 31, 2009
   2. December 31, 2010
b. Describe the income statement impact from the December 31, 2010, journal entry.

EX 13-16
Financial statement
disclosure, trading
investments

obj. 4

The income statement for Harris Company was as follows:

Harris Company
Income Statement (selected items)
For the Year Ended December 31, 2010

Income from operations	$345,000
Less unrealized loss on trading investments	23,000
Net income	$322,000

The balance sheet dated December 31, 2009, showed a Retained Earnings balance of $823,000 and a Valuation Allowance for Trading Investments debit balance of $68,000. The company paid $43,000 in dividends during 2010.

a. Determine the December 31, 2010, Retained Earnings balance.
b. Determine the December 31, 2010, Valuation Allowance for Trading Investments balance.

EX 13-17
Missing statement items, available-for-sale securities

obj. **4**

✔ f. ($6,000)

Oceanic Airways makes investments in available-for-sale securities. Selected income statement items for the years ended December 31, 2010 and 2011, plus selected items from comparative balance sheets, are as follows:

Oceanic Airways
Selected Income Statement Items
For the Years Ended December 31, 2010 and 2011

	2010	2011
Operating income	a.	g.
Gain (loss) from sale of investments	$4,000	$ (8,000)
Net income	b.	(11,000)

Oceanic Airways
Selected Balance Sheet Items
December 31, 2009, 2010, and 2011

	Dec. 31, 2009	Dec. 31, 2010	Dec. 31, 2011
Assets			
Available-for-sale investments, at cost	$ 78,000	$ 68,000	$95,000
Valuation allowance for available-for-sale investments	5,000	(6,000)	h.
Available-for-sale investments, at fair value	c.	e.	i.
Stockholders' Equity			
Unrealized gain (loss) on available-for-sale investments	d.	f.	(7,000)
Retained earnings	$164,000	$232,000	j.

There were no dividends.
Determine the missing lettered items.

EX 13-18
Fair value journal entries, available-for-sale investments

obj. **4**

✔ b. Dec. 31, 2010, Unrealized gain (loss) on available-for-sale investments, ($70,000)

The investments of Charter Inc. include 10,000 shares of Wallace Inc. common stock purchased on January 10, 2010, for $30 per share. These shares were classified as available-for-sale securities. As of the December 31, 2010, balance sheet date, assume that the share price declined to $23 per share. As of the December 31, 2011, balance sheet date, assume that the share price rose to $27 per share. The investment was held through December 31, 2011.

a. Journalize the entries to record the adjustment of the Wallace Inc. investment to fair value on December 31, 2010, and December 31, 2011.
b. What is the balance of Unrealized Gain (Loss) on Available-for-Sale Investments for December 31, 2010, and December 31, 2011?
c. Where is Unrealized Gain (Loss) on Available-for-Sale Investments disclosed on the financial statements?

EX 13-19
Fair value journal entries, available-for-sale investments

objs. **3, 4**

Lipscomb Inc. purchased a portfolio of available-for-sale securities in 2009, its first year of operations. The cost and fair value of this portfolio on December 31, 2009, was as follows:

Name	Number of Shares	Total Cost	Total Fair Value
Loomis, Inc.	600	$ 9,000	$10,000
Parker Corp.	900	21,000	22,800
Smithfield Corp.	1,800	32,500	31,000
Total		$62,500	$63,800

On May 10, 2010, Lipscomb purchased 700 shares of Nova Inc. at $50 per share plus a $150 brokerage fee. On December 31, 2010, the available-for-sale security portfolio had the following cost and fair value:

Name	Number of Shares	Total Cost	Total Fair Value
Loomis, Inc.	600	$ 9,000	$ 12,300
Nova, Inc.	700	35,150	36,100
Parker Corp.	900	21,000	20,000
Smithfield Corp.	1,800	32,500	33,100
Total		$97,650	$101,500

Provide the journal entries to record the following:

a. The adjustment of the available-for-sale security portfolio to fair value on December 31, 2009.
b. The May 10, 2010, purchase of Nova Inc. stock.
c. The adjustment of the available-for-sale security portfolio to fair value on December 31, 2010.

EX 13-20
Fair value journal entries, available-for-sale investments

obj. 4

Nantahla, Inc., purchased the following available-for-sale securities during 2009, its first year of operations:

Name	Number of Shares	Cost
Barns Electronics, Inc.	1,500	$ 42,500
Ryan Co.	400	28,200
Sharon Co.	2,200	66,100
Total		$136,800

The market price per share for the available-for-sale security portfolio on December 31, 2009, and December 31, 2010 was as follows:

	Market Price per Share	
	Dec. 31, 2009	Dec. 31, 2010
Barns Electronics, Inc.	$31.00	$28.00
Ryan Co.	77.00	67.00
Sharon Co.	29.00	26.00

a. Provide the journal entry to adjust the available-for-sale security portfolio to fair value on:
   1. December 31, 2009
   2. December 31, 2010
b. Describe the income statement impact from the December 31, 2010, journal entry.

EX 13-21
Balance sheet presentation of available-for-sale investments

obj. 4

During 2010, its first year of operations, Myron Company purchased two available-for-sale investments as follows:

Security	Shares Purchased	Cost
Olson Products, Inc.	700	$29,000
Reynolds Co.	1,900	41,000

Assume that as of December 31, 2010, the Olson Products, Inc., stock had a market value of $49 per share and the Reynolds Co. stock had a market value of $20 per share. Myron Company had net income of $225,000, and paid no dividends for the year ending December 31, 2010.

a. Prepare the Current Assets section of the balance sheet presentation for the available-for-sale investments.
b. Prepare the Stockholders' Equity section of the balance sheet to reflect the earnings and unrealized gain (loss) for the available-for-sale investments.

EX 13-22
Balance sheet presentation of available-for-sale investments

obj. 4

During 2010, Toney Corporation held a portfolio of available-for-sale securities having a cost of $190,000. There were no purchases or sales of investments during the year. The market values at the beginning and end of the year were $225,000 and $180,000, respectively. The net income for 2010 was $175,000, and no dividends were paid during the year. The Stockholders' Equity section of the balance sheet was as follows on December 31, 2009:

Toney Corporation
Stockholders' Equity
December 31, 2009

Common stock	$ 40,000
Paid-in capital in excess of par value	300,000
Retained earnings	395,000
Unrealized gain (loss) on available-for-sale investments	35,000
Total	$770,000

Prepare the Stockholders' Equity section of the balance sheet for December 31, 2010.

Appendix 1
EX 13-23
Bond premium
amortization

On January 2, 2010, Patel Company purchased $80,000, 10-year, 7%, government bonds at 104, including the brokerage commission. January 2 is an interest payment date.

a. Journalize the entry to record the bond purchase.
b. Journalize the entry to amortize the bond premium on December 31, 2010.
c. What is the relationship between the market rate of interest and the coupon rate on the bond investment acquisition date?

Appendix 1
EX 13-24
Bond discount
amortization

On September 1, 2010, Longstreet Company purchased $150,000 of 20-year, 6%, Marvin Company bonds at 97, including the brokerage commission. September 1 is an interest payment date.

a. Journalize the entry to record the bond purchase.
b. Journalize the entry to amortize the bond discount on December 31, 2010.
c. What is the relationship between the market rate of interest and the coupon rate on the bond investment acquisition date?

Appendix 1
EX 13-25
Bond interest
and premium
amortization
entries

On May 1, 2010, Starmaker Machinery, Inc., purchased $60,000 of 10-year, 5% government bonds at 103, including the brokerage commission. The interest is received semiannually on May 1 and November 1.

a. Journalize the entry to record the May 1, 2010, bond purchase.
b. Journalize the semiannual interest received on November 1, 2010.
c. Journalize the accrued interest adjustment on December 31, 2010.
d. Journalize the premium amortization adjustment on December 31, 2010.
e. Journalize the receipt of the face amount of the bonds on the bond maturity date, May 1, 2020.

Appendix 1
EX 13-26
Bond interest
and discount
amortization
entries

On June 1, 2010, Firefly, Inc., purchased $120,000 of 10-year, 6% Barron Company bonds at 98, including the brokerage commission. The interest is payable semiannually on June 1 and December 1.

a. Journalize the entry to record the June 1, 2010, bond purchase.
b. Journalize the semiannual interest received on December 1, 2010.
c. Journalize the accrued interest adjustment on December 31, 2010.
d. Journalize the discount amortization adjustment on December 31, 2010.
e. Journalize the receipt of the face amount of the bonds on the bond maturity date, June 1, 2020.

Appendix 2
EX 13-27
Comprehensive
income

On April 23, 2010, Albert Co. purchased 1,500 shares of Conover, Inc., for $55 per share including the brokerage commission. The Conover investment was classified as an available-for-sale security. On December 31, 2010, the fair value of Conover, Inc., was $65 per share. The net income of Albert Co. was $70,000 for 2010.

Prepare a statement of comprehensive income for Albert Co. for the year ended December 31, 2010.

Appendix 2
EX 13-28
Comprehensive
income

On December 31, 2009, Phoenix Co. had the following available-for-sale investment disclosure within the Current Assets section of the balance sheet:

Available-for-sale investments (at cost)	$105,000
Plus valuation allowance for available-for-sale investments	15,000
Available-for-sale investments (at fair value)	$120,000

There were no purchases or sales of available-for-sale investments during 2010. On December 31, 2010, the fair value of the available-for-sale investment portfolio was $101,000. The net income of Phoenix Co. was $135,000 for 2010.

Prepare a statement of comprehensive income for Phoenix Co. for the year ended December 31, 2010.

EX 13-29
Dividend yield

At the market close on January 29, 2008, Bank of America Corporation had a closing stock price of $41.84. In addition, Bank of America had a dividend per share of $2.40. Determine Bank of America's dividend yield. (Round to one decimal place.)

EX 13-30
Dividend yield

The market price for Microsoft Corporation closed at $29.86 and $35.60 on December 29, 2006, and December 31, 2007, respectively. The dividends per share were $0.37 for 2006 and $0.41 for 2007.

✔ a. Dec. 29, 2006, 1.24%

a. Determine the dividend yield for Microsoft on December 29, 2006, and December 31, 2007. (Round percentages to two decimal places.)
b. Interpret these measures.

EX 13-31
Dividend yield

eBay Inc. developed a Web-based marketplace at **http://www.ebay.com**, in which individuals can buy and sell a variety of items. eBay also acquired PayPal, an online payments system that allows businesses and individuals to send and receive online payments securely. In a recent annual report, eBay published the following dividend policy:

We have never paid cash dividends on our stock and currently anticipate that we will continue to retain any future earnings for the foreseeable future.

Given eBay's dividend policy, why would an investor be attracted to its stock?

Problems Series A

PR 13-1A
Stock investment transactions, equity method and available-for-sale securities

objs. 3, 4

Roman Products, Inc., is a wholesaler of men's hair products. The company began operations on January 1, 2010. The following transactions relate to securities acquired by Roman Products, Inc., which has a fiscal year ending on December 31:

2010
Jan. 3. Purchased 3,000 shares of Whalen Inc. as an available-for-sale investment at $46 per share, including the brokerage commission.
July 6. Split Whalen Inc. stock 2 for 1 and received the regular cash dividend of $0.60 per share on the Whalen Inc. stock after the split.
Oct. 14. Sold 900 shares of Whalen Inc. stock at $25 per share, less a brokerage commission of $50.
Dec. 9. Received the regular cash dividend of $0.60 per share.
   31. Whalen Inc. is classified as an available-for-sale investment and is adjusted to a fair value of $21 per share. Use the Valuation Allowance for Available-for-Sale Investments account in making the adjustment.

2011
Jan. 5. Purchased an influential interest in Tasmania Co. for $620,000 by purchasing 60,000 shares directly from the estate of the founder of Tasmania. There are 150,000 shares of Tasmania Co. stock outstanding.
July 8. Received the regular cash divided of $0.70 per share on Whalen Inc. stock.
Dec. 8. Received the regular cash dividend of $0.70 per share plus an extra dividend of $0.15 per share on Whalen Inc. stock.
   31. Received $18,000 of cash dividends on Tasmania Co. stock. Tasmania Co. reported net income of $74,000 in 2011. Roman Products uses the equity method of accounting for its investment in Tasmania Co.
   31. Whalen Inc. is classified as an available-for-sale investment and is adjusted to a fair value of $26 per share. Use the Valuation Allowance for Available-for-Sale Investments account in making the adjustment.

Instructions
1. Journalize the entries to record the preceding transactions.
2. Prepare the investment-related asset and stockholders' equity balance sheet disclosures for Roman Products, Inc., on December 31, 2011, assuming the Retained Earnings balance on December 31, 2011, is $455,000.

PR 13-2A
Stock investment transactions, trading securities

objs. **3, 4**

Western Capital Inc. is a regional investment company that began operations on January 1, 2010. The following transactions relate to trading securities acquired by Western Capital Inc., which has a fiscal year ending on December 31:

2010

Feb.	3.	Purchased 2,500 shares of Titan Inc. as a trading security at $35 per share plus a brokerage commission of $500.
Mar.	12.	Purchased 1,200 shares of Quick Tyme Inc. as a trading security at $14 per share plus a brokerage commission of $240.
May	15.	Sold 600 shares of Titan Inc. for $36 per share less a $80 brokerage commission.
June	12.	Received an annual dividend of $0.12 per share on Titan Inc. stock.
Dec.	31.	The portfolio of trading securities was adjusted to fair values of $15 and $39 per share for Quick Tyme Inc. and Titan Inc., respectively.

2011

Apr.	9.	Purchased 1,100 shares of Aspire Inc. as a trading security at $41 per share plus a $165 brokerage commission.
June	15.	Received an annual dividend of $0.15 per share on Titan Inc. stock.
Aug.	20.	Sold 200 shares of Aspire Inc. for $35 per share less a $60 brokerage commission.
Dec.	31.	The portfolio of trading securities was adjusted to fair value using the following fair values per share for the trading securities:

Aspire Inc.	$31
Quick Tyme Inc.	16
Titan Inc.	37

The portfolio of trading securities was adjusted to fair value.

Instructions
1. Journalize the entries to record these transactions.
2. Prepare the investment-related current asset balance sheet disclosures for Western Capital Inc. on December 31, 2011.
3. How are unrealized gains or losses on trading investments disclosed on the financial statements of Western Capital Inc.?

PR 13-3A
Debt investment transactions, available-for-sale valuation

objs. **2, 4**

✔ 2. Available-for-sale investments (at fair value), $147,640

Dollar-Mart Inc. is a general merchandise retail company that began operations on January 1, 2010. The following transactions relate to debt investments acquired by Dollar-Mart Inc., which has a fiscal year ending on December 31:

2010

May	1.	Purchased $60,000 of Elkin City 4%, 10-year bonds at face value plus accrued interest of $400. The bond is classified as an available-for-sale investment. The bonds pay interest semiannually on March 1 and September 1.
June	16.	Purchased $112,000 of Morgan Co. 6%, 12-year bonds at face value plus accrued interest of $280. The bond is classified as an available-for-sale investment. The bonds pay interest semiannually on June 1 and December 1.
Sept.	1.	Received semiannual interest on the Elkin City bonds.
Oct.	1.	Sold $24,000 of Elkin City bonds at 103 plus accrued interest of $80.
Dec.	1.	Received semiannual interest on Morgan Co. bonds.
	31.	Accrued $480 interest on Elkin City bonds.
	31.	Accrued $560 interest on Morgan Co. bonds.
	31.	The available-for-sale bond portfolio was adjusted to fair values of 102 and 101 for Elkin City and Morgan Co. bonds, respectively.

2011
Mar. 1. Received semiannual interest on the Elkin City bonds.
June 1. Received semiannual interest on the Morgan Co. bonds.
(Assume that there are no more purchases or sales of bonds during 2011. Also assume all subsequent interest transactions for 2011 have been recorded properly.)
Dec. 31. The available-for-sale bond portfolio was adjusted to fair values of 99 and 100 for Elkin City and Morgan Co. bonds, respectively.

Instructions
1. Journalize the entries to record these transactions.
2. Prepare the investment-related current asset and stockholders' equity balance sheet disclosures for Dollar-Mart Inc. on December 31, 2011, assuming the Retained Earnings balance on December 31, 2011, is $310,000.

PR 13-4A
Investment reporting
objs. 2, 3, 4

✔ 1. b. $6,115

Miranda, Inc., manufactures and sells commercial and residential security equipment. The comparative unclassified balance sheets for December 31, 2011 and 2010 are provided below. Selected missing balances are shown by letters.

Miranda, Inc.
Balance Sheet
December 31, 2011 and 2010

	Dec. 31, 2011	Dec. 31, 2010
Cash	$104,000	$ 98,000
Accounts receivable (net)	71,000	67,500
Available-for-sale investments (at cost)—Note 1	$ a.	$ 36,000
Plus valuation allowance for available-for-sale investments	b.	4,000
Available-for-sale investments (fair value)	$ c.	$ 40,000
Interest receivable	$ d.	—
Investment in Denver Co. stock—Note 2	e.	$ 48,000
Office equipment (net)	60,000	65,000
Total assets	$ f.	$318,500
Accounts payable	$ 56,900	$ 51,400
Common stock	50,000	50,000
Excess of issue price over par	160,000	160,000
Retained earnings	g.	53,100
Plus unrealized gain (loss) on available-for-sale investments	h.	4,000
Total liabilities and stockholders' equity	$ i.	$318,500

Note 1. Investments are classified as available for sale. The investments at cost and fair value on December 31, 2010, are as follows:

	No. of Shares	Cost per Share	Total Cost	Total Fair Value
Tyndale Inc. Stock	600	$24	$14,400	$16,000
UR-Smart Inc. Stock	1,200	18	21,600	24,000
			$36,000	$40,000

Note 2. The Investment in Denver Co. stock is an equity method investment representing 36% of the outstanding shares of Denver Co.

The following selected investment transactions occurred during 2011:

2011
Apr. 21. Purchased 300 shares of Vegas Resorts, Inc., at $20 per share plus a $45 brokerage commission.
June 12. Dividends of $1 per share are received on the UR-Smart Inc. stock investment.
Sept. 9. Dividends of $8,900 are received on the Denver Co. investment.

Oct. 1.   Purchased $8,000 of Vita-Mighty Co. 7%, 10-year bonds at 100. The bonds are classified as available for sale. The bonds pay interest on October 1 and April 1.

Dec. 31.   Denver Co. reported a total net income of $40,000 for 2011. Miranda recorded equity earnings for its share of Denver Co. net income.

    31.   Accrued interest on Vita-Mighty bonds purchased on October 1.

    31.   Adjusted the available-for-sale investment portfolio to fair value using the following fair value per share amounts:

Available-for-Sale Investments	Fair Value
Tyndale Inc. stock	$28 per share
UR-Smart Inc. stock	$20 per share
Vegas Resorts, Inc., stock	$24 per share
Vita-Mighty Co. bonds	102 per $1,000 of face value

    31.   Closed the Miranda, Inc., net income of $18,685 for 2011. Miranda paid no dividends during 2011.

Instructions

Determine the missing letters in the unclassified balance sheet. Provide appropriate supporting calculations.

Problems Series B

● ● ● ● ●

PR 13-1B
Stock investment transactions, equity method and available-for-sale securities

objs. **3, 4**

Broadway Arts Inc. produces and sells theater set designs and costumes. The company began operations on January 1, 2010. The following transactions relate to securities acquired by Broadway Arts Inc., which has a fiscal year ending on December 31:

2010

Jan. 10.   Purchased 5,000 shares of Crystal Inc. as an available-for-sale security at $36 per share, including the brokerage commission.

Mar. 12.   Received the regular cash dividend of $0.80 per share.

Sept. 9.   Split Crystal Inc. stock 2 for 1 and received the regular cash dividend of $0.40 per share on the Crystal Inc. stock.

Oct. 14.   Sold 1,000 shares of Crystal Inc. stock at $15 per share, less a brokerage commission of $100.

Dec. 31.   Crystal Inc. is classified as an available-for-sale investment and is adjusted to a fair value of $19 per share. Use the Valuation Allowance for Available-for-Sale Investments account in making the adjustment.

2011

Jan.   5.   Purchased an influential interest in Bulls Eye Inc. for $410,000 by purchasing 50,000 shares directly from the estate of the founder of Bulls Eye Inc. There are 200,000 shares of Bulls Eye Inc. stock outstanding.

Mar. 8.   Received the regular cash divided of $0.45 per share on Crystal Inc. stock.

Sept. 10.   Received the regular cash dividend of $0.45 per share plus an extra dividend of $0.10 per share on Crystal Inc. stock.

Dec. 31.   Received $35,000 of cash dividends on Bulls Eye Inc. stock. Bulls Eye Inc. reported net income of $126,000 in 2011. Broadway Arts Inc. uses the equity method of accounting for its investment in Bulls Eye Inc.

    31.   Crystal Inc. is classified as an available-for-sale investment and is adjusted to a fair value of $15 per share. Use the Valuation Allowance for Available-for-Sale Investments account in making the adjustment.

Instructions

1. Journalize the entries to record these transactions.
2. Prepare the investment-related asset and stockholders' equity balance sheet disclosures for Broadway Arts Inc. on December 31, 2011, assuming the Retained Earnings balance on December 31, 2011, is $390,000.

PR 13-2B
Stock investment transactions, trading securities

objs. 3, 4

Jupiter Insurance Co. is a regional insurance company that began operations on January 1, 2010. The following transactions relate to trading securities acquired by Jupiter Insurance Co., which has a fiscal year ending on December 31:

2010
Feb. 21. Purchased 3,000 shares of Loral Inc. as a trading security at $25 per share plus a brokerage commission of $600.

Mar. 2. Purchased 900 shares of Monarch Inc. as a trading security at $52 per share plus a brokerage commission of $180.

May 3. Sold 800 shares of Loral Inc. for $23.50 per share less a $80 brokerage commission.

June 8. Received an annual dividend of $0.18 per share on Loral Inc. stock.

Dec. 31. The portfolio of trading securities was adjusted to fair values of $24 and $48 per share for Loral Inc. and Monarch Inc., respectively.

2011
May 11. Purchased 1,600 shares of Echelon Inc. as a trading security at $18 per share plus a $160 brokerage commission.

June 11. Received an annual dividend of $0.20 per share on Loral Inc. stock.

Aug. 14. Sold 400 shares of Echelon Inc. for $20 per share less a $80 brokerage commission.

Dec. 31. The portfolio of trading securities was adjusted to fair value using the following fair values per share for the trading securities:

Echelon Inc.	$22
Loral Inc.	23
Monarch Inc.	49

The portfolio of trading securities was adjusted to fair value.

Instructions
1. Journalize the entries to record these transactions.
2. Prepare the investment-related current asset balance sheet disclosures for Jupiter Insurance Co. on December 31, 2011.
3. How are unrealized gains or losses on trading investments disclosed on the financial statements of Jupiter Insurance Co.?

PR 13-3B
Debt investment transactions, available-for-sale valuation

objs. 2, 4

✔ 2. Available-for-sale investments (at fair value), $156,000

Eclipse Inc. is an athletic footwear company that began operations on January 1, 2010. The following transactions relate to debt investments acquired by Eclipse Inc., which has a fiscal year ending on December 31:

2010
Mar. 1. Purchased $80,000 of Noble Co. 6%, 10-year bonds at face value plus accrued interest of $400. The bond is classified as an available-for-sale investment. The bonds pay interest semiannually on February 1 and August 1.

Apr. 16. Purchased $105,000 of Mason City 4%, 15-year bonds at face value plus accrued interest of $175. The bond is classified as an available-for-sale investment. The bonds pay interest semiannually on April 1 and October 1.

Aug. 1. Received semiannual interest on the Noble Co. bonds.

Sept. 1. Sold $30,000 of Noble Co. bonds at 99 plus accrued interest of $150.

Oct. 1. Received semiannual interest on Mason City bonds.

Dec. 31. Accrued $1,250 interest on Noble Co. bonds.

31. Accrued $1,050 interest on Mason City bonds.

31. The available-for-sale bond portfolio was adjusted to fair values of 98 and 99 for Mason City and Noble Co. bonds, respectively.

2011
Feb. 1. Received semiannual interest on the Noble Co. bonds.

Apr. 1. Received semiannual interest on the Mason City bonds.

(Assume that there are no more purchases or sales of bonds during 2011. Also assume all subsequent interest transactions for 2011 have been recorded properly.)

Dec. 31. The available-for-sale bond portfolio was adjusted to fair values of 100 and 102 for Mason City and Noble Co. bonds, respectively.

Instructions
1. Journalize the entries to record these transactions.
2. Prepare the investment-related current asset and stockholders' equity balance sheet disclosures for Eclipse Inc. on December 31, 2011, assuming the Retained Earnings balance on December 31, 2011, is $490,000.

PR 13-4B
Investment reporting

objs. 2, 3, 4

✔ 1. b. ($6,040)

Scholar House, Inc., is a book publisher. The comparative unclassified balance sheets for December 31, 2011 and 2010 are provided below. Selected missing balances are shown by letters.

Scholar House, Inc.
Balance Sheet
December 31, 2011 and 2010

	Dec. 31, 2011	Dec. 31, 2010
Cash	$178,000	$157,000
Accounts receivable (net)	106,000	98,000
Available-for-sale investments (at cost)—Note 1	$ a.	$ 53,400
Less valuation allowance for available-for-sale investments	b.	2,400
Available-for-sale investments (fair value)	$ c.	$ 51,000
Interest receivable	$ d.	—
Investment in Nahum Co. stock—Note 2	e.	$ 64,000
Office equipment (net)	90,000	95,000
Total assets	$ f.	$465,000
Accounts payable	$ 56,900	$ 51,400
Common stock	50,000	50,000
Excess of issue price over par	160,000	160,000
Retained earnings	g.	206,000
Less unrealized gain (loss) on available-for-sale investments	h.	(2,400)
Total liabilities and stockholders' equity	$ i.	$465,000

Note 1. Investments are classified as available for sale. The investments at cost and fair value on December 31, 2010, are as follows:

	No. of Shares	Cost per Share	Total Cost	Total Fair Value
Barns Co. Stock	1,600	$12	$19,200	$18,000
Dynasty Co. Stock	900	38	34,200	33,000
			$53,400	$51,000

Note 2. The investment in Nahum Co. stock is an equity method investment representing 32% of the outstanding shares of Nahum Co.

The following selected investment transactions occurred during 2011:

2011
May   5.   Purchased 500 shares of High-Star, Inc., at $29 per share plus a $100 brokerage commission.
June 12.   Dividends of $1.25 per share are received on the Dynasty Co. stock investment.
Aug. 9.   Dividends of $5,700 are received on the Nahum Co. investment.
Sept. 1.   Purchased $18,000 of Opus Co. 5%, 10-year bonds at 100. The bonds are classified as available for sale. The bonds pay interest on September 1 and March 1.
Dec. 31.   Nahum Co. reported a total net income of $60,000 for 2011. Scholar House recorded equity earnings for its share of Nahum Co. net income.
      31.   Accrued 4 months of interest on the Opus bonds.
      31.   Adjusted the available-for-sale investment portfolio to fair value using the following fair value per share amounts:

Available-for-Sale Investments	Fair Value
Barns Co. stock	$10 per share
Dynasty Co. stock	$35 per share
High-Star Inc. stock	$30 per share
Opus Co. bonds	97 per $1,000 of face value

Dec. 31. Closed the Scholar House Inc. net income of $64,900 for 2011. Miranda paid no dividends during 2011.

Instructions
Determine the missing letters in the unclassified balance sheet. Provide appropriate supporting calculations.

Comprehensive Problem 4

Selected transactions completed by Jordan Products Inc. during the fiscal year ending December 31, 2010, were as follows:

a. Issued 14,500 shares of $30 par common stock at $48, receiving cash.
b. Issued 8,000 shares of $120 par preferred 6% stock at $130, receiving cash.
c. Issued $8,000,000 of 10-year, 7% bonds at 110, with interest payable semiannually.
d. Declared a dividend of $0.65 per share on common stock and $1.80 per share on preferred stock. On the date of record, 120,000 shares of common stock were outstanding, no treasury shares were held, and 22,500 shares of preferred stock were outstanding.
e. Paid the cash dividends declared in (d).
f. Purchased 12,000 shares of Avocado Corp. at $31 per share, plus a $2,400 brokerage commission. The investment is classified as an available-for-sale investment.
g. Purchased 9,500 shares of treasury common stock at $52 per share.
h. Purchased 340,000 shares of Amigo Co. stock directly from the founders for $21 per share. Amigo has 1,000,000 shares issued and outstanding. Jordan Products Inc. treated the investment as an equity method investment.
i. Declared a 2% stock dividend on common stock and a $1.80 cash dividend per share on preferred stock. On the date of declaration, the market value of the common stock was $55 per share. On the date of record, 120,000 shares of common stock had been issued, 9,500 shares of treasury common stock were held, and 22,500 shares of preferred stock had been issued.
j. Issued the stock certificates for the stock dividends declared in (h) and paid the cash dividends to the preferred stockholders.
k. Received $272,000 dividend from Amigo Co. investment in (h).
l. Purchased $86,000 of Game Gear Inc. 10-year, 6% bonds, directly from the issuing company at par value, plus accrued interest of $950. The bonds are classifed as a held-to-maturity long-term investment.
m. Sold, at $59.50 per share, 3,800 shares of treasury common stock purchased in (g).
n. Received a dividend of $1.45 per share from the Avocado Corp. investment in (f).
o. Sold 2,000 shares of Avocado Corp. at $32.80, including commission.
p. Recorded the payment of semiannual interest on the bonds issued in (c) and the amortization of the premium for six months. The amortization was determined using the straight-line method.
q. Accrued interest for three months on the Game Gear Inc. bonds purchased in (l).
r. Amigo Co. recorded total earnings of $478,000. Jordan Products recorded equity earnings for its share of Amigo Co. net income.
s. The fair value for Avocado Corp. stock was $28.50 per share on December 31, 2010. The investment is adjusted to fair value using a valuation allowance account. Assume the Valuation Allowance for Available-for-Sale Investments account had a beginning balance of zero.

Instructions
1. Journalize the selected transactions.
2. After all of the transactions for the year ended December 31, 2010, had been posted [including the transactions recorded in part (1) and all adjusting entries], the data below and on the following page were taken from the records of Jordan Products Inc.
   a. Prepare a multiple-step income statement for the year ended December 31, 2010, concluding with earnings per share. In computing earnings per share,

assume that the average number of common shares outstanding was 120,000 and preferred dividends were $162,000. (Round earnings per share to the nearest cent.)

b. Prepare a retained earnings statement for the year ended December 31, 2010.
c. Prepare a balance sheet in report form as of December 31, 2010.

Income statement data:

Advertising expense	$ 125,000
Cost of merchandise sold	3,240,000
Delivery expense	29,000
Depreciation expense—office buildings and equipment	26,000
Depreciation expense—store buildings and equipment	95,000
Dividend revenue	17,400
Gain on sale of investment	3,200
Income from Amigo Co. investment	162,520
Income tax expense	306,700
Interest expense	384,000
Interest revenue	1,650
Miscellaneous administrative expense	7,500
Miscellaneous selling expense	13,750
Office rent expense	50,000
Office salaries expense	140,000
Office supplies expense	10,000
Sales	5,580,000
Sales commissions	182,000
Sales salaries expense	345,000
Store supplies expense	22,000

Retained earnings and balance sheet data:

Accounts payable	195,000
Accounts receivable	543,000
Accumulated depreciation—office buildings and equipment	1,580,000
Accumulated depreciation—store buildings and equipment	4,126,000
Allowance for doubtful accounts	8,150
Available-for-sale investments (at cost)	312,000
Bonds payable, 7%, due 2020	8,000,000
Cash	240,000
Common stock, $30 par (400,000 shares authorized; 122,210 shares issued, 116,510 outstanding)	3,666,300
Dividends:	
Cash dividends for common stock	316,310
Cash dividends for preferred stock	162,000
Stock dividends for common stock	121,550
Goodwill	510,000
Income tax payable	40,000
Interest receivable	1,290
Investment in Amigo Co. stock (equity method)	7,030,520
Investment in Game Gear Inc. bonds (long term)	86,000
Merchandise inventory (December 31, 2010), at lower of cost (FIFO) or market	780,000
Office buildings and equipment	4,320,000
Paid-in capital from sale of treasury stock	28,500
Paid-in capital in excess of par—common stock	842,000
Paid-in capital in excess of par—preferred stock	150,000
Preferred 6% stock, $120 par (30,000 shares authorized; 22,500 shares issued)	2,700,000
Premium on bonds payable	760,000
Prepaid expenses	26,500
Retained earnings, January 1, 2010	4,420,800
Store buildings and equipment	12,560,000
Treasury stock (5,700 shares of common stock at cost of $52 per share)	296,400
Unrealized gain (loss) on available-for-sale investments	(27,000)
Valuation allowance for available-for-sale investments	(27,000)

Special Activities

SA 13-1
Benefits of fair value

On August 16, 1995, Parson Corp. purchased 20 acres of land for $300,000. The land has been held for a future plant site until the current date, December 31, 2010. On December 5, 2010, Mobile Air, Inc., purchased 20 acres of land for $2,000,000 to be used for a distribution center. The Mobile Air land is located next to the Parson Corp. land. Thus, both Parson Corp. and Mobile Air, Inc., own nearly identical pieces of land.

1. What are the valuations of land on the balance sheets of Parson Corp. and Mobile Air, Inc., using generally accepted accounting principles?
2. How might fair value accounting aid comparability when evaluating these two companies?

SA 13-2
International fair value accounting

International Accounting Standard No. 16 provides companies the option of valuing property, plant, and equipment at either historical cost or fair value. If fair value is selected, then the property, plant, and equipment must be revalued periodically to fair value. Under fair value, if there is an increase in the value of the property, plant, and equipment over the reporting period, then the increase is credited to stockholders' equity. However, if there is a decrease in fair value, then the decrease is reported as an expense for the period.

1. Why do International Accounting Standards influence U.S. GAAP?
2. What would be some of the disadvantages of using fair value accounting for property, plant, and equipment?
3. Why are there different treatments for increases and decreases in the fair value of property, plant, and equipment over a period?

SA 13-3
Ethics and fair value measurement

Financial assets include stocks and bonds. These are fairly simple securities that can often be valued using quoted market prices. However, Wall Street has created many complex and exotic securities that do not have quoted market prices. These securities, such as structured investment vehicles (SIVs), must still be valued on the balance sheet at fair value. Generally accepted accounting principles require that the reporting entity use assumptions in valuing investments when market prices or critical valuation inputs are unobservable.

What are the ethical considerations in making subjective valuations of complex and exotic investments?

SA 13-4
Warren Buffett and "look-through" earnings

Berkshire Hathaway, the investment holding company of Warren Buffett, reports its "less than 20% ownership" investments according to generally accepted accounting principles. However, it also provides additional disclosures that it terms "look-through" earnings.

Warren Buffett states,

Many of these companies (in the less than 20% owned category) pay out relatively small proportions of their earnings in dividends. This means that only a small proportion of their earning power is recorded in our own current operating earnings. But, while our reported operating earnings reflect only the dividends received from such companies, our economic well-being is determined by their earnings, not their dividends.

The value to Berkshire Hathaway of retained earnings (of our investees) is not determined by whether we own 100%, 50%, 20%, or 1% of the businesses in which they reside. . . . Our perspective on such "forgotten-but-not-gone" earnings is simple: the way they are accounted for is of no importance, but their ownership and subsequent utilization is all-important. We care not whether the auditors hear a tree fall in the forest; we do care who owns the tree and what's next done with it.

I believe the best way to think about our earnings is in terms of "look-through" results, calculated as follows: Take $250 million, which is roughly our share of the operating earnings retained by our investees (<20% ownership holdings); subtract . . . incremental taxes we would have owed had that $250 million been paid to us in dividends; then add the remainder,

$220 million, to our reported earnings of $371 million. Thus our, "look-through" earnings were about $590 million.

Source: Warren Buffett, *The Essays of Warren Buffett: Lessons for Corporate America*, edited by Lawrence A. Cunningham, pp. 180–183 (excerpted).

1. What are "look-through" earnings?
2. Why does Warren Buffett favor "look-through" earnings?

SA 13-5
Reporting
investments

Group Project

Internet Project

In groups of three or four, find the latest annual report for Microsoft Corporation. The annual report can be found on the company's Web site at **http://www.microsoft.com/msft/default.mspx**.

The notes to the financial statements include details of Microsoft's investments. Find the notes that provide details of its investments (Note 3) and the income from its investments (Note 4).

From these disclosures, answer the following questions:

1. What is the total cost of investments?
2. What is the fair value of investments?
3. What is the total unrealized gain from investments?
4. What is the total unrealized loss from investments?
5. What percent of total investments are:
   a. Cash and equivalents
   b. Short-term investments
   c. Equity and other investments (long term)
6. What was the total combined dividend and interest revenue?
7. What was the realized net gain or loss from sale of investments?
8. What was the total income (loss) from equity investees?

Answers to Self-Examination Questions

1. **B**   ($50,000 × 5% × 54/360)
2. **C**

Proceeds (800 shares × $20) − $50	$15,950
Cost (800 shares × $23.05*)	18,440
Loss on sale of investment	$ 2,490

$$\frac{*(1,400 \text{ shares} \times \$23) + \$70}{1,400 \text{ shares}}$$

3. **B**

Income from Barnwell Inc. ($200,000 × 40%)	$80,000
Barnwell Inc. dividend ($60,000 × 40%)	24,000
Increase in Investment in Barnwell Inc. Stock	$56,000

4. **A**   Answer C is the valuation allowance balance on December 31, 2010, but not the adjustment to arrive at the balance. Answer D incorrectly adds the beginning and ending debit balances of the valuation allowance. Answer B incorrectly interprets the credit adjustment as an unrealized gain. The adjustment is the net decrease in the debit balance, or answer A, as shown below.

Valuation allowance for trading investments, January 1, 2011		$32,000	Dr.
Trading investments at cost, December 31, 2011	$500,000		
Trading investments at fair value, December 31, 2011	520,000		
Valuation allowance for trading investments, December 31, 2011		20,000	Dr.
Adjustment		$12,000	Cr.

5. **A**   There is no income statement recognition of changes in the fair value of the available-for-sale portfolio; thus, answers B, C, and D are incorrect. The accumulated change in fair value for the available-for-sale portfolio is recognized in the Stockholders' Equity section of the balance sheet.

Financial Statements for Mornin' Joe

The financial statements of Mornin' Joe are provided in the following pages. Mornin' Joe is a fictitious coffeehouse chain featuring drip and espresso coffee in a café setting. The financial statements of Mornin' Joe are provided to illustrate the complete financial statements of a corporation using the terms, formats, and reporting illustrated throughout this text. In addition, excerpts of the Mornin' Joe financial statements are used to illustrate the financial reporting presentation for the topics discussed in Chapters 7–15. Thus, you can refer to the complete financial statements shown here or the excerpts in Chapters 7–15. A set of real world financial statements by Nike, Inc., is provided in Appendix F.

Mornin' Joe
Income Statement
For the Year Ended December 31, 2010

Revenue from sales:			
Sales		$5,450,000	
Less: Sales returns and allowances	$ 26,500		
Sales discounts	21,400	47,900	
Net sales			$5,402,100
Cost of merchandise sold			2,160,000
Gross profit			$3,242,100
Operating expenses			
Selling expenses:			
Wages expense	$825,000		
Advertising expense	678,900		
Depreciation expense—buildings	124,300		
Miscellaneous selling expense	26,500		
Total selling expenses		$1,654,700	
Administrative expenses:			
Office salaries expense	$325,000		
Rent expense	425,600		
Payroll tax expense	110,000		
Depreciation expense—office equipment	68,900		
Bad debt expense	14,000		
Amortization expense	10,500		
Total administrative expenses		954,000	
Total operating expenses			2,608,700
Income from operations			$ 633,400
Other income and expense:			
Interest revenue		$ 18,000	
Interest expense		(136,000)	
Loss on disposal of fixed asset		(23,000)	
Unrealized gain on trading investments		5,000	
Equity income in AM Coffee		57,000	(79,000)
Income before income taxes			$ 554,400
Income tax expense			132,800
Net income			$ 421,600
Basic earnings per share [($421,600 − $30,000)/44,000 shares issued and outstanding]			$ 8.90

Mornin' Joe
Balance Sheet
December 31, 2010

Assets

Current assets:

Cash and cash equivalents		$ 235,000
Trading investments (at cost)	$ 420,000	
Plus valuation allowance for trading investments	45,000	465,000
Accounts receivable	$ 305,000	
Less allowance for doubtful accounts	12,300	292,700
Merchandise inventory—at lower of cost (first-in, first-out method) or market		120,000
Prepaid insurance		24,000
Total current assets		$1,136,700

Investments:

Investment in AM Coffee (equity method)		565,000

Property, plant, and equipment:

Land		$1,850,000
Buildings	$2,650,000	
Less accumulated depreciation	420,000	2,230,000
Office equipment	$ 350,000	
Less accumulated depreciation	102,000	248,000
Total property, plant, and equipment		4,328,000

Intangible assets:

Patents		140,000
Total assets		$6,169,700

Liabilities

Current liabilities:

Accounts payable		$ 133,000
Notes payable (current portion)		200,000
Salaries and wages payable		42,000
Payroll taxes payable		16,400
Interest payable		40,000
Total current liabilities		$ 431,400

Long-term liabilities:

Bonds payable, 8%, due December 31, 2030	$ 500,000	
Less unamortized discount	16,000	$ 484,000
Notes payable		1,400,000
Total long-term liabilities		$1,884,000
Total liabilities		$2,315,400

Stockholders' Equity

Paid-in capital:

Preferred 10% stock, $50 par (6,000 shares authorized and issued)	$ 300,000	
Excess of issue price over par	50,000	$ 350,000
Common stock, $20 par (50,000 shares authorized, 45,000 shares issued)	$ 900,000	
Excess of issue price over par	1,450,000	2,350,000
Total paid-in capital		$2,700,000
Retained earnings		1,200,300
Total		$3,900,300
Deduct treasury stock (1,000 shares at cost)		46,000
Total stockholders' equity		$3,854,300
Total liabilities and stockholders' equity		$6,169,700

Mornin' Joe
Retained Earnings Statement
For the Year Ended December 31, 2010

Retained earnings, January 1, 2010			$ 852,700
Net income		$421,600	
Less dividends:			
Preferred stock	$30,000		
Common stock	44,000	74,000	
Increase in retained earnings			347,600
Retained earnings, December 31, 2010			$1,200,300

Mornin' Joe
Statement of Stockholders' Equity
For the Year Ended December 31, 2010

	Preferred Stock	Common Stock	Additional Paid-In Capital	Retained Earnings	Treasury Stock	Total
Balance, January 1, 2010	$300,000	$800,000	$1,325,000	$ 852,700	$(36,000)	$3,241,700
Net income				421,600		421,600
Dividends on preferred stock				(30,000)		(30,000)
Dividends on common stock				(44,000)		(44,000)
Issuance of additional common stock		100,000	175,000			275,000
Purchase of treasury stock					(10,000)	(10,000)
Balance, December 31, 2010	$300,000	$900,000	$1,500,000	$1,200,300	$(46,000)	$3,854,300

Statement of Cash Flows

JONES SODA CO.

Suppose you were to receive $100 as a result of some event. Would it make a difference what the event was? Yes, it would! If you received $100 for your birthday, then it's a gift. If you received $100 as a result of working part time for a week, then it's the result of your effort. If you received $100 as a loan, then it's money that you will have to pay back in the future. If you received $100 as a result of selling your iPod, then it's the result of giving up something tangible. Thus, the same $100 received can be associated with different types of events, and these events have different meanings to you. You would much rather receive a $100 gift than take out a $100 loan. Likewise, company stakeholders would also view events such as these differently.

Companies are required to report information about the events causing a change in cash over a period of time. This information is reported in the statement of cash flows. One such company is Jones Soda Co. Jones began in the late 1980s as an alternative beverage company, known for its customer-provided labels, unique flavors, and support for extreme sports. You have probably seen Jones Soda at Barnes & Noble, Panera Bread, or Starbucks, or maybe sampled some of its unique flavors, such as Fufu Berry®, Blue Bubblegum®, or Lemon Drop®. As with any company, cash is important to Jones Soda. Without cash, Jones would be unable to expand its brands, distribute its product, support extreme sports, or provide a return for its owners. Thus, its managers are concerned about the sources and uses of cash.

In previous chapters, we have used the income statement, balance sheet, retained earnings statement, and other information to analyze the effects of management decisions on a business's financial position and operating performance. In this chapter, we focus on the events causing a change in cash by presenting the preparation and use of the statement of cash flows.

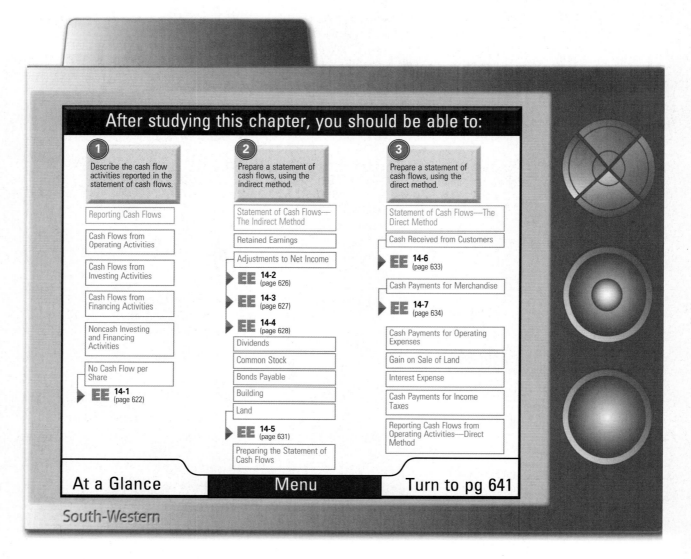

After studying this chapter, you should be able to:

1 Describe the cash flow activities reported in the statement of cash flows.

Reporting Cash Flows

Cash Flows from Operating Activities

Cash Flows from Investing Activities

Cash Flows from Financing Activities

Noncash Investing and Financing Activities

No Cash Flow per Share

EE 14-1 (page 622)

2 Prepare a statement of cash flows, using the indirect method.

Statement of Cash Flows— The Indirect Method

Retained Earnings

Adjustments to Net Income

EE 14-2 (page 626)

EE 14-3 (page 627)

EE 14-4 (page 628)

Dividends

Common Stock

Bonds Payable

Building

Land

EE 14-5 (page 631)

Preparing the Statement of Cash Flows

3 Prepare a statement of cash flows, using the direct method.

Statement of Cash Flows—The Direct Method

Cash Received from Customers

EE 14-6 (page 633)

Cash Payments for Merchandise

EE 14-7 (page 634)

Cash Payments for Operating Expenses

Gain on Sale of Land

Interest Expense

Cash Payments for Income Taxes

Reporting Cash Flows from Operating Activities—Direct Method

At a Glance   Menu   Turn to pg 641

South-Western

1 Describe the cash flow activities reported in the statement of cash flows.

Reporting Cash Flows

The **statement of cash flows** reports a company's cash inflows and outflows for a period.[1] The statement of cash flows provides useful information about a company's ability to do the following:

1. Generate cash from operations
2. Maintain and expand its operating capacity
3. Meet its financial obligations
4. Pay dividends

The statement of cash flows is used by managers in evaluating past operations and in planning future investing and financing activities. It is also used by external users such as investors and creditors to assess a company's profit potential and ability to pay its debt and pay dividends.

The statement of cash flows reports three types of cash flow activities as follows:

1. **Cash flows from operating activities** are cash flows from transactions that affect the net income of the company.

    Example: Purchase and sale of merchandise by a retailer.

---

1 As used in this chapter, *cash* refers to cash and cash equivalents. Examples of cash equivalents include short-term, highly liquid investments, such as money market accounts, bank certificates of deposit, and U.S. Treasury bills.

2. **Cash flows from investing activities** are cash flows from transactions that affect investments in noncurrent assets of the company.

> Example: Sale and purchase of fixed assets, such as equipment and buildings.

3. **Cash flows from financing activities** are cash flows from transactions that affect the debt and equity of the company.

> Example: Issuing or retiring equity and debt securities.

The cash flows are reported in the statement of cash flows as follows:

Cash flows from operating activities	$XXX
Cash flows from investing activities	XXX
Cash flows from financing activities	XXX
Net increase or decrease in cash for the period	$XXX
Cash at the beginning of the period	XXX
Cash at the end of the period	$XXX

The ending cash on the statement of cash flows equals the cash reported on the company's balance sheet.

Exhibit 1 illustrates the sources (increases) and uses (decreases) of cash by each of the three cash flow activities. A *source* of cash causes the cash flow to increase and is called a *cash inflow*. A *use* of cash causes cash flow to decrease and is called *cash outflow*.

> **The statement of cash flows reports cash flows from operating, investing, and financing activities.**

Exhibit 1

Cash Flows

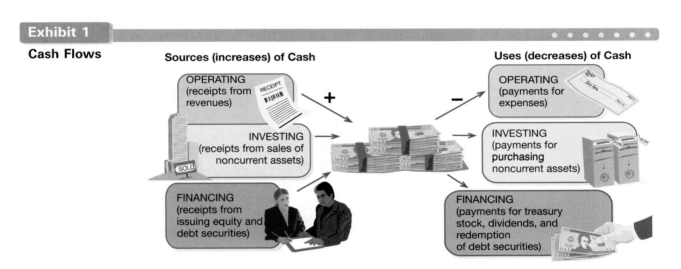

Cash Flows from Operating Activities

There are two methods for reporting cash flows from operating activities in the statement of cash flows. These methods are as follows:

1. Direct method
2. Indirect method

The **direct method** reports operating cash inflows (receipts) and cash outflows (payments) as follows:

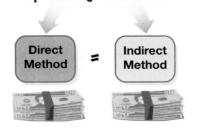

Cash Flows from Operating Activities

Direct Method = Indirect Method

Cash flows from operating activities:		
Cash received from customers		$XXX
Less: Cash payments for merchandise	$XXX	
Cash payments for operating expenses	XXX	
Cash payments for interest	XXX	
Cash payments for income taxes	XXX	XXX
Net cash flows from operating activities		$XXX

The primary operating cash inflow is cash received from customers. The primary operating cash outflows are cash payments for merchandise, operating expenses, interest, and income tax payments. The cash received less the cash payments is the net cash flow from operating activities.

The primary advantage of the direct method is that it *directly* reports cash receipts and payments in the statement of cash flows. Its primary disadvantage is that these data may not be readily available in the accounting records. Thus, the direct method is normally more costly to use and, as a result, is used by less than 1% of companies.[2]

The **indirect method** reports operating cash flows by beginning with net income and adjusting it for revenues and expenses that do not involve the receipt or payment of cash as follows:

Cash flows from operating activities:
Net income $XXX
Adjustments to reconcile net income to net
   cash flow from operating activities XXX
Net cash flow from operating activities $XXX

The adjustments to reconcile net income to net cash flow from operating activities include such items as depreciation and gains (or losses) on fixed assets. Changes in current operating assets and liabilities such as accounts receivable or accounts payable are also added or deducted depending on their effect on cash flows. In effect, these additions and deductions adjust net income, which is reported on an accrual accounting basis, to cash flows from operating activities, which uses a cash basis.

A primary advantage of the indirect method is that it reconciles the differences between net income and net cash flows from operations. In doing so, it shows how net income is related to the ending cash balance that is reported on the balance sheet.

Because the data are readily available, the indirect method is less costly to use than the direct method. As a result, over 99% of companies use the indirect method of reporting cash flows from operations.

Exhibit 2 illustrates the Cash Flows from Operating Activities section of the statement of cash flows for **NetSolutions**. Exhibit 2 shows the direct and indirect methods using the **NetSolutions** data from Chapter 1. As Exhibit 2 illustrates, both methods report the same amount of net cash flow from operating activities, $2,900.

enetsolutions

Exhibit 2

Cash Flow from Operations: Direct and Indirect Methods—NetSolutions

Direct Method

Cash flows from operating activities:
Cash received from customers	$7,500
Deduct cash payments for expenses	
and payments to creditors	4,600
Net cash flow from operating activities	$2,900

Indirect Method

Cash flows from operating activities:
Net income	$3,050
Add increase in accounts payable	400
	$3,450
Deduct increase in supplies	550
Net cash flow from operating activities	$2,900

the same

In Chapter 1, the direct method was used to report NetSolutions' statement of cash flows. This is because the indirect method requires an understanding of the accrual accounting concepts such as depreciation, which had yet to be covered in Chapter 1.

2 *Accounting Trends & Techniques*, AICPA, 2007 edition.

The Walt Disney Company recently invested $1.1 billion in parks, resorts, and other properties, including two new cruise ships and new attractions at Disneyland.

Cash Flows from Investing Activities

Cash flows from investing activities are reported on the statement of cash flows as follows:

Cash flows from investing activities:		
Cash inflows from investing activities	$XXX	
Less cash used for investing activities	XXX	
Net cash flows from investing activities		$XXX

Cash inflows from investing activities normally arise from selling fixed assets, investments, and intangible assets. Cash outflows normally include payments to purchase fixed assets, investments, and intangible assets.

Cash Flows from Financing Activities

Cash flows from financing activities are reported on the statement of cash flows as follows:

Cash flows from financing activities:		
Cash inflows from financing activities	$XXX	
Less cash used for financing activities	XXX	
Net cash flows from financing activities		$XXX

Cash inflows from financing activities normally arise from issuing debt or equity securities. For example, issuing bonds, notes payable, preferred stock, and common stock creates cash inflows from financing activities. Cash outflows from financing activities include paying cash dividends, repaying debt, and acquiring treasury stock.

Google disclosed the issuance of over $25 million in common stock for business acquisitions in its statement of cash flows as a noncash investing and financing activity.

Noncash Investing and Financing Activities

A company may enter into transactions involving investing and financing activities that do not *directly* affect cash. For example, a company may issue common stock to retire long-term debt. Although this transaction does not directly affect cash, it does eliminate future cash payments for interest and for paying the bonds when they mature. Because such transactions *indirectly* affect cash flows, they are reported in a separate section of the statement of cash flows. This section usually appears at the bottom of the statement of cash flows.

Business Connection

TOO MUCH CASH!

Is it possible to have too much cash? Clearly, most of us would answer no. However, a business views cash differently than an individual. Naturally, a business needs cash to develop and launch new products, expand markets, purchase plant and equipment, and acquire other businesses. However, some businesses have built up huge cash balances beyond even these needs. For example, both Microsoft Corporation and Dell Inc. have accumulated billions of dollars in cash and temporary investments, totaling in excess of 60% of their total assets. Such large cash balances can lower the return on total assets. As stated by one analyst, "When a company sits on cash (which earns 1% or 2%) and leaves equity outstanding . . ., it is tantamount to taking a loan at 15% and investing in a passbook savings account that earns 2%—it destroys value." So while having too much cash is a good problem to have, companies like Microsoft, Cisco Systems, Inc., IBM, Apple Computer Inc., and Dell are under pressure to pay dividends or repurchase common stock. For example, Microsoft declared a $32 billion special dividend to return cash to its shareholders.

No Cash Flow per Share

Cash flow per share is sometimes reported in the financial press. As reported, cash flow per share is normally computed as *cash flow from operations per share*. However, such reporting may be misleading because of the following:

1. Users may misinterpret cash flow per share as the per-share amount available for dividends. This would not be the case if the cash generated by operations is required for repaying loans or for reinvesting in the business.
2. Users may misinterpret cash flow per share as equivalent to (or better than) earnings per share.

For these reasons, the financial statements, including the statement of cash flows, should not report cash flow per share.

Example Exercise 14-1   Classifying Cash Flows   1

Identify whether each of the following would be reported as an operating, investing, or financing activity in the statement of cash flows.

a. Purchase of patent   d. Cash sales
b. Payment of cash dividend   e. Purchase of treasury stock
c. Disposal of equipment   f. Payment of wages expense

Follow My Example 14-1

a. Investing   d. Operating
b. Financing   e. Financing
c. Investing   f. Operating

For Practice: PE 14-1A, PE 14-1B

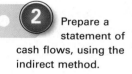

Prepare a statement of cash flows, using the indirect method.

Statement of Cash Flows— The Indirect Method

The indirect method of reporting cash flows from operating activities uses the logic that a change in any balance sheet account (including cash) can be analyzed in terms of changes in the other balance sheet accounts. Thus, by analyzing changes in non-cash balance sheet accounts, any change in the cash account can be *indirectly* determined.

To illustrate, the accounting equation can be solved for cash as shown below.

Assets = Liabilities + Stockholders' Equity
Cash + Noncash Assets = Liabilities + Stockholders' Equity
Cash = Liabilities + Stockholders' Equity − Noncash Assets

Therefore, any change in the cash account can be determined by analyzing changes in the liability, stockholders' equity, and noncash asset accounts as shown below.

Change in Cash = *Change* in Liabilities + *Change* in Stockholders' Equity
 − *Change* in Noncash Assets

Under the indirect method, there is no order in which the balance sheet accounts must be analyzed. However, net income (or net loss) is the first amount reported on the statement of cash flows. Since net income (or net loss) is a component of any change in Retained Earnings, the first account normally analyzed is Retained Earnings.

To illustrate the indirect method, the income statement and comparative balance sheets for Rundell Inc. shown in Exhibit 3 are used. Ledger accounts and

Exhibit 3

Income Statement and Comparative Balance Sheet

Rundell Inc.
Income Statement
For the Year Ended December 31, 2010

Sales		$1,180,000
Cost of merchandise sold		790,000
Gross profit		$ 390,000
Operating expenses:		
Depreciation expense	$ 7,000	
Other operating expenses	196,000	
Total operating expenses		203,000
Income from operations		$ 187,000
Other income:		
Gain on sale of land	$ 12,000	
Other expense:		
Interest expense	8,000	4,000
Income before income tax		$ 191,000
Income tax expense		83,000
Net income		$ 108,000

Rundell Inc.
Comparative Balance Sheet
December 31, 2010 and 2009

	2010	2009	Increase Decrease*
Assets			
Cash	$ 97,500	$ 26,000	$ 71,500
Accounts receivable (net)	74,000	65,000	9,000
Inventories	172,000	180,000	8,000*
Land	80,000	125,000	45,000*
Building	260,000	200,000	60,000
Accumulated depreciation—building	(65,300)	(58,300)	7,000
Total assets	$618,200	$537,700	$ 80,500
Liabilities			
Accounts payable (merchandise creditors)	$ 43,500	$ 46,700	$ 3,200*
Accrued expenses payable (operating expenses)	26,500	24,300	2,200
Income taxes payable	7,900	8,400	500*
Dividends payable	14,000	10,000	4,000
Bonds payable	100,000	150,000	50,000*
Total liabilities	$191,900	$239,400	$ 47,500*
Stockholders' Equity			
Common stock ($2 par)	$ 24,000	$ 16,000	$ 8,000
Paid-in capital in excess of par	120,000	80,000	40,000
Retained earnings	282,300	202,300	80,000
Total stockholders' equity	$426,300	$298,300	$128,000
Total liabilities and stockholders' equity	$618,200	$537,700	$ 80,500

other data supporting the income statement and balance sheet are presented as needed.[3]

Retained Earnings

The comparative balance sheet for Rundell Inc. shows that retained earnings increased $80,000 during the year. The retained earnings account shown below indicates how this change occurred.

Account Retained Earnings				Account No.		
					Balance	
Date	**Item**	**Debit**	**Credit**	**Debit**	**Credit**	
2010						
Jan. 1	Balance				202,300	
Dec. 31	Net income		108,000		310,300	
31	Cash dividends	28,000			282,300	

The retained earnings account indicates that the $80,000 ($108,000 − $28,000) change resulted from net income of $108,000 and cash dividends of $28,000. The net income of $108,000 is the first amount reported in the Cash Flows from Operating Activities section.

Adjustments to Net Income

The net income of $108,000 reported by Rundell Inc. does not equal the cash flows from operating activities for the period. This is because net income is determined using the accrual method of accounting.

Under the accrual method of accounting, revenues and expenses are recorded at different times from when cash is received or paid. For example, merchandise may be sold on account and the cash received at a later date. Likewise, insurance premiums may be paid in the current period, but expensed in a following period.

Thus, under the indirect method, adjustments to net income must be made to determine cash flows from operating activities. The typical adjustments to net income are shown in Exhibit 4.[4]

Net income is normally adjusted to cash flows from operating activities using the following steps:

Step 1. Expenses that do not affect cash are added. Such expenses decrease net income, but did not involve cash payments and, thus, are added to net income.

Examples: *Depreciation* of fixed assets and *amortization* of intangible assets are added to net income.

---

3 An appendix that discusses using a spreadsheet (work sheet) as an aid in assembling data for the statement of cash flows is presented at the end of this chapter. This appendix illustrates the use of this spreadsheet in reporting cash flows from operating activities using the indirect method.

4 Other items that also require adjustments to net income to obtain cash flows from operating activities include amortization of bonds payable discounts (add), losses on debt retirement (add), amortization of bonds payable premiums (deduct), and gains on retirement of debt (deduct).

Exhibit 4

Adjustments to Net Income (Loss) Using the Indirect Method

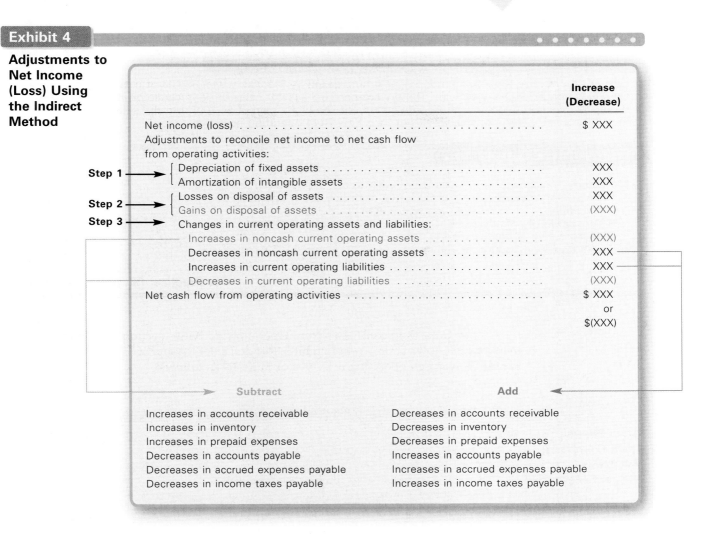

	Increase (Decrease)
Net income (loss)	$ XXX
Adjustments to reconcile net income to net cash flow from operating activities:	
Step 1 → Depreciation of fixed assets	XXX
Amortization of intangible assets	XXX
Step 2 → Losses on disposal of assets	XXX
Gains on disposal of assets	(XXX)
Step 3 → Changes in current operating assets and liabilities:	
Increases in noncash current operating assets	(XXX)
Decreases in noncash current operating assets	XXX
Increases in current operating liabilities	XXX
Decreases in current operating liabilities	(XXX)
Net cash flow from operating activities	$ XXX
	or
	$(XXX)

Subtract	Add
Increases in accounts receivable	Decreases in accounts receivable
Increases in inventory	Decreases in inventory
Increases in prepaid expenses	Decreases in prepaid expenses
Decreases in accounts payable	Increases in accounts payable
Decreases in accrued expenses payable	Increases in accrued expenses payable
Decreases in income taxes payable	Increases in income taxes payable

Step 2. Losses and gains on disposal of assets are added or deducted. The disposal (sale) of assets is an investing activity rather than an operating activity. However, such losses and gains are reported as part of net income. As a result, any *losses* on disposal of assets are *added* back to net income. Likewise, any *gains* on disposal of assets are *deducted* from net income.

Example: Land costing $100,000 is sold for $90,000. The loss of $10,000 is added back to net income.

Step 3. Changes in current operating assets and liabilities are added or deducted as follows:

Increases in noncash current operating assets are deducted.
Decreases in noncash current operating assets are added.
Increases in current operating liabilities are added.
Decreases in current operating liabilities are deducted.

Example: A sale of $10,000 on account increases accounts receivable by $10,000. However, cash is not affected. Thus, an increase in accounts receivable of $10,000 is deducted. Similar adjustments are required for the changes in the other current asset and liability accounts such as inventory, prepaid expenses, accounts payable, accrued expenses payable, and income taxes payable as shown in Exhibit 4.

Example Exercise 14-2 Adjustments to Net Income—Indirect Method

Omni Corporation's accumulated depreciation increased by $12,000, while, $3,400 of patents were amortized between balance sheet dates. There were no purchases or sales of depreciable or intangible assets during the year. In addition, the income statement showed a gain of $4,100 from the sale of land. Reconcile a net income of $50,000 to net cash flow from operating activities.

Follow My Example 14-2

Net income	$50,000
Adjustments to reconcile net income to net cash flow from operating activities:	
Depreciation.	12,000
Amortization of patents	3,400
Gain from sale of land	(4,100)
Net cash flow from operating activities	$61,300

For Practice: PE 14-2A, PE 14-2B

To illustrate, the Cash Flows from Operating Activities section of Rundell's statement of cash flows is shown in Exhibit 5. Rundell's net income of $108,000 is converted to cash flows from operating activities of $100,500 as follows:

Exhibit 5

Cash Flows from Operating Activities— Indirect Method

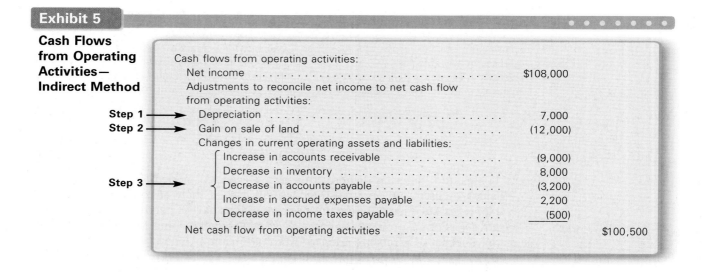

Cash flows from operating activities:		
Net income		$108,000
Adjustments to reconcile net income to net cash flow from operating activities:		
Step 1 →	Depreciation	7,000
Step 2 →	Gain on sale of land	(12,000)
	Changes in current operating assets and liabilities:	
	Increase in accounts receivable	(9,000)
	Decrease in inventory	8,000
Step 3 →	Decrease in accounts payable	(3,200)
	Increase in accrued expenses payable	2,200
	Decrease in income taxes payable	(500)
	Net cash flow from operating activities	$100,500

Step 1. Add depreciation of $7,000.

Analysis: The comparative balance sheet in Exhibit 3 indicates that Accumulated Depreciation—Building increased by $7,000. The account, shown below, indicates that depreciation for the year was $7,000 for the building.

Account Accumulated Depreciation—Building					Account No.	
					Balance	
Date		**Item**	**Debit**	**Credit**	**Debit**	**Credit**
2010						
Jan.	1	Balance				58,300
Dec.	31	Depreciation for year		7,000		65,300

Step 2. Deduct the gain on the sale of land of $12,000.

Analysis: The income statement in Exhibit 3 reports a gain from the sale of land of $12,000. The proceeds, which include the gain, are reported in the Investing section of the statement of cash flows.[5] Thus, the gain of $12,000 is deducted from net income in determining cash flows from operating activities.

Step 3. Add and deduct changes in current operating assets and liabilities.

Analysis: The increases and decreases in the current operating asset and current liability accounts are shown below.

Accounts	December 31 2010	December 31 2009	Increase Decrease*
Accounts Receivable (net)	$ 74,000	$ 65,000	$9,000
Inventories	172,000	180,000	8,000*
Accounts Payable (merchandise creditors)	43,500	46,700	3,200*
Accrued Expenses Payable (operating expenses)	26,500	24,300	2,200
Income Taxes Payable	7,900	8,400	500*

Accounts receivable (net): The $9,000 increase is deducted from net income. This is because the $9,000 increase in accounts receivable indicates that sales on account were $9,000 more than the cash received from customers. Thus, sales (and net income) includes $9,000 that was not received in cash during the year.

Inventories: The $8,000 decrease is added to net income. This is because the $8,000 decrease in inventories indicates that the cost of merchandise *sold* exceeds the cost of the merchandise *purchased* during the year by $8,000. In other words, cost of merchandise sold includes $8,000 that was not purchased (used cash) during the year.

Ford Motor Company had a net loss of $12.6 billion but a positive cash flow from operating activities of $3.3 billion. This difference was mostly due to $16.5 billion of depreciation expenses.

Accounts payable (merchandise creditors): The $3,200 decrease is deducted from net income. This is because a decrease in accounts payable indicates that the cash *payments* to merchandise creditors exceeds the merchandise *purchased on account* by $3,200. Therefore, cost of merchandise sold is $3,200 less than the cash paid to merchandise creditors during the year.

Accrued expenses payable (operating expenses): The $2,200 increase is added to net income. This is because an increase in accrued expenses payable indicates that operating expenses exceed the cash payments for operating expenses by $2,200. In other words, operating expenses reported on the income statement include $2,200 that did not require a cash outflow during the year.

Income taxes payable: The $500 decrease is deducted from net income. This is because a decrease in income taxes payable indicates that taxes paid exceed the amount of taxes incurred during the year by $500. In other words, the amount reported on the income statement for income tax expense is less than the amount paid by $500.

Example Exercise 14-3   Changes in Current Operating Assets and Liabilities—Indirect Method

Victor Corporation's comparative balance sheet for current assets and liabilities was as follows:

	Dec. 31, 2011	Dec. 31, 2010
Accounts receivable	$ 6,500	$ 4,900
Inventory	12,300	15,000
Accounts payable	4,800	5,200
Dividends payable	5,000	4,000

Adjust net income of $70,000 for changes in operating assets and liabilities to arrive at cash flows from operating activities.

(continued)

5 The reporting of the proceeds (cash flows) from the sale of land as part of investing activities is discussed later in this chapter.

Follow My Example 14-3

Net income	$70,000
Adjustments to reconcile net income to net cash flow from operating activities:	
Changes in current operating assets and liabilities:	
Increase in accounts receivable	(1,600)
Decrease in inventory	2,700
Decrease in accounts payable	(400)
Net cash flow from operating activities	$70,700

For Practice: PE 14-3A, PE 14-3B

Using the preceding analyses, Rundell's net income of $108,000 is converted to cash flows from operating activities of $100,500 as shown in Exhibit 5, on page 626.

Exercise 14-4   Cash Flows from Operating Activities— Indirect Method

•••••••• > 2

Omicron Inc. reported the following data:

Net income	$120,000
Depreciation expense	12,000
Loss on disposal of equipment	15,000
Increase in accounts receivable	5,000
Decrease in accounts payable	2,000

Prepare the Cash Flows from Operating Activities section of the statement of cash flows using the indirect method.

Follow My Example 14-4

Cash flows from operating activities:		
Net income		$120,000
Adjustments to reconcile net income to net cash flow from operating activities:		
Depreciation expense		12,000
Loss on disposal of equipment		15,000
Changes in current operating assets and liabilities:		
Increase in accounts receivable		(5,000)
Decrease in accounts payable		(2,000)
Net cash flow from operating activities		$140,000

Note: The change in dividends payable impacts the cash paid for dividends, which is disclosed under financing activities.

For Practice: PE 14-4A, PE 14-4B

Integrity, Objectivity, and Ethics in Business

CREDIT POLICY AND CASH FLOW

One would expect customers to pay for products and services sold on account. Unfortunately, that is not always the case. Collecting accounts receivable efficiently is the key to turning a current asset into positive cash flow. Most entrepreneurs would rather think about the exciting aspects of their business—such as product development, marketing, sales, and advertising—rather than credit collection. This can be a mistake. Hugh McHugh of Overhill Flowers, Inc., decided that he would have no more trade accounts after dealing with Christmas

orders that weren't paid for until late February, or sometimes not paid at all. As stated by one collection service, "One thing business owners always tell me is that they never thought about [collections] when they started their own business." To the small business owner, the collection of accounts receivable may mean the difference between succeeding and failing.

Source: Paulette Thomas, "Making Them Pay: The Last Thing Most Entrepreneurs Want to Think About Is Bill Collection; It Should Be One of the First Things," *The Wall Street Journal*, September 19, 2005, p. R6.

Dividends

The retained earnings account of Rundell Inc., shown on page 624, indicates cash dividends of $28,000 during the year. However, the dividends payable account, shown below, indicates that only $24,000 of the dividends was paid during the year.

Account Dividends Payable					Account No.	
					Balance	
Date	**Item**	**Debit**	**Credit**	**Debit**	**Credit**	
2010						
Jan. 1	Balance				10,000	
10	Cash paid	10,000		—	—	
June 20	Dividends declared		14,000		14,000	
July 10	Cash paid	14,000		—	—	
Dec. 20	Dividends declared		14,000		14,000	

Since dividend payments are a financing activity, the dividend payment of $24,000 is reported in the Financing Activities section of the statement of cash flows, as shown below.

Cash flows from financing activities:
    Cash paid for dividends $24,000

XM Satellite Radio has had negative cash flows from operations for most of its young corporate life. However, it has been able to grow by obtaining cash from the sale of common stock and issuing debt.

Common Stock

The common stock account increased by $8,000, and the paid-in capital in excess of par—common stock account increased by $40,000, as shown below. These increases were from issuing 4,000 shares of common stock for $12 per share.

Account Common Stock					Account No.	
					Balance	
Date	**Item**	**Debit**	**Credit**	**Debit**	**Credit**	
2010						
Jan. 1	Balance				16,000	
Nov. 1	4,000 shares issued for cash		8,000		24,000	

Account Paid-In Capital in Excess of Par—Common Stock					Account No.	
					Balance	
Date	**Item**	**Debit**	**Credit**	**Debit**	**Credit**	
2010						
Jan. 1	Balance				80,000	
Nov. 1	4,000 shares issued for cash		40,000		120,000	

This cash inflow is reported in the Financing Activities section as follows:

Cash flows from financing activities:
    Cash received from sale of common stock $48,000

Bonds Payable

The bonds payable account decreased by $50,000, as shown below. This decrease is from retiring the bonds by a cash payment for their face amount.

Account Bonds Payable						Account No.
					Balance	
Date	Item	Debit	Credit	Debit	Credit	
2010						
Jan. 1	Balance				150,000	
June 30	Retired by payment of cash at face amount	50,000			100,000	

This cash outflow is reported in the Financing Activities section as follows:

Cash flows from financing activities:
Cash paid to retire bonds payable $50,000

Building

The building account increased by $60,000, and the accumulated depreciation—building account increased by $7,000, as shown below.

Account Building						Account No.
					Balance	
Date	Item	Debit	Credit	Debit	Credit	
2010						
Jan. 1	Balance			200,000		
Dec. 27	Purchased for cash	60,000		260,000		

Account Accumulated Depreciation—Building						Account No.
					Balance	
Date	Item	Debit	Credit	Debit	Credit	
2010						
Jan. 1	Balance				58,300	
Dec. 31	Depreciation for the year		7,000		65,300	

The purchase of a building for cash of $60,000 is reported as an outflow of cash in the Investing Activities section as follows:

Cash flows from investing activities:
Cash paid for purchase of building $60,000

The credit in the accumulated depreciation—building account represents depreciation expense for the year. This depreciation expense of $7,000 on the building was added to net income in determining cash flows from operating activities, as reported in Exhibit 5, on page 626.

Land

The $45,000 decline in the land account was from two transactions, as shown below.

Account *Land*						Account No.	
					Balance		
Date		**Item**	**Debit**	**Credit**	**Debit**	**Credit**	
2010							
Jan.	1	Balance			125,000		
June	8	Sold for $72,000 cash		60,000	65,000		
Oct.	12	Purchased for $15,000 cash	15,000		80,000		

The June 8 transaction is the sale of land with a cost of $60,000 for $72,000 in cash. The $72,000 proceeds from the sale are reported in the Investing Activities section, as follows:

Cash flows from investing activities:
    Cash received from sale of land $72,000

The proceeds of $72,000 include the $12,000 gain on the sale of land and the $60,000 cost (book value) of the land. As shown in Exhibit 5, on page 626, the $12,000 gain is deducted from net income in the Cash Flows from Operating Activities section. This is so that the $12,000 cash inflow related to the gain is not included twice as a cash inflow.

The October 12 transaction is the purchase of land for cash of $15,000. This transaction is reported as an outflow of cash in the Investing Activities section, as follows:

Cash flows from investing activities:
    Cash paid for purchase of land $15,000

Example Exercise 14-5   Land Transactions on the Statement of Cash Flows

Alpha Corporation purchased land for $125,000. Later in the year, the company sold land with a book value of $165,000 for $200,000. How are the effects of these transactions reported on the statement of cash flows?

Follow My Example 14-5

The gain on sale of land is deducted from net income as shown below.
    Gain on sale of land . . . . $ (35,000)

The purchase and sale of land is reported as part of cash flows from investing activities as shown below.
    Cash received for sale of land   200,000
    Cash paid for purchase of land . . . .   (125,000)

· ·

For Practice: PE 14-5A, PE 14-5B

Preparing the Statement of Cash Flows

The statement of cash flows for Rundell Inc. using the indirect method is shown in Exhibit 6. The statement of cash flows indicates that cash increased by $71,500 during the year. The most significant increase in net cash flows ($100,500) was from operating activities. The most significant use of cash ($26,000) was for financing activities. The ending balance of cash on December 31, 2010, is $97,500. This ending cash balance is also reported on the December 31, 2010, balance sheet shown in Exhibit 3, on page 623.

Exhibit 6

Statement of Cash Flows— Indirect Method

Rundell Inc.
Statement of Cash Flows
For the Year Ended December 31, 2010

Cash flows from operating activities:			
Net income			$108,000
Adjustments to reconcile net income to net cash flow from operating activities:			
Depreciation			7,000
Gain on sale of land			(12,000)
Changes in current operating assets and liabilities:			
Increase in accounts receivable			(9,000)
Decrease in inventory			8,000
Decrease in accounts payable			(3,200)
Increase in accrued expenses payable			2,200
Decrease in income taxes payable			(500)
Net cash flow from operating activities			$100,500
Cash flows from investing activities:			
Cash from sale of land			$ 72,000
Less: Cash paid to purchase land		$15,000	
Cash paid for purchase of building		60,000	75,000
Net cash flow used for investing activities			(3,000)
Cash flows from financing activities:			
Cash received from sale of common stock			$ 48,000
Less: Cash paid to retire bonds payable		$50,000	
Cash paid for dividends		24,000	74,000
Net cash flow used for financing activities			(26,000)
Increase in cash			$ 71,500
Cash at the beginning of the year			26,000
Cash at the end of the year			$ 97,500

3 Prepare a statement of cash flows, using the direct method.

Statement of Cash Flows— The Direct Method

The direct method reports cash flows from operating activities as follows:

Cash flows from operating activities:		
Cash received from customers		$XXX
Less: Cash payments for merchandise	$XXX	
Cash payments for operating expenses	XXX	
Cash payments for interest	XXX	
Cash payments for income taxes	XXX	XXX
Net cash flows from operating activities		$XXX

The Cash Flows from Investing and Financing Activities sections of the statement of cash flows are the same under the direct and indirect methods. The amount of cash flows from operating activities is also the same.

Under the direct method, the income statement is adjusted to cash flows from operating activities as follows:

Income Statement	Adjusted to	Cash Flows from Operating Activities
Sales	→	Cash received from customers
Cost of merchandise sold	→	Cash payments for merchandise
Operating expenses:		
Depreciation expense	N/A	N/A
Other operating expenses	→	Cash payments for operating expenses
Gain on sale of land	N/A	N/A
Interest expense	→	Cash payments for interest
Income tax expense	→	Cash payments for income taxes
Net income	→	Cash flows from operating activities

N/A—Not applicable

    As shown above, depreciation expense is not adjusted or reported as part of cash flows from operating activities. This is because depreciation expense does not involve a cash outflow. The gain on sale of land is also not adjusted or reported as part of cash flows from operating activities. This is because the sale of land is reported as an investing activity rather than an operating activity.

    To illustrate the direct method, the income statement and comparative balance sheet for Rundell Inc. shown in Exhibit 3, on page 623, are used.

Cash Received from Customers

The income statement (shown in Exhibit 3) of Rundell Inc. reports sales of $1,180,000. To determine the *cash received from customers*, the $1,180,000 is adjusted for any increase or decrease in accounts receivable. The adjustment is summarized below.

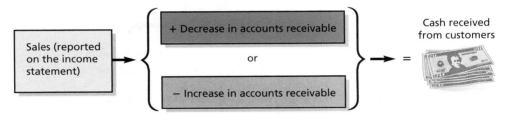

The cash received from customers is $1,171,000, computed as follows:

Sales	$1,180,000
Less increase in accounts receivable	9,000
Cash received from customers	$1,171,000

    The increase of $9,000 in accounts receivable (shown in Exhibit 3) during 2010 indicates that sales on account exceeded cash received from customers by $9,000. In other words, sales include $9,000 that did not result in a cash inflow during the year. Thus, $9,000 is deducted from sales to determine the *cash received from customers*.

Example Exercise 14-6   Cash Received from Customers— Direct Method

Sales reported on the income statement were $350,000. The accounts receivable balance declined $8,000 over the year. Determine the amount of cash received from customers.

Follow My Example 14-6

Sales	$350,000
Add decrease in accounts receivable	8,000
Cash received from customers	$358,000

For Practice: PE 14-6A, PE 14-6B

Cash Payments for Merchandise

The income statement (shown in Exhibit 3) for Rundell Inc. reports cost of merchandise sold of $790,000. To determine the *cash payments for merchandise*, the $790,000 is adjusted for any increases or decreases in inventories and accounts payable. Assuming the accounts payable are owed to merchandise suppliers, the adjustment is summarized below.

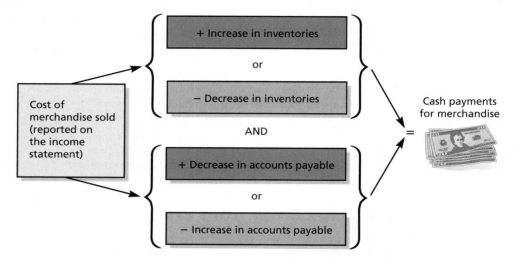

The cash payments for merchandise are $785,200, computed as follows:

Cost of merchandise sold	$790,000
Deduct decrease in inventories	(8,000)
Add decrease in accounts payable	3,200
Cash payments for merchandise	$785,200

The $8,000 decrease in inventories (from Exhibit 3) indicates that the merchandise sold exceeded the cost of the merchandise purchased by $8,000. In other words, cost of merchandise sold includes $8,000 that did not require a cash outflow during the year. Thus, $8,000 is deducted from the cost of merchandise sold in determining the *cash payments for merchandise*.

The $3,200 decrease in accounts payable (from Exhibit 3) indicates that cash payments for merchandise were $3,200 more than the purchases on account during 2010. Therefore, $3,200 is added to the cost of merchandise sold in determining the *cash payments for merchandise*.

Example Exercise 14-7 Cash Payments for Merchandise— Direct Method •••••••• 3

Cost of merchandise sold reported on the income statement was $145,000. The accounts payable balance increased $4,000, and the inventory balance increased by $9,000 over the year. Determine the amount of cash paid for merchandise.

Follow My Example 14-7

Cost of merchandise sold	$145,000
Add increase in inventories.	9,000
Deduct increase in accounts payable	(4,000)
Cash paid for merchandise	$150,000

....

For Practice: PE 14-7A, PE 14-7B

Cash Payments for Operating Expenses

The income statement (from Exhibit 3) for Rundell Inc. reports total operating expenses of $203,000, which includes depreciation expense of $7,000. Since depreciation expense does not require a cash outflow, it is omitted from *cash payments for operating expenses*.

To determine the *cash payments for operating expenses*, the other operating expenses (excluding depreciation) of $196,000 ($203,000 − $7,000) are adjusted for any increase or decrease in accrued expenses payable. Assuming that the accrued expenses payable are all operating expenses, this adjustment is summarized below.

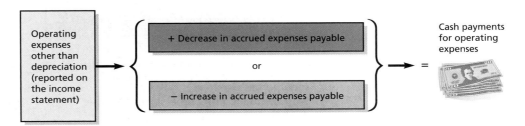

The cash payments for operating expenses is $193,800, computed as follows:

Operating expenses other than depreciation	$196,000
Deduct increase in accrued expenses payable	(2,200)
Cash payments for operating expenses	$193,800

The increase in accrued expenses payable (from Exhibit 3) indicates that the cash payments for operating expenses were $2,200 less than the amount reported for operating expenses during the year. Thus, $2,200 is deducted from the operating expenses in determining the *cash payments for operating expenses*.

Gain on Sale of Land

The income statement for Rundell Inc. (from Exhibit 3) reports a gain of $12,000 on the sale of land. The sale of land is an investing activity. Thus, the proceeds from the sale, which include the gain, are reported as part of the cash flows from investing activities.

Interest Expense

The income statement (from Exhibit 3) for Rundell Inc. reports interest expense of $8,000. To determine the *cash payments for interest*, the $8,000 is adjusted for any increases or decreases in interest payable. The adjustment is summarized below.

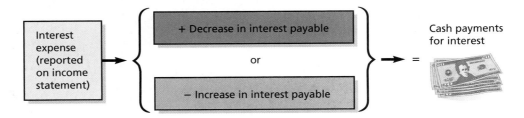

The comparative balance sheet of Rundell Inc. in Exhibit 3 indicates no interest payable. This is because the interest expense on the bonds payable is paid on June 1 and December 31. Since there is no interest payable, no adjustment of the interest expense of $8,000 is necessary.

Cash Payments for Income Taxes

The income statement (from Exhibit 3) for Rundell Inc. reports income tax expense of $83,000. To determine the *Cash payments for income taxes*, the $83,000 is adjusted for any increases or decreases in income taxes payable. The adjustment is summarized below.

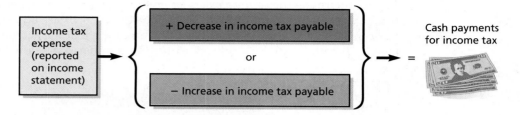

The cash payments for income taxes are $83,500, computed as follows:

Income tax expense	$83,000
Add decrease in income taxes payable	500
Cash payments for income taxes	$83,500

The $500 decrease in income taxes payable (from Exhibit 3) indicates that the cash payments for income taxes were $500 more than the amount reported for income tax expense during 2010. Thus, $500 is added to the income tax expense in determining the *cash payments for income taxes*.

Reporting Cash Flows from Operating Activities—Direct Method

The statement of cash flows for Rundell Inc. using the direct method for reporting cash flows from operating activities is shown in Exhibit 7. The portions of the

---

Exhibit 7

Statement of Cash Flows— Direct Method

Rundell Inc.
Statement of Cash Flows
For the Year Ended December 31, 2010

Cash flows from operating activities:			
Cash received from customers		$1,171,000	
Deduct: Cash payments for merchandise	$785,200		
Cash payments for operating expenses	193,800		
Cash payments for interest	8,000		
Cash payments for income taxes	83,500	1,070,500	
Net cash flow from operating activities			$100,500
Cash flows from investing activities:			
Cash from sale of land		$ 72,000	
Less: Cash paid to purchase land	$ 15,000		
Cash paid for purchase of building	60,000	75,000	
Net cash flow used for investing activities			(3,000)
Cash flows from financing activities:			
Cash received from sale of common stock		$ 48,000	
Less: Cash paid to retire bonds payable	$ 50,000		
Cash paid for dividends	24,000	74,000	
Net cash flow used for financing activities			(26,000)
Increase in cash			$ 71,500
Cash at the beginning of the year			26,000
Cash at the end of the year			$ 97,500

(continued)

Exhibit 7

(concluded)

Schedule Reconciling Net Income with Cash Flows from Operating Activities:

Cash flows from operating activities:	
Net income	$108,000
Adjustments to reconcile net income to net cash flow from operating activities:	
Depreciation	7,000
Gain on sale of land	(12,000)
Changes in current operating assets and liabilities:	
Increase in accounts receivable	(9,000)
Decrease in inventory	8,000
Decrease in accounts payable	(3,200)
Increase in accrued expenses payable	2,200
Decrease in income taxes payable	(500)
Net cash flow from operating activities	$100,500

statement that differ from those prepared under the indirect method are highlighted in color.

Exhibit 7 also includes the separate schedule reconciling net income and net cash flow from operating activities. This schedule is included in the statement of cash flows when the direct method is used. This schedule is similar to the Cash Flows from Operating Activities section prepared under the indirect method.

Financial Analysis and Interpretation

A valuable tool for evaluating the cash flows of a business is free cash flow. **Free cash flow** is a measure of operating cash flow available for corporate purposes after providing sufficient fixed asset additions to maintain current productive capacity. Thus, free cash flow can be calculated as follows:

Cash flow from operating activities	$XXX
Less: Investments in fixed assets to maintain current production	XXX
Free cash flow	$XXX

Analysts often use free cash flow, rather than cash flows from operating activities, to measure the financial strength of a business. Many high-technology firms must aggressively reinvest in new technology to remain competitive. This can reduce free cash flow. For example, Verizon Communications Inc.'s free cash flow is less than 30% of the cash flow from operating activities. In contrast, The Coca-Cola Company's free cash flow is approximately 75% of the cash flow from operating activities. Three nonfinancial companies with large free cash flows for a recent year were as follows:

	Free Cash Flow (in millions)
General Electric Company	$13,996
ExxonMobil Corporation	33,824
Microsoft Corporation	15,532

To illustrate, the cash flow from operating activities for Intuit Inc., the developer of TurboTax®, was $727 million in a recent fiscal year. The statement of cash flows indicated that the cash invested in property, plant, and equipment was $105 million. Assuming that the amount invested in property, plant, and equipment maintained existing operations, free cash flow would be calculated as follows (in millions):

Cash flow from operating activities	$727
Less: Investments in fixed assets to maintain current production	105
Free cash flow	$622

During this period, Intuit generated free cash flow in excess of $600 million, which was 86% of cash flows from operations and over 23% of sales.

Positive free cash flow is considered favorable. A company that has free cash flow is able to fund internal growth, retire debt, pay dividends, and enjoy financial flexibility. A company with no free cash flow is unable to maintain current productive capacity. Lack of free cash flow can be an early indicator of liquidity problems. As stated by one analyst, "Free cash flow gives the company firepower to reduce debt and ultimately generate consistent, actual income."[6]

Source: "CFO Free Cash Flow Scorecard," *CFO Magazine*, January 1, 2005.

6 Jill Krutick, *Fortune*, March 30, 1998, p. 106.

f·a·i

APPENDIX

Spreadsheet (Work Sheet) for Statement of Cash Flows— The Indirect Method

A spreadsheet (work sheet) may be used in preparing the statement of cash flows. However, whether or not a spreadsheet (work sheet) is used, the concepts presented in this chapter are not affected.

The data for Rundell Inc., presented in Exhibit 3, are used as a basis for illustrating the spreadsheet (work sheet) for the indirect method. The steps in preparing this spreadsheet (work sheet), shown in Exhibit 8, are as follows:

Step 1. List the title of each balance sheet account in the Accounts column.

Step 2. For each balance sheet account, enter its balance as of December 31, 2009, in the first column and its balance as of December 31, 2010, in the last column. Place the credit balances in parentheses.

Step 3. Add the December 31, 2009 and 2010 column totals, which should total to zero.

Step 4. Analyze the change during the year in each noncash account to determine its net increase (decrease) and classify the change as affecting cash flows from operating activities, investing activities, financing activities, or noncash investing and financing activities.

Step 5. Indicate the effect of the change on cash flows by making entries in the Transactions columns.

Step 6. After all noncash accounts have been analyzed, enter the net increase (decrease) in cash during the period.

Step 7. Add the Debit and Credit Transactions columns. The totals should be equal.

Analyzing Accounts

In analyzing the noncash accounts (Step 4), try to determine the type of cash flow activity (operating, investing, or financing) that led to the change in account. As each noncash account is analyzed, an entry (Step 5) is made on the spreadsheet (work sheet) for the type of cash flow activity that caused the change. After all noncash accounts have been analyzed, an entry (Step 6) is made for the increase (decrease) in cash during the period.

The entries made on the spreadsheet are not posted to the ledger. They are only used in preparing and summarizing the data on the spreadsheet.

The order in which the accounts are analyzed is not important. However, it is more efficient to begin with Retained Earnings and proceed upward in the account listing.

Retained Earnings

The spreadsheet (work sheet) shows a Retained Earnings balance of $202,300 at December 31, 2009, and $282,300 at December 31, 2010. Thus, Retained Earnings increased $80,000 during the year. This increase is from the following:

1. Net income of $108,000
2. Declaring cash dividends of $28,000

To identify the cash flows from these activities, two entries are made on the spreadsheet.

The $108,000 is reported on the statement of cash flows as part of "cash flows from operating activities." Thus, an entry is made in the Transactions columns on the spreadsheet as follows:

(a) Operating Activities—Net Income 108,000
  Retained Earnings 108,000

The preceding entry accounts for the net income portion of the change to Retained Earnings. It also identifies the cash flow in the bottom portion of the spreadsheet as related to operating activities.

Exhibit 8

End-of-Period Spreadsheet (Work Sheet) for Statement of Cash Flows—Indirect Method

Step 2

	A	B	C	D	E	F	G
1	Rundell Inc.						
2	End-of-Period Spreadsheet (Work Sheet) for Statement of Cash Flows						
3	For the Year Ended December 31, 2010						
4	Accounts	Balance,	Transactions				Balance,
5		Dec. 31, 2009	Debit		Credit		Dec. 31, 2010
6	Cash	26,000	(o)	71,500			97,500
7	Accounts receivable (net)	65,000	(n)	9,000			74,000
8	Inventories	180,000			(m)	8,000	172,000
9	Land	125,000	(k)	15,000	(l)	60,000	80,000
10	Building	200,000	(j)	60,000			260,000
11	Accumulated depreciation—building	(58,300)			(i)	7,000	(65,300)
12	Accounts payable (merchandise creditors)	(46,700)	(h)	3,200			(43,500)
13	Accrued expenses payable (operating expenses)	(24,300)			(g)	2,200	(26,500)
14	Income taxes payable	(8,400)	(f)	500			(7,900)
15	Dividends payable	(10,000)			(e)	4,000	(14,000)
16	Bonds payable	(150,000)	(d)	50,000			(100,000)
17	Common stock	(16,000)			(c)	8,000	(24,000)
18	Paid-in capital in excess of par	(80,000)			(c)	40,000	(120,000)
19	Retained earnings	(202,300)	(b)	28,000	(a)	108,000	(282,300)
20	Totals	0		237,200		237,200	0
21	Operating activities:						
22	Net income		(a)	108,000			
23	Depreciation of building		(i)	7,000			
24	Gain on sale of land				(l)	12,000	
25	Increase in accounts receivable				(n)	9,000	
26	Decrease in inventories		(m)	8,000			
27	Decrease in accounts payable				(h)	3,200	
28	Increase in accrued expenses payable		(g)	2,200			
29	Decrease in income taxes payable				(f)	500	
30	Investing activities:						
31	Sale of land		(l)	72,000			
32	Purchase of land				(k)	15,000	
33	Purchase of building				(j)	60,000	
34	Financing activities:						
35	Issued common stock		(c)	48,000			
36	Retired bonds payable				(d)	50,000	
37	Declared cash dividends				(b)	28,000	
38	Increase in dividends payable		(e)	4,000			
39	Net increase in cash				(o)	71,500	
40	Totals			249,200		249,200	

Step 1

Step 3 → (row 20, col B) Step 3 ← (row 20, col G)

Steps 4–7

The $28,000 of dividends is reported as a financing activity on the statement of cash flows. Thus, an entry is made in the Transactions columns on the spreadsheet as follows:

| (b) | Retained Earnings | 28,000 | |
| | Financing Activities—Declared Cash Dividends | | 28,000 |

The preceding entry accounts for the dividends portion of the change to Retained Earnings. It also identifies the cash flow in the bottom portion of the spreadsheet as related to financing activities. The $28,000 of declared dividends will be adjusted later for the actual amount of cash dividends paid during the year.

Other Accounts

The entries for the other noncash accounts are made in the spreadsheet in a manner similar to entries (a) and (b). A summary of these entries is as follows:

(c)	Financing Activities—Issued Common Stock	48,000	
	Common Stock		8,000
	Paid-In Capital in Excess of Par—Common Stock		40,000
(d)	Bonds Payable	50,000	
	Financing Activities—Retired Bonds Payable		50,000
(e)	Financing Activities—Increase in Dividends Payable	4,000	
	Dividends Payable		4,000
(f)	Income Taxes Payable	500	
	Operating Activities—Decrease in Income Taxes Payable		500
(g)	Operating Activities—Increase in Accrued Expenses Payable	2,200	
	Accrued Expenses Payable		2,200
(h)	Accounts Payable	3,200	
	Operating Activities—Decrease in Accounts Payable		3,200
(i)	Operating Activities—Depreciation of Building	7,000	
	Accumulated Depreciation—Building		7,000
(j)	Building	60,000	
	Investing Activities—Purchase of Building		60,000
(k)	Land	15,000	
	Investing Activities—Purchase of Land		15,000
(l)	Investing Activities—Sale of Land	72,000	
	Operating Activities—Gain on Sale of Land		12,000
	Land		60,000
(m)	Operating Activities—Decrease in Inventories	8,000	
	Inventories		8,000
(n)	Accounts Receivable	9,000	
	Operating Activities—Increase in Accounts Receivable		9,000
(o)	Cash	71,500	
	Net Increase in Cash		71,500

After all the balance sheet accounts are analyzed and the entries made on the spreadsheet (work sheet), all the operating, investing, and financing activities are identified in the bottom portion of the spreadsheet. The accuracy of the entries is verified by totaling the Debit and Credit Transactions columns. The totals of the columns should be equal.

Preparing the Statement of Cash Flows

The statement of cash flows prepared from the spreadsheet is identical to the statement in Exhibit 6. The data for the three sections of the statement are obtained from the bottom portion of the spreadsheet.

1 Describe the cash flow activities reported in the statement of cash flows.

Key Points	Key Learning Outcomes	Example Exercises	Practice Exercises
The statement of cash flows reports cash receipts and cash payments by three types of activities: operating activities, investing activities, and financing activities. Investing and financing for a business may be affected by transactions that do not involve cash. The effect of such transactions should be reported in a separate schedule accompanying the statement of cash flows.	• Classify transactions that either provide or use cash into either operating, investing, or financing activities.	**14-1**	14-1A, 14-1B

2 Prepare a statement of cash flows, using the indirect method.

Key Points	Key Learning Outcomes	Example Exercises	Practice Exercises
The changes in the noncash balance sheet accounts are used to develop the statement of cash flows, beginning with the cash flows from operating activities.			
Determine the cash flows from operating activities using the indirect method by adjusting net income for expenses that do not require cash and for gains and losses from disposal of fixed assets.	• Adjust net income for noncash expenses and gains and losses from asset disposals under the indirect method.	**14-2**	14-2A, 14-2B
Determine the cash flows from operating activities using the indirect method by adjusting net income for changes in current operating assets and liabilities.	• Adjust net income for changes in current operating assets and liabilities under the indirect method.	**14-3**	14-3A, 14-3B
Report cash flows from operating activities under the indirect method.	• Prepare the cash flows from operating activities under the indirect method in proper form.	**14-4**	14-4A, 14-4B
Report investing and financing activities on the statement of cash flows.	• Prepare the remainder of the statement of cash flows by reporting investing and financing activities.	**14-5**	14-5A, 14-5B

3 Prepare a statement of cash flows, using the direct method.

Key Points	Key Learning Outcomes	Example Exercises	Practice Exercises
The direct method reports cash flows from operating activities by major classes of operating cash receipts and cash payments. The difference between the major classes of total operating cash receipts and total operating cash payments is the net cash flow from operating activities. The investing and financing activities sections of the statement are the same as under the indirect method.	• Prepare the cash flows from operating activities and the remainder of the statement of cash flows under the direct method.	**14-6** **14-7**	14-6A, 14-6B 14-7A, 14-7B

Key Terms

cash flow per share (622)

cash flows from financing activities (619)

cash flows from investing activities (619)

cash flows from operating activities (618)

direct method (619)

free cash flow (637)

indirect method (620)

statement of cash flows (618)

Illustrative Problem

The comparative balance sheet of Dowling Company for December 31, 2010 and 2009, is as follows:

Dowling Company
Comparative Balance Sheet
December 31, 2010 and 2009

	2010	2009
Assets		
Cash	$ 140,350	$ 95,900
Accounts receivable (net)	95,300	102,300
Inventories	165,200	157,900
Prepaid expenses	6,240	5,860
Investments (long-term)	35,700	84,700
Land	75,000	90,000
Buildings	375,000	260,000
Accumulated depreciation—buildings	(71,300)	(58,300)
Machinery and equipment	428,300	428,300
Accumulated depreciation—machinery and equipment	(148,500)	(138,000)
Patents	58,000	65,000
Total assets	$1,159,290	$1,093,660
Liabilities and Stockholders' Equity		
Accounts payable (merchandise creditors)	$ 43,500	$ 46,700
Accrued expenses payable (operating expenses)	14,000	12,500
Income taxes payable	7,900	8,400
Dividends payable	14,000	10,000
Mortgage note payable, due 2021	40,000	0
Bonds payable	150,000	250,000
Common stock, $30 par	450,000	375,000
Excess of issue price over par—common stock	66,250	41,250
Retained earnings	373,640	349,810
Total liabilities and stockholders' equity	$1,159,290	$1,093,660

The income statement for Dowling Company is shown here.

Dowling Company
Income Statement
For the Year Ended December 31, 2010

Sales		$1,100,000
Cost of merchandise sold		710,000
Gross profit		$ 390,000
Operating expenses:		
Depreciation expense	$ 23,500	
Patent amortization	7,000	
Other operating expenses	196,000	
Total operating expenses		226,500
Income from operations		$ 163,500
Other income:		
Gain on sale of investments	$ 11,000	
Other expense:		
Interest expense	26,000	(15,000)
Income before income tax		$ 148,500
Income tax expense		50,000
Net income		$ 98,500

An examination of the accounting records revealed the following additional information applicable to 2010:

a. Land costing $15,000 was sold for $15,000.
b. A mortgage note was issued for $40,000.
c. A building costing $115,000 was constructed.
d. 2,500 shares of common stock were issued at 40 in exchange for the bonds payable.
e. Cash dividends declared were $74,670.

Instructions

1. Prepare a statement of cash flows, using the indirect method of reporting cash flows from operating activities.
2. Prepare a statement of cash flows, using the direct method of reporting cash flows from operating activities.

Solution

1.

Dowling Company Statement of Cash Flows—Indirect Method For the Year Ended December 31, 2010			
Cash flows from operating activities:			
Net income		$ 98,500	
Adjustments to reconcile net income to net cash flow from operating activities:			
Depreciation		23,500	
Amortization of patents		7,000	
Gain on sale of investments		(11,000)	
Changes in current operating assets and liabilities:			
Decrease in accounts receivable		7,000	
Increase in inventories		(7,300)	
Increase in prepaid expenses		(380)	
Decrease in accounts payable		(3,200)	
Increase in accrued expenses payable		1,500	
Decrease in income taxes payable		(500)	
Net cash flow from operating activities			$115,120
Cash flows from investing activities:			
Cash received from sale of:			
Investments	$60,000		
Land	15,000	$ 75,000	
Less: Cash paid for construction of building		115,000	
Net cash flow used for investing activities			(40,000)
Cash flows from financing activities:			
Cash received from issuing mortgage note payable		$ 40,000	
Less: Cash paid for dividends		70,670*	
Net cash flow used for financing activities			(30,670)
Increase in cash			$ 44,450
Cash at the beginning of the year			95,900
Cash at the end of the year			$140,350
Schedule of Noncash Investing and Financing Activities:			
Issued common stock to retire bonds payable			$100,000
*$70,670 = $74,670 − $4,000 (increase in dividends)			

2.

Dowling Company
Statement of Cash Flows—Direct Method
For the Year Ended December 31, 2010

Cash flows from operating activities:			
Cash received from customers[1]		$1,107,000	
Deduct: Cash paid for merchandise[2]	$720,500		
Cash paid for operating expenses[3]	194,880		
Cash paid for interest expense	26,000		
Cash paid for income tax[4]	50,500	991,880	
Net cash flow from operating activities			$115,120
Cash flows from investing activities:			
Cash received from sale of:			
Investments	$ 60,000		
Land	15,000	$ 75,000	
Less: Cash paid for construction of building		115,000	
Net cash flow used for investing activities			(40,000)
Cash flows from financing activities:			
Cash received from issuing mortgage note payable		$ 40,000	
Less: Cash paid for dividends[5]		70,670	
Net cash flow used for financing activities			(30,670)
Increase in cash			$ 44,450
Cash at the beginning of the year			95,900
Cash at the end of the year			$140,350
Schedule of Noncash Investing and			
Financing Activities:			
Issued common stock to retire bonds payable			$100,000
Schedule Reconciling Net Income with Cash Flows			
from Operating Activities[6]			

Computations:

[1]$1,100,000 + $7,000 = $1,107,000
[2]$710,000 + $3,200 + $7,300 = $720,500
[3]$196,000 + $380 − $1,500 = $194,880
[4]$50,000 + $500 = $50,500

[5]$74,670 + $10,000 − $14,000 = $70,670
[6]The content of this schedule is the same as the Operating Activities section of part (1) of this solution and is not reproduced here for the sake of brevity.

Self-Examination Questions (Answers at End of Chapter)

1. An example of a cash flow from an operating activity is:
   A. receipt of cash from the sale of stock.
   B. receipt of cash from the sale of bonds.
   C. payment of cash for dividends.
   D. receipt of cash from customers on account.

2. An example of a cash flow from an investing activity is:
   A. receipt of cash from the sale of equipment.
   B. receipt of cash from the sale of stock.
   C. payment of cash for dividends.
   D. payment of cash to acquire treasury stock.

3. An example of a cash flow from a financing activity is:
   A. receipt of cash from customers on account.
   B. receipt of cash from the sale of equipment.
   C. payment of cash for dividends.
   D. payment of cash to acquire land.

4. Which of the following methods of reporting cash flows from operating activities adjusts net income for revenues and expenses not involving the receipt or payment of cash?
   A. Direct method   C. Reciprocal method
   B. Purchase method   D. Indirect method

5. The net income reported on the income statement for the year was $55,000, and depreciation of fixed assets for the year was $22,000. The balances of the current asset and current liability accounts at the beginning and end of the year are shown below.

	End	Beginning
Cash	$ 65,000	$ 70,000
Accounts receivable	100,000	90,000
Inventories	145,000	150,000
Prepaid expenses	7,500	8,000
Accounts payable (merchandise creditors)	51,000	58,000

The total amount reported for cash flows from operating activities in the statement of cash flows, using the indirect method, is:

A. $33,000. C. $65,500.
B. $55,000. D. $77,000.

Eye Openers

1. What is the principal disadvantage of the direct method of reporting cash flows from operating activities?
2. What are the major advantages of the indirect method of reporting cash flows from operating activities?
3. A corporation issued $500,000 of common stock in exchange for $500,000 of fixed assets. Where would this transaction be reported on the statement of cash flows?
4. A retail business, using the accrual method of accounting, owed merchandise creditors (accounts payable) $300,000 at the beginning of the year and $340,000 at the end of the year. How would the $40,000 increase be used to adjust net income in determining the amount of cash flows from operating activities by the indirect method? Explain.
5. If salaries payable was $90,000 at the beginning of the year and $70,000 at the end of the year, should $20,000 be added to or deducted from income to determine the amount of cash flows from operating activities by the indirect method? Explain.
6. A long-term investment in bonds with a cost of $60,000 was sold for $72,000 cash. (a) What was the gain or loss on the sale? (b) What was the effect of the transaction on cash flows? (c) How should the transaction be reported in the statement of cash flows if cash flows from operating activities are reported by the indirect method?
7. A corporation issued $6,000,000 of 20-year bonds for cash at 104. How would the transaction be reported on the statement of cash flows?
8. Fully depreciated equipment costing $100,000 was discarded. What was the effect of the transaction on cash flows if (a) $24,000 cash is received, (b) no cash is received?
9. For the current year, Bearings Company decided to switch from the indirect method to the direct method for reporting cash flows from operating activities on the statement of cash flows. Will the change cause the amount of net cash flow from operating activities to be (a) larger, (b) smaller, or (c) the same as if the indirect method had been used? Explain.
10. Name five common major classes of operating cash receipts or operating cash payments presented on the statement of cash flows when the cash flows from operating activities are reported by the direct method.
11. In a recent annual report, eBay Inc. reported that during the year it issued stock of $128 million for acquisitions. How would this be reported on the statement of cash flows?

Practice Exercises

PE 14-1A
Classifying cash flows
obj. 1
EE 14-1   p. 622

Identify whether each of the following would be reported as an operating, investing, or financing activity in the statement of cash flows.

a. Issuance of common stock
b. Purchase of land
c. Payment of accounts payable

d. Retirement of bonds payable
e. Payment for administrative expenses
f. Cash received from customers

PE 14-1B
Classifying cash flows
obj. 1
EE 14-1   p. 622

Identify whether each of the following would be reported as an operating, investing, or financing activity in the statement of cash flows.

a. Payment for selling expenses
b. Issuance of bonds payable
c. Disposal of equipment

d. Cash sales
e. Purchase of investments
f. Collection of accounts receivable

PE 14-2A
Adjustments to net income—indirect method
obj. 2
EE 14-2   p. 626

Choi Corporation's accumulated depreciation—furniture increased by $7,000, while $2,600 of patents were amortized between balance sheet dates. There were no purchases or sales of depreciable or intangible assets during the year. In addition, the income statement showed a gain of $15,000 from the sale of land. Reconcile a net income of $140,000 to net cash flow from operating activities.

PE 14-2B
Adjustments to net income—indirect method
obj. 2
EE 14-2   p. 626

Singh Corporation's accumulated depreciation—equipment increased by $6,000, while $2,200 of patents were amortized between balance sheet dates. There were no purchases or sales of depreciable or intangible assets during the year. In addition, the income statement showed a loss of $3,200 from the sale of investments. Reconcile a net income of $86,000 to net cash flow from operating activities.

PE 14-3A
Changes in current operating assets and liabilities—indirect method
obj. 2
EE 14-3   p. 627

Watson Corporation's comparative balance sheet for current assets and liabilities was as follows:

	Dec. 31, 2010	Dec. 31, 2009
Accounts receivable	$30,000	$24,000
Inventory	58,000	49,500
Accounts payable	46,000	34,500
Dividends payable	14,000	18,000

Adjust net income of $320,000 for changes in operating assets and liabilities to arrive at net cash flow from operating activities.

PE 14-3B
Changes in current operating assets and liabilities—indirect method
obj. 2
EE 14-3   p. 627

Chopra Corporation's comparative balance sheet for current assets and liabilities was as follows:

	Dec. 31, 2010	Dec. 31, 2009
Accounts receivable	$15,000	$18,000
Inventory	10,000	8,600
Accounts payable	9,000	7,900
Dividends payable	27,500	29,500

Adjust net income of $115,000 for changes in operating assets and liabilities to arrive at net cash flow from operating activities.

PE 14-4A
Cash flows from operating activities— indirect method
obj. 2
EE 14-4   p. 628

Trahan Inc. reported the following data:

Net income	$175,000
Depreciation expense	30,000
Loss on disposal of equipment	12,200
Increase in accounts receivable	10,800
Increase in accounts payable	5,600

Prepare the Cash Flows from Operating Activities section of the statement of cash flows using the indirect method.

PE 14-4B
Cash flows from operating activities— indirect method
obj. 2
EE 14-4   p. 628

Daly Inc. reported the following data:

Net income	$225,000
Depreciation expense	25,000
Gain on disposal of equipment	20,500
Decrease in accounts receivable	14,000
Decrease in accounts payable	3,600

Prepare the Cash Flows from Operating Activities section of the statement of cash flows using the indirect method.

PE 14-5A
Land transactions on the statement of cash flows
obj. 2
EE 14-5   p. 631

Slocum Corporation purchased land for $600,000. Later in the year, the company sold land with a book value of $360,000 for $410,000. How are the effects of these transactions reported on the statement of cash flows?

PE 14-5B
Land transactions on the statement of cash flows
obj. 2
EE 14-5   p. 631

Verplank Corporation purchased land for $340,000. Later in the year, the company sold land with a book value of $145,000 for $110,000. How are the effects of these transactions reported on the statement of cash flows?

PE 14-6A
Cash received from customers—direct method
obj. 3
EE 14-6   p. 633

Sales reported on the income statement were $46,200. The accounts receivable balance decreased $3,400 over the year. Determine the amount of cash received from customers.

PE 14-6B
Cash received from customers—direct method
obj. 3
EE 14-6   p. 633

Sales reported on the income statement were $521,000. The accounts receivable balance increased $56,000 over the year. Determine the amount of cash received from customers.

PE 14-7A
Cash payments for merchandise—direct method
obj. 3
EE 14-7   p. 634

Cost of merchandise sold reported on the income statement was $130,000. The accounts payable balance increased $6,200, and the inventory balance increased by $11,400 over the year. Determine the amount of cash paid for merchandise.

PE 14-7B
Cash payments for merchandise—direct method

obj. 3

EE 14-7   p. 634

Cost of merchandise sold reported on the income statement was $420,000. The accounts payable balance decreased $22,500, and the inventory balance decreased by $26,000 over the year. Determine the amount of cash paid for merchandise.

Exercises

EX 14-1
Cash flows from operating activities—net loss

obj. 1

On its income statement for a recent year, Continental Airlines, Inc. reported a net *loss* of $68 million from operations. On its statement of cash flows, it reported $457 million of cash flows from operating activities.

➤ Explain this apparent contradiction between the loss and the positive cash flows.

EX 14-2
Effect of transactions on cash flows

obj. 1

✔ c. Cash receipt, $500,000

State the effect (cash receipt or payment and amount) of each of the following transactions, considered individually, on cash flows:

a. Sold a new issue of $200,000 of bonds at 99.
b. Purchased 4,000 shares of $35 par common stock as treasury stock at $70 per share.
c. Sold 10,000 shares of $20 par common stock for $50 per share.
d. Purchased a building by paying $60,000 cash and issuing a $100,000 mortgage note payable.
e. Retired $250,000 of bonds, on which there was $2,500 of unamortized discount, for $260,000.
f. Purchased land for $320,000 cash.
g. Paid dividends of $2.00 per share. There were 25,000 shares issued and 4,000 shares of treasury stock.
h. Sold equipment with a book value of $50,000 for $72,000.

EX 14-3
Classifying cash flows

obj. 1

Identify the type of cash flow activity for each of the following events (operating, investing, or financing):

a. Issued common stock.
b. Redeemed bonds.
c. Issued preferred stock.
d. Purchased patents.
e. Net income.
f. Paid cash dividends.
g. Purchased treasury stock.
h. Sold long-term investments.
i. Sold equipment.
j. Purchased buildings.
k. Issued bonds.

EX 14-4
Cash flows from operating activities—indirect method

obj. 2

Indicate whether each of the following would be added to or deducted from net income in determining net cash flow from operating activities by the indirect method:

a. Decrease in accounts receivable
b. Increase in notes payable due in 90 days to vendors
c. Decrease in salaries payable
d. Decrease in prepaid expenses
e. Gain on retirement of long-term debt
f. Decrease in accounts payable
g. Increase in notes receivable due in 90 days from customers
h. Depreciation of fixed assets
i. Increase in merchandise inventory
j. Amortization of patent
k. Loss on disposal of fixed assets

EX 14-5
Cash flows from operating activities— indirect method

obj. 2

✔ Net cash flow from operating activities, $153,920

The net income reported on the income statement for the current year was $132,000. Depreciation recorded on store equipment for the year amounted to $21,800. Balances of the current asset and current liability accounts at the beginning and end of the year are as follows:

	End of Year	Beginning of Year
Cash	$52,300	$48,200
Accounts receivable (net)	37,500	35,600
Merchandise inventory	51,200	54,220
Prepaid expenses	6,000	4,600
Accounts payable (merchandise creditors)	49,000	45,600
Wages payable	26,800	29,800

Prepare the Cash Flows from Operating Activities section of the statement of cash flows, using the indirect method.

EX 14-6
Net cash flow from operating activities— indirect method

objs. 1, 2

✔ Cash flows from operating activities, $258,950

The net income reported on the income statement for the current year was $210,000. Depreciation recorded on equipment and a building amounted to $62,500 for the year. Balances of the current asset and current liability accounts at the beginning and end of the year are as follows:

	End of Year	Beginning of Year
Cash	$ 56,000	$ 59,500
Accounts receivable (net)	71,000	73,400
Inventories	140,000	126,500
Prepaid expenses	7,800	8,400
Accounts payable (merchandise creditors)	62,600	66,400
Salaries payable	9,000	8,250

a. Prepare the Cash Flows from Operating Activities section of the statement of cash flows, using the indirect method.

b. ━━━▶ If the direct method had been used, would the net cash flow from operating activities have been the same? Explain.

EX 14-7
Net cash flow from operating activities— indirect method

objs. 1, 2

✔ Cash flows from operating activities, $328,700

The income statement disclosed the following items for 2010:

Depreciation expense	$ 36,000
Gain on disposal of equipment	21,000
Net income	317,500

Balances of the current assets and current liability accounts changed between December 31, 2009, and December 31, 2010, as follows:

Accounts receivable	$5,600
Inventory	3,200*
Prepaid insurance	1,200*
Accounts payable	3,800*
Income taxes payable	1,200
Dividends payable	850

*Decrease

Prepare the Cash Flows from Operating Activities section of the statement of cash flows, using the indirect method.

EX 14-8
Determining cash payments to stockholders

obj. 2

The board of directors declared cash dividends totaling $152,000 during the current year. The comparative balance sheet indicates dividends payable of $42,000 at the beginning of the year and $38,000 at the end of the year. What was the amount of cash payments to stockholders during the year?

EX 14-9
Reporting changes in equipment on statement of cash flows
obj. 2

An analysis of the general ledger accounts indicates that office equipment, which cost $67,000 and on which accumulated depreciation totaled $22,500 on the date of sale, was sold for $38,600 during the year. Using this information, indicate the items to be reported on the statement of cash flows.

EX 14-10
Reporting changes in equipment on statement of cash flows
obj. 2

An analysis of the general ledger accounts indicates that delivery equipment, which cost $96,000 and on which accumulated depreciation totaled $42,100 on the date of sale, was sold for $46,500 during the year. Using this information, indicate the items to be reported on the statement of cash flows.

EX 14-11
Reporting land transactions on statement of cash flows
obj. 2

On the basis of the details of the following fixed asset account, indicate the items to be reported on the statement of cash flows:

ACCOUNT *Land*   ACCOUNT NO.

Date		Item	Debit	Credit	Balance Debit	Balance Credit
2010						
Jan.	1	Balance			1,200,000	
Feb.	5	Purchased for cash	380,000		1,580,000	
Oct.	30	Sold for $210,000		180,000	1,400,000	

EX 14-12
Reporting stockholders' equity items on statement of cash flows
obj. 2

On the basis of the following stockholders' equity accounts, indicate the items, exclusive of net income, to be reported on the statement of cash flows. There were no unpaid dividends at either the beginning or the end of the year.

ACCOUNT *Common Stock, $10 par*   ACCOUNT NO.

Date		Item	Debit	Credit	Balance Debit	Balance Credit
2010						
Jan.	1	Balance, 60,000 shares				1,200,000
Feb.	11	15,000 shares issued for cash		300,000		1,500,000
June	30	2,200-share stock dividend		44,000		1,544,000

ACCOUNT *Paid-In Capital in Excess of Par—Common Stock*   ACCOUNT NO.

Date		Item	Debit	Credit	Balance Debit	Balance Credit
2010						
Jan.	1	Balance				200,000
Feb.	11	15,000 shares issued for cash		480,000		680,000
June	30	Stock dividend		79,200		759,200

ACCOUNT *Retained Earnings*   **ACCOUNT NO.**

Date		Item	Debit	Credit	Balance Debit	Balance Credit
2010						
Jan.	1	Balance				1,000,000
June	30	Stock dividend	123,200			876,800
Dec.	30	Cash dividend	115,800			761,000
	31	Net income		720,000		1,481,000

EX 14-13
Reporting land acqui-
sition for cash and
mortgage note on
statement of cash
flows

obj. 2

On the basis of the details of the following fixed asset account, indicate the items to be reported on the statement of cash flows:

ACCOUNT *Land*   **ACCOUNT NO.**

Date		Item	Debit	Credit	Balance Debit	Balance Credit
2010						
Jan.	1	Balance			260,000	
Feb.	10	Purchased for cash	410,000		670,000	
Nov.	20	Purchased with long-term				
		mortgage note	540,000		1,210,000	

EX 14-14
Reporting issuance
and retirement of
long-term debt

obj. 2

On the basis of the details of the following bonds payable and related discount accounts, indicate the items to be reported in the Financing section of the statement of cash flows, assuming no gain or loss on retiring the bonds:

ACCOUNT *Bonds Payable*   **ACCOUNT NO.**

Date		Item	Debit	Credit	Balance Debit	Balance Credit
2010						
Jan.	1	Balance				500,000
	3	Retire bonds	100,000			400,000
July	30	Issue bonds		300,000		700,000

ACCOUNT *Discount on Bond Payable*   **ACCOUNT NO.**

Date		Item	Debit	Credit	Balance Debit	Balance Credit
2010						
Jan.	1	Balance			22,500	
	3	Retire bonds		8,000	14,500	
July	30	Issue bonds	20,000		34,500	
Dec.	31	Amortize discount		1,750	32,750	

EX 14-15
**Determining net
income from net
cash flow from
operating activities**

obj. 2

✔ Net income,
$155,350

Sanhueza, Inc., reported a net cash flow from operating activities of $162,500 on its statement of cash flows for the year ended December 31, 2010. The following information was reported in the Cash Flows from Operating Activities section of the statement of cash flows, using the indirect method:

Decrease in income taxes payable	$ 3,500
Decrease in inventories	8,700
Depreciation	13,400
Gain on sale of investments	6,000
Increase in accounts payable	2,400
Increase in prepaid expenses	1,350
Increase in accounts receivable	6,500

Determine the net income reported by Sanhueza, Inc., for the year ended December 31, 2010.

EX 14-16
**Cash flows from
operating activities—
indirect method**

obj. 2

✔ Net cash flow
from operating
activities, $3,048

Selected data derived from the income statement and balance sheet of Jones Soda Co. for a recent year are as follows:

Income statement data (in thousands):

Net earnings	$4,574
Depreciation expense	256
Stock-based compensation expense (noncash)	1,196

Balance sheet data (in thousands):

Increase in accounts receivable	$3,214
Increase in inventory	1,089
Increase in prepaid expenses	566
Increase in accounts payable	1,891

a. Prepare the Cash Flows from Operating Activities section of the statement of cash flows using the indirect method for Jones Soda Co. for the year.
b. ━━━▶ Interpret your results in part (a).

EX 14-17
**Statement of cash
flows—indirect
method**

obj. 2

✔ Net cash flow
from operating
activities, $30

The comparative balance sheet of Tru-Built Construction Inc. for December 31, 2010 and 2009, is as follows:

	Dec. 31, 2010	Dec. 31, 2009
Assets		
Cash	$ 98	$ 32
Accounts receivable (net)	56	40
Inventories	35	22
Land	80	90
Equipment	45	35
Accumulated depreciation—equipment	(12)	(6)
Total	$302	$213
Liabilities and Stockholders' Equity		
Accounts payable (merchandise creditors)	$ 35	$ 32
Dividends payable	6	—
Common stock, $1 par	20	10
Paid-in capital in excess of par—common stock	50	25
Retained earnings	191	146
Total	$302	$213

The following additional information is taken from the records:
a. Land was sold for $25.
b. Equipment was acquired for cash.
c. There were no disposals of equipment during the year.
d. The common stock was issued for cash.
e. There was a $65 credit to Retained Earnings for net income.
f. There was a $20 debit to Retained Earnings for cash dividends declared.

Prepare a statement of cash flows, using the indirect method of presenting cash flows from operating activities.

EX 14-18
Statement of cash flows—indirect method

obj. 2

List the errors you find in the following statement of cash flows. The cash balance at the beginning of the year was $100,320. All other amounts are correct, except the cash balance at the end of the year.

Devon Inc.
Statement of Cash Flows
For the Year Ended December 31, 2010

Cash flows from operating activities:			
Net income		$148,080	
Adjustments to reconcile net income to net cash flow			
from operating activities:			
Depreciation		42,000	
Gain on sale of investements		7,200	
Changes in current operating assets and liabilities:			
Increase in accounts receivable		11,400	
Increase in inventories		(14,760)	
Increase in accounts payable		(4,440)	
Decrease in accrued expenses payable		(1,080)	
Net cash flow from operating activities			$188,400
Cash flows from investing activities:			
Cash received from sale of investments		$102,000	
Less: Cash paid for purchase of land	$108,000		
Cash paid for purchase of equipment	180,200	288,200	
Net cash flow used for investing activities			(186,200)
Cash flows from financing activities:			
Cash received from sale of common stock		$128,400	
Cash paid for dividends		54,000	
Net cash flow provided by financing activities			182,400
Increase in cash			$184,600
Cash at the end of the year			126,300
Cash at the beginning of the year			$310,900

EX 14-19
Cash flows from operating activities—direct method

obj. 3

✔ a. $728,500

The cash flows from operating activities are reported by the direct method on the statement of cash flows. Determine the following:
a. If sales for the current year were $685,000 and accounts receivable decreased by $43,500 during the year, what was the amount of cash received from customers?
b. If income tax expense for the current year was $46,000 and income tax payable decreased by $5,200 during the year, what was the amount of cash payments for income tax?

EX 14-20
Cash paid for merchandise purchases

obj. 3

The cost of merchandise sold for Kohl's Corporation for a recent year was $9,891 million. The balance sheet showed the following current account balances (in millions):

	Balance, End of Year	Balance, Beginning of Year
Merchandise inventories	$2,588	$2,238
Accounts payable	934	830

Determine the amount of cash payments for merchandise.

EX 14-21
Determining selected amounts for cash flows from operating activities—direct method

obj. 3

✔ b. $77,870

Selected data taken from the accounting records of Lachgar Inc. for the current year ended December 31 are as follows:

	Balance, December 31	Balance, January 1
Accrued expenses payable (operating expenses)	$ 5,590	$ 6,110
Accounts payable (merchandise creditors)	41,730	46,020
Inventories	77,350	84,110
Prepaid expenses	3,250	3,900

During the current year, the cost of merchandise sold was $448,500, and the operating expenses other than depreciation were $78,000. The direct method is used for presenting the cash flows from operating activities on the statement of cash flows.

Determine the amount reported on the statement of cash flows for (a) cash payments for merchandise and (b) cash payments for operating expenses.

EX 14-22
Cash flows from operating activities— direct method

obj. 3

✔ Net cash flow from operating activities, $69,760

The income statement of Kodiak Industries Inc. for the current year ended June 30 is as follows:

Sales		$364,800
Cost of merchandise sold		207,200
Gross profit		$157,600
Operating expenses:		
Depreciation expense	$28,000	
Other operating expenses	73,920	
Total operating expenses		101,920
Income before income tax		$ 55,680
Income tax expense		15,440
Net income		$ 40,240

Changes in the balances of selected accounts from the beginning to the end of the current year are as follows:

	Increase Decrease*
Accounts receivable (net)	$8,400*
Inventories	2,800
Prepaid expenses	2,720*
Accounts payable (merchandise creditors)	5,760*
Accrued expenses payable (operating expenses) . .	880
Income taxes payable	1,920*

Prepare the Cash Flows from Operating Activities section of the statement of cash flows, using the direct method.

EX 14-23
Cash flows from operating activities— direct method

obj. 3

✔ Net cash flow from operating activities, $56,490

The income statement for M2 Pizza Pie Company for the current year ended June 30 and balances of selected accounts at the beginning and the end of the year are as follows:

Sales		$202,400
Cost of merchandise sold		70,000
Gross profit		$132,400
Operating expenses:		
Depreciation expense	$17,500	
Other operating expenses	52,400	
Total operating expenses		69,900
Income before income tax		$ 62,500
Income tax expense		18,000
Net income		$ 44,500

	End of Year	Beginning of Year
Accounts receivable (net)	$16,300	$14,190
Inventories	41,900	36,410
Prepaid expenses	6,600	7,260
Accounts payable (merchandise creditors)	30,690	28,490
Accrued expenses payable (operating expenses) . . .	8,690	9,460
Income taxes payable	1,650	1,650

Prepare the Cash Flows from Operating Activities section of the statement of cash flows, using the direct method.

EX 14-24
Free cash flow

Morrocan Marble Company has cash flows from operating activities of $300,000. Cash flows used for investments in property, plant, and equipment totaled $65,000, of which 75% of this investment was used to replace existing capacity.

Determine the free cash flow for Morrocan Marble Company.

EX 14-25
Free cash flow

The financial statements for Nike, Inc., are provided in Appendix F at the end of the text.

Determine the free cash flow for the year ended May 31, 2007. Assume that 90% of additions to property, plant and equipment were used to maintain productive capacity.

Problems Series A

PR 14-1A
Statement of cash flows—indirect method

obj. 2

✔ Net cash flow from operating activities, $49,520

The comparative balance sheet of Mavenir Technologies Inc. for December 31, 2010 and 2009, is shown as follows:

	Dec. 31, 2010	Dec. 31, 2009
Assets		
Cash	$ 312,880	$ 292,960
Accounts receivable (net)	113,920	104,480
Inventories	320,880	308,560
Investments	0	120,000
Land	164,000	0
Equipment	352,560	276,560
Accumulated depreciation—equipment	(83,200)	(74,000)
	$1,181,040	$1,028,560
Liabilities and Stockholders' Equity		
Accounts payable (merchandise creditors)	$ 214,240	$ 202,480
Accrued expenses payable (operating expenses)	21,120	26,320
Dividends payable	12,000	9,600
Common stock, $10 par	64,000	48,000
Paid-in capital in excess of par—common stock	240,000	140,000
Retained earnings	629,680	602,160
	$1,181,040	$1,028,560

The following additional information was taken from the records:

a. The investments were sold for $140,000 cash.
b. Equipment and land were acquired for cash.
c. There were no disposals of equipment during the year.
d. The common stock was issued for cash.
e. There was a $75,520 credit to Retained Earnings for net income.
f. There was a $48,000 debit to Retained Earnings for cash dividends declared.

Instructions

Prepare a statement of cash flows, using the indirect method of presenting cash flows from operating activities.

PR 14-2A
Statement of cash
flows—indirect
method

obj. 2

✔ Net cash flow
from operating
activities, $169,600

The comparative balance sheet of Amelia Enterprises, Inc. at December 31, 2010 and 2009, is as follows:

	Dec. 31, 2010	Dec. 31, 2009
Assets		
Cash	$ 73,300	$ 89,900
Accounts receivable (net).	112,300	121,000
Merchandise inventory.	160,800	149,600
Prepaid expenses	6,700	4,800
Equipment	327,500	268,500
Accumulated depreciation—equipment	(85,400)	(66,100)
	$595,200	$567,700
Liabilities and Stockholders' Equity		
Accounts payable (merchandise creditors)	$125,100	$118,800
Mortgage note payable	0	168,000
Common stock, $1 par.	24,000	12,000
Paid-in capital in excess of par—common stock. . . .	288,000	160,000
Retained earnings	158,100	108,900
	$595,200	$567,700

Additional data obtained from the income statement and from an examination of the accounts in the ledger for 2010 are as follows:

a. Net income, $126,000.
b. Depreciation reported on the income statement, $41,700.
c. Equipment was purchased at a cost of $81,400, and fully depreciated equipment costing $22,400 was discarded, with no salvage realized.
d. The mortgage note payable was not due until 2013, but the terms permitted earlier payment without penalty.
e. 7,000 shares of common stock were issued at $20 for cash.
f. Cash dividends declared and paid, $76,800.

Instructions

Prepare a statement of cash flows, using the indirect method of presenting cash flows from operating activities.

PR 14-3A
Statement of cash
flows—indirect
method

obj. 2

✔ Net cash flow
from operating
activities, ($92,000)

The comparative balance sheet of Putnam Cycle Co. at December 31, 2010 and 2009, is as follows:

	Dec. 31, 2010	Dec. 31, 2009
Assets		
Cash	$ 510,000	$ 536,000
Accounts receivable (net).	460,500	423,300
Inventories	704,700	646,100
Prepaid expenses	16,300	19,500
Land	175,500	266,500
Buildings	812,500	500,500
Accumulated depreciation—buildings	(227,000)	(212,400)
Equipment	284,600	252,600
Accumulated depreciation—equipment	(78,500)	(88,200)
	$2,658,600	$2,343,900
Liabilities and Stockholders' Equity		
Accounts payable (merchandise creditors)	$ 512,500	$ 532,400
Bonds payable	150,000	0
Common stock, $1 par.	75,000	65,000
Paid-in capital in excess of par—common stock. . . .	520,000	310,000
Retained earnings	1,401,100	1,436,500
	$2,658,600	$2,343,900

The noncurrent asset, noncurrent liability, and stockholders' equity accounts for 2010 are as follows:

ACCOUNT *Land*   ACCOUNT NO.

Date		Item	Debit	Credit	Balance Debit	Balance Credit
2010						
Jan.	1	Balance			266,500	
Apr.	20	Realized $84,000 cash from sale		91,000	175,500	

ACCOUNT *Buildings*   ACCOUNT NO.

Date		Item	Debit	Credit	Balance Debit	Balance Credit
2010						
Jan.	1	Balance			500,500	
Apr.	20	Acquired for cash	312,000		812,500	

ACCOUNT *Accumulated Depreciation—Buildings*   ACCOUNT NO.

Date		Item	Debit	Credit	Balance Debit	Balance Credit
2010						
Jan.	1	Balance				212,400
Dec.	31	Depreciation for year		14,600		227,000

ACCOUNT *Equipment*   ACCOUNT NO.

Date		Item	Debit	Credit	Balance Debit	Balance Credit
2010						
Jan.	1	Balance			252,600	
	26	Discarded, no salvage		26,000	226,600	
Aug.	11	Purchased for cash	58,000		284,600	

ACCOUNT *Accumulated Depreciation—Equipment*   ACCOUNT NO.

Date		Item	Debit	Credit	Balance Debit	Balance Credit
2010						
Jan.	1	Balance				88,200
	26	Equipment discarded	26,000			62,200
Dec.	31	Depreciation for year		16,300		78,500

ACCOUNT *Bonds Payable*   ACCOUNT NO.

Date		Item	Debit	Credit	Balance Debit	Balance Credit
					Debit	**Credit**
2010						
May	1	Issued 20-year bonds		150,000		150,000

ACCOUNT *Common Stock, $1 par*   ACCOUNT NO.

Date		Item	Debit	Credit	Balance Debit	Balance Credit
					Debit	**Credit**
2010						
Jan.	1	Balance				65,000
Dec.	7	Issued 10,000 shares of common stock for $22 per share		10,000		75,000

ACCOUNT *Paid-In Capital in Excess of Par—Common Stock*   ACCOUNT NO.

Date		Item	Debit	Credit	Balance Debit	Balance Credit
					Debit	**Credit**
2010						
Jan.	1	Balance				310,000
Dec.	7	Issued 10,000 shares of common stock for $22 per share		210,000		520,000

ACCOUNT *Retained Earnings*   ACCOUNT NO.

Date		Item	Debit	Credit	Balance Debit	Balance Credit
					Debit	**Credit**
2010						
Jan.	1	Balance				1,436,500
Dec.	31	Net loss	17,400			1,419,100
	31	Cash dividends	18,000			1,401,100

Instructions

Prepare a statement of cash flows, using the indirect method of presenting cash flows from operating activities.

PR 14-4A
Statement of cash flows—direct method

obj. 3

✔ Net cash flow from operating activities, $146,800

The comparative balance sheet of Rucker Photography Products Inc. for December 31, 2011 and 2010, is as follows:

	Dec. 31, 2011	Dec. 31, 2010
Assets		
Cash	$ 321,700	$ 339,700
Accounts receivable (net).	283,400	273,700
Inventories	505,500	491,400
Investments	0	120,000
Land	260,000	0
Equipment	440,000	340,000
Accumulated depreciation	(122,200)	(100,200)
	$1,688,400	$1,464,600

Liabilities and Stockholders' Equity

Accounts payable (merchandise creditors)	$ 385,900	$ 374,200
Accrued expenses payable (operating expenses) . . .	31,700	35,400
Dividends payable.	4,400	3,200
Common stock, $1 par.	20,000	16,000
Paid-in capital in excess of par—common stock	208,000	96,000
Retained earnings	1,038,400	939,800
	$1,688,400	$1,464,600

The income statement for the year ended December 31, 2011, is as follows:

Sales		$2,990,000
Cost of merchandise sold		1,226,000
Gross profit		$1,764,000
Operating expenses:		
Depreciation expense	$ 22,000	
Other operating expenses	1,550,000	
Total operating expenses		1,572,000
Operating income		$ 192,000
Other expense:		
Loss on sale of investments		(32,000)
Income before income tax		$ 160,000
Income tax expense		51,400
Net income		$ 108,600

The following additional information was taken from the records:

a. Equipment and land were acquired for cash.
b. There were no disposals of equipment during the year.
c. The investments were sold for $88,000 cash.
d. The common stock was issued for cash.
e. There was a $10,000 debit to Retained Earnings for cash dividends declared.

Instructions

Prepare a statement of cash flows, using the direct method of presenting cash flows from operating activities.

PR 14-5A
Statement of cash flows—direct method applied to PR 14-1A

obj. 3

✔ Net cash flow from operating activities, $49,520

The comparative balance sheet of Mavenir Technologies Inc. for December 31, 2010 and 2009, is as follows:

	Dec. 31, 2010	Dec. 31, 2009
Assets		
Cash	$ 312,880	$ 292,960
Accounts receivable (net).	113,920	104,480
Inventories	320,880	308,560
Investments	0	120,000
Land	164,000	0
Equipment	352,560	276,560
Accumulated depreciation—equipment	(83,200)	(74,000)
	$1,181,040	$1,028,560
Liabilities and Stockholders' Equity		
Accounts payable (merchandise creditors)	$ 214,240	$ 202,480
Accrued expenses payable (operating expenses) . . .	21,120	26,320
Dividends payable.	12,000	9,600
Common stock, $10 par.	64,000	48,000
Paid-in capital in excess of par—common stock	240,000	140,000
Retained earnings	629,680	602,160
	$1,181,040	$1,028,560

The income statement for the year ended December 31, 2010, is as follows:

Sales		$1,950,699
Cost of merchandise sold		1,200,430
Gross profit		$ 750,269
Operating expenses:		
Depreciation expense	$ 9,200	
Other operating expenses	635,202	
Total operating expenses		644,402
Operating income		$ 105,867
Other income:		
Gain on sale of investments		20,000
Income before income tax		$ 125,867
Income tax expense		50,347
Net income		$ 75,520

The following additional information was taken from the records:

a. The investments were sold for $140,000 cash.
b. Equipment and land were acquired for cash.
c. There were no disposals of equipment during the year.
d. The common stock was issued for cash.
e. There was a $48,000 debit to Retained Earnings for cash dividends declared.

Instructions

Prepare a statement of cash flows, using the direct method of presenting cash flows from operating activities.

Problems Series B

PR 14-1B
Statement of cash flows—indirect method

obj. 2

✔ Net cash flow from operating activities, $86,600

The comparative balance sheet of House Construction Co. for June 30, 2010 and 2009, is as follows:

	June 30, 2010	June 30, 2009
Assets		
Cash	$ 41,600	$ 28,200
Accounts receivable (net)	121,900	110,700
Inventories	175,600	170,500
Investments	0	60,000
Land	174,000	0
Equipment	258,000	210,600
Accumulated depreciation	(58,300)	(49,600)
	$712,800	$530,400
Liabilities and Stockholders' Equity		
Accounts payable (merchandise creditors)	$121,000	$114,200
Accrued expenses payable (operating expenses)	18,000	15,800
Dividends payable	15,000	12,000
Common stock, $1 par	67,200	60,000
Paid-in capital in excess of par—common stock	264,000	120,000
Retained earnings	227,600	208,400
	$712,800	$530,400

The following additional information was taken from the records of House Construction Co.:

a. Equipment and land were acquired for cash.
b. There were no disposals of equipment during the year.
c. The investments were sold for $54,000 cash.
d. The common stock was issued for cash.
e. There was a $79,200 credit to Retained Earnings for net income.
f. There was a $60,000 debit to Retained Earnings for cash dividends declared.

Instructions

Prepare a statement of cash flows, using the indirect method of presenting cash flows from operating activities.

PR 14-2B
Statement of cash
flows—indirect
method

obj. 2

✔ Net cash flow
from operating
activities, $200,500

The comparative balance sheet of TorMax Technology, Inc. at December 31, 2010 and 2009, is as follows:

	Dec. 31, 2010	Dec. 31, 2009
Assets		
Cash	$ 158,300	$ 128,900
Accounts receivable (net)	237,600	211,500
Inventories	317,100	365,200
Prepaid expenses	11,300	9,000
Land	108,000	108,000
Buildings	612,000	405,000
Accumulated depreciation—buildings	(166,500)	(148,050)
Machinery and equipment	279,000	279,000
Accumulated depreciation—machinery & equipment	(76,500)	(68,400)
Patents	38,200	43,200
	$1,518,500	$1,333,350
Liabilities and Stockholders' Equity		
Accounts payable (merchandise creditors)	$ 299,100	$ 331,100
Dividends payable	11,700	9,000
Salaries payable	28,200	31,100
Mortgage note payable, due 2017	80,000	—
Bonds payable	—	140,000
Common stock, $1 par	23,000	18,000
Paid-in capital in excess of par—common stock	180,000	45,000
Retained earnings	896,500	759,150
	$1,518,500	$1,333,350

An examination of the income statement and the accounting records revealed the following additional information applicable to 2010:

a. Net income, $184,150.
b. Depreciation expense reported on the income statement: buildings, $18,450; machinery and equipment, $8,100.
c. Patent amortization reported on the income statement, $5,000.
d. A building was constructed for $207,000.
e. A mortgage note for $80,000 was issued for cash.
f. 5,000 shares of common stock were issued at $28 in exchange for the bonds payable.
g. Cash dividends declared, $46,800.

Instructions Prepare a statement of cash flows, using the indirect method of presenting cash flows from operating activities.

PR 14-3B
Statement of cash
flows—indirect
method

obj. 2

✔ Net cash flow
from operating
activities, $7,800

The comparative balance sheet of Cantor Industries, Inc. at December 31, 2010 and 2009, is as follows:

	Dec. 31, 2010	Dec. 31, 2009
Assets		
Cash	$ 50,100	$ 56,300
Accounts receivable (net)	117,400	101,600
Inventories	153,100	144,300
Prepaid expenses	3,100	4,400
Land	165,000	231,000
Buildings	330,000	165,000
Accumulated depreciation—buildings	(66,200)	(61,000)
Equipment	110,100	88,300
Accumulated depreciation—equipment	(22,200)	(27,000)
	$840,400	$702,900
Liabilities and Stockholders' Equity		
Accounts payable (merchandise creditors)	$ 99,000	$105,200
Income taxes payable	4,400	3,600
Bonds payable	55,000	0
Common stock, $1 par	36,000	30,000
Paid-in capital in excess of par—common stock	195,000	135,000
Retained earnings	451,000	429,100
	$840,400	$702,900

The noncurrent asset, noncurrent liability, and stockholders' equity accounts for 2010 are as follows:

ACCOUNT *Land*   **ACCOUNT NO.**

Date		Item	Debit	Credit	Balance Debit	Balance Credit
2010						
Jan.	1	Balance			231,000	
Apr.	20	Realized $76,000 cash from sale		66,000	165,000	

ACCOUNT *Buildings*   **ACCOUNT NO.**

Date		Item	Debit	Credit	Balance Debit	Balance Credit
2010						
Jan.	1	Balance			165,000	
Apr.	20	Acquired for cash	165,000		330,000	

ACCOUNT *Accumulated Depreciation—Buildings*   **ACCOUNT NO.**

Date		Item	Debit	Credit	Balance Debit	Balance Credit
2010						
Jan.	1	Balance				61,000
Dec.	31	Depreciation for year		5,200		66,200

ACCOUNT *Equipment*   **ACCOUNT NO.**

Date		Item	Debit	Credit	Balance Debit	Balance Credit
2010						
Jan.	1	Balance			88,300	
	26	Discarded, no salvage		11,000	77,300	
Aug.	11	Purchased for cash	32,800		110,100	

ACCOUNT *Accumulated Depreciation—Equipment*   **ACCOUNT NO.**

Date		Item	Debit	Credit	Balance Debit	Balance Credit
2010						
Jan.	1	Balance				27,000
	26	Equipment discarded	11,000			16,000
Dec.	31	Depreciation for year		6,200		22,200

ACCOUNT *Bonds Payable*   **ACCOUNT NO.**

Date		Item	Debit	Credit	Balance Debit	Balance Credit
2010						
May	1	Issued 20-year bonds		55,000		55,000

ACCOUNT *Common Stock, $1 par*   ACCOUNT NO.

Date		Item	Debit	Credit	Balance Debit	Balance Credit
2010						
Jan.	1	Balance				30,000
Dec.	7	Issued 6,000 shares of common stock for $11 per share		6,000		36,000

ACCOUNT *Paid-In Capital in Excess of Par—Common Stock*   ACCOUNT NO.

Date		Item	Debit	Credit	Balance Debit	Balance Credit
2010						
Jan.	1	Balance				135,000
Dec.	7	Issued 6,000 shares of common stock for $11 per share		60,000		195,000

ACCOUNT *Retained Earnings*   ACCOUNT NO.

Date		Item	Debit	Credit	Balance Debit	Balance Credit
2010						
Jan.	1	Balance				429,100
Dec.	31	Net income		35,100		464,200
	31	Cash dividends	13,200			451,000

Instructions

Prepare a statement of cash flows, using the indirect method of presenting cash flows from operating activities.

PR 14-4B
Statement of cash flows—direct method

obj. 3

✔ Net cash flow from operating activities, $169,740

The comparative balance sheet of Lim Garden Supplies Inc. for December 31, 2010 and 2011, is as follows:

	Dec. 31, 2011	Dec. 31, 2010
Assets		
Cash	$ 220,640	$ 227,700
Accounts receivable (net).	330,880	304,800
Inventories	464,800	454,600
Investments	0	144,000
Land	320,000	0
Equipment	408,000	328,000
Accumulated depreciation	(160,500)	(122,800)
	$1,583,820	$1,336,300
Liabilities and Stockholders' Equity		
Accounts payable (merchandise creditors)	$ 360,000	$ 322,200
Accrued expenses payable (operating expenses) . . .	22,600	26,400
Dividends payable	33,600	30,400
Common stock, ...	16,000	8,000
Paid-in capital in excess of par—common stock	320,000	160,000
Retained earnings	831,620	789,300
	$1,583,820	$1,336,300

The income statement for the year ended December 31, 2011, is as follows:

Sales		$1,504,000
Cost of merchandise sold		784,000
Gross profit		$ 720,000
Operating expenses:		
Depreciation expense	$ 37,700	
Other operating expenses	448,280	
Total operating expenses		485,980
Operating income		$ 234,020
Other income:		
Gain on sale of investments		52,000
Income before income tax		$ 286,020
Income tax expense		99,700
Net income		$ 186,320

The following additional information was taken from the records:

a. Equipment and land were acquired for cash.
b. There were no disposals of equipment during the year.
c. The investments were sold for $196,000 cash.
d. The common stock was issued for cash.
e. There was a $144,000 debit to Retained Earnings for cash dividends declared.

Instructions

Prepare a statement of cash flows, using the direct method of presenting cash flows from operating activities.

PR 14-5B
Statement of cash flows—direct method applied to PR 14-1B

obj. 3

✔ Net cash flow from operating activities, $86,600

The comparative balance sheet of House Construction Co. for June 30, 2010 and 2009, is as follows:

	June 30, 2010	June 30, 2009
Assets		
Cash	$ 41,600	$ 28,200
Accounts receivable (net)	121,900	110,700
Inventories	175,600	170,500
Investments	0	60,000
Land	174,000	0
Equipment	258,000	210,600
Accumulated depreciation	(58,300)	(49,600)
	$712,800	$530,400
Liabilities and Stockholders' Equity		
Accounts payable (merchandise creditors)	$121,000	$114,200
Accrued expenses payable (operating expenses)	18,000	15,800
Dividends payable	15,000	12,000
Common stock, $1 par	67,200	60,000
Paid-in capital in excess of par—common stock	264,000	120,000
Retained earnings	227,600	208,400
	$712,800	$530,400

The income statement for the year ended June 30, 2010, is as follows:

Sales		$1,134,900
Cost of merchandise sold		698,400
Gross profit		$ 436,500
Operating expenses:		
Depreciation expense	$ 8,700	
Other operating expenses	289,800	
Total operating expenses		298,500
Operating income		$ 138,000
Other expenses:		
Loss on sale of investments		(6,000)
Income before income tax		$ 132,000
Income tax expense		52,800
Net income		$ 79,200

The following additional information was taken from the records:

a. Equipment and land were acquired for cash.
b. There were no disposals of equipment during the year.
c. The investments were sold for $54,000 cash.
d. The common stock was issued for cash.
e. There was a $60,000 debit to Retained Earnings for cash dividends declared.

Instructions

Prepare a statement of cash flows, using the direct method of presenting cash flows from operating activities.

Special Activities

SA 14-1
Ethics and professional conduct in business

Kelly Tough, president of Tu-Rock Industries Inc., believes that reporting operating cash flow per share on the income statement would be a useful addition to the company's just completed financial statements. The following discussion took place between Kelly Tough and Tu-Rock controller, Tripp Kelso, in January, after the close of the fiscal year.

Kelly: I have been reviewing our financial statements for the last year. I am disappointed that our net income per share has dropped by 10% from last year. This is not going to look good to our shareholders. Isn't there anything we can do about this?

Tripp: What do you mean? The past is the past, and the numbers are in. There isn't much that can be done about it. Our financial statements were prepared according to generally accepted accounting principles, and I don't see much leeway for significant change at this point.

Kelly: No, no. I'm not suggesting that we "cook the books." But look at the cash flow from operating activities on the statement of cash flows. The cash flow from operating activities has increased by 20%. This is very good news—and, I might add, useful information. The higher cash flow from operating activities will give our creditors comfort.

Tripp: Well, the cash flow from operating activities is on the statement of cash flows, so I guess users will be able to see the improved cash flow figures there.

Kelly: This is true, but somehow I feel that this information should be given a much higher profile. I don't like this information being "buried" in the statement of cash flows. You know as well as I do that many users will focus on the income statement. Therefore, I think we ought to include an operating cash flow per share number on the face of the income statement—someplace under the earnings per share number. In this way, users will get the complete picture of our operating performance. Yes, our earnings per share dropped this year, but our cash flow from operating activities improved! And all the information is in one place where users can see and compare the figures. What do you think?

Tripp: I've never really thought about it like that before. I guess we could put the operating cash flow per share on the income statement, under the earnings per share. Users would really benefit from this disclosure. Thanks for the idea—I'll start working on it.

Kelly: Glad to be of service.

How would you interpret this situation? Is Tripp behaving in an ethical and professional manner?

SA 14-2
Using the statement of cash flows

You are considering an investment in a new start-up company, Steamboat IQ Inc., an Internet service provider. A review of the company's financial statements reveals a negative retained earnings. In addition, it appears as though the company has been running a negative cash flow from operating activities since the company's inception.

How is the company staying in business under these circumstances? Could this be a good investment?

SA 14-3
Analysis of
statement of cash
flows

Jim Walker is the president and majority shareholder of Tech Trends Inc., a small retail store chain. Recently, Walker submitted a loan application for Tech Trends Inc. to Yadkin National Bank. It called for a $200,000, 9%, 10-year loan to help finance the construction of a building and the purchase of store equipment, costing a total of $250,000, to enable Tech Trends Inc. to open a store in Yadkin. Land for this purpose was acquired last year. The bank's loan officer requested a statement of cash flows in addition to the most recent income statement, balance sheet, and retained earnings statement that Walker had submitted with the loan application.

As a close family friend, Walker asked you to prepare a statement of cash flows. From the records provided, you prepared the following statement:

Tech Trends Inc.
Statement of Cash Flows
For the Year Ended December 31, 2010

Cash flows from operating activities:			
Net income		$100,000	
Adjustments to reconcile net income to net cash flow			
from operating activities:			
Depreciation		28,000	
Gain on sale of investments		(10,000)	
Changes in current operating assets and liabilities:			
Decrease in accounts receivable		7,000	
Increase in inventories		(14,000)	
Increase in accounts payable		10,000	
Decrease in accrued expenses payable		(2,000)	
Net cash flow from operating activities			$119,000
Cash flows from investing activities:			
Cash received from investments sold	$ 60,000		
Less cash paid for purchase of store equipment	(40,000)		
Net cash flow provided by investing activities			20,000
Cash flows from financing activities:			
Cash paid for dividends	$ 42,000		
Net cash flow used for financing activities			(42,000)
Increase in cash			$ 97,000
Cash at the beginning of the year			36,000
Cash at the end of the year			$133,000

Schedule of Noncash Financing and Investing Activities:

Issued common stock for land	$ 80,000

After reviewing the statement, Walker telephoned you and commented, "Are you sure this statement is right?" Walker then raised the following questions:

1. "How can depreciation be a cash flow?"
2. "Issuing common stock for the land is listed in a separate schedule. This transaction has nothing to do with cash! Shouldn't this transaction be eliminated from the statement?"
3. "How can the gain on sale of investments be a deduction from net income in determining the cash flow from operating activities?"
4. "Why does the bank need this statement anyway? They can compute the increase in cash from the balance sheets for the last two years."

After jotting down Walker's questions, you assured him that this statement was "right." But to alleviate Walker's concern, you arranged a meeting for the following day.

a.   ▬▬▶ How would you respond to each of Walker's questions?
b.   ▬▬▶ Do you think that the statement of cash flows enhances the chances of Tech Trends Inc. receiving the loan? Discuss.

SA 14-4
Analysis of cash flow from operations

The Retailing Division of Most Excellent Purchase Inc. provided the following information on its cash flow from operations:

Net income	$ 540,000
Increase in accounts receivable	(648,000)
Increase in inventory	(720,000)
Decrease in accounts payable	(108,000)
Depreciation	120,000
Cash flow from operating activities	$(816,000)

The manager of the Retailing Division provided the accompanying memo with this report:

From: Senior Vice President, Retailing Division

I am pleased to report that we had earnings of $540,000 over the last period. This resulted in a return on invested capital of 10%, which is near our targets for this division. I have been aggressive in building the revenue volume in the division. As a result, I am happy to report that we have increased the number of new credit card customers as a result of an aggressive marketing campaign. In addition, we have found some excellent merchandise opportunities. Some of our suppliers have made some of their apparel merchandise available at a deep discount. We have purchased as much of these goods as possible in order to improve profitability. I'm also happy to report that our vendor payment problems have improved. We are nearly caught up on our overdue payables balances.

➤ Comment on the senior vice president's memo in light of the cash flow information.

SA 14-5
Statement of cash flows

Group Project

Internet Project

This activity will require two teams to retrieve cash flow statement information from the Internet. One team is to obtain the most recent year's statement of cash flows for Johnson & Johnson, and the other team the most recent year's statement of cash flows for AMR Corp.

The statement of cash flows is included as part of the annual report information that is a required disclosure to the Securities and Exchange Commission (SEC). SEC documents can be retrieved using the EdgarScan™ service at **http://www.sec.gov/edgar/searchedgar/webusers.htm**.

To obtain annual report information, type in a company name in the appropriate space. EdgarScan will list the reports available to you for the company you've selected. Select the most recent annual report filing, identified as a 10-K or 10-K405. EdgarScan provides an outline of the report, including the separate financial statements. You can double-click the income statement and balance sheet for the selected company into an Excel™ spreadsheet for further analysis.

As a group, compare the two statements of cash flows.

a. How are Johnson & Johnson and AMR Corp. similar or different regarding cash flows?
b. Compute and compare the free cash flow for each company, assuming additions to property, plant, and equipment replace current capacity.

Answers to Self-Examination Questions

1. **D** Cash flows from operating activities affect transactions that enter into the determination of net income, such as the receipt of cash from customers on account (answer D). Receipts of cash from the sale of stock (answer A) and the sale of bonds (answer B) and payments of cash for dividends (answer C) are cash flows from financing activities.

2. **A** Cash flows from investing activities include receipts from the sale of noncurrent assets, such as equipment (answer A), and payments to acquire noncurrent assets. Receipts of cash from

the sale of stock (answer B) and payments of cash for dividends (answer C) and to acquire treasury stock (answer D) are cash flows from financing activities.

3. **C** Payment of cash for dividends (answer C) is an example of a financing activity. The receipt of cash from customers on account (answer A) is an operating activity. The receipt of cash from the sale of equipment (answer B) is an investing activity. The payment of cash to acquire land (answer D) is an example of an investing activity.

4. **D** The indirect method (answer D) reports cash flows from operating activities by beginning with net income and adjusting it for revenues and expenses not involving the receipt or payment of cash.

5. **C** The Cash Flows from Operating Activities section of the statement of cash flows would report net cash flow from operating activities of $65,500, determined as follows:

Cash flows from operating activities:

Net income	$ 55,000
Adjustments to reconcile net income to net cash flow from operating activities:	
Depreciation	22,000
Changes in current operating assets and liabilities:	
Increase in accounts receivable	(10,000)
Decrease in inventories	5,000
Decrease in prepaid expenses	500
Decrease in accounts payable	(7,000)
Net cash flow from operating activities	$65,500

Reversing Entries

Some of the adjusting entries recorded at the end of the accounting period affect transactions that occur in the next period. In such cases, a reversing entry may be used to simplify the recording of the next period's transactions.

To illustrate, an adjusting entry for accrued wages expense affects the first payment of wages in the next period. Without using a reversing entry, Wages Payable must be debited for the accrued wages at the end of the preceding period. In addition, Wages Expense must also be debited for only that portion of the payroll that is an expense of the current period.

Using a reversing entry, however, simplifies the analysis and recording of the first wages payment in the next period. As the term implies, a *reversing entry* is the exact opposite of the related adjusting entry. The amounts and accounts are the same as the adjusting entry, but the debits and credits are reversed.

@netsolutions   Reversing entries are illustrated by using the accrued wages for NetSolutions presented in Chapter 3. These data are summarized in Exhibit 1.

Exhibit 1

Accrued Wages

1. Wages are paid on the second and fourth Fridays for the two-week periods ending on those Fridays. The payments were $950 on December 13 and $1,200 on December 27.

2. The wages accrued for Monday and Tuesday, December 30 and 31, are $250.

3. Wages paid on Friday, January 10, total $1,275.

4. Wages expense, January 1–10, $1,025.

December

S	M	T	W	T	F	S
1	2	3	4	5	6	7
8	9	10	11	12	13	14
15	16	17	18	19	20	21
22	23	24	25	26	27	28
29	30	31				

1. Wages expense (paid), $950

1. Wages expense (paid), $1,200

2. Wages expense (accrued), $250

January

				1	2	3	4
5	6	7	8	9	10	11	

3. Wages expense (paid), $1,275

4. Wages expense (Jan. 1–10), $1,025

The adjusting entry for the accrued wages of December 30 and 31 is as follows:

2009					
Dec.	31	Wages Expense	51	250	
		Wages Payable	22		250
		Accrued wages.			

After the adjusting entry is recorded, Wages Expense will have a debit balance of $4,525 ($4,275 + $250), as shown on the top of page B-3. Wages Payable will have a credit balance of $250, as shown on page B-3.

After the closing entries are recorded, Wages Expense will have a zero balance. However, since Wages Payable is a liability account, it is not closed. Thus, Wages Payable will have a credit balance of $250 as of January 1, 2010.

Without recording a reversing entry, the payment of the $1,275 payroll on January 10 would be recorded as follows:

2010					
Jan.	10	Wages Payable	22	250	
		Wages Expense	51	1,025	
		Cash	11		1,275

As shown above, to record the January 10 payroll correctly Wages Payable must be debited for $250. This means that the employee who records the January 10 payroll must refer to the December 31, 2009, adjusting entry or to the ledger to determine the amount to debit Wages Payable.

Because the January 10 payroll is not recorded in the normal manner, there is a greater chance that an error may occur. This chance of error is reduced by recording a reversing entry as of the first day of the next period. For example, the reversing entry for the accrued wages expense would be recorded on January 1, 2010, as follows:

2010					
Jan.	1	Wages Payable	22	250	
		Wages Expense	51		250
		Reversing entry.			

The preceding reversing entry transfers the $250 liability from Wages Payable to the credit side of Wages Expense. The nature of the $250 is unchanged—it is still a liability. However, because of its unusual nature, an explanation is written under the reversing entry.

When the payroll is paid on January 10, the following entry is recorded:

Jan.	10	Wages Expense	51	1,275	
		Cash	11		1,275

After the January 10 payroll is recorded, Wages Expense has a debit balance of $1,025. This is the wages expense for the period January 1–10, 2010.

Wages Payable and Wages Expense after posting the adjusting, closing, and reversing entries are shown on the next page.

Account Wages Payable   Account No. 22

Date		Item	Post. Ref.	Debit	Credit	Balance Debit	Balance Credit
2009 Dec.	31	Adjusting	5		250		250
2010 Jan.	1	Reversing	7	250		—	—

Account Wages Expense   Account No. 51

Date		Item	Post. Ref.	Debit	Credit	Balance Debit	Balance Credit
2009 Nov.	30		1	2,125		2,125	
Dec.	13		3	950		3,075	
	27		3	1,200		4,275	
	31	Adjusting	5	250		4,525	
	31	Closing	6		4,525	—	—
2010 Jan.	1	Reversing	7		250		250
	10		7	1,275		1,025	

In addition to accrued expenses (accrued liabilities), reversing entries are also used for accrued revenues (accrued assets). To illustrate, the reversing entry for NetSolutions' accrued fees earned as of December 31, 2009, is as follows:

Jan.	1	Fees Earned	41	500	
		Accounts Receivable	12		500
		Reversing entry.			

The use of reversing entries is optional. However, in computerized accounting systems, data entry employees often input routine accounting entries. In such cases, reversing entries may be useful in avoiding errors.

....

EX B-1
Adjusting and
reversing entries

On the basis of the following data, (a) journalize the adjusting entries at December 31, the end of the current fiscal year, and (b) journalize the reversing entries on January 1, the first day of the following year.

1. Sales salaries are uniformly $17,375 for a five-day workweek, ending on Friday. The last payday of the year was Friday, December 26.
2. Accrued fees earned but not recorded at December 31, $19,850.

....

EX B-2
Adjusting and
reversing entries

On the basis of the following data, (a) journalize the adjusting entries at June 30, the end of the current fiscal year, and (b) journalize the reversing entries on July 1, the first day of the following year.

1. Wages are uniformly $25,900 for a five-day workweek, ending on Friday. The last payday of the year was Friday, June 27.
2. Accrued fees earned but not recorded at June 30, $36,100.

EX B-3
Entries posted to the
wages expense
account

Portions of the wages expense account of a business are shown below.

a. Indicate the nature of the entry (payment, adjusting, closing, reversing) from which each numbered posting was made.
b. Journalize the complete entry from which each numbered posting was made.

Account	**Wages Expense**					Account No. **53**	
						Balance	
Date	**Item**	**Post. Ref.**	**Dr.**	**Cr.**		**Dr.**	**Cr.**
2009							
Dec. 26	(1)	49	27,000			1,400,000	
31	(2)	50	16,200			1,416,200	
31	(3)	51		1,416,200		—	—
2010							
Jan. 1	(4)	52		16,200			16,200
2	(5)	53	27,000			10,800	

EX B-4
Entries posted to the
salaries expense
account

Portions of the salaries expense account of a business are shown below.

Account	**Salaries Expense**					Account No. **53**	
						Balance	
Date	**Item**	**Post. Ref.**	**Dr.**	**Cr.**		**Dr.**	**Cr.**
2009							
Dec. 27	(1)	29	17,500			910,000	
31	(2)	30	7,000			917,000	
31	(3)	31		917,000		—	—
2010							
Jan. 1	(4)	32		7,000			7,000
2	(5)	33	17,500			10,500	

a. Indicate the nature of the entry (payment, adjusting, closing, reversing) from which each numbered posting was made.
b. Journalize the complete entry from which each numbered posting was made.

Special Journals and Subsidiary Ledgers

In the beginning chapters of this text, the transactions for NetSolutions were manually recorded in an all-purpose (two-column) journal. The journal entries were then posted individually to the accounts in the ledger. Such a system is simple to use and easy to understand when there are a small number of transactions. However, when a business has a large number of *similar* transactions, using an all-purpose journal is inefficient and impractical. For example, in a given day, a company might earn fees on account from 20 customers. Recording each fee earned by debiting Accounts Receivable and crediting Fees Earned would be inefficient. Also, a record of the amount each customer owes must be kept. In such cases, subsidiary ledgers and special journals are useful. Although the manual use of subsidiary ledgers and special journals is described and illustrated, the basic principles also apply to computerized systems.

Subsidiary Ledgers

An accounting system should be designed to provide information on the amounts due from various customers (accounts receivable) and amounts owed to various creditors (accounts payable). A separate account for each customer and creditor could be added to the ledger. However, as the number of customers and creditors increases, the ledger would become awkward.

A large number of individual accounts with a common characteristic can be grouped together in a separate ledger called a *subsidiary ledger*. The primary ledger, which contains all of the balance sheet and income statement accounts, is then called the *general ledger*. Each subsidiary ledger is represented in the general ledger by a summarizing account, called a *controlling account*. The sum of the balances of the accounts in a subsidiary ledger must equal the balance of the related controlling account. Thus, a subsidiary ledger is a secondary ledger that supports a controlling account in the general ledger.

Common subsidiary ledgers are:

1. The *accounts receivable subsidiary ledger,* or *customers ledger* lists the individual customer accounts in alphabetical order. The controlling account in the general ledger is Accounts Receivable.
2. The *accounts payable subsidiary ledger,* or *creditors ledger* lists individual creditor accounts in alphabetical order. The controlling account in the general ledger is Accounts Payable.
3. The *inventory subsidiary ledger,* or *inventory ledger,* lists individual inventory by item (bar code) number. The controlling account in the general ledger is Inventory. An inventory subsidiary ledger is used in a perpetual inventory system.

The relationship between the general ledger and the accounts receivable, accounts payable, and inventory subsidiary ledgers is illustrated in Exhibit 1.

Special Journals

One method of processing data more efficiently in a manual accounting system is to expand the all-purpose two-column journal to a multicolumn journal. Each column in a multicolumn journal is used only for recording transactions that affect a certain account.

Exhibit 1

General Ledger and Subsidiary Ledgers

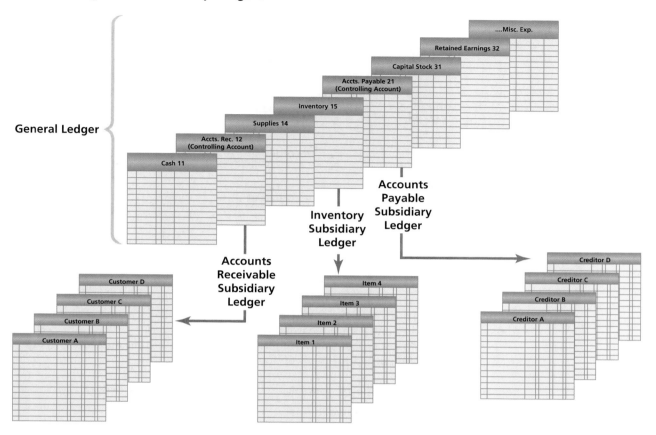

For example, a special column could be used only for recording debits to the cash account. Likewise, another special column could be used only for recording credits to the cash account. The addition of the two special columns would eliminate the writing of *Cash* in the journal for every receipt and every payment of cash. Also, there would be no need to post each individual debit and credit to the cash account. Instead, the *Cash Dr.* and *Cash Cr.* columns could be totaled periodically and only the totals posted. In a similar way, special columns could be added for recording credits to Fees Earned, debits and credits to Accounts Receivable and Accounts Payable, and for other entries that are repeated.

An all-purpose multicolumn journal may be adequate for a small business that has many transactions of a similar nature. However, a journal that has many columns for recording many different types of transactions is impractical for larger businesses.

> **Special journals are a method of summarizing transactions.**

The next logical extension of the accounting system is to replace the single multicolumn journal with several *special journals.* Each special journal is designed to be used for recording a single kind of transaction that occurs frequently. For example, since most businesses have many transactions in which cash is paid out, they will likely use a special journal for recording cash payments. Likewise, they will use another special journal for recording cash receipts. Special journals are a method of summarizing transactions, which is a basic feature of any accounting system.

The format and number of special journals that a business uses depends on the nature of the business. A business that gives credit might use a special journal designed for recording only revenue from services provided on credit. In contrast, a business that does not give credit would have no need for such a journal.

The transactions that occur most often in a small service business and the special journals in which they are recorded are as follows:

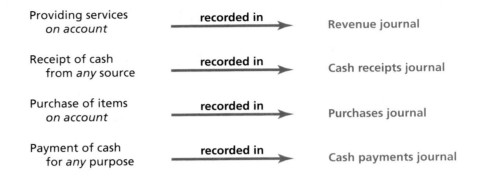

The all-purpose two-column journal, called the *general journal* or simply the *journal,* can be used for entries that do not fit into any of the special journals. For example, adjusting and closing entries are recorded in the general journal.

@netsolutions

Next, the following types of transactions, special journals, and subsidiary ledgers are described and illustrated for NetSolutions:

Transaction	Special Journal	Subsidiary Ledger
Fees earned on account	Revenue journal	Accounts receivable subsidiary ledger
Cash receipts	Cash receipts journal	Accounts receivable subsidiary ledger
Purchases on account	Purchases journal	Accounts payable subsidiary ledger
Cash payments	Cash payments journal	Accounts payable subsidiary ledger

As shown above, transactions that are recorded in the revenue and cash receipts journals will affect the accounts receivable subsidiary ledger. Likewise, transactions that are recorded in the purchases and cash payments journals will affect the accounts payable subsidiary ledger.

Assume that NetSolutions has the following selected general ledger balances on March 1, 2010:

Account Number	Account	Balance
11	Cash	$6,200
12	Accounts Receivable	3,400
14	Supplies	2,500
18	Office Equipment	2,500
21	Accounts Payable	1,230

Revenue Journal

Fees earned on account would be recorded in the *revenue journal. Cash fees earned* would be recorded in the cash receipts journal.

To illustrate the efficiency of using a revenue journal, an example for NetSolutions is used. Specifically, assume that NetSolutions recorded the following four revenue transactions for March in its general journal:

2010					
Mar.	2	Accounts Receivable—Accessories By Claire	12/✓	2,200	
		Fees Earned	41		2,200
	6	Accounts Receivable—RapZone	12/✓	1,750	
		Fees Earned	41		1,750
	18	Accounts Receivable—Web Cantina	12/✓	2,650	
		Fees Earned	41		2,650
	27	Accounts Receivable—Accessories By Claire	12/✓	3,000	
		Fees Earned	41		3,000

For the above entries, NetSolutions recorded eight account titles and eight amounts. In addition, NetSolutions made twelve postings to the ledgers—four to Accounts Receivable in the general ledger, four to the accounts receivable subsidiary ledger (indicated by each check mark), and four to Fees Earned in the general ledger.

The preceding revenue transactions could be recorded more efficiently in a revenue journal, as shown in Exhibit 2. In each revenue transaction, the amount of the debit to Accounts Receivable is the same as the amount of the credit to Fees Earned. Thus, only a single amount column is necessary. The date, invoice number, customer name, and amount are entered separately for each transaction.

Revenues are normally recorded in the revenue journal when the company sends an invoice to the customer. An **invoice** is the bill that is sent to the customer by the company. Each invoice is normally numbered in sequence for future reference.

To illustrate, assume that on March 2 NetSolutions issued Invoice No. 615 to Accessories By Claire for fees earned of $2,200. This transaction is entered in the revenue journal, shown in Exhibit 2, by entering the following items:

1. Date column: *Mar. 2*
2. Invoice No. column: *615*
3. Account Debited column: *Accessories By Claire*
4. Accts. Rec. Dr./Fees Earned Cr. column: *2,200*

The process of posting from a revenue journal, shown in Exhibit 3, is as follows:

1. Each transaction is posted individually to a customer account in the accounts receivable subsidiary ledger. Postings to customer accounts should be made on a

Exhibit 2

Revenue Journal

Revenue Journal   Page 35

Date		Invoice No.	Account Debited	Post. Ref.	Accts. Rec. Dr. Fees Earned Cr.
2010					
Mar.	2	615	Accessories By Claire		2,200
	6	616	RapZone		1,750
	18	617	Web Cantina		2,650
	27	618	Accessories By Claire		3,000
	31				9,600

Exhibit 3

Revenue Journal and Postings

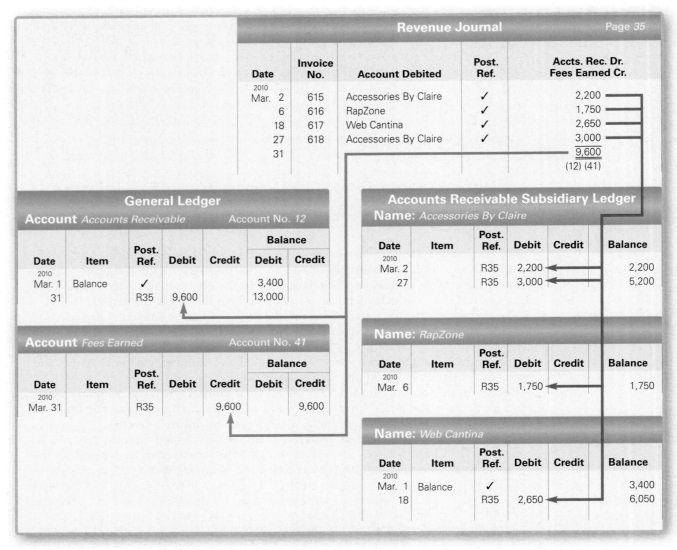

regular basis. In this way, the customer's account will show a current balance. Since the balances in the customer accounts are usually debit balances, the three-column account form is shown in Exhibit 3.

To illustrate, Exhibit 3 shows the posting of the $2,200 debit to Accessories By Claire in the accounts receivable subsidiary ledger. After the posting, Accessories By Claire has a debit balance of $2,200.

2. To provide a trail of the entries posted to the subsidiary and general ledger, the source of these entries is indicated in the Posting Reference column of each account by inserting the letter R (for revenue journal) and the page number of the revenue journal.

To illustrate, Exhibit 3 shows that after $2,200 is posted to Accessories By Claire's account, R35 is inserted into the Post. Ref. column of the account.

3. To indicate that the transaction has been posted to the accounts receivable subsidiary ledger, a check mark (✓) is inserted in the Post. Ref. column of the revenue journal, as shown in Exhibit 3.

To illustrate, Exhibit 3 shows that a check mark (✓) has been inserted in the Post. Ref. column next to Accessories By Claire in the revenue journal to indicate that the $2,200 has been posted.

4.   A single monthly total is posted to Accounts Receivable and Fees Earned in the general ledger. This total is equal to the sum of the month's debits to the individual accounts in the subsidiary ledger. It is posted in the general ledger as a debit to Accounts Receivable and a credit to Fees Earned, as shown in Exhibit 3. The accounts receivable account number (12) and the fees earned account number (41) are then inserted below the total in the revenue journal to indicate that the posting is completed.

To illustrate, Exhibit 3 shows the monthly total of $9,600 was posted as a debit to Accounts Receivable (12) and as a credit to Fees Earned (41).

Exhibit 3 illustrates the efficiency gained by using the revenue journal rather than the general journal. Specifically, all of the transactions for fees earned during the month are posted to the general ledger only once—at the end of the month.

Cash Receipts Journal

All transactions that involve the receipt of cash are recorded in a *cash receipts journal*. The cash receipts journal for NetSolutions is shown in Exhibit 4.

The cash receipts journal shown in Exhibit 4 has a Cash Dr. column. The kinds of transactions in which cash is received and how often they occur determine the titles of the other columns. For example, NetSolutions often receives cash from customers on account. Thus, the cash receipts journal in Exhibit 4 has an Accounts Receivable Cr. column.

To illustrate, on March 28 Accessories By Claire made a payment of $2,200 on its account. This transaction is recorded in the cash receipts journal, shown in Exhibit 4, by entering the following items:

1.   Date column: *Mar. 28*
2.   Account Credited column: *Accessories By Claire*
3.   Accounts Receivable Cr. column: *2,200*
4.   Cash Dr. column: *2,200*

The Other Accounts Cr. column in Exhibit 4 is used for recording credits to any account for which there is no special credit column. For example, NetSolutions received cash on March 1 for rent. Since no special column exists for Rent Revenue, Rent Revenue is entered in the Account Credited column. Thus, this transaction is recorded in the cash receipts journal, shown in Exhibit 4, by entering the following items:

1.   Date column: *Mar. 1*
2.   Account Credited column: *Rent Revenue*
3.   Other Accounts Cr. column: *400*
4.   Cash Dr. column: *400*

At the end of the month, all of the amount columns are totaled. The debits must equal the credits. If the debits do not equal the credits, an error has occurred. Before proceeding further, the error must be found and corrected.

The process of posting from the cash receipts journal, shown in Exhibit 4, is as follows:

1.   Each transaction involving the receipt of cash on account is posted individually to a customer account in the accounts receivable subsidiary ledger. Postings to customer accounts should be made on a regular basis. In this way, the customer's account will show a current balance.

To illustrate, Exhibit 4 shows on March 19 the receipt of $3,400 on account from Web Cantina. The posting of the $3,400 credit to Web Cantina in the accounts receivable subsidiary ledger is shown in Exhibit 4. After the posting, Web Cantina has a debit balance of $2,650. If a posting results in a customer's account with a credit balance, the credit balance

Exhibit 4

Exhibit 4

Cash Receipts Journal and Postings

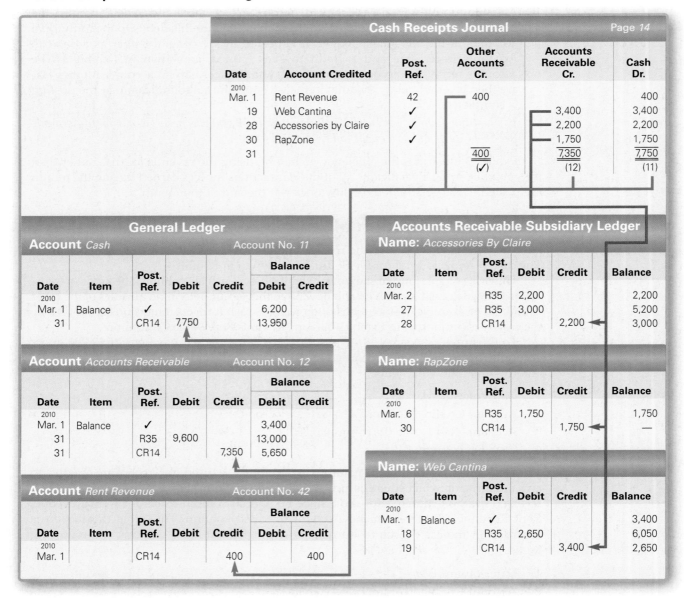

is indicated by an asterisk or parentheses in the Balance column. If an account's balance is zero, a line may be drawn in the Balance column.

2. To provide a trail of the entries posted to the subsidiary ledger, the source of these entries is indicated in the Posting Reference column of each account by inserting the letter CR (for cash receipts journal) and the page number of the cash receipts journal.

    To illustrate, Exhibit 4 shows that after $3,400 is posted to Web Cantina's account in the accounts receivable subsidiary ledger, CR14 is inserted into the Post. Ref. column of the account.

3. To indicate that the transaction has been posted to the accounts receivable subsidiary ledger, a check mark (✓) is inserted in the Posting Reference column of the cash receipts journal, as shown in Exhibit 4.

    To illustrate, Exhibit 4 shows that a check mark (✓) has been inserted in the Post. Ref. column next to Web Cantina to indicate that the $3,400 has been posted.

4. A single monthly total of the Accounts Receivable Cr. column is posted to the accounts receivable general ledger account. This is the total cash received on account and is posted as a credit to Accounts Receivable. The accounts receivable account number (12) is then inserted below the Accounts Receivable Cr. column to indicate that the posting is complete.

    To illustrate, Exhibit 4 shows the monthly total of $7,350 was posted as a credit to Accounts Receivable (12).

5. A single monthly total of the Cash Dr. column is posted to the cash general ledger account. This is the total cash received during the month and is posted as a debit to Cash. The cash account number (11) is then inserted below the Cash Dr. column to indicate that the posting is complete.

    To illustrate, Exhibit 4 shows the monthly total of $7,750 was posted as a debit to Cash (11).

6. The accounts listed in the Other Accounts Cr. column are posted on a regular basis as a separate credit to each account. The account number is then inserted in the Post. Ref. column to indicate that the posting is complete. Because accounts in the Other Accounts Cr. column are posted individually, a check mark is placed below the column total at the end of the month to show that no further action is needed.

    To illustrate, Exhibit 4 shows that $400 was posted as a credit to Rent Revenue (42). Also, at the end of the month a check mark (✓) is entered below the Other Accounts Cr. column to indicate that no further action is needed.

Accounts Receivable Control Account and Subsidiary Ledger

After all posting has been completed for the month, the balances in the accounts receivable subsidiary ledger should be totaled. This total should then be compared with the balance of the accounts receivable controlling account in the general ledger. If the controlling account and the subsidiary ledger do not agree, an error has occurred. Before proceeding further, the error must be located and corrected.

The total of NetSolutions' accounts receivable subsidiary ledger is $5,650. This total agrees with the balance of its accounts receivable control account on March 31, 2010, as shown below.

Accounts Receivable (Control)		NetSolutions Accounts Receivable Subsidiary Ledger March 31, 2010	
Balance, March 1, 2010	$ 3,400	Accessories By Claire	$3,000
Total debits (from revenue journal)	9,600	RapZone	0
Total credits (from cash receipts journal)	(7,350)	Web Cantina	2,650
Balance, March 31, 2010	$ 5,650	Total accounts receivable	$5,650

Purchases Journal

All *purchases on account* are recorded in the *purchases journal. Cash purchases would be recorded in the cash payments journal.* The purchases journal for NetSolutions is shown in Exhibit 5.

The amounts purchased on account are recorded in the purchases journal in an Accounts Payable Cr. column. The items most often purchased on account determine the titles of the other columns. For example, NetSolutions often purchases supplies on account. Thus, the purchases journal in Exhibit 5 has a Supplies Dr. column.

To illustrate, on March 3 NetSolutions purchased $600 of supplies on account from Howard Supplies. This transaction is recorded in the purchases journal, shown in Exhibit 5, by entering the following items:

1. Date column: *Mar. 3*
2. Account Credited column: *Howard Supplies*

3.   Accounts Payable Cr. column: *600*
4.   Supplies Dr. column: *600*

The Other Accounts Dr. column in Exhibit 5 is used to record purchases, on account, of any item for which there is no debit column. The title of the account to be debited is entered in the Other Accounts Dr. column, and the amount is entered in the Amount column.

Exhibit 5
Purchases Journal and Postings

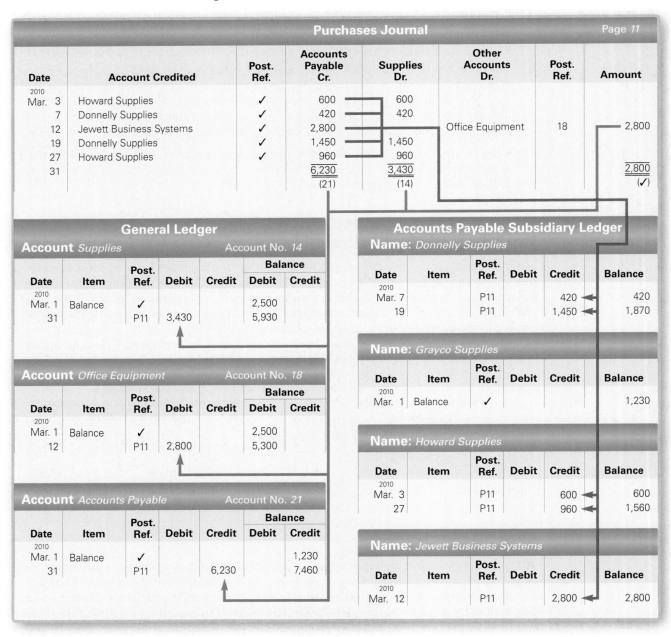

To illustrate, on March 12 NetSolutions purchased office equipment on account from Jewett Business Systems for $2,800. This transaction is recorded in the purchases journal shown in Exhibit 5 by entering the following items:

1.   Date column: *Mar. 12*
2.   Account Credited column: *Jewett Business Systems*

3.   Accounts Payable Cr. column: *2,800*

4.   Other Accounts Dr. column: *Office Equipment*

5.   Amount column: *2,800*

At the end of the month, all of the amount columns are totaled. The debits must equal the credits. If the debits do not equal the credits, an error has occurred. Before proceeding further, the error must be found and corrected.

The process of posting from the purchases journal shown in Exhibit 5 is as follows:

1.   Each transaction involving a purchase on account is posted individually to a creditor's account in the accounts payable subsidiary ledger. Postings to creditor accounts should be made on a regular basis. In this way, the creditor's account will show a current balance.

To illustrate, Exhibit 5 shows on March 3 the purchase of supplies of $600 on account from Howard Supplies. The posting of the $600 credit to Howard Supplies accounts payable subsidiary ledger is shown in Exhibit 5. After the posting, Howard Supplies has a credit balance of $600.

2.   To provide a trail of the entries posted to the subsidiary and general ledger, the source of these entries is indicated in the Posting Reference column of each account by inserting the letter P (for purchases journal) and the page number of the purchases journal.

To illustrate, Exhibit 5 shows that after $600 is posted to Howard Supplies' account, P11 is inserted into the Post. Ref. column of the account.

3.   To indicate that the transaction has been posted to the accounts payable subsidiary ledger, a check mark (✓) is inserted in the Posting Reference column of the purchases journal, as shown in Exhibit 5.

To illustrate, Exhibit 5 shows that a check mark (✓) has been inserted in the Post. Ref. column next to Howard Supplies to indicate that the $600 has been posted.

4.   A single monthly total of the Accounts Payable Cr. column is posted to the accounts payable general ledger account. This is the total amount purchased on account and is posted as a credit to Accounts Payable. The accounts payable account number (21) is then inserted below the Accounts Payable Cr. column to indicate that the posting is complete.

To illustrate, Exhibit 5 shows the monthly total of $6,230 was posted as a credit to Accounts Payable (21).

5.   A single monthly total of the Supplies Dr. column is posted to the supplies general ledger account. This is the total supplies purchased on account during the month and is posted as a debit to Supplies. The supplies account number (14) is then inserted below the Supplies Dr. column to indicate that the posting is complete.

To illustrate, Exhibit 5 shows the monthly total of $3,430 was posted as a debit to Supplies (14).

6.   The accounts listed in the Other Accounts Dr. column are posted on a regular basis as a separate debit to each account. The account number is then inserted in the Post. Ref. column to indicate that the posting is complete. Because accounts in the Other Accounts Dr. column are posted individually, a check mark is placed below the column total at the end of the month to show that no further action is needed.

To illustrate, Exhibit 5 shows that $2,800 was posted as a debit to Office Equipment (18). Also, at the end of the month, a check mark (✓) is entered below the Amount column to indicate that no further action is needed.

Cash Payments Journal

All transactions that involve the payment of cash are recorded in a *cash payments journal*. The cash payments journal for NetSolutions is shown in Exhibit 6.

The cash payments journal shown in Exhibit 6 has a Cash Cr. column. The kinds of transactions in which cash is paid and how often they occur determine the titles of the

Exhibit 6

Cash Payments Journal and Postings

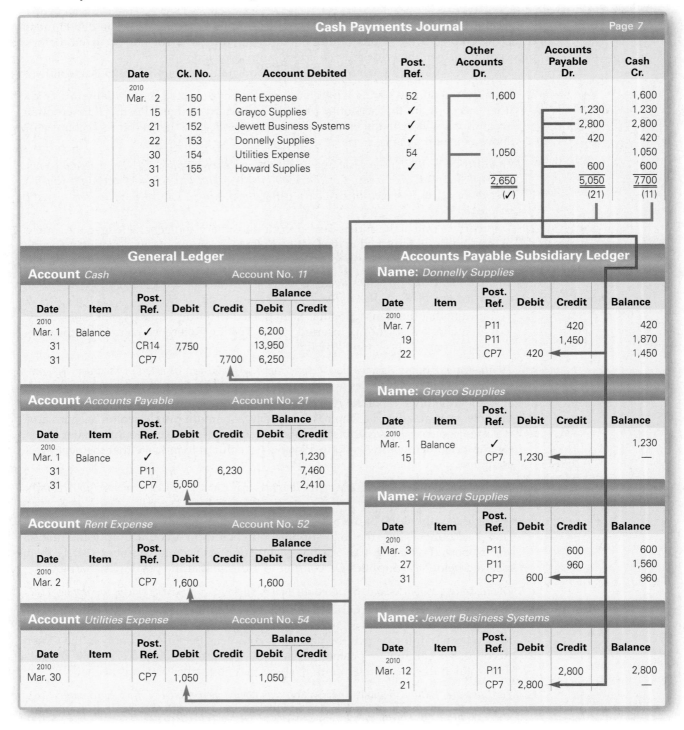

Cash Payments Journal — Page 7

Date	Ck. No.	Account Debited	Post. Ref.	Other Accounts Dr.	Accounts Payable Dr.	Cash Cr.
2010						
Mar. 2	150	Rent Expense	52	1,600		1,600
15	151	Grayco Supplies	✓		1,230	1,230
21	152	Jewett Business Systems	✓		2,800	2,800
22	153	Donnelly Supplies	✓		420	420
30	154	Utilities Expense	54	1,050		1,050
31	155	Howard Supplies	✓		600	600
31				2,650	5,050	7,700
				(✓)	(21)	(11)

General Ledger

Account Cash   Account No. 11

Date	Item	Post. Ref.	Debit	Credit	Balance Debit	Balance Credit
2010						
Mar. 1	Balance	✓			6,200	
31		CR14	7,750		13,950	
31		CP7		7,700	6,250	

Account Accounts Payable   Account No. 21

Date	Item	Post. Ref.	Debit	Credit	Balance Debit	Balance Credit
2010						
Mar. 1	Balance	✓				1,230
31		P11		6,230		7,460
31		CP7	5,050			2,410

Account Rent Expense   Account No. 52

Date	Item	Post. Ref.	Debit	Credit	Balance Debit	Balance Credit
2010						
Mar. 2		CP7	1,600		1,600	

Account Utilities Expense   Account No. 54

Date	Item	Post. Ref.	Debit	Credit	Balance Debit	Balance Credit
2010						
Mar. 30		CP7	1,050		1,050	

Accounts Payable Subsidiary Ledger

Name: Donnelly Supplies

Date	Item	Post. Ref.	Debit	Credit	Balance
2010					
Mar. 7		P11		420	420
19		P11		1,450	1,870
22		CP7	420		1,450

Name: Grayco Supplies

Date	Item	Post. Ref.	Debit	Credit	Balance
2010					
Mar. 1	Balance	✓			1,230
15		CP7	1,230		—

Name: Howard Supplies

Date	Item	Post. Ref.	Debit	Credit	Balance
2010					
Mar. 3		P11		600	600
27		P11		960	1,560
31		CP7	600		960

Name: Jewett Business Systems

Date	Item	Post. Ref.	Debit	Credit	Balance
2010					
Mar. 12		P11		2,800	2,800
21		CP7	2,800		—

other columns. For example, NetSolutions often pays cash to creditors on account. Thus, the cash payments journal in Exhibit 6 has an Accounts Payable Dr. column. In addition, NetSolutions makes all payments by check. Thus, a check number is entered for each payment in the Ck. No. (Check Number) column to the right of the Date column. The check numbers are helpful in controlling cash payments and provide a useful cross-reference.

To illustrate, on March 15 NetSolutions issued Check No. 151 for $1,230 to Grayco Supplies for payment on its account. This transaction is recorded in the cash payments journal shown in Exhibit 6 by entering the following items:

1. Date column: *Mar. 15*
2. Ck. No. column: *151*
3. Account Debited column: *Grayco Supplies*
4. Accounts Payable Dr. column: *1,230*
5. Cash Cr. column: *1,230*

The Other Accounts Dr. column in Exhibit 6 is used for recording debits to any account for which there is no special debit column. For example, NetSolutions issued Check No. 150 on March 2 for $1,600 in payment of the March rent. This transaction is recorded in the cash payments journal, shown in Exhibit 6, by entering the following items:

1. Date column: *Mar. 2*
2. Ck. No. column: *150*
3. Account Debited column: *Rent Expense*
4. Other Accounts Dr. column: *1,600*
5. Cash Cr. column: *1,600*

At the end of the month, all of the amount columns are totaled. The debits must equal the credits. If the debits do not equal the credits, an error has occurred. Before proceeding further, the error must be found and corrected.

The process of posting from the cash payments journal, shown in Exhibit 6, is as follows:

1. Each transaction involving the payment of cash on account is posted individually to a creditor account in the accounts payable subsidiary ledger. Postings to creditor accounts should be made on a regular basis. In this way, the creditor's account will show a current balance.

   To illustrate, Exhibit 6 shows on March 22 the payment of $420 on account to Donnelly Supplies. The posting of the $420 debit to Donnelly Supplies in the accounts payable subsidiary ledger is shown in Exhibit 6. After the posting, Donnelly Supplies has a credit balance of $1,450.

2. To provide a trail of the entries posted to the subsidiary and general ledger, the source of these entries is indicated in the Posting Reference column of each account by inserting the letter CP (for cash payments journal) and the page number of the cash payments journal.

   To illustrate, Exhibit 6 shows that after $420 is posted to Donnelly Supplies' account, CP7 is inserted into the Post. Ref. column of the account.

3. To indicate that the transaction has been posted to the accounts payable subsidiary ledger, a check mark (✓) is inserted in the Posting Reference column of the cash payments journal, as shown in Exhibit 6.

   To illustrate, Exhibit 6 shows that a check mark (✓) has been inserted in the Post. Ref. column next to Donnelly Supplies to indicate that the $420 has been posted.

4. A single monthly total of the Accounts Payable Dr. column is posted to the accounts payable general ledger account. This is the total cash paid on account and is posted as a debit to Accounts Payable. The accounts payable account number (21) is then inserted below the Accounts Payable Dr. column to indicate that the posting is complete.

   To illustrate, Exhibit 6 shows the monthly total of $5,050 was posted as a debit to Accounts Payable (21).

5. A single monthly total of the Cash Cr. column is posted to the cash general ledger account. This is the total cash payments during the month and is posted as a credit to Cash. The cash account number (11) is then inserted below the Cash Cr. column to indicate that the posting is complete.

To illustrate, Exhibit 6 shows the monthly total of $7,700 was posted as a credit to Cash (11).

6. The accounts listed in the Other Accounts Dr. column are posted on a regular basis as a separate debit to each account. The account number is then inserted in the Post. Ref. column to indicate that the posting is complete. Because accounts in the Other Accounts Dr. column are posted individually, a check mark is placed below the column total at the end of the month to show that no further action is needed.

To illustrate, Exhibit 6 shows that $1,600 was posted as a debit to Rent Expense (52) and $1,050 was posted as a debit to Utilities Expense (54). Also, at the end of the month, a check mark (✓) is entered below the Other Accounts Dr. column to indicate that no further action is needed.

Accounts Payable Control Account and Subsidiary Ledger

After all posting has been completed for the month, the balances in the accounts payable subsidiary ledger should be totaled. This total should then be compared with the balance of the accounts payable controlling account in the general ledger. If the controlling account and the subsidiary ledger do not agree, an error has occurred. Before proceeding, the error must be located and corrected.

The total of NetSolutions' accounts payable subsidiary ledger is $2,410. This total agrees with the balance of its accounts payable control account on March 31, 2010, as shown below.

Accounts Payable (Control)		NetSolutions Accounts Payable Subsidiary Ledger March 31, 2010	
Balance, March 1, 2010	$ 1,230	Donnelly Supplies	$1,450
Total credits (from purchases journal)	6,230	Grayco Supplies	0
Total debits		Howard Supplies	960
(from cash payments journal)	(5,050)	Jewett Business Systems	0
Balance, March 31, 2010	$ 2,410	Total	$2,410

Exercises

EX C-1
Identify journals

Assuming the use of a two-column (all-purpose) general journal, a revenue journal, and a cash receipts journal as illustrated in this chapter, indicate the journal in which each of the following transactions should be recorded:

a. Receipt of cash from sale of office equipment.
b. Sale of office supplies on account, at cost, to a neighboring business.
c. Providing services for cash.
d. Closing of the dividends account at the end of the year.
e. Adjustment to record accrued salaries at the end of the year.
f. Receipt of cash refund from overpayment of taxes.
g. Receipt of cash on account from a customer.
h. Receipt of cash for rent.
i. Investment of cash in the business by the owner in exchange for capital stock.
j. Providing services on account.

EX C-2
Identify journals

Assuming the use of a two-column (all-purpose) general journal, a purchases journal, and a cash payments journal as illustrated in this chapter, indicate the journal in which each of the following transactions should be recorded:

a. Payment of six months' rent in advance.
b. Adjustment to record depreciation at the end of the month.
c. Adjustment to prepaid insurance at the end of the month.
d. Purchase of office equipment for cash.
e. Advance payment of a one-year fire insurance policy on the office.
f. Purchase of office supplies for cash.
g. Adjustment to record accrued salaries at the end of the period.
h. Adjustment to prepaid rent at the end of the month.
i. Purchase of office supplies on account.
j. Purchase of services on account.
k. Purchase of an office computer on account.

EX C-3
**Identify postings
from revenue journal**

Using the following revenue journal for Alpha Services Inc., identify each of the posting references, indicated by a letter, as representing (1) posting to general ledger accounts or (2) posting to subsidiary ledger accounts.

REVENUE JOURNAL

Date	Invoice No.	Account Debited	Post. Ref.	Accounts Rec. Dr. Fees Earned Cr.
2010				
Nov. 1	112	Environmental Safety Co.	(a)	$2,625
10	113	Jenkins Co.	(b)	1,050
18	114	Eco-Systems	(c)	1,600
27	115	TEK Corp.	(d)	965
30				$6,240
				(e)

EX C-4
**Identify transactions
in accounts
receivable ledger**

The debits and credits from three related transactions are presented in the following customer's account taken from the accounts receivable subsidiary ledger.

NAME   *Insite Design*
ADDRESS   *1319 Elm Street*

Date	Item	Post. Ref.	Debit	Credit	Balance
2010					
Nov. 3		R36	740		740
6		J11		80	660
13		CR47		660	—

Describe each transaction, and identify the source of each posting.

EX C-5
**Identify postings
from purchases
journal**

Using the following purchases journal, identify each of the posting references, indicated by a letter, as representing (1) a posting to a general ledger account, (2) a posting to a subsidiary ledger account, or (3) that no posting is required.

PURCHASES JOURNAL   Page *49*

Date	Account Credited	Post. Ref.	Accounts Payable Cr.	Store Supplies Dr.	Office Supplies Dr.	Other Accounts Dr.	Post. Ref.	Amount
2010								
Sept. 4	Amex Supply Co.	(a)	4,000		4,000			
6	Coastal Equipment Co.	(b)	5,325			Warehouse Equipment	(c)	5,325
11	Office Warehouse	(d)	2,000			Office Equipment	(e)	2,000
13	Taylor Products	(f)	1,875	1,600	275			
20	Office Warehouse	(g)	6,000			Store Equipment	(h)	6,000
27	Miller Supply Co.	(i)	2,740	2,740				
30			21,940	4,340	4,275			13,325
			(j)	(k)	(l)			(m)

EX C-6
Identify postings from cash payments journal

Using the following cash payments journal, identify each of the posting references, indicated by a letter, as representing (1) a posting to a general ledger account, (2) a posting to a subsidiary ledger account, or (3) that no posting is required.

CASH PAYMENTS JOURNAL Page *46*

Date	Ck. No.	Account Debited	Post. Ref.	Other Accounts Dr.	Accounts Payable Dr.	Cash Cr.
2010						
Jan. 3	611	Aquatic Systems Co.	(a)		4,000	4,000
5	612	Utilities Expense	(b)	310		310
10	613	Prepaid Rent	(c)	3,200		3,200
17	614	Advertising Expense	(d)	640		640
20	615	Flowers to Go, Inc.	(e)		1,250	1,250
22	616	Office Equipment	(f)	3,600		3,600
25	617	Office Supplies	(g)	250		250
27	618	Evans Co.	(h)		5,500	5,500
31	619	Salaries Expense	(i)	1,750		1,750
31				9,750	10,750	20,500
				(j)	(k)	(l)

EX C-7
Identify transactions in accounts payable ledger account

The debits and credits from three related transactions are presented in the following creditor's account taken from the accounts payable ledger.

NAME Madison Co.
ADDRESS 101 W. Stratford Ave.

Date	Item	Post. Ref.	Debit	Credit	Balance
2010					
Oct. 6		P39		11,900	11,900
11		J12	300		11,600
16		CP56	11,600		—

Describe each transaction, and identify the source of each posting.

Problems

PR C-1
Revenue journal; accounts receivable and general ledgers

✔ 1. Revenue journal, total fees earned, $2,025

Guardian Security Services was established on August 15, 2010, to provide security services. The services provided during the remainder of the month are listed below.

Aug. 18. Issued Invoice No. 1 to Jacob Co. for $325 on account.
20. Issued Invoice No. 2 to Qwik-Mart Co. for $260 on account.
22. Issued Invoice No. 3 to Hawke Co. for $545 on account.
27. Issued Invoice No. 4 to Carson Co. for $450 on account.
28. Issued Invoice No. 5 to Bower Co. for $100 on account.
28. Provided security services, $80, to Qwik-Mart Co. in exchange for supplies.
30. Issued Invoice No. 6 to Qwik-Mart Co. for $115 on account.
31. Issued Invoice No. 7 to Hawke Co. for $230 on account.

Instructions
1. Journalize the transactions for August, using a single-column revenue journal and a two-column general journal. Post to the following customer accounts in the accounts receivable ledger, and insert the balance immediately after recording each entry: Bower Co.; Carson Co.; Hawke Co.; Jacob Co.; Qwik-Mart Co.

2. Post the revenue journal to the following accounts in the general ledger, inserting the account balances only after the last postings:

> 12   Accounts Receivable
> 14   Supplies
> 41   Fees Earned

3. a. What is the sum of the balances of the accounts in the subsidiary ledger at August 31?
    b. What is the balance of the controlling account at August 31?

PR C-2
Revenue and cash receipts journals; accounts receivable and general ledgers

obj. 2

✔ 3. Total cash receipts, $6,630

Transactions related to revenue and cash receipts completed by Sterling Engineering Services during the period November 2–30, 2010, are as follows:

Nov. 2. Issued Invoice No. 717 to Yee Co., $810.
     3. Received cash from AGI Co. for the balance owed on its account.
     7. Issued Invoice No. 718 to Phoenix Development Co., $400.
    10. Issued Invoice No. 719 to Ridge Communities, $1,940.
         Post revenue and collections to the accounts receivable subsidiary ledger.
    14. Received cash from Phoenix Development Co. for the balance owed on November 1.
    16. Issued Invoice No. 720 to Phoenix Development Co., $275.
         Post revenue and collections to the accounts receivable subsidiary ledger.
    19. Received cash from Yee Co. for the balance due on invoice of November 2.
    20. Received cash from Phoenix Development Co. for invoice of November 7.
    23. Issued Invoice No. 721 to AGI Co., $670.
    30. Recorded cash fees earned, $3,400.
    30. Received office equipment of $1,500 in partial settlement of balance due on the Ridge Communities account.
         Post revenue and collections to the accounts receivable subsidiary ledger.

Instructions
1. Insert the following balances in the general ledger as of November 1:

> | 11 | Cash | $17,240 |
> |----|------|---------|
> | 12 | Accounts Receivable | 2,020 |
> | 18 | Office Equipment | 31,500 |
> | 41 | Fees Earned | — |

2. Insert the following balances in the accounts receivable subsidiary ledger as of November 1:

> | AGI Co. | $1,340 |
> |---------|--------|
> | Phoenix Development Co. | 680 |
> | Ridge Communities | — |
> | Yee Co. | — |

3. Prepare a single-column revenue journal and a cash receipts journal. Use the following column headings for the cash receipts journal: Fees Earned Cr., Accounts Receivable Cr., and Cash Dr. The Fees Earned column is used to record cash fees. Insert a check mark (✔) in the Post. Ref. column.
4. Using the two special journals and the two-column general journal, journalize the transactions for November. Post to the accounts receivable subsidiary ledger, and insert the balances at the points indicated in the narrative of transactions. Determine the balance in the customer's account before recording a cash receipt.
5. Total each of the columns of the special journals, and post the individual entries and totals to the general ledger. Insert account balances after the last posting.
6. Determine that the subsidiary ledger agrees with the controlling account in the general ledger.

PR C-3

Purchases, accounts payable account, and accounts payable ledger

✔ 3. Total accounts payable credit, $20,950

GW Surveyors provides survey work for construction projects. The office staff use office supplies, while surveying crews use field supplies. Purchases on account completed by GW Surveyors during October 2010 are as follows:

Oct. 1. Purchased field supplies on account from Wendell Co., $2,505.
3. Purchased office supplies on account from Lassiter Co., $260.
8. Purchased field supplies on account from Sure Measure Supplies, $3,600.
12. Purchased field supplies on account from Wendell Co., $2,850.
15. Purchased office supplies on account from J-Mart Co., $375.
19. Purchased office equipment on account from Eskew Co., $6,780.
23. Purchased field supplies on account from Sure Measure Supplies, $1,910.
26. Purchased office supplies on account from J-Mart Co., $170.
30. Purchased field supplies on account from Sure Measure Supplies, $2,500.

Instructions

1. Insert the following balances in the general ledger as of October 1:

14	Field Supplies	$ 5,100
15	Office Supplies	1,170
18	Office Equipment	17,200
21	Accounts Payable	4,375

2. Insert the following balances in the accounts payable subsidiary ledger as of October 1:

Eskew Co.	$3,400
J-Mart Co.	580
Lassiter Co.	395
Sure Measure Supplies	—
Wendell Co.	—

3. Journalize the transactions for October, using a purchases journal similar to the one illustrated in this chapter. Prepare the purchases journal with columns for Accounts Payable, Field Supplies, Office Supplies, and Other Accounts. Post to the creditor accounts in the accounts payable ledger immediately after each entry.
4. Post the purchases journal to the accounts in the general ledger.
5. a. What is the sum of the balances in the subsidiary ledger at October 31?
    b. What is the balance of the controlling account at October 31?

PR C-4

Purchases and cash payments journals; accounts payable and general ledgers

✔ 1. Total cash payments, $243,460

Black Gold Tea Exploration Co. was established on March 15, 2010, to provide oil-drilling services. Black Gold Tea uses field equipment (rigs and pipe) and field supplies (drill bits and lubricants) in its operations. Transactions related to purchases and cash payments during the remainder of March are as follows:

Mar. 16. Issued Check No. 1 in payment of rent for the remainder of March, $5,000.
16. Purchased field equipment on account from PMI Sales Inc., $29,400.
17. Purchased field supplies on account from Culver Supply Co., $9,320.
18. Issued Check No. 2 in payment of field supplies, $2,180, and office supplies, $450.
20. Purchased office supplies on account from A-One Office Supply Co., $1,110.
Post the journals to the accounts payable subsidiary ledger.
24. Issued Check No. 3 to PMI Sales Inc., in payment of March 16 invoice.
26. Issued Check No. 4 to Culver Supply Co. in payment of March 17 invoice.
28. Issued Check No. 5 to purchase land, $170,000.
28. Purchased office supplies on account from A-One Office Supply Co., $2,670.
Post the journals to the accounts payable subsidiary ledger.
30. Purchased the following from PMI Sales Inc. on account: field supplies, $22,340 and office equipment, $12,200.
30. Issued Check No. 6 to A-One Office Supply Co. in payment of March 20 invoice.

Mar. 30.   Purchased field supplies on account from Culver Supply Co., $11,900.
   31.   Issued Check No. 7 in payment of salaries, $26,000.
   31.   Rented building for one year in exchange for field equipment having a cost of $12,000.
   Post the journals to the accounts payable subsidiary ledger.

Instructions

1. Journalize the transactions for March. Use a purchases journal and a cash payments journal, similar to those illustrated in this chapter, and a two-column general journal. Set debit columns for Field Supplies, Office Supplies, and Other Accounts in the purchases journal. Refer to the following partial chart of accounts:

11	Cash	18	Office Equipment
14	Field Supplies	19	Land
15	Office Supplies	21	Accounts Payable
16	Prepaid Rent	61	Salary Expense
17	Field Equipment	71	Rent Expense

At the points indicated in the narrative of transactions, post to the following accounts in the accounts payable ledger:

A-One Office Supply Co.
Culver Supply Co.
PMI Sales Inc.

2. Post the individual entries (Other Accounts columns of the purchases journal and the cash payments journal; both columns of the general journal) to the appropriate general ledger accounts.
3. Total each of the columns of the purchases journal and the cash payments journal, and post the appropriate totals to the general ledger. (Because the problem does not include transactions related to cash receipts, the cash account in the ledger will have a credit balance.)
4. Prepare an accounts payable subsidiary ledger.

PR C-5

All journals and general ledger; trial balance

✔ 2. Total cash receipts, $73,230

The transactions completed by Over-Nite Express Company during May 2010, the first month of the fiscal year, were as follows:

May 1.   Issued Check No. 205 for May rent, $1,000.
   2.   Purchased a vehicle on account from McIntyre Sales Co., $22,300.
   3.   Purchased office equipment on account from Office Mate Inc., $520.
   5.   Issued Invoice No. 91 to Martin Co., $5,200.
   6.   Received check for $5,610 from Baker Co. in payment of invoice.
   7.   Issued Invoice No. 92 to Trent Co., $8,150.
   9.   Issued Check No. 206 for fuel expense, $670.
   10.   Received check for $8,920 from Sanchez Co. in payment of invoice.
   10.   Issued Check No. 207 to Office City in payment of $490 invoice.
   10.   Issued Check No. 208 to Bastille Co. in payment of $1,350 invoice.
   11.   Issued Invoice No. 93 to Jarvis Co., $6,540.
   11.   Issued Check No. 209 to Porter Co. in payment of $325 invoice.
   12.   Received check for $5,200 from Martin Co. in payment of invoice.
   13.   Issued Check No. 210 to McIntyre Sales Co. in payment of $22,300 invoice.
   16.   Cash fees earned for May 1–16, $18,900.
   16.   Issued Check No. 211 for purchase of a vehicle, $22,400.
   17.   Issued Check No. 212 for miscellaneous administrative expense, $4,100.
   18.   Purchased maintenance supplies on account from Bastille Co., $1,680.
   18.   Received check for rent revenue on office space, $2,000.
   19.   Purchased the following on account from Master Supply Co.: maintenance supplies, $1,950, and office supplies, $2,050.
   20.   Issued Check No. 213 in payment of advertising expense, $7,250.

May 20. Used maintenance supplies with a cost of $2,400 to repair vehicles.
   21. Purchased office supplies on account from Office City, $710.
   24. Issued Invoice No. 94 to Sanchez Co., $7,890.
   25. Received check for $11,900 from Baker Co. in payment of invoice.
   25. Issued Invoice No. 95 to Trent Co., $5,030.
   26. Issued Check No. 214 to Office Mate Inc. in payment of $520 invoice.
   27. Issued Check No. 215 as a dividend, $3,240.
   30. Issued Check No. 216 in payment of driver salaries, $27,690.
   31. Issued Check No. 217 in payment of office salaries, $18,600.
   31. Issued Check No. 218 for office supplies, $450.
   31. Cash fees earned for May 17–31, $20,700.

Instructions

1. Enter the following account balances in the general ledger as of May 1:

11	Cash	$ 61,300	33	Dividends	—
12	Accounts Receivable	26,430	41	Fees Earned	—
14	Maintenance Supplies	6,580	42	Rent Revenue	—
15	Office Supplies	3,150	51	Driver Salaries Expense	—
16	Office Equipment	15,390	52	Maintenance Supplies Expense	—
17	Accum. Depr.—Office Equip.	3,450	53	Fuel Expense	—
18	Vehicles	57,000	61	Office Salaries Expense	—
19	Accum. Depr.—Vehicles	15,460	62	Rent Expense	—
21	Accounts Payable	2,165	63	Advertising Expense	—
31	Capital Stock	100,000	64	Miscellaneous Administrative Exp.	—
32	Retained Earnings	48,775			

2. Journalize the transactions for May 2010, using the following journals similar to those illustrated in this chapter: single-column revenue journal, cash receipts journal, purchases journal (with columns for Accounts Payable, Maintenance Supplies, Office Supplies, and Other Accounts), cash payments journal, and two-column general journal. Assume that the daily postings to the individual accounts in the accounts payable ledger and the accounts receivable ledger have been made.
3. Post the appropriate individual entries to the general ledger.
4. Total each of the columns of the special journals, and post the appropriate totals to the general ledger; insert the account balances.
5. Prepare a trial balance.
6. Verify the agreement of each subsidiary ledger with its controlling account. The sum of the balances of the accounts in the subsidiary ledgers as of May 31 are as follows:

Accounts Receivable	$27,610
Accounts Payable	6,390

Appendix D

End-of-Period Spreadsheet (Work Sheet) for a Merchandising Business

A merchandising business may use an end-of-period spreadsheet (work sheet) for preparing financial statements and adjusting and closing entries. This appendix illustrates such a spreadsheet for the perpetual inventory system.

The end-of-period spreadsheet in Exhibit 1 is for NetSolutions on December 31, 2011. Exhibit 1 was prepared using the following steps that are described and illustrated in the appendix to Chapter 4.

Step 1.   Enter the Title.
Step 2.   Enter the Unadjusted Trial Balance.
Step 3.   Enter the Adjustments.
Step 4.   Enter the Adjusted Trial Balance.
Step 5.   Extend the Accounts to the Income Statement and Balance Sheet columns.
Step 6.   Total the Income Statement and Balance Sheet columns, compute the Net Income or Net Loss, and complete the spreadsheet.

The data needed for adjusting the accounts of NetSolutions are as follows:

Physical merchandise inventory on December 31, 2011		$62,150
Office supplies on hand on December 31, 2011		480
Insurance expired during 2011		1,910
Depreciation during 2011 on: Store equipment		3,100
Office equipment		2,490
Salaries accrued on December 31, 2011: Sales salaries	$780	
Office salaries	360	1,140
Rent earned during 2011		600

There is no required order for analyzing the adjustment data and the accounts in the spreadsheet. However, the accounts are normally analyzed in the order in which they appear in the spreadsheet. Using this approach, the adjustment for merchandise inventory shrinkage is listed first as entry (a), followed by the adjustment for office supplies used as entry (b), and so on.

After all the adjustments have been entered, the Adjustments columns are totaled to prove the equality of debits and credits. The adjusted trial balance is entered by combining the adjustments with the unadjusted balances for each account.[1] The Adjusted Trial Balance columns are then totaled to prove the equality of debits and credits. The adjusted balances are then extended to the statement columns. The four statement columns are totaled, and the net income or net loss is determined.

For NetSolutions, the difference between the Credit and Debit columns of the Income Statement section is $75,400, the amount of the net income. The difference between the Debit and Credit columns of the Balance Sheet section is also $75,400, which is the increase in retained earnings as a result of the net income.

1 Some accountants prefer to eliminate the Adjusted Trial Balance columns and to extend the adjusted balances directly to the statement columns. Such a spreadsheet (work sheet) is often used if there are only a few adjustment items.

Exhibit 1

End-of-Period Spreadsheet (Work Sheet) for a Merchandising Business Using Perpetual Inventory System

	A	B	C	D	E	F	G	H	I	J	K
1		NetSolutions									
2		End-of-Period Spreadsheet (Work Sheet)									
3		For the Year Ended December 31, 2011									
4		Unadjusted				Adjusted		Income			
5	Account Title	Trial Balance		Adjustments		Trial Balance		Statement		Balance Sheet	
6		Dr.	Cr.	Dr.	Cr.	Dr.	Cr.	Dr.	Cr.	Dr.	Cr.
7	Cash	52,950				52,950				52,950	
8	Accounts Receivable	91,080				91,080				91,080	
9	Merchandise Inventory	63,950			(a)1,800	62,150				62,150	
10	Office Supplies	1,090			(b) 610	480				480	
11	Prepaid Insurance	4,560			(c)1,910	2,650				2,650	
12	Land	20,000				20,000				20,000	
13	Store Equipment	27,100				27,100				27,100	
14	Accum. Depr.—Store Equipment		2,600		(d)3,100		5,700				5,700
15	Office Equipment	15,570				15,570				15,570	
16	Accum. Depr.—Office Equipment		2,230		(e)2,490		4,720				4,720
17	Accounts Payable		22,420				22,420				22,420
18	Salaries Payable				(f)1,140		1,140				1,140
19	Unearned Rent		2,400	(g) 600			1,800				1,800
20	Notes Payable										
21	(final payment due 2019)		25,000				25,000				25,000
22	Capital Stock		25,000				25,000				25,000
23	Retained Earnings		128,800				128,800				128,800
24	Dividends	18,000				18,000				18,000	
25	Sales		720,185				720,185		720,185		
26	Sales Returns and Allowances	6,140				6,140		6,140			
27	Sales Discounts	5,790				5,790		5,790			
28	Cost of Merchandise Sold	523,505		(a)1,800		525,305		525,305			
29	Sales Salaries Expense	52,650		(f) 780		53,430		53,430			
30	Advertising Expense	10,860				10,860		10,860			
31	Depr. Exp.—Store Equipment			(d)3,100		3,100		3,100			
32	Delivery Expense	2,800				2,800		2,800			
33	Miscellaneous Selling Expense	630				630		630			
34	Office Salaries Expense	20,660		(f) 360		21,020		21,020			
35	Rent Expense	8,100				8,100		8,100			
36	Depr. Exp.—Office Equipment			(e)2,490		2,490		2,490			
37	Insurance Expense			(c)1,910		1,910		1,910			
38	Office Supplies Expense			(b) 610		610		610			
39	Misc. Administrative Expense	760				760		760			
40	Rent Revenue				(g) 600		600		600		
41	Interest Expense	2,440				2,440		2,440			214,580
42		928,635	928,635	11,650	11,650	935,365	935,365	645,385	720,785	289,980	75,400
43	Net income							75,400			289,980
44								720,785	720,785	289,980	

(a) Merchandise inventory shrinkage for period, $1,800 ($63,950 − $62,150).
(b) Office supplies used, $610 ($1,090 − $480).
(c) Insurance expired, $1,910.
(d) Depreciation of store equipment, $3,100.
(e) Depreciation of office equipment, $2,490.
(f) Salaries accrued but not paid (sales salaries, $780; office salaries, $360), $1,140.
(g) Rent earned from amount received in advance, $600.

The income statement, retained earnings statement, and balance sheet can be prepared from the spreadsheet (work sheet). These financial statements are shown in Exhibits 1, 4, and 5 in Chapter 6. The Adjustments columns in the spreadsheet (work sheet) may be used as the basis for journalizing the adjusting entries. NetSolutions' adjusting entries at the end of 2011 are shown at the top of the following page.

Date		Description	Post. Ref.	Debit	Credit
		Journal			Page *28*
		Adjusting Entries			
2011 Dec.	31	Cost of Merchandise Sold	510	1,800	
		Merchandise Inventory	115		1,800
		Inventory shrinkage.			
	31	Office Supplies Expense	534	610	
		Office Supplies	116		610
		Supplies used.			
	31	Insurance Expense	533	1,910	
		Prepaid Insurance	117		1,910
		Insurance expired.			
	31	Depr. Expense—Store Equipment	522	3,100	
		Accumulated Depr.—Store Equipment	124		3,100
		Store equipment depreciation.			
	31	Depr. Expense—Office Equipment	532	2,490	
		Accumulated Depr.—Office Equipment	126		2,490
		Office equipment depreciation.			
	31	Sales Salaries Expense	520	780	
		Office Salaries Expense	530	360	
		Salaries Payable	211		1,140
		Accrued salaries.			
	31	Unearned Rent	212	600	
		Rent Revenue	610		600
		Rent earned.			

The Income Statement columns of the work sheet may be used as the basis for preparing the closing entries. The closing entries for NetSolutions at the end of 2011 are shown on page 232 of Chapter 5.

After the closing entries have been prepared and posted to the accounts, a post-closing trial balance may be prepared to verify the debit-credit equality. The only accounts that should appear on the post-closing trial balance are the asset, contra asset, liability, and stockholders' accounts with balances. These are the same accounts that appear on the end-of-period balance sheet.

PR D-1
End-of-period spreadsheet (work sheet), financial statements, and adjusting and closing entries for perpetual inventory system

✔ 2. Net income: $38,800

The accounts and their balances in the ledger of Rack Saver Co. on December 31, 2010, are as follows:

Cash	$ 12,000	Sales	$800,000
Accounts Receivable	72,500	Sales Returns and Allowances	11,900
Merchandise Inventory	170,000	Sales Discounts	7,100
Prepaid Insurance	9,700	Cost of Merchandise Sold	500,000
Store Supplies	4,200	Sales Salaries Expense	96,400
Office Supplies	2,100	Advertising Expense	25,000
Store Equipment	360,000	Depreciation Expense—	
Accumulated Depreciation—		Store Equipment	—
Store Equipment	60,300	Store Supplies Expense	—
Office Equipment	70,000	Miscellaneous Selling Expense	1,600
Accumulated Depreciation—		Office Salaries Expense	64,000
Office Equipment	17,200	Rent Expense	16,000
Accounts Payable	46,700	Insurance Expense	—
Salaries Payable	—	Depreciation Expense—	
Unearned Rent	3,000	Office Equipment	—
Note Payable		Office Supplies Expense	—
(final payment due 2018)	180,000	Miscellaneous Administrative	
Capital Stock	150,000	Expense	1,650
Retained Earnings	202,750	Rent Revenue	—
Dividends	25,000	Interest Expense	10,800
Income Summary	—		

The data needed for year-end adjustments on December 31 are as follows:

Physical merchandise inventory on December 31		$162,500
Insurance expired during the year		3,600
Supplies on hand on December 31:		
Store supplies		1,050
Office supplies		600
Depreciation for the year:		
Store equipment		6,000
Office equipment		3,000
Salaries payable on December 31:		
Sales salaries	$1,800	
Office salaries	1,200	3,000
Unearned rent on December 31		2,000

Instructions
1. Prepare an end-of-period spreadsheet (work sheet) for the fiscal year ended December 31, 2010. List all accounts in the order given.
2. Prepare a multiple-step income statement.
3. Prepare a retained earnings statement.
4. Prepare a report form of balance sheet, assuming that the current portion of the note payable is $36,000.
5. Journalize the adjusting entries.
6. Journalize the closing entries.

PR D-2
End-of-period spreadsheet (work sheet), financial statements, and adjusting and closing entries for perpetual inventory system

✔ 1. Net income: $38,450

The accounts and their balances in the ledger of Quality Sports Co. on December 31, 2010, are as follows:

Cash	$ 18,000	Sales Returns and Allowances	$ 13,900
Accounts Receivable	42,500	Sales Discounts	7,100
Merchandise Inventory	218,000	Cost of Merchandise Sold	557,000
Prepaid Insurance	8,000	Sales Salaries Expense	101,400
Store Supplies	4,200	Advertising Expense	45,000
Office Supplies	2,100	Depreciation Expense—	
Store Equipment	282,000	Store Equipment	—
Accumulated Depreciation—		Delivery Expense	6,000
Store Equipment	70,300	Store Supplies Expense	—
Office Equipment	60,000	Miscellaneous Selling Expense	1,600
Accumulated Depreciation—		Office Salaries Expense	64,000
Office Equipment	17,200	Rent Expense	25,200
Accounts Payable	26,700	Insurance Expense	—
Salaries Payable	—	Depreciation Expense—	
Unearned Rent	2,500	Office Equipment	—
Note Payable (final payment, 2018)	175,000	Office Supplies Expense	—
Capital Stock	50,000	Miscellaneous Administrative	
Retained Earnings	236,450	Expense	1,650
Dividends	10,000	Rent Revenue	—
Sales	900,000	Interest Expense	10,500

The data needed for year-end adjustments on December 31 are as follows:

Merchandise inventory on December 31		$211,000
Insurance expired during the year		5,000
Supplies on hand on December 31:		
Store supplies		1,150
Office supplies		750
Depreciation for the year:		
Store equipment		7,500
Office equipment		3,800
Salaries payable on December 31:		
Sales salaries	$1,500	
Office salaries	1,000	2,500
Unearned rent on December 31		500

Instructions
1. Prepare an end-of-period spreadsheet (work sheet) for the fiscal year ended December 31, listing all accounts in the order given.
2. Prepare a multiple-step income statement.
3. Prepare a retained earnings statement.
4. Prepare a report form of balance sheet, assuming that the current portion of the note payable is $25,000.
5. Journalize the adjusting entries.
6. Journalize the closing entries.

Appendix E

Accounting for Deferred Income Taxes[1]

A corporation determines its taxable income according to the tax laws and files a corporate tax return. In contrast, a corporation prepares its financial statements using generally accepted accounting principles (GAAP). As a result, *taxable income* normally differs from *income before taxes* reported on the income statement.

Temporary Differences

Some differences between *taxable income* and *income before income taxes* are created because items are recognized in one period for tax purposes and in another period for income statement purposes. Such differences, called *temporary differences*, reverse or turn around in later years. Examples of items that create temporary differences include:

1. Revenues or gains that are taxed *after* they are reported in the income statement.

   Example: In some cases, companies make sales under an installment plan in which customers make periodic payments over future time periods. In such cases, the company recognizes revenue for financial reporting purposes when a sale is made but recognizes revenue for tax purposes when the cash is collected.

2. Expenses or losses that are deducted in determining taxable income *after* they are reported in the income statement.

   Example: Product warranty liability expense is estimated and reported in the year of the sale for financial statement reporting but is deducted for tax reporting when paid.

3. Revenues or gains that are taxed *before* they are reported in the income statement.

   Example: Cash received in advance for magazine subscriptions is included in taxable income when received but included in the income statement only when earned in a future period.

4. Expenses or losses that are deducted in determining taxable income *before* they are reported in the income statement.

   Example: MACRS depreciation is used for tax purposes, and the straight-line method is used for financial reporting purposes.

Since temporary differences reverse in later years, they do not change or reduce the total amount of taxable income over the life of a business. Exhibit 1 illustrates the reversing nature of temporary differences.

In Exhibit 1, a corporation uses MACRS depreciation for tax purposes and straight-line depreciation for financial statement purposes. MACRS recognizes more depreciation in the early years and less depreciation in the later years. However, the total depreciation expense is the same for both methods over the life of the asset.

As Exhibit 1 illustrates, temporary differences affect only the timing of when revenues and expenses are reported for tax purposes. The total amount of taxes paid does not change. In other words, only the timing of the payment of taxes is affected.

---

1 Accounting for deferred income taxes is a complex topic that is treated in greater detail in advanced accounting texts. The treatment here provides a general overview and conceptual understanding of the topic.

Exhibit 1

Temporary Differences

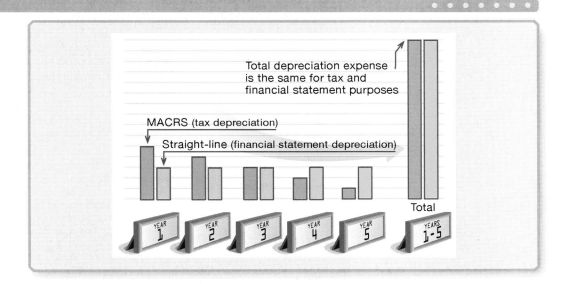

Most corporations use tax-planning methods that delay or defer the payment of taxes to later years. As a result, at the end of each year, most corporations will have two tax liabilities as follows:

1. Current income tax liability, which is due on the current year's taxable income.
2. Postponed or deferred tax liability, which is due in the future when the temporary differences reverse.

To illustrate, assume the following data for the first year of a corporation's operations:

Income before income taxes (income statement)	$ 300,000
Temporary differences	(200,000)
Taxable income (tax return)	$ 100,000
Income tax rate	40%

Based on the preceding data, the income tax expense reported on the income statement is $120,000 ($300,000 × 40%).[2] However, the current income tax liability (income tax due for the year) and reported on the corporate tax return is only $40,000 ($100,000 × 40%). The $80,000 ($120,000 − $40,000) difference is the deferred tax liability that will be paid in future years as shown below.

Income tax expense based on $300,000 reported income at 40%	$120,000
Income tax payable based on $100,000 taxable income at 40%	40,000
Income tax deferred to future years	$ 80,000

On the income statement, income tax expense of $120,000 ($300,000 × 40%) must be reported. This is done so that the current year's expenses (including income tax) are properly matched against the current year's revenue. The entry to record the income tax expense of $120,000 is as shown below.

Income Tax Expense	120,000	
Income Tax Payable		40,000
Deferred Income Tax Payable		80,000
Record income tax expense for the year.		

2 For purposes of illustration, the 40% rate is assumed to include all federal, state, and local income taxes.

The income tax expense reported on the income statement is the total tax, $120,000. Of this amount, $40,000 is currently due and $80,000 will be due in (deferred to) future years.

As the temporary differences reverse and the taxes become due in future years, the $80,000 in *Deferred Income Tax Payable* will be transferred to *Income Tax Payable*. To illustrate, assume that $48,000 of the deferred tax reverses and becomes due in the second year. The journal entry in the second year would be as follows:

Deferred Income Tax Payable	48,000	
Income Tax Payable		48,000
Record income tax payable.		

Reporting Deferred Taxes

The balance of *Deferred Income Tax Payable* at the end of a year is reported as a liability.[3] The amount due within one year is classified as a current liability. The remainder is classified as a long-term liability or reported in a Deferred Credits section following the Long-Term Liabilities section.[4]

Permanent Differences

Differences between taxable income and income (before taxes) reported on the income statement may also arise because of the following:

1. Some revenues are exempt from tax.
2. Some expenses are not deductible in determining taxable income.

The preceding differences, which will not reverse with the passage of time, are called *permanent differences*. For example, interest income on municipal bonds is exempt from federal taxation.

Permanent differences create no special financial reporting problems. This is because the amount of income tax determined according to the tax laws is the *same* amount reported on the income statement.

Interest from investments in municipal bonds is also tax exempt for individual taxpayers.

3 In some cases, a deferred tax asset may arise for tax benefits to be received in the future. Such deferred tax assets are reported as either current or long-term assets, depending on when the benefits are expected to be realized.

4 Additional note disclosures for deferred income taxes are also required. These are discussed in advanced accounting texts.

EX E-1
Deferred tax entries

Ramsey Inc. has $600,000 of income before income taxes, a 35% tax rate, and $320,000 of taxable income. Provide the journal entry for the current year's taxes.

EX E-2
Deferred tax entries

Downstairs Corp. has $180,000 of income before income taxes, a 40% tax rate, and $90,000 of taxable income. Provide the journal entry for the current year's taxes.

EX E-3
Deferred income taxes

Mattress Systems Inc. recognized service revenue of $500,000 on its financial statements in 2009. Assume, however, that the Tax Code requires this amount to be recognized for tax purposes in 2010. The taxable income for 2009 and 2010 is $1,800,000 and $2,400,000, respectively. Assume a tax rate of 40%.

Prepare the journal entries to record the tax expense, deferred taxes, and taxes payable for 2009 and 2010, respectively.

PR E-1
Deferred taxes

✔ 1. Year-end balance, 3rd year, $30,000

Differences between the accounting methods applied to accounts and financial reports and those used in determining taxable income yielded the following amounts for the first four years of a corporation's operations:

	First Year	Second Year	Third Year	Fourth Year
Income before income taxes	$625,000	$750,000	$1,250,000	$1,000,000
Taxable income	500,000	700,000	1,350,000	1,075,000

The income tax rate for each of the four years was 40% of taxable income, and each year's taxes were promptly paid.

Instructions
1. Determine for each year the amounts described by the following captions, presenting the information in the form indicated:

Year	Income Tax Deducted on Income Statement	Income Tax Payments for the Year	Deferred Income Tax Payable	
			Year's Addition (Deduction)	Year-End Balance

2. Total the first three amount columns.

PR E-2
Deferred taxes

✔ 1. Year-end balance, 3rd year, $12,600

Differences between the accounting methods applied to accounts and financial reports and those used in determining taxable income yielded the following amounts for the first four years of a corporation's operations:

	First Year	Second Year	Third Year	Fourth Year
Income before income taxes	$150,000	$195,000	$270,000	$300,000
Taxable income	105,000	180,000	294,000	336,000

The income tax rate for each of the four years was 35% of taxable income, and each year's taxes were promptly paid.

Instructions
1. Determine for each year the amounts described by the following captions, presenting the information in the form indicated:

Year	Income Tax Deducted on Income Statement	Income Tax Payments for the Year	Deferred Income Tax Payable	
			Year's Addition (Deduction)	Year-End Balance

2. Total the first three amount columns.

FORM 10-K

NIKE INC - NKE

Filed: July 27, 2007 (period: May 31, 2007)

Annual report which provides a comprehensive overview of the company for the past year

Nike Inc. Form 10-K – Annual report [Section 13 or 15(d)] of The Securities Exchange Act of 1934 for the fiscal year ended May 31, 2007.

REPORT OF INDEPENDENT REGISTERED PUBLIC ACCOUNTING FIRM

To the Board of Directors and
Shareholders of NIKE, Inc.:

We have completed integrated audits of NIKE, Inc.'s consolidated financial statements and of its internal control over financial reporting as of May 31, 2007, in accordance with the standards of the Public Company Accounting Oversight Board (United States). Our opinions, based on our audits, are presented below.

Consolidated financial statements and financial statement schedule

In our opinion, the consolidated financial statements listed in the index appearing under Item 15(a)(1) present fairly, in all material respects, the financial position of NIKE, Inc. and its subsidiaries at May 31, 2007 and 2006, and the results of their operations and their cash flows for each of the three years in the period ended May 31, 2007 in conformity with accounting principles generally accepted in the United States of America. In addition, in our opinion, the financial statement schedule listed in the index appearing under Item 15(a)(2) presents fairly, in all material respects, the information set forth therein when read in conjunction with the related consolidated financial statements. These financial statements and financial statement schedule are the responsibility of the Company's management. Our responsibility is to express an opinion on these financial statements and financial statement schedule based on our audits. We conducted our audits of these statements in accordance with the standards of the Public Company Accounting Oversight Board (United States). Those standards require that we plan and perform the audit to obtain reasonable assurance about whether the financial statements are free of material misstatement. An audit of financial statements includes examining, on a test basis, evidence supporting the amounts and disclosures in the financial statements, assessing the accounting principles used and significant estimates made by management, and evaluating the overall financial statement presentation. We believe that our audits provide a reasonable basis for our opinion.

As discussed in Note 1 to the consolidated financial statements, effective June 1, 2006, the Company changed the manner in which it accounts for stock-based compensation in accordance with the Statement of Financial Accounting Standards No. 123R "Share-Based Payment."

Internal control over financial reporting

Also, in our opinion, management's assessment, included in "Management's Annual Report on Internal Control Over Financial Reporting" appearing under Item 8, that the Company maintained effective internal control over financial reporting as of May 31, 2007 based on criteria established in *Internal Control — Integrated Framework* issued by the Committee of Sponsoring Organizations of the Treadway Commission ("COSO"), is fairly stated, in all material respects, based on those criteria. Furthermore, in our opinion, the Company maintained, in all material respects, effective internal control over financial reporting as of May 31, 2007, based on criteria established in *Internal Control — Integrated Framework* issued by the COSO. The Company's management is responsible for maintaining effective internal control over financial reporting and for its assessment of the effectiveness of internal control over financial reporting. Our responsibility is to express opinions on management's assessment and on the effectiveness of the Company's internal control over financial reporting based on our audit. We conducted our audit of internal control over financial reporting in accordance with the standards of the Public Company Accounting Oversight Board (United States). Those standards require that we plan and perform the audit to obtain reasonable assurance about whether effective internal control over financial reporting was maintained in all material respects. An audit of internal control over financial reporting includes obtaining an understanding of internal control over financial reporting, evaluating management's assessment, testing and evaluating the design and operating effectiveness of internal control, and performing such other procedures as we consider necessary in the circumstances. We believe that our audit provides a reasonable basis for our opinions.

A company's internal control over financial reporting is a process designed to provide reasonable assurance regarding the reliability of financial reporting and the preparation of financial statements for external purposes in

48

accordance with generally accepted accounting principles. A company's internal control over financial reporting includes those policies and procedures that (i) pertain to the maintenance of records that, in reasonable detail, accurately and fairly reflect the transactions and dispositions of the assets of the company; (ii) provide reasonable assurance that transactions are recorded as necessary to permit preparation of financial statements in accordance with generally accepted accounting principles, and that receipts and expenditures of the company are being made only in accordance with authorizations of management and directors of the company; and (iii) provide reasonable assurance regarding prevention or timely detection of unauthorized acquisition, use, or disposition of the company's assets that could have a material effect on the financial statements.

Because of its inherent limitations, internal control over financial reporting may not prevent or detect misstatements. Also, projections of any evaluation of effectiveness to future periods are subject to the risk that controls may become inadequate because of changes in conditions, or that the degree of compliance with the policies or procedures may deteriorate.

/s/ PRICEWATERHOUSECOOPERS LLP

Portland, Oregon
July 26, 2007

49

NIKE, INC.
CONSOLIDATED STATEMENTS OF INCOME

	Year Ended May 31,		
	2007	2006	2005
	(In millions, except per share data)		
Revenues	$16,325.9	$14,954.9	$13,739.7
Cost of sales	9,165.4	8,367.9	7,624.3
Gross margin	7,160.5	6,587.0	6,115.4
Selling and administrative expense	5,028.7	4,477.8	4,221.7
Interest (income) expense, net (Notes 1, 6 and 7)	(67.2)	(36.8)	4.8
Other (income) expense, net (Notes 5 and 16)	(0.9)	4.4	29.1
Income before income taxes	2,199.9	2,141.6	1,859.8
Income taxes (Note 8)	708.4	749.6	648.2
Net income	$ 1,491.5	$ 1,392.0	$ 1,211.6
Basic earnings per common share (Notes 1 and 11)	$ 2.96	$ 2.69	$ 2.31
Diluted earnings per common share (Notes 1 and 11)	$ 2.93	$ 2.64	$ 2.24
Dividends declared per common share	$ 0.71	$ 0.59	$ 0.475

The accompanying notes to consolidated financial statements are an integral part of this statement.

50

NIKE, INC.
CONSOLIDATED BALANCE SHEETS

	May 31,	
	2007	**2006**
	(In millions)	
ASSETS		
Current assets:		
Cash and equivalents	$ 1,856.7	$ 954.2
Short-term investments	990.3	1,348.8
Accounts receivable, net	2,494.7	2,382.9
Inventories (Note 2)	2,121.9	2,076.7
Deferred income taxes (Note 8)	219.7	203.3
Prepaid expenses and other current assets	393.2	380.1
Total current assets	8,076.5	7,346.0
Property, plant and equipment, net (Note 3)	1,678.3	1,657.7
Identifiable intangible assets, net (Note 4)	409.9	405.5
Goodwill (Note 4)	130.8	130.8
Deferred income taxes and other assets (Note 8)	392.8	329.6
Total assets	$ 10,688.3	$ 9,869.6
LIABILITIES AND SHAREHOLDERS' EQUITY		
Current liabilities:		
Current portion of long-term debt (Note 7)	$ 30.5	$ 255.3
Notes payable (Note 6)	100.8	43.4
Accounts payable (Note 6)	1,040.3	952.2
Accrued liabilities (Notes 5 and 16)	1,303.4	1,276.0
Income taxes payable	109.0	85.5
Total current liabilities	2,584.0	2,612.4
Long-term debt (Note 7)	409.9	410.7
Deferred income taxes and other liabilities (Note 8)	668.7	561.0
Commitments and contingencies (Notes 14 and 16)	—	—
Redeemable Preferred Stock (Note 9)	0.3	0.3
Shareholders' equity:		
Common stock at stated value (Note 10):		
Class A convertible — 117.6 and 127.8 shares outstanding	0.1	0.1
Class B — 384.1 and 384.2 shares outstanding	2.7	2.7
Capital in excess of stated value	1,960.0	1,447.3
Accumulated other comprehensive income (Note 13)	177.4	121.7
Retained earnings	4,885.2	4,713.4
Total shareholders' equity	7,025.4	6,285.2
Total liabilities and shareholders' equity	$ 10,688.3	$ 9,869.6

The accompanying notes to consolidated financial statements are an integral part of this statement.

51

NIKE, INC.
CONSOLIDATED STATEMENTS OF CASH FLOWS

	Year Ended May 31,		
	2007	2006	2005
		(In millions)	
Cash provided (used) by operations:			
Net income	$ 1,491.5	$ 1,392.0	$ 1,211.6
Income charges not affecting cash:			
Depreciation	269.7	282.0	257.2
Deferred income taxes	34.1	(26.0)	21.3
Stock-based compensation (Notes 1 and 10)	147.7	11.8	4.9
Amortization and other	0.5	(2.9)	25.6
Income tax benefit from exercise of stock options	—	54.2	63.1
Changes in certain working capital components and other assets and liabilities:			
Increase in accounts receivable	(39.6)	(85.1)	(93.5)
Increase in inventories	(49.5)	(200.3)	(103.3)
(Increase) decrease in prepaid expenses and other current assets	(60.8)	(37.2)	71.4
Increase in accounts payable, accrued liabilities and income taxes payable	85.1	279.4	112.4
Cash provided by operations	1,878.7	1,667.9	1,570.7
Cash provided (used) by investing activities:			
Purchases of short-term investments	(2,133.8)	(2,619.7)	(1,527.2)
Maturities of short-term investments	2,516.2	1,709.8	1,491.9
Additions to property, plant and equipment	(313.5)	(333.7)	(257.1)
Disposals of property, plant and equipment	28.3	1.6	7.2
Increase in other assets, net of other liabilities	(4.3)	(34.6)	(28.0)
Acquisition of subsidiary, net of cash acquired	—	—	(47.2)
Cash provided (used) by investing activities	92.9	(1,276.6)	(360.4)
Cash provided (used) by financing activities:			
Proceeds from issuance of long-term debt	41.8	—	—
Reductions in long-term debt, including current portion	(255.7)	(6.0)	(9.2)
Increase (decrease) in notes payable	52.6	(18.2)	(81.7)
Proceeds from exercise of stock options and other stock issuances	322.9	225.3	226.8
Excess tax benefits from share-based payment arrangements	55.8	—	—
Repurchase of common stock	(985.2)	(761.1)	(556.2)
Dividends — common and preferred	(343.7)	(290.9)	(236.7)
Cash used by financing activities	(1,111.5)	(850.9)	(657.0)
Effect of exchange rate changes	42.4	25.7	6.8
Net increase (decrease) in cash and equivalents	902.5	(433.9)	560.1
Cash and equivalents, beginning of year	954.2	1,388.1	828.0
Cash and equivalents, end of year	$ 1,856.7	$ 954.2	$ 1,388.1
Supplemental disclosure of cash flow information:			
Cash paid during the year for:			
Interest, net of capitalized interest	$ 60.0	$ 54.2	$ 33.9
Income taxes	601.1	752.6	585.3
Dividends declared and not paid	92.9	79.4	65.3

The accompanying notes to consolidated financial statements are an integral part of this statement.

52

NIKE, INC.
CONSOLIDATED STATEMENTS OF SHAREHOLDERS' EQUITY

	Common Stock Class A Shares	Class A Amount	Class B Shares	Class B Amount	Capital in Excess of Stated Value	Accumulated Other Comprehensive Income (Loss)	Retained Earnings	Total
					(In millions, except per share data)			
Balance at May 31, 2004	155.2	$ 0.1	371.0	$ 2.7	$ 882.3	$ (86.3)	$ 3,982.9	$ 4,781.7
Stock options exercised			8.8		272.2			272.2
Conversion to Class B Common Stock	(11.4)		11.4					—
Repurchase of Class B Common Stock			(13.8)		(8.3)		(547.9)	(556.2)
Dividends on Common stock ($0.475 per share)							(249.4)	(249.4)
Issuance of shares to employees			1.0		21.9			21.9
Stock-based compensation (Note 10):					4.9			4.9
Forfeiture of shares from employees					(1.5)		(0.7)	(2.2)
Comprehensive income (Note 13):								
Net income							1,211.6	1,211.6
Other comprehensive income (net of tax expense of $40.2):								
Foreign currency translation						70.1		70.1
Adjustment for fair value of hedge derivatives						89.6		89.6
Comprehensive income						159.7	1,211.6	1,371.3
Balance at May 31, 2005	143.8	$ 0.1	378.4	$ 2.7	$ 1,171.5	$ 73.4	$ 4,396.5	$ 5,644.2
Stock options exercised			8.0		253.7			253.7
Conversion to Class B Common Stock	(16.0)		16.0					—
Repurchase of Class B Common Stock			(19.0)		(11.3)		(769.9)	(781.2)
Dividends on Common stock ($0.59 per share)							(304.9)	(304.9)
Issuance of shares to employees			1.0		26.9			26.9
Stock-based compensation (Note 10):					11.8			11.8
Forfeiture of shares from employees			(0.2)		(5.3)		(0.3)	(5.6)
Comprehensive income (Note 13):								
Net income							1,392.0	1,392.0
Other comprehensive income (net of tax benefit of $37.8):								
Foreign currency translation						87.1		87.1
Adjustment for fair value of hedge derivatives						(38.8)		(38.8)
Comprehensive income						48.3	1,392.0	1,440.3
Balance at May 31, 2006	127.8	$ 0.1	384.2	$ 2.7	$ 1,447.3	$ 121.7	$ 4,713.4	$ 6,285.2
Stock options exercised			10.7		349.7			349.7
Conversion to Class B Common Stock	(10.2)		10.2					—
Repurchase of Class B Common Stock			(22.1)		(13.2)		(962.0)	(975.2)
Dividends on Common stock ($0.71 per share)							(357.2)	(357.2)
Issuance of shares to employees			1.2		30.1			30.1
Stock-based compensation (Note 10):					147.7			147.7
Forfeiture of shares from employees			(0.1)		(1.6)		(0.5)	(2.1)
Comprehensive income (Note 13):								
Net income							1,491.5	1,491.5
Other comprehensive income (net of tax benefit of $0.5):								
Foreign currency translation						84.6		84.6
Adjustment for fair value of hedge derivatives						(16.7)		(16.7)
Comprehensive income						67.9	1,491.5	1,559.4
Adoption of FAS 158 (net of tax benefit of $5.4) (Note 12):						(12.2)		(12.2)
Balance at May 31, 2007	117.6	$ 0.1	384.1	$ 2.7	$ 1,960.0	$ 177.4	$ 4,885.2	$ 7,025.4

The accompanying notes to consolidated financial statements are an integral part of this statement.

53

NIKE, INC.
NOTES TO CONSOLIDATED FINANCIAL STATEMENTS

Note 1 — Summary of Significant Accounting Policies

Basis of Consolidation

The consolidated financial statements include the accounts of NIKE, Inc. and its subsidiaries (the "Company"). All significant intercompany transactions and balances have been eliminated.

Stock Split

On February 15, 2007 the Board of Directors declared a two-for-one stock split of the Company's Class A and Class B common shares, which was effected in the form of a 100% common stock dividend distributed on April 2, 2007. All references to share and per share amounts in the consolidated financial statements and accompanying notes to the consolidated financial statements have been retroactively restated to reflect the two-for-one stock split.

Recognition of Revenues

Wholesale revenues are recognized when the risks and rewards of ownership have passed to the customer, based on the terms of sale. This occurs upon shipment or upon receipt by the customer depending on the country of the sale and the agreement with the customer. Retail store revenues are recorded at the time of sale. Provisions for sales discounts, returns and miscellaneous claims from customers are made at the time of sale.

Shipping and Handling Costs

Shipping and handling costs are expensed as incurred and included in cost of sales.

Advertising and Promotion

Advertising production costs are expensed the first time the advertisement is run. Media (TV and print) placement costs are expensed in the month the advertising appears.

A significant amount of the Company's promotional expenses result from payments under endorsement contracts. Accounting for endorsement payments is based upon specific contract provisions. Generally, endorsement payments are expensed on a straight-line basis over the term of the contract after giving recognition to periodic performance compliance provisions of the contracts. Prepayments made under contracts are included in prepaid expenses or other assets depending on the period to which the prepayment applies.

Through cooperative advertising programs, the Company reimburses its retail customers for certain of their costs of advertising the Company's products. The Company records these costs in selling and administrative expense at the point in time when it is obligated to its customers for the costs, which is when the related revenues are recognized. This obligation may arise prior to the related advertisement being run.

Total advertising and promotion expenses were $1,912.4 million, $1,740.2 million, and $1,600.7 million for the years ended May 31, 2007, 2006 and 2005, respectively. Prepaid advertising and promotion expenses recorded in prepaid expenses and other assets totaled $253.0 million and $177.1 million at May 31, 2007 and 2006, respectively.

Cash and Equivalents

Cash and equivalents represent cash and short-term, highly liquid investments with maturities of three months or less at date of purchase. The carrying amounts reflected in the consolidated balance sheet for cash and equivalents approximate fair value.

54

NIKE, INC.

NOTES TO CONSOLIDATED FINANCIAL STATEMENTS — (Continued)

Short-term Investments

Short-term investments consist of highly liquid investments, primarily U.S. Treasury debt securities, with maturities over three months from the date of purchase. Debt securities which the Company has the ability and positive intent to hold to maturity are carried at amortized cost. Available-for-sale debt securities are recorded at fair value with any net unrealized gains and losses reported, net of tax, in other comprehensive income. Realized gains or losses are determined based on the specific identification method. The Company holds no investments considered to be trading securities. Amortized cost of both available-for-sale and held-to-maturity debt securities approximates fair market value due to their short maturities. Substantially all short-term investments held at May 31, 2007 have remaining maturities of 180 days or less. Included in interest (income) expense, net for the years ended May 31, 2007, 2006, and 2005, was interest income of $116.9 million, $87.3 million and $34.9 million, respectively, related to short-term investments and cash and equivalents.

Allowance for Uncollectible Accounts Receivable

Accounts receivable consists principally of amounts receivable from customers. We make ongoing estimates relating to the collectibility of our accounts receivable and maintain an allowance for estimated losses resulting from the inability of our customers to make required payments. In determining the amount of the allowance, we consider our historical level of credit losses and make judgments about the creditworthiness of significant customers based on ongoing credit evaluations. Accounts receivable with anticipated collection dates greater than twelve months from the balance sheet date and related allowances are considered non-current and recorded in other assets. The allowance for uncollectible accounts receivable was $71.5 million and $67.6 million at May 31, 2007 and 2006, respectively, of which $33.3 million and $29.2 million was recorded in other assets.

Inventory Valuation

Inventories related to our wholesale operations are stated at lower of cost or market and valued on a first-in, first-out ("FIFO") or moving average cost basis. Inventories related to our retail operations are stated at the lower of average cost or market using the retail inventory method. Under the retail inventory method, the valuation of inventories at cost is calculated by applying a cost-to-retail ratio to the retail value inventories. Permanent and point of sale markdowns, when recorded, reduce both the retail and cost components of inventory on hand so as to maintain the already established cost-to-retail relationship.

Property, Plant and Equipment and Depreciation

Property, plant and equipment are recorded at cost. Depreciation for financial reporting purposes is determined on a straight-line basis for buildings and leasehold improvements over 2 to 40 years and for machinery and equipment over 2 to 15 years. Computer software (including, in some cases, the cost of internal labor) is depreciated on a straight-line basis over 3 to 10 years.

Impairment of Long-Lived Assets

The Company estimates the future undiscounted cash flows to be derived from an asset to assess whether or not a potential impairment exists when events or circumstances indicate the carrying value of a long-lived asset may be impaired. If the carrying value exceeds the Company's estimate of future undiscounted cash flows, the Company then calculates the impairment as the excess of the carrying value of the asset over the Company's estimate of its fair market value.

55

NIKE, INC.

NOTES TO CONSOLIDATED FINANCIAL STATEMENTS — (Continued)

Identifiable Intangible Assets and Goodwill

Goodwill and intangible assets with indefinite lives are not amortized but instead are measured for impairment at least annually in the fourth quarter, or when events indicate that an impairment exists. As required by Statement of Financial Accounting Standards ("SFAS") No. 142, "Goodwill and other Intangible Assets" ("FAS 142"), in the Company's impairment test of goodwill, the Company compares the fair value of the applicable reporting unit to its carrying value. The Company estimates the fair value of its reporting units by using a combination of discounted cash flow analysis and comparisons with the market values of similar publicly traded companies. If the carrying value of the reporting unit exceeds the estimate of fair value, the Company calculates the impairment as the excess of the carrying value of goodwill over its implied fair value. In the impairment tests for indefinite-lived intangible assets, the Company compares the estimated fair value of the indefinite-lived intangible assets to the carrying value. The Company estimates the fair value of indefinite-lived intangible assets and trademarks using the relief from royalty approach, which is a standard form of discounted cash flow analysis used for the valuation of trademarks. If the carrying value exceeds the estimate of fair value, the Company calculates impairment as the excess of the carrying value over the estimate of fair value.

Intangible assets that are determined to have definite lives are amortized over their useful lives and are measured for impairment only when events or circumstances indicate the carrying value may be impaired.

Foreign Currency Translation and Foreign Currency Transactions

Adjustments resulting from translating foreign functional currency financial statements into U.S. dollars are included in the foreign currency translation adjustment, a component of accumulated other comprehensive income in shareholders' equity.

Transaction gains and losses generated by the effect of foreign exchange rates on recorded assets and liabilities denominated in a currency different from the functional currency of the applicable Company entity are recorded in other (income) expense, net, in the period in which they occur.

Accounting for Derivatives and Hedging Activities

The Company uses derivative financial instruments to limit exposure to changes in foreign currency exchange rates and interest rates. The Company accounts for derivatives pursuant to SFAS No. 133, "Accounting for Derivative Instruments and Hedging Activities," as amended and interpreted ("FAS 133"). FAS 133 establishes accounting and reporting standards for derivative instruments and requires that all derivatives be recorded at fair value on the balance sheet. Changes in the fair value of derivative financial instruments are either recognized in other comprehensive income (a component of shareholders' equity) or net income depending on whether the derivative is being used to hedge changes in cash flows or fair value.

See Note 16 for more information on the Company's Risk Management program and derivatives.

Stock-Based Compensation

On June 1, 2006, the Company adopted SFAS No. 123R "Share-Based Payment" ("FAS 123R") which requires the Company to record expense for stock-based compensation to employees using a fair value method. Under FAS 123R, the Company estimates the fair value of options granted under the NIKE, Inc. 1990 Stock Incentive Plan (the "1990 Plan") (see Note 10) and employees' purchase rights under the Employee Stock Purchase Plans ("ESPPs") using the Black-Scholes option pricing model. The Company recognizes this fair value, net of estimated forfeitures, as selling and administrative expense in the Consolidated Statements of Income over the vesting period using the straight-line method.

56

NIKE, INC.

NOTES TO CONSOLIDATED FINANCIAL STATEMENTS — (Continued)

The Company has adopted the modified prospective transition method prescribed by FAS 123R, which does not require the restatement of financial results for previous periods. In accordance with this transition method, the Company's Consolidated Statement of Income for the year ended May 31, 2007 includes (1) amortization of outstanding stock-based compensation granted prior to, but not vested, as of June 1, 2006, based on the fair value estimated in accordance with the original provisions of SFAS No. 123, "Accounting for Stock-Based Compensation" ("FAS 123") and (2) amortization of all stock-based awards granted subsequent to June 1, 2006, based on the fair value estimated in accordance with the provisions of FAS 123R.

The following table summarizes the effects of applying FAS 123R during the year ended May 31, 2007. The resulting stock-based compensation expense primarily relates to stock options.

(in millions, except per share data)	
Addition to selling and administrative expense	$141.9
Reduction to income tax expense	(45.2)
Reduction to net income[1]	$ 96.7
Reduction to earnings per share:	
Basic	$ 0.19
Diluted	$ 0.18

[1] In accordance with FAS 123R, stock-based compensation expense reported during the year ended May 31, 2007, includes $24.2 million, net of tax, or $0.04 per diluted share, of accelerated stock-based compensation expense recorded for employees eligible for accelerated stock option vesting upon retirement.

Prior to the adoption of FAS 123R, the Company used the intrinsic value method to account for stock options and ESPP shares in accordance with Accounting Principles Board Opinion No. 25, "Accounting for Stock Issued to Employees" as permitted by FAS 123. If the Company had instead accounted for stock options and ESPP shares issued to employees using the fair value method prescribed by FAS 123 during the years ended May 31, 2006 and 2005 the Company's pro forma net income and pro forma earnings per share would have been reported as follows:

	Year Ended May 31,	
	2006	2005
	(In millions, except per share data)	
Net income as reported	$ 1,392.0	$ 1,211.6
Add: Stock option expense included in reported net income, net of tax	0.2	0.6
Deduct: Total stock option and ESPP expense under fair value based method for all awards, net of tax[1]	(76.8)	(64.1)
Pro forma net income	$ 1,315.4	$ 1,148.1
Earnings per share:		
Basic — as reported	$ 2.69	$ 2.31
Basic — pro forma	2.54	2.19
Diluted — as reported	2.64	2.24
Diluted — pro forma	2.50	2.14

[1] Accelerated stock-based compensation expense for options subject to accelerated vesting due to employee retirement is not included in the pro forma figures shown above for the years ended May 31, 2006 and 2005. This disclosure reflects the expense of such options ratably over the stated vesting period or upon actual employee retirement. Had the Company recognized the fair value for such stock options on an accelerated

57

NIKE, INC.

NOTES TO CONSOLIDATED FINANCIAL STATEMENTS — (Continued)

basis in this pro forma disclosure, the Company would have recognized additional stock-based compensation expense of $17.5 million, net of tax, or $0.03 per diluted share for the year ended May 31, 2006 and $21.8 million, net of tax, or $0.04 per diluted share for the year ended May 31, 2005.

To calculate the excess tax benefits available for use in offsetting future tax shortfalls as of the date of implementation, the Company is following the alternative transition method discussed in FASB Staff Position No. 123R-3, "Transition Election Relating to Accounting for the Tax Effects of Share-Based Payment Awards."

See Note 10 for more information on the Company's stock programs.

Income Taxes

The Company accounts for income taxes using the asset and liability method. This approach requires the recognition of deferred tax assets and liabilities for the expected future tax consequences of temporary differences between the carrying amounts and the tax basis of assets and liabilities. United States income taxes are provided currently on financial statement earnings of non-U.S. subsidiaries that are expected to be repatriated. The Company determines annually the amount of undistributed non-U.S. earnings to invest indefinitely in its non-U.S. operations. See Note 8 for further discussion.

Earnings Per Share

Basic earnings per common share is calculated by dividing net income by the weighted average number of common shares outstanding during the year. Diluted earnings per common share is calculated by adjusting weighted average outstanding shares, assuming conversion of all potentially dilutive stock options and awards. See Note 11 for further discussion.

Management Estimates

The preparation of financial statements in conformity with generally accepted accounting principles requires management to make estimates, including estimates relating to assumptions that affect the reported amounts of assets and liabilities and disclosure of contingent assets and liabilities at the date of financial statements and the reported amounts of revenues and expenses during the reporting period. Actual results could differ from these estimates.

Reclassifications

Certain prior year amounts have been reclassified to conform to fiscal year 2007 presentation. These changes had no impact on previously reported results of operations or shareholders' equity.

Recently Issued Accounting Standards

In June 2006, the Financial Accounting Standards Board ("FASB") ratified the consensus reached on Emerging Issues Task Force ("EITF") Issue No. 06-3, "How Taxes Collected from Customers and Remitted to Governmental Authorities Should Be Presented in the Income Statement (That Is, Gross versus Net Presentation)" ("EITF 06-3"). EITF 06-3 requires disclosure of the method of accounting for the applicable assessed taxes and the amount of assessed taxes that are included in revenues if they are accounted for under the gross method. EITF 06-3 was adopted in the fourth quarter ended May 31, 2007; however, since the Company presents revenues net of any taxes collected from customers, no additional disclosures were required.

58

NIKE, INC.

NOTES TO CONSOLIDATED FINANCIAL STATEMENTS — (Continued)

In September 2006, the FASB issued SFAS No. 158, "Employers' Accounting for Defined Benefit Pension and Other Postretirement Plans" ("FAS 158"). FAS 158 requires employers to fully recognize the obligations associated with single-employer defined benefit pension, retiree healthcare and other postretirement plans in their financial statements. The Company adopted the provisions of FAS 158 in the fourth quarter ended May 31, 2007. See Note 12 for additional details.

In September 2006, the SEC staff issued Staff Accounting Bulletin No. 108, "Considering the Effects of Prior Year Misstatements when Quantifying Misstatements in Current Year Financial Statements" ("SAB 108"). SAB 108 requires public companies to quantify errors using both a balance sheet and income statement approach and evaluate whether either approach results in quantifying a misstatement as material, when all relevant quantitative and qualitative factors are considered. The adoption of SAB 108 at May 31, 2007 did not have a material impact on the Company's consolidated financial position or results of operations.

In June 2006, the FASB issued FASB Interpretation No. 48, "Accounting for Uncertainty in Income Taxes" ("FIN 48"). FIN 48 clarifies the accounting for uncertainty in income taxes recognized in the Company's financial statements in accordance with FASB Statement No. 109, "Accounting for Income Taxes". The provisions of FIN 48 are effective for the fiscal year beginning June 1, 2007. The Company has evaluated the impact of the provisions of FIN 48 and does not expect that the adoption will have a material impact on the Company's consolidated financial position or results of operations.

In June 2006, the FASB ratified the consensus reached on EITF Issue No. 06-2, "Accounting for Sabbatical Leave and Other Similar Benefits Pursuant to FASB Statement No. 43" ("EITF 06-2"). EITF 06-2 clarifies recognition guidance on the accrual of employees' rights to compensated absences under a sabbatical or other similar benefit arrangement. The provisions of EITF 06-2 are effective for the fiscal year beginning June 1, 2007 and will be applied through a cumulative effect adjustment to retained earnings. The Company has evaluated the provisions of EITF 06-2 and does not expect that the adoption will have a material impact on the Company's consolidated financial position or results of operations.

In September 2006, the FASB issued SFAS No. 157, "Fair Value Measurements" ("FAS 157"). FAS 157 defines fair value, establishes a framework for measuring fair value in accordance with generally accepted accounting principles, and expands disclosures about fair value measurements. The provisions of FAS 157 are effective for the fiscal year beginning June 1, 2008. The Company is currently evaluating the impact of the provisions of FAS 157.

In February 2007, the FASB issued SFAS No. 159, "The Fair Value Option for Financial Assets and Financial Liabilities — Including an Amendment of FASB Statement No. 115" ("FAS 159"). FAS 159 permits entities to choose to measure many financial instruments and certain other items at fair value. Unrealized gains and losses on items for which the fair value option has been elected will be recognized in earnings at each subsequent reporting date. The provisions of FAS 159 are effective for the fiscal year beginning June 1, 2008. The Company is currently evaluating the impact of the provisions of FAS 159.

Note 2 — Inventories

Inventory balances of $2,121.9 million and $2,076.7 million at May 31, 2007 and 2006, respectively, were substantially all finished goods.

59

NIKE, INC.

NOTES TO CONSOLIDATED FINANCIAL STATEMENTS — (Continued)

Note 3 — Property, Plant and Equipment

Property, plant and equipment includes the following:

	May 31,	
	2007	**2006**
	(In millions)	
Land	$ 193.8	$ 195.9
Buildings	840.9	842.6
Machinery and equipment	1,817.2	1,661.7
Leasehold improvements	672.8	626.7
Construction in process	94.4	81.4
	3,619.1	3,408.3
Less accumulated depreciation	1,940.8	1,750.6
	$ 1,678.3	$ 1,657.7

Capitalized interest was not material for the years ended May 31, 2007, 2006 and 2005.

Note 4 — Identifiable Intangible Assets and Goodwill:

The following table summarizes the Company's identifiable intangible assets and goodwill balances as of May 31, 2007 and May 31, 2006:

	May 31, 2007			May 31, 2006		
	Gross Carrying Amount	Accumulated Amortization	Net Carrying Amount	Gross Carrying Amount	Accumulated Amortization	Net Carrying Amount
	(In millions)					
Amortized intangible assets:						
Patents	$ 44.1	$ (12.3)	$ 31.8	$ 34.1	$ (10.5)	$ 23.6
Trademarks	49.8	(17.5)	32.3	46.4	(11.8)	34.6
Other	21.6	(17.3)	4.3	21.5	(15.7)	5.8
Total	$115.5	$ (47.1)	$ 68.4	$102.0	$ (38.0)	$ 64.0
Unamortized intangible assets — Trademarks			$ 341.5			$ 341.5
Total			$ 409.9			$ 405.5
Goodwill			$ 130.8			$ 130.8

Amortization expense of identifiable assets with definite lives, which is included in selling and administrative expense, was $9.9 million, $9.8 million and $9.3 million for the years ended May 31, 2007, 2006, and 2005, respectively. The estimated amortization expense for intangible assets subject to amortization for each of the years ending May 31, 2008 through May 31, 2012 is as follows: 2008: $9.7 million; 2009: $8.7 million; 2010: $8.2 million; 2011: $7.7 million; 2012: $6.9 million.

60

NIKE, INC.

NOTES TO CONSOLIDATED FINANCIAL STATEMENTS — (Continued)

Note 5 — Accrued Liabilities

Accrued liabilities include the following:

	May 31,	
	2007	2006
	(In millions)	
Compensation and benefits, excluding taxes	$ 451.6	$ 427.2
Endorser compensation	139.9	124.7
Taxes other than income taxes	133.4	115.1
Dividends payable	92.9	79.5
Fair value of derivatives	90.5	111.2
Import and logistics costs	81.4	63.3
Advertising and marketing	70.6	75.4
Converse arbitration[1]	—	51.9
Other[2]	243.1	227.7
	$ 1,303.4	$ 1,276.0

[1] The Converse arbitration relates to a charge taken during the fourth quarter ended May 31, 2006 as a result of a contract dispute between Converse and a former South American licensee. The dispute was settled during the first quarter ended August 31, 2006.

[2] Other consists of various accrued expenses and no individual item accounted for more than $50 million of the balance at May 31, 2007 or 2006.

Note 6 — Short-Term Borrowings and Credit Lines

Notes payable to banks and interest-bearing accounts payable to Sojitz Corporation of America ("Sojitz America") as of May 31, 2007 and 2006, are summarized below:

	May 31,				
	2007			2006	
	Borrowings	Interest Rate		Borrowings	Interest Rate
		(In millions)			
Notes payable:					
U.S. operations	$ 14.6	0.00%[1]		$ 21.0	0.00%[1]
Non-U.S. operations	86.2	9.85%		22.4	7.72%
	$ 100.8			$ 43.4	
Sojitz America	$ 44.6	6.09%		$ 69.7	5.83%

[1] Weighted average interest rate includes non-interest bearing overdrafts.

The carrying amounts reflected in the consolidated balance sheet for notes payable approximate fair value.

The Company purchases through Sojitz America certain athletic footwear, apparel and equipment it acquires from non-U.S. suppliers. These purchases are for the Company's operations outside of the United States, the Europe, Middle East, and Africa Region and Japan. Accounts payable to Sojitz America are generally due up to 60 days after shipment of goods from the foreign port. The interest rate on such accounts payable is the 60-day London Interbank Offered Rate ("LIBOR") as of the beginning of the month of the invoice date, plus 0.75%.

61

NIKE, INC.

NOTES TO CONSOLIDATED FINANCIAL STATEMENTS — (Continued)

The Company had no borrowings outstanding under its commercial paper program at May 31, 2007 and 2006.

In December 2006, the Company entered into a $1 billion multi-year credit facility that replaced the Company's previous $750 million facility. The facility matures in December 2011, and can be extended for one additional year on both the first and second anniversary date for a total extension of two years. Based on the Company's current long-term senior unsecured debt ratings, the interest rate charged on any outstanding borrowings would be the prevailing LIBOR plus 0.15%. The facility fee is 0.05% of the total commitment. Under this agreement, the Company must maintain, among other things, certain minimum specified financial ratios with which the Company was in compliance at May 31, 2007. No amounts were outstanding under these facilities as of May 31, 2007 or 2006.

In January 2007, one of the Company's Japanese subsidiaries entered into a 3.0 billion yen (approximately $24.7 million as of May 31, 2007) loan facility that replaced certain intercompany borrowings. The interest rate on the facility is based on the six-month Japanese Yen LIBOR plus a spread, resulting in an all-in rate of 0.805% at May 31, 2007. The facility expires December 31, 2007 unless both parties agree to an extension.

Note 7 — Long-Term Debt

Long-term debt includes the following:

	May 31, 2007	2006
	(In millions)	
5.5% Corporate Bond, payable August 15, 2006	$ —	$249.3
4.8% Corporate Bond, payable July 9, 2007	25.0	24.7
5.375% Corporate Bond, payable July 8, 2009	24.8	24.6
5.66% Corporate Bond, payable July 23, 2012	24.8	24.6
5.4% Corporate Bond, payable August 7, 2012	14.6	14.4
4.7% Corporate Bond, payable October 1, 2013	50.0	50.0
5.15% Corporate Bonds, payable October 15, 2015	99.6	98.2
4.3% Japanese yen note, payable June 26, 2011	86.4	93.8
1.5% Japanese yen note, payable February 14, 2012	41.1	—
2.6% Japanese yen note, maturing August 20, 2001 through November 20, 2020	51.2	59.7
2.0% Japanese yen note, maturing August 20, 2001 through November 20, 2020	22.9	26.6
Other	—	0.1
Total	440.4	666.0
Less current maturities	30.5	255.3
	$409.9	$410.7

The fair value of long-term debt is estimated using discounted cash flow analyses, based on the Company's incremental borrowing rates for similar types of borrowing arrangements. The fair value of the Company's long-term debt, including current portion, is approximately $443.2 million at May 31, 2007 and $674.0 million at May 31, 2006.

The Company had interest rate swap agreements with the same notional amount and maturity dates as the $250.0 million corporate bond that matured on August 15, 2006, whereby the Company received fixed interest payments at the same rate as the bond and paid variable interest payments based on the three-month LIBOR plus a spread. The interest rate payable on these swap agreements was approximately 6.6% at May 31, 2006.

62

NIKE, INC.

NOTES TO CONSOLIDATED FINANCIAL STATEMENTS — (Continued)

The Company has an effective shelf registration statement with the Securities and Exchange Commission for $1 billion of debt securities. The Company has a medium-term note program under the shelf registration ("medium-term note program") that allows the Company to issue up to $500 million in medium-term notes. The Company has issued $240 million in medium-term notes under this program. During the years ended May 31, 2007 and 2006, no notes were issued under the medium-term note program. The issued notes have coupon rates that range from 4.70% to 5.66%. The maturities range from July 9, 2007 to October 15, 2015. For each of these notes, except for the swap for the $50 million note maturing October 1, 2013, the Company has entered into interest rate swap agreements whereby the Company receives fixed interest payments at the same rate as the notes and pays variable interest payments based on the three-month or six-month LIBOR plus a spread. Each swap has the same notional amount and maturity date as the corresponding note. The swap for the $50 million note maturing October 1, 2013, expired October 2, 2006. At May 31, 2007, the interest rates payable on these swap agreements range from approximately 5.2% to 5.9%.

In June 1996, one of the Company's Japanese subsidiaries, NIKE Logistics YK, borrowed 10.5 billion Japanese yen in a private placement with a maturity of June 26, 2011. Interest is paid semi-annually. The agreement provides for early retirement after year ten.

In July 1999, NIKE Logistics YK assumed 13.0 billion in Japanese yen loans as part of its agreement to purchase a distribution center in Japan, which serves as collateral for the loans. These loans mature in equal quarterly installments during the period August 20, 2001 through November 20, 2020. Interest is also paid quarterly.

In February 2007, NIKE Logistics YK entered into a 5.0 billion yen (approximately $41.1 million at May 31, 2007) term loan maturing February 14, 2012 that replaces certain intercompany borrowings. The interest rate on the loan is approximately 1.5% and interest is paid semi-annually.

Amounts of long-term debt maturities in each of the years ending May 31, 2008 through 2012 are $30.5 million, $5.5 million, $30.5 million, $5.5 million and $133.0 million, respectively.

Note 8 — Income Taxes

Income before income taxes is as follows:

	Year Ended May 31,		
	2007	2006	2005
		(In millions)	
Income before income taxes:			
United States	$ 805.1	$ 838.6	$ 755.5
Foreign	1,394.8	1,303.0	1,104.3
	$ 2,199.9	$ 2,141.6	$ 1,859.8

63

NIKE, INC.

NOTES TO CONSOLIDATED FINANCIAL STATEMENTS — (Continued)

The provision for income taxes is as follows:

	Year Ended May 31,		
	2007	2006	2005
		(In millions)	
Current:			
United States			
Federal	$352.6	$359.0	$279.6
State	59.6	60.6	50.7
Foreign	261.9	356.0	292.5
	674.1	775.6	622.8
Deferred:			
United States			
Federal	38.7	(4.2)	21.9
State	(4.8)	(6.8)	(5.3)
Foreign	0.4	(15.0)	8.8
	34.3	(26.0)	25.4
	$708.4	$749.6	$648.2

Deferred tax (assets) and liabilities are comprised of the following:

	May 31,	
	2007	2006
	(In millions)	
Deferred tax assets:		
Allowance for doubtful accounts	$ (12.4)	$ (10.9)
Inventories	(45.8)	(43.9)
Sales return reserves	(42.1)	(39.4)
Deferred compensation	(132.5)	(110.6)
Stock-based compensation	(30.3)	—
Reserves and accrued liabilities	(46.2)	(50.6)
Property, plant, and equipment	(16.3)	(28.6)
Foreign loss carryforwards	(37.5)	(29.2)
Foreign tax credit carryforwards	(3.4)	(9.5)
Hedges	(26.2)	(25.5)
Other	(33.0)	(29.1)
Total deferred tax assets	(425.7)	(377.3)
Valuation allowance	42.3	36.6
Total deferred tax assets after valuation allowance	(383.4)	(340.7)
Deferred tax liabilities:		
Undistributed earnings of foreign subsidiaries	232.6	135.3
Property, plant and equipment	66.1	91.4
Intangibles	97.2	96.8
Hedges	2.5	7.8
Other	17.8	12.5
Total deferred tax liabilities	416.2	343.8
Net deferred tax liability	$ 32.8	$ 3.1

64

NIKE, INC.

NOTES TO CONSOLIDATED FINANCIAL STATEMENTS — (Continued)

A reconciliation from the U.S. statutory federal income tax rate to the effective income tax rate follows:

| | Year Ended May 31, | | |
	2007	2006	2005
Federal income tax rate	35.0%	35.0%	35.0%
State taxes, net of federal benefit	1.6	1.5	1.8
Foreign earnings	(4.1)	(1.5)	(2.8)
Other, net	(0.3)	—	0.9
Effective income tax rate	32.2%	35.0%	34.9%

The effective tax rate for the year ended May 31, 2007 of 32.2% has decreased from the fiscal 2006 effective tax rate of 35%. The decrease is primarily due to a European tax agreement entered into during the three months ended November 30, 2006. The Company recorded a retroactive benefit for the European tax agreement during the year ended May 31, 2007.

During the quarter ended November 30, 2005, the Company's CEO and Board of Directors approved a domestic reinvestment plan as required by the American Jobs Creation Act of 2004 (the "Act") to repatriate $500 million of foreign earnings in fiscal 2006. The Act created a temporary incentive for U.S. multinational corporations to repatriate accumulated income earned outside the U.S. by providing an 85% dividend received deduction for certain dividends from controlled foreign corporations. A $500 million repatriation was made during the quarter ended May 31, 2006 comprised of both foreign earnings for which U.S. taxes have previously been provided and foreign earnings that had been designated as permanently reinvested. Accordingly, the provisions made did not have a material impact on the Company's income tax expense or effective tax rate for the years ended May 31, 2007, 2006 and 2005.

The Company has indefinitely reinvested approximately $1,185.0 million of the cumulative undistributed earnings of certain foreign subsidiaries. Such earnings would be subject to U.S. taxation if repatriated to the U.S. The amount of unrecognized deferred tax liability associated with the permanently reinvested cumulative undistributed earnings was approximately $248.3 million as of May 31, 2007.

Deferred tax assets at May 31, 2007 and 2006 were reduced by a valuation allowance relating to tax benefits of certain foreign subsidiaries with operating losses where it is more likely than not that the deferred tax assets will not be realized.

During the years ended May 31, 2007, 2006, and 2005, income tax benefits attributable to employee stock-based compensation transactions of $56.6 million, $54.2 million, and $63.1 million, respectively, were allocated to shareholders' equity.

Note 9 — Redeemable Preferred Stock

Sojitz America is the sole owner of the Company's authorized Redeemable Preferred Stock, $1 par value, which is redeemable at the option of Sojitz America or the Company at par value aggregating $0.3 million. A cumulative dividend of $0.10 per share is payable annually on May 31 and no dividends may be declared or paid on the common stock of the Company unless dividends on the Redeemable Preferred Stock have been declared and paid in full. There have been no changes in the Redeemable Preferred Stock in the three years ended May 31, 2007, 2006 and 2005. As the holder of the Redeemable Preferred Stock, Sojitz America does not have general voting rights but does have the right to vote as a separate class on the sale of all or substantially all of the assets of the Company and its subsidiaries, on merger, consolidation, liquidation or dissolution of the Company or on the sale or assignment of the NIKE trademark for athletic footwear sold in the United States.

65

NIKE, INC.

NOTES TO CONSOLIDATED FINANCIAL STATEMENTS — (Continued)

Note 10 — Common Stock

The authorized number of shares of Class A Common Stock, no par value, and Class B Common Stock, no par value, are 350 million and 1.5 billion, respectively. Each share of Class A Common Stock is convertible into one share of Class B Common Stock. Voting rights of Class B Common Stock are limited in certain circumstances with respect to the election of directors.

In 1990, the Board of Directors adopted, and the shareholders approved, the NIKE, Inc. 1990 Stock Incentive Plan (the "1990 Plan"). The 1990 Plan provides for the issuance of up to 132 million previously unissued shares of Class B Common Stock in connection with stock options and other awards granted under the plan. The 1990 Plan authorizes the grant of non-statutory stock options, incentive stock options, stock appreciation rights, stock bonuses and the issuance and sale of restricted stock. The exercise price for non-statutory stock options, stock appreciation rights and the grant price of restricted stock may not be less than 75% of the fair market value of the underlying shares on the date of grant. The exercise price for incentive stock options may not be less than the fair market value of the underlying shares on the date of grant. A committee of the Board of Directors administers the 1990 Plan. The committee has the authority to determine the employees to whom awards will be made, the amount of the awards, and the other terms and conditions of the awards. The committee has granted substantially all stock options and restricted stock at 100% of the market price on the date of grant. Substantially all stock option grants outstanding under the 1990 plan were granted in the first quarter of each fiscal year, vest ratably over four years, and expire 10 years from the date of grant.

The weighted average fair value per share of the options granted during the years ended May 31, 2007, 2006 and 2005, as computed using the Black-Scholes pricing model, was $8.80, $9.68 and $13.95, respectively. The weighted average assumptions used to estimate these fair values are as follows:

	Year Ended May 31,		
	2007	2006	2005
Dividend yield	1.6%	1%	1%
Expected volatility	19%	21%	42%
Weighted average expected life (in years)	5.0	4.5	5.0
Risk-free interest rate	5.0%	4.0%	3.7%

For the years ended May 31, 2007 and 2006, the Company estimated the expected volatility based on the implied volatility in market traded options on the Company's common stock with a term greater than one year, along with other factors. For the year ended May 31, 2005, the Company estimated the expected volatility based on the historical volatility of the Company's common stock. The weighted average expected life of options is based on an analysis of historical and expected future exercise patterns. The interest rate is based on the U.S. Treasury (constant maturity) risk-free rate in effect at the date of grant for periods corresponding with the expected term of the options.

66

NIKE, INC.

NOTES TO CONSOLIDATED FINANCIAL STATEMENTS — (Continued)

The following summarizes the stock option transactions under the plan discussed above:

	Shares (In millions)	Weighted Average Option Price
Options outstanding May 31, 2004	37.6	$ 23.71
Exercised	(8.8)	23.17
Forfeited	(0.9)	26.33
Granted	10.8	36.96
Options outstanding May 31, 2005	38.7	27.49
Exercised	(8.0)	24.68
Forfeited	(1.8)	35.75
Granted	11.5	43.68
Options outstanding May 31, 2006	40.4	32.31
Exercised	(10.7)	27.55
Forfeited	(1.6)	37.17
Granted	11.6	39.54
Options outstanding May 31, 2007	39.7	$ 35.50
Options exercisable at May 31,		
2005	14.7	$ 23.01
2006	16.6	25.68
2007	15.3	29.52

The weighted average contractual life remaining for options outstanding and options exercisable at May 31, 2007 was 7.2 years and 5.4 years, respectively. The aggregate intrinsic value for options outstanding and exercisable at May 31, 2007 was $843.7 million and $417.0 million, respectively. The aggregate intrinsic value was the amount by which the market value of the underlying stock exceeded the exercise price of the options. The total intrinsic value of the options exercised during the years ended May 31, 2007, 2006 and 2005 was $204.9 million, $144.0 million and $145.7 million, respectively.

As of May 31, 2007, the Company had $132.4 million of unrecognized compensation costs from stock options, net of estimated forfeitures, to be recognized as selling and administrative expense over a weighted average period of 2.1 years.

In addition to the 1990 Plan, the Company gives employees the right to purchase shares at a discount to the market price under employee stock purchase plans ("ESPPs"). Employees are eligible to participate through payroll deductions up to 10% of their compensation. At the end of each six-month offering period, shares are purchased by the participants at 85% of the lower of the fair market value at the beginning or the ending of the offering period. During the years ended May 31, 2007, 2006 and 2005, employees purchased 0.8 million, 0.8 million and 0.6 million shares, respectively.

From time to time, the Company grants restricted stock and unrestricted stock to key employees under the 1990 Plan. The number of shares granted to employees during the years ended May 31, 2007, 2006 and 2005 were 345,000, 141,000 and 229,000 with weighted average prices of $39.38, $43.38 and $44.65, respectively. Recipients of restricted shares are entitled to cash dividends and to vote their respective shares throughout the period of restriction. The value of all of the granted shares was established by the market price on the date of grant.

67

NIKE, INC.

NOTES TO CONSOLIDATED FINANCIAL STATEMENTS — (Continued)

The following table summarizes the Company's total stock-based compensation expense recognized in selling and administrative expense:

	Year Ended May 31,		
	2007	2006	2005
	(in millions)		
Stock options	$134.9	$ 0.3	$1.0
ESPPs	7.0	—	—
Restricted stock [(1)]	5.8	11.5	3.9
Total stock-based compensation expense	$147.7	$11.8	$4.9

[(1)] The expense related to restricted stock awards was included in selling and administrative expense in prior years and was not affected by the adoption of FAS 123R.

During the years ended May 31, 2007, 2006 and 2005, the Company also granted shares of stock under the Long-Term Incentive Plan ("LTIP"), adopted by the Board of Directors and approved by shareholders in September 1997. The LTIP provides for the issuance of up to 2.0 million shares of Class B Common Stock. Under the LTIP, awards are made to certain executives in their choice of either cash or stock, based on performance targets established over three-year time periods. Once performance targets are achieved, cash or shares of stock are issued. The shares are immediately vested upon grant. The value of the shares is established by the market price on the date of issuance. Under the LTIP, 3,000, 6,000 and 8,000 shares with a price of $38.84, $40.79 and $34.85, respectively, were issued during the years ended May 31, 2007, 2006 and 2005 for the plan years ended May 31, 2006, 2005 and 2004, respectively. The Company recognized nominal expense related to the shares issued during the years ended May 31, 2007 and 2006, and $0.1 million during the year ended May 31, 2005. The Company recognized $30.0 million, $21.7 million and $22.1 million of selling and administrative expense related to the cash awards during the years ended May 31, 2007, 2006 and 2005, respectively. During the year ended May 31, 2007, LTIP participants agreed to amend their grant agreements to eliminate the ability to receive payments in shares of stock, so shares of stock are no longer awarded. Beginning with the plan year ended May 31, 2007, cash will be awarded if performance targets are achieved.

Note 11 — Earnings Per Share

The following represents a reconciliation from basic earnings per share to diluted earnings per share. Options to purchase an additional 9.5 million, 11.3 million and 0.5 million shares of common stock were outstanding at May 31, 2007, 2006 and 2005, respectively, but were not included in the computation of diluted earnings per share because the options were antidilutive.

	Year Ended May 31,		
	2007	2006	2005
	(In millions, except per share data)		
Determination of shares:			
Weighted average common shares outstanding	503.8	518.0	525.2
Assumed conversion of dilutive stock options and awards	6.1	9.6	15.4
Diluted weighted average common shares outstanding	509.9	527.6	540.6
Basic earnings per common share	$ 2.96	$ 2.69	$ 2.31
Diluted earnings per common share	$ 2.93	$ 2.64	$ 2.24

68

NIKE, INC.

NOTES TO CONSOLIDATED FINANCIAL STATEMENTS — (Continued)

Note 12 — Benefit Plans

The Company has a profit sharing plan available to most U.S.-based employees. The terms of the plan call for annual contributions by the Company as determined by the Board of Directors. A subsidiary of the Company also has a profit sharing plan available to its U.S.-based employees. The terms of the plan call for annual contributions as determined by the subsidiary's executive management. Contributions of $31.8 million, $33.2 million, and $29.1 million were made to the plans and are included in selling and administrative expenses in the consolidated financial statements for the years ended May 31, 2007, 2006 and 2005, respectively. The Company has various 401(k) employee savings plans available to U.S.-based employees. The Company matches a portion of employee contributions with common stock or cash. Company contributions to the savings plans were $24.9 million, $22.5 million, and $20.3 million for the years ended May 31, 2007, 2006 and 2005, respectively, and are included in selling and administrative expenses.

The Company has pension plans in various countries worldwide. The pension plans are only available to local employees and are generally government mandated. Upon adoption of FAS 158, "Employers' Accounting for Defined Benefit Pension and Other Postretirement Plans" on May 31, 2007, the Company recorded a liability of $17.6 million related to the unfunded pension liabilities of the plans.

Note 13 — Comprehensive Income

Comprehensive income is as follows:

	Year Ended May 31,		
	2007	2006	2005
		(In millions)	
Net income	$1,491.5	$1,392.0	$1,211.6
Other comprehensive income:			
Change in cumulative translation adjustment and other (net of tax (expense) benefit of ($5.4) in 2007, $19.7 in 2006, and $3.9 in 2005)	84.6	87.1	70.1
Changes due to cash flow hedging instruments (Note 16):			
Net loss on hedge derivatives (net of tax benefit of $9.5 in 2007, $2.8 in 2006 and $28.7 in 2005)	(38.1)	(5.6)	(54.0)
Reclassification to net income of previously deferred losses and (gains) related to hedge derivatives (net of tax expense (benefit) of ($3.6) in 2007, $15.3 in 2006 and ($72.8) in 2005)	21.4	(33.2)	143.6
Other comprehensive income	67.9	48.3	159.7
Total comprehensive income	$1,559.4	$1,440.3	$1,371.3

The components of accumulated other comprehensive income are as follows:

	May 31,	
	2007	2006
	(In millions)	
Cumulative translation adjustment and other[1]	$234.3	$161.9
Net deferred loss on hedge derivatives	(56.9)	(40.2)
	$177.4	$121.7

---

[1]   Cumulative translation adjustment and other for the year ended May 31, 2007 includes a $12.2 million net-of-tax adjustment relating to the adoption of FAS 158. See Note 12 for additional details.

69

NIKE, INC.
NOTES TO CONSOLIDATED FINANCIAL STATEMENTS — (Continued)

Note 14 — Commitments and Contingencies

The Company leases space for certain of its offices, warehouses and retail stores under leases expiring from one to twenty-seven years after May 31, 2007. Rent expense was $285.2 million, $252.0 million and $232.6 million for the years ended May 31, 2007, 2006 and 2005, respectively. Amounts of minimum future annual rental commitments under non-cancelable operating leases in each of the five years ending May 31, 2008 through 2012 are $260.9 million, $219.9 million, $183.3 million, $156.7 million, $128.4 million, respectively, and $587.0 million in later years.

As of May 31, 2007 and 2006, the Company had letters of credit outstanding totaling $165.9 million and $347.6 million, respectively. These letters of credit were generally issued for the purchase of inventory.

In connection with various contracts and agreements, the Company provides routine indemnifications relating to the enforceability of intellectual property rights, coverage for legal issues that arise and other items that fall under the scope of FASB Interpretation No. 45, "Guarantor's Accounting and Disclosure Requirements for Guarantees, Including Indirect Guarantees of Indebtedness of Others." Currently, the Company has several such agreements in place. However, based on the Company's historical experience and the estimated probability of future loss, the Company has determined that the fair value of such indemnifications is not material to the Company's financial position or results of operations.

In the ordinary course of its business, the Company is involved in various legal proceedings involving contractual and employment relationships, product liability claims, trademark rights, and a variety of other matters. The Company does not believe there are any pending legal proceedings that will have a material impact on the Company's financial position or results of operations.

Note 15 — Acquisitions

In August 2004, the Company acquired 100% of the equity interests in Official Starter LLC and Official Starter Properties LLC (collectively "Official Starter"). The Exeter Brands Group LLC, a wholly-owned subsidiary of the Company, was formed soon thereafter to develop the Company's business in retail channels serving value-conscious consumers and to operate the Official Starter business. The acquisition was accounted for under the purchase method of accounting. The cash purchase price, including acquisition costs net of cash acquired, was $47.2 million. All assets and liabilities of Exeter Brands Group were initially recorded in the Company's Consolidated Balance Sheet based on their estimated fair values at the date of acquisition. The results of Exeter Brands Group's operations have been included in the consolidated financial statements since the date of acquisition as part of the Company's Other operating segment. The pro forma effect of the acquisition on the combined results of operations was not significant.

Note 16 — Risk Management and Derivatives

The Company is exposed to global market risks, including the effect of changes in foreign currency exchange rates and interest rates. The Company uses derivatives to manage financial exposures that occur in the normal course of business. The Company does not hold or issue derivatives for trading purposes.

The Company formally documents all relationships between hedging instruments and hedged items, as well as its risk-management objective and strategy for undertaking hedge transactions. This process includes linking all derivatives to either specific assets and liabilities on the balance sheet or specific firm commitments or forecasted transactions.

70

NIKE, INC.

NOTES TO CONSOLIDATED FINANCIAL STATEMENTS — (Continued)

Substantially all derivatives outstanding as of May 31, 2007 and 2006 are designated as either cash flow or fair value hedges. All derivatives are recognized on the balance sheet at their fair value. Unrealized gain positions are recorded as other current assets or other non-current assets, depending on the instrument's maturity date. Unrealized loss positions are recorded as accrued liabilities or other non-current liabilities. All changes in fair values of outstanding cash flow hedge derivatives, except the ineffective portion, are recorded in other comprehensive income, until net income is affected by the variability of cash flows of the hedged transaction. Fair value hedges are recorded in net income and are offset by the change in fair value of the underlying asset or liability being hedged.

Cash Flow Hedges

The purpose of the Company's foreign currency hedging activities is to protect the Company from the risk that the eventual cash flows resulting from transactions in foreign currencies, including revenues, product costs, selling and administrative expenses, investments in U.S. dollar-denominated available-for-sale debt securities and intercompany transactions, including intercompany borrowings, will be adversely affected by changes in exchange rates. It is the Company's policy to utilize derivatives to reduce foreign exchange risks where internal netting strategies cannot be effectively employed.

Derivatives used by the Company to hedge foreign currency exchange risks are forward exchange contracts and options. Hedged transactions are denominated primarily in euros, British pounds, Japanese yen, Korean won, Canadian dollars and Mexican pesos. The Company hedges up to 100% of anticipated exposures typically twelve months in advance, but has hedged as much as 32 months in advance. When intercompany loans are hedged, it is typically for their expected duration.

Substantially all foreign currency derivatives outstanding as of May 31, 2007 and 2006 qualify for and are designated as foreign-currency cash flow hedges, including those hedging foreign currency denominated firm commitments.

Changes in fair values of outstanding cash flow hedge derivatives, except the ineffective portion, are recorded in other comprehensive income, until net income is affected by the variability of cash flows of the hedged transaction. In most cases amounts recorded in other comprehensive income will be released to net income some time after the maturity of the related derivative. The consolidated statement of income classification of effective hedge results is the same as that of the underlying exposure. Results of hedges of revenue and product costs are recorded in revenue and cost of sales, respectively, when the underlying hedged transaction affects net income. Results of hedges of selling and administrative expense are recorded together with those costs when the related expense is recorded. Results of hedges of anticipated purchases and sales of U.S. dollar-denominated available-for-sale securities are recorded in other (income) expense, net when the securities are sold.

Results of hedges of anticipated intercompany transactions are recorded in other (income) expense, net when the transaction occurs. Hedges of recorded balance sheet positions are recorded in other (income) expense, net currently together with the transaction gain or loss from the hedged balance sheet position. Net foreign currency transaction gains and losses, which includes hedge results captured in revenues, cost of sales, selling and administrative expense and other (income) expense, net, were a $27.9 million loss, a $49.9 million gain, and a $217.8 million loss for the years ended May 31, 2007, 2006, and 2005, respectively.

Premiums paid on options are initially recorded as deferred charges. The Company assesses effectiveness on options based on the total cash flows method and records total changes in the options' fair value to other comprehensive income to the degree they are effective.

71

NIKE, INC.

NOTES TO CONSOLIDATED FINANCIAL STATEMENTS — (Continued)

As of May 31, 2007, $52.8 million of deferred net losses (net of tax) on both outstanding and matured derivatives accumulated in other comprehensive income are expected to be reclassified to net income during the next twelve months as a result of underlying hedged transactions also being recorded in net income. Actual amounts ultimately reclassified to net income are dependent on the exchange rates in effect when derivative contracts that are currently outstanding mature. As of May 31, 2007, the maximum term over which the Company is hedging exposures to the variability of cash flows for all forecasted and recorded transactions is 18 months.

The Company formally assesses, both at a hedge's inception and on an ongoing basis, whether the derivatives that are used in the hedging transaction have been highly effective in offsetting changes in the cash flows of hedged items and whether those derivatives may be expected to remain highly effective in future periods. When it is determined that a derivative is not, or has ceased to be, highly effective as a hedge, the Company discontinues hedge accounting prospectively.

The Company discontinues hedge accounting prospectively when (1) it determines that the derivative is no longer highly effective in offsetting changes in the cash flows of a hedged item (including hedged items such as firm commitments or forecasted transactions); (2) the derivative expires or is sold, terminated, or exercised; (3) it is no longer probable that the forecasted transaction will occur; or (4) management determines that designating the derivative as a hedging instrument is no longer appropriate.

When the Company discontinues hedge accounting because it is no longer probable that the forecasted transaction will occur in the originally expected period, the gain or loss on the derivative remains in accumulated other comprehensive income and is reclassified to net income when the forecasted transaction affects net income. However, if it is probable that a forecasted transaction will not occur by the end of the originally specified time period or within an additional two-month period of time thereafter, the gains and losses that were accumulated in other comprehensive income will be recognized immediately in net income. In all situations in which hedge accounting is discontinued and the derivative remains outstanding, the Company will carry the derivative at its fair value on the balance sheet, recognizing future changes in the fair value in other (income) expense, net. Any hedge ineffectiveness is recorded in other (income) expense, net. Effectiveness for cash flow hedges is assessed based on forward rates.

For each of the years ended May 31, 2007, 2006 and 2005, the Company recorded in other (income) expense, net an insignificant loss representing the total ineffectiveness of all derivatives. Net income for each of the years ended May 31, 2007, 2006 and 2005 was not materially affected due to discontinued hedge accounting.

Fair Value Hedges

The Company is also exposed to the risk of changes in the fair value of certain fixed-rate debt attributable to changes in interest rates. Derivatives currently used by the Company to hedge this risk are receive-fixed, pay-variable interest rate swaps.

Substantially all interest rate swap agreements are designated as fair value hedges of the related long-term debt and meet the shortcut method requirements under FAS 133. Accordingly, changes in the fair values of the interest rate swap agreements are exactly offset by changes in the fair value of the underlying long-term debt. No ineffectiveness has been recorded to net income related to interest rate swaps designated as fair value hedges for the years ended May 31, 2007, 2006 and 2005.

As discussed in Note 7, during the year ended May 31, 2004, the Company issued a $50 million medium-term note maturing October 1, 2013 and simultaneously entered into a receive-fixed, pay-variable interest rate swap with the same notional amount and fixed interest rate as the note. However, the swap expired

72

NIKE, INC.

NOTES TO CONSOLIDATED FINANCIAL STATEMENTS — (Continued)

October 2, 2006. This interest rate swap was not accounted for as a fair value hedge. Accordingly, changes in the fair value of the swap were recorded to net income each period as a component of other (income) expense, net. The change in the fair value of the swap was not material for the years ended May 31, 2007, 2006 and 2005.

In fiscal 2003, the Company entered into an interest rate swap agreement related to a Japanese yen denominated intercompany loan with one of the Company's Japanese subsidiaries. The Japanese subsidiary pays variable interest on the intercompany loan based on 3-month LIBOR plus a spread. Under the interest rate swap agreement, the subsidiary pays fixed interest payments at 0.8% and receives variable interest payments based on 3-month LIBOR plus a spread based on a notional amount of 8 billion Japanese yen. This interest rate swap is not accounted for as a fair value hedge. Accordingly, changes in the fair value of the swap are recorded to net income each period as a component of other (income) expense, net. The change in the fair value of the swap was not material for the years ended May 31, 2007, 2006 and 2005.

The fair values of all derivatives recorded on the consolidated balance sheet are as follows:

	May 31,	
	2007	2006
	(In millions)	
Unrealized Gains:		
Foreign currency exchange contracts and options	$ 43.5	$ 75.7
Interest rate swaps	0.5	0.9
Unrealized (Losses):		
Foreign currency exchange contracts and options	(90.6)	(122.2)
Interest rate swaps	(2.6)	(6.0)

Concentration of Credit Risk

The Company is exposed to credit-related losses in the event of non-performance by counterparties to hedging instruments. The counterparties to all derivative transactions are major financial institutions with investment grade credit ratings. However, this does not eliminate the Company's exposure to credit risk with these institutions. This credit risk is generally limited to the unrealized gains in such contracts should any of these counterparties fail to perform as contracted. To manage this risk, the Company has established strict counterparty credit guidelines that are continually monitored and reported to senior management according to prescribed guidelines. The Company utilizes a portfolio of financial institutions either headquartered or operating in the same countries the Company conducts its business. As a result of the above considerations, the Company considers the risk of counterparty default to be minimal.

In addition to hedging instruments, the Company is subject to concentrations of credit risk associated with cash and equivalents and accounts receivable. The Company places cash and equivalents with financial institutions with investment grade credit ratings and, by policy, limits the amount of credit exposure to any one financial institution. The Company considers its concentration risk related to accounts receivable to be mitigated by the Company's credit policy, the significance of outstanding balances owed by each individual customer at any point in time and the geographic dispersion of these customers.

Note 17 — Operating Segments and Related Information

Operating Segments. The Company's operating segments are evidence of the structure of the Company's internal organization. The major segments are defined by geographic regions for operations participating in NIKE brand sales activity excluding NIKE Golf and NIKE Bauer Hockey. Each NIKE brand geographic segment operates predominantly in one industry: the design, production, marketing and selling of sports and fitness

73

NIKE, INC.

NOTES TO CONSOLIDATED FINANCIAL STATEMENTS — (Continued)

footwear, apparel, and equipment. The "Other" category shown below represents activities of Cole Haan, Converse, Exeter Brands Group (beginning August 11, 2004), Hurley, NIKE Bauer Hockey, and NIKE Golf, which are considered immaterial for individual disclosure based on the aggregation criteria in SFAS No. 131 "Disclosures about Segments of an Enterprise and Related Information".

Where applicable, "Corporate" represents items necessary to reconcile to the consolidated financial statements, which generally include corporate activity and corporate eliminations.

Net revenues as shown below represent sales to external customers for each segment. Intercompany revenues have been eliminated and are immaterial for separate disclosure. The Company evaluates performance of individual operating segments based on pre-tax income. On a consolidated basis, this amount represents income before income taxes as shown in the Consolidated Statements of Income. Reconciling items for pre-tax income represent corporate costs that are not allocated to the operating segments for management reporting including corporate activity, certain currency exchange rate gains and losses on transactions and intercompany eliminations for specific income statement items in the Consolidated Statements of Income.

Additions to long-lived assets as presented in the following table represent capital expenditures.

74

NIKE, INC.

NOTES TO CONSOLIDATED FINANCIAL STATEMENTS — (Continued)

Accounts receivable, inventories and property, plant and equipment for operating segments are regularly reviewed by management and are therefore provided below.

Certain prior year amounts have been reclassed to conform to fiscal 2007 presentation.

	Year Ended May 31,		
	2007	2006	2005
		(In millions)	
Net Revenue			
United States	$ 6,107.1	$ 5,722.5	$ 5,129.3
Europe, Middle East and Africa	4,723.3	4,326.6	4,281.6
Asia Pacific	2,283.4	2,053.8	1,897.3
Americas	952.5	904.9	695.8
Other	2,259.6	1,947.1	1,735.7
	$16,325.9	$14,954.9	$13,739.7
Pre-tax Income			
United States	$ 1,300.3	$ 1,244.5	$ 1,127.9
Europe, Middle East and Africa	1,000.7	960.7	917.5
Asia Pacific	483.7	412.5	399.8
Americas	187.4	172.6	116.5
Other	303.7	153.6	154.8
Corporate	(1,075.9)	(802.3)	(856.7)
	$ 2,199.9	$ 2,141.6	$ 1,859.8
Additions to Long-lived Assets			
United States	$ 67.3	$ 59.8	$ 54.8
Europe, Middle East and Africa	94.9	73.6	38.8
Asia Pacific	20.7	16.8	22.0
Americas	5.3	6.9	6.8
Other	36.0	33.2	31.3
Corporate	89.3	143.4	103.4
	$ 313.5	$ 333.7	$ 257.1
Depreciation			
United States	$ 45.4	$ 54.2	$ 49.0
Europe, Middle East and Africa	47.4	46.9	45.2
Asia Pacific	25.2	28.4	28.3
Americas	6.1	6.4	4.0
Other	28.2	29.0	28.5
Corporate	117.4	117.1	102.2
	$ 269.7	$ 282.0	$ 257.2

75

NIKE, INC.

NOTES TO CONSOLIDATED FINANCIAL STATEMENTS — (Continued)

	Year Ended May 31,		
	2007	2006	2005
	(In millions)		
Accounts Receivable, net			
United States	$ 806.8	$ 717.2	$ 627.0
Europe, Middle East and Africa	739.1	703.3	711.4
Asia Pacific	296.6	319.7	309.8
Americas	184.1	174.5	168.7
Other	404.9	410.0	394.0
Corporate	63.2	58.2	39.0
	$ 2,494.7	$ 2,382.9	$2,249.9
Inventories			
United States	$ 796.0	$ 725.9	$ 639.9
Europe, Middle East and Africa	554.5	590.1	496.5
Asia Pacific	214.1	238.3	228.9
Americas	132.0	147.6	96.8
Other	378.7	330.5	316.2
Corporate	46.6	44.3	32.8
	$ 2,121.9	$ 2,076.7	$1,811.1
Property, Plant and Equipment, net			
United States	$ 232.7	$ 219.3	$ 216.0
Europe, Middle East and Africa	325.4	266.6	230.0
Asia Pacific	326.1	354.8	380.4
Americas	16.9	17.0	15.7
Other	103.6	98.2	93.4
Corporate	673.6	701.8	670.3
	$ 1,678.3	$ 1,657.7	$1,605.8

Revenues by Major Product Lines. Revenues to external customers for NIKE brand products are attributable to sales of footwear, apparel and equipment. Other revenues to external customers primarily include external sales by Cole Haan Holdings Incorporated, Converse Inc., Exeter Brands Group LLC (beginning August 11, 2004), Hurley International LLC, NIKE Bauer Hockey Corp., and NIKE Golf.

	Year Ended May 31,		
	2007	2006	2005
	(In millions)		
Footwear	$ 8,514.0	$ 7,965.9	$ 7,299.7
Apparel	4,576.5	4,168.0	3,879.4
Equipment	975.8	873.9	824.9
Other	2,259.6	1,947.1	1,735.7
	$ 16,325.9	$ 14,954.9	$ 13,739.7

Revenues and Long-Lived Assets by Geographic Area. Geographical area information is similar to that shown previously under operating segments with the exception of the Other activity, which has been allocated to the geographical areas based on the location where the sales originated. Revenues derived in the United States were $7,593.7 million, $7,019.0 million, and $6,284.5 million, for the years ended May 31, 2007, 2006, and

76

NIKE, INC.

NOTES TO CONSOLIDATED FINANCIAL STATEMENTS — (Continued)

2005, respectively. The Company's largest concentrations of long-lived assets are in the United States and Japan. Long-lived assets attributable to operations in the United States, which are comprised of net property, plant & equipment were $991.3 million, $998.2 million, and $956.6 million at May 31, 2007, 2006, and 2005, respectively. Long-lived assets attributable to operations in Japan were $260.6 million, $296.3 million, and $321.0 million at May 31, 2007, 2006, and 2005, respectively.

Major Customers. During the years ended May 31, 2007, 2006 and 2005, revenues derived from Foot Locker, Inc. represented 10 percent, 10 percent and 11 percent of the Company's consolidated revenues, respectively. Sales to this customer are included in all segments of the Company.

Item 9. *Changes In and Disagreements with Accountants on Accounting and Financial Disclosure*

There has been no change of accountants nor any disagreements with accountants on any matter of accounting principles or practices or financial statement disclosure required to be reported under this Item.

Item 9A. *Controls and Procedures*

We maintain disclosure controls and procedures that are designed to ensure that information required to be disclosed in our Exchange Act reports is recorded, processed, summarized and reported within the time periods specified in the Securities and Exchange Commission's rules and forms and that such information is accumulated and communicated to our management, including our Chief Executive Officer and Chief Financial Officer, as appropriate, to allow for timely decisions regarding required disclosure. In designing and evaluating the disclosure controls and procedures, management recognizes that any controls and procedures, no matter how well designed and operated, can provide only reasonable assurance of achieving the desired control objectives, and management is required to apply its judgment in evaluating the cost-benefit relationship of possible controls and procedures.

We carry out a variety of on-going procedures, under the supervision and with the participation of our management, including our Chief Executive Officer and Chief Financial Officer, to evaluate the effectiveness of the design and operation of our disclosure controls and procedures. Based on the foregoing, our Chief Executive Officer and Chief Financial Officer concluded that our disclosure controls and procedures were effective at the reasonable assurance level as of May 31, 2007.

"Management's Annual Report on Internal Control Over Financial Reporting" and the related attestation report of PricewaterhouseCoopers LLP are included in Item 8 on pages 46-49 of this Report.

There has been no change in our internal control over financial reporting during our most recent fiscal quarter that has materially affected, or is reasonable likely to materially affect, our internal control over financial reporting.

Item 9B. *Other Information*

No disclosure is required under this Item.

77

International Financial Reporting Standards

Within the United States, Generally Accepted Accounting Principles (GAAP) are used to prepare financial reports. The Financial Accounting Standards Board (FASB) has the primary responsibility for developing U.S. GAAP. Outside of the United States, however, most countries use International Financial Reporting Standards (IFRS). IFRS are developed by the International Accounting Standards Board (IASB), which is a multinational body similar to the FASB.

The IASB and FASB have been working together to reduce the differences between IFRS and GAAP in order to create a single set of accounting principles that can be used around the world. The effort began in 2002 when the FASB and IASB agreed to a process called *convergence*. In August 2008, the U.S. Securities and Exchange Commission (SEC) accelerated this process, proposing to allow large U.S. multinational companies to use IFRS beginning in 2010. In addition, the SEC's plan proposes requiring all U.S. companies to use IFRS by 2014. While the SEC proposal was not final at the time of this printing, it appears that the convergence of IFRS and GAAP will occur in the near future.

Key conceptual similarities between IFRS and GAAP include:

- The objective of providing meaningful information for the decision-making needs of external financial statement users
- The use of the accrual basis of accounting
- The use of the business entity concept to record transactions
- The reporting of the four primary financial statements:
  - Balance sheet
  - Income statement
  - Statement of stockholders' equity (referred to in IFRS as the statement of recognized income and expense)
  - Statement of cash flows

Although IFRS and GAAP are similar, key differences arise in the form of the financial statements and the amounts reported in those statements.

Some of the key differences are summarized in Exhibit 1 on the next page.

Exhibit 1

GAAP and IFRS

	GAAP	IFRS	Text Reference
Balance Sheet Items:			
Inventory—LIFO	LIFO allowed.	LIFO prohibited.	Ch. 6; LO 3, 4, 5
Inventory—Cost Method	No requirement that similar inventories use a consistent cost method.	A consistent cost method must be used for all similar inventories.	Ch. 6; LO 6
Inventory—Reversal of inventory write-downs	Prohibited.	Required under certain circumstances.	Ch. 6; LO 6
Property, plant, and equipment: Fair value	May not be revalued to fair value.	May be revalued to fair value on a regular basis.	Ch. 9; LO 1
Capital and revenue expenditures	Different treatments for ordinary repairs and maintenance, asset improvement, and extraordinary repairs.	Typically included as part of the cost of the asset if future economic benefit is probable and can be reliably measured.	Ch. 9; LO 1
Revaluation of intangible assets	Not permitted.	Allowed if the intangible asset trades in an active market.	Ch. 9; LO 5
Investments	Treated as held for use or sale and recorded at historical cost.	May be accounted for on a historical cost basis or on a fair value basis with changes in fair value recognized through profit and loss.	Ch. 9; LO 1
Income Statement Items:			
Classification of expenses on income statement	Companies normally present expenses by function (e.g., cost of goods sold, selling, administrative).	Expenses may be presented based on either function (e.g., cost of goods sold, selling) or nature of expense (e.g., wages expense, interest expense).	Ch. 5; LO 1
Extraordinary items	Allowed for items that are both unusual in nature and infrequent in occurrence.	Prohibited.	Ch. 15; Appendix
Earnings per share	Report separately for income from continuing operations, discontinued operations, extraordinary items, and net income.	Report separately for income from continuing operations, and net profit or loss.	Ch. 15; Appendix
Cash Flow Statement Items:			
Classification of interest payments	Treated as an operating activity.	May be treated as either an operating or a financing activity.	Ch. 14; LO 3

A

absorption costing The reporting of the costs of manufactured products, normally direct materials, direct labor, and factory overhead, as product costs. (906)

accelerated depreciation method A depreciation method that provides for a higher depreciation amount in the first year of the asset's use, followed by a gradually declining amount of depreciation. (402)

account An accounting form that is used to record the increases and decreases in each financial statement item. (52)

account form The form of balance sheet that resembles the basic format of the accounting equation, with assets on the left side and Liabilities and Stockholders' Equity sections on the right side. (20, 215)

account payable The liability created by a purchase on account. (12)

account receivable A claim against the customer created by selling merchandise or services on credit. (12, 64, 350)

accounting An information system that provides reports to stakeholders about the economic activities and condition of a business. (3)

accounting cycle The process that begins with analyzing and journalizing transactions and ends with the post-closing trial balance. (158)

accounting equation Assets = Liabilities + Owner's Equity. (10)

accounting period concept The accounting concept that assumes that the economic life of the business can be divided into time periods. (102)

accounts payable subsidiary ledger The subsidiary ledger containing the individual accounts with suppliers (creditors). (218)

accounts receivable analysis A company's ability to collect its accounts receivable. (681)

accounts receivable subsidiary ledger The subsidiary ledger containing the individual accounts with customers. (218)

accounts receivable turnover The relationship between net sales and accounts receivable, computed by dividing the net sales by the average net accounts receivable; measures how frequently during the year the accounts receivable are being converted to cash. (366, 681)

accrual basis of accounting Under this basis of accounting, revenues and expenses are reported in the income statement in the period in which they are earned or incurred. (102)

accrued expenses Expenses that have been incurred but not recorded in the accounts. (105)

accrued revenues Revenues that have been earned but not recorded in the accounts. (105)

accumulated depreciation The contra asset account credited when recording the depreciation of a fixed asset. (113)

accumulated other comprehensive income The cumulative effects of other comprehensive income items reported separately in the Stockholders' Equity section of the balance sheet. (588)

activity analysis The study of employee effort and other business records to determine the cost of activities. (1231)

activity base (driver) A measure of activity that is related to changes in cost. Used in analyzing and classifying cost behavior. Activity bases are also used in the denominator in calculating the predetermined factory overhead rate to assign overhead costs to cost objects. (774, 860, 1181)

activity cost pools Cost accumulations that are associated with a given activity, such as machine usage, inspections, moving, and production setups. (1179)

activity rate The cost of an activity per unit of activity base, determined by dividing the activity cost pool by the activity base. (1181)

activity-based costing (ABC) method A cost allocation method that identifies activities causing the incurrence of costs and allocates these costs to products (or other cost objects), based on activity drivers (bases). (774, 1108, 1179)

adjusted trial balance The trial balance prepared after all the adjusting entries have been posted. (120)

adjusting entries The journal entries that bring the accounts up to date at the end of the accounting period. (103)

adjusting process An analysis and updating of the accounts when financial statements are prepared. (103)

administrative expenses (general expenses) Expenses incurred in the administration or general operations of the business. (215)

aging the receivables The process of analyzing the accounts receivable and classifying them according to various age groupings, with the due date being the base point for determining age. (357)

Allowance for Doubtful Accounts The contra asset account for accounts receivable. (353)

allowance method The method of accounting for uncollectible accounts that provides an expense for uncollectible receivables in advance of their write-off. (351)

amortization The periodic transfer of the cost of an intangible asset to expense. (409)

annuity A series of equal cash flows at fixed intervals. (542, 1139)

appraisal costs Costs to detect, measure, evaluate, and audit products and processes to ensure that they conform to customer requirements and performance standards. (1231)

assets The resources owned by a business. (9, 54)

available-for-sale securities Securities that management expects to sell in the future but which are not actively traded for profit. (578)

average inventory cost flow method The method of inventory costing that is based on the assumption that costs should be charged against revenue by using the weighted average unit cost of the items sold. (266)

average rate of return A method of evaluating capital investment proposals that focuses on the expected profitability of the investment. (1135)

B

backflush accounting Simplification of the accounting system by eliminating accumulation and transfer of costs as products move through production. (1228)

bad debt expense The operating expense incurred because of the failure to collect receivables. (351)

balance of the account The amount of the difference between the debits and the credits that have been entered into an account. (53)

balance sheet A list of the assets, liabilities, and stockholders' equity as of a specific date, usually at the close of the last day of a month or a year. (17)

balanced scorecard A performance evaluation approach that incorporates multiple performance dimensions by combining financial and nonfinancial measures. (1060)

bank reconciliation The analysis that details the items responsible for the difference between the cash balance reported in the bank statement and the balance of the cash account in the ledger. (319)

bank statement A summary of all transactions mailed to the depositor or made available online by the bank each month. (316)

bond A form of an interest-bearing note used by corporations to borrow on a long-term basis. (525)

bond indenture The contract between a corporation issuing bonds and the bondholders. (528)

book value The cost of a fixed asset minus accumulated depreciation on the asset. (402)

book value of the asset (or net book value) The difference between the cost of a fixed asset and its accumulated depreciation. (114)

boot The amount a buyer owes a seller when a fixed asset is traded in on a similar asset. (415)

break-even point The level of business operations at which revenues and expired costs are equal. (869)

budget An accounting device used to plan and control resources of operational departments and divisions. (956)

budget performance report A report comparing actual results with budget figures. (1006)

budgetary slack Excess resources set within a budget to provide for uncertain events. (958)

budgeted variable factory overhead The standard variable overhead for the actual units produced. (1014)

business An organization in which basic resources (inputs), such as materials and labor, are assembled and processed to provide goods or services (outputs) to customers. (2)

business combination A business making an investment in another business by acquiring a controlling share, often greater than 50%, of the outstanding voting stock of another corporation by paying cash or exchanging stock. (573)

business entity concept A concept of accounting that limits the economic data in the accounting system to data related directly to the activities of the business. (8)

business transaction An economic event or condition that directly changes an entity's financial condition or directly affects its results of operations. (10)

C

capital expenditures The costs of acquiring fixed assets, adding to a fixed asset, improving a fixed asset, or extending a fixed asset's useful life. (396)

capital expenditures budget The budget summarizing future plans for acquiring plant facilities and equipment. (975)

capital investment analysis The process by which management plans, evaluates, and controls long-term capital investments involving property, plant, and equipment. (1134)

capital leases Leases that include one or more provisions that result in treating the leased assets as purchased assets in the accounts. (398)

capital rationing The process by which management plans, evaluates, and controls long-term capital investments involving fixed assets. (1149)

capital stock The portion of a corporation's stockholders' equity contributed by investors (owners) in exchange for shares of stock. (11)

carrying amount The balance of the bonds payable account (face amount of the bonds) less any unamortized discount or plus any unamortized premium. (534)

cash Coins, currency (paper money), checks, money orders, and money on deposit that is available for unrestricted withdrawal from banks and other financial institutions. (312)

cash basis of accounting Under this basis of accounting, revenues and expenses are reported in the income statement in the period in which cash is received or paid. (102)

cash budget A budget of estimated cash receipts and payments. (972)

cash dividend A cash distribution of earnings by a corporation to its shareholders. (492)

cash equivalents Highly liquid investments that are usually reported with cash on the balance sheet. (325)

cash flow per share Normally computed as cash flow from operations per share. (622)

cash flows from financing activities The section of the statement of cash flows that reports cash flows from transactions affecting the equity and debt of the business. (619)

cash flows from investing activities The section of the statement of cash flows that reports cash flows from transactions affecting investments in noncurrent assets. (619)

cash flows from operating activities The section of the statement of cash flows that reports the cash transactions affecting the determination of net income. (618)

cash payback period The expected period of time that will elapse between the date of a capital expenditure and the complete recovery in cash (or equivalent) of the amount invested. (1136)

cash short and over account An account which has recorded errors in cash sales or errors in making change causing the amount of actual cash on hand to differ from the beginning amount of cash plus the cash sales for the day. (314)

Certified Public Accountant (CPA) Public accountants who have met a state's education, experience, and examination requirements. (7)

chart of accounts A list of the accounts in the ledger. (54)

clearing account Another name for the income summary account because it has the effect of clearing the revenue and expense accounts of their balances. (153)

closing entries The entries that transfer the balances of the revenue, expense, and drawing accounts to the owner's capital account. (152)

closing process The transfer process of converting temporary account balances to zero by transferring the revenue and expense account balances to Income Summary, transferring the income summary account balance to the retained earnings account, and transferring the dividends account to the retained earnings account. (152)

closing the books The process of transferring temporary accounts balances to permanent accounts at the end of the accounting period. (152)

common stock The stock outstanding when a corporation has issued only one class of stock. (487)

common-sized statement A financial statement in which all items are expressed only in relative terms. (676)

compensating balance A requirement by some banks requiring depositors to maintain minimum cash balances in their bank accounts. (325)

consigned inventory Merchandise that is shipped by manufacturers to retailers who act as the manufacturer's selling agent. (279)

consignee The name for the retailer in a consigned inventory arrangement. (279)

consignor The name for the manufacturer in a consigned inventory arrangement. (279)

consolidated financial statements Financial statements resulting from combining parent and subsidiary statements. (573)

contingent liabilities Liabilities that may arise from past transactions if certain events occur in the future. (456)

continuous budgeting A method of budgeting that provides for maintaining a 12-month projection into the future. (959)

continuous process improvement A management approach that is part of the overall total quality management philosophy. The approach requires all employees to constantly improve processes of which they are a part or for which they have managerial responsibility. (734)

contra account (or contra asset account) An account offset against another account. (113)

contract rate The periodic interest to be paid on the bonds that is identified in the bond indenture; expressed as a percentage of the face amount of the bond. (528)

contribution margin Sales less variable costs and variable selling and administrative expenses. (866, 907)

contribution margin analysis The systematic examination of the differences between planned and actual contribution margins. (922)

contribution margin ratio The percentage of each sales dollar that is available to cover the fixed costs and provide an operating income. (866)

control environment The overall attitude of management and employees about the importance of controls. (308)

controllable costs Costs that can be influenced (increased, decreased, or eliminated) by someone such as a manager or factory worker. (916)

controllable expenses Costs that can be influenced by the decisions of a manager. (1050)

controllable revenues Revenues earned by the profit center. (1050)

controllable variance The difference between the actual amount of variable factory overhead cost incurred and the amount of variable factory overhead budgeted for the standard product. (1014)

controller The chief management accountant of a division or other segment of a business. (733)

controlling A phase in the management process that consists of monitoring the operating results of implemented plans and comparing the actual results with the expected results. (734)

controlling account The account in the general ledger that summarizes the balances of the accounts in a subsidiary ledger. (219)

conversion costs The combination of direct labor and factory overhead costs. (739, 1227)

copyright An exclusive right to publish and sell a literary, artistic, or musical composition. (410)

corporation A business organized under state or federal statutes as a separate legal entity. (8)

correcting journal entry An entry that is prepared when an error has already been journalized and posted. (72)

cost A payment of cash (or a commitment to pay cash in the future) for the purpose of generating revenues. (736)

cost accounting system A branch of managerial accounting concerned with accumulating manufacturing costs for financial reporting and decision-making purposes. (767)

cost allocation The process of assigning indirect cost to a cost object, such as a job. (774)

cost behavior The manner in which a cost changes in relation to its activity base (driver). (860)

cost center A decentralized unit in which the department or division manager has responsibility for the control of costs incurred and the authority to make decisions that affect these costs. (1048)

cost concept A concept of accounting that determines the amount initially entered into the accounting records for purchases. (8)

cost method A method of accounting for equity investments representing less than 20% of the outstanding shares of the investee. The purchase is at original cost, and any gains or losses upon sale are recognized by the difference between the sale proceeds and the original cost. (569)

cost object The object or segment of operations to which costs are related for management's use, such as a product or department. (736)

cost of finished goods available for sale The beginning finished goods inventory added to the cost of goods manufactured during the period. (743)

cost of goods manufactured The total cost of making and finishing a product. (743)

cost of goods sold The cost of finished goods available for sale minus the ending finished goods inventory. (743)

cost of goods sold budget A budget of the estimated direct materials, direct labor, and factory overhead consumed by sold products. (969)

cost of merchandise purchased The cost of net purchases plus transportation costs. (213)

cost of merchandise sold The cost that is reported as an expense when merchandise is sold. (211, 742)

cost of production report A report prepared periodically by a processing department, summarizing (1) the units for which the department is accountable and the disposition of those units and (2) the costs incurred by the department and the allocation of those costs between completed and incomplete production. (815)

cost of quality report A report summarizing the costs, percent of total, and percent of sales by appraisal, prevention, internal failure, and external failure cost of quality categories. (1233)

cost per equivalent unit The rate used to allocate costs between completed and partially completed production. (820)

cost price approach An approach to transfer pricing that uses cost as the basis for setting the transfer price. (1065)

cost variance The difference between actual cost and the flexible budget at actual volumes. (1006)

costs of quality The cost associated with controlling quality (prevention and appraisal) and failing to control quality (internal and external failure). (1231)

cost-volume-profit analysis The systematic examination of the relationships among selling prices, volume of sales and production, costs, expenses, and profits. (865)

cost-volume-profit chart A chart used to assist management in

understanding the relationships among costs, expenses, sales, and operating profit or loss. (874)

credit Amount entered on the right side of an account. (53)

credit memorandum (credit memo) A form used by a seller to inform the buyer of the amount the seller proposes to credit to the account receivable due from the buyer. (222)

credit period The amount of time the buyer is allowed in which to pay the seller. (221)

credit terms Terms for payment on account by the buyer to the seller. (221)

cumulative preferred stock Stock that has a right to receive regular dividends that were not declared (paid) in prior years. (488)

currency exchange rate The rate at which currency in another country can be exchanged for local currency. (1148)

current assets Cash and other assets that are expected to be converted to cash or sold or used up, usually within one year or less, through the normal operations of the business. (151)

current liabilities Liabilities that will be due within a short time (usually one year or less) and that are to be paid out of current assets. (151)

current position analysis A company's ability to pay its current liabilities. (679)

current ratio A financial ratio that is computed by dividing current assets by current liabilities. (679)

currently attainable standards Standards that represent levels of operation that can be attained with reasonable effort. (1003)

D

debit Amount entered on the left side of an account. (53)

debit memorandum (debit memo) A form used by a buyer to inform the seller of the amount the buyer proposes to debit to the account payable due the seller. (225)

debt securities Notes and bond investments that provide interest revenue over a fixed maturity. (566)

decision making A component inherent in the other management

processes of planning, directing, controlling, and improving. (734)

defined benefit plan A pension plan that promises employees a fixed annual pension benefit at retirement, based on years of service and compensation levels. (454)

defined contribution plan A pension plan that requires a fixed amount of money to be invested for the employee's behalf during the employee's working years. (454)

depletion The process of transferring the cost of natural resources to an expense account. (408)

depreciate To lose usefulness as all fixed assets except land do. (113)

depreciation The systematic periodic transfer of the cost of a fixed asset to an expense account during its expected useful life. (113, 398)

depreciation expense The portion of the cost of a fixed asset that is recorded as an expense each year of its useful life. (113)

differential analysis The area of accounting concerned with the effect of alternative courses of action on revenues and costs. (1091)

differential cost The amount of increase or decrease in cost expected from a particular course of action compared with an alternative. (1091)

differential income (or loss) The difference between the differential revenue and the differential costs. (1091)

differential revenue The amount of increase or decrease in revenue expected from a particular course of action as compared with an alternative. (1091)

direct costs Costs that can be traced directly to a cost object. (736)

direct labor cost The wages of factory workers who are directly involved in converting materials into a finished product. (738)

direct labor cost budget Budget that estimates direct labor hours and related costs needed to support budgeted production. (967)

direct labor rate variance The cost associated with the difference between the standard rate and the actual rate paid for direct labor used in producing a commodity. (1011)

direct labor time variance The cost associated with the difference between the standard hours and the actual hours of direct labor spent producing a commodity. (1011)

direct materials cost The cost of materials that are an integral part of the finished product. (737)

direct materials price variance The cost associated with the difference between the standard price and the actual price of direct materials used in producing a commodity. (1009)

direct materials purchases budget A budget that uses the production budget as a starting point to budget materials purchases. (966)

direct materials quantity variance The cost associated with the difference between the standard quantity and the actual quantity of direct materials used in producing a commodity. (1009)

direct method A method of reporting the cash flows from operating activities as the difference between the operating cash receipts and the operating cash payments. (619)

direct write-off method The method of accounting for uncollectible accounts that recognizes the expense only when accounts are judged to be worthless. (351)

directing The process by which managers, given their assigned level of responsibilities, run day-to-day operations. (734)

discount The interest deducted from the maturity value of a note or the excess of the face amount of bonds over their issue price. (489, 528)

dishonored note receivable A note that the maker fails to pay on the due date. (364)

dividend yield A ratio, computed by dividing the annual dividends paid per share of common stock by the market price per share at a specific date, that indicates the rate of return to stockholders in terms of cash dividend distributions. (692)

dividends Distribution of a corporation's earning to stockholders. (14, 54)

dividends per share Measures the extent to which earnings are being distributed to common shareholders. (692)

double-declining-balance method A method of depreciation that provides periodic depreciation expense based on the declining book value of a fixed asset over its estimated life. (402)

double-entry accounting system A system of accounting for recording transactions, based on recording increases and decreases in accounts so that debits equal credits. (55)

DuPont formula An expanded expression of return on investment determined by multiplying the profit margin by the investment turnover. (1055)

E

earnings per common share (EPS) Net income per share of common stock outstanding during a period. (507)

earnings per share (EPS) on common stock The profitability ratio of net income available to common shareholders to the number of common shares outstanding. (526, 690)

effective interest rate method The method of amortizing discounts and premiums that provides for a constant rate of interest on the carrying amount of the bonds at the beginning of each period; often called simply the "interest method." (531)

effective rate of interest The market rate of interest at the time bonds are issued. (528)

electronic data interchange (EDI) An information technology that allows different business organizations to use computers to communicate orders, relay information, and make or receive payments. (1225)

electronic funds transfer (EFT) A system in which computers rather than paper (money, checks, etc.) are used to effect cash transactions. (315)

elements of internal control The control environment, risk assessment, control activities, information and communication, and monitoring. (307)

employee fraud The intentional act of deceiving an employer for personal gain. (307)

employee involvement A philosophy that grants employees the responsibility and authority to make their own decisions about their operations. (1224)

employee's earnings record A detailed record of each employee's earnings. (449)

engineering change order (ECO) A document that initiates a change in the specification or a product or process. (1180)

enterprise resource planning (ERP) An integrated business and information system used by companies to plan and control both internal and supply chain operations. (1225)

equity method A method of accounting for an investment in common stock by which the investment account is adjusted for the investor's share of periodic net income and cash dividends of the investee. (571)

equity securities The common and preferred stock of a firm. (566)

equivalent units of production The number of production units that could have been completed within a given accounting period, given the resources consumed. (817)

ethics Moral principles that guide the conduct of individuals. (4)

expenses Assets used up or services consumed in the process of generating revenues. (12, 55)

external failure costs The costs incurred after defective units or services have been delivered to consumers. (1231)

F

factory burden Another term for manufacturing overhead or factory overhead. (738)

factory overhead cost All of the costs of producing a product except for direct materials and direct labor. (738)

factory overhead cost budget Budget that estimates the cost for each item of factory overhead needed to support budgeted production. (968)

factory overhead cost variance report Reports budgeted and actual costs for variable and fixed factory overhead along with the related controllable and volume variances. (1017)

fair value The price that would be received for selling an asset or paying off a liability, often the market price for an equity or debt security. (574)

favorable cost variance A variance that occurs when the actual cost is less than standard cost. (1006)

feedback Measures provided to operational employees or managers on the performance of subunits of the organization. These measures are used by employees to adjust a process or a behavior to achieve goals. See management by exception. (734)

fees earned Revenue from providing services. (12)

FICA tax Federal Insurance Contributions Act tax used to finance federal programs for old-age and disability benefits (social security) and health insurance for the aged (Medicare). (443)

financial accounting The branch of accounting that is concerned with recording transactions using generally accepted accounting principles (GAAP) for a business or other economic unit and with a periodic preparation of various statements from such records. (4, 731)

Financial Accounting Standards Board (FASB) The authoritative body that has the primary responsibility for developing accounting principles. (7)

financial statements Financial reports that summarize the effects of events on a business. (16)

finished goods inventory The direct materials costs, direct labor costs, and factory overhead costs of finished products that have not been sold. (741)

finished goods ledger The subsidiary ledger that contains the individual accounts for each kind of commodity or product produced. (779)

first-in, first-out (FIFO) inventory cost flow method The method of inventory costing based on the assumption that the costs of merchandise sold should be charged against revenue in the order in which the costs were incurred. (266, 815)

fiscal year The annual accounting period adopted by a business. (170)

fixed asset turnover ratio The number of dollars of sales that are generated from each dollar of average fixed assets during the year, computed by dividing the net sales by the average net fixed assets. (414)

fixed assets (or plant assets) Long-term or relatively permanent tangible assets such as equipment, machinery, and buildings that are used in the normal business operations and that depreciate over time. (113, 151, 393)

fixed costs Costs that tend to remain the same in amount, regardless of variations in the level of activity. (862)

flexible budget A budget that adjusts for varying rates of activity. (960)

FOB (free on board) destination Freight terms in which the seller pays the transportation costs from the shipping point to the final destination. (227)

FOB (free on board) shipping point Freight terms in which the buyer pays the transportation costs from the shipping point to the final destination. (227)

free cash flow The amount of operating cash flow remaining after replacing current productive capacity and maintaining current dividends. (637)

freight in Costs of transportation. (213)

fringe benefits Benefits provided to employees in addition to wages and salaries. (453)

future value The estimated worth in the future of an amount of cash on hand today invested at a fixed rate of interest. (540)

G

general ledger The primary ledger, when used in conjunction with subsidiary ledgers, that contains all of the balance sheet and income statement accounts. (218)

general-purpose financial statements A type of financial accounting report that is distributed to external users. The term "general purpose" refers to the wide range of decision-making needs that the reports are designed to serve. (4)

generally accepted accounting principles (GAAP) Generally accepted guidelines for the preparation of financial statements. (7)

goal conflict A condition that occurs when individual objectives conflict with organizational objectives. (958)

goodwill An intangible asset that is created from such favorable factors as location, product quality, reputation, and managerial skill. (411)

gross pay The total earnings of an employee for a payroll period. (441)

gross profit Sales minus the cost of merchandise sold. (211)

gross profit method A method of estimating inventory cost that is based on the relationship of gross profit to sales. (284)

H

held-to-maturity securities Investments in bonds or other debt securities that management intends to hold to their maturity. (577)

high-low method A technique that uses the highest and lowest total costs as a basis for estimating the variable cost per unit and the fixed cost component of a mixed cost. (864)

horizontal analysis Financial analysis that compares an item in a current statement with the same item in prior statements. (73, 673)

I

ideal standards Standards that can be achieved only under perfect operating conditions, such as no idle time, no machine breakdowns, and no materials spoilage; also called theoretical standards. (1003)

in arrears Cumulative preferred stock dividends that have not been paid in prior years are said to be in arrears. (488)

income from operations (operating income) Revenues less operating expenses and service department charges for a profit or an investment center. (215)

income statement A summary of the revenue and expenses for a specific period of time, such as a month or a year. (17)

Income Summary An account to which the revenue and expense account balances are transferred at the end of a period. (153)

indirect costs Costs that cannot be traced directly to a cost object. (736)

indirect method A method of reporting the cash flows from operating activities as the net income from operations adjusted for all deferrals of past cash receipts and payments and all accruals of expected future cash receipts and payments. (620)

inflation A period when prices in general are rising and the purchasing power of money is declining. (1148)

installment note A debt that requires the borrower to make equal periodic payments to the lender for the term of the note. (536)

intangible assets Long-term assets that are useful in the operations of a business, are not held for sale, and are without physical qualities. (409)

interest revenue Money received for interest. (12)

internal controls The policies and procedures used to safeguard assets, ensure accurate business information, and ensure compliance with laws and regulations. (305)

internal failure costs The costs associated with defects that are discovered by the organization before the product or service is delivered to the consumer. (1231)

internal rate of return (IRR) method A method of analysis of proposed capital investments that uses present value concepts to compute the rate of return from the net cash flows expected from the investment. (1143)

International Accounting Standards Board (IASB) An organization that issues International Financial Reporting Standards for many countries outside the United States. (7)

inventory analysis A company's ability to manage its inventory effectively. (682)

inventory shrinkage (inventory shortage) The amount by which the merchandise for sale, as indicated by the balance of the merchandise inventory account, is larger than the total amount of merchandise counted during the physical inventory. (231)

inventory subsidiary ledger A ledger containing individual accounts with a common characteristic. (218, 265)

inventory turnover The relationship between the volume of goods sold and inventory, computed by dividing the cost of goods sold by the average inventory. (282, 683)

investee The company whose stock is purchased by the investor. (569)

investment center A decentralized unit in which the manager has the responsibility and authority to make decisions that affect not only costs and revenues but also the fixed assets available to the center. (1054)

investment turnover A component of the rate of return on investment, computed as the ratio of sales to invested assets. (1055)

investments The balance sheet caption used to report long-term investments in stocks not intended as a source of cash in the normal operations of the business. (566)

investor The company investing in another company's stock. (569)

invoice The bill that the seller sends to the buyer. (221)

J

job cost sheet An account in the work in process subsidiary ledger in which the costs charged to a particular job order are recorded. (770)

job order cost system A type of cost accounting system that provides for a separate record of the cost of each particular quantity of product that passes through the factory. (767)

journal The initial record in which the effects of a transaction are recorded. (57)

journal entry The form of recording a transaction in a journal. (58)

journalizing The process of recording a transaction in the journal. (58)

just-in-time (JIT) processing A processing approach that focuses on eliminating time, cost, and poor quality within manufacturing and nonmanufacturing processes. (830, 1218)

L

last-in, first-out (LIFO) inventory cost flow method A method of inventory costing based on the assumption that the most recent merchandise inventory costs should be charged against revenue. (266)

lead time The elapsed time between starting a unit of product into the beginning of a process and its completion. (1219)

ledger A group of accounts for a business. (54)

liabilities The rights of creditors that represent debts of the business. (9, 54)

limited liability company (LLC) A business form consisting of one or more persons or entities filing an operating agreement with a state to conduct business with limited liability to the owners, yet treated as a partnership for tax purposes. (8)

line department A unit that is directly involved in the basic objectives of an organization. (732)

long-term liabilities Liabilities that usually will not be due for more than one year. (151)

lower-of-cost-or-market (LCM) method A method of valuing inventory that reports the inventory at the lower of its cost or current market value (replacement cost). (277)

M

management (or managerial) accounting The branch of accounting that uses both historical and estimated data in providing information that management uses in conducting daily operations, in planning future operations, and in developing overall business strategies. (4, 731)

management by exception The philosophy of managing which involves monitoring the operating results of implemented plans and comparing the expected results with the actual results. This feedback allows management to isolate significant variations for further investigation and possible remedial action. (734)

management process The five basic management functions of (1) planning, (2) directing, (3) controlling, (4) improving, and (5) decision making. (733)

Management's Discussion and Analysis (MD&A) An annual report disclosure that provides management's analysis of the results of operations and financial condition. (694)

managerial accounting The branch of accounting that uses both historical and estimated data in providing information that management uses in conducting daily operations, in planning future operations, and in developing overall business strategies. (731)

manufacturing business A type of business that changes basic inputs into products that are sold to individual customers. (3)

manufacturing cells A grouping of processes where employees are cross-trained to perform more than one function. (831)

manufacturing margin The variable cost of goods sold deducted from sales. (907)

manufacturing overhead Costs, other than direct materials and direct labor costs, that are incurred in the manufacturing process. (738)

margin of safety Indicates the possible decrease in sales that may occur before an operating loss results. (882)

market price approach An approach to transfer pricing that uses the price at which the product or service transferred could be sold to outside buyers as the transfer price. (1062)

market rate of interest The rate determined from sales and purchases of similar bonds. (528)

market segment A portion of business that can be assigned to a manager for profit responsibility. (917)

markup An amount that is added to a "cost" amount to determine product price. (1101)

master budget The comprehensive budget plan linking all the individual budgets related to sales, cost of goods sold, operating expenses, projects, capital expenditures, and cash. (963)

matching concept (or matching principle) A concept of accounting in which expenses are matched with the revenue generated during a period by those expenses. (17, 102)

materials inventory The cost of materials that have not yet entered into the manufacturing process. (741)

materials ledger The subsidiary ledger containing the individual accounts for each type of material. (769)

materials requisition The form or electronic transmission used by a manufacturing department to authorize materials issuances from the storeroom. (770)

maturity value The amount that is due at the maturity or due date of a note. (363)

merchandise available for sale The cost of merchandise available for sale to customers calculated by adding the beginning merchandise inventory to net purchases. (213, 742)

merchandise inventory Merchandise on hand (not sold) at the end of an accounting period. (211)

merchandising business A type of business that purchases products from other businesses and sells them to customers. (3)

mixed cost A cost with both variable and fixed characteristics, sometimes called a semivariable or semifixed cost. (862)

mortgage notes An installment note that may be secured by a pledge of the borrower's assets. (536)

multiple production department factory overhead rate method A method that allocated factory overhead to product by using factory overhead rates for each production department. (1175)

multiple-step income statement A form of income statement that contains several sections, subsections, and subtotals. (212)

N

natural business year A fiscal year that ends when business activities have reached the lowest point in an annual operating cycle. (170)

negotiated price approach An approach to transfer pricing that allows managers of decentralized units to agree (negotiate) among themselves as to the transfer price. (1063)

net income or net profit The amount by which revenues exceed expenses. (17)

net loss The amount by which expenses exceed revenues. (17)

net pay Gross pay less payroll deductions; the amount the employer is obligated to pay the employee. (441)

net present value method A method of analysis of proposed capital investments that focuses on the present value of the cash flows expected from the investments. (1141)

net purchases Determined when purchases returns and allowances and the purchases discounts are deducted from the total purchases. (213)

net realizable value The estimated selling price of an item of inventory less any direct costs of disposal, such as sales commissions. (278, 353)

net sales Revenue received for merchandise sold to customers less any sales returns and allowances and sales discounts. (213)

noncontrollable cost Cost that cannot be influenced (increased, decreased, or eliminated) by someone such as a manager or factory worker. (916)

nonfinancial measure A performance measure that has not been stated in dollar terms. (1230)

nonfinancial performance measure A performance measure expressed in units rather than dollars. (1022)

non-value-added activity The cost of activities that are perceived as unnecessary from the customer's perspective and are thus candidates for elimination. (1234)

non-value-added lead time The time that units wait in inventories, move unnecessarily, and wait during machine breakdowns. (1220)

normal balance of an account The normal balance of an account can be either a debit or a credit depending on whether increases in the account are recorded as debits or credits. (56)

notes receivable A customer's written promise to pay an amount and possibly interest at an agreed-upon rate. (151, 350)

number of days' sales in inventory The relationship between the volume of sales and inventory, computed by dividing the inventory at the end of the year by the average daily cost of goods sold. (282, 683)

number of days' sales in receivables The relationship between sales and accounts receivable, computed by dividing the net accounts receivable at the end of the year by the average daily sales. (366, 682)

number of times interest charges are earned A ratio that measures creditor margin of safety for interest payments, calculated as income before interest and taxes divided by interest expense. (539, 685)

O

objectives (goals) Developed in the planning stage, these reflect the direction and desired outcomes of certain courses of action. (734)

objectivity concept A concept of accounting that requires accounting records and the data reported in financial statements to be based on objective evidence. (9)

operating leases Leases that do not meet the criteria for capital leases and thus are accounted for as operating expenses. (398)

operating leverage A measure of the relative mix of a business's variable costs and fixed costs, computed as contribution margin divided by operating income. (880)

operational planning The development of short-term plans to achieve goals identified in a business's strategic plan. Sometimes called tactical planning. (734)

opportunity cost The amount of income forgone from an alternative to a proposed use of cash or its equivalent. (1097)

other expense Expenses that cannot be traced directly to operations. (215)

other income Revenue from sources other than the primary operating activity of a business. (215)

outstanding stock The stock in the hands of stockholders. (487)

overapplied factory overhead The amount of factory overhead applied in excess of the actual factory overhead costs incurred for production during a period. (776)

owner's equity The owner's right to the assets of the business. (9)

P

par The monetary amount printed on a stock certificate. (487)

parent company The corporation owning all or a majority of the voting stock of the other corporation. (573)

Pareto chart A bar chart that shows the totals of a particular attribute for a number of categories, ranked left to right from the largest to smallest totals. (1233)

partnership An unincorporated business form consisting of two or more persons conducting business as co-owners for profit. (8)

patents Exclusive rights to produce and sell goods with one or more unique features. (409)

payroll The total amount paid to employees for a certain period. (441)

payroll register A multicolumn report used to assemble and summarize payroll data at the end of each payroll period. (446)

pension A cash payment to retired employees. (454)

period costs Those costs that are used up in generating revenue during the current period and that are not involved in manufacturing a product, such as selling, general, and administrative expenses. (739, 780)

periodic inventory system The inventory system in which the inventory records do not show the amount available for sale or sold during the period. (214)

perpetual inventory system The inventory system in which each purchase and sale of merchandise is recorded in an inventory account. (214)

petty cash fund A special cash fund to pay relatively small amounts. (323)

physical inventory A detailed listing of merchandise on hand. (265)

planning A phase of the management process whereby objectives are outlined and courses of action determined. (734)

posting The process of transferring the debits and credits from the journal entries to the accounts. (61)

predetermined factory overhead rate The rate used to apply factory overhead costs to the goods man-ufactured. The rate is determined by dividing the budgeted overhead cost by the estimated activity usage at the beginning of the fiscal period. (774)

preferred stock A class of stock with preferential rights over common stock. (487)

premium The excess of the issue price of a stock over its par value or the excess of the issue price of bonds over their face amount. (489, 528)

prepaid expenses Items such as supplies that will be used in the business in the future. (12, 104)

present value The estimated worth today of an amount of cash to be received (or paid) in the future. (540)

present value concept Cash to be received (or paid) in the future is not the equivalent of the same amount of money received at an earlier date. (1138)

present value index An index computed by dividing the total present value of the net cash flow to be received from a proposed capital investment by the amount to be invested. (1142)

present value of an annuity The sum of the present values of a series of equal cash flows to be received at fixed intervals. (542, 1139)

prevention costs Costs incurred to prevent defects from occurring during the design and delivery of products or services. (1231)

price factor The effect of a difference in unit sales price or unit cost on the number of units sold. (922)

price-earnings (P/E) ratio The ratio of the market price per share of common stock, at a specific date, to the annual earnings per share. (691)

prime costs The combination of direct materials and direct labor costs. (739)

prior period adjustments Corrections of material errors related to a prior period or periods, excluded from the determination of net income. (500)

private accounting The field of accounting whereby accountants are employed by a business firm or a not-for-profit organization. (4)

process A sequence of activities linked together for performing a particular task. (1023, 1235)

process cost system A type of cost system that accumulates costs for each of the various departments within a manufacturing facility. (768, 809)

process manufacturers Manufacturers that use large machines to process a continuous flow of raw materials through various stages of completion into a finished state. (809)

process-oriented layout Organizing work in a plant or administrative function around processes (tasks). (1223)

product cost concept A concept used in applying the cost-plus approach to product pricing in which only the costs of manufacturing the product, termed the product cost, are included in the cost amount to which the markup is added. (1104)

product costing Determining the cost of a product. (1172)

product costs The three components of manufacturing cost: direct materials, direct labor, and factory overhead costs. (739)

production bottleneck A condition that occurs when product demand exceeds production capacity. (1109)

production budget A budget of estimated unit production. (965)

production department factory overhead rates Rates determined by dividing the budgeted production department factory overhead by the budgeted allocation base for each department. (1176)

product-oriented layout Organizing work in a plant or administrative function around products; sometimes referred to as product cells. (1223)

profit The difference between the amounts received from customers for goods or services provided and the amounts paid for the inputs used to provide the goods or services. (2)

profit center A decentralized unit in which the manager has the responsibility and the authority to make decisions that affect both costs and revenues (and thus profits). (1050)

profit margin A component of the rate of return on investment, computed as the ratio of income from operations to sales. (1055)

profit-volume chart A chart used to assist management in understanding the relationship between profit and volume. (876)

profitability The ability of a firm to earn income. (678)

proprietorship A business owned by one individual. (8)

public accounting The field of accounting where accountants and their staff provide services on a fee basis. (7)

pull manufacturing A just-in-time method wherein customer orders trigger the release of finished goods, which triggers production, which triggers release of materials from suppliers. (1224)

purchase order The purchase order authorizes the purchase of the inventory from an approved vendor. (265)

purchases discounts Discounts taken by the buyer for early payment of an invoice. (213)

purchases returns and allowances From the buyer's perspective, returned merchandise or an adjustment for defective merchandise. (213)

push manufacturing Materials are released into production and work in process is released into finished goods in anticipation of future sales. (1224)

Q

quantity factor The effect of a difference in the number of units sold, assuming no change in unit sales price or unit cost. (922)

quick assets Cash and other current assets that can be quickly converted to cash, such as marketable securities and receivables. (459, 680)

quick ratio A financial ratio that measures the ability to pay current liabilities with quick assets (cash, marketable securities, accounts receivable). (459, 680)

R

radio frequency identification devices (RFID) Electronic tags (chips) placed on or embedded within products that can be read by radio waves that allow instant monitoring or production location. (1225)

rate earned on common stockholders' equity A measure of profitability computed by dividing net income, reduced by preferred dividend requirements, by common stockholders' equity. (689)

rate earned on stockholders' equity A measure of profitability computed

by dividing net income by total stockholders' equity. (688)

rate earned on total assets A measure of the profitability of assets, without regard to the equity of creditors and stockholders in the assets. (687)

rate of return on investment (ROI) A measure of managerial efficiency in the use of investments in assets, computed as income from operations divided by invested assets. (1055)

ratio of fixed assets to long-term liabilities A leverage ratio that measures the margin of safety of long-term creditors, calculated as the net fixed assets divided by the long-term liabilities. (684)

ratio of liabilities to stockholders' equity A comprehensive leverage ratio that measures the relationship of the claims of creditors to stockholders' equity. (684)

ratio of net sales to assets Ratio that measures how effectively a company uses its assets, computed as net sales divided by average total assets. (686)

Raw and In Process (RIP) Inventory The capitalized cost of direct materials purchases, labor, and overhead charged to the production cell. (1227)

real (permanent) accounts Term for balance sheet accounts because they are relatively permanent and carried forward from year to year. (152)

receivables All money claims against other entities, including people, business firms, and other organizations. (350)

receiving report The form or electronic transmission used by the receiving personnel to indicate that materials have been received and inspected. (265, 769)

relevant range The range of activity over which changes in cost are of interest to management. (860)

rent revenue Money received for rent. (12)

report form The form of balance sheet with the Liabilities and Owner's Equity sections presented below the Assets section. (216)

residual income The excess of divisional income from operations over a "minimum" acceptable income from operations. (1058)

residual value The estimated value of a fixed asset at the end of its useful life. (399)

responsibility accounting The process of measuring and reporting operating data by areas of responsibility. (1047)

responsibility center An organizational unit for which a manager is assigned responsibility over costs, revenues, or assets. (957)

restrictions Amounts of retained earnings that have been limited for use as dividends. (499)

retail inventory method A method of estimating inventory cost that is based on the relationship of gross profit to sales. (283)

retained earnings Net income retained in a corporation. (15)

retained earnings statement A summary of the changes in the retained earnings in a corporation for a specific period of time, such as a month or a year. (17)

revenue Increase in owner's equity as a result of selling services or products to customers. (12, 55)

revenue expenditures Costs that benefit only the current period or costs incurred for normal maintenance and repairs of fixed assets. (396)

revenue recognition concept The accounting concept that supports reporting revenues when the services are provided to customers. (102)

rules of debit and credit In the double-entry accounting system, specific rules for recording debits and credits based on the type of account. (55)

S

sales The total amount charged customers for merchandise sold, including cash sales and sales on account. (12, 213)

sales budget One of the major elements of the income statement budget that indicates the quantity of estimated sales and the expected unit selling price. (964)

sales discounts From the seller's perspective, discounts that a seller may offer the buyer for early payment. (213)

sales mix The relative distribution of sales among the various products available for sale. (879, 919)

sales returns and allowances From the seller's perspective, returned merchandise or an adjustment for defective merchandise. (213)

Sarbanes-Oxley Act of 2002 An act passed by Congress to restore public confidence and trust in the financial statements of companies. (305)

Securities and Exchange Commission (SEC) An agency of the U.S. government that has authority over the accounting and financial disclosures for companies whose shares of ownership (stock) are traded and sold to the public. (7)

selling expenses Expenses that are incurred directly in the selling of merchandise. (215)

service business A business providing services rather than products to customers. (3)

service department charges The costs of services provided by an internal service department and transferred to a responsibility center. (1050)

setup Changing the characteristics of a machine to produce a different product. (1180)

single plantwide factory overhead rate method A method that allocates all factory overhead to products by using a single factory overhead rate. (1173)

single-step income statement A form of income statement in which the total of all expenses is deducted from the total of all revenues. (216)

Six-Sigma A quality improvement process developed by Motorola Corporation consisting of five steps: define, measure, analyze, improve, and control (DMAIC). (1224)

slide An error in which the entire number is moved one or more spaces to the right or the left, such as writing $542.00 as $54.20 or $5,420.00. (71)

solvency The ability of a firm to pay its debts as they come due. (678)

special-purpose fund A cash fund used for a special business need. (324)

specific identification inventory cost flow method Inventory method in

which the unit sold is identified with a specific purchase. (264)

staff department A unit that provides services, assistance, and advice to the departments with line or other staff responsibilities. (733)

standard cost A detailed estimate of what a product should cost. (1002)

standard cost systems Accounting systems that use standards for each element of manufacturing cost entering into the finished product. (1002)

standards Performance goals, often relating to how much a product should cost. (1002)

statement of cash flows A summary of the cash receipts and cash payments for a specific period of time, such as a month or a year. (17, 618)

statement of cost of goods manufactured The income statement of manufacturing companies. (743)

statement of stockholders' equity A summary of the changes in the stockholders' equity in a corporation that have occurred during a specific period of time. (500)

static budget A budget that does not adjust to changes in activity levels. (960)

stock Shares of ownership of a corporation. (484)

stock dividend A distribution of shares of stock to its stockholders. (494)

stock split A reduction in the par or stated value of a common stock and the issuance of a proportionate number of additional shares. (502)

stockholders The owners of a corporation. (484)

stockholders' equity The owners' equity in a corporation. (11, 54)

straight-line method A method of depreciation that provides for equal periodic depreciation expense over the estimated life of a fixed asset. (400)

strategic planning The development of a long-range course of action to achieve business goals. (734)

strategies The means by which business goals and objectives will be achieved. (734)

subsidiary company The corporation that is controlled by a parent company. (573)

subsidiary ledger A ledger containing individual accounts with a common characteristic. (218)

sunk cost A cost that is not affected by subsequent decisions. (1091)

supply chain management The coordination and control of materials, services, information, and finances as they move in a process from supplier, through the manufacturer, wholesaler, and retailer to the consumer. (1225)

T

T account The simplest form of an account. (52)

target costing The target cost is determined by subtracting a desired profit from a market method determined price. The resulting target cost is used to motivate cost improvements in design and manufacture. (1108)

temporary (nominal) accounts Accounts that report amounts for only one period. (152)

theory of constraints (TOC) A manufacturing strategy that attempts to remove the influence of bottlenecks (constraints) on a process. (1109)

time tickets The form on which the amount of time spent by each employee and the labor cost incurred for each individual job, or for factory overhead, are recorded. (771)

time value of money concept The concept that an amount of money invested today will earn income. (1135)

total cost concept A concept used in applying the cost-plus approach to product pricing in which all the costs of manufacturing the product plus the selling and administrative expenses are included in the cost amount to which the markup is added. (1101)

total manufacturing cost variance The difference between total standard costs and total actual costs for units produced. (1007)

trade discounts Discounts from the list prices in published catalogs or special discounts offered to certain classes of buyers. (229)

trade-in allowance The amount a seller allows a buyer for a fixed asset that is traded in for a similar asset. (415)

trademark A name, term, or symbol used to identify a business and its products. (410)

trading securities Securities that management intends to actively trade for profit. (574)

transfer price The price charged one decentralized unit by another for the goods or services provided. (1061)

transposition An error in which the order of the digits is changed, such as writing $542 as $452 or $524. (71)

treasury stock Stock that a corporation has once issued and then reacquires. (495)

trial balance A summary listing of the titles and balances of accounts in the ledger. (70)

U

unadjusted trial balance A summary listing of the titles and balances of accounts in the ledger prior to the posting of adjusting entries. (70)

underapplied factory overhead The amount of actual factory overhead in excess of the factory overhead applied to production during a period. (776)

unearned revenue The liability created by receiving revenue in advance. (62, 104)

unfavorable cost variance A variance that occurs when the actual cost exceeds the standard cost. (1006)

unit contribution margin The dollars available from each unit of sales to cover fixed costs and provide operating profits. (867)

unit of measure concept A concept of accounting requiring that economic data be recorded in dollars. (9)

units-of-production method A method of depreciation that provides for depreciation expense based on the expected productive capacity of a fixed asset. (401)

unrealized gain or loss Changes in the fair value of equity or debt securities for a period. (574)

V

value-added activity The cost of activities that are needed to meet customer requirements. (1234)

value-added lead time The time required to manufacture a unit of product or other output. (1219

value-added ratio The ratio of the value-added lead time to the total lead time. (1220)

variable cost concept A concept used in applying the cost-plus approach to product pricing in which only the variable costs are included in the cost amount to which the markup is added. (1105)

variable cost of goods sold Consists of direct materials, direct labor, and variable factory overhead for the units sold. (907)

variable costing The concept that considers the cost of products manufactured to be composed only of those manufacturing costs that increase or decrease as the volume of production rises or falls (direct materials, direct labor, and variable factory overhead). (865, 907)

variable costs Costs that vary in total dollar amount as the level of activity changes. (861)

vertical analysis An analysis that compares each item in a current statement with a total amount within the same statement. (675)

volume variance The difference between the budgeted fixed overhead at 100% of normal capacity and the standard fixed overhead for the actual production achieved during the period. (1015)

voucher A special form for recording relevant data about a liability and the details of its payment. (315)

voucher system A set of procedures for authorizing and recording liabilities and cash payments. (315)

W

whole units The number of units in production during a period, whether completed or not. (817)

work in process inventory The direct materials costs, the direct labor costs, and the applied factory overhead costs that have entered into the manufacturing process but are associated with products that have not been finished. (741)

working capital The excess of the current assets of a business over its current liabilities. (679)

Y

yield A measure of materials usage efficiency. (829)

Z

zero-based budgeting A concept of budgeting that requires all levels of management to start from zero and estimate budget data as if there had been no previous activities in their units. (959)

Company Index

Global Economic Crisis

Impact on Accounting

SOUTH-WESTERN
CENGAGE Learning

Australia • Brazil • Japan • Korea • Mexico • Singapore • Spain • United Kingdom • United States

Building Up to the Current Crisis

Learning Objectives.

By the end of this chapter, you will be able to:

- Explain the important financial market regulation that came out of the Great Depression of the 1930s.

- Describe why the rise of American consumerism took place after World War II.

- Elaborate on why the Savings and Loan crisis took place.

- Describe why there was a drive for mortgage-backed securities during the first decade of the 21st century.

- Delineate how all of these historical events have led up to the current financial crisis.

In January 2007, everything seemed to be going right for the U.S. economy and, by extension, U.S. financial markets. On January 24, 2007, the Dow Jones Industrial Index ended the day at 12,621. This was the first time ever the Dow had climbed above 12,600[1]. As stock prices continued to increase, the Federal Reserve worried that the U.S. economy might be growing too quickly. The Federal Reserve had raised its target for the Fed Funds Rate from 5.25 percent to 5.50 percent six months earlier, in the hopes of cooling a red hot U.S. economy. Even with the higher interest rates, the economy was growing at faster than 4 percent a year, a rate many economists believed was unsustainable for an economy the size of the United States.

By the fall of 2008, things had changed drastically. By November 12, 2008, the Dow had fallen to 8,282, a 41 percent drop from its high of 14,164 on October 9, 2007. The Federal Reserve had cut its target for the Fed Funds rate to a mere 1 percent, in a desperate attempt to keep the economy from sliding into a deep recession.

What on earth happened? How could such a highly successful economy like that of the United States in January 2007 find itself on the brink of a severe recession a mere few months later? At this point, we must ask ourselves: Where is the U.S. economy headed? As the old saying goes, "If you want to know where you are going, you have to understand where you have been." To learn why the current financial crisis occurred and where the global economy is headed, we need to determine how we got here. In fact, to fully grasp how we got to where we are, we have to travel back over seventy years to the

---

1 See http://www.mdleasing.com/djia.htm.

Great Depression of the 1930s. As the American society was coming to grips with the economic catastrophe of the Great Depression, there was a call for greater regulation of our financial markets. Many of these regulations are still in place, and understanding them helps to frame the structure of the current financial crisis.

From the economic despair of the Great Depression, we moved to the post–World War II economic expansion with its boom in the housing market. One of the main players in this post-war housing boom is the Federal National Mortgage Association and later the Federal Home Loan Mortgage Corporation, or as they are better known, Fannie Mae and Freddie Mac, respectfully. The financial troubles of Fannie and Freddie are a centerpiece of the current financial crisis.

The current financial crisis is not the first crisis to have centered on the American mortgage market. Over twenty years ago, the Savings & Loan crisis also focused on entities that lent money to households to buy their homes. The outfall from the Savings & Loan crisis sets the groundwork for the current global financial crisis. While our current crisis has roots dating back over seven decades ago with the Great Depression of the 1930s, the picture is by no means complete. Updates on this discussion can be found on the web page that accompanies this booklet.

THE EARLY CALL FOR REGULATION OF FINANCIAL MARKETS: THE 1930S

From Flappers to Breadlines

The 1920s was a glamorous decade. The "Roaring '20s," as they were called, saw the rise of American consumerism, with American households buying a wide range of goods and services from new automobiles and household appliances to radios and other electrical devices. Americans were able to buy these consumer goods thanks, in great part, to the booming stock market of the times. The New York Times index of 25 industrial stocks was at 110 in 1924[2]; by June 1929, it had risen to 338, and by September 1929, it stood at 452. Thus, someone buying the index in 1924 would have seen his or her investment grow by over 400 percent by September 1929.[3] The flappers with their trendy dresses, flashy zoot suits, and dancing the Charleston all night long epitomized the carefree decade. However, the good times could not last forever. By the end of the decade, the party that had been the Roaring '20s would collapse into the Great Depression of the 1930s.

---

2 Gary Walton and Hugh Rockoff, "History of the American Economy," South-Western College Publishing, 2004.

3 Charles Kindlegerger, *The World in Depression, 1929–1939*, Berkeley: University of California Press, 1973.

The Depression witnessed the once vibrant American economy seemingly imploding overnight. As the previously dynamic and ever-expanding economy contracted, unemployment across the economy increased dramatically. No sector of the economy seemed to be spared of the growing massive unemployment of the 1930s. The unemployment of unskilled workers, skilled craftsmen, farmers, businesspeople, and even executives increased rapidly. The unemployment rate that stood at only 4 percent for much of the 1920s increased to 25 percent by 1932.

The carefree dancing flappers of the 1920s were replaced with long breadlines and soup kitchens feeding the growing masses of unemployed of the 1930s. The once booming stock market seemed to evaporate and take the rest of the economy with it. The fall in the stock market was so dramatic that stocks lost 40 percent of their value in just two months. The stock market crash caused increased uncertainty over future income and employment translated into a reduction of household spending on durable goods such as automobiles and radios. [4]

The Call for Reform

As the economy contracted and unemployment rose, there were cries from the American people for their elected leaders to "do something" about the economic crisis. The election of President Franklin Delano Roosevelt in 1932 marked a dramatic change in how the federal government would approach the crisis. Roosevelt and his fellow Democrats believed that the Depression and the resulting rise in unemployment was due to the rampant speculation in the stock market and financial markets in general.

Even before Roosevelt was sworn in, Senator Ferdinand Pecora had begun hearings to examine the role the financial markets played in triggering the Depression. The Pecora Hearings, as they became known, resulted in sweeping new regulations of the financial markets. Within weeks of taking office, the Roosevelt Administration called for a bank holiday that would close all of the commercial banks in the country for seven days; passed and signed the Securities Act of 1933; and, perhaps most importantly, passed the Glass-Steagall Act or Banking Act of 1933.

The Glass-Steagall Act accomplished three key things:

- It separated commercial banks (i.e., those entities that take deposits and make loans) from investment banks (i.e., those entities involved with underwriting and selling stocks and bonds).

- It created bank deposit insurance.

- It gave the Federal Reserve the power to limit the interest rates commercial banks could pay on deposits.

The Glass-Steagall Act's separation of commercial and investment banking was based on the premise that if commercial banks were allowed to be involved in the selling of

---

[4] Christina Romer, "The Great Crash and the Onset of the Depression," *Quarterly Journal of Economics,* August 1990, Vol. 105, no. 3.

stocks and bonds, a conflict of interest could exist and ultimately make commercial banks less safe.

The creation of deposit insurance was also designed to make commercial banks more stable. With the advent of government deposit insurance, depositors at insured banks could be confident that their savings were secure. Even if an insured bank failed, the government's deposit insurance would be there to ensure that savers would not lose their money. However, in order to make certain that banks were not taking on too much risk, government deposit insurance prompted the need for government regulation or oversight of the banking system.

In addition, Regulation Q of the Glass-Steagall Act was enacted to give the Federal Reserve the power to limit interest rates paid on deposits and to make the banking system more stable by limiting the amount of competition between banks. The drafters of the bill feared that if commercial banks competed for deposits, they would ultimately engage in destructive competitive behavior. Thus, to limit the amount of competition, banks were not allowed to pay interest on demand deposits (checking accounts) and had a cap on what interest rates they could pay on savings accounts.

As time went by, other legislation was passed that increased and expanded the government regulation of U.S. financial markets. The Securities Act of 1933 and the Securities Exchange Act of 1934 created the Securities and Exchange Commission, or the SEC, which is still today the main regulator of the bond and stock markets. In 1938, Congress created the Federal National Mortgage Association, or Fannie Mae, to help stabilize the home mortgage market. See the boxed feature for details.

Fannie Mae & Freddie Mac:
Government Entities to "Semi-Private" Financial Intermediaries

A mortgage loan uses real estate as collateral for the loan. Collateral is the pledge of an asset to ensure repayment by the borrower. Collateral serves as protection for the lender in case of default or nonpayment by the borrower. If a person borrows money and pledges something as collateral and does not repay as promised, the lenders allowed to take the collateral in lieu of the payment. So, a home mortgage loan, or what we will simply refer to as a home mortgage, is when the borrower pledges a house as collateral on a loan. A first mortgage is when a lender agrees to loan money to a family or an individual so that they can purchase a house.

Until the 20th century, mortgages were usually short term, lasting only about five to seven years. During those years, the borrower would have to pay interest on the money borrowed and repay the entire amount at the end of the period. Thus, at the end of the mortgage, the borrower would have to try to find someone or some entity to lend them the money again.

During the Great Depression, many people lost their jobs and could not afford to make their monthly mortgage payment, leaving the borrower to foreclose on them and have the family evicted from their home. With the federal government creation of the Federal National Mortgage Association (i.e., Fannie Mae), borrowers were encouraged to lend money to families over a period of 30 years. Over these 30 years, both interest and the loan principle would be paid. At the end of the 30-year mortgage, the borrower would own the home outright.

To entice lenders to loan money for home mortgages, Fannie Mae would agree to buy certain "qualified" mortgages from banks. Fannie Mae would then either hold the mortgages or sell them to interested investors. In doing so, Fannie Mae would free up funds for the lender to loan on new mortgages.

Due to budget constraints, President Johnson privatized Fannie Mae in 1968. In order to ensure that Fannie Mae did not have a monopoly in the mortgage securitizing business, the federal government created the Federal Home Loan Mortgage Corporation (i.e., Freddie Mac) in 1970.

Since both of these entities were created by the Federal government, many in the financial markets believed that Fannie and Freddie enjoyed a government guarantee against failure. Because of this "implied" government guarantee, Fannie and Freddie could borrow money at very low interest rates in financial markets.

The financial market regulation that came out of the Great Depression seemed to work very well. As the U.S. economy recovered from the Depression, financial markets remained stable and the number of banking failures dropped significantly. During World War II, the U.S. financial markets allowed the government to issue war bonds to finance the wars in Europe and the Pacific.

BUILDING THE AMERICAN DREAM: U.S. HOUSING BOOM IN POST-WAR AMERICA

Pent Up Consumption During World War II

The Second World War was a very hard time for American consumers. While household income increased, household spending decreased significantly. This reduction in household spending was in part necessary, as scarce consumer goods were diverted for the war effort. Many consumer goods, including sugar, meat, gasoline, tires, and even clothes, were rationed during the war. To buy these rationed goods, a family would need not only cash but a government-issued ration coupon. Even having a ration coupon did not guarantee that a consumer could find the good available for sale on store shelves. Shortages of popular goods, especially sugar, were commonplace during the war.

While consumer goods were scarce during the war, one thing was not in short supply: jobs. Workers were needed to build the tanks, ships, and arms that were critical to the war effort. The production of many consumer goods was suspended so that resources could be used for the war effort. For example, there were no new automobiles built in the United States between the end of 1942 and 1946, since the factories that built automobiles were converted into plants for making tanks, aircraft, artillery, etc., for the war. Similarly, no new farm tractors were built during the war, as those factories were likewise converted for the war effort. But these factories needed workers to produce war-related products. Because many young males had joined the military to fight in the war, workers were in short supply. For the first time in U.S. history, large numbers of women entered the labor force.

As employment increased during the war, American households saw their incomes increase. However, with the war rationing in effect, households had very few things on which to spend this new income. Instead, scores of Americans saved their money during the War, waiting and hoping for a better future.

Unleashing American Spending

The end of the Second World War saw a return of American consumerism in grand style. The long years of economic hardship of the Great Depression were behind them, as were the days of sacrifice during World War II. The American consumer had pent up spending power that was being unleashed. For military personnel who were returning from fighting the war overseas as well as those who had "fought the war on the home front," the end of the war created an opportunity to capture the "American Dream." A big part of that post-war "American Dream" was home ownership. In 1940, just 44 percent of families owned their own home; by the end of the 1950s, three out of five families owned their home (according to a U.S. Census). This remarkable increase in homeownership was due, in great part, to the expansion of the Savings and Loan industry.

Savings and Loans are depository institutions that take deposits, mostly from households, and make loans mostly to consumers; these loans are often home mortgages. While the Savings and Loan industry has a long history in the United States going back to the 19th century (the forerunners were called Building & Loans), a number of Savings and Loans failed during the depression. As a result, in 1932, Congress passed the Federal Home Loan Bank Act of 1932, which created the Federal Home Loan Bank Board to lend money to Savings and Loans that found themselves short of funds. In 1934, Congress created the Federal Savings and Loan Insurance Corporation (FSLIC), which would offer government deposit insurance to savers at Savings and Loans.[5]

Expansion of the Savings and Loan Industry

During the post–World War II era, the Savings and Loan industry thrived. The first decade after the Second World War saw the Savings & Loan industry grow at its fastest rate ever. The expansion of American suburbs during the late 1940s and 1950s increased the demand for home mortgages that the Savings and Loans were prepared to offer. In addition, the Savings and Loan trade association worked with the managers of the S&Ls

---

5 David Mason, "From Building and Loans to Bail-outs," Cambridge University Press, 2004.

showing them how to advertise their services and focus on providing a high level of consumer service. As a result, the size and reach of the Savings and Loan industry expanded greatly.

Government regulation of the Savings and Loan industry also played a large role in the industry's expansion. Thanks to Regulation Q, which the Savings and Loans became subject to in 1966, the Savings and Loans faced a cap on their cost of funds. At the same time, government regulations were changing, making it easier for the Savings and Loans to offer even more mortgages and grow even more quickly. These were very successful times for the Savings and Loans. Managers of the Savings and Loans lived by the "3-6-3 Rule," that is, pay 3 percent on deposits, lend the money at 6 percent on mortgages, and be on the golf course by 3:00 pm.

The "3-6-3 Rule" illustrates why the Savings and Loans were so profitable. When a depository institution pays 3 percent for deposits and lends the money out at 6 percent, the difference between the two is what economists call the "interest rate spread." For the Savings and Loans, the 3 percentage point interest rate spread is how they paid their expenses and generated a profit. During the decades after the Second World War, the Savings and Loans were very profitable indeed. These profits allowed existing Savings and Loans to expand and drew in a large number of new S&Ls. By 1965, the Savings and Loan industry held 26 percent of all consumer savings and provided 46 percent of the single-family mortgages in the United States. Unfortunately, the good times would not last forever.

The Savings & Loan Crisis of the 1980s

Inflation and Interest Rates

During the 1970s, the U.S. economy suffered from increased rates of inflation. Inflation is defined as the continuous increase in the general level of prices. A high rate of inflation mean the cost of living for households increases and the cost of operations for firms increase. In addition, as the rate of inflation increases, market interest rates also increase.

To see why this happens, think about how you would feel if you were a lender of money and prices increased. Suppose I ask you to lend me $2 so that I can buy a bottle of diet Coke from a vending machine and agree to repay you tomorrow. . Essentially you are lending me enough resources, the two dollars, to purchase an entire bottle of diet Coke. Now assume the person who refills the vending machine changes the price of a bottle of diet Coke from $2 to $3. Tomorrow comes and I give you $2. You say, "Wait a minute-- I gave you enough resources to buy an entire bottle of diet Coke, and yet you pay me back with resources that can now only buy two-thirds of a bottle of diet Coke!"
Notice what happened: When prices increase, or there is inflation, lenders get paid back in money that simply no longer buys as much. As a result, if lenders think there is going to be inflation, they are going to demand to be compensated for the difference and thus demand a higher interest rate before they will lend their money.

This is what happened during the 1970s. As the inflation rate in the United States increased, market interest rates also increased. Thus, interest rates on Treasury bills, corporate bonds, and other types of debt increased higher and higher as U.S. inflation got worse and worse.

The Problem of Disintermediation

One set of interest rates that did not increase during the 1970s was that paid by the Savings and Loans. Remember that during this time, the Savings and Loans were subject to Regulation Q, the law that stated the maximum interest rate that could be paid on deposits. Thus, while the market interest rates on regular passbook savings accounts could be no higher than 5.5 percent, the yield on a 1-year Treasury bill was over 12 percent by February 1980. As a result of these interest rate differences, savers started to pull their money out of the Savings and Loans in favor of higher paying money market mutual funds. The process of funds moving from one financial intermediary to another is what economists call disintermediation.

To combat disintermediation, the Savings and Loans looked for ways around Regulation Q. One "invention" was the creation of NOW, or negotiable orders of withdrawal. NOW accounts were essentially demand deposits that paid a market rate of interest. Initially the NOW accounts were of questionable legality, since they were violating the premise of Regulation Q that prohibited the paying of interest on demand deposits or checking accounts. But the operators of Savings and Loans thought they had little choice but to offer the NOW accounts. If they did not offer NOW accounts, they would see more and more deposits leave their institutions. If the disintermediation were allowed to go on unchecked, it would lead to a collapse of the Savings and Loan industry, since a depository institution with no deposits simply can not function. Clearly, something needed to change.

DIDMCA: The Solution that Did Not Work

The Savings and Loan industry turned to Washington for help with disintermediation. In response to the growing financial market difficulties, after much debate, Congress passed, and President Carter signed, the Depository Institutions Deregulation and Monetary Control Act (DIDMCA) in 1980. The DIDMCA was the Carter Administration's attempt to bring about some type of financial market reform. Four years earlier, Carter had campaigned on the promise that his administration would bring about such reform, but by 1980, little to nothing had changed in terms of financial market regulation. DIDMCA was about to change all of that.

Two of DIDMCA's major reforms were that it set up for the complete repeal of Regulation Q over six years and it would make it legal for Savings & Loans to offer NOW accounts in order to fend off the disintermediation immediately. While DIDMCA allowed the Savings and Loans to compete with the money market mutual funds for deposits, it created a whole new set of problems. Savings and Loans generated most of their income off the 30-year fixed interest rate mortgages that they had written in the past. The vast majority of these mortgages paid the Savings and Loan a 6 to 8 percent annual rate of interest. When the Savings and Loans were paying 3 to 5.5 percent on deposits, they enjoyed a positive interest rate spread. With the passage of DIDMCA, the Savings and Loans would now be paying upwards of 14 percent on their NOW accounts. That meant that the Savings and Loans would be paying 14 percent for funds while earning only 6 to 8 percent on funds. Thus, the Savings and loans were suffering from a negative interest rate spread.

Garn-St. Germain: Making a Bad Problem Worse

To get relief from their negative interest rate spread, the Savings and Loans returned to Congress in 1981 and 1982 seeking help. In response to the industry's cry for help, Congress passed the Garn-St. Germain Depository Institutions Act of 1982. Garn-St. Germain allowed the Savings and Loans to diversify their lending away from traditional 30-year fixed rate home loans and into shorter term, more profitable business loans. The Act allowed the Savings and Loans to hold up to 40 percent of their assets in commercial mortgages and up to 11 percent of their assets in secured or unsecured commercial loans. In addition, many states, including California and Texas, significantly reduced the amount of regulations on their respective state-chartered Savings and Loans.

As a result of these reduced regulations and a desire to diversify their loan portfolios, the Savings and Loans set off a business lending spree. The Savings and Loans wrote a dizzying array of commercial real estate loans, include loans for high-rise office buildings, massive suburban shopping mall developments, and retail strip mall developments. In addition, many Savings and Loans started lending money for alternative energy development such as windmill farms in the Texas panhandle. One issue with this new lending is that many Savings and Loan lenders had little to no experience in making such loans. As a result, many loans were written where risk was mispriced. Numerous office buildings were built that simply were not needed. Many shopping centers never found enough tenants because they knew shopping centers were not needed. For example, by 1986, nearly one-third of the office space in Houston, Texas, sat unoccupied. As these spaces went unrented, the real estate developers who built these buildings could not pay the loans they had taken out from the Savings and Loans.

The Zombie Savings and Loans

By the late 1980s, the Savings and Loan industry was riddled with insolvent institutions. These institutions had written so many bad loans that they simply did not have enough assets to make good on all of their deposits. These insolvent institutions, sometimes called "Zombie institutions" because they were financially "dead," should have been closed down by their regulators. These regulators, which included the Federal Home Loan Bank and FSLIC, instead chose to suspend the regulatory rules and allowed these Zombie institutions to continue to function. This suspension of the regulatory rules, called "Capital Forbearance," allowed the Zombie institutions to continue in operation and make more and more risky loans.

As the Zombie institutions were allowed to continue in operation, many of the Zombies "infected" the healthy, well run institutions. A Zombie institution would compete with a healthy institution for a loan customer by offering the customer a loan on very favorable terms with a low interest rate and/or easy repayment terms. To compete, the healthy institution would have to offer the loan customer similar terms or face being locked out of the market. Thus, the healthy institution would have to behave like the Zombie institution and essentially "become" a Zombie institution.

One question that has been raised is: why did the regulators allow the Zombie institutions to continue in operation? One answer to this question is that the regulators simply did not have the resources to close all of the Zombie institutions. Closing all of the Zombie institutions would have required perhaps hundreds of billions of dollars to pay insured depositors. Since the regulators did have the resources to close all of these Zombie institutions, they allowed them to continue in operation.

A second potential explanation to why the regulators allowed the Zombie institutions to continue in operation was the political power some of the savings and loan operators wielded. See the box below for one of the more infamous examples of political influence in the savings and loan crisis.

Charles Keating and the Keating 5

One reason many of the Savings and Loan regulators practiced capital forbearance was the political influence of the Savings and Loan operators. An example of this is what became known as the Keating 5. An Arizona real estate developer by the name of Charles Keating was allowed to buy a Savings and Loan in California called Lincoln Savings and Loan. When Lincoln Savings and Loan started to suffer from disintermediation, Keating promised depositors that he could offer them a "special account" that would pay an interest rate much above what money market mutual funds would pay.

Many of Lincoln's depositors were elderly, and they questioned Keating as to the safety of the "special accounts." Keating reassured his elderly customers that the special accounts were fully insured by the federal government. In fact, they were not. The special accounts were actual shares in his real estate development in Arizona.

The regulators of Lincoln Savings and Loan at the Federal Home Bank Board became concerned about the growing riskiness of Lincoln. But Charles Keating did not want the regulators to interfere in his operations. Keating had made large campaign contributions to five key U.S. Senators. Keating now called on these five Senators to intervene with the regulators on his behalf. The five Senators basically did what Keating requested. As a result, Keating was allowed to continue to operate Lincoln Savings and Loan as he saw fit.

In 1989, Lincoln Savings and Loan failed, costing taxpayers $1.3 billion, and more importantly, more than 22,000 depositors/bondholders at Lincoln Savings and Loan lost their savings since they were not in government-insured accounts. Charles Keating eventually was convicted of bank fraud and served four and a half years in prison. What happened to those five Senators known as the Keating 5? Basically, nothing. All were allowed to continue serving in the U.S.

Senate, and two of the Keating 5 went on to run for President of the United States despite their questionable ethical dealings with Charles Keating.

As the 1980s moved on, the Savings and Loan problem grew significantly. In 1988, the FSLIC had closed over 200 Savings and Loans that were insolvent. The problem, however, was that by the end of 1988, over 500 insolvent Savings and Loans continued to operate. Clearly, the current system had failed.

In August 1989, President George H. Bush signed the Financial Institutions Reform Recovery and Enforcement Act. FIRREA was the first dramatic step to resolve the Savings and Loan crisis. Among other things, FIRREA forced the absorption of the FSLIC into the FDIC. In addition, the Federal Home Loan Banks' independence was stripped away and it was taken over by the Office of Thrift Supervision within the Treasury Department. Perhaps most importantly, FIRREA created the Resolution Trust Corporation (RTC), which was to close the insolvent Savings and Loans and sell off their assets.

The once proud Savings and Loan industry that had helped to build the American suburbs after the Second World War was now a mere shadow of itself. The inability or unwillingness of the Savings and Loan operators to measure the riskiness of their loans problem greatly contributed to the industry's demise. The regulators such as the Federal Home Loan Bank and FSLIC arguably did not do their job correctly, and these entities were either stripped of their powers or completely eliminated.

THE SEEKING OF RETURN: 2002–2006

One of the lessons learned from the Savings and Loan crisis is that depository institutions that rely on the interest rate spread between what they earn on long-term loans and what they pay on short-term deposits can suffer greatly when market interest rates increase. The Savings and Loans suffered from negative interest rate spreads throughout the late 1970s and early 1980s, and these negative spreads triggered a series of chain reactions that ultimately led to the current financial crisis.

Banks and Fee Income

In an attempt to avoid a repeat of the Savings and Loan crisis, commercial banks in the United States during the 1990s and throughout the first decade of the 21st century attempted to end their reliance on interest rate spreads. Instead of depending on the spread as a source of profits, commercial banks envisioned themselves as providers of financial services who earned fees for their services. Since fee income was independent of changes in market interest rates, commercial banks saw it as a much more stable source of income and profits.

Commercial banks looked in a variety of places to generate fees. They charged fees for use of ATMs (automated teller machines), for use of the bank lobby, and for printing checks, and they looked at offering new services where they could generate new fees. One expanding market that caught the banks' attention was the home mortgage market. Traditionally, when a depository institution wrote a home mortgage loan, the depository institution would hold the mortgage, collect payment, or service the mortgage for 30 years until the household borrower paid off the mortgage. However, in their desire to earn fees, commercial banks were turning more and more to the securitization of home mortgages.

Securitization

Securitization is the pooling or combining of loans, such as mortgages, into one big bundle. This bundle is then used to create a new financial instrument or bond whose cash flows are the original loans in the pool. For example, the securitization of home mortgages entails the purchase of a large number of home mortgages and the creation of a mortgage-backed security, or MBS. The mortgaged-backed securities are paid the cash flow received from the households as they make their mortgage payments.

Securitization takes place with other loans in addition to home mortgages. Commercial mortgages are also securitized into their own version of securitized securities called Commercial Mortgaged-Backed Assets. Student Loans are also securitized. If you have borrowed money for a student loan, once you signed your promise to repay the loan, the bank or financial institution that lent you the money took your student loan, bundled it with other student loans, and created an Asset-Backed Security, or ABS. In 2006, $79 billion of new student-loan-backed ABS were issued, with the total market size estimated to exceed $350 billion in 2007.

Fannie Mae and Freddie Mac: Their Great Demise

Fannie Mae and Freddie Mac were originally created by Congress to provide liquidity to the mortgage market, and they were very successful. They did so by buying "qualified" mortgages and securitizing them, or bundling them and selling the bundles to investors. The two "government-sponsored entities," or GSEs, came to dominate the mortgage market. Together they hold or guarantee over $5 trillion in mortgages. By comparison, the entire U.S. economy is just over $13 trillion and the total entire outstanding mortgages in the United States amount to $12 trillion.

However, in 2007 and 2008, both Fannie Mae and Freddie Mac ran into a great deal of financial trouble. Both Fannie and Freddie had purchased mortgages without carefully examining the default risks associated with those mortgages. As a result, in 2008, the federal government had to take over both Fannie and Freddie to keep them from failing.

When a commercial bank writes a loan that will be bundled up or securitized, the bank earns a fee from the entity that does the bundling. The "bundler" or securitizer may be an investment bank, a Government-Sponsored Entity (such as Fannie Mae, Freddie Mac, or Sallie Mae--for student loans), or a Special Investment Vehicle, which is created by commercial banks. The bundler then sells the newly created asset, such as a mortgage-backed security, to an institutional investor, such as an insurance company, pension fund, or an endowment.

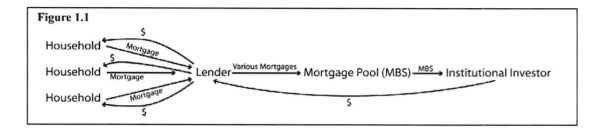

Figure 1.1

Over time, the market for mortgage-backed securities increased. The loan originators, oftentimes commercial banks, liked the process of making mortgage loans and earning a fee and then servicing the mortgage and earning more fees. They could generate fee income and move the long-term mortgages off their balance sheet, so they no longer had to worry about interest rate spreads. The process was appealing too because it enabled the mortgage bundlers to charge a fee for bundling the mortgages together and then selling them to institutional investors.

As time went on, new inventions in the mortgage market came about. One issue that arose was that not all institutional investors had the same desire for risk. Some institutional investors didn't want any risk of default. That is, they wanted to be sure that they received the payments they were expecting. At the same time, other institutional investors were more willing to take on some risk, as long as they were compensated for this increased risk by being paid a higher interest rate.

To meet the differing needs of these institutional investors, the bundlers of Mortgage-Backed Securities decided to slice the MBSs into different pieces. The first slice would be paid first, as the households made their mortgage payments. The next slice would be paid after the first slice was paid, if there was still money left over, meaning if there were only a few or no defaults. Each of the remaining slices would then be paid in descending order. These slices of the MBSs are called *tranches*, from the French word *tranch*, which means slice.

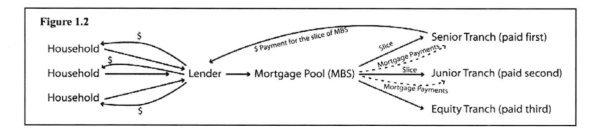

Figure 1.2

In reality, there could be more than just three tranches, but the logic remains the same: the senior tranche gets paid first and so on down the line. Some of the lower tranches, the last to be paid and thus the most risky, the lenders (including commercial banks) held onto the mortgages since they could be very difficult to sell to institutional investors. But, as long as there are no defaults on mortgages, all of the tranches get paid.

Historically, home mortgage defaults were very low, only around 2 percent, so the buyers of the Mortgage-Backed Assets felt fairly safe that they would receive their payments as promised. Thus, the securitized mortgage market grew.

Falling Market Interest Rates

In 2001, in a response to a slowing U.S. economy, the Federal Reserve set out to lower interest rates to stimulate the economy. The collapse of the dot.com boom in 2001 had brought about a significant reduction in the amount of household and business spending. To encourage more borrowing and spending by households and firms, the Federal Reserve cut interest rates throughout 2001, 2002, and 2003. By 2003, market interest rates in the United States were the lowest they had been in forty years.

In response to these falling market interest rates, institutional investors' interest rates in the home mortgage market increased significantly. While other market interest rates had dropped significantly due to the Federal Reserve's actions, the interest rates on home mortgages, and thus the return on mortgage-backed securities, had not fallen as much. Thus, there was a growing interest by institutional investors to buy these mortgage-backed securities.

The mortgage lenders, including commercial banks, were desperate to the meet the growing demand for mortgage-backed assets. But in order to create more mortgage-backed assets, these lenders needed to write more and more mortgages. The problem these lenders faced was that in order to write more mortgages, they would need to go beyond "traditional" borrowers. That is, the lenders needed to lower their lending standards so that more people could qualify for mortgages.

Traditionally, if a family wanted to borrow money to buy a house, they needed to have 20 percent of the purchase price in cash. The family could then borrow the remaining 80 percent of the purchase price of the house via a mortgage. But, as the demand for mortgage-backed assets increased, mortgage lenders began writing "zero-down" mortgages where the borrower puts no money down and borrows 100 percent of the purchase price.

One potential problem with "zero-down" mortgages is that they can result in much higher default rates. In the traditional 20-percent down mortgage, the borrower has some of their own money in the house, or as the saying goes, they have "their skin in the game." If times become financially difficult for the borrower, they would work hard to stay current on their mortgage payments, since defaulting on the mortgage or being foreclosed on would cause the borrower to lose the money they had used to purchase the house. However, with zero-down mortgages, the borrower doesn't have any "skin in the game" or any financial interest in the house. Under this setting, if financial times become difficult, the borrower is much more likely to simply walk away from the house and have the lender foreclose on the house.

Thus, the advent of the zero-down mortgage greatly increased the probability of default by the borrowers. The problem is, many in the financial markets ignored these increasing risks in the mortgage market. Instead, they continued to believe that mortgage default rates would stay exactly as they always had been. In other words, there was a major mispricing of risk occurring in the U.S. mortgage markets.

Heads I Win, Tales the Government Loses

As depository institutions such as Savings and Loans or commercial banks take on more risk, either through writing risky loans or holding risky assets, depositors usually "punish" this behavior by withdrawing their deposits. Depositors do this because if the depository institution fails due to too many of its risky assets failing to pay out as planned, the depositor will lose all of the money they have on deposit. In these cases, the depositors essentially "watch over" the depository institution and help to ensure that Savings and Loans or commercial banks do not engage in excessive risky behavior.

However, deposit insurance changes all of this. With government-sponsored deposit insurance, the depositor knows that even if the depository institution fails, the depositor will not lose any of their money. If the institution fails, all the depositor has to do is go to the government to get a check equal to the amount of the government insurance.

On the other hand, if the depository institution engages in holding risk assets and these risky assets pay off, the institution can "share" these high payoffs with the depositor in the form of higher interest rates on deposits. This is what economists call the "moral hazard" of deposit insurance. A moral hazard is the existence of a contract that can alter behavior by changing incentives.

With the creation of government deposit insurance, the incentives and behavior of depositors change. Depositors no longer "watch over" depository institutions to "keep them safe" and instead have an incentive to push lenders to hold very risky assets. If those risky assets pay off as planned, the depositor benefits, as the institution shares with them the high returns generated by the risky assets. Conversely, if the risky assets fail to pay off as planned and the depository institution fails, the depositor turns to the government to be made whole again. From the point of view of the depositor, government-sponsored deposit insurance creates a situation where the depositor can say "head I win, tails the government loses."

BRINGING IT ALL TOGETHER

The current financial crisis that centers on the home mortgage markets has its roots in the evolution of the U.S. financial markets. Many economists argue that the deposit insurance that was created during the Great Depression of the 1930s may have contributed to the excessive risk taking and the mispricing of risk in the home mortgage market during the first decade of the 21st century. What contributed to this mispricing of risk in the home mortgage market was the rapid expansion of the securitizing of home mortgages, which was an outcome of the Savings and Loan crisis of the 1980s. But this securitization would not have been possible without the rapid expansion of the U.S. housing market in the decades following the Second World War.

But the synopsis of the current financial crisis is not complete. In the next chapter, we will examine in more depth the issues of the current crisis. Updates on the current status of the crisis can be found on the web page www.cengage.com/gec that accompanies this booklet. It will be very interesting and informative to watch this crisis unfold.

Accounting and the Global Financial Crisis

Chapter Outline

Major Events in the Global Financial Crisis
Accounting and the Global Financial Crisis
Change in Holding Mortgages to Securitizing Mortgages
    Accounting for Securitizations
    Investment Losses Grow
    Accounting's Role in the Crisis: Fair Value Accounting

Learning Goals

After reading this chapter, you should be able to answer these questions:
1. What led to the global financial crisis?
2. Why do banks securitize mortgages?
3. How do we account for securitization transactions?
4. What role did leverage play in the crisis?
5. What is fair value accounting?

MAJOR EVENTS IN THE GLOBAL CRISIS

The global financial crisis is the result of cascading effects. Trouble in the housing market led to trouble for home building companies and companies associated with housing, such as furniture companies and home improvement companies. In addition, the downturn in housing created problems for mortgage lending companies, forcing almost 300 to close down in 2007 and 2008. As more homeowners began experiencing fiscal difficulties, the financial companies that held the mortgages started to suffer financially—some ultimately collapsing or going bankrupt. This downturn in the mortgage securities market ultimately affected the stock market, which tumbled more than 40 percent during 2008. With a declining stock market and houses losing value, consumers became more prudent, especially about buying large-ticket items such as automobiles. As retail sales declined, many companies announced layoffs and additional cutbacks. Together, these effects led into one of the deepest recessions in recent memory. This chapter discusses these issues with a special focus on the accounting issues present in the global financial crisis.

The evolving global financial crisis brought a number of accounting issues to the attention of policymakers, business people, and the media. These accounting issues that affect financial institutions making mortgage loans, financial institutions securitizing mortgages, and investors in mortgage-related assets, including securitization, investment impairment, fair value accounting, and pensions, are discussed in this chapter

ACCOUNTING AND THE GLOBAL FINANCIAL CRISIS

Change in Holding Mortgages to Securitizing Mortgages

The origins of the financial crisis can be found in the increase in homeownership and changes in the way in which financial institutions manage mortgages. Mortgages are simply loans backed by real property and are the normal method through which individuals purchase their homes. Traditionally, an individual would pay 10–20 percent of the home price up front and then sign a mortgage for the balance of the funds. This mortgage would then be paid off over a long period, normally 30 years. Mortgage financing changed greatly in the late 1990s when homeownership started increasing above its long-term average as shown in the following graph.

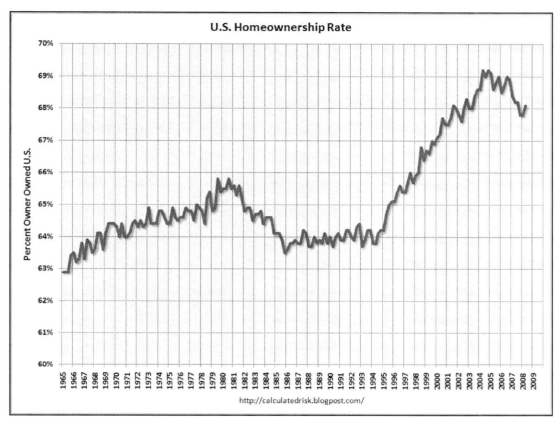

U.S. Homeownership Rate

http://calculatedrisk.blogpost.com/

One reason for this increase in homeownership is the process by which financial institutions started treating mortgages after origination. In the traditional mortgage process, a bank or other financial institution would make a mortgage loan and then hold the mortgage to maturity. However, this process tied up funds for the bank and prevented it from making additional loans. To solve this problem, bankers created a process called securitization.

Securitization, a profitable yet obscure part of the financial world, would soon become more familiar to the public. Securitization is the process of packaging and reselling mortgages, credit card receivables, and other cash flows into securities that are then sold. Securitization can reduce risk, but in the case of securitization of mortgages, a breakdown in the market exploded the risk. Securitization and the financial crisis also reminded people of the special-purpose entity, which was associated with the Enron scandal.

Securitization transfers receivables, either individually or pooled, to a special-purpose corporation in which investors may purchase shares that entitle them to receive cash as the receivables are paid. In most cases, companies that securitize receivables are large financial institutions such as investment banks, mortgage lenders, credit card companies, and leasing companies. The securitization process began with mortgages, but has grown to include numerous types of cash flows, such as credit card receivables, auto loans, and home equity loans. By securitizing its receivables, a financial institution can transfer a large amount of mortgages from its balance sheet.

One of the more familiar types of securitization transactions is called a Bowie bond. The transaction involved rock star David Bowie who securitized his catalog of music. In the transaction, Bowie transferred his music catalog to a trust, which then received all of the royalties from future sales. Based on Bowie's past history of record sales that generated royalty payments, investors in the trust could estimate future royalty payments and then discount the cash flows to determine the current value of the future royalty stream. The amount invested in the trust was Bowie's payment. Since this transaction, many musicians and authors have completed securitizations.

The securitization market, which began in the late 1970s, grew into a huge market, largely on the foundation of mortgage securitization. A simple securitization transaction would work as shown in the illustration below.

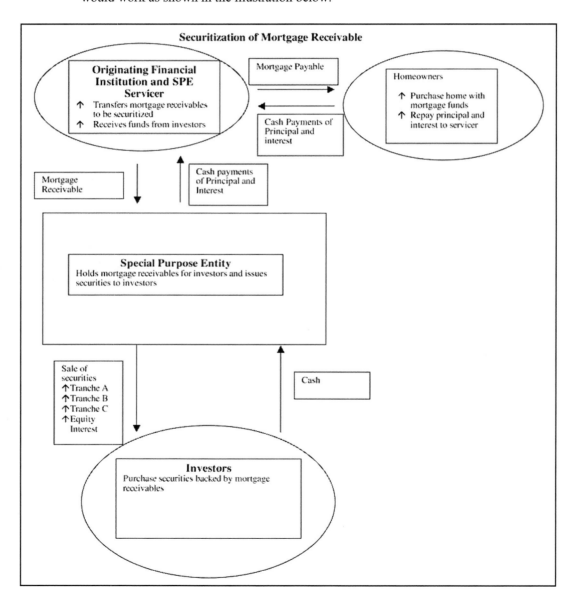

In this transaction the financial institution originates the mortgage when it assesses the borrower's credit worthiness and takes care of the loan application. This step may also be conducted by a mortgage broker who specializes in mortgages and then submits a group of loans to a financial institution for securitization. Additionally, in this example, the financial institution is the servicer of the mortgage, which means that it is responsible for sending out mortgage statements to the borrower and collecting payments. The servicer also remits property taxes, and most importantly, the servicer is responsible for taking care of late payments and foreclosures as necessary. These services are often provided by the originating financial institution but may be outsourced or sold to another company.

The special-purpose entity is a subsidiary of the sponsoring financial institution. In accounting it is the most important and controversial part of the securitization transaction. As discussed in the next section, if the special-purpose entity is organized properly as a bankruptcy remote corporation, it is exempt from taxation. The transfer of mortgage receivables from the sponsor may then be treated as a sale of receivables, and the subsidiary does not have to be consolidated. The investors in mortgage securitizations are normally large institutions such as hedge funds, insurance companies, investment banks, and pension funds. These companies hold the securities and receive principal and interest payments as the original homeowners repay their mortgages.

ENRON AND SPECIAL-PURPOSE ENTITIES

The Enron Scandal

Almost ten years ago, a financial scandal involving the Enron Corporation brought national attention to the term special-purpose entity. In August 2000, Enron Corporation had grown to be the fifth-largest corporation in the United States in terms of market capitalization and one of the most talked-about corporations on Wall Street. Enron was also known as a company that had transformed itself from a slow-growth energy distribution company into a rapidly growing energy trading firm. Enron was able to do much of its transformation through business transactions involving special-purpose entities. The special-purpose entities allowed Enron to keep debt and assets off its balance sheet and appear more profitable and continue its rapid growth. The use of special-purpose entities and rapid growth were not the only thing that Enron had in common with many financial institutions involved in the current financial crisis. In addition, Enron declared bankruptcy in 2001.

The Reasons for Special-Purpose Entities

Special-purpose entities are created for two main purposes. The first is to create a subsidiary that borrows money in order to fund the construction a plant (or other large asset) or to operate a service. If the special-purpose entity is created properly, the debt will not have to be recorded on the corporate balance sheet, which is especially good for a company that already has a high amount of debt. For the most part, Enron used this type of special-purpose entities. A secondary purpose is to securitize receivables. Financial institutions engaged in this type of special-purpose entities.

In both types of transactions, special-purpose entities are created to carry out a specific business transaction or series of transactions. When the purpose is complete the special-purpose entity is expected to be terminated. Another unique feature of special-purpose entities is that they normally do not have any independent employees; all administrative functions are handled by employees who work for the sponsor or an outside party. In addition, a special-purpose entity's balance sheet consists mostly of assets that have been transferred to it by the sponsor and debt that has been purchased by investors in the special-purpose entity. In this situation, the special-purpose entity creates little stockholders' equity.

Accounting for Securitizations

The securitization transaction provides two main advantages from a financial institution's perspective. The first is that the financial institution is able to convert the mortgage receivables from its balance sheet into cash so that they are able to make more mortgage loans. The other great advantage of securitization for financial institutions is that under SFAS No. 140, Accounting for Transfers and Servicing of Financial Assets and Extinguishment of Liabilities, financial institutions have the ability to recognize a sale when the mortgage receivables are transferred to the special-purpose corporation. In many cases of mortgage receivables, the sale entry results in a gain for the financial institution.

The ability to treat the transaction as a sale, given that the financial institution created the special-purpose entity, seems unusual given that accounting rules normally require a company to consolidate all of its subsidiaries in which it has a controlling financial interest. Again this issue is important with special-purpose entities because if the sponsor is forced to consolidate the subsidiary and not record a sale, the advantages of the transaction are lost. In normal cases, control is determined when a company owns 50 percent or more of the voting stock of the subsidiary. However, the accounting for special-purpose entities is more complicated. Another issue that arises with securitization transactions is how the financial institution should account for the servicing rights to the receivables that they maintain in order to keep a customer relationship with the homeowner.

Accounting Rules Covering Securitization

The accounting for special-purpose entities has changed greatly as a result of the Enron scandal. Initially, the accounting for special-purpose entities was covered under consolidation rules and only required that an outside interest own at least 3 percent of the special-purpose entity in order for the sponsor to not have to consolidate the special-purpose entity. In response to the Enron scandal, the FASB released SFAS No. 125, Accounting for Transfer and Servicing of Financial Assets and Extinguishment of Liabilities. The standard updated accounting rules and provided guidance on which types of special-purpose entities would not have to be consolidated, referred to as qualifying special-purpose entities (QSPE). Even though this standard appeared adequate at the time, many financial institutions were able to find ambiguities that allowed them to avoid consolidating special-purpose entities that they controlled even when they did not own 50 percent of the stock of the special-purpose entity.

In response to the problems associated with SFAS No. 125, the FASB released SFAS No. 140 in September 2000 to replace SFAS No. 125. The main requirements to qualify for sale accounting under SFAS No. 140 include the following:

- Transferred receivables are isolated from the transferring financial institution.

- The special-purpose corporation to which assets are transferred has the right to sell or pledge the receivables.

- The transferring financial institution does not maintain control over the receivables through a repurchase agreement.

If these conditions are met, the financial institution would be able to remove the mortgage receivables from its balance sheet, through QSPEs, and not have to consolidate the special-purpose entity.

Sale Accounting and Additional Disclosure

SFAS No. 140 also provided the direction for determining the amount of gain that a sponsor could recognize in a securitization transaction. A gain would be recognized when the financial components of the transaction that were sold were less than the proceeds of the transaction. In these cases, a fair value would need to be placed on each component of the securitization transaction, such as the servicing rights and the different securities. If the fair value of what was received was greater than the fair value of what was sold, then a gain was recorded.

SFAS No. 140 also greatly increased the disclosures required by sponsors of securitization transactions that are accounted for as a sale and do not have to be consolidated. For these cases, companies must disclose the following:

- The cash flows between the company and the special-purpose entity

- The projected and actual losses as a percentage of the original balance of assets securitized

- An analysis of the assumptions used to determine fair value of any retained interest, such as servicing rights

- A summary of delinquencies at end of the period, credit losses during the period, and principal amounts outstanding at the end of the period.

An interpretation to SFAS No. 140 titled FIN 46 R, Consolidation of Variable Interest Entities, provides more stringent rules regarding consolidation of special-purpose entities and introduces the term variable interest entity (VIE). Even though a QSPE was still not required to be consolidated under FIN 46 R, other types of special-purpose entities would need further analysis.

FIN 46 R was put in place to require consolidation of subsidiaries that a company controls even though it owns less than 50 percent of the voting stock. Under this rule, if a corporation receives the majority of the variable interest entities' expected returns, or incurs the majority of expected losses or has the ability to make economic decisions for the VIE, then the VIE should be consolidated.

Securitization transactions of mortgages met these requirements and in most cases financial institutions were not required to consolidate the special-purpose corporations from their securitization transactions. However, as more homeowners had trouble paying their mortgages, financial institutions were forced to violate the requirements for sale accounting of SFAS No. 140 and FIN 46 R. These violations resulted in financial institutions having to consolidate the QSPEs back onto their balance sheets and recognize large losses from transactions that most analysts believed were separated from the financial institution.

During 2008, the FASB put forth an exposure draft, Accounting for Transfers of Financial Assets, to amend SFAS No. 140. The proposed amendments would change securitization accounting by greatly reducing the number of special-purpose entities that are not required to be consolidated. In these cases, financial institutions would no longer be able to record a sale when mortgage receivables are transferred in a securitization transaction. The FASB will vote on a final amendment in 2009.

From an investor's perspective, the advantage of the securitization transaction is that they are purchasing a share of a pool of mortgages as opposed to an individual mortgage. In theory, this pooling reduces risks in that if one mortgage in the group of loans securitized went bankrupt it would only cause a small loss for the entire transaction, whereas if an investor owned an individual mortgage and it went bankrupt the entire investment would be lost. In addition, the individual securities from the trust are split into various types, called tranches. Each tranche has a different level of risk. Senior securities have the lowest risk and are often divided into various classes such as Senior A, Senior B, and so on. Junior securities carry higher levels of risk and are also divided into various classes: A, B, C. Senior securities present lower risk , because, as payments come into the securitization trust, senior securities are paid first, followed by lower-level securities based on the amounts remaining. If not enough cash comes into the securitization trust, junior securities suffer losses first.

In most securitization transactions, the pool of mortgages would include a range of credit risk, from very safe mortgages (with a low probability that the homeowner would not repay) to more risky mortgages (with a higher probability of default). Risky mortgages—in which the borrower has a higher probability of default—are referred to subprime mortgages. By including mortgages of various credit risk, securitizing institutions believed that defaults would not reduce the value of the securitization transaction.

Investment Losses Grow

The breakdown in securitization markets was a result of higher-than-expected defaults by homeowners. Default percentages and late payments increased along the entire spectrum of mortgages from prime (or safe) mortgages to high-risk subprime mortgages. As more individuals defaulted on their mortgages, home prices began to decrease, putting additional pressure on other homeowners. The defaults also began to damage the value of the securitization transaction securities, leaving investors in the mortgages with heavy losses.